PASO A PASO

Teacher's Edition

3

Myriam Met
Coordinator of Foreign Languages
Montgomery County Public Schools
Rockville, MD

Richard S. Sayers
Longmont, CO

Carol Eubanks Wargin
Glen Crest Junior High School
Glen Ellyn, IL

220859

Prentice Hall

Glenview, Illinois
Needham, Massachusetts
Upper Saddle River, New Jersey

Visit our Web site at http://www.pasoapaso.com

ADDITIONAL WRITERS AND CONTRIBUTORS

The following individuals contributed their expertise and creativity in developing the many notes and features in this Teacher's Edition.

Peggy Boyles
Foreign Language Coordinator
Putnam City Schools
Oklahoma City, OK

Mary Louise Carey
Natick (MA) High School

JoAnn DiGiandomenico
Natick (MA) High School

Susan Dobinsky
Niles North High School
Skokie, IL

Marjorie Hall Haley, Ph. D.
George Mason University
Fairfax, VA

Thomasina Pagán Hannum
Albuquerque, NM

Lucía Nuñez
Stanford University
Stanford, CA

Craig Reubelt
University of Chicago (IL)
Laboratory Schools

Bernadette M. Reynolds
Parker, CO

Luz Nuncio Schick
Naperville, IL

Michael S. Werner
University of Chicago (IL)

ACKNOWLEDGMENTS

Photographs
25A: ©David R. Frazier Photolibrary; **57A:** ©Joel Gordon; **91A:** ©Mary Altier;
123A: ©Robert Frerck / Odyssey / Chicago; **157A:** ©Sergio Dorantes / Sygma;
189A: ©David R. Frazier Photolibrary; **221A:** Courtesy Habitat for Humanity /
Photography Kimberly Prenda; **253A:** ©Donald Nausbaum / Tony Stone Images;
289A: ©David R. Frazier Photolibrary; **323A:** ©Michael Newman / PhotoEdit;
361A: ©Chip & Rosa Maria de la Cueva Peterson; **395A:** ©Bob Daemmrich /
The Image Works

ISBN: 0-673-58927-7

4 5 6 7 8 9 10 DOW 03 02

Prentice Hall
Upper Saddle River, New Jersey 07458

TABLE OF CONTENTS

PHILOSOPHY OF THE PROGRAM

Welcome to *PASO A PASO!*

This program is based on the belief that the purpose of learning Spanish is to communicate with the people who speak it and to understand their cultures. *PASO A PASO* is designed to help your students achieve that goal by getting them to communicate right from the start. In *PASO A PASO 1* and *PASO A PASO 2,* students learn to communicate about topics or in situations they are likely to encounter. In *PASO A PASO 3,* chapters are organized around important, intriguing questions for which there are no simple or quick answers. Thus, students go beyond talking about themselves to talking about important ideas that affect themselves, their society, and their world.

PASO A PASO reflects the most current thinking in the foreign language field. It reflects state-of-the-art research on how students learn languages and what teachers and materials need to do to help them become proficient language users, whether they are using their new language for oral or written communication.

Let's take a look at some basic premises about language and language learning, the components of *PASO A PASO,* and how each of these components contributes to developing language proficiency.

What is communication?

Communication is an authentic exchange of information for a real purpose between two or more people. By this we mean that people tell each other (through speech or writing) something the other person doesn't already know.

Communicating meaning has several aspects. Students need to learn to listen to and read Spanish in order to interpret intended meanings, to express meaning by conveying their own messages for a purpose and to a real audience, and to negotiate meaning through the natural give-and-take involved in understanding and in making oneself understood (Savignon, 1991). Research tells us that classroom activities must provide students practice in interpreting, expressing, and negotiating meaning through extensive and frequent peer interactions, preferably in pairs or small groups.

Communication is driven not only by meaning, but also by purpose. In real life, people communicate to get things done. They may communicate to transact business, to get to know someone else, or to find out something they really need to know. In authentic communication, people give and get new ideas or information. The information that one partner has and the other doesn't is often called an *information gap* or an *opinion gap.* How unlike the classrooms of old, where we typically asked students questions to which we (and everyone else) already knew the answer, questions such as, "Tom, what's your name?" and "Sally, are you a boy or a girl?" These questions are not heard in real life because they lack a communicative purpose: There is no information or opinion gap.

PASO A PASO is organized around the principle that just as meaning and purpose drive all language use, so too should they drive all language learning. Students are engaged in understanding messages, in sending their own messages, and thus in communicating on every page of every chapter. Because *PASO A PASO* structures almost all activities for pair or group interaction, students find themselves active participants in every lesson, every day. They communicate real ideas and real meanings for real purposes. Every component of *PASO A PASO* is designed with the goal of communication in mind.

Interpreting meaning

In the last decade we have learned more than ever before about how language is acquired. We know that students learn best when they have ample opportunities to internalize meanings before they have to produce them. That is, we know that comprehension precedes production. Many teachers will be familiar with the term "comprehensible input," first used by Stephen

Krashen, who suggests that learners acquire language by understanding what they hear. Students need many opportunities to match what they hear with visual cues (pictures, video, or teacher pantomime) or experiences (physical actions) so that they can associate meanings with forms. This is as true for comprehending language structure and syntax as it is for vocabulary development.

In keeping with research on the importance of matching language with meaning, *PASO A PASO* gives students many opportunities to comprehend new language before producing it. Numerous activities for providing comprehensible input are suggested in this Teacher's Edition, activities that involve visuals (transparencies and pictures) and that physically engage students as they acquire new language. Whenever possible, in the pupil's text, vocabulary is visualized, providing examples of language in context. The video provides opportunities for students to develop skills in interpreting meaning using authentic footage drawn from the Spanish-speaking world. It also reinforces the issues and ideas presented in the chapter.

What kind of practice promotes communication skills?

The first and most critical step in the language development process is getting meaning—learning to understand by matching what is heard with what is seen or experienced. But by itself, understanding is not enough. Students also need to use their new knowledge.

Research tells us that students need extensive practice in using their new language to create and convey their own messages. While there may be a legitimate role for simply drilling new structures or vocabulary, the most valuable practice comes from using them to send messages that have meaning for the learner and serve a legitimate communicative purpose. When teachers (or texts) structure activities so there is only one right answer, clearly students are sending messages that convey someone else's thoughts, not their own, and are serving someone else's communicative purpose. In these kinds of activities students are *practicing* language, but they are not really *using* language to communicate.

In contrast, when the answers are determined by the students themselves—and are therefore unpredictable, with no single correct response—students are involved in authentic communication. In these information- or opinion-gap activities, answers will vary. Research suggests that these types of activities are extremely important. After all, if the purpose of learning Spanish is to communicate, then students will need practice in doing just that! In contrast, if practice consists only (or mainly) of producing right answers determined by others, students will have difficulty spontaneously creating their own messages when needed. Thus language activities and tasks should not proceed from rote or de-contextualized to meaningful practice. All practice should be meaningful, with a predominance of activities that are truly communicative, activities in which students' answers will vary.

Research also tells us that pair and group language practice is far more effective than student-teacher practice alone. Cooperative learning and pair and group work both provide increased time for communicative language practice and promote the give-and-take necessary for negotiating meaning.

Working with a partner to make and share meaning lies at the heart of *PASO A PASO*. Everything students learn in each chapter is tied together in a meaningful way. The parts of language are taught and practiced (with a partner) within the context of the whole, with vocabulary and related grammar closely intertwined. Students use language in context to convey meaning and for a real purpose. All activities involve meaning, and most allow students to choose the meanings they want to convey. These are the kinds of information- and opinion-gap events that are characteristic of real-life communication. Even in structured activities designed to provide specific practice of forms and to elicit certain responses, teachers will find that students may still respond in ways that are personal and true for them. The activities are, however, focused, and you will often find "answers will vary, but look for correct use of ..." in the answer keys.

To promote the development of communicative ability, *PASO A PASO* integrates vocabulary and grammar. They are then re-integrated continually, with gradually increasing complexity. In addition to the personalized and open-ended responses found in the vocabulary and grammar sections of the chapter, the *Sopa de actividades* feature specifically focuses on weaving together newly learned material with material from previous chapters. It promotes the use of all the language students have learned to that point, in oral tasks and through reading and writing. These tasks require greater integration and are more complex than the communicative exercises students encounter in other parts of the chapter.

Teaching for understanding:
The whole is greater than the parts

In many academic disciplines today, instructional practices are based on constructivist theory, which suggests that learners are more likely to be successful when instruction focuses on making meaning, on students' pursuing their natural inclination to try to make sense of what they are experiencing, and on ensuring that the parts are carefully integrated. In foreign languages, we traditionally taught the parts (grammar rules, vocabulary, pronunciation) hoping that eventually students would have the opportunity and ability to integrate them into the "whole" of communicating their own ideas. Today, integration of the parts of language takes place right from the start. It has been suggested that the relationship between learning the parts vs. integration with the whole is like learning to play a musical instru-

ment. The focus is always on making music, and from the outset, learners need to have many experiences producing it. But they can't learn to play an instrument without knowing something about how to produce sounds (e.g., use the violin bow or play scales) or without practice.

Just as students learn the specific skills they need to produce a piece of music in learning to play an instrument, in language-learning we proceed today by identifying the learner's communicative needs (that is, the "music" they want to be able to produce) and then identifying the vocabulary, structures, and cultural skills needed to accomplish their purpose. Vocabulary and grammar are thus taught in the context of the situations in which students will be communicating or the topics they will be communicating about. Everything ties together naturally.

All effective learning is rooted in a meaningful context. We know from research that information is most likely to be retained when it is connected to other information in a meaningful way. Thus, language learning is more successful and retention more likely when we present new language organized into topics or by situations. This also means that some things we have taught in the past may not get taught at the same point or in the same way. For example, students may need to learn the use of the subjunctive with *cuando* to discuss how to be successful in the work place. However, since the subjunctive with *para que* may not naturally fit into this theme, it may not be introduced until another theme or situation arises that will logically involve its use.

PASO A PASO is organized into thematic chapters tied to a key question and related issues that students explore. All material—vocabulary, grammar, culture—is rooted in a context and used meaningfully. All the elements of a chapter tie together. Students learn the vocabulary related to the theme, the grammar they need to communicate about the theme, and the information that helps anchor language in its cultural context.

The questions have been chosen to stimulate student interest and provoke thoughtful exploration. And the end-of-chapter vocabulary list is organized to reflect how the new words are used to create and convey meaning.

Critical thinking: Understanding and making meaning

We know from research that language learners are active makers of meaning. They learn by creating their own understandings, not by memorizing ours. This means that students are more likely to remember vocabulary when they have acquired it by figuring out its meaning in a logical context (video situation, visual, teacher pantomime). Grammar is most likely to be understood and rules applied when students have been guided to discover underlying patterns or have formulated the rules for themselves. In contrast, retention and applicability are greatly reduced when students simply memorize lists or rules without real understanding.

In order for students to construct their own understandings and generate rules of language usage, they need to be guided through interaction with teacher and text. Strategic questioning (in the text or by the teacher) plays an important role in this process, a process that is not at all the same as groping blindly to make a random discovery. Rather, through well-chosen examples and appropriate, inductive questioning, students can be led to make significant discoveries on their own, leading to a deep understanding that is much more likely to stay with them and be reflected in their own language use.

Understanding grammar

Understanding and critical thinking are reflected throughout *PASO A PASO*. This text is unique in its approach to the development of grammar skills, emphasizing as it does the critical roles that comprehensible input and student construction of knowledge play in language learning. New structures are foreshadowed through lexical presentation in the vocabulary section prior to the grammar presentation. Vocabulary activities familiarize students with new grammar before it is formally presented, allowing them to construct their own understanding.

To further facilitate grammar learning, students observe patterns of use in the comprehensible input that introduces the grammar section. This is done through a visualized context and strategic inductive questions. Through interaction with the teacher and the text, observation and analysis lead students to understand grammar, not merely to memorize formulas to be applied in rote fashion.

Understanding culture

Guided discovery is also an effective means of helping students construct an understanding of culture. Not only do we want our students to know about the cultures of the people who speak Spanish, we also want them to understand the cultural framework that determines what people say or do. In other words, we want students to understand the *why* of culture that determines the *what*. Whenever and wherever students may encounter speakers of Spanish, they will likely confront cultural practices and behaviors that are new to them. Cultural understanding begins with developing sensitivity to the possibility that people vary in how they think, live, and behave. Students must learn to observe other cultures without judging and to use what they see to help them discover the meanings that underlie cultural practices or behaviors. Specific information provides knowledge that aids in understanding the system of attitudes, values, and beliefs that frames cultural practices or behaviors. Students also need to understand other cultures in relation to their own, so that they may gain a deeper understanding of why they think, live, and behave as they do.

Background knowledge can serve as an important tool for the construction of meaning. It may be contextual (What normally happens in a restaurant?), topical (What are some typical leisure activities?), linguistic (What words do I already know that look like this new word?), or cultural (I know that interpersonal relationships are very important in Hispanic cultures, so that may be why people put so much value on greeting one another). This can serve to help students interpret new cultural information or contrast that information with values and practices common to their own culture. Students should be encouraged to understand the close relationship between language and culture.

PASO A PASO develops important cultural understandings through a unique guided-discovery approach and provides students with a progression of activities that lead them from thoughtful observation to knowledge and understanding of Hispanic cultures and then to reflection on their own culture. A photo or realia essay with strategic inductive questions leads them to reflect on what they are observing. Extended captions provide cultural information or insights that expand upon the visual information and allow students to validate or reject the ideas they formulated at the beginning. They are then asked thought-provoking questions to lead to reflection upon their own cultural perspectives.

Strategies for success

Effective learners not only construct their own understanding of new concepts, they also know how to help themselves be successful learners. One way they do this is by using specific problem-solving strategies. When confronted with unknown words in a reading passage, successful learners don't run for a dictionary or just give up. They know how to get around that obstacle.

PASO A PASO teaches students to use strategies to be effective listeners, readers, and writers. Each reading selection takes students through a multi-step process (Phillips, 1984). Before reading, they are encouraged to use their background knowledge to help them predict or anticipate information they are likely to encounter in the text. A first reading helps them focus on general ideas (gist) without getting mired in details or dif-

ficult expressions. Reading closely for specific information, with specific strategies for dealing with difficult aspects of a text, is a strategy frequently emphasized in the reading sections. Students are then encouraged to use what they have learned in the reading by applying it in a new way. Thus, from the start, students are empowered to deal with authentic print materials. Effective writing is promoted through a process approach in *PASO A PASO*. In the pre-writing stage, students think about the topic, generate needed language, and organize their ideas. They then write a first draft. Reviewing this draft with a peer yields insights into needed revisions or clarification and results in a revision that may be published or placed in a portfolio. This approach is consistent with the ways in which many students are learning to write in their English classes. It also provides them with a strategy or model for independent writing.

Authenticity in language learning

Language teaching today places great value on authenticity. The content that students are expected to learn and how they practice it (objectives and tasks) should be authentic to the learner's interests and to real-life uses. Tasks should require an authentic exchange of meaning (an information or opinion gap) and should have an authentic purpose. Students should be taught authentic, not "textbook," language. Most important, information and, to the extent possible, materials should be culturally authentic.

PASO A PASO opens authentic avenues to communication and culture. Students continually engage in authentic communicative tasks. Pair and group activities in which students fill information or opinion gaps constitute the great majority of exercises. These activities allow students to express their own views on topics and questions of interest to them. The language presented is culturally accurate. Videos, photos, realia, and readings provide authentic contacts with the cultures of Spanish speakers.

PASO A PASO and the student

PASO A PASO is a learner-friendly series. It is friendly to the interests of students and provides extensive opportunities for them to talk about themselves, to explore with peers, and to be engaged, thoughtful learners. Each chapter opens with clearly stated communicative objectives that help focus on what students are expected to learn. Knowing what's expected of them makes students more comfortable.

Because we know that it is impossible for students to learn all the vocabulary related to a given theme at one time, and because we know that it is unusual for students to "master" the grammar the first time they are exposed to it, *PASO A PASO 1* and *2* are each organized around the same set of themes. *PASO A PASO 3* integrates and reviews these themes in key questions of interest to students. However, the review is not simply repetition, re-entry, or recycling. Rather, our approach is recursive: Each review allows students to expand to new levels of achievement, so that their language becomes more refined, more elaborate, and more complex. Students will find comfort in knowing that there is more than one chance to learn the material and that they don't need to know everything perfectly all at once. *PASO A PASO* is a program in which students are continually getting better at communicating in Spanish and are regularly made aware of their progress at specific points in every chapter.

The student book and tests convey a powerful message. Both emphasize knowledge in action. Students are asked to use what they know to communicate real messages to a real audience for a real purpose. Practice activities make it clear to students that they are expected to learn to communicate in the language. End-of-chapter tests reinforce the message, assessing students' ability to use what they have learned for receptive and productive purposes and allowing them to demonstrate their understanding of related aspects of Hispanic cultures.

We know more today than ever about how foreign languages are learned. Using that knowledge to help students become proficient communicators, and to acquire an understanding and appreciation of other cultures, can be facilitated by appropriate instructional materials. *PASO A PASO* is based on solid research on second-language acquisition, on accepted theories about the teaching of culture, and on sound pedagogical practices that are common to all disciplines. We are sure that you and your students will find this an exciting, engaging, and enormously successful approach to learning Spanish.

Bibliography

Adair-Hauck, Bonnie, Richard Donato and Philomena Cumo. 1994. "Using a Whole Language Approach to Teach Grammar," in Eileen Glisan and Judith Shrum, Eds. *Contextualized Language Instruction,* Boston: Heinle and Heinle Publishers. pp. 90–111.

Brooks, Jacqueline and Martin G. Brooks. 1993. *In Search of Understanding: The Case for Constructivist Classrooms.* Alexandria, VA: Association for Supervision and Curriculum Development.

Doughty, Catherine and Teresa Pica. 1986. "Information Gap Tasks: Do They Facilitate Second Language Acquisition?" *TESOL Quarterly.* 20:3, 305–325.

Ellis, Rod. 1993. "The Structural Syllabus and Second Language Acquisition." *TESOL Quarterly.* 27:1, 91–112.

Kagan, Spencer. 1992. *Cooperative Learning.* San Juan Capistrano, CA: Resource for Teachers Inc.

Krashen, Stephen. 1982. *Principles and Practice in Second Language Acquisition.* Oxford: Pergamon Press.

Nunan, D. 1991. "Communicative Tasks and the Language Curriculum." *TESOL Quarterly.* 25:2, 279–295.

Phillips, June K. "Practical Implication of Recent Research in Reading." *Foreign Language Annals* 17:4 (September 1984), 285–299.

Resnick, Lauren B. 1989. *Knowing, Learning, and Instruction: Essays in Honor of Robert Glaser.* Hillsdale, New Jersey: Lawrence Erlbaum Associates, Publishers.

Savignon, S. J. 1991. "Communicative Language Teaching: State of the Art." *TESOL Quarterly.* 25:2, 261–277.

Swain, Merrill. 1985. "Communicative Competence: Some Roles of Comprehensible Input and Comprehensible Output in Its Development." In Susan Gass and Madden, C. (Eds.) *Input in Second Language Acquisition.* Rowley, MA: Newbury House.

PASO A PASO AND THE NATIONAL STANDARDS

National standards provide an important and useful framework to guide the teaching and learning of foreign languages. This framework should result in a new generation of language learners prepared to meet the demand for competence in other languages that our nation will face as we move toward an increasingly interdependent world. The work of teachers and students will be facilitated by instructional resources aligned with the National Standards. *PASO A PASO* provides these resources. The program at all levels, with its rich array of ancillary materials (including print and technological resources), is designed to help students develop the competencies delineated in the *Standards for Foreign Language Learning*.

Goal 1. Communication

Communicate in Languages Other than English

Standard 1.1:	Students engage in conversations, provide and obtain information, express feelings and emotions, and exchange opinions.
Standard 1.2:	Students understand and interpret written and spoken language on a variety of topics.
Standard 1.3:	Students present information, concepts, and ideas to an audience of listeners or readers on a variety of topics.

From the very first oral activity in *PASO A PASO,* students work with a partner. They use language to convey meaning and for a real purpose that allows them to choose the meanings *they* want to convey, which is the basic characteristic of real-life communication. Even in structured activities designed to provide practice of specific forms, students may still interact with partners to exchange real information.

PASO A PASO gives students many opportunities to comprehend new language before producing it. The video allows students to hear native speakers using new vocabulary and grammar in a context that makes the meanings clear. Numerous activities for providing comprehensible input are suggested in this Teacher's Edition, including

hands-on activities that physically engage students as they acquire new language. In the student book, vocabulary is visualized, rather than translated or buried in cartoons or *fotonovelas,* so that print and video materials provide different but complementary examples of language in context.

An important characteristic of both the audio and video materials is that they do not repeat material from the text, but rather extend it. Simply hearing what they read does not develop students' ability to understand Spanish when it is spoken, because spoken language and written language are not alike. Even more important, students need to develop the ability to understand the spoken message without being able to predict every word they will hear.

Reading activities can also be found in every chapter and at every level of *PASO A PASO.* As students begin to gain control of new chapter material, they are presented with short reading passages. Later in the chapter, more extensive reading selections are presented, along with strategies that empower students to be successful independent readers. In Book 2, cultural essays are presented in Spanish. As students progress through the program, reading selections increase in challenge level, culminating in a 68-page *Fondo literario* in Book 3. The various Web-based activities at www.pasoapaso.com provide still more opportunities for reading authentic materials.

The presentational mode (Standard 1.3) differs from the interpersonal mode (Standard 1.1) in that the opportunity for direct interaction (conversational give-and-take) between speaker and listener (or reader and writer) is absent. Examples of the former include leaving messages and giving speeches. At the earliest stages of language development, students are more likely to engage in the presentational mode in writing than in speaking. Nonetheless, students have many opportunities for making oral presentations in the *Puntos de vista* sections at the end of each chapter. As they move through the program, the presentational speaking activities become more frequent and more challenging.

Various challenge levels of writing occur throughout each chapter of *PASO A PASO*. Initial writing tasks are limited in scope and audience, but at the end of every chapter at every level a more extended and comprehensive writing task requires student communication on the chapter topic. Because writing always has an intended audience and purpose, these are made clear in each writing task, with suggestions for ways in which students can publish their writing.

Goal 2. Cultures

Gain Knowledge and Understanding of Other Cultures

Standard 2.1:	Students demonstrate an understanding of the relationship between the practices and perspectives of the culture studied.
Standard 2.2:	Students demonstrate an understanding of the relationship between the products and perspectives of the culture studied.

Cultural understanding is at the heart of Goal 2. Cultural information (knowing about the practices and products of other cultures) is important. However, it is equally important for students to understand that the perspectives of a culture (its attitudes, values, beliefs) both determine that culture's practices and products and may in turn be influenced by them. Resources for teaching toward Goal 2 of the Standards are found throughout the student books in cultural photo essays *(Anticipación)* and cultural readings *(Álbum cultural)*. There are also culture notes throughout this Teacher's Edition. Significant cultural information abounds in the video program.

Too often in teaching foreign languages, it is easier to focus on the informational aspects of culture and to ignore the perspectives that underlie them. *PASO A PASO* helps students know about the cultures of the people who speak Spanish, but it also highlights the cultural framework that determines what people say or do. In other words, we want students to understand the *why* of culture that determines the *what*.

These important cultural understandings are developed through guided discovery, an approach unique to *PASO A PASO*. The program provides students with a progression of activities that lead them from thoughtful observation, to knowledge and understanding of Hispanic cultures, as well as to reflection on their own culture. A photo essay in the opening section of the textbook chapter along with strategic inductive questions lead students to reflect on what they are observing. An informative cultural reading provides information and insights that expand upon the visual information in the photo essay and allows students to validate or reject the ideas they formulated earlier. Most important, students are asked thought-provoking questions for reflection upon the cultural perspectives they have encountered.

Goal 3. Connections

Connect with Other Disciplines and Acquire Information

Standard 3.1:	Students reinforce and further their knowledge of other disciplines through the foreign language.
Standard 3.2:	Students acquire information and recognize the distinctive viewpoints that are only available through the foreign language and its cultures.

Certain chapter themes (the environment, health, art) directly relate to the content of the school curriculum. The Internet-based activities found at www.pasoapaso.com provide activities that connect to other curriculum areas as well as access to information that is available only through the Spanish language. In the Teacher's Editions of Books 1–3, cross-curricular connections are noted at the beginning of each chapter, including suggestions for student activities.

Another important way in which *PASO A PASO* connects with other disciplines is through the development of learning strategies, learning processes, and higher order thinking skills. We teach students to use strategies to be effective readers, listeners, and writers. For example, the *Para leer* takes students through a multi-step process similar to the strategic approach they may be using in their language arts courses. Similarly, effective writing is promoted through a process approach. In the pre-writing stage, students think about the topic, generate needed language, and organize their ideas. They then write a first draft. Reviewing this draft with a peer results in a revision, which may be published or placed in a portfolio. This approach is not only consistent with the ways in which many students are learning to write effectively in their English classes, but it also provides them with a strategy or model for independent writing.

Higher order thinking skills are emphasized throughout, with suggestions for developing critical thinking and for enrichment activities included in the Teacher's Edition. In addition, deep understanding, rather than rote memorization, is a key feature of grammar and culture instruction. *PASO A PASO* is unique in its approach to the development of grammar understanding. It emphasizes the critical roles that comprehensible input and the construction of knowledge play in language learning. To provide comprehensible input, new structures are foreshadowed through lexical presentation in the vocabulary section, for example, by the use of first- and second-person singular verb forms in vocabulary practice prior to the grammar presentation. Both the video and vocabulary activities familiarize students with new grammar before it is formally presented, allowing students to construct their own understanding. Students then discuss with a partner the grammatical patterns under observation. This is done through actual or simulated realia highlighted by inductive questions in the text. This approach of observation and analysis leads students to *understand* the grammar, eventually leading to a more consistently correct use of the structures being studied.

Goal 4. Comparisons

Gain Insight into the Nature of Language and Culture

Standard 4.1:	Students demonstrate understanding of the nature of language through comparisons of the language studied and their own.
Standard 4.2:	Students demonstrate understanding of the concept of culture through comparisons of the cultures studied and their own.

Myriad opportunities exist in *PASO A PASO* for students to compare their own language and culture to Spanish and to Hispanic cultures. Take, for example, the very first chapter of Books A and 1. Students are introduced to the concept that most adjectives change if they are describing a boy or a girl. They note how this can help them as a reading strategy (was the self-descriptive poem "Yo" written by a male or a female?). They learn the very different cultural connotations of the supposedly equivalent words *amigo(a)* and "friend."

Such comparisons between the student's own language and culture and the target language and culture(s) are found in every chapter. Guided discovery is a prime feature of *PASO A PASO* as a means to help students gain insight into language and culture. For example, at the end of every culture section, students are asked to reflect upon what they have read from their own cultural perspective. This heightened consciousness of their own language and cultural beliefs and practices can only evoke a deeper understanding of those being studied.

Goal 5. Communities

Participate in Multilingual Communities at Home and Around the World

Standard 5.1:	Students use the language both within and beyond the school setting.
Standard 5.2:	Students show evidence of becoming life-long learners by using the language for personal enjoyment and enrichment.

Of the five goals in the National Standards, Goal 5 involves application of Goals 1–4, and is most closely aligned with experiences that take place outside the classroom. These experiences may be within the school itself, but are also likely to be in the community and even beyond the student's enrollment in a given course.

For students with direct access to Spanish speakers in their school or community, there are many suggestions in *PASO A PASO* that address Standard 5.1. Many of these are found in the Teacher's Edition (labeled "Spanish in Your Community"). Other opportunities to use Spanish in or beyond the school setting are included in suggestions for publishing student writing, in activities that involve collecting information from the local community, and in chapters related to the environment (Books A-B, 1, and 2) and community service (Book 3). In fact, two chapters in Book 3 directly address Standard 5.1: a chapter on community service and another on the importance of knowing another language. Indeed, the latter chapter also addresses Standard 5.2, for the personal enrichment derived from knowing Spanish is highlighted. Each chapter provides at least two Internet links that take students into the Spanish-speaking world.

As for Standard 5.2, it is hard to do much more than promote this Standard, for it is neither text- nor schoolroom-based. However, users of the first edition of *PASO A PASO* share with us their students' enthusiasm for the study of Spanish, of going beyond the textbook, of wanting to interact with Spanish speakers both in school and in the community. And we also know that the award-winning *telenovela, La Catrina,* that accompanies *PASO A PASO 2* moves students toward achieving Standard 5.2, for we have seen the essays, reports, and taped sequels that it has prompted individuals and small groups of students to create.

Page-by-Page Correlations to the Standards

In this Teacher's Edition, you will find page-by-page correlations to the Standards. These are located in the bottom left- or right-hand corner of each page. All material in the Teacher's Edition pages and in the reduced Student Edition are correlated. So when the audio program is listed in the margin of the Teacher's Edition, Standard 1.2 will be noted; if a video activity asks students to compare cultures, Standard 4.2 is noted, and so on.

Each chapter supports the Standards, but not all Standards are supported on every page. Some pages contain no correlations, because the material on those pages is not Standard-specific. It is important to recognize that not every activity in a textbook or ancillary component supports a Standard, and we have been very strict in our interpretation. For example, a fill-in-the-blank exercise designed for skill-building writing practice is a valid activity, but it is *not* aimed at fulfilling a Standard.

COMPONENTS OF THE PROGRAM

PASO A PASO is a complete, three-level series with a full range of ancillary components that allow you to tailor the materials to the needs of your students and to your teaching style.

Student's Edition

Presentation material begins with maps of Spanish-speaking countries and *Pasodoble,* a unique magazine-format contextual review of basic Book 2 material (irregular verbs, stem-changing verbs, preterite tense, and the like). This is followed by twelve thematic chapters, a set of optional reading selections, and an appendix offering verb charts, Spanish-English / English-Spanish vocabularies, and a grammar index.

Teacher's Edition

This Teacher's Edition contains the student text in slightly reduced form, with answers, teaching suggestions, and cross references to ancillary materials. Each chapter presents an extensive array of Teacher Notes that includes:

- a scope and sequence chart with communicative, cultural, and grammar objectives

- an overview of components available for use in the chapter

- on-page cultural information for photos and realia

- correlations to the National Standards

- on-page suggestions for Spanish-speaking students, students needing extra help, enrichment, multiple intelligences, extended written practice / homework, cooperative learning, multicultural perspectives, cross-curricular activities, using the video, critical thinking, class starter reviews, reteaching / reviewing, and re-entering / recycling.

Ancillaries
Multisensory / Technology

 Overheads: A package of 64 full-color overhead visuals that reproduce the vocabulary-teaching illustrations without labels or captions. Also included are maps, a pronoun chart, the realia from selected *Gramática en contexto* sections, and additional teaching transparencies. Suggestions for use are provided in a separate booklet.

 Audio Cassettes / CDs: A set of eight 60-minute audio tapes on cassette or CD containing listening activities for each chapter and separate tapes for assessment and pronunciation and vocabulary. The primary focus is on developing listening comprehension, with secondary emphasis on supporting the advanced stages of speaking, including practice with pronunciation of new words and some focused speaking opportunities.

 Vocabulary Art Blackline Masters for Hands-On Learning / CD ROM: All teaching vocabulary art reproduced on blackline masters and available on the Resource Pro® CD-ROM, ideal for making manipulatives or flashcards.

 Classroom Crossword: A wall-size crossword puzzle to be completed over the course of the school year.

 Realidades: A video series consisting of authentic footage from several locations in the Hispanic world. Available on both tape and disc, *Realidades* incorporates the chapter themes into an engaging series suitable for students at Level 3 and above. A Teacher's Guide is included with complete transcriptions, cultural information, teaching suggestions, and reduced reproductions of the Video Activities pages *(see next page)* with overprinted answers.

Multisensory / Technology (*continued*)

 Internet-based activities at www.pasoapaso.com: Chapter-by-chapter support for the culture and content of each chapter through engaging internet-based activities. Students can explore sites from around the Spanish-speaking world via selected web sites and can interact with the information provided at each while expanding language skills and cultural understanding. Additional chapter-by-chapter activities provide games and drill-and-skill practice with vocabulary and grammar.

Print

 Practice Workbook: (with separate Teacher's Answer Key): Worksheets for basic, one-step writing practice for all vocabulary and grammar sections of the student text. Exercises include the support of learning strategies. Each chapter also has an Organizer that allows students to record and keep track of new vocabulary and structures.

 Writing, Audio & Video Activities: Writing Activities provide chapter-by-chapter practice that is at the same level as (or slightly higher level than) that in the student text. Audio Activities offer exercises necessary to focus attention on listening comprehension as students work with the audio tapes. Video Activities focus attention as students view the video. Follow-up activities verify and extend their understanding of what they have seen.

Teacher's Edition: Writing, Audio & Video Activities: Student material with overprinted answers and a complete tapescript of the audio tapes and CDs.

 Communicative Activities Blackline Masters (Pair and Small-Group Activities with Situation Cards): Oral activities for pair and group practice.

Assessment

 Assessment Program: Blackline master quizzes *(Pruebas)* for each vocabulary section and each grammar topic in the student text; twelve chapter quizzes *(Pruebas cumulativas);* twelve chapter proficiency tests *(Exámenes de habilidades);* a chapter test for *Pasodoble (Prueba Pasodoble);* and *Bancos de ideas,* several sets of cumulative proficiency sections for use in creating mid-term and special end-of-year tests to highlight teachers' own objectives or areas of concern. Suggestions for administering and scoring proficiency tests are included.

 ¿Lo sabes bien? Video Quiz: This end-of-chapter video quiz provides ten multiple-choice questions that review key concepts. The questions appear on the monitor and are read aloud.

 Test Generator: A multiple-choice test generator. Teachers can add their own questions to the question bank.

Teacher's Resource File: This convenient, desk-top organizer contains the Teacher's Edition of the Writing, Audio & Video Activities, the Assessment Program, and the Communicative Activities Blackline Masters.

RESOURCE PRO®

Resource Pro®: Teachers have complete support for developing lesson plans through this multipurpose CD-ROM. The Teaching Resources Library allows teachers to view and print out all print ancillaries. Planning Express builds complete lesson plans for regular and block scheduling with objectives and correlations to local and national standards. The Vocabulary Clip Art Library contains clip art for all visualized vocabulary in all levels of the program. Teacher and students can copy and use images for manipulatives and flashcards.

CHAPTER ORGANIZATION

Organization of the Text

PASO A PASO 3 contains a review section *(Pasodoble)* and 12 thematically organized chapters in which students learn to communicate about their own lives and how to interact with Hispanic cultures. A section consisting of optional reading selections is found at the end of the book. This supplementary text compliments the chapter themes:

CAPÍTULO 1   **Identity and Self-Perception**

CAPÍTULO 2   **Rural and Urban Life**

CAPÍTULO 3   **Art**

CAPÍTULO 4   **Television**

CAPÍTULO 5   **Mayan Civilization**

CAPÍTULO 6   **Communication Technology**

CAPÍTULO 7   **Community Service**

CAPÍTULO 8   **Myths and Legends**

CAPÍTULO 9   **The Workforce**

CAPÍTULO 10   **Controlling Violence**

CAPÍTULO 11   **Multiculturalism**

CAPÍTULO 12   **Learning Another Language**

Using *Pasodoble*

The magazine-format review, *Pasodoble,* is designed to help students recall certain major vocabulary sets and structure taught in Chapters 1–12 of *PASO A PASO 2.* Previously taught concepts are uniquely integrated to provide meaningful communication combined with purposeful review.

Chapter organization

The 12 chapters follow a consistent organization that increases student confidence while allowing for easy classroom management. Chapters are organized according to the latest research on how students learn a second language and follow a clear pedagogical model:

1 Introduce/Preview   **4** Apply

2 Present   **5** Summarize/Assess

3 Practice

![E]ach chapter follows this model:

Chapter Sections	Pedagogical Support
Objetivos	Introduce
Anticipación	Preview
Vocabulario para comunicarse	
• *Visualized vocabulary*	Present
• También necesitas . . .	Present
• Empecemos a conversar	Practice
• ¿Y qué piensas tú?	Apply
Tema para investigar	Practice
• ¿Comprendiste?	Practice
• ¿Y qué piensas tú?	Apply
• ¿Qué sabes ahora?	Practice / Assess
Álbum cultural	Preview / Present
• Reacción personal	Apply
Gramática en contexto	Preview / Present / Practice
• Ahora lo sabes	Practice / Assess
Puntos de vista	
• Sopa de actividades	Apply
• Para leer	Apply
• Para escribir	Apply
Repaso: ¿Lo sabes bien?	Apply / Assess
Resumen del vocabulario	Summarize

CAPÍTULO 6

OBJETIVOS

Al terminar este capítulo vas a poder responder a la pregunta clave:

¿Cómo nos podemos comunicar mejor?

También vas a poder:
- escribir y enviar una carta
- hablar de diferentes medios de comunicac
- dar tu opinión sobre las comunicaciones en el futuro
- explicar el impacto de la tecnología en la vida diaria de los países hispanos

Radiotelescopios cerca de Socorro, Nuevo México

USING A CHAPTER

Chapter Opener (Introduce)

The chapter theme is introduced through a photograph and related communicative and cultural objectives.

Teaching ideas for the Chapter Opener

Wrap-around notes give many suggestions. Here are a few basic ideas for these two pages:

1 Prior to discussing the objectives, have students look at the photos and skim the chapter. Ask them to suggest objectives based upon what they have seen. Write these on the chalkboard and see if they compare with those listed.

2 Show additional pictures, posters, videos, or slides that preview the chapter theme.

Objetivos:
Relate to real-life, purposeful communication and relevant cultural information. These will be referred to throughout the chapter so that students can monitor their own progress. Chapter assessment is based on the objectives.

VISTA
www.pasoapaso.com

CAPÍTULO 2

OBJETIVOS

Al terminar este capítulo vas a poder responder a la pregunta clave:

¿Prefieres vivir en la ciudad o en el campo?

También vas a poder:

- describir cómo es la vida en un lugar
- comparar la vida de antes con la vida de ahora
- indicar las ventajas y las desventajas de vivir en cierto lugar
- comparar la vida de la ciudad con la vida del campo en los países hispanos

Vista aérea de Taxco, México

Pregunta clave:
The chapter title is a "key" critical thinking question. At the end of the chapter, the key will appear to indicate an opportunity for students to provide their own thoughtful answer to this question.

Anticipación *(Preview)*

This section continues to preview the chapter theme. Students use their own experiences and background information to interact with the photographs.

Teaching ideas for *Anticipación*

1 Ask students to study the photographs and to suggest as many words, phrases, or short sentences as they can about them. Focus on previously taught vocabulary.

2 Use the inductive questions to elicit the similarities and differences. Focus on the similarities.

3 At the end of the chapter, return to these photos. See how extensively students can describe the pictures. Choose a photo and have students bring it to life by acting out the situation.

Questions:
Students use critical thinking to answer inductive questions.

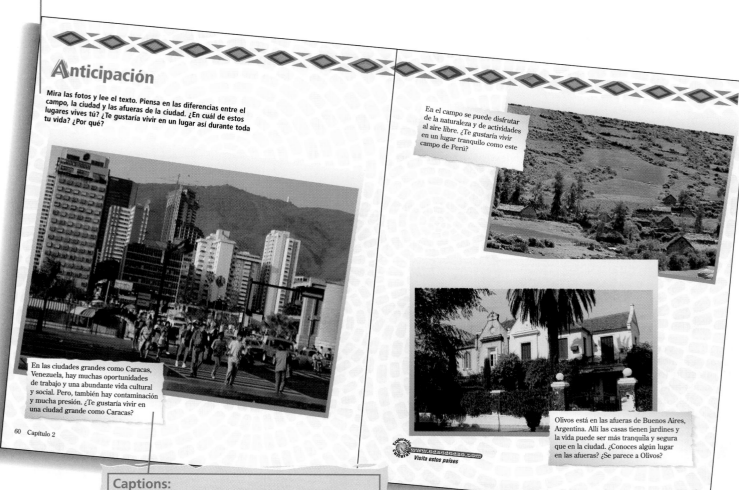

Anticipación

Mira las fotos y lee el texto. Piensa en las diferencias entre el campo, la ciudad y las afueras de la ciudad. ¿En cuál de estos lugares vives tú? ¿Te gustaría vivir en un lugar así durante toda tu vida? ¿Por qué?

En las ciudades grandes como Caracas, Venezuela, hay muchas oportunidades de trabajo y una abundante vida cultural y social. Pero, también hay contaminación y mucha presión. ¿Te gustaría vivir en una ciudad grande como Caracas?

60 Capítulo 2

En el campo se puede disfrutar de la naturaleza y de actividades al aire libre. ¿Te gustaría vivir en un lugar tranquilo como este campo de Perú?

Olivos está en las afueras de Buenos Aires, Argentina. Allí las casas tienen jardines y la vida puede ser más tranquila y segura que en la ciudad. ¿Conoces algún lugar en las afueras? ¿Se parece a Olivos?

Exploración cultural
www.pasoapaso.com
Visita estos países

61

Captions:
Easy-to-read captions provide information about the chapter's key question and get students to begin thinking and forming their responses. Previously taught vocabulary is recycled.

Vocabulario para comunicarse (Present, Practice & Apply)

New vocabulary is presented in two sections. The first set of vocabulary is in a visualized context. The second set is presented in an informative, narrative reading called the *Tema para investigar.*

Teaching ideas

1 Use the Overheads, the Vocabulary Audio Tape, and /or the Vocabulary Art Blackline Masters/ CD-ROM to introduce the new vocabulary.

2 Combine auditory, visual, and kinesthetic activities. Present the vocabulary using comprehensible input. Here are several suggestions:

Getting ready to speak: *Vocabulario para comunicarse*

The following activities are to be done prior to the first vocabulary section.

A. Getting meaning from comprehensible input

The purpose of these activities is to allow students to match new language with its meaning.

- Using the Overhead, point to pictures as you simply and clearly name and talk about them in Spanish. Students should be able to understand new vocabulary from your body language and gestures. For example: *Éste es el centro de una ciudad. Las aceras están al lado de la calle. La gente camina sobre las aceras. En una ciudad, hay edificios muy altos. Aquí hay unos rascacielos.* You may also wish to pantomime new vocabulary when appropriate.

- As you progress through *PASO A PASO 3,* your descriptions of new vocabulary may become more expansive and elaborate as you include language from previous levels and chapters.

Vocabulario pa...

¿Dónde te gustaría vivir?
Aquí tienes palabras y expresiones nec
vida en la ciudad, en las afueras y en e
y practícalas con un(a) compañero(a) e... las páginas siguientes.

la ciudad

el rascacielos,
pl. los rascacielos

el sendero

el campo

el peaje

el puente

la granja

la acera

el atasco

el peatón,
pl. los peatones

las afueras

la cerca

el camino

la autopista

el jardín, *pl.*
los jardines

También necesitas . . . :
Non-visualizable vocabulary and lexical preview of grammar. Do *not* treat these *as grammar*. The more students can master without explanation, the more easily and thoroughly they will learn it.

También necesitas . . .

aislado, -a	isolated	el ruido	noise
animado, -a	lively	sano, -a	healthy
bello, -a	beautiful	seguro, -a	safe
lleno, -a de gente	crowded	tardar (en)	to take time (to)
oír*	to hear	¡Una maravilla!	Wonderful!

¿Y qué quiere decir . . . ?

conveniente	peligroso, -a	situado, -a
cultivar	rápido, -a	

* *Oír* has a *y* in all of its present-tense forms except the *yo* form which ends in -go, and the *nosotros* and *vosotros* forms, which have an accent on the *i: oigo, oyes, oye, oímos, oís, oyen.* It also has a *y* in the *Ud. /él / ella* and the *Uds./ ellos /ellas* forms of the preterite.

Visualized vocabulary:
Research indicates that we learn best in logical sets or categories and through immediately associating words with objects.

¿Y qué quiere decir . . . ?:
Cognates and word families are the focus of this section.

B. Demonstrating comprehension through physical response

The purpose of these activities is to allow students to demonstrate their comprehension non-verbally.

■ After presenting two or three pictures of new language, review by asking *sí / no* questions: *¿Es una calle? ¿Es una acera? ¿Son bajos los rascacielos? ¿Hay rascacielos en nuestra ciudad?* Students may respond as a group with thumbs up / down *(sí / no)*. Individual students may also be asked to respond in this way.

■ As students become more proficient, vocabulary from previous levels and chapters can be used in these questions: *¿Es peligroso ser peatón en una ciudad? ¿Dónde están las fábricas en nuestra ciudad? Hay más contaminación en el centro de una ciudad o en las afueras?*

■ Continue to alternate steps A and B until all new vocabulary has been presented.

■ Distribute the Vocabulary Art BLMs or make photocopies from the CD-ROM printout. As you name each new vocabulary item, point to it on the transparency. Have students point to the corresponding picture on their worksheet. After a while, ask students to point to *el puente, el sendero,* and *el campo.* This time, do not point to the picture on the transparency until after students have pointed to it on their worksheet. Confirm student responses on the transparency.

■ Have students open their books to pp. 62–63. Have them point to pictures you name or describe.

■ Have students pantomime vocabulary as appropriate.

■ Have students respond to the commands you give: *Señalen la acera. Señalen la contaminación.*

■ Provide each student with a picture worksheet of new vocabulary from the Vocabulary Art BLMs/CD-ROM. Direct them to cut out each picture. Have students move the pictures as you direct: *Pongan los peatones en la acera. Pongan los rascacielos en el centro de la ciudad y las casas en las afueras.* Or, students may use the pictures to "make your sentence true." For example: *En el centro de esta ciudad hay rascacielos y fábricas. Hay muchos coches y peatones en las calles.*

C. Limited verbal response

Once students have had an opportunity to internalize meaning and to physically demonstrate comprehension of new language, they may respond verbally.

■ Ask *sí / no* or true / false questions: *¿Te gustaría ser ciclista en el centro de la ciudad? Hay muchos atascos en el campo.*

■ Ask questions which require comprehension of new vocabulary, but do not require using it in the answer. Responses will use language from previous chapters: *¿Adónde va toda la gente en las aceras de la ciudad? ¿Y la gente en los coches?*

■ Ask students questions in which the correct answer is embedded: *¿Es un sendero o una acera?*

■ Have students open their books to the new vocabulary and repeat after you for pronunciation practice.

3 On subsequent days, add details by recycling previously learned vocabulary. Retell an earlier narration without visual support. Ask students to draw their own visual representation of what has been said.

Empecemos a conversar (Practice)

Students practice the new vocabulary in paired activities that provide models for real-life language.

Teaching ideas for *Empecemos a conversar*

1 Place students in pairs. (There are many ways of doing this.) You may want to pair students of different abilities. Assign "study buddies" for each week or chapter. They are not only pair-practice partners, but they also keep track of each other's papers and assignments. (Be sure they exchange phone numbers.) You might award extra credit for partners who work well together and show improvement.

2 Always model the pair practice. Quickly review the vocabulary so that students can be more successful.

3 Set a time limit. Finish an activity when approximately three fourths of the class have finished. Walk around the class, listening for areas of difficulty such as pronunciation or grammar. Focus on these at a later time.

4 Ask pairs of students to do selected items for the whole class.

5 Have students work in pairs to answer the questions, then with another group to compare responses. Ask individuals to write this section as homework. Use the more open-ended questions as one-on-one questions with students or as topics for class discussion.

6 See the list of ancillaries for additional resources to help students work with the new vocabulary.

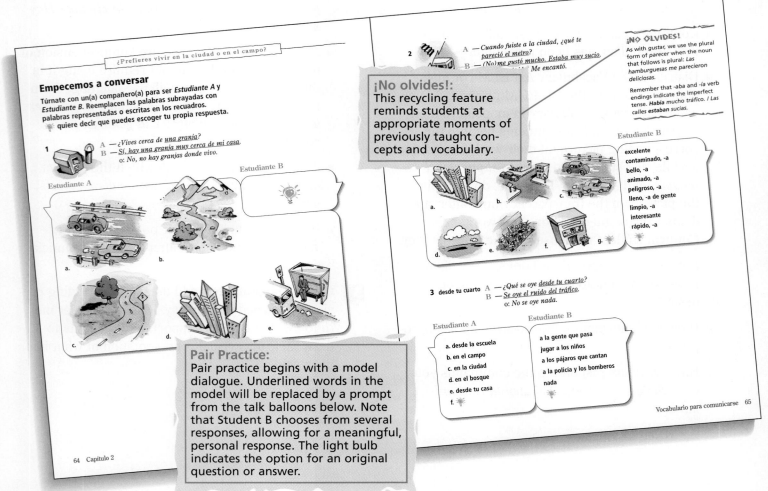

¡No olvides!:
This recycling feature reminds students at appropriate moments of previously taught concepts and vocabulary.

Pair Practice:
Pair practice begins with a model dialogue. Underlined words in the model will be replaced by a prompt from the talk balloons below. Note that Student B chooses from several responses, allowing for a meaningful, personal response. The light bulb indicates the option for an original question or answer.

Empecemos a conversar / ¿Y qué piensas tú? (Practice / Apply)

Vocabulary practice continues with more paired practice. The next section called *¿Y qué piensas tú?* provides personalized questions and critical thinking activities that apply the new vocabulary.

Teaching ideas

Continue following the guidelines for paired practice. Students can work with the *¿Y qué piensas tú?* questions in a variety of ways.

1 Have students respond in writing for homework. In groups the next day, students can share their answers.

2 Have students discuss possible answers in pairs or small groups. One student can record the responses and share with the class or hand them in for the group.

3 Students can interview each other and write up their report in a magazine style.

4 You can write each of these questions on index cards and use them as oral questions with students in a one-on-one situation. These conversations can become part of an informal or formal speaking assessment.

> **¿Y qué piensas tú?:**
> Vocabulary practice and application continue with personalized questions for speaking and writing.

> **También se dice:**
> Variations in usage throughout the Spanish-speaking world.

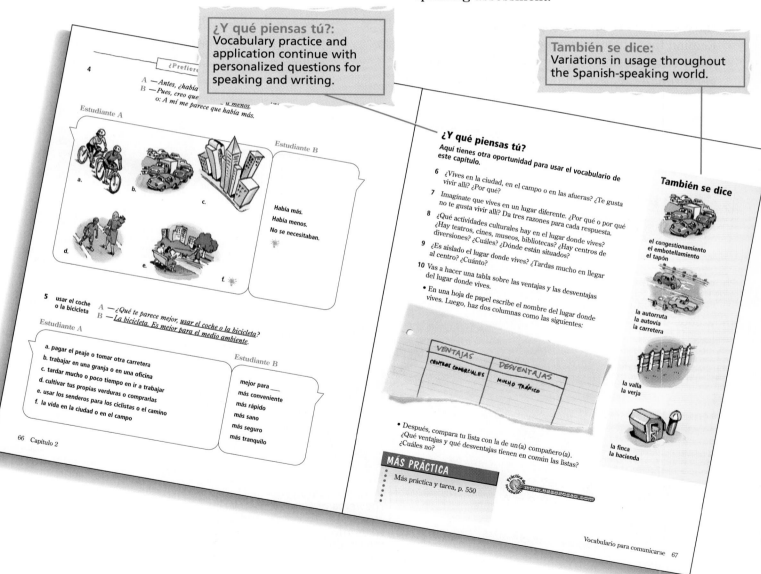

4   ¿Prefiere

A — Antes, ¿había
B — Pues, creo que
o: A mí me parece que había más.

_ o menos.

Estudiante A

a.
b.
c.
d.
e.
f.

Estudiante B

Había más.
Había menos.
No se necesitaban.

5   usar el coche
o la bicicleta

A — ¿Qué te parece mejor, usar el coche o la bicicleta?
B — La bicicleta. Es mejor para el medio ambiente.

Estudiante A

a. pagar el peaje o tomar otra carretera
b. trabajar en una granja o en una oficina
c. tardar mucho o poco tiempo en ir a trabajar
d. cultivar tus propias verduras o comprarlas
e. usar los senderos para los ciclistas o el camino
f. la vida en la ciudad o en el campo

Estudiante B

mejor para ___
más conveniente
más rápido
más sano
más seguro
más tranquilo

66   Capítulo 2

¿Y qué piensas tú?

Aquí tienes otra oportunidad para usar el vocabulario de este capítulo.

6   ¿Vives en la ciudad, en el campo o en las afueras? ¿Te gusta vivir allí? ¿Por qué?

7   Imagínate que vives en un lugar diferente. ¿Por qué o por qué no te gusta vivir allí? Da tres razones para cada respuesta.

8   ¿Qué actividades culturales hay en el lugar donde vives? ¿Hay teatros, cines, museos, bibliotecas? ¿Hay centros de diversiones? ¿Cuáles? ¿Dónde están situados?

9   ¿Es aislado el lugar donde vives? ¿Tardas mucho en llegar al centro? ¿Cuánto?

10   Vas a hacer una tabla sobre las ventajas y las desventajas del lugar donde vives.

• En una hoja de papel escribe el nombre del lugar donde vives. Luego, haz dos columnas como las siguientes:

VENTAJAS	DESVENTAJAS
CENTROS COMERCIALES	MUCHO TRÁFICO

• Después, compara tu lista con la de un(a) compañero(a). ¿Qué ventajas y qué desventajas tienen en común las listas? ¿Cuáles no?

MÁS PRÁCTICA

Más práctica y tarea, p. 550

www.pasoapaso.com

También se dice

el congestionamiento
el embotellamiento
el tapón

la autorruta
la autovía
la carretera

la valla
la verja

la finca
la hacienda

Vocabulario para comunicarse   67

Tema para investigar *(Present)*

Getting ready to speak: *Tema para investigar*

The *Tema para investigar* serves two purposes. It is designed to help students explore important ideas related to the chapter question. It is also a vehicle for presenting new vocabulary in a meaningful context. Unlike the vocabulary presented in the *Vocabulario para comunicarse,* the *Tema* vocabulary is more abstract and cannot be visualized or pictured. Students will need to learn the meanings from context and by using strategies as described below.

Have students read through the *Tema* silently. Remind them before they begin that they know many strategies for reading that will help them get through the text. Students should read through once just for the gist. On the second reading, encourage them to look for main ideas.

Remind students that the *Tema* presents new vocabulary and that they have learned a number of strategies for coping with unknown words.

- Students may try to use context clues to deduce the meaning of new words.

- Students should determine whether the unknown word is a cognate or similar to an English word they know.

- Students should think about whether the new word is related to Spanish words they already know, or whether prefixes in Spanish give clues to the meaning.

- Students should verify their decisions by consulting the vocabulary list that follows the *Tema*.

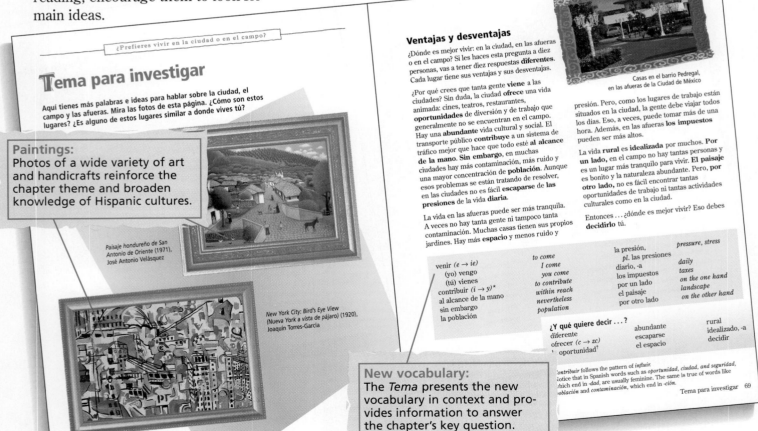

Paintings:
Photos of a wide variety of art and handicrafts reinforce the chapter theme and broaden knowledge of Hispanic cultures.

New vocabulary:
The *Tema* presents the new vocabulary in context and provides information to answer the chapter's key question.

Emphasize that it is important that they try to deduce the meaning of unknown words on their own before consulting the vocabulary list that follows. Using strategies is an important way for students to become successful independent readers of Spanish.

Prior to doing the follow-up questions and activities that follow the *Tema,* you may also wish to do one or more of the following vocabulary development activities:

- Copy the *Tema* on an overhead transparency or a worksheet, leaving spaces where you omit the new vocabulary words. Provide a word bank at the bottom of the page. With their books closed, students determine which word belongs in each of the blanks.

- Define one of the new words. Have students point to the vocabulary item in their book or on an overhead transparency. Later, you may wish to reverse roles.

- Give several examples of words that are similar to a new vocabulary item, or words which might fit in the same category. Have students point to the vocabulary item in their book or on an overhead transparency.

- Provide sentences with a word missing. Have students point to the vocabulary item in their book or on an overhead transparency that completes the sentence.

- Give a vocabulary item and its definition. Students indicate a thumbs up if your definition is correct, thumbs down if incorrect: *Un impuesto es el dinero que uno paga al gobierno.*

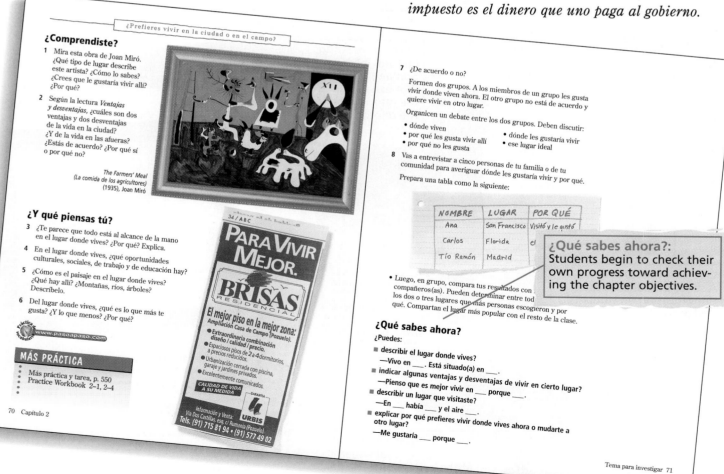

Álbum cultural (Preview, Present & Apply)

This section offers a unique perspective into understanding the richness of Hispanic cultures. Using a combination of photographs and captions, it asks students to think about culture in such a way as to develop real cross-cultural understanding and sensitivity. It also provides insights and useful information in answering the key chapter question.

Teaching ideas for the *Álbum cultural*

1 Have students answer the inductive questions as a whole-class or small-group activity. Write their responses on the board. This will activate background information, prompt and recycle related vocabulary, and show that, even in their own class, they will find a variety of customs and traditions.

2 Use the photos to encourage students to make observations about the cultural perspective. Have them describe the photos in Spanish.

3 Have students add any personal knowledge about the cultural topic. Ask Spanish speakers to share family traditions.

4 In small groups or as a whole class, have students answer the questions in the *Reacción personal*. This is your best opportunity for helping students understand their own culture and the beliefs and attitudes they have formed.

5 Ask students to use the cultural insight gained to reflect on their own culture. For example, ask students to provide examples of U.S. locations that are similar to those in the photo essay.

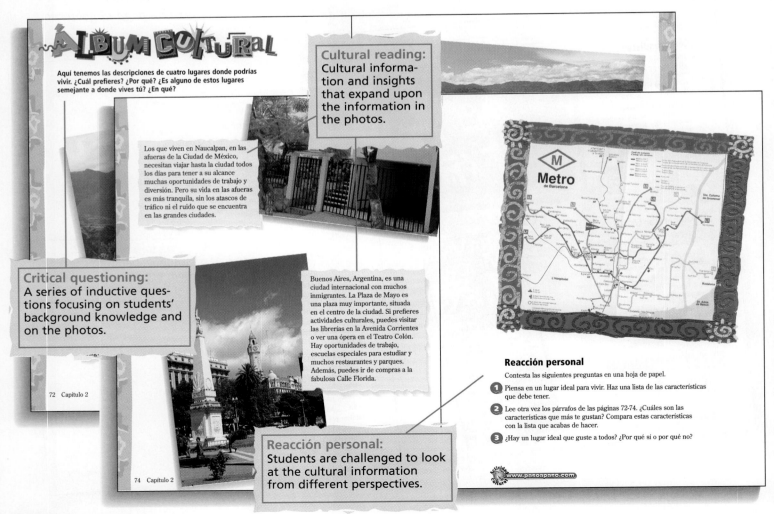

ÁLBUM CULTURAL

Aquí tenemos las descripciones de cuatro lugares donde podrías vivir. ¿Cuál prefieres? ¿Por qué? ¿Es alguno de estos lugares semejante a donde vives tú? ¿En qué?

Cultural reading: Cultural information and insights that expand upon the information in the photos.

Los que viven en Naucalpan, en las afueras de la Ciudad de México, necesitan viajar hasta la ciudad todos los días para tener a su alcance muchas oportunidades de trabajo y diversión. Pero su vida en las afueras es más tranquila, sin los atascos de tráfico ni el ruido que se encuentra en las grandes ciudades.

Critical questioning: A series of inductive questions focusing on students' background knowledge and on the photos.

Buenos Aires, Argentina, es una ciudad internacional con muchos inmigrantes. La Plaza de Mayo es una plaza muy importante, situada en el centro de la ciudad. Si prefieres actividades culturales, puedes visitar las librerías en la Avenida Corrientes o ver una ópera en el Teatro Colón. Hay oportunidades de trabajo, escuelas especiales para estudiar y muchos restaurantes y parques. Además, puedes ir de compras a la fabulosa Calle Florida.

72   Capítulo 2

74   Capítulo 2

Reacción personal: Students are challenged to look at the cultural information from different perspectives.

M Metro de Barcelona

Reacción personal

Contesta las siguientes preguntas en una hoja de papel.

1 Piensa en un lugar ideal para vivir. Haz una lista de las características que debe tener.

2 Lee otra vez los párrafos de las páginas 72-74. ¿Cuáles son las características que más te gustan? Compara estas características con la lista que acabas de hacer.

3 ¿Hay un lugar ideal que guste a todos? ¿Por qué sí o por qué no?

www.pasoapaso.com

Gramática en contexto *(Preview, Present & Practice)*

A realia-based reading provides comprehensible input for the new grammar. This gives students meaningful understanding of the structures by letting them intuit the rules. This inductive approach allows students to internalize and gain a deeper understanding of the grammar. Students were shown these structures in the vocabulary presentation and have practiced using them. They should not be uncomfortable with the structures themselves.

Teaching ideas for *Gramática en contexto*

1 Activate students' own experience by asking questions such as: How many students have studied Spanish architecture? Do any of them know about the Arabic influence in Spain?

2 Have students read the captions and study the pictures. Have them answer the questions individually or in pairs. Let them verify their answers with another pair or as a whole-class activity.

As students generate explanations, write them on the chalkboard along with examples from the reading.

Realia-based reading:
The reading combines cognates and previously learned vocabulary with the chapter's key grammar concepts.

Easy-to-understand grammar explanations:
Rules developed by the student are reinforced in easily understood explanations. Grammar terminology is kept to a minimum.

¿Prefieres vivir en la ciudad o en el campo?

Gramática en contexto

Mira esta guía turística de Sevilla, donde se describen algunas de sus principales obras de arquitectura. ¿Qué piensas que vas a encontrar en una guía como ésta?

Una Guía turística de Sevilla, España

Le añadieron a la torre una estatua llamada el Triunfo de la Fe. Esta estatua gira movida por el viento y por eso los sevillanos la llaman La Giralda.

La Torre del Oro, situada al lado del río Guadalquivir, se usaba en el siglo XIII para controlar el paso de los barcos que iban por el río. Originalmente estaba unida a otra torre similar que había en la orilla opuesta del río. Antiguamente la torre estaba decorada con azulejos dorados y de ahí viene su nombre.

La torre de la catedral, construida durante la ocupación árabe de Sevilla, era una maravilla. La torre original, que tenía 250 pies de altura, estaba rematada por cuatro globos. Después,

A Find the forms of the verbs *tener* and *estar* in the first description and of *usar* and *haber* in the second. What are their endings? Find the form of the verb *ser* in the first description and of *ir* in the second. Are these verbs used to describe the towers in the present or in the past?

B In the first description you find the word *construida*. The infinitive that is related to this adjective is *construir* ("to build," "to

construct"). In the tourist guide you also find the words *llamada* and *movida*. What do you think the related infinitives of these adjectives are? What do you think the adjective form that relates to *dormir* is?

C In the second description you find the words *decorada*, *situada*, and *dorados*. What do you think are the related infinitives of these adjectives? What do you think the adjective form that relates to *cerrar* is?

76 Capítulo 2

Repaso: El imperfecto

You have learned that we use the imperfect tense to talk about that happened repeatedly in the past. In English we often say or "would always" to express this idea.

Antes, mis parientes **vivían** y **trabajaban** en una granja.
*In the past, my relatives **used to live** and **work** on a farm.*

Remember that in Spanish we have *-ar*, *-er*, and *-ir* verbs. To form the imperfect tense we add to the stem one set of endings for *-ar* verbs and another set for both *-er* and *-ir* verbs. Here are all the forms of *estar*, *tener*, and *vivir* in the imperfect.

estar *(-ar)*		tener *(-er)*		vivir *(-ir)*	
estaba	estábamos	tenía	teníamos	vivía	vivíamos
estabas	estabais	tenías	teníais	vivías	vivíais
estaba	estaban	tenía	tenían	vivía	vivían

There are three irregular verbs in the imperfect. Here are their forms.

ir		ser		ver	
iba	íbamos	era	éramos	veía	veíamos
ibas	ibais	eras	erais	veías	veíais
iba	iban	era	eran	veía	veían

• Remember that we use only one form of *haber* in the imperfect tense, *había* ("there was / were, there used to be").

En el pasado, no **había** tanto tráfico en las calles.
Hace veinte años **había** menos autopistas.

¡NO OLVIDES!
Expressions such as *generalmente*, *a menudo*, *muchas veces*, *todos los días*, *siempre*, and *nunca* can cue us to use the imperfect.

Gramática en contexto 77

Inductive questions:
Students scan for information that leads them to produce their own explanation for the structures used.

In a truly thematic approach, grammar is tied to the communicative objectives. What is not relevant is not presented. Here, for example, students work with understanding and using the imperfect in describing things in the past. Students focus on content relevant to the theme. Students will, in later chapters, continue to work with the imperfect as related to other themes. This thematic approach builds in regular review and recycling as students are reminded of structures and vocabulary sets through the *¡No olvides!* feature. There are three to four grammar topics per chapter, each followed by a variety of activities.

Ahora lo sabes (Assess):
Students continue assessing their progress toward achieving the chapter objectives.

6 Túrnate con tu compañero(a) para formar frases sobre estos lugares. Usen elementos de las dos columnas.

el correo / cerrar *El correo está cerrado por la tarde.*

las escuelas
el correo cerca del centro
la cama
los centros comerciales
los lagos y ríos
las calles durante las fiestas

contaminar
decorar
animar
situar
hacer
aislar

¡NO OLVIDES!
You already know many adjectives that are actually past participles: *ocupado, callado, cansado, divorciado, ordenado, aburrido, divertido,* and many more.

Ahora lo sabes

¿Puedes:

■ hablar de acciones que ocurrían repetidamente en el pasado?
—Mis abuelos ___ en una granja en Kansas.

■ describir a personas, lugares y situaciones en el pasado?
—Las carreteras de la ciudad ___ muy peligrosas.

■ describir condiciones de personas y cosas en el presente y el pasado?
—Antes el agua ___ menos contaminada.

De compras en Caracas, Venezuela

Carrera de bicicletas en Texcoco (1938), Antonio M. Ruiz

Gramática en contexto 83

¿Prefieres vivir en la ciudad

3 Imagina que tu compañero(a) y tú visitaron esta ciudad. están tratando de recordar lo que vieron. Usen el dibujo preguntar y contestar.

aire / estar contaminado

A —*El aire estal*
B —*No, no esta*

a. puente de peaje / ser bastan
b. nosotros / tener que pagar
c. muchas personas / querer
d. peatones / caminar por el
e. haber / una policía en el
f. ciclistas / montar en bici
g. todos los ciclistas / ser
h. hacer frío / aquel día
i. calles / estar lleno(a) de ge...

80 Capítulo 2

¿Prefi

1 Haz una encuesta entre los era su vida cuando eran pec compañeros para hacer un

A —¡Juga
B —Sí, ju
o: N

jugar

a. ser

d. ir

Usando las resp escribiste, prep sobre tus comp

Tres estudiante al parque de d eran pequeños y yo teníamos peluche. Dos frutas y verd estudiante e

Padre e hijo jugando basqu...

78 Capítulo 2

Puntos de vista *(Apply)*

Puntos de vista is composed of three integrative sections: *Sopa de actividades, Para leer,* and *Para escribir.*

Para decir más:
These optional vocabulary suggestions enable students to personalize the activities.

Teaching ideas for *Sopa de actividades*

1 To complement what students have learned up to this point, use the video *Realidades.* (See pp. T50–T51 for details.) See the Teacher's Guide that accompanies the video program for teaching suggestions.

2 You may want to use different activities for different ability groupings. Better students might work together on Ex. 3 while others do either Ex. 1 or 2. Assess students on their effort, completion of the task, creativity, and ability to communicate rather than on accuracy.

3 Use activities for performance-based assessment. Refer to the section in the Assessment Program book on the development and use of rubrics to evaluate student performance.

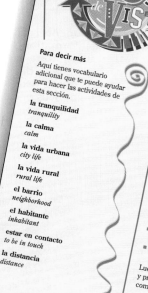

Para decir más

Aquí tienes vocabulario adicional que te puede ayudar para hacer las actividades de esta sección.

la tranquilidad
tranquility

la calma
calm

la vida urbana
city life

la vida rural
rural life

el barrio
neighborhood

el habitante
inhabitant

estar en contacto
to be in touch

la distancia
distance

¿Prefieres vivir en la ciudad o en el campo?

Esta sección te ofrece la oportunidad de combinar lo que aprendiste en este capítulo con lo que ya sabes para responder a la pregunta clave.

Sopa de actividades

1 En un montaje, muestra el lugar donde vives o donde te gustaría vivir. Usa fotos, tarjetas postales, o fotos de revistas y periódicos para ilustrarlo. Indica:

- cómo es
- dónde está situado
- cuántos habitantes tiene
- cuáles son los principales puntos de interés y dónde están situados
- cómo es el paisaje
- qué se ve y qué se oye allí
- cuáles son las ventajas y las desventajas de vivir allí
- cómo era antes y cómo es ahora

Luego prepara un informe oral y preséntalo a un grupo de compañeros(as).

Buenos Aires, Argentina

Caracas, Venezuela

2 Entre toda la clase van a escoger cinco lugares diferentes donde les gustaría vivir. Pueden ser: el campo, las montañas, las afueras y una o dos ciudades grandes. Cada uno de los lugares escogidos va a estar representado por un lugar de la clase.

Ve al lugar donde más te gustaría vivir. En tu nuevo grupo, prepara con tus compañeros(as) cinco frases para explicar por qué prefieren vivir en ese lugar. Por ejemplo:

El aire del campo es fresco y no está contaminado.

o:

Por la noche la ciudad está muy animada y puedes hacer muchas cosas.

Cada grupo lee sus frases a la clase y escribe las ideas de los demás grupos. Después deben decir lo que piensan de las ideas de los otros grupos. Por ejemplo:

Por un lado es divertido vivir en la ciudad porque está muy animada por la noche. Por otro lado, la ciudad puede ser muy violenta y peligrosa.

3 Prepara con los demás estudiantes de la clase una comparación entre la vida de tu ciudad o región en el pasado y en el presente. Primero, decidan qué categorías quieren comparar. Pueden incluir información sobre:

- la naturaleza de la región y el clima
- la población y el tamaño del área
- la economía (fábricas, trabajos, etc.)
- los lugares de interés y la vida social
- las fiestas celebradas por la comunidad

Después, pueden asignar cada categoría a un grupo diferente. Pueden buscar información en libros, periódicos y revistas; también pueden preguntar a personas mayores o buscar información en una sociedad histórica local. Preparen una presentación oral con fotos y dibujos. Por ejemplo:

Hace 50 años el agua del río no estaba contaminada, pero ahora no podemos nadar allí.

En el pasado había sólo una autopista. Ahora hay cinco.

84 Capítulo 2

Sopa de actividades 85

Sopa de actividades *(Apply)*:
Pick and choose from among these activities.

Para leer (Apply)

Students learn how to become efficient readers through a four-step process. Real comprehension is achieved through strategies, questions, and activities in the *Infórmate* and *Aplicación*. Students encounter unknown vocabulary, but gain confidence by realizing they don't need to know every word to read successfully.

Teaching ideas

1 *Antes de leer:* Use the questions to help students activate background knowledge and anticipate the story.

2 *Mira la lectura:* Have students work individually or in groups and report back to the class. Compare their answers to what they brainstormed in *Antes de leer.*

3 *Infórmate:* This can be done individually or in pairs.

4 *Aplicación:* Students will complete this activity successfully because of the careful structuring of the early steps in the reading process. You might have students work in pairs or small groups.

• Step 1
Antes de leer: Activates students' background knowledge to help them predict or anticipate.

• Step 2
Mira la lectura: Pre-reading section focusing on a specific reading strategy.

• Step 3
Infórmate: Students read for specific information or details, using strategies for dealing with difficult aspects of the text. Questions help focus on key information.

• Step 4
Aplicación: Students use what they have learned by applying it in a different way.

PUNTOS DE VISTA

Actividad cultural www.pasoapaso.com

Para leer

Antes de leer

STRATEGY ▸ Using titles and pictures to predict

Esta selección trata de las visitas que hace una joven a un pueblo español. ¿De qué temas se va a tratar? Usa las fotos como ayuda para añadir, por lo menos, dos más a esta lista.

A. el tiempo   B. la gente

Mira la lectura

STRATEGY ▸ Skimming

Lee la selección rápidamente sólo para ver cuáles de los temas de tu lista están en la selección. Compara los resultados con los de un(a) compañero(a).

Benvinguts a Cálig

Cuando Patricia y su familia llegaron a su casa de Cálig en la provincia de Castellón el verano pasado, había un letrero en la puerta que decía: *Benvinguts* a Cálig. Ella estaba tan contenta de estar otra vez en este pequeño pueblo agrícola de España que quería correr por el pueblo saludando a todos. Después de cinco veranos ella se sentía muy aceptada.

Cálig es un lugar ideal para las vacaciones. Han pasado ya cinco veranos allí. Es un pueblo tranquilo y sin contaminación, situado cerca del mar y la montaña. No hay miedo de robos ni de atracos como en las grandes ciudades. La gente los trata muy bien en la calle y en las pequeñas tiendas donde hacen sus compras. Y por supuesto, toda la familia participa en las fiestas tradicionales del pueblo.

Al principio Patricia no estaba contenta. Tenía once años y echaba de menos a sus amigas de los Estados Unidos. No podía ir con ellas a los grandes centros comerciales a comprar como solía hacer los sábados. Además no hablaba mucho español y en este pueblo hablaban también valenciano, una lengua que ella no comprendía. Quería volver a su casa en St. Louis, Missouri, y lo más pronto posible.

Con los años fue teniendo cada vez más amigos caligenses. Salía con ellos todas las tardes, primero a la piscina, después a tomar refrescos y charlar. Por la noche volvían a salir después de cenar. A veces iban a una discoteca para bailar. Algunas noches simplemente paseaban por las calles estrechas de este pueblo medieval.

Algunos días Patricia hacía excursiones con su familia a los pueblos cercanos de la montaña, pueblos mejor conservados, con casas hechas de piedra, una iglesia vieja y una ermita en las afueras. Les gustaban mucho las colinas rocosas de la montaña y los campos de olivos y algarrobos. Otros días pasaban la tarde en la playa. Aunque le agradaban a Patricia esas excursiones con sus padres, ella prefería estar con los amigos, sobre todo con un tal David, un chico muy guapo y muy divertido.

Cuando llegó el momento de salir para los Estados Unidos, ella se sentía muy triste porque no quería dejar a sus amigos. Ya se había acostumbrado tanto a la vida del pueblo que la vida de la ciudad le parecía muy sofocante. No podría ir a pie a las tiendas ni saludar a todos en la calle como lo hacía en Cálig. No podría quedarse en la calle con los amigos hasta la medianoche. Además iba a echar mucho de menos la comida: el pan con tomate, la paella, el brazo gitano.† Ahora ella pasa el invierno en St. Louis soñando con el verano en Cálig.

* *Benvinguts* Palabra valenciana que quiere decir ¡Bienvenidos!

† *brazo gitano* Pastel hecho de bizcocho *(sponge cake)* con relleno de crema o nata *(whipped cream).*

86 Capítulo 2

De paseo por las calles de Cálig

Un mercado de Cálig

Infórmate

STRATEGY ▸ Identifying supporting details

Ahora lee la selección con cuidado.

1 Describe la actitud de Patricia hacia Cálig (a) después de un año de visitar el pueblo, (b) después de dos o tres años y (c) después de cinco años. Luego muéstrale a un(a) compañero(a) la evidencia del texto para justificar tu opinión.

2 Imagina que eres un(a) joven caligense y estás pasando un verano en St. Louis u otra ciudad grande de los Estados Unidos. Escribe una carta breve a tu familia explicándoles lo que sientes.

Una vista de Cálig desde la carretera

Aplicación

En grupo hagan un cartel turístico para una ciudad grande o para un pueblo pequeño de un país hispano. Incluyan las características más atractivas del lugar. Después, escojan el lugar que la clase prefiere visitar.

Para leer 87

Para escribir (Apply)

As with reading, students develop effective writing through a process approach consistent with the way they are learning to write in their English classes. It also provides a strategy or model for writing independently. Each writing task provides a creative, personalized opportunity to expand the chapter theme.

> **• Step 1**
> Pre-writing questions have students think about the topic, generate needed language, and organize their ideas. They then write the first draft.

> **• Steps 2 & 3**
> Through peer review students gain insights into needed revisions or clarifications for preparing the final draft.

Teaching ideas

1 This may be done in class or as homework. Students can work individually, in pairs, or in small groups to brainstorm the topic and needed vocabulary. Be sure to review the model interviews that accompany the photographs. They can jot down answers to the questions and share them with other students. They then use the questions and responses as a starting point for writing their first draft. Have students skip lines on the first draft so that there is room for comments during the peer review.

2 Have students share their first draft with one or more partners. Peer reviewers should check for thoroughness and comprehensibility, as well as for errors in spelling, grammar, and punctuation. (Each reviewer should say at least one good thing about the writing sample.)

3 Students may want to include final drafts in their writing portfolios.

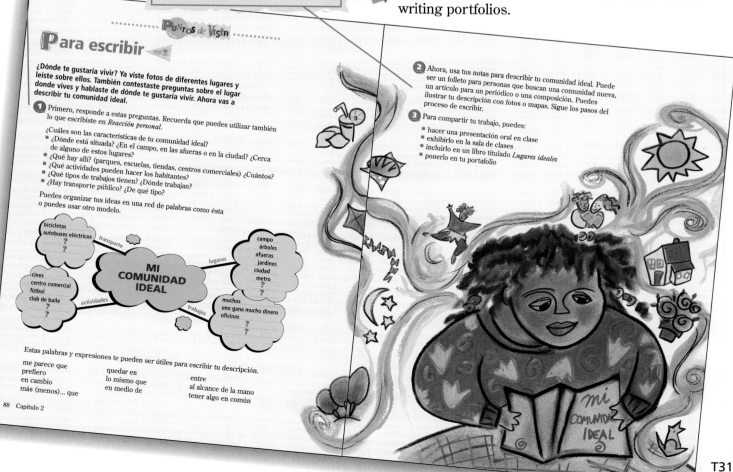

Repaso: ¿Lo sabes bien? (Apply, Assess & Summarize)

In this section students practice tasks similar to those they will encounter on the *Examen de habilidades.* They focus on the chapter objectives and show what they can do with the language.

Teaching ideas

1 Point out how this pre-test and the vocabulary on the following page prepare for the *Examen de habilidades.*

2 Do this as a whole-class activity or have pairs complete the sections at home and then compare their responses with those of a partner. Or, with a partner, they can work through each section in class and then compare their answers with those of another pair.

3 Students who do well should feel confident about performing well on the test. Those having difficulty will know where they need to focus attention as they study for the test.

Resumen del vocabulario (*Summarize*)

This section organizes the chapter vocabulary to reflect how it can be used to meet the communicative objectives. The objectives were stated in the chapter overview, and students have been given regular opportunities to assess their progress in the *¿Qué sabes ahora?, Ahora lo sabes,* and *Repaso: ¿Lo sabes bien?*

CAPÍTULO 2

Repaso ¿Lo sabes bien?

Esta sección te ayudará a prepararte para el examen de habilidades, donde tendrás que hacer tareas semejantes.

Listening
¿Puedes entender una descripción de cómo es la vida en un lugar? Escucha mientras el (la) profesor(a) lee un ejemplo semejante al que vas a oír en el examen. ¿Dónde vive esta persona? ¿Cómo lo sabes? ¿Dónde prefiere vivir? ¿Por qué no vive allí?

Reading
¿Puedes leer un anuncio sobre un lugar de vacaciones y fijarte bien en los detalles para saber de qué lugar se trata?

¡NO PIERDA LA OPORTUNIDAD DE ENCONTRAR EL PARAÍSO EN LA TIERRA! En Valle Azul, rodeado de montañas, puede encontrar el aire puro y la tranquilidad que busca. Sin coches, ni ruido, ni contaminación. Y por la noche ¡disfrute de sus calles estrechas y silenciosas!

Writing
¿Puedes escribir un párrafo para tu clase de español sobre el lugar donde vivías de niño(a)? Aquí tienes un ejemplo:

Recuerdo mucho la casa en donde vivía cuando era niño. Tenía una cerca blanca y un jardín con flores muy bonitas. Estaba situada cerca de un sendero de árboles que terminaba en el bosque. El aire era puro y no estaba contaminado. Aunque vivía aislada y lejos de la ciudad, era feliz con mis amigos, los animalitos del campo y los pájaros.

Culture
¿Puedes comparar tu vida con la de otros jóvenes que viven en el Altiplano de Perú?

Un grupo de personas en el Altiplano peruano

Speaking
Con un(a) compañero(a), ¿puedes comparar la vida de la ciudad con la vida del campo? Aquí tienes un ejemplo:

A —*¿Qué prefieres, vivir en la ciudad o en el campo?*
B —*Me gusta más la ciudad porque todo está al alcance de la mano y tiene más centros de diversiones. ¿Y a ti?*
A —*Creo que me gusta más vivir en el campo. Hay menos contaminación, menos tráfico y menos ruido.*
B —*Sí, pero en el campo hay menos oportunidades de trabajo, ¿no?*

www.pasoapaso.com

90 Capítulo 2

Teaching ideas

1 Have pairs review the vocabulary. They might make up a sentence or dialogue in each category. For example, *Hay contaminación en muchas ciudades* or:
> —¿*Vivías en una granja?*
> —*No, nunca vivía allí.*

2 If students have created flashcards, have them organize these according to the communicative categories.

3 Have students quiz each other using the list in the book or their flashcards. Ask them to indicate any words their partner had trouble with by writing them on a sheet of paper or placing a check on the flashcard. This will focus their test preparation on problem areas.

Assessment options

1 The *Prueba cumulativa* is a prochievement instrument that focuses on students' knowledge of the chapter vocabulary and grammar in a communicative context.

2 The *Examen de habilidades* is a proficiency-oriented instrument that focuses on what students can do with the language in a real-world context.

3 The Test Generator provides a test bank of multiple-choice questions to which you can add your own questions.

At this point, you may elect to use one of the optional readings:

Capítulo 1: El valor de las opiniones

Capítulo 2: El vendedor de globos

Capítulo 3: La persistencia de la memoria: El arte viviente

Capítulo 4: La sexta tele

Capítulo 5: Quetzal no muere nunca

Capítulo 6: Una carta a Dios / Apocalipsis

Capítulo 7: La pobreza

Capítulo 8: La herencia

Capítulo 9: Naranjas

Capítulo 10: Espuma y nada más

Capítulo 11: Balada de los dos abuelos

Capítulo 12: Las salamandras

Resumen del vocabulario

Usa el vocabulario de este capítulo para:
- responder a la pregunta clave: ¿Prefieres vivir en la ciudad o en el campo?
- describir cómo es la vida en un lugar
- comparar la vida de antes con la vida de ahora
- indicar las ventajas y las desventajas de vivir en cierto lugar

para describir cómo es la vida en la ciudad
el atasco
el /la ciclista
la contaminación
el peatón, *pl.* los peatones
la población
la presión, *pl.* las presiones
el rascacielos, *pl.* los rascacielos
el ruido

para describir cómo es la vida en el campo
cultivar
la granja
idealizado, -a
el paisaje
rural

para describir cómo es la vida en las afueras
las afueras, *pl.*
la cerca
el jardín, *pl.* los jardines

para hablar de las ventajas y desventajas de los tres
abundante
aislado, -a
animado, -a
bello, -a
contribuir *(i → y)*
conveniente
decidir
diario, -a
escaparse
el espacio
los impuestos, *pl.*
lleno, -a de gente
ofrecer *(c → zc)*
la oportunidad
peligroso, -a
rápido, -a
sano, -a
seguro, -a
situado, -a
tardar (en)

para hablar sobre cómo viajamos a diario
la acera
la autopista
el camino
el peaje
el puente
el sendero

otras palabras y expresiones útiles
al alcance de la mano
diferente
oír
por un lado
por otro lado
sin embargo
¡Una maravilla!
venir *(e → ie)*
    (yo) vengo
    (tú) vienes

Resumen 91

USING THE TEACHER'S EDITION

This Teacher's Edition provides all the support needed to work with the wide range of students in today's Spanish classes.

Each teacher chapter begins with a spread that provides organizational and cultural information for instructional planning.

Additional information and insight into the chapter's cultural theme

List of the chapter communication, culture, and grammar objectives

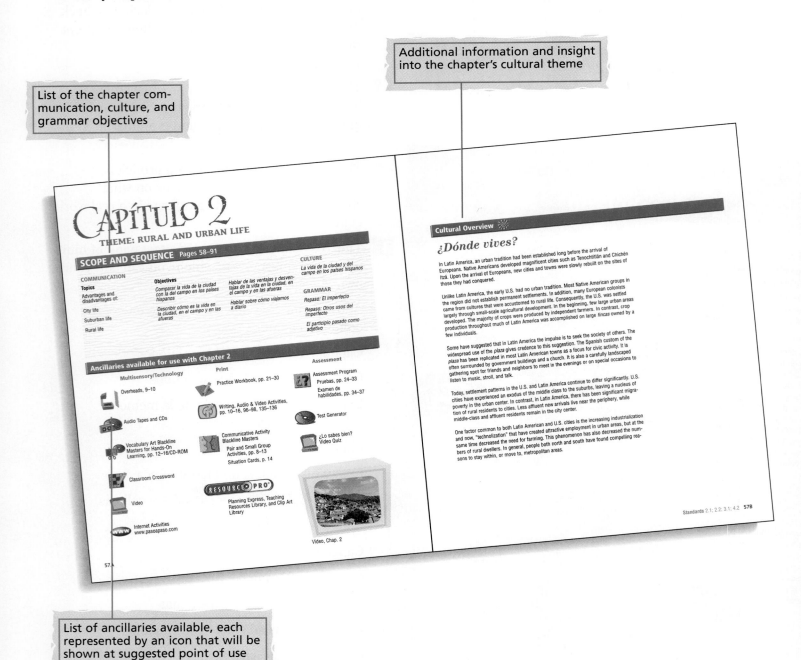

List of ancillaries available, each represented by an icon that will be shown at suggested point of use

This Teacher's Edition is organized to provide for maximum ease of use. The student page is slightly reduced. Teacher notes appear regularly in the same place on the page.

Sidenotes are organized around the five-step pedagogical model used throughout *PASO A PASO:*

- ■ **Introduce / Preview**
- ■ **Present**
- ■ **Practice**
- ■ **Apply**
- ■ **Summarize / Assess**

Notes provide answers, teaching suggestions, ancillary cross-references, recycling references, and other useful information.

Previously taught vocabulary sets that are re-entered in the chapter

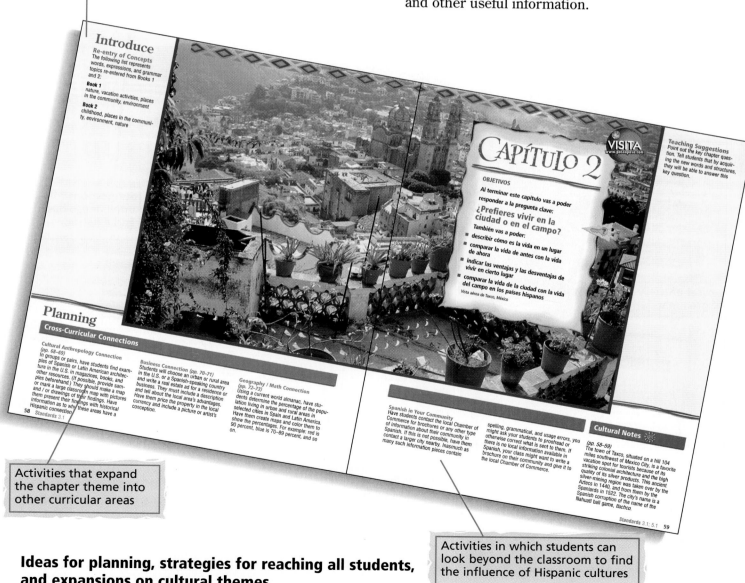

Introduce

Re-entry of Concepts
The following list represents words, expressions, and grammar topics re-entered from Books 1 and 2:

Book 1
nature, vacation activities, places in the community, environment

Book 2
childhood, places in the community, environment, nature

Planning

Cross-Curricular Connections

Cultural Anthropology Connection
(pp. 68–69)
In groups or pairs, have students find examples of Spanish or Latin American architecture in the U.S. in magazines, books, and other resources. (If possible, provide samples beforehand.) They should make a map or mark a large classroom map with pictures and / or drawings of their findings. Have them present their findings. Have information as to why these areas have a Hispanic connection.
58 Standards 3.1

Business Connection (pp. 70–71)
Students will choose an urban or rural area in the U.S. or a Spanish-speaking country and write a real estate ad for a residence or business. They must include a description and tell about the local area's advantages. Have them price the property in the local currency and include a picture or artist's conception.

Geography / Math Connection
(pp. 72–73)
Using a current world almanac, have students determine the percentage of the population living in urban and rural areas in selected cities in Spain and Latin America. Have them create maps and color them to show the percentages. For example: red is 90 percent, blue is 70–89 percent, and so on.

CAPÍTULO 2

VISITA
www.pasoapaso.com

OBJETIVOS
Al terminar este capítulo vas a poder responder a la pregunta clave:
¿Prefieres vivir en la ciudad o en el campo?
También vas a poder:

■ describir cómo es la vida en un lugar

■ comparar la vida de antes con la vida de ahora

■ indicar las ventajas y las desventajas de vivir en cierto lugar

■ comparar la vida de la ciudad con la vida del campo en los países hispanos
Vista aérea de Taxco, México

Teaching Suggestions
Point out the key chapter question. Tell students that by acquiring the new words and structures, they will be able to answer this key question.

Spanish in Your Community
Have students contact the local Chamber of Commerce for brochures or any other type of information about their community in Spanish. If this is not possible, have them contact a larger city nearby. Inasmuch as many such information pieces contain spelling, grammatical, and usage errors, you might ask your students to proofread or otherwise correct what is sent to them. If there is no local information available in Spanish, your class might want to write a brochure on their community and give it to the local Chamber of Commerce.

Cultural Notes ☀
(pp. 58–59)
The town of Taxco, situated on a hill 104 miles southwest of Mexico City, is a favorite vacation spot for tourists because of its striking colonial architecture and the high quality of its silver products. This ancient silver-mining region was taken over by the Aztecs in 1440, and from them by the Spaniards in 1522. The city's name is a Spanish corruption of the name of the Nahuatl ball game, *tlachco.*

Standards 3.1; 5.1 59

Activities that expand the chapter theme into other curricular areas

Activities in which students can look beyond the classroom to find the influence of Hispanic cultures

Ideas for planning, strategies for reaching all students, and expansions on cultural themes

References to help with planning and instruction

Chapter theme

Communicative objectives

Icons for ancillary references

Ideas for recycling previous-ly taught material

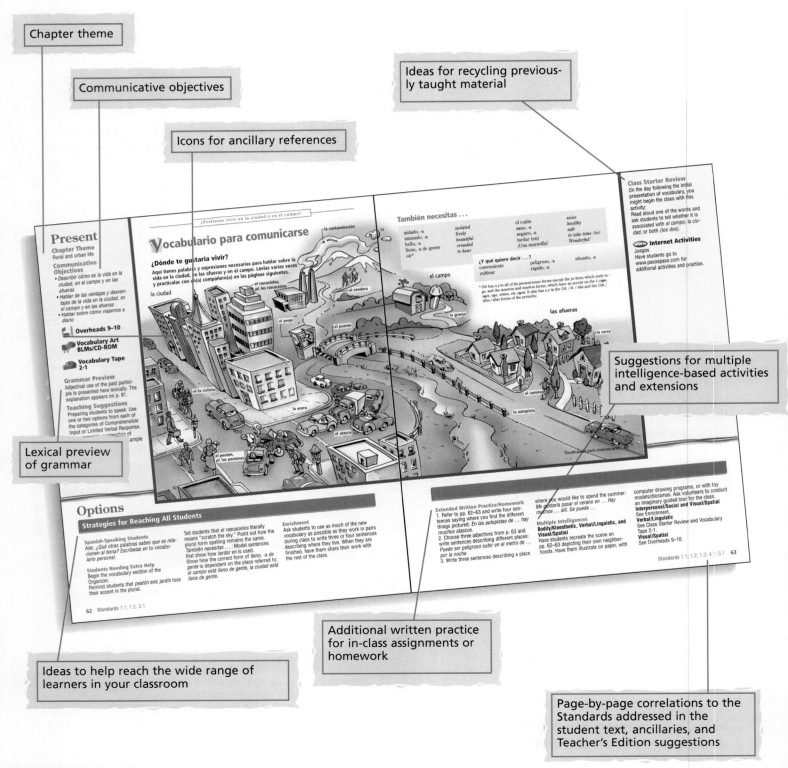

Suggestions for multiple intelligence-based activities and extensions

Lexical preview of grammar

Ideas to help reach the wide range of learners in your classroom

Additional written practice for in-class assignments or homework

Page-by-page correlations to the Standards addressed in the student text, ancillaries, and Teacher's Edition suggestions

CLASSROOM MANAGEMENT AND LESSON PLANS

PASO A PASO 3 has been carefully developed to provide the instructional materials for one school year. The authors had as a goal the development of a realistically paced and easy-to-manage program that would relieve teacher and student frustration. There is flexibility and choice among the textbook activities and ancillaries. To help work with the wide variety of learners in your classroom, *PASO A PASO 3* offers unprecedented support on every page. We developed the Scope and Sequence to give students the tools needed to communicate about their interests. Thematic chapter organization allows for real integration of vocabulary, grammar, and culture, while avoiding unneeded grammatical content.

We present vocabulary in logical sets and, when possible, with visuals. Research shows that both of these approaches lead to more efficient and more permanent learning. Above all, lexical and contextual introduction of grammar allows students to learn structures in a truly natural way. *Tendría* is not "the first-person singular conditional of the verb *tener*," but, quite simply, "I would have"—a concept that presents no difficulty. (This is particularly true for students who neither know nor care that "I would have" is a conditional-tense form of the verb "to have.")

We would urge you to allow this process to unfold. Avoid explanations in the vocabulary section. Allow students to use the words naturally. By the time they reach the explanations they will feel confident in their ability to use the language.

Management and Lesson Plans for the Traditional Class Schedule

Teachers working in a traditional class schedule (meeting daily for approximately 40–50 minutes) should complete *PASO A PASO 3* in one year.

Pacing for *Pasodoble*

The *Pasodoble* contains 14 theme-based review sections that recycle the vocabulary and grammar of Chapters 1–12 of *PASO A PASO 2*. Study the overview of *Pasodoble* on pages 1A–B to see the thematic review, recycling, and ancillary support. We suggest that you incorporate the review gradually into the first few weeks of instruction. Spend the first three days of school on it, and then move into Chapter 1. Return to *Pasodoble* sections throughout the first chapter (or the first few chapters) as a warm-up activity. You will find that students remember the key concepts and that the *Pasodoble*'s integrated review will help them move easily into *PASO A PASO 3*.

Pacing for Chapters 1–12

We suggest that approximately 11–13 instructional days be spent on each chapter, including assessment. This time will vary based upon the amount of instructional time and the range of students in the class.

As you begin teaching with *PASO A PASO 3,* you will sense a rhythm, a flow within each chapter that helps students move smoothly and successfully. The thematic integration and spiraling within a chapter, the extensive use of context and comprehensible input for vocabulary and grammar, the inductive questioning that leads to real understanding, and the recycling of previously taught material are part of the carefully thought-out chapter design. You should be able to move quickly through the chapters in the suggested time period.

The following Lesson Plans show how Chapter 1 might be organized for instruction. Feel free to adapt these sample lessons to your teaching style, students, and schedule. As you become more familiar with the program, you will find many more ways to use all of the *PASO A PASO* components.

Pasodoble
Capítulo 1 ¿Quién soy yo en realidad?

	Instructional Process	Tasks/Activities	Components
Day # 1	Preview	Explanation of *Pasodoble* review	Text, p. 1
	Presentation/Practice	*Pasodoble* review	Text, pp. 2–3
	Practice	Vocabulary review and practice	Level 2 Overheads 6–7, 13–14
	Application	Writing Activity	WAVA: Writing Activity PD-A
	Closing/Assignments	Review day's objectives and tasks to be done Preview Day #2	Practice Wkbk. PD-1, PD-2
Day # 2	Introduction/Review	Review homework	Practice Wkbk. PD-1, PD-2
	Presentation/Practice	*Pasodoble* review Vocabulary review	Text, pp. 4–5 Level 2 Vocabulary Art BLMs pp. 13–15 or Communicative Activity BLMs 2-1, 2-2, 2-3
	Application	*Pasodoble* review	Text, pp. 8–9
	Closing/Assignments	Review day's objectives and tasks to be done Preview Day #3	Text, p. 5, Writing Extensions

	Instructional Process	Tasks/Activities	Components
Day # 3	Introduction/Review	Review homework	Text, p. 5
	Presentation/Practice	*Pasodoble* review Vocabulary review	Text, p. 10 Level 2 Overheads 21–24 or Vocabulary Art BLMs, pp. 23–27
	Application	Writing Activity	WAVA: Writing Activity PD-B
	Closing/Assignments	Review day's objectives and tasks to be done Preview Day #4	Practice Wkbk. PD-4
Day # 4	Introduction/Review	Review homework	Practice Wkbk. PD-4
	Presentation/Practice	*Pasodoble* review Vocabulary review	Text, pp. 12–13 Level 2 Overheads 35–38 or Communicative Activity BLMs 7-1
	Presentation	*Capítulo 1* Cultural Overview, Objectives	Text, pp. 25B–27
	Presentation/Practice	*Anticipación*	Text, pp. 28–29
	Closing/Assignments	Review day's objectives and tasks to be done Preview Day #5	WAVA: Writing Activity PD-D
Day # 5	Introduction/Review	Review homework Audio Activities	WAVA: Writing Activity PD-D WAVA: Audio Activities P.1–P.2
	Presentation	Vocabulary presentation / Input	Text, p. 30 Overhead 7 Vocabulary Art BLMs
	Practice	Paired practice	Text, p. 32
	Presentation	*También necesitas …*	Text, p. 31
	Closing/Assignments	Review day's objectives and tasks to be done Preview Day #6	Vocabulary Art BLMs Text, p. 35, *¿Y qué piensas tú?* 9–10

	Instructional Process	Tasks/Activities	Components
Day # 6	Introduction/Review	Vocabulary Review Class Starter Review Pronunciation Review Review homework	Vocabulary Art BLMs Text, p. 31 Pronunciation Tape 1-1 Text, p. 35
	Practice	Audio Activity	WAVA: Audio Activity P.3
	Practice	Paired practice	Text, pp. 33–34
	Closing/Assignments	Review day's objectives and tasks to be done Preview Day #7	Text, p. 35, *¿Y qué piensas tú?* 1–8
Day # 7	Introduction/Review	Review homework Review vocabulary	Text, p. 35 Text, pp. 30–31
	Presentation/Practice	*Pasodoble* review Vocabulary review	Text, pp. 6–7 Level 2 Overheads 16–17 or Communicative Activity BLMs 5-2
	Application	Writing Activities	WAVA: Writing Activities 1-A, 1-B
	Closing/Assignments	Review day's objectives and tasks to be done Preview Day #8	Practice Wkbk. 1-1, 1-2
Day # 8	Introduction/Review	Review homework	Practice Wkbk. 1-1, 1-2
	Practice	Communicative Activity	Communicative Activity BLMs 1-1
	Application	Audio Activity	WAVA: Audio Activity 1.1
	Assessment	Quiz	Prueba 1-1
	Closing/Assignments	Review day's objectives and tasks to be done Preview Day #9	Text, pp. 30–31

	Instructional Process	Tasks/Activities	Components
Day # 9	Assessment	Quiz	*Prueba* 1-2
	Presentation/Practice	*Gramática en contexto*	Text, pp. 44–45 Overhead 8
	Practice	Paired practice Review grammar	Text, p. 45 Level 1 Communicative Activity BLMs 13-2
	Presentation	Vocabulary presentation / Input	Text, pp. 36–37
	Closing/Assignments	Review day's objectives and tasks to be done Preview Day #10	Practice Wkbk. 1-3, 1-5
Day # 10	Introduction/Review	Review vocabulary Class Starter Review	Text, pp. 36–37 Text, p. 37
	Review	Pronunciation Review Review homework	Pronunciation Tape 1-2 Practice Wkbk. 1-3, 1-5
	Practice	*¿Comprendiste?, ¿Y qué piensas tú?*	Text, p. 38
	Application	Writing Activities	WAVA: Writing Activities 1-C, 1-D
	Closing/Assignments	Review day's objectives and tasks to be done Preview Day #11	Practice Wkbk. 1-4
Day # 11	Introduction/Review	Review homework	Practice Wkbk. 1-4
	Assessment	Quizzes	*Pruebas* 1-3, 1-5
	Presentation/Practice	*Gramática en contexto* Paired practice	Text, p. 46 Text, p. 47
	Application	Using Documents Self-Assessment	Text, p. 39 Text, p. 39, *¿Qué sabes ahora?*
	Closing/Assignments	Review day's objectives and tasks to be done Preview Day #12	

	Instructional Process	Tasks/Activities	Components
Day # 12	Assessment	Quizzes	*Pruebas* 1-4, 1-6
	Application	Audio Activity	WAVA: Audio Activity 1.2
	Practice	Paired practice	Text, p. 48
	Practice	Communicative Activity	Communicative Activity BLMs 1-3
	Closing/Assignments	Review day's objectives and tasks to be done Preview Day #13	Practice Wkbk. 1-6, 1-7
Day # 13	Introduction/Review	Review homework	Practice Wkbk. 1-6, 1-7
	Presentation/Practice	*Álbum cultural*	Text, pp. 40–43
	Presentation/Practice	*Gramática en contexto* Paired practice	Text, p. 48 Text, p. 49
	Closing/Assignments	Review day's objectives and tasks to be done Preview Day #14	Practice Wkbk. 1-8, 1-9
Day # 14	Introduction/Review	Review homework	Practice Wkbk. 1-8, 1-9
	Practice	Communicative Activity Writing Activities	Communicative Activity BLMs 1-2 WAVA: Writing Activities 1-E, 1-F
	Assessment	Quizzes	*Pruebas* 1-7, 1-8
	Closing/Assignments	Review day's objectives and tasks to be done Preview Day #15	Practice Wkbk. Organizer, p. 20
Day # 15	Introduction/Review	Review homework	Practice Wkbk. Organizer, p. 20
	Application	*Puntos de vista*	Text, pp. 50–51
	Presentation	*Para escribir*	Text, pp. 54–55
	Closing/Assignments	Review day's objectives and tasks to be done Preview Day #16	Text, p. 54, Exs. 1–2

	Instructional Process	Tasks/Activities	Components
Day # 16	Introduction/Review	Review homework Peer editing	Text, p. 54
	Presentation/Practice	*Para leer*	Text, pp. 52–53
	Application	Video Activity	*Realidades,* Episode 1 WAVA: Video Activities, pp. 133–134, A–C
	Closing/Assignments	Review day's objectives and tasks to be done Preview Day #17	Text, p. 54, *Para escribir*
Day # 17	Introduction/Review	Display homework	Text, p. 54
	Application	Choose from: *Actividades en grupo* Audio Activities Writing Activities	Communicative Activity BLMs 1-4 WAVA: Audio Activities 1.4–1.5 WAVA: Writing Activities 1-G, 1-H
	Application	*Repaso: ¿Lo sabes bien?*	Text, p. 56
	Closing/Assignments	Review for Chapter Test	
Day # 18	Assessment	Chapter Test	Assessment Program: Choose from *Prueba cumulativa* or *Examen de habilidades* (or) Use components such as: Situation Cards, Communicative Activity BLMs, p. 7; Test Generator
	Presentation/Practice	Choose from: *Pasodoble* *Fondo literario*	Text, p. 11 Text, pp. 430–435
	Closing/Assignments	Preview Day #1 of *Capítulo 2*	Text, pp. 58–59

Management and Lesson Plans for the Block Schedule

PASO A PASO is ideal for the block schedule. The theme-based approach in each chapter allows for a more holistic presentation of content. Since the vocabulary, grammar, and culture are based upon the theme and recycle naturally throughout the chapter, there is flexibility in the way the material can be presented. The wide range of activities in the student book and the many ancillary components allow for individual, paired, and small group activities, as well as for the incorporation of different learning modalities. A variety of formal and informal assessment options are provided.

For teachers using the block schedule (85–90 minutes of instructional time), you should comfortably reach between Chapters 10–12 in one block.

Do not spend more than two days on the *Pasodoble* review. While students will need to recognize the vocabulary through listening and reading, they will not need spelling mastery at this point. Use this chapter to let students learn the beginning communication tools, cultural insights, and learning strategies. All of the concepts presented will be recycled throughout the text.

We suggest approximately 6–8 instructional days for each chapter. Start planning by looking at the year as a whole. Determine how many class periods you will have for instruction and how these are grouped around grading periods, testing, and vacation. Determine what your goals will be and then develop a general plan for the entire year using the following sample lesson plans as a guide. To develop a daily lesson plan, you might want to divide each day into a five- or six-step instructional sequence: Introduction/Review; Preview/Presentation; Practice; Application; Assessment; and Closing/Assignments. The amount of time devoted to each and how it is sequenced each day will vary based upon daily goals. You will notice variations in these sample plans. Feel free to adapt them to your teaching style, students, and class schedule. As you become more familiar with the program, you will find many more ways to use all of the *PASO A PASO* components.

Pasodoble
Capítulo 1 ¿Quién soy yo en realidad?

	Instructional Process	Tasks/Activities	Components
Day # 1	Preview	Explanation of *Pasodoble* review	Text, p. 1
	Presentation/Practice	*Pasodoble* review	Text, pp. 2–3
	Practice	Vocabulary review and practice	Level 2 Overheads 6–7, 13–14
	Presentation/Practice	*Pasodoble* review Vocabulary review	Text, pp. 4–5 Level 2 Vocabulary Art BLMs, pp. 13–15
	Application	Writing Activity	WAVA: Writing Activity PD-A
	Closing/Assignments	Review day's objectives and tasks to be done Preview Day #2	Practice Wkbk. PD-1, PD-2

	Instructional Process	Tasks/Activities	Components
Day # 2	Introduction/Review	*Pasodoble* review Review homework	Text, pp. 8–9 Practice Wkbk. PD-1, PD-2
	Presentation/Practice	*Pasodoble* review Vocabulary review	Text, p. 10 Level 2 Overheads 21–24 or Vocabulary Art BLMs pp. 23–27
	Application	Writing Activity	WAVA: Writing Activity PD-B
	Presentation/Practice	*Pasodoble* review Vocabulary review	Text, pp. 12–13 Level 2 Overheads 35–38 or Communicative Activity BLMs 7-1
	Application	Writing Activity	WAVA: Writing Activity PD-D
	Presentation	*Capítulo 1* Cultural Overview, Objectives *Anticipación*	Text, pp. 25B–27 Text, pp. 28–29
	Closing/Assignments	Review day's objectives and tasks to be done Preview Day #3	Practice Wkbk. PD-4
Day # 3	Introduction/Review	Audio Activities Review homework	WAVA: Audio Activities P.1–P.2 Practice Wkbk. PD-4
	Presentation	Vocabulary presentation / Input	Text, p. 30 Overhead 7 Vocabulary Art BLMs
	Practice	Paired practice	Text, p. 32
	Presentation	*También necesitas …*	Text, p. 31
	Practice	Paired practice	Text, p. 33
	Closing/Assignments	Review day's objectives and tasks to be done Preview Day #4	Vocabulary Art BLMs Text, p. 35, *¿Y qué piensas tú?* 9–10

	Instructional Process	Tasks/Activities	Components
Day # 4	Introduction/Review	Audio Activity Class Starter Review Vocabulary Review Pronunciation Review Review homework	WAVA: Audio Activity P.3 Text, p. 31 Vocabulary Art BLMs Pronunciation Tape 1-1 Text, p. 35
	Presentation/Practice	*Pasodoble* review Vocabulary review	Text, pp. 6–7 Level 2 Overheads 16–17 or Communicative Activity BLMs 5-2
	Practice	Paired practice	Text, pp. 34–35
	Practice	*¿Y qué piensas tú?*	Text, p. 35, 1–8
	Application	Writing Activities	WAVA: Writing Activities 1-A, 1-B
	Closing/Assignments	Review day's objectives and tasks to be done Preview Day #5	Practice Wkbk. 1-1, 1-2
Day # 5	Introduction/Review	Review homework Review vocabulary	Practice Wkbk. 1-1, 1-2 Text, pp. 30–31
	Practice	Communicative Activity	Communicative Activity BLMs 1-1
	Application	Audio Activity	WAVA: Audio Activity 1.1
	Assessment	Quiz	*Prueba* 1-1
	Presentation/Practice	*Gramática en contexto* Paired practice	Overhead 8 Text, pp. 44–45
	Closing/Assignments	Review day's objectives Assign vocabulary for quiz Preview Day #6	Practice Wkbk. 1-5
Day # 6	Assessment	Quiz	*Prueba* 1-2
	Introduction/Review	Review homework Review grammar	Practice Wkbk. 1-5 Level 1 Communicative Activity BLMs 13-2
	Presentation	Vocabulary presentation / Input	Text, pp. 36–37
	Practice	*¿Comprendiste?* *¿Y qué piensas tú?*	Text, p. 38
	Closing	Review day's objectives and tasks to be done Preview Day #7	Practice Wkbk. 1-3, 1-4

	Instructional Process	Tasks/Activities	Components
Day # 7	Introduction/Review	Vocabulary Review Class Starter Review Pronunciation Review Review homework	Text, pp. 36–37 Text, p. 37 Pronunciation Tape 1-2 Practice Wkbk. 1-3, 1-4
	Practice	Writing Activities	WAVA: Writing Activities 1-C, 1-D
	Present/Practice	*Gramática en contexto* Paired practice	Text, p. 46 Text, p. 47
	Application	Audio Activity Using Documents Self-Assessment	WAVA: Audio Activity 1.2 Text, p. 39 Text, p. 39, *¿Qué sabes ahora?*
	Assessment	Quizzes	*Pruebas* 1-3, 1-5
	Closing/Assignments	Review day's objectives and tasks to be done Preview Day #8	Practice Wkbk. 1-6, 1-7
Day # 8	Introduction/Review	Review homework Paired practice	Practice Wkbk. 1-6, 1-7 Text, p. 48
	Assessment	Quizzes	*Pruebas* 1-4, 1-6
	Practice	Communicative Activity	Communicative Activities BLMs 1-3
	Presentation/Practice	*Álbum cultural*	Text, pp. 40–43
	Presentation/Practice	*Gramática en contexto* Paired practice *Ahora lo sabes*	Text, p. 48 Text, p. 49 Text, p. 49
	Closing/Assignments	Review day's objectives and tasks to be done Preview Day #9	Practice Wkbk. 1-8, 1-9
Day # 9	Introduction/Review	Review homework	Practice Wkbk. 1-8, 1-9
	Practice	Communicative Activity Writing Activities	Communicative Activity BLMs 1-2 WAVA: Writing Activities 1-E, 1-F
	Assessment	Quizzes	*Pruebas* 1-6, 1-8
	Application	*Puntos de vista*	Text, pp. 50–51
	Presentation	*Para escribir*	Text, pp. 54–55
	Closing/Assignments	Review day's objectives and tasks to be done Preview Day #10	Text, p. 54, Exs. 1–2

	Instructional Process	Tasks/Activities	Components
Day # 10	Introduction/Review	Review homework Peer editing	Text, p. 54
	Presentation/Practice	*Para leer*	Text, pp. 52–53
	Application	Video Activity	*Realidades:* Episode 1 WAVA: Video Activities, pp. 133–134, A–C
	Application	*Repaso: ¿Lo sabes bien?* Choose from: *Actividades en grupo* Audio Activities Writing Activities	Text, p. 56 Communicative Activity BLMs 1-4 WAVA: Audio Activities 1.4–1.5 WAVA: Writing Activities 1-G, 1-H
	Closing/Assignments	Review for Chapter Test	Text, p. 54, *Para escribir*
Day # 11	Assessment	Chapter Test	Assessment Program: Choose from *Prueba cumulativa* or *Examen de habilidades* (or) Use other components such as: Situation Cards, Communicative Activities BLMs, p. 7; Test Generator
	Presentation/Practice	Choose from: *Pasodoble* review *Fondo literario*	Text, p. 11, or Practice Wkbk. PD-5 Text, pp. 430–435
	Closing/Assignments	Preview Day #1 of *Capítulo 2*	Text, pp. 58–59

Bridging to *PASO A PASO 3*

As students move into *PASO A PASO 3,* it is expected that they will have completed the content in Chapters 1–12 of Book 2. The grammar and vocabulary in Chapters 13–14 will be retaught as if new in *PASO A PASO 3.*

Review and reteaching

As students move into *PASO A PASO 3,* they will continually be exposed to material they will have learned in the preceding books.

PASO A PASO 3 begins with a lively, communicative magazine-like section entitled *Pasodoble* that reactivates the major vocabulary sets and structures of the early chapters of *PASO A PASO 2.*

The chart on the following page shows the reteaching and expansion of specific grammar points from book to book.

Grammar	PASO A PASO 2	PASO A PASO 3
ir	*Pasodoble*	*Pasodoble*
hacer	*Pasodoble*	*Pasodoble*
tener	*Pasodoble*, 1*	*Pasodoble*
comparatives / superlatives	*Pasodoble*, **1, 3**	*Pasodoble*
demonstratives	**3**	*Pasodoble*
ser	*Pasodoble*, **4, 5, 7**	*Pasodoble*
possession	*Pasodoble*, **7**	*Pasodoble*
estar	*Pasodoble*, **8**	*Pasodoble*
direct object pronouns	**1**, 9	**1, 6**
indirect object pronouns	2, 3, 5, 9	**1, 6**
reflexive verbs	**2, 4, 6, 8**	*Pasodoble*
stem-changing verbs: $e \rightarrow i$	**2, 6**	**8**
preterite	**3, 4, 6, 9, 10**	*Pasodoble*, **3, 4,** 11, 12
imperfect	**5, 6, 10**	*Pasodoble*, **2**
negatives	**8**	*Pasodoble*
present progressive	**8**, 9	**5**
imperfect progressive	**9**	**3**
future	**11**	**6**
tú commands	**12, 13**, 14	*Pasodoble*, **1**, 9
subjunctive	**13, 14**	**7, 8, 9, 10, 11, 12**

*Lightface numbers represent lexical introduction or quick review;
boldface numbers represent presentation of the grammar point.

NTEGRATING TECHNOLOGY IN THE *PASO A PASO* CLASSROOM

PASO A PASO provides a complete, state-of-the-art technology package for each chapter at all levels, including Internet-based activities, award-winning video programs, lively audio activities, easy-to-use test generators, and vocabulary art on CD-ROM. *PASO A PASO* also provides extensive overheads that build upon the time-tested approach of presenting vocabulary visually.

Throughout this Teacher's Edition, there are clear cross-references to the various technology components. The following chart shows how to integrate these in a chapter.

Chapter section	Technology component
Vocabulario para comunicarse	Audio program
	www.pasoapaso.com
	Vocabulary Art CD-ROM
	Overheads
Álbum cultural	www.pasoapaso.com
	Realidades video
Gramática en contexto	Overheads
	Audio program
Puntos de vista: Sopa de actividades	*Realidades* video
Puntos de vista: Para leer	www.pasoapaso.com
Resumen: Exámenes	Audio program
	Test generator

Internet-based Activities: www.pasoapaso.com
Standards: 1.2; 1.3; 2.1; 2.2; 3.1; 3.2; 4.1; 4.2; 5.1; 5.2

A quick trip via cyberspace to www.pasoapaso.com provides access to a wide range of activities, from authentic sources and cultural resources found on web sites to vocabulary and grammar games and extra drill-and-skill opportunities. All chapters in *PASO A PASO* have specific activities that integrate vocabulary, grammar, and culture. You will also find addition-

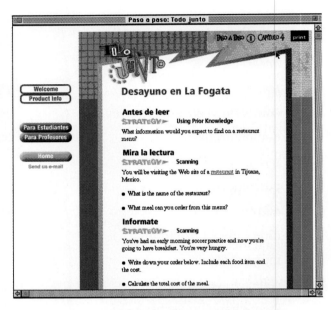

al resources, articles, updates, teaching ideas, and ways to network with other *PASO A PASO* users.

Realidades Video Program
Standards: 1.2; 2.1; 2.2; 3.1; 3.2; 4.1; 4.2; 5.1; 5.2

Realidades (available on videocassettes or videodiscs) is integrated throughout each chapter in *PASO A PASO 3*. Student activity sheets are found in the Writing, Audio & Video Activities workbook. An extensive Teacher's Guide offers many suggestions for use of the video.

Realidades consists of authentic footage such as excerpts from news broadcasts and documentaries, interviews, and commercials. Segments run from three to four minutes in length and are designed to expand the theme of the textbook chapter. You might find it most productive to show *Realidades* as students begin working with the *Puntos de vista* section of the chapter. At that point, they are well acquainted with the issues under examination and should have sufficient familiarity with the topical vocabulary. In this way students continually reaffirm and build upon language they already know.

As you work with *Realidades,* we suggest that you use the material in the video section of the Writing, Audio & Video Activities, which contains both pre- and post-viewing activities. Before viewing, you might want to ask students to share what information they already have about the segment they are about to see.

Let students watch a given segment several times. You might want to break the segment up and show it over a period of days. The first viewing might be with the sound off so that students become acquainted first with the surroundings and visual focus of the situation. This also cuts down significantly on stress, as the felt need to understand is strictly limited. Let students watch the segment two or three more times as they work through the post-viewing activities. After completing these, students might re-view the video in order to have a class discussion about it. Encourage students to note any cultural insights they are developing. All of this should enable them to work with the *Puntos de vista* section of the chapter with greater confidence and understanding.

While it is certainly possible to teach *PASO A PASO 3* without using *Realidades,* you will nonetheless find it an unequaled tool in promoting the development of the skills and understanding basic to functioning outside the sheltered environment of the classroom.

Vocabulary Art CD-ROM
Standards: 1.1; 1.2

This clip art (part of the Resource Pro® CD-ROM) includes all visualized vocabulary from Books 1–3 of *PASO A PASO.* Teachers can modify the clip art to create a variety of hands-on learning tools, such as flashcards, posters, and games.

Audio Program
Standards: 1.2; 3.1

Each chapter contains a variety of audio activities, including vocabulary/pronunciation practice, contextualized listening activities, songs, and listening comprehension tests. The audio activities help students learn the vocabulary and grammar of each chapter. Student activity sheets appear in the Writing, Audio & Video Activities workbook.

Test Generator
Standards: 1.2; 1.3; 2.1; 2.2; 4.2

Teachers can access ready-made tests for each chapter that contain multiple choice, true/false, matching, fill-in-the-blank, short answer, and essay questions. You can integrate these as intra-chapter quizzes, prepare end-of-chapter tests, or combine questions from various chapters to create semester or year-end tests. The templates can also be used to create your own questions.

Overheads
Standards: 1.1; 1.2

Each chapter provides complete overheads for vocabulary and grammar presentation and practice.

STRATEGIES FOR REACHING ALL STUDENTS

PASO A PASO 3 provides teachers the support and strategies needed to reach all students in the Spanish classroom. We offer an unprecedented commitment to providing materials that help meet the realities of today's classroom. This article focuses on strategies from *PASO A PASO 3* that will help you and all of your students enjoy a successful year learning Spanish . . . step by step!

1 Material that builds upon students' experiences

Language students learn best by using what they know, by building new knowledge on old, and by experiencing and doing. As you use the text, you will see that *PASO A PASO 3* provides for an authentic, meaningful experience for the learner. The twelve chapter themes were developed by asking, "What do students want to talk about?" The vocabulary taught is high-frequency language that students want to learn. The grammar supports communication and is practiced communicatively. The cultural content provides a means toward understanding and a global perspective that will be meaningful to all students. The activities ask students to interact, to become active participants in the learning process, and to express real ideas and real meanings for real purposes.

2 A multisensory approach to learning

Each student enters the Spanish classroom with different learning styles and abilities. Some work best with an aural / oral approach; others need a strong visual approach. Many need to touch and be physically involved in learning. An approach that addresses the needs and strengths of each student lays the groundwork for reaching all.

PASO A PASO 3 provides a strong multisensory approach to language learning. Students have varied opportunities for success by working with

activities that recognize different learning styles and employ more than one modality. The *Sopa de actividades* offers activities that involve different learning skills and interests (creating a collage, preparing a skit, participating in a debate).

The cornerstone of success in Scott Foresman's foreign language programs has always been our strong visual approach. We have expanded this in *PASO A PASO 3*. Each chapter opens with culturally authentic photographs *(Anticipación)* that call upon students' background knowledge in discussing the chapter theme. Vocabulary presentation is facilitated by contextual visualization that is then recycled in the practice activities to reinforce learning. This approach is supported by the Overheads and the Vocabulary Art Blackline Masters/CD-ROM. We have enhanced the visual approach through a photo essay in the *Álbum cultural*. A new, realia-based approach offers students an opportunity to study grammar in a real-life context. And reading and writing practice are made more accessible through the strong use of visual cues.

The multisensory approach is further expanded through use of the chapter-by-chapter audio tapes and video. The video program brings the culture and everyday themes to students in a truly authentic context.

3 Learning strategies

PASO A PASO 3 reinforces the strategies and skill-building techniques that students are using in their other classes. Some of these may be new to you but are easily implemented in the Spanish classroom. Strategies include building on background knowledge and experience, making lists or webs to organize their learning, inductive questioning, and consistent application of reading strategies and process writing.

Higher-order and inductive thinking

It sometimes seems that every day researchers are discovering new facts about the workings of the brain. We now know that information is stored in many areas of the brain and connected by a rich network of neurons. The goal of instruction should be to maximize the use of this network by helping students make connections and to learn information from a variety of perspectives and in a variety of ways. Activities aimed toward this goal are inherently interesting and motivating.

Students learn more successfully when they create their own understanding. Throughout *PASO A PASO 3* you will find activities that ask students to do just this. Inductive questions, for example, are the starting point of the following chapter features: *Anticipación, Álbum cultural, Gramática en contexto,* and *Para leer.* Activities that engage students in higher-level thinking skills are the initial focus in each of these sections, as well as in the *Sopa de actividades* and *Para escribir.* We sequence these activities so that all students can be successful.

Another important learning strategy, informed guessing, is embedded in the vocabulary section entitled *¿Y qué quiere decir . . . ?* and is focused on in the inductive questions about photographs, as well as in the process reading and writing sections of each chapter.

 Multiple learning opportunities

We know that students will improve at different rates and will be stronger in some areas than in others. In addition, developing proficiency takes time for everyone, no matter how gifted. Therefore, instruction must provide multiple opportunities for learning and improvement.

PASO A PASO 3 offers these opportunities. New vocabulary is presented, practiced, and recycled throughout a chapter and in subsequent chapters.

Students are first exposed to grammar lexically, use it as they practice, and have some degree of understanding and control of it before it is presented and practiced as grammar. It is presented in easy-to-deal-with increments. The adjectival use of the past participle, for example, is first explained in Chapter 2, with additional information and new tenses using the past participle presented in Chapters 4, 5, 7, and 8. In addition, recursive themes from one level to the next allow for regular review, expansion, and elaboration.

Throughout the text you will find reminder notes to students entitled *¡No olvides!* These focus on previously learned concepts that students will need in order to do a particular exercise or to understand better an extension of a given structure. These reminders are not crutches, but rather important tools for mastery.

 Additional opportunities for students who need them

A regular on-page feature of this Teacher's Edition entitled "Strategies for Reaching All Students" provides you support for working with:

- Spanish-speaking students
- those having difficulty learning
- the gifted
- cooperative learning groups
- students needing extra practice
- multiple intelligences

Notes under the heading "Students Needing Extra Help" suggest adaptations of the textbook activities or grammar explanations for those with real learning difficulties. Enrichment suggestions allow students who are capable of doing so to move beyond the textbook.

7 Varied assessment options

Students will do better in assessment situations if they have a clear understanding of the objectives and of how they will be assessed, and if they are assessed in such a way as to focus on their strengths.

PASO A PASO 3 offers a variety of options. Besides the *Pruebas* and *Exámenes de habilidades* in the Assessment Program, the *Sopa de actividades* in the integrative *Puntos de vista* offer you different types of opportunities for assessment, asking students to draw upon auditory, visual, and kinesthetic strengths. The Communicative Activities Blackline Masters include Situation Cards that are ideal for use in assessing speaking proficiency. (For additional ideas, see the article on assessment, pp. T58–T62, and the Introduction to the Assessment Program itself.)

Through the clearly stated objectives at the beginning of each chapter and the mini-assessments within the chapter *(¿Qué sabes ahora?* and *Ahora lo sabes),* students are able to monitor their own progress. In addition, the end-of-chapter pretest *(Repaso: ¿Lo sabes bien?)* gives them a clear picture of how they will be assessed on the *Examen de habilidades.*

PASO A PASO 3 is committed to helping every teacher reach every student in the Spanish class. By providing materials that are strategy-based and that have built-in teacher support, we believe that we are enabling both you and your students to experience real enjoyment and unparalleled success.

Multiple Intelligences

Education, like most institutions, has weathered storms of quick fix-it methodologies or theories that look promising on paper but have little or no practical application or realistic hope of success in an actual classroom. The Multiple Intelligences Theory is in no way intended to be a quick fix-it approach for teaching second languages, yet it is easily applicable in any classroom with careful planning and reflection on the teacher's part. Additionally, the Multiple Intelligences Theory does not demand that you teach in a certain way or falsely promise an easy ten-step process which, if followed precisely, will transform the entire class into straight A students! However, what the theory does do is remind us of what we already know: Everyone learns in different ways, and if you present new material in a variety of formats, then more students will likely learn and be able to demonstrate proficiency with the new material.

The notion that a person's intellectual worth can be based on a narrowly focused standardized test was challenged in 1983 by Howard Gardner in his book, *Frames of Mind,* which proposed the theory of Multiple Intelligences. Gardner believes that a person has many different ways of both acquiring and demonstrating intelligence (Armstrong, 1994). For instance, some students can remember just about anything as long as it is learned to the tune of a jingle, while someone else may be able to grasp an idea, concept, or grammatical form provided it is presented visually in the form of a graph, chart, or picture. Gardner has identified and labeled eight main styles of acquiring and demonstrating knowledge; those eight intelligences are Verbal/Linguistic, Visual/Spatial, Bodily/Kinesthetic, Logical/Mathematical, Interpersonal/Social, Intrapersonal/Introspective, Musical/Rhythmic, and Naturalist. Allowing students the opportunity to learn and acquire knowledge in the manner in which they are most receptive maximizes their potential to become successful students (Armstrong, 1994; Beckman, 1998).

When Gardner introduced his theory of Multiple Intelligences in 1983, he marked a new trend in cognitive psychology, broadening perspectives on human brain functions and views on human potential in terms of learning, and facilitating attempts to explain human differences. Gardner presents the notion that there is no "general intelligence," but rather that the mind is organized around distinct functional capacities, which he defines as "intelligences." Though each of the intelligences is developed independently of the others over the course of a lifetime, they usually work together and do not often appear in isolation.

In this Teacher's Edition you will find frequent specific suggestions for accommodating and teaching to the Multiple Intelligences. This is not meant to be construed as a paradigm for labeling every student in your class. On the contrary, we must continue to recognize each student as unique, complex, and highly individualistic. Therefore, we must regard students holistically and as individuals, recognizing that they are intelligent in many ways and that their overall "intelligence" is based on the sum of all of their intelligences.

Given the nature of the subject, foreign language teachers traditionally work most often with the **Verbal/Linguistic Intelligence.** Individuals who demonstrate strength in this area think and express themselves through words and have a strong ability to understand and use language to communicate effectively (Chapman, 1993). They enjoy reading, writing, telling stories, playing word games, and often excel in memorizing.

Musical/Rhythmic Intelligence is reflected in an individual's ability to analyze or create musical compositions. This intelligence can be used in a foreign language classroom in a variety of ways, such as teaching about culture through music or having students create their own raps or jingles to enhance vocabulary/grammar learning. It is important to note that Gardner does not believe that music played in the background during an activity or test is necessarily engaging the Musical Intelligence. If it is merely background music, its function is "unlikely to be different from that of a dripping faucet or a humming fan" (Gardner, 1995). The following are opportunities for accommodating this intelligence: Students research Spanish dances and are prepared to discuss them and teach them to the class; students compose a song about traveling and favorite places to visit; students make up rhymes to practice vocabulary; students create and demonstrate an aerobic exercise routine.

Interpersonal/Social Intelligence operates primarily through person-to-person relationships and communication. A common misconception is that it applies only to extroverted individuals (Gardner, 1995). One of the most effective ways to utilize this intelligence is through pair, group, and cooperative learning activities.

Intrapersonal/Introspective Intelligence is the ability to understand oneself and to think introspectively. Such students often enjoy working alone, being allowed to pursue their own interests, being provided with individualized projects and self-paced instruction. The following activities will provide opportunities to accommodate this intelligence: Students write poems describing themselves; students write a report on their views about recycling; students write a personal agenda for improving the environment.

Bodily/Kinesthetic Intelligence is related to physical movement and the ability to manipulate objects. These students enjoy most physical activities, e.g., moving, touching, body language, jumping, and running. Learning Spanish Through Action provides a wide variety of activities that accommodate this intelligence. Other production activities include role-playing, drama, creative movements, and gross motor and whole body activities.

Visual/Spatial Intelligence relies on the sense of sight and being able to visualize an object through mental images or pictures. These students enjoy opportunities to work with art and construction materials and to create projects. The use of video, movies, slides, imagination games, mazes, and puzzles will accommodate this intelligence.

Logical/Mathematical Intelligence deals with inductive and deductive reasoning, numbers, and the recognition of abstract patterns. Individuals who enjoy analyzing similarities and differences and manipulating numbers and graphs are strong in this intelligence. These students will perform well by working with numbers, exploring patterns and relationships, and using manipulatives. The following activities will provide opportunities to accommodate this intelligence: Students use a Venn diagram to compare Spanish and U.S. homes; students create a survey to determine what one should do to prevent catching a cold and display the results in a graph or chart; students use a logic puzzle to figure out which primary colors combine to produce the secondary colors on their TV screen.

Naturalist Intelligence is the latest intelligence added by Gardner. It includes the capacity to recognize flora and fauna, to make distinctions in the natural world, and to use this ability productively in activities such as gardening, farming, and biological science. This intelligence involves the ability to see the natural world from a larger perspective—an understanding of how nature interacts with civilization, the symbiotic relationships inherent in nature, and the life cycles of nature. Students exhibiting this intelligence will learn best through working in nature, exploring living things, learning about plants and natural events.

It should be stressed that the eight intelligences were not designed to be used as a new set of labels for teachers to assign to students (Edwards, 1998). Instead, by identifying a student's preferred intelligence, you can encourage the learning process while also fostering the other intelligences through appropriate activities. As a rule, the eight intelligences should not be thought of as independent and isolated approaches, but rather should be intertwined and used in conjunction with each other to create the best possible learning experience for all students (Armstrong, 1994).

Integrating the use of Multiple Intelligences into the classroom does not require a major overhaul of lesson plans or a reworking of the curriculum. Generally, all that is required is supplementing and enhancing already existing lesson plans with a few creative and imaginative activities (Campbell, 1997). Some first-hand accounts are reassuring because many teachers find that in a very short time thinking and planning within the framework of the eight intelligences becomes second nature and quite painless (Campbell, 1989). Another suggestion from veteran Multiple Intelligences teachers is to team teach or team plan with teachers who have strengths in the intelligences that complement your own (Campbell, 1997).

The idea of Multiple Intelligences is a wonderful concept because it recognizes and validates the fact that every person is an individual who acquires and demonstrates knowledge through different means. However inclined, students should all be given the same opportunity to function in the manner in which they are most receptive and proficient. Some of those students may even discover that they actually enjoy learning—and that is the goal of every teacher: to instill the love of learning for learning itself.

References

Armstrong, Thomas. *Multiple Intelligences in the Classroom.* State of Virginia: Association for Supervision and Curriculum Development (1994).

Beckman, Marian S. *Multiple Ways of Knowing: Howard Gardner's Theory of Multiple Intelligences Extend and Enhance Student Learning.* http://www.earlychildhood.com/articles/artmi.html (1998).

Campbell, Bruce. "Multiplying Intelligences in the Classroom." New Horizons for Learning: *On the Beam,* IX, No. 2, (Winter 1989).

Campbell, Linda. "Variations on a Theme: How Teachers Interpret MI Theory." *Educational Leadership,* Vol. 55, No. 1 (September 1997).

Campbell, L., B. Campbell, and D. Dickinson. *Teaching and Learning Through Multiple Intelligences.* Tucson, AZ: Zephyr Press (1996).

Chapman, C. *If the Shoe Fits . . . How to Develop Multiple Intelligences in the Classroom.* Palatine, IL: IRI/Skylight (1993).

Edwards, Jack. *Multiple Intelligences and Technology.* http://www.firn.edu/~face/about/dec95/multi_int.html (1995).

Gardner, Howard. *Frames of Mind: The Theory of Multiple Intelligences.* New York: Basic Books (1983).

————. *Multiple Intelligences: The Theory in Practice: A Reader.* New York: Basic Books (1993).

ASSESSMENT

Various methods of assessment are appropriate in a standards-driven classroom. Chapter tests, student conferences, teacher notes, checklists, portfolios, and performance demonstrations are all part of a well-rounded assessment program. All have advantages and disadvantages, and to use any one method exclusively would block your view of the total student picture. *PASO A PASO 3* offers a multi-faceted assessment program based on the premise that the main purpose of learning a language is to communicate in a meaningful and culturally appropriate way. As you begin to use the assessment program, you might want to start by asking yourself a few key questions: What do I expect my students to learn? What do I want them to be able to do? and How can I assess what I am looking for in student performance? Your answers to these questions can help define your philosophy in regard to assessment.

Self-Assessment of Chapter Objectives

Essential to any assessment program is the inclusion of self-assessment opportunities, which allow students to become independent evaluators of their own progress and to take more responsibility for their own learning. They engage students in the process of learning and promote greater involvement and reflection. The *chapter objectives* offer the basis for a self-assessment checklist of what each student should be able to do at the end of the chapter. The stated objectives can be rewritten by you and distributed as "I can . . ." statements to be used as a checklist as students move through the chapter. For example, a checklist for *Capítulo 1* might look like this:

Student Checklist		*Capítulo 1*
Usando lo que he aprendido . . .	**Sí**	**No**
1. Puedo describirme.	☐	☐
2. Puedo describir a otras personas.	☐	☐
3. Puedo hablar sobre cómo me relaciono con otras personas.	☐	☐
4. Puedo hablar sobre las cualidades de una persona a quien admiro.	☐	☐
5. Puedo hablar sobre actividades en las que participo o en que podría participar.	☐	☐
6. Puedo hablar de lo mejor y de lo peor de mi familia o de mi escuela.	☐	☐
7. Puedo hablar sobre mi papel en la sociedad (e.g., trabajos comunitarios o voluntarios).	☐	☐
8. Puedo describir a quién le hago algo (e.g., ayudar con la tarea, prestar dinero).	☐	☐
9. Puedo dar razones por qué sí o por qué no estoy de acuerdo con mis amigos o con mis padres.	☐	☐
10. Puedo describir lo que les gusta hacer a los jóvenes en España e Hispanoamérica.	☐	☐

Two Types of Assessment

Both traditional and authentic assessment are part of the *PASO A PASO 3* program. *Traditional assessments* test knowledge of limited materials presented in a given chapter, and therefore are achievement based. *Authentic assessments* evaluate what learners can *do* with the language being learned, and are therefore competency-based. Both have a valid place in today's classroom. While the former assess for "coverage," the latter assess for "uncoverage." In other words, it is important to know that students can prove mastery of the material covered, but it is also important to "uncover" how they can use this language to express their own meanings.

PASO A PASO 3 offers you opportunities to assess the students' knowledge of specific vocabulary and grammar points through the use of several *pruebas* provided for each chapter. These prompt the student to progress from simple vocabulary recognition to limited production of a specific grammatical structure. The *prueba cumulativa* can be used as a final quiz to assess students' ability to apply learned material in a new context. The *Test Generator,* a bank of multiple-choice questions, offers yet another option for end of chapter assessment. It serves especially well as a make-up assessment for those who were unable to attend class on final quiz day.

A unique assessment tool in *PASO A PASO 3,* the *Examen de habilidades,* provides a vehicle for evaluating students' ability to apply what they have learned in a realistic, yet controlled context. For example, students may be asked to role-play a situation in which they are buying clothes. These more revealing, performance-based assessments provide engaging tasks from which to evaluate students' ability to use acquired language more creatively. Both the *Test Generator* and the *Banco de ideas* section offer additional test questions and assessment tasks, providing students opportunities to demonstrate real-life applications of the language they are learning.

Many of the activities in the *Sopa de actividades* and *Para escribir* sections of the textbook provide the basis for *performance demonstrations,* such as individual writing projects, small group presentations, and paired conversations. Such performance assessments allow you to see the students' actual use of language in several types of tasks. Another source of mini-performance assessments can be found in the *Communicative Activity Blackline Masters,* which offer small group tasks, paired activities, and situation cards.

Grading Performance Assessments

Because many teachers find it difficult and time consuming to establish grading criteria for performance-based assessment, *PASO A PASO 3* provides you with several templates for *scoring rubrics.* These include numerical values associated with performance levels, such as Below Average (1 point), Average (3 points), and Good (5 points). The criteria are precisely defined in terms of what students actually do to demonstrate performance at that level and they reflect what are considered to be appropriate communication skills and strategies. These criteria can be changed at any time to reflect a different emphasis. A rubric should be explained in advance to the students so that they have a clear understanding of what is expected of them and the level of performance needed to receive the highest score.

Grading a Paired Conversation

Throughout *PASO A PASO 3,* there are many activities that can serve as a basis for a performance assessment. For example, in the *¿Lo sabes bien?* section of Chapter 4, students ask each other questions about their favorite TV programs. What would your expectations be for your students in this activity? How can you be consistent in the way you grade performances? The following rubric can serve as a template for this paired activity, as well as for many similar tasks in any chapter:

Paired Conversation Rubric

	1 point	3 points	5 points
Language Use	Relies on memorized phrases and short sentences. May use English when attempting to communicate beyond the chapter vocabulary.	Pauses frequently to search for words, but tries to use familiar vocabulary in a new situation.	Uses language confidently, with ease, and with few pauses.
Ability to Sustain Conversation	Can only answer partner's direct questions.	Can both ask and answer questions.	Can state opinions and give reasons for them.
Conversational Interaction	Interaction is nonexistent. No conversational reaction to what is said by partner.	Limited conversational reaction to what is said by partner. Responds, but quickly moves to next question.	Natural interaction between partners. Each responds by following up on what the other person says.

15 pts. = A; 11–13 pts. = B; 7–9 pts. = C; 3–5 pts. = D

This particular rubric makes clear to students that getting their message across to their partners and maintaining a conversational flow are your top priorities at this point.

Although performance levels will vary greatly, your expectations are firmly anchored in the rubric's descriptors and in the models you give as examples of the different levels. For example, *Prefiero las películas terror porque me gusta estar ... frightened* is an example of *language use* at the 1-point level, whereas *Prefiero las películas de terror porque, cómo se dice ... me gusta miedo, no ... me gustar tener miedo* is at the 3-point level. *Prefiero las películas de terror porque me gusta tener miedo* is at the 5-point level because the student is using previously learned vocabulary confidently and without hesitation. A student able both to answer and ask questions would receive 3 points for *ability to sustain conversation*. To perform at the 5-point level in this category, the student would respond with a reason for his or her statement by saying something such as *Me gustan mucho las películas de terror porque todas me dan miedo, especialmente las de Steven Spielberg.*

Conversational interaction focuses on whether the partners are listening and responding appropriately. For example, after hearing that one's partner really likes horror movies, the student responds at the 1-point level by ignoring the information and begins to talk about his or her favorite sitcom. At the 3-point level, the student might respond with *A mí me gustan también.* A performance at the 5-point level would elicit a response such as *No puedo dormir si veo una película de terror.*

Grading a Writing Sample

Throughout *PASO A PASO 3,* students are led through the writing process to enable them to organize both their thinking and writing. There are several writing tasks strategically placed in each chapter's *Para escribir* sections. These can serve as stand-alone writing assessments, or as writing assignments for homework. In either case, you want to be able to grade the sample objectively and fairly. For example, students are asked in Chapter 3 to imagine that they are reporters and are to write a personal reaction as a review of a work of art. Using the process writing approach, the review is to include the artist's background, reactions to the painting itself, and the student's own interpretation of the work of art. The following rubric could be used for this activity and many similar writing tasks in the program:

Writing Rubric

Criteria	1 point	3 points	5 points
Use of pre-writing strategies	Only turns in final product.	Turns in lists or planning notes along with final product.	Turns in planning notes, first draft, and final product.
Accuracy	Many spelling errors and repeated patterns of subject/verb agreement errors.	Several spelling errors and repeated patterns of subject/verb agreement errors.	Few spelling or subject/verb agreement errors.
Content	Gives no examples or details.	Gives a few examples or details.	Consistently adds examples and/or details.

15 pts. = A; 11–13 pts. = B; 7–9 pts. = C; 3–5 pts. = D

Assessment of Cultural Awareness

Both the *Foreign Language Standards* and *PASO A PASO 3* emphasize the importance of students' using their language and cultural understanding outside of the classroom in order to connect to and reflect on their own and the target culture. At several points in each chapter, students are called upon to reflect about the products, practices, and perspectives of people in the Spanish-speaking world, and as they progress through the program, they gain increasing awareness of Hispanic influences around them.

In the *Examen de habilidades,* students are consistently asked to compare their own culture to that of the Spanish-speaking world and to reflect upon the differences and similarities. For example, merely stating that more women are in the workplace in the United States and that more men stay home with the children would earn the student points. Reflecting upon how that fact would change many long-held attitudes of the Spanish-speaking world would earn additional points. Rather than awarding points for a "correct" reflection, you are awarding points for going through the process and showing evidence of reflective thinking.

Personal Culture Logs

In order to encourage cultural awareness, you might want to ask students to keep a log of at least ten instances in which they have encountered the target language or target culture in their own communities. Their entries might include chance meetings with Spanish speakers, snippets of conversation in movies or TV programs, street or store signs, product information, references noted from other classes where Spanish culture or language was mentioned, or any other experience in which students realized that "something Spanish" was going on.

Each of the ten entries would be graded as 2-point, 4-point, or 6-point entries. The following rubric could be distributed to students and used for giving an objective grade to their log entries. The rubric guides students to go beyond the recognition level to a more reflective level of thinking about culture and language. The following is an example of a student entry in a culture log that would earn six points because of the evidence of reflection:

Personal Language and Culture Log

Date	Recognition—2 points "Hey, that's Spanish!"	Comprehension—4 points "Hey, that's Spanish and I know what it means!"	Reflection—6 points "Hey, that's Spanish and I think I know why they did that!"
1.			We went to the arts festival in the city's Paseo District. *Paseo* means "walk" in Spanish. I bet they named it that because it is one of the few places where there are sidewalks for people who like to walk!

Portfolios

A portfolio is a purposeful collection that exhibits a student's performance efforts, progress, and achievement over a period of time. Some teachers, especially those working on a block schedule, have found that portfolios have given their students an avenue to pursue some things outside of class that they don't have time to develop in the class period. For example, students could compare the reporting of a major international news story in newspapers from around the Spanish-speaking world to that in the United States by accessing foreign newspapers on the Internet outside of class. Portfolios can allow students to document aspects of their learning that do not show up well in traditional assessments, yet are part of the overall assessment program.

One of the most common uses of portfolios is to showcase the students' favorite examples of their work. This type of portfolio can include both assigned and student-selected projects. Since the student chooses some of the work to be showcased, the portfolio can link the student personally to his or her own assessment in a way that traditional assessment can never create. The final portfolio can then be shared with parents, friends, and other teachers.

Another type of portfolio might have the focus of documenting student progress over time. You could collect baseline samples of work, such as the first piece of writing for the year and the first oral interview, and then regularly update and add to the portfolio. It can be a unique opportunity for your students to monitor and evaluate their own progress.

INDEX OF CULTURAL REFERENCES

PASO A PASO

3

Una carreta de bueyes típica de Costa Rica

(p. II and back cover, photos)
Sarchí, Costa Rica. Brilliantly hand-painted and handmade oxcarts are the form of folk art most identified with Costa Rica. They were first used by peasant farmers in the mid-nineteenth century to transport the coffee bean crop from the mountains to the ports. This crop was new to Costa Rica. It had been imported from Cuba in 1808. The brightly colored, elaborate designs of the oxcarts are traditional and identify the carts as belonging to a particular family.

PASO A PASO

3

Myriam Met
Coordinator of Foreign Languages
Montgomery County Public Schools
Rockville, MD

Richard S. Sayers
Longmont, CO

Carol Eubanks Wargin
Glen Crest Junior High School
Glen Ellyn, IL

Prentice Hall

Glenview, Illinois
Needham, Massachusetts
Upper Saddle River, New Jersey

Visit our Web site at http://www.pasoapaso.com

ISBN: 0-673-58924-2

3 4 5 6 7 8 9 10 DOC 03 02 01 00

Prentice Hall
Upper Saddle River, New Jersey 07458

Contributing Writers

Margaret Juanita Azevedo
Stanford University
Palo Alto, CA

Thomasina Pagán Hannum
Albuquerque, NM

Martha E. Heard
Río Rancho Public Schools
Río Rancho, NM

Mary Mosley, Ph.D.
Fulton, MO

Craig Reubelt
The University of Chicago
  Laboratory Schools
Chicago, IL

Reader Consultants

The authors and editors would like to express our heartfelt thanks to the following team of reader consultants. Each of them read the manuscript, chapter-by-chapter, offering suggestions and providing encouragement. Their contribution has been invaluable.

Rosario Martínez-Cantú
Northside Health Careers High School
San Antonio, TX

Greg Duncan
InterPrep
Marietta, GA

Walter Kleinmann
Sewanhaka Central High School District
New Hyde Park, NY

Bernadette M. Reynolds
Parker, CO

Rudolf L. Schonfeld, Ph.D.
Parsippany-Troy Hills School District
Parsippany, NJ

Edra Staffieri
North Central High School
Indianapolis, IN

Connie Johnson Vargas
Apple Valley High School
Apple Valley, CA

Marcia Payne Wooten
Starmount High School
Boonville, NC

Tabla de materias

PASODOBLE
Una revista escolar para los jóvenes

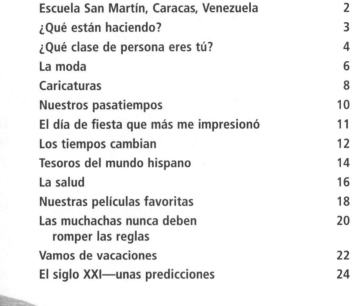

VI

Tabla de materias VII

CAPÍTULO 5   ¿Cómo se relacionan el pasado y el presente?   159

Tema

► La civilización maya

Objetivos

► Describir las características de la civilización maya

► Hablar de las contribuciones de la civilización maya

► Explicar cómo nos han influido otras civilizaciones

► Identificar lo que sigue existiendo de la civilización maya en la vida de hoy

CAPÍTULO 6   ¿Cómo nos podemos comunicar mejor?   191

Tema

► Tecnología y comunicación

Objetivos

► Escribir y enviar una carta

► Hablar de diferentes medios de comunicación

► Dar tu opinión sobre las comunicaciones en el futuro

► Explicar el impacto de la tecnología en la vida diaria de los países hispanos

CAPÍTULO 9   Cómo tener éxito en el mundo del trabajo

291

Tema

▶ El trabajo

Objetivos

▶ Hablar de diferentes tipos de trabajo

▶ Describir las cualidades y habilidades que se necesitan para realizar un trabajo

▶ Explicar los pasos necesarios para buscar y conseguir trabajo

▶ Hablar sobre cómo ha cambiado el mundo del trabajo en los países hispanos

|---|---|
Anticipación	292
Vocabulario para comunicarse *¿Necesitas un buen trabajo?* 294	
Tema para investigar *¿Cómo te estás preparando?* 300	
Álbum cultural	304
Gramática en contexto	308
Repaso: Mandatos afirmativos y negativos con tú 309 *El subjuntivo en cláusulas adjetivas* 311 *El subjuntivo con* cuando 312	
Puntos de vista: *Sopa de actividades*	314
Para leer: *¿Qué tipo de inteligencia tienes?*	316
Para escribir	320
Repaso: *¿Lo sabes bien?*	322
Resumen del vocabulario	323

CAPÍTULO 10   ¿Cómo se puede controlar la violencia?

325

Tema

▶ El control de la violencia

Objetivos

▶ Describir un hecho de violencia

▶ Hablar de las causas de la violencia y de sus efectos en la sociedad

▶ Dar tu opinión sobre diferentes medidas para controlar la violencia

▶ Dar ejemplos del control de la violencia en los países de habla hispana y en los Estados Unidos

|---|---|
Anticipación	326
Vocabulario para comunicarse *La violencia en nuestra vida* 328	
Tema para investigar *La violencia y la justicia* 334	
Álbum cultural	338
Gramática en contexto	342
Mandatos afirmativos y negativos con Ud. *y* Uds. 343 *El subjuntivo con expresiones de emoción* 346	
Puntos de vista: *Sopa de actividades*	350
Para leer: *Hasta aclarar el misterio*	352
Para escribir	358
Repaso: *¿Lo sabes bien?*	360
Resumen del vocabulario	361

Tabla de materias XI

XI

FONDO LITERARIO

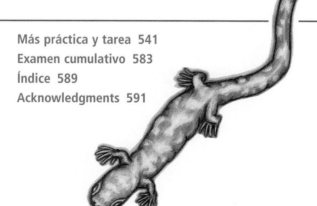

Tabla de materias XIII

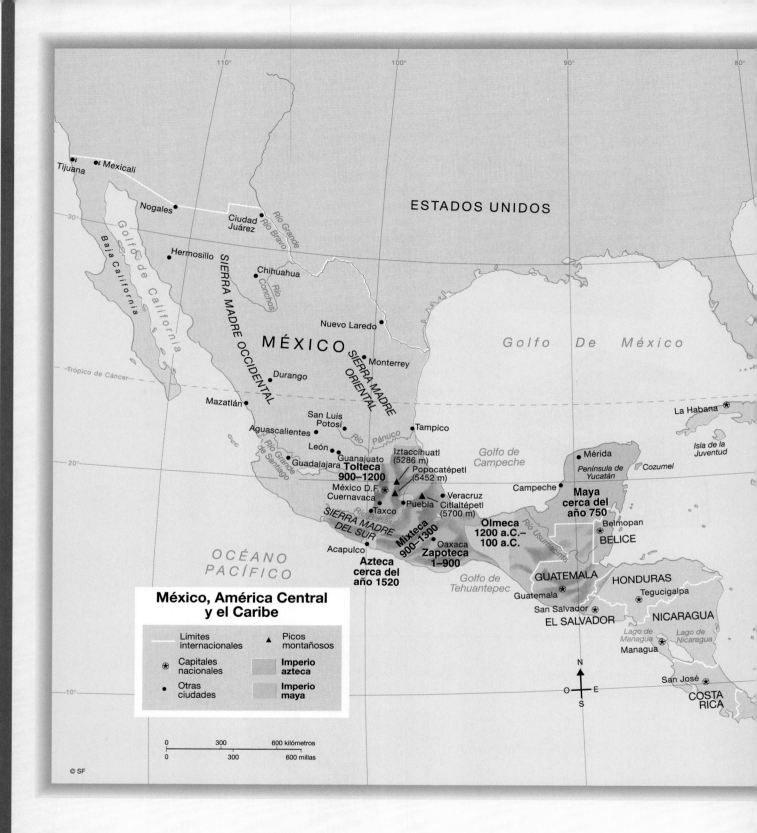

México, América Central y el Caribe

Límites internacionales

Capitales nacionales

Otras ciudades

Picos montañosos

Imperio azteca

Imperio maya

0 300 600 kilómetros
0 300 600 millas

© SF

ESTADOS UNIDOS

MÉXICO

SIERRA MADRE OCCIDENTAL

SIERRA MADRE ORIENTAL

SIERRA MADRE DEL SUR

Golfo de California

Baja California

Trópico de Cáncer

Río Grande
Río Bravo

Río Conchos

Río Pánuco

Río Grande de Santiago

Río Balsas

Río Usumacinta

OCÉANO PACÍFICO

Golfo De México

Golfo de Campeche

Golfo de Tehuantepec

Tijuana
Mexicali
Nogales
Ciudad Juárez
Hermosillo
Chihuahua
Nuevo Laredo
Monterrey
Durango
Mazatlán
San Luis Potosí
Aguascalientes
Tampico
León
Guanajuato
Guadalajara
Tolteca 900–1200
Iztaccíhuatl (5286 m)
Popocatépetl (5452 m)
México D.F.
Cuernavaca
Taxco
Puebla
Veracruz
Citlaltépetl (5700 m)
Mixteca 900–1300
Acapulco
Oaxaca
Zapoteca 1–900
Azteca cerca del año 1520
Olmeca 1200 a.C.– 100 a.C.
Maya cerca del año 750
Mérida
Campeche
Península de Yucatán
Cozumel
Belmopan
BELICE
GUATEMALA
Guatemala
San Salvador
EL SALVADOR
HONDURAS
Tegucigalpa
NICARAGUA
Lago de Managua
Lago de Nicaragua
Managua
San José
COSTA RICA
La Habana
Isla de la Juventud

N
O E
S

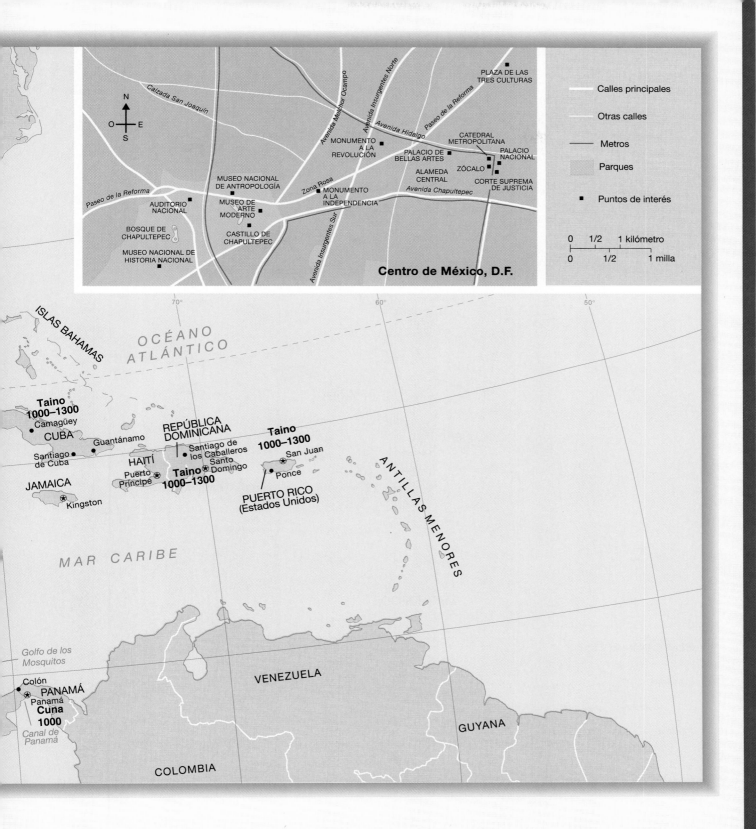

Centro de México, D.F.

Calles principales
Otras calles
Metros
Parques
Puntos de interés

PLAZA DE LAS TRES CULTURAS
CATEDRAL METROPOLITANA
MONUMENTO A LA REVOLUCIÓN
PALACIO DE BELLAS ARTES
PALACIO NACIONAL
ZÓCALO
ALAMEDA CENTRAL
CORTE SUPREMA DE JUSTICIA
MUSEO NACIONAL DE ANTROPOLOGÍA
Zona Rosa
MONUMENTO A LA INDEPENDENCIA
AUDITORIO NACIONAL
MUSEO DE ARTE MODERNO
BOSQUE DE CHAPULTEPEC
CASTILLO DE CHAPULTEPEC
MUSEO NACIONAL DE HISTORIA NACIONAL

Calzada San Joaquín
Paseo de la Reforma
Avenida Melchor Ocampo
Avenida Insurgentes Norte
Avenida Hidalgo
Paseo de la Reforma
Avenida Chapultepec
Avenida Insurgentes Sur

0   1/2   1 kilómetro
0   1/2   1 milla

ISLAS BAHAMAS
OCÉANO ATLÁNTICO

Taino 1000–1300
Camagüey
CUBA
Guantánamo
Santiago de Cuba
JAMAICA
Kingston

REPÚBLICA DOMINICANA
Santiago de los Caballeros
HAITÍ
Puerto Príncipe
Taino 1000–1300
Santo Domingo

Taino 1000–1300
San Juan
Ponce
PUERTO RICO (Estados Unidos)

ANTILLAS MENORES

MAR CARIBE

Golfo de los Mosquitos
Colón
PANAMÁ
Panamá
Cuna 1000
Canal de Panamá

VENEZUELA

GUYANA

COLOMBIA

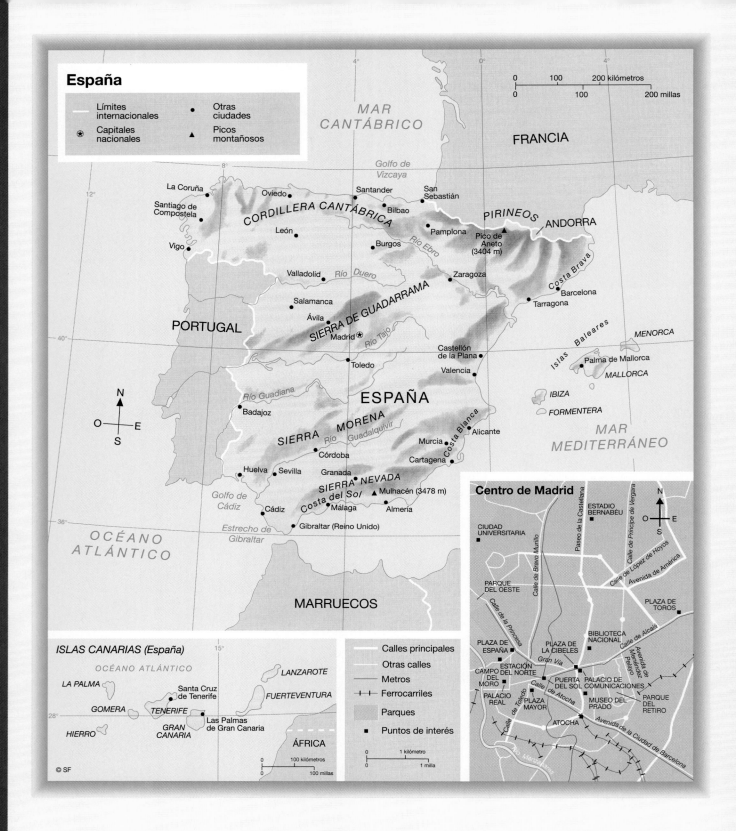

España

- Límites internacionales
- Capitales nacionales
- Otras ciudades
- Picos montañosos

MAR CANTÁBRICO

FRANCIA

Golfo de Vizcaya

La Coruña
Oviedo
Santander
San Sebastián
Santiago de Compostela
Bilbao
PIRINEOS
ANDORRA
CORDILLERA CANTÁBRICA
León
Pamplona
Pico de Aneto (3404 m)
Vigo
Burgos
Río Ebro
Valladolid
Río Duero
Zaragoza
Costa Brava
Salamanca
Barcelona
SIERRA DE GUADARRAMA
Ávila
Tarragona
PORTUGAL
Madrid
Río Tajo
Islas Baleares
MENORCA
Castellón de la Plana
Palma de Mallorca
Toledo
Valencia
MALLORCA
ESPAÑA
IBIZA
Río Guadiana
FORMENTERA
Badajoz
SIERRA MORENA
Costa Blanca
MAR MEDITERRÁNEO
Río Guadalquivir
Alicante
Murcia
Córdoba
Cartagena
Huelva
Sevilla
Granada
SIERRA NEVADA
Mulhacén (3478 m)
Golfo de Cádiz
Costa del Sol
Almería
Cádiz
Málaga
Gibraltar (Reino Unido)
OCÉANO ATLÁNTICO
Estrecho de Gibraltar

MARRUECOS

Centro de Madrid

- Calles principales
- Otras calles
- Metros
- Ferrocarriles
- Parques
- Puntos de interés

ESTADIO BERNABÉU
CIUDAD UNIVERSITARIA
Paseo de la Castellana
Calle de Príncipe de Vergara
Calle de López de Hoyos
Avenida de América
PARQUE DEL OESTE
Calle de la Princesa
PLAZA DE TOROS
PLAZA DE ESPAÑA
BIBLIOTECA NACIONAL
Calle de Alcalá
PLAZA DE LA CIBELES
Gran Vía
ESTACIÓN DEL NORTE
CAMPO DEL MORO
PUERTA DEL SOL
PALACIO DE COMUNICACIONES
Avenida de Menéndez Pelayo
PALACIO REAL
Calle de Atocha
MUSEO DEL PRADO
PARQUE DEL RETIRO
PLAZA MAYOR
Calle de Toledo
ATOCHA
Avenida de la Ciudad de Barcelona
Río Manzanares

ISLAS CANARIAS (España)

OCÉANO ATLÁNTICO
LA PALMA
LANZAROTE
Santa Cruz de Tenerife
FUERTEVENTURA
GOMERA
TENERIFE
Las Palmas de Gran Canaria
HIERRO
GRAN CANARIA
ÁFRICA

© SF

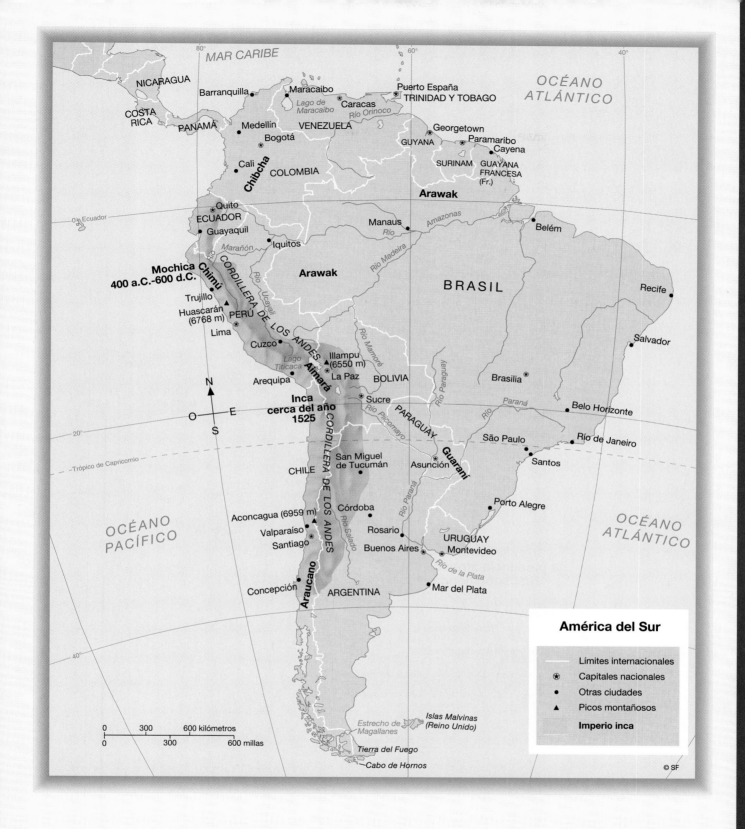

MAR CARIBE

OCÉANO ATLÁNTICO

NICARAGUA

Barranquilla

Maracaibo

Puerto España
TRINIDAD Y TOBAGO

COSTA
RICA

Lago de
Maracaibo

Caracas
Río Orinoco

PANAMÁ

Medellín

VENEZUELA

Georgetown

Bogotá

GUYANA

Paramaribo
Cayena

Cali

Chibcha

COLOMBIA

SURINAM

GUAYANA
FRANCESA
(Fr.)

Arawak

Quito
ECUADOR

Manaus

Amazonas

Belém

0° Ecuador

Guayaquil

Marañón

Iquitos

Río

Mochica Chimú
400 a.C.-600 d.C.

Arawak

Río Madeira

BRASIL

CORDILLERA DE LOS ANDES

Río Ucayali

Recife

Trujillo

Huascarán
(6768 m)

PERÚ

Río Mamoré

Lima

Salvador

Cuzco

Illampu
(6550 m)

Lago
Titicaca

Aimará

La Paz

BOLIVIA

Brasilia

Arequipa

Río Paraguay

Inca
cerca del año
1525

Sucre

Río Pilcomayo

PARAGUAY

Paraná

Río

Belo Horizonte

20°

São Paulo

Río de Janeiro

Trópico de Capricornio

San Miguel
de Tucumán

CHILE

Guaraní

Asunción

Santos

Río Paraná

Aconcagua (6959 m)

Córdoba

Porto Alegre

OCÉANO
PACÍFICO

Valparaíso

Río Salado

Rosario

URUGUAY

OCÉANO
ATLÁNTICO

Santiago

Buenos Aires

Montevideo

Río de la Plata

Araucano

Concepción

ARGENTINA

Mar del Plata

40°

N
O   E
S

CORDILLERA DE LOS ANDES

0   300   600 kilómetros
0   300   600 millas

Estrecho de
Magallanes

Islas Malvinas
(Reino Unido)

Tierra del Fuego

Cabo de Hornos

© SF

América del Sur

Límites internacionales

⊛ Capitales nacionales

• Otras ciudades

▲ Picos montañosos

Imperio inca

Mapas   XVII

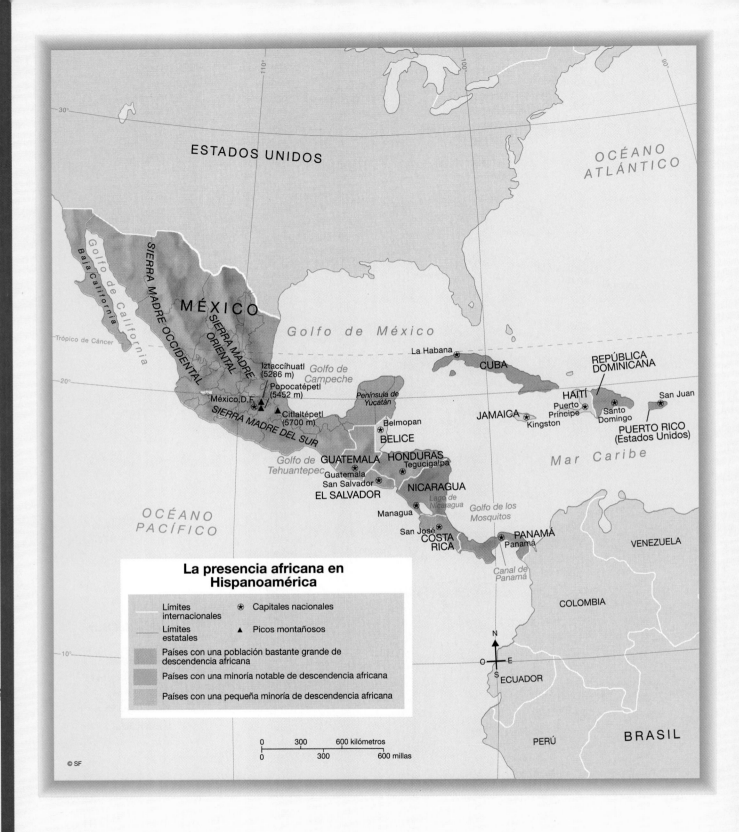

La presencia africana en Hispanoamérica

Límites internacionales
Límites estatales
Países con una población bastante grande de descendencia africana
Países con una minoría notable de descendencia africana
Países con una pequeña minoría de descendencia africana
⊛ Capitales nacionales
▲ Picos montañosos

0   300   600 kilómetros
0   300   600 millas

© SF

ESTADOS UNIDOS

OCÉANO ATLÁNTICO

Golfo de California

Baja California

SIERRA MADRE OCCIDENTAL

SIERRA MADRE ORIENTAL

MÉXICO

Golfo de México

Trópico de Cáncer

Iztaccíhuatl (5286 m)
Popocatépetl (5452 m)
México D.F.
Citlaltépetl (5700 m)

SIERRA MADRE DEL SUR

Golfo de Campeche

Península de Yucatán

Belmopan
BELICE

Golfo de Tehuantepec

GUATEMALA
Guatemala
San Salvador
EL SALVADOR

HONDURAS
Tegucigalpa

NICARAGUA
Lago de Nicaragua
Managua

Golfo de los Mosquitos

San José
COSTA RICA

PANAMÁ
Panamá

Canal de Panamá

OCÉANO PACÍFICO

La Habana

CUBA

JAMAICA
Kingston

HAITÍ
Puerto Príncipe

REPÚBLICA DOMINICANA
Santo Domingo

San Juan
PUERTO RICO (Estados Unidos)

Mar Caribe

COLOMBIA

VENEZUELA

N
O   E
S
ECUADOR

PERÚ   BRASIL

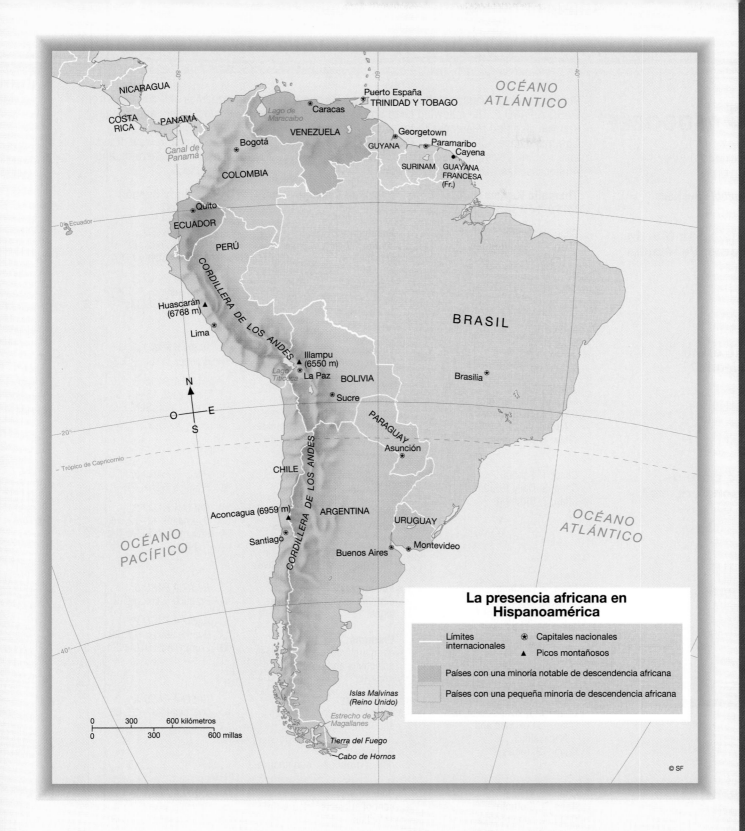

La presencia africana en Hispanoamérica

— Límites internacionales
⊛ Capitales nacionales
▲ Picos montañosos

Países con una minoría notable de descendencia africana

Países con una pequeña minoría de descendencia africana

© SF

NICARAGUA

COSTA RICA

PANAMÁ

Canal de Panamá

Puerto España
TRINIDAD Y TOBAGO
Lago de Maracaibo
Caracas
VENEZUELA
Bogotá
Georgetown
GUYANA
Paramaribo
Cayena
SURINAM
GUAYANA FRANCESA (Fr.)
COLOMBIA

Quito
ECUADOR
0° Ecuador

PERÚ

CORDILLERA DE LOS ANDES

Huascarán (6768 m) ▲
Lima

BRASIL

Illampu (6550 m) ▲
Lago Titicaca
La Paz
BOLIVIA
Sucre
Brasilia

N
O E
S

20°
Trópico de Capricornio

PARAGUAY
Asunción

CHILE

CORDILLERA DE LOS ANDES

Aconcagua (6959 m) ▲
Santiago

ARGENTINA

URUGUAY
Buenos Aires
Montevideo

OCÉANO PACÍFICO

OCÉANO ATLÁNTICO

OCÉANO ATLÁNTICO

40°

Islas Malvinas (Reino Unido)

Estrecho de Magallanes

0   300   600 kilómetros
0   300   600 millas

Tierra del Fuego
Cabo de Hornos

Mapas   XIX

PASODOBLE

This motivating, magazine-style section recycles some of the major themes and concepts from *PASO A PASO 2*. The following chart shows the integrative review of vocabulary and grammar. You will also find references to the ancillary materials for *Pasodoble*. Some of the Communicative Activities from *PASO A PASO 2* are listed to provide additional review. If available, you may wish to use the *Pasos vivos 2* CD-ROM, *La Catrina* video, Test Generator, and Audiocassettes/CDs for further review.

Pasodoble Sections	Thematic Review from *PASO A PASO 2*	Recycled Concepts	Ancillary Support Materials
Escuela San Martín, Caracas, Venezuela	Chap. 1: School Chap. 4: Leisure-time Activities	**Vocabulary:** school subjects, leisure-time activities **Grammar:** *salir, tener, traer, conocer,* superlatives, direct object pronouns	*PASO A PASO 3:* Practice Wkbk. PD-1 Writing Activity PD-A *PASO A PASO 2:* Overheads 6–7, 13–14 Comm. Act. BLMs 1-1, 1-3
¿Qué están haciendo?	Chap. 1: School Chap. 3: Clothing Chap. 4: Leisure-time Activities Chap. 6: Special Occasions Chap. 7: Luxuries and Necessities Chap. 8: Shopping	**Vocabulary:** leisure-time activities, special occasions **Grammar:** superlatives, *ir a / tener que / deber / poder* + inf., comparatives, use of adjectives with *ser,* present progressive	*PASO A PASO 3:* Practice Wkbk. PD-2 *PASO A PASO 2:* Overheads 13–14, 38 Comm. Act. BLM 8-2
¿Qué clase de persona eres tú?	Chap. 1: School Chap. 2: Daily Routine Chap. 3: Clothing	**Vocabulary:** daily routine **Grammar:** *para* + inf., reflexive verbs, *depender de, antes de / después de* + inf., stem-changing verbs, comparatives	*PASO A PASO 3:* Practice Wkbk. PD-3 *PASO A PASO 2:* Overheads 11–12, 15 Comm. Act. BLMs 2-1, 2-2, 2-3
La moda	Chap. 3: Clothing Chap. 5: Childhood Chap. 8: Shopping Chap. 11: The Future	**Vocabulary:** clothing, shopping, professions **Grammar:** comparatives, demonstrative adjectives and pronouns, imperfect	*PASO A PASO 3:* Practice Wkbk. PD-3 *PASO A PASO 2:* Overheads 16–17, 29 Comm. Act. BLMs 3-1, 5-2
Caricaturas	Chap. 1: School Chap. 6: Special Occasions Chap. 7: Luxuries and Necessities Chap. 13: Meals	**Vocabulary:** holidays, home appliances and furnishings **Grammar:** object pronouns, subjunctive	*PASO A PASO 2:* Overheads 32–33, 66
Nuestros pasatiempos	Chap. 1: School Chap. 3: Clothing Chap. 4: Leisure-time Activities	**Vocabulary:** school subjects, leisure-time activities **Grammar:** object pronouns, regular and irregular preterite	*PASO A PASO 3:* Practice Wkbk. PD-4 Writing Activity PD-B *PASO A PASO 2:* Overheads 21–24 Comm. Act. BLMs 3-3, 4-2, 4-3

Pasodoble Sections	Thematic Review from *PASO A PASO 2*	Recycled Concepts	Ancillary Support Materials
El día de fiesta que más me impresionó	Chap. 1: School Chap. 2: Daily Routine Chap. 3: Clothing Chap. 5: Childhood Chap. 6: Special Occasions Chap. 10: Movies and Television Chap. 13: Meals	**Vocabulary:** clothing, toys, holidays and special occasions, food **Grammar:** personal *a,* object pronouns, reflexive pronouns, preterite of stem-changing verbs and *dar,* negative expressions, preterite vs. imperfect	*PASO A PASO 3:* Practice Wkbk. PD-5 Writing Activity PD-C *PASO A PASO 2:* Overheads 16–17, 32–34, 62–65 Comm. Act. BLMs 6-1, 6-2, 6-3, 10-2
Los tiempos cambian	Chap. 7: Luxuries and Necessities	**Vocabulary:** home appliances and furnishings **Grammar:** possessive pronouns	*PASO A PASO 3:* Practice Wkbk. PD-6 Writing Activity PD-D *PASO A PASO 2:* Overheads 35–38 Comm. Act. BLM 7-1
Tesoros del mundo hispano	Chap. 3: Clothing Chap. 7: Luxuries and Necessities Chap. 8: Shopping	**Vocabulary:** material **Grammar:** preterite, demonstrative adjectives, impersonal *se*	*PASO A PASO 3:* Practice Wkbk. PD-6 *PASO A PASO 2:* Overhead 20
La salud	Chap. 9: Accidents and Illness	**Vocabulary:** parts of the body, illness **Grammar:** imperfect progressive vs. preterite	*PASO A PASO 3:* Practice Wkbk. PD-7 *PASO A PASO 2:* Overheads 44–47 Comm. Act. BLMs 9-1, 9-2
Nuestras películas favoritas	Chap. 1: School Chap. 4: Leisure-time Activities Chap. 10: Movies and Television	**Vocabulary:** types of movies **Grammar:** personal *a, saber,* preterite vs. imperfect	*PASO A PASO 3:* Practice Wkbk. PD-8 *PASO A PASO 2:* Overheads 48–49, 51 Comm. Act. BLMs 10-1, 10-3
Las muchachas nunca deben romper las reglas	Chap. 2: Daily Routine Chap. 3: Clothing Chap. 8: Shopping	**Vocabulary:** clothing **Grammar:** *antes de / después de* + inf., preterite, impersonal *se,* negative expressions	*PASO A PASO 3:* Practice Wkbk. PD-9 *PASO A PASO 2:* Overheads 15, 43 Comm. Act. BLM 8-3
Vamos de vacaciones	Chap. 12: Travel	**Vocabulary:** travel **Grammar:** affirmative and negative *tú* commands, object pronouns with *tú* commands, reflexive *tú* commands	*PASO A PASO 3:* Practice Wkbk. PD-9 Writing Activity PD-E *PASO A PASO 2:* Overheads 59–60 Comm. Act. BLMs 12-2, 12-3
El siglo XXI—unas predicciones	Chap. 11: The Future	**Vocabulary:** professions, technology **Grammar:** future tense	*PASO A PASO 3:* Practice Wkbk. PD-10 Writing Activity PD-F *PASO A PASO 2:* Overheads 52–53, 56 Comm. Act. BLMs 11-2, 11-3

Present

Pasodoble is a motivating, magazine-style recycling of major themes and concepts from *PASO A PASO 2*. Its purpose is to help students bridge the time gap between Levels 2 and 3 and to give teachers interesting and purposeful materials to use during the first days of a course when class rosters may continue to change. There are different ways in which *Pasodoble* can be used, depending on student needs. Here are some options to consider:

1 Complete all sections of *Pasodoble* before beginning Chapter 1. In order to ensure appropriate pacing, this use of *Pasodoble* should last no longer than two weeks on a schedule of daily 45- to 50-minute classes.

2 Choose five to six sections of *Pasodoble* to use during the first days of class. The chart on pp. 1A–1B, which lists the recycling of *PASO A PASO 2* themes, vocabulary, and grammar, is useful in making those choices. After approximately one week, on a schedule of 45- to 50-minute classes, begin Chapter 1. Keep track of the *Pasodoble* sections that were not used and introduce them at appropriate times during the year. For example, *El día de fiesta que más me impresionó* can be used with Chapter 2 to practice

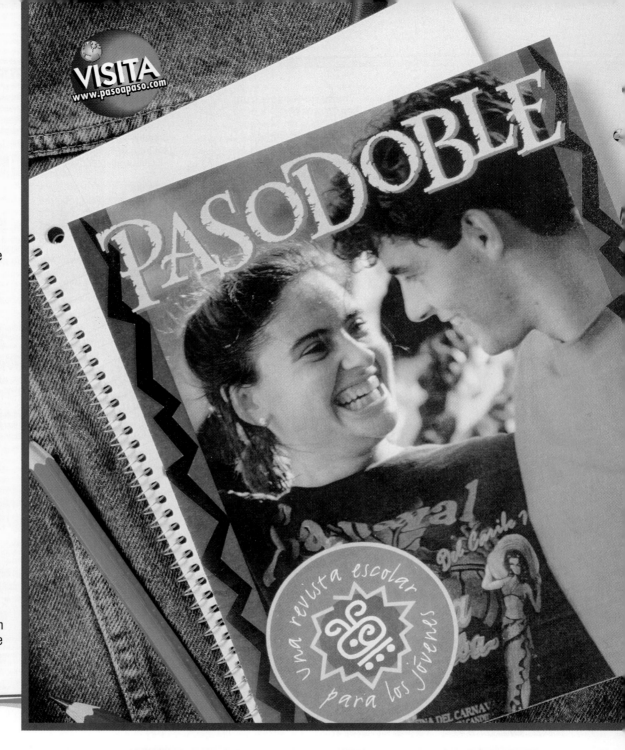

Options

Strategies for Reaching All Students

Students Needing Extra Help
Students may not recognize the format as being that of a magazine. Point out that just as magazines or newspapers sometimes reprint popular articles to celebrate an anniversary or a histroical event, that is what the publisher has done here.

Enrichment
Tell students that the *pasodoble,* a familiar ballroom dance, actually refers to the dramatic march music played at bullfights, military processions, and other public events in Spain. Each measure of its music consists of eight beats in 2/4 time, creating an even rhythm. Although the term literally means "two-step," the dance is a march step accentuated by movements reminiscent of the *torero.* The popular meaning came into use as professional dancers of the 1920s and '30s used the music to improvise encores after classical dance performances.

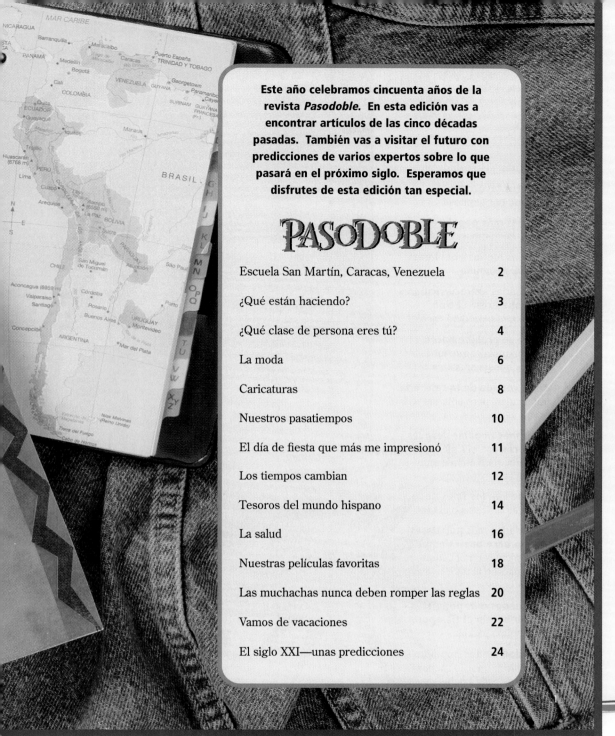

Este año celebramos cincuenta años de la revista *Pasodoble*. En esta edición vas a encontrar artículos de las cinco décadas pasadas. También vas a visitar el futuro con predicciones de varios expertos sobre lo que pasará en el próximo siglo. Esperamos que disfrutes de esta edición tan especial.

PASODOBLE

the imperfect. Use *La salud* with Chapter 3 to introduce or practice the imperfect progressive. Use other sections to complement chapter themes, such as *Tesoros del mundo hispano* with Chapter 5 and *Nuestras películas favoritas* with Chapter 4. You might reserve some *Pasodoble* sections for days when a substitute teacher is in class.

3 Begin Chapter 1 within the first week of class. During the first two weeks, develop lessons in which you combine *Pasodoble* sections with elements of Chapter 1 on a daily basis. Sections that are not used now can be introduced later (see option #2).

The *Pasodoble* articles can be complemented by ancillary support materials from *PASO A PASO 1* and *2*. These provide additional practice of vocabulary and grammar, as well as development of language skills, for classroom use or as homework. Refer to pp. 1A–B for a listing of these support materials.

Review

Recycled Concepts from
PASO A PASO 2
School subjects, *salir, tener, traer,
conocer,* superlatives, direct object
pronouns (Chap. 1); leisure-time
activities (Chap. 4)

**Ancillaries available for
use with** *Pasodoble*

 Practice Wkbk. PD-1

**Ancillaries suggested
from** *PASO A PASO 2*

 **Overheads 6–7,
13–14**

 **Comm. Act. BLMs
1-1, 1-3**

Activate Prior Knowledge
As a class, brainstorm answers
appropriate to your school for
each category.

Writing Extensions

 **Writing Activity
PD-A**

ESCUELA SAN MARTÍN
Caracas, Venezuela

Población: 340 estudiantes

Deportes favoritos:
el fútbol, por supuesto

Materias más populares:
literatura, idiomas, biología

Materias menos populares:
historia, geografía

**Actividades extracurriculares
más populares:** el club
literario, el periódico escolar

Lo que se prohibe hacer:
usar maquillaje; que los
muchachos usen aretes

Mejor comida de la cafetería:
empanadas, pero sólo las
sirven los viernes

**Lugar más popular después
de las clases:** el Café
Conchita, para comer una
merienda

**Adónde van los fines de
semana:** a fiestas o al cine

**Actividades más populares
cuando hace buen tiempo:**
hacer picnics en el campo,
ir a la plaza o al parque con
amigos

**Actividades más populares
cuando hace mal tiempo:**
jugar bolos, patinar

Actividad menos popular:
hacer tarea (¡por lo menos
dos horas cada noche!)

2   Pasodoble

*Antes de
repasar el
pasado, vamos
a averiguar
cómo son unos
estudiantes
de hoy.*

MÁS PRÁCTICA

- Más práctica y tarea, p. 541
- Practice Workbook PD–1

Options

Strategies for Reaching All Students

Spanish-Speaking Students
Escuela San Martín, Caracas, Venezuela:
Have students respond in writing to the
following: *Piensa en tu escuela y en tus
compañeros. ¿Cómo responderías a las
categorías que dan para la Escuela San
Martín en tu propia situación?*

¿Qué están haciendo?: Have students write
the answers to the following questions:
*Imagina que vas a hacer un álbum de fotos
del año pasado en tu escuela. ¿De quiénes
serían las fotos? ¿Qué eventos incluirías?
¿Por qué?*

Students Needing Extra Help
Escuela San Martín, Caracas, Venezuela:
Review school subjects and comparative
adjectives. If available, use the vocabulary
section of the Book 2, Chap. 1 Organizer.
Have students fill in the categories with their
own preferences.

de la edición de enero de 1995

¿Qué están haciendo?

Los estudiantes de la Escuela San Martín nos enviaron fotos de algunas de sus actividades durante este año escolar. Nos parece que todos se divirtieron mucho.

¿Nunca vas a terminar este proyecto, Carlos? Como siempre, ¡vas a terminarlo mañana!

Juan y Alberto antes del partido contra los Leones. ¡Qué partido tan emocionante!

Ramiro y Elena caminando después de la escuela. ¿Quieren un helado?

Carmen y Pablo planeando la fiesta del sábado. ¡Vamos a bailar toda la noche!

Juan Gabriel se prepara para su papel en la producción de *La barca sin pescador*—un éxito fabuloso, ¿no?

¡A Javier le encanta tocar la flauta!

También nos enviaron los resultados de su encuesta sobre quién es el / la más artístico(a), divertido(a), etc. de la clase. ¿Qué título crees que recibió cada persona que ves aquí? (Los títulos que "ganaron" se encuentran abajo.)

Carlos: el estudiante más desordenado Ramiro y Elena: los más sociables Juan y Alberto: los más deportistas Juan Gabriel: el más artístico Carmen y Pablo: los más divertidos Javier: el mejor músico

MÁS PRÁCTICA

- Más práctica y tarea, pp. 541–542
- Practice Workbook PD–1

3

Review

Recycled Concepts from *PASO A PASO 2*
Superlatives, *ir a / tener que / deber / poder* + inf., (Chap. 1); comparatives (Chap. 3); leisure-time activities (Chap. 4); special occasions (Chap. 6); use of adjectives with *ser* (Chap. 7); present progressive (Chap. 8)

Ancillaries available for use with *Pasodoble*

Practice Wkbk. PD-2

Ancillaries suggested from *PASO A PASO 2*

Overheads 13–14, 38

Comm. Act. BLM 8-2

Activate Prior Knowledge
Tell students to list as many adjectives as they can in one minute to describe the people in the photos. Combine students' lists on the chalkboard to create a master list for them to use in answering the questions.

Answers
Answers will vary. Students may check their answers at the bottom of the page.

Enrichment
Escuela San Martín, Caracas, Venezuela: Conduct a class discussion about your school, profiling it and its student body as is done here.

Multiple Intelligences
Visual/Spatial
See Activate Prior Knowledge; Practice Wkbk. PD-1 and PD-2; Writing Activity PD-A; Overheads 6–7, 13–14, and 38 (from Book 2); and Comm. Act. BLMs 1-1, 1-3, and 8-2 (from Book 2).

Review

Recycled Concepts from *PASO A PASO 2*

Para + inf. (Chap. 1); reflexive verbs, daily routine, *depender de, antes de / después de* + inf., stem-changing verbs (Chap. 2); comparatives (Chap. 3)

Ancillaries available for use with *Pasodoble*

 Practice Wkbk. PD-3

Ancillaries suggested from *PASO A PASO 2*

 Overheads 11–12, 15

 Comm. Act. BLMs 2-1, 2-2, 2-3

¿Qué clase de persona eres tú?

1. Generalmente me despierto

a. temprano para hacer ejercicio antes de salir para la escuela.

b. justo a tiempo para no llegar tarde a la escuela.

c. cuando la profesora me hace una pregunta.

2. ¿Cómo te despiertas cada día?

a. Con un despertador

b. Me despierto a la misma hora todos los días sin despertador.

c. Cuando el perro y el gato tienen hambre

3. Los fines de semana me levanto

a. a la misma hora que los otros días.

b. una hora o más después de despertarme.

c. alrededor del mediodía (a tiempo para almorzar).

4. Me cepillo los dientes

a. tres veces al día después de las comidas.

b. por lo menos una vez al día.

c. cuando recuerdo hacerlo.

5. Para estar limpio(a) prefiero

a. bañarme.

b. ducharme.

c. lavarme la cara de vez en cuando.

6. ¿Cuánto tiempo necesitas para vestirte por la mañana?

a. Más de una hora

b. Depende de adónde voy a ir

c. Cinco minutos o menos

7. ¿Cuánto tiempo necesitas para peinarte cada día?

a. Media hora o más

b. Un cuarto de hora más o menos

c. Diez segundos

MÁS PRÁCTICA

Más práctica y tarea, p. 542

4 Pasodoble

Options

Strategies for Reaching All Students

Spanish-Speaking Students
Have students survey the class and use the results to answer the following questions in writing: *Haz una encuesta en tu clase. ¿Cuántas personas salieron con un tanteo de 0–5, según la prueba? ¿De 6–12? ¿De 13–20? Piensa en las personas de cada grupo. ¿Crees que esta prueba da una verdadera idea de cómo son? Explica tu respuesta.*

Students Needing Extra Help
Point out the stem-changing verbs among the reflexive verbs. If available, use the vocabulary section of the Book 2, Chap. 2 Organizer.

Enrichment
As an in-class assignment, have students create three more questions for this questionnaire, then share them with the class.

8. Los días de semana, ¿a qué hora te acuestas?

a. A las nueve y media o antes
b. A las diez o más tarde
c. Depende de cuándo termino mi tarea

9. Generalmente me despierto

a. de buen humor.
b. bastante perezoso(a).
c. queriendo matar a la primera persona que me habla.

10. De éstos, lo que más me gustaría hacer los fines de semana es

a. trabajar como voluntario(a) en un hospital.
b. cuidar niños para ganar dinero.
c. ir a fiestas, bailar y escuchar música.

Tu tanteo

Cada respuesta a = 0 puntos

Cada respuesta b = 1 punto

Cada respuesta c = 2 puntos

Si tu tanteo es 0–5, eres demasiado serio(a). Necesitas divertirte más.

Si tu tanteo es 6–12, estás bastante bien equilibrado(a), pero puedes divertirte un poco más también.

Si tu tanteo es 13–20, ¿no mientes? Si no, probablemente tratas de ser demasiado divertido(a). Necesitas ser un poco <u>más</u> serio(a).

Compara tus respuestas con las de un(a) compañero(a). ¿Qué clase de persona eres? ¿Qué clase de persona es él o ella? ¿En qué son Uds. similares o diferentes?

Activate Prior Knowledge

As a class, brainstorm verbs associated with daily routine, and write them on the chalkboard. In small groups, have students tell each other at what time they do the activities listed. Students should take notes on what their group members say, so that they can report it to the class.

Answers

Student responses will vary, but you might want to keep track of how many students fall into each point total category.

Writing Extensions

As a homework assignment, have students write a short paragraph about their family's morning routine. Tell them to include the times at which various family members get up, shower, dress, eat breakfast, brush their teeth, and leave the house.

Multiple Intelligences

Bodily/Kinesthetic and Visual/Spatial

1) Have students write descriptions of themselves, including what they are wearing. The papers are shuffled and redistributed, making sure that no one gets his or her own description. Students walk around the room and ask each other questions in order to find the person described on their papers. If Student A has found Student B, but Student B has not yet found the person described on his or her paper, Student A must help Student B with the search. The initial "finders" continue to help with other searches until everyone has been found.
2) Have students create a poster in which they illustrate themselves and their daily routines. Display the posters around the room. If available, use computer software to create a slide show.

Interpersonal/Social
See Spanish-Speaking Students and Enrichment.

Interpersonal/Social and Verbal/Linguistic
See Activate Prior Knowledge.

Visual/Spatial
See Writing Extensions; Practice Wkbk. PD-3; Overheads 11–12 and 15 (from Book 2); and Comm. Act. BLMs 2-1, 2-2, and 2-3 (from Book 2).

Review

LA MODA

¿Qué ropa usaron tus padres y tus abuelos? En estas páginas encontrarás la ropa que estaba de moda durante cada década de nuestra publicación. ¿Qué década prefieres? ¿Por qué? ¿Podrías pensar en otras modas para jóvenes que te gustarían más?

LOS 50

En estos años los poetas y otros escritores eran héroes. Y el color negro era su favorito.

Claro que sí, había modas más conservadoras.

LOS 60

Durante esos años teníamos el pelo un poco más largo y la ropa era mucho más imaginativa.

MÁS PRÁCTICA

Más práctica y tarea, p. 542
Practice Workbook PD-3

6   Pasodoble

Options

Strategies for Reaching All Students

Spanish-Speaking Students
Ask students: *¿Cómo crees que se vestirán los jóvenes en los próximos cinco años? ¿Volverán a un estilo del pasado o promoverán algún "look" nuevo?*

Students Needing Extra Help
Review clothing and demonstrative adjectives. If available, use the Book 2, Chap. 3 Organizer.
Brainstorm responses to the *¿Por qué?* question.

Enrichment
Have students survey their family members by answering the following questions and then reporting to class the next day: *¿Qué música, libros y películas les gustaron a tus padres cuando eran jóvenes? ¿A tus abuelos? ¿Qué piensas tú de sus gustos?*

de la edición de marzo de 1992

LOS 70

Ésa era la época de la ropa exagerada. El pelo largo todavía estaba de moda.

En esa década las diferencias entre la ropa para caballeros y para damas empezaban a desaparecer.

LOS 80

Éstos eran años en los que todos querían ser hombres o mujeres de negocios, o por lo menos trataban de vestirse así.

LOS 90

Y en los 90 . . . Bueno, ¿cómo nos vestimos hoy?

7

Activate Prior Knowledge
Have magazine pictures of various fashions available. Call on individuals to express their opinion about the clothing pictured, using demonstrative adjectives: *¿Qué prefieres, esta falda gris o esa falda negra? / Prefiero esa falda negra porque . . . .*

Answers
Answers to introductory paragraph questions will vary.

Writing Extensions
As an in-class assignment, have pairs of students write a fashion review of one of the decades pictured here. Tell them to include a detailed description of both outfits for each period, as well as a critique.

Multiple Intelligences
Bodily/Kinesthetic and Verbal/Linguistic
Have students stage a fashion show in which they model a style from their choice of decades. Each student chooses another student to be the narrator when he or she models.
Interpersonal/Social
See Enrichment.

Visual/Spatial
See Writing Extensions, Practice Wkbk. PD-3, Overheads 16–17 and 29 (from Book 2), and Comm. Act. BLMs 3-1 and 5-2 (from Book 2).
Visual/Spatial and Verbal/Linguistic
See Activate Prior Knowledge.

Recycled Concepts from
PASO A PASO 2
Object pronouns (Chap. 1);
holidays (Chap. 6); home appliances and furnishings (Chap. 7);
subjunctive (Chap. 13)

Ancillaries suggested
from *PASO A PASO 2*

 Overheads 32–33,
66

8 Pasodoble

Options

Strategies for Reaching All Students

Spanish-Speaking Students
*¿Cuál de las caricaturas crees que es la más
cómica? ¿Por qué?*

Students Needing Extra Help
Ask students what they think *socorro*
means. If necessary, point out that it is
a synonym for *ayuda.*

Multiple Intelligences
Bodily/Kinesthetic and Visual/Spatial
Have students write a dialogue based on the
cartoon on p. 9 and act it out in front of the
class.
Visual/Spatial
See Activate Prior Knowledge, Writing
Extensions, and Overheads 32–33 and 66
(from Book 2).

—Perdona, querido . . . , pero . . . ¿estás seguro de que sabes arreglar el televisor?

MÁS PRÁCTICA

Más práctica y tarea, p. 543

Activate Prior Knowledge
Bring in some one-panel cartoons from the local newspaper and discuss with students how artists convey their message using both art and text—or even text alone.

Writing Extensions
Students or student pairs might enjoy drawing their own cartoons and writing captions for them.

9

Review

Recycled Concepts from
PASO A PASO 2
School subjects, object pronouns
(Chap. 1); preterite (Chap. 3);
leisure-time activities, irregular
preterite (Chap. 4)

Ancillaries available for
use with *Pasodoble*

 Practice Wkbk. PD-4

Ancillaries suggested
from *PASO A PASO 2*

 Overheads 21–24

 Comm. Act. BLMs
3-3, 4-2, 4-3

Activate Prior Knowledge
Brainstorm other leisure-time
activities *(pasear en bote, dibujar,
hablar por teléfono, jugar videojuegos, escuchar música, sacar
fotos,* etc.) and ask students if
they did those things last week.

Answers
Answers to introductory
paragraph questions will vary.

Writing Extensions

 Writing Activity
PD-B

de la edición de abril de 1960

NUESTROS PASATIEMPOS

Hicimos una encuesta a nuestros lectores sobre sus pasatiempos favoritos y los más aburridos. Éstos fueron los resultados. ¿Estás de acuerdo con ellos o son diferentes a tus propios pasatiempos? ¿Cuándo fue la última vez que tú hiciste estas actividades? ¿Cuáles de éstas hiciste la semana pasada?

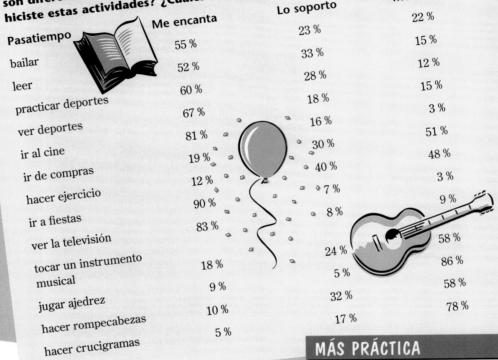

Pasatiempo	Me encanta	Lo soporto	Me aburre
bailar	55 %	23 %	22 %
leer	52 %	33 %	15 %
practicar deportes	60 %	28 %	12 %
ver deportes	67 %	18 %	15 %
ir al cine	81 %	16 %	3 %
ir de compras	19 %	30 %	51 %
hacer ejercicio	12 %	40 %	48 %
ir a fiestas	90 %	7 %	3 %
ver la televisión	83 %	8 %	9 %
tocar un instrumento musical	18 %	24 %	58 %
jugar ajedrez	9 %	5 %	86 %
hacer rompecabezas	10 %	32 %	58 %
hacer crucigramas	5 %	17 %	78 %

MÁS PRÁCTICA

Más práctica y tarea, p. 543
Practice Workbook PD–4

10   Pasodoble

Options

Strategies for Reaching All Students

Spanish-Speaking Students
Nuestros pasatiempos: Tell students: *Pon
estas actividades en orden según la importancia que les das tú. Explica por qué has
decidido en ese orden.*
El día de fiesta que más me impresionó:
Ask: ¿*Cuál es tu día de fiesta favorito? ¿Qué
es lo que te gusta de la celebración? ¿Lo
celebra tu familia de alguna manera especial? Descríbela.*

Students Needing Extra Help
Nuestros pasatiempos: Review pastimes.
Brainstorm others that are not on the list. If
available, use the Book 2, Chap. 4 Organizer.
Review the preterite of *ver, ir, hacer,* and
-car, -gar, -zar verbs.

El día de fiesta que más me impresionó:
Review *lo que,* negatives, personal *a,* and
object pronouns. Review the less frequently
used names for family members. If available,
use the Book 2, Chap. 6 Organizer. Review
reading strategies.
Have students work in pairs or groups to
create their own story. Limit it to a specific
number of lines.

10   Standards 1.1; 1.2; 3.1

El día de fiesta que más me impresionó

Les hicimos una pregunta a nuestros lectores sobre los días de fiesta que mejor recuerdan. Aquí están algunas de las respuestas más interesantes.

Paco Lo que más recuerdo es la boda de mi primo porque a mí no me gustan las ocasiones en las que tengo que ponerme traje y corbata. Toda la familia—bisabuelos, abuelos, primos, tíos, nietos, sobrinos— estaba en la iglesia, pero mi primo no llegaba. Pues, hubo un accidente en la carretera y no podía hacer nada. Cuando llegó, la novia y su mamá lloraban y su papá estaba muy enojado porque creían que no iba a llegar a tiempo. Luego, cuando las niñas encendían las velas, el pelo de una de ellas se encendió también y mi primo tuvo que apagarlo. Por fin se casaron y todos los invitados los felicitaron. Imagino que nadie podrá olvidar esa boda nunca.

Roberto La Navidad es mi fiesta favorita. Recuerdo que una vez, cuando era pequeño, pedí un perro de peluche especial pero no había ninguno en las tiendas. Por fin, la Nochebuena, me compraron otra clase de animal de peluche. Cuando abrí el regalo yo estaba muy triste. Esa tarde, cuando llegaron mis tíos, tío Enrique llegó con regalos para todos y él me dio el perro que quería. ¡Qué contento estaba entonces!

Carmen Recuerdo el día de mi santo cuando yo tenía 8 años. Tengo cinco hermanos. Mi mamá bañó y vistió a los pequeños y Anita y yo, las mayores, nos bañamos y nos vestimos. Después, mientras esperábamos a los menores, Ana y yo fuimos al patio para jugar. Cuando mamá nos llamó para salir, estábamos sucias de cabeza a pie. Por supuesto, no había tiempo para bañarnos otra vez. Sólo nos lavamos la cara y las manos, y fuimos a la fiesta con los vestidos sucios. Teníamos miedo de lo que papá iba a decir, pero cuando nos vio, nos dijo que las fiestas eran para celebrar. Mi padre es un hombre muy comprensivo. Ni Anita ni yo olvidaremos nunca lo que nos dijo esa tarde.

MÁS PRÁCTICA

- Más práctica y tarea, pp. 543–544
- Practice Workbook PD–5

11

Review

Recycled Concepts from PASO A PASO 2
Personal *a*, object pronouns (Chap. 1); reflexive pronouns (Chap. 2); clothing (Chap. 3); toys (Chap. 5); holidays and special occasions, preterite of stem-changing verbs and *dar* (Chap. 6); negative expressions (Chap. 8); preterite vs. imperfect (Chap. 10); food (Chap. 13)

Ancillaries available for use with *Pasodoble*

 Practice Wkbk. PD-5

Ancillaries suggested from PASO A PASO 2

 Overheads 16–17, 32–34, 62–65

 Comm. Act. BLMs 6-1, 6-2, 6-3, 10-2

Activate Prior Knowledge
To prepare students for this reading, have them write a short paragraph about a holiday or special occasion they remember from their childhood. Ask for volunteers to share their stories with the class.

Writing Extensions

 Writing Activity PD-C

Enrichment
Nuestros pasatiempos: Review this list as a class activity, keeping a tally of students' opinions.
El día de fiesta que más me impresionó: As an in-class assignment, have students describe the most memorable celebration of their childhood. Call on individuals to read their work to the class.

Multiple Intelligences
Logical/Mathematical and Verbal/Linguistic
See Enrichment.
Visual/Spatial
See Practice Wkbk. PD-4 and PD-5; Overheads 16–17, 21–24, 32–34, and 62–65 (from Book 2); Comm. Act. BLMs 3-3, 4-2, 4-3, 6-1, 6-2, 6-3, and 10-2 (from Book 2); Activate Prior Knowledge; and Writing Activities PD-B and PD-C.

Review

Recycled Concepts from
PASO A PASO 2
Home appliances and furnishings,
possessive pronouns (Chap. 7)

**Ancillaries available for
use with** *Pasodoble*

 Practice Wkbk. PD-6

**Ancillaries suggested
from** *PASO A PASO 2*

 Overheads 35–38

 Comm. Act. BLM 7-1

de la edición de junio de 1991

Los tiempos cambian

Les preguntamos a nuestros lectores qué aparatos
y otros productos creían que eran lujos y cuáles
necesidades. Aquí están dos de las respuestas que
recibimos. ¿Estás de acuerdo con ellas? Haz tus
propias listas. Luego, haz esta pregunta a alguien
que tenga cuarenta o cincuenta años más que tú.
¿Sus respuestas son diferentes de las tuyas? (¡Estas
listas son muy diferentes de las nuestras!)

La lista de Antonio

LUJOS:

el televisor

el tocacintas

la lavadora

la secadora

la aspiradora

la calefacción central

el aire acondicionado

NECESIDADES:

la estufa

el refrigerador

el radio

el fregadero

los libros

el coche

el reloj pulsera

el calentador

el ventilador

12   Pasodoble

Options

Strategies for Reaching All Students

Spanish-Speaking Students
Ask: *¿Cómo crees que cambiará tu lista de
necesidades cuando tengas tu propia casa
y tengas que comprar todo tú mismo(a)?
¿Habrá más o menos en ella? ¿Por qué?*

Students Needing Extra Help
Review the meanings of the words in the list
and possessive pronouns. If available, use
the Book 2, Chap. 7 Organizer.
Remind students to conduct the interview in
English, but to report back to the class in
Spanish. Specify the number of items
required on students' lists.
Have students discuss the reasons for the
differences in the lists of the two age
groups. They may need some help with
the vocabulary.

Enrichment
Review these lists together with your students as a class activity, asking for their
opinion as to whether a particular item is
a luxury or a necessity.

12   Standards 1.1; 1.2; 3.1; 5.1

La lista de María

LUJOS:

el aire acondicionado

el secador de pelo

el microondas

el lavaplatos

el televisor con control remoto

la videocasetera

las joyas

la secadora

el coche

NECESIDADES:

el tostador

la lavadora

la estufa

el refrigerador

los cuchillos, los tenedores y
las cucharas

el detector de humo

el extinguidor de incendios

la computadora

la bicicleta

MÁS PRÁCTICA

Más práctica y tarea, p. 544

13

Activate Prior Knowledge
As a class, brainstorm things that people now consider a necessity, but that were uncommon or unknown 20, or even ten, years ago.

Answers
Answers to introductory paragraph questions will vary.

Writing Extensions

Writing Activity PD-D

Multiple Intelligences
Interpersonal/Social
See Activate Prior Knowledge.
Visual/Spatial
See Practice Wkbk. PD-6, Overheads 35–38 (from Book 2), Comm. Act. BLM 7-1 (from Book 2), and Writing Activity PD-D.

Review

Recycled Concepts from
PASO A PASO 2
Preterite, demonstrative adjectives (Chap. 3); materials (Chap. 7); impersonal *se* (Chap. 8)

Ancillaries suggested from *PASO A PASO 2*

 Overhead 20

TESOROS DEL MUNDO HISPANO

VIAJAMOS POR TODAS PARTES PARA TRAERLES LOS TESOROS MÁS BELLOS DEL MUNDO HISPANO. AQUÍ SE MUESTRA LO QUE ENCONTRAMOS.

▶ Descubrimos esta botella de oro en el Museo de América de Madrid. Es parte del Tesoro de los Quimbaya, indígenas de Colombia.

▶ Encontraron estos cuchillos de piedra en las excavaciones del Templo Mayor en la Ciudad de México. Los adornos son de turquesa, obsidiana y concha.

14   Pasodoble

MÁS PRÁCTICA

Más práctica y tarea, p. 544
Practice Workbook PD–6

Options

Strategies for Reaching All Students

Spanish-Speaking Students
Have students respond in writing to the following: *Los "tesoros" de una familia son cosas que tienen mucha importancia para la familia. No es necesario que tengan gran valor monetario. ¿Hay algo en tu familia que se considere un "tesoro"? ¿Qué es? ¿Quién lo tiene? ¿Se pasa de generación en generación? ¿Por qué crees que tiene importancia?*

Students Needing Extra Help
Review impersonal *se*. Brainstorm other materials. If available, use the Book 2, Chap. 3 Organizer. Have students describe something in a museum that appealed to them.

Multiple Intelligences
Visual/Spatial
See Overhead 20 (from Book 2), Activate Prior Knowledge, and Writing Extensions.

Cultural Notes ☼

(p. 14, bottom left photo)
These personified sacrificial knives, made of flint with pieces of obsidian, turquoise, and shell to form teeth and eyes, were found at the ruins of the Aztec Templo Mayor in Mexico City. Like many other such discoveries, they were uncovered by accident during a construction project in 1978.
(p. 14, top right photo)
This elegant, beautifully proportioned flask with female figures in relief on both sides was made by the Quimbaya Indians of

◀ Esta figura de Xiuhtecuhtli, el Señor de Turquesa, está hecha de piedra, y conserva la pintura original de las figuras aztecas. Se encuentra en el Museo Nacional de Antropología de México.

▲ Este objeto de cerámica de Cholula se encuentra en el Museo del Templo Mayor de México. Representa a Chicomecoatl, diosa azteca de la vegetación, de un lado y a Tlaloc, dios de la lluvia, del otro.

▶ Este platillo de cerámica de Cholula es parte de la colección del Museo Nacional de Antropología de México.

Activate Prior Knowledge
As a class, generate a list of what students perceive as U.S. national treasures (the original Declaration of Independence or Constitution, Monticello, the Wright brothers' airplane, the Apollo spacecraft, a certain painting or sculpture, a famous bridge or building, etc.). Discuss how these things are similar to the Mexican and Colombian national treasures seen here.

Writing Extensions
As a homework assignment, tell students to choose one of the U.S. treasures they listed in the Activate Prior Knowledge section. Have them list five to ten reasons why they consider that item to be a national treasure.

Colombia, one of that country's many pre-Columbian cultures. It is part of a collection of 121 items that were found in 1891 in two grave sites. The most beautiful objects made by the Quimbaya date from between A.D. 400 and 1000.
(p. 15, top left photo)
This stone with polychrome statue of Xuihtecuhtli, Aztec god of fire, is part of the phenomenally rich and varied collection of the Museo Nacional de Antropología in Mexico City. The disks on either side of the

statue's head represent wooden beams that were rubbed together to make fire. Like most other Aztec sculptures, the statue was originally painted.
(p. 15, top right photo)
This ceramic vessel is one of a pair found in a chamber of Mexico City's Templo Mayor. It shows Chicomecóatl, the goddess of sustenance, on one side, and Tlaloc, the god of rain, on the other. Tlaloc is also represented on the painted lid, holding his arms out as if scattering water from a pot. This vessel was

among the 6,000 pieces of pottery, jewelry, wall hangings, and human and animal remains uncovered at the site.
(p. 15, bottom photo)
Mexico City's world-famous Museo Nacional de Antropología, where this ceramic plate is displayed, was opened in 1964. It covers eleven acres in Chapultepec Park, and consists of two floors: one devoted to archaeology, the other to ethnography. The displays contain artifacts covering approximately 10,000 years.

Review

Recycled Concepts from PASO A PASO 2
Parts of the body, illness, imperfect progressive vs. preterite (Chap. 9)

Ancillaries available for use with Pasodoble

 Practice Wkbk. PD-7

Ancillaries suggested from PASO A PASO 2

 Overheads 44–47

 Comm. Act. BLMs 9-1, 9-2

Activate Prior Knowledge
Have students recall a time when they or someone they know was injured. Ask them to describe the circumstances surrounding the injury as well as the injury itself.

La salud

Muchas personas tienen accidentes u otros problemas durante las vacaciones. Aquí están algunos de los eventos desafortunados que ocurrieron este verano. ¿Qué estaban haciendo estas personas? ¿Qué ocurrió? ¿Qué debían hacer para protegerse?

Antes

Después

Antes

Después

16   Pasodoble

Options

Strategies for Reaching All Students

Spanish-Speaking Students
Tell students: *Escribe cinco recomendaciones que deben seguir los jóvenes para evitar problemas y mantener la salud durante las actividades al aire libre.*

Students Needing Extra Help
Review vocabulary related to health, accidents, injuries, and illness, as well as the imperfect progressive. If available, use the Book 2, Chap. 9 Organizer. Model the first scene.

Multiple Intelligences
Verbal/Linguistic
See Activate Prior Knowledge.
Visual/Spatial
See Practice Wkbk. PD-7, Overheads 44–47 (from Book 2), Comm. Act. BLMs 9-1 and 9-2 (from Book 2), and Writing Extensions.

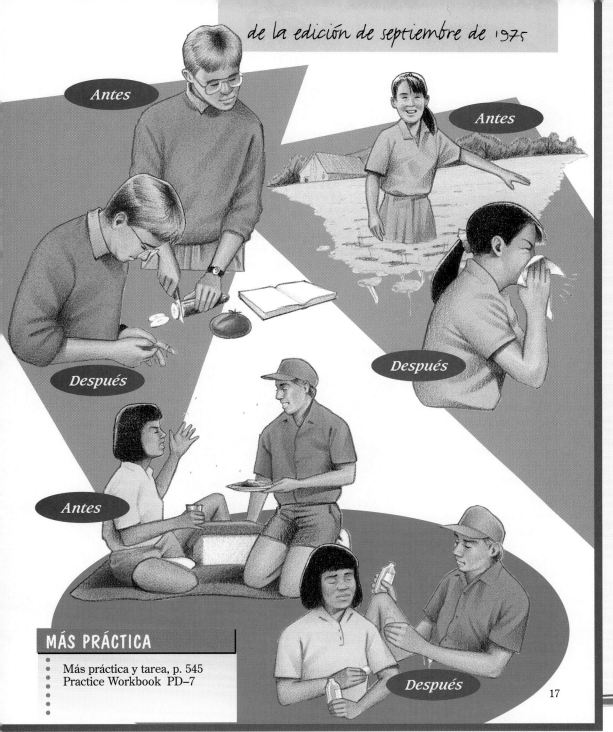

de la edición de septiembre de 1975

Antes

Después

Antes

Después

Antes

Después

MÁS PRÁCTICA

- Más práctica y tarea, p. 545
- Practice Workbook PD–7

17

Answers
Answers will vary, but may include:

Answers
Answers will vary, but may include:
La mujer estaba pintando, y después se cayó la lata. Debía tener más cuidado con la lata.

El muchacho estaba jugando tenis, y después se lastimó la pierna. Debía hacer ejercicio para prepararse antes de jugar tenis.

El joven estaba cortando un pepino, y a la vez estaba leyendo un libro de cocina. Se cortó el dedo. Debía prestar más atención a lo que estaba haciendo.

La muchacha estaba caminando entre las flores, y después tuvo alergia. Debía tomar algo para la alergia.

Los jóvenes estaban comiendo, y después unos mosquitos los picaron. Ellos debían ponerse repelente.

Writing Extensions
Tell students to think of one specific event during the past week. Have them write five sentences using the imperfect progressive, stating what five family members or friends were doing when that event occurred.

Review

Recycled Concepts from
PASO A PASO 2
Personal *a* (Chap. 1); *saber*
(Chap. 4); types of movies,
preterite vs. imperfect (Chap. 10)

**Ancillaries available for
use with *Pasodoble***

 Practice Wkbk. PD-8

**Ancillaries suggested
from *PASO A PASO 2***

 **Overheads 48–49,
51**

 **Comm. Act. BLMs
10-1, 10-3**

NUESTRAS PELÍCULAS FAVORITAS

ANA Y JUAN

Para esta edición de aniversario nuestros editores Juan y
Ana escogieron sus películas favoritas en varias
categorías. Aquí nos dicen por qué les gustan.

PELÍCULA ROMÁNTICA

Titanic

Ana: Me encantó *Titanic,* especialmente por las actuaciones de los actores
principales, Leonardo DiCaprio y Kate Winslet.
Creo que todas mis amigas se
enamoraron del personaje
Jack porque tiene todas las
características del galán
romántico perfecto—es pobre
pero guapo, artístico, gracioso,
inteligente . . . ¡ah, y también
maravillosamente atrevido!

Juan: A mí también me gustó,
pero no por el romance
exactamente. Para mí, los
efectos especiales son lo mejor
de *Titanic.* Realmente ayudan
a la gente a entender cómo pasó
este desastre. También me gustó
cómo el guión presenta muchos
argumentos a la vez, y con mucho
suspenso—el argumento del amor
entre Jack y Rose, el del desastre,
y el del científico que busca el collar de joyas de Rose.

18   Pasodoble

Options

Strategies for Reaching All Students

Spanish-Speaking Students
Ask: *Piensa en las películas que has visto en
el año pasado. ¿Cuál fue tu favorita? ¿En
qué categoría la pondrías? ¿Por qué te
gustó?*

Students Needing Extra Help
Review words related to the movies and the
uses of the preterite vs. the imperfect. If
available, use the Book 2, Chap. 10
Organizer. Be prepared to give a brief summary of the films pictured. Have students
discuss aspects of their favorite movies.

Enrichment
As a homework assignment, students can
write reviews of movies in these or other
categories. Call on individuals to share their
reviews with the class. You might first want
to discuss movies about which students
have differences of opinion, as is done here.
Pairs of students could then write conflict-
ing reviews.

PELÍCULA DE CIENCIA FICCIÓN

E.T.

Juan: E.T. es mi película favorita de ciencia ficción. El personaje principal era este pequeño extraterrestre (por eso lo llaman E.T., claro) que llegó a la Tierra y fue a vivir con un niño. El niño y sus hermanos lo escondieron de su mamá y de la policía. Todo es bueno en esta película—la actuación, los personajes, el guión, el argumento. Es una película para toda la familia.

Ana: Sé que probablemente soy la única persona del mundo a quien no le gustó E.T. Los efectos especiales sí eran buenos, especialmente cuando E.T. montó en bicicleta, pero tiene que haber algo más que efectos especiales si voy a divertirme en el cine.

PELÍCULA DE TERROR

Parque jurásico

Ana: Generalmente no me gustan las películas de terror, pero *Parque jurásico* me encantó. Unos científicos crearon dinosaurios para un parque de diversiones y luego los dinosaurios empezaron a matar a la gente. Era una película de terror clásica, con monstruos que parecían reales. ¡Mucho mejor que los monstruos del cine del pasado! Creo que fue tan popular porque nos enseñó una lección—que no debemos molestar a la naturaleza.

Juan: Pues, a mí no me gustó porque había demasiada violencia. Además, los científicos eran los malos y, como quiero ser científico, no me gustó nada ese aspecto.

MÁS PRÁCTICA

- Más práctica y tarea, p. 545
- Practice Workbook PD–8

19

Activate Prior Knowledge

As a class, brainstorm three popular current movies. Call on individuals to answer questions about each film. Questions might include: *¿Quiénes fueron los actores y las actrices en la película? ¿Cuál fue el argumento? ¿Por qué (no) te gustó la película?*

Writing Extensions

As an in-class assignment, have pairs of students choose one of the three photos and write a dialogue for the scene shown. Call on pairs to enact their dialogues in front of the class.

Multiple Intelligences
Bodily/Kinesthetic, Verbal/Linguistic, and Visual/Spatial
See Writing Extensions.
Verbal/Linguistic
See Activate Prior Knowledge.
Visual/Spatial
See Practice Wkbk. PD-8, Overheads 48–49 and 51 (from Book 2), and Comm. Act. BLMs 10-1 and 10-3 (from Book 2).
Visual/Spatial and Verbal/Linguistic
See Enrichment.

Review

Recycled Concepts from
PASO A PASO 2

Antes de / después de + inf.
(Chap. 2); clothing, preterite
(Chap. 3); impersonal *se*, nega-
tive expressions (Chap. 8)

**Ancillaries available for
use with** *Pasodoble*

 **Practice Wkbk.
PD-9**

**Ancillaries suggested
from** *PASO A PASO 2*

 Overheads 15, 43

 Comm. Act. BLM 8-3

Estas reglas son del tiempo de tus abuelos. ¿Cuáles de ellas se rompen hoy? ¿Hay algunas que todavía son iguales? ¿Hay reglas nuevas hoy? ¿Cuáles son?

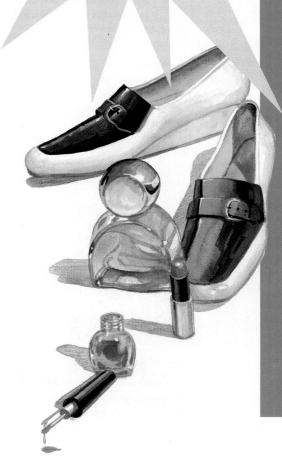

20 Pasodoble

Las muchachas nunca deben romper las reglas

Todas nosotras conocemos estas reglas para el uso del maquillaje, la moda y la etiqueta. ¿Quién será bastante atrevida para romperlas?

1. El lápiz de labios siempre debe ser de un color que vaya con tu ropa.

2. El esmalte de uñas siempre debe ser del mismo color que el lápiz de labios.

3. Las jóvenes de menos de quince años pueden usar lápiz de labios de color claro, pero sólo después de las clases.

4. Ningún muchacho quiere tener maquillaje en la camisa. Por eso, cuando salgas con tu novio, nunca uses demasiado maquillaje.

5. Se debe usar muy poco maquillaje antes de las cinco de la tarde. Tampoco debes ponerte demasiadas joyas.

6. El perfume también se debe usar con cuidado— una gota en cada muñeca, otras dos en el cuello.

7. Nadie usa zapatos blancos antes de Pascua ni después del primero de septiembre. Tampoco se usan guantes ni sombreros blancos excepto en el verano.

8. Todas sabemos que los zapatos de tacón alto generalmente no son cómodos. Pero si quieres estar de moda, debes llevarlos.

Options

Strategies for Reaching All Students

Spanish-Speaking Students
Have students respond in writing to the following: *Habla con algunas personas que
sean mayores que tus padres. Pregúntales
sobre las reglas de etiqueta que ellos
recuerdan. Haz una lista de por lo menos
cinco reglas de esa época.*

Students Needing Extra Help
Review vocabulary related to personal care.
If available, use the vocabulary section of
the Book 2, Chap. 8 Organizer. As a class,
brainstorm some new rules of etiquette.

Enrichment
After reviewing this section as a class, discuss why rules are made and observed.
Include rules of fashion as well as behavior,
encouraging debate and discussion.

de la edición de octubre de 1947

Y no olvides que . . .

- Un joven bien educado siempre se afeita todos los días.

- Ningún muchacho debe usar calcetines blancos con un traje.

- Si un joven no lleva corbata cuando sale contigo por primera vez . . . bueno, no vale la pena. ¡Sigue buscando!

21

MÁS PRÁCTICA

Más práctica y tarea, pp. 545–546

Review

Recycled Concepts from
PASO A PASO 2
Affirmative and negative *tú* commands, object and reflexive pronouns with *tú* commands, travel (Chap. 12)

Ancillaries available for use with *Pasodoble*

 Practice Wkbk. PD-9

Ancillaries suggested from *PASO A PASO 2*

 Overheads 59–60

 Comm. Act. BLMs 12-2, 12-3

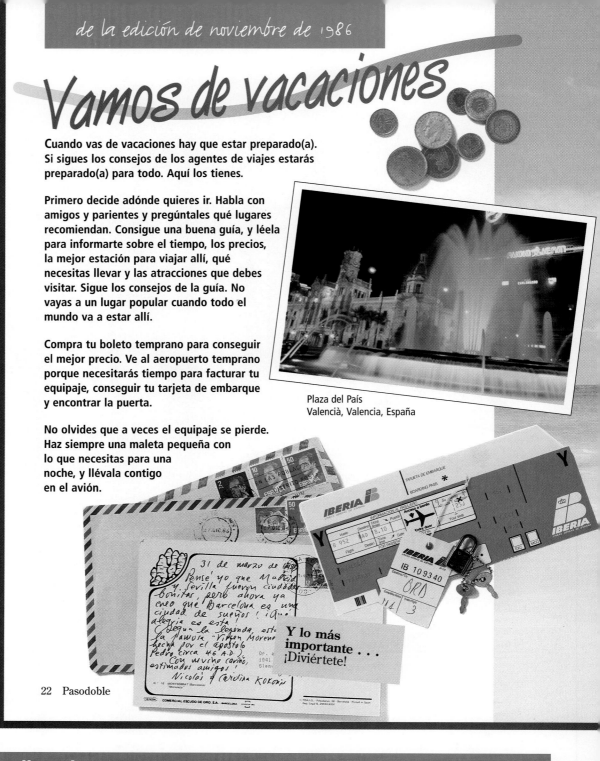

de la edición de noviembre de 1986

Vamos de vacaciones

Cuando vas de vacaciones hay que estar preparado(a). Si sigues los consejos de los agentes de viajes estarás preparado(a) para todo. Aquí los tienes.

Primero decide adónde quieres ir. Habla con amigos y parientes y pregúntales qué lugares recomiendan. Consigue una buena guía, y léela para informarte sobre el tiempo, los precios, la mejor estación para viajar allí, qué necesitas llevar y las atracciones que debes visitar. Sigue los consejos de la guía. No vayas a un lugar popular cuando todo el mundo va a estar allí.

Compra tu boleto temprano para conseguir el mejor precio. Ve al aeropuerto temprano porque necesitarás tiempo para facturar tu equipaje, conseguir tu tarjeta de embarque y encontrar la puerta.

Plaza del País
Valencià, Valencia, España

No olvides que a veces el equipaje se pierde. Haz siempre una maleta pequeña con lo que necesitas para una noche, y llévala contigo en el avión.

Y lo más importante . . . ¡Diviértete!

22   Pasodoble

Options

Strategies for Reaching All Students

Spanish-Speaking Students
Ask: *¿Cuál de las recomendaciones es más importante para asegurar un buen viaje? ¿Por qué?*

Students Needing Extra Help
Review commands and travel-related vocabulary. If available, use the Book 2, Chap. 12 Organizer. Brainstorm other practical advice for going to a concert, looking for a job, going camping, etc.

Multiple Intelligences
Bodily/Kinesthetic and Visual/Spatial
Have students use the Internet to find pictures from at least two Spanish-speaking countries which they would like to visit. Have them write a description or caption for each one.

Verbal/Linguistic
See Activate Prior Knowledge.
Visual/Spatial
See Practice Wkbk. PD-9, Overheads 59–60 (from Book 2), Comm. Act. BLMs 12-2 and 12-3 (from Book 2), and Writing Activity PD-E.

Si viajas a otro país...

No traigas demasiado equipaje. Trae sólo lo que puedes llevar.

Recuerda el "jet lag." No trates de hacer ni ver demasiado los primeros días. Tienes que acostumbrarte al tiempo, a la altitud, a la hora y a la cultura.

Es una buena idea beber sólo agua en botellas. Y ten cuidado con las comidas. No comas demasiado, especialmente por la noche.

Escribe tarjetas postales a tus amigos y parientes. Pero no olvides que hay que comprar sellos del país de donde las envías.

Siempre sé amable con todos. No seas mal(a) embajador(a) de tu país.

No seas tímido(a). Trata de hablar siempre la lengua del país. No es importante que la hables bien. A la gente le gustará que hagas el esfuerzo. Recuerda: ¡No todo el mundo habla inglés!

La iglesia de Santa Prisca en la plaza de Borda en Taxco, México

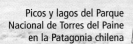

Picos y lagos del Parque Nacional de Torres del Paine en la Patagonia chilena

En lugares donde hace mucho sol...

Prepárate. Trae bronceador, anteojos de sol y un sombrero. Ponte el sombrero si vas a pasar mucho tiempo al sol. Bebe agua para no deshidratarte. No pases mucho tiempo en la playa la primera semana, y siempre usa bronceador para no quemarte.

MÁS PRÁCTICA

Más práctica y tarea, p. 546
Practice Workbook PD–9

23

Activate Prior Knowledge
As a class, brainstorm things to tell a new exchange student to prepare him or her for the trip from a given Spanish-speaking country to your community.

Writing Extensions

 Writing Activity PD-E

Cultural Notes

(p. 22, photo)
The port city of Valencia is Spain's third largest and one of its most ancient. Due to its strategic location (roughly halfway down the Mediterranean coast), as well as to its extremely fertile soil, Valencia has seen many conflicts among peoples who have wanted to establish themselves there. It was founded as a Greek colony, then passed to the Carthaginians, Romans, Visigoths, Arabs, and was finally incorporated into Spain in the fourteenth century.

(p. 23, top photo)
Taxco's Catedral de Santa Prisca is one of the finest in Mexico. Founded in the sixteenth century, it was almost entirely renovated in the Baroque style in the mid-eighteenth century at the request of silver baron José de la Borda. Among its features are its rose-colored façade with inverted columns, its brilliant, blue-tiled dome, and two elaborately carved towers. Inside, one can view a gilded altar and two paintings by the Mexican colonial artist, Miguel Cabrera (1695–1768).

(p. 23, bottom photo)
Patagonia consists of the southern third of Argentina and Tierra del Fuego, the island shared by Argentina and Chile. Its landscape is varied, with mountains, lakes, rain forests, and a flat desert shrub land. The area was first visited by Europeans in 1520, when Portuguese navigator Magellan explored it for the Spanish crown. The name originated with the Spaniards' mistaken notion that the natives, who wore animal pelts on their feet, were big-footed *(patagones)*.

Review

Recycled Concepts from
PASO A PASO 2
Professions, technology, future tense (Chap. 11)

Ancillaries available for use with *Pasodoble*

Practice Wkbk. PD-10

Ancillaries suggested from *PASO A PASO 2*

Overheads 52–53, 56

Comm. Act. BLMs 11-2, 11-3

---

de la edición de diciembre de 1989

El siglo XXI–unas predicciones

Javier Gómez —científico

Con la tecnología sabremos resolver muchos de los problemas del mundo de hoy. Todos sabrán usar la computadora, y la comunicación será más rápida y mejor que ahora. Con teléfonos con video podremos tener conferencias con gente en otras partes del mundo, y los veremos en pantallas gigantes. No habrá oficinas porque todos tendrán computadora en casa y no necesitarán perder tiempo viajando a una oficina todos los días.

Cuando empezó la última década del siglo XX, varios expertos nos ofrecieron sus predicciones sobre el futuro. ¿Qué piensas tú? ¿Estás de acuerdo o no? ¿Por qué? Haz tus propias predicciones.

David Vélez —cocinero

¿Qué comeremos en el futuro? Primero, tendremos que cambiar nuestra dieta. No comeremos tanta carne, porque no habrá suficiente y será muy cara. Aprenderemos a comer proteína vegetal—¡y nos gustará! Nuestra comida será más sana y viviremos más años.

Alberta García–Peña —médica

Sabremos curar muchas de las enfermedades de hoy, por ejemplo, el cáncer, pero habrá más enfermedades que todavía no conocemos. (¡No olvides que el SIDA es una enfermedad muy nueva!) Cuando veamos el papel que tiene la contaminación

en las enfermedades, por fin trabajaremos para limpiar el medio ambiente. Lo que nunca sabremos hacer es curar el resfriado.

24   Pasodoble

Options

Strategies for Reaching All Students

Spanish-Speaking Students
Have students respond in writing to the following: *¿Cuáles son tus propias predicciones para el futuro? ¿Cómo crees que serán las escuelas y las familias?*

Students Needing Extra Help
Review vocabulary related to the future as well as the future tense. If available, use the Book 2, Chap. 11 Organizer. Have students predict what a young person will do in the future regarding jobs, clothing, pastimes, etc. Have them brainstorm how occupations will be different in the future.

Enrichment
As an in-class writing assignment, have students make three predictions about the future. Call on them to share their predictions with the class. Create a list on the chalkboard to discover the most common predictions. Let the class vote on the three that they think most likely will occur.

**Gloria Ramos
—diseñadora**

La ropa será más práctica. Usaremos sólo materiales modernos como el plástico. Los bolsos para mujeres desaparecerán porque no tendrán ni tiempo ni paciencia para llevarlos y, además, es demasiado fácil robarlos. Por eso, toda la ropa femenina tendrá bolsillos. Aquí hay uno de mis vestidos.

**Lola Villas
—agente de viajes**

Los viajeros podrán ver por televisión los lugares que quieran visitar. Además tendrán la opción de pagar todos los gastos del viaje electrónicamente. No tendrán que ir al banco a cambiar dinero. El ecoturismo seguirá ganando popularidad.

**Alfredo Pérez
—arquitecto**

Nuestras ciudades deberán cambiar mucho porque si no, nadie podrá vivir allí. Habrá lugares verdes—parques y senderos—por todas partes y menos edificios grandes. Las casas estarán situadas en grupos con un área de césped común. Y serán más pequeñas, más cómodas y más fáciles de mantener porque nadie querrá perder tiempo limpiándolas.

MÁS PRÁCTICA

- Más práctica y tarea, p. 546
- Practice Workbook PD–10

25

Activate Prior Knowledge
As a class, brainstorm a list of occupations. Call on students to tell how they perceive they will change in the future and why.

Answers
Responses will vary.

 Audio Activities P.1, P.2, P.3, P.4

Writing Extensions

 Writing Activity PD-F

 Internet Activities
Have students go to www.pasoapaso.com for additional activities and practice.

Assessment

 Prueba Pasodoble

Internet Activities
Self-Test

**Multiple Intelligences
Logical/Mathematical and Verbal/Linguistic**
See Enrichment.
Musical/Rhythmic
Tell students you will play a song which makes a prediction about life in the future. Ask them to take note of any words or phrases that they recognize. Afterwards, have students share their lists and try to determine what the songwriter is predicting.

Use the song "Días de amar" (see Writing, Audio & Video Activities, p. 140), or another song that makes a prediction about the future.
Verbal/Linguistic
See Audio Activities P.1, P.2, P.3, and P.4.
Visual/Spatial
See Practice Wkbk. PD-10, Overheads 52–53 and 56 (from Book 2), Comm. Act. BLMs 11-2 and 11-3 (from Book 2), and Writing Activity PD-F.

CAPÍTULO 1
THEME: IDENTITY

SCOPE AND SEQUENCE   Pages 26–57

COMMUNICATION

Topics
Personal characteristics

Conflicts and solutions

Extracurricular activities

After-school jobs

Objectives
Comparar las relaciones que tienes con la familia, amigos y compañeros con las que tienen los jóvenes hispanos

Describirte a ti mismo(a) y a otras personas

Hablar sobre cómo te relacionas con otras personas

Hablar sobre actividades en las que puedes participar

CULTURE

La relación entre familia y amigos en países hispanos

GRAMMAR

Repaso: Los mandatos afirmativos con tú

Repaso: Los complementos directos e indirectos

Otros usos de lo

Ancillaries available for use with Chapter 1

Multisensory/Technology

 Overheads, 7–8

 Audio Tapes and CDs

 Vocabulary Art Blackline Masters for Hands-On Learning, pp. 8–11/CD-ROM

 Classroom Crossword

 Video

 Internet Activities www.pasoapaso.com

Print

 Practice Workbook, pp. 11–20

 Writing, Audio & Video Activities, pp. 5–9, 93–95, 133–134

 Communicative Activity Blackline Masters
   Pair and Small Group Activities, pp. 1–6
   Situation Cards, p. 7

RESOURCE PRO

Planning Express, Teaching Resources Library, and Clip Art Library

Assessment

 Assessment Program
   Pruebas, pp. 9–19
   Examen de habilidades, pp. 20–23

 Test Generator

 ¿Lo sabes bien? Video Quiz

Video, Chap. 1

¿Quién soy yo en realidad?

¿Quién soy yo en realidad? is a multi-faceted question: How do I look? Who is my family? Who are my friends? How do I feel about things? Self may be defined through family or religious affiliation, ethnic identity, personal qualities, and other factors. Identity is often compared to an onion—the outer layer being only the most visible; when the onion is peeled, the inner layers are revealed.

Gender and physical attributes are the most visible traits of an individual's identity. Teenagers, in particular, regard appearance as an important part of self-identity. In much of Latin America, as in the U.S., young people dress to express themselves, paying close attention to fashion trends.

In many Spanish-speaking cultures, families often provide a strong identity and social network for their members. Young people often form close relationships with cousins or other relatives *(parientes)*. *Confianza* is the basis of all these relationships. To have *confianza,* however, is not just to regard that person with trust. Rather, it signifies a relationship of special importance involving respect and intimacy. When two people share *confianza,* they confide in each other, offer advice and support, and keep in close communication. Good friends may, of course, also have *confianza* with one another.

Religious affiliation is often another important aspect of identity. The majority of Spanish-speaking people identify themselves as Catholic. However, many Latin American cities or towns have significant Jewish or Protestant populations. Indigenous and non-western religions, such as *santería,* which originated in Africa, are also practiced.

Ethnicity is an important part of how some people perceive themselves. In the *cono sur* (southern cone countries of Argentina, Uruguay, and Chile) some people maintain their European ethnic identities (most often German, Italian, Portuguese, or Spanish). The infusion of varied cultural backgrounds can often be seen in major cities in Argentina, for example. There are cultural and religious centers for the Jewish population, where the language is preserved through Hebrew schools or classes. People in other Latin American countries commonly preserve an indigenous identity, such as Huichol, Zapotec, Mayan, or Incan.

Introduce

Re-entry of Concepts
The following list represents words, expressions, and grammar topics re-entered from Books 1 and 2:

Book 1
calendar expressions, likes and preferences, sports, colors, community activities, physical descriptions, adjective agreement, friendship, expressions of frequency, family members, personality characteristics, direct and indirect object pronouns

Book 2
school personnel, after-school activities, extracurricular activities, sports, affirmative commands with *tú*

Critical Thinking: Synthesizing
Divide the class into groups of three or four. Appoint one person in each group to be a recorder. Have recorders ask each student to list three adjectives that describe the qualities of a famous person *(you supply the name)* with whom they are all familiar. Have them tally the results and write the three most commonly mentioned adjectives on the chalkboard. Discuss the results.

Planning

Cross-Curricular Connections

Literature Connection *(p. 35)*
Using the Cinquain format (a verse form consisting of five lines of two, four, six, eight, and two syllables respectively) or free verse, have students choose their favorite color and write a poem depicting it. After corrections are made, have students write their poems on large sheets of paper, decorating them as they wish.

Business Education Connection *(pp. 44–45)*
In pairs or small groups, have students prepare an ad for a product of their choice using affirmative *tú* commands. You may want to bring in examples from Spanish-language newspapers or magazines to show as a model.

Spanish in Your Community
If possible, have students visit a shop in their community and look for cards in Spanish that refer to friendship and relationships. Ask them, if they would like to, to purchase some and share them with the class. Using them as examples, have students create their own cards.

CAPÍTULO 1

OBJETIVOS

Al terminar este capítulo vas a poder responder a la pregunta clave:

¿Quién soy yo en realidad?

También vas a poder:

- describir las cualidades de una persona
- describir cómo te relacionas con los demás
- hablar sobre cuál es tu papel en la sociedad
- comparar tus relaciones con la familia, amigos y compañeros con las de los jóvenes hispanos

Unos promotores de salud de Clínica del Pueblo, *Latin American Youth Center*, Washington, D.C.

VISITA
www.pasoapaso.com

Teaching Suggestions
Point out the key chapter question *(la pregunta clave del capítulo)*. Tell students that, by working through the activities and tasks, and by acquiring the new words and structures of this chapter, they will be able to answer this key question: *¿Quién soy yo en realidad?*

Cultural Notes ☼

(pp. 26–27, photo)
Health care for Hispanics in the U.S. is complicated by the language barrier as well as by a reluctance to visit the doctor until it is absolutely necessary. As a result, such problems as AIDS and diabetes are affecting Hispanics at a higher per capita rate. Bilingual and bicultural health workers such as these trainees at la Clínica del Pueblo in Washington, D.C., are vital to the Hispanic community.

Preview

Cultural Objective

- *Comparar las actividades de los jóvenes estadounidenses con las de los jóvenes hispanos*

Teaching Suggestions

To help students remember previously learned vocabulary, have them list all the objects and / or activities they see in the photographs for which they know the Spanish words.

Answers: Anticipación

Answers will vary.

Anticipación

Mira las fotos. ¿Cómo son estos jóvenes hispanos? ¿Adónde les gusta ir y qué les gusta hacer? Y a ti, ¿adónde te gusta ir y qué te gusta hacer?

"Las estudiantes de la banda de la escuela nos sentimos muy orgullosas cuando marchamos por las calles."

Muchos estudiantes de primaria y secundaria son parte de las bandas de música. Los jóvenes de la foto marchan en las calles de Laredo, Texas para celebrar el cumpleaños de George Washington. ¿Qué instrumentos incluye la banda de música de tu escuela? ¿Perteneces o te gustaría pertenecer a la banda?

28   Capítulo 1

Options

Strategies for Reaching All Students

Spanish-Speaking Students

Ask: *¿Cómo eres con tus parientes y tus amigos? ¿Eres igual con todo el mundo? ¿Qué influye en tu relación con la gente? ¿Trabajas o sirves de voluntario(a) después de las clases?*

Students Needing Extra Help

Remind students that the photos are merely a tool for thinking about the theme. Many of the questions require students to think about their own experiences. Be alert to the fact that some students may come from families where affection is limited. Be careful that the discussion does not turn to inappropriate topics.

Multiple Intelligences

Bodily/Kinesthetic and Musical/Rhythmic
Have volunteers bring a musical instrument to class and give a demonstration on how to play it, step by step. If students know any performers of Latin American or Spanish music personally, ask them to invite those artists to class to demonstrate and explain their art.

"Cada año, los que pertenecemos a la familia Limón celebramos el cumpleaños de la abuela. Aquí estamos en su casa, en Austin, Texas."

¿Cómo son las celebraciones de tu familia? Las familias hispanoamericanas se reúnen para la Navidad o para el Año Nuevo. Ellos prefieren tener sus reuniones en la casa de las personas de mayor edad, los abuelos. ¿Visitas a tus abuelos frecuentemente? ¿Eres cariñoso(a) con ellos? ¿Cómo son tus abuelos?

"Después de las clases, nos gusta ir a un restaurante al aire libre."

¿Qué te gusta hacer después de la escuela? ¿Tienes que trabajar, o tienes tiempo para divertirte un poco? A los jóvenes hispanos les gusta estar con sus amigos cuando pueden. Pero esto no quiere decir que no les guste estar con su familia. Frecuentemente, sus hermanos también son sus amigos íntimos.

www.pasoapaso.com
Exploración Cultural
Visita estos países

29

Cultural Notes ☼

(p. 28, photo)
These members of the United High School Marching Band in Laredo, Texas, are performing in the Washington's Birthday parade. The high school also has a drill team, the Lariats, whose name comes from the Spanish *la reata* (rope).

(p. 29, bottom photo)
Mexican *elotes*—corn on the cob slathered with mayonnaise, sprinkled with cheese, dusted with cayenne pepper, and served on a stick—are a great alternative to greasier types of fast food. These Puerto Rican teens are enjoying a quick bite to eat Mexican style, including *elotes* and *tacos*.

Present

Chapter Theme
Friendship

Communicative Objectives
• *Describirte a ti mismo(a) y a otras personas*
• *Hablar sobre cómo te relacionas con otras personas*

 Overhead 7

 Vocabulary Art BLMs/CD-ROM

 Vocabulary Tape 1-1

Grammar Preview
Uses of *lo* are previewed here lexically. The grammar explanation appears on p. 48, but avoid explanations at this point. As students use the new structures lexically in this controlled context, they will begin to develop an understanding of their use. It will make the later presentation and explanation of the grammar easier both for you and for them.

Teaching Suggestions
Preparing students to speak: Use one or two options from each of the categories of Comprehensible Input or Limited Verbal Response. For a complete explanation of these categories and some sample activities, see pp. T20–T21.

Vocabulario para comunicarse

¿Cómo eres?

Aquí tienes palabras y expresiones necesarias para hablar sobre ti mismo(a) y sobre tus amigos. Léelas varias veces y practícalas con un(a) compañero(a) en las páginas siguientes.

modesto, -a

vanidoso, -a

comprensivo, -a

incomprensivo, -a

tranquilo, -a

nervioso, -a

compartir

quejarse (de)

mudarse

30   Capítulo 1

Options

Strategies for Reaching All Students

Spanish-Speaking Students
Ask: *¿Qué otras palabras usas para describir a otras personas o para describirte a ti mismo(a)? Empieza un vocabulario personal y escribe esas palabras.*

Enrichment
Engage the class in a discussion by calling on students to answer the following questions: *Para ti, ¿qué cosas indican que una persona es sincera (modesta, vanidosa, comprensiva)?*

Students Needing Extra Help
Begin the vocabulary section of the Organizer.
These emotions are rather subtle. The pictures may have to be explained.
Give examples of *quejarse de.*
También necesitas. . . : Show the connection between *amistad* and *amigo.*
Conjugate the verbs in all the tenses students have learned so far. This is a good review since it includes reflexive verbs, stem-changing verbs, and irregular verbs.

Emphasize that *íntimo(a)* is used with close, personal relationships, not closeness in terms of proximity. Remind them of the English word "intimate."
For *hacer caso a,* give an example in a complete sentence.
Give examples of *lo más / menos* + adjective and *lo mejor / lo peor.*
¿Y qué quiere decir. . . ?: Give complete sentence examples of *dar un consejo, tener en común,* and *resolver un problema.*

También necesitas . . .

la amistad, *pl.* las amistades	*friendship*	íntimo, -a	*close*
apoyar(se)	*to support (each other)*	llevarse (bien / mal)	*to get along (well / badly)*
los demás	the others	lo más / menos (+ *adj.*)	*the most / least (+ adj.) (thing)*
discutir	*to argue, discuss*	lo mejor / lo peor	*the best / the worst (thing)*
enojarse	to get angry		
entender(se) (e → ie)	*to understand (each other)*	¡Qué va!	*Not at all!*
hacer caso a	*to pay attention to*	relacionar(se) con	*to relate to*

¿Y qué quiere decir . . . ?

admirar
el conflicto
el consejo
considerado, -a
dar un consejo*
la discusión, *pl.* las discusiones
frecuentemente

mantener *(e → ie)*†
  (yo) mantengo
  (tú) mantienes
resolver *(o → ue)*
respetar
responsable
el sentido del humor
sincero, -a
tener en común

* *Dar un consejo* refers to giving a specific piece of advice. We use the plural *dar consejos* to refer to giving advice in general.
† *Mantener* follows the pattern of *tener.*

Vocabulario para comunicarse 31

Practice

Answers: Empecemos a conversar

1 ESTUDIANTE A
a. Eres vanidoso(a), ¿verdad?
b. ...incomprensivo(a), ...
c. ...generoso(a), ...
d. ...tranquilo(a), ...
e. ...tacaño(a), ...
f. ...nervioso(a), ...
g. ...modesto(a), ...
h. Questions will vary.
ESTUDIANTE B
a.–h. Answers will vary, but look for agreement of adjectives.

Empecemos a conversar

Túrnate con un(a) compañero(a) para ser *Estudiante A* y *Estudiante B*. Reemplacen las palabras subrayadas con palabras representadas o escritas en los recuadros. 💡 quiere decir que puedes escoger tu propia respuesta.

1

A — *Eres comprensivo(a), ¿verdad?*
B — *¡Claro que sí!, soy (muy) comprensivo(a).*
 o: *¡Qué va!, no lo soy.*
 o: *Sí, a veces.*

Estudiante A   Estudiante B

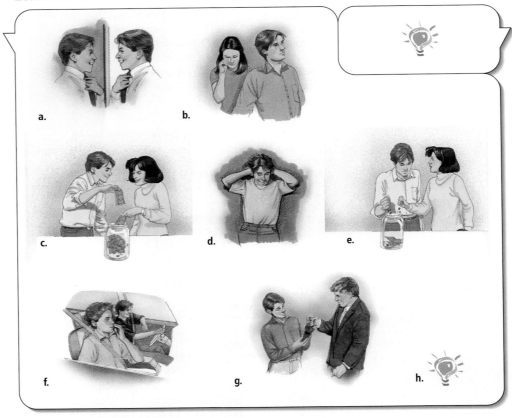

a.   b.

c.   d.   e.

f.   g.   h.

32   Capítulo 1

Options

Strategies for Reaching All Students

Spanish-Speaking Students
Exs. 1–4: If possible, pair bilingual and non-bilingual students for all activities.

Students Needing Extra Help
Ex. 1: Review the possible *Estudiante B* responses.
Ex. 2: Point out that *los* replaces *a tus amigos*.

Enrichment
Ex. 1: *Estudiante B* can make a statement supporting or illustrating what he or she says. Example: *¡Claro que sí! Soy muy tranquilo(a). Me parece que no vale la pena tener conflictos con nadie.*
Ex. 2: *Estudiante A* can ask for reasons if *Estudiante B* answers negatively.

Extended Written Practice/Homework
1. Choose four verbs from pp. 30–31 and write sentences describing your relationship with other people: *Los chicos en el equipo de béisbol y yo nos apoyamos siempre.*
2. Write three sentences telling how to accomplish the following: *mantener una amistad, resolver un conflicto, llevarse bien con los demás. Para mantener una amistad, hay que ...*

2 respetar

A — *¿Respetas a tus amigos?*
B — *Sí, los respeto siempre.*
  o: *A veces sí y a veces no.*

Estudiante A

a. apoyar
b. entender
c. ver
d. ayudar
e. admirar
f.

Estudiante B

siempre
nunca
frecuentemente
a menudo

El joven de la garibaldina roja
(autorretrato) (1919), Joan Miró

Vocabulario para comunicarse   33

---

2 ESTUDIANTE A
a. ¿Apoyas a tus amigos?
b. ¿Entiendes . . .
c. ¿Ves . . .
d. ¿Ayudas . . .
e. ¿Admiras . . .
f. Questions will vary.

ESTUDIANTE B
Answers will vary, but may include the following pattern:
a. Sí, los apoyo + *adverb*.
b. Sí, los entiendo . . .
c. Sí, los veo . . .
d. Sí, los ayudo . . .
e. Sí, los admiro . . .
f. Answers will vary.

Using Photos
Ask: *Mira el autorretrato de Joan Miró. ¿Cómo es su personalidad?*

---

3. Write three sentences telling when you (or another person) moved and what you did to develop new friendships.

Multiple Intelligences
Verbal/Linguistic
1) See Exs. 1–4.
2) Have students create a poem or a story inspired by the Miró portrait on p. 33. Ask volunteers to read their work aloud.

Cultural Notes

(p. 33, photo)
This self-portrait was painted by Joan Miró (1893–1983) in 1919, the same year he moved from his native Barcelona to Paris. This move was instrumental in shaping the dreamlike, whimsical style that identifies his later work. Miró felt a strong affinity with André Breton and other French surrealist poets, and sought to make his paintings as exuberant and anarchic as their poems.

Practice & Apply

Answers: Empecemos a conversar

3 ESTUDIANTE A
a. ¿Es callado(a) tu mejor amigo(a)?
b. ¿Es deportista ...
c. ¿Es responsable ...
d. ¿Es gracioso(a) ...
e. ¿Es perezoso(a) ...
f. Questions will vary.

ESTUDIANTE B
Answers will vary, but may include the following:
a. Sí, nunca habla mucho.
b. Sí, todos los días nada por una hora.
c. Sí, siempre hace su tarea.
d. Sí, tiene sentido del humor.
e. Sí, siempre se levanta tarde.
f. Answers will vary.

4 ESTUDIANTE A
a. ¿Cómo te llevas con tus compañeros?
b. ...tus profesores?
c. ...tus padres?
d. ...tus vecinos?
e. ...los demás?
f. Questions will vary.

ESTUDIANTE B
a.–f. Answers will vary.

34

Standards 1.1; 4.1

¿Quién soy yo en realidad?

3 desordenado,-a A — ¿*Es desordenado(a) tu mejor amigo(a)?*
B — *Sí, nunca encuentra nada.*
o: *No, es ordenado(a).*

Estudiante A

a. callado,-a

b. deportista

c. responsable

d. gracioso,-a

e. perezoso,-a

f.

Estudiante B

siempre se levanta tarde

siempre hace su tarea

nunca habla mucho

todos los días nada por una hora

tiene sentido del humor

4 tus amigas A — ¿*Cómo te llevas con tus amigas?*
B — *Generalmente me llevo muy bien.*
o: *Depende, a veces me llevo bien, a veces nos enojamos.*

Estudiante A

a. tus compañeros

b. tus profesores

c. tus padres

d. tus vecinos

e. los demás

f.

Estudiante B

mal

regular

discutimos mucho

nos entendemos bien

a veces nos enojamos

¡NO OLVIDES!

We can use the reflexive pronouns *se* and *nos* to express the idea of "(to) each other." *Mis amigos nunca **se** enojan. Nosotros no **nos** hablamos frecuentemente.*

34 Capítulo 1

Options

Strategies for Reaching All Students

Spanish-Speaking Students
Exs. 5–6: Have Spanish-speaking students write the answer to this question: *¿Qué características crees que admiran tus amigos en ti? ¿Por qué?*
Ex. 6: Have Spanish-speaking students write the answer to this question: *¿Cómo te influyen tu familia y tus amigos?*

Students Needing Extra Help
Ex. 3: Give students time to match the responses before they start to manipulate the language.
Ex. 4: Remind students of the meaning of *llevarse.* They may not recognize its conjugated form.
¡No olvides!: Give additional examples.
Exs. 5–10: If necessary, brainstorm appropriate vocabulary for answers.
Ex. 5: Remind students that *discusiones* can mean "arguments" or "discussions."

Brainstorm constructive ways to deal with conflicts.
Ex. 6: Review the expressions *dar consejos* and *hacer caso a.*
Ex. 7: Students usually have a lot to say regarding friendships. Insist that they respond in Spanish.
Ex. 8: Use the vocabulary section of the Organizer.
Students may need help with the structure *lo mejor* and *lo peor,* and with articulating their response to the *¿Por qué?* question.

¿Y qué piensas tú?

Aquí tienes otra oportunidad para usar el vocabulario de este capítulo.

5 ¿Con quién o en qué situaciones te enojas más? ¿Con quién tienes discusiones? ¿Qué haces para resolver un problema?

6 ¿Quiénes te dan consejos, tus amigos o alguien de tu familia? ¿Haces caso generalmente a los consejos que te dan?

7 ¿Cómo se puede mantener una amistad con una persona que se muda lejos de ti? ¿Qué es lo más importante para ti en una amistad? ¿Y lo menos importante?

8 ¿Cómo te relacionas con tus amigos? ¿Qué es lo mejor de una amistad? ¿Y lo peor? ¿Por qué?

9 Piensa en la persona a quien más admiras. ¿Cuáles son cuatro adjetivos para describirlo(la)? ¿Y tres sustantivos *(nouns)*? Sigue las siguientes instrucciones para hacer un poema sobre esa persona.

- Escribe su nombre.
- Escribe dos de los adjetivos.
- Escribe los tres sustantivos.
- Escribe los otros dos adjetivos.
- Escribe su nombre otra vez.

Juan
sincero, tranquilo
estudiante, atleta, amigo
responsable, considerado
Juan

Ahora puedes hacer un poema sobre ti mismo(a) o sobre una persona famosa.

10 Brevemente, describe cómo eres tú. Piensa qué dicen tus amigos, hermanos y profesores sobre ti e inclúyelo en tu descripción.

Juan estudia la preparatoria en Puerto Vallarta, México.

Práctica de vocabulario · www.pasoapaso.com

MÁS PRÁCTICA

- Más práctica y tarea, p. 547
- Practice Workbook 1–1, 1–2

Vocabulario para comunicarse 35

Answers: ¿Y qué piensas tú?
5–10 Answers will vary.

 Practice Wkbk. 1-1, 1-2

 Audio Activity 1.1

 Writing Activities 1-A, 1-B

 Pruebas 1-1, 1-2

 Comm. Act. BLM 1-1

Strategies for Reaching All Students

MULTIPLE INTELLIGENCES
Bodily/Kinesthetic and Logical/Mathematical
See Cooperative Learning.
Interpersonal/Social
See Enrichment.
Intrapersonal/Introspective
See Exs. 5–10.
Verbal/Linguistic
See Audio Activity 1.1.
Visual/Spatial
See Practice Wkbk. 1-1 and 1-2, Writing Activities 1-A and 1-B, and Comm. Act. BLM 1-1.

Ex. 9: Brainstorm the nouns.
Ex. 10: Students are not always aware of how other people perceive them. You may need to preface this activity with some discussion about the idea of self-perception vs. how others see us.
Do a complete model and let students know how many sentences you expect.
Describe yourself. Then, if you are willing to take the risk, have another student or Spanish teacher describe you as well.

Enrichment
Have pairs of students work on a melodramatic story to read aloud to the rest of the class. Story topics can be either *Así empezó una buena amistad* or *Así terminó una buena amistad*. Encourage students to be imaginative as they invent the turn of events that made or broke a wonderful friendship.

Cooperative Learning
Divide the class into groups of three. Using the vocabulary for characteristics in Exs. 1 and 3 on pp. 32 and 34, have one student list positive qualities and another, negative qualities. Have the third student list the names of movies, TV shows, or book characters. From the two lists, have groups describe the characters. Ask several groups to share information with the class.

Present

Chapter Theme
Activities and community involvement

Communicative Objectives
- *Describirte a ti mismo(a) y a otras personas*
- *Hablar sobre cómo te relacionas con otras personas*
- *Hablar sobre actividades en las que puedes participar*

 Vocabulary Tape 1-2

Teaching Suggestions
Tell students that the new vocabulary in this section appears in boldface.

Getting ready to speak:
Remind students of the reading strategies that they learned (getting meaning from context and coping with unknown words) to help them understand the *Tema para investigar.* For further details and some sample activities, see pp. T24–T25.

¿Quién soy yo en realidad?

Tema para investigar

Aquí tienes más palabras e ideas que te ayudarán a conocerte mejor. Mira las ilustraciones y las fotos de esta página. ¿En qué actividades participan estos jóvenes? Y tú, ¿participas en alguna de estas actividades o en otras?

36

Options

Strategies for Reaching All Students

Students Needing Extra Help
Have students take notes.
You may wish to go over the vocabulary words that follow the reading before students actually read it.
Emphasize that this section is really the second vocabulary, but it is presented in text as opposed to list or picture form. Be sure stu-

dents understand that they are responsible for the vocabulary in boldface.
Write out the verb paradigms for *influir* and give examples of *influir en* and *influir sobre.* Have students practice these verbs both in spoken and written forms.
Give examples of how *adquirir* is used.

Extended Written Practice/Homework
1. Write three sentences telling who is a fan of different sports or activities.
2. Write four sentences using the vocabulary on p. 37 to tell in which kinds of activities and jobs you and your friends are involved: *Mi amiga trabaja como voluntaria en un asilo.*
3. Write three sentences telling who or what influences the ideas of young people: *Los programas de televisión influyen mucho en las opiniones de los jóvenes.*

¿Cuál es tu papel en la sociedad?

En los países hispanos, al igual que en los Estados Unidos, los estudiantes participan en varias actividades extracurriculares.
Mientras **los aficionados** a la música o al teatro tocan en una banda o **se inscriben** en un club de teatro, hay otros que prefieren practicar deportes que no ofrecen en la escuela como, por ejemplo, las artes marciales o **la esgrima.** Si les gusta la literatura y escribir, pueden participar en el club literario, o en **la redacción** de la revista literaria de la escuela.

Aunque en los países hispanos esto no está muy generalizado, algunos jóvenes quieren trabajar para ganar dinero extra. Pueden trabajar después de las clases, aunque lo más común es que traten de encontrar un trabajo para los fines de semana. Generalmente, cuidan niños, trabajan en un supermercado o en una tienda, reparten periódicos, **dan clases particulares** o son **ayudantes** de biblioteca.

Diferentes cosas nos **influyen** a escoger un trabajo, pero los trabajos comunitarios están **adquiriendo** una gran popularidad entre los jóvenes hispanos. Pueden trabajar como voluntarios en **campañas** de reciclaje y de **higiene.** A otros jóvenes les gusta pasar parte de su fin de semana en guarderías infantiles, **orfanatos** y **asilos.**

Y tú, ¿qué haces después de las clases?

Una clase de karate en la Ciudad de México

el (la) aficionado(a)	*fan, enthusiast*	influir (en / sobre):*	*to influence:*
inscribirse	*to enroll, to sign up*	(yo) influyo	*I influence*
la esgrima	*fencing*	(tú) influyes	*you influence*
la redacción	*editing*	adquirir *(i → ie)*	*to become, to acquire*
aunque	*although*	la campaña	*campaign*
dar clases particulares	*to give private lessons, to tutor*	la higiene	*hygiene*
		el orfanato	*orphanage*
el / la ayudante	*aide, assistant*	el asilo	*nursing home*

*Influir follows the pattern of *incluir.*

Tema para investigar   37

Answers: Tema para investigar
Answers will vary, but may include: *Estos jóvenes practican deportes, ayudan a otras personas, reparten el periódico, etc.* / Answers will vary.

After students have read the *Tema para investigar,* return to these questions and see if they now can use the new vocabulary to answer differently.

Class Starter Review
On the day following the presentation of the *Tema para investigar,* you might begin the class with this activity:
Using the vocabulary from this section, prepare several statements to be read aloud. They should be things that describe several students in the class. For example: *Me gusta ser ayudante en la escuela. Trabajo bien cuando tengo muchos quehaceres. Siempre ayudo a los demás en la clase de español.* Students then try to guess who is being described.

www Internet Activities
Juegos
Have students go to www.pasoapaso.com for additional activities and practice.

Cultural Notes

Multiple Intelligences
Bodily/Kinesthetic and Verbal/Linguistic
Ask for volunteers to explain and demonstrate a karate movement or a series of positions.
Verbal/Linguistic
1) See Vocabulary Tape 1-2 and Class Starter Review.
2) Have students write personal interview questions that would be appropriate for any of the photos on p. 36.

(p. 37, photo)
Karate's popularity in the U.S. has spread to Mexico, due in great part to the influence of American TV programs and films featuring Asian martial arts.

Practice & Apply

Answers: ¿Comprendiste?

1 Possible answers:
a. En los países hispanos, como en los Estados Unidos, los estudiantes participan en varias actividades extracurriculares.
b. cierta
c. Algunos jóvenes tratan de encontrar un trabajo para los fines de semana.
d. Muchos jóvenes hispanos hacen trabajo comunitario.

2 Prefieren trabajar los fines de semana porque no tienen clases. / (Reasons will vary.)

Answers: ¿Y qué piensas tú?

3–6 Answers will vary.

¿Comprendiste?

1 Según la lectura, ¿cuáles de las siguientes frases son ciertas? Cambia las que no sean ciertas.

   a. En los países hispanos los estudiantes no participan en actividades extracurriculares.
   b. Algunos estudiantes prefieren practicar deportes que no hay en la escuela.
   c. Es común tratar de encontrar un trabajo los fines de semana si ellos quieren ganar dinero extra.
   d. Los trabajos comunitarios casi nunca son populares entre los jóvenes hispanos.

2 ¿Cuándo es más común que trabajen los jóvenes hispanos, después de las clases o los fines de semana? ¿Por qué crees que es así?

¿Y qué piensas tú?

3 ¿En qué actividades participas? ¿Eres miembro de alguna banda o grupo de teatro? ¿Prefieres participar en los deportes de la escuela o en otros? ¿En cuáles?

4 ¿Te gusta escribir? ¿Hay una revista literaria en tu escuela? ¿Cómo se llama? ¿Participas en su redacción?

5 ¿Trabajas para ganar dinero extra? ¿En qué trabajas? ¿Trabajas después de las clases o los fines de semana? ¿Por qué?

6 ¿Qué clases de trabajos comunitarios son populares entre los estudiantes que conoces? ¿Qué oportunidades hay en tu comunidad para trabajar como voluntario? ¿Participas en algún trabajo voluntario o comunitario? ¿En cuál?

Un artista haciendo un dibujo en el Parque del Retiro en Madrid, España

Práctica de vocabulario · www.pasoapaso.com

MÁS PRÁCTICA

Más práctica, p. 548
Practice Workbook 1–3, 1–4

Options

Strategies for Reaching All Students

Spanish-Speaking Students
Ex. 6: Tell Spanish-speaking students: *Haz un cartel que dé información sobre un lugar en tu comunidad que necesite voluntarios. Anima a los estudiantes de tu escuela a que trabajen de voluntario(a).*

Students Needing Extra Help
Ex. 1: Remind students that here, *ciertas* is the same as answering with *verdad*. Tell them to go back to the reading (pp. 36–37) to find the information they need.
Ex. 2: Again, have students refer to the *Tema para investigar* to see how the questions could be answered.
Ex. 4: If students are unaware of your school's literary magazine, bring in some samples.

Ex. 6: The term *popular* may not be the descriptor that best fits the idea of community service. In many schools, it is a requirement. If this causes confusion, simply ask if their friends are or are not involved in community service.
Brainstorm possible verb choices.
Write a model on the chalkboard.
¿Qué sabes ahora?: Have students write this so that they can record their progress.

¡Vivan los voluntarios!

En Panamá, los jóvenes son super activos en cuanto a la ecología. Todos los meses, varias fundaciones, tanto nacionales como privadas, organizan proyectos para la reforestación, la limpieza de las playas y la protección de animales en los bosques.

Uno de los proyectos requiere que los voluntarios pasen el fin de semana en las montañas. La misión: desarmar las trampas que ponen los cazadores. Dice Ana Smith, de 17 años, «Me encanta ser parte de este proyecto. Tenemos que aprender a conservar el medio ambiente para el futuro».

¿Qué sabes ahora?

¿Puedes:

- describirte a ti mismo(a)?
  —Soy ___ y ___ . (No) me gusta ___ .
- describir a tu mejor amigo(a)?
  —Mi mejor amigo(a) es ___ y ___ . Le gusta ___ .
- decir cómo te llevas con los demás y por qué?
  —Mi hermano y yo siempre ___ . Él es muy ___ .
- hablar sobre tu papel en la sociedad?
  —Los viernes, después de las clases, ___ .

En una academia de
baile en Caracas, Venezuela

Tema para investigar   39

Answers: ¿Qué sabes ahora?
• All answers will vary, but look for use of new vocabulary that is appropriate to the statements.

Using Documents
Ask students if they can understand the gist of the article about volunteers at the top of this page.

 Practice Wkbk. 1-3, 1-4

 Audio Activity 1.2

 Writing Activity 1-C

 Pruebas 1-3, 1-4

Strategies for Reaching All Students
MULTIPLE INTELLIGENCES
Intrapersonal/Introspective
See Exs. 3–6 and ¿Qué sabes ahora?
Verbal/Linguistic
See Audio Activity 1.2.
Visual/Spatial
See Exs. 1–2, Cooperative Learning, Practice Wkbk. 1-3 and 1-4, and Writing Activity 1-C.

Cultural Notes

Cooperative Learning
Divide the class into groups of three, four, or five. Following the directions in Ex. 9, p. 35, have students decide on a group name and characteristics they have in common. Have them construct a poem about themselves, using the guidelines given in the exercise. Post their poems around the classroom.

(p. 38, photo)
Sidewalk painters and other street artists are a familiar sight in Madrid's scenic Parque del Retiro, particularly on weekends, when hundreds of families come to enjoy the park's many attractions. Exhibitions of modern art are regularly held in two buildings in the Retiro gardens, the Palacio de Cristal, a huge glass conservatory, and the Palacio de Velázquez, both designed by Ricardo Velázquez Bosco for the Philippines Exhibition of 1887.

(p. 39, bottom photo)
A benefit of Venezuela's 1958 democratic revolution was the government's promotion of all kinds of artistic expression, including folk art. Venezuela's national dance, the jiglike joropo, has received particular attention, and is now often a part of the classical ballet curriculum at dance academies such as this one in Caracas. The joropo is typically accompanied by the cuatro (a four-string guitar), a 32-string harp, and maracas.

Standards 1.2; 1.3; 3.1; 3.2   **39**

Present & Apply

ÁLBUM CULTURAL

¿Qué les gusta hacer a los adolescentes
en España e Hispanoamérica? ¿Cómo se
relacionan con los amigos y con la familia?
¿Cuáles son sus preocupaciones?
¿Cómo son ellos?

En Barcelona, muchos jóvenes prefieren
salir con un grupo de amigos. Un lugar
de reunión es el café Parc Güell. Ahí los
jóvenes hablan sobre la escuela, sobre
una película o sobre el último juego de
su equipo favorito de fútbol, el Barça.
Dice Leticia, "Me gusta estar con las
personas que me aceptan tal como soy.
Eso me hace sentir bien."

40   Capítulo 1

Options

Strategies for Reaching All Students

Students Needing Extra Help
Have students take notes for use in the
¿Lo sabes bien? section.

Multiple Intelligences
Bodily/Kinesthetic and Visual/Spatial
Have students create a rough draft of a
class mural that depicts how learning
Spanish has broadened their vision of the
world. Words may be included as well as
images.
Verbal/Linguistic and Visual/Spatial
Have students compare the boy's room in
the photo on p. 41 to their room (or the
room in which they prefer to study).

Eduardo es un joven catalán que estudia en la universidad. Está tomando un curso de biología. "Me considero un muchacho estudioso," dice Eduardo. "A veces me quejo porque no tengo mucho tiempo para ir al cine o escuchar música, pero en general me gusta mucho estudiar biología." Eduardo puede estudiar en la biblioteca de la universidad, pero prefiere la tranquilidad de su cuarto.

Los jóvenes del mural *Song of Unity* están tocando música y trabajando juntos para mejorar la vida de la comunidad. Un grupo de artistas pintó este mural en una de las paredes de La Peña Cultural Center en Berkeley, California para unir las diferentes culturas representadas allí.

Álbum cultural 41

Cultural Notes

(p. 40, top photo)
Like many parks across Spain's cities, Barcelona's Parc Güell features outdoor cafés such as this one, where customers enjoy the usual daily break for socializing and refreshments. Yet Parc Güell itself, built between 1900 and 1914 by the eccentric, modernist architect Antonio Gaudí, is far from usual in its layout and structures. Named for Gaudí's patron, the industrialist

Eusebio Güell, the park features dreamlike stairways, buildings, and other structures with sinuous, organic lines, and curved surfaces covered with polychromatic pieces of ceramic tile.
Ask students: Imagine that the architecture of your school were like Parc Güell and other structures designed by Gaudí. How might that affect the attitudes and behavior of students?

(pp. 40–41, photo)
This mural, aptly entitled "Song of Unity," was painted by a group of artists of varying ethnic backgrounds at the La Peña Cultural Center in Berkeley, California. Artists Ray Patlan, Osha Neumann, Brian Thiele, Anna de León, and Joanne Cooke have combined their efforts to create a work that is popular in the great tradition of Mexican mural art.

Present & Apply

Multicultural Perspectives

Nuyorican. Puertorriqueño. Boricua. Puerto Ricans both on the island and in the U.S. face the question of identity. For the generations of Puerto Ricans living in the U.S., the self-determined label of *Nuyorican* (the combination of New York and Puerto Rican) exemplifies the blending between two cultures. Other immigrant groups face similar dilemmas of balancing the values, belief systems, and customs of two or more cultures. Ask students to investigate and report back about other cultures experiencing similar situations.

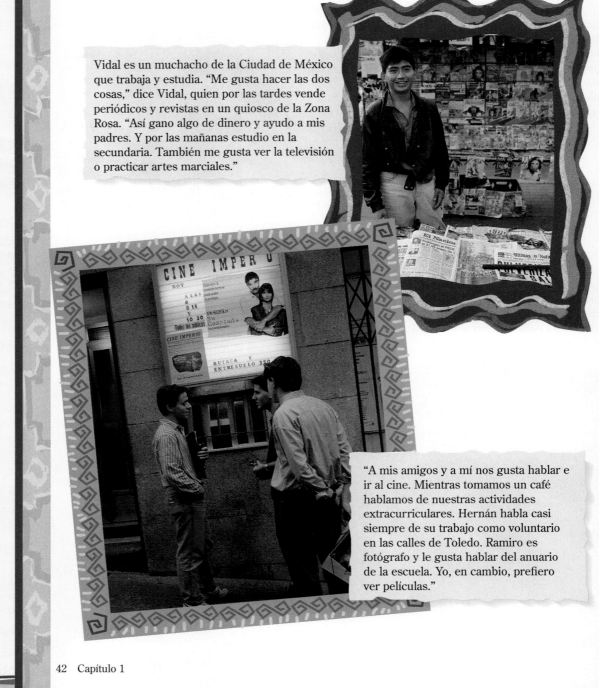

Vidal es un muchacho de la Ciudad de México que trabaja y estudia. "Me gusta hacer las dos cosas," dice Vidal, quien por las tardes vende periódicos y revistas en un quiosco de la Zona Rosa. "Así gano algo de dinero y ayudo a mis padres. Y por las mañanas estudio en la secundaria. También me gusta ver la televisión o practicar artes marciales."

"A mis amigos y a mí nos gusta hablar e ir al cine. Mientras tomamos un café hablamos de nuestras actividades extracurriculares. Hernán habla casi siempre de su trabajo como voluntario en las calles de Toledo. Ramiro es fotógrafo y le gusta hablar del anuario de la escuela. Yo, en cambio, prefiero ver películas."

42   Capítulo 1

Options

Strategies for Reaching All Students

Spanish-Speaking Students
Ask: *¿Cómo son las reuniones de tu familia? ¿Quiénes asisten? ¿Qué hacen? ¿Quién(es) prepara(n) la comida? ¿Qué valor tienen estas reuniones para ti? ¿Crees que tu generación continuará las reuniones cuando sea mayor? ¿Por qué?*

Students Needing Extra Help
Ex. 1: Remind students what a "characteristic" is. Make a list of characteristics that they share with other teenagers.
Ex. 2: Discuss or explain the term *la interacción.* Be aware that some students may have families that do not interact well.

Multiple Intelligences
Intrapersonal/Introspective
See Exs. 1–3.

"Las personas más comprensivas se encuentran en mi misma familia," dice Magda. " Sí, nuestros parientes son nuestros mejores amigos." Cada año la familia de Magda se reúne en Río Grande, Texas. Ahí tienen una casa muy grande que pertenece a toda la familia. Magda también dice que para cada reunión su abuela prepara un plato especial. "Por las noches nos sentamos a comer y compartir experiencias de nuestra vida," dice Magda.

Reacción personal

Contesta las siguientes preguntas en una hoja de papel.

1 Mira las fotos y lee el texto de cada una de ellas para ver cuáles son las características de los jóvenes hispanos. ¿Qué tienes en común con ellos? ¿Cuáles son las diferencias entre tú y ellos?

2 ¿Cuándo te reúnes tú con tu familia? ¿Y con tus amigos? Cuando te reúnes con ellos(as), ¿adónde van?

3 ¿Cuáles son las actividades en que participan las personas en las fotos? ¿Participas en las mismas actividades? ¿En qué actividades participas o te gustaría participar?

Álbum cultural 43

Answers: Reacción personal

1–2 Answers will vary.

3 Answers will vary, but may include:
Descansan en un café. / Estudia. (Hace la tarea.) / Vende periódicos. / Van al cine. / Participan en una fiesta. (Bailan.)

www Internet Activities
Álbum cultural
Have students go to www.pasoapaso.com for additional activities and practice.

Cultural Notes

(p. 42, top photo)
Mexico City residents have an abundance of newspapers and magazines to choose from to keep them informed and entertained. In addition to the highly popular sports daily *Esto* (400,000 circulation), the capital has about thirty dailies (500,000 total circulation) spanning a broad range of political views. Spanish-language versions of *Reader's Digest (Selecciones), Cosmopolitan, Good Housekeeping,* and *Popular Mechanics* are also very popular.

Ask students: Do most newspapers in the U.S. have distinct and recognizable political views? Does your local newspaper operate from a certain viewpoint, or does it present issues from a variety of angles? Give examples.

(p. 42, bottom photo)
Moviegoing is only the latest in Toledo's vast, ancient, and ethnically diverse store of cultural attractions. Located 44 miles south of Madrid, Toledo has been declared a national treasure by the Spanish government. The architectural gems that line its streets reflect the magnificence of the Arabic, Christian, and Jewish cultures that flourished there from the eighth to the fifteenth centuries.

Preview

Overhead 8

Teaching Suggestions

A Ask students how the *tú* command forms differ from the *tú* present tense forms. Review if necessary.

B Students may need help with the infinitives for irregular command forms. Have them apply reading strategies they have learned. They should make logical choices and, if necessary, make guesses. Ask: Which infinitive is *di* most likely from, *dar* or *decir?* Why?

C Remind students that they have seen the expression *lo* + adjective in the vocabulary section.

Answers

Answers will vary.

A *Escucha, respeta, explica,* and *sugiere / Resuelve el problema.*

B *Haz, sé,* and *di / hacer, ser,* and *decir*

C (2) lo que *dice,* (5) *explica* lo que *pasó; lo que* refers to an action

Gramática en contexto

Mira este cartel donde se dan siete pasos sobre cómo resolver un problema. ¿Qué haces para resolver un conflicto? Ahora lee el cartel.

A In this poster, the first words in each sentence tell you what to do to resolve a conflict. In steps 2, 3, 5, and 6, what verbs indicate a command? Using *resolver*, complete the sentence: "... el problema."

B In numbers 1, 4, and 7 there are other commands. What are they? What are the infinitives of these verbs?

C *Lo que* appears twice, in steps 2 and 5. In these examples, does *lo que* refer to an object, an action, or a person?

44   Capítulo 1

Options

Strategies for Reaching All Students

Students Needing Extra Help
Begin the grammar section of the Organizer. If available, refer to the grammar section of the Organizers *(Practice Workbook)* from Book 1, Chap. 13, and Book 2, Chaps. 12 and 13.
Students may confuse the command form of *ser* with the *yo* form of *saber* in the present tense. Explain that the context usually makes this clear.
C: Students might get frustrated with the

subtlety of this grammar point. If so, move quickly to the explanation.
Repaso: Los mandatos afirmativos con tú: Give additional examples of the regular *tú* commands.
Give at least two examples of each of the irregular commands in sentences and two more examples of attaching the object pronoun to the command form.
Ex. 1: Remind students that there are regular and irregular verbs in this exercise.

Enrichment
Repaso: Los mandatos afirmativos con tú: As a homework assignment, have students write a command or commands from a well-known folk tale in which a character or animal is ordered to do something. Folk tales that lend themselves well to this exercise are *The Story of the Fisherman and His Wife, Snow White, The Sorcerer's Apprentice,* and *Cinderella.*

Repaso: Los mandatos afirmativos con *tú*

Remember that to give an affirmative *tú* command, we use the same form as the *Ud./él/ella* form of the present tense.

Juanito, **comparte** tus juguetes con los otros niños.
Resuelve rápido tus problemas con los demás.

• Certain verbs have irregular affirmative command forms.

tener	**ten**	poner	**pon**
hacer	**haz**	decir	**di**
ser	**sé**	ir	**ve**
salir	**sal**		

• When we use an affirmative *tú* command with a direct or indirect object pronoun, we attach the pronoun to the verb. If the command form has more than two syllables, we must add an accent mark to show that the stress remains in the same place.

Dime la verdad siempre.
Explícale a tu padre por qué llegaste tarde.

Dos jóvenes se dan la mano en un parque de la Ciudad de México.

1 ¿Qué consejos puedes darle a un(a) compañero(a) que tiene los siguientes problemas?

A —*Nunca llego a tiempo.*
B —*Sal de casa más temprano.*

Estudiante A

a. Me peleo con todo el mundo.
b. Siempre doy excusas.
c. Nunca ayudo en casa.
d. No hago nada los viernes por la noche.
e. Soy bastante vanidoso.
f. Nunca sé cuáles son las tareas.
g.

Estudiante B

Preguntarle a un(a) compañero(a).
Ir al cine con tu hermano(a).
Ser más amable.
Decir la verdad.
Pensar también en los demás.
Poner la mesa esta noche.

Gramática en contexto   45

Present & Practice

Class Starter Review
On the day following the review of affirmative *tú* commands, you might begin the class with this activity:
Tell one student to do several things. Continue until he or she makes a mistake. At that point, ask a volunteer to correctly carry out the command. Allow Spanish-speaking students to give commands to their classmates.

Reteach / Review
Los mandatos afirmativos con tú: Ask volunteers to follow your instructions. Example: *Ven aquí. Ahora ve a la ventana. Pon el libro en el suelo. Ahora sé amable y levanta el libro del suelo. Ponlo en mi escritorio.*

Answers
1 a. Sé más amable.
b. Di la verdad.
c. Pon la mesa esta noche.
d. Ve al cine con tu hermano(a).
e. Piensa también en los demás.
f. Pregúntale a un(a) compañero(a).
g. Statements and responses will vary.

 Practice Wkbk. 1-5

 Writing Activity 1-D

 Pruebas 1-5, 1-6

Extended Written Practice/Homework
1. Write four commands telling another person what to do to get along well with others: *Sé sincera y di la verdad.*
2. Write three commands telling another person which volunteer activity to choose: *Trabaja como voluntario(a) en un hospital.*
3. Write three commands telling another person what to do to get along well at home: *Arregla tu cuarto y haz la cama todos los días.*

Multiple Intelligences
Bodily/Kinesthetic
See Class Starter Review.
Interpersonal/Social and Logical/Mathematical
Have students conduct an opinion survey on the top five ways to resolve a conflict. Display the tallied results.
Visual/Spatial
See Exs. A–C, Overhead 8, Enrichment, Practice Wkbk. 1-5, and Writing Activity 1-D.

Cultural Notes

(p. 45, photo)
Mexicans perform a certain ritual when they greet and leave each other that is much more physical and formal than most Americans are accustomed to. Even when they are only casual acquaintances, adults and even very young teenagers of both sexes always shake hands on greeting and taking leave. Among friends, men often greet each other with an embrace as well as a handshake, while women kiss each other on the cheek while shaking hands.

Present & Practice

Class Starter Review

On the day following the review of direct and indirect object pronouns, you might begin the class with this activity:

Give a sentence containing a direct object and have students restate it, replacing the noun with a pronoun. (For those students who are visual learners, use the actual items.) For example: *Necesito el libro. (Lo necesito.)*

Answers

2 ESTUDIANTE A

a. ¿Invitas a tus amigos(as) a tu casa?

b. ¿Admiras a tu profesor(a) de ___?

c. ¿Conoces bien al director (a la directora) de la escuela?

d. ¿Obedeces a tus padres?

e. ¿Entiendes siempre a tus hermanos(as)?

f. ¿Respetas a los demás estudiantes de tu escuela?

g. ¿Visitas frecuentemente a otras personas de tu familia?

h. Questions will vary.

Repaso: Los complementos directos e indirectos

Remember that direct object pronouns tell who or what receives the action of the verb, and indirect object pronouns indicate to whom or for whom an action is performed. Here are all the direct and indirect object pronouns:

Pronombres de complemento directo

me	nos
te	os
lo / la	los / las

Pronombres de complemento indirecto

me	nos
te	os
le	les

- These pronouns go before the main verb or are attached to an infinitive, a present participle, or an affirmative command.

  La influencia de los amigos **nos puede** causar problemas.
  La influencia de los amigos puede **causarnos** problemas.
  Creo que nuestros amigos están **influyéndonos**.
  Dale buenos consejos a tu amigo.

- When we attach an object pronoun to a present participle or to a command that has more than one syllable, we must add an accent mark to preserve the original stress.

  Es un buen amigo. **Respétalo.**

- When we use a noun as an indirect object, we usually also use the indirect object pronoun.

  ¿Siempre **les** haces caso **a tus padres**?

46   Capítulo 1

detalle de *Autorretrato* (1794–1795), Francisco de Goya

¡NO OLVIDES!

When the direct object is a definite person or group of people, we use the personal *a* before it: *Suelo ayudar a mis amigos.*

Options

Strategies for Reaching All Students

Students Needing Extra Help

Repaso: Los complementos directos e indirectos: If available, refer to the grammar section of the Organizers from Book 1, Chaps. 6, 8, and 11. In Book 2, refer to the Chap. 12 Organizer.

Give additional examples of the two ways of placing pronouns when there is a verb followed by an infinitive, and of replacing the indirect object noun with a pronoun.

Ex. 2: Brainstorm possible explanations for each response. For example: *Sí, los invito a mi casa. Escuchamos música.* Remind students that the verb forms will vary in this dialogue.

Ex. 3: Remind students that they shouldn't go straight across the columns when formulating the dialogues.

Extended Written Practice/Homework

1. Write three pairs of sentences describing different people and indicating whether or not you respect or admire them: *El consejero es muy comprensivo. Lo respeto mucho.*

2. Using verbs such as *explicar, entender, ayudar, dar, respetar,* and *apoyar,* write three sentences telling how people treat you and your classmates: *La profesora de álgebra nos explica bien las tareas y los problemas.*

3. Write two sentences telling what or who influences you.

2 Pregúntale a tu compañero(a) sobre sus relaciones con los demás. Explica tus respuestas.

ver a tu mejor amigo(a) todos los días

A — *¿Ves a tu mejor amigo(a) todos los días?*
B — *Sí, lo (la) veo todos los días. Tenemos las mismas clases.*
   o: *No, no lo (la) veo todos los días. Va a otra escuela.*

a. invitar a tus amigos(as) a tu casa
b. admirar a tu profesor(a) de ___
c. conocer bien al director (a la directora) de la escuela
d. obedecer a tus padres
e. entender siempre a tus hermanos(as)
f. respetar a los demás estudiantes de tu escuela
g. visitar frecuentemente a otras personas de tu familia
h.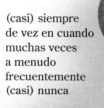

3 Pregúntale a tu compañero(a) qué hacen otras personas por él (ella). Usa expresiones de las tres columnas en las preguntas y en las respuestas.

ayudar con la tarea

A — *¿Tu mejor amigo(a) te ayuda con la tarea?*
B — *Sí, me ayuda frecuentemente.*
   o: *No, nunca me ayuda.*

a. tus padres	apoyar	(casi) siempre
b. tus abuelos	llamar por teléfono	de vez en cuando
c. tus amigos(as)	hacer caso	muchas veces
d. tus compañeros(as)	escribir cartas	a menudo
e. tu mejor amigo(a)	prestar dinero	frecuentemente
f. tu profesor(a) de ___	dar consejos	(casi) nunca
g.	dar clases particulares	

47

ESTUDIANTE B
a.–h. Answers will vary, but look for correct use of *yo* forms and direct object pronouns:
a. . . . los (las) invito . . .
b. . . . lo (la) admiro . . .
c. . . . lo (la) conozco . . .
d. . . . los obedezco . . .
e. . . . los (las) entiendo . . .
f. . . . los respeto . . .
g. . . . las visito . . .
h. Answers will vary.

3 ESTUDIANTE A
Questions will vary, but should begin with the following:
a. ¿Tus padres te . . .
b. ¿Tus abuelos te . . .
c. ¿Tus amigos(as) te . . .
d. ¿Tus compañeros(as) te . . .
e. ¿Tu mejor amigo(a) te . . .
f. ¿Tu profesor(a) de ___ te . . .
g. Questions will vary.
ESTUDIANTE B
a.–g. Answers will vary, but should include the pronoun *me* and an adverbial expression.

Comm. Act. BLM 1-2

Cultural Notes

Multiple Intelligences
Interpersonal/Social and Verbal/Linguistic
See Exs. 2–3.
Verbal/Linguistic
See Class Starter Review.
Visual/Spatial
See Comm. Act. BLM 1-2.

(p. 46, photo)
One of the world's master artists, Francisco José de Goya y Lucientes was born on March 30, 1746, in the northern Spanish village of Fuendetodos, and died in Bordeaux, France, on April 16, 1828. Goya is widely considered to be the first of the modern artists for his bold, realistic paintings and for the dark and satiric style of his etchings.

Present & Practice

Class Starter Review

On the day following the presentation of uses of *lo,* you might begin the class with this activity:
Write on the chalkboard the following expressions: *lo peor, lo mejor, lo más interesante,* and *lo más difícil.* Have students use one of these expressions to give an opinion or a piece of advice about studying Spanish.

Answers

4 ESTUDIANTE A

a. Me gusta decirle la verdad a mi profesor(a) de español.
b. ...darles clases particulares a otros estudiantes.
c. ...prestarle mis apuntes a mi compañero(a) de clase.
d. ...escuchar al profesor (a la profesora) de ___.
e. ...ayudar a mi madre en casa.
f. ...llamar a mis abuelos(as).
g. Statements will vary, but look for correct use of personal *a.*

ESTUDIANTE B

a.–g. Responses will vary, but look for correct use of the indirect object pronouns *le / les.*

 Practice Wkbk. 1-6, 1-7

 Writing Activity 1-E

 Prueba 1-7

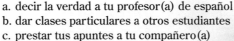

¿Quién soy yo en realidad?

4 Dile a tu compañero(a) qué te gusta hacer por los demás.
Tu compañero(a) te puede decir si le gusta hacer lo mismo o no.

preparar su plato favorito a tu padre (madre)

A —*Me gusta prepararle su plato favorito a mi padre.*
B —*A mí no. No me gusta cocinar. Nunca le preparo nada.*
   o: *A mí también. Generalmente le preparo un bistec con papas fritas.*

a. decir la verdad a tu profesor(a) de español
b. dar clases particulares a otros estudiantes
c. prestar tus apuntes a tu compañero(a) de clase
d. escuchar al profesor (a la profesora) de ___
e. ayudar a tu madre en casa
f. llamar a tus abuelos(as)
g. 💡

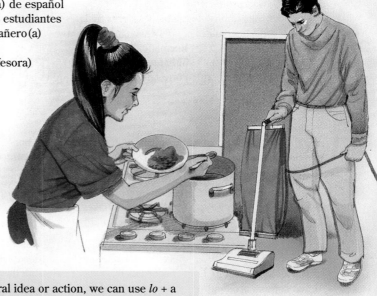

Otros usos de *lo*

When we want to refer to a general idea or action, we can use *lo* + a masculine singular adjective to make it into a noun or noun phrase. The English equivalent often includes the word "thing" or "part."

Lo peor que puedes hacer es decir mentiras a tus compañeros.
***The worst thing** you can do is to tell lies to your friends.*

Lo más importante es ser sincero.
***The most important thing** is to be sincere.*

• We use *lo que* to refer to a situation, action, or object not yet identified. The English equivalent is usually "what."

Lo que debes hacer es no escucharlo.
***What** you should do is not to listen to him.*

No entendemos **lo que** ellos dicen.
*We don't understand **what** they're saying.*

48 Capítulo 1

Options

Strategies for Reaching All Students

Students Needing Extra Help
Ex. 4: Show students that they are using the indirect object pronoun *le* or *les* to clarify the indirect object in the *Estudiante A* statement.
Brainstorm responses to complete the sentences.

Otros usos de lo: Show students that there is no Spanish word in the examples that means "thing." Give further examples.
The "what" idea may be difficult for students to grasp. Help them create examples with you.
Ahora lo sabes: Have students write this so that they can record their progress.

Enrichment
Ex. 4: Assign this exercise as written homework before having pairs of students do it in class.

48 Standards 1.1; 4.1

5 Completa las frases de una manera original.
Después compáralas con las de un(a) compañero(a).

Lo bueno de este año escolar es…
Lo bueno de este año escolar es que me gustan mis clases.

Lo que mis amigos dicen…
Lo que mis amigos dicen me influye mucho.

a. Lo peor que una persona
   puede hacer es…
b. Lo mejor que un(a) amigo(a)
   puede hacer es…
c. En una amistad, lo más
   difícil es…
d. Lo que mis padres piensan…
e. Lo peor que un(a) compañero(a)
   puede hacer es…
f. Lo que mis tíos(as) hacen…

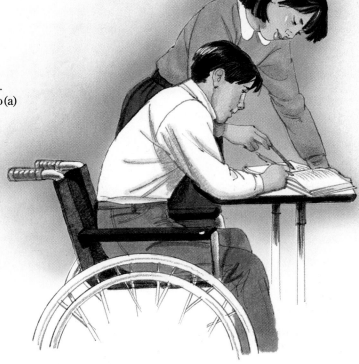

Ahora lo sabes

¿Puedes:

■ darle un consejo a un(a) amigo(a)?
   —Por favor, ___ lo que dice la profesora.

■ decir a quién o para quién se hace algo?
   —Mi mejor amigo ___ llama por teléfono siempre.
   Yo ___ ayudo con la tarea.

■ hablar de algo todavía no identificado?
   —No sé ___ ___ me va a regalar para mi cumpleaños.

> ### MÁS PRÁCTICA
>
> • Más práctica y tarea, pp. 548–549
> • Practice Workbook 1–5, 1–9

Gramática en contexto   49

Answers
5 a.–f. Statements will vary, but should be logical.

Answers: Ahora lo sabes
• Answers will vary, but may include: *escucha, haz.*
• me, le
• lo que

Practice Wkbk. 1-8, 1-9

Audio Activities 1.3, 1.4, 1.5

Writing Activity 1-F

Prueba 1-8

Comm. Act. BLM 1-3

Cooperative Learning
Divide the class into groups of four. Have groups brainstorm situations in which one might receive "good news, bad news" at the same time. Assign specific topics to groups and instruct them to construct four good / bad items utilizing *lo bueno, lo mejor, lo malo,* and *lo peor.*

Extended Written Practice/Homework
1. Using expressions such as *decir la verdad, dar consejos,* and *hacer caso a,* write sentences telling how you relate to others: *Le doy consejos a mi hermano menor sobre las clases y los deportes.*
2. Copy these phrases and complete them according to your opinion: *Lo más importante en una amistad es… No entiendo lo que …*

Multiple Intelligences
Logical/Mathematical
See Cooperative Learning.
Verbal/Linguistic
See Exs. 4–5, Class Starter Review, and Audio Activities 1.3, 1.4, and 1.5.
Visual/Spatial
See Practice Wkbk. 1-6, 1-7, 1-8, and 1-9; Writing Activities 1-E and 1-F; Comm. Act. BLM 1-3; and Enrichment.

Apply

Completing these activities will help students answer the key chapter question: *¿Quién soy yo en realidad?* You may select one, two, or all three of them, time permitting.

Ex. 2: Allow students about four minutes to make their lists. Compile a master list by asking each student to tell you one verb that he or she has written down. When students have guessed their partner's "lie," they can change partners and repeat the activity. You may want to conclude the activity by choosing students to tell you something they've learned about a classmate: *María trabaja en un asilo después de las clases.*

Answers: Sopa de actividades
1–3 Responses will vary.

Para decir más

Aquí tienes vocabulario adicional que te puede ayudar para hacer las actividades de esta sección.

orgulloso(a)
proud

talentoso(a)
talented

sensible
sensitive

sensato(a)
sensible

idealista
idealist

perfeccionista
perfectionist

optimista
optimist

pesimista
pessimist

**el ciudadano,
la ciudadana**
citizen

50   Capítulo 1

¿Quién soy yo en realidad?

Esta sección te ofrece la oportunidad de combinar lo que aprendiste en este capítulo con lo que ya sabes para responder a la pregunta clave.

Sopa de actividades

1. Haz una descripción de ti mismo(a) en un montaje *(collage)*. Usa fotos tuyas o de una revista y palabras claves para indicar:

- cómo eres
- qué te gusta hacer y qué no
- cuáles son tus intereses
- cómo son tus amigos(as)
- cómo te llevas con ellos
- por qué te consideras un(a) buen(a) amigo(a), estudiante, ciudadano(a)

Luego prepara un informe oral con esos datos y preséntalo a un grupo de tus compañeros(as).

Options

Strategies for Reaching All Students

Spanish-Speaking Students
Ex. 3: *Escucha el debate de uno de los grupos. ¿Quién crees que presentó mejor su argumento? ¿Por qué?*

Students Needing Extra Help
If time is a factor, or depending on the ability of the class, do Exs. 1 and 2.
Ex. 1: Model, then have students brainstorm other adjectives to use in describing themselves and their friends.
Remind students to write down this information in preparation for writing a more formal report to present to the class.
Help with the vocabulary and structures needed to answer the question about being a good friend.

Ex. 2: After completing the four statements, students may be tempted to show the list to their partner instead of reading it. Encourage them to work through the assignment completely.
Ex. 3: Do as a whole class and give a specific number of hours that the school might enforce if it were to adopt this policy. This gives students something concrete.

Using Documents

See if students can get the meaning of *chupas negras* (black leather jackets) through visual and written context clues.

Chapter 1: Play

Step

 Video Activities B–C

 Writing Activities 1-G, 1-H

 Comm. Act. BLMs 1-4, 1-5

2 Trabaja con un(a) compañero(a) y haz una lista de verbos. Por ejemplo: *montar, dibujar, ir al campo.*

Ahora escribe cuatro frases que te describen a ti. Tres de las frases son verdaderas y una es falsa. Por ejemplo:

> *Me encanta practicar la esgrima.*
> *Trabajo en un asilo los fines de semana.*
> *Toco el clarinete en la orquesta*
>   *de la escuela.*
> *Escribo artículos para el periódico*
>   *escolar.*

Lee las cuatro frases a un(a) compañero(a).
Tu compañero(a) debe identificar la frase falsa.
Por ejemplo:

A —*No tocas el clarinete en la orquesta*
  de la escuela.
B —*Tienes razón. No toco el clarinete.*
  o: *Sí, toco el clarinete en*
  la orquesta.

¡Al concierto!

¿Qué hacen los jóvenes en Barcelona un sábado por la noche? ¡Van a los conciertos de rock!

«Primero, vamos a casa de alguien y escuchamos la música del cantante o del grupo», dice Jordi Tarrida. «Después, con nuestras chupas negras, vamos en grupo al concierto. Si la música lo permite, bailamos. Después del concierto, el grupo termina la noche en un café o en una discoteca».

3 Nuestro trabajo nos ayuda a conocernos mejor.
Pero los estudiantes no pueden trabajar muchas horas.
En grupos de cuatro, discutan sobre si la escuela debe limitar el número de horas que pueden trabajar los estudiantes.

- Den cinco razones por qué sí o por qué no están de acuerdo.
- En una tabla, escriban un contraargumento para cada una de ellas.
- Dos estudiantes de cada grupo deben trabajar con otros dos estudiantes de otro grupo con un punto de vista diferente para debatir el tema.
- Reporten los resultados a su grupo.

Sopa de actividades 51

Require only three reasons. Students may be hard-pressed to generate five different reasons because their focus might be on the need for more money.
Model the advice that could be given and brainstorm other problems and solutions.

Multiple Intelligences
Bodily/Kinesthetic and Visual/Spatial
See Ex. 1.
Interpersonal/Social and Intrapersonal/Introspective
See Ex. 2.

Interpersonal/Social and Verbal/Linguistic
See Ex. 3.
Visual/Spatial
See Writing Activities 1-G and 1-H and Comm. Act. BLMs 1-4 and 1-5.

Apply

Process Reading

Make sure students understand the four headings in this section and the tasks they represent:

- *Antes de leer:* pre-reading activity for activating prior knowledge
- *Mira la lectura:* scanning / skimming for general ideas or information, emphasis on one or more strategies for identifying the general idea of the text or for focusing only on the specific information required
- *Infórmate:* closer reading for text comprehension, identifying details, interpreting the writer's intent
- *Aplicación:* using the information, new vocabulary, or strategy learned in the reading for a new task or purpose

Teaching Suggestions

Working through the *Para leer* section will help students answer the key chapter question.

Encourage students to use the strategies to understand the ideas presented in the reading. Remind them that they do not need to understand each word, but can use cognates, word families, and familiar vocabulary to get the main idea.

Puntos de Vista

Para leer

Antes de leer

STRATEGY Using heads, subheads, and illustrations

En la Edad Media, cada uno de los elementos: el fuego, el aire, el agua y la tierra, se asociaba con colores y características personales. ¿Qué piensas tú? En una hoja de papel, escribe los colores y características de cada elemento.

Mira la lectura

STRATEGY Scanning

Lee la selección una vez rápidamente sólo para ver si los colores y las características de tu lista corresponden a los de la selección.

El color de tu personalidad

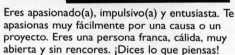

Tu grupo es:
FUEGO

Eres apasionado(a), impulsivo(a) y entusiasta. Te apasionas muy fácilmente por una causa o un proyecto. Eres una persona franca, cálida, muy abierta y sin rencores. ¡Dices lo que piensas!

Si eres "fuego," prefieres:

El rojo: Entusiasta y espontáneo(a), exteriorizas fácilmente tus sentimientos, a veces con pasión.

El anaranjado: Eres una persona generosa, afectuosa y muy abierta.

El amarillo: Tu carácter es orgulloso y firme. No aceptas los compromisos.

52   Capítulo 1

Tu grupo es:
AIRE

Lucidez y vigor son tus características principales. Haces amistades con facilidad y te encanta discutir. No te gusta estar solo(a).

Si eres "aire," prefieres:

El violeta: Eres sentimental e idealista. Tienes tendencia a soñar mucho.

El blanco: Eres muy franco(a) y prefieres las situaciones claras.

El azul cielo: Soñador(a) y sensible, buscas el gran amor y lo imposible.

Options

Strategies for Reaching All Students

Spanish-Speaking Students

Have Spanish-speaking students write:
¿Estás de acuerdo con estas descripciones?
¿Tienes características que correspondan a más de un elemento o a más de un color?
¿Cuáles?

Students Needing Extra Help

Antes de leer: Explain the Middle Ages reference and review the imperfect tense. Students have probably not given this idea a lot of thought. Discuss if necessary. Since you are just beginning the school year, take the time now to review reading strategies. Have students skim the reading the first time through just for a sense of the article. Assure them that they don't need to know every word.

Infórmate: Remind students to answer with a color for sections 2 and 3.
Aplicación: For the second activity, have students brainstorm as a class another classification system to replace *fuego, aire, agua,* and *tierra.*

Tu grupo es:
AGUA

Tienes mucha imaginación y eres muy romántico(a). Las emociones te dominan y buscas refugio en los sueños.

Si eres "agua," prefieres:

El azul oscuro: En busca de lo absoluto, eres misterioso(a) y discreto(a).

El turquesa: Enfrentas cualquier obstáculo para obtener tu ideal.

El verde claro: Eres sentimental, tienes mucho encanto y fantasía.

Infórmate

STRATEGY Reading for details

Ahora lee todo el artículo prestando atención a los detalles.

1 ¿Una persona a quien le gusta el rojo se lleva bien con una persona a quien le gusta el marrón? ¿Por qué?

2 ¿Con qué "color" te gustaría ir a una fiesta? ¿Por qué?

3 ¿Qué "color" sería buen actor o actriz? ¿Por qué?

Tu grupo es:
TIERRA

Eres una persona estable, práctica y sólida, que no tiene miedo a las responsabilidades. Eres perfeccionista y paciente y también reservado(a).

Si eres "tierra," prefieres:

El beige: Eres alegre, afectuoso(a) y te gusta divertirte.

El marrón: Eres muy reservado(a). Buscas la tranquilidad y la serenidad.

El negro: Eres tímido(a) y no muestras tus sentimientos. Tienes perseverancia.

Aplicación

1 Escribe un párrafo explicando qué elemento eres tú o qué elemento es una persona famosa y por qué piensas así.

2 Inventa otro sistema para clasificar los colores y haz un cartel que lo explique.

Para leer   53

Apply

Teaching Suggestions

Point out the key chapter question. Working through the *Para escribir* section will help students answer this question.

Remind students about correct accent placement, question marks, and exclamation points. For spelling checks, tell students that they may always refer back to the vocabulary sections or the *Resumen del capítulo* at the end of the chapter.

Before beginning this exercise, you may want to review the five steps of process writing with your students.

Process Writing

Inform students in advance that their work will be kept in a portfolio of their writing. If necessary, explain that their portfolio will help them keep a record of their progress through the year.

Portfolios represent a systematic process involving both learner and teacher. They document progress toward specific standards by applying clearly stated criteria in selecting, monitoring, and evaluating significant products and performance. (For a more detailed explanation of portfolio writing and assessment, see pp. T31 and T58–T62.)

Answers

Writing selections will vary.

Para escribir

Vamos a hacer un autorretrato *(self-portrait)* con palabras.

1 Piensa en ti mismo(a) y responde a estas preguntas.

- ¿Qué soy yo? ¿Soy hijo(a), nieto(a), amigo(a), estudiante?
- ¿Cómo soy yo cuando estoy solo(a)? ¿Y con mi familia? ¿Con amigos(as) o compañeros(as)? ¿En el trabajo?
- ¿Qué o quién influye en las decisiones que tomo?
- ¿Cómo ayudo a mi familia? ¿Qué hago por mis amigos, la escuela, la comunidad?
- ¿En qué actividades participo? ¿Cómo me relaciono con las personas en mi trabajo?
- ¿Cuáles de mis características admiro? ¿Cuáles me gustaría cambiar? ¿Por qué?

2 Ahora, usa tus notas para escribir tu autorretrato. Puedes ilustrarlo con dibujos, fotos o diseños. Sigue los pasos del proceso de escribir.

3 Para distribuir tu trabajo, puedes:

- presentar un informe a la clase
- exhibirlo en la sala de clases
- incluirlo en un libro titulado *Así somos*
- ponerlo en tu portafolio

¡NO OLVIDES!

Hay cinco pasos en el proceso de escribir.
1. Primero piensa en el tema *(topic)* y escribe tus ideas.
2. Luego escribe el primer borrador *(draft)*.
3. Comparte tu borrador con un(a) compañero(a) y pídele recomendaciones o ideas. Escribe el segundo borrador.
4. Revisa tu trabajo para corregir los errores de ortografía y puntuación.
5. Ahora, distribuye tu trabajo entre las personas a quienes pueda interesar, y guarda otra copia en tu portafolio.

Autorretrato con mono (1940), Frida Kahlo

54   Capítulo 1

Options

Strategies for Reaching All Students

Students Needing Extra Help

Step 1: Students may be alarmed at the number of questions, not the level of difficulty. Keep them focused by doing one question at a time.
Remind them that they will need the answers to these questions in order to write the self-portrait.
If available, use the vocabulary sections of Organizers from Books 1 and 2 to review possible adjectives. Otherwise, brainstorm.

Students may need help articulating their responses to the final *¿Por qué?* question.
Step 2: Have a model ready to share with students and review process writing.
Step 3: Be clear on your expectations. Let students know how much you expect them to write, whether the assignment will be private or shared, how it will be graded, whether structured writing will be expected or if free-flowing thoughts will be acceptable, and so on.

Multiple Intelligences
Intrapersonal/Introspective
See steps 1–3.

Multicultural Perspectives

The process of discovering one's identity and all the factors influencing it is the theme of a number of literary works by Latina women. *How the García Girls Lost Their Accents,* by the Dominican Julia Álvarez, relates the experiences of four sisters growing up in the U.S. yet maintaining strong ties with the Dominican Republic. (An excerpt appears in Chap. 12, pp. 422–423.) Cuban American writer Cristina García describes three generations of women in one family as they struggle with issues of identity, the generation gap, and politics in the novel *Dreaming in Cuban.* The writings of Sandra Cisneros provide the Chicana perspective on growing up in the U.S. Ask students to select one of these or other Latina writers to research. You may want them to read one of these or other novels for a special class project or extra-credit assignment.

Cultural Notes ☼

(p. 54, photo)
Mexican painter Frida Kahlo did not have a major exhibition of her own until 1953, one year before her death. During her lifetime she was known as a leftist activist and the wife of artist Diego Rivera. Today she is world-famous for her surreal, tormented paintings, of which she is most often the subject. Kahlo was born in 1907 in Coyoacán, Mexico City, where her house stands as a museum donated by Rivera to the Mexican people.

Assess & Summarize

Test Preparation

You may want to assign parts of this section as written homework or as an in-class writing activity prior to administering the *Examen de habilidades.*

Answers

Listening

—La familia se mudó de California hace un mes. Él está en mi clase de matemáticas. Se lleva bien con todos. No se queja de nada, y no se enoja con los otros estudiantes menos considerados de la clase. Ayer me olvidé el dinero para comprar el almuerzo y me dijo que le encantaría compartir su almuerzo conmigo.
Es una persona simpática y generosa. Se lleva bien con todos y no se queja de nada. / Answers will vary.

Reading

Answers will vary.

Writing

Writing selections will vary.

Culture

A los jóvenes hispanos les gusta salir con amigos, ver la televisión, practicar deportes e ir al cine. / *Answers will vary.*

Speaking

Dialogues will vary.

Esta sección te ayudará a prepararte para el examen de habilidades, donde tendrás que hacer tareas semejantes *(similar).*

Listening

¿Puedes entender una descripción de las cualidades de una persona? Escucha mientras el (la) profesor(a) lee un ejemplo semejante al que vas a oír en el examen. ¿Cómo es la persona según la descripción? ¿Te gustaría ser su amigo(a)? ¿Por qué?

Reading

¿Puedes leer una nota en una revista y prestar atención a los detalles para entender la relación que muestra entre los elementos y la personalidad?

> Si eres una
> persona apasionada,
> impulsiva, franca
> y dices siempre
> lo que piensas, tu
> grupo es el **fuego**.

Writing

¿Puedes escribir en tu diario algo semejante a lo que Manuel escribió en el suyo?

Diario de Manuel

Mi mejor amigo, Claudio, se va a mudar a otra ciudad y me siento muy triste. Me llevo bien con los demás, pero no tengo nada en común con ellos. Lo que más me gusta de Claudio es que siempre me ayuda a resolver mis problemas. A veces discutimos, pero lo más importante es que los dos tenemos sentido del humor y nos respetamos mucho. No sé si mis nuevos amigos me van a entender como Claudio.

Cantando en una escuela de música en Zaragoza, España

Culture

¿En qué actividades les gusta participar a los jóvenes hispanos? Y a ti, ¿en cuáles te gusta participar? ¿Qué tienes en común con ellos?

Speaking

Con un(a) compañero(a) habla sobre cómo eres y qué te gusta hacer.

A —*A ti te gusta cuidar niños, ¿verdad?*
B —*Sí, me llevo muy bien con ellos. Nos entendemos muy bien. Además les encanta mi sentido del humor. ¿Y tú? Eres muy tranquilo, ¿verdad?*
A —*¡Qué va! Los sábados doy clases de inglés a dos niños pequeños y los domingos trabajo como voluntario en una campaña de reciclaje. También soy muy aficionado al teatro.*

www.pasoapaso.com

Options

Strategies for Reaching All Students

Students Needing Extra Help

Remind students that this is just a sample, not the real exam.

Since this is the first time that they are seeing this review in the target language, take them through it step by step. The time you spend now will pay off in later chapters. Even for those students who know this approach from Books 1 and 2, it may seem new to them.

Listening: Read more than once. Remind students that they need to listen only for select pieces of information. Brainstorm the types of words for which they should be listening.

Reading: Have students discuss the images that come to mind when they think of fire. Then have them apply those ideas to people. Review the use of cognates, context clues, and word families.

Writing: Have students use the Organizer and write a sample diary entry as practice before the test. This section of the test (for this chapter and subsequent ones) could be a separate grade, scored in accordance with the fact that they could use their books and Organizers.

Discuss other situations that would cause students to write about a friend's personality: an award he or she won that was well deserved; his or her thoughtfulness in helping through a hard time; an argument that they hope doesn't ruin a friendship; appreciation of someone they've known for a long time, and so on.

Resumen del vocabulario

Usa el vocabulario de este capítulo para:

■ responder a la pregunta clave: ¿Quién soy yo en realidad?
■ describir las cualidades de una persona
■ describir cómo te relacionas con los demás
■ hablar sobre cuál es tu papel en la sociedad

Assessment

 Prueba cumulativa

 Examen de habilidades

 Test Generator

Additional Assessment Options

 Comm. Act. BLMs

Small Group Activities
Situation Cards

 ¿Lo sabes bien? Video Quiz

www Internet Activities
Self-Test

para describirte a ti mismo(a) y a otras personas
el (la) aficionado(a)
comprensivo, -a
considerado, -a
incomprensivo, -a
modesto, -a
nervioso, -a
responsable
sincero, -a
tranquilo, -a
vanidoso, -a
el sentido del humor

para hablar sobre cómo te relacionas con otras personas
admirar
la amistad, *pl.* las amistades
apoyar(se)
compartir
el conflicto
el consejo
dar un consejo
los demás

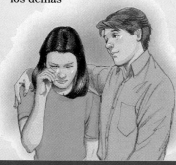

la discusión, *pl.* las discusiones
discutir
enojar(se)
entender(se) *(e → ie)*
hacer caso a
influir (en / sobre) *(i → y):*
   (yo) influyo
   (tú) influyes
íntimo, -a
llevarse (bien / mal)
mantener *(e → ie)*
   (yo) mantengo
   (tú) mantienes
quejarse (de)
relacionar(se) con
resolver *(o → ue)*
respetar
tener en común

para hablar sobre actividades en las que puedes participar
adquirir *(i → ie)*
el asilo
el /la ayudante
la campaña
dar clases particulares
la esgrima
la higiene
inscribirse
el orfanato
la redacción

otras palabras y expresiones útiles
aunque
frecuentemente
lo más / menos *(+ adj.)*
lo mejor / lo peor
mudarse
¡Qué va!

Resumen 57

Cultural Notes ☀

Culture: Have students review any notes they took from the *Álbum cultural* reading. Refer to the *Tema para investigar* for further information.
Speaking: Use the vocabulary section of the Organizer.
Limit the number of lines of dialogue.
Refer students to the grammar section if necessary.

(p. 56, photo)
This girl is singing in a music class in Zaragoza, Spain. Named for Caesar Augustus, who founded the city in 19 B.C., Zaragoza lies halfway between Madrid and Barcelona in the region of Aragón. This ancient city has a current population of over one million, and is home to a major university and the Spanish headquarters for General Motors. The traditional music and dance of Aragón is the jiglike *jota,* which is as identified with Spain as is flamenco.

CAPÍTULO 2

THEME: RURAL AND URBAN LIFE

SCOPE AND SEQUENCE   Pages 58–91

COMMUNICATION

Topics

Advantages and disadvantages of:

City life

Suburban life

Rural life

Objectives

Comparar la vida de la ciudad con la del campo en los países hispanos

Describir cómo es la vida en la ciudad, en el campo y en las afueras

Hablar de las ventajas y desventajas de la vida en la ciudad, en el campo y en las afueras

Hablar sobre cómo viajamos a diario

CULTURE

La vida de la ciudad y del campo en los países hispanos

GRAMMAR

Repaso: El imperfecto

Repaso: Otros usos del imperfecto

El participio pasado como adjetivo

Ancillaries available for use with Chapter 2

Multisensory/Technology	Print	Assessment

 Overheads, 9–10

 Practice Workbook, pp. 21–30

 Assessment Program
   Pruebas, pp. 24–33
   Examen de habilidades, pp. 34–37

 Audio Tapes and CDs

 Writing, Audio & Video Activities, pp. 10–16, 96–98, 135–136

 Test Generator

 Vocabulary Art Blackline Masters for Hands-On Learning, pp. 12–16/CD-ROM

 Communicative Activity Blackline Masters
   Pair and Small Group Activities, pp. 8–13
   Situation Cards, p. 14

 ¿Lo sabes bien? Video Quiz

 Classroom Crossword

 Video

RESOURCE PRO®

Planning Express, Teaching Resources Library, and Clip Art Library

 Internet Activities www.pasoapaso.com

Video, Chap. 2

¿Dónde vives?

In Latin America, an urban tradition had been established long before the arrival of Europeans. Native Americans developed magnificent cities such as Tenochtitlán and Chichén Itzá. Upon the arrival of Europeans, new cities and towns were slowly rebuilt on the sites of those they had conquered.

Unlike Latin America, the early U.S. had no urban tradition. Most Native American groups in the region did not establish permanent settlements. In addition, many European colonists came from cultures that were accustomed to rural life. Consequently, the U.S. was settled largely through small-scale agricultural development. In the beginning, few large urban areas developed. The majority of crops were produced by independent farmers. In contrast, crop production throughout much of Latin America was accomplished on large *fincas* owned by a few individuals.

Some have suggested that in Latin America the impulse is to seek the society of others. The widespread use of the *plaza* gives credence to this suggestion. The Spanish custom of the *plaza* has been replicated in most Latin American towns as a focus for civic activity. It is often surrounded by government buildings and a church. It is also a carefully landscaped gathering spot for friends and neighbors to meet in the evenings or on special occasions to listen to music, stroll, and talk.

Today, settlement patterns in the U.S. and Latin America continue to differ significantly. U.S. cities have experienced an exodus of the middle class to the suburbs, leaving a nucleus of poverty in the urban center. In contrast, in Latin America, there has been significant migration of rural residents to cities. Less affluent new arrivals live near the periphery, while middle-class and affluent residents remain in the city center.

One factor common to both Latin American and U.S. cities is the increasing industrialization and now, "technolization" that have created attractive employment in urban areas, but at the same time decreased the need for farming. This phenomenon has also decreased the numbers of rural dwellers. In general, people both north and south have found compelling reasons to stay within, or move to, metropolitan areas.

Introduce

The following list represents words, expressions, and grammar topics re-entered from Books 1 and 2:

Book 1
nature, vacation activities, places in the community, environment

Book 2
childhood, places in the community, environment, nature

Planning

Cross-Curricular Connections

Cultural Anthropology Connection *(pp. 68–69)*
In groups or pairs, have students find examples of Spanish or Latin American architecture in the U.S. in magazines, books, and other resources. (If possible, provide samples beforehand.) They should make a map or mark a large classroom map with pictures and / or drawings of their findings. Have them present their findings with historical information as to why these areas have a Hispanic connection.

Business Connection *(pp. 70–71)*
Students will choose an urban or rural area in the U.S. or a Spanish-speaking country and write a real estate ad for a residence or business. They must include a description and tell about the local area's advantages. Have them price the property in the local currency and include a picture or artist's conception.

Geography / Math Connection *(pp. 72–73)*
Using a current world almanac, have students determine the percentage of the population living in urban and rural areas in selected cities in Spain and Latin America. Have them create maps and color them to show the percentages. For example: red is 90 percent, blue is 70–89 percent, and so on.

CAPÍTULO 2

OBJETIVOS

Al terminar este capítulo vas a poder responder a la pregunta clave:

¿Prefieres vivir en la ciudad o en el campo?

También vas a poder:

- describir cómo es la vida en un lugar
- comparar la vida de antes con la vida de ahora
- indicar las ventajas y las desventajas de vivir en cierto lugar
- comparar la vida de la ciudad con la vida del campo en los países hispanos

Vista aérea de Taxco, México

59

Spanish in Your Community
Have students contact the local Chamber of Commerce for brochures or any other type of information about their community in Spanish. If this is not possible, have them contact a larger city nearby. Inasmuch as many such information pieces contain spelling, grammatical, and usage errors, you might ask your students to proofread or otherwise correct what is sent to them. If there is no local information available in Spanish, your class might want to write a brochure on their community and give it to the local Chamber of Commerce.

Cultural Notes ☼

(pp. 58–59)
The town of Taxco, situated on a hill 104 miles southwest of Mexico City, is a favorite vacation spot for tourists because of its striking colonial architecture and the high quality of its silver products. This ancient silver-mining region was taken over by the Aztecs in 1440, and from them by the Spaniards in 1522. The city's name is a Spanish corruption of the name of the Nahuatl ball game, *tlachco*.

Preview

Cultural Objective
• Hablar sobre las diferencias entre la vida del campo, de la ciudad y de las afueras

Critical Thinking: Formulating Appropriate Questions

Divide the class into groups of four. Tell students to imagine that they are investigators helping a family find an ideal community in which to live. As part of their investigation, they will need to ask a number of relevant questions that will help them develop a sense of what the family considers "ideal." Have each group compile a list of five questions they would ask. Collect the lists and combine them into a questionnaire. Leave space at the bottom under the heading *Recomendaciones.* Save a copy of the questionnaire from each class for the activity on p. 66.

Answers: Anticipación
Answers will vary.

(pp. 60–61, photos) Answers will vary.

Anticipación

Mira las fotos y lee el texto. Piensa en las diferencias entre el campo, la ciudad y las afueras de la ciudad. ¿En cuál de estos lugares vives tú? ¿Te gustaría vivir en un lugar así durante toda tu vida? ¿Por qué?

En las ciudades grandes como Caracas, Venezuela, hay muchas oportunidades de trabajo y una abundante vida cultural y social. Pero, también hay contaminación y mucha presión. ¿Te gustaría vivir en una ciudad grande como Caracas?

60   Capítulo 2

Options

Strategies for Reaching All Students

Spanish-Speaking Students
Ask: *¿A cuál de estos lugares se parece tu comunidad? Si has vivido en otro lugar, ¿cómo era? Descríbelo.*

Multiple Intelligences
Interpersonal/Social and Logical/Mathematical
See Critical Thinking.

En el campo se puede disfrutar de la naturaleza y de actividades al aire libre. ¿Te gustaría vivir en un lugar tranquilo como este campo de Perú?

Olivos está en las afueras de Buenos Aires, Argentina. Allí las casas tienen jardines y la vida puede ser más tranquila y segura que en la ciudad. ¿Conoces algún lugar en las afueras? ¿Se parece a Olivos?

Exploración Cultural
www.pasoapaso.com
Visita estos países

Cultural Notes ☼

(p. 60, photo)
Caracas is one of the world's largest producers of oil. *La ciudad de las autopistas* (City of Highways), as it is often called, has grown over 300 percent in the last 45 years. Because of this growth, the city experienced massive traffic problems and installed a modern subway system. Commuters also rely on buses, taxis, and collective cars called *por puestos,* which travel along set routes.

(p. 61, top photo)
Approximately 31 percent of Peru's population of 23 million lives in rural areas, where the large indigenous population has conserved much of the culture of their pre-Columbian ancestors. Farming, weaving, traditional music, and spirituality are very much alive. Rural coalitions have formed to address the economic and social disadvantages that they face.

(p. 61, bottom photo)
Buenos Aires has many distinctive neighborhoods. Olivos, pictured here, is one of the more prestigious, with many city officials and businesspeople having homes there. The San Telmo neighborhood, with cobbled streets and some of the few remaining colonial buildings in the city, is an artistic center. La Boca, a neighborhood known for its colorful houses, is also home to many artists.

Present

Chapter Theme
Rural and urban life

Communicative Objectives
- *Describir cómo es la vida en la ciudad, en el campo y en las afueras*
- *Hablar de las ventajas y desventajas de la vida en la ciudad, en el campo y en las afueras*
- *Hablar sobre cómo viajamos a diario*

 Overheads 9–10

 Vocabulary Art BLMs/CD-ROM

 Vocabulary Tape 2-1

Grammar Preview
Adjectival use of the past participle is presented here lexically. The explanation appears on p. 81.

Teaching Suggestions
Preparing students to speak: Use one or two options from each of the categories of Comprehensible Input or Limited Verbal Response. For a complete explanation of these categories and some sample activities, see pp. T20–T21.

Vocabulario para comunicarse

¿Dónde te gustaría vivir?

Aquí tienes palabras y expresiones necesarias para hablar sobre la vida en la ciudad, en las afueras y en el campo. Léelas varias veces y practícalas con un(a) compañero(a) en las páginas siguientes.

la ciudad

la contaminación

el rascacielos, *pl.* los rascacielos

el sendero

el peaje

el puente

el/la ciclista

la acera

el atasco

el peatón, *pl.* los peatones

62

Options

Strategies for Reaching All Students

Spanish-Speaking Students
Ask: *¿Qué otras palabras sabes que se relacionen al tema? Escríbelas en tu vocabulario personal.*

Students Needing Extra Help
Begin the vocabulary section of the Organizer.
Remind students that *peatón* and *jardín* lose their accent in the plural.

Tell students that *el rascacielos* literally means "scratch the sky." Point out how the plural form spelling remains the same. *También necesitas . . . :* Model sentences that show how *tardar en* is used.
Show how the correct form of *lleno, -a de gente* is dependent on the place referred to: *el campo está lleno de gente, la ciudad está llena de gente.*

Enrichment
Ask students to use as much of the new vocabulary as possible as they work in pairs during class to write three or four sentences describing where they live. When they are finished, have them share their work with the rest of the class.

También necesitas . . .

aislado, -a	*isolated*	el ruido	*noise*
animado, -a	*lively*	sano, -a	*healthy*
bello, -a	*beautiful*	seguro, -a	*safe*
lleno, -a de gente	*crowded*	tardar (en)	*to take time (to)*
oír*	*to hear*	¡Una maravilla!	*Wonderful!*

¿Y qué quiere decir . . . ?

conveniente	peligroso, -a	situado, -a
cultivar	rápido, -a	

* *Oír* has a y in all of its present-tense forms except the *yo* form which ends in -*go*, and the *nosotros* and *vosotros* forms, which have an accent on the *i: oigo, oyes, oye, oímos, oís, oyen*. It also has a y in the *Ud. /él / ella* and the *Uds./ ellos / ellas* forms of the preterite.

el campo

la granja

las afueras

la cerca

el camino

el jardín, *pl.* los jardines

la autopista

Vocabulario para comunicarse   63

Class Starter Review
On the day following the initial presentation of vocabulary, you might begin the class with this activity:
Read aloud one of the words and ask students to tell whether it is associated with *el campo, la ciudad,* or both *(los dos).*

www **Internet Activities**
Juegos
Have students go to www.pasoapaso.com for additional activities and practice.

Extended Written Practice/Homework
1. Refer to pp. 62–63 and write four sentences saying where you find the different things pictured: *En las autopistas de … hay muchos atascos.*
2. Choose three adjectives from p. 63 and write sentences describing different places: *Puede ser peligroso subir en el metro de … por la noche.*
3. Write three sentences describing a place where you would like to spend the summer: *Me gustaría pasar el verano en … Hay muchos … allí. Se puede …*

Multiple Intelligences
Bodily/Kinesthetic, Verbal/Linguistic, and Visual/Spatial
Have students recreate the scene on pp. 62–63 depicting their own neighborhoods. Have them illustrate on paper, with computer drawing programs, or with toy models/dioramas. Ask volunteers to conduct an imaginary guided tour for the class.
Interpersonal/Social and Visual/Spatial
See Enrichment.
Verbal/Linguistic
See Class Starter Review and Vocabulary Tape 2-1.
Visual/Spatial
See Overheads 9–10.

Practice

Reteach / Review: Vocabulary

Ex. 1: As a variation on this exercise, have *Estudiante A* ask *Estudiante B* if he or she would like to live near the place in question. After *Estudiante B* has answered, *Estudiante A* can follow up by asking why.

Answers: Empecemos a conversar

1 ESTUDIANTE A

a. ¿Vives cerca de una autopista (carretera)?

b. ...un sendero?

c. ...un camino?

d. ...unos rascacielos?

e. ...una parada de autobús?

ESTUDIANTE B

a.–e. Answers will vary.

Empecemos a conversar

Túrnate con un(a) compañero(a) para ser *Estudiante A* y *Estudiante B*. Reemplacen las palabras subrayadas con palabras representadas o escritas en los recuadros.

💡 **quiere decir que puedes escoger tu propia respuesta.**

1 A —¿*Vives cerca de una granja?*
B —*Sí, hay una granja muy cerca de mi casa.*
o: *No, no hay granjas donde vivo.*

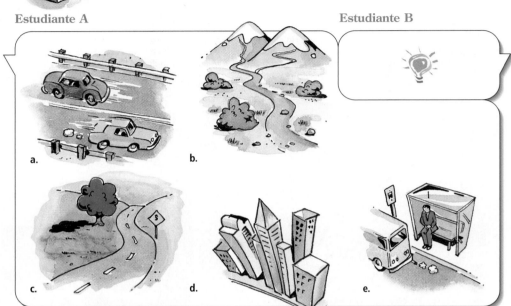

Estudiante A

Estudiante B

a.

b.

c.

d.

e.

64 Capítulo 2

Options

Strategies for Reaching All Students

Spanish-Speaking Students
Ex. 2: Pair bilingual and non-bilingual students, if possible.

Students Needing Extra Help
Ex. 2: Explain that *pareció* is a preterite form of *parecer*. Show another model using *rascacielos,* because it will require the third-person plural form of the verbs.

Enrichment
Ex. 2: To extend this exercise, have *Estudiante A* ask *Estudiante B* for additional reasons why he or she liked or disliked the particular item. Encourage students to use as much of the new vocabulary as possible.
Ex 3: Have *Estudiante A* ask what can be seen from the place in question.

2

A —*Cuando fuiste a la ciudad, ¿qué te parecío el metro?*

B —*(No) me gustó mucho. Estaba muy sucio.*
o: *¡Muy rápido! Me encantó.*
o: *No lo vi.*

¡NO OLVIDES!

As with *gustar,* we use the plural form of *parecer* when the noun that follows is plural: *Las hamburguesas me parecieron deliciosas.*

Remember that *-aba* and *-ía* verb endings indicate the imperfect tense. **Había** *mucho tráfico. / Las calles* **estaban** *sucias.*

Estudiante A

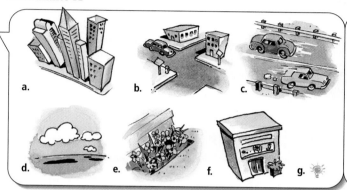

a.
b.
c.
d.
e.
f.
g.

Estudiante B

excelente
contaminado, -a
bello, -a
animado, -a
peligroso, -a
lleno, -a de gente
limpio, -a
interesante
rápido, -a

3 desde tu cuarto

A —*¿Qué se oye desde tu cuarto?*

B —*Se oye el ruido del tráfico.*
o: *No se oye nada.*

Estudiante A

a. desde la escuela
b. en el campo
c. en la ciudad
d. en el bosque
e. desde tu casa
f.

Estudiante B

a la gente que pasa
jugar a los niños
a los pájaros que cantan
a la policía y los bomberos
nada

2 ESTUDIANTE A
a. Cuando fuiste a la ciudad, ¿qué te parecieron los rascacielos?
b. ...parecieron las calles?
c. ...pareció la autopista (carretera)?
d. ...pareció el aire?
e. ...parecieron los jardines?
f. ...parecieron los almacenes?
g. Questions will vary.
ESTUDIANTE B
a.–g. Answers will vary, but look for adjective and verb agreement.

3 ESTUDIANTE A
a. ¿Qué se oye desde la escuela?
b. ...en el campo?
c. ...en la ciudad?
d. ...en el bosque?
e. ...desde tu casa?
f. Questions will vary.
ESTUDIANTE B
a.–f. Answers will vary, but should be logical.

Extended Written Practice/Homework
1. For each place, write an advantage of living in *las afueras, el campo,* or *la ciudad: Una ventaja de vivir en la ciudad son los restaurantes fantásticos.*
2. For each place, write a disadvantage of living there: *las afueras, el campo, la ciudad.*
3. Write three sentences telling about a place where you went, what you saw there, and what you did: *El verano pasado fui a ... Vi ... Visité ...*

Multiple Intelligences
Verbal/Linguistic
See Exs. 1–3.

Practice & Apply

Critical Thinking: Evaluating Information

Photocopy the questionnaire from the Critical Thinking activity on p. 60 and distribute to students. Tell them to ask their family or a friend's family to fill it out. The next day, have students evaluate their questionnaires and fill in the *Recomendaciones* section by naming one or two communities that they think might best fit the respondents' definition of "ideal." Have them share their questionnaires with the class.

Answers: Empecemos a conversar

4 ESTUDIANTE A

a. Antes, ¿había tantos ciclistas como ahora?

b. . . . tantos atascos . . .

c. . . . tantos rascacielos . . .

d. . . . tantos peatones . . .

e. . . . tantos parques . . .

f. Questions will vary.

ESTUDIANTE B

a.–f. Answers will vary.

4

A —Antes, ¿había *tantos puentes* como ahora?
B —Pues, creo que no. *Había menos.*
  o: *A mí me parece que había más.*

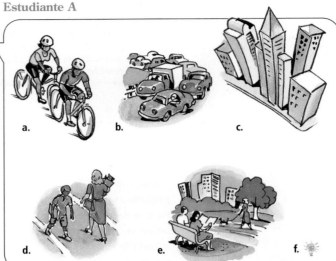

Estudiante A   Estudiante B

a.   b.   c.

d.   e.   f.

Había más.

Había menos.

No se necesitaban.

5 usar el coche
      o la bicicleta

A —¿Qué te parece mejor, *usar el coche o la bicicleta*?
B —*La bicicleta. Es mejor para el medio ambiente*.

Estudiante A

a. pagar el peaje o tomar otra carretera

b. trabajar en una granja o en una oficina

c. tardar mucho o poco tiempo en ir a trabajar

d. cultivar tus propias verduras o comprarlas

e. usar los senderos para los ciclistas o el camino

f. la vida en la ciudad o en el campo

Estudiante B

mejor para ___

más conveniente

más rápido

más sano

más seguro

más tranquilo

Options

Strategies for Reaching All Students

Spanish-Speaking Students
Ex. 8: Ask: *¿En cuáles participas o te gustaría participar? ¿Por qué?*

Students Needing Extra Help
Ex. 4: Review the *tantos(as) . . . como* construction and its meaning.
Ex. 5: Explain the *mejor para* response. Model another response to the questions using the expressions suggested.

Ex. 10: Have students work with a partner to create the list. Then they can compare their list with that of another pair.

Enrichment
Ex. 4: Ask students to write about one thing where they live that has increased or decreased in number over time, telling why they think this change has occurred. For example: more people, fewer gardens; more students, fewer teachers, etc.

Exs. 6–10: Ask: *En diez or quince años, ¿dónde quieres vivir? ¿Por qué? ¿Crees que es más importante conocer bien la ciudad o el campo? ¿Por qué?*
Ex. 9: As a homework assignment, students can write about the advantages and disadvantages of living in an isolated place.

¿Y qué piensas tú?

Aquí tienes otra oportunidad para usar el vocabulario de este capítulo.

6. ¿Vives en la ciudad, en el campo o en las afueras? ¿Te gusta vivir allí? ¿Por qué?

7. Imagínate que vives en un lugar diferente. ¿Por qué o por qué no te gusta vivir allí? Da tres razones para cada respuesta.

8. ¿Qué actividades culturales hay en el lugar donde vives? ¿Hay teatros, cines, museos, bibliotecas? ¿Hay centros de diversiones? ¿Cuáles? ¿Dónde están situados?

9. ¿Es aislado el lugar donde vives? ¿Tardas mucho en llegar al centro? ¿Cuánto?

10. Vas a hacer una tabla sobre las ventajas y las desventajas del lugar donde vives.

   - En una hoja de papel escribe el nombre del lugar donde vives. Luego, haz dos columnas como las siguientes:

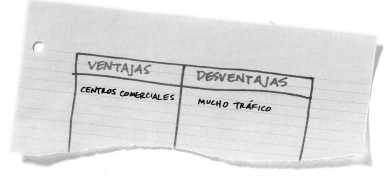

VENTAJAS	DESVENTAJAS
CENTROS COMERCIALES	MUCHO TRÁFICO

   - Después, compara tu lista con la de un(a) compañero(a). ¿Qué ventajas y qué desventajas tienen en común las listas? ¿Cuáles no?

MÁS PRÁCTICA

www.pasoapaso.com

Más práctica y tarea, p. 550

Vocabulario para comunicarse   67

También se dice

el congestionamiento
el embotellamiento
el tapón

la autorruta
la autovía
la carretera

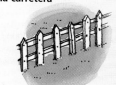

la valla
la verja

la finca
la hacienda

Present

Chapter Theme
Advantages and disadvantages of urban and rural living

Communicative Objectives
• *Describir cómo es la vida en la ciudad, en las afueras y en el campo*
• *Hablar de las ventajas y desventajas de la vida en la ciudad, en las afueras y en el campo*

 Vocabulary Tape 2-2

Teaching Suggestions
Getting ready to speak: Remind students of the reading strategies that they learned (getting meaning from context and coping with unknown words) to help them understand the *Tema para investigar*. For further details and some sample activities, see pp. T24–T25.

Answers: Tema para investigar
Answers will vary.

Tema para investigar

Aquí tienes más palabras e ideas para hablar sobre la ciudad, el campo y las afueras. Mira las fotos de esta página. ¿Cómo son estos lugares? ¿Es alguno de estos lugares similar a donde vives tú?

Paisaje hondureño de San Antonio de Oriente (1971), José Antonio Velásquez

New York City: Bird's Eye View (Nueva York a vista de pájaro) (1920), Joaquín Torres-García

68   Capítulo 2

Options

Strategies for Reaching All Students

Spanish-Speaking Students
Ask: *¿Qué otras ventajas y desventajas puedes añadir? ¿Dónde prefieres vivir tú? ¿Crees que tiene más ventajas que desventajas? Da ejemplos.*

Students Needing Extra Help
Have students conjugate *ofrecer* and compare it to *conocer* or *obedecer*.

Multiple Intelligences
Intrapersonal/Introspective and Verbal/Linguistic
Have students select a piece of art work from this chapter or the following and describe why they like or dislike it to the class.
Verbal/Linguistic
See Vocabulary Tape 2-2.
Verbal/Linguistic and Visual/Spatial
See Class Starter Review.

Cultural Notes

(p. 68, top photo)
Honduran artist José Antonio Velásquez, born in La Caridad in 1906, is one of Latin America's most renowned painters. The style of this self-taught artist is often labeled primitive and childlike, although Velásquez himself prefers to call it realistic and photographic.

Ventajas y desventajas

¿Dónde es mejor vivir: en la ciudad, en las afueras o en el campo? Si les haces esta pregunta a diez personas, vas a tener diez respuestas **diferentes**. Cada lugar tiene sus ventajas y sus desventajas.

¿Por qué crees que tanta gente **viene** a las ciudades? Sin duda, la ciudad **ofrece** una vida animada: cines, teatros, restaurantes, **oportunidades** de diversión y de trabajo que generalmente no se encuentran en el campo. Hay una **abundante** vida cultural y social. El transporte público **contribuye** a un sistema de tráfico mejor que hace que todo esté **al alcance de la mano**. **Sin embargo**, en muchas ciudades hay más contaminación, más ruido y una mayor concentración de **población**. Aunque esos problemas se están tratando de resolver, en las ciudades no es fácil **escaparse** de **las presiones** de la vida **diaria**.

La vida en las afueras puede ser más tranquila. A veces no hay tanta gente ni tampoco tanta contaminación. Muchas casas tienen sus propios jardines. Hay más **espacio** y menos ruido y

Casas en el barrio Pedregal,
en las afueras de la Ciudad de México

presión. Pero, como los lugares de trabajo están situados en la ciudad, la gente debe viajar todos los días. Eso, a veces, puede tomar más de una hora. Además, en las afueras **los impuestos** pueden ser más altos.

La vida **rural** es **idealizada** por muchos. **Por un lado,** en el campo no hay tantas personas y es un lugar más tranquilo para vivir. **El paisaje** es bonito y la naturaleza abundante. Pero, **por otro lado,** no es fácil encontrar tantas oportunidades de trabajo ni tantas actividades culturales como en la ciudad.

Entonces . . . ¿dónde es mejor vivir? Eso debes **decidirlo** tú.

venir *(e → ie)*	*to come*	la presión,	*pressure, stress*
(yo) vengo	*I come*	*pl.* las presiones	
(tú) vienes	*you come*	diario, -a	*daily*
contribuir *(i → y)**	*to contribute*	los impuestos	*taxes*
al alcance de la mano	*within reach*	por un lado	*on the one hand*
sin embargo	*nevertheless*	el paisaje	*landscape*
la población	*population*	por otro lado	*on the other hand*

¿Y qué quiere decir . . . ?

diferente	abundante	rural
ofrecer *(c → zc)*	escaparse	idealizado, -a
la oportunidad†	el espacio	decidir

* *Contribuir* follows the pattern of *influir.*
† Notice that in Spanish words such as *oportunidad, ciudad, and seguridad,* which end in *-dad,* are usually feminine. The same is true of words like *población* and *contaminación,* which end in *-ción.*

Tema para investigar 69

Class Starter Review
On the day following the presentation of the *Tema para investigar,* you might begin the class with this activity:
Make several statements regarding life in the city, country, or suburbs. Have students tell whether they view each as an advantage or a disadvantage of living there. They can then take turns making statements to which the others respond. You may wish to write the statements on the chalkboard, and take a poll to see where most students would prefer to live.

www Internet Activities
Juegos
Have students go to www.pasoapaso.com for additional activities and practice.

(p. 68, bottom photo)
This 1920 painting by the influential Uruguayan artist Joaquín Torres-García (1874–1949) was executed early in the period of his artistic training, which he received in post-World War I Europe and New York. A forerunner of abstract art in Latin America, Torres-García founded a workshop for student artists upon his return to Montevideo in 1932, as well as a publication, *Círculo y cuadrado.* Through these, and through his paintings, he stressed the mastery of artistic technique as a means to express a vision of a world in which order, equilibrium, and reason prevail.

(p. 69, photo)
Mexico City's Pedregal district, built on the lava fields of a long-dormant volcano, is home to some of the country's most powerful families. Developed in the 1950s, and given this name meaning "stony ground," it is located in the southern part of the city, near the complex of the Universidad Nacional Autónoma de México.

Practice & Apply

Answers: ¿Comprendiste?

1 Answers will vary, but may include:

El artista describe un lugar en el campo (una granja). / Hay animales de la granja. / *Answers will vary.*

2 Answers will vary, but may include the following:

Las ventajas de vivir en la ciudad incluyen: vida animada, oportunidades de diversión y de trabajo, abundante vida cultural y social y transporte público.

Las desventajas de vivir en la ciudad incluyen: contaminación, ruido, concentración de la población y que no es fácil escaparse de las presiones de la vida diaria.

Las ventajas de vivir en las afueras incluyen: vida más tranquila, menos gente y menos contaminación, más jardines y más espacio, menos ruido, paisaje bonito y naturaleza abundante.

Las desventajas de vivir en las afueras incluyen: hay que viajar a los lugares de trabajo, impuestos más altos, menos oportunidades de encontrar trabajo y de actividades culturales que en la ciudad. / *Opinions will vary.*

¿Comprendiste?

1 Mira esta obra de Joan Miró. ¿Qué tipo de lugar describe este artista? ¿Cómo lo sabes? ¿Crees que le gustaría vivir allí? ¿Por qué?

2 Según la lectura *Ventajas y desventajas,* ¿cuáles son dos ventajas y dos desventajas de la vida en la ciudad? ¿Y de la vida en las afueras? ¿Estás de acuerdo? ¿Por qué sí o por qué no?

The Farmers' Meal
(La comida de los agricultores)
(1935), Joan Miró

¿Y qué piensas tú?

3 ¿Te parece que todo está al alcance de la mano en el lugar donde vives? ¿Por qué? Explica.

4 En el lugar donde vives, ¿qué oportunidades culturales, sociales, de trabajo y de educación hay?

5 ¿Cómo es el paisaje en el lugar donde vives? ¿Qué hay allí? ¿Montañas, ríos, árboles? Descríbelo.

6 Del lugar donde vives, ¿qué es lo que más te gusta? ¿Y lo que menos? ¿Por qué?

www.pasoapaso.com

MÁS PRÁCTICA

- Más práctica y tarea, p. 550
- Practice Workbook 2–1, 2–4

70   Capítulo 2

Options

Strategies for Reaching All Students

Students Needing Extra Help
Ex. 5: Do as a whole group. Tell students what length will be acceptable.
Ex. 7: Brainstorm other places where students might want to live. Then decide on one place to compare to the place where they live now. Require a minimum number of reasons from each group.

Ex. 8: Remind students that they can interview in English but must record the results in Spanish.
¿Qué sabes ahora?: Have students write this so that they can record their progress.

Enrichment
Ex. 3: Ask: *¿Crees que todo debe estar al alcance de la mano en el lugar donde uno vive? Explica tu respuesta.*

Cooperative Learning
Have students work in groups of four to create a brochure for a new housing development in either the city, suburbs, or country. Have them brainstorm reasons why people would want to live there. Ask each student to write one sentence designed to attract prospective tenants. Students may wish to illustrate their brochures with drawings or by using magazine pictures.

7 ¿De acuerdo o no?

Formen dos grupos. A los miembros de un grupo les gusta vivir donde viven ahora. El otro grupo no está de acuerdo y quiere vivir en otro lugar.

Organicen un debate entre los dos grupos. Deben discutir:

- dónde viven
- por qué les gusta vivir allí
- por qué no les gusta
- dónde les gustaría vivir
- ese lugar ideal

8 Vas a entrevistar a cinco personas de tu familia o de tu comunidad para averiguar dónde les gustaría vivir y por qué.

Prepara una tabla como la siguiente:

NOMBRE	LUGAR	POR QUÉ
Ana	San Francisco	Visitó y le gustó mucho
Carlos	Florida	el clima
Tío Ramón	Madrid	

- Luego, en grupo, compara tus resultados con los de tus compañeros(as). Pueden determinar entre todos cuáles son los dos o tres lugares que más personas escogieron y por qué. Compartan el lugar más popular con el resto de la clase.

¿Qué sabes ahora?

¿Puedes:

- describir el lugar donde vives?

  —Vivo en ___. Está situado(a) en ___.
- indicar algunas ventajas y desventajas de vivir en cierto lugar?

  —Pienso que es mejor vivir en ___ porque ___.
- describir un lugar que visitaste?

  —En ___ había ___ y el aire ___.
- explicar por qué prefieres vivir donde vives ahora o mudarte a otro lugar?

  —Me gustaría ___ porque ___.

Tema para investigar 71

Present & Apply

Cultural Objective
• *Comparar la vida de la ciudad con la vida del campo en los países hispanos*

Critical Thinking: Making Comparisons
Have small groups of students prepare lists of four advantages and disadvantages of living in the country and the city. Ask volunteers from each group to write their responses on the chalkboard. Ask each student: *¿Prefieres vivir en la ciudad o en el campo?* Record answers on the chalkboard. Then ask students to complete these sentences: *Lo mejor de vivir en la ciudad es ___. Lo mejor de vivir en el campo es ___.*

Answers
Answers will vary.

Aquí tenemos las descripciones de cuatro lugares donde podrías vivir. ¿Cuál prefieres? ¿Por qué? ¿Es alguno de estos lugares semejante a donde vives tú? ¿En qué?

El Altiplano de Bolivia es un lugar fantástico si te gusta vivir en armonía con la tierra. Nunca hace calor por la altitud. Si te gustan los deportes, hay muchas opciones como escalar montañas o jugar fútbol. Aquí puedes trabajar cultivando papa o haciendo ropa y artesanía. La música de los Andes también es muy popular. Hay festivales locales donde puedes aprender sobre la cultura indígena de esta región.

Options

Strategies for Reaching All Students

Spanish-Speaking Students
Ask: *¿Qué atrae a la gente a tu comunidad? ¿Por qué vives tú aquí? ¿Crees que es lo mismo para todos los que se mudan a tu comunidad?*

Enrichment
Ask: *¿Qué es lo más importante que debe aprender una persona que llega a la ciudad del campo? ¿Qué es lo más importante que debe aprender una persona que llega al campo de la ciudad?*

Multiple Intelligences
Interpersonal/Social, Logical/Mathematical, and Visual/Spatial
See Critical Thinking.

Migration from rural to urban areas is a continuing trend in much of Latin America. People are leaving agricultural life in search of a better future, higher wages, educational opportunities, and a higher standard of living. As a result, Latin American cities are growing at incredible rates. Squatter settlements—known as *barrios, pueblos jóvenes,* or *tugu-rios*—are evidence of this growth. These spontaneous settlements often go without water or electrical services. Inhabitants build their own homes from whatever materials they can find. In Monterrey, Mexico, for example, people living in the *colonia* Tierra y Libertad have not only built their own homes, but have formed their own police force, block clubs, and other community organizations.

San José de Costa Rica es un lugar ideal para vivir. Es famosa por su hospitalidad y por su excelente clima. Se dice que San José tiene una primavera eterna. Aunque San José es la capital y la ciudad más grande de Costa Rica, es, a la vez, una ciudad muy grande y un pueblo. Sin tener una gran concentración de gente como en otras ciudades, hay muchas oportunidades de trabajo y, también, atracciones.

Álbum cultural 73

Cultural Notes ☼

(p. 72, photo)
About 46 percent of all Bolivian workers are farmers. Those who live in the highlands, or on the Altiplano (often referred to as *alti-plánicos),* grow potatoes and wheat and raise alpacas and llamas for their wool. The Indians of the Altiplano are *los aymaras.* Together with *los quechua,* they make up the largest segment of Bolivia's population.

(p. 73, photo)
San José has been the capital of Costa Rica since 1823, two years after the country gained its independence from Spain. Situated at an altitude of 3,800 feet above sea level on a plateau in the central mountains, the city has an ideal climate. Temperatures there average 70 degrees year-round. San José is also the country's largest city, home to approximately 285,000 people.

Present & Apply

Los que viven en Naucalpan, en las afueras de la Ciudad de México, necesitan viajar hasta la ciudad todos los días para tener a su alcance muchas oportunidades de trabajo y diversión. Pero su vida en las afueras es más tranquila, sin los atascos de tráfico ni el ruido que se encuentra en las grandes ciudades.

Buenos Aires, Argentina, es una ciudad internacional con muchos inmigrantes. La Plaza de Mayo es una plaza muy importante, situada en el centro de la ciudad. Si prefieres actividades culturales, puedes visitar las librerías en la Avenida Corrientes o ver una ópera en el Teatro Colón. Hay oportunidades de trabajo, escuelas especiales para estudiar y muchos restaurantes y parques. Además, puedes ir de compras a la fabulosa Calle Florida.

Options

Strategies for Reaching All Students

Students Needing Extra Help
Ex. 1: Give students a definite number of characteristics to list.

Multiple Intelligences
Bodily/Kinesthetic and Visual/Spatial
Have students create a map similar to the one on p. 75 showing the main routes of a public transportation system with which they are familiar. Or, if they would prefer, have them draw a street map of their own neighborhood.
Intrapersonal/Introspective
See Exs. 1–3.
Visual/Spatial
See Using Realia.

Cultural Notes

(p. 74, top photo)
Another attractive suburban area of Mexico City is Naucalpan. Shown here is one of the typical modern residences that can be found in the area.

Metro
de Barcelona

Reacción personal

Contesta las siguientes preguntas en una hoja de papel.

1 Piensa en un lugar ideal para vivir. Haz una lista de las características que debe tener.

2 Lee otra vez los párrafos de las páginas 72-74. ¿Cuáles son las características que más te gustan? Compara estas características con la lista que acabas de hacer.

3 ¿Hay un lugar ideal que guste a todos? ¿Por qué sí o por qué no?

Using Realia
Giving start and end points on the *metro* map of Barcelona, have students tell how one would travel to reach the destination point you have indicated. For example: *Navas (línea 1) hasta Lesseps (línea 3)*. Have them include what *línea* they should take and indicate any *estaciones de enlace* they must use in order to change trains. Remind them that all the station names are in *catalán*.

www Internet Activities
Álbum cultural
Have students go to www.pasoapaso.com for additional activities and practice.

(p. 74, bottom photo)
The heart of Buenos Aires is its principal square, the Plaza de Mayo, which measures one block wide and two blocks long. It is surrounded by colonial religious and government buildings. Named in honor of the date of independence from the Spanish viceroy, May 25, 1910, the Plaza de Mayo has been the scene of many political gatherings in Argentinean history. The *Abuelas de mayo* who courageously demonstrated during Argentina's last military regime to gain information about their disappeared loved ones continue to gather here every Thursday at 3:00 P.M.

(p. 75, realia)
Barcelona's clean, safe, and efficient *metro* system runs along five lines that link the city center with its suburban outskirts. As in many places in Barcelona, signs in the *metro* are in *catalán* only. Its continuously expanding lines offer the quickest, most economical commute available to the 4.7 million people who live in the metropolitan area.

Preview

Teaching Suggestions

A Review regular imperfect verb endings. Ask how the perfect verb forms of *ser* and *ir* are different from regular verb forms.

B Ask how each adjective is similar to and different from the related infinitive (the stem, the ending). / Ask what endings are used to make the adjective form (*-ada, -ida*).

C Point out that these words function as adjectives. / Ask students to identify the nouns to which each adjective refers and how it agrees with that noun.

Answers

Answers will vary to inductive question.

A The forms are *tenía, estaba, usaba,* and *había.* Their endings are *-ía* and *-aba.* / The forms of *ser* and *ir* are *era* and *iban.* / past

B *llamar* and *mover* / *dormido* / Give students the meanings of the infinitives, if necessary, and have them guess the meanings of the adjectives.

C *decorar, situar,* and *dorar* / *cerrado* / Have students guess the meanings of *situar* and *dorar* / *dorados.* If necessary, remind them of the known word *oro.* Tell them the legend of the golden city, El Dorado.

Gramática en contexto

Mira esta guía turística de Sevilla, donde se describen algunas de sus principales obras de arquitectura. ¿Qué piensas que vas a encontrar en una guía como ésta?

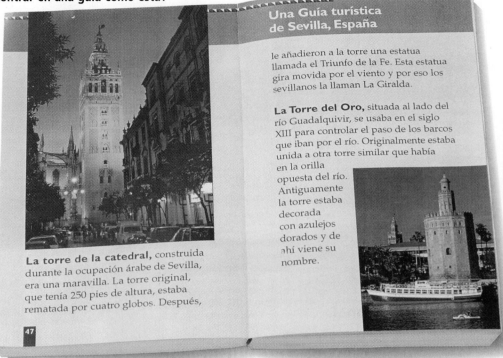

Una Guía turística de Sevilla, España

le añadieron a la torre una estatua llamada el Triunfo de la Fe. Esta estatua gira movida por el viento y por eso los sevillanos la llaman La Giralda.

La Torre del Oro, situada al lado del río Guadalquivir, se usaba en el siglo XIII para controlar el paso de los barcos que iban por el río. Originalmente estaba unida a otra torre similar que había en la orilla opuesta del río. Antiguamente la torre estaba decorada con azulejos dorados y de ahí viene su nombre.

La torre de la catedral, construida durante la ocupación árabe de Sevilla, era una maravilla. La torre original, que tenía 250 pies de altura, estaba rematada por cuatro globos. Después,

47

A Find the forms of the verbs *tener* and *estar* in the first description and of *usar* and *haber* in the second. What are their endings? Find the form of the verb *ser* in the first description and of *ir* in the second. Are these verbs used to describe the towers in the present or in the past?

B In the first description you find the word *construida.* The infinitive that is related to this adjective is *construir* ("to build," "to construct"). In the tourist guide you also find the words *llamada* and *movida.* What do you think the related infinitives of these adjectives are? What do you think the adjective form that relates to *dormir* is?

C In the second description you find the words *decorada, situada,* and *dorados.* What do you think are the related infinitives of these adjectives? What do you think the adjective form that relates to *cerrar* is?

76   Capítulo 2

Options

Strategies for Reaching All Students

Students Needing Extra Help
Begin the grammar section of the Organizer. *Repaso: El imperfecto:* If available, review the grammar sections of the Organizers from Book 2, Chaps. 5, 9, and 10. Emphasize placement of accents. Give further examples using *había.* Students should be taking notes on this information. They should keep running lists of words and expressions that cue the imperfect. (You may want to post a list of these words in the classroom for reference.)

Extended Written Practice/Homework
1. Write four sentences describing the type of child that you were. Verbs that you might use are: *portarse bien/mal, obedecer, mentir, llorar, pelearse, ser,* and *compartir.*
2. Write four sentences telling the type of activities that you and your friends liked when you were children: *Cuando éramos niños, mis amigos y yo patinábamos en las aceras cerca de mi casa.*

3. Choose a person from the past and write three sentences describing what he or she was like and what he or she used to do.

Repaso: El imperfecto

You have learned that we use the imperfect tense to talk about actions that happened repeatedly in the past. In English we often say "used to" or "would always" to express this idea.

Antes, mis parientes **vivían** y **trabajaban** en una granja.
In the past, my relatives used to live and work on a farm.

Remember that in Spanish we have *-ar, -er,* and *-ir* verbs. To form the imperfect tense we add to the stem one set of endings for *-ar* verbs and another set for both *-er* and *-ir* verbs. Here are all the forms of *estar, tener,* and *vivir* in the imperfect.

estar *(-ar)*		tener *(-er)*		vivir *(-ir)*	
estaba	estábamos	tenía	teníamos	vivía	vivíamos
estabas	estabais	tenías	teníais	vivías	vivíais
estaba	estaban	tenía	tenían	vivía	vivían

There are three irregular verbs in the imperfect. Here are their forms.

ir		ser		ver	
iba	íbamos	era	éramos	veía	veíamos
ibas	ibais	eras	erais	veías	veíais
iba	iban	era	eran	veía	veían

- Remember that we use only one form of *haber* in the imperfect tense, *había* ("there was/were, there used to be").

En el pasado, no **había** tanto tráfico en las calles.
Hace veinte años **había** menos autopistas.

¡NO OLVIDES!

Expressions such as *generalmente, a menudo, muchas veces, todos los días, siempre,* and *nunca* can cue us to use the imperfect.

Gramática en contexto   77

Present & Practice

Answers

1 **ESTUDIANTE A**

a. ¿Eras tranquilo(a) cuando eras pequeño(a)?

b. ¿Tenías animales de peluche . . .

c. ¿Te gustaban los trenes eléctricos . . .

d. ¿Ibas a los parques de diversiones . . .

e. ¿Veías dibujos animados . . .

f. ¿Comías verduras y frutas. . . .

ESTUDIANTE B

a.–f. Answers will vary, but look for the *yo* form of the verb in the imperfect.

Student reports will vary. Look for correct use of the imperfect.

1 Haz una encuesta entre los estudiantes de tu clase para ver cómo era su vida cuando eran pequeños. Escribe las respuestas de tus compañeros para hacer un informe después.

A —*¿Jugabas con muñecos cuando eras pequeño(a)?*
B —*Sí, jugaba con muñecos.*
    o: *No, cuando era pequeño(a) jugaba béisbol.*

jugar

a. ser

b. tener

c. gustar

d. ir

e. ver

f. comer

Usando las respuestas que escribiste, prepara un informe sobre tus compañeros.

Tres estudiantes de esta clase iban al parque de diversiones cuando eran pequeños. Nueve estudiantes y yo teníamos animales de peluche. Dos estudiantes comían frutas y verduras y un estudiante era tranquilo.

Padre e hijo jugando básquetbol

78   Capítulo 2

Options

Strategies for Reaching All Students

Students Needing Extra Help
Ex. 1: Students should make a chart to fill in as their classmates respond. List the activities and let students check them off. Remind them to ask the questions in the *tú* form, to respond in the *yo* form, and to report in the third person. You may want to give students more practice with further examples.
Ex. 2: As a class, complete this model. This will show students that *Estudiante A* begins

with one descriptive sentence. Then *Estudiante B* asks questions about that place, one at a time, as *Estudiante A* responds. Review ¿*Cómo es?* to help students make the connection to ¿*Cómo era?* Brainstorm words to complete the sentences. For example, *ver . . . a tus parientes, estar . . . aburrido,* etc.
Repaso: Otros usos del imperfecto: Give additional examples.

Enrichment
Ex. 1: Remind students to use the frequency expressions in *¡No olvides!* on p. 77 in the sentences they create for this exercise.
As a homework assignment, have students describe a person (or themselves) from their childhood. Encourage them to give details about the person's physical appearance and personality as well as to tell what the person used to do, play, say, etc.

2 Describe la vida en un lugar que recuerdes de tu infancia *(childhood)*. Comienza tu descripción: *De mi infancia, recuerdo bien . . .* (Nueva York, la granja de mis abuelos, etc.) Luego, tu compañero(a) va a hacerte preguntas usando los verbos de la lista.

ser   A —*De mi infancia, recuerdo bien la granja de mis tíos en Nebraska.*
            B —*¿Era muy grande la granja?*
            A —*No, era bastante pequeña.*

a. vivir   e. tener
b. ir   f. ver
c. trabajar   g. estar
d. haber   h. 💡

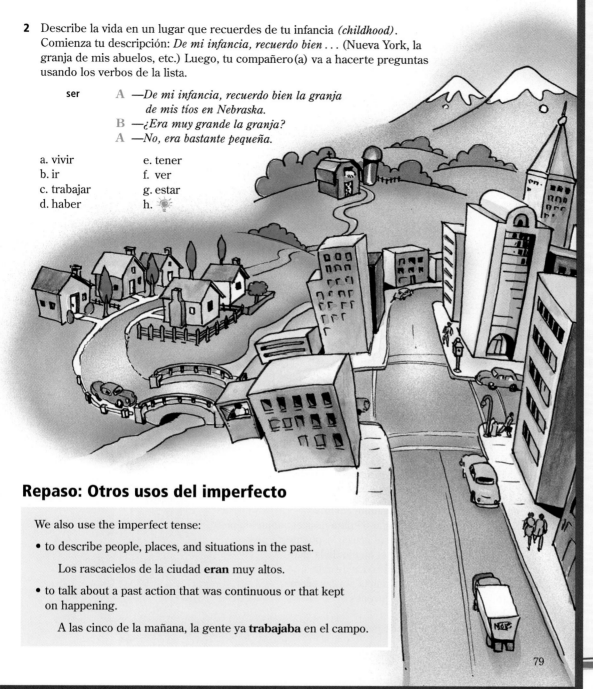

Repaso: Otros usos del imperfecto

We also use the imperfect tense:

• to describe people, places, and situations in the past.

    Los rascacielos de la ciudad **eran** muy altos.

• to talk about a past action that was continuous or that kept on happening.

    A las cinco de la mañana, la gente ya **trabajaba** en el campo.

79

2 Questions and answers will vary, but look for correct use of the imperfect.

 Practice Wkbk. 2-5, 2-6

 Writing Activity 2-D

 Prueba 2-5

 Comm. Act. BLM 2-2

Extended Written Practice/Homework
1. Write three sentences describing a place that you visited: *En julio fui a . . . Las autopistas estaban . . . Había . . .*
2. Write three sentences describing a vacation spot that you remember from your childhood: *Cuando tenía nueve años fuimos a un lago en . . . El lago era . . . Muchas personas allí tenían . . .*
3. Write three sentences describing what your elementary school and the people there were like.

Multiple Intelligences
Verbal/Linguistic
See Exs. 1–2.
Visual/Spatial
See Practice Wkbk. 2-5 and 2-6, Writing Activity 2-D, and Comm. Act. BLM 2-2.

Present & Practice

Answers

3 ESTUDIANTE A

a. El puente de peaje era bastante corto, ¿verdad?

b. Teníamos que pagar $5 para usar el puente de peaje ...

c. Muchas personas querían cruzar el puente de peaje ...

d. Los peatones caminaban por el medio de la calle ...

e. Había una policía en el cruce de calles ...

f. Los ciclistas montaban en bicicleta por las aceras ...

g. Todos los ciclistas eran jóvenes ...

h. Hacía frío aquel día ...

i. Las calles estaban llenas de gente ...

ESTUDIANTE B

a. Sí, el puente de peaje era bastante corto.

b. No, teníamos que pagar $3.00.

c. Sí, muchas personas querían cruzar el puente de peaje.

d. No, los peatones caminaban por las aceras.

e. Sí, había una policía en el cruce de calles.

f. No, los ciclistas montaban en bicicleta por las calles.

g. No, los ciclistas eran jóvenes y viejos.

h. No, aquel día hacía calor.

i. Sí, las calles estaban llenas de gente.

3 Imagina que tu compañero(a) y tú visitaron esta ciudad. Ahora, están tratando de recordar lo que vieron. Usen el dibujo para preguntar y contestar.

aire / estar contaminado

A — *El aire estaba contaminado, ¿verdad?*
B — *No, no estaba contaminado.*

a. puente de peaje / ser bastante corto

b. nosotros / tener que pagar $5 para usar el puente de peaje

c. muchas personas / querer cruzar el puente de peaje

d. peatones / caminar por el medio de la calle

e. haber / una policía en el cruce de calles

f. ciclistas / montar en bicicleta por las aceras

g. todos los ciclistas / ser jóvenes

h. hacer frío / aquel día

i. calles / estar lleno(a) de gente

80   Capítulo 2

Options

Strategies for Reaching All Students

Students Needing Extra Help
Ex. 3: Remind students to use the imperfect form of the verb and to answer according to the picture.
Ex. 4: Brainstorm other useful description words, and words that describe the activities in those places.

El participio pasado como adjetivo: Give further examples of past participles, using the imperfect and the present tenses of *estar.* Have students practice forming the past participle from a list of infinitives that you provide.

Multiple Intelligences
Verbal/Linguistic
See Exs. 3–4 and Class Starter Review.
Visual/Spatial
See Practice Wkbk. 2-7, Writing Activity 2-E, and Comm. Act. BLM 2-3.

4 Describe una excursión (verdadera o imaginaria) a una ciudad, una granja o las afueras. Túrnate con tu compañero(a) para hacer preguntas. Puedes usar estos verbos u otros.

ser	haber
tener	estar
hacer	

A — *Yo fui a (nombre del lugar).*
B — *¿Cómo ___ ?*
A — *Muy bello.*
B — *¿Qué había?*
A — *Un parque, ___ y ___ .*
B — *¿Qué tiempo ___ ?*

El jardín de Kahlo (1990),
Alfredo Arreguín

El participio pasado como adjetivo

Many adjectives that we use in Spanish are actually the verb form called the past participle. We form the past participle of most -*ar* verbs by adding -*ado* to the stem. For most -*er* and -*ir* verbs, we form the past participle by adding -*ido* to the stem. For example:

contaminar	**contaminado**
dormir	**dormido**
situar	**situado**
esconder	**escondido**

Some verbs have irregular past participles. You already know some of these adjectives. For example:

hacer	**hecho**
romper	**roto**

When we use past participles as adjectives they must agree in gender and number with the noun or pronoun they refer to. We frequently use *estar* with the past participle to describe a condition that exists now or existed in the past.

El aire del campo no **está** muy **contaminado**.
La torre **estaba situada** en la orilla del río.
Las luces de la ciudad **estaban apagadas** a esa hora.

Gramática en contexto   81

 Practice Wkbk. 2-7

 Writing Activity 2-E

 Prueba 2-6

 Comm. Act. BLM 2-3

Class Starter Review
On the day following the presentation of adjectival use of the past participle, you might begin the class with this activity:
Make several statements using the preterite. Students will take turns giving the result of your statement, using the past participle. For example: *Cerré la puerta. / La puerta está cerrada.* Students can then take turns stating the first sentence.

Cultural Notes

(p. 81, photo)
Mexican-born painter Alfredo Arreguín (b. 1935) has received international acclaim for his intricate works, which feature stylized human and animal figures on a background of fine, interlocking lines. Born in the state of Michoacán, Arreguín has lived in Seattle since 1957. He frequently remembers his native land in such works as *Jardín de Kahlo,* which honors both Frida Kahlo and the natural beauty of Mexico that inspired her.

Practice

Answers

5 a. El espejo estaba roto.
b. La cena estaba servida.
c. Las luces estaban apagadas.
d. La mesa estaba decorada.
e. El televisor estaba encendido.
f. Los gatos estaban dormidos.
g. Las ventanas estaban cerradas.

5 Imagina que eres el (la) detective encargado(a) de investigar un robo. Describe la escena que está en esta página.

el bolso / esconder

El bolso estaba escondido.

a. el espejo   cerrar
b. la cena   decorar
c. las luces   dormir
d. la mesa   encender
e. el televisor   romper
f. los gatos   apagar
g. las ventanas   servir

82   Capítulo 2

Options

Strategies for Reaching All Students

Students Needing Extra Help
Ex. 5: Remind students to use the picture in order to form the statements. Be sure they realize that they have to search for the correct verb to use as a participle.
Give an example using a plural noun.
Ex. 6: Remind students to use the present tense of *estar.*
Ahora lo sabes: Have students write this so that they can record their progress.

Extended Written Practice/Homework
1. Describe different places using the following past participles as adjectives: *aislado, contaminado, animado, situado. Los ríos en algunos lugares están contaminados.*
2. Refer to the list of verbs in Ex. 5 on p. 82 and write three sentences describing what your house was like when you returned yesterday: *Todas las luces estaban apagadas.*

Multiple Intelligences
Verbal/Linguistic
See Ex. 6 and Audio Activities 2.3, 2.4, and 2.5.
Verbal/Linguistic and Visual/Spatial
1) See Ex. 5.
2) In pairs, have students draw their own scene similar to the one on p. 82. Then have them exchange scenes and describe each other's.
Visual/Spatial
See Practice Wkbk. 2-8 and 2-9 and Writing Activity 2-F.

82

6 Túrnate con tu compañero(a) para formar frases sobre estos lugares. Usen elementos de las dos columnas.

el correo / cerrar *El correo está cerrado por la tarde.*

las escuelas	contaminar
el correo cerca del centro	decorar
la cama	animar
los centros comerciales	situar
los lagos y ríos	hacer
las calles durante las fiestas	aislar

Ahora lo sabes

¿Puedes:

■ hablar de acciones que ocurrían repetidamente en el pasado?
  —Mis abuelos ____ en una granja en Kansas.

■ describir a personas, lugares y situaciones en el pasado?
  —Las carreteras de la ciudad ____ muy peligrosas.

■ describir condiciones de personas y cosas en el presente y el pasado?
  —Antes el agua ____ menos contaminada.

MÁS PRÁCTICA

- Más práctica y tarea, pp. 551–552
- Practice Workbook 2–5, 2–9

De compras en Caracas, Venezuela

¡NO OLVIDES!

You already know many adjectives that are actually past participles: *ocupado, callado, cansado, divorciado, ordenado, aburrido, divertido,* and many more.

Carrera de bicicletas en Texcoco (1938), Antonio M. Ruiz

Gramática en contexto   83

6 Answers may vary:
Las escuelas no están animadas los fines de semana.
El correo está situado cerca del centro.
La cama está hecha.
Los centros comerciales están aislados.
Los lagos y ríos están contaminados desde hace dos años.
Las calles están decoradas durante las fiestas.

Answers: Ahora lo sabes
• trabajaban *(Answers will vary.)*
• eran
• estaba

 Practice Wkbk. 2-8, 2-9

 Audio Activities 2.3, 2.4, 2.5

 Writing Activity 2-F

 Prueba 2-7

Cultural Notes ☀

(p. 83, top photo)
Sabana Grande in Caracas is a busy, mile-long boulevard open only to pedestrians. One of the city's leading shopping districts, Sabana Grande is also a place to enjoy theater, fast food restaurants, and sidewalk cafés.

(p. 83, bottom photo)
Painter Antonio Ruiz (1897–1964) belongs to a large group of Mexican artists whose works were somewhat eclipsed during their lifetime by the grander and more obviously nationalistic art of their contemporaries, Rivera, Orozco, and Siqueiros. Yet Ruiz's work, as shown in this 1938 oil on canvas, is also unmistakably Mexican.

Ask students: Contrast the dress of the people seated on the victory stand with the figures sitting on the wall and standing by the road. How might you interpret the meaning of this? (Those who attain official positions have adopted European styles; those who maintain traditional dress remain outsiders.)

Apply

Teaching Suggestions

Point out the key chapter question. Tell students that completing these activities will help them answer this key question. You may select one, two, or all three of these activities, as time permits.

Answers: Sopa de actividades

1–3 Responses will vary, but encourage use of a wide variety of vocabulary.

Strategies for Reaching All Students

MULTIPLE INTELLIGENCES
Interpersonal/Social and Visual/Spatial
See Ex. 2.
Verbal/Linguistic and Visual/Spatial
See Ex. 3.
Visual/Spatial
See Cooperative Learning and Writing Activities 2-G and 2-H.

¿Prefieres vivir en la ciudad o en el campo?

Esta sección te ofrece la oportunidad de combinar lo que aprendiste en este capítulo con lo que ya sabes para responder a la pregunta clave.

Sopa de actividades

Para decir más

Aquí tienes vocabulario adicional que te puede ayudar para hacer las actividades de esta sección.

la tranquilidad
tranquility

la calma
calm

la vida urbana
city life

la vida rural
rural life

el barrio
neighborhood

el habitante
inhabitant

estar en contacto
to be in touch

la distancia
distance

1 En un montaje, muestra el lugar donde vives o donde te gustaría vivir. Usa fotos, tarjetas postales, o fotos de revistas y periódicos para ilustrarlo. Indica:

- cómo es
- dónde está situado
- cuántos habitantes tiene
- cuáles son los principales puntos de interés y dónde están situados
- cómo es el paisaje
- qué se ve y qué se oye allí
- cuáles son las ventajas y las desventajas de vivir allí
- cómo era antes y cómo es ahora

Luego prepara un informe oral y preséntalo a un grupo de compañeros(as).

Buenos Aires, Argentina

Caracas, Venezuela

84 Capítulo 2

Options

Strategies for Reaching All Students

Spanish-Speaking Students

Ex. 2: *Estudia los diferentes grupos. ¿Cuál tiene más personas, menos personas? Pregúntales a tus compañeros(as) por qué se juntaron a un grupo en particular. Luego, escribe dos o tres párrafos que expliquen por qué escogieron cada lugar.*

Students Needing Extra Help

If time is a factor, Exs. 1 and 2 compliment each other. Ex. 3 can be done without the other two. You may want to divide the class into two groups: one to do Exs. 1 and 2, the other to do Ex. 3.
Ex.1: Have magazines, newspapers, travel brochures, etc. available. Set guidelines for the minimum and maximum amounts of information that will be acceptable. Allow students to use their notes for the report. Use the vocabulary section of the Organizer.

Ex. 2: Use the vocabulary section of the Organizer. Be sure one student from each group is recording the statements, that another person is ready to present them to the class, and that a third student is recording the statements from the other groups.
Ex. 3: Limit the amount of research students need to do. Remind them that they will be using the imperfect and the present tenses of the verbs.

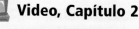

2 Entre toda la clase van a escoger cinco lugares diferentes donde les gustaría vivir. Pueden ser: el campo, las montañas, las afueras y una o dos ciudades grandes. Cada uno de los lugares escogidos va a estar representado por un lugar de la clase.

Ve al lugar donde más te gustaría vivir. En tu nuevo grupo, prepara con tus compañeros(as) cinco frases para explicar por qué prefieren vivir en ese lugar. Por ejemplo:

> *El aire del campo es fresco y no está contaminado.*
> o:
> *Por la noche la ciudad está muy animada y puedes hacer muchas cosas.*

Cada grupo lee sus frases a la clase y escribe las ideas de los demás grupos. Después deben decir lo que piensan de las ideas de los otros grupos. Por ejemplo:

> *Por un lado es divertido vivir en la ciudad porque está muy animada por la noche. Por otro lado, la ciudad puede ser muy violenta y peligrosa.*

3 Prepara con los demás estudiantes de la clase una comparación entre la vida de tu ciudad o región en el pasado y en el presente. Primero, decidan qué categorías quieren comparar. Pueden incluir información sobre:

- la naturaleza de la región y el clima
- la población y el tamaño del área
- la economía (fábricas, trabajos, etc.)
- los lugares de interés y la vida social
- las fiestas celebradas por la comunidad

Después, pueden asignar cada categoría a un grupo diferente. Pueden buscar información en libros, periódicos y revistas; también pueden preguntar a personas mayores o buscar información en una sociedad histórica local. Preparen una presentación oral con fotos y dibujos. Por ejemplo:

> *Hace 50 años el agua del río no estaba contaminada, pero ahora no podemos nadar allí.*

> *En el pasado había sólo una autopista. Ahora hay cinco.*

Sopa de actividades   85

 Video Activity A

 Video, Capítulo 2

Chapter 2: Play

Step

 Video Activities B–C

 Writing Activities 2-G, 2-H

Comm. Act. BLMs 2-4, 2-5

Cooperative Learning

Divide the class into groups of four and write on the chalkboard a list of infinitives. Instruct students to think about a childhood friend—real or imaginary. Tell them that they are going to create a character for a children's story from a composite of all of their childhood friends. Have two students list personality traits. Have the other two list physical characteristics.

Instruct groups to write descriptive sentences using either their own verbs or those from the chalkboard, and to include the personality traits and physical characteristics they have listed. Have students write descriptive sentences so that each group member has written at least one sentence. Call on specific groups to read their descriptions while the groups listening draw the characters described.

Cultural Notes

(p. 84, top photo)
Including its suburbs, greater Buenos Aires has a population of approximately 12.5 million people. Most of the city's buildings, built at the beginning of the twentieth century, imitate the architectural styles seen in Paris. This photo also shows the wide boulevards and parks, which, along with the many theaters, cafés, and museums, help to give the city its distinctive European feel.
(p. 84, bottom photo: see p. 61)

Apply

Process Reading
For a description of process reading, see p. 52.

Teaching Suggestions
Point out the key chapter question *(la pregunta clave del capítulo)*. Tell students that working through the *Para leer* section will help them answer this key question.

Encourage students to use the strategies given in the text to help them understand the reading. Emphasize that they do not need to understand every word.

Para leer

Antes de leer

STRATEGY ➤ Using titles and pictures to predict

Esta selección trata de las visitas que hace una joven a un pueblo español. ¿De qué temas se va a tratar? Usa las fotos como ayuda para añadir, por lo menos, dos más a esta lista.

A. el tiempo   B. la gente

Mira la lectura

STRATEGY ➤ Skimming

Lee la selección rápidamente sólo para ver cuáles de los temas de tu lista están en la selección. Compara los resultados con los de un(a) compañero(a).

Benvinguts a Cálig

Cuando Patricia y su familia llegaron a su casa de Cálig en la provincia de Castellón el verano pasado, había un letrero en la puerta que decía: *Benvinguts* a Cálig*. Ella estaba tan contenta de estar otra vez en este pequeño pueblo agrícola de España que quería correr por el pueblo saludando a todos. Después de cinco veranos ella se sentía muy aceptada.

Cálig es un lugar ideal para las vacaciones. Han pasado ya cinco veranos allí. Es un pueblo tranquilo y sin contaminación, situado cerca del mar y la montaña. No hay miedo de robos ni de atracos como en las grandes ciudades. La gente los trata muy bien en la calle y en las pequeñas tiendas donde hacen sus compras. Y por supuesto, toda la familia participa en las fiestas tradicionales del pueblo.

Al principio Patricia no estaba contenta. Tenía once años y echaba de menos a sus amigas de

los Estados Unidos. No podía ir con ellas a los grandes centros comerciales a comprar como solía hacer los sábados. Además no hablaba mucho español y en este pueblo hablaban también valenciano, una lengua que ella no comprendía. Quería volver a su casa en St. Louis, Missouri, y lo más pronto posible.

Con los años fue teniendo cada vez más amigos caligenses. Salía con ellos todas las tardes, primero a la piscina, después a tomar refrescos y charlar. Por la noche volvían a salir después de cenar. A veces iban a una discoteca para bailar. Algunas noches simplemente paseaban por las calles estrechas de este pueblo medieval.

Algunos días Patricia hacía excursiones con su familia a los pueblos cercanos de la montaña, pueblos mejor conservados, con casas hechas de piedra, una iglesia vieja y una ermita en las afueras. Les gustaban mucho las colinas rocosas de la montaña y los campos de olivos y algarrobos. Otros días pasaban la tarde en la playa. Aunque le agradaban a Patricia esas excursiones con sus padres, ella prefería estar con los amigos, sobre todo con un tal David, un chico muy guapo y muy divertido.

Cuando llegó el momento de salir para los Estados Unidos, ella se sentía muy triste porque no quería dejar a sus amigos. Ya se había acostumbrado tanto a la vida del pueblo que la vida de la ciudad le parecía muy sofocante. No podría ir a pie a las tiendas ni saludar a todos en la calle como lo hacía en Cálig. No podría quedarse en la calle con los amigos hasta la medianoche. Además iba a echar mucho de menos la comida: el pan con tomate, la paella, el brazo gitano.[†] Ahora ella pasa el invierno en St. Louis soñando con el verano en Cálig.

* *Benvinguts* Palabra valenciana que quiere decir ¡Bienvenidos!

[†] *brazo gitano* Pastel hecho de bizcocho *(sponge cake)* con relleno de crema o nata *(whipped cream)*.

Options

Strategies for Reaching All Students

Spanish-Speaking Students
Ask: *Imagina que llegas a un lugar donde no conoces a nadie y que no hablas su idioma. ¿Podrías acostumbrarte a vivir allí? ¿Qué harías para integrarte a la comunidad lo más pronto posible?*

Students Needing Extra Help
Antes de leer: Make a list as a class.
Mira la lectura: Review reading strategies.
Aplicación: Use the vocabulary section of the Organizer.

Enrichment
Remind students that the writer's feelings for Cálig are colored by the fact that she was there on vacation, and not attending school. Ask students to discuss whether or not they would feel differently about where they live if they were only there on vacation.

De paseo por las calles de Cálig

Un mercado de Cálig

Una vista de Cálig desde la carretera

Infórmate

STRATEGY> Identifying supporting details

Ahora lee la selección con cuidado.

1 Describe la actitud de Patricia hacia Cálig (a) después de un año de visitar el pueblo, (b) después de dos o tres años y (c) después de cinco años. Luego muéstrale a un(a) compañero(a) la evidencia del texto para justificar tu opinión.

2 Imagina que eres un(a) joven caligense y estás pasando un verano en St. Louis u otra ciudad grande de los Estados Unidos. Escribe una carta breve a tu familia explicándoles lo que sientes.

Aplicación

En grupo hagan un cartel turístico para una ciudad grande o para un pueblo pequeño de un país hispano. Incluyan las características más atractivas del lugar. Después, escojan el lugar que la clase prefiere visitar.

Para leer   87

Cultural Notes

Multiple Intelligences
Bodily/Kinesthetic, Interpersonal/Social, and Visual/Spatial
See *Aplicación.*
Visual/Spatial
See *Infórmate.*

(p. 87, photos)
The town of Cálig lies in Spain's Aragón region, in the province of Teruel, which shows a strong Muslim influence in its art, architecture, and town names. The architectural style known as *mudéjar* is particularly striking in the provincial capital, which is also named Teruel. This style combines elements of Moorish ornamentation with Christian art.

Apply

Process Writing
For information regarding writing portfolios, see p. 54.

Teaching Suggestions
Tell students that working through the *Para escribir* section will help them answer the key chapter question.

Answers
Descriptions will vary.

Para escribir

¿Dónde te gustaría vivir? Ya viste fotos de diferentes lugares y leíste sobre ellos. También contestaste preguntas sobre el lugar donde vives y hablaste de dónde te gustaría vivir. Ahora vas a describir tu comunidad ideal.

1 Primero, responde a estas preguntas. Recuerda que puedes utilizar también lo que escribiste en *Reacción personal*.

¿Cuáles son las características de tu comunidad ideal?
- ¿Dónde está situada? ¿En el campo, en las afueras o en la ciudad? ¿Cerca de alguno de estos lugares?
- ¿Qué hay allí? (parques, escuelas, tiendas, centros comerciales) ¿Cuántos?
- ¿Qué actividades pueden hacer los habitantes?
- ¿Qué tipos de trabajos tienen? ¿Dónde trabajan?
- ¿Hay transporte público? ¿De qué tipo?

Puedes organizar tus ideas en una red de palabras como ésta o puedes usar otro modelo.

Estas palabras y expresiones te pueden ser útiles para escribir tu descripción.

me parece que	quedar en	entre
prefiero	lo mismo que	al alcance de la mano
en cambio	en medio de	tener algo en común
más (menos)... que		

88   Capítulo 2

Options

Strategies for Reaching All Students

Students Needing Extra Help
Step 1: Be aware that word maps may be confusing for many students. Give them the option of making columns or outlines. Point out the different categories that the questions include: people, jobs, places, transportation, etc. This activity may at first seem overwhelming. Limit the number for each category and give examples.

Emphasize that students don't have to use all the words on this list. You may want to choose two or three that are commonly used.
Step 2: Remind students that the final product can be a pamphlet, a newspaper article, or a composition. Let them choose the format that is most comfortable for them.

Multiple Intelligences
Intrapersonal/Introspective and Visual/Spatial
See Exs. 1–3.
Verbal/Linguistic and Visual/Spatial
See Critical Thinking.

2 Ahora, usa tus notas para describir tu comunidad ideal. Puede ser un folleto para personas que buscan una comunidad nueva, un artículo para un periódico o una composición. Puedes ilustrar tu descripción con fotos o mapas. Sigue los pasos del proceso de escribir.

3 Para compartir tu trabajo, puedes:

- hacer una presentación oral en clase
- exhibirlo en la sala de clases
- incluirlo en un libro titulado *Lugares ideales*
- ponerlo en tu portafolio

Assess & Summarize

Test Preparation

You may want to assign parts of this section as written homework or as an in-class writing activity prior to administering the *Examen de habilidades*.

Answers

Listening

—*Por un lado, donde vivo ahora todo está al alcance de la mano. Hay una abundante vida cultural y social con cines, museos y restaurantes de muchas clases. Pero, por otro lado, uno no se puede escapar ni de los atascos ni de la contaminación. Prefiero vivir en una granja. Todo es más sano y no tan peligroso. Sin embargo, no hay muchas oportunidades de trabajo. Por eso vivo aquí.*

Esta persona vive en una ciudad. Lo sabemos porque describe los lugares de una ciudad. / Prefiere vivir en una granja. No vive allí porque no hay muchas oportunidades de trabajo.

Reading

Answers may vary, but students might say:
Se trata de un lugar en las afueras.

Writing

Paragraphs will vary.

Esta sección te ayudará a prepararte para el examen de habilidades, donde tendrás que hacer tareas semejantes.

Listening

¿Puedes entender una descripción de cómo es la vida en un lugar? Escucha mientras el (la) profesor(a) lee un ejemplo semejante al que vas a oír en el examen. ¿Dónde vive esta persona? ¿Cómo lo sabes? ¿Dónde prefiere vivir? ¿Por qué no vive allí?

Reading

¿Puedes leer un anuncio sobre un lugar de vacaciones y fijarte bien en los detalles para saber de qué lugar se trata?

> **¡NO PIERDA LA OPORTUNIDAD DE ENCONTRAR EL PARAÍSO EN LA TIERRA!** En Valle Azul, rodeado de montañas, puede encontrar el aire puro y la tranquilidad que busca. Sin coches, ni ruido, ni contaminación. Y por la noche ¡disfrute de sus calles estrechas y silenciosas!

Writing

¿Puedes escribir un párrafo para tu clase de español sobre el lugar donde vivías de niño(a)? Aquí tienes un ejemplo:

> Recuerdo mucho la casa en donde vivía cuando era niño. Tenía una cerca blanca y un jardín con flores muy bonitas. Estaba situada cerca de un sendero de árboles que terminaba en el bosque. El aire era puro y no estaba contaminado. Aunque vivía aislada y lejos de la ciudad, era feliz con mis amigos, los animalitos del campo y los pájaros.

Culture

¿Puedes comparar tu vida con la de otros jóvenes que viven en el Altiplano de Perú?

Un grupo de personas en el Altiplano peruano

Speaking

Con un(a) compañero(a), ¿puedes comparar la vida de la ciudad con la vida del campo? Aquí tienes un ejemplo:

A —*¿Qué prefieres, vivir en la ciudad o en el campo?*
B —*Me gusta más la ciudad porque todo está al alcance de la mano y tiene más centros de diversiones. ¿Y a ti?*
A —*Creo que me gusta más vivir en el campo. Hay menos contaminación, menos tráfico y menos ruido.*
B —*Sí, pero en el campo hay menos oportunidades de trabajo, ¿no?*

Self Test www.pasoapaso.com

90 Capítulo 2

Options

Strategies for Reaching All Students

Students Needing Extra Help
Have students write this exercise so that they can check off what they have mastered. Remind students that this is just a sample of what the real test will be like.
Listening: Read more than once. Write the four questions on the chalkboard. Remind students that they need listen for only four pieces of information. Students may think they will be hearing the name of a specific town or city. Tell them that this is

not so. Brainstorm words that they should be listening for in terms of categories, e.g., city words, country words, etc. Refer to the vocabulary section of the Organizer.
Reading: Remind students that they don't need to know every word. Review strategies for finding cognates, context clues, and word families.
Again, remind students that they are not looking for a specific place, but rather what type of place it is.

Writing: Have students use the Organizer and write a sample paragraph as practice before the test.
Culture: Make a two-column chart so students can write their comparisons. Brainstorm categories of comparisons, e.g., clean air vs. pollution, buildings vs. trees and flowers, etc.
Speaking: Use the vocabulary section of the Organizer. Limit the number of lines of dialogue.

Resumen del vocabulario

Usa el vocabulario de este capítulo para:

- responder a la pregunta clave: ¿Prefieres vivir en la ciudad o en el campo?
- describir cómo es la vida en un lugar
- comparar la vida de antes con la vida de ahora
- indicar las ventajas y las desventajas de vivir en cierto lugar

para describir cómo es la vida en la ciudad
el atasco
el / la ciclista
la contaminación
el peatón, *pl.* los peatones
la población
la presión, *pl.* las presiones
el rascacielos, *pl.* los rascacielos
el ruido

para describir cómo es la vida en el campo
cultivar
la granja
idealizado, -a
el paisaje
rural

para describir cómo es la vida en las afueras
las afueras, *pl.*
la cerca
el jardín, *pl.* los jardines

para hablar de las ventajas y desventajas de los tres
abundante
aislado, -a
animado, -a
bello, -a
contribuir *(i → y)*
conveniente
decidir
diario, -a
escaparse
el espacio
los impuestos, *pl.*
lleno, -a de gente
ofrecer *(c → zc)*
la oportunidad
peligroso, -a
rápido, -a
sano, -a
seguro, -a
situado, -a
tardar (en)

para hablar sobre cómo viajamos a diario
la acera
la autopista
el camino
el peaje
el puente
el sendero

otras palabras y expresiones útiles
al alcance de la mano
diferente
oír
por un lado
por otro lado
sin embargo
¡Una maravilla!
venir *(e → ie)*
    (yo) vengo
    (tú) vienes

Resumen 91

Assessment

 Prueba cumulativa

 Examen de habilidades

 Test Generator

Additional Assessment Options

 Comm. Act. BLMs

Small Group Activities
Situation Cards

 ¿Lo sabes bien? Video Quiz

Internet Activities
Self-Test

Cultural Notes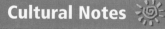

(p. 90, photo)
Peru's Altiplano, or high plains, is a vast area of flatlands at high altitudes in the Andes Mountains. Highland Indians live at elevations reaching 15,000 feet, subsisting by farming and raising livestock, such as llamas and sheep, in the grassy valleys of the area. Peru's Indian population is one of the largest of all South America, comprising nearly half of its total population.

CAPÍTULO 3
THEME: ART

COMMUNICATION

Topics

Types of paintings

Art materials

Art movements

Objectives

Identificar algunos de los principales pintores del mundo hispano

Hablar sobre un artista y su obra

Describir una obra de arte

Hablar de diferentes tipos de pinturas

Describir los colores de una pintura

Discutir la escena de una pintura

Referirse a estilos de pintura

CULTURE

Pintores del mundo hispano

GRAMMAR

Repaso: El pretérito del verbo poner

El pretérito de los verbos influir y contribuir

Repaso: El imperfecto progresivo/El uso del imperfecto progresivo y del pretérito

Ancillaries available for use with Chapter 3

Multisensory/Technology

Overheads, 11–13

Audio Tapes and CDs

Vocabulary Art Blackline Masters for Hands-On Learning, pp. 17–22/CD-ROM

Classroom Crossword

Video

Internet Activities
www.pasoapaso.com

Print

Practice Workbook, pp. 31–40

Writing, Audio & Video Activities, pp. 17–22, 99–101, 137–138

Communicative Activity Blackline Masters

   Pair and Small Group Activities, pp. 15–20

   Situation Cards, p. 21

RESOURCE PRO®

Planning Express, Teaching Resources Library, and Clip Art Library

Assessment

Assessment Program
   Pruebas, pp. 38–48
   Examen de habilidades, pp. 49–52

Test Generator

¿Lo sabes bien?
Video Quiz

Video, Chap. 3

Modern Latin American Art

Latin American art can be categorized by three stages: pre-Columbian, colonial, and modern. Work of the two earlier stages was largely defined by religious belief and social convention. Art of the twentieth century, on the other hand, is more often a personal statement and a reflection of the artists' vision of life.

The beginning of the twentieth century was marked by a return to native subject matter even as artists continued to work in European styles of painting. Painters such as Dr. Atl (Geraldo Murillo Cornado, 1875–1964) and José Maria Velasco (1840–1920) explored Mexican landscapes in monumental paintings that anticipated the Mexican mural movement. Dr. Atl chose his professional name, a Nahuatl word meaning "water", in honor of his Indian heritage. In Uruguay, Pedro Figari (1861–1938) was an important public and political figure as well as an accomplished artist. he painted Uruguayan domestic and street scenes, as well as historical and Brazilian Creole subjects.

Modernism appeared throughout Latin America in the late 1920s. Argentinian Xul Solar (Schultz Solar, 1897–1963), influenced by Cubism and Dadaism, produced drawings that included lettering and graphic signs. Amelia Peláez (1896–1968), of Cuba, painted abstract still lifes, often showing Cuban tropical fruits and stained-glass windows typical of older Cuban houses.

Surrealism is another important phase of twentieth-century art in Latin America. Mexican artists Frida Kahlo (1907–1954) and María Izquierdo (1902–1955) both produced important surrealist paintings, drawing upon their own lives and experiences to shape the intensely personal imagery in their paintings.

Contemporary Latin American artists display diverse influences in their work. Francisco Toledo (b. 1940) of Mexico refers to Mayan myths in his richly colored paintings. Chilean Gonzalo Díaz (b. 1947) produced avant-garde installations incorporating photography, electronics, neon, and print. The titles of his works are often puns giving double meanings to the work.

Hispanic American artists are making important contributions to the U.S. art scene. Their work can be found in many museums and galleries, notably the Museum of Contemporary Hispanic Art and the Museum del Barrio in New York City, the Galería de la Raza in San Francisco, the Cuban Museum of Art and Culture in Miami, and the Mexican Fine Arts Center Museum in Chicago.

Introduce

Re-entry of Concepts

The following represents a list of words, expressions, and grammar topics re-entered from Book 1, Book 2, and Book 3 (Chap. 1):

Book 1

gustar expressions, personality traits, *estar,* family members, physical characteristics, colors, clothing, personal possessions, furniture, direction words, direct object pronouns

Book 2

impersonal *se,* preterite, imperfect

Chapter 1

personality traits

Planning

Cross-Curricular Connections

Art Connection *(pp. 102–103)*
Have students create a work of art, using the same style and techniques that are used by a famous Hispanic artist of their choice. Works can be in any medium or genre, including photos, drawings, sculpture, jewelry, decorative accessories, etc. Have students be prepared to explain how the artist influenced what they did. They should then affix a price and display the work in a gallery area that you can set up. Classmates could bid for the items in an imaginary art auction or write critiques for an art review.

Art History Connection *(pp. 102, 104)*
Bring in prints or slides of Picasso's different periods, or styles (blue period, cubist, etc.). Show them in random order. In groups, ask students to put them in chronological order. Discuss their answers and then show the correct sequence (which might surprise most students). Ask them to tell what Picasso might have been feeling or experiencing during each period.

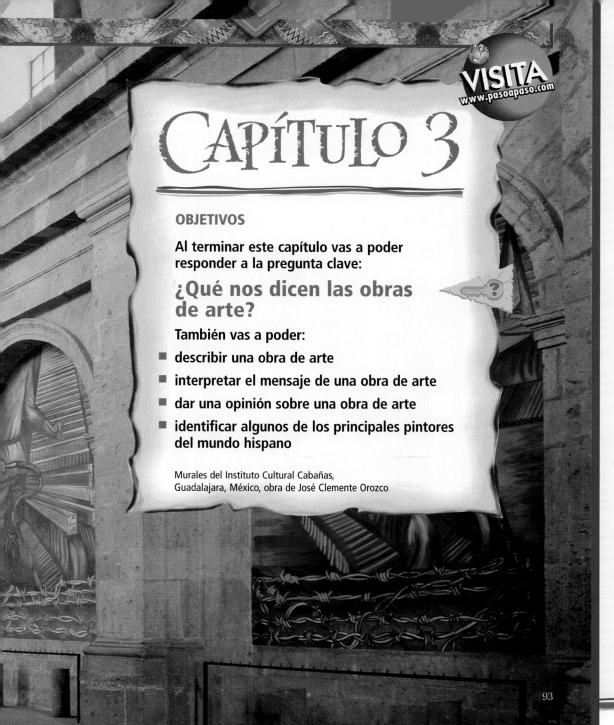

CAPÍTULO 3

OBJETIVOS

Al terminar este capítulo vas a poder responder a la pregunta clave:

¿Qué nos dicen las obras de arte?

También vas a poder:

- describir una obra de arte
- interpretar el mensaje de una obra de arte
- dar una opinión sobre una obra de arte
- identificar algunos de los principales pintores del mundo hispano

Murales del Instituto Cultural Cabañas, Guadalajara, México, obra de José Clemente Orozco

93

Teaching Suggestions
Point out the key chapter question (la pregunta clave del capítulo). Remind students that by acquiring the new words and structures of this chapter, they will be able to answer this key question.

Speech Connection (pp. 104–105)
Bring in slides of famous artworks that have been studied or chosen by students as their favorites. For homework, have them look up information about these works or the artists who created them. Project each slide on the wall as large as possible. As you project them, have volunteers provide commentary for the slides, as an art museum guide might do.

Spanish in Your Community
If possible, have students visit a local art museum and inquire about any works of art on exhibit done by Hispanic painters. Ask them to view the works and report to the class about them and the painter. If there is no local museum or gallery, have students visit the school or local library and bring to class books about Hispanic art or painters. Have them choose an artist or painting to describe to the class.

Cultural Notes

(pp. 92–93, photo)
The frescos on the walls and ceiling of the former chapel of the neoclassical Instituto Cultural Cabañas in Guadalajara are considered by many to be the masterpiece of José Clemente Orozco (1883–1949). It took the entire year of 1938 to paint these scenes, which vividly depict the encounter between Mexico's indigenous peoples and the Spaniards who conquered them. Table-size benches are provided for patrons to lie on and view the magnificent scenes on the ceiling.

Preview

Answers: Anticipación
Answers will vary.

Anticipación

Mira las fotos de estas páginas y lee el texto. ¿Cuándo fue la última vez que fuiste a un museo? ¿Has participado alguna vez en un proyecto de arte? Si no lo has hecho, ¿en cuál te gustaría participar?

"Cuando viajamos a Madrid, nos gusta visitar los museos."

En el Museo del Prado de Madrid hay exposiciones permanentes y otras que duran sólo unos meses. Aquí presentan obras de arte de artistas españoles y de todo el mundo. Algunos artistas españoles como Velázquez, El Greco y Goya tienen la mayor parte de sus obras en este museo.

94   Capítulo 3

Options

Strategies for Reaching All Students

Spanish-Speaking Students
Ask: *Piensa en el arte que ves en diferentes lugares en tu comunidad (iglesias, museos, escuelas, parques, etc.). ¿Qué te gusta o te atrae? ¿Qué no te gusta? ¿Por qué?*

Multiple Intelligences
Visual/Spatial
Have students access the Internet to visit various websites of Spanish and Latin American museums.

Students Needing Extra Help
Inform the art teacher of the contents of this chapter and see what he or she can do to help you.
Tell students that one of the requirements for this chapter is to visit an art gallery, art museum, or library. The experience will provide them with information that will be helpful in the *Para escribir* section. If this is not possible, provide students with videos about Hispanic art or artists.
Be prepared with visuals and anecdotes of painters and works of art to spark students' interest. Remind students of their elementary school years when they made works of art from papier-mâché, craft sticks, etc. Remind them of the many different art media.

"El mural que estamos pintando trata de la historia de nuestra comunidad."

Los grandes muralistas mexicanos tienen mucha influencia sobre algunos artistas hispanos de California y del suroeste de los Estados Unidos. Hoy la gente puede entender más de su historia con la ayuda del arte.

"Me llamo León López. Me gusta seguir la tradición de mis padres y abuelos. Por eso traigo mis pinturas al Mercado español tradicional."

Cada año, los jóvenes y niños hispanos del norte de Nuevo México participan en una exposición de arte. Aquí ellos pueden mostrar sus pinturas y otros objetos artísticos. En 1992, León López ganó el primer premio.

www.pasoapaso.com
Visita estos países

95

One of the most influential periods in artistic expression in Latin America began after the Mexican Revolution in 1910. A national style emerged that expressed the social issues of the time as Mexico was forming a new independent nation. Diego Rivera, José Clemente Orozco, and David Alfaro Siqueiros were part of the muralist school. Started as the Sindicato de Obreros Técnicos, Pintores y Escultores at the Escuela Nacional Preparatoria in Mexico in the 1920s, these muralists began a movement whose impact is still visible today in works of contemporary Mexican and Mexican American artists.

Cultural Notes

(p. 94, photo)
Madrid's Museo del Prado ranks as one of Europe's finest museums. It has a collection of 8,000 paintings, of which only 1,500 are displayed. Built at the end of the eighteenth century, its galleries are filled with master pieces by Velázquez, Goya, and El Greco, as well as paintings by Venetian and Flemish masters. Charles I, a Hapsburg who came to the Spanish throne in 1516 and was later elected Holy Roman Emperor, is credited with starting the magnificent collection housed in the Prado.

(p. 95, top photo)
Mural painting is an ancient art form in Latin America, developed by the Mayas and Aztecs. Revived after the Mexican Revolution of 1910, it continues to be tremendously popular both there and in Mexican American neighborhoods in the U.S. Folk art representing holy images is another traditional art form. It flourished in New Mexico during the late eighteenth and early nineteenth centuries, and continues to thrive today.

Standards 1.2; 2.2; 3.1   **95**

Present

Chapter Theme
Paintings

Communicative Objectives
* Hablar sobre un artista y su obra
* Describir una pintura
* Hablar de diferentes tipos de pinturas
* Describir los colores de una pintura
* Discutir la escena de una pintura
* Referirse a estilos de pintura

 Overheads 11–12

 Vocabulary Art BLMs/CD-ROM

 Vocabulary Tape 3-1

Teaching Suggestions
Preparing students to speak: Use one or two options from each of the categories of Comprehensible Input or Limited Verbal Response. For a complete explanation of these categories and some sample activities, see pp. T20–T21.

Explain that we say *en primer plano* (in the foreground) and *al fondo* (in the background).

Vocabulario para comunicarse

¿Qué tipo de arte prefieres?

Aquí tienes palabras y expresiones para hablar sobre obras de arte. Léelas varias veces y practícalas con un(a) compañero(a) en las páginas siguientes.

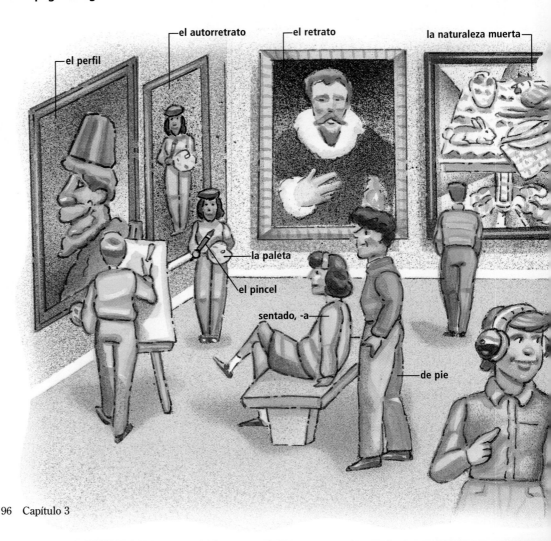

el perfil — el autorretrato — el retrato — la naturaleza muerta — la paleta — el pincel — sentado, -a — de pie

96   Capítulo 3

Options

Strategies for Reaching All Students

Spanish-Speaking Students
¿Qué otras palabras sabes que puedes usar para describir una obra de arte? Escríbelas en tu vocabulario personal.

Students Needing Extra Help
Begin the vocabulary section of the Organizer. Give examples using *sentado,-a* and *de pie* in a context other than a museum, e.g., in a classroom, at a baseball game, at the mall, etc. Make a distinction between a portrait and a profile. Write out the complete paradigms of *atraer* and *fijarse*. Have students practice both written and spoken forms of these verbs.

Enrichment
To help present this vocabulary, you may want to bring art books to show students examples of different types of paintings. Take time to describe some paintings in detail, modeling as much of the vocabulary as possible. Ask students if they can name several famous examples of each kind of painting.

También necesitas . . .

la obra (de arte)	*work (of art)*	junto a	*next to*
el tema	*subject*	reflejado, -a	*reflected*
el primer plano	*foreground*	vivo, -a	here: *bright*
el fondo	*background*	apagado, -a	here: *dull*
la figura	*form, shape*	atraer*	*to attract*
arriba	*on top*	fijarse (en)	*to pay attention (to)*
abajo	*below*		

¿Y qué quiere decir . . . ?

el / la artista	la galería
el centro	interpretar
el estilo	pastel
la forma	el tono

*Atraer follows the pattern of traer.

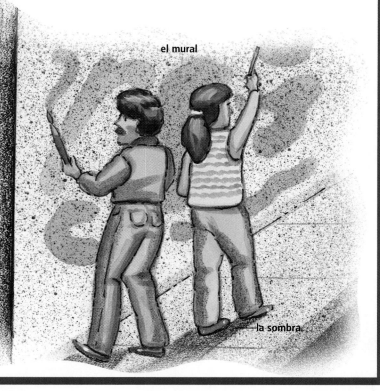

—la pintura

el mural

la sombra

Class Starter Review
On the day following the presentation of the vocabulary, you may want to begin the class with this activity:
Give an oral definition (in Spanish) of several of the vocabulary words. Then have students name the word you are defining. For example: *¿Qué se usa para pintar? (el pincel); ¿Cómo se llama una pintura hecha sobre una pared? (un mural)*

🌐 Internet Activities
Juegos
Have students go to www.pasoapaso.com for additional activities and practice.

Extended Written Practice/Homework
1. Imagine you just visited the art gallery on pp. 96–97. Write four sentences telling what you saw: *En la galería había un retrato de ...*
2. Describe the painting of the landscape on p. 97. Include the following: *el primer plano, el fondo, el centro.*
3. Write sentences telling your likes and dislikes of the paintings in the art gallery and explaining why: *Me atrae el autorretrato porque ...*

Multiple Intelligences
Musical/Rhythmic
Have students bring in various types of music which they feel match the style of different artists' work, e.g., Picasso, Goya, and Velázquez.
Verbal/Linguistic
See Vocabulary Tape 3-1 and Class Starter Review.
Visual/Spatial
See Overheads 11–12 and the Vocabulary Art BLMs/CD-ROM.

Practice

Reteach / Review: Vocabulary

Ex. 1: As a variation on this exercise, have pairs of students take different positions in the classroom and describe to each other what they see in the foreground, background, etc. from where they are standing.

Answers: Empecemos a conversar

1 ESTUDIANTE A

a. No veo la paleta. ¿Dónde está?

b. ...el retrato. ...está?

c. ...la naturaleza muerta. ...está?

d. ...la pintura. ...está?

e. ...el autorretrato. ...está?

f. ...las diapositivas. ...están?

g. Statements and questions will vary.

ESTUDIANTE B

a.–g. Answers may vary, but look for the correct use of *está / están* and the appropriate direct object pronoun. Encourage students to practice a variety of expressions in their responses.

a. Está a la derecha (de los pinceles). ¿No la ves?

b. Está allí arriba. ...lo...

c. Está allí abajo. ...la...

d. Está al fondo. ...la...

e. Está a la izquierda. ...lo...

f. Están junto al proyector. ...las...

g. Statements and questions will vary.

Empecemos a conversar

Túrnate con un(a) compañero(a) para ser *Estudiante A* y *Estudiante B.* Reemplacen las palabras subrayadas con palabras representadas o escritas en los recuadros.

💡 quiere decir que puedes escoger tu propia respuesta.

1

A —No veo *los pinceles*. ¿Dónde *están*?

B —*Están en el centro*. ¿No *los* ves?

Estudiante A   **Estudiante B**

a.   b.   c.

d.   e.   f.   g.

allí arriba

allí abajo

al fondo

a la derecha

a la izquierda

junto a ____

98   Capítulo 3

Options

Strategies for Reaching All Students

Spanish-Speaking Students

Exs. 1–4: Pair Spanish-speaking students, if possible.

Students Needing Extra Help

Ex. 1: Study the pictured artist's studio carefully with students, identifying the objects in the room as a class. Show students that *está(n)* and the direct object pronoun will change according to the object(s) being named.

Ex. 2: Review *¿Qué se ve?*

98   Standards 1.1; 3.2; 4.2

Enrichment

Ex. 1: As a written, in-class assignment, have students describe in detail a specific work of art that you show them. Tell them to include the name of the artist and work as they write their description, and to tell why they do or do not like it.

Extended Written Practice/Homework

1. Write three sentences naming objects that have different colors using *vivo, apagado,* and *pastel: El mural de la biblioteca tiene un azul muy vivo.*

2. Write three sentences describing a work of art in your home or school: *En nuestra sala hay una obra de arte que ...*

3. Write three sentences telling what you notice most when you look at a work of art: *Cuando miro una obra de arte, me fijo más en ...*

Para este ejercicio, mira la pintura de abajo.

2 abajo, a   A —*¿Qué se ve abajo, a la derecha?*
   la derecha   B —*Se ve la figura de un perro.*

Estudiante A

a. en primer plano
b. en el centro, a la izquierda
c. al fondo
d. en el espejo
e. a la izquierda de la niña
f. en la pared del fondo, arriba
g.

Estudiante B

dos personas reflejadas

una muchacha, de perfil, ofreciéndole agua

un hombre en la puerta

una niña rubia de pelo largo

dos cuadros

el pintor, de pie, con los pinceles y la paleta

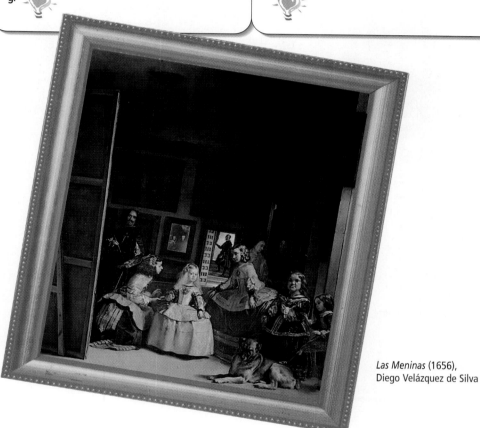

Las Meninas (1656),
Diego Velázquez de Silva

99

Practice & Apply

Answers: Empecemos a conversar

3 ESTUDIANTE A
a. Fíjate en el artista. ¿Lo ves?
b. ... las montañas. ¿Las ves?
c. ... los animales. ¿Los ves?
d. ... la esposa del presidente. ¿La ves?
e. ... el general. ¿Lo ves?
f. ... el avión. ¿Lo ves?
g. Questions will vary.

ESTUDIANTE B
a.–g. Answers will vary, but should be logical and, if negative, include correct use of the direct object pronoun. If *Estudiante B* responds in the negative, *Estudiante A* should answer *Estudiante B*'s question.

Strategies for Reaching All Students

MULTIPLE INTELLIGENCES

Bodily/Kinesthetic and Visual/Spatial
Have students create their own brochure to announce an art show in their community or school.

Intrapersonal/Introspective
See Exs. 5–9.

Logical/Mathematical
See Cooperative Learning.

Verbal/Linguistic
See Exs. 3–4 and Audio Activity 3.1.

Visual/Spatial
See Practice Wkbk. 3-1 and 3-2 and Writing Activity 3-A.

La familia presidencial (1967), Fernando Botero

3 la madre del presidente

A — *Fíjate en la madre del presidente. ¿La ves?*
B — *Sí, claro, es la figura sentada, a la izquierda.*
   o: *No, no la veo. ¿Dónde está?*

Estudiante A

a. el artista
b. las montañas
c. los animales
d. la esposa del presidente
e. el general
f. el avión
g.

Estudiante B

100   Capítulo 3

Options

Strategies for Reaching All Students

Spanish-Speaking Students
Ex. 9: Ask: *¿Dónde pintarías tu mural? ¿Por qué?*

Students Needing Extra Help
Ex. 3: Remind students that they have to use location words in order to answer the question. Model a response to *¿Dónde está?*
Ex. 4: Brainstorm other possible responses. If available, refer to the Book 1, Chap. 11 vocabulary section of the Organizer. Present a complete model.
Ex. 5: For students who have never been to an art exhibit, bring in newspaper reviews

and have them do the same. Students may need more direction and / or more vocabulary to answer *¿Qué tipo ....*
Ex. 7: Students may need help with the vocabulary for the *¿Por qué?* question.
Ex. 8: Students will need some help sorting out their impressions of a painting and with naming its theme or style.
Ex. 9: Brainstorm possible themes for the mural.

4 Conversa con tu compañero(a). Sigue el modelo y da tu propia opinión.

  A — *¿Te gusta la obra de Botero?*
  B — *Pues, me atrae mucho porque . . .*
     o: *Pues, no me atrae nada porque . . .*

¿Y qué piensas tú?

Aquí tienes otra oportunidad para usar el vocabulario de este capítulo.

5 ¿Cuándo fue la última vez que fuiste a una exposición de arte? ¿Qué tipo de arte era? ¿Fue en una galería o en un museo?

6 ¿Cuál de las obras de arte que vimos te atrae más? Después, comenta tu respuesta con un(a) compañero(a).

Puedes usar estas palabras y expresiones u otras:

¡Qué va!	sin embargo
¡Una maravilla!	por un lado
por supuesto	por otro lado
además	¿verdad?
también	tampoco

7 ¿Te parece más fácil interpretar la pintura clásica o la moderna? ¿Por qué?

8 ¿Qué tipo de pinturas te gusta más, retratos, paisajes o naturalezas muertas? ¿Qué es lo que más te gusta ver en una pintura? (temas, estilos, formas, colores).

9 Imagínate que estás haciendo un mural para la clase de arte. ¿Cuál es el tema de tu mural? ¿Por qué? ¿Qué tonos vas a usar?

MÁS PRÁCTICA

- Más práctica y tarea, p. 553
- Practice Workbook 3–1, 3–2

LA UNIDAD DE PROMOCIÓN CULTURAL Y ACERVO PATRIMONIAL DE LA SECRETARÍA DE HACIENDA Y CRÉDITO PÚBLICO

invita a los

TALLERES CULTURALES

CENTRO CULTURAL
Guatemala 8, Centro Histórico
Tel. 521 55 66 y 510 00 12

Vocabulario para comunicarse   101

4 Dialogues will vary.

Answers: ¿Y qué piensas tú?

5–9 Answers will vary.

 Practice Wkbk. 3-1, 3-2

 Audio Activity 3.1

 Writing Activity 3-A

 Pruebas 3-1, 3-2

Cultural Notes

Cooperative Learning
Using the questions in Ex. 6, have pairs of students survey the class within a set time limit. Make groups of four from the pairs and tell them to create a graph representative of responses. Have each group present their information to the class and discuss possible reasons for any differences in the graphs.

(p. 100, photo)
Colombian artist Fernando Botero was born in Medellín in 1932 and studied art in Spain, Germany, and Italy. A highly versatile artist, he has produced a great number of drawings (his principal medium), paintings, and sculptures. His paintings alone number about 1,000; those from the early 1960s on, such as *La familia presidencial* (1967), feature "vast bodies"—the fat, full figures that characterize his distinctive style.

(p. 101, realia)
The Guatemalan government has recently begun efforts to preserve and promote the culture of its indigenous peoples which comprise nearly half its population of ten million. In addition to sponsoring the cultural workshops advertised here, the government began a ten-year project in 1989 to record the music of 24 Guatemalan ethnic groups for both research and commercial use.

Present

Chapter Theme
Artistic movements

Communicative Objectives
• *Hablar sobre un artista y su obra*
• *Describir una pintura*
• *Referirse a estilos de pintura*

 Vocabulary Tape 3-2

Grammar Preview
The preterite of *contribuir* is previewed lexically. Its explanation appears in the grammar section on p. 112.

Teaching Suggestions
Getting ready to speak:
Remind students of the reading strategies that they learned (getting meaning from context and coping with unknown words) to help them understand the *Tema para investigar*. For further details and some sample activities, see pp. T24–T25.

Answers: Tema para investigar
Answers will vary.

Tema para investigar

Aquí tienes más palabras e ideas que te ayudarán a hablar sobre arte. Mira las fotos de esta página. ¿Son estilos de arte diferentes? ¿Cuál te gusta más? ¿Por qué?

Composición surrealista (1927), Salvador Dalí

Paisaje Juan les Pins (1920), Pablo Picasso

102   Capítulo 3

Options

Strategies for Reaching All Students

Spanish-Speaking Students
Tell students: *Escribe oraciones originales con el vocabulario de esta sección.*

Students Needing Extra Help
Discuss each of these periods or styles of art according to students' prior knowledge. Use visuals to represent the different types of art.
Be sure that students take notes on the different artistic styles and periods for use in other parts of the chapter.
Give examples using *la época*.

Enrichment
To enhance this reading, ask students to go to the library and prepare brief written reports on other works of art by Picasso and Dalí. Ask them to include the basic facts regarding the works about which they choose to write (name, date, artist, style) and to tell what feelings they think the artist was trying to convey. You may want to prepare some historical background information about the artists to give students beforehand.

La pintura en el siglo XX

A principios del **siglo** XX, Pablo Picasso, un pintor español que estaba entonces viviendo en París, contribuyó* a crear un nuevo estilo que rompió† con las tradiciones artísticas de esa **época**. El artista encontró **inspiración** en el arte de África y de las islas del Pacífico. En sus obras, los objetos y las personas **se transformaban** en formas casi **abstractas**. Picasso **trataba de** presentar sus **imágenes** desde más de un **punto de vista**. Este estilo recibió el nombre de **cubismo**. Un buen ejemplo es la pintura de Picasso *Juan les Pins* que ven a la izquierda.

Una de **las etapas** más importantes en el desarrollo del arte ocurrió cuando los artistas abandonaron **el realismo**, es decir, no pintaron más las cosas como las veían. Los pintores del **movimiento impresionista** trataron de reproducir las sensaciones creadas por el color y la luz. Luego, los pintores del **surrealismo** empezaron a explorar temas de su propia **imaginación**. Capturaron ideas e imágenes del **subconsciente**, como las que vemos en **sueños**. **Quisieron**†† hacer, como dijo el pintor español del surrealismo Salvador Dalí (1904-1989), "fotos de sueños, pintadas a mano." La obra de Dalí *Composición surrealista* es un ejemplo de este estilo.

¿Cómo se puede saber qué obras tienen **valor** y cuáles no? ¿Y cuál es **el mensaje** de una obra de arte? No es nada fácil **criticar** el arte, porque cada persona que mira una obra de arte tiene su propio punto de vista y le da a cada obra un valor diferente.

el siglo	century	el movimiento	movement, school
la época	time, age	el subconsciente	subconscious
tratar de	to try to	el sueño	dream
la imagen,	image	quisieron††	they wanted to
pl. las imágenes		el valor	value
el punto de vista	point of view	el mensaje	message
la etapa	stage		

¿Y qué quiere decir . . . ?

la inspiración	impresionista
transformar(se)	el surrealismo
abstracto, -a	la imaginación
el cubismo	criticar *(c → qu)*
el realismo	

MUSEO THYSSEN-BORNEMISZA
PASEO DEL PRADO, 8. 28014 MADRID. TEL.(91) 420 39 44

* *Contribuir* is similar to *oír* in the preterite.
† You already know the reflexive verb *romperse* "to break." Here it is used in its nonreflexive form.
†† *Quisieron* is the preterite *Uds. / ellos / ellas* form of *querer*.

Tema para investigar 103

Cultural Notes

(p. 102, top photo)
While an art student in Madrid in the 1920s, Salvador Dalí (1904–1989) was influenced by the writings of Sigmund Freud and of the French surrealists on dreams and the subconscious. Dalí's personal experience and these writings combined to determine the bizarre subject matter and style he chose for his art. One example is this haunting ink on paper drawing, *Composición surrealista* (1927).

(p. 102, bottom photo)
From early in his career, Pablo Picasso (1881–1973) kept various pieces that he had created. *Paisaje Juan les Pins* (1920) was one of 50,000 such works that he owned at the time of his death. The collection then passed into the hands of his heirs and the French government.

(p. 103, realia)
Madrid's Museo Thyssen-Bornemisza houses a private collection of Old Master's paintings that is second only to that of Queen Elizabeth II of Britain. The collection belongs to Baron Hans Heinrich Thyssen-Bornemisza. It was begun by his father and today includes works by the more modern schools, including the French Impressionists and the German Expressionists.

Practice & Apply

Answers: ¿Comprendiste?

1 a. 3.
b. 1.
c. 2.
d. 3.
e. 2.

2 Descriptions will vary. / *Pertenece al cubismo (al movimiento cubista).*

Answers: ¿Y qué piensas tú?

3–6 Answers will vary.

Strategies for Reaching All Students

MULTIPLE INTELLIGENCES
Intrapersonal/Introspective
See Exs. 3–6.
Verbal/Linguistic
See Audio Activity 3.2.
Visual/Spatial
See Exs. 1–2, Practice Wkbk. 3-3 and 3-4, Writing Activities 3-B and 3-C, and Comm. Act. BLM 3-1.

¿Comprendiste?

1 Según la lectura, completa estas frases de una forma correcta.

a. Picasso era
   1. un pintor francés que vivía en España.
   2. un pintor español que vivía en España.
   3. un pintor español que vivía en Francia.

b. Picasso se inspiró en
   1. el arte de África y de las islas del Pacífico.
   2. el arte español de su época.
   3. el arte francés.

c. En el cubismo
   1. las imágenes se ven como son en realidad.
   2. las imágenes se transforman en formas casi abstractas.
   3. las imágenes están llenas de color y de luz.

d. Los pintores del surrealismo
   1. usan métodos e ideas realistas.
   2. no exploran temas de su imaginación.
   3. pintan imágenes del subconsciente.

e. Los pintores realistas
   1. quisieron pintar lo que veían en su imaginación.
   2. pintaban las cosas como las veían.
   3. presentaban sus imágenes desde más de un punto de vista.

2 Mira la escultura *(sculpture)* de arriba. Descríbela. Según lo que leíste en *La pintura en el siglo XX,* ¿a qué movimiento artístico pertenece *(does it belong)*?

Violín (1915), Pablo Picasso

¿Y qué piensas tú?

3 De los movimientos artísticos mencionados, cubismo, realismo, impresionismo y surrealismo, ¿cuál es el que más te interesa? ¿Por qué?

4 ¿Cuál es la obra de arte que más te gusta? ¿Quién es el (la) artista? ¿Cuándo y dónde la viste? ¿En un museo, en una galería de arte, en un libro?

5 ¿Qué valor tiene para ti la obra de arte que mencionaste? Explica por qué te gusta. Puedes hablar del tema, del estilo, del mensaje, de los colores.

104   Capítulo 3

MÁS PRÁCTICA

- Más práctica y tarea, p. 554
- Practice Workbook 3-3, 3-4

Options

Strategies for Reaching All Students

Spanish-Speaking Students
Exs. 4–5: Have students write these exercises.

Students Needing Extra Help
Ex. 3: Have some visuals available for reference. Remind students to refer to their notes taken at the beginning of this section. These are sophisticated concepts that probably will not be cemented until the end of the chapter. Brainstorm possible answers to the *¿Por qué?* question.

Ex. 4: Remind students that this can be any work of art they have enjoyed, not just paintings.
Ex. 5: Present the *¿Qué valor...* question as rhetorical. Focus on the *Explica por qué...* response.
Brainstorm the message of a particular piece of art.
Ex. 6: Answer the introductory question as a class.
¿Qué sabes ahora?: Have students write this so that they can record their progress.

Enrichment
Additional question regarding Dalí's *La persistencia de la memoria: En tu opinión, ¿qué imágenes de esta obra son del subconsciente?* (Guide student responses.)

6 *La persistencia de la memoria* es una pintura de la etapa surrealista de Salvador Dalí. Escribe lo que ves y lo que sientes. Comparte tus respuestas con tu compañero(a). ¿Están ustedes de acuerdo o no?

a. ¿Qué ves en la pintura? ¿En primer plano? ¿Al fondo?
b. ¿Qué se ve a la izquierda?
c. ¿Cómo son las formas? ¿Y los colores? ¿Qué tipo de arte es?
d. ¿Cómo te hace sentir? ¿Te gusta? ¿Por qué?

La persistencia de la memoria (1931), Salvador Dalí

¿Qué sabes ahora?

¿Puedes:

■ describir una obra de arte?

—En ___ se ve la figura de ___, y al fondo hay ___.

■ dar tu opinión sobre una obra de arte?

—Lo que me atrae de una pintura es ___.

■ hablar sobre diferentes movimientos artísticos?

—Los artistas ___ pintaban las cosas como las ___.

Answers: ¿Qué sabes ahora?
• Answers will vary.

Multicultural Perspectives
Of the painters of the surrealistic movement, one of the most colorful characters was Frida Kahlo. True to the surrealistic tradition, her paintings reflected her subconscious—the pain and suffering she endured all her life from a near-fatal accident as a young woman was a constant theme in many of her works. Her marriage to Diego Rivera was highly publicized. Their home was a center for intellectuals and artists. Ask students to discuss the style of their favorite artist.

 Practice Wkbk. 3-3, 3-4

 Audio Activity 3.2

 Writing Activities 3-B, 3-C

 Pruebas 3-3, 3-4

 Comm. Act. BLM 3-1

Cultural Notes ☀

Extended Written Practice/Homework
1. Write sentences explaining what an artist of each movement tries to do: *cubismo, realismo, impresionismo, surrealismo. En el surrealismo, el (la) artista trata de …*
2. Choose a painter and write three sentences describing him or her. You might include: *siglo, época, etapa, punto de vista, mensaje, movimiento. Goya pintó durante los siglos 18 y 19. Su primer movimiento artístico fue el realismo. Tuvo otras etapas diferentes también.*

(p. 104, photo)
Picasso's *Violín* (1915) dates from his Cubist period, when he worked closely with French artist Georges Braque to create a style called "Analytic Cubism." This style breaks away from traditional perspective, "analyzing" objects by fracturing them so that multiple perspectives are achieved.

(p. 105, photo)
Dalí's *La persistencia de la memoria* (1931) is probably the most famous of all surrealist paintings. Like many of Dalí's works, it creates a bizarre, compelling whole by blending elements from reality and dreams. In addition to paintings, Dalí's extensive creative output includes two surrealist films with Spanish film maker Luis Buñuel, book illustrations, jewelry and stage set designs, poetry, fiction, and an autobiography.

Present & Apply

Cultural Objective
• *Hablar de algunos de los principales pintores del mundo hispano*

Critical Thinking: Synthesizing
Have each student write a poem or short piece of prose to accompany their favorite piece of art in the *Álbum cultural.* Have them share their pieces with the class.

Answers
Answers will vary.

El pintor comunica con imágenes lo que el escritor comunica con palabras. Aquí tenemos cinco obras de arte de artistas hispanoamericanos del siglo XX. ¿Qué mensaje piensas que quiere comunicar cada artista?

Uno de los objetivos del artista mexicano Diego Rivera es revitalizar el interés y el respeto por la gente indígena y por las clases económicas más bajas de México. En esta obra, la expresión de los personajes muestra su dedicación al trabajo.

Día de flores (1925), Diego Rivera

Mujer en violeta (1938), Wifredo Lam

Wifredo Lam es un artista cubano. Su padre era chino y su madre afrocubana. Por esta razón, una característica de sus pinturas es mostrar la diversidad de razas. En *Mujer en violeta* podemos ver la influencia del arte africano por la forma de la cara y de los ojos del personaje.

106   Capítulo 3

Options

Strategies for Reaching All Students

Spanish-Speaking Students
Have students describe one of the paintings: *Describe una de las pinturas que ves aquí. Usa las preguntas del número seis, pág. 105, como guía.*

Students Needing Extra Help
Have students take notes for use in the *¿Lo sabes bien?* section at the end of the chapter.

Multiple Intelligences
Verbal/Linguistic and Visual/Spatial
1) See Critical Thinking.
2) If possible, have students bring in a piece of art (or a book containing a photo of the piece) and ask them to explain its cultural significance or what it means to them.

Fernando Botero, pintor y escultor *(sculptor)* colombiano, es conocido por las grandes dimensiones de sus obras. En *Reclining Woman,* algunos rasgos *(features)* como la cabeza y los ojos son exagerados, mientras que otros son más delicados y finos.

Reclining Woman (1984),
(Mujer recostada)
Fernando Botero

Cultural Notes

(p. 106, left photo)
Although Diego Rivera (1886–1957) is best known as the leader of the Mexican muralist school that emerged after the Mexican Revolution of 1910, his work also includes a large number of drawings, paintings, and prints. *Día de flores* (1925) is representative of Rivera's stylized, loving depiction of Mexican Indians' daily lives. Rivera worked sometimes 10 to 14 hours a day throughout his life, to render his vision of the forces that shaped Mexican history and society.

(p. 106, right photo)
One of the major Latin American artists of the twentieth century, Wilfredo Lam (1902–1982), was born in Cuba. At age 21 he traveled to Europe, where he remained until 1940. Lam's early work was profoundly influenced by Picasso and the French surrealist author, André Breton. His later work, however, is distinctly Afrocuban and original in both style and content, depicting jungle scenes containing primitive human figures and deities.

(p. 107, photo)
Fernando Botero's *Reclining Woman* (1984) was one of 17 of his massive bronze sculptures displayed in an outdoor exhibition in Chicago's Grant Park in 1994. Like the sculptures themselves, whose total weight came to 25,500 pounds, the task of mounting the exhibition was monumental, requiring a helicopter and ground crew to carefully place each enormous piece exactly above a load-bearing column of the park's underground garage.

Present & Apply

Composición constructiva núm. 548 (1932), Joaquín Torres-García

El artista uruguayo Joaquín Torres-García usó elementos del arte africano y precolombino con los principios griegos para hacer un nuevo arte abstracto. En esta composición, Torres-García usa símbolos universales además de una gran variedad de colores que expresan otros mensajes.

El alhajero (1942), María Izquierdo

No todo el arte tiene mensajes políticos. María Izquierdo, una artista mexicana, pintó esta naturaleza muerta que incluye artículos personales. Los artículos que están encima de una silla y una mesa forman la base de esta obra, y también se ven en otras de sus pinturas y en fotografías de la artista.

108   Capítulo 3

Options

Strategies for Reaching All Students

Artistas Latinoamericanos del Siglo XX

6 JUNIO–7 SEPTIEMBRE, 1993

THE MUSEUM OF MODERN ART
NEW YORK

Mediada la década de los veinte y en años posteriores, la política se convirtió en tema predominante para los artistas a lo largo y ancho de las Américas y particularmente en México. Las revoluciones mexicana y rusa, la subida del fascismo y la depresión económica mundial, así como las condiciones sociales de los años treinta, afectaron profundamente la obra de Rivera, David Alfaro Siqueiros y José Clemente Orozco. Para ellos el arte era un arma contundente para educar a la gente en la política. Eligieron trabajar con un poderoso realismo; sus enormes murales, a menudo subvencionados por el gobierno, sostienen explícitas afirmaciones políticas en una escala épica.

Pinceladas de dramáticos colores terrosos, violentas y entrecortadas, se mezclan con poderosas diagonales en el cuadro de Orozco, *Barricada*, 1931, donde nos transmite la experiencia de la batalla: tensión, temor, extenuación, la futilidad de la guerra. En este caso poco hay que identifique las tensas figuras como mexicanas. Sus rostros, o no son visibles, o están vagamente indicados; sus ropas están mínimamente descritas. Lo que más se destaca son quizá las armas: un cuchillo en el primer plano y un rifle apuntando a la barricada.

Hacia los años treinta, el realismo social de los muralistas mexicanos, como así fueron llamados, se extendió por América del Sur y del Norte. Véase *Café*, 1935, un enorme cuadro realizado por el artista brasileño Cândido Portinari, o incluso *Desocupados* de Antonio Berni, argentino, una ponderada reflexión de 1914 sobre la Depresión. La escala de las obras de Orozco y de Rivera, al igual que el más agresivo, vigoroso estilo de Siqueiros, influenciaron a muchos pintores norteamericanos, incluido Jackson Pollock. Sin embargo, con el giro de la política, el tratamiento de los muralistas mexicanos empezó a sentirse como opresivo ya que servía entonces al status-quo post-revolucionario.

José Clemente Orozco, Barricada, 1931. Óleo sobre lienzo, 55 x 45". The Museum of Modern Art, New York. Donación anónima, 1937. Foto: S. Sunami. The Museum of Modern Art, New York.

Reacción personal

Contesta las siguientes preguntas en una hoja de papel.

1 ¿Cuál de las obras de Álbum cultural te atrae más? ¿Qué es lo que te atrae: el color, las formas, el estilo?

2 Los escritores comunican sus historias con palabras. Los artistas usan elementos como el color, la forma y el tema. Describe el color, la forma y el tema de cada obra e interpreta lo que quieren decir.

3 Las características del cubismo son las formas geométricas y las formas abstractas. ¿Crees que estas obras son cubistas? ¿Por qué? ¿Qué quieren decirnos los artistas de estas obras?

Actividad cultural · www.pasoapaso.com

Álbum cultural 109

Cultural Notes

(p. 108, top photo)
The Uruguayan Joaquín Torres-García (1874–1949) played a major role in the development of twentieth century Latin American art as an artist, thinker, teacher, and writer. He received his art training in post-World War I New York and Europe.

He returned to Montevideo in 1932. Torres-García created a style called *universalismo constructivo,* which declares that artistic creations should go beyond the purely visual and be a meaningful expression of our relationship with the universe.

(p. 108, bottom photo)
The style of painter María Izquierdo (1902–1955), as seen in the still life *El alhajero* (1942), is direct and ingenious. It is quite distinct from the fantastic, intensely personal work of the better-known Mexican female artist of her generation, Frida Kahlo. Izquierdo worked with the leading Mexican artists of her time, including Rufino Tamayo, who, from the late 1920s to the early 1930s, was her teacher at la Escuela Nacional de Bellas Artes.

Preview

🖨 **Overhead 13**

Teaching Suggestions

A Remind students that *estaba mirando* is the imperfect progressive. Have them give you their own eyewitness report of the robbery.

B Have students think of the regular preterite *-er* verb endings for *tú* and *ellos.* Then have them apply these endings to the irregular preterite stem of *poner.* Review the remaining forms if necessary.

C Ask students to tell you the present participles of other regular *-er* and *-ir* verbs.

Answers

A *estaba mirando / Quitó, puso,* and *salió* tell what he did next. The verbs in the other reports include *estaba leyendo, levantar, tomó, puso, sé, fue; vi, estaba mirando, quitó, puso, salió; estaba dibujando, quitó, puso, caminó.* The imperfect progressive is used to tell what the person was doing at the time of the robbery, and the preterite is used to tell what the person did at a specific moment.

B The verb used to tell where each suspect put the painting is *puso.* Its infinitive form is *poner.*

C *Leyendo* is spelled with a *y* instead of an *i. /* The present participle of *incluir* is *incluyendo.*

¿Qué nos dicen las obras de arte?

𝒢ramática en contexto

Lee este reportaje sobre un robo en una galería de arte. Hay tres versiones distintas. ¿Cuál piensas que es la verdadera?

Robo en una galería de arte

Anoche, en una exposición, robaron un pequeño cuadro pintado por Emilia Rodríguez. Tres personas vieron el robo, pero sus versiones son muy diferentes.

Vi a un joven que estaba mirando el cuadro. De repente, quitó el cuadro de la pared y lo puso bajo su chaqueta. Luego, salió entre un grupo de turistas.

Al lado del cuadro una mujer estaba leyendo un folleto. Sin levantar los ojos del folleto, tomó el cuadro y lo puso en su bolso. Después, no sé adónde fue.

Un hombre de barba negra estaba dibujando en un cuaderno. Rápidamente quitó el cuadro, lo puso debajo del cuaderno y caminó hacia la salida.

A In the first eyewitness report, the person uses the verbs *estaba mirando, quitó, puso,* and *salió.* Which of these verbs tells what the thief was doing before taking the painting? Which tell what he did next? Identify the verbs in the other eyewitness reports. In all the reports, is the imperfect progressive or the preterite used to tell what the person was doing at the time of the robbery? Which tense is used to tell what the person did at a particular moment in time?

B Each suspected thief put the painting somewhere. What verb is used to tell this? What is the infinitive of this verb?

C How does the spelling of *leyendo* differ from the present participle of other *-er* and *-ir* verbs? What would you guess the present participle of *incluir* is?

110 Capítulo 3

Options

Strategies for Reaching All Students

Students Needing Extra Help
Begin the grammar section of the Organizer. Be sure that students focus on the artwork in order to help with their comprehension.
B: Students may be confused because the activities go quickly from imperfect progressive to the preterite of *poner.* Write the preterite forms of *poner* on the chalkboard to help them organize their thoughts.

C: If students are having difficulty identifying the *y* in *leyendo,* review the present participle of *comer* and other *-er* and *-ir* verbs. *Repaso: El pretérito del verbo* poner: Review *hacer* in the preterite.
Give additional examples of the use of *ponerse.* If available, refer to the grammar section of the Organizer for Book 2, Chap. 9. Ex. 1: Study the artist's studio carefully with students, identifying the objects in the room. Review object pronouns.

Extended Written Practice/Homework
1. Write four sentences saying where different members of your family put their belongings yesterday: *Mi papá puso sus llaves sobre la mesa.*
2. Write three sentences saying what different people put on and why: *Nos pusimos chaquetas porque hacía mucho viento.*

110 Standards 1.2; 3.1; 4.1

Repaso: El pretérito del verbo *poner*

Review the preterite forms of *poner*.

puse	**pusimos**
pusiste	**pusisteis**
puso	**pusieron**

- As with the preterite of *hacer*, there are no accent marks in the preterite forms of *poner*.

- The reflexive forms of *poner* have a special meaning: "to put on" and "to become."

> Paula **se puso** el abrigo antes de salir.
> *Paula **put on** an overcoat before going out.*

> Los turistas **se pusieron** serios cuando vieron la obra de Picasso.
> *The tourists **became serious** when they saw Picasso's work.*

¡NO OLVIDES!

Remember the preterite forms of *hacer: hice, hiciste, hizo, hicimos, hicisteis, hicieron.*

1 El pintor Federico González tiene mala memoria. No recuerda dónde puso sus cosas. Con un(a) compañero(a), hagan los papeles de Federico y de la persona que lo ayuda, y traten de encontrar dónde dejó sus cosas.

A — *¿Dónde puse mis llaves?*
B — *Las pusiste debajo del sofá.*

Class Starter Review

On the day following the review of the preterite forms of *poner*, you may want to begin the class with the following activity:
Say aloud several words or groups of words that would require the use of either *poner* or *ponerse*. Students will say a sentence using the correct preterite form of the verb. For example: *los libros sobre la mesa / Yo puse los libros sobre la mesa,* or: *el abrigo / Ella se puso el abrigo.*

Answers

1 ESTUDIANTE A
(Questions and answers will vary.)
¿Dónde puse mis pinceles?
. . . mi taza de café?
. . . mis zapatos?
. . . mi cepillo de dientes?
. . . mi mochila?

ESTUDIANTE B
Los puso sobre el sillón.
La puso debajo del sillón.
Los puso detrás de la mesa.
Lo puso sobre la mesa.
La puso debajo de la mesa.

Multiple Intelligences
Verbal/Linguistic
See Ex. 1 and Class Starter Review.
Visual/Spatial
See Overhead 13 and Exs. A–C.

Present & Practice

Answers

2 Answers will vary, but should begin as shown. Look for the correct preterite form of *ponerse* and adjective agreement. Remind students that they also need to supply the correct preterite form of *ver*.

a. Cuando vi la pintura, me puse ...

b. ... viste el mar, te pusiste ...

c. ... los turistas vieron la exposición de arte, se pusieron ...

d. ... mis amigos y yo vimos el desfile, nos pusimos ...

e. ... (nombre) vio el atasco, se puso ...

f. Statements will vary.

 Practice Wkbk. 3-5

 Writing Activity 3-D

 Prueba 3-5

Reteach / Review: Preterite

You may want to review preterite forms of the verbs covered in this section by doing a quick drill in which you give the personal pronoun and the appropriate present-tense conjugation of a given verb, and ask students to give the appropriate preterite form.

---

2 Describe la reacción de diferentes personas cuando vieron ciertas cosas. Forma frases usando el pretérito de *ponerse* y estos adjetivos u otros: *alegre, animado(a), furioso(a), impaciente, romántico(a)* y *triste.*

Cuando vieron el campo, mis padres se pusieron alegres.

a. yo

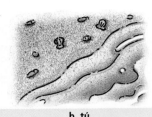
b. tú

c. los turistas

d. mis amigos y yo

e. (nombre)

f.

El pretérito de los verbos *influir* y *contribuir*

Here are the preterite forms of *influir.* *

influí	influimos
influiste	influisteis
influyó	influyeron

• Note that the *i* becomes *y* in the *Ud. /él /ella* and *Uds. / ellos /ellas* forms.

• *Contribuir* follows the same pattern. Other verbs, such as *leer,*† *creer, oír,* and *caerse,* follow a similar pattern. In these four verbs, the *i* is accented in all forms.

  —¿**Leíste** la biografía de Pablo Picasso?
  —Sí, mi amigo y yo la **leímos.**

* Verbs ending in *-uir,* such as *influir* and *contribuir,* have an accented *i* only in the preterite *yo* form.
† Here are the preterite forms of *leer: leí, leíste, leyó, leímos, leísteis, leyeron.*

112 Capítulo 3

Options

Strategies for Reaching All Students

Students Needing Extra Help

Ex. 2: If necessary, present an additional model.

El pretérito de los verbos influir *y* contribuir: Emphasize the *y* and the accent marks. Write out complete paradigms of *contribuir, leer, creer, oír,* and *caerse,* emphasizing the *y* and the accents.

Ex. 3: Give students time to match the responses before they form their answers.

Repaso: El imperfecto progresivo: If avail-able, use the grammar section of the Book 2, Chap. 10 Organizer.

Give further examples, using regular *-ar, -er,* and *-ir* verbs. Give examples using more of the verbs whose stems end in a vowel: *creer, traer, oír,* etc. Present a complete model, using the imperfect of *estar.* Give several examples of the *-ir* stem-changing verbs: *servir, seguir,* etc.

¡No olvides!: Give additional examples of attaching the object pronouns to the end of the present participle.

Enrichment

Ex. 3: As a homework assignment, have students create sentences using all forms of *contribuir* in the preterite.

Extended Written Practice/Homework

1. Write three sentences saying what differ-ent people read in the last week: *Mi entre-nador leyó la sección deportiva del periódi-co.*

3 Con un(a) compañero(a) formen frases con los elementos de las dos columnas usando el pretérito de *influir*.

Los sueños influyeron en la obra de los artistas surrealistas.

a. Su cultura
b. El mal tiempo
c. Los turistas
d. Mis hermanos y yo
e. Tú, con tus consejos
f.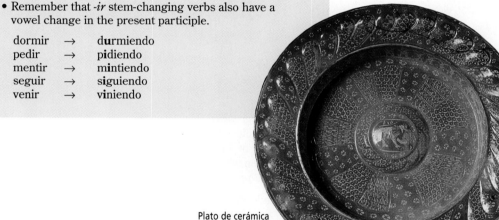

en nuestra amistad
en la decisión de nuestros padres
en el juego de Luis
en la economía del país
en los artistas hispanoamericanos

Repaso: El imperfecto progresivo

To describe something that was taking place at a certain time in the past, we use the imperfect progressive. We form this tense by using the imperfect tense forms of *estar* and the present participle.

En esa época, Velázquez **estaba pintando** retratos para la familia de Felipe IV.

• Certain verbs have irregular present participles. When the stem of an *-er* or *-ir* verb ends in a vowel, the *i* of *-iendo* usually changes to *y*.

leer → leyendo
incluir → incluyendo

• Remember that *-ir* stem-changing verbs also have a vowel change in the present participle.

dormir → d**u**rmiendo
pedir → p**i**diendo
mentir → m**i**ntiendo
seguir → s**i**guiendo
venir → v**i**niendo

Plato de cerámica española del siglo XVI

113

¡NO OLVIDES!

Do you remember the present-tense forms of *influir*?

influyo	influimos
influyes	influís
influye	influyen

¡NO OLVIDES!

Remember that direct and indirect object pronouns can go before the main verb or be attached to the end of the present participle: *Yo no **le** estaba hablando a él; estaba leyéndo**lo**.*

Answers
3 a. Su cultura influyó en los artistas hispanoamericanos.
b. El mal tiempo influyó en el juego de Luis.
c. Los turistas influyeron en la economía del país.
d. Mis hermanos y yo influimos en la decisión de nuestros padres.
e. Tú, con tus consejos, influiste en nuestra amistad.
f. Statements will vary.

Practice Wkbk. 3-6

Writing Activity 3-E

Prueba 3-6

Comm. Act. BLM 3-2

---

2. Choose three artists discussed in this chapter or whom you are familiar with and write sentences saying to which artistic movements they contributed.
3. Write three sentences describing a situation that you observed. Tell what different people were doing: *Cuando llegué a la escuela, mi novia estaba poniendo sus libros en el armario. Mis amigos estaban …*

Multiple Intelligences
Verbal/Linguistic
See Exs. 2–3.
Visual/Spatial
See Practice Wkbk. 3-5 and 3-6, Writing Activities 3-D and 3-E, and Comm. Act. BLM 3-2.

Cultural Notes

Cultural Notes

(p. 113, realia)
Spain is well known for the beauty and variety of its traditional handicrafts. Most pieces were originally intended to be functional, but became increasingly specialized and lavishly decorated. This plate, dating from the sixteenth century, demonstrates the intricacy and delicacy of patterns that are typical of crafts from the Iberian peninsula. These types of plates were first produced under Moorish rule in the thirteenth and fourteenth centuries.

Standards 1.1; 2.2; 3.1   **113**

Present & Practice

Answers

4 ESTUDIANTE A

a. ¿Qué estaban haciendo los artistas?

b. ¿Qué estaba haciendo el joven?

c. ¿Qué estaba haciendo la familia?

d. ¿Qué estaba haciendo la mujer con el bebé?

e. ¿Qué estaban haciendo los dos hombres?

f. ¿Qué estaban haciendo las dos niñas?

ESTUDIANTE B

(Answers may vary.)

a. Estaban pintando un mural.

b. Estaba dibujando.

c. Estaba mirando un retrato.

d. Estaba leyendo.

e. Estaban llevando algo a los artistas.

f. Estaban jugando.

 Practice Wkbk. 3-7, 3-8

 Writing Activity 3-F

 Prueba 3-7

 Comm. Act. BLM 3-3

4 Imagina que estabas ayer en una galería de arte con un(a) compañero(a). Pregúntale qué estaban haciendo las demás personas.

la señora de pelo canoso

A — *¿Qué estaba haciendo la señora de pelo canoso?*

B — *Estaba hablando con su esposo.*

a. los artistas
b. el joven
c. la familia
d. la mujer con el bebé
e. los dos hombres
f. las dos niñas

Repaso: El uso del pretérito y del imperfecto progresivo

We often use the preterite and the imperfect progressive together. The preterite is used to indicate a specific action that had a definite beginning and end. The imperfect progressive is used to give information about what was going on when the action happened, with no indication of a beginning or end.

El pintor **estaba terminando** su obra cuando su hija **llegó**.
*The painter **was finishing** his work when his daughter **arrived**.*

114   Capítulo 3

Options

Strategies for Reaching All Students

Students Needing Extra Help

Repaso: El uso del pretérito y del imperfecto progresivo: Give further examples.
Ex. 5: Review the placement of the pronouns and the present participle.
Point out the pronouns in a. and d.
Ex. 6: Brainstorm what each person in the painting might have been doing ten minutes before the artist started to paint.
Ahora lo sabes: Have students write this so that they can record their progress.

Enrichment

Ex. 5: Have pairs of students work together to create the beginning of a suspense story in which they set up a background situation using the imperfect progressive and then, using the preterite, have something happen that will change the situation.

Extended Written Practice/Homework

1. Write three sentences telling what people were doing when something else occurred: *Tomás estaba subiendo las escaleras cuando se cayó.*
2. Write three sentences telling what you were doing when you heard or saw different things: *Estaba duchándome cuando oí …*

5 Habla con un(a) compañero(a) sobre lo que estabas haciendo cuando ocurrieron estas cosas.

llamar amiga

A — *¿Qué estabas haciendo cuando te llamó tu amiga?*
B — *Estaba viendo la televisión.*

a. (alguien) invitarte a salir

b. (alguien) entrar en el cuarto

c. oír un ruido extraño

d. caerse

e. (alguien) volver del trabajo

6 Imagina que estabas en el taller *(workshop)* de Velázquez diez minutos antes de que el pintor comenzara a pintar *Las Meninas.* (Ve la página 99.) Describe con tu compañero(a) lo que estaba haciendo cada una de las personas.

La niña rubia de pelo largo estaba jugando cuando Velázquez comenzó a pintar.

Ahora lo sabes

¿Puedes:

■ decir dónde alguien puso algo o cómo se sintió?

—(Yo) me ___ muy triste cuando vi ese cuadro.

■ decir quién influyó a alguien o en algo?

—Norman Rockwell ___ mucho en la pintura de los Estados Unidos.

■ hablar de lo que estaba pasando cuando algo ocurrió?

—Cuando (nosotros) ___ unos cuadros, el pintor ___ a la galería.

> ### MÁS PRÁCTICA
> Más práctica y tarea, pp. 554–555
> Practice Workbook 3–5, 3–9

Gramática en contexto   115

---

5 ESTUDIANTE A
a. ¿Qué estabas haciendo cuando (nombre) te invitó a salir?
b. ...(nombre) entró en el cuarto?
c. ...oíste un ruido extraño?
d. ...te caíste?
e. ...(nombre) volvió del trabajo?
ESTUDIANTE B
a. Estaba leyendo.
b. ...durmiendo.
c. ...hablando por teléfono.
d. ...jugando fútbol.
e. ...poniendo la mesa.

6 Answers will vary, but look for correct use of the preterite and the imperfect progressive.

Answers: Ahora lo sabes
• puse
• influyó
• *(Answers may vary.)* estábamos mirando / llegó

 Practice Wkbk. 3-9

 Audio Activities 3.3, 3.4, 3.5

 Prueba 3-8

---

3. Write three sentences saying what an artist was experiencing when he or she painted a work of art: *Frida Kahlo estaba divorciándose de Diego Rivera cuando pintó* Las dos Fridas.

Multiple Intelligences
Verbal/Linguistic
See Exs. 4–6 and Audio Activities 3.3, 3.4, and 3.5.
Verbal/Linguistic and Visual/Spatial
Have students write "bubble" conversations which they imagine might be taking place in the picture on p. 114.
Visual/Spatial
See Practice Wkbk. 3-7, 3-8, and 3-9; Writing Activity 3-F; Comm. Act. BLM 3-3; and Enrichment.

Apply

Point out the key chapter question *(la pregunta clave del capítulo)*. Tell students that completing these activities will help them answer this key question. You may select one, two, or all three of these activities, as time permits.

Ex. 1: This activity can be done individually, in pairs, or in small groups. You might want to convert your classroom into an art gallery in which students play the roles of visitors to the gallery or experts who describe the paintings.

Ex. 3: To extend this exercise, have students go to the library and look for a painting they like by a Spanish or Latin American artist. Have them photocopy the painting and write a brief paragraph describing it and why they like it.

Answers: Sopa de actividades
1–3 Responses will vary, but encourage use of a wide variety of chapter vocabulary.

¿Qué nos dicen las obras de arte?

Esta sección te ofrece la oportunidad de combinar lo que aprendiste en este capítulo con lo que ya sabes para responder a la pregunta clave.

Sopa de actividades

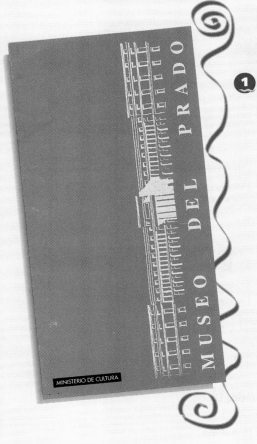

1. Prepara una presentación oral sobre una obra de arte. La obra puede ser tuya, de un amigo o de otro artista. Puedes incluir esta información:

   - el nombre del artista (o tu nombre si la obra es tuya)
   - lo que usó el artista (o usaste tú) para crear la obra (lápiz, pintura, etc.)
   - lo que se ve en el cuadro (en primer plano, al fondo, en el centro, etc.)
   - el estilo y los colores
   - en qué deben fijarse especialmente los que ven la obra
   - qué es lo que quiere decir el artista (o lo que quieres decir tú) en esta obra
   - si te gusta la obra o no
   - Si la obra es tuya, ¿qué te pareció más difícil de pintar? ¿Cómo te gustaría poder pintar?

   Si es posible, trae la obra de arte o una foto de ella a la clase. Haz una presentación para la clase o para un grupo de estudiantes.

116   Capítulo 3

Options

Strategies for Reaching All Students

Spanish-Speaking Students
Ex. 2: Have students do a variation on this exercise. *Trae dos o tres tiras cómicas (sin palabras) a clase. Escribe lo que ocurrió en una de las tiras y luego díselo a tus compañeros. Ellos deben adivinar de cuál hablas.*

Students Needing Extra Help
If time is a factor, assign either Ex. 1 or 3 in addition to Ex. 2.
Ex. 1: Students may have difficulty expressing the message of the artist. Help them with the vocabulary.
Ex. 2: Remind students that they have to use the imperfect progressive and the preterite together. Present a complete model. After adding more details, students may be ready to move on. It may not be necessary to exchange cartoons.

Cooperative Learning
In groups of four, have students imagine that they are the people in one of the paintings in the chapter, or in one of their own choosing. Have them imagine what the people were doing ten minutes before the moment captured in the painting. While some students create a physical tableau to illustrate, the group spokesperson explains the tableau to the class.

2 Busca en un periódico o libro una tira cómica *(comic strip)* que
muestre algo que estaba pasando cuando ocurrió otra cosa. Luego:

- Quita de la tira cómica todas las palabras y tráela a la clase.
- Muéstrasela a un(a) compañero(a) y explícale lo que estaba
pasando y lo que ocurrió.
- Tu compañero(a) va a hacerte preguntas sobre lo que dices
o va a añadir algo más.
- Cambia tiras cómicas con tu compañero(a) y explícale a otro(a)
estudiante qué pasa en tu nueva tira cómica.

   A —*Luisita estaba patinando. Al mismo tiempo estaba
   escuchando su tocacintas y no estaba mirando la acera.
   Un perro cruzó enfrente de ella y ella se cayó.*

   B —*Y fue al hospital con un brazo roto.*
   o: ¿Se rompió algún hueso cuando se cayó?

3 Trae a la clase una obra de arte tuya o de algún artista que
te guste. Descríbesela a un(a) compañero(a), pero no le digas
el movimiento artístico al que pertenece. Tu compañero(a) debe
adivinar a qué movimiento artístico pertenece.

Pablo Picasso decorando una
pieza de cerámica en su estudio

El pintor Rufino Tamayo
en su estudio

Sopa de actividades   117

Video Activity A

Video, Capítulo 3

Chapter 3: Play

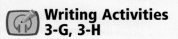

Step

Video Activities B–C

**Writing Activities
3-G, 3-H**

**Comm. Act. BLMs
3-4, 3-5**

Cultural Notes

Multiple Intelligences
Bodily/Kinesthetic and Verbal Linguistic
See Cooperative Learning.
Verbal/Linguistic
See Exs. 1 and 3.
Visual/Spatial
See Ex. 2, Writing Activities 3-G and 3-H,
and Comm. Act. BLMs 3-4 and 3-5.

(p. 117, left photo)
Considered by many to be the most influential artist of the twentieth century, Picasso
produced an enormously varied body of
work that includes paintings, drawings,
engravings, sculpture, theater designs, and
poetry. Picasso was born in Málaga in 1881
and was encouraged early to pursue art by
his father who was a professor of drawing.
The latter half of his life was spent in exile
from Spain as a protest against the dictator
Francisco Franco.

(p. 117, right photo)
Throughout his long and distinguished
career, Mexican artist Rufino Tamayo
(1899–1991) produced paintings, murals,
drawings, lithographs, and engravings in a
powerful, unique style that blended elements from pre-Columbian indigenous art
and modern, international art. Shown here
in his Mexico City studio, Tamayo continued
to work full days until a few months before
his death.

Apply

Process Reading
For a description of process reading, see p. 52.

Teaching Suggestions
Point out the key chapter question (la pregunta clave del capítulo). Tell students that working through the *Para leer* section will help them answer this question.

Encourage students to use the strategies given in the text to help them understand the reading. Remind them that they do not need to understand every word.

Tell students that, in the interview, they will see *el arte* and *las artes*. Point out that this word is masculine in the singular form, but feminine in the plural.

Bring library books on the great Mexican painters of the twentieth century to give a context to this interview. Check the audio-visual department for films or videos on twentieth-century Hispanic artists or art movements.

Answers
Antes de leer
Answers will vary, but students may mention:
La pintura *Mandolinas y piñas* es más realista porque las cosas son más o menos como los ve el artista. *Ciurana, el sendero* y *León y caballo* son más cubistas porque las formas son geométricas.

Para leer

Antes de leer

STRATEGY Using prior knowledge

Antes de leer esta entrevista, prepárate relacionando cada cuadro de abajo con el movimiento artístico que representa.

Explícale tus decisiones a un(a) compañero(a). Luego mira las respuestas en la página 103.

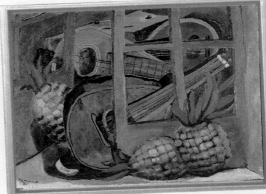

Mandolins and Pineapples (Mandolinas y piñas), (1930), Rufino Tamayo

Mira la lectura

STRATEGY Making predictions

Mira bien la obra de Tamayo de la izquierda. ¿Cómo crees que Tamayo responderá a estas preguntas? Escribe tus respuestas.

¿Dónde encuentra su inspiración?
¿En qué sentido le ayuda la naturaleza?
¿Cómo se definiría como pintor?

Ciurana, le sentier (Ciurana, el sendero), (1917), Joan Miró

Entrevista con Rufino Tamayo

A.S.   **Maestro, ¿cómo comenzó a pintar?**

R.T.   Después de la muerte de mi madre en 1907, me mudé con mi familia de Oaxaca a la Ciudad de México cuando tenía once años. En la gran ciudad comencé a dibujar copiando tarjetas postales. Fue entonces cuando, en 1917, entré en la Escuela Nacional de Bellas Artes.

A.S.   **¿Le gustaba asistir a la Escuela de Bellas Artes?**

R.T.   No, en absoluto. Era terriblemente académica. Nos enseñaban a copiar con exactitud

los modelos, y eso va en contra de toda creación. Después de tres años abandoné la Escuela y me puse a pintar por mi cuenta. En ese tiempo descubrí que en las artes populares mexicanas y en ese gran arte precolombino estaban mis raíces.

A.S.   **¿Cómo fue su vida en Nueva York?**

R.T.   Realicé mi primera exposición fuera de México en la Weybe Gallery en Nueva York, en 1926. Al principio fue muy difícil. No tenía qué comer, no hablaba el idioma, no tenía amigos; pero seguí trabajando. Mi éxito, en realidad, comenzó en la década de 1930. Nueva York (donde viví veinte años)

118   Capítulo 3

Options

Strategies for Reaching All Students

Spanish-Speaking Students
Aplicación: Have students write: *Imagina que entevistas a un(a) pintor(a) cuya obra te gusta. Escribe las preguntas que le harías. Luego, investiga la vida del (de la) pintor(a) para poder responder a las preguntas. Completa la entrevista.*

Students Needing Extra Help
Antes de leer: Review the *Tema para investigar* if necessary.

Mira la lectura: Remind students of cognates, word families, and other reading strategies that they have practiced. Remind them that they don't have to know what every word means, and that the questions in the interview should be their guide as to what the major themes are. At the end of each paragraph, have students decide its essential point. Have them take notes to reinforce what they have read.
Aplicación: Review the list of characteristics before students break into groups.

Multiple Intelligences
Interpersonal/Social
See *Aplicación.*
Visual/Spatial
See *Mira la lectura* and *Infórmate.*

Lion and Horse (León y caballo), (1942), Rufino Tamayo

me dio dos cosas importantes: en Nueva York pude ver arte de todo el mundo, y además, fue en Nueva York donde fui inicialmente reconocido internacionalmente. Más aún, fue allí donde por primera vez se notó y se habló de mi "sello mexicano": los colores, las proporciones, mi manera de representar la figura humana, todo el drama, si se puede decir así, que contiene mi obra.

A.S. **¿Dónde encuentra su inspiración?**

R.T. Considero que la naturaleza me da los elementos a partir de los cuales realizo mi obra, particularmente el hombre. El hombre es la esencia de mi trabajo.

A.S. **¿En qué sentido le ayuda la naturaleza?**

R.T. La naturaleza proporciona a los pintores todos los elementos: formas, espacios, colores . . . pero somos nosotros, los pintores, los que los transformamos, en mi caso, para hacer poesía. Considero que el color, por ejemplo, es importante en mi obra. Esos colores—el blanco de la cal, el ocre de la tierra, el siena—son los que usaban los pueblos precolombinos . . . y esos son mis colores mexicanos.

Ahora bien, para pintar las frutas necesito colores muy jugosos, tales como los anaranjados, los amarillos, los rojos, pero los rojos simples. Durante mi infancia vivía entre frutas. Ésta es la diferencia entre mis dos paletas: una es muy calma, la otra es muy luminosa.

A.S. **¿Cómo se definiría como pintor?**

R.T. Soy un realista, pero en una manera poética. Soy un realista porque en mi pintura se reconocen las formas, los objetos, pero con ellos hago poemas . . . No copio el árbol que veo en la naturaleza. Creo mi árbol. Lo mismo ocurre con la figura humana. Simplifico las cosas pero sigo comunicándome con el público. Me afectan profundamente los problemas de los seres humanos y trato de expresarlos a mi manera.

Infórmate

STRATEGY ➤ Identifying supporting details

1 Ahora lee la selección con cuidado. ¿Aparecen las frases que escribiste en las respuestas de Tamayo?

¿Cuáles de estas frases reflejan el punto de vista de Rufino Tamayo?

- El/la artista debe copiar la naturaleza.
- México influye mucho en mi arte.
- Mis obras reflejan a mi manera los problemas de los seres humanos.
- Soy un artista surrealista.
- La cosa más importante de mi trabajo es la fruta.
- Algunos de los colores que uso están inspirados en los del pueblo mexicano precolombino.

2 Mira el cuadro de arriba. ¿Qué características del estilo de Tamayo se encuentran en él?

Aplicación

Trabajen en grupos para ver cuáles de estas características se encuentran en las obras de Tamayo. Usen el texto como referencia.

- colores muy jugosos
- la naturaleza muerta
- el realismo
- el cubismo
- colores apagados
- la paleta calma
- la figura humana

Para leer 119

Mira la lectura
Answers will vary, but students may mention:
Tamayo encuentra su inspiración en la naturaleza. / La naturaleza le ayuda a decidir qué formas o colores puede usar en sus pinturas, por ejemplo, los colores de la tierra. / Se definiría como un pintor bastante realista.

Infórmate
1 *Answers will vary.* / Las frases que reflejan el punto de vista de Tamayo son: México influye mucho en mi arte. Mis obras reflejan a mi manera los problemas de los seres humanos. Algunos de los colores que uso están inspirados en los del pueblo mexicano precolombino.

2 Answers will vary, but students may mention:
Se encuentra la naturaleza, pero no en forma muy realista.

Aplicación
Se encuentran todas estas características en las obras de Tamayo.

Fondo literario
La persistencia de la memoria: El arte viviente (pp. 440–443)

www **Internet Activities**
Have students go to www.pasoapaso.com for additional activities and practice.

Standards 1.2; 2.2; 3.1; 5.1; 5.2   **119**

Apply

Process Writing
For information regarding writing portfolios, see p. 54.

Teaching Suggestions
Tell students that working through the *Para escribir* section will help them answer the key chapter question.

Answers
Articles will vary.

Para escribir

Imagina que eres un(a) reportero(a) de tu periódico escolar o de la página de los jóvenes del periódico de tu comunidad. Debes asistir a una exposición de arte y escribir sobre una de las obras que ves.

1 Primero, escoge una pintura que te gusta. Puede ser una de las pinturas incluidas en este capítulo o una de tu artista favorito(a). Luego, contesta estas preguntas. Lo que escribiste en *Reacción personal* puede servirte de ayuda.

- El (la) artista

¿Quién es?
¿Es contemporáneo o vivió en otro siglo?
¿Tuvo o tiene influencia de otros pintores? ¿De quiénes?
¿En qué estilo(s) pintó?

- La pintura

¿Qué título le puso el (la) artista?
¿Cómo es? Descríbela. Menciona detalles *(details)* específicos.
¿Qué ves en primer plano? ¿En el centro? ¿Al fondo?
¿Qué colores usó el (la) artista? ¿Son vivos, oscuros, etc.?

- La interpretación de la pintura

¿Cómo te afecta esta pintura? ¿Crees que el (la) artista tenía un motivo social o político cuando la hizo?
¿Cuál es el tema de la obra?
¿Crees que el título es apropiado? Si no, ¿qué título crees que debe tener?

Puedes usar estas palabras u otras:

a la derecha	cariño	luz
a la izquierda	claro	sombra
agitado	confuso	tranquilo
alegre	emocional	
apagado	indiferencia	

2 Ahora, usa tus notas y apuntes para escribir tu artículo. Ilústralo con una foto, una tarjeta postal o una fotocopia de la pintura. Sigue los pasos del proceso de escribir.

Options

Strategies for Reaching All Students

Students Needing Extra Help
Step 1: Assign this ahead of time so that students have ample opportunity to find something that they like. The expression *es contemporáneo* may be unfamiliar to students. Give examples. Students may have difficulty with the two tenses of *tener* used in the third question.

Refer to the *Para leer* and *Tema para investigar* for help with the questions about the influences of other painters.
Remind students that they did something similar in Ex. 6 of *¿Y qué piensas tú?* (p. 105) and in Ex. 1 in *Sopa de actividades* (p. 116). Have them review these exercises for help with the questions in *La interpretación*.

Multiple Intelligences
Bodily/Kinesthetic and Visual/Spatial
See step 2.
Visual/Spatial
See step 1.

3 Para compartir tu trabajo, puedes:

- enviarlo al periódico escolar o a un periódico publicado en español
- incluirlo en un periódico publicado en clase
- exhibirlo en la sala de clases
- incluirlo en un libro titulado *Pinturas favoritas*
- ponerlo en tu portafolio

Para escribir 121

Assess & Summarize

Test Preparation

You may want to assign parts of this section as written homework or as an in-class writing activity prior to administering the *Examen de habilidades.*

Answers

Listening

—Fíjate en este cuadro. ¿Te atrae el estilo?
—¡Qué va! Es demasiado abstracto para mí. Sólo veo muchos colores y formas que no entiendo.
—Pues, hay artistas que pintan imágenes que son del subconsciente y de los sueños. ¿No ves el perfil del artista en el fondo? Es un autorretrato desde su punto de vista.
—¡Ah, sí! ¡Claro! Ahora lo veo.
La conversación ocurre en una galería o en un museo. / Están hablando de una pintura abstracta. / El movimiento es el surrealismo.

Reading

Los primeros cuadros de Goya son de personas que conocía y de paisajes tranquilos. Pero cuando vio los problemas políticos y sociales en España, como la pobreza y la vanidad de la aristocracia, empezó a pintar escenas con colores apagados y figuras entre sombras.

Repaso ¿Lo sabes bien?

Esta sección te ayudará a prepararte para el examen de habilidades, donde tendrás que hacer tareas semejantes.

Listening

¿Puedes entender la descripción de una obra de arte? Escucha mientras el (la) profesor(a) lee un ejemplo semejante al que vas a oír en el examen. ¿Dónde ocurre esta conversación? ¿De qué tipo de pintura están hablando? ¿De qué movimiento artístico es?

Reading

Lee el siguiente folleto sobre Francisco de Goya para ayudarte a identificar algunos detalles de su obra. ¿Cuáles fueron los temas de sus primeros cuadros? ¿Qué aspectos influyeron después para cambiar la obra del artista?

Los primeros cuadros de Francisco de Goya son de personajes conocidos y de paisajes tranquilos. Le atraían las costumbres y la vida del campo. Pero las circunstancias sociales y políticas en las que se encontraba España, la vanidad de la aristocracia, la pobreza de su país y la hipocresía de la humanidad influyeron en su vida y en sus obras. En los cuadros que pintó después, Goya comenzó a usar tonos apagados y figuras que se ven entre sombras. Goya contribuyó al arte universal e influyó en los pintores de los siglos XIX y XX.

Los fusilamientos del 3 de mayo de 1808 (1814)

Writing

¿Puedes escribir un comentario semejante al que Mirasol escribió para su clase de arte?

El pintor español Salvador Dalí vivió de 1904 a 1989. Sus primeros cuadros eran impresionistas, realistas y cubistas. En algunos de estos cuadros podemos ver la influencia de Pablo Picasso. Pero él quería encontrar su propio estilo. Cuando Dalí vivía en Francia encontró inspiración en el surrealismo. Empezó a explorar temas del subconsciente. Pintó imágenes de sus propios sueños, a veces usando colores apagados y a veces colores vivos.

122 Capítulo 3

Culture

¿Cuáles son algunos temas de las obras de Diego Rivera?

Speaking

¿Puedes hablar con un(a) compañero(a) sobre una obra de arte? Aquí tienes un ejemplo:

A —*¿Cuál de los cuadros que vimos en la galería te atrae más?*

B —*El de la naturaleza muerta. Prefiero el realismo. Y a ti, ¿cuál te gustó?*

A —*Pues, el retrato abstracto de las figuras en colores vivos. ¡Me encanta el surrealismo! Sus temas me fascinan.*

B —*Pero con el realismo siempre sabemos lo que el artista quiere decir. Sin embargo, el arte abstracto . . .*

Self Test — www.pasoapaso.com

Options

Strategies for Reaching All Students

Students Needing Extra Help

Remind students that this is just a sample of what the real test will be like.
Listening: Read more than once. Write the three questions on the chalkboard.
Remind students that they need to listen for only three pieces of information.
Have them use the notes they took in the *Tema para investigar* to help them identify the artistic movement.
Reading: Remind students that they don't need to know every word.

Review strategies for finding cognates, context clues, and word families.
Have students read the questions before they start the reading.
You may want to list the questions on the chalkboard or overhead.
Writing: Have students use the Organizer and write a sample paragraph before the test as practice.
Because students did a thorough writing sample in the *Para escribir,* have them use that and summarize the information.

Culture: Have students review the notes they took in the *Álbum cultural.*
Speaking: Use the vocabulary section of the Organizer.
Limit the number of lines of dialogue.
Finish the model so that students know how to end the conversation.

Resumen del vocabulario

Usa el vocabulario de este capítulo para:

- responder a la pregunta clave: ¿Qué nos dicen las obras de arte?
- describir una obra de arte
- interpretar el mensaje de una obra de arte
- dar una opinión sobre una obra de arte

**para hablar sobre un artista
y su obra**
el /la artista
atraer
criticar *(c → qu)*
la galería
la inspiración
el mensaje
la obra (de arte)
la paleta
el pincel
la pintura
el valor

**para describir una obra
de arte**
el centro
la figura
el fondo
la forma
la imagen,
  pl. las imágenes
el primer plano
reflejado, -a
la sombra

**para hablar de diferentes
tipos de pinturas**
el autorretrato
el mural
la naturaleza muerta
el perfil
la pintura
el retrato

**para describir los colores de
una pintura**
apagado, -a
pastel
el tono
vivo, -a

**para discutir la escena de
una pintura**
abajo
arriba
de pie
junto a
sentado, -a

**para referirse a estilos
de pintura**
abstracto, -a
el cubismo
la época
el estilo
la etapa
impresionista
el movimiento
el punto de vista
el realismo
el siglo
el surrealismo
el tema

**otras palabras y
expresiones útiles**
fijarse (en)
la imaginación
interpretar
querer:
  (ellos) quisieron
el subconsciente
el sueño
transformar(se)
tratar de

Resumen 123

Cultural Notes ☀

(p. 122, photo)
Francisco Goya's (1746–1828) *El tres de
mayo de 1808* is one of the Spanish artist's
most powerful works. He expresses the sav-
agery of war he witnessed from his home
during the revolt of the *madrileños* against
French invaders at the Puerta del Sol. In one
luminous section, which dominates the
otherwise dark painting, a condemned man
raises his arms and waits to be shot, his
face contorted by terror.

CAPÍTULO 4

THEME: TELEVISION

SCOPE AND SEQUENCE Pages 124–157

COMMUNICATION

Topics
TV programs

Censorship

Objectives
Comparar la influencia de la televisión en los países hispanos con la que tiene en los Estados Unidos

Hablar de la televisión

Describir un programa de televisión

Explicar quién puede ver los programas

Discutir la influencia de la televisión

CULTURE

La influencia de la televisión en los países hispanos

GRAMMAR

El presente perfecto

Los participios pasados irregulares

Repaso: El pretérito de poder, tener, estar, decir *y* dar

Ancillaries available for use with Chapter 4

Multisensory/Technology	Print	Assessment

 Overheads, 14–15

 Audio Tapes and CDs

 Vocabulary Art Blackline Masters for Hands-On Learning, pp. 23–25/CD-ROM

 Classroom Crossword

 Video

 Internet Activities
www.pasoapaso.com

 Practice Workbook, pp. 41–50

 Writing, Audio & Video Activities, pp. 23–28, 102–104, 139–140

 Communicative Activity Blackline Masters
Pair and Small Group Activities, pp. 22–27
Situation Cards, p. 28

RESOURCE PRO®

Planning Express, Teaching Resources Library, and Clip Art Library

 Assessment Program
Pruebas, pp. 53–63
Examen de habilidades, pp. 64–67

 Test Generator

 **¿Lo sabes bien?
Video Quiz**

Video, Chap. 4

123A

La ventana que da al mundo

Since the 1950s television has greatly influenced cultures throughout the world. Documentaries and travelogues have long served as an important educational and cultural tool. Today, as the influence of Hispanic American culture grows, all types of Spanish-language programming produced in the U.S. are exerting considerable cultural influence both within and outside the U.S.

Many U.S.-produced shows are exported for viewing outside the country. "Padrísimo," a music program hosted by Raquelín González, features a variety of music styles *(Tejano, Banda, Quebradita,* and *Techno-Banda)* and is seen in several Latin American countries. The show travels to different parts of the U.S. to interview popular disc jockeys and to cover concerts.

A popular *telenovela* produced for export is "Señora Tentación," starring Lucía Méndez and including cast members from Latin America. The story, set in the fictional country of San Marcos, is filmed on location in Puerto Rico, Mexico, and the U.S.

Spanish-language television within the U.S. has been dominated by three networks: Univisión, the Telemundo Group, and Galavisión. Univisión and Telemundo focus on the needs and interests of Hispanic Americans from all regions of the U.S. Galavisión broadcasts primarily west of the Mississippi, concentrating on an audience of Mexican and Central American origin, and provides both U.S.- and Mexican-produced programming.

On December 1, 1994, Telemundo, together with Antena 3 of Spain, Artear of Argentina, and Reuters Television, launched TeleNoticias, the first 24-hour Spanish-language television news network. This network reaches approximately 8.2 million broadcast and cable viewers in Latin America. According to Gustavo Pupo-Mayo, president of TeleNoticias, their goal is "to provide Spanish-speaking people throughout the world with news and information presented from their own perspective, with the highest standards of reporting and production possible." Produced at its new facilities in Miami, TeleNoticias employs writers, reporters, technical staff, and producers from nearly every Spanish-speaking country.

Introduce

Re-entry of Concepts

The following list represents words, expressions, and grammar topics re-entered from Books 1, 2, and 3 (Chap. 3):

Book 1

numbers, time-telling, *tener que,* object pronouns, preterite, TV shows and movies, comparatives, superlatives, expressions of frequency

Book 2

imperfect, TV shows and movies

Chapter 3

past participles

Planning

Strategies for Reaching All Students

Math Connection (*pp. 134–135*)

Conduct class surveys on one or more of the following topics: violence on TV, establishing a rating system for TV, censorship for minors, and parental control over TV viewing for children. Use the survey results to calculate the percentage of students who agree or disagree with each topic. Have them display the results on different types of graphs (bar, pie).

Journalism Connection (*pp. 148–149*)

In pairs, have students write a review of the current list of movie or TV hits. Prepare a *Telerevista* or a *Cinerevista.*

Spanish in Your Community

Have students view Spanish-language television shows and commercials. Ask them to report back to class how they feel these programs may influence viewers. Then have them compare this to how English-language programs shown on U.S. networks affect their viewers.

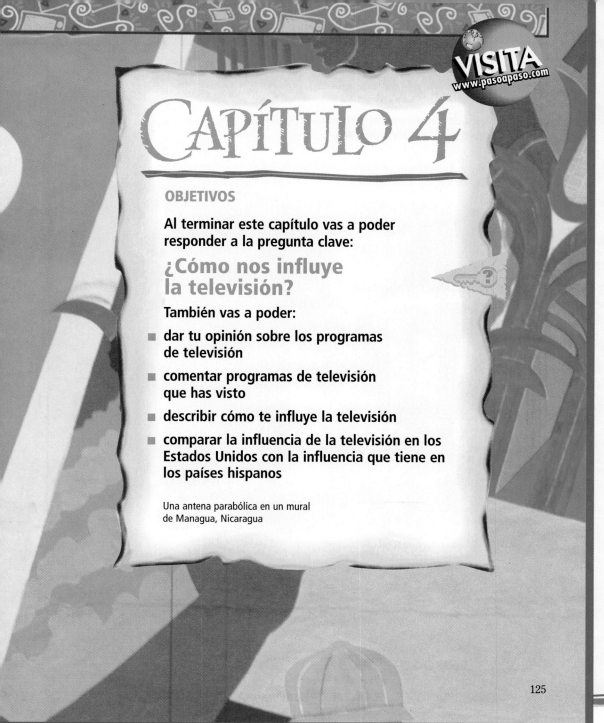

Teaching Suggestions
Point out the key chapter question *(la pregunta clave del capítulo)*. Tell students that by acquiring the new words and structures of this chapter, they will be able to answer this question.

CAPÍTULO 4

OBJETIVOS

Al terminar este capítulo vas a poder responder a la pregunta clave:

¿Cómo nos influye la televisión?

También vas a poder:

- **dar tu opinión sobre los programas de televisión**

- **comentar programas de televisión que has visto**

- **describir cómo te influye la televisión**

- **comparar la influencia de la televisión en los Estados Unidos con la influencia que tiene en los países hispanos**

Una antena parabólica en un mural de Managua, Nicaragua

125

Cultural Notes

(pp. 124–125, photo)
Mural art, particularly from twentieth-century Latin America, has traditionally had a purpose when painted by the artist. It gives a specific impression or message that educates the public about significant people, places, or events. This mural in the Nicara-guan capital of Managua uses people and a satellite dish to intermingle the past with the present.

Preview

Cultural Objective
• *Comparar la influencia de la televisión en los países hispanos con la que tiene en los Estados Unidos*

Critical Thinking: Making Comparisons
Ask students to think of as many positive and negative aspects of television as they can. Record answers under plus and minus signs on the chalkboard. Discuss the results.

Answers: Anticipación
Answers will vary, but students may mention:
Se puede alquilar videos, jugar videojuegos o ver programas de televisión por vía satélite.

Answers will vary for questions in caption text.

Using Photos
(p. 126, photo)
Ask students what they think *más adelante* means if they saw this phrase in a scene change in a television program or movie.

Anticipación

Mira las fotos. Además de ver los programas regulares, ¿cómo se puede usar la televisión?

Hoy en día muchos jóvenes pasan su tiempo libre viendo la televisión. Muchas personas creen que es mejor para los jóvenes usar ese tiempo en otras actividades, como estar con amigos o leer. ¿Cuántas horas ves tú la televisión? ¿Piensas que son demasiadas o no? ¿Por qué?

Options

Strategies for Reaching All Students

Spanish-Speaking Students
Ask: *¿Te gusta ver la televisión? ¿Qué tipos de programas prefieres? ¿Alquilas muchas películas? ¿Cuáles te gustan más, las películas románticas, las aventuras u otras?*

Students Needing Extra Help
If available, use the vocabulary sections of the Book 1, Chap. 11, and Book 2, Chap. 10 Organizers.
Encourage students to see suitable foreign films. Explain that some are dubbed, but many will have subtitles.

Multiple Intelligences
Logical/Mathematical
See Critical Thinking.

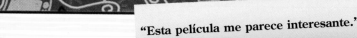

"Esta película me parece interesante."

Alquilar videos, como está haciendo este joven en una tienda de Caracas, Venezuela, también ha ganado popularidad en los países hispanos. Es posible alquilar videos de películas producidas en los Estados Unidos, pero dobladas, es decir, con los diálogos traducidos, o con subtítulos en español, además de películas producidas en países hispanos. ¿Has visto alguna película doblada o con subtítulos? ¿Cuál? ¿Por qué crees que a la gente le interesa alquilar películas con subtítulos?

Tradicionalmente, las plazas en los países hispanos son lugares públicos con bonitos jardines, fuentes y senderos. La gente va allí para caminar y conversar tranquilos y al aire libre. Pero en esta plaza en Nazca, Perú, hay cosas que no son tradicionales. ¿Qué cambios ves aquí? ¿Qué piensas de estos cambios?

Exploración cultural
www.pasoapaso.com
Visita estos países

127

Cultural Notes ☀

(p. 127, top photo)
Video stores in Venezuela are much like those in the U.S., with perhaps one great difference—the majority of movies on videotape would be in Spanish. Videos in English and other foreign languages are also available, particularly if they were hits at the box office. In most cases, these videos are released in Venezuela at the same time as in the U.S.

(p. 127, bottom photo)
The *plaza* is the nerve center of most Latin American communities, where people can find work, recruits for a political cause, or even a sweetheart—all under the watchful eyes of family and community elders. It is also the place where news is shared and discussed, be it local gossip or world events, but scenes such as the one shown in this photo are quite rare. Ask students: How might the installation of TVs in outdoor public spaces affect life in your community?

Present

Chapter Theme
Television

Communicative Objectives
- *Hablar de la televisión*
- *Describir un programa de televisión*
- *Explicar quién puede ver los programas*

 Overheads 14–15

 Vocabulary Art BLMs/CD-ROM

 Vocabulary Tape 4-1

Grammar Preview
The present perfect tense is presented here lexically. Its explanation is found on pp. 143–144.

Teaching Suggestions
Preparing students to speak: Use one or two options from each of the categories of Comprehensible Input or Limited Verbal Response. For a complete explanation of these categories and some sample activities, see pp. T20–T21.

Remind students that they learned *el comentario* in Book 2, Chap. 10.

Vocabulario para comunicarse

¿Qué programas grabas?

Aquí tienes palabras y expresiones necesarias para hablar sobre la televisión. Después de leerlas varias veces, practícalas con un(a) compañero(a).

el noticiero

cambiar de canal

el comentario

"En mi opinión..."

500 GRAMOS
400 GRAMOS
200 GRAMOS

bostezar (z → c)*

reírse (e → i)

* Remember that verbs ending in *-zar* have a spelling change *(z → c)* in the *yo* form of the preterite: *bostecé*.

128   Capítulo 4

Options

Strategies for Reaching All Students

Spanish-Speaking Students
¿Qué significan los círculos en cada cartel? ¿Son importantes? ¿Por qué sí o no? ¿Por qué crees que tienen esa clasificación?

Students Needing Extra Help
Begin the vocabulary section of the Organizer. Point out cognates and word families: *el noticiero (la noticia)*. Write out the paradigms for the different tenses of *bostezar* and *reírse*.
También necesitas . . . : Emphasize the meanings of *dieron* and *he / has visto* rather than the conjugations. Give example sentences with *la multa*.
¿Y qué quiere decir . . . ?: Explain the concept for the terms *objetivo* and *subjetivo*.

Enrichment
Discuss students' TV and video viewing habits. Sample questions might include: *¿Qué noticiero ves todos los días? ¿Por qué te gusta ese noticiero? ¿Quiénes son los locutores? ¿Alquilas videos frecuentemente? ¿Dónde los alquilas?*

También necesitas . . .

demasiado, -a	here: *too many*	la multa	*fine*
dieron (*from:* dar)	*they gave*	recientemente	*recently*
emocionarse	*to be moved, touched*	el reportaje	*report*
he visto } (*from:* ver)	*I have seen,*		
has visto	*you have seen*		

¿Y qué quiere decir . . . ?

informativo, -a
negativo, -a
positivo, -a
objetivo, -a

subjetivo, -a
la televisión por cable
la televisión por satélite

la antena parabólica

Prohibida para menores

"uno, dos, tres..."

Se recomienda discreción

grabar

Sólo para mayores

Apta para toda la familia

alquilar

VIDEOS $4 POR DÍA

Extended Written Practice/Homework
1. Write sentences telling why you like or do not like certain types of TV programs: *No me gustan los programas de entrevistas porque son demasiado subjetivos.*
2. Write two pairs of sentences naming programs or movies that they showed on TV. Tell how you reacted to them: *Anoche dieron un programa educativo sobre las serpientes. Me interesó mucho.*

3. Write sentences saying if you did the following recently: *grabar una película, alquilar un video, pagar una multa.*

Practice

Answers: Empecemos a conversar

1 ESTUDIANTE A
Para ti, ¿qué programas son los más . . . ? *(Answers will vary, but may include:* divertidos, informativos, objetivos, subjetivos, positivos, negativos, violentos.*)*

ESTUDIANTE B
Answers will vary. Suggested items include:
los dibujos animados, las comedias, los programas de entrevistas, las telenovelas, los noticieros, las películas de aventuras

2 ESTUDIANTE A
a. ¿Vemos la entrevista con el presidente o el reportaje sobre África?
b. . . . el documental sobre gatos o la telenovela?
c. . . . el pronóstico del tiempo o el fútbol?
d. . . . el comentario o el programa educativo?
e. . . . el noticiero o el programa musical?
f. Questions will vary.

ESTUDIANTE B
a.–f. Answers will vary, but look for logical responses and correct adjective agreement.

Empecemos a conversar

Túrnate con un(a) compañero(a) para ser *Estudiante A* y *Estudiante B*. Reemplacen las palabras subrayadas con palabras representadas o escritas en los recuadros.
🔆 quiere decir que puedes escoger tu propia respuesta.

1 A —*Para ti, ¿qué programas son los más <u>violentos</u>?*
  B —*Las películas de terror y, algunas veces, los noticieros.*

Estudiante A

divertido, -a
informativo, -a
objetivo, -a
subjetivo, -a
positivo, -a
negativo, -a
violento, -a

Estudiante B

2 la comedia / el noticiero
  A —*¿Vemos <u>la comedia</u> o <u>el noticiero</u>?*
  B —*<u>La comedia</u>. Me gustan los programas <u>divertidos</u>.*
  A —*<u>Podemos grabar el noticiero, si quieres</u>.*

Estudiante A

a. la entrevista con el presidente / el reportaje sobre África
b. el documental sobre gatos / la telenovela
c. el pronóstico del tiempo / el fútbol
d. el comentario / el programa educativo
e. el noticiero / el programa musical
f.

Estudiante B

130 Capítulo 4

Options

Strategies for Reaching All Students

Spanish-Speaking Students
Exs. 1–4: Pair bilingual and non-bilingual students, if possible.

Students Needing Extra Help
Ex. 1: Review adjective endings.
Ex. 2: Brainstorm possibilities for the *Estudiante B* response.
Ex. 3: Review the meaning of the rating system. Brainstorm responses for movies with one and three dots. Determine if students would prefer another rating system and allow them to create one.
Ex. 4: Review preterite forms. Remind students that the object pronoun *la* will change according to the program being discussed.

Enrichment
Ex. 1: To extend this exercise, have students ask each other about specific programs they like within each type of program.
Ex. 4: As a homework assignment, have students write about one of the kinds of programs that they have seen recently. Have them begin by telling their reaction to the program and then go into as much detail as possible regarding the program's content and why they reacted to it as they did.

3

El hombre
de dos cabezas

A — *Voy a alquilar El hombre de dos cabezas.*
B — *No puedes, es prohibida para menores.*

Estudiante A

La guerra de los planetas

El gato travieso

a.

b.

Amor de verano

c.

¡DESAPARECIDO!

d.

EL VIEJO OESTE

e.

Estudiante B

4

El tío Pepito

A — *¿Qué te pareció la comedia que dieron anoche?*
B — *Muy aburrida. Bostecé todo el tiempo.*
  o: *Excelente. Me reí mucho.*
  o: *No la vi. Vi el comentario.*

¡NO OLVIDES!

Remember that *reírse* is similar to *pedir* in the preterite. Both verbs have stem changes in the *Ud./él/ella* and *Uds./ellos/ellas* forms: *Los muchachos se rieron durante la película.*

Estudiante A

Romance de primavera

a.

Los mejores días

b.

¡S.O.S.!

c.

"En mi opinión..."

d.

AVENTURA en las RUINAS

e.

Hablando con Olivia

f.

g.

Estudiante B

bostezar

cambiar de canal

divertirse

emocionarse

llorar

reírse

g.

Vocabulario para comunicarse   131

---

3 ESTUDIANTE A
a. Voy a alquilar *La guerra de los planetas.*
b. ... *El gato travieso.*
c. ... *Amor de verano.*
d. ... *¡Desaparecido!*
e. ... *El viejo oeste.*

ESTUDIANTE B
a. No puedes, se recomienda discreción.
b. Bueno, es apta para toda la familia.
c. No puedes, es prohibida para menores.
d. No puedes, es sólo para mayores.
e. No puedes, se recomienda discreción.

4 ESTUDIANTE A
a. ¿Qué te pareció la película romántica que dieron anoche?
b. ... la telenovela ...
c. ... el programa de hechos de la vida real ...
d. ... el comentario ...
e. ... la película de aventuras ...
f. ... el programa de entrevistas ...
g. Questions will vary.

ESTUDIANTE B
a.–g. Answers will vary, but look for logical responses, correct verb forms, and adjective agreement.

Extended Written Practice/Homework
1. Write sentences naming a current movie of each classification shown on p. 129. Indicate whether or not you have seen the movie.
2. Write sentences telling when you do the following while watching TV or movies: *cambiar de canal, bostezar, emocionarse, reírse.*

Multiple Intelligences
Verbal/Linguistic
See Exs. 1–4.
Visual/Spatial
1) See Enrichment Ex. 4.

2) Make lists of movies made in the U.S. and of the titles that are used in the Spanish translations of the same movies. *(My Best Friend's Wedding/La boda de mi mejor amigo; Home Alone/Solo en casa; As Good as It Gets/Mejor, imposible).* Have students match movies with their Spanish counterparts. Explain that titles are not always translated literally.

Practice & Apply

Teaching Suggestions
Ex. 5: Make sure students refer to the TV listings on p. 132.

Answers: Empecemos a conversar

5 ESTUDIANTE A
Statements will vary. Students may choose from the following: un documental, un reportaje, una película de terror, un noticiero, un video musical, un pronóstico del tiempo.

ESTUDIANTE B
Questions or statements will vary.

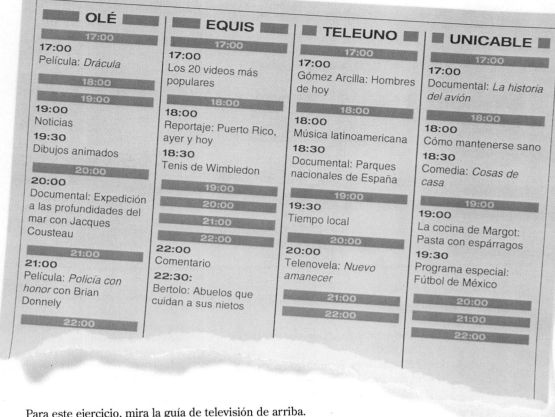

OLÉ

17:00
17:00
Película: *Drácula*

18:00

19:00
19:00
Noticias
19:30
Dibujos animados

20:00
20:00
Documental: Expedición a las profundidades del mar con Jacques Cousteau

21:00
21:00
Película: *Policía con honor* con Brian Donnely

22:00

EQUIS

17:00
17:00
Los 20 videos más populares

18:00
18:00
Reportaje: Puerto Rico, ayer y hoy
18:30
Tenis de Wimbledon

19:00

20:00

21:00

22:00
22:00
Comentario
22:30:
Bertolo: Abuelos que cuidan a sus nietos

TELEUNO

17:00
17:00
Gómez Arcilla: Hombres de hoy

18:00
18:00
Música latinoamericana
18:30
Documental: Parques nacionales de España

19:00
19:30
Tiempo local

20:00
20:00
Telenovela: *Nuevo amanecer*

21:00

22:00

UNICABLE

17:00
17:00
Documental: *La historia del avión*

18:00
18:00
Cómo mantenerse sano
18:30
Comedia: *Cosas de casa*

19:00
19:00
La cocina de Margot: Pasta con espárragos
19:30
Programa especial: Fútbol de México

20:00

21:00

22:00

Para este ejercicio, mira la guía de televisión de arriba.

5 A — *Quisiera ver <u>un programa deportivo</u>.*
   B — *¿Por qué no ves <u>el fútbol de México a las 19:30 en UNICABLE</u>?*
       o: No dan lo que quieres ver en ningún canal esta noche.

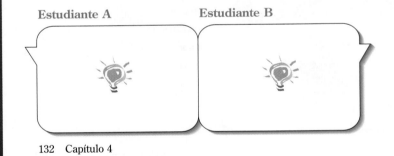

Estudiante A

Estudiante B

132   Capítulo 4

Options

Strategies for Reaching All Students

Spanish-Speaking Students
Ex. 5: Ask: *¿Qué haces primero, ver la televisión o estudiar? ¿Te limitan la televisión tus padres? ¿Por qué?*

Students Needing Extra Help
Ex. 5: Read through the TV listing as a class before beginning the activity. Show students that there is more than one choice for some of the program categories.

Cooperative Learning
In groups of four, assign each student one of the ratings: *Apta para toda la familia, Prohibida para menores, Se recomienda discreción, Sólo para mayores.* Ask them to think of one or two movies or television shows that fit their category. Have individuals briefly describe the movie or show and tell the category. Have other groups then guess the title based on the description and category name.

¿Y qué piensas tú?

Aquí tienes otra oportunidad para usar el vocabulario de este capítulo.

6 ¿Cuál es el mejor programa de televisión que has visto recientemente? ¿Lo grabaste? ¿Y el peor? ¿Qué clase de programas eran?

7 ¿Cuál es tu canal favorito? ¿Qué clase de programas ofrece? ¿Por qué te gusta tanto? ¿Les gusta también a tus padres o prefieren otro? ¿Por qué?

8 ¿Qué clase de películas te gusta alquilar? ¿Las alquilas frecuentemente? ¿Tienes que pagar una multa si no devuelves un video a tiempo? ¿Cuánto?

9 ¿Cuál es el peor anuncio que has visto recientemente? ¿Cómo es? ¿Por qué no te gusta?

10 ¿Cuántas horas ves la televisión cada día? ¿Cuántas horas crees que son demasiadas? ¿Por qué?

11 En grupos de tres hablen sobre los programas de televisión que vieron anoche o durante el fin de semana. Pueden hablar de qué canales vieron, qué clase de programas eran y qué les parecieron. ¿Hay alguien en tu grupo que pueda ver la televisión por satélite? Si la respuesta es sí, ¿le gusta? ¿Qué tipo de programas dan?

También se dice

las noticias
el noticiario

Para todo público
Para todos los públicos
Tolerada

Sólo para adultos

www.pasoapaso.com

MÁS PRÁCTICA

Más práctica y tarea, p. 556
Practice Workbook 4–1, 4–2

133

Cultural Notes

Multiple Intelligences
Intrapersonal/Introspective
See Exs. 6–11.
Verbal/Linguistic
See Ex. 5 and Audio Activity 4.1.
Verbal/Linguistic and Interpersonal/Social
See Cooperative Learning.
Visual/Spatial
See Students Needing Extra Help, Practice Wkbk. 4-1 and 4-2, and Writing Activities 4-A and 4-B.

(p. 133, realia)
This ad for a clothing store in Spain catches the reader's attention both visually and by its play on words, *"mono / stereo."*

Standards 1.1; 1.2   **133**

Present

Chapter Theme
The influence of television

Communicative Objectives
• *Explicar quién puede ver los programas*
• *Discutir la influencia de la televisión*

 Vocabulary Tape 4-2

Teaching Suggestions
Getting ready to speak:
Remind students of the reading strategies that they learned (getting meaning from context and coping with unknown words) to help them understand the *Tema para investigar.* For further details and some sample activities, see pp. T24–T25.

Answers: Tema para investigar
Answers will vary, but may include:
una comedia, un programa educativo, etc.

Tema para investigar

Aquí tienes más palabras e ideas que te ayudarán a hablar sobre la televisión. Mira las ilustraciones. ¿Qué clase de programas se muestran? ¿Cuáles ves tú con más frecuencia?

134   Capítulo 4

Options

Strategies for Reaching All Students

Spanish-Speaking Students
Tell students: *Escribe oraciones originales con diez de las palabras del vocabulario de esta sección.*

Students Needing Extra Help
Be sure students understand that they are responsible for the vocabulary in boldface. Remind students to use the reading strategies they know when reading the *Tema para investigar* before consulting the end Vocabulary.

¿Y qué quiere decir . . . ?: Point out that the accent in *opinión* is dropped in the plural. Write the present-tense forms of *evaluar* on the chalkboard or overhead transparency: *evalúo, evalúas, evalúa; evaluamos, evaluáis, evalúan.*

Extended Written Practice/Homework
1. Write three sentences saying how different types of programs affect TV viewers: *Los programas deportivos entretienen a los aficionados de los deportes.*

2. Write three sentences saying if you and your friends or family do the following: *analizar los anuncios y noticieros, evaluar las películas recientes, tener derecho a escoger los programas.*
3. Write three sentences saying what you consider to be the benefits or harm related to watching TV and movies.

134 Standards 3.1; 4.2

La televisión y tú

Con el tiempo, la televisión se ha convertido en el medio principal de recibir información. Como resultado, su influencia en la forma de reportar las noticias, en los productos que compramos y en los candidatos políticos que escogemos es cada vez mayor. ¿De qué otras maneras nos influye la televisión?

Muchas personas piensan que la televisión es una mala influencia, especialmente los programas violentos. **Se ha dicho** que estos programas **hacen daño**, y que los jóvenes que los ven son más violentos. También se ha dicho que la televisión ofrece programas que simplemente **entretienen**, pero que no reflejan la vida **tal como** es. Muchos aceptan lo que les muestra la televisión sin pensar en más. Por ejemplo, algunos programas de entrevistas y algunos anuncios tratan de **manipular** al **público** y contribuyen a formar una **opinión** negativa.

Hay personas que consideran que la televisión es uno de los medios más efectivos para la educación en la sociedad de hoy, y por lo tanto les gustaría incluir clases sobre el uso de la televisión como parte del currículum. Estas clases enseñarán a los estudiantes a ver la televisión de una manera más **crítica**, **analizando** los programas, anuncios y noticieros, y los mensajes que éstos presentan. Clases como éstas ofrecen una forma de **evaluar** cómo lo que los jóvenes ven en la televisión influye en su **percepción** del mundo y les enseña a formar su propia opinión.

Otras personas creen que nadie **ha comprobado** la relación entre la violencia y la televisión. Además, ¿quién va a decidir qué programas son violentos y cómo van a **clasificarlos**? A este grupo **la censura** le da tanto miedo como los programas violentos. Piensan que el público debe tener **derecho** a escoger los programas que quiere ver. Dicen que hay que darles a los padres la información que necesitan para decidir qué van a ver ellos y sus hijos.

Posiblemente lo que se debe **controlar** es cuánto tiempo se ve la televisión y el tipo de programas que debemos ver. ¿Qué crees tú? ¿Piensas que la televisión tiene aspectos positivos y negativos? ¿Cómo te influye a ti?

se ha dicho (*from:* decir)	*it has been said*	crítico, -a	*critical*
hacer daño	here: *to be harmful*	comprobar *(o → ue)*	*to prove*
entretener(se) *(e → ie)**	*to amuse (oneself)*	la censura	*censorship*
tal como	*such as*	el derecho	*right*
el público	*viewers, public*		

¿Y qué quiere decir . . . ?

manipular	la percepción
la opinión, *pl.* las opiniones	clasificar *(c → qu)*
analizar *(z → c)*	controlar
evaluar *(u → ú)*†	

*Entretener follows the pattern of tener.
†Evaluar follows the pattern of actuar.

Class Starter Review
On the day following the presentation of the *Tema para investigar,* you might want to begin the class with this activity:
Give oral definitions in Spanish of the new vocabulary words. Have students guess the word. For example: *Cuando digo lo que pienso, doy mi ___ (opinión).* After you have given several examples, have students take turns giving definitions.

www Internet Activities
Juegos
Have students go to www.pasoapaso.com for additional activities and practice.

Cultural Notes ☼

Multiple Intelligences
Musical/Rhythmic
Have students in pairs select a well-known television program and, without having to change the melody, write a theme song for the show.
Verbal/Linguistic
See Vocabulary Tape 4-2 and Class Starter Review.
Visual/Spatial
See *Tema para investigar.*

(p. 134, top right photo)
This educational television program comes from Palma, the capital of the Spanish island of Mallorca. One of Spain's wealthiest cities, Palma is famous for its sophisticated nightlife which, along with the island's spectacular scenery, helps make it a favorite vacation spot for Europeans. It is also renowned for its Old Quarter, where buildings from as early as the thirteenth century, including a Gothic cathedral, have been well preserved.

(p. 134, top left photo)
The situation comedy *Corte Tropical* is produced for Univisión, one of the leading U.S. Spanish-language television networks. Univisión broadcasts continually and offers mainly *telenovelas,* news programs, and talk, variety, and comedy shows. About 44 percent of Univisión's programs are based in the U.S. This percentage is expected to rise with the network's continuing success and expansion.

Practice & Apply

Answers: ¿Comprendiste?

1–2 Answers will vary, but students may mention the following: La televisión nos influye en la forma de reportar las noticias, en los productos que compramos y en los candidatos políticos que escogemos. / *Answers will vary.*

Answers: ¿Y qué piensas tú?

3 Answers will vary, but may include the following; La televisión nos divierte con las comedias, nos informa con las noticias y nos enseña con los programas educativos.

4–7 Answers will vary.

¿Comprendiste?

1 Según la lectura, ¿de qué formas nos influye la televisión? ¿Estás de acuerdo? ¿Por qué?

2 ¿Cuáles son otros aspectos de la televisión? Para ti, ¿cuál es el más importante? ¿Por qué?

¿Y qué piensas tú?

Aquí tienes otra oportunidad para usar el vocabulario de este capítulo.

3 ¿Con qué clase de programas nos divierte la televisión? ¿Con qué clase de programas nos informa? ¿Cómo nos la televisión?

4 ¿Cuáles son los programas de televisión más violentos que puedes ver donde vives? ¿Cómo te influyen? ¿Crees que existe una relación entre la televisión y la violencia? ¿Por qué?

5 ¿Se debe tener derecho a controlar los programas que ven los jóvenes? ¿Crees que los niños deben tener derecho a decidir qué programas van a ver o son los padres los que deben escoger?

6 Describe un noticiero o un reportaje que has visto recientemente y di por qué crees que fue o no fue objetivo.

MÁS PRÁCTICA

- Más práctica y tarea, p. 557
- Practice Workbook 4–3, 4–4

UNIDOS POR LA ONDA MUSICAL

SON LAS TRES DE LA mañana en Santo Domingo, en Asunción o en cualquier ciudad de América Latina. La abuelita está desvelada y enciende el televisor. Aparece Madonna cantando *Justify my love* en medio de unas escenitas que le quitan el sueño a cualquiera. La abuelita se espanta y cambia el canal, pero a esa hora no hay más nada, así que regresa al que la había asustado. Y como de alguna forma hay que pasar la noche, despierta al abuelito para verla juntos.

¿Increíble? Pues no... A partir de octubre, MTV inaugurará una cadena en español que transmitirá 24 horas diarias a Latinoamérica y EE UU. Estará ubicada en Miami y su objetivo no será la abuelita, sino el grupo de televidentes entre 12 y 34 años.

"La situación de la televisión por cable en América Latina es similar a la de EE UU hace 10 años", dice Barbara Corcoran, productora ejecutiva de MTV Internacional y una persona clave del nuevo proyecto. "Queremos entrar temprano a ese mercado", señala. Los planes inmediatos son alcanzar 3 millones de casas en Latinoamérica—en especial en Argentina y México—que ya tienen cable.

"Nuestro mercado principal será América Latina", dice Corcoran. También quieren llegar a los hispanos en EE UU, y contratarán a 35 personas en Miami ("todos hispanos") y reporteros en América Latina.

Tendrán una mezcla de música en español y en inglés, conciertos y especiales desde Latinoamérica. Esto dará, dice Corcoran, oportunidades a artistas latinoamericanos—de los de la nueva ola, no de los que le devolverían el sueño a la abuelita.

—*Albor Ruiz*

Options

Strategies for Reaching All Students

Spanish-Speaking Students
Exs. 3–4: Have students write these exercises.

Students Needing Extra Help
Ex. 1: Have students make a two-column chart for the positive and negative points of view. Accept simple responses to the *¿Por qué?* question.

Ex. 3: If available, use the vocabulary sections of the Book 1, Chap. 11, and Book 2, Chap. 10 Organizers.
Ex. 4: If students have difficulty with the *¿Por qué?* question, refer them to the reading.
Ex. 6: You might want to have students respond as a class, to include those who do not regularly watch the news.

Ex. 7: (item d.) Students are not always aware when they are being manipulated. Discuss how some talk shows try to do this. *¿Qué sabes ahora?:* Have students write this so that they can record their progress.

Enrichment
Ex. 4: Have students work in groups of three or four to act out the worst commercials they have seen. Allow time for students to discuss how they will present each commercial, assign roles, etc.

7 Un canal de televisión quiere saber qué clase de programas les gusta más a los jóvenes.

- Haz una encuesta entre tus compañeros de clase sobre sus programas favoritos. Luego, escribe los resultados en la pizarra. Puedes hacer una tabla como la siguiente con los resultados.

Programa	De qué se trata	Por qué nos gusta

- Haz lo mismo con los peores programas.

- Con las respuestas a estas preguntas, escribe un informe sobre los resultados de la encuesta y envíalo al canal.

a. ¿Cuál es el programa más popular?

b. ¿Qué clase de programas son más populares? ¿Por qué?

c. ¿Qué programas informan al público? ¿Son tan populares como los que no informan al público?

d. En tu opinión, ¿cuáles son los programas que manipulan al público?

e. ¿Qué clase de programas son menos populares? ¿Por qué?

f. ¿Son todos de la misma clase o hay varias clases de programas?

¿Qué sabes ahora?

¿Puedes:

- decir lo que hace la televisión?

  —La televisión nos ___ con programas ___ .

- decir lo que debe hacer la televisión?

  —Pienso que la televisión debe ___ y no debe ___ .

- describir cómo te influye la televisión?

  —La televisión tiene una influencia ___ en mí porque ___ .

- describir un programa de televisión que has visto?

  —He visto ___ . Trataba de ___ . (No) Me gustó porque ___ .

¡NO OLVIDES!

Remember that we say *dar un programa / una película*.

Giselle Fernandez, presentadora del programa de entrevistas *Café Olé*

Tema para investigar   137

Answers: ¿Qué sabes ahora?

• All answers will vary.

 Practice Wkbk. 4-3, 4-4

 Audio Activity 4.2

 Writing Activity 4-C

 Pruebas 4-3, 4-4

 Comm. Act. BLM 4-1

Cultural Notes ☼

Multiple Intelligences
Bodily/Kinesthetic and Verbal/Linguistic
See Enrichment.
Verbal/Linguistic
See Audio Activity 4.2.
Visual/Spatial
See Practice Wkbk. 4-3 and 4-4, Writing Activity 4-C, and Comm. Act. BLM 4-1.

(p. 136, realia)
MTV Internacional is a one-hour mix of Spanish- and English-language rock videos, interviews with musicians, and concert clips. Seen in North and South America by millions of viewers every week, the program was launched in 1988 by Telemundo. Based on the tremendous success of this program, MTV's 24-hour Spanish cable network, announced in this article, should also do very well.

(p. 137, photo)
Starting as a local anchorperson in Chicago, Giselle Fernandez rose through the ranks of the CBS news system and later NBC, earning five Emmies for her international news coverage. She currently co-hosts *Access Hollywood* on NBC as well as *Café Olé*, the first English-language talk show on the Hispanic cable network Galavisión. Fernandez also is developing her own production company, where she hopes to produce shows that appeal to both Hispanic and Anglo audiences.

Present & Apply

Cultural Objective

• *Comparar la influencia de la televisión en los países hispanos con la que tiene en los Estados Unidos*

Critical Thinking: Formulating Appropriate Questions

Divide the class into groups of three or four. Tell students that they are television programming executives who need to gather information about teenage viewers and their viewing habits so that they can plan several new shows for their network. Have each group devise a short questionnaire that will help them make their programming decisions. (Provide a model or several ideas.) Students should then ask several friends to fill out the questionnaires. Remind them that they can interview in English, but must present the information in Spanish.

Using Realia

Ask students to scan the television listings in *TV CABLE INTERCOM* on this page. What shows, if any, are they familiar with? What programs are shown from other foreign countries? *(televisión italiana, ... francesa, ... argentina, ... alemana)*

ÁLBUM CULTURAL

Gracias a la televisión por cable y vía satélite podemos saber en poco tiempo lo que ocurre en cualquier parte del mundo. ¿De qué manera influye en nuestra manera de pensar el poder ver tantos programas diferentes?

138   Capítulo 4

Options

Strategies for Reaching All Students

Students Needing Extra Help
When talking about cable TV, VCRs, and so on, be aware that some students may come from families who cannot afford these items or services.

Multiple Intelligences
Logical/Mathematical
See Critical Thinking.
Visual/Spatial
See Using Realia.

Los programas de televisión de Venezuela son muy populares en otros países hispanos. En los estudios de televisión de Caracas se producen comedias, telenovelas y otros programas para públicos de todo el continente.

In some Spanish-speaking countries, the influence of television and radio is totally or partially controlled by the government. In Cuba, for example, television and radio broadcasts on all channels are government-controlled and are subject to strict censorship laws. In Spain, most television stations are owned by the State, but the number of private channels is growing. The latter is subject to uniform broadcast standards, but not censorship. Peruvian radio and television are almost equally divided between privately owned and government-owned channels. By contrast, Paraguayan broadcasting is completely privatized, as in the U.S. It is guaranteed free from censorship by the Paraguayan Constitution. Discuss with students how they think U.S. television would change if it were controlled by the government.

La televisión por cable es cada día más popular en todo el mundo. En Chile, el sistema TV Cable Intercom permite que el público vea programas de otros países como España, Italia, Francia y Alemania, además de los producidos en Chile. También pueden recibir programas de estaciones de los Estados Unidos, como *HBO Olé, MTV Internacional* y *Discovery.*

Álbum cultural 139

Cultural Notes ☀

(p. 139, photo)
Television commercials in Hispanic countries, such as this one being filmed in Caracas, are often as slick as those produced in the U.S. Yet perhaps the most sophisticated Hispanic commercials are those shown on the Spanish-language networks in the U.S. These often feature evocative music and appealing actors, who are presented as assimilated yet still proudly Hispanic.

Present & Apply

Critical Thinking: Evaluating Information

Have the groups from the activity on p. 138 compile the results of the surveys. Ask each group what types of shows would be of interest to teenagers. If time permits, have each group use the results of their surveys to develop a title and short description of a new show for their network.

Answers: Reacción personal

1 Answers will vary, but students may mention:
Las ventajas de recibir programas de televisión de otros países son: se puede escuchar español y ver programas de otras culturas. / *Answers will vary.*

2 Los candidatos pueden hablar al público. / *Answers will vary.*

3 Answers will vary.

www Internet Activities

Álbum cultural
Have students go to www.pasoapaso.com for additional activities and practice.

Hispasat, primer satélite español.

APUESTA POR EL SATELITE

ALGUNOS «LOCOS» FANtásticos se han empeñado en demostrar que el futuro de las comunicaciones no está en el cable de fibra óptica ni en la telefonía celular, sino en los satélites. El banco de inversiones británico Baring Securities estima que en el año 2005 las comunicaciones por satélite generarán un negocio superior a los seis billones de pesetas. Los dos proyectos de comunicaciones por satélite más ambiciosos (pretenden transmitir, además de voz, imagen y datos), son éstos:
Teledesic: Tiene como padrino financiero a Bill Gates, primera fortuna personal de Estados Unidos, creador y presidente de Microsoft, líder mundial en *software*. Le acompaña en la aventura Craig McCaw, fundador de MacCaw Cellular Communications, primera operadora en telefonía móvil. Con 840 satélites que cubran todo el globo terráqueo a partir del año 2001, Teledesic pretende dar servicio de telefonía, datos, imagen, telemedicina y teleeducación. La odisea costará más de un billón de pesetas.
Iridium: Es un proyecto más modesto que Teledesic en cuanto a inversión: cerca de 500.000 millones, pero más realista. Sus servicios de telefonía global (voz, datos, fax y radiobúsqueda) se comercializarán a partir de 1998. Liderado por Motorola, primer fabricante de teléfonos móviles, con la participación de otras 14 multinacionales, Iridium emplea ya a 600 personas.

Hispasat, el primer satélite español para comunicaciones, fue lanzado en septiembre de 1992 y ha llevado programas de televisión y otros servicios a distintos países. Algunas personas piensan que los satélites tendrán más influencia en las telecomunicaciones del futuro que la televisión por cable. Proyectos como *Teledesic* e *Iridium* exploran las distintas posibilidades para el uso del satélite.

140   Capítulo 4

Options

Strategies for Reaching All Students

Students Needing Extra Help
Reacción personal: If necessary, help students with the double infinitive phrase in question 1.

Multiple Intelligences
Intrapersonal/Introspective
See Exs. 1–3.

La televisión en Colombia fue muy importante para los candidatos en las elecciones presidenciales de 1998, que fueron muy reñidas *(hard fought)*. Aquí ves a Andrés Pastrana, el candidato del partido *(party)* conservador, que fue elegido presidente con el 50.6 por ciento de los votos en una segunda vuelta *(round)* electoral entre él y Horacio Serpa, el candidato del partido liberal.

La televisión no sólo nos muestra campañas políticas, sino cualquier tipo de elección donde se decida sobre un asunto importante para el país. Por ejemplo, estas mujeres en Santiago, Chile, esperan para votar en el plebiscito del 5 de octubre de 1988. Un plebiscito es una elección especial para decidir cosas de importancia.

Reacción personal

Contesta las siguientes preguntas en una hoja de papel.

1 ¿Qué ventajas tiene poder recibir programas de televisión de otros países? ¿Te gustaría poder recibir estos programas? ¿Por qué?

2 ¿Por qué o por qué no crees que los satélites tendrán más influencia que la televisión por cable? ¿Qué otros usos podrán tener los satélites?

3 ¿Cómo se usa la televisión en una campaña *(campaign)* electoral? ¿Crees que la televisión influye en el resultado de esas campañas? ¿Cómo? ¿Conoces alguna elección especial? ¿Qué se decidía en esa elección? ¿Cómo se usó la televisión en esa elección?

Álbum cultural 141

Cultural Notes ☼

(p. 141, top photo)
Andrés Pastrana was elected president in June 1998, ending the Liberal Party's twelve-year grip on the presidency. Much of Pastrana's campaign hinged on incumbent president Ernesto Samper's alleged ties to the Cali drug cartel, but decades of political scandal, economic crisis, and bloody civil war also had undermined Pastrana's own Conservative Party.

(p. 141, bottom photo)
During the October, 1988 plebiscite, voters in Santiago, Chile, rejected the rule of General Augusto Pinochet and his military *junta* (council). All Chilean citizens over 18 who meet a certain literacy qualification are eligible to vote. Candidates for the Chilean presidency must be native-born and at least 30 years old.

Preview

Teaching Suggestions

A Ask students what verb they have used before with *emociona-do*. Explain that sometimes *está* is used with the past participle; sometimes *ha*. Give them the sentence: *Este documental ___ premios recientemente en seis diferentes ciudades.* Ask them if they would complete the sentence with *ha recibido* or *está recibido*. Explain why.

B Point out the irregular forms *escrito* and *dicho*. Ask: How do you know they are past participles? (They are used with *haber*.) How do they differ from regular past participles? (The forms do not end in *-ado* or *-ido*.) What are the infinitives of these two irregular past participles? *(escribir, decir)*

Answers

A The subject is *un magnífico ejemplo de generosidad.* / The subject is *sus autores.* / The subject is *nosotros.* / No, there was no change in the past participle. / *el público ha mirado (ha asistido), los admiradores han mirado (han asistido), nosotros hemos mirado (hemos asistido) / yo he mirado (he asistido), tú has mirado (has asistido)*

B They have been put before the two words in the verb form. / *Mis padres (no) me han comprado un nuevo video.*

Gramática en contexto

En este momento van a dar un premio al mejor documental. ¿Has visto recientemente algún programa al que le dieron un premio? ¿Qué tipo de programa era? ¿Qué información piensas que vas a encontrar aquí?

Premios a los mejores documentales

Voluntarios y víctimas, documental sobre las personas que dieron su tiempo y dinero para ayudar a las víctimas del terremoto, muestra un magnífico ejemplo de generosidad que nos ha emocionado a todos.

En *Regreso a la buena tierra,* un documental sobre la ayuda médica en San Cristóbal, Chiapas, sus autores nos han mostrado un aspecto poco conocido de nuestra sociedad.

Éstos son los programas que más han sobresalido este año. Para el premio hemos escogido a *Voluntarios y víctimas* de Rafael González y Teresa Anaya.

"Gracias a todos los que nos han apoyado, y también a las personas que nos han escrito y nos han dicho cuánto les ha gustado nuestro trabajo."

A In the first description, the presenter says *nos ha emocionado a todos*. What is the subject of the verb in this expression? About *Regreso a la buena tierra,* the presenter says, *nos han mostrado un aspecto* . . . What is the subject of the verb in this expression? Later the presenter says, *hemos escogido* . . . What is the subject of this verb? One of these verbs has a singular subject; the others have plural subjects. Has there been any change in the past participle with a plural subject? Take a piece of paper and make a chart showing how to say that someone has watched or attended something. Give the forms of *mirar* and *asistir* for the subjects: *el público, los admiradores,* and *nosotros.* Can you also give the forms for *yo* and *tú* of these verbs?

B The recipients of the award say, *nos han apoyado, nos han escrito, nos han dicho,* and *les ha gustado.* Where have the object pronouns *nos* and *les* been put in relationship to the two words in the verb form? Tell a classmate where you would put the pronoun *me* in the following sentence: *Mis padres han comprado un nuevo video.* Where do you think you would put *no* in the same sentence?

142 Capítulo 4

Options

Strategies for Reaching All Students

Students Needing Extra Help
Begin the grammar section of the Organizer.
A: Show students that *nos* is an object pronoun, not the subject of *ha emocionado*.
B: Help students see the relationship between *escribir* and *escrito,* and *decir* and *dicho*.
El presente perfecto: Show students how past participles used as adjectives are used with *estar,* but when used as a verb they are used with *haber*. Review the present perfect tense in English. Present additional models, emphasizing meaning. Have students make two lists of the double-vowel words: those that require accents and those that do not. Present some negative examples, using only *no* at first, then other negative words. Give examples using object pronouns and reflexives. Combine those with negatives.

Extended Written Practice/Homework
1. Write three sentences telling what people have done to help the environment. Use: *ahorrar, apagar, reciclar, reparar, separar, conservar. Hemos reciclado botellas y latas.*
2. Write three questions you can ask concerning what people have eaten and drunk. Use: *comer, beber, pedir. ¿Has pedido paella en un restaurante español alguna vez?*

El presente perfecto

In English we form the present perfect tense by combining **have** or **has** with the past participle of a verb: *he has seen, have you tried?, they haven't eaten.*

You have already learned to form the past participle of a verb in Spanish by adding *-ado* to the stem of *-ar* verbs and *-ido* to the stem of most *-er* and *-ir* verbs. To form the present-perfect tense, we combine this past participle with the present tense of the verb *haber*.

We generally use the Spanish present perfect in the same way we use its English equivalent. Here are all the present-perfect forms of *alquilar, escoger,* and *decidir.*

he	alquilado escogido decidido	hemos	alquilado escogido decidido
has	alquilado escogido decidido	habéis	alquilado escogido decidido
ha	alquilado escogido decidido	han	alquilado escogido decidido

No **he alquilado** un video hoy.
I haven't rented a video today.

¿Qué programa **han escogido**?
What program have they chosen?

- Notice that when the past participle is used with forms of *haber,* the final *-o* never changes.

  Ricardo **ha grabado** su película favorita.
  Sus hermanos **han grabado** una telenovela.

- Certain verbs that have a double vowel in the infinitive form (except those with the double vowel *ui)* require an accent mark on the *i* in the past participle. For example:

  caer → ca**í**do   oír → o**í**do
  leer → le**í**do   creer → cre**í**do

Class Starter Review
On the day following the presentation of the present perfect tense, you may want to begin the class with this activity:
Toss a small rubber ball to a student, asking a question using the present perfect. The student must catch the ball, answer the question, and throw it to another student, asking another question, etc.

3. Write sentences telling who has done the following: *dirigir una película, actuar en una película de terror, ser víctima de un crimen en una película.*

Multiple Intelligences
Verbal/Linguistic
See Class Starter Review.
Visual/Spatial
See Exs. A–B.

Present & Practice

Answers

1 ESTUDIANTE A

a. ¿Has buceado en el mar alguna vez?

b. ¿Has esquiado en las montañas . . .

c. ¿Has ido de pesca al mar . . .

d. ¿Has viajado a otro país . . .

e. ¿Has explorado una selva . . .

f. ¿Has subido pirámides . . .

g. ¿Has alquilado una casa en la playa . . .

ESTUDIANTE B

Answers will vary, but should begin in the following manner:

a. Sí (No, no) he buceado . . .

b. . . . he esquiado . . .

c. . . . he ido . . .

d. . . . he viajado . . .

e. . . . he explorado . . .

f. . . . he subido . . .

g. . . . he alquilado . . .

Summaries will vary, but look for the *ellos* form of the present perfect and the correct past participle.

• Notice that we place *no* and other negative words, object pronouns, and reflexive pronouns directly in front of the form of the verb *haber*.

— ¿Has alquilado esa película alguna vez?
— No, **no la** he alquilado nunca.

1 Haz una encuesta entre los estudiantes de tu clase para ver qué cosas interesantes han hecho durante las vacaciones. Apunta sus respuestas para presentar un informe después.

visitar un zoológico grande

A — *¿Has visitado un zoológico grande alguna vez?*
B — *Sí, he visitado un zoológico grande dos veces. He visitado el zoológico de San Diego y el de St. Louis.*

a. bucear en el mar
b. esquiar en las montañas
c. ir de pesca al mar
d. viajar a otro país
e. explorar una selva
f. subir pirámides
g. alquilar una casa en la playa

Usando las respuestas de tus compañeros, di lo que ustedes han hecho.

Tres estudiantes han visitado zoológicos grandes. Tomás y yo hemos visitado los zoológicos de San Diego y de St. Louis. Sara nunca ha visitado un zoológico grande.

Haciendo un programa en un estudio de televisión en Caracas, Venezuela

144 Capítulo 4

Options

Strategies for Reaching All Students

Students Needing Extra Help
Ex. 1: Have students make a chart with seven columns, so they can keep track of which activities their classmates were involved in. Review *haber*. Before beginning this exercise, see if students can form the past participles correctly.
Ex. 2: As a class, discuss the two columns and decide which descriptions go together.

Remind them to use each answer only once. *Los participios pasados irregulares:* Before reviewing the examples in the book, create some very simple sentences on the chalkboard. First, write affirmative sentences; then negative examples, using only *no* at first, then other negative words. Give examples using object pronouns and reflexives. Combine those with negatives.

Enrichment
Ex. 2: As a homework assignment, ask students to write about how a specific program or character from a program has influenced their lives and why.

Extended Written Practice/Homework
1. Write four sentences using *hacer* and the following expressions to tell who has done these activities: *esquí acuático, moto acuático, surf, surf de vela.*

2 Discute con un(a) compañero(a) tus opiniones sobre cómo la televisión y las películas han influido en nuestras vidas.

La antena parabólica ha traído mejores programas a nuestras casas.

a.   b.   c.

d.   e.   f.   g.

- traer mejores programas a nuestras casas
- divertir mucho
- manipular la presentación de las noticias
- ayudar a los niños en sus tareas
- influir a los niños
- presentar los hechos objetivamente
- contribuir a controlar la violencia

Los participios pasados irregulares

Just as in English, many Spanish verbs have irregular past participles. You have already learned some of these:

decir	→	**dicho**	romper(se)	→	**roto**
hacer	→	**hecho**	ver	→	**visto**
morir(se)	→	**muerto**			

¿Qué ha **dicho** ella sobre el noticiero?
*What has she **said** about the newscast?*

No hemos **hecho** la tarea todavía.
*We haven't **done** the homework yet.*

Sus peces se han **muerto**.
*Her fish have **died**.*

Nunca me he **roto** un hueso.
*I've never **broken** a bone.*

Gramática en contexto   145

Reteach / Review: Vocabulary

Ex. 2: Before beginning this activity, you may want to review ways to express opinions: *Creo, Me parece, Pienso*, etc. Brainstorm vocabulary for TV programs and movies. Refer to Book 1, Chap. 11, and Book 2, Chap. 10.

2 Statements will vary, but may include:
a. La televisión ha traído mejores programas a nuestras casas.
b. Las películas violentas han contribuido a controlar la violencia.
c. Las comedias han divertido mucho.
d. Los programas educativos han ayudado a los niños en sus tareas.
e. Los noticieros no han presentado los hechos objectivamante.
f. Los dibujos animados han influido mucho a los niños.
g. Statements will vary.

Strategies for Reaching All Students
MULTIPLE INTELLIGENCES
Interpersonal/Social and Verbal/Linguistic
See Exs. 1–2.
Visual/Spatial
See Enrichment, Practice Wkbk. 4-5, and Writing Activity 4-D.

Practice Wkbk. 4-5

Writing Activity 4-D

Prueba 4-5

Cultural Notes

2. Write three sentences telling who has not seen a certain movie yet: *Mis padres no han visto* Titanic *todavía.*
3. Choose four of these expressions and write sentences telling who has had bad things happen to them: *romperse un hueso, ponerse muy enfermo(a), quemarse, cortarse, tener una infección.*

(p. 144, photo)
Venezuelan law requires that 50 percent of television programming be broadcast live or recorded locally in studios, such as this one in Caracas. This helps the government maintain tight control. It has also made Venezuela a leader in production of *telenovelas,* game shows, and other programs viewed throughout Latin America.

Ask students: In the U.S., what factors control what is shown on TV? (advertisers, viewers, ratings) Is there government control? If so, of what type? Do you think there should be more or less control?

Present & Practice

Answers

3 ESTUDIANTE A
a. Ya he ayudado a ... ¿Y tú? /
b. ... hecho la tarea de ... / c. ...
visto un video ... / d. ... terminado ... / e. ... devuelto ... / f. ...
escrito ... / g. ... resuelto un
problema con ... / h. ... puesto ...

ESTUDIANTE B
a.–h. Answers will vary. Look for
correct use of the present perfect
and placement of object pronouns.

4 ESTUDIANTE A
a. ¿Han grabado Uds. un programa recientemente?
b. ¿Han visto Uds. un programa
educativo ...
c. ¿Han alquilado Uds. una
película ...
d. ¿Han participado Uds. en un
programa de concursos ...
e. ¿Se han peleado Uds. por el
canal que querían ver ...
f. ¿Se han emocionado Uds. con
algún programa ...
g. ¿Se han reído Uds. viendo la
televisión ...
h. Questions will vary.

 Practice Wkbk. 4-6, 4-7

 Writing Activity 4-E

 Prueba 4-6

 Comm. Act. BLM 4-2

¿Has **visto** la película nueva?
*Have you **seen** the new movie?*

Other verbs that have irregular past participles are:

abrir	→	**abierto**	poner	→	**puesto**
devolver	→	**devuelto**	resolver	→	**resuelto**
escribir	→	**escrito**			

3 Habla con un(a) compañero(a) sobre las diferentes cosas que (no) han hecho recientemente en la escuela.

leer ...
A — *Ya he leído tres capítulos de* Moby Dick. *¿Y tú?*
B — *No, no los he leído todavía.*
    o: *Sí, yo también los he leído.*

a. ayudar a ...
b. hacer la tarea de ...
c. ver un video ...
d. terminar ...
e. devolver ...
f. escribir ...
g. resolver un problema con ...
h. poner ...

4 La televisión y las películas son parte de la vida diaria de muchas personas. Conversa con un(a) compañero(a) sobre cosas que has hecho recientemente relacionadas con la televisión o las películas.

pagar una multa por un video
A — *¿Han pagado Uds. una multa por un video recientemente?*
B — *Sí, hemos pagado tres dólares por un video que no devolvimos a tiempo.*
    o: *No, no hemos pagado ninguna multa recientemente.*

a. grabar un programa
b. ver un programa educativo
c. alquilar una película
d. participar en un programa de concursos
e. pelearse por el canal que querían ver
f. emocionarse con algún programa
g. reírse viendo la televisión
h. 🔆

146 Capítulo 4

¡NO OLVIDES!

Remember that to agree with a negative statement we use *no ... tampoco.* To disagree with a negative statement, we can use *Yo sí.*:
A—*No he leído nada de* Moby Dick *todavía.* B—*No he leído nada tampoco,* o: *Yo sí, he leído cien páginas ya.*

¡NO OLVIDES!

The reflexive pronouns are: *me, te, se, nos, os, se.*

Options

Strategies for Reaching All Students

Students Needing Extra Help
Ex. 3: Before beginning this exercise, complete the sentences in the list of activities.
Ex. 4: Brainstorm the *Estudiante B* responses. Point out the reflexives and irregular verbs in the list.

Repaso: El pretérito de poder, tener *y* estar: Write the regular preterite endings on the chalkboard, as well as the *hacer* and *poner* paradigms, so students can contrast the two. Point out that *anoche* and *ayer* indicate a specific past time. Give other expressions that indicate the preterite.

Ex. 5: Brainstorm reasons why people couldn't watch the show. Review the preterite forms of *ver*. Review object pronouns and their use with *gustar*. Remind students how to manipulate the pronoun when answering the questions. Remind them that the forms of *poder* and *tener (estar)* will also change.

Repaso: El pretérito de *poder, tener* y *estar*

Here are the preterite forms of *poder, tener,* and *estar.*

poder		tener		estar	
pude	pudimos	tuve	tuvimos	estuve	estuvimos
pudiste	pudisteis	tuviste	tuvisteis	estuviste	estuvisteis
pudo	pudieron	tuvo	tuvieron	estuvo	estuvieron

- Notice that, as with *hacer* and *poner,* none of the verb forms has an accent.

- As you know, the imperfect tense forms of these verbs are used to describe people, places, and situations in the past and to tell how things *used to be.* The preterite forms, on the other hand, are used to talk about situations at a specific time in the past.

> Anoche **tuve** que salir y no **pude** ver mi programa favorito.
> Ayer **estuvo** lloviendo y no **vimos** el sol en todo el día.

5 Habla con un(a) compañero(a) y explícale por qué ciertas personas no pudieron ver un programa de televisión.

tu hermano

> A —¿*Vio tu hermano la película de aventuras anoche?*
> B —*No, no pudo. Tuvo que . . . /Estuvo en . . .*
>   *o: Sí, le gustó mucho. Estuvo en . . .*

Estudiante A   Estudiante B

a. tu papá (tu mamá)   b. tus amigos(as)

c. (nombre) y tú   d. (nombre)   e. tú   f. (dos nombres)

 Practice Wkbk. 4-8

 Writing Activity 4-F

 Prueba 4-7

Extended Written Practice/Homework
1. Write three sentences telling why different people could not see a movie or TV program: *Mi hermano menor no pudo ver la película de terror porque fue prohibida para menores.*
2. Write three sentences telling what you and your classmates had to do for different classes recently.

3. Write three sentences telling how long different people were in a place: *Mi padre estuvo en un atasco en la autopista por tres horas.*

Multiple Intelligences
Verbal/Linguistic
See Exs. 3–5.
Visual/Spatial
See Practice Wkbk. 4-6, 4-7, and 4-8; Writing Activities 4-E and 4-F; and Comm. Act. BLM 4-2.

Present & Practice

Reteach / Review: Preterite and imperfect

As an in-class assignment, have students write sentences using the present, preterite, and imperfect forms of *decir*. Tell them to include the chapter vocabulary. (You may wish to have them work with a partner so that they can check each other's work.) Call on individuals to read one or more of their sentences to the class.

Teaching Suggestions

Ex. 6: The follow-up to this activity is important in the development of the *pregunta clave* since it asks students to evaluate the type of things being said on television.

Answers

6 Dialogues will vary, but look for the correct preterite forms of *decir* and *dar*. Summaries should include the preterite forms *dieron* and *dijeron*.

Repaso: El pretérito de *decir* y *dar*

Here are the preterite forms of *decir*.

dije	dijimos
dijiste	dijisteis
dijo	dijeron

• Remember that the *Uds. / ellos / ellas* form of *decir* does not have an *i* in the ending.

Here are the preterite forms of *dar*.

di	dimos
diste	disteis
dio	dieron

• Remember that the preterite endings of *dar* are the same as those of -*er* and -*ir* verbs.

6 Con otros(as) compañeros(as), habla de las noticias, opiniones, chismes *(gossip)* y otras cosas que han oído en la televisión recientemente. Apunta lo que dicen tus compañeros.

A —*Anoche dieron (un programa de entrevistas) en la televisión.*
B —*¿Qué dijo (el locutor)?*
A —*Dijo que los niños no deben ver películas violentas.*
B —*¿Qué más dijo?*
A — ...

Después hablen de lo que dijeron los locutores. ¿Era informativo, negativo, subjetivo ...?

En los programas que dieron en la televisión recientemente, muchos locutores dijeron que .... Creo que sus ideas eran informativas pero bastante subjetivas.

148   Capítulo 4

Options

Strategies for Reaching All Students

Students Needing Extra Help
Repaso: El pretérito de decir *y* dar: Drill these forms frequently to avoid confusion. Point out the bullet that emphasizes the spelling of the third person plural form of *decir*.
Ex. 6: Have students take notes on what their friends are saying. Complete the model, including the second section, where

they summarize their findings. Have them take notes on the model, and, as a class, do a second example. Brainstorm possible responses to the *¿Qué más dijo?* question. Remind them to use verbs in the *ellos* form when summarizing.
Ahora lo sabes: Have students write this so that they can record their progress.

Extended Written Practice/Homework
1. Write three sentences telling what people said about different movies: *Mis amigas dijeron que* Titanic *fue muy triste.*
2. Write two sentences telling where different people went hiking: *Mis amigos y yo dimos una caminata en el bosque.*
3. Write three sentences naming movies or TV shows that scared you or other people: *La película* Psycho *me dio miedo.*

Un fotógrafo y una reportera
en Caracas, Venezuela

CONCURSO

EL GRAN JUEGO de la OCA

De Oca a Oca

EL GRAN JUEGO de la OCA

'94

Vuelve el programa
concurso de mayor éxito.

'95

▲ Antena 3 Televisión

Ahora lo sabes

¿Puedes:

- decir lo que alguien ha hecho o no ha hecho?

  —Mi hermano y yo no ___ esa película todavía pero queremos verla pronto.

- hablar de situaciones que ocurren en un momento del pasado?

  —Mi mamá no ___ ver las noticias anoche porque ___ que llevar a mi hermano a una clase de tenis.

- hablar de lo que alguien dijo?

  —Los locutores ___ que el aeropuerto no iba a abrir hasta la primavera.

MÁS PRÁCTICA

Más práctica y tarea, pp. 557–558
Practice Workbook 4–5, 4–9

Gramática en contexto   149

Cultural Notes ☼

Multiple Intelligences
Verbal/Linguistic
See Audio Activities 4.3, 4.4, and 4.5.
Visual/Spatial
See Practice Wkbk. 4-9, Writing Activity 4-G, and Comm. Act. BLM 4-3.
Visual/Spatial and Verbal/Linguistic
See Reteach/Review.

(p. 149, photo)
Caracas is the press center of Venezuela, and its newspapers are distributed throughout the country. Unlike television, most newspapers are independent and generally free from government intervention. Venezuela's two leading dailies are *Últimas Noticias* and *Meridiano*. Approximately 60 other newspapers are published every day. Weekly newsmagazines that rely heavily on photographs also help keep Venezuelans informed.

(p. 149, realia)
Ad for the Spanish game show *El gran juego de la oca* (The Great Goose Game). *Antena 3 Televisión*, one of Spain's public TV stations, broadcasts this relatively new program that is based on a traditional board game called *la oca*. Participants are asked to perform certain activities on stage in a specific time period and compete for prizes.

Apply

Teaching Suggestions

Point out the key chapter question *(la pregunta clave del capítulo).* Tell students that completing these activities will help them answer this question. You may select one, two, or all three of these activities, as time permits.

Ex. 1: You might want to have pairs of students choose programs from different categories in order to have a variety of types of programs to evaluate. Guide them through the activity by selecting an example and modeling it.

Ex. 3: Students should think through their ideas carefully before beginning the debate in order to avoid the use of English.

Answers: Sopa de actividades

1–3 Responses will vary.

Puntos de Vista

¿Cómo nos influye la televisión?

Esta sección te ofrece la oportunidad de combinar lo que aprendiste en este capítulo con lo que ya sabes para responder a la pregunta clave.

Sopa de actividades

1. Preparen una lista de categorías de programas de televisión. Den ejemplos de programas que conocen en cada categoría. En parejas, escojan un programa que les interese y preparen una crítica. La crítica debe incluir:

a. Descripción del programa

- clase de programa
- argumento, elementos, situación, etc.
- actores, actrices, personajes, locutores, etc.
- hora, día, canal de televisión

b. Evaluación del programa

- qué es interesante en el programa
- si el programa está bien escrito, filmado, dirigido, etc.
- qué piensan sobre los actores, locutores, etc.
- si el programa es diferente a otros

c. Recomendación sobre el programa

- quiénes deben o no deben verlo y por qué

150   Capítulo 4

Options

Strategies for Reaching All Students

Spanish-Speaking Students
Include Spanish-speaking students in each group, if possible.
Ex. 1: Form a group of bilingual students and have them present their critique to the class. This can also be used as a listening comprehension activity.

Students Needing Extra Help
Depending on the level of the class, Exs. 1 and 2 may be sufficient.
Ex. 1: Brainstorm categories as a class. If available, use the vocabulary section of the Organizer from Book 1, Chap. 11, and Book 2, Chap. 10.

Ex. 2: Brainstorm possible themes for new programs. Have the class create the three awards: a no-homework night, bonus points on a quiz, etc.
Ex. 3: As a class, write the five sentences. Students will need help with the vocabulary to express their opinions.

2 En grupos de dos o tres, hagan un nuevo programa de televisión. Anuncien el programa. Pueden incluir un cartel con distintos elementos del programa e información sobre:

- qué clase de programa es
- quiénes participan
- por qué hay que dar un programa como éste
- dónde y cuándo van a filmarlo
- a quiénes va a interesar
- cuándo y a qué hora deben darlo
- por qué va a tener éxito

Cada grupo va a presentar su anuncio a la clase. Al final, cada persona (o grupo) de la clase puede escoger los tres programas mejores. Den premios a los programas más populares.

3 Prepárate para participar en una discusión sobre la televisión.

- En grupos de cuatro escriban cinco frases sobre la televisión. Por ejemplo:

Sólo deben dar programas violentos tarde por la noche.

Se debe controlar más los programas de televisión.

Debe haber más programas educativos los fines de semana.

- Traten de anticipar si habrá opiniones contrarias a las del grupo y cuáles serán. Piensen también cómo se puede responder a alguien que piensa de una forma diferente, como, por ejemplo:

Debe haber más programas de hechos de la vida real.

- Lean sus ideas a otro grupo. Luego voten a favor o en contra de cada idea. Escriban los resultados.
- Para discutir cada punto de vista, formen dos grupos (a favor y en contra) según los resultados de la discusión.
- Cada grupo va a tratar de convencer a sus oponentes de lo que piensa.
- Para finalizar pueden escoger los puntos de vista más interesantes de toda la clase.

LA ESTRELLA

La televisión contribuye a la violencia entre los jóvenes

Video Activity A

Video, Capítulo 4

Chapter 4: Play

Step

Video Activities B–C

Writing Activities 4-H, 4-I

Comm. Act. BLMs 4-4, 4-5

Enrichment
Ex. 1: Tape and show a popular program from one of the Spanish television networks. Then ask groups to prepare a critique of the program following the guidelines given here.
Ex. 3: Ask students to give their opinions on cable television and pay-per-view programs *(la programación pagada por adelantado).*

Cooperative Learning
In groups of three, ask students to design an ad or poster for a movie of their choice. Have group members be responsible for a particular task: description of the movie, rating, show dates, etc. Encourage use of chapter grammar. When finished, display the ads or posters around the classroom.

Multiple Intelligences
Bodily/Kinesthetic and Visual/Spatial
See Cooperative Learning.

Interpersonal/Social, Verbal/Linguistic, and Visual/Spatial
See Ex. 2.
Logical/Mathematical and Interpersonal/Social
See Ex. 1.
Verbal/Linguistic
See Ex. 3.
Visual/Spatial
See Writing Activities 4-H and 4-I and Comm. Act. BLMs 4-4 and 4-5.

Apply

Process Reading
For a description of process reading, see p. 52.

Teaching Suggestions
Tell students that working through the *Para leer* section will help them answer the key chapter question.

Encourage students to use the strategies given to them in the text to help them understand the reading. Remind them that they do not need to understand every word.

Answers
Antes de leer
Statements will vary.

Mira la lectura
Students' responses will vary.

Para leer ?

www.pasoapaso.com

Jugando videojuegos

Antes de leer

STRATEGY ► Using prior knowledge

Vas a leer una entrevista con Alejandra Vallejo-Nágera, hija de un psiquiatra y escritor español famoso. Ella ha escrito un libro sobre el efecto de la televisión en los niños.

Existen muchas opiniones diferentes sobre el efecto de la televisión en los niños. Aquí hay tres. Cópialas y escribe tres más.

- Algunos programas ayudan a los niños a aprender a leer.
- Los niños que ven mucha televisión necesitan más imágenes para aprender a leer.
- Si se ve demasiada televisión, se pierde la imaginación.

Mira la lectura

STRATEGY ► Scanning

Lee la selección rápidamente sólo para ver si están mencionados los efectos que escribiste en tu lista. Pon una cruz delante de los que encuentras.

152 Capítulo 4

Cómo usar la televisión

Revista Tiempo. Dice en su libro que no existe ninguna otra generación en la que un factor como la televisión haya podido influir tan directa, rápida y pasivamente en los niños.

Alejandra Vallejo-Nágera. Un niño cuando ve la televisión no deja de recibir estímulos para los que necesita respuestas que no se las ofrece este medio. El niño tiene que aprender a hablar con la familia, tiene que aprender a leer, a jugar, y todas estas actividades las necesita para su desarrollo y su sistema psicológico. ¿Qué está pasando ahora? Los niños no saben leer y, si lo hacen, necesitan constantemente de la ayuda de imágenes. Recuerdo que mis libros de infancia eran de autores como Salgari o Emily Bronte y sus páginas no contenían dibujo alguno.

T. ¿La televisión siempre es dañina?

A.V.-N. Depende de cómo se utilice. Si se abusa, es mala; pero si se usa de forma inteligente, resulta buena. La televisión ha hecho, por ejemplo, mucho bien al deporte. Nunca se había conocido a tantos deportistas como hasta ahora y todo es gracias a la pequeña pantalla.

T. ¿Cómo se usa inteligentemente?

A.V.-N. Hoy en día uno de los grandes problemas de los padres con sus hijos es la incomunicación total que existe entre ellos, y la culpa, en parte, es de la televisión y del abuso que se hace de ella.

T. ¿Quién tiene más culpa, los padres por permitir que sus hijos vean la televisión o los responsables de las cadenas por no emitir programas adecuados a la infancia?

A.V.-N. Los padres. Si hay una demanda por parte de la audiencia, es normal que exista una

---

Options

Strategies for Reaching All Students

Spanish-Speaking Students
Have students respond to the following in writing: *Piensa en tus hermanitos, tus primitos u otros niñitos que conozcas. ¿Pasan mucho tiempo viendo la televisión? ¿Quién decide cuántos programas o cuántas horas van a poder ver? ¿Qué tipos de programas crees que deben poder ver o no ver? ¿Por qué? Cuando tengas niños, ¿vas a permitirles pasar mucho tiempo viendo televisión o vas a limitarlo? ¿Por qué?*

Students Needing Extra Help
Antes de leer: Students may need help with vocabulary in order to write their opinions.
Mira la lectura: Students might be looking for exactly the same words that they wrote. Point out that they should look for a similar idea, and that it might be written slightly different.
Be prepared to read through the text section by section.
Paragraph 1: Point out that *haya podido* is from *poder.*

Paragraph 2: If necessary, help students with the first sentence. Discuss the idea that television itself doesn't answer the questions that enter a child's mind as he or she watches a program.
Paragraph 3: See if students can figure out *dañina* from *hacer daño.*
Paragraph 4: Many students may not be aware of the popularity of radio before the television age. Discuss the idea that sports, soap operas, etc. were all radio broadcasts at one time.

respuesta por parte de los jefes de los canales. El problema no está en el uso de la televisión sino en el abuso que se hace de ella.

T.   ¿Estas teorías las lleva a la práctica?

A.V.-N.   Lo llevo a rajatabla, pero no me cuesta mucho esfuerzo porque como lo he hecho desde que eran pequeñas, mis hijas no la echan de menos.

T.   La actriz americana Debra Winger declaraba recientemente en una entrevista que a su hijo sólo le deja ver películas en vídeo. ¿Esa medida le parece correcta?

A.V.-N.   Como me gusta mucho el cine, procuro ver vídeos con ellas, hablar de la iluminación, del maquillaje, de la música, los decorados, el vestuario, e intento que esa actividad sedentaria, como es ver la televisión, se convierta en un momento compartido.

T.   ¿Hasta dónde puede llegar el poder de seducción de la televisión?

A.V.-N.   Es ilimitado. Es muy tentador para un adulto llegar a casa y no tener que pensar ni tomar decisiones. El problema es que el niño necesita aprender a defenderse y a desarrollarse en el mundo que le ha tocado vivir.

T.   En su libro asegura que según aumentan las cifras de espectadores entre los niños que empiezan su aprendizaje, menos es la atención que aquéllos prestan en el colegio y más baja es su preparación a la hora de enfrentarse a las asignaturas.

A.V.-N.   ¿No es evidente que a los niños les cuesta muchísimo aprender a leer? Si echamos marcha atrás, nosotros sabíamos leer con 4 años, y hoy en día, con 6 años no sólo no saben sino que además les cuesta trabajo fijarse en las letras y unir las palabras.

Infórmate

STRATEGY ⟩ Reading for detail

Ahora lee todo el artículo con cuidado.

1 ¿Cómo pueden los padres abusar de la televisión?

2 ¿Qué edad piensas que tienen las hijas de la autora? ¿Por qué piensas así?

3 ¿Qué actividades piensas que hacen las hijas de la autora en vez de ver la televisión?

4 ¿Qué hace la autora cuando ve una película con sus hijas? ¿Por qué lo hace?

5 ¿Piensas que la autora cambiará de actitud cuando sus hijas tengan tu edad? ¿Por qué piensas que sí o que no?

Aplicación

1 Con tu familia, pasa un fin de semana sin ver la televisión. Escribe en tu diario qué pasó y cuál fue tu reacción y la de tu familia.

2 Clasifica los programas de televisión utilizando estas categorías:

- apta para toda la familia
- se recomienda discreción
- prohibida para menores
- sólo para mayores

Luego da tres ejemplos de programas de cada categoría.

Para leer   153

Apply

Process Writing
For information regarding writing portfolios, see p. 54.

Teaching Suggestions
Tell students that working through the *Para escribir* section will help them answer the key question.

Answers
Interview results will vary.

Puntos de Vista

Para escribir

Casi todos pasamos varias horas a la semana viendo la televisión. Hace años que hacemos esto y, por eso, hemos visto muchos tipos de programas diferentes. Hay personas que creen que la televisión tiene una influencia enorme en nuestras vidas. ¿Qué crees tú?

1 La pregunta clave, "¿Cómo nos influye la televisión?," te presenta la oportunidad de aprender lo que piensan algunas personas sobre este tema. Vas a entrevistar a adultos, a jóvenes y a niños, y luego vas a hacer un informe con los resultados.

■ Primero, decide qué preguntas vas a hacer. Por ejemplo:

¿Tiene la televisión una influencia positiva o negativa? ¿Por qué?
¿Qué aspectos positivos tiene?
¿Cuáles son los efectos negativos?

Puedes usar estas preguntas o escribir otras.

■ Luego, escoge a las personas que vas a entrevistar. Trata de entrevistar a algunas personas que hablan español. Debes incluir a tres o a cuatro en cada categoría:

adultos (profesores, policías, padres, consejeros, etc.)
jóvenes (amigos, compañeros de clase, compañeros de trabajo, etc.)
niños (hermanos, primos, vecinos, etc.)

Hazles las preguntas y anota sus respuestas. Si quieres, puedes usar una grabadora para las entrevistas y escribir las respuestas más tarde.

■ Revisa lo que dijeron las personas y trata de organizar los resultados lógicamente.

¿Quiénes dijeron que la influencia de la televisión es positiva?
¿Qué ejemplos te dieron de los aspectos positivos? ¿Por qué piensan que es así?
¿Quiénes dijeron que la influencia de la televisión es negativa?
¿Qué ejemplos te dieron? ¿Por qué piensan que es así?
¿Con qué grupo estás de acuerdo? ¿Por qué?

154   Capítulo 4

Options

Strategies for Reaching All Students

Students Needing Extra Help
You may want to do this activity in pairs or small groups. Assign the category of people to be interviewed: one group would interview only adults, and so on. As a class, create a bank of questions to use while interviewing. Some may need to be simplified while addressing children. Remind students that they can interview in English but must report their findings in Spanish. Once the class has decided on the questions, make a separate chart for each question, with a column along the left side for students to indicate who they have interviewed, and a corresponding space large enough for the response.

¿Tiene la televisión una influencia positiva o negativa?	
Mi abuelo	
Mi vecina	
Mi primo	

Have students use a tape recorder for help with the summaries. Point out that *quiénes* refers to categories of people, not individual names. Highlight the people on the charts who gave positive opinions. Try to keep the theme of the activity in mind through each element.

2 Escribe el primer borrador de tu artículo usando tus notas y lo que escribiste para las otras actividades. Consulta con un(a) compañero(a) y sigue los pasos del proceso de escribir. Luego, haz tu versión final.

Aquí tienes algunas palabras y expresiones que te pueden ser útiles.

(no) estar de acuerdo	por un lado
al contrario	por otro lado
(no) tener razón	

3 Para compartir tu trabajo, puedes:

- enviarlo a un periódico
- mandarlo a un canal de televisión local
- exhibirlo en la sala de clases o en la biblioteca escolar
- incluirlo en el boletín que se envía a los padres
- incluirlo en tu portafolio

155

Assess & Summarize

Test Preparation

You may want to assign parts of this section as written homework or as an in-class writing activity prior to administering the *Examen de habilidades.*

Answers

Listening

—*¿Entretenerme con la tele? Pues, las películas me hacen bostezar y las telenovelas me hacen reír. Me parece que el reportaje del noticiero es bastante subjetivo y los comentarios que he visto recientemente no son interesantes. Además, creo que los anuncios manipulan al público. Por ejemplo, en casa tenemos siete tipos de cereales que nadie come. Mi hermano menor vio los anuncios mientras veía los dibujos animados. Él tiene mucha influencia sobre mamá en el supermercado. Sin embargo, no estoy de acuerdo con la censura, y creo que la gente debe tener el derecho de escoger los programas que quiere ver.*

La persona tiene una opinión negativa de los programas en la televisión. / La televisión le influye al hermano menor.

CAPÍTULO 4

Repaso ¿Lo sabes bien?

Esta sección te ayudará a prepararte para el examen de habilidades, donde tendrás que hacer tareas semejantes.

Listening

¿Puedes entender un comentario sobre la televisión? Escucha mientras el (la) profesor(a) lee un ejemplo semejante al que vas a oír en el examen. ¿Tiene esta persona una opinión positiva o negativa de los programas en la televisión? ¿A quién(es) en la familia de esta persona le(s) influye la televisión?

Reading

Lee estas descripciones con cuidado para saber qué describe la teleguía. ¿Para cuál de los tres programas se recomienda discreción probablemente? ¿Cuál deben ver los más pequeños?

> **15:00**
> El programa de *Balance semanal.* La política durante seis años de una investigación.
>
> **18:00**
> Película "El último boy scout" con Bruce Willis y Damon Wayans. Una bella mujer…un crimen…una investigación que puede resultar explosiva.
>
> **22:00**
> **NUBELUZ** "Viaje al futuro." En este episodio nuestros héroes viajan a un planeta desconocido.

156   Capítulo 4

Writing

¿Puedes escribir un breve resumen de las opiniones que tienen algunas personas sobre cómo nos influye la televisión? Aquí tienes un ejemplo.

> Diario de Manuel
> He entrevistado a adultos y a jóvenes sobre cómo nos influye la televisión. Todos han expresado diferentes opiniones. Algunos adultos piensan que sólo deben dar programas de violencia tarde por la noche. Piensan que estos programas han tenido una influencia negativa sobre los jóvenes. Algunos jóvenes dijeron que no les influye y que deben tener derecho a escoger los programas que quieren ver. Ellos dicen que son bastante inteligentes para no ser manipulados por la televisión. Los dos grupos expresaron diferentes opiniones pero casi todos estaban de acuerdo en su opinión sobre la televisión y los niños. Piensan que los padres deben controlar más los programas que sus hijos menores ven, porque sí les influye mucho.

Culture

¿Qué tipo de programas pueden ver los hispanoamericanos a través de la televisión por cable?

Speaking

Habla con otra persona sobre la clase de programas que prefieres ver en la televisión.

A —*¿Qué clase de programas prefieres ver?*
B —*Prefiero los programas informativos. ¿Y tú?*
A —*Para mí los programas informativos son muy aburridos. Me gustan más las películas de terror.*
B —*¿Las películas de terror? Pero hay mucha violencia en esas películas. ¿No te parece que hay demasiada violencia en la televisión?*
A —*Pues, en mi opinión …*

Self Test   www.pasoapaso.com

Options

Strategies for Reaching All Students

Students Needing Extra Help
Have students write this exercise so that they can check off what they have mastered. Remind them that this is just a sample of what the test will be like.
Listening: Read more than once. Remind students that they need to listen only for certain pieces of information. Be sure that they understand the final question.

Reading: Remind students that they don't need to know every word in the reading. They may have difficulty recognizing the shows that are to be viewed with discretion. Help them accordingly.
Writing: Have students use the Organizer and write a sample summary before the test. Have them refer to the *Tema para investigar, Sopa de actividades,* and *Para escribir* for ideas.

Culture: Have students review the notes they took in the *Álbum cultural.*
Speaking: Use the vocabulary section of the Organizer. Limit the number of lines of dialogue and complete the model given in the text.

Resumen del vocabulario

Usa el vocabulario de este capítulo para:

- responder a la pregunta clave: ¿Cómo nos influye la televisión?
- dar tu opinión sobre los programas de televisión
- comentar programas de televisión que has visto
- describir cómo te influye la televisión

para hablar de la televisión
alquilar
la antena parabólica
cambiar de canal
dieron (*from:* dar)
grabar
el comentario
el noticiero
el público
el reportaje
la televisión por cable
la televisión por satélite

para describir un programa de televisión
bostezar *(z → c)*
crítico, -a
emocionarse
entretener(se) *(e → ie)*
he visto; has visto (*from:* ver)
informativo, -a
negativo, -a
objetivo, -a
positivo, -a
reírse *(e → i)*
subjetivo, -a

para explicar quién puede ver los programas
la censura
clasificar *(c → qu)*
Apta para toda la familia
Prohibida para menores
Se recomienda discreción
Sólo para mayores

para discutir la influencia de la televisión
analizar *(z → c)*
comprobar *(o → ue)*
controlar
el derecho
evaluar *(u → ú)*
hacer daño
manipular
la opinión,
  pl. las opiniones
la percepción

otras palabras y expresiones útiles
demasiado, -a
la multa
recientemente
se ha dicho (*from:* decir)
tal como

Resumen 157

Reading
"El último boy scout." / Los más pequeños deben ver NUBELUZ.

Writing
Summaries will vary.

Culture
Answers will vary, but may include:
Los hispanoamericanos pueden ver todo tipo de programas de otros países.

Speaking
Dialogues will vary.

Assessment

¿? **Prueba cumulativa**

¿? **Examen de habilidades**

Test Generator

Additional Assessment Options

Comm. Act. BLMs

Small Group Activities
Situation Cards

¿Lo sabes bien? Video Quiz

www **Internet Activities**
Self-Test

CAPÍTULO 5
THEME: MAYAN CIVILIZATION

COMMUNICATION

Topics

Mayan cities

Archaeology

Mayan contributions

Objectives

Hablar de la civilización maya en el presente y en el pasado

Describir la civilización maya

Identificar lo que sigue existiendo de la civilización maya

Describir otras culturas del pasado

Hablar del presente y del pasado

CULTURE

La civilización maya

GRAMMAR

Hace . . . que / Hacía . . . que

El pluscuamperfecto

El verbo seguir *y el presente progresivo*

Ancillaries available for use with Chapter 5

Multisensory/Technology

 Overheads, 16–18

 Audio Tapes and CDs

 Vocabulary Art Blackline Masters for Hands-On Learning, pp. 26–29/CD-ROM

 Classroom Crossword

 Video

 Internet Activities www.pasoapaso.com

Print

 Practice Workbook, pp. 51–60

 Writing, Audio & Video Activities, pp. 29–34, 105–107, 141–142

 Communicative Activity Blackline Masters
  Pair and Small Group Activities, pp. 29–34
  Situation Cards, p. 35

RESOURCE PRO

Planning Express, Teaching Resources Library, and Clip Art Library

Assessment

 Assessment Program
  Pruebas, pp. 68–77
  Examen de habilidades, pp. 78–81

 Test Generator

 ¿Lo sabes bien? Video Quiz

Video, Chap. 5

157A

Native Peoples of the Americas

Descendants of prominent pre-Columbian civilizations continue to live throughout the Americas. Communities of Aztec, Maya, Tarascan, Huichol, and other native peoples are concentrated in Mexico. Guatemala is still home to thriving Mayan cultures, in spite of persecution, poverty, and isolation. Quechua (Incan) *pueblos* still flourish in rural areas of Peru and Bolivia.

Approximately 25 million people in Latin America speak indigenous languages, such as Nahuatl, Caxchiquel, Mam, Guaraní, Quechua, and Aymara. In Mexico alone, more than a million people speak only their native indigenous language, and nearly eight million others speak Spanish as a second language.

Recently, leaders in the Americas have begun to speak out about political and economic empowerment for indigenous peoples. Intercontinental alliances have been formed through such organizations as the World Council of Indigenous Peoples, the Coordinating Commission of Indigenous Nations and Organizations of the Continent (CONIC), and Indigenous Peoples Alliance (IPA). Since these descendants of the original inhabitants are often out of the mainstream, they are sometimes referred to as "marginalized" *(los marginados)*. It is considered key to the success of democracy throughout Latin America to represent these citizens in elected governments.

In an effort to acknowledge Bolivia's multiethnic population, Vice President Víctor Hugo Cárdenas gave his 1993 inaugural speech in Spanish, Aymara, Quechua, and Guaraní. This was an historic gesture in Latin America, where indigenous people have rarely participated in national elections. In Guatemala, for example, nearly 60 percent of the country's 10 million people are of Mayan descent, yet in 1994, there were only six indigenous members of the Guatemalan congress. In Ecuador, during the same year, there was only one such congressman; while in Bolivia, only three out of the 130 members of parliament were members of indigenous groups.

On Human Rights Day, December 10, 1994, the United Nations General Assembly declared the following ten years to be the "Decade of Indigenous Peoples." The goals are to strengthen international cooperation for the solution of problems faced by native peoples in areas such as human rights, the environment, economic development, education, and health.

Introduce

Re-entry of Concepts

The following list represents words, expressions, and grammar topics re-entered from Books 1, 2, and 3 (Chaps. 3 and 4):

Book 1
numbers, holidays, food, family members, clothing, location words, preterite, superlatives, present progressive

Book 2
clothing, imperfect, special occasions, pharmacy items

Chapter 3
past participles

Chapter 4
irregular past participles

Planning

Cross-Curricular Connections

History Connection *(pp. 168–169)*
In pairs or groups, have students role play archaeologists who have just uncovered a previously unknown building in a Mayan city. Have them draw the building in its ancient setting and prepare a written or oral report describing its features, its importance to the community, and the activities that occurred there.

Social Studies Connection *(pp. 182–183)*
In groups of four, have students role play ancient Mayans who have been transported to the present in a time machine. They should create a symbol for their city and explain it to the class. Have students present an additional oral report on what they have observed in our civilization and how it relates to what they had done in their own time.

Spanish in Your Community
Have students compile a list of Hispanic traditions celebrated in their community. Is there a Catholic church with ceremonies in Spanish for a baptism or a *quinceañera?* Does a church celebrate Mass in Spanish? Is the *posada* performed locally? They might want to attend if possible. Or, invite someone from the community, such as a priest, to visit the class to discuss various celebrations.

CAPÍTULO 5

OBJETIVOS

Al terminar este capítulo vas a poder responder a la pregunta clave:

¿Cómo se relacionan el pasado y el presente?

También vas a poder:

- describir las características de la civilización maya

- hablar de las contribuciones de la civilización maya

- explicar cómo nos han influido otras civilizaciones

- identificar lo que sigue existiendo de la civilización maya en la vida de hoy

Mural maya en las ruinas de Bonampak, México

159

VISITA
www.pasoapaso.com

Cultural Notes

(pp. 158–159, photo)
The murals at the Mayan site of Bonampak in Chiapas, Mexico, are the most complete and lavish of the known art from the ancient Americas. Found in three rooms of one of the larger ruins, the murals depict scenes from royal life between A.D. 790 and 792. In this mural, a new heir is presented to powerful lords who honor him with a sumptuous feast. The overall violent content of the Bonampak murals radically changed the previous scholarly view of the ancient Mayas as peaceable and priestly.

Preview

Cultural Objective
- *Hablar de la civilización maya en el presente y en el pasado*

Critical Thinking: Expressing Problems and Issues

Divide the class into groups of three or four. Have each group write several paragraphs that either support or refute this statement: *Para entender mejor la civilización actual, hay que entender las civilizaciones antiguas.* If necessary, help students get started by supplying ideas or examples. Have volunteers from each group read their paragraphs to the class. Discuss.

Answers

Answers will vary, but may include:
la arquitectura, la vida diaria / Hay muchos detalles en la pared. / Usan cosas modernas para coser.

Answers will vary for questions in caption text.

Anticipación

Mira las fotos. ¿Qué aspectos de la vida maya representan?
¿Cómo muestra su arquitectura que era una civilización avanzada?
¿Cómo combinan los mayas de hoy sus tradiciones con la vida moderna?

"Me gusta trabajar en estas ruinas mayas de Copán, Honduras."

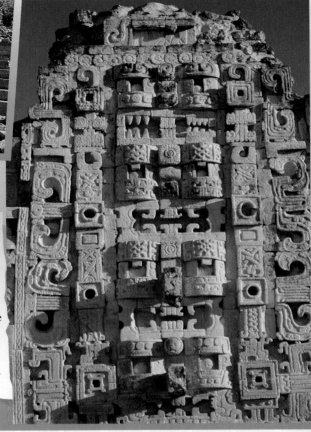

Los mayas dejaron muestras de una civilización muy avanzada en el sur de México y en Centroamérica. Las ruinas de Copán, Honduras, y las de Uxmal, Yucatán, México, como la Casa de las monjas que se ve a la derecha, son dos de los lugares donde los arqueólogos siguen encontrando restos de esta civilización. ¿Has oído hablar de algún lugar donde hay excavaciones arqueológicas? ¿Dónde?

160   Capítulo 5

Options

Strategies for Reaching All Students

Spanish-Speaking Students
Ask: *¿Te gustaría visitar uno de estos lugares? ¿Por qué? ¿Qué crees que aprenderías?*

Students Needing Extra Help
Students may not be aware of any recent archaeological digs. Be prepared with this information beforehand.

Cultural Notes ☀

(p. 160, left photo)
The Mayan ruins in Copán, Honduras, are world famous for their beauty, detail, and sheer abundance of ornamentation. Particularly impressive is the Hieroglyphic Stairway, dedicated in A.D. 755, whose ornate balustrades and remaining 63 steps recount the history of the site through 2,500 glyphs. The Copán ruins were declared a UNESCO World Heritage Site in 1980 and every year attract more than 30,000 visitors from throughout the world.

Hoy en día los mayas se dedican a la agricultura y la artesanía, haciendo ropas y tejidos. Algunos son miembros de cooperativas, como esta tejedora *(weaver)* de Zunil, Guatemala, y con su trabajo benefician a la comunidad. ¿Sabes de algún tipo de artesanía que todavía use métodos antiguos?

(see note, p. 163).

Multicultural Perspectives

The four greatest centers of Mayan civilization were Tikal in Guatemala, Palenque and Calakmul in Mexico, and Copán in northwestern Honduras. Copán flourished around 900 B.C. The rich soil in that area encouraged the growth of a large city. The Mayas there cultivated maize, practiced hierarchical religion, and prospered through trade with other cultures. The remaining ruins, artifacts, and monuments continue to fascinate archaeologists. The long reign of Humo Jaguar, the twelfth king of Copán, is known today by the many sculpted stelae he left behind (see note, p. 163). Copán has one of the most complete ruins of a ball court, where a life-and-death combination of soccer and handball was played by Mayan warriors. Bring books and articles on each of the Mayan cities. As an extra credit assignment, have groups of students choose one city to research and present their findings to the class.

Aunque muchos continúan usando los mismos métodos que sus antepasados, algunos mayas de hoy usan máquinas *(machines)* modernas, como esta costurera *(seamstress)* cerca de Chichén Itzá, Yucatán. ¿Por qué crees que esta costurera ha decidido usar máquinas modernas en su trabajo?

Exploración Cultural   www.pasoapaso.com
Visita estos países

161

(p. 160, right photo)
Uxmal, one of Mexico's best-preserved Mayan sites, is renowned for the beauty and elegant proportions of its buildings which offer the best examples of pure, Puuc (Classic Mayan) architecture. Like nearby Kabah, Uxmal flourished during the Late Classic period. It was the most important city in the region. Its splendid buildings are decorated with masks of Chac, the ninth-century king and last-known ruler.

(p. 161, top photo)
Many Mayan weavers in Zunil, Guatemala, produce and sell their work through cooperatives. These organizations can include hundreds of women from dozens of villages and are devoted to keeping alive ancient designs, as well as weaving and natural dyeing techniques. In addition to preserving their identity and tradition, these cooperatives bring needed income to the indigenous population.

(p. 161, bottom photo)
The traditional garment worn by this Mayan woman near Chichén Itzá is called a *huipil,* a Nahuatl word. As worn in the Yucatán peninsula, a *huipil* is a loose, white cotton dress, all one width from top to bottom. It usually has brilliant embroidery at its square neckline and hem. In the Guatemalan highlands, a *huipil* is a short, rectangularly-shaped blouse that is woven in a design unique to the community to which the wearer belongs.

Standards 1.2; 2.1; 3.1; 5.1   **161**

Present

Chapter Theme
Past and present

Communicative Objectives
- *Describir la civilización maya*
- *Identíficar lo que sigue existiendo de la civilización maya*
- *Describir otras culturas del pasado*
- *Hablar del presente y del pasado*

 Overheads 16–17

 Vocabulary Art BLMs/CD-ROM

 Vocabulary Tape 5-1

Teaching Suggestions
Preparing students to speak: Use one or two options from each of the categories of Comprehensible Input or Limited Verbal Response. For a complete explanation of these categories and some sample activities, see pp. T20–T21.

Vocabulario para comunicarse

El pasado y el presente

Aquí tienes palabras y expresiones necesarias para hablar sobre la relación entre el pasado y el presente. Léelas varias veces y practícalas con un(a) compañero(a) en las páginas siguientes.

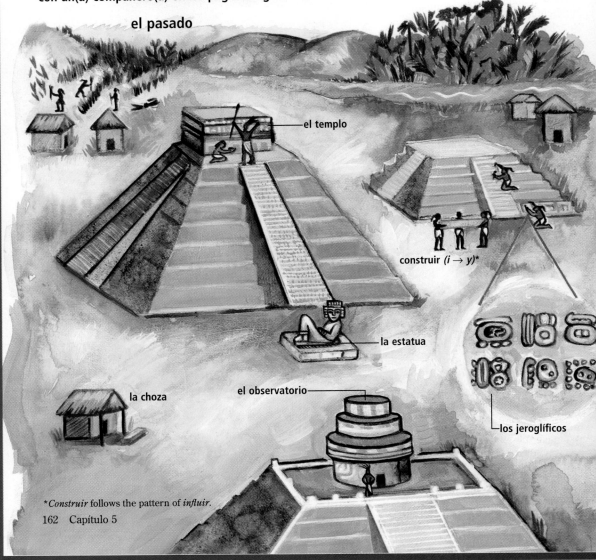

el pasado

el templo

construir *(i → y)**

la estatua

el observatorio

la choza

los jeroglíficos

*Construir follows the pattern of *influir*.

162   Capítulo 5

Options

Strategies for Reaching All Students

Spanish-Speaking Students
Tell students: *Escribe oraciones originales con diez de las palabras del vocabulario.*

Students Needing Extra Help
Begin the vocabulary section of the Organizer. Write out the complete paradigms of all tenses of *construir*. Point out the *en* and *terra* in *enterrado*, "in the earth." *También necesitas...:* Drill *la costumbre* if students confuse it with "costume." Explain the concept of hieroglyphics to those who do not understand it.

Extended Written Practice/Homework
1. Write sentences telling what people with each of the professions on p. 163 do: *Los arquitectos construyen ...*
2. Write three sentences describing the village in the drawing on pp. 162–163: *En el centro había ...*
3. Refer to p. 163. Write four sentences telling what the archaeologists discovered in the jungle.

También necesitas . . .

la costumbre	*custom*	heredar	*to inherit*
el descubrimiento	*discovery*	sagrado, -a	*sacred*
el dios, *pl.* los dioses	*god*	el significado	*meaning*
la escritura	*writing*		

el presente

¿Y qué quiere decir . . . ?

aceptar
el antropólogo, la antropóloga
el arquitecto, la arquitecta
el astrónomo, la astrónoma
la ceremonia
la civilización,
    pl. las civilizaciones
la cultura

los mayas
el objeto
el origen, *pl.* los orígenes
la religión,
    pl. las religiones
la tradición,
    pl. las tradiciones

descubrir
la arqueóloga
el arqueólogo
enterrado, -a
la escultura
el cuenco
la tumba
la vasija
el jade

Vocabulario para comunicarse 163

Multicultural Perspectives
La estela is an anthropological term used to describe a statuelike monument Mayan kings ordered built in their honor. Hieroglyphs inscribed on these monuments tell about the king's ancestry, his role as a shaman and family patriarch, and his accomplishments. When the king died, or was defeated, his stelae were destroyed or defaced. At Copán, the son of Humo Jaguar failed to destroy his father's monuments, which is why archaeologists were able to find them. Two other unusual stelae are found there as well. One is of a woman, the other of a bearded man—perhaps a trader from another city. Ask students to discuss how past and present leaders record their accomplishments. What do they create to document their time as leaders?

www Internet Activities
Juegos

Multiple Intelligences
Verbal/Linguistic
1) Have students write a paragraph comparing the two scenes on pp. 162–163.
2) See Vocabulary Tape 5-1.
Visual/Spatial
See Overheads 16–17 and the Vocabulary Art BLMs/CD-ROM.

Practice

Reteach / Review: Prepositions

Ex. 1: For additional practice, have the entire class play a game in which one student places an object in a certain part of the room and the other students have to describe its location. Include the student placing the object by asking ¿Dónde pusiste el / la / los / las ___?

Answers: Empecemos a conversar

1 ESTUDIANTE A
a. Dónde descubrió el arqueólogo el templo?
b. ...la pirámide?
c. ...la choza?
d. ...la tumba?
e. ...la pared?
f. ...el observatorio?
g. Questions will vary.

ESTUDIANTE B
a.–g. Answers will vary, but look for correct use of direct object pronouns and logical choices of prepositions.

Empecemos a conversar

Túrnate con un(a) compañero(a) para ser *Estudiante A* y *Estudiante B*. Reemplacen las palabras subrayadas con palabras representadas o escritas en los recuadros. ☀ quiere decir que puedes escoger tu propia respuesta.

Para el ejercicio 1, mira el mapa de arriba.

1
A —¿Dónde descubrió el arqueólogo *la estatua*?
B —*La* descubrió en *el centro de la plaza*.

Estudiante A

a.   b.   c.   d.

e.   f.   g.

Estudiante B

al fondo
a la derecha
junto a
al lado de
enfrente de
detrás de
delante de
entre

164   Capítulo 5

Options

Strategies for Reaching All Students

Students Needing Extra Help
Ex. 1: Review location words.
Ex. 3: Review the preterite tense of *-ar* verbs and *construir*.

Enrichment
Ex. 2: Bring several books on the past or present Mayas with photographs or drawings showing the objects listed in the exercise. Have pairs of students choose a photograph or drawing that they can describe in detail to the class.

Ex. 3: As a homework assignment, ask students to write a few sentences answering these questions: ¿Cuál es el trabajo más importante que puede hacer un(a) arqueólogo(a)? ¿Por qué crees que es importante este trabajo?

2

A —¿Qué había en *las chozas*?
B —Había *unos cuencos*.

Estudiante A

Estudiante B

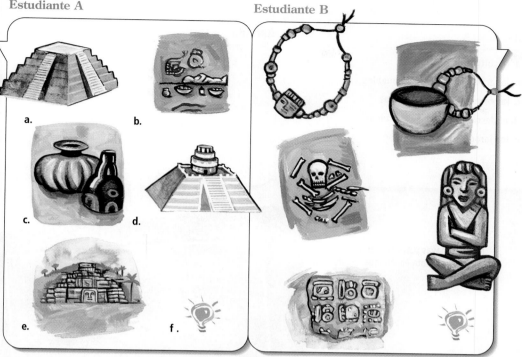

a.

b.

c.

d.

e.

f.

2 **ESTUDIANTE A**
a. ¿Qué había en la pirámide?
b. . . . la tumba?
c. . . . las vasijas?
d. . . . el observatorio?
e. . . . la pared?
f. Questions will vary.

ESTUDIANTE B
(Answers may vary.)
a. Había una escultura.
b. . . . huesos.
c. . . . jade.
d. . . . una escultura.
e. . . . jeroglíficos.
f. Answers will vary

3 **ESTUDIANTE A**
a. ¿Qué hizo la profesora?
b. . . . el obrero?
c. . . . el astrónomo?
d. . . . la antropóloga?
e. . . . el guía?
f. Questions will vary.

ESTUDIANTE B
a. Explicó el significado de los jeroglíficos.
b. Construyó el templo.
c. Estudió los planetas.
d. Investigó el origen de la civilización.
e. Mostró los objetos sagrados.
f. Answers will vary.

3 la arqueóloga

A —¿Qué hizo *la arqueóloga*?
B —*Investigó las ruinas enterradas*.

Estudiante A

a. la profesora
b. el obrero
c. el astrónomo
d. la antropóloga
e. el guía
f.

Estudiante B

estudiar los planetas
explicar el significado de los jeroglíficos
construir el templo
mostrar los objetos sagrados
investigar el origen de la civilización

Vocabulario para comunicarse   165

Extended Written Practice/Homework
1. Write three sentences naming the aspects of a culture or civilization that interest anthropologists: *A los antropólogos les interesan . . .*
2. Write three sentences describing customs or traditions of your family or community in the present or in the past: *Una costumbre de mi comunidad es dar conciertos en el parque en el verano.*

Multiple Intelligences
Verbal/Linguistic
See Exs. 1–3.
Verbal/Linguistic and Visual/Spatial
See Enrichment.

Practice & Apply

Answers: Empecemos a conversar

4 ESTUDIANTE A

a. ¿Qué es lo que más te interesa de la cultura de los mayas?

b. ... de las tradiciones de otros pueblos?

c. ... de las ceremonias de los mayas?

d. ... del descubrimiento de las ruinas?

e. ... de los jeroglíficos?

f. Questions will vary.

ESTUDIANTE B

a.–f. Answers will vary.

¿Cómo se relacionan el pasado y el presente?

4 las religiones antiguas   A — ¿Qué es lo que más te interesa de _las religiones antiguas_?
B — _Sus dioses._

Estudiante A

a. la cultura de los mayas

b. las tradiciones de otros pueblos

c. las ceremonias de los mayas

d. el descubrimiento de las ruinas

e. los jeroglíficos

f.

Estudiante B

Mujeres mayas participan en la procesión de Semana Santa en Antigua, Guatemala

Ensayando un baile tradicional en Chiapas, México

Options

Strategies for Reaching All Students

Spanish-Speaking Students
Ex. 6: Ask: _¿Es importante que tus nietos continúen estas tradiciones? ¿Por qué?_

Students Needing Extra Help
Ex. 4: Brainstorm examples for the _Estudiante B_ responses.
Ex. 6: Assign this activity in advance so that students have time to discuss this with their families.
Ex. 7: Remind students of the meaning of _guardar una caja._ Limit the number of items.

Ex. 8: Assign this activity in advance.

Enrichment
Ex. 4: Bring in books and articles that give more detail on the day-to-day lives of the modern Mayas. Assign an article or book to pairs of students so that they can prepare a class presentation on these questions: _¿En qué es diferente la vida de los mayas de hoy de la vida de sus antepasados hace cinco siglos? ¿En qué es diferente de la vida en nuestra sociedad?_

Cooperative Learning
As a class, develop a list of ten items students could bring to class that represent the culture in your area today. Plan a specific day for them to bring the items, and place them in numbered boxes. Ask students to form groups of five, draw a number, and take the appropriate box. Tell them to imagine they are archaeologists from the year 2500. Have groups develop five statements (one per group member) about the culture the item represents, then discuss as a class.

¿Y qué piensas tú?

Aquí tienes otra oportunidad para usar el vocabulario de este capítulo.

5 ¿La ciudad o el pueblo donde vives es antigua(o) o moderna(o)? Describe algo viejo y algo nuevo que hay en el lugar donde vives.

6 ¿Cuáles son algunas de las ceremonias que celebramos hoy? ¿En qué se parecen y en qué se diferencian de las ceremonias que celebraban tus abuelos? ¿Cuáles crees que van a heredar tus nietos?

7 Imagina que vas a guardar una caja con cosas importantes que usas en tu vida diaria. Si alguien descubre esa caja en el futuro, ¿qué encontrará?

8 Entrevista a un pariente mayor o a personas mayores de tu comunidad. ¿Cuáles eran algunos de sus valores cuando eran jóvenes? ¿Cuáles son algunos de los valores de los jóvenes de ahora? ¿Han cambiado? Comparte las respuestas con el resto de la clase.

Práctica de vocabulario www.pasoapaso.com

MÁS PRÁCTICA

- Más práctica y tarea, p. 559
- Practice Workbook 5–1, 5–2

Vocabulario para comunicarse 167

Answers: ¿Y qué piensas tú?

5–8 Answers will vary, but should include a variety of verb tenses.

 Practice Wkbk. 5-1, 5-2

 Audio Activity 5.1

 Writing Activities 5-A, 5-B

 Pruebas 5-1, 5-2

Cultural Notes ☀

Multiple Intelligences
Intrapersonal/Introspective
See Ex. 7.
Logical/Mathematical and Visual/Spatial
See Cooperative Learning.
Verbal/Linguistic
See Ex. 4 and Audio Activity 5.1.
Visual/Spatial
See Practice Wkbk. 5-1 and 5-2 and Writing Activities 5-A and 5-B.

(p. 166, left photo)
A showcase of beautiful Spanish colonial architecture, the city of San Cristóbal de las Casas in Chiapas, Mexico, was founded in 1528. Indigenous dress, beliefs, rituals, and forms of entertainment, such as this dance, are still prominent in the city. Five Mayan languages are spoken here, along with Spanish, the official language.

(p. 166, right photo)
The daily religious processions during *Semana Santa* in Antigua, Guatemala, involve hundreds of the city's 30,000 residents and attract tourists from all over the world. Many locals dress in deep purple robes to play the part of Israelites in the ceremonial marches. The streets on which processions will pass are carpeted with colored sawdust and flower petals arranged in elaborate, vivid designs.

Present

Chapter Theme
Mayan contributions

Communicative Objectives
- *Describir la civilización maya*
- *Identificar lo que sigue existiendo de la civilización maya*
- *Describir otras culturas del pasado*
- *Hablar del presente y del pasado*

 Overhead 18

 Vocabulary Tape 5-2

Grammar Preview
Seguir + present participle is presented lexically. Its presentation appears on p. 180.

Teaching Suggestions
Getting ready to speak:
Remind students of the reading strategies that they learned (getting meaning from context and coping with unknown words) to help them understand the *Tema para investigar*. For further details and some sample activities, see pp. T24–T25.

Answers: Tema para investigar
Answers will vary.

Tema para investigar

Aquí tienes más palabras e ideas para hablar sobre el pasado y el presente. Mira el mapa de esta página. ¿Dónde puedes visitar otras ruinas? ¿Las has visitado?

168   Capítulo 5

Options

Strategies for Reaching All Students

Spanish-Speaking Students
Haz una investigación sobre una de las ciudades de los mayas mencionadas en este artículo. Prepara una presentación oral para tus compañeros con un mapa, dibujos o fotos. Puedes usar materiales que hay en tu sala de clases o en la biblioteca escolar.

Students Needing Extra Help
Point out the relationship between *descubiertas* and *descubrir*.
If necessary, explain the term *precolombino* (pre-Columbian): anything belonging to or representative of the period in the 1400s before the arrival of Columbus in the Americas.

Extended Written Practice/Homework
1. Based on the reading on p. 169, write three sentences naming different items that were developed by the Mayas. Use: *desarrollar, contribución, crear*.
2. Write four sentences naming important aspects of the Mayan way of life: *El estudio de las estrellas era muy importante*.
3. Write three sentences telling what scientists have done to learn more about the Mayan civilization. Use: *excavar, descubrir, estudiar*.

Los mayas de antes y de hoy

En México se pueden visitar las ruinas de las famosas ciudades de Chichén Itzá, Uxmal, Cobá y Palenque. En Guatemala se encuentra la magnífica ciudad de Tikal, y en Honduras están todavía **excavando** las ruinas de Copán, **descubiertas** en 1839. Todas ellas son obras de los mayas, una civilización que ya **existía** unos mil años antes de Cristo y que todavía no ha **desaparecido**.

Gracias al descubrimiento del significado de **los símbolos**, sabemos ahora que los mayas **desarrollaron** el sistema de escritura más **avanzado** de la América **precolombina**. Era un sistema que tenía cerca de 800 símbolos. Algunos símbolos representaban palabras; otros, sólo **sílabas**. La mayor parte de los jeroglíficos describían la vida de los grandes **líderes**, las guerras, las ceremonias religiosas y otros hechos históricos. Aunque ya no se usa este sistema de escritura, su idioma, **el quiché**, todavía se **sigue hablando**, especialmente en ciertos lugares de México, como en la Península de Yucatán, y en ciertos lugares de Guatemala y Honduras.

Las matemáticas eran muy importantes para los mayas. Ellos fueron los primeros que entendieron y usaron el cero como número. Se dice que ésta es su **contribución** más importante en este **campo**. Además, desarrollaron un sistema avanzado de astronomía. Siguiendo el movimiento de **las estrellas** que veían desde sus observatorios astronómicos, crearon dos **calendarios** distintos: uno, sagrado, que indicaba las fiestas religiosas; otro, solar, de 365 días que era casi tan exacto como el que usamos hoy. Sus ceremonias religiosas se relacionaban principalmente con **la siembra** y **la cosecha**.

Aunque la cultura maya **actual** no tiene **el esplendor** que tenía hace más de 1500 años, los mayas de hoy todavía conservan muchas de las tradiciones y ceremonias de sus **antepasados**. Muchos mayas todavía viven en pueblos pequeños donde se dedican a **la agricultura**, y mantienen el **rico legado** que heredaron de sus antepasados.

desaparecido, -a	*disappeared*	la estrella	*star*
desarrollar	*to develop*	la siembra	*planting, sowing*
el quiché	*Mayan language*	la cosecha	*harvest*
seguir *(e → i)* + present participle	*to continue* + verb + *-ing*	actual	*present-day*
		los antepasados	*ancestors*
el campo	here: *field, area*	el legado	*legacy*

¿Y qué quiere decir . . . ?

excavar	la sílaba
descubierto, -a	el / la líder
existir	la contribución, *pl.* las contribuciones
gracias a	el calendario
el símbolo	el esplendor
avanzado, -a	la agricultura
precolombino, -a	rico, -a

Tema para investigar   169

Practice & Apply

Teaching Suggestions
(p. 171) Point out that the symbols in the drawing represent Mayan hieroglyphs for numbers. Explain that this system using dot-and-bar combinations was positional like the decimal system, but was based on 20 instead of 10.

Answers: ¿Comprendiste?
1 Answers will vary, but students may mention the following: Siguen hablando quiché. Todavía conservan muchas de las tradiciones y ceremonias de sus antepasados. Muchos mayas todavía viven en pueblos pequeños. / Se dedican a la agricultura y a mantener el legado de sus antepasados.

2 Responses will vary.

Answers: ¿Y qué piensas tú?
3–6 Answers will vary.

¿Comprendiste?

1 Según la lectura *Los mayas de antes y de hoy,* ¿cómo son hoy? ¿A qué se dedican?

2 Inventa dos jeroglíficos para representar dos de las contribuciones más importantes de los mayas. Compara tus jeroglíficos con los de tus compañeros(as) de clase.

¿Y tú qué piensas?

Aquí tienes otra oportunidad para usar el vocabulario de este capítulo.

3 En tu opinión, ¿cuál de las contribuciones de los mayas es la más interesante? ¿Por qué?

4 ¿Qué existe hoy de la antigua civilización maya? ¿Qué ha desaparecido? ¿Qué aspectos de nuestra civilización moderna crees que permanecerán en mil años?

5 En un diagrama de Venn, escribe palabras que describan las contribuciones de los mayas. Luego, escribe palabras que describan las contribuciones de nuestra cultura actual. ¿Qué contribuciones tienen en común? Compara tu diagrama con el de un(a) compañero(a).

jeroglíficos | agricultura arquitectura | computadoras

Mujer maya llevando verduras en el mercado de Almolonga, Guatemala

MÁS PRÁCTICA
- Más práctica y tarea, p. 560
- Practice Workbook 5–3, 5–4

170   Capítulo 5

Options

Strategies for Reaching All Students

Spanish-Speaking Students
Ex. 4: *¿Por qué crees que permanecerán estos aspectos de la civilización moderna? ¿Qué aprenderán las civilizaciones futuras de nosotros y de nuestro modo de vivir?*

Students Needing Extra Help
Ex. 1: Brainstorm possible responses to the question.
Ex. 3: Students will need help with the vocabulary for the *¿Por qué?* question.
Ex. 4: Name several aspects of today's civilization, allowing students to choose which ones they think will survive.
Ex. 5: Discuss the idea of "contributions" as a class.
¿Qué sabes ahora?: Have students write this so that they can record their progress.

Cooperative Learning
As a class, brainstorm ten contributions that our civilization of the last hundred years has made to the future. In groups of four, tell pairs of students to create hieroglyphics representing any five of these. Within each group, tell pairs to exchange hieroglyphics, and try to guess which contributions they represent.

6 Lee las palabras siguientes. Cada una de ellas representa un concepto que era importante en la sociedad maya.

| contribuciones | valores | religión | costumbres | tradiciones |

- Piensa en el significado que tiene cada uno de estos conceptos en tu vida.
- Decide qué conceptos son los más importantes para ti y cuáles tienen menos importancia.
- Haz una gráfica como la de la derecha.
- Escribe cada una de las palabras bajo el número apropiado.
- Luego, compara tu gráfica con las de tus compañeros de clase.

menos importante

0
1
2
3
4
5

más importante

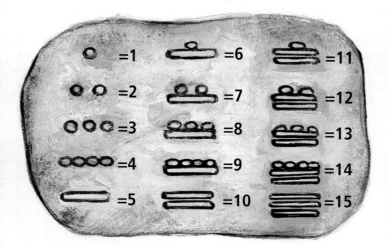

¿Qué sabes ahora?

¿Puedes:

■ describir las contribuciones de la civilización maya?

—Los mayas estudiaron el _____ de las estrellas. También fueron los primeros que usaron el _____ como número.

■ hablar de lo que nos ha quedado de la civilización maya?

—Los mayas de hoy ___ y ___.

■ hablar de algunas de las contribuciones mayas a nuestra civilización?

—Los mayas hicieron importantes contribuciones en el campo de ___ y de ____.

Tema para investigar   171

Cultural Notes

Multiple Intelligences
Interpersonal/Social, Visual/Spatial, and Verbal/Linguistic
See Cooperative Learning.
Verbal/Linguistic
1) Have students simulate an interview with an ancient Maya.
2) See Audio Activity 5.2.
Visual/Spatial
See Practice Wkbk. 5-3 and 5-4, Writing Activity 5-C, and Comm. Act. BLM 5-1.

(p. 170, photo)
A woman carries vegetables to the market in Almolonga, Guatemala. Guatemala's economy is heavily dependent on agriculture, which employs over half of the active work force. Yet while some people may own small parcels of mountain land on which they raise vegetables such as these, the most fertile land, producing coffee and other important exports, belongs to a mere two percent of the landowners.

Present & Apply

Cultural Objective
• *Hablar de la civilización maya en el presente y en el pasado*

Critical Thinking: Determining Relevant Information
Ask students: *¿Cuáles son cinco cosas (objetos) que representen a nuestra civilización en los Estados Unidos?* Have each student write down their items. Collect and write the items on the chalkboard. Discuss students' reasoning behind their choices.

Answers
Answers will vary, but may include:
Sus intereses principales eran la agricultura, la arquitectura, la literatura y la artesanía.

ÁLBUM CULTURAL

En estas páginas vas a ver diferentes aspectos del legado de la civilización maya. También vas a ver aspectos de la vida de los mayas de hoy y cómo siguen conservando sus tradiciones. Según estas ilustraciones y fotos, ¿cuáles eran sus intereses principales?

Los mayas se establecieron *(settled)* en Yucatán, Guatemala y Honduras alrededor *(circa)* del año 2000 a.C. y empezaron a cultivar maíz y frijoles. Para el año 250 a.C., su civilización había recibido la influencia de los olmecas y habían fundado ciudades como Tikal y El Mirador, en Guatemala. En el período clásico (300 d.C. a 900 d.C.) los mayas construyeron las ciudades de Palenque y Bonampak, en México, y Copán, en Honduras. Después del 900 d.C., los mayas recibieron la influencia de los toltecas. En este período, llamado posclásico, construyeron las ciudades de Chichén Itzá y Uxmal, en Yucatán. Las ruinas de estas ciudades nos muestran el sorprendente legado de los mayas.

LOS MAYAS

Período formativo
2000 a.C.-300 d.C.

Período clásico
300 d.C.-900 d.C.

172   Capítulo 5

Options

Strategies for Reaching All Students

Students Needing Extra Help
Remind students to take notes for use in the *¿Lo sabes bien?* section at the end of the chapter.
Explain the use of *a.C.* and *d.C. (antes de Cristo* and *después de Cristo)* for B.C. and A.D.

Multiple Intelligences
Bodily/Kinesthetic
Have students build a model of a pyramid.
Musical/Rhythmic
As extra credit, have students research various types of music from Yucatán, Guatemala, and Honduras and see if there are connections to the Mayan civilization.
Visual/Spatial and Verbal/Linguistic
See Critical Thinking.

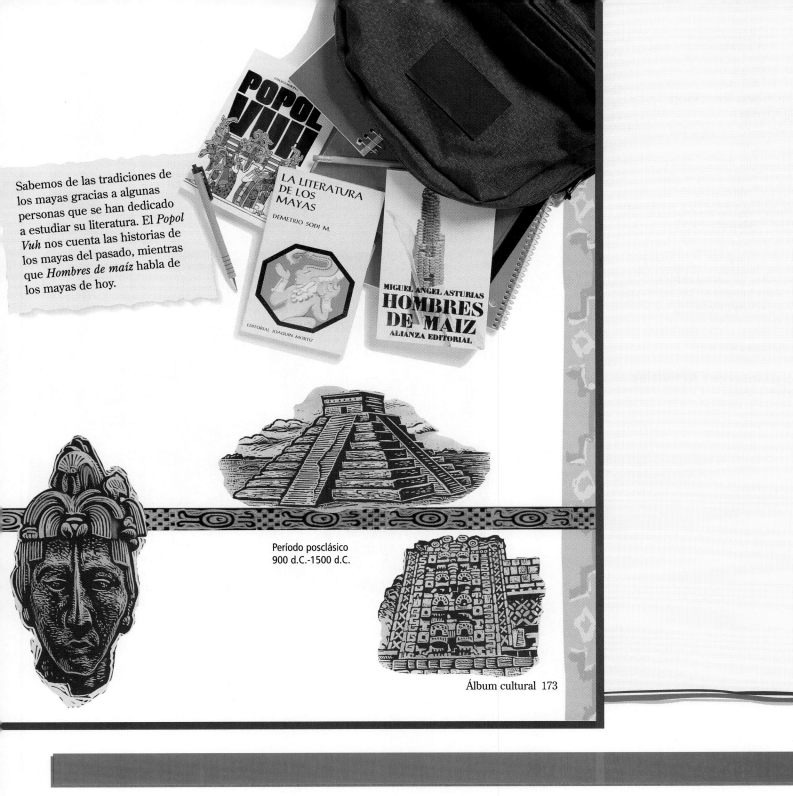

Sabemos de las tradiciones de los mayas gracias a algunas personas que se han dedicado a estudiar su literatura. El *Popol Vuh* nos cuenta las historias de los mayas del pasado, mientras que *Hombres de maíz* habla de los mayas de hoy.

Período posclásico
900 d.C.-1500 d.C.

Álbum cultural 173

Present & Apply

Answers: Reacción personal

1 Answers will vary, but students may mention:
La literatura nos ayuda a saber de las tradiciones porque puede decirnos cómo empezaron. También nos ayuda a entenderlas mejor. / *Answers will vary.*

2 Podemos observar la influencia de los olmecas en las ruinas (las ciudades) de Tikal y El Mirador, y la de los toltecas en las ruinas (las ciudades) de Chichén Itzá y Uxmal.

3 Answers will vary.

www Internet Activities
Álbum cultural

Entre los productos agrícolas, el maíz es el más importante para los mayas. Desde jóvenes aprenden a sembrar y cosechar maíz, frijoles y otros productos, teniendo siempre respeto por la tierra.

Options

Strategies for Reaching All Students

Students Needing Extra Help
Reacción personal: In question 3, be aware that some students may not have older family members who will be passing on traditions.

Multiple Intelligences
Verbal/Linguistic
See Exs. 1–3.

La tradición de hacer y pintar artículos de artesanía ha pasado de padres a hijos por varias generaciones. Estas vasijas de Amatenango, México, son decoradas con escenas de la vida diaria. Algunas reflejan la admiración de los mayas por la naturaleza.

Reacción personal

Contesta las siguientes preguntas en una hoja de papel.

1 ¿Cómo nos ayuda la literatura a saber de las tradiciones de otras civilizaciones? ¿Te parece interesante aprender de otras civilizaciones del pasado? ¿Por qué?

2 Los olmecas y los toltecas influyeron en la civilización maya. ¿En qué podemos observar su influencia?

3 ¿Por qué es importante para los mayas de hoy conservar las tradiciones de sus antepasados? ¿Cuáles son algunas maneras de pasar una tradición de una generación a otra?

Actividad cultural · www.pasoapaso.com

Álbum cultural 175

Cultural Notes ☀

(p. 174, photo)
The living conditions for poor Indian women in Guatemala are among the worst in Latin America. In rural areas, they live in the poverty suffered by many of the country's indigenous people. If they elect to go to the city to work—most likely as maids—they may be paid as little as $40.00 per month.

(p. 175, photo)
The women of the Tzeltal Mayan village of Amatenango del Valle, in Chiapas, Mexico, are known for the traditional pottery they produce. It is especially remarkable because it is fired using the pre-Columbian method of burning a wood fire around the pieces rather than using a kiln. Today, younger women have begun making delicate, appealing *animalitos,* primarily for the tourist trade. This woman is wearing a dress typical of the area.

Preview

Teaching Suggestions

A Have students explain how they've used this combination before. / Review the present perfect with questions such as: *¿Qué películas has visto recientemente?* / Ask if *había* refers to the past, present, or future. / Explain the idea of something that had taken place prior to another action taking place. Ask students to draw a timeline to illustrate this point.

B Ask students to identify other verb forms that are similar to *disminuyendo*. / Have them identify the present participle endings for *-ar, -er,* and *-ir* verbs. / Review the present progressive with questions such as: *¿Qué están haciendo tus amigos?*

Answers

A This combination was used before with the present perfect. / imperfect (past tense) / The meaning changes from "have" to "had" (done something). / These actions refer to something that already had taken place in the past.

B Verbs like *disminuyendo* have been used before with a form of *estar.* / *Siguen comiendo* would be a better choice, because the use of *están* implies that they are actually eating right now, as opposed to the meaning "they continue to eat" (an action started in the past and is still continuing in the present).

Gramática en contexto

Mira las fotos y lee el texto. La descripción de abajo te ayudará a adivinar el nombre de un bonito pájaro.

¿Cómo se llama?

Lee la descripción de este pájaro. ¿Cómo se llama?

A In the first and second paragraphs, these verbs are used: *habían adorado* and *habían creído*. These use a form of *haber* + the past participle. How have you used this combination before? What is the tense of *había(n)?* How do you think this changes the meaning of *haber* + the past participle from the way you used it before? Explain to a partner why *habían,* instead of *han,* is the correct form of *haber* in these paragraphs.

B In the third paragraph, *sigue disminuyendo* is used. You have used verb forms like *disminuyendo* before. What verb did you use them with? Consider this sentence: *Antiguamente comían tortillas de maíz, y en muchas partes todavía comen tortillas de maíz.* Which of the following would be a better replacement for *todavía comen* without changing the meaning of the sentence: *están comiendo /siguen comiendo?* Explain to a partner why you think this is a better choice.

¿Cómo se llama?

Antiguamente, los habitantes de Guatemala habían creído que este pájaro no podía vivir en cautiverio; era un símbolo de libertad. Por eso los guatemaltecos decidieron ponerlo en su bandera y dar su nombre al dinero del país.

Los mayas y aztecas habían adorado a un dios que llevaba una prenda en la cabeza adornada con plumas de este pájaro.

Mucha gente en Guatemala quema y destruye las selvas para producir tierras de cultivo. Por eso, el número de estos pájaros que vive allí sigue disminuyendo.

176   Capítulo 5

Options

Strategies for Reaching All Students

Students Needing Extra Help

Begin the grammar section of the Organizer. *Hace . . . que / Hacía . . . que:* Emphasize the idea that with *hace . . . que* the action started in the past and is still going on. With *hacía . . . que,* the action that started in the past has now ended. Give further examples.
Ex. 1: Brainstorm words to complete the questions to be asked from the verb list.

Extended Written Practice/Homework

1. Write three sentences telling how long a famous person has been doing what they are known for: *Hace . . . años que Gloria Estefan canta . . .*
2. Write three sentences telling how long you or others had done something when something happened: *Hacía nueve años que vivíamos en San Agustín cuando nos mudamos a Tampa.*

Multiple Intelligences

Interpersonal/Social and Verbal/Linguistic
See Ex. 1.
Verbal/Linguistic
See Class Starter Review.

Hace . . . que / Hacía . . . que

Remember that we use the following construction to tell how long something has been going on:

hace + period of time + **que** + present tense

Hace tres años **que** los astrónomos **estudian** el calendario maya.
The astronomers have been studying the Mayan calendar for three years.

- To tell how long something had been going on in the past, we use the same construction with the imperfect tense:

hacía + period of time + **que** + imperfect tense

Hacía dos siglos **que** los mayas **vivían** en aquella región.
The Mayas had been living in that region for two centuries.

- To find out how long something has or had been going on, we ask:

¿Cuánto tiempo hace que + present tense?

¿Cuánto tiempo hacía que + imperfect tense?

¿Cuánto tiempo hace que cultivan maíz en ese campo?
How long have they been growing corn in that field?

¿Cuánto tiempo hacía que tenían esas tradiciones?
How long had they had those traditions?

1 Pregúntale a un(a) compañero(a) cuánto tiempo hace que hace algo.

tocar   A —*¿Cuánto tiempo hace que tocas el violín?*
          B —*Hace ocho años que toco el violín.*

a. conocer   e. saber
b. estudiar   f. vivir
c. jugar   g. 🔆
d. participar

Present & Practice

Class Starter Review
On the day following the presentation of *hace . . . que / hacía . . . que,* you might begin the class with this activity:
Think of events, either historical or recent, and ask students: *¿Cuánto tiempo hace que . . . ?* Be sure to use both present and imperfect tenses, and have students answer in complete sentences.

Answers
1 ESTUDIANTE A
Questions will vary, but may begin in the following manner:
a. ¿Cuánto tiempo hace que conoces . . .
b. . . . estudias . . .
c. . . . juegas . . .
d. . . . participas . . .
e. . . . sabes . . .
f. . . . vives . . .
g. Questions will vary.
ESTUDIANTE B
Answers will vary, but may begin in the following manner:
a. Hace ____ años que conozco . . .
b. . . . estudio . . .
c. . . . juego . . .
d. . . . participo . . .
e. . . . sé . . .
f. . . . vivo . . .
g. Answers will vary.

Cultural Notes ☀

(p. 176, top left inset photo)
The rare, resplendent *quetzal,* Guatemala's national bird, is found only in that country's northern highland rain forests, which are home to more than 700 bird species—as many as in the U.S. and Canada combined. In 1988, the governments of Mexico, Guatemala, Belize, Honduras, and El Salvador joined in a plan called *La ruta maya,* designed to protect and develop these areas in a low-impact, ecologically responsible way.

(p. 176, bottom inset photo)
The colorful, complex featherwork of the costumes of these dancers in Puebla, Mexico, indicates the high value placed on beautiful feathers for adornment by indigenous peoples throughout the Americas. Only a few such examples have survived from central Mexico. No examples have been found of ancient Mayan featherwork, the most striking of which included the long, iridescent blue-green tailfeathers of the *quetzal,* which were worn exclusively by royalty.

Present & Practice

Re-enter / Recycle

Ex. 3–4: past participles from Chap. 3, irregular past participles from Chap. 4

Answers

2 ESTUDIANTE A

a. Los mayas ya vivían en la selva cuando llegaron los españoles, ¿no?

b. ...resolvían problemas de matemáticas...

c. ...escribían con jeroglíficos...

d. ...tenían un calendario exacto...

e. ...eran buenos astrónomos...

f. ...cultivaban las tierras...

g. Statements will vary.

ESTUDIANTE B

Answers will vary, but should follow this pattern:

a. Sí, hacía + *time expression* + que vivían en la selva.

b. ...resolvían problemas de matemáticas.

c. ...escribían con jeroglíficos.

d. ...tenían un calendario exacto.

e. ...eran buenos astrónomos.

f. ...cultivaban las tierras.

g. Statements will vary.

 Practice Wkbk. 5-5, 5-6

 Writing Activity 5-D

 Prueba 5-5

---

2 Habla con otra persona sobre la historia de los mayas en Yucatán.

vivir en Yucatán   A —*Los mayas ya vivían en Yucatán cuando llegaron los españoles ¿no?*
   B —*Sí, hacía muchos siglos que vivían allí.*

Estudiante A

a. vivir en la selva
b. resolver problemas de matemáticas
c. escribir con jeroglíficos
d. tener un calendario exacto
e. ser buenos astrónomos
f. cultivar las tierras
g.

Estudiante B

muchos siglos
cientos de años
más de 500 años
mucho tiempo
unos siglos

El pluscuamperfecto

We use the pluperfect tense to describe an action in the past that occurred *before* another action in the past. Its English equivalent is *had* + the past participle: *they had built, we had seen, had you heard?* To form the pluperfect we use the imperfect of *haber* + a past participle. Here are all of the pluperfect tense forms of *construir*.

había construido	habíamos construido
habías construido	habíais construido
había construido	habían construido

Cuando llegaron los españoles, los mayas ya **habían construido** muchas ciudades.
*When the Spaniards arrived, the Mayas **had** already **built** many cities.*

• *Descubrir* has an irregular past participle: *descubierto*.

Los arqueólogos ya **habían descubierto** algunos objetos antes de encontrar las ruinas.

¡NO OLVIDES!

To form the past participle of a verb in Spanish we add *-ado* to the stem of *-ar* verbs (*mirar* → *mirado*) and *-ido* to the stem of most *-er* and *-ir* verbs (*escoger* → *escogido*). Here are some irregular past participles: *abierto, devuelto, escrito, hecho, muerto, puesto, resuelto, roto, visto*.

178   Capítulo 5

Options

Strategies for Reaching All Students

Students Needing Extra Help
El pluscuamperfecto: Review the concept of an action in the past occuring before another past action. Give more examples.
¡No olvides!: Give additional examples of regular past participles. Refer to the list of irregular past participles that students started in Chap. 4.

¡No olvides!: Give further examples of the placement of negative words and object pronouns. Include examples using the pluperfect.
Ex. 4: Brainstorm words to complete the verb list. Complete the first two as a class. Point out that the list includes some irregular verbs.

Extended Written Practice/Homework
1. Write sentences telling what someone had done before another action occurred: *Antes de trabajar como médica, mi tía había estudiado en la Universidad de Colorado.*
2. Write three sentences telling what an individual or group had accomplished at some point in time: *Cuando ganaron el campeonato, los ... habían ganado ... partidos consecutivos.*

3 ¿Qué había pasado en la civilización maya antes del año 1000 a.C.?*
Trabaja con un(a) compañero(a) para expresar estas ideas.

Antes del año 1000, los mayas ya habían construido pirámides.

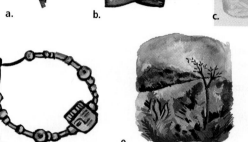

a.

b.

c.

d.

e.

f.

hacer

explorar

cultivar

descubrir el uso de

usar

construir

4 Dile a un(a) compañero(a) algo que hiciste durante el año pasado. Luego, dile si habías hecho lo mismo antes.

visitar   A —*El año pasado visité una ciudad maya.*
          B —*¿Habías visitado antes una ciudad maya?*
          A —*No, nunca. Pero, había leído sobre ellas.*
              o: *Sí, ya la había visitado antes.*

a. escribir   d. leer   g. ver
b. hacer   e. participar   h. 🔆
c. ir   f. estudiar

¡NO OLVIDES!

We put *no* and other negative words, object pronouns, and reflexive pronouns directly in front of the verb *haber: ¿Has visitado ya esas ruinas? No, no las he visitado todavía.*

*In Spanish, *a.C.* and *d.C.* are abbreviated forms for **antes de Cristo** and **después de Cristo**.

Gramática en contexto   179

Present & Practice

Reteach / Review: Vocabulary

As you present *seguir* + present participle, review weather expressions with *hacer* and personal expressions with *tener* by having students complete statements that you make. For example: *Hacía frío esta mañana y sigue ___. / Yo tenía dolor de cabeza hace dos horas y lo sigo ___ ahora.*

Teaching Suggestions

Tell students that another way to express an action that keeps on happening is with *continuar* + present participle: *Mi familia continúa observando las costumbres de nuestros abuelos.*

El verbo *seguir* y el presente progresivo

The verb *seguir*, "to follow, to continue," is an $e \rightarrow i$ stem-changing verb. You have already learned its present-tense forms:

(yo)	sigo	(nosotros) (nosotras)	seguimos
(tú)	sigues	(vosotros) (vosotras)	seguís
Ud. (él) (ella)	sigue	Uds. (ellos) (ellas)	siguen

- We use *seguir* + present participle to indicate that an action that began in the past is still continuing or that it happens regularly. When we use *seguir* this way, it means "to keep on, to go on, to continue (doing something)."

> Mis abuelos siempre celebraban el Día de los Enamorados con una fiesta. Mi familia lo **sigue celebrando** así.
> *My grandparents always used to celebrate Valentine's Day with a party. My family continues celebrating it that way.*

Fiesta de los Reyes Magos, el 6 de enero, en la Ciudad de México

180   Capítulo 5

Options

Strategies for Reaching All Students

Students Needing Extra Help
El verbo seguir *y el presente progresivo:* Give additional examples.
Ex. 5: Be sure that students have some verbs associated with their ideas. They will need them in order to do the second part of the activity.
Ahora lo sabes: Have students write this so that they can record their progress.

Extended Written Practice/Homework
1. Based on the readings on pp. 169, 174, and 175, write four sentences naming customs that the Mayas of today continue to practice.
2. Write three sentences telling what customs and traditions different people continue to practice: *Mi abuela sigue cosiendo ropa para los pobres de mi comunidad.*

Multiple Intelligences
Interpersonal/Social
See Ex. 5.
Verbal/Linguistic
See Audio Activities 5.3, 5.4, and 5.5.
Visual/Spatial
See Practice Wkbk. 5-9, Writing Activity 5-F, and Comm. Act. BLM 5-3.

5 Haz una lista de tradiciones, costumbres, celebraciones, etc., que tenían tus antepasados o que había en tu pueblo o ciudad. Puedes incluir ideas sobre:

- la comida
- los días festivos
- la religión
- los valores de la familia
- el trabajo
- la ropa

Después, lee la lista a un(a) compañero(a). Pregúntale si todavía se mantienen esas costumbres.

A —*Mis abuelos siempre preparaban paella para celebrar los cumpleaños.*

B —*¿Siguen Uds. preparándola?*

A —*Sí, todavía seguimos preparándola.*
o: *No, ya no la preparamos. Generalmente,...*

Celebrando un cumpleaños en California

Ahora lo sabes

¿Puedes:

■ decir cuánto tiempo hace que algo ocurre o cuánto tiempo hacía que algo ocurría?

—___ dos años que la arqueóloga ___ la estatua maya.

■ describir una acción que ocurrió antes que otra acción en el pasado?

—Cuando los españoles llegaron a la ciudad, los mayas ya ___ una gran ciudad.

■ describir algo que empezó en el pasado y que todavía ocurre hoy?

—En Guatemala los mayas hablaban quiché y todavía ___ hablándolo.

MÁS PRÁCTICA

- Más práctica y tarea, pp. 560–561
- Practice Workbook 5–5, 5–9

Gramática en contexto   181

Cultural Notes ☼

(p. 180, photo)
El Día de los Tres Reyes Magos, known in the U.S. as Epiphany, is celebrated on January 6. Traditionally in Mexico, the most important Christmas gifts are given on this day. Children believe that the Three Wise Men bring them gifts, just as they did for the Christ child. Yet increasingly, this custom is fading. Many Mexican children now expect Santa Claus to bring presents on Christmas Eve.

Ask students: Do you think that customs, such as Santa Claus or the birthday cake, should become more universal, or do you like the idea of maintaining distinct regional customs and diversity? Why?

Apply

Teaching Suggestions

Point out the key chapter question. Remind students that completing these activities will help them answer it. You may select one, two, or all three of these activities, as time permits.

Answers: Sopa de actividades

1–2 Responses will vary.

3 Responses will vary, but students may mention:
Similarities: The Egyptians built pyramids and used a hieroglyphic writing system. The Greeks made many advances in math and astronomy, and the Romans built large cities.
Differences: The Greeks and Romans used an alphabet rather than hieroglyphics, and were more interested in expanding their territories.
Contributions: The Egyptians perfected papyrus, the first paper; the Greeks shaped the study of basic algebra and geometry; the Romans improved architecture and sanitation.

Para decir más

Aquí tienes vocabulario adicional que te puede ayudar para hacer las actividades de esta sección.

crecer *(c —> zc)*
to grow up

por completo
completely

asombroso, -a
amazing

impresionante
impressive

escondido, -a
hidden

el conocimiento
knowledge

el sacerdote
priest

los egipcios
Egyptians

los griegos
Greeks

los romanos
Romans

182   Capítulo 5

¿Cómo se relacionan el pasado y el presente?

Esta sección te ofrece la oportunidad de combinar lo que aprendiste en este capítulo con lo que ya sabes para responder a la pregunta clave.

Sopa de actividades

1 Busca una foto tuya del año pasado y otras fotos tuyas sacadas a edades diferentes. Prepara un cartel y una presentación oral para demostrar y explicar lo que habías hecho a cada edad. Explica cuánto tiempo hacía que hacías estas cosas.

Aquí estoy yo junto a mi bicicleta. Hacía sólo un mes que la tenía.
Ésta es mi escuela primaria. Hacía 4 años que estudiaba allí.

Options

Strategies for Reaching All Students

Students Needing Extra Help
Give students ample time to prepare and complete these activities. You may want to choose just one or two of them.
Ex. 1: Allow students to use whatever examples they are most comfortable with. Present a model using yourself. Stress the concept of time duration.

Ex. 2: Emphasize the idea of the Mayan descendants being compared to the early Mayans. Assign a topic to each group, rather than having all groups do all topics.
Ex. 3: Set some limits for this presentation: length of time, number of sentences, the amount of information, etc. Present several models.

Enrichment
Ex. 2: Additional topics: *la vida diaria, la vida escolar, el trabajo que hacían los hombres / las mujeres / los niños.*

2. ¿Cuáles son algunas de las contribuciones de la civilización actual? ¿En qué se parecen y en qué se diferencian de las contribuciones de los mayas? En grupos de cuatro pueden hablar de las contribuciones en:

- el trabajo
- la arquitectura
- el idioma
- la escritura
- la salud
- la religión
- la ropa
- la comida

Luego preparen una presentación oral para explicar sus resultados a la clase.

Video Activity A

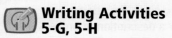
Video, Capítulo 5

Chapter 5: Play

Step

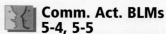
Video Activities B–C

Writing Activities 5-G, 5-H

Comm. Act. BLMs 5-4, 5-5

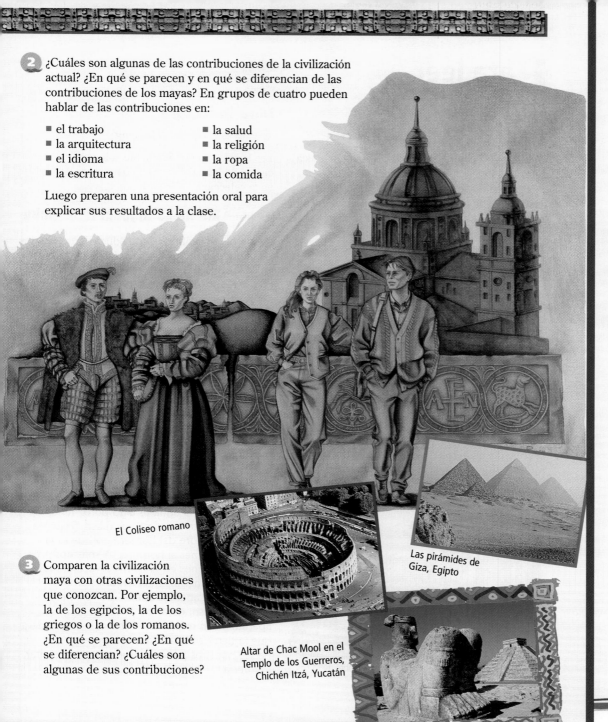

El Coliseo romano

Las pirámides de Giza, Egipto

Altar de Chac Mool en el Templo de los Guerreros, Chichén Itzá, Yucatán

3. Comparen la civilización maya con otras civilizaciones que conozcan. Por ejemplo, la de los egipcios, la de los griegos o la de los romanos. ¿En qué se parecen? ¿En qué se diferencian? ¿Cuáles son algunas de sus contribuciones?

Cooperative Learning
In groups of five, have students compare the answers they gave to the questions in Ex. 4, p. 179. Have them create group responses using the present perfect and pluperfect tenses.

Multiple Intelligences
Bodily/Kinesthetic and Visual/Spatial
See Ex. 1.
Interpersonal/Social and Verbal/Linguistic
See Cooperative Learning.
Verbal/Linguistic
See Exs. 2–3.
Visual/Spatial
See Writing Activities 5-G and 5-H and Comm. Act. BLMs 5-4 and 5-5.

Cultural Notes

(p. 183, bottom photo)
Chichén Itzá is the most famous ancient Mayan city in Yucatán, Mexico. It was first settled by the Mayas approximately A.D. 550 to 900, invaded soon thereafter by the Toltecs of central Mexico, and abandoned in the fourteenth century. The reclining *Chac Mool* sculpture in the foreground presumably held human hearts and is Toltec, as is the Temple of the Warriors atop which it lies.

Apply

Teaching Suggestions

Point out the key chapter question. Tell students that working through the *Para leer* section will help them answer this key question.

Encourage them to use the strategies given in the text to help them understand the reading. Remind them that they do not need to understand every word.

Process Reading

For a description of process reading, see p. 52.

Answers
Antes de leer
Answers will vary.

Mira la lectura

Students' lists may vary, but should include items 1, 3, 4, 5, 7, and 10.

Para leer

Antes de leer

STRATEGY ➤ Using prior knowledge

Rigoberta Menchú es una activista guatemalteca del grupo indígena quiché, actuales descendientes de los mayas. La señora Menchú ganó el Premio Nóbel de la Paz en 1992. En este fragmento de su libro *Me llamo Rigoberta Menchú*, la autora nos habla de la importancia que tiene la naturaleza para los descendientes de los mayas. ¿Cuáles de estas palabras piensas que vas a encontrar en la selección?

1. el agua
2. jugar
3. respetar
4. la tierra
5. el campo
6. la radio
7. la naturaleza
8. vender
9. el teléfono
10. desperdiciar *(to waste)*

Escribe los números de las que escogiste y compara tu lista con la de un(a) compañero(a).

Rigoberta Menchú recibiendo el Premio Nóbel de la Paz

184   Capítulo 5

www.pasoapaso.com

Mira la lectura

STRATEGY ➤ Skimming

Lee la selección rápidamente sólo para ver cuáles de las palabras de tu lista aparecen en la selección.

Fragmento de **Me llamo Rigoberta Menchú**

Desde niños recibimos una educación diferente de la que tienen los blancos, los ladinos. Nosotros, los indígenas, tenemos más contacto con la naturaleza. Por eso nos dicen politeístas. Pero, sin embargo, no somos politeístas... o, si lo somos, sería bueno, porque es nuestra cultura, nuestras costumbres. De que nosotros adoramos, no es que adoremos, sino que respetamos una serie de cosas de la naturaleza, las cosas más importantes para nosotros. Por ejemplo, el agua es algo sagrado. La explicación que nos dan nuestros padres desde niños es que no hay que desperdiciar el agua... El agua es algo puro, es algo limpio y es algo que da vida al hombre. Sin el agua no se puede vivir, tampoco hubieran podido vivir nuestros antepasados. Entonces, el agua la tenemos como algo sagrado y eso está en la mente desde niños y nunca se le quita a uno de pensar que el agua es algo puro. Tenemos la tierra. Nuestros padres nos dicen "Hijos, la tierra es la madre del hombre porque es la que da de comer al hombre." Y más nosotros, que nos basamos en el cultivo. Nosotros los indígenas comemos maíz, frijol y yerba del campo y no sabemos comer, por ejemplo, jamón o queso, cosas compuestas con aparatos, con máquinas. Entonces se considera que la tierra es la madre del hombre. Y de hecho nuestros padres nos enseñan a respetar esa tierra.

Options

Strategies for Reaching All Students

Spanish-Speaking Students
Ask: *¿Qué piensas de la actitud de Rigoberta Menchú hacia la naturaleza? ¿Son tan importantes el agua y la tierra hoy en este país? ¿Por qué?*

Students Needing Extra Help
To keep students focused, divide the reading into thirds, reviewing the previous sentences before continuing.

Multiple Intelligences
Verbal/Linguistic, Visual/Spatial, and Bodily/Kinesthetic
See *Aplicación* Exs. 1–2.

Infórmate

STRATEGIES Identifying the main idea
Identifying supporting details

Ahora lee la selección con cuidado.

1 De estas ideas, ¿cuáles son las dos ideas principales de la selección?

- El agua es algo sagrado.
- El campo es mejor que la ciudad.
- Los indígenas prefieren vivir en el campo.
- La tierra es la madre de todos los seres humanos.

2 ¿Cuáles de estos detalles no se encuentran en la selección?

- A los indígenas no les gusta comer comida hecha con aparatos.
- Los dioses viven en las montañas.
- La agricultura es muy importante para los indígenas.
- El agua hace posible la vida.
- La gente de la ciudad no respeta la naturaleza.
- El respeto a la naturaleza de los indígenas se debe a los padres.

Indícale a un(a) compañero(a) dónde encontraste los detalles que sí aparecen en la selección.

Aplicación

1 Imagina un diálogo entre un(a) joven norteamericano(a) y un(a) joven quiché sobre uno de estos temas.

- el ecoturismo
- el reciclaje
- la energía solar

2 Compara sus ideas. ¿Cuáles dice el (la) joven norteamericano(a)? ¿Cuáles dice el (la) joven quiché? ¿Cuáles dicen los dos? En una hoja de papel, haz un diagrama de Venn y escribe las ideas en el espacio apropiado.

Haz un cartel con dibujos que muestren la relación entre la gente quiché y la naturaleza.

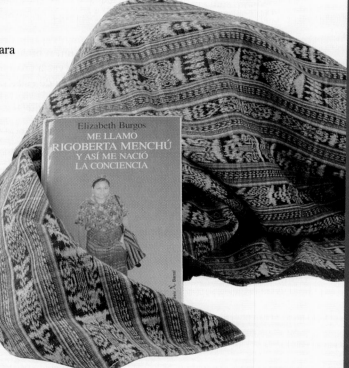

Para leer   185

Infórmate

1 Las dos ideas principales de la selección son: El agua es algo sagrado y la tierra es la madre de todos los seres humanos.

2 Estos detalles no se encuentran en la selección:
A los indígenas no les gusta comer comida hecha con aparatos. Los dioses viven en las montañas. La gente de la ciudad no respeta la naturaleza.

Estos detalles sí aparecen en la selección:
La agricultura es muy importante para los indígenas (línea 21).
El agua hace posible la vida (línea 15).
El respeto a la naturaleza de los indígenas se debe a los padres (línea 30).

Aplicación

1–2 Dialogues and drawings will vary.

Fondo literario

Quetzal no muere nunca
(pp. 454–457)

www **Internet Activities**

Cultural Notes ☀

(p. 184, photo)
Guatemalan Indian rights activist Rigoberta Menchú was awarded the 1992 Nobel Peace Prize for her crusade to bring international attention to the repression of over 46,000 Indians by the Guatemalan military over the previous 30 years. Her autobiography, *Me llamo Rigoberta Menchú,* was published in 1983 and has been translated into 12 languages. Menchú, a Quiché Indian with no formal education, first learned to speak Spanish when she was 19 years old.

Apply

Teaching Suggestions
Point out the key chapter question. Tell students that working through the *Para escribir* section will help them answer it.

Process Writing
For information regarding writing portfolios, see p. 54.

Answers
Presentations will vary.

Para escribir

¿Te hablan tus padres de cómo era la vida cuando eran jóvenes? ¿Por qué lo hacen? Puede que sea para enseñarte sobre el pasado y las experiencias que tuvieron. Para responder a la pregunta clave y para aprender algo del pasado, vas a investigar una civilización o un evento del pasado. Luego vas a preparar una presentación para la clase.

1 Primero, debes decidir si quieres referirte a un evento en particular o a una civilización en general.

- Si es un evento, piensa cuándo, dónde y por qué ocurrió, y cómo afectó a la gente de esa época. También indica cómo sigue afectándonos ahora. ¿Crees que nos afectará en el futuro?

- Si es una civilización antigua, tendrás que decir cuándo y dónde existió, cuál era su estructura social y política y cuáles fueron sus contribuciones importantes. ¿Nos sigue influyendo todavía esta civilización?

2 Puedes pedir ayuda a tu profesor(a) o a un(a) bibliotecario(a). Debes organizar los datos y decidir cómo vas a presentarle la información a la clase. Puedes preparar una de estas cosas:

- un cartel con mapas, ilustraciones (fotos, dibujos) y texto
- una ilustración con una narración
- un video con mapas, fotos, dibujos y una narración
- una serie de diapositivas con la narración grabada

3 Escribe el primer borrador del texto o de la narración. Consulta con un(a) compañero(a) para revisar tu trabajo. Sigue los pasos del proceso de escribir. Luego, haz tu versión final y prepara tu presentación para la clase. No te olvides de ponerlo en tu portafolio.

El acueducto romano de Tarragona, España

186   Capítulo 5

Options

Strategies for Reaching All Students

Students Needing Extra Help
Encourage students to concentrate on a specific event. Have them use the questions as guidelines while they do their research. Students will probably need help with the vocabulary.

Para escribir 187

(p. 186, photo)
This two-tiered aqueduct, known as Pont del Diable or Pont de les Ferreres, is just one of the several Roman structures in Tarragona, a coastal city in Cataluña. The Roman conquest of the Iberian Peninsula began in the second century B.C. and was based in Tarragona, which later became a provincial capital and one of the empire's most splendid cities.

Assess & Summarize

Test Preparation

You may want to assign parts of this section as written homework or as an in-class writing activity prior to administering the *Examen de habilidades.*

Answers

Listening

—*Gracias a los arqueólogos y sus descubrimientos, sabemos mucho más de esta civilización. Por los observatorios que construyeron para estudiar las estrellas, sabemos que fueron buenos astrónomos y arquitectos. Por sus jeroglíficos hemos descubierto que desarrollaron el sistema de escritura más avanzado de la América precolombina. Las vasijas y cuencos de jade enterrados en sus tumbas también nos dan más información sobre sus costumbres, su agricultura y su religión. Hablamos de una civilización desaparecida. Sin embargo, el legado que los mayas de hoy heredaron de sus antepasados es muy rico.*

Se refiere a los mayas. / Sabemos que fueron buenos astrónomos y arquitectos. / Su sistema de escritura era el más avanzado de la América precolombina.

Repaso ¿Lo sabes bien?

Esta sección te ayudará a prepararte para el examen de habilidades, donde tendrás que hacer tareas semejantes.

Listening

¿Puedes entender una descripción de otra cultura? Escucha mientras el (la) profesor(a) lee un ejemplo semejante al que vas a oír en el examen. ¿A qué civilización se refiere la descripción? ¿Qué sabemos de sus estudios de las estrellas? ¿Cómo era su sistema de escritura?

Reading

Lee con cuidado este folleto de un museo. De estas ideas, ¿cuál es la principal?

a. el esplendor de una civilización
b. el descubrimiento de una civilización

Cuando los arqueólogos descubrieron esta civilización, ya hacía más de veinte siglos que no existía. En sus excavaciones encontraron unas ruinas y unas estatuas que parecían tener un significado sagrado. No se sabe por qué esta civilización desapareció.

Writing

¿Puedes escribir un breve informe sobre la civilización maya? Aquí tienes un ejemplo.

La civilización maya no ha desaparecido. Se pueden encontrar restos de ella en México, Honduras y Guatemala. Aunque tenían un sistema de escritura muy avanzado, sus mayores contribuciones fueron en el campo de las matemáticas y de la astronomía.

Culture

¿Qué estudian los antropólogos y arqueólogos para saber más sobre las culturas precolombinas? ¿Qué nos queda hoy de esas culturas?

Un grupo de arqueólogos en una excavación en Chiapas, México

Speaking

¿Puedes hablar con otra persona sobre un descubrimiento arqueológico reciente?

A —*¡Qué fascinante! Un arqueólogo descubrió una tumba antigua en Guatemala.*
B —*¿De verdad? ¿Y qué había en la tumba?*
A —*Unas vasijas, unos cuencos y la escultura de un jaguar.*
B —*Pues, a mí no me interesan mucho los objetos antiguos. Prefiero estudiar el presente.*
A —*Pero, debemos estudiar el pasado porque . . .*

self Test www.pasoapaso.com

Options

Strategies for Reaching All Students

Students Needing Extra Help
Have students write this exercise so that they can check off what they have mastered. Remind students that this is just a sample of what the test will be like.
Listening: Read more than once. Remind students that they need to listen for only certain pieces of information. Brainstorm the words for which they should be listening. Write the questions on the chalkboard or allow students to keep their books open.

Point out that the information is not given in the same order as the questions.
Reading: Remind students that they don't need to know every word in the text.
Writing: Have students use the Organizer and write a sample paragraph as practice before the test.
Have them refer to the *Tema para investigar, Álbum cultural,* and Ex. 2 in the *Sopa de actividades.*

Culture: Have students review the notes they took from the *Álbum cultural.* Guide them with the first question, as they may be thinking of classes for the answer, instead of literature, ruins, and so on.
Speaking: Use the vocabulary section of the Organizer. Complete the model and limit the number of lines of dialogue. Brainstorm recent archaeological discoveries.

Resumen del vocabulario

Usa el vocabulario de este capítulo para:

- responder a la pregunta clave: ¿Cómo se relacionan el pasado y el presente?
- describir las características de la civilización maya
- hablar de las contribuciones de la civilización maya
- explicar cómo nos han influido otras civilizaciones

para describir la civilización maya

el astrónomo, la astrónoma
el calendario
la estrella
el jade
los jeroglíficos
los mayas
el observatorio
la sílaba
el símbolo

para identificar lo que sigue existiendo de la civilización maya

la agricultura
la choza
la cosecha
la cultura
la escultura
la estatua
el objeto
el quiché
la siembra
el templo

para describir otras culturas del pasado

el arquitecto, la arquitecta
avanzado, -a
la ceremonia
la civilización, pl. las civilizaciones
el cuenco
descubierto, -a
el descubrimiento
descubrir
el dios, pl. los dioses
enterrado, -a
la escritura
el esplendor
existir
el / la líder
la religión, pl. las religiones
sagrado, -a
el significado
la tumba
la vasija

para hablar del presente y del pasado

actual
los antepasados
el antropólogo, la antropóloga
el arqueólogo, la arqueóloga
la costumbre
desaparecido, -a
heredar
el legado
el origen, pl. los orígenes
el pasado
precolombino, -a
el presente
rico, -a
la tradición, pl. las tradiciones

otras palabras y expresiones útiles

aceptar
el campo
construir (i → y)
la contribución, pl. las contribuciones
desarrollar
excavar
gracias a
seguir (e → i) + present participle

Resumen 189

Cultural Notes

(p. 188, photo)
Much of the archaeological work in the Mexican state of Chiapas concentrates on the Mayan civilization, which reached its peak in that region during the Classic Mayan period of A.D. 300 to 900. Nonetheless, houses such as this one from 1500 B.C. are also being excavated, revealing the slow development of early village life and the agricultural methods needed to support it in this difficult and diverse terrain.

CAPÍTULO 6
THEME: COMMUNICATION TECHNOLOGY

SCOPE AND SEQUENCE Pages 190–221

COMMUNICATION

Topics

Methods of communication

Technology

Objectives

Explicar el impacto de la tecnología en la vida diaria de los países hispanos

Hablar de los diferentes medios de comunicación

Hacer una llamada telefónica

Hablar por teléfono

Escribir y enviar algo por correo

Hablar de la tecnología del futuro

CULTURE

La tecnología en los países hispanos

GRAMMAR

Repaso: El futuro

El futuro: Continuación

Uso de los complementos directos e indirectos

Ancillaries available for use with Chapter 6

Multisensory/Technology

 Overheads, 19–21

 Audio Tapes and CDs

 Vocabulary Art Blackline Masters for Hands-On Learning, pp. 30–32/CD-ROM

 Classroom Crossword

 Video

 Internet Activities
www.pasoapaso.com

Print

 Practice Workbook, pp. 61–70

 Writing, Audio & Video Activities, pp. 35–40, 108–110, 143–144

 Communicative Activity Blackline Masters

    Pair and Small Group Activities, pp. 36–41

    Situation Cards, p. 42

RESOURCE PRO®

Planning Express, Teaching Resources Library, and Clip Art Library

Assessment

 Assessment Program

    Pruebas, pp. 82–92

    Examen de habilidades, pp. 93–96

 Test Generator

 ¿Lo sabes bien?
Video Quiz

Video, Chap. 6

Communication Today

The rapid development of technology has radically affected communication worldwide. Land and sea mail systems have served us for hundreds of years, but this type of service often takes days, weeks, or months. Today, however, we can quickly communicate across the globe using the telephone, fax machine, and computer e-mail.

The telephone is central to most state-of-the-art communications systems. Its innovation was to allow people to speak directly to each other regardless of distance. The answering machine has changed the way people communicate, allowing them to talk to each other any time of the day without speaking to each other directly. Cellular phones have freed users from a fixed instrument attached to a physical wire, allowing the user to call from virtually any location. Telephone lines also make it possible to send fax messages, offering almost simultaneous transmission of documents from one party to another. A person in an office in Kansas, for example, can send a fax to a ship captain at sea in the Pacific Ocean, who can then fax back a reply, all within minutes.

Phone lines also allow computers to communicate via e-mail. Some experts believe that e-mail has created a resurgence of the long-lost written word as a means of communication, in a style conducive to today's fast-paced, efficiency-oriented lifestyle. Someone composing an e-mail message may omit the introduction and the closing and not use complete sentence structure, elements considered essential to a letter writer in the eighteenth century, who might receive one or two letters a year from someone in a faraway country.

Answering machines, cellular phones, faxes, and e-mail have all made inroads in Latin America. These means of rapid, efficient communication are most commonly used by professionals, academics, and relatively well-off people. The Internet, a worldwide network of computers, has many users in Latin America. In fact, U.S. Internet users can explore "bulletin boards" and other postings in Spanish by "traveling" to Latin America on the Internet.

Unfortunately, the infrastructure necessary to allow widespread electronic communication is often limited in Latin America. The electricity available to cities and towns may be subject to brownouts and surges, which pose a danger to electrical equipment. The devices that make electronic communication possible are generally more expensive in Latin America than in the U.S., and less prosperous local economies often prevent installation of the requisite number of telephone lines. Because of inadequate traditional telephone systems, cellular phones have become popular in places such as Mexico City or San Salvador.

Instead of owning their own telephone, some households in Latin America use local public telephone centers to place a call. These centers may contain a dozen or so telephones. The user can deposit coins directly into a pay phone or, in some instances, pay a cashier after completing a call. Especially in the case of long distance calls, it may take up to an hour to get a connection after dialing—a far cry from the instantaneous communication available to e-mail users!

Introduce

Re-entry of Concepts

The following list represents words, expressions, and grammar topics re-entered from Books 1, 2, and 3 (Chaps. 4 and 5):

Book 1
numbers, time-telling, family members, demonstrative adjectives, direct object pronouns, indirect object pronouns, preterite, comparatives

Book 2
personal possessions, professions, future

Chapter 4
present perfect

Chapter 5
seguir + present participle

Planning

Cross-Curricular Connections

History Connection *(pp. 200–201)*
Have students choose a historical figure from the Hispanic world or of Hispanic origin, and write a letter to the class pretending to be that person. They should write their latest news and ask questions related to their needs. Have students exchange letters and answer them. Responses should include questions students would like to know about the historical figure. This can continue for two or more rounds, and can be presented to the whole class.

Computer Science Connection *(pp. 214–215)*
In groups, have students take turns role playing the sales presentation of a computer, fax, or other modern machine. Presentations should include explaining how this machine can assist them in their daily social and work-related tasks, and what specific equipment will be used. Encourage use of the future tense and object pronouns.

Spanish in Your Community
If possible, have students call Directory Assistance and speak with the Spanish-speaking operator. Another activity would be to assign students different Spanish-speaking countries and have them determine how they would make a long distance phone call to that country and what it would cost for three minutes.

CAPÍTULO 6

OBJETIVOS

Al terminar este capítulo vas a poder responder a la pregunta clave:

¿Cómo nos podemos comunicar mejor?

También vas a poder:

- escribir y enviar una carta
- hablar de diferentes medios de comunicación
- dar tu opinión sobre las comunicaciones en el futuro
- explicar el impacto de la tecnología en la vida diaria de los países hispanos

Radiotelescopios cerca de Socorro, Nuevo México

VISITA
www.pasoapaso.com

Teaching Suggestions
Point out the key chapter question. Remind students that by acquiring the new words and structures, they will be able to answer this question.

Cultural Notes ☼

(pp. 190–191, photo)
27 antennas, some of which are seen here, make up the VLA (Very Large Array) at the National Radio Astronomy Observatory in Socorro, New Mexico. These radio telescopes were constructed during the 1970s and began operating in 1981. They collect radio waves from space which are then processed by computers to form images for scientific study. A site for international research, the array attracts visiting scientists from all over the world. At the Visitors' Center, an automated slide show presents information about accomplishments in the field of astronomy by the three cultures that make up New Mexico today: U.S., Hispanic, and Native American.

• *Explicar el impacto de la tecnología en la vida diaria de los países hispanos*

Critical Thinking: Expressing Problems and Issues

Divide the class into groups of three or four. Have each group cooperatively write several paragraphs that either support or refute this statement: *La palabra escrita es la forma más importante para comunicarse.* Have volunteers from each group read their paragraphs to the class. Discuss.

Answers: Anticipación

Answers will vary. / el telegrama, el correo, el teléfono

Anticipación

Mira las fotos. Los medios de comunicación han cambiado con el tiempo, pero su fin sigue siendo el mismo: ayudar a comunicarnos mejor. ¿Cuántos de estos medios de comunicación conoces? ¿Cuáles son?

En la Plaza de la Cibeles en Madrid, España, se encuentra el Palacio de Comunicaciones, que es la oficina central de correos de la ciudad. Aquí, igual que en la oficina de Correos y Telégrafos de Caracas, Venezuela, se pueden mandar y recibir telegramas, comprar sellos y preparar y mandar paquetes a todo el mundo. ¿Cómo es el correo en tu país? ¿Qué servicios ofrece?

192   Capítulo 6

Options

Strategies for Reaching All Students

Spanish-Speaking Students
Ask: *¿Cómo te comunicas con tus compañeros y tu familia? ¿Sabes usar la nueva tecnología?*

Students Needing Extra Help
Although students may be familiar with the telephone and fax as means of communication, stress the importance of the post office and mail system.

Cultural Notes

(p. 192, top left photo)
Access to advanced technology is common nowadays, yet communication by telegram is still efficient and convenient for many people, as seen in the telegraph section of a Caracas post office. Venezuelan cities and towns hold 91 percent of the country's population, so most people are close to post offices providing telegraph service.

"Por favor, ¿podría comunicarme con el 555-4517?"

Para hacer llamadas locales y de larga distancia desde un teléfono público en Venezuela puedes usar monedas. Sin embargo, en otros países hispanos los teléfonos públicos sólo aceptan fichas. Si quieres hacer una llamada desde un teléfono público en tu país, ¿qué tienes que usar, monedas o fichas? ¿Cómo puedes hacer una llamada de larga distancia desde un teléfono público?

"El Sr. Navarro tendrá esta información inmediatamente."

El desarrollo de nuevas tecnologías hace más fácil comunicarnos. Gracias al teléfono celular, este hombre de negocios en Caracas, Venezuela, no necesita estar en su oficina para comunicarse con sus clientes. ¿Qué ventajas tiene un teléfono celular?

Exploración Cultural
www.pasoapaso.com
Visita estos países

193

(p. 192, right photo)
Madrid's imposing central post office, El Palacio de Comunicaciones, is located in the heart of the city, in the Plaza de la Cibeles. Inaugurated in 1919, the post office is open seven days a week and offers the various kinds of mail services available in most major cities around the world, along with telephone, fax, telex, and telegraph services.

(p. 193, top photo)
Like other public services in Caracas, pay phones are modern and convenient. For most of the latter half of the twentieth century, Venezuela has enjoyed economic prosperity and modernization due to consistently high prices for oil, its main export. In spite of a drop in oil prices at the end of the 1970s, Venezuela's yearly per capita income of approximately $2,500 is still one of the highest in South America.

(p. 193, bottom photo)
As Venezuela's urban population continues to grow, so does the number of telephones in use. In 1991, there were approximately 1.8 million, an increase of 36,000 from the previous year, four times the amount of increase the preceding year.

Present

Chapter Theme
Methods of communication

Communicative Objectives
- *Hablar de los diferentes medios de comunicación*
- *Hacer una llamada telefónica*
- *Hablar por teléfono*
- *Escribir y enviar algo por correo*

 Overheads 19–20

 Vocabulary Art BLMs/CD-ROM

 Vocabulary Tape 6-1

Teaching Suggestions
Preparing students to speak: Use one or two options from each of the categories of Comprehensible Input or Limited Verbal Response. For a complete explanation of these categories and some sample activities, see pp. T20–T21.

Point out that *¡Aló!* is only one way to answer the phone in Spanish-speaking countries. Although it is used in Nicaragua, Argentina, and Uruguay, in other countries they use different words. In Cuba, it is common to hear *Oigo,* in Mexico and Venezuela, *Bueno,* and in Spain, *Diga.*

Vocabulario para comunicarse

¿Cómo nos comunicamos?

Aquí tienes palabras y expresiones necesarias para hablar sobre las distintas formas de comunicarnos. Léelas varias veces y practícalas con un(a) compañero(a) en las páginas siguientes.

194   Capítulo 6

Options

Strategies for Reaching All Students

Spanish-Speaking Students
Ask: *¿A quién(es) llamas por teléfono? ¿Haces llamadas de larga distancia? ¿Qué información tienes que proveer? ¿A quién(es) escribes? ¿Cómo mandas tus cartas?*

Students Needing Extra Help
Begin the vocabulary section of the Organizer. Divide vocabulary into small sections by scenes or theme (telephone-related material, post office, and mail material). Write out complete paradigms of *envolver, descolgar,* and *colgar* in the present, as well as *marcar* in the preterite.

También necesitas . . . : Write out the entire phrases for "to make a collect call" and "to make a long-distance call." Write out the complete present-tense paradigms of *sonar, equivocarse,* and *volver.*

También necesitas . . .

hacer una llamada	*to make a call*	equivocado, -a	*wrong*
___ a cobro revertido	*to make a collect call*	dejar	*to leave*
___ de larga distancia	*to make a long-distance call*	el recado	*message*
la ficha††	*token*	volver (o → ue) a + inf.	*to do (something) again*
el tono	here: *dial tone*	mandar	*to send*
sonar (o → ue)	*to ring*	por correo urgente	*by special delivery*
¡Aló!	*Hello* (on the telephone)	querido, -a	*dear*
¿De parte de quién?	*Who's calling?*	Cariños	*Love (as a closing in a letter)*
en voz alta / baja	*in a loud / soft voice*	lento, -a	*slow*
equivocarse (c → qu)†	*to make a mistake, be mistaken*	entonces	*then*

¿Y qué quiere decir . . . ?

el fax · por vía aérea

la línea · el telegrama

* In the preterite, the *g* of the *yo* form of *colgar* and *descolgar* changes to gu: *colgué, descolgué.*

† In the preterite, the *c* of the *yo* form in *marcar* and *equivocarse* changes to qu: *marqué, me equivoqué.*

†† In many Spanish-speaking countries, tokens are used in pay telephones.

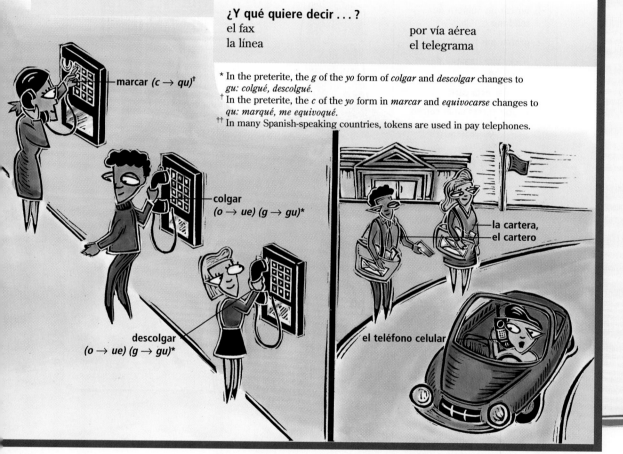

marcar (c → qu)†

colgar (o → ue) (g → gu)*

descolgar (o → ue) (g → gu)*

la cartera, el cartero

el teléfono celular

Class Starter Review
On the day following the presentation of vocabulary, you might begin the class with this activity: Play a game of charades with the class. Act out one of the words and have students guess which one it is. Whoever guesses the word correctly will act out the next word, and so on.

www Internet Activities
Juegos

Extended Written Practice/Homework
1. Write four sentences naming means of communication that you use in different situations: *Cuando hago mi tarea, a veces uso un teléfono inalámbrico para hablar con mis amigos.*
2. Write sentences explaining the use of: *un apartado postal, un fax, una llamada a cobro revertido, el (la) operador(a). Se usa un apartado postal . . .*

Multiple Intelligences
Bodily/Kinesthetic
See Class Starter Review.
Mathematical/Logical
Have students who are familiar with cellular phones write basic instructions for using one.
Verbal/Linguistic
See Vocabulary Tape 6-1.
Visual/Spatial
See Overheads 19–20 and the Vocabulary Art BLMs/CD-ROM.

Practice

**Answers: Empecemos
a conversar**

1 ESTUDIANTE A
a. Quiero hacer una llamada
desde el jardín.
b. ...buscar un número de teléfono.
c. ...grabar mis recados.
d. ...hacer una llamada desde mi
coche.
e. ...mandar esta carta.
f. ...recibir cartas en el correo.
g. ...usar el teléfono público.
h. Statements will vary.
ESTUDIANTE B
Answers will vary, but may
include:
a. Entonces necesitas un teléfono
inalámbrico. Está ...
b. ...una guía telefónica. Está ...
c. ...un contestador automático.
Está ...
d. ...un teléfono celular. Está ...
e. ...un buzón. Está ...
f. ...un apartado postal. Está ...
g. ...monedas. Están ...
h. Statements will vary.

Empecemos a conversar

Túrnate con un(a) compañero(a) para ser *Estudiante A* y
Estudiante B. Reemplacen las palabras subrayadas con palabras
representadas o escritas en los recuadros. 💡 quiere decir que
puedes escoger tu propia respuesta.

1

A — *Quiero escribir una carta.*
B — *Entonces necesitas papel y un bolígrafo.*
Están sobre tu escritorio.

escribir una carta

Estudiante A

a. hacer una llamada desde el
   jardín

b. buscar un número de
   teléfono

c. grabar mis recados

d. hacer una llamada desde
   mi coche

e. mandar esta carta

f. recibir cartas en el correo

g. usar el teléfono público

h. 💡

Estudiante B

196   Capítulo 6

Options

Strategies for Reaching All Students

Spanish-Speaking Students
Exs. 1–3: Pair bilingual with non-bilingual
students, if possible.

Students Needing Extra Help
Ex. 1: Brainstorm the location of the object.
Ex. 2: Brainstorm the *pero* part of the
Estudiante B response.
Ex. 3: Brainstorm possible answers for
Estudiante B.

Enrichment
Ex. 1: As homework, ask students to create
a short message for their own answering
machines. Encourage them to be imaginative as they provide the information typical
of these messages (phone number reached,
apology for unavailability, request for a message, promise to return the call).

2 mandar una carta / hacer una llamada

A —¿Qué es más caro, _mandar una carta o hacer una llamada_?

B —_Claro que una llamada es más cara, pero es más rápida._

Estudiante A

a. mandar una carta por correo urgente / por vía aérea

b. llamar por teléfono inalámbrico / mandar un telegrama

c. enviar un fax / mandar una carta por correo urgente

d. marcar el número / llamar al (a la) operador(a)

Estudiante B

3 el teléfono suena y nadie contesta

A —¿Qué haces si _el teléfono suena y nadie contesta_?

B —_Vuelvo a llamar más tarde._

Estudiante A

a. tienes un número equivocado

b. quieres hacer una llamada pero no tienes dinero

c. la persona con quien hablas no puede oírte

d. la línea está ocupada

e. quieres hacer una llamada de larga distancia

f. no sabes el número de teléfono

g. la persona con quien quieres hablar no está en casa

h. no oyes el tono

Estudiante B

También se dice

la planilla

la postdata
el post scriptum

discar

el teléfono portátil

el apartado de correos
la casilla postal

el / la telefonista

la máquina contestadora

a. ¿Qué es más caro, mandar una carta por correo urgente o por vía aérea?
b. . . . llamar por teléfono inalámbrico o mandar un telegrama?
c. . . . enviar un fax o mandar una carta por correo urgente?
d. . . . marcar el número o llamar al (a la) operador(a)?
ESTUDIANTE B
a.–d. Answers will vary, but should be logical and focus on the issue of expense vs. speed.

3 ESTUDIANTE A
a. ¿Qué haces si tienes un número equivocado?
b. . . . quieres hacer una llamada pero no tienes dinero?
c. . . . la persona con quien hablas no puede oírte?
d. . . . la línea está ocupada?
e. . . . quieres hacer una llamada de larga distancia?
f. . . . no sabes el número de teléfono?
g. . . . la persona con quien quieres hablar no está en casa?
h. . . . no oyes el tono?
ESTUDIANTE B
a.–h. Answers will vary, but look for correct use of verb tenses.

Extended Written Practice/Homework
1. Write four sentences saying what you or another person did to communicate with others: _Dejé un recado en el contestador automático de mi amiga Luisa._
2. Write four sentences giving advice concerning how to communicate effectively with others: _Siempre escribe el nombre y la dirección en el remitente del sobre._

Multiple Intelligences
Verbal/Linguistic
See Enrichment.
Verbal/Linguistic and Interpersonal/Social
See Exs. 1–3.

Standards 1.1   **197**

Practice & Apply

¿Y qué piensas tú?

Aquí tienes otra oportunidad para usar el vocabulario de este capítulo.

4 Imagina que una persona acaba de llegar a los Estados Unidos y no sabe hacer una llamada en el teléfono público. Explícale cómo hacerlo. Usen las frases de abajo en el orden correcto.

— *Primero, busca el número de teléfono en la guía telefónica. Después . . . .*

a. Decir "Adiós."
b. Decir "¡Aló!"
c. Descolgar.
d. Colgar.
e. Hablar o dejar un recado.
f. Escuchar para ver si hay tono.
g. Buscar el número de teléfono en la guía telefónica.
h. Conseguir una moneda.
i. Marcar el número.

5 ¿Cuánto tiempo hablas por teléfono cada día? ¿Hasta qué hora puedes recibir llamadas? ¿Haces llamadas de larga distancia? ¿Adónde llamas? ¿A quién?

6 ¿Tienes tu propia línea de teléfono? ¿Crees que todos los jóvenes deben tener su propia línea? ¿Por qué?

7 ¿Por qué se alquilan apartados postales?

8 ¿Qué te parecen los contestadores automáticos? ¿Tienes uno? ¿Cuáles son sus ventajas y sus desventajas?

Práctica de vocabulario www.pasoapaso.com

MÁS PRÁCTICA

Más práctica y tarea, p. 562
Practice Workbook 6–1, 6–2

"Voy a ver quién me ha llamado hoy."

198 Capítulo 6

Options

Strategies for Reaching All Students

Spanish-Speaking Students
Ex. 10: After this exercise, tell students: *Sigue el modelo y escríbele a un(a) pariente o a un(a) amigo(a). Dile algo que has hecho o de un lugar que has visitado.*

Students Needing Extra Help
Ex. 4: Remind students to use the *tú* command forms.
Ex. 7: Discuss possible reasons why people rent post office boxes.
Ex. 8: Brainstorm the vocabulary needed to express the advantages and disadvantages of answering machines.
Ex. 9: As a class, complete the first dialogue. Emphasize the expressions that are being practiced rather than the content of the call.

Cooperative Learning
In pairs, have each student list the methods of communication in Ex. 2 on p. 197. One student will list them according to speed, the other according to cost. Have each pair combine their lists, considering both speed and cost, to discover the best and worst values in communication. Call on pairs to tell which methods they prefer, and why.

9 Con un(a) compañero(a), completa y continúa estos diálogos telefónicos hasta terminar la conversación. Puedes usar estas expresiones u otras.

llamada de larga distancia
¿De parte de quién?
grabar un recado
estar ocupado
hablar en voz alta / baja

número equivocado
llamada a cobro revertido
equivocarse
sonar, pero no contesta nadie
volver a llamar

A —*¿Aló?*
B —*Por favor, quisiera hablar con ___.*
A — ....

A —*Con ___, por favor.*
B —*¿Cómo? No puedo oírle. ¿Puede ___?*
A — ....

A —*Operador(a).*
B —*Quiero hacer una ___.*
A —*El número, por favor.*
B — ....

10 Después de mirar el sobre y leer la carta, contesta estas preguntas con un(a) compañero(a).

a. ¿Quién es la destinataria de la carta? ¿Cuál es su dirección?
b. ¿Quién es el remitente? ¿Cuál es su dirección?
c. ¿Por qué clase de correo va la carta?
   ¿Cómo empieza y cómo termina?
d. ¿Por qué escribió Esteban una posdata?

Esteban Suárez   Rodríguez San Pedro, 49
Madrid, 28003 España

VIA AÉREA

Ana Suárez
Avenida Vallarta, 8
Guadalajara, México

Madrid, 3 de julio

Querida mamá,

Llegué a Madrid hace tres días. Me estoy divirtiendo muchísimo, aunque dejé mi tarjeta de crédito en Barcelona. Al día siguiente fui al Banco Hispano y llené un formulario para pedir una nueva. Creo que va a llegar en el correo de hoy.

Te llamaré para tu cumpleaños. Ya te he comprado el regalo, sólo tengo que envolver el paquete. ¡El cartero está aquí! No puedo seguir escribiendo.

Cariños,

Esteban

P.D. ¿Puedes mandarme dinero? Hay lugares que no aceptan tarjetas de crédito.

Vocabulario para comunicarse   199

10 a. Ana Suárez es la destinataria; Su dirección es Avenida Vallarta, 8; Guadalajara, México.
b. Esteban Suárez es el remitente; Su dirección es Rodríguez San Pedro, 49; 28003 Madrid, España.
c. La carta va por vía aérea; La carta empieza con "Querida mamá" y termina con "Cariños."
or: Empieza con el lugar y la fecha y termina con la posdata.
d. La escribió porque necesitaba dinero.

 Practice Wkbk. 6-1, 6-2

 Audio Activity 6.1

 Writing Activities 6-A, 6-B

 Pruebas 6-1, 6-2

Present

Chapter Theme
Communication technology

Communicative Objectives
- *Hablar de los diferentes medios de comunicación*
- *Hablar de la tecnología del futuro*

 Overhead 21

 Vocabulary Tape 6-2

Grammar Preview
Querremos is previewed here lexically. The presentation of irregular verbs in the future tense appears on p. 211.

Teaching Suggestions
Getting ready to speak:
Remind students of the reading strategies that they learned (getting meaning from context and coping with unknown words) to help them understand the *Tema para investigar*. For further details and some sample activities, see pp. T24–T25.

Answers: Tema para investigar
Answers will vary.

Tema para investigar

Aquí tienes más palabras e ideas que te ayudarán a hablar sobre las diferentes formas de comunicarnos. Mira las ilustraciones. ¿Qué medios de comunicación usas tú? ¿Cómo ha cambiado la comunicación en los últimos años? ¿Y cómo va a cambiar en el futuro?

Options

Strategies for Reaching All Students

Spanish-Speaking Students
Usa el vocabulario de esta lista para escribir cinco oraciones originales. En cada oración, usa dos de las palabras o expresiones de la lista.

Extended Written Practice/Homework
1. Using the vocabulary on pp. 194–195 and 201, write four sentences describing the technology of communication in your region at the present time: *Hoy en día, en la oficina de mi mamá, se usa el fax cada vez más.*
2. Write three sentences describing how different people have reacted to changes in technology: *Mi abuela tiene 62 años pero ella y sus amigas se comunican mucho usando el correo electrónico.*

Multiple Intelligences
Bodily/Kinesthetic and Verbal/LInguistic
Have students design a new telephone for the future and explain how it will be used.
Verbal/Linguistic
See Vocabulary Tape 6-2 and Class Starter Review.
Visual/Spatial
See Overhead 21.

Comunicación y tecnología

¿Cuál es el mejor **medio de comunicación hoy en día?** Hace unos años no había tantas opciones. Existían el teléfono, el telégrafo y el correo. Luego **inventaron** el radio, la televisión y la computadora. Estos **inventos** hicieron muy fácil la comunicación. Antes teníamos que **esperar aproximadamente** una semana para recibir una carta. Pero ahora con el fax y **el correo electrónico** ya no tenemos que esperar. ¡**Comunicarse** es **cada vez más** fácil!

Y en el futuro la comunicación será todavía más rápida. Aunque ya usamos computadoras **interactivas**, para el siglo XXI no habrá computadoras que no lo sean. Podremos usarlas para conseguir información de bibliotecas y tiendas, para ver el menú de un restaurante, para leer periódicos y revistas, y también para pagar los impuestos. En el próximo siglo, **las conferencias por video,** que nos permitirán ver a la persona con quien hablamos por teléfono, serán algo de todos los días.

Por suerte, no es necesario ser científicos para usar toda esta tecnología. Pero, ¿podremos usarla para comunicarnos realmente mejor?

Cada vez se **fabrican** más productos nuevos, y esos nuevos inventos traen nuevos problemas. Al mismo tiempo que **cualquiera** puede obtener información sobre nuestra vida **privada,** el contacto personal sigue perdiendo importancia. Con esta nueva tecnología, recibiremos información con **rapidez,** pero también **querremos** respuestas cada vez más rápidas. Esto, según algunas personas, **creará** más presión en nuestras vidas. ¿Qué piensas tú? ¿Cómo cambiarán nuestras vidas estos nuevos productos?

hoy en día	*nowadays*	querremos	*we will want*
esperar	*here: to wait*	(*from:* querer)	
cada vez más	*more and more*	(*e → ie*)	
fabricar *(c → qu)*	*to manufacture*	creará (*from:* crear)	*it will create*
cualquiera	*anybody*		

¿Y qué quiere decir...?

el medio de comunicación	comunicar(se) *(c → qu)*
inventar	interactivo, -a
el invento	la conferencia por video
aproximadamente	privado, -a
el correo electrónico	la rapidez

Class Starter Review

On the day following the presentation of the *Tema para investigar,* you might begin the class with this activity:
Define one of the vocabulary words in Spanish. Have students guess which word it is. Whoever guesses correctly will define the next word, and so on.

www Internet Activities
Juegos

Practice & Apply

Re-enter / Recycle
Exs. 1 and 6: present perfect from Chap. 4

Answers: ¿Comprendiste?
1 Estas ideas están incluidas en el tema: a, b, d, f.

2 Answers will vary.

Answers: ¿Y qué piensas tú?
3–7 Answers will vary.

¿Comprendiste?

1 ¿Cuáles de estas ideas están incluidas en el tema y cuáles no?

a. En el pasado había sólo tres medios de comunicación.
b. Recientemente han inventado cosas que hacen la comunicación más fácil y más rápida.
c. Hoy en día una carta tarda aproximadamente dos días en llegar al destinatario.
d. En el próximo siglo, será posible tener conferencias por video.
e. Tendremos que pagar más impuestos para tener mejores medios de comunicación.
f. Otras personas podrán obtener información sobre nuestra vida privada.

2 Nombra tres inventos. ¿Qué problemas resolvieron? ¿Qué problemas causaron?

¿Y qué piensas tú?

Aquí tienes otra oportunidad para usar el vocabulario de este capítulo.

3 ¿Cuál crees que será la función más importante de las computadoras interactivas? ¿Crees que te gustarán? ¿Por qué?

4 ¿Cuáles son las ventajas y desventajas de poder ver a las personas con quienes hablas por teléfono? ¿Te gustaría tener conferencias por video? ¿Por qué?

5 Cada año se fabrican muchas cosas que no necesitamos. ¿Cuáles son algunas de las cosas que crees que no necesitamos?

202   Capítulo 6

MÁS PRÁCTICA

- Más práctica y tarea, p. 563
- Practice Workbook 6–3, 6–4

Options

Strategies for Reaching All Students

Spanish-Speaking Students
Ex. 7: After this exercise, have students answer in writing: *En tu opinión, ¿cuál es el mejor medio de comunicación? ¿Por qué?*

Students Needing Extra Help
Ex. 5: Brainstorm unnecessary inventions. *¿Qué sabes ahora?:* Have students write this so that they can record their progress.

Enrichment
Additional questions: *¿Tienes o te gustaría tener un teléfono celular en tu coche? ¿Por qué?*
Ex. 6: As homework, ask students to write a few sentences describing how one of the following places has changed in the last fifty years due to inventions or innovations in communications: a doctor's office, a public library, a bank, a gas station, or a movie theater. For an alternate assignment, ask students to list the kinds of businesses or services related to communications that are common now but that were not common or didn't even exist when they were born.

6 En grupos de tres o cuatro, decidan cuáles son los tres o cuatro inventos más importantes del siglo XX. Luego digan:

- ¿Para qué sirven?
- ¿Por qué son tan importantes?
- ¿Qué influencia han tenido en nuestras vidas? ¿Ha sido negativa o positiva?

7 En grupos de tres o cuatro, piensen en cuatro medios de comunicación que no se usarán en el futuro. ¿Qué se usará en su lugar? Hagan una tabla como la siguiente y luego comparen sus resultados con los de los otros grupos.

MEDIO DE COMUNICACIÓN	LO QUE SE USARÁ
El correo	El correo electrónico

Usando un videoteléfono

¿Qué sabes ahora?

¿Puedes:

- escribir y enviar una carta a alguien?
  —**En el sobre siempre escribo mi ___, el nombre del (de la) ___ y su ___.**
- hacer una llamada telefónica?
  —**Busco el número en ___, ___ el número y digo ___.**
- hablar de diferentes medios de comunicación?
  —**Creo que el mejor medio de comunicación es ___ porque ___.**
- dar tu opinión sobre las comunicaciones en el futuro?
  —**En el futuro, la comunicación será ___ porque ___.**

Tema para investigar   203

Present & Apply

ÁLBUM CULTURAL

La nueva tecnología hace más fácil las comunicaciones. ¿Qué nuevos inventos conoces que nos ayudan a comunicarnos mejor?

¡La Moda es estar en Contacto!
MEMO EXPRESS

Entre los nuevos inventos que nos ayudan a comunicarnos mejor están los *beepers* o "buscapersonas". Aunque al principio los usaban sólo los médicos, hoy en día muchos los tienen para uso personal. Los nuevos modelos son del tamaño de una tarjeta de crédito y permiten recibir varios mensajes cada vez.

El teléfono celular también es popular en muchos países hispanos. Una de sus ventajas es que permite ponerse en contacto con otros desde cualquier lugar. Los que usan el teléfono celular dicen que así pueden usar mejor su tiempo.

204   Capítulo 6

Options

Además, te ofrecemos la posibilidad de remitir envíos certificados, asegurados, contrareembolso o con acuse de recibo.

Tú eliges la rapidez, nosotros te ponemos los medios.

Correos y Telégrafos es ante todo un servicio público, que está y estamos al ALCANCE DE TODOS. Mejorar día a día nuestro servicio, es sin duda alguna, nuestro principal objetivo; por eso queremos dar respuesta a tus posibles preguntas.

Puedes pedir más información en cualquiera de nuestras oficinas.

CORREOS Y TELÉGRAFOS

Correos y Telégrafos

Mandar una carta es el medio de comunicación más tradicional y a veces el más económico. El servicio de correos de España tiene una tarifa *(rate)* para los países del Mercado Común Europeo, además de otras según el lugar a donde se manda la carta. Se puede comprar sellos en la oficina de correos o en otros lugares llamados estancos.

Álbum cultural 205

Cultural Notes

(p. 204, realia)
As in the U.S., daily life in Hispanic countries is being transformed by the proliferation of high-technology personal communication devices. Pagers, beepers, and cellular phones are becoming ever lighter, slimmer, and more efficient. Motorola, a world leader in communication technology, is promoting two of these devices in the ads.

(p. 205, realia)
This advertisement is for Spain's postal service, Correos y Telégrafos. Although customers do have a choice as to the speed with which they want or need materials delivered, the most economical and reliable rapid means of written communication in Spain is the telegram, which customers may send by phone or by going to the telegraph services section of any post office.

Present & Apply

Answers: Reacción personal

1–2 Answers will vary.

3 Answers will vary, but students may mention:
Las oficinas de Correos y Telégrafos ofrecen servicio de correos. También se venden sellos. / *Answers will vary.* / Se puede comprar sellos en super-mercados.

4–5 Answers will vary.

 **Internet Activities**
Álbum cultural

H oy es la palabra de moda. Mañana será moneda de consumo corriente. Todo el mundo habla de lo interacti-vo: televisión interactiva, disco compacto interactivo, videojue-gos interactivos, museos inte-ractivos y realidad virtual como la expresión máxima de lo inte-ractivo. Gracias a esta técnica, cada vez más bienes y servicios están al alcance del ciudadano. Interactivo es todo diálogo en-tre una máquina y el hombre. Comunicación bidireccional. Mu-chos de los servicios que ofrece la televisión por cable de fibra óptica son interactivos. Por ejemplo, a través del ordenador se puede comunicar con el su-permercado, ver en la pantalla los géneros y las ofertas del día, con todo tipo de información adicional, y encargar la compra. Es la telecompra, con servicio, naturalmente, a domicilio.
Disco compacto digital: Uno de los soportes más populares y con más futuro de la interactividad. Se presenta en dos versiones: CD-I, con mando a distancia, y CD-ROM, de uso informático. Destinados fundamentalmente a aplica-ciones educativas y de ocio, estos aparatos hacen las funciones del vídeo doméstico, el proyector de diapositivas, el disco com-pacto de audio y la consola de videojuegos. Permiten almacenar 300.000 páginas de texto, más de 7.000 imágenes, 19 horas de audio y vídeo y 16 millones de variaciones de color, además de di-versos programas de ordenador. En un CD-ROM se puede meter casi todo: desde la Biblia y los 890 pergaminos del Mar Muerto,

Nº 1.208 · 16 ENERO 1995 · CAMBIO16

Realidad virtual: imágenes tridimensionales.

INTERACTIVO

hasta los cuadros de El Pra-do y las actuaciones Joan Manuel Serrat.
Realidad virtual: Es aquí donde la interactividad pre-senta los desarrollos tecno-lógicos más avanzados. Consiste en la representa-ción de escenarios virtua-les, con imágenes en tres dimensiones y de apariencia real. Es la exaltación del vínculo humano con el orde-nador. Con un casco o ga-fas especiales, uno se su-merge en múltiples expe-riencias y mundos imagina-rios, con sonido estereofóni-co y objetos palpables. Sólo la imaginación y la ética son los límites de esta tec-nología.
Televisión a la carta: La pe-queña pantalla no podría sustraerse a la interactivi-dad. Diseñar un telediario a capricho del espectador, es-coger el ángulo de visión o ver sólo el final de una película, es de-cir, elegir en cada momento lo que se quiera ver, ya es posible en España. Por ahora, queda reservado a unos pocos privilegiados. En el próximo milenio esto será el pan nuestro de cada día. Para entonces ya se comercializará la televisión de alta defini-ción, que prácticamente duplica las 625 líneas de los aparatos actuales. Será como tener el cine en casa, con una calidad de imagen y sonido superior a una película de 35 milímetros. Se cal-cula que este negocio representará en el mercado europeo unas ventas de 15 billones de pesetas al año a partir del 2000. ∎

Los aparatos electrónicos interactivos son cosa de todos los días y están en todas partes. Hoy en día se pueden hacer compras a través de la computadora, sin salir de casa y es posible obtener toda clase de información por medio de la red electrónica o usando el CD-ROM. No está lejos el día en el que podamos diseñar nuestros propios programas de televisión.

206   Capítulo 6

Options

Strategies for Reaching All Students

Students Needing Extra Help
If necessary, help students with the caption text on p. 207 by dividing it into sections.
Reacción personal: Make sure that the first question doesn't turn into an inappropriate topic.

Multiple Intelligences
Interpersonal/Social
Have students make a list of problems stu-dents may face in the year 2040 and then suggest possible solutions.
Mathematical/Logical
1) Have students create a new electronic money system to be used in the future.

2) Have students create a time line for the years 2000–3000 indicating how they think technology will change.
Visual/Spatial
See Exs. 1–5.

Entre los inventos que encontraremos en el futuro estarán los aparatos electrónicos inteligentes, que harán toda clase de trabajos en la casa, desde regular la temperatura del aire acondicionado en el lugar donde están las personas hasta calcular *(calculate)* la potencia *(power)* que necesita usar la aspiradora. Habrá también robots que harán otros trabajos.

EL HOGAR INTELIGENTE

En Japón ya se comercializan los electrodomésticos inteligentes: sistemas de aire acondicionado que calientan o enfrían adecuadamente la parte de la habitación donde se hallan las personas; lavadoras que analizan la ropa para establecer ciclos de lavado y secado; microondas que determinan si los alimentos necesitan ser descongelados antes o simplemente calentarlos; aspiradoras que miden la cantidad de polvo de succionan con el fin de ajustar su potencia... Ello gracias a unos sensores y microprocesadores capaces de medir y procesar cualquier elemento físico o ambiental.

Sensores y microprocesadores que, debidamente programados y conectados a un ordenador personal, permiten a distancia llenar la bañera de agua, encender el horno o activar el riego automático del jardín. Basta con telefonear a la casa y decir la clave correspondiente. El ordenador dará las órdenes oportunas a los sensores para que cumplan lo mandado.

Junto a estos artilugios, en el hogar convivirán otros más reconocibles: los robots domésticos. Para éstos quedarán reservadas funciones como el barrer, poner la mesa o servir las copas, además de jugar con los niños. El robot será uno más de la familia, como un empleado que no se cansa, que no reivindica nada y que obedece a la voz de su amo.

El hogar se convertirá, además, en un centro de trabajo y comunicaciones telemáticas. Bastará tener el teléfono y el televisor conectados con el ordenador personal para que se abran, sin salir de casa, casi todas las puertas imaginables: desde la telecompra al telediagnóstico, pasando por la realidad virtual y el acceso a las autopistas de la información.

El robot será uno más de la familia.

Reacción personal

Contesta las siguientes preguntas en una hoja de papel.

1 ¿Crees que es necesario tener un *beeper* para uso personal? ¿Por qué o por qué no?

2 ¿Tiene tu familia un teléfono inalámbrico o celular? ¿En qué clase de trabajo es práctico tener un teléfono celular?

3 ¿Qué servicios ofrecen las oficinas de Correos y Telégrafos de España? ¿Son como los que ofrece el servicio de correos de tu país? Explica.

4 ¿Qué otros aparatos interactivos conoces además de las computadoras? ¿Qué es lo que te parece más interesante de los aparatos interactivos?

5 ¿Qué es lo que más te atrae de los aparatos electrónicos inteligentes? ¿Qué ventajas crees que tendrán estos aparatos? ¿Qué trabajos piensas que podría hacer un robot?

www.pasoapaso.com

Álbum cultural 207

Preview

Teaching Suggestions

A Ask students if the verb forms *ayudará* and *permitirá* refer to actions in the past, present, or future. Have them tell you if these endings for *-ar* and *-ir* verbs are the same or different.

B Ask students to explain how *tener, poner,* and *saber* are irregular in the future tense. Have them also tell if the endings to these verbs are regular or irregular.

Answers

Answers to inductive questions will vary, but students may mention size, features, price, or optional equipment such as extra batteries, etc.

A *-á* / the infinitive / The ending for the *yo* form should be *-é*, the ending for the *Ud. / él / ella* form should be *-á*.

B The ending for the *nosotros* form is *-emos*, the ending for the *Uds. / ellos / ellas* form is *-án*. The chart for *tener: yo tendré, tú tendrás, Ud. / él / ella tendrá, nosotros tendremos, Uds. / ellos / ellas tendrán.* / *Poner* and *saber* would have regular future-tense endings, but their stems would be *pondr-* and *sabr-*.

C *Se* refers to María, and *lo* refers to *el teléfono*.

Gramática en contexto

Mira la foto y lee lo que este estudiante les envía a sus padres. ¿Qué información esperas encontrar sobre este teléfono?

El teléfono del futuro

Queridos padres:

Como en el teléfono habrá memoria para 90 números, grabaré los números de la familia y de todos mis amigos. Podré programarlo para casos de emergencia.

Si alguien me llama cuando no esté en casa, el teléfono me pondrá en contacto inmediatamente con la persona que llame; no tendré que esperar.

Esto les ayudará mucho a Uds. porque así sabrán dónde estoy en cualquier momento. Podremos comunicarnos mejor. El teléfono les permitirá llamarme cuando quieran y podrán hablar conmigo con frecuencia.

El teléfono del futuro

El teléfono habrá memori.

Se lo prestaré a María si lo necesita.

A In his note, the student says *Esto les ayudará* and *El teléfono les permitirá*. What ending has been added to both verbs? Was the ending added to a stem or to the infinitive? On a piece of paper, make a chart that shows the endings used when the subject is *yo* or *el teléfono*. Leave space to add other subjects and endings to your chart.

B Look at the third paragraph and fill in the chart showing the endings for *nosotros* and *Uds.* Now make a chart showing the stem and endings for *tener* in the future tense. What do you think the chart would look like for the verb *poner*? and for *saber*?

C In the self-adhesive note, it says *Se lo prestaré*. To what or whom does the pronoun *se* refer? To what or whom does the pronoun *lo* refer?

208 Capítulo 6

Options

Strategies for Reaching All Students

Students Needing Extra Help
Begin the grammar section of the Organizer.
B: As students come up with the future-tense forms of the irregular verbs, write them in chart form on the chalkboard.
C: Review the indirect object pronouns. Rewrite the sentence as *prestaré el teléfono,* then as *lo prestaré,* then as *le prestaré el teléfono a María.* Finally, rewrite it as *se lo prestaré a María.*
Repaso: El futuro: If available, use the Organizer from Book 2, Chap. 11. Model the future tense of another *-er* and *-ir* verb, such as *comer* and *escribir.*

Enrichment
Ex. 1: As a class, discuss well-known personalities and what they will probably *never* do. Encourage the class to be imaginative, as in these examples: *Madonna nunca será profesora. / Jon Secada nunca venderá coches usados.*

Repaso: El futuro

You have learned that we can express the future in Spanish in three ways: by using *ir* + *a* + infinitive, the present tense, or the future tense.

Remember that when we use the future tense, all verbs have the same endings. For most verbs we attach the endings to the infinitive. Here are all the future-tense forms of *enviar, ver,* and *ir.*

enviar		ver		ir	
enviar**é**	enviar**emos**	ver**é**	ver**emos**	ir**é**	ir**emos**
enviar**ás**	enviar**éis**	ver**ás**	ver**éis**	ir**ás**	ir**éis**
enviar**á**	enviar**án**	ver**á**	ver**án**	ir**á**	ir**án**

Les **enviaré** una carta a mis abuelos mañana.
En diciembre **iremos** a Santiago y **veremos** los últimos modelos de teléfonos.

1 Con un(a) compañero(a), habla de lo que harán diferentes personas que Uds. conocen.

A — *¿Crees que Alejandra será astrónoma algún día?*

B — *Sí, y estudiará los planetas.*

(nombre)

¡NO OLVIDES!

Remember that there is an accent mark on all but the *nosotros* form.

You have already seen that the future is often used with *si* (if) and a verb in the present or in the present progressive tense.
*Si no **tengo** dinero **llamaré** a cobro revertido.*

Estudiante A

a. tú

b. (dos nombres)

c. (nombre)

d. Uds.

e. tu primo(a)

f.

Estudiante B

cuidar a los enfermos

investigar en un laboratorio

estudiar civilizaciones antiguas

hablar con personas famosas

llevar el correo a todas las casas

Gramática en contexto 209

Present & Practice

Class Starter Review
On the day following the review of the future tense, you might begin the class with this activity:
Ask students to tell what they are going to do later that day or tomorrow using *ir a* + inf. *(Susan, ¿qué vas a hacer esta noche? / Voy a ver la tele.)* As a follow-up activity, have other students report what their classmates will do using the future tense *(Susan verá la tele esta noche.).*

Answers
1 ESTUDIANTE A
a. ¿Crees que tú serás locutor(a) algún día?
b. ...(dos nombres) serán arqueólogos(as) ...
c. ...(nombre) será cartero(a) ...
d. ...Uds. serán científicos(as) ...
e. ...tu primo(a) será enfermero(a) ...
f. Questions will vary.
ESTUDIANTE B
Answers will vary, but may include:
a. Sí, y hablaré con personas famosas.
b. ...estudiarán civilizaciones antiguas.
c. ...llevará el correo a todas las casas.
d. ...investigarán en un laboratorio.
e. ...cuidará a los enfermos.
f. Answers will vary.

Extended Written Practice/Homework
1. Choose four verbs and write sentences saying what you think will take place in your community in the future: *construir, fabricar, eliminar, reducir, ofrecer, vivir, ser, resolver.*
2. Write three pairs of sentences telling what different people like to do or do well now. Tell what they will do in the future: *A mi hermano le encanta dibujar. En el futuro trabajará para una compañía que crea películas de dibujos animados.*

Multiple Intelligences
Intrapersonal/Introspective
Have students make a list of ten things they are currently learning that may help them in the future.
Verbal/Linguistic
See Ex. 1, Enrichment, and Class Starter Review.

Present & Practice

Re-enter / Recycle

Ex. 2: *seguir* + present participle from Chap. 5
Ex. 3: present perfect from Chap. 4

Answers

2 ESTUDIANTE A
a.–i. Statements will vary, but look for the correct future-tense form of *seguir* plus the present participle.

ESTUDIANTE B
a.–i. Responses will vary, but look for the correct use of the future tense.

3 a.–f. Statements will vary, but should include a wide variety of vocabulary and correct use of the future tense.

 Practice Wkbk. 6-5

 Writing Activity 6-D

 Prueba 6-5

---

2 Dile a un(a) compañero(a) qué piensas que seguirán haciendo estas personas en el futuro. Tu compañero(a) te dirá si está de acuerdo o no.

tu actor o actriz favorito(a)

A —*Mi actriz favorita, (nombre), seguirá apareciendo en la misma telenovela.*
B —*No estoy de acuerdo. Creo que esa telenovela terminará después de este año.*

a. yo
b. mi mejor amigo(a)
c. los carteros
d. los profesores
e. el presidente de los Estados Unidos
f. mis amigos y yo
g. mi familia
h. los atletas profesionales
i. 💡

3 Con un(a) compañero(a) digan qué medios de comunicación usarán en las situaciones siguientes. Usen el futuro.

En el pueblo no hay teléfonos públicos y necesitas dinero.

Les mandaré un telegrama a mis padres para pedir dinero.

a. Tu hermana va a asistir a una boda pero no ha traído sus zapatos nuevos. Tienes que mandárselos.
b. Estás en casa y quieres hablar con tu primo(a) en otro estado.
c. Tienes una computadora y quieres mandarle un recado a un(a) compañero(a) que también tiene una.
d. Quieres comunicarte con un(a) amigo(a) en Uruguay, pero no tienes dinero para hacer una llamada.
e. Llamas a tu amigo(a) y su contestador automático contesta el teléfono.
f. Estás de vacaciones y quieres decirles a tus amigos dónde estás.

210   Capítulo 6

Options

Strategies for Reaching All Students

Students Needing Extra Help
Ex. 2: Brainstorm phrases to complete the *Estudiante A* statements and *Estudiante B* responses.
El futuro: Continuación: If available, use the Organizer from Book 2, Chap. 11.

Continue (or begin) a list of the irregular future-tense verbs.
Ex. 3: Brainstorm different means of communication.
Ex. 4: Brainstorm phrases to complete the statements regarding what students do now and what they will do in the future.

Enrichment
Ex. 2: As homework, ask students to describe a personal habit, outlook, or trait that has a positive effect in their daily lives and that they hope always to maintain.

El futuro: Continuación

You have already learned that certain verbs have irregular stems in the future tense. However, their future endings (-é, -ás, -á, -emos, -éis, -án) are the same as for regular verbs.

saber	→	**sabr-**
tener	→	**tendr-**
poder	→	**podr-**
hacer	→	**har-**
haber	→	**habr-**

Si vas a España, ya **sabrás** usar el teléfono público.
Pronto **tendrán** un teléfono celular y **podrán** llamar desde el jardín.
¿Qué **haremos** si no nos llaman?
Algún día **habrá** teléfonos inalámbricos en todas las casas.

• Other verbs that have irregular stems in the future tense are:

venir	→	**vendr-**
decir	→	**dir-**
poner	→	**pondr-**
salir	→	**saldr-**
querer	→	**querr-**

Vendrás a casa y me **dirás** lo que pasó durante la película.
Primero **pondremos** el cuarto en orden y luego **saldremos**.
Mis padres nunca **querrán** comprar un contestador automático.

4 Túrnate con un(a) compañero(a) para describir cómo es la vida de ustedes ahora y cómo será en el futuro.

> vivir   *Ahora vivo con mis padres. En el futuro, viviré con unos amigos en un apartamento cerca de la universidad.*

a. salir con mis amigos
b. (no) poder (+ infinitivo)
c. (no) tener que (+ infinitivo)
d. decirles a mis padres
e. querer tener

f. (no) saber (+ infinitivo)
g. (no) hacer
h. (no) haber
i. (no) venir
j. 💡

Extended Written Practice/Homework
1. Write four sentences telling how you believe the technology of communication in your region will change in twenty years. Include the verbs *saber, tener, poder, hacer, haber, venir, decir, poner, salir, querer.*
2. Write four sentences describing a typical house in the future. Include the verbs *saber, tener, poder, hacer, haber, venir, decir, poner, salir, querer.*

3. Write three sentences telling what you will observe about your classmates when you attend your twentieth class reunion.

Multiple Intelligences
Intrapersonal/Introspective
See Enrichment.
Visual/Spatial
See Practice Wkbk. 6-5 and Writing Activities 6-D.

Present & Practice

Teaching Suggestions
Before beginning this exercise, have students review the vocabulary from Book 2, Chap. 11.

Answers
5 a.–g. Answers will vary.

 Practice Wkbk. 6-6

 Writing Activity 6-E

 Prueba 6-6

 Comm. Act. BLM 6-2

6 ESTUDIANTE A
a. ¿Quién te envió esa tarjeta de cumpleaños?
b. ... esa carta?
c. ... esas tarjetas postales?
d. ... esos paquetes?
e. ... esos regalos?
ESTUDIANTE B
Answers will vary, but may include:
a. Mis abuelos me la enviaron / No me las envió nadie. Yo la compré.
b. ... me la ...
c. ... me las ...
d. ... me los ...
e. ... me los ...

5 Imagina que vives diez años en el futuro. Con un(a) compañero(a), digan qué medios de comunicación usarán en situaciones como las siguientes.

a. Es muy tarde y estás listo para salir del trabajo.
b. Tu familia vive muy lejos de ti y quieres saber cómo están.
c. Es el cumpleaños de un(a) amigo(a) que está en otro país.
d. Estás de vacaciones y necesitas dinero inmediatamente.
e. Quieres saber cómo será el tiempo la semana próxima.
f. Quieres jugar ajedrez con un(a) amigo(a) en otro estado.
g. Necesitas una copia de un documento muy importante inmediatamente.

Puedes usar estos verbos u otros en tu respuesta:

llamar	no haber ...	poder (mandar,	tener que
mandar	no hacer	llamar ...)	usar

Uso de los complementos directos e indirectos
You already know the direct and indirect object pronouns in Spanish:

Direct object pronouns:	**me, te, lo, la, nos, os, los, las**
Indirect object pronouns:	**me, te, le, nos, os, les**

• When we use a direct and an indirect object pronoun together, we place the indirect object pronoun before the direct object pronoun.

—¿Quién **te** enviará el artículo?
—Mi tía **me lo** enviará.
Si no tienes el dinero, yo **te lo** presto.

• When the indirect object pronoun *le* or *les* comes before the direct object pronoun *lo, la, los,* or *las,* we change *le* or *les* to *se.* In these cases, we sometimes add the prepositional phrase *a Ud., a él, a ella,* etc. or *a* + a noun or a person's name for clarification.

Marisa y Tere necesitan estos sellos. ¿Quieres **dárselos**?
— ¿A quién **le** enviarás el paquete?
— **Se lo** enviaré **a mi prima**.

• When we attach two object pronouns to an infinitive, a command, or a present participle, we must add an accent mark to preserve the original stress.

Necesito llenar ese formulario. **Dámelo**, por favor.
Lo siento, no puedo **dártelo** porque es el último formulario que tengo.
¿Me enviaste el fax?
Estoy **enviándotelo** ahora.

212   Capítulo 6

Options

Strategies for Reaching All Students

Students Needing Extra Help
Uso de los complementos directos e indirectos: Model sentences using direct and indirect object pronouns, emphasizing the difference between them. Give further examples.
If students are having difficulty with the order, show them visually that they should find the subject, then jump to the verb, and then work backwards, going from the direct object to the indirect object.
Remind students that *le* and *les* will always become *se.* Give additional examples.
Separate the concepts: for example, placement of object pronouns, attachment to infinitive, attachment to commands, *le* and *les* becoming *se,* and use of accents. Have students take notes.
Ex. 6: Tell students to look at the pictures first, deciding what object pronoun will replace them. Brainstorm who will send these things to them. Point out all the changes in the dialogue: *te* becomes *me, esas fotos* becomes *las,* etc.
Have students do the exercise twice, once using only positive responses, the second time using negative responses.
Ex. 7: Brainstorm a list of items, as well as to whom they will give the gift(s).

6 Habla con un(a) compañero(a) sobre lo que te enviaron otras personas.

   A —¿*Quién te envió esas fotos?*
   B —*Mis abuelos me las enviaron.*
      o: *No me las envió nadie. Yo las saqué.*

Estudiante A

a.

Querida Ana:

Cariños,
Marta
P.D.

b.

c.

d.

e.

Estudiante B

7 Imagina que ganaste la lotería y puedes reemplazar *(replace)* todas tus posesiones con otras nuevas y mejores. Haz una lista de las cosas que ya no quieres. Tu compañero(a) va a preguntarte a quién se las darás.

una cadena
de oro

   A —¿*A quién le darás la cadena de oro?*
   B —*Se la daré a mi hermana.*

Ahora lo sabes

¿Puedes:

- **describir una acción que ocurrirá en el futuro?**

  —**El verano próximo, mis padres ___ a Argentina para visitar a mis tíos.**

- **decir cómo nos comunicaremos en el futuro?**

  —**Ahora podemos comunicarnos bien, pero en el futuro ___ comunicarnos todavía más rápidamente.**

- **responder sin repetir palabras?**

  —**Por favor, mamá, ¿me envuelves este paquete?**

  —**Claro, hijo, espera y yo ___ envuelvo.**

MÁS PRÁCTICA

   Más práctica y tarea, pp. 563–564
   Practice Workbook 6–5, 6–9

Gramática en contexto   213

Apply

Teaching Suggestions
Point out that completing these activities will help students answer the key chapter question. You may select one, two, or all three of these activities, as time permits.

Answers: Sopa de actividades
1–3 Responses will vary, but look for a wide use of chapter vocabulary, as well as correct use of the future tense and direct and indirect object pronouns.

¿Cómo nos podemos comunicar mejor?

Esta sección te ofrece la oportunidad de combinar lo que aprendiste en este capítulo con lo que ya sabes para responder a la pregunta clave.

Sopa de actividades

1. Formen grupos de tres o cuatro estudiantes. Cada grupo va a escoger un aspecto de la vida diaria para describirlo en el pasado, en el presente y en el futuro. Por ejemplo, pueden hablar de:

- la comida
- las diversiones
- los medios de comunicación
- los viajes
- la ropa
- la salud

Preparen una presentación oral para la clase y usen fotos de revistas, dibujos, ilustraciones, etc. para mostrar las diferencias o semejanzas que hay entre el pasado, el presente y el futuro.

Después de ver cada presentación, pueden discutir en grupo las ventajas y desventajas de cada época. Por ejemplo:

- ¿Será el futuro más cómodo y eficiente?
- ¿Es mejor nuestra vida ahora o era mejor en el pasado?

214

Options

Strategies for Reaching All Students

Spanish-Speaking Students
Ex. 3: Instead of this exercise, have students write: *Escribe un párrafo que responda a estas preguntas: ¿Qué necesitarás saber en el futuro para comunicarte mejor? ¿Cómo lo aprenderás?*

Students Needing Extra Help
If time is a factor, you may want to do only one or two of these exercises, or assign a different exercise to each group of students. Exs. 1 and 2 are similar in focus (the future), while Ex. 3 emphasizes object pronouns.

Ex. 1: Review verb tenses. Have each group make a chart with three columns, labeled for each time period. Have them write their ideas in the appropriate column. Give a specific number of ideas for each time period.
Ex. 2: Allow students to use the same category they used in Ex. 1. Have them act out what they have already prepared.

2 En grupos de tres o cuatro, preparen su propio video o dramatización de "Regreso al futuro."

- Consideren los aspectos de la vida del futuro que quieren presentar.
- En la primera escena un científico les habla a un grupo de jóvenes sobre lo que encontrarán al llegar al futuro.
- Los jóvenes están ahora en el futuro. Ustedes pueden mostrar aquí lo que pasará en el futuro.
- Después de cada presentación, los demás estudiantes pueden decir si están de acuerdo o no con las predicciones que cada grupo ha hecho y explicar por qué.

3 A veces podemos escoger el medio para comunicarnos con otros. Trabaja con un(a) compañero(a). Para cada una de las situaciones siguientes, escribe una ventaja y una desventaja de los medios de comunicación indicados. Comparen sus respuestas con las de otra pareja y luego decidan, en grupo, qué medio de comunicación van a recomendar.

- Es el cumpleaños de tu abuela y no le mandaste una tarjeta. Ella no está en su casa ahora.
- Tu amiga está enojada contigo.
- Necesitas conseguir un trabajo para el verano, pero los documentos deben llegar hoy.
- No trajiste tu tarea a la clase.

Dejar un recado en el contestador automático
Enviar un mensaje por correo electrónico
Explicar la situación en persona
Escribir una nota / una carta
Mandar los documentos / la carta / la tarjeta por fax

Sopa de actividades   215

Video Activity A

Video, Capítulo 6

Chapter 6: Play

Step

Video Activities B–C

Writing Activities 6-G, 6-H

Comm. Act. BLMs 6-4, 6-5

Apply

Teaching Suggestions
Tell students that working through the *Para leer* section will help them answer the key question.

Encourage students to use the strategies given to them in the text to help them understand the reading. Remind them that they do not need to understand every word.

Process Reading
For a description of process reading, see p. 52.

Answers
Antes de leer
a. los términos técnicos
b. los términos de negocios
c. las expresiones de tiempo

Mira la lectura
Los nombres de los tres aparatos son: el videoteléfono, el teléfono inteligente, el comunicador personal inteligente.

Para leer

Antes de leer

STRATEGY ➤ Using prior knowledge

Estas palabras y expresiones aparecen en la selección "El mejor amigo del hombre." Con un(a) compañero(a), decide en qué grupo están los términos técnicos, los términos de negocios y las expresiones de tiempo.

a. semiconductores
receptor de mensajes electrónicos
ondas radiofónicas
de señal y proceso

b. mercados financieros
compañía
empresas

c. por primera vez
hoy en día
muy pronto

216   Capítulo 6

Mira la lectura

STRATEGY ➤ Scanning

La selección trata de tres nuevos aparatos electrónicos. Lee la selección sólo para encontrar los nombres de los aparatos.

El mejor amigo del hombre

El mejor amigo del hombre siempre ha sido el perro… sin duda. Pero en estos tiempos de revolución tecnológica la tradicional fidelidad de un animal de 4 patas ha sido superada por un "aparato": el teléfono. Y es que el ser humano puede vivir sin la compañía de un perro, ¡pero ya es imposible vivir sin un teléfono alrededor! "Este es el modo como la gente quiere comunicarse", opinó Robert Kavner, ejecutivo de la AT&T, mostrando el videoteléfono, el aparato que ha marcado una etapa en la historia de las telecomunicaciones, y que trabaja como un teléfono común y corriente, con la excepción de que se puede ver en su pequeña pantalla la imagen a todo color del interlocutor. Su precio hoy en día en Estados Unidos es de menos de 1.000 dólares (y sigue bajando). Claro, se necesitan 2 para que ambos usuarios se vean en la pantalla.

AT&T, la compañía de teléfonos más grande del mundo, fabrica estos aparatos siguiendo el mismo principio básico que Graham Bell inventó hace 117 años, y combinándolo con la más moderna tecnología en servicios de telecomunicaciones. El videoteléfono es la forma más avanzada de las ultramodernas técnicas llamadas de señal y proceso, que salen al aire usando la misma tecnología de la televisión.

Pero eso no es todo en materia de "revolución". AT&T introducirá muy pronto en el mercado el "teléfono inteligente", que también poseerá una

Options

Strategies for Reaching All Students

Students Needing Extra Help
Antes de leer: Remind students of word families and cognates.
Mira la lectura: Point out that students need to find the names of the three *new* forms of communication.

For those students who may not be technically oriented, help them with the reading as needed.
Infórmate: If students have difficulty determining some of the functions, brainstorm key words or expressions that would help cue the information.

nuevos aparatos de telecomunicación

_____

_____

_____

pantalla con una combinación de funciones, la que permitirá transacciones bancarias. Su costo: 500 dólares. Pero el "comunicador personal inteligente" será, sin duda, el teléfono del año 2000, que marcará un hito en los servicios mundiales de telecomunicaciones.

Para comenzar, Apple Computer Inc., AT&T, Matsushita Electric Industrial Co., Motorola Inc., Philips NV y Sony Corp., se han unido por primera vez en una empresa mixta llamada General Magic Inc. Su objetivo...fabricar una "cajita" que sirva de teléfono, computadora, fax y receptor de mensajes electrónicos que funcionará a través de ondas radiofónicas y vía satélite y será parte de una red de telecomunicaciones que proporcionará todo tipo de información, desde los mercados financieros a las tarifas de hoteles de todas las capitales del mundo.

Apple está encargada del sistema con un *software* llamado *telescript,* con el cual las computadoras podrán comunicarse en el mismo lenguaje. AT&T construirá la red de comunicaciones en que se incorporará el *telescript.* Motorola proporcionará los semiconductores y junto con Sony y Philips desarrollarán los comunicadores personales inteligentes. Su precio: 2.000 dólares. Pero los analistas creen que con el "comunicador" pasará lo mismo que con el fax, que en 7 años bajó su precio de 7.000 a 300 dólares.

Infórmate

STRATEGY Using graphic organizers

Ahora lee la selección con cuidado.

1 Copia la gráfica organizadora de arriba y úsala como ayuda para entender el artículo. Primero escribe los nombres de los nuevos aparatos electrónicos. Luego escribe por lo menos dos funciones para dos de los aparatos. Sólo encontrarás una función para el tercero.

2 ¿Cuáles de estas ideas *no* aparecen en el texto?

- El teléfono es el mejor amigo del hombre.
- Uno va a poder enviar un fax con el teléfono inteligente.
- El videoteléfono usa la misma tecnología que la televisión.
- Uno podrá recibir información sobre los mercados financieros a través del comunicador personal inteligente.
- Se pueden ver películas en video con el videoteléfono.
- Es probable que el precio del comunicador personal inteligente baje.

Aplicación

1 Mira la gráfica organizadora otra vez. Para cada aparato, escribe una frase que explique por qué te gustaría tener uno o por qué no.

2 Lee el primer párrafo de nuevo. ¿Qué opinión expresa el escritor? ¿Estás de acuerdo? ¿Por qué?

Para leer   217

Infórmate

1 Answers may vary:
el videoteléfono: para comunicarse y ver a los interlocutores; el teléfono inteligente: para comunicarse y hacer transacciones bancarias; el comunicador personal inteligente: para servir de teléfono, computadora, fax y receptor de mensajes electrónicos

2 Estas ideas no aparecen en el texto:
Uno va a poder enviar un fax con el teléfono inteligente.
Se pueden ver películas en video con el videoteléfono.

Aplicación

1 Statements will vary.

2 El escritor dice que es imposible vivir sin un teléfono. / *Answers will vary.*

Fondo literario
Una carta a Dios (pp. 458–461) / *Apocalipsis* (pp. 462–463)

 **Internet Activities**

Apply

Teaching Suggestions
Tell students that working through the *Para escribir* section will help them answer the key chapter question.

Process Writing
For information regarding writing portfolios, see p. 54.

Answers
Students' responses will vary.

Para escribir

Todos usamos en la vida diaria diferentes medios de comunicación. Pero, ¿cómo podemos comunicarnos mejor? Antes de responder, lee las preguntas que siguen y luego escribe un corto trabajo para explicar tu opinión.

1 Primero, piensa en estas preguntas y escribe tus ideas.

- ¿Con quién(es) tienes que comunicarte?
- ¿Qué medios de comunicación usas?
- ¿Cuál(es) de estos medios hace(n) mejor la interacción entre las personas? ¿Cuál(es) la hace(n) peor? ¿Por qué?
- ¿Qué es para ti la "buena comunicación"?
- ¿Cómo crees que te comunicarás en el futuro? ¿Habrá más comunicación personal o menos?

2 Ahora, usa tus ideas y tus notas sobre esas preguntas para escribir tu trabajo.

Aquí tienes algunas palabras y expresiones que te pueden ayudar.

al mismo tiempo	generalmente	por un lado
a veces	mientras	por otro lado
entonces	parece que	sin embargo
	por eso	

Cuando termines el primer borrador, consulta con un(a) compañero(a) y sigue los pasos del proceso de escribir. Luego, escribe tu versión final.

218

Options

Strategies for Reaching All Students

Students Needing Extra Help
Brainstorm all the aspects that the paper needs to include. Set a specific length you will accept.

Multiple Intelligences
Bodily/Kinesthetic, Verbal/Linguistic, and Visual/Spatial
See step 3.

3 Para compartir tu trabajo, puedes:

- exhibirlo en la sala de clases
- hacer un debate entre los estudiantes que tienen opiniones diferentes
- incluirlo en un libro llamado *Cómo nos comunicamos*
- ponerlo en tu portafolio

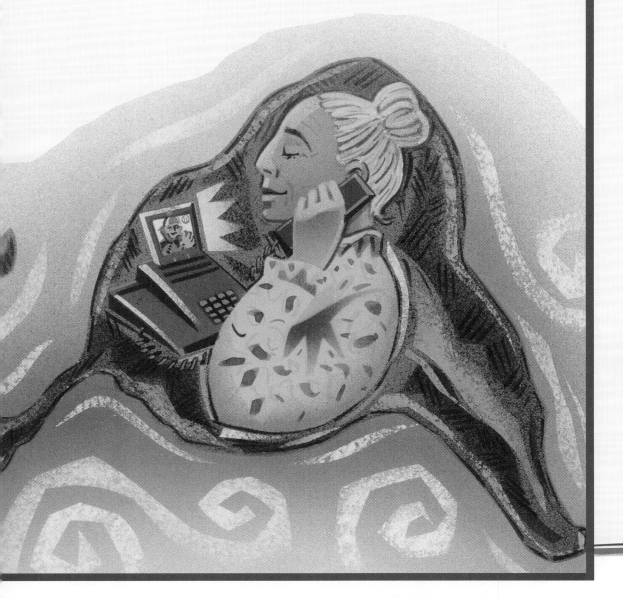

Assess & Summarize

Test Preparation
You may want to assign parts of this section as written homework or as an in-class writing activity prior to administering the *Examen de habilidades*.

Answers
Listening
—*Pues no te comunicaste porque pusiste una moneda. Tendrás que conseguir unas fichas en algún quiosco. No cuestan mucho. Primero descolgarás, pondrás una ficha y escucharás para ver si hay tono. Entonces podrás marcar el número. Si la persona que contesta no es la persona con quien quieres hablar, te preguntará, "¿De parte de quién?" Le dirás tu nombre, y te dirá si la persona está o no. Claro, si no está, podrás dejar un recado. Ahora, recuerda que con cada ficha podrás hablar sólo por tres minutos o tendrás que poner más fichas para seguir la conversación. La persona que quiere hacer la llamada telefónica tiene que comprar unas fichas. / La persona puede hablar por tres minutos.*

Esta sección te ayudará a prepararte para el examen de habilidades, donde tendrás que hacer tareas semejantes.

Listening
¿Puedes entender una conversación sobre cómo hacer una llamada telefónica en otro país? Escucha mientras el (la) profesor(a) lee un ejemplo semejante al que vas a oír en el examen. ¿Qué tiene que hacer la persona que quiere hacer la llamada? ¿Por cuánto tiempo puede hablar cada vez?

Reading
Lee el anuncio y haz una gráfica organizadora con esta información: ¿Qué vende el anuncio? ¿A quiénes les interesará?

¿Da su despacho la impresión de estar todavía en la época prehistórica?
Comunicarse es cada vez más fácil con todos los medios que podría tener al alcance de la mano. Con una visita a TALLER ELECTRÓNICO tendrá más éxito en sus negocios gracias a las más recientes invenciones que se hayan fabricado. ¡Piense en las posibilidades! Podrá recibir un recado por correo electrónico o por fax en segundos, comunicarse con otra persona en cualquier país usando computadoras interactivas, mejorar su negocio usando un teléfono inalámbrico, un teléfono celular o un contestador automático. Todo lo encontrará en TALLER ELECTRÓNICO a los mejores precios. ¡Comuníquese con nosotros hoy!

Writing
¿Puedes escribir una carta semejante a la que escribió Juliana?

Queridos padres:

¡No lo van a creer! Esta mañana descubrí que dejé mis cheques de viajero en casa. Les hice muchas llamadas pero no contestaron. No pude dejarles un recado porque no tenemos contestador automático, así que les estoy escribiendo por correo urgente. Por suerte tengo suficiente dinero para unos días más, pero tendrán que mandarme los cheques de viajero pronto. Como nuestro grupo visitará diferentes ciudades esta semana, tendré que ir al correo esta tarde para conseguir un apartado postal. Podrán mandarme cualquier carta o paquete al apartado, pero todavía no tengo la dirección. Les volveré a llamar y también les escribiré otra carta con el número del apartado.

Cariños,

Juliana

P.D. También dejé mi llavero sobre la mesa de noche. ¿Me lo podrán incluir en el paquete con los cheques?

Culture
¿Prefieres un teléfono celular o uno inalámbrico? ¿Por qué?

Speaking
Habla con otra persona por teléfono.

A —*Aló, ¿operadora? Quisiera hacer una llamada a cobro revertido.*

B —*Bueno. ¿Con quién quiere usted comunicarse y de parte de quién?*

A —*Con los señores Gutiérrez, al teléfono 645-9900, de parte de su hijo Francisco.*

B —*Muchas gracias . . . Lo siento, pero no contestan.*

A —*¡No contestan! ¿Qué haré? Ya no tengo más fichas. ¿Podría usted volver a marcar? Necesito ponerme en contacto con ellos.*

B —*¡Cómo no! Pero si no contestan usted tendrá que . . .*

self Test www.pasoapaso.com

Una joven con un teléfono inalámbrico

Options

Strategies for Reaching All Students

Students Needing Extra Help
Have students write this exercise so that they can check off what they have mastered. Remind students that this is just a sample of what the test will be like.
Listening: Read more than once. Remind students that they need to listen only for certain pieces of information. Brainstorm the words for which students should be listening.

Students may think that coins and tokens are interchangeable. Explain this difference. Help them with the passage and, if necessary, explain who is asking *¿De parte de quién?*
Reading: Remind students that they don't need to know every word to answer the questions. Tell them that another word for *despacho* is *oficina.*

Writing: Have students use the Organizer and write a sample letter as practice. Be specific about the amount of text that you will accept.
Culture: Have students review the notes they took in the *Álbum cultural.*
Speaking: Use the vocabulary section of the Organizer. Complete the model and limit the number of lines in the dialogue.

Resumen del vocabulario

Usa el vocabulario de este capítulo para:

- responder a la pregunta clave: ¿Cómo nos podemos comunicar mejor?
- escribir y enviar una carta
- hablar de diferentes medios de comunicación
- dar tu opinión sobre las comunicaciones en el futuro

para hablar de los diferentes medios de comunicación

comunicar(se) *(c → qu)*
la conferencia por video
el contestador automático
el correo electrónico
el fax
interactivo, -a
el medio de
    comunicación
por correo urgente
por vía aérea
el teléfono celular
el teléfono inalámbrico
el telegrama

para hacer una llamada telefónica

hacer una llamada
    a cobro revertido
    de larga distancia
la ficha
la línea
el operador,
    la operadora
el tono
marcar *(c → qu)*
sonar *(o → ue)*
colgar *(o → ue) (g → gu)*
descolgar *(o → ue) (g → gu)*

para hablar por teléfono

¡Aló!
¿De parte de quién?
dejar
en voz baja / alta
equivocarse *(c → qu)*
equivocado, -a
el recado
volver *(o → ue)* a + *inf.*

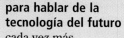

para escribir y enviar algo por correo

el apartado postal
Cariños
el cartero, la cartera
el destinatario, la destinataria
envolver *(o → ue)*
el formulario
llenar un formulario
mandar
el paquete
la posdata
querido, -a
el / la remitente
el sobre

para hablar de la tecnología del futuro

cada vez más
creará *(from:* crear*)*
fabricar *(c → qu)*
inventar
el invento
la rapidez

otras palabras y expresiones útiles

aproximadamente
cualquiera
entonces
esperar
hoy en día
lento, -a
privado, -a
querremos *(from:* querer*)*
    (e → ie)

Resumen 221

Assessment

¿? **Prueba cumulativa**

¿? **Examen de habilidades**

Test Generator

Additional Assessment Options

Comm. Act. BLMs
Small Group Activities
Situation Cards

¿Lo sabes bien? Video Quiz

www Internet Activities
Self-Test

CAPÍTULO 7

THEME: COMMUNITY SERVICE

COMMUNICATION

Topics

Volunteer work

Civic responsibilities

Objectives

Hablar del trabajo voluntario en los países hispanos y en los Estados Unidos

Describir las oportunidades de trabajo voluntario que hay en tu comunidad

Hablar de tus responsabilidades

Expresar tu opinión

Decir qué puedes hacer por la sociedad

CULTURE

El trabajo voluntario en los países hispanos

GRAMMAR

Repaso: El subjuntivo

El subjuntivo: Continuación

La voz pasiva: Ser + participio pasado

Ancillaries available for use with Chapter 7

Multisensory/Technology

 Overheads, 22–24

 Audio Tapes and CDs

 Vocabulary Art Blackline Masters for Hands-On Learning, pp. 33–37/CD-ROM

 Classroom Crossword

 Video

 Internet Activities www.pasoapaso.com

Print

 Practice Workbook, pp. 71–80

 Writing, Audio & Video Activities, pp. 41–46, 111–113, 145–146

 Communicative Activity Blackline Masters

    Pair and Small Group Activities, pp. 43–48

    Situation Cards, p. 49

 RESOURCE PRO®

Planning Express, Teaching Resources Library, and Clip Art Library

Assessment

 Assessment Program

    Pruebas, pp. 97–106

    Examen de habilidades, pp. 107–110

 Test Generator

 ¿Lo sabes bien? Video Quiz

Video, Chap. 7

221A

People Helping People

A characteristic common to all human beings is their desire to help each other. While economic realities often force us to work for monetary profit, most of us have a desire to act altruistically. Young people in particular tend to dedicate time for the benefit of society. In the U.S., for example, many work with Habitat for Humanity or join the Peace Corps to help with development projects in foreign countries. Others seek employment with or do volunteer work for non-profit organizations working with the poor.

The concept of public service has a long tradition in Latin America. Spanish-speaking countries of the Americas were profoundly shaped by the actions of the Catholic clergy who arrived with the first colonists. Beginning in the early sixteenth century, the Church began establishing a chain of missions stretching from Argentina to California. These missions often administered schools, provided basic health care, and cultivated food crops. Local craftsmen and laborers, working in conjunction with the parish, constructed public buildings, tilled gardens, and carried out other community enterprises.

Today, important social commitments are still made by people throughout Latin America. In many cities, for example, volunteers staff local fire departments. Buenos Aires, for example, is divided into *colonias,* each having its own volunteer fire department. *Los bomberos voluntarios de la Boca* augment official funds by holding fundraising events to help finance their department.

The service tradition is also maintained by universities and other educational institutions in Latin America. Upon completion of a medical degree in Mexico, doctors are required to work for a year in a rural clinic of the IMSS (Instituto Mexicano de Seguro Social). Since tuition in Mexico's public universities is free of charge, this is a way for medical professionals to repay their debt to society. This system also helps the Mexican government in its struggle to bring medical care to isolated communities.

While much volunteer work in Latin America is linked to formal institutions such as the Church or the Red Cross, probably the great majority of those who volunteer do so informally. Countless individuals donate time to helping an elderly or infirm neighbor, or to tutoring a child they know. Whether an individual gets involved with a beneficent organization or simply takes the time to help a neighbor, the beneficiary is always the community at large.

Introduce

Re-entry of Concepts

The following list represents words, expressions, and grammar topics re-entered from Books 1, 2, and 3 (Chaps. 2–5):

Book 1
school subjects, preterite, recycling, environment

Book 2
school subjects, preterite, impersonal *se,* environment, subjunctive

Chapter 2
past participles

Chapter 4
present perfect tense

Chapter 5
archaeology

Planning

Cross-Curricular Connections

Business Education Connection
(pp. 228–229)
In groups, have students create an organization to address one major world problem. They need to generate a name, logo, slogan, and a poster-size ad for their organization. Students can then either write a short essay on the goals and functions of their organization, or act out a commercial for recruiting volunteers. Display the posters or videotape the commercials.

Spanish in Your Community
Have students contact a local charity organization, such as the Red Cross or the United Way, and ask for information in Spanish about the organization. Have students share the information with the class. Create a bulletin board to display the information they have obtained.

If possible, have students inquire about organizations that provide services specifically for the Spanish-speaking population in their community. Ask them to determine if this is an area where they could not only provide assistance, but also might have the opportunity to practice their speaking skills while learning about Hispanic culture.

CAPÍTULO 7

OBJETIVOS

Al terminar este capítulo vas a poder responder a la pregunta clave:

¿Debes servir a la comunidad para graduarte?

También vas a poder:

- hablar de cuáles son tus responsabilidades en la sociedad

- expresar tu opinión sobre el trabajo voluntario

- describir las oportunidades de trabajo voluntario que existen en tu comunidad

- comparar el trabajo voluntario en los países de habla hispana y en los Estados Unidos

Voluntarios en New Braunfels, Texas

223

Teaching Suggestions
Point out that by acquiring the new words and structures of the chapter, students will be able to answer the key question.

Cultural Notes

(pp. 222–223, photo)
These volunteers are participating in a clean-up project in New Braunfels, Texas, which lies in the hill country between Austin and San Antonio. Amid the lovely rolling landscape lie meticulously restored towns, originally built in the 1850s by German and Eastern European immigrants. Their music is the source of one of the most popular kinds of Mexican music today—*norteña,* which features polka rhythms with accordion and guitar accompaniment.

Preview

- *Hablar del trabajo voluntario en los países hispanos y en los Estados Unidos*

Critical Thinking: Summarizing Information

Have pairs of students choose a photo from pp. 224–225 and summarize what they see. Tell them that the summaries should include who is in the photo, what they are doing, and how students think their actions will help the community in which they live. Discuss as a class.

Answers: Anticipación

Answers will vary, but students may mention:
Están ayudando a otras personas en la comunidad. / Algunas personas están limpiando el medio ambiente. Una persona le está poniendo una inyección a un niño. / *Answers will vary.*

Answers will vary for questions in caption text.

Anticipación

Mira las fotos. ¿A quiénes están ayudando las personas de las fotografías? ¿Qué crees que están haciendo? ¿Cuáles de estas actividades se pueden hacer en tu comunidad?

"Este trabajo voluntario nos ayuda a aprender sobre otras culturas."

Estas jóvenes voluntarias en Magdalena Teitipac, México, participan en un programa de intercambio cultural con los indígenas zapotecas de la región. Además de la experiencia que obtengan en sus trabajos, este tipo de intercambio las ayudará a conocer personas de otras culturas. ¿Conoces alguna organización que participe en programas de intercambio? ¿Cuál? ¿Es una organización local o internacional?

224   Capítulo 7

Options

Strategies for Reaching All Students

Spanish-Speaking Students
Ask: *¿Has trabajado como voluntario(a) en tu comunidad? ¿Qué has hecho? ¿Es importante trabajar como voluntario(a)? ¿Por qué?*

Students Needing Extra Help
Have information available about student exchange programs.
If necessary, explain about community service programs. Have students investigate the ones offered in your area.

Multiple Intelligences
Intrapersonal/Introspective
Have students write a paragraph about a community service project they participate in or would like to join.
Visual/Spatial and Verbal/Linguistic
See Critical Thinking.

"Ayudamos a mantener limpia nuestra comunidad."

La organización voluntaria *Clean and Green*, en Los Angeles, California, ayuda a mantener limpia la comunidad recogiendo la basura después de algún evento como este festival hispano en 1992. ¿A qué otras actividades puede dedicarse un grupo como éste? ¿Hay en tu comunidad una organización parecida? ¿Cómo se llama?

"Es importante vacunarse para evitar enfermedades."

La Cruz Roja en El Salvador dirige programas de inmunización contra varias enfermedades. También mantiene clínicas para ayudar a los pobres con sus problemas de salud. ¿Conoces otras actividades de la Cruz Roja? ¿Cuáles? ¿Qué organización hay en tu comunidad que dirija programas de inmunización como éstos?

Exploración cultural www.pasoapaso.com
Visita estos países

225

Cultural Notes ☀

(p. 224, photo)
The Zapotecs of Mexico's Oaxaca valley have dominated life in that fertile area, which lies between the central valley of Mexico and the south, since 1500 B.C. Today's valley Zapotecs are surprisingly open to modern ways in comparison with other indigenous groups in the region. Yet ancient religious beliefs and rituals still thrive, and are especially evident in the Zapotec medicinal and agricultural practices.

(p. 225, top photo)
Founded in 1781 by Spaniards as El Pueblo de Nuestra Señora la Reina de los Ángeles de Porciúncula, Los Angeles remains a city with a strong Hispanic presence. An estimated 18 percent of all Hispanics in the U.S. live in Los Angeles. The city's largest Spanish-speaking groups are Mexican, Salvadoran, and Guatemalan. The city's population of these groups is exceeded only by that of their respective capitals: Mexico City, San Salvador, and Guatemala City.

(p. 225, bottom photo)
Throughout 1995, El Salvador's public health ministry conducted an aggressive nationwide immunization campaign against polio, diphtheria, whooping cough, measles, tetanus, and tuberculosis. This campaign, which primarily targeted children under five and women of child-bearing age, was carried out with help from the U.S. Agency for Development, the United Nations, and other international health organizations.

Present

Chapter Theme
Volunteer work

Communicative Objectives
- *Describir las oportunidades de trabajo voluntario que hay en tu comunidad*
- *Hablar de tus responsabilidades*
- *Expresar tu opinión*
- *Decir qué puedes hacer por la sociedad*

 Overheads 22–23

 Vocabulary Art BLMs/CD-ROM

 Vocabulary Tape 7-1

Teaching Suggestions
Preparing students to speak: Use one or two options from each of the categories of Comprehensible Input or Limited Verbal Response. For a complete explanation of these categories and some sample activities, see pp. T20–T21.

Vocabulario para comunicarse

El servicio a la comunidad

Aquí tienes palabras y expresiones necesarias para hablar sobre lo que puedes hacer por tu comunidad. Léelas varias veces y practícalas con un(a) compañero(a) en las páginas siguientes.

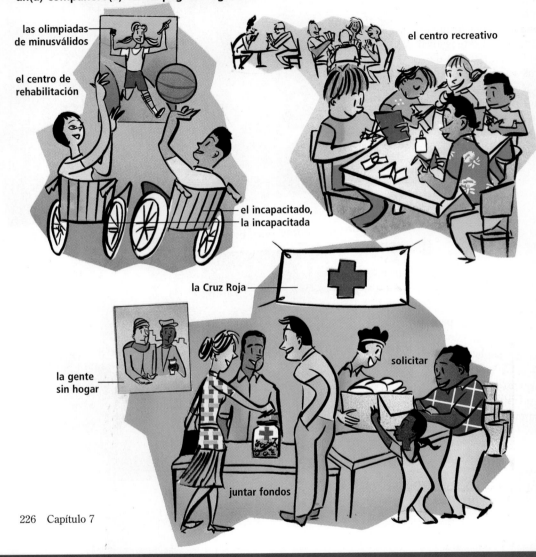

las olimpiadas de minusválidos

el centro de rehabilitación

el centro recreativo

el incapacitado, la incapacitada

la Cruz Roja

la gente sin hogar

solicitar

juntar fondos

226   Capítulo 7

Options

Strategies for Reaching All Students

Spanish-Speaking Students
Ask: *¿Qué otras palabras sabes que se relacionan con el tema? Agrégalas a tu vocabulario personal.*

Students Needing Extra Help
Have information available regarding the community service requirements for your school and / or that of surrounding communities.
Begin the vocabulary section of the Organizer. Point out the difference between *juntar fondos* and *solicitar.* Present all the vocabulary words that have cognates that

students will recognize: *el candidato, solicitar,* etc.
También necesitas…: Point out the word *ciudad* within *ciudadano.* Write out the complete *exigir* paradigm.
¿Y qué quiere decir…?: Define "to collaborate" in English. Model sentences using *colaborar con.* Drill the spelling of *responsabilidad.*

También necesitas . . .

el anciano, la anciana	*older person*	el partido político	*political party*
beneficiar(se)	*to benefit*	los pobres *(pl.)*	*poor people*
el centro de la comunidad	*community center*	por	here: *on behalf of*
el ciudadano, la ciudadana	*citizen*	prometer	*to promise*
exigir *(g → j)*: (yo) exijo	*to demand: I demand*	el refugio	*shelter*
(tú) exiges	*you demand*	sin fines de lucro	*nonprofit*
el gobierno	*government*		

¿Y qué quiere decir . . . ?
la campaña electoral

colaborar (con)

donar

la organización

la responsabilidad

el servicio social

el trabajo

votar

el candidato, la candidata

protestar

el comedor de beneficencia

Vocabulario para comunicarse 227

Class Starter Review
On the day following the presentation of vocabulary, you might begin the class with this activity: In pairs, have one student define the new vocabulary words in Spanish, and the other identify which word is being defined.

www Internet Activities
Juegos

Extended Written Practice/Homework
1. Write three sentences naming places where people can get help in your community: *Hay un comedor de beneficencia en el centro donde la gente puede encontrar comida.*
2. Write three sentences describing ways in which people can help others: *Se puede trabajar como voluntario(a) en un asilo.*
3. Write three sentences saying what the responsibilities are of: *un(a) ciudadano(a), el gobierno, los políticos.*

Multiple Intelligences
Verbal/Linguistic
1) Have students discuss reasons for the importance of registering and voting.
2) See Vocabulary Tape 7-1.
Verbal/Linguistic and Interpersonal/Social
See Class Starter Review.
Visual/Spatial
See Overheads 22–23.

Standards 1.1; 1.2; 4.1; 5.1 227

Practice & Apply

Re-enter / Recycle

Ex. 5: present perfect from Chap. 4

Answers: Empecemos a conversar

1 **ESTUDIANTE A**

a. ¿Te gustaría trabajar para la gente sin hogar?

b. ...un centro recreativo?

c. ...un(a) candidato(a)?

d. ...las olimpiadas de minusváli-dos?

e. ...un comedor de bene-ficencia?

f. Questions will vary.

ESTUDIANTE B

a.–f. Answers will vary.

2 **ESTUDIANTE A**

a. ¿Qué necesita el centro de la comunidad?

b. ¿Qué necesita la campaña electoral?

c. ¿Qué necesitan los partidos políticos?

d. ¿Qué necesitan las organizaciones sin fines de lucro?

e. ¿Qué necesitan los pobres?

f. ¿Qué necesita el gobierno?

g. ¿Qué necesitan los asilos de ancianos?

h. Questions will vary.

ESTUDIANTE B

a.–h. Answers will vary, but should begin: *Necesita(n) ....*

Empecemos a conversar

Túrnate con un(a) compañero(a) para ser *Estudiante A* y *Estudiante B*. Reemplacen las palabras subrayadas con palabras representadas o escritas en los recuadros. 💡 quiere decir que puedes escoger tu propia respuesta.

1

A — ¿Te gustaría trabajar para <u>la Cruz Roja</u>?

B — ¡Claro que sí! Quiero <u>trabajar como voluntario(a)</u>.
o: ¡De ninguna manera! Ya tengo muchas responsabilidades.

Estudiante A

a.

b.

c.

d.

e.

f. 💡

Estudiante B

juntar fondos

solicitar dinero

dar algo de tu tiempo

ayudar a los incapacitados

servir comida a los pobres

trabajar como voluntario(a)

💡

2 la gente sin hogar

A — ¿Qué <u>necesita la gente sin hogar</u>?

B — <u>Necesita más refugios</u>.

Estudiante A

a. el centro de la comunidad

b. la campaña electoral

c. los partidos políticos

d. las organizaciones sin fines de lucro

e. los pobres

f. el gobierno

g. los asilos de ancianos

h. 💡

Estudiante B

💡

228   Capítulo 7

Options

Strategies for Reaching All Students

Spanish-Speaking Students
Exs. 1–3: Pair bilingual and non-bilingual students, if possible.
Ex. 4: After this exercise, tell students: *Habla con tus compañeros(as) sobre sus listas. ¿Cuáles son los grupos que se mencionan más? ¿Qué sugerencias dan para ayudarles? Escribe un artículo para el periódico escolar u otro en la comunidad sobre este tema.*

Students Needing Extra Help
Conduct a class discussion on the general idea of a community service graduation requirement.
Ex. 1: Remind students that the choices can be matched in more than one way.
Ex. 2: Brainstorm possible *Estudiante B* responses. Point out that the verb form may change depending on the subject.

Ex. 3: Brainstorm possible *Estudiante B* responses.
Ex. 4: Have information available on the variety of services offered in your community. You may want to have someone from the community come in to talk to the class. Brainstorm possible responses to the *¿Por qué?* question.

3

A — *¿Qué podría hacer yo por el centro recreativo?*
B — *Podrías dar algo de tu tiempo.*

Estudiante A   Estudiante B

a.   b.   c.

d.   e.   f.   g.

¿Y qué piensas tú?

Aquí tienes otra oportunidad para usar el vocabulario de este capítulo.

4 ¿Qué servicios sociales hay en la comunidad donde vives? En tu opinión, ¿cuál es el más importante? ¿Por qué?

5 ¿En cuál(es) de esos servicios sociales participas o has participado? Si no has participado en ninguno, ¿en cuál(es) te gustaría participar?

6 Explícale a tu compañero(a) por qué o por qué no estás de acuerdo con las frases siguientes.

a. La Cruz Roja es algo necesario para nuestra sociedad.
b. Los centros recreativos no benefician a la comunidad.
c. Los candidatos prometen muchas cosas durante sus campañas pero no las hacen.
d. Si uno no está de acuerdo con el gobierno tiene que protestar.
e. El gobierno debe exigir que todos los ciudadanos hagan algún trabajo voluntario.

MÁS PRÁCTICA

- Más práctica y tarea, p. 565
- Practice Workbook 7-1, 7-2

Vocabulario para comunicarse   229

Present

Chapter Theme
Required community service

Communicative Objectives
- *Hablar de tus responsabilidades*
- *Expresar tu opinión*
- *Decir qué puedes hacer por la sociedad*

 Vocabulary Tape 7-2

Grammar Preview
The present subjunctive form *hagan* is previewed lexically. The explanation of certain irregular verbs in the subjunctive appears on p. 241.

Teaching Suggestions
Getting ready to speak:
Remind students of the reading strategies that they learned (getting meaning from context and coping with unknown words) to help them understand the *Tema para investigar.* For further details and some sample activities, see pp. T24–T25.

If students ask, tell them that the left photo is a painting of the Boston Tea Party.

Tema para investigar

Aquí tienes más palabras e ideas para hablar sobre el trabajo voluntario. Mira la ilustración y las fotos de esta página. ¿Cuáles de los trabajos que ves aquí son voluntarios? ¿Cuáles no?

Tu voto cuenta

El futuro está en tus manos

Tu partido te necesita

230   Capítulo 7

Options

Strategies for Reaching All Students

Spanish-Speaking Students
Tell students: *Responde por escrito a las preguntas de estas dos páginas.*

Students Needing Extra Help
Have students read one paragraph at a time. Explain that *sino* is used only after a negative phrase. Emphasize differences in spelling and meaning between *ciudadanía* and *ciudadano.*
¿Y qué quiere decir . . . ?: Model several sentences using *justo(a),* emphasizing the meaning.

Extended Written Practice/Homework
1. Write two pairs of sentences naming rights that our laws guarantee or protect. Give an example of how we depend on these rights.
2. Write three sentences naming different causes for which people protest, or have marches or demonstrations. Tell if you have participated in any of these.

¿Debe ser obligatorio o no?

Gracias al trabajo que los voluntarios han hecho, tenemos hoy en día **leyes justas** que nos **garantizan** a todos los mismos derechos. Garantizan también **elecciones** en las que decidimos quiénes nos van a **gobernar**. Durante la guerra de independencia, los hombres no **se presentaban** al **ejército** por obligación, **sino** porque creían en una **causa** común. Esa misma causa fue la que **unió** a la comunidad para protestar contra leyes **injustas** y para formar un nuevo gobierno democrático.

Actualmente el trabajo voluntario sigue teniendo gran importancia. Muchos grupos organizan **marchas** para juntar fondos para una causa. Otros grupos ofrecen ayuda a los inmigrantes para **obtener** su **ciudadanía**, otros hacen **manifestaciones a favor** o **en contra** de diferentes causas. Todos estos grupos siguen una tradición que hace más rica y fuerte **la sociedad** en que vivimos.

Todos nos beneficiamos del trabajo voluntario. Pero, ¿cuáles son las razones para exigir que los estudiantes **completen** un número de horas de servicio voluntario a la comunidad antes de graduarse?

Es importante que los estudiantes **hagan** trabajos voluntarios para aprender cuáles son las responsabilidades de un buen ciudadano.

Además, los servicios a la comunidad son una buena ocasión para explorar diferentes profesiones como la medicina, las leyes o los servicios sociales. Se **espera** que los estudiantes que participan en trabajos voluntarios sean aceptados en una universidad y puedan conseguir ayuda **financiera** más fácilmente.

Pero también hay opiniones contrarias: por ejemplo, que la principal responsabilidad de los estudiantes es estudiar; los servicios voluntarios que uno tiene que hacer no son nada voluntarios; los estudiantes son demasiado jóvenes para entender los problemas de la sociedad. ¿Qué piensas tú?

la ley, *pl.* las leyes	*law*	obtener *(e → ie)*[†]	*to obtain*
garantizar *(z → c)**	*to guarantee*	la ciudadanía	*citizenship*
presentar(se)	*to join*	la manifestación,	*demonstration*
el ejército	*army*	*pl.* las manifestaciones	
sino	*but*	a favor (de)	*in favor (of)*
unir	*to unite*	en contra (de)	*against*
actualmente	*at present*	hagan *(from:* hacer)	here: *to perform*
la marcha	*walk; hike*	esperar	here: *to hope*

¿Y qué quiere decir . . . ?

obligatorio, -a	gobernar *(e → ie)*	la sociedad
justo, -a	la causa	completar
la elección,	injusto, -a	financiero, -a
pl. las elecciones		

* *Garantizar* follows the pattern of *analizar*.
[†] *Obtener* follows the pattern of *tener*.

Answers: Tema para investigar
Answers will vary, but may include:
Protestar y ayudar a los ancianos son trabajos voluntarios. Votar no es obligatorio, sino una responsabilidad.

Class Starter Review
On the day following the presentation of the *Tema para investigar,* you might begin the class with this activity:
Say a sentence in Spanish describing or defining one of the vocabulary words, omitting the actual word. Have students finish the sentence with the appropriate word. For example: *Si quiero participar en una elección, tengo que _____. / Si quiero participar en una elección, tengo que <u>votar</u>.*

www Internet Activities
Juegos

---

3. Write two pairs of sentences identifying problems in our society and suggesting solutions for these problems. Tell if you would like to be a part of the solutions.

Multiple Intelligences
Interpersonal/Social and Visual/Spatial
Have students create a list of community service projects in which friends or family members are involved.
Verbal/Linguistic
See Vocabulary Tape 7-2 and Class Starter Review.

Cultural Notes ☀

(p. 230, bottom right photo)
Supporters of El Salvador's ARENA (Alianza Republicana Nacionalista) party on election night, March 20, 1994. They had reason to celebrate when their candidate for president, Armando Calderón Sol, was declared victorious with 68.3 percent of the total vote.

Practice & Apply

Re-enter / Recycle
Ex. 3: present perfect from
Chap. 4

Answers: ¿Comprendiste?
1–2 Answers will vary.

Answers: ¿Y qué piensas tú?
3–5 Answers will vary.

¿Comprendiste?

1 Imagina que eres miembro del consejo estudiantil. Da dos razones por las que el trabajo voluntario debe ser obligatorio para graduarse y dos por las que no debe ser obligatorio.

2 ¿Qué otro título se puede dar a la lectura de la página 231? Haz una lista de tres posibles títulos y discútelos con tu compañero(a).

¿Y qué piensas tú?

3 ¿Qué personas de tu comunidad han necesitado alguna vez la ayuda de un grupo de voluntarios? ¿Por qué? ¿Quiénes ayudaron? ¿Cómo y cuándo ayudaron?

4 ¿Qué tipo de trabajo voluntario te interesa más? ¿Por qué? ¿Tienes que hacer algún trabajo voluntario para graduarte de la escuela secundaria?

5 Vas a entrevistar a cinco personas de tu comunidad o profesores de tu escuela para averiguar si piensan que el servicio a la comunidad debe ser obligatorio y por qué.

- Prepara una tabla como la siguiente:

NOMBRE	SÍ O NO	POR QUÉ
Rosario	sí	para ser mejores ciudadanos
José Luis	No	los estudiantes sólo deben estudiar
Abuela	sí	

- Luego, compara tu tabla con la de otros(as) compañeros(as). ¿Cuántas personas han dicho que sí? ¿Y que no? ¿Qué razones han dado?

¡NO OLVIDES!

Remember these words:
el huracán
la erupción
el terremoto
la tormenta
el derrumbe
la inundación

www.pasoapaso.com

MÁS PRÁCTICA

- Más práctica y tarea, p. 566
- Practice Workbook 7-3, 7-4

Options

Strategies for Reaching All Students

Students Needing Extra Help
Ex. 1: Tell students to refer to the *Tema* for ideas.
Ex. 3: Accept any logical answer to the *¿Por qué?* question.
Ex. 5: Assign this exercise in advance. Remind students that they can ask the questions in English, but must report in Spanish. *¿Qué sabes ahora?:* Have students write this so that they can record their progress.

Enrichment
Additional questions: *En el Tema para investigar, dicen que hay personas que piensan que los estudiantes son demasiado jóvenes para entender los problemas de la sociedad. ¿Estás de acuerdo con esta opinión? ¿Cuáles son algunos problemas de la sociedad que afectan mucho a los jóvenes? ¿Hay problemas que sólo afectan a los jóvenes?*

Cooperative Learning
In groups of four, tell students to imagine that a grant of $10,000 will be awarded to a group of volunteers with the best plan for addressing a school or community problem. Instruct each group to name the problem and plan the approach to solving it, and then name the organization and itemize how the grant would be spent. Discuss group scenarios as a class, and vote on which group should receive the grant.

Votando en la elección en Guazapa,
El Salvador, 1994

¿Qué sabes ahora?

¿Puedes:

- hablar de algunas de las organizaciones de voluntarios en tu comunidad?

  —En mi comunidad hay varios grupos de voluntarios como ___ y ___ .

- hablar de la importancia de esos grupos de voluntarios?

  —Pienso que ___ es la organización más importante porque ___ .

- decir qué clase de trabajo voluntario te gustaría hacer y por qué?

  —Me gustaría trabajar para ___ porque ___ .

- explicar cómo la tradición del trabajo voluntario en los Estados Unidos nos beneficia a todos hoy en día?

  —En los Estados Unidos, los ___ han contribuido mucho a la sociedad de hoy porque ___ .

Tema para investigar   233

Answers: ¿Qué sabes ahora?
• All answers will vary.

 Practice Wkbk. 7-3, 7-4

 Audio Activity 7.2

 Writing Activities 7-B, 7-C

 Pruebas 7-3, 7-4

Cultural Notes ☀

Multiple Intelligences
Interpersonal/Social
See Cooperative Learning.
Verbal/Linguistic
See Exs. 1–2 and Audio Activity 7.2.
Visual/Spatial
See Practice Wkbk. 7-3 and 7-4 and Writing Activities 7-B and 7-C.

(p. 233, photo)
El Salvador's Frente Farabundo Martí de Liberación Nacional (FMLN) is one of the few political groups in the world that has successfully transformed itself from an armed revolutionary movement into an electoral party. The FMLN was able to enter the electoral arena following a United Nations-mediated peace settlement in 1992. In the 1998 elections the FMLN won in fifty municipalities, representing nearly half of the Salvadoran population.

Standards 1.2; 3.1; 5.1   **233**

Cultural Objective

• *Hablar del trabajo voluntario en los países hispanos y en los Estados Unidos*

Critical Thinking: Hypothesizing

Tell students to predict what will happen to the places or people pictured in the *Álbum cultural* as a result of the community services being performed. Call on individuals to share their predictions with the class.

Answers

Answers to inductive questions will vary.

ÁLBUM CULTURAL

Existen muchas organizaciones que tienen proyectos para voluntarios que quieren mejorar la comunidad. ¿Qué piensas tú de estas organizaciones? ¿De qué otra manera se puede ayudar a la comunidad?

En los países hispanos, por lo general la familia y los amigos se encargan de ayudar a los incapacitados. Este joven estudiante universitario en Caracas, Venezuela, ayuda a un compañero empujando su silla de ruedas.

234   Capítulo 7

Strategies for Reaching All Students

Spanish-Speaking Students
Ask: *¿A quiénes ayudan los voluntarios en tu comunidad? ¿Quiénes son las personas que prestan servicio voluntario?*

Students Needing Extra Help
Have students take notes for use in the *¿Lo sabes bien?* section at the end of the chapter.
Explain about civil defense if students are not familiar with this type of program.

Multiple Intelligences
Verbal/Linguistic and Visual/Spatial
See Critical Thinking.

La comunidad necesita de todos sus miembros, especialmente en momentos de crisis. Después de un terremoto en Pereira, Colombia, los vecinos, la policía y miembros de la Cruz Roja y la Defensa Civil ayudaron a sacar a los heridos. Los voluntarios que forman estas organizaciones están siempre preparados para estas emergencias, y gracias a su ayuda se salvaron muchas vidas.

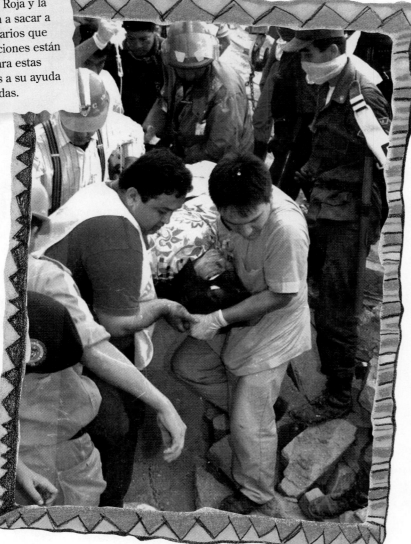

Multicultural Perspectives

The Peace Corps was officially created on March 1, 1961, when Congress passed the Peace Corps Act. President John F. Kennedy conceived of the Corps as a group of volunteers who would travel abroad, acting both as "diplomats" and as free labor. Volunteers must be at least 18 years old, provide several character references, and fill out a detailed application. Those who are accepted undergo a rigorous eight- to fourteen-week training course, including intensive language and cultural study of their assigned country. Latin American destinations include Bolivia, Chile, Colombia, Costa Rica, Dominican Republic, Ecuador, El Salvador, Guatemala, Honduras, Peru, Uruguay, and Venezuela. Ask students how they think spending time in the Peace Corps would help them in later life.

Cultural Notes ☀

(p. 234, photo)
Although progress is being made to raise awareness of the needs of disabled people in Hispanic countries, access can still be very difficult for them. In Caracas, for example, they may have relatively easy access to modern buildings and facilities, but many city streets are extremely narrow and are often blocked by street vendor posts. There are many stairways and few wheelchair ramps in public places. The *metro* stations, although built in the 1980s, have neither elevators nor ramps.

(p. 235, photo)
Rescue workers helping victims of the earthquake that shook Pereira, Colombia on February 8, 1995. News stories of earthquakes and other disasters in Hispanic counties are followed closely by Hispanics in the U.S. Telethons broadcast on U.S. Spanish-language television have become a popular means of raising funds for disaster victims.

Present & Apply

Answers: Reacción personal

1 Answers will vary, but students may mention:
Los miembros de la comunidad pueden ayudar a los heridos, limpiar las calles o donar comida y ropa a las víctimas. / La Cruz Roja y la FEMA *(Federal Emergency Management Administration)* son dos organizaciones que ayudan en caso de emergencias. Estas organizaciones dan comida, ropa y dinero a las víctimas de un desastre.

2 Answers will vary.

www Internet Activities
Álbum cultural

El trabajo voluntario ofrece la oportunidad de adquirir experiencia mientras se estudia en la escuela secundaria. Estos jóvenes muralistas de Austin, Texas, tendrán más oportunidad de ser admitidos a una universidad o escuela de arte gracias a su experiencia. Además, el trabajo voluntario enseña a trabajar en equipo y a formar buenos hábitos que les ayudarán en cualquier trabajo o profesión.

236

Options

Strategies for Reaching All Students

Students Needing Extra Help
Reacción personal: In section 1, bring in newspaper or magazine reports of national coverage of these disasters for discussion. Remind students of the meaning of *clase* (kind, type) in this context.
In section 2, give students time to think of what opportunities are open to them if they'd like to volunteer for a particular organization.

Multiple Intelligences
Intrapersonal/Introspective
See Ex. 2.

En muchas partes del mundo la gente necesita lugares para vivir. Los voluntarios de *Habitat for Humanity*, como este joven en San Juan Ostuncalco, Guatemala, construyen casas para personas que no tienen mucho dinero. Trabajar como voluntario en esta organización es una oportunidad ideal para los que quieren dedicarse a una profesión relacionada con la construcción.

Reacción personal

Contesta las siguientes preguntas en una hoja de papel.

1 ¿Cómo pueden ayudar los miembros de la comunidad en caso de desastres como terremotos y huracanes? ¿Qué organizaciones conoces que ayudan en estas situaciones? ¿Qué clase de ayuda ofrecen?

2 Muchas organizaciones internacionales tienen voluntarios que trabajan en diferentes proyectos en todo el mundo. ¿Qué oportunidades pueden tener los jóvenes que participan en uno de estos proyectos? ¿Te gustaría participar en alguno? ¿Por qué?

Álbum cultural 237

(p. 236, photos)
Chicano murals, such as the one being painted here in Austin, Texas, are found throughout the U.S. wherever there are established Mexican American communities. During the 1970s, an especially rich period of Chicano mural painting, many outstanding murals were created in *barrios* in the Southwest, Pacific Southwest, and the Great Lakes region. The greatest concentration of them is in Los Angeles, which has several hundred.

(p. 237, photo)
This young worker is helping to build a house in San Juan Ostuncalco, Guatemala, with the support of Habitat for Humanity International. This organization was founded in the 1970s to fight poor living conditions and homelessness throughout the world. Headquartered in Americus, Georgia, Habitat for Humanity has helped people build homes for themselves in all 50 U.S. states and in over 40 countries.

Preview

 **Overhead 24**

Teaching Suggestions

A Have students look for a common idea (demands, needs, desires) with *exige que* and *es necesario que.*

B Ask: In what way does *tenga* resemble *tengo?* Is *-a* an ending you usually find on present-tense *-er* verbs?

C Ask what the ending is for these verbs. Have them summarize what the present subjuntive *él / ella / Ud.* endings are for *-ar, -er,* and *-ir* verbs.

Answers

Que tenga 18 años y que sea ciudadano(a).

A The expressions introduce a "demand" and "need" for someone to do something. / *quiere, voten*

B *tengo* / You would drop the *-o* of the present indicative *yo* form *(pongo)* and add the subjunctive ending *-a* to form *ponga.*

C You would drop the *-o* of the present indicative *yo* form and then add *-a.*

D *Será (publicada)* is the verb. / *Una lista* is the subject. / No. / *Las organizaciones comunitarias y los periódicos locales* "do" the action.

Repaso: El subjuntivo

You know that we use the indicative to talk about facts or actual events. We use the subjunctive to say what one person asks, hopes, tells, insists or requires someone else to do.

Indicative	Subjunctive
Los pobres **necesitan** comida y ropa.	La Cruz Roja **nos pide que donemos** comida y ropa a los pobres.
Al centro recreativo **van** varios incapacitados.	El jefe del centro recreativo siempre les **dice** a los voluntarios **que ayuden** a los incapacitados.
Los ciudadanos **deben respetar** las leyes y **pagar** los impuestos.	El gobierno **insiste en que respetemos** las leyes. También **exige que paguemos** los impuestos.

- To form the present subjunctive of most verbs we drop the *-o* of the present indicative *yo* form and add the subjunctive endings. Here are the present subjunctive forms of regular *-ar, -er,* and *-ir* verbs.

votar

que vote	que vot**emos**	que promet**a**	que promet**amos**	que recib**a**	que recib**amos**
que vot**es**	que vot**éis**	que promet**as**	que promet**áis**	que recib**as**	que recib**áis**
que vote	que vot**en**	que promet**a**	que promet**an**	que recib**a**	que recib**an**

prometer   **recibir**

- Remember that a sentence that includes the subjunctive form has two parts connected by the word *que.*

> **Espero que votes** en las elecciones.
> El presidente del consejo estudiantil **nos pide que participemos** en la manifestación.

Present

Teaching Suggestions
You may want to present the subjunctive as new material.

Multicultural Perspectives
(See previous page.)
In some Latin American countries, voting ballots are produced so that illiterate people can use them as well as those who can read. The ballots are specially designed to indicate the color or flag of a particular party. Photographs of the candidates are often included to make sure people can identify the candidate of their choice. As an extra-credit assignment, have pairs of students create a ballot for a national or local election that can be used by someone who is illiterate.

Using Realia
(See previous page.)
By using context and visual clues in the ad and voter's registration card, see if students can determine what two countries these documents are from. (The ad is from the U.S. and the voter's registration card is from Mexico.)

Strategies for Reaching All Students
MULTIPLE INTELLIGENCES
Visual/Spatial
See Overhead 24, Students Needing Extra Help, and Using Realia.

Emphasize that each sentence will have two different subjects and two different actions, connected by a *que.*
Present these columns carefully. Show the difference in the subjects and the meaning. Write out this comparison on the chalkboard:

> *Donamos comida y ropa a los pobres.*
> *La Cruz Roja nos pide que donemos comida y ropa a los pobres.*

Repeat with other examples.
Give additional examples of regular and stem-changing verbs in the subjunctive. Have lists ready of the verbs that students know that fall into the *-car, -gar,* and *-zar* categories. Emphasize those that are both stem-changing and spelling-changing verbs, such as *jugar, empezar,* etc.
Drill all of these forms as frequently as possible, and provide practice in oral and written exercises.

Cultural Notes

(p. 238, realia)
Mexico's August 1994 elections were the most closely scrutinized ever held. Over 80,000 national and international observers were stationed around the country to help prevent voter fraud. This special voting card was devised by the Instituto Federal Electoral (IFE), an organization that coordinates the electoral process in Mexico. Among the various security mechanisms, the plastic card includes a photo and fingerprint of the voter, a hologram, and a magnetic band.

Present & Practice

Answers

1 ESTUDIANTE A

a. ¿Qué dicen los voluntarios?

b. ¿Qué esperan . . .

c. ¿Qué piden . . .

d. ¿Qué quieren . . .

e. ¿Qué recomiendan . . .

f. ¿Qué sugieren . . .

ESTUDIANTE B

Answers will vary, but may include:

Dicen que todos los ciudadanos voten.

Esperan que nosotros hagamos fila.

Piden que los pobres (no) protesten.

Quieren que Uds. monten en bicicleta.

Recomiendan que tú y yo reciclemos botellas y latas.

Sugieren que . . . *(Answers will vary.)*

• Stem-changing *-ar* and *-er* verbs have the stem change in all except the *nosotros* and *vosotros* forms.

que enc**ue**ntre	que encontremos
que enc**ue**ntres	que encontréis
que enc**ue**ntre	que enc**ue**ntren

Queremos **que encuentren** una solución para el problema de la contaminación del aire.

La organización nos pide **que encontremos** más voluntarios.

• Verbs whose infinitives end in *-car, -gar,* and *-zar* have a spelling change in all of their present subjunctive forms to keep the same sound. Here are some examples with the verbs *explicar, pagar,* and *empezar*.

Mis amigos me piden **que les explique** mis opiniones políticas.

Exigen **que paguemos** impuestos.

Esperamos **que** la campaña **empiece** pronto.

1 Con un(a) compañero(a), di lo que quieren los voluntarios.

A — *¿Qué recomiendan los voluntarios?*

B — *Recomiendan que juntemos fondos.*

nosotros

Estudiante A

a. decir   d. querer

b. esperar   e. recomendar

c. pedir   f. sugerir

Estudiante B

Uds.

todos los ciudadanos

nosotros

los pobres

tú y yo

Options

Strategies for Reaching All Students

Students Needing Extra Help

Ex. 1: Remind students that *Estudiante B* can answer using the art in any order.

Ex. 2: Brainstorm phrases that are needed to complete the thought of the verbs in the final column. For example: *leer un libro, escribir un informe,* etc.

El subjuntivo: Continuación: Give students the following formula to add to their list:

ES +	importante				
	mejor	+ QUE +	*different*	+	*subjunctive*
	necesario		*subject*		

2 ¿Exigen mucho tus profesores? Usa elementos de cada columna para formar frases.

Algunos de mis profesores exigen que escribamos siempre con bolígrafo.

Mi profesor(a) de___	exigir	los estudiantes	aprender
	decir	yo	(no) dormir
Algunos(as) de mis	insistir en	tú	empezar
profesores(as)	pedir	nosotros	entregar
	querer	ustedes	escribir
Todos(as) mis			leer
profesores(as)			pensar
			(no) perder
			practicar
			recoger
			recordar

El subjuntivo: Continuación

We also use the subjunctive after impersonal expressions to specify *who* should do something. Some of these expressions are *es mejor, es necesario,* and *es importante.*

Creen que es mejor **que su tía viva** en un asilo para ancianos.
Es necesario **que obedezcamos** todas las leyes.
Es importante **que los políticos nos digan** la verdad.

- Since the subjunctive is formed from the present indicative *yo* form, irregular verbs whose *yo* form ends in *-o* keep the change in all of their present subjunctive forms. Here are some examples with the verbs *hacer, conocer,* and *contribuir.*

Mi padre piensa que es importante **que todos hagan** el servicio militar.
Es necesario **que conozcan** bien a los candidatos antes de las elecciones.
Espero **que contribuyas** a la campaña.

- Irregular verbs whose *yo* form does not end in *-o* don't follow this pattern.

Infinitivo	Presente del indicativo (yo)	Presente del subjuntivo
dar	doy	dé
estar	estoy	esté
ir	voy	vaya
saber	sé	sepa
ser	soy	sea

Gramática en contexto   241

2 Statements will vary, but may begin in the following manner:

Mi profesor(a) de ___ exige que + subject from third column + subjunctive of verb in fourth column

Algunos(as) de mis profesores(as) insisten en que + subject from third column + subjunctive of verb in fourth column

Todos(as) mis profesores(as) dicen que + subject from third column + subjunctive of verb in fourth column

Strategies for Reaching All Students
MULTIPLE INTELLIGENCES
Verbal/Linguistic
See Ex. 1.
Visual/Spatial
See Enrichment, Practice Wkbk. 7-5 and 7-6, Writing Activity 7-D, and Comm. Act. BLM 7-2.

 Practice Wkbk. 7-5, 7-6

 Writing Activity 7-D

 Prueba 7-5

 Comm. Act. BLM 7-2

Write the three model sentences on the chalkboard. Underline *viva, obedezcamos,* and *digan.* Have students identify the infinitive for each. Emphasize that these are *-er* and *-ir* verbs. Create a new sentence, leaving a blank for students to fill in the correct form of the verb.
Brainstorm verbs that have irregular *yo* forms. Ask students to give the subjunctive form of those verbs.

Enrichment
Ex. 2: As homework, ask students to list three things that their families insist that they do. Students who work or volunteer can mention three things that their supervisors require that they do.

Extended Written Practice/Homework
1. Write three sentences saying what you recommend that people do to help the environment. You might include: *respetar, fabricar, ahorrar, reciclar, usar, apagar.*
2. Write three sentences telling what the government demands: *El gobierno exige que paguemos impuestos.*
3. Write three sentences saying what you and your friends and family hope will happen in our society: *Esperamos que todos los ciudadanos voten en las elecciones.*

Present & Practice

Teaching Suggestions

Ex. 3: Point out that *Estudiante A* uses the infinitive and *Estudiante B* uses *que* + the subjunctive. Tell *Estudiante A* to use the expressions in both columns.

Answers

3 ESTUDIANTE A
Statements will vary, but should begin in the following manner: *Me gustaría / Quisiera / Espero / Necesito / Quiero* + inf. from second column

ESTUDIANTE B
Statements will vary, but may begin in the following manner: *Pues, es importante (mejor / necesario) que / Espero (Recomiendo / Sugiero) que* + *tú* form of the verb in subjunctive

4 Statements will vary, but should include correct use of the subjunctive.

 Practice Wkbk. 7-7, 7-8

 Writing Activity 7-E

 Prueba 7-6

3 Se ha mudado a tu barrio un(a) joven de tu edad. Con tu compañero(a) di qué le dices para que tenga éxito en la comunidad.

A — *Quisiera salir con otros jóvenes.*
B — *Pues, es importante que conozcas a todos los jóvenes en este edificio de apartamentos.*

Estudiante A

Me gustaría	colaborar
Quisiera	conocer
Espero	contribuir
Necesito	decir
Quiero	hacer
	ir
	saber
	ser
	tener
	venir

Estudiante B

Es importante
Es mejor
Es necesario
Esperar
Recomendar
Sugerir

4 En tu opinión, ¿qué es necesario para ser un miembro responsable de una comunidad? Escribe tres de las cosas más importantes.

Es necesario que donemos nuestro tiempo y dinero a las organizaciones sin fines de lucro.

• Luego, haz una encuesta en tu clase para conocer la opinión de los demás estudiantes. Comparte los resultados con el resto de la clase.

Seis estudiantes piensan que es necesario que contribuyamos nuestro tiempo o dinero a diferentes organizaciones.

242 Capítulo 7

Options

Strategies for Reaching All Students

Students Needing Extra Help
Ex. 3: Brainstorm possible expressions to complete the *Estudiante A* statements. Remind students that in the *Estudiante B* list, the last three verbs have to be put into the *yo* form. Brainstorm possible expressions that will complete the phrases and match the *Estudiante A* statement. Emphasize the subjunctive as students create their dialogues. You may want to act as *Estudiante A* and have the class as a whole respond as *Estudiante B*.

La voz pasiva: Ser + participio pasado: Present further examples before beginning the grammatical explanation. Review past participles, emphasizing agreement with the subject of the sentence. Tell students that *por* is an indicator of who or what does the action. Give additional examples. If necessary, emphasize that expressions with *se* are also in the passive voice, but do not use the *por* expression. Give further examples.

Extended Written Practice/Homework
1. Write three sentences telling what one should do to be successful in school, sports, music, art, or extracurricular activities. Use: *es importante, es mejor, es necesario.*
2. Choose three verbs and tell what you want or do not want to take place in your community: *construir, ser, ofrecer, poner, hacer, tener. Quiero que ofrezcan más actividades culturales.*

La voz pasiva: *Ser* + participio pasado

The subject of the verb usually performs the action. This is called *active voice*.

Los partidos políticos *The political parties* (the "doer" of the action)	organizaron *organized* (the action)	las campañas electorales. *the election campaigns.* (the "receiver" of the action)

Sometimes, the subject of the verb does not "do" the action but rather has the action "done to it" or receives the action. This is called *passive voice*. Contrast the following sentence with the sentence above.

Las campañas electorales *The election campaigns* (the "receiver" of the action)	fueron organizadas por *were organized by* (the action)	los partidos políticos. *the political parties.* (the "doer" of the action)

- In Spanish, as in English, we form the passive voice by using *ser* + past participle. Since the past participle is an adjective, it agrees in number and gender with the subject.

    Mucha ropa **fue donada** por los miembros de la comunidad.
    *A lot of clothing **was donated** by members of the community.*

    Varios programas **fueron creados** por el nuevo gobierno.
    *Several programs **were created** by the new government.*

    Notice that if we mention who or what performs the action, we use *por* to mean "by."

- Remember that we often use the impersonal *se* to express passive voice in Spanish.

    Se necesitan más voluntarios en el refugio.
    *More volunteers **are needed** in the shelter.*

Un asilo de ancianos en la
Ciudad de México

Gramática en contexto   243

Cultural Notes

(p. 243, photo)
Most of the elderly in Hispanic countries confront circumstances that are quite different from those faced by aging people in the U.S., who have a solid social welfare system to turn to for the income and care they require. While Hispanic cultures teach respect and compassion for the elderly, their governments have generally done little to provide adequate housing, high-quality medical care, or nutrition programs for their aging citizens. This government-sponsored home for the elderly in Mexico City is an exception, but many more will be needed as Mexico's large, currently young population ages.
Ask students: In Latin America, older people are traditionally cared for in the homes of their children or other relatives. Do you think that is a good idea or, when you grow old, would you prefer to live in a retirement community? Why?

Practice

Re-enter / Recycle

Ex. 5: past participles from Chap. 2
Ex. 6: archaeology from Chap. 5

Answers

5 Answers will vary, but students may mention:
a. Esta campaña electoral fue organizada por un partido político.
b. Este dinero fue donado por unos hombres de negocios.
c. Esta organización para servir a <u>los ancianos</u> fue creada por el gobierno.
d. Este comedor de beneficencia para <u>los minusválidos</u> fue reparado por un grupo de estudiantes.
e. Estas botellas y latas fueron recicladas por todos los niños de la comunidad.
f. Estos refugios para <u>la gente sin hogar</u> fueron construidos por los voluntarios.
g. El presidente fue elegido por la gente que votó.
h. Statements will vary.

5 Con un(a) compañero(a) describe por quién o quiénes fueron hechos los siguientes trabajos en tu comunidad.

ropa / donar

Esta ropa fue donada a la Cruz Roja por varias familias.

a. campaña electoral / organizar
b. dinero / donar
c. organización para servir a ___ / crear
d. comedor de beneficencia ___ / reparar
e. botellas y latas / reciclar
f. refugios para ___ / construir
g. (nombre) / elegir
h. 💡

CRUZ ROJA VENEZOLANA

La vida es un regalo.
¡Dona sangre!

¡NO OLVIDES!

Remember that *por* has many English equivalents:
for: *¿Qué se puede hacer por los minusválidos? / ¿Cuánto pagaste por este libro?*
for + time: *por dos años*
by: *Envié la carta por vía aérea. / El refugio fue construido por los voluntarios.*

Options

Strategies for Reaching All Students

Students Needing Extra Help

¡No olvides!: Have students create a chart illustrating the various uses of *por*.
Ex. 6: Show students that in the model, *fue* refers to *este templo,* and *construido* matches accordingly.
Remind students that the artwork will determine these two points.
Ahora lo sabes: Have students write this so that they can record their progress.

Enrichment

Ex. 5: Ask pairs of students to repeat this exercise, using the impersonal *se,* leaving out the agent, and creating new endings to complete their sentences. For example: *ropa / donar: En esta comunidad se donó mucha ropa para las víctimas del huracán.*

Extended Written Practice/Homework

1. Write three sentences telling what activities or events in your school or community were organized by different people: *El baile del invierno fue organizado por los estudiantes del tercer año.*
2. Write three sentences telling when or by whom different buildings were built: *La iglesia de San Pedro fue construida en 1915.*

6 Imagina que un(a) guía lleva a unos turistas a visitar unas ruinas. Trabaja con un(a) compañero(a) para hacer los papeles del (de la) guía y del (de la) turista.

construir

A —¿Quién(es) construyó(eron) este templo?
B —Fue construido por los mayas.

Estudiante A

a. descubrir
b. estudiar
c. hacer
d. romper
e. excavar
f. encontrar

Estudiante B

un arqueólogo francés

unos niños del pueblo

unos antropólogos

un profesor de la universidad

un grupo de turistas

los mayas

un artista del pasado

Ahora lo sabes

¿Puedes:

■ explicar lo que alguien espera, sugiere o exige que se haga?
—En esta comunidad exigen que (nosotros) ___ a los pobres.

■ describir por quién fue hecho algo?
—Las manifestaciones ___ por grupos de estudiantes.

■ decir a favor de quién o de qué se hace algo?
—Vamos a juntar fondos ___ el centro recreativo.

MÁS PRÁCTICA

Más práctica y tarea, pp. 566–567
Practice Workbook 7–5, 7–9

Apply

Teaching Suggestions
Point out the key chapter question, telling students that completing these activities will help them answer it. You may select one, two, or all three of these activities, as time permits.

Ex. 2: To enhance this discussion, bring information on academic grants and awards that require volunteer work as well as academic performance.

Answers: Sopa de actividades
1–3 Responses will vary.

Strategies for Reaching All Students
MULTIPLE INTELLIGENCES
Interpersonal/Social
See Exs. 1–3.
Interpersonal/Social and Bodily/Kinesthetic
See Ex. 3.
Logical/Mathematical
Have students make a chart contrasting the reasons supporting and opposing obligatory volunteer work as discussed in Ex. 2.
Verbal/Linguistic, Interpersonal/Social, and Bodily/Kinesthetic
See Cooperative Learning.
Visual/Spatial
See Writing Activities 7-G and 7-H and Comm. Act. BLMs 7-4 and 7-5.

PUNTOS de VISTA

Para decir más

Aquí tienes vocabulario adicional que te puede ayudar para hacer las actividades de esta sección.

la pobreza
poverty

el huérfano, la huérfana
orphan

el analfabeto, la analfabeta
illiterate man, illiterate woman

el analfabetismo
illiteracy

los necesitados, *pl.*
needy people

¿Qué se puede hacer por...?

246   Capítulo 7

¿Debes servir a la comunidad para graduarte?

Esta sección te ofrece la oportunidad de combinar lo que aprendiste en este capítulo con lo que ya sabes para responder a la pregunta clave.

Sopa de actividades

1 En grupos de tres o cuatro van a escoger uno de estos temas. Luego hagan recomendaciones para ayudar a estas personas.

- los pobres
- la gente sin hogar
- los analfabetos
- los ancianos que viven en asilos
- las víctimas del SIDA (Síndrome de Inmuno-Deficiencia Adquirida)

Después, van a compartir sus ideas con los otros grupos de la clase y decir si están o no están de acuerdo con sus ideas. Por ejemplo:

A —*Ustedes escogieron a los ancianos que viven en asilos. ¿Qué se puede hacer por ellos?*
B —*Recomendamos que se organicen visitas de las escuelas primarias.*
A —*Estamos de acuerdo. Este programa no costará mucho y los ancianos estarán muy contentos.*

Options

Strategies for Reaching All Students

Spanish-Speaking Students
Ex. 3: After this exercise, ask: *¿Has visto una manifestación alguna vez? ¿Por qué protestaban o qué apoyaban las personas? ¿Crees que tenían razón? ¿Por qué?*

Students Needing Extra Help
If time is a factor, Exs. 1 and 2 are the most easily completed.
Ex. 1: Have students write two recommendations. Model a situation where Group A disagrees with the recommendation. Allow students enough time to organize their thoughts.
Ex. 2: Refer students to the *Tema para investigar* for examples of reasons why

community service shouldn't be obligatory. Allow sufficient time for students to respond to the argument made by the other group.
Ex. 3: You may want to offer this as a group extra credit assignment, done either live or on video. Have students create questions and answers for the news reporters and the protesters.

2 Dividan la clase en dos grupos. Uno cree que el trabajo voluntario debe ser obligatorio para graduarse; el otro piensa que no. Cada grupo debe tratar de convencer al otro. Pueden hablar sobre:

- tipos de trabajo
- el tiempo que se debe dedicar al trabajo
- cuándo debe hacerse (después de las clases, los fines de semana, etc.)
- si debe ser parte del currículum o no
- las ventajas que pueden tener para el futuro
- si los estudiantes deben dedicar su tiempo sólo a estudiar

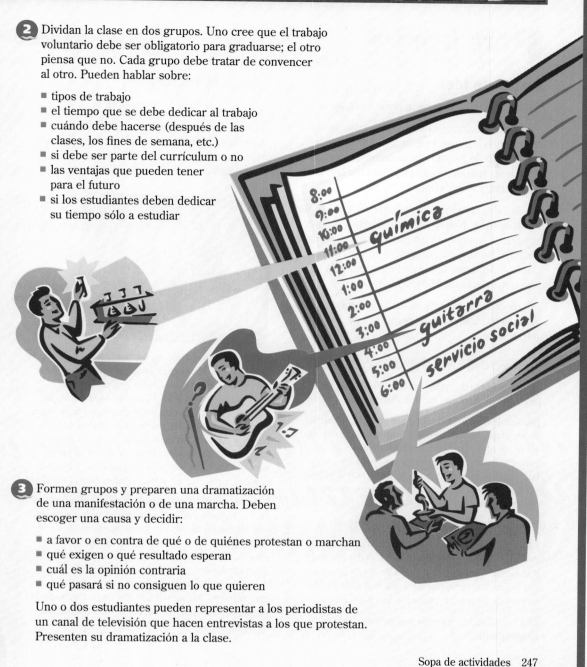

3 Formen grupos y preparen una dramatización de una manifestación o de una marcha. Deben escoger una causa y decidir:

- a favor o en contra de qué o de quiénes protestan o marchan
- qué exigen o qué resultado esperan
- cuál es la opinión contraria
- qué pasará si no consiguen lo que quieren

Uno o dos estudiantes pueden representar a los periodistas de un canal de televisión que hacen entrevistas a los que protestan. Presenten su dramatización a la clase.

Sopa de actividades   247

Visual/Spatial and Bodily/Kinesthetic
Have students in groups create a video presentation based on community service in their school or neighborhood.

 Video Activity A

 Video, Capítulo 7

Chapter 7: Play

Step

 Video Activities B–C

 Writing Activities 7-G, 7-H

 Comm. Act. BLMs 7-4, 7-5

Cooperative Learning
In groups of three, have students create a public service announcement for television or radio. Have them brainstorm the cause or charity for which they would like to campaign, and divide the announcement into three segments: an explanation of the problem, what is currently being done to solve it, and how the public can help. Encourage use of chapter vocabulary and grammar. Individuals should write their own portion and exchange it within the group for editing. When completed, each group presents the announcements to the class. You may want to tape the presentations.

Apply

Teaching Suggestions

Tell students that working through the *Para leer* section will help them answer the key chapter question.

Encourage students to use the strategies given to them in the text to help them understand the reading. Remind them they do not need to understand every word.

If students request more information on *Amigos de las Américas,* you or they can write or call:

Amigos de las Américas
5618 Star Lane
Houston, TX 77057
Phone: 1-800-231-7796

Process Reading

For a description of process reading, see p. 52.

Answers
Antes de leer
Answers will vary.

Mira la lectura

Answers will vary, but students may mention:
Al principio extrañó no tener comodidades, pero se acostumbró después de unos días.

Para leer

Antes de leer

STRATEGY Using prior knowledge

El programa Amigos de las Américas manda voluntarios a trabajar en América Latina por un período de seis a ocho semanas. Trabajan en varios campos, como en el de la salud, la educación y la agricultura.

Jessica Ramos es una estudiante de 17 años de Albuquerque, Nuevo México. Participó en el programa Amigos de las Américas en el verano de 1994. Su trabajo era ayudar con la higiene pública. Aquí nos habla de su experiencia en una entrevista con Martha Heard.

¿Cómo reaccionas tú a la falta de comodidades *(comforts)*? Escribe una respuesta de una a tres frases.

Mira la lectura

STRATEGY Scanning

Lee la entrevista rápidamente sólo para averiguar cómo reaccionó Jessica a la falta de comodidades. Con un(a) compañero(a), compara su reacción a San Fernando con la tuya.

Jessica Ramos,
Ecuador, 1994

Entrevista con una Amiga

Martha Heard **¿Por qué te interesó el programa Amigos de las Américas?**

Jessica Ramos Un día unos Amigos hablaron en mi clase. Yo nunca había viajado fuera del país y me pareció una oportunidad extraordinaria para conocer otro país y otra manera de vivir. En Albuquerque yo había trabajado con la gente sin hogar, pero eso era diferente porque después de darles de cenar, yo volvía a casa.

M.H. **¿Cuándo supiste adónde irías?**

J.R. En la primavera supe que iría a Ecuador, pero no supe a qué pueblo hasta el día anterior a la salida. Cuando llegamos a Ambato tuvimos cuatro días de orientación y allí nos dijeron que cuatro de nosotros iríamos a San Fernando.

M.H. **¿Cuáles fueron tus primeras impresiones?**

J.R. San Fernando es un pueblo de la montaña donde viven 35 familias en casas de ladrillo o de barro. El padre de mi familia era carpintero. Además de los padres y sus tres hijas vivían allí cuatro primos, los tíos y los abuelos. Había niños y animales por todas partes. Los suelos eran de barro y las paredes de madera. Al principio me extrañó no tener alfombras en el suelo; pero después de unos días me acostumbré, y cuando regresé a mi casa en Albuquerque quería quitarlas.

Nuestro proyecto en San Fernando tuvo que ver con la higiene pública. En parte, nuestro trabajo era motivar a la gente y convencerlos de la importancia de la sanidad. Dimos charlas sobre este tema y enseñamos a los niños a cepillar sus dientes. Además teníamos una lista de la gente que necesitaba letrinas, una casita al aire libre con retrete.[1] Nosotros participamos tomando las medidas para las letrinas, pero ellos mismos las

[1] outdoor toilet

Options

Strategies for Reaching All Students

Students Needing Extra Help
Mira la lectura: Be sure that students understand the second question asked by the interviewer.
If students ask, explain any unfamiliar words or expressions.
Aplicación: You may want to point out to students that they could use the sentences they wrote in section 1 as a basis for a script in section 2.

Multiple Intelligences
Verbal/Linguistic
See *Aplicación* Ex. 2.
Visual/Spatial and Bodily/Kinesthetic
Have students make a group mural or collage illustrating a community service project.

Infórmate

STRATEGY ➤ Reading for detail

¿Cuáles de estas frases piensas que podría decir Jessica Ramos? ¿Cuáles podría decir al principio, cuando llegó allí? ¿Y al final? Escribe las frases en dos listas.

Luego, compara tu lista con la de un(a) compañero(a). Usa el texto para verificar tus decisiones.

- Puedo vivir sin las comodidades que tenía en los Estados Unidos.
- No sé si puedo vivir sin agua corriente.
- ¿Por qué no cubren el suelo?
- La gente del pueblo nos quiere mucho.
- La gente sabe mucho sobre la nutrición.
- Necesito enseñarle a la gente la importancia de la sanidad.
- No puedo comunicarme bien.

construyeron. Nuestra organización donó los materiales: el retrete, el cemento y las puertas. Plantamos árboles y hablamos de la importancia de tener árboles en el pueblo. También dimos clases informales de inglés.

M.H. ¿Cómo te aceptaron?

J.R. Al principio fue difícil. Me parecía que querían más a los voluntarios del año anterior. No siempre entendía y, a veces, no podía expresarme como quería. Pero después de las dos primeras semanas lo pasé mejor. Jugábamos con los niños y participábamos en las actividades de la comunidad. Comíamos en las casas donde trabajábamos y así conocimos a más familias. Al final del proyecto todo el pueblo nos dio una fiesta de despedida.

M.H. ¿Cambiaron tus ideas después de pasar un tiempo allí?

J.R. Yo fui con la idea de que tenía que enseñarles todo sobre la salud, pero una vez

Aplicación

1 Jessica Ramos quiere usar su experiencia como voluntaria del programa Amigos de las Américas para conseguir un trabajo. Escribe tres frases que expliquen cómo esa experiencia le ayudará a ser una buena empleada.

2 Prepara un anuncio comercial para el programa Amigos de las Américas. Puede ser un cartel o el guión de un anuncio para la radio.

Jessica Ramos con dos jóvenes en Ecuador, 1994

allí vi que tenían muy buena salud y no tuvimos que hablar de la nutrición. Ellos comían muy bien: papas, arroz, maíz, pan dulce, huevos y pollo. Al principio todo me pareció muy primitivo. Después se acostumbra uno. Al final era totalmente normal.

M.H. ¿Qué aprendiste?

J.R. Aprendí a tener confianza en mí misma. Ahora sé que puedo vivir de otra manera, sin algunas comodidades como agua corriente y alfombras en el suelo. La vida es mucho más que estas cosas.

M.H. ¿Te gustaría regresar?

J.R. Quiero volver dentro de 5 años.

Infórmate

Podría decir estas frases al principio:
No sé si puedo vivir sin agua corriente.
¿Por qué no cubren el suelo?
Necesito enseñarle a la gente la importancia de la sanidad.
No puedo comunicarme bien.

Podría decir estas frases al final:
Puedo vivir sin las comodidades que tenía en los Estados Unidos.
La gente del pueblo nos quiere mucho.
La gente sabe mucho de la nutrición.

Aplicación

1 Sentences will vary.

2 Ads will vary.

Fondo literario
La pobreza (pp. 464–467)

 **Internet Activities**

Cultural Notes ☀

(pp. 248–249, photos)
Amigos de las Américas is an international non-profit volunteer organization through which North American young people work to improve community health in Latin America. Over 17,000 volunteers have been placed by the organization since its founding in 1965. It serves in ongoing public health projects throughout Latin America.

Ask students: Would you be interested in someday doing volunteer work in Latin America? What kind of work might you choose?

Apply

Para escribir

¿Qué necesitas para graduarte? ¿Piensas que el trabajo voluntario debe ser parte del currículum? Vas a escribir un artículo sobre los trabajos voluntarios que te gustaría hacer, y si deben ser obligatorios o no para graduarse.

1 Primero, investiga qué trabajos voluntarios les gustaría hacer a tus compañeros(as) de clase:

- ¿Con qué grupos y organizaciones se puede trabajar?
- ¿A quiénes benefician esas organizaciones? ¿A los ancianos? ¿A los niños? ¿A los pobres? ¿A otras personas?
- ¿Qué programas tienen? ¿Para qué son esos programas? ¿Para enseñar inglés como segundo idioma? ¿Para proteger el medio ambiente? ¿Para ofrecer servicios médicos a los enfermos? ¿Qué otros programas se necesitan?

2 Ahora, discutan si los trabajos voluntarios deberían ser obligatorios o no para graduarse. Hablen sobre:

- si deben formar parte del currículum o no
- quiénes se benefician con ese tipo de trabajos
- si les ayuda a los estudiantes a conseguir ayuda financiera
- si les ayuda a explorar diferentes tipos de trabajo
- si les hace más responsables
- si los estudiantes son demasiado jóvenes para tratar con los problemas de la comunidad o no
- si deben usar todo su tiempo para sus estudios

¡Hola Profesor

250

Options

Strategies for Reaching All Students

3 Usa esta información para escribir tu primer borrador. Revisa tu trabajo con un(a) compañero(a) y sigue los pasos del proceso de escribir. Para compartir tu trabajo puedes:

- enviar el artículo a un periódico hispano
- exhibirlo y distribuirlo en tu escuela
- ofrecer esta información a las organizaciones que necesitan voluntarios
- enviarlo al consejo estudiantil de tu escuela
- incluirlo en tu portafolio

Assess & Summarize

Test Preparation
You may want to assign parts of this section as written homework or as an in-class writing activity prior to administering the *Examen de habilidades*.

Answers
Listening
—*En el centro de la comunidad, tendrás oportunidad de ayudar a otros. Hay mucha gente sin hogar que viene aquí a buscar refugio, o que usa el comedor de beneficencia de nuestro centro. En el centro de rehabilitación, los incapacitados practican cada fin de semana para las olimpiadas de minusválidos, que este año prometen ser muy buenas. Los ancianos también colaboran con el centro recreativo. ¡Hay tantos pobres que se benefician del servicio social que ofrecemos aquí! Somos una organización sin fines de lucro, y esperamos que nos ayuden a juntar fondos. Esperamos también que puedas servir con nosotros como voluntario.*

Answers will vary, but students may mention:
La persona está hablando con un posible voluntario. El centro de la comunidad ofrece programas para la gente sin hogar, los ancianos y los incapacitados. Es una organización sin fines de lucro.

Esta sección te ayudará a prepararte para el examen de habilidades, donde tendrás que hacer tareas semejantes.

Listening
¿Puedes entender la descripción de los servicios que ofrece este centro? Escucha mientras el (la) profesor(a) lee un ejemplo semejante al que vas a oír en el examen. ¿Con quién está hablando esta persona? ¿Qué servicios sociales ofrece este centro de la comunidad? ¿Qué clase de organización es?

Reading
Lee este artículo con cuidado para saber de qué se trata. Según el artículo, ¿por qué es importante participar en las elecciones? ¿Qué pueden hacer los jóvenes? ¿Cuál es una de las responsabilidades de todos los ciudadanos?

VOTA EN LA PRÓXIMA CAMPAÑA

Votar es una responsabilidad de todo ciudadano para garantizar que tengamos un gobierno que nos represente. Aunque siempre habrá opiniones contrarias sobre si una ley es justa o injusta, es importante participar en las elecciones para decidir a favor o en contra de los que nos gobiernan. Se espera que los jóvenes, al cumplir dieciocho años, voten, participen en la campaña electoral y colaboren con el partido político que prefieren.

www.pasoapaso.com

Self Test

252   Capítulo 7

Writing
¿Puedes escribir un artículo breve como el que escribió Claudio para el periódico de su escuela?

Este año escolar los estudiantes podrán obtener crédito por su trabajo de servicio a la comunidad. Conocerán mejor cuáles son los problemas de la sociedad y no les quitará tiempo para sus estudios. Podrán conseguir un trabajo que les guste, por ejemplo juntar fondos para la Cruz Roja o ayudar en el comedor de beneficencia. Si quieren más información, pónganse en contacto con su consejero. Una lista de los trabajos que ofrece la comunidad será publicada cada dos semanas.

Culture
¿Qué hacen los jóvenes en los países hispanos para ayudar a la comunidad?

Speaking
Habla con otra persona sobre la posibilidad de ayudar en la comunidad.

A — *¡Hay tantas personas con problemas hoy! Quisiera participar en algún servicio social en mi tiempo libre, pero no sé qué hacer.*

B — *Pues, hay muchas organizaciones sin fines de lucro que ayudan a la comunidad. ¿Qué trabajo te interesa más?*

A — *Me gustaría enseñar algún deporte a los incapacitados o trabajar en el centro recreativo. Y a ti, ¿qué te gustaría hacer? Ya no tienes que practicar fútbol y podrías ayudar a alguna organización.*

B — *¿Yo? ¡De ninguna manera! Es necesario que ...*

Options

Strategies for Reaching All Students

Students Needing Extra Help
Have students write this exercise so that they can check off what they have mastered. Remind them that this is just a sample of what the test will be like.
Listening: Read more than once. Remind students that they need to listen for only certain pieces of information. Tell them to be aware that the answers may not be given in the same order as the questions.

Reading: Remind students that they don't need to know every word to understand the reading. As in the Listening section, tell students that they might not find the answers in the same order as the questions.
Writing: Have students use the Organizer and write a brief sample article as practice before the test. Refer them to the *Tema para investigar* and *Para escribir* sections for ideas. Be specific about the amount of text that you are willing to accept.

Culture: Have students review the notes they took when they read the *Álbum cultural*.
Speaking: Have students use the vocabulary section of the Organizer. Complete the model and limit the number of lines of dialogue. Brainstorm other phrases to begin the conversation.

Resumen del vocabulario

Usa el vocabulario de este capítulo para:

- responder a la pregunta clave: ¿Debes servir a la comunidad para graduarte?
- hablar de cuáles son tus responsabilidades en la sociedad
- expresar tu opinión sobre el trabajo voluntario
- describir las oportunidades de trabajo voluntario que existen en tu comunidad

para describir las oportunidades de trabajo voluntario que hay en tu comunidad

el anciano, la anciana
la campaña electoral
el centro de la comunidad
el centro de rehabilitación
el centro recreativo
el comedor de beneficencia
la Cruz Roja
financiero, -a
la gente sin hogar
el incapacitado,
    la incapacitada
las olimpiadas
    de minusválidos
la organización
el partido político
el refugio
el servicio social
sin fines de lucro

para hablar de tus responsabilidades

el candidato, la candidata
la ciudadanía
el ciudadano, la ciudadana
completar
el ejército
la elección, *pl.* las elecciones
garantizar *(z → c)*
gobernar *(e → ie)*
el gobierno
la ley, *pl.* las leyes
obligatorio, -a
la responsabilidad
el trabajo

para expresar tu opinión

a favor (de)
beneficiar(se)
en contra (de)
exigir *(g → j)*
injusto, -a
justo, -a
protestar
votar

para decir qué puedes hacer por la sociedad

la causa
colaborar (con)
donar
juntar fondos
la manifestación, *pl.* las
    manifestaciones
la marcha
obtener *(e → ie)*
los pobres
por
la sociedad
solicitar

otras palabras y expresiones útiles

actualmente
esperar
hagan *(from:* hacer)
presentar(se)
prometer
sino
unir

Resumen 253

Reading

Answers will vary, but students may mention:
Es importante participar en las elecciones porque tenemos que escoger a las personas que nos gobiernan. Los jóvenes, al cumplir dieciocho años, pueden votar, participar en la campaña electoral y colaborar con el partido político que prefieren. Una de las responsabilidades de todos los ciudadanos es votar.

Writing

Articles will vary.

Culture

Students may mention:
Ayudan a los incapacitados, ayudan a la gente en momentos de crisis, hacen trabajo voluntario, etc.

Speaking

Dialogues will vary.

Assessment

 Prueba cumulativa

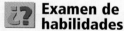 **Examen de habilidades**

 Test Generator

Additional Assessment Options

 Comm. Act. BLMs

Small Group Activities
Situation Cards

(continued from above)

 ¿Lo sabes bien? Video Quiz

www Internet Activities
Self-Test

CAPÍTULO 8
THEME: MYTHS AND LEGENDS

SCOPE AND SEQUENCE Pages 254–289

COMMUNICATION

Topics

Mysterious phenomena and their possible explanations

Measurement

Objectives

Comparar algunos mitos y leyendas hispanos con los de los Estados Unidos

Identificar fenómenos extraordinarios

Describir objetos

Dar tu opinión

Indicar si dudas de algo

CULTURE

Mitos y leyendas hispanos

GRAMMAR

El subjuntivo con expresiones de duda

El subjuntivo: Verbos irregulares

El presente perfecto del subjuntivo

Ancillaries available for use with Chapter 8

Multisensory/Technology

 Overheads, 25–26

 Audio Tapes and CDs

 Vocabulary Art Blackline Masters for Hands-On Learning, pp. 38–41/CD-ROM

 Classroom Crossword

 Video

 Internet Activities
www.pasoapaso.com

Print

 Practice Workbook, pp. 81–90

 Writing, Audio & Video Activities, pp. 47–52, 114–116, 147–148

 Communicative Activity Blackline Masters

Pair and Small Group Activities, pp. 50–55

Situation Cards, p. 56

 RESOURCE PRO®

Planning Express, Teaching Resources Library, and Clip Art Library

Assessment

 Assessment Program

Pruebas, pp. 111–120

Examen de habilidades, pp. 121–124

 Test Generator

 ¿Lo sabes bien? Video Quiz

Video, Chap. 8

In Search of Understanding

Human beings are driven to understand the problems and mysteries that surround them. A biologist, for example, might spend days camped in a rain forest observing rare species of plants. The forest might be dangerous, the weather inclement, and the living conditions extremely uncomfortable, yet the scientist will accept these circumstances even though, in the end, he or she may fail to discover the answers.

Scientists are not the only people driven to seek knowledge. A backyard mechanic may spend weeks examining an automobile engine, searching for the source of a disturbing noise. Discovering and eliminating the sound may not improve the car's performance, but the mechanic, just like the biologist, is compelled to determine the cause.

The discoveries made by the biologist or auto mechanic may have practical applications. The biologist may discover a plant whose medicinal value eases human suffering. The mechanic may improve understanding of how all motors are engineered. Yet even if these individuals did not derive a clear-cut benefit from their investigations, they would probably continue their search. This is because we receive satisfaction from the *pursuit* of knowledge as well as from its actual attainment.

Some phenomena, however, seem to defy our best efforts, however diligently we search. In Nazca, Peru, for example, enormous drawings were traced into the earth. These figures make little sense upon close observation, but appear as clear renderings of animal and human figures when seen from an airplane. Scientists and philosophers have been unable to explain how these tracings were planned, let alone why.

Similarly, it is largely a mystery why native peoples of Mexico carved enormous stone heads that stand some six feet in height. Even less obvious is how these figures were moved about, given that the people who made them did not use the wheel. The famous stone carvings of Easter Island in the Pacific Ocean also defy explanation. Their meaning and how they were constructed and put in place continue to confound us.

These mysteries humble us, accustomed as we are to finding an answer to everything. They demonstrate that our modern knowledge contains huge gaps. It may be centuries before we achieve a real understanding of these mysterious phenomena. But we can be confident of one thing: our compulsive search for answers promises that we stand a good chance of eventually developing explanations that satisfy our curiosity.

Introduce

Re-entry of Concepts
The following list represents words, expressions, and grammar topics re-entered from Books 1, 2, and 3 (Chaps. 4–6):

Book 1
numbers, family members, nature

Book 2
impersonal *se,* household chores, nature

Chapter 4
present perfect

Chapter 5
archaeology

Chapter 6
communication technology

Planning

Cross-Curricular Connections

Literature Connection *(pp. 266–267)*
Tell students to choose a story from their favorite science fiction, horror, or thriller novel or film. Have them recount the plot, adding themselves as a character, and show how they would change what actually happened.

History Connection *(pp. 280–281)*
In small groups, tell students to choose four symbols of our civilization and draw them as they would appear five thousand years in the future. After providing a written description of their symbols, tell them to list at least four scientific questions about them, using the *¿Comprendiste?* (p. 266) section as a guide. Have groups exchange papers to answer each other's questions. Ask groups to share their conclusions with the class.

Spanish in Your Community
Have students visit the local library and research any articles, short stories, or novels that focus on Hispanic legends. They might want to look in the children's collections as well as the adult section of the library. Have them share a legend with the class. Compile these resources into a reading list for students wanting extra credit.

CAPÍTULO 8

OBJETIVOS

Al terminar este capítulo vas a poder responder a la pregunta clave:

¿Cómo se explica...?

También vas a poder:

- **identificar y describir algunos fenómenos extraordinarios**
- **dar tu opinión sobre esos fenómenos**
- **indicar si estás seguro(a) o si dudas de algo**
- **comparar algunos mitos y leyendas de los países hispanos con los que existen en los Estados Unidos**

Gigantescas estatuas de Ahu Nau Nau, en la Isla de Pascua, Chile

VISITA
www.pasoapaso.com

Preview

Cultural Objective
• *Hablar de algunos fenómenos*

Critical Thinking:
Drawing Conclusions
Discuss the images seen in the photos and ask students how they think these objects were created.

Answers: Anticipación
Answers will vary for inductive questions and those in the caption text.

Anticipación

Mira las fotos. ¿Cuáles de estas imágenes conoces?
¿Qué representan? ¿En dónde están?

El enorme círculo de piedra de Stonehenge está cerca de Salisbury, Inglaterra. Su construcción empezó alrededor del año 2100 a.C. y nadie sabe para qué fue construido. Es probable que haya sido un observatorio solar, aunque algunos creen que era un centro religioso. ¿Qué crees tú? ¿Por qué?

256   Capítulo 8

Options

Strategies for Reaching All Students

Spanish-Speaking Students
Tell students: *Escribe una descripción de cada foto.*

Students Needing Extra Help
Students may not be aware of the contributions made by early civilizations. Discuss as needed.
Be prepared to answer questions that students may have regarding the photo content on these pages.

Multiple Intelligences
Visual/Spatial and Verbal/Linguistic
See Critical Thinking.

Chichén Itzá fue un importante centro político y religioso de la civilización maya entre los siglos IV y XV, cuando sus habitantes la abandonaron. Es posible que las guerras con otros pueblos *(peoples)* hayan obligado a los mayas a dejar Chichén Itzá, pero esto sigue siendo un misterio para los arqueólogos. ¿Por qué crees tú que los mayas abandonaron Chichén Itzá?

En el fondo *(bottom)* del mar cerca de la isla de Bimini se han encontrado los restos de un antiguo camino de piedra. Nadie sabe cuándo ni por quién fue construido, pero algunas personas creen que son restos de la Atlántida *(Atlantis)*, el continente perdido. ¿Crees que ese continente existió? ¿Por qué o por qué no?

www.pasoapaso.com
Visita estos países

257

Cultural Notes ☀

(p. 257, top photo)
This pyramid, at 82 feet high, is the largest temple at the renowned Mayan site of Chichén Itzá. Known as *El castillo,* it is actually a precise representation of the ancient Mayan calendar, through combinations of its total number of steps, panels, platforms, and other architectural features. *El castillo* is perhaps best known for the show of architectural precision seen every year during the spring and autumn equinoxes. Light and shadow on its north staircase simulate the creep of a serpent, ascending in March and descending in September.

(p. 257, bottom photo)
The Bimini Islands, consisting of tiny North and South Bimini, encompass nearly nine square miles, including a few islets and cays. They are part of the Bahamian chain of islands, and lie only 50 miles from the coast of Florida. The first settlers are believed to have been Arawak Indians. Spanish explorers, among them Juan Ponce de León, who landed at Bimini in 1512, soon realized that the islands offered none of the wealth they sought, and paid little attention to them.

Present

Chapter Theme
Mysteries

Communicative Objectives
- *Identificar fenómenos extraordinarios*
- *Describir objetos*
- *Dar tu opinión*
- *Indicar si dudas de algo*

 Overheads 25–26

 Vocabulary Art BLMs/CD-ROM

 Vocabulary Tape 8-1

Teaching Suggestions

Preparing students to speak: Use one or two options from each of the categories of Comprehensible Input or Limited Verbal Response. For a complete explanation of these categories and some sample activities, see pp. T20–T21.

Point out that *geométrico, -a* is a cognate that refers to the relationship between points and lines in space. Remind students of what is studied in a geometry class.

Vocabulario para comunicarse

¿Cómo se explica . . . ?

Aquí tienes palabras y expresiones necesarias para hablar de lo inexplicable. Léelas varias veces y practícalas con un(a) compañero(a) en las páginas siguientes.

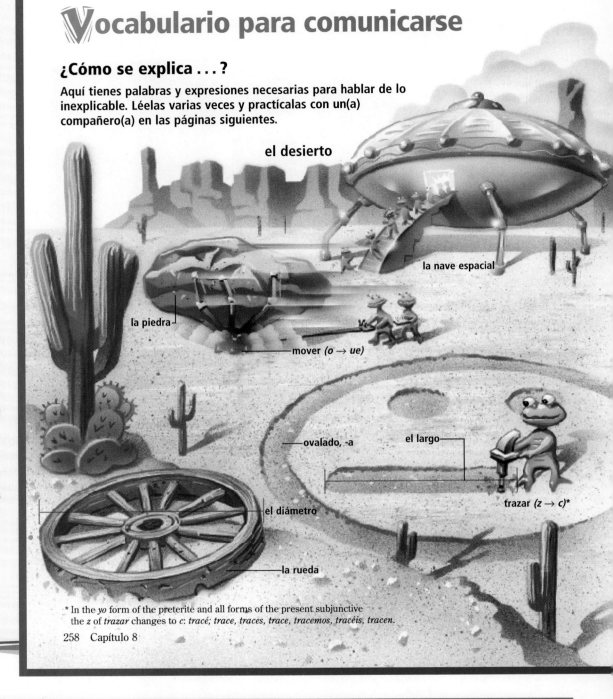

el desierto

la nave espacial

la piedra

mover *(o → ue)*

ovalado, -a

el largo

el diámetro

trazar *(z → c)**

la rueda

* In the *yo* form of the preterite and all forms of the present subjunctive the *z* of *trazar* changes to *c*: *tracé; trace, traces, trace, tracemos, tracéis, tracen.*

258   Capítulo 8

Options

Strategies for Reaching All Students

Spanish-Speaking Students
Tell students: *Usa diez de las palabras del vocabulario para escribir un párrafo sobre un evento imaginario.*

Students Needing Extra Help
Begin the vocabulary section of the Organizer. Point out the vocabulary words that may cause spelling difficulties: *la nave espacial* might be confused with *especial*, *largo* looks like "large" instead of "length." Write out the complete paradigms for *mover* and *medir.*

También necesitas . . . : Model sentences using the *medir . . . de* expressions. Write out the complete paradigms for *aparecer* and *servir*. Emphasize how *encantado, -a* is used in this chapter.

También necesitas . . .

aparecer $(c \rightarrow zc)$	to appear	medir . . . de alto	to be / measure . . . high
cierto, -a	true, certain	de ancho	to be / measure . . . wide
dudar	to doubt	de diámetro	to be / measure . . . in
el diseño	design		diameter
el fantasma	ghost	de largo	to be / measure . . . long
encantado, -a	here: haunted	servir $(e \rightarrow i)$ para	to be used for
estar seguro, -a	to be sure	¿Para qué sirve?	What's it used for?
extraño, -a	strange	el Yeti	the abominable
increíble	unbelievable		snowman
la prueba	here: proof		

¿Y qué quiere decir . . . ?

enorme	el peso
falso, -a	posible
geométrico, -a	imposible
gigantesco, -a	probable
misterioso, -a	improbable

medir $(e \rightarrow i)$

el ancho

el alto

el centímetro

la geóloga

calcular

$$\frac{X + Y}{2} = 2R^2$$

la huella

el geólogo

pesar

Vocabulario para comunicarse · 259

Class Starter Review
On the day following the vocabulary presentation, you might begin the class with this activity: Prepare a brief paragraph in which you use the vocabulary to describe a UFO sighting or any other unexplained occurrence. Have students draw the object that you describe, making sure they include details that you provide (for example: *La nave espacial medía 50 pies de ancho y 20 pies de alto.*).

www **Internet Activities**
Juegos

Extended Written Practice/Homework
1. Imagine that you came upon the scene on pp. 258–259. Write three sentences describing what was happening: *Unos extraterrestres estaban bajando de una nave espacial.*
2. Write three sentences telling the measurements of different items in your home: *Mi cama mide . . .*
3. Write three questions asking what different items and appliances are used for: *¿Para qué sirve el control remoto?*

Multiple Intelligences
Verbal/Linguistic
See Vocabulary Tape 8-1.
Verbal/Linguistic and Interpersonal/Social
Have students create a dialogue between a reporter and scientists studying one of the sites in the photos on pp. 256–257, discussing possible theories behind its origins and purposes. Have them present the dialogues to the class.

Verbal/Linguistic and Visual/Spatial
See Class Starter Review.
Visual/Spatial
See Overheads 25–26.

Practice

Re-enter / Recycle
Ex. 3: present perfect from Chap. 4

Answers: Empecemos a conversar

1 ESTUDIANTE A
Answers will vary, but should begin in the following manner:
a. La rueda es ... , ¿no?
b. El desierto es ...
c. El dibujo es ...
d. Las huellas son ...
e. La piedra es ...
f. El casco es ...
g. Statements will vary.

ESTUDIANTE B
a.–g. Answers will vary, but should be logical and agree with the picture.

2 ESTUDIANTE A
a. ¿Cuánto mide la nave espacial?
b. ... el dibujo?
c. ... la piedra?
d. ... la rueda?
e. ... la pizarra?
f. Questions will vary.

ESTUDIANTE B
a. Mide doscientos metros de ancho y setenta y cuatro metros de alto.
b. Mide trescientos metros de ancho y cien metros de alto.
c. Mide ochenta metros de ancho y treinta metros de alto.
d. Mide un metro de diámetro.
e. Mide tres metros de largo.
f. Answers will vary.

¿Cómo se explica . . . ?

Empecemos a conversar

Túrnate con un(a) compañero(a) para ser *Estudiante A* y *Estudiante B*. Reemplacen las palabras subrayadas en el modelo con palabras representadas o escritas en los recuadros.
💡 quiere decir que puedes escoger tu propia respuesta.

¡NO OLVIDES!
Other words and expressions that you've already learned related to the theme of this chapter are: *el dibujo, el extraterrestre, el planeta, la Tierra, la Luna, el espacio, el sendero, la sombra*

1
A —*La nave espacial es redonda, ¿no?*
B —*¡Qué va! Es ovalada.*

redondo, -a

Estudiante A

Estudiante B

redondo, -a
ovalado, -a
pequeño, -a
enorme
geométrico, -a
gigantesco, -a
cuadrado, -a

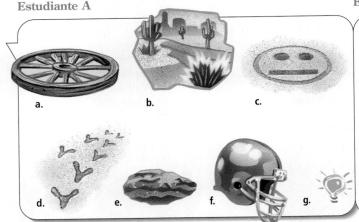

a.   b.   c.
d.   e.   f.   g.

2
2 m
3 m
A —*¿Cuánto mide la piedra?*
B —*Mide tres metros de ancho y dos metros de alto.*

Estudiante A

Estudiante B

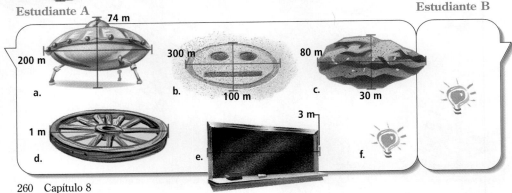

74 m
200 m
300 m   100 m
80 m   30 m
a.   b.   c.
1 m
3 m
d.   e.   f.

Options

Strategies for Reaching All Students

Spanish-Speaking Students
Exs. 1–3: Pair bilingual with non-bilingual students, if possible.

Students Needing Extra Help
¡No olvides!: If available, refer to the vocabulary sections of the Organizers for Book 2, Chaps. 11 and 14.
Ex. 2: Show students that the model is referring to width and height. Remind them that other measurements will be used in the remaining items.

Enrichment
Ex. 1: To continue this exercise, *Estudiante A* can choose classroom objects, make obviously accurate or inaccurate statements about their size and shape, and *Estudiante B* can respond to the statements.
Ex. 2: Have students bring in tape measures and then work in pairs to measure each other's height metrically. When this activity is done, ask each student to report his or her partner's height, and record this information on the chalkboard to determine the tallest in

the class. As students report information to you, ask questions reviewing as much vocabulary as possible: *¿Estás seguro(a)? ¿Es posible (imposible, probable, improbable, cierto, falso, increíble) lo que dice (nombre)?*

3

A — *Oí que <u>los extraterrestres se comunican con nosotros</u>. ¿Qué piensas?*

B — *<u>Puede ser, pero lo dudo</u>.*
    o: *¡Es imposible!*

se comunican
con nosotros

Estudiante A

a. apareció cerca de mi casa

b. calculó el diámetro de la piedra

c. de Sahara ha desaparecido

d. descubrió huellas del Yeti

e. trazaron diseños en el jardín de la escuela

f.

Estudiante B

¿Qué dices? Me parece increíble.

¡No, es imposible!

Bueno, es probable.

No sé, pero me parece improbable.

¡Por supuesto! Estoy seguro(a).

Ésa es una noticia falsa.

Puede ser, pero lo dudo.

Me parece que es cierto.

Gillian Anderson y David Duchovny
en la película *Expediente X*

261

---

3 ESTUDIANTE A

a. Oí que la nave espacial apareció cerca de mi casa. ¿Qué piensas?

b. ...la geóloga calculó el diámetro de la rueda. ...

c. ...el desierto de Sahara ha desaparecido. ...

d. ...un arqueólogo descubrió huellas del Yeti. ...

e. ...los extraterrestres trazaron diseños en el jardín de la escuela. ...

f. Statements will vary.

ESTUDIANTE B

a.–f. Statements will vary.

Using Photos

Ask students to create a story (aloud or in writing) to describe what is happening in the photo on this page.

Extended Written Practice/Homework
1. Write three sentences saying what you are sure will take place in the future: *Estoy seguro(a) de que tendremos un presidente diferente después de la próxima elección.*
2. Write three sentences naming different movies, TV shows, or books that you think are strange.

3. Choose three adjectives from p. 259 and write sentences describing different people, places, or things: *Las cabezas de los presidentes en Mount Rushmore son gigantescas.*

Multiple Intelligences
Logical/Mathematical
See Enrichment Ex. 2.
Verbal/Linguistic
See Exs. 1–3.

Practice & Apply

Re-enter / Recycle
Ex. 4: technology from Chap. 6
Exs. 5–6: present perfect from Chap. 4

Answers: Empecemos a conversar

4 ESTUDIANTE A
a. ¿Para qué sirve un pincel?
b. ...un casco?
c. ...un cuenco?
d. ...un teléfono inalámbrico?
e. ...un contestador automático?
f. Questions will vary.

ESTUDIANTE B
a.–f. Answers will vary, but should be logical and begin *Sirve para* + inf.

Answers: ¿Y qué piensas tú?
5–10 Answers will vary.

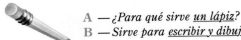

¿Cómo se explica . . . ?

4

A — ¿Para qué sirve *un lápiz*?
B — Sirve para *escribir y dibujar*.

Estudiante A   Estudiante B

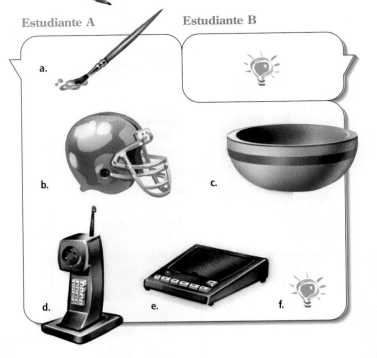

a.

b.

c.

d.

e.

f.

¿Y qué piensas tú?

Aquí tienes otra oportunidad para usar el vocabulario de este capítulo.

5 ¿Has visto alguna vez una nave espacial? ¿Dónde? ¿En una película? ¿En la televisión? ¿En algún museo? ¿Cuándo? ¿Cómo era?

6 ¿Crees que en la Tierra han aterrizado naves espaciales de otros planetas? ¿Por qué? ¿Qué pruebas tienes? Describe cómo te imaginas un extraterrestre. ¿Crees que existen? ¿Por qué sí o no?

www.pasoapaso.com

MÁS PRÁCTICA

Más práctica y tarea, p. 568
Practice Workbook 8–1, 8–2

262   Capítulo 8

Options

Strategies for Reaching All Students

Spanish-Speaking Students
Ex. 7: After this exercise, have students respond in writing: *Imagina que vas a diseñar una casa encantada para un carnaval en tu escuela. ¿Qué debes incluir? Describe la casa y las cosas que van a asustar y a asombrar a la gente que entre. Di por qué has incluido cada cosa.*

Students Needing Extra Help
Ex. 6: Brainstorm responses to the *¿Por qué?* and *¿Qué pruebas tienes?* questions.
Ex. 7: Have research material about haunted houses on hand, or have students use an imaginary house and its history.
Ex. 9: Have students jot down the color, size, shape, etc. of their object.
Ex. 10: Brainstorm topics that lend themselves to true / false statements: haunted houses, aliens, Mayans, the homeless, and so on.

Enrichment
Ex. 9: As a homework assignment, have students write sentences telling the uses of the different objects.

7 ¿Qué casas encantadas conoces? ¿Se encuentran en un parque de diversiones o son reales? ¿Cuál es su historia? ¿Tienen fantasmas?

8 Mide tres objetos de la sala de clases y dile a un(a) compañero(a) cuánto miden y cuánto piensas que pesan.

9 Debes escoger un objeto de la sala de clases sin decir qué es. Tu compañero(a) debe decir en qué objeto estás pensando. Puede preguntarte: ¿De qué color es? ¿Cuánto mide? ¿Cuánto pesa? ¿Para qué sirve?

10 Túrnate con un(a) compañero(a) para decir diez frases verdaderas o falsas, por ejemplo: "Costa Rica está en Suramérica," o "Hay personas en la Luna." Tu compañero(a) va a decidir si las frases son verdaderas o falsas. Puedes usar las siguientes expresiones u otras:

¡Qué va! Eso no es cierto.
¡No me digas! Yo no creo que . . .
Sí, por supuesto, . . .

Si tu compañero(a) tiene razón, recibe un punto. Si no, tú recibes un punto. La persona que recibe más puntos gana.

También se dice

la altura

la anchura

Para *encantado* también se dice:
hechizado

Para *prueba* tambien se dice:
evidencia
indicio
muestra
señal

 Practice Wkbk. 8-1, 8-2

 Audio Activity 8.1

 Writing Activities 8-A, 8-B

 Pruebas 8-1, 8-2

La casa misteriosa de la familia Addams

Vocabulario para comunicarse   263

Cooperative Learning
Have students think about how well they know their school building: how large they think it is, how large the different classrooms and halls are, etc. Provide pairs of students with tape measures and assign them specific areas of the building to measure: Spanish classroom, gym, library, cafeteria, etc. The following day, have one student from each pair draw the assigned area, including measurements. The other student should estimate the number of square meters in the room and figure out how many square meters of space are available per person if 20 people are in the room. Post the drawings and discuss.

Multiple Intelligences
Interpersonal/Social and Logical/Mathematical
See Cooperative Learning.
Verbal/Linguistic
See Audio Activity 8.1.
Visual/Spatial
See Enrichment, Practice Wkbk. 8-1 and 8-2, and Writing Activities 8-A and 8-B.

Present

Chapter Theme
Inexplicable phenomena

Communicative Objectives
- *Identificar fenómenos extraordinarios*
- *Describir objetos*
- *Dar tu opinión*
- *Indicar si dudas de algo*

 Vocabulary Tape 8-2

Grammar Preview
The present perfect subjunctive is presented here lexically. The explanation appears on p. 277.

Teaching Suggestions
Getting ready to speak:
Remind students of the reading strategies that they learned (getting meaning from context and coping with unknown words) to help them understand the *Tema para investigar*. For further details and some sample activities, see pp. T24–T25.

Point out that the Spanish prefixes *des-* and *in-* are equivalent to the English "un-" or "in-."

Answers: Tema para investigar
Answers will vary.

Tema para investigar

Aquí tienes más palabras e ideas que te ayudarán a hablar de lo inexplicable. Mira las fotos de esta página. ¿Por qué crees que se consideran extraordinarios estos fenómenos? Aquí tienes algunas teorías que tratan de explicarlos.

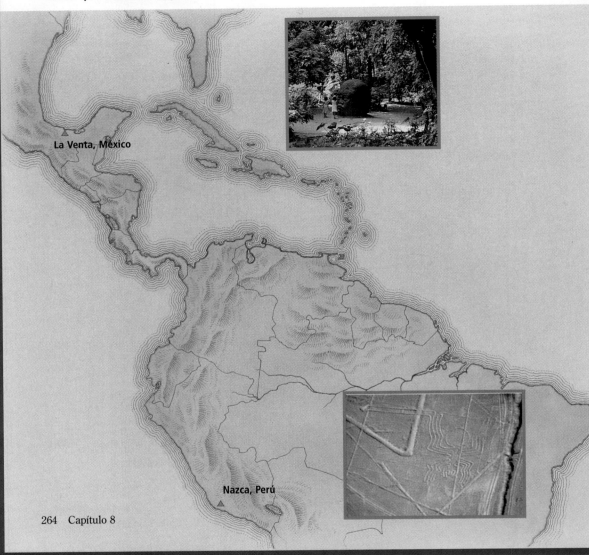

La Venta, México

Nazca, Perú

264   Capítulo 8

Options

Strategies for Reaching All Students

Students Needing Extra Help
Point out the vocabulary words that students may have difficulty spelling: *la tonelada* (may be confused with "tunnel"), *a pesar de* (students just learned *pesar* with a very different meaning), and *el mito*.
¿Y qué quiere decir . . .?: Review the English meaning of "to affirm."

Multiple Intelligences
Verbal/Linguistic
See Vocabulary Tape 8-2 and Class Starter Review.

¿Cómo lo podemos saber?

En La Venta, cerca de la costa del Golfo de México, se han encontrado ruinas de una antigua civilización. Entre ellas se han descubierto cabezas gigantescas de piedra. Estas enormes cabezas miden entre dos o tres metros de alto y pesan entre 11 y 24 **toneladas**. Lo **extraordinario** es que no existen piedras tan grandes en esa región de México; entonces **se supone** que los olmecas, **los habitantes** de esta región, tuvieron que moverlas ... ¡más de 80 millas! **A pesar de que** conocían la rueda, parece que no la usaban para el transporte. ¡Nadie puede explicar cómo movieron piedras tan pesadas!

En el desierto de Perú encontramos otro **fenómeno inexplicable**. En un lugar que se llama Nazca, se ven diseños misteriosos en la tierra. Hay cientos de figuras geométricas y treinta dibujos enormes—las figuras de un **mono** y una araña entre otros. Pero los dibujos son tan grandes que los diseños completos sólo pueden verse desde el aire. Se supone que sus

creadores **pertenecían** a una antigua civilización **desconocida**. Pero si ellos no podían **volar**, ¿cómo podían ver lo que creaban? ¿Para qué servían las líneas y por qué las trazaron?

Existen varias **teorías** que tratan de explicar estos misteriosos dibujos. Según una de ellas, los diseños eran un gran calendario que indicaba las estaciones, los eclipses y los movimientos de las estrellas.

Hay otra teoría que **afirma** que los dioses que aparecen en **los mitos** y **leyendas** hispanoamericanos eran en realidad extraterrestres. Esta **afirmación** está basada en **la "evidencia"** de que los dioses de la mitología indígena llegaban a la Tierra acompañados frecuentemente de fuego. A pesar de que algunos creen en esta teoría, los arqueólogos tienen muchas **dudas** sobre la misma. No existen **datos** suficientes; por eso no creen que **el misterio** se **haya resuelto** todavía. ¿Qué piensas tú?

la tonelada	ton	pertenecer (c → zc)	to belong
suponer: (yo) supongo*	to suppose: I suppose	volar (o → ue)	to fly
(tú) supones	you suppose	el mito	myth
a pesar de (que)	in spite of (the fact that)	los datos	data, information
el mono	monkey	haya resuelto	has solved
		(from: resolver)	

¿Y qué quiere decir ... ?

extraordinario, -a	afirmar
el /la habitante	la leyenda
el fenómeno	la afirmación
inexplicable	la evidencia
el creador, la creadora	la duda
desconocido, -a	el misterio
la teoría	

* *Suponer* follows the pattern of *poner*.

Tema para investigar   265

Class Starter Review
Start a chain story by saying a sentence using one of the vocabulary words. Have a student add another sentence to the story, also using one of the vocabulary words. Continue until as many new words as possible are used.

Multicultural Perspectives
The Nazca civilization flourished between 1,500 and 2,000 years ago. Today, they are known for the designs called the Nazca lines. Maria Reiche, a mathematician, has spent many years in Peru studying *las líneas de Nazca*. The most accepted theory is that they were part of some kind of calendar.

Most ancient civilizations, including the Nazca, were more advanced than originally thought. To enhance their agricultural production, the Nazca built aqueducts to store water from rainfall and mountain runoff. They wove wool and cotton garments with elaborate designs. Nazca pottery is distinguished by bright colors, intricate drawings, and paint on the inside as well as the outside of the vessel. Provide books and articles about the ancient civilizations of Latin America (Olmecs, Toltecs, Nazca) for further discussion.

www Internet Activities
Juegos

Cultural Notes ☀

(p. 264, top photo)
The first great civilization in Mexico, that of the Olmec Indians of the southern Gulf Coast, flourished between 1200 and 100 B.C. Among other achievements, the Olmecs developed a counting system, calendar, and impressive carving techniques for jade and massive stone statues. The reasons for the demise of the Olmec civilization are unknown, but it is believed that they were gradually edged out of power by civilizations arising in nearby regions, particularly Oaxaca.

(p. 264, bottom photo)
The lines on the desert plain at Nazca, Peru, representing birds, animals, and geometric figures up to 1,000 feet across, have been the subject of intense inquiry since their discovery in 1939 by the American scientist Paul Kosok during a flight over the arid region. Before Kosok viewed them from the air and noted the distinct patterns they make, the lines were believed to be part of a

pre-Incan irrigation system. The German mathematician Maria Reiche (1903–1998), who initially acted as Kosok's translator, devoted her life to research on Nazca, proposing that the lines were made by ancient Peruvians for viewing by their gods. Reiche, a solitary and enigmatic figure that local people rarely understood, received a hero's funeral when she died in Nazca in June of 1998.

Practice & Apply

Answers: ¿Comprendiste?

1 Hechos: a, b, d, e, g
Teorías: c, f

2 Las cabezas enormes de piedra en México y las líneas de Nazca en Perú. / *Answers will vary.*

Answers: ¿Y qué piensas tú?

3–7 Answers will vary.

¿Comprendiste?

1 Con un(a) compañero(a) decide cuáles de las siguientes frases son hechos y cuáles son teorías según la lectura.

   a. Los olmecas eran los habitantes de una región de México.
   b. Las cabezas de piedra de los olmecas pesan unas 20 toneladas.
   c. Las líneas de Nazca son un gran calendario.
   d. Los creadores de los diseños del mono y de la araña pertenecían a una civilización desconocida.
   e. Las leyendas y los mitos hispanoamericanos hablan de dioses que llegaban acompañados de fuego.
   f. Los dioses de los mitos hispanoamericanos eran extraterrestres.
   g. No hay datos suficientes para explicar el origen de los dibujos.

2 ¿De qué fenómenos inexplicables se habla aquí? ¿Estás de acuerdo con las teorías para explicarlos? ¿Por qué?

¿Y qué piensas tú?

3 Se piensa que puede haber habitantes en otros planetas. ¿Qué crees tú? ¿Qué evidencia hay? ¿Cómo crees que podemos comunicarnos con ellos?

4 ¿Crees que hay pruebas de visitas de extraterrestres a la Tierra? ¿Por qué? ¿Cuáles son las pruebas?

5 ¿Qué fenómenos extraordinarios conoces de la región o del país donde vives? ¿De otras partes del mundo? Descríbelos.

6 ¿Por qué son misteriosas las líneas de Nazca? ¿Cuál crees que es la mejor teoría para explicarlas? Crea tu propia teoría y explícasela a tus compañeros(as).

7 Busca una leyenda o un mito hispanoamericano en la biblioteca y cuéntaselo a la clase. ¿De qué se trata? ¿Quiénes son los personajes?

Detalle del Templo de los Danzantes, Monte Albán, México

www.pasoapaso.com

MÁS PRÁCTICA

- Más práctica y tarea, p. 569
- Practice Workbook 8–3, 8–4

266   Capítulo 8

Options

Strategies for Reaching All Students

Spanish-Speaking Students
Ex. 3: After this exercise, ask: *Si tuvieras la oportunidad de visitar otros planetas, ¿irías? ¿Por qué?*

Students Needing Extra Help
Ex. 1: Emphasize that this exercise is trying to distinguish between fact and theory, not true / false statements.
Ex. 4: Brainstorm possible responses to the *¿Por qué?* question.

Ex. 5: Have materials available about regional / national / international phenomena.
Ex. 7: Have books and materials reserved in advance in the library.
¿Qué sabes ahora?: Have students write this so that they can record their progress.

Cooperative Learning
In pairs within groups of four, have students compare the theories they created for Ex. 6.

Each pair should choose the best theory and write a paragraph explaining it. Pairs within the group exchange paragraphs, and write a critique of the other pair's theory. Return critiques, and adjust the original theory to compensate for the weaknesses found. As a group, choose one of the revised theories to present to the class. When all theories have been presented, the class will vote on the most plausible.

Leyendas latinoamericanas

ARGENTINA
BOLIVIA
COLOMBIA
GUATEMALA
HONDURAS
MEXICO
PARAGUAY
PERU
PUERTO RICO
VENEZUELA

Genevieve
Barlow

También se dice

Para *mono* también se dice:
mico

Para *leyenda* también se dice:
tradición

 Practice Wkbk. 8-3, 8-4

 Audio Activity 8.2

 Writing Activity 8-C

 Pruebas 8-3, 8-4

 Comm. Act. BLM 8-1

¿Qué sabes ahora?

¿Puedes:

■ hablar sobre fenómenos inexplicables que se encuentran en los países hispanos?

—Parece que los ___, que no sabían usar la ___, pudieron mover piedras gigantescas.

■ describir un fenómeno inexplicable?

—Las líneas de Nazca son ___. Se cree que fueron hechas por ___.

■ expresar tu opinión sobre la existencia de fenómenos inexplicables?

—Creo que las ___ sobre las líneas de Nazca son ___.

Tema para investigar   267

Extended Written Practice/Homework
1. Write three sentences naming different different groups of people who had legends or myths: *Los incas tenían leyendas sobre las personas que iban a conquistarlos.*
2. Write three sentences naming the organizations or groups that different people belong to: *Pertenezco a un club deportivo.*
3. Write two pairs of sentences describing different extraordinary phenomena and indicating how much evidence there is for them.

Multiple Intelligences
Interpersonal/Social and Visual/Spatial
See Cooperative Learning.
Verbal/Linguistic
See Exs. 1–2 and Audio Activity 8.2.
Visual/Spatial
See Practice Wkbk. 8-3 and 8-4, Writing Activity 8-C, and Comm. Act. BLM 8-1.

Cultural Notes

(p. 266, photo)
This dancing figure is found at Monte Albán, the magnificent mountaintop capital of the ancient Zapotec civilization of Oaxaca, Mexico, which flourished from 700 B.C. to A.D. 900. The Monte Albán complex, consisting of pyramids, tombs, temples, and other impressive buildings, appears to have been occupied only by priests and administrators. The general population of approximately 26,000 lived on the surrounding terraced slopes.

Standards 1.1; 1.2; 1.3; 3.1   **267**

Critical Thinking: Making Comparisons
Ask students to look at the photos on these two pages. Remind them that the stone objects were created long ago by people using tools available at that time. Ask if these objects can be compared to any present-day monuments or structures (Mount Rushmore, skyscrapers, suspension bridges, etc.).

Answers
Answers will vary for inductive question.

ÁLBUM CULTURAL

En muchas partes del mundo se encuentran fenómenos inexplicables, como las ruinas de Machu Picchu o el monstruo de Loch Ness. Diferentes civilizaciones han tratado de explicar algunos fenómenos usando mitos y leyendas. Y tú, ¿qué fenómenos inexplicables conoces?

Tula, en la zona central de México, fue la capital de la civilización tolteca durante el período posclásico, entre los años 950 a 1150 d.C. Estas columnas, que representan guerreros, son conocidas como los Atlantes, y se encuentran en la pirámide principal. La luz del atardecer los hace parecer vivos y ha dado lugar *(has given rise)* a la leyenda de que caminan por las noches.

268   Capítulo 8

Options

Strategies for Reaching All Students

Spanish-Speaking Students
Ask: *¿Qué otros misterios incluirías entre estas fotos? ¿Por qué?*

Students Needing Extra Help
Ask students to take notes for use in the *¿Lo sabes bien?* section at the end of the chapter.

Multiple Intelligences
Visual/Spatial and Logical/Mathematical
See Critical Thinking.

Cultural Notes ☼

(p. 268, photo)
The Toltecs had the next great civilization in Mexico after the fall of the Mayas and Zapotecs around A.D. 900. They established their capital at Tula, north of present-day Mexico City. The Toltecs worshipped the feathered serpent god Quetzalcóatl. Their dominance lasted only until around 1200, when they were invaded by nomadic tribes, including the Aztecs. The reclining warrior god Chac Mool, found in ruins throughout Mexico and Central America, dates to the Toltecs.

Estas esferas de piedra perfectamente redondas deben pesar varias toneladas. No se sabe nada de su origen. Se cree que fueron hechas por los indígenas de Costa Rica.

En las ruinas de Monte Albán, centro de la civilización zapoteca, en Oaxaca, México, se encuentran estas figuras de piedra en el Templo de los Danzantes. Las más antiguas son del año 300 a.C. Nadie sabe qué significan estas figuras deformes. Tampoco se sabe por qué los habitantes de Monte Albán abandonaron la ciudad alrededor del año 800 d.C.

Ask students: A winged serpent is an unusual image. In mythology and religion, are there other examples of earthbound creatures that can fly? (dragons, Cupid, angels)

(p. 269, top photo)
Perfectly round, smoothly finished stones such as this one have been found in Costa Rica, the product of indigenous sculptors. Made from granite, they range in size from a few inches to seven feet in diameter and were placed in specific rows and groupings. Similar stone spheres have been found in Los Alamos, New Mexico, and in Jalisco, Mexico, but they were proven to be naturally formed.

(p. 269, bottom photo)
Built around 500 B.C. near the present-day city of Oaxaca, Mexico, the so-called *danzantes* monument shown in this photo is believed to include one of the earliest examples of writing in the Americas. Although anthropologists and linguists initially tended to dismiss ancient American cultures as pre-literate or even illiterate, more recent scholarship has shown that their writing systems were sophisticated means for conveying certain kinds of ideas and information—not unlike road signs, maps, scientific notation, and musical scores in our own culture.

Present & Apply

Answers: Reacción personal
1–3 Answers will vary.

www Internet Activities
Álbum cultural

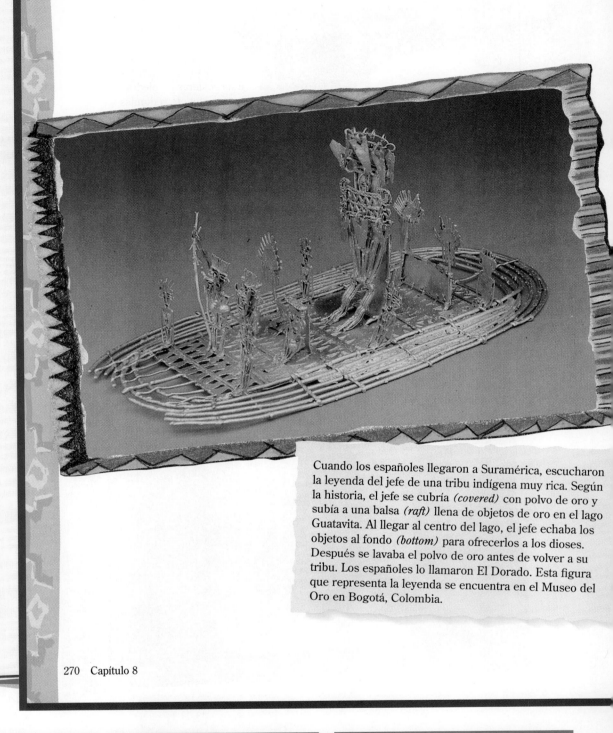

Cuando los españoles llegaron a Suramérica, escucharon la leyenda del jefe de una tribu indígena muy rica. Según la historia, el jefe se cubría *(covered)* con polvo de oro y subía a una balsa *(raft)* llena de objetos de oro en el lago Guatavita. Al llegar al centro del lago, el jefe echaba los objetos al fondo *(bottom)* para ofrecerlos a los dioses. Después se lavaba el polvo de oro antes de volver a su tribu. Los españoles lo llamaron El Dorado. Esta figura que representa la leyenda se encuentra en el Museo del Oro en Bogotá, Colombia.

270   Capítulo 8

Options

Strategies for Reaching All Students

Students Needing Extra Help
Reacción personal: Have materials regarding this subject available.
Ex. 2: Students may have difficulty formulating a theory. You may wish to offer a model so that they can see which grammar structures are needed to express their thoughts. Brainstorm a list of possible phrases that students can use in their sentences.

Multiple Intelligences
Intrapersonal/Introspective
See Exs. 1–3.

Cultural Notes ☀

(p. 270, photo)
The legend of El Dorado has come to be thought of as referring to the kingdom of gold and jewels long sought by Spanish explorers in the perilous terrain of South America. In the original ritual of the Chibcha Indians of Colombia, however, El Dorado

Reacción personal

Contesta las siguientes preguntas en una hoja de papel.

1 Describe algo que hayas oído o leído sobre un fenómeno inexplicable. ¿Dónde lo oíste o leíste?

2 De los fenómenos inexplicables que se describen en las páginas 268–271, ¿cuál te parece más interesante? Crea tu propia teoría para explicar ese fenómeno.

3 ¿Qué leyenda conoces? ¿De dónde es? Explícasela a un(a) compañero(a).

La leyenda es un tipo de literatura que habla de las tradiciones y la mitología de diferentes pueblos *(peoples)*. Muchas de ellas cuentan *(tell)* fenómenos inexplicables. Los libros de esta página incluyen leyendas de España, cuentos indígenas e historias del período colonial, y nos enseñan el rico legado cultural de los países hispanos.

was their chief, who once a year was dusted from head to toe with powdered gold and rowed out to the center of Lake Guatavita. The chief would then dive into the water, leaving the gold dust from his body, as well as a gold and emerald mask he wore, as offerings to the goddess of the lake.

(p. 271, photo)
The legends and myths of ancient civilizations have inspired some of the world's great writers. American author Washington Irving (1783–1859) lived in Spain for several years. Fascinated by the legends of Granada and the Moors, he wrote *Leyendas de la Alhambra.* Mexican writer Ermilio Abreu Gómez (1894–1971) turned to legends from his own country for his material in *Leyendas y consejas del antiguo Yucatán,* as did Guatemalan author and winner of the 1967 Nobel Prize Miguel Ángel Asturias (1899–1974) in *Leyendas de Guatemala.*

Preview

Gramática en contexto

Mira este anuncio sobre la Isla de Pascua. ¿Qué tipo de fenómeno inexplicable se encuentra allí?

A los que visitan nuestra isla por primera vez siempre les parece difícil creer lo que ven sus ojos. No dudan que algunas de estas cabezas enormes pesan hasta 90 toneladas. Pero lo misterioso es que nadie sabe su origen. ¿Es posible que las esculturas representen alguna construcción religiosa o que estén en estas colinas por razones astronómicas? Los científicos dudan que las hayan hecho los extraterrestres. Se duda también que los escultores hayan tenido poderes sobrenaturales; pero sí sabemos que conocían bien la ingeniería y la astronomía.

La misteriosa Isla de Pascua
¡Más de 500 esculturas gigantescas! Pero, ¿de dónde son? —y ¿cómo han llegado allí? ¡Visítenos! Estamos seguros de que Ud. se llevará un recuerdo inolvidable del misterio de la Isla de Pascua

¡Visítenos! Quizás Ud. encontrará la respuesta.
Póngase en contacto con el Servicio de Turismo de Chile, donde se ofrece toda la información necesaria sobre el viaje.

A The bottom, left paragraph of the ad says *Estamos seguros de que.* Does this express certainty or doubt? Is the verb that follows *que* in the indicative or the subjunctive? What form of *ser* would you use in this sentence: *No estoy segura de que la estatua . . . de piedra?*

B In the ad the following expressions are used: *no dudan que, es posible que,* and *se duda también que.* Which of these express certainty? Which express doubt? Can you explain to a partner when to use the subjunctive and when to use the indicative with these expressions?

C The ad says *los científicos dudan que las hayan hecho los extraterrestres* and *sabemos que conocían.* Do these statements refer to present or past situations? In which sentence is *que* followed by the subjunctive? Is this consistent with the explanation you gave in B?

272   Capítulo 8

Options

Strategies for Reaching All Students

El subjuntivo con expresiones de duda

We have been using the subjunctive in statements in which a person tells someone else to do something. We also use the subjunctive after verbs and expressions that indicate doubt or uncertainty.

> Mi mamá **duda que** los extraterrestres **existan**.
> **Es posible que** los científicos **tengan** otra teoría.
> **Es improbable que** los extraterrestres **se comuniquen** con nosotros.

• Other expressions that indicate doubt or uncertainty are:

no creer que	es probable que
no estar seguro(a) de que	no es cierto que
es imposible que	es increíble que

• When the expression indicates certainty, we use the indicative, not the subjunctive.

> **Estamos seguros de que** eso **puede** explicarse.
> **Creo que** la estatua **mide** diez metros de alto.
> **Es cierto que** los dibujos **son** geométricos.

Piedra funeral indígena en el Museo de Arqueología, San José, Costa Rica

Gramática en contexto   273

Present

Class Starter Review

On the day following the presentation of the subjunctive with expressions of doubt, you might want to begin the class with this activity:
State one of the expressions of doubt presented in the text *(dudo que . . . , es imposible que . . . ,* etc.). Then point to a student and have him or her finish the sentence using the present subjunctive. He or she will then state another expression of doubt and point to the next student, and so on. Continue until everyone has had a turn.

Cultural Notes ☀️

Multiple Intelligences
Verbal/Linguistic
See Class Starter Review.
Visual/Spatial
See Enrichment.

(p. 272, photo)
Easter Island, or Isla de Pascua, was so named by the Dutch explorer Jacob Roggeveen, who landed there on Easter Sunday, 1722. To its Polynesian natives the remote island is *Rapa Nui,* or "Navel of the World." The population today numbers about 2,000, up considerably from the 111 counted in 1871.

(p. 273, photo)
One of Latin America's most cosmopolitan cities, the Costa Rican capital of San José offers three dozen museums, several of which feature fine collections of pre-Columbian art and artifacts such as the massive stone sphere shown here.

Present & Practice

Re-enter / Recycle
Ex. 1: archaeology from Chap. 5

Answers

1 a. *(certainty)* conocen

b. *(doubt)* existan

c. *(certainty)* estudian

d. *(certainty)* hay

e. *(uncertainty)* descubran

f. *(doubt)* se construyan

2 Statements will vary. Look for correct use of the subjunctive and indicative.

 Practice Wkbk. 8-5, 8-6

 Writing Activity 8-D

 Prueba 8-5

 Comm. Act. BLM 8-2

1 Lee las frases siguientes. Primero decide si vas a usar el indicativo o el subjuntivo y explica por qué. Luego, completa las frases con la forma correcta del verbo en paréntesis.

a. Creo que los arqueólogos (conocer) el origen de estas esculturas.

b. Los científicos dudan que (existir) extraterrestres.

c. Estoy seguro(a) de que los geólogos (estudiar) la composición de estas piedras.

d. Es cierto que (haber) fenómenos inexplicables.

e. Es posible que los arqueólogos (descubrir) otras ciudades escondidas.

f. Dudo que (construirse) más pirámides.

2 Trabaja con un(a) compañero(a) para formar frases completas con elementos de las tres columnas.

Creo que las líneas de Nazca representan un calendario.

o: No creo que las líneas de Nazca representen un calendario.

(no) Dudar que	los científicos	descubrir más cabezas enormes
Es (im)posible que	la piedra	
Es (im)probable que	el dibujo	medir dos metros de diámetro
(no) Creer que	las líneas de Nazca	
(no) Estar seguro (a) de que	los arqueólogos	pesar dos toneladas
(no) Es cierto que		representar un calendario
		trazar las líneas

Estudiando una cabeza olmeca en el Museo Nacional de Antropología de México

274   Capítulo 8

Options

Strategies for Reaching All Students

Students Needing Extra Help

El subjuntivo: Verbos irregulares: Give additional examples of regular and stem-changing verbs in the subjunctive. Write out the complete paradigms on the chalkboard. Review the list of stem-changing verbs in the subjunctive from Chap. 7. Write out a complete paradigm of all those listed, high-

lighting the changes with colored chalk or pens. Emphasize and drill these forms daily. Present a complete paradigm of *seguir* in the present subjunctive. Point out that if students know the *yo* form of the irregular verbs and of the *e → i* stem-changing verbs, they can do the whole paradigm.

Extended Written Practice/Homework

1. Write three sentences telling what you hope or doubt will continue to happen: *Dudo que sigan cultivando maíz en los campos cerca de esta ciudad.*

2. Choose expressions from p. 273 and verbs from p. 275 and write four sentences expressing your doubts or uncertainty: *Es improbable que vayamos de vacaciones este verano.*

El subjuntivo: Verbos irregulares

Remember that in the present subjunctive, -*ar* and -*er* stem-changing verbs have the stem change in all forms except the *nosotros* and *vosotros* forms. For example:

mover

que m**ue**va	que movamos
que m**ue**vas	que mováis
que m**ue**va	que m**ue**van

- -*Ir* stem-changing verbs have a stem change in *all* of their present subjunctive forms. Here are the present subjunctive forms of *mentir, dormir,* and *medir.*

mentir   **dormir**   **medir**

que m**ie**nta	que m**i**ntamos	que d**ue**rma	que d**u**rmamos	que m**i**da	que m**i**damos
que m**ie**ntas	que m**i**ntáis	que d**ue**rmas	que d**u**rmáis	que m**i**das	que m**i**dáis
que m**ie**nta	que m**ie**ntan	que d**ue**rma	que d**ue**rman	que m**i**da	que m**i**dan

- Other -*ir* stem-changing verbs you know that follow these patterns are:

  e → i: despedirse, pedir, reírse, seguir, servir, vestirse
  e → ie: divertirse, hervir, preferir, sentirse

- The following verbs are irregular in all their present subjunctive forms:

dar   **estar**   **haber**

que **dé**	que **demos**	que **esté**	que **estemos**	que **haya**	que **hayamos**
que **des**	que **deis**	que **estés**	que **estéis**	que **hayas**	que **hayáis**
que **dé**	que **den**	que **esté**	que **estén**	que **haya**	que **hayan**

ir   **saber**   **ser**

que **vaya**	que **vayamos**	que **sepa**	que **sepamos**	que **sea**	que **seamos**
que **vayas**	que **vayáis**	que **sepas**	que **sepáis**	que **seas**	que **seáis**
que **vaya**	que **vayan**	que **sepa**	que **sepan**	que **sea**	que **sean**

Gramática en contexto   275

Cultural Notes

Multiple Intelligences
Interpersonal/Social
See Ex. 2.
Visual/Spatial
See Ex. 1, Practice Wkbk. 8-5 and 8-6, Writing Activity 8-D, and Comm. Act. BLM 8-2.
Visual/Spatial and Verbal/Linguistic
See Class Starter Review.

(p. 274, photo)
This colossal stone head at Mexico's Museo Nacional de Antropología is an example of the distinctive sculpting style of the Olmecs, the first Mesoamerican people to work with large blocks of stone. They carved huge, helmeted heads with high foreheads, flaring nostrils, and thick, down-turned lips. The Museo Nacional de Antropología, opened in 1964, contains 23 exhibition halls packed with treasures from Mexico's ancient and current cultures.

Present & Practice

Answers

3 a. Quieren que hagamos un dibujo de los animales de la región.
b. Quieren que midamos el alto de los árboles.
c. Quieren que calculemos la distancia al río.
d. Quieren que pesemos las piedras.
e. Statements will vary.

4 ESTUDIANTE A
a. Dice que se siente mal.
b. Nunca sabe cuáles son las tareas.
c. No hace el trabajo que el (la) profesor(a) le da.
d. No recuerda nada sobre el arte de los olmecas.
e. Tiene mucho sueño en la clase.
f. Tiene un examen mañana.
g. Debe hablar con el profesor.
h. Llega tarde a clase.

ESTUDIANTE B
Answers may vary, but should contain the subjunctive.
a. ...vaya a la enfermería.
b. ...le haga caso al (a la) profesor(a).
c. ...sea más responsable.
d. ...pida información en la biblioteca.
e. ...duerma más por la noche.
f. ...esté tranquilo(a).
g. ...sepa dónde está su oficina.
h. ...dé una excusa al (a la) profesor(a).

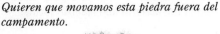
¿Cómo se explica . . . ?

3 Imagina que tú y tu compañero(a) reciben instrucciones. Trabajen para formar frases lógicas.

mover esta piedra

Quieren que movamos esta piedra fuera del campamento.

a. hacer un dibujo de los animales de la región

b. medir el alto de los árboles

c. calcular la distancia al río

d. pesar las piedras

e.

4 Un(a) amigo(a) tiene problemas en su clase de español. Trabaja con un(a) compañero(a) para sugerirle qué puede hacer. Usen las expresiones que siguen.

Le sugiero que   Es importante que
Le recomiendo que   Es necesario que
Espero que   Es mejor que

no entender   A — *(nombre) no entiende cómo hacer las actividades.*
cómo hacer las   B — *Le recomiendo que siga las instrucciones.*
actividades

Estudiante A

a. decir que se siente mal
b. nunca saber cuáles son las tareas
c. no hacer el trabajo que el (la) profesor(a) le da
d. no recordar nada sobre el arte de los olmecas
e. tener mucho sueño en la clase
f. tener un examen mañana
g. deber hablar con el profesor
h. llegar tarde a clase

Estudiante B

(dormir) más por la noche
(ir) a la enfermería
(estar) tranquilo(a)
(pedir) información en la biblioteca
(dar) una excusa al (a la) profesor(a)
(ser) más responsable
(saber) dónde está su oficina
(hacerle) caso al (a la) profesor(a)

276   Capítulo 8

Options

Strategies for Reaching All Students

Students Needing Extra Help
Ex. 4: Be sure that students are aware that the right-hand list uses the subjunctive. *El presente perfecto del subjuntivo:* Review formation of past participles. Refer to the Chap. 4 Organizer. Write a separate paradigm for *mover*.

Enrichment
Ex. 4: Ask students to redo this exercise making recommendations (when appropriate) about what *not* to do in each situation or making alternative recommendations about what to do.

Extended Written Practice/Homework
1. Write three sentences saying what you hope or doubt has happened: *Espero que mi profesor de español ya haya leído mi composición.*
2. Write three sentences expressing your beliefs, doubts, and uncertainties about different extraordinary phenomena: *Es posible que unos extraterrestres hayan creado las cabezas grandes en la Isla de Pascua.*

El presente perfecto del subjuntivo

When we want to express our hopes, doubts, disbelief, or uncertainty about actions **in the past**, we use the present-perfect subjunctive. We form it by using the present subjunctive of *haber* + past participle. Here are all the present perfect subjunctive forms of *trazar*.

trazar

que **haya** trazado	que **hayamos** trazado
que **hayas** trazado	que **hayáis** trazado
que **haya** trazado	que **hayan** trazado

Dudo que los extraterrestres **hayan trazado** las líneas de Nazca.
Esperamos que hayan movido la piedra.

* Remember to put negative words and object or reflexive pronouns before the form of *haber:*

Mariana iba a escribir una carta pero no creo que **lo haya hecho**.
Dudo que **nunca hayan visto** una película de terror.
Mario no habló con nosotros. Es posible que **se haya enojado**.

La noche del cometa (1992),
Roberto Márquez

 Practice Wkbk. 8-7, 8-8

 Writing Activity 8-E

¿? Prueba 8-6

Class Starter Review
On the day following the presentation of the present perfect subjunctive, you might want to begin the class with this activity:
Using the present perfect subjunctive, ask students to create sentences in which they doubt or disbelieve something of their classmates. For example: *Dudo que María haya comido tamales azules.* Call on individuals to read their sentences. Then, as a review of the present perfect tense, ask the student in question to respond: *María, ¿has comido alguna vez tamales azules?* As an extension activity, have other students ask the follow-up questions.

Cultural Notes ☀

Multiple Intelligences
Verbal/Linguistic
See Exs. 3–4.
Visual/Spatial
1) Have students write a paragraph describing or analyzing the painting on p. 277.
2) See Practice Wkbk. 8-7 and 8-8 and Writing Activity 8-E.
Visual/Spatial and Verbal/Linguistic
See Class Starter Review.

(p. 277, photo)
This dreamlike, compelling painting by artist Roberto Márquez (b. 1959), is an example of the highly individualistic art being produced in Mexico today. Art critic Teresa del Conde has noted the variety and uniqueness of recent Mexican painting, with some artists revisiting the baroque style and others using imagery from Mexico's ancient cultures as they develop their own innovative styles.

Practice

Answers

5 Statements will vary, but all the expressions should be followed by the present perfect subjunctive.

a. ...mis hijos hayan ido al supermercado.

b. ...mi hijo mayor haya hecho la cama.

c. ...mi hija haya pasado la aspiradora.

d. ...mi hijo menor haya sacudido los muebles.

e. ...todos hayan hecho ejercicio.

f. ...mi hija y mi hijo mayor hayan sacado la basura.

g. Statements will vary.

5 Imagina que tu padre o madre regresa a casa después de hacer un viaje. Forma frases para decir lo que él o ella está pensando. Usa las expresiones de la lista.

Dudo que	Espero que
No creo que	Es posible que

Espero que mi hija haya lavado los platos todos los días.

mi hija

| a. mis hijos | b. mi hijo mayor | c. mi hija |

| d. mi hijo menor | e. todos | f. mi hija y mi hijo mayor | g. |

278   Capítulo 8

Options

Strategies for Reaching All Students

Students Needing Extra Help
Ahora lo sabes: Have students write this so that they can record their progress.

Multiple Intelligences
Verbal/Linguistic
See Audio Activities 8.3, 8.4, and 8.5.
Verbal/Linguistic and Bodily/Kinesthetic
Using the drawings in items a.–f. in Ex. 5, have groups of students write dialogues and present them to the class.
Verbal/Linguistic and Visual/Spatial
See Ex. 5.
Visual/Spatial
See Practice Wkbk. 8-9, Writing Activity 8-F, and Comm. Act. BLM 8-3.

6 Algunos(as) de tus amigos(as) no recuerdan muy bien las cosas que tienen que hacer. Forma frases según el modelo.

Roberto iba a alquilar un video pero no creo que lo haya alquilado todavía.

Roberto / alquilar

a. Andrea y tú / escribir

b. Manuel y Raúl / depositar

c. Ud. / comprar

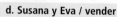

d. Susana y Eva / vender

e. tú / devolver

f.

Ahora lo sabes

¿Puedes:

■ hablar sobre algo de lo que estás seguro(a)?
  —Estoy seguro(a) de que ___ muchas cosas misteriosas en el mundo.

■ hablar sobre algo de lo que dudas o no estás seguro(a)?
  —Dudamos que la teoría ___ verdadera.

■ decir lo que esperas o dudas que haya ocurrido?
  —Es posible que los habitantes ___ las pirámides para estar más cerca de sus dioses.

MÁS PRÁCTICA

• Más práctica y tarea, pp. 569–570
• Practice Workbook 8–5, 8–9

Gramática en contexto   279

Apply

Point out the key chapter question. Remind students that completing these activities will help them answer it. You may select one, two, or all three of these activities, as time permits.

Answers: Sopa de actividades
1–3 Responses will vary.

¿Cómo se explica...?

Esta sección te ofrece la oportunidad de combinar lo que aprendiste en este capítulo con lo que ya sabes para responder a la pregunta clave.

Para decir más

Aquí tienes vocabulario adicional que te puede ayudar para hacer las actividades de esta sección.

el universo
universe

el marciano, la marciana
Martian

el platillo volador
flying saucer

el O.V.N.I. (Objeto volador no identificado)
UFO

el rastro
trace, trail

la aparición
apparition, appearance

el rayo
ray

centellear
to sparkle, to flicker

emitir
to emit

la señal
signal

280 Capítulo 8

Sopa de actividades

1. En grupos de cuatro o cinco van a investigar uno de los misterios que estudiaron en este capítulo u otros fenómenos inexplicables, como el monstruo de Loch Ness o el triángulo de las Bermudas. Deben:

- investigar los datos específicos (fecha, lugar, características) en periódicos, revistas o libros
- describir las teorías populares sobre ese misterio
- incluir las explicaciones científicas para él
- dar la opinión que ustedes tienen sobre ese misterio
- presentar sus conclusiones a la clase

Para la presentación pueden usar fotos de periódicos, libros o revistas sobre el misterio.

El monstruo de
Loch Ness

Options

Strategies for Reaching All Students

Spanish-Speaking Students
Ex. 2: Instead of this exercise, tell students: *Estudia la tabla que ha hecho cada grupo. Prepara un artículo periodístico sobre los misterios extraordinarios que se conocen en la comunidad. Incluye un resumen de los misterios, los datos y las explicaciones. Revísalo y envíalo a un periódico o una revista que se publica en español.*

Students Needing Extra Help
If time is a factor, eliminate Ex. 3.
Ex. 1: Have research materials available, or reserve materials in the library.
Point out the specific guidelines given for this report.
Ex. 2: Remind students that they can ask the questions in English, but must record the answers in Spanish.
Ex. 3: Complete this exercise as a whole class, or assign students to the debate groups.

Enrichment
Ex. 1: Have students answer these questions in writing: *¿Cuál de estos misterios te gustaría más resolver? ¿Por qué?*

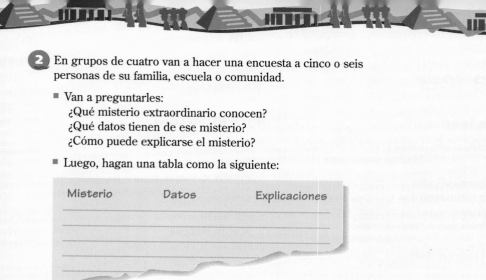

2 En grupos de cuatro van a hacer una encuesta a cinco o seis personas de su familia, escuela o comunidad.

- Van a preguntarles:
  ¿Qué misterio extraordinario conocen?
  ¿Qué datos tienen de ese misterio?
  ¿Cómo puede explicarse el misterio?

- Luego, hagan una tabla como la siguiente:

Misterio	Datos	Explicaciones

- Compartan sus resultados con los de la clase.

3 En grupos de cuatro o cinco van a hacer un debate sobre los "Misterios inexplicables del mundo." Cada grupo debe escoger un misterio. Puede ser uno de los misterios de este capítulo u otro que ustedes conozcan.

- Den tres razones por las que piensen que este misterio es inexplicable y tres que lo expliquen.
- En una tabla escriban un contraargumento o una explicación posible para cada una de ellas.
- Dos estudiantes de cada grupo deben emparejarse con dos estudiantes de otro grupo con un punto de vista diferente para discutir el tema.
- Compartan los resultados con su grupo y luego con la clase.

 Video Activity A

 Video, Capítulo 8

Chapter 8: Play

Step

 Video Activities B–C

 Writing Activities 8-G, 8-H

 Comm. Act. BLMs 8-4, 8-5

Cooperative Learning
Tell groups of four students to brainstorm things they may or may not have done in the past. Instruct groups to write a sentence expressing a real or fictitious accomplishment for each member of the group on butcher paper. Each item must use the person's name. Assign groups to comment on each other's lists, with each member expressing belief, doubt, or certainty about the stated fact.

Multiple Intelligences
Interpersonal/Social
See Cooperative Learning.
Interpersonal/Social and Logical/Mathematical
See Exs. 2–3.
Interpersonal/Social and Verbal/Linguistic
See Ex. 1.
Visual/Spatial
See Writing Activities 8-G and 8-H and Comm. Act. BLMs 8-4 and 8-5.

Apply

Process Reading
For a description of process reading, see p. 52.

Teaching Suggestions
Point out the key chapter question. Tell students that working through the *Para leer* section will help them answer this question.

Encourage students to use the strategies given in the text to help them understand the reading. Remind them that they do not need to understand every word.

Answers
Antes de leer
Answers will vary.

Mira la lectura
Most students would agree that the answer is item b.

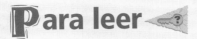

Antes de leer
STRATEGIES Using prior knowledge
Making predictions

¿Conoces algunos cuentos que expliquen un aspecto de la naturaleza? Por ejemplo, algunos cuentos explican cómo el mono llegó a tener una cola. Mira la foto de los volcanes Iztaccíhuatl y Popocatépetl. ¿Qué piensas que va a explicar este cuento?

Mira la lectura
STRATEGY Skimming

Lee el cuento rápidamente sólo para familiarizarte con él. Ahora, imagínate que es una película. ¿Qué tipo de película es?

a. película de terror
b. película de amor
c. película de ciencia ficción

El Iztaccíhuatl y el Popocatépetl

Hace mucho tiempo, en la gran ciudad de Teotihuacán, había un rey tolteca que tenía una hija muy hermosa. El pelo de la princesa era tan negro y suave como una noche de verano, sus ojos eran grandes y oscuros como las aguas de un lago secreto y su sonrisa era tan bonita que decían que el sol miraba por las montañas todas las mañanas para ser el primero en verla.

Muchos príncipes ricos y famosos venían de todas partes de la región tolteca para ganar el amor de la princesa, pero ella no se enamoraba de ninguno. El rey, que quería para su hija un esposo rico de buena posición en la sociedad tolteca, ya estaba impaciente. A veces le preguntaba a la princesa qué esperaba.

—No sé—contestaba la muchacha—. Sólo sé que mi esposo será alguien que amaré desde el principio y para siempre.

Un día llegó a la ciudad un príncipe chichimeca. Los chichimecas no tenían una civilización tan espléndida como la de los toltecas. Vivían de la caza y la pesca en las montañas. Los toltecas pensaban que los chichimecas vivían como

282 Capítulo 8

Options

Strategies for Reaching All Students

Students Needing Extra Help
Antes de leer: Encourage students to be creative in their responses.
Mira la lectura: Students may have difficulty with skimming a reading of this length. Encourage them to skim the text until they find the answer.
If students ask, help them with unknown words or expressions that may cause confusion. For example: *el principio* vs. *el príncipe.*

perros, y se reían de ellos.

El príncipe chichimeca venía para visitar el gran mercado de Teotihuacán, donde vendían hermosísimos objetos de oro, ropa de brillantes colores, animales exóticos y muchas otras cosas.

Ese mismo día, la princesa tolteca estaba en el mercado, comprando canastas, telas y alfombras para su palacio. Pasó que, de repente, entre toda la gente y el ruido del mercado, el príncipe y la princesa se fijaron uno en el otro. Sin una palabra, desde el principio y para siempre, el príncipe y la princesa se enamoraron.

Los dos sabían muy bien que su amor era prohibido. Cada uno debía casarse con alguien de su pueblo y su clase—la princesa tolteca con un príncipe tolteca y el príncipe chichimeca con una princesa chichimeca.

Las señoras que acompañaban a la princesa se dieron cuenta de lo que pasaba, y rápidamente llevaron a la princesa a su palacio. El príncipe también regresó al suyo en las montañas. Trató de olvidar a la bella princesa, pero no pudo.

Después de un tiempo, el príncipe decidió volver a Teotihuacán, a pedir la mano de la princesa. Un día se vistió de su ropa más fina y fue al palacio del rey tolteca. Allí mandó a

sus mensajeros a hablar con el rey para pedirle a su hija como esposa.

Cuando oyó las palabras de los mensajeros del príncipe, el rey tembló de furia y gritó: —¡Mi hija sólo se casará con un príncipe tolteca, nunca con un chichimeca que vive en las montañas como un animal!

El cráter del volcán Popocatépetl visto desde un avión

Para leer   283

 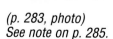
(p. 283, photo)
See note on p. 285.

Apply

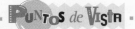

Answers
Infórmate
Summaries will vary, but students may mention:
Una princesa tolteca y un príncipe chichimeca se enamoraron. Cuando sus padres supieron que querían casarse, dijeron que los jóvenes tenían que vivir en las montañas. Poco a poco el príncipe y la princesa estaban muriéndose. Cada uno fue a una montaña diferente; la princesa a la montaña más baja, y el príncipe a la más alta. Allí se murieron, donde hoy hay ruidos desde una de las montañas. Se cree que es el príncipe llorando por su princesa.

Aplicación
Summaries and suggestions will vary.

Fondo literario
La herencia (pp. 468–475)

 **Internet Activities**

Los volcanes Popocatépetl e Iztaccíhuatl

Cuando la princesa oyó todo esto, se sintió muy triste. Le tenía mucho respeto a su papá, pero sabía que no podía vivir sin el amor del príncipe chichimeca. Salió de su palacio y se reunió con el príncipe para decirle que sí quería casarse con él. Se fueron a las montañas, y esa noche se casaron.

Al día siguiente, la princesa regresó a Teotihuacán y le dijo a su padre que ya era la esposa del príncipe chichimeca. Le pidió perdón y esperó la comprensión de su padre.

Pero el rey estaba furioso. —¿Cómo pudiste hacerme esto?—le preguntó a su hija—. ¡Vete de aquí y no vuelvas nunca! ¡Y no le pidas ni comida ni casa a ningún tolteca, que no te dará nada! ¡Lo prohíbo!

Lo mismo le pasó al príncipe cuando volvió a su palacio. Su padre le gritó—: ¿Te casaste con una tolteca? ¡Ya no eres mi hijo, ni eres chichimeca! ¡No esperes nunca la ayuda de ningún chichimeca!

Con el corazón muy triste, el príncipe y la princesa se reunieron y empezaron a buscar dónde vivir en las montañas. Nadie los quería ayudar o darles un lugar para descansar y refugiarse de los vientos fríos. Comían sólo hierbas y frutas, porque el príncipe no tenía nada con qué cazar o pescar. Poco a poco, los esposos se estaban muriendo.

Una noche muy fría y larga, el príncipe se dio cuenta de que pronto se iban a morir los dos. Estaban en un valle pequeño desde donde podían ver la gran ciudad de Teotihuacán. La princesa pensaba en su casa, y el príncipe la miraba con tristeza y amor, sabiendo lo que pensaba.

284   Capítulo 8

Options

Strategies for Reaching All Students

Students Needing Extra Help
Infórmate: If necessary, explain the term *los protagonistas.*
Aplicación: You may wish to have students create dialogues from the characters' thoughts and convert them into conversations for the play.

Multiple Intelligences
Visual/Spatial
See *Infórmate.*
Visual/Spatial and Bodily/Kinesthetic
Have students create a drawing, mural, or other type of art piece inspired by the story on pp. 282–285.

—Mi bella princesa—le dijo—, ya nos vamos a morir. Nos vamos a separar ahora en este mundo para estar juntos para siempre en el otro. Duerme por última vez en mis brazos esta noche. En la mañana, tú te irás a la montaña más baja que mira sobre tu ciudad, y yo me iré a la montaña más alta que también mira sobre tu ciudad. Allí descansaremos, allí te cuidaré para siempre y nuestros espíritus serán un solo espíritu.

Al día siguiente los dos se separaron, y cada uno empezó a subir su montaña. La princesa subió la montaña Iztaccíhuatl y el príncipe subió la montaña Popocatépetl. Cuando la princesa llegó a la cumbre de su montaña, se durmió y la nieve la cubrió. El príncipe se puso de rodillas, mirando hacia la princesa y la nieve también lo cubrió.

De esta manera podemos ver hoy al príncipe y a la princesa, en la cumbre del Iztaccíhuatl y el Popocatépetl. A veces hay grandes ruidos desde muy dentro del Popocatépetl. Es el príncipe llorando por su princesa.

Infórmate

STRATEGY ➤ Using graphic organizers

Lee el cuento con cuidado. Copia la gráfica organizadora de la derecha para ayudarte a entender el argumento. Lee el cuento y llena los espacios de la gráfica. Por ejemplo, en el primer espacio, escribe *los nombres* de los protagonistas. En el segundo, escribe lo que *querían* hacer. En el tercero, escribe *el resultado* de lo que querían hacer. De la misma manera, llena todos los espacios.

Cuando termines, escribe un resumen del cuento basado en la gráfica organizadora.

El argumento
alguien _____
quería _____
por eso _____
pero _____
por eso _____
al fin _____

Aplicación

Imagina que vas a adaptar el cuento para una obra de teatro. Divide el argumento en tres actos y escribe un resumen de cada uno. Sugiere algunos actores para los papeles principales. ¿Qué música vas a incluir?

Cultural Notes ☀

(p. 284, photo)
According to ancient Mexican Indian legends, the two snow-covered volcanoes near Mexico City, Iztaccíhuatl and Popocatépetl, are actually tragic human lovers. They were transformed into these majestic natural formations by the greatness of their love and fidelity to one another. There are many variations of the story of the couple's forbidden love, but all end with Prince Popocatépetl, as the taller peak, keeping eternal watch over Princess Itzaccíhuatl, the lower peak.

Ask students: The names *Popocatépetl* and *Iztaccíhuatl* are *náhuatl* words meaning "smoking mountain" and "sleeping woman." Are there any places with Native American names in your area? What do they mean?

Apply

Teaching Suggestions

Remind students that working through the *Para escribir* section will help them answer the key chapter question.

Process Writing

For information regarding writing portfolios, see p. 54.

Answers

Stories will vary.

Para escribir

Desde que éramos pequeños, todos nosotros hemos conocido eventos o cosas que no se pueden explicar. En este capítulo has visto algunos fenómenos inexplicables. Ahora tendrás la oportunidad de usar tu imaginación para hablar sobre algo misterioso o fantástico.

1 Primero, decide si vas a contar una historia real o si vas a inventar un misterio. Piensa en:

- la situación
- los personajes (reales o fantásticos)
- el lugar
- la época

2 Escribe una versión corta de tu historia.

Puedes usar algunas de estas palabras u otras.

a pesar de que	aunque	hasta ahora
además	en seguida	por eso
antes	entonces	sin embargo

Si escribes sobre algo que has oído, no te olvides de decir quién te lo dijo. Trata de mantener el suspense de la historia. No expliques el misterio hasta el final.

Luego, da tu propia explicación de cómo crees que ocurre u ocurrió el fenómeno. Si quieres, puedes ilustrar tu versión final.

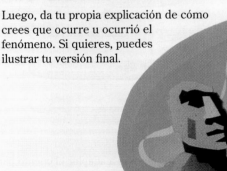

Options

Strategies for Reaching All Students

Students Needing Extra Help

Step 1: Model a suspenseful story. Divide students into two large groups, according to their story preference. Have each group brainstorm possible storylines.

Step 2: Give students a specific number of sentences to write. Review the suggested expressions. Repeat the story you told at the beginning of the activity. Ask which words or expressions helped create a feeling of suspense. Be sure students understand that after they have told the story, they need to write an explanation of the event.

3 Consulta con un(a) compañero(a) para revisar tu trabajo. Sigue los pasos del proceso de escribir.

Para compartir tu trabajo, puedes:

- incluirlo en un libro llamado *Misterios*
- exhibirlo en la sala de clases
- ponerlo en tu portafolio

Para escribir   287

Answers
Listening
—*Hoy en la clase de historia vimos un video de fenómenos inexplicables. ¿Has visto alguna vez las gigantescas cabezas de la civilización olmeca?*

—*Sí, en un video en la clase de español. Vimos una que pesa más de quince toneladas. Es increíble porque no había piedras donde vivían los olmecas. Tuvieron que traerlas de otro lugar, y sin usar la rueda.*

—*También vimos las figuras geométricas y misteriosas de las líneas de Nazca. Hay enormes dibujos de una araña y un mono en el desierto del Perú. Lo misterioso es que algunas figuras miden hasta ochocientos metros de largo y cien metros de ancho.*

—*Creo que hemos visto el mismo video.*

Answers will vary, but students may mention:
Los dos estudiantes hablan de las gigantescas cabezas olmecas y las figuras de los nazcas. Parecen increíbles porque las cabezas son

Esta sección te ayudará a prepararte para el examen de habilidades, donde tendrás que hacer tareas semejantes.

Listening
¿Puedes entender una conversación sobre fenómenos inexplicables? Escucha mientras el(la) profesor(a) lee un ejemplo semejante al que vas a oír en el examen. ¿Puedes describir los fenómenos de los que hablan estos estudiantes? ¿Por qué parecen increíbles?

Reading
Lee este artículo de una revista científica. Haz una gráfica organizadora con esta información: Según el artículo, ¿qué es el *Ulama*? ¿Dónde se han encontrado campos de este juego? ¿Con qué creen que se relacionaba el *Ulama*?

Aunque no se haya resuelto completamente el misterio del *Ulama,* los arqueólogos siguen descubriendo evidencia sobre este extraño juego de pelota que se practicaba en México y Centroamérica desde hace más de dos mil años. Los jugadores usaban una pelota de látex del tamaño de una pelota de fútbol. Estudios de esculturas, cerámica y murales indican que el juego tenía un significado religioso y que probablemente se relacionaba con la siembra y la cosecha. Hasta ahora los arqueólogos han encontrado 1,200 campos de juego de *Ulama* en México, las Antillas, Centroamérica y el sur de los Estados Unidos.

Writing
Escribe un artículo breve como el que escribió Carmela.

Aunque parece improbable que los O.V.N.I. u objetos voladores no identificados existan, a veces aparecen en los periódicos noticias de fenómenos increíbles. En Perú, unos campesinos vieron unos objetos voladores pequeños y luminosos. En los Estados Unidos alguien sacó fotos de unas naves espaciales ovaladas de seis metros de diámetro. En las Islas Canarias, una persona creyó ver una luz que se movía sobre su casa. ¿Cómo se explican estos fenómenos? Una organización que investiga la existencia de los O.V.N.I. informa que menos del ocho por ciento de los objetos que la gente ve son reales.

Culture
¿Puedes describir algunos fenómenos inexplicables de la época precolombina?

Speaking
Habla con otra persona sobre la posibilidad de fenómenos misteriosos.

A —*Oí que una nave espacial apareció en el desierto de Arizona.*

B —*¿Qué dices? ¡Me parece imposible!*

A —*A mí también me parece increíble, pero dicen que descubrieron las huellas de los extraterrestres que llegaron en la nave.*

B —*¡Qué va! Tiene que ser una noticia falsa, porque...*

www.pasoapaso.com

288 Capítulo 8

Strategies for Reaching All Students

Students Needing Extra Help
Have students write this exercise so that they can check off what they have mastered. Remind students that this is just a sample of what the test will be like.
Listening: Read more than once. Inform students that two phenomena will be described.
To help answer the questions, tell them to listen for descriptive words and opinions. Review the chapter vocabulary and reread the *Tema para investigar,* if necessary.

Reading: Remind students they don't need to know every word in the reading.
Writing: You may wish to have materials ready beforehand that deal with UFOs. Have students use the Organizer and write a brief sample article before the test. Refer them to the *Sopa de actividades* for ideas. Be specific about the amount of information that you expect to be included in the article. If students are having difficulty, create a sample as a class and point out essential grammar structures to be used.

Culture: Have students review the notes they took when they read the *Álbum cultural.*
Speaking: Have students use the vocabulary section of the Organizer. Complete the model and limit the number of lines of dialogue.

Resumen del vocabulario

Usa el vocabulario de este capítulo para:

- responder a la pregunta clave: ¿Cómo se explica . . . ?
- identificar y describir algunos fenómenos extraordinarios
- dar tu opinión sobre esos fenómenos
- indicar si estás seguro(a) o si dudas de algo

para identificar fenómenos extraordinarios
aparecer *(c → zc)*
desconocido, -a
encantado, -a
enorme
extraño, -a
extraordinario, -a
el fantasma
el fenómeno
gigantesco, -a
la huella
inexplicable
la leyenda
el misterio
misterioso, -a
el mito
la nave espacial
la teoría
el Yeti

para describir objetos
el alto
el ancho
calcular
el centímetro
el diámetro

el diseño
geométrico, -a
el largo
medir *(e → i)*
    de alto
    de ancho
    de diámetro
    de largo
mover *(o → ue)*
ovalado, -a
pertenecer *(c → zc)*
pesar
el peso
servir *(e → i)* para
    ¿Para qué sirve?
la tonelada

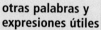

para dar tu opinión
la afirmación
afirmar
cierto, -a
los datos
estar seguro, -a
la evidencia
haya resuelto
    (*from:* resolver)
la prueba
suponer: (yo) supongo
    (tú) supones

para indicar si dudas de algo
la duda
dudar
falso, -a
imposible
improbable
increíble
posible
probable

otras palabras y expresiones útiles
a pesar de (que)
el creador, la creadora
el desierto
el geólogo, la geóloga
el /la habitante
el mono
la piedra
la rueda
trazar *(z → c)*
volar *(o → ue)*

Resumen 289

---

muy grandes y no había piedras donde vivían los olmecas. También algunas figuras nazcas son enormes.

Reading
El *Ulama* era un juego de pelota que se practicaba en México y América Central. / Se han encontrado campos de este juego en México, las Antillas, América Central y el sur de los Estados Unidos. / Creen que el *Ulama* se relacionaba con la siembra y la cosecha.

Writing
Articles will vary.

Culture
Answers will vary, but students may include descriptions of *las líneas de Nazca* and *las cabezas olmecas.*

Speaking
Dialogues will vary.

Assessment

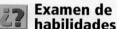 **Prueba cumulativa**

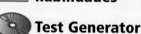 **Examen de habilidades**

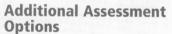 **Test Generator**

Additional Assessment Options

 Comm. Act. BLMs

Small Group Activities
Situation Cards

(continued from above)

 ¿Lo sabes bien? Video Quiz

Internet Activities
Self-Test

CAPÍTULO 9

THEME: THE WORKFORCE

SCOPE AND SEQUENCE Pages 290–323

COMMUNICATION

Topics

Types of employment

Job qualifications

The job search

Objectives

Hablar sobre cómo ha cambiado el mundo del trabajo en los países de habla hispana

Hablar de distintos trabajos

Describir las cualidades necesarias para un trabajo

Explicar los requisitos de un trabajo

Buscar y conseguir trabajo

CULTURE

El mundo del trabajo en los países de habla hispana

GRAMMAR

Repaso: Mandatos afirmativos y negativos con tú

El subjuntivo en cláusulas adjetivas

El subjuntivo con cuando

Ancillaries available for use with Chapter 9

Multisensory/Technology

 Overheads, 27–29

 Audio Tapes and CDs

 Vocabulary Art Blackline Masters for Hands-On Learning, pp. 42–45/CD-ROM

 Classroom Crossword

 Video

 Internet Activities www.pasoapaso.com

Print

 Practice Workbook, pp. 91–100

 Writing, Audio & Video Activities, pp. 53–58, 117–119, 149–150

 Communicative Activity Blackline Masters

  Pair and Small Group Activities, pp. 57–62

  Situation Cards, p. 63

 RESOURCE PRO®

Planning Express, Teaching Resources Library, and Clip Art Library

Assessment

 Assessment Program

  Pruebas, pp. 125–134

  Examen de habilidades, pp. 135–138

Test Generator

¿Lo sabes bien? Video Quiz

Video, Chap. 9

The Latin American Job Market

Until comparatively recently, most individuals worked at one job for their entire lifetime. Many families held a common occupation, with every family member contributing in some way to the family business. Young people usually received their career training through apprenticeships with their parents, or with townspeople who could teach them other skills that helped them increase their occupational knowledge.

In recent decades, an increasing number of workers have been affected by major shifts in the kind of employment they hold during their lifetime. Often, the new career directions that people take are made possible only through further education. The kind of education we receive today is crucial to our ability to adapt to the shifting opportunities in the job market.

The amount of education that a person receives usually determines his or her employment opportunities. College graduates generally earn more than those without a college degree. In fact, in the U.S., people with a bachelor's degree earn nearly twice as much as those who do not have formal education beyond high school, according to a study by the U.S. Department of Commerce.

The relationship between education and employment is as true in Latin America as it is in the U.S. Many young people in Latin America compete to obtain an advanced education, hoping for improved opportunities in the job market. The economies of most Latin American nations, however, tend to offer more limited opportunities for success than the U.S.

After a period of apparent strength and stability, in early 1995 the Mexican *peso* suffered a sharp devaluation in comparison with other world currencies. This meant that the average Mexican faced sharply higher prices for imported goods and even for domestic products. Businesses found it difficult to borrow money to pay for raw materials, expansion, and the creation of jobs. The crash of the *peso* had a chilling effect on the nation's short-term economic future.

The underlying causes of the weaker Latin American economies are complicated, and vary from nation to nation. Inflation is a common problem, with the prices of even basic food items climbing significantly upward each year. Unemployment is often high, and the phenomenon of "underemployment" is widespread. Underemployed people are able to find work, but the work is sporadic or amounts to only a few hours each day. Full-time, year-round employment can be more difficult to find.

In recent years, Latin American nations have taken steps to create more jobs. A highly visible example of this is Mexico's entry into the North American Free Trade Agreement (NAFTA) with the U.S. and Canada. Other countries, such as Chile, have experimented with far-ranging plans to loosen government restrictions on businesses in an attempt to stimulate their economies.

Introduce

Re-entry of Concepts
The following list represents words, expressions, and grammar topics re-entered from Books 1, 2, and 3 (Chaps. 4 and 8):

Book 1
calendar expressions, leisure-time activities, clothing, places in a community, affirmative and negative commands, professions

Book 2
reflexive verbs, clothing, impersonal *se,* professions

Chapter 4
present perfect

Chapter 8
present perfect subjunctive

Planning

Cross-Curricular Connections

Marketing Connection *(pp. 314–315)*
Tell groups of three students to prepare TV or print ads for three jobs for the class of 2099. Describe the tasks, qualifications, and compensation for each job. Refer students to Book 2, Chap. 11, and Book 3, Chap. 6 for additional vocabulary. Encourage creative answers that reflect students' perception of what the world will be like at the end of the century.

Civics Connection *(pp. 318–319)*
In pairs or groups, tell students to imagine that they are a candidate for president of a country of their choice. Have them prepare a 30- to 60-second speech detailing how they will help the economy and create more jobs. If possible, videotape the speeches and have students conduct an election.

Spanish in Your Community
Have students look for job opportunities that require Spanish. They can compile these into a bulletin board or create a collage. They might want to follow up with a particular company and obtain employment information as well as an application in Spanish. You may want to invite a representative from a Human Resources department to visit the class to discuss the importance of Spanish in his or her company.

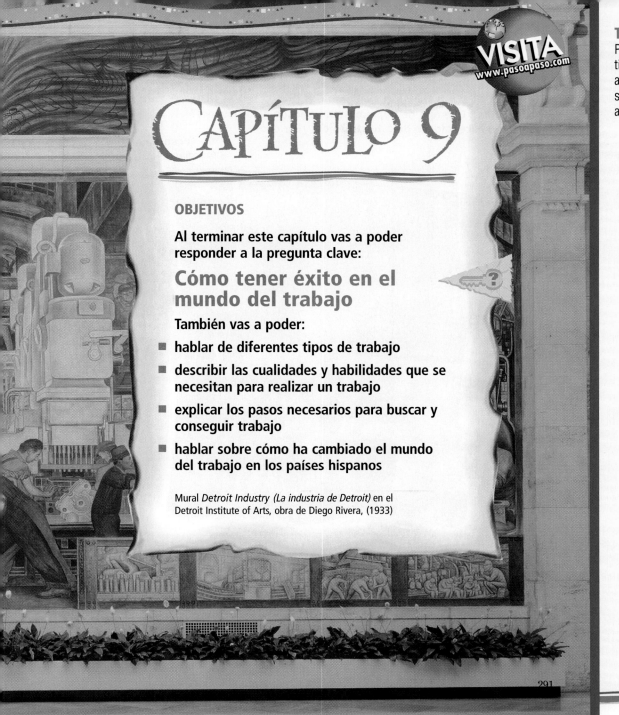

CAPÍTULO 9

OBJETIVOS

Al terminar este capítulo vas a poder responder a la pregunta clave:

Cómo tener éxito en el mundo del trabajo

También vas a poder:

- hablar de diferentes tipos de trabajo
- describir las cualidades y habilidades que se necesitan para realizar un trabajo
- explicar los pasos necesarios para buscar y conseguir trabajo
- hablar sobre cómo ha cambiado el mundo del trabajo en los países hispanos

Mural *Detroit Industry (La industria de Detroit)* en el Detroit Institute of Arts, obra de Diego Rivera, (1933)

291

Cultural Notes

(pp. 290–291, photo)
In the spring of 1931, Diego Rivera (1886–1957) was commissioned by Edsel Ford and the Detroit Arts Commission to paint *La industria de Detroit* at the Detroit Institute of Arts. Rivera, a labor sympathizer and a fervent admirer of technology, approached the project with intensity and conviction. Working 15 hours a day, seven days a week, he completed the series of 27 panels in March of 1933. Although the work was criticized by some for "obscenity" and threats were made to destroy it, 86,000 people came to view it on opening day and it remains one of the city's greatest treasures.

Preview

Anticipación

Visita estos países

Mira las fotos. ¿Qué tipo de trabajo están haciendo estos jóvenes? ¿Te gustaría hacer alguno de estos trabajos? ¿Por qué?

"Nos encanta mostrar a otras personas esta hacienda antigua."

Los turistas que visitan la Hacienda Buena Vista, una antigua plantación de café en Puerto Rico, reciben ayuda de estas jóvenes guías del Fideicomiso de Conservación de Puerto Rico. Para este trabajo se necesita tener buenos modales y ser amable. ¿Por qué son importantes estas cualidades?

292   Capítulo 9

Options

Strategies for Reaching All Students

"Quiero ahorrar dinero para comprarme una bicicleta nueva."

Algunos jóvenes hispanos, como éstos en Chile, trabajan en supermercados los fines de semana y durante las vacaciones para ganar dinero extra. Así desarrollan su sentido de responsabilidad y otras cualidades que les serán útiles no sólo ahora, sino también en el futuro. ¿Qué cualidades personales puedes desarrollar en un trabajo?

"Sembrar árboles ayuda a conservar la naturaleza."

Estos jóvenes trabajan en el vivero (nursery) de un programa de siembra de árboles en Ecuador. Para este tipo de trabajo se necesita tener habilidad para sembrar e interés por las plantas. ¿Qué otras habilidades e intereses crees que serán útiles para trabajar en un programa como éste?

Exploración cultural www.pasoapaso.com
Visita estos países

293

(p. 292, right photo)
These guides work for El Fideicomiso de Conservación de Puerto Rico, an organization founded in 1968 to preserve sites of natural and historical interest on the island. Two of the Trust's properties are Cabezas de San Juan on the island's northeastern corner, and Bahía Fosforescente on its southern coast. They consist of rare bodies of water in which so many bioluminescent microscopic organisms exist that they light up the water's surface when they are disturbed.

(p. 293, top photo)
Cashiers at a supermarket in Chile. In 1990, when Chilean president Patricio Aylwin Azócar took office, he launched an intensive anti-poverty program. Within two years nearly anyone who wanted a job could find one. Unemployment, which had been running at 25 percent, dropped to four percent, and inflation decreased dramatically, from 26 to 12.7 percent.

(p. 293, bottom photo)
High numbers of tourists on "ecotourism" packages have endangered some of Ecuador's most prized nature sites. These tourists and their guides alter animal behavior patterns and destroy fragile plants when they stray from designated paths to be "closer to nature." Although there is a strict policy that all naturalist guides be licensed by the government, the 87,000 permits issued each year far exceeds the 25,000 experts have recommended as safe for the environment.

Present

Chapter Theme
Employment

Communicative Objectives
- *Hablar de distintos trabajos*
- *Describir las cualidades necesarias para un trabajo*
- *Explicar los requisitos de un trabajo*
- *Buscar y conseguir trabajo*

 Overheads 27–28

 Vocabulary Art BLMs/CD-ROM

 Vocabulary Tape 9-1

Teaching Suggestions
Preparing students to speak: Use one or two options from each of the categories of Comprehensible Input or Limited Verbal Response. For a complete explanation of these categories and some sample activities, see pp. T20–T21.

Vocabulario para comunicarse

¿Necesitas un buen trabajo?

Aquí tienes palabras y expresiones necesarias para hablar sobre el mundo del trabajo. Léelas varias veces y practícalas con un(a) compañero(a) en las páginas siguientes.

294   Capítulo 9

Options

Strategies for Reaching All Students

Spanish-Speaking Students
Ask: *¿Qué otras palabras sabes para hablar sobre el mundo del trabajo? Escríbelas en tu vocabulario personal.*
Escribe una conversación en la recepción del hotel o en la tienda. ¿Qué crees que dicen estas personas? Debes incluir por lo menos tres interacciones entre las personas.

Students Needing Extra Help
Begin the vocabulary section of the Organizer. Point out the features and / or objects that will help students make the distinction between these occupations. If available, have students refer to the vocabulary section of the Book 2, Chap. 11 Organizer. Write out the complete paradigm for *atender*.

Remind students of word families: *repartir (repartidor)*.
También necesitas . . . : Model how to use *me conviene, cumplir con, encargarse de,* and *realizar*. Emphasize the meaning of these expressions.

También necesitas . . .

administrar	*to manage (a business)*	maduro, -a	*mature*
atender *(e → ie)* (a)	*to attend (to)*	los modales, *pl.*	*manners*
capaz, *pl.* capaces	*capable*	realizar *(z → c)*	*to perform*
la cita	*appointment*	el requisito	*requirement*
convenir *(e → ie):*	*to be convenient; to*	la solicitud	*application*
me conviene*	*suit: it suits me*	el sueldo	*salary*
cuidadoso, -a	*careful*	la tarea	here: *task*
cumplir con	*to fulfill*	(de) tiempo completo	*full-time*
encargarse *(g → gu)* (de)	*to take charge (of)*	(de) tiempo parcial	*part-time*
el entrenamiento	*training*	tratar (bien / mal)	*to treat (well /*
la habilidad	*skill*		*badly)*

¿Y qué quiere decir . . . ?

ambicioso, -a   productivo, -a
los anuncios clasificados   puntual
la cualidad   la recomendación,
la experiencia   *pl.* las recomendaciones
honesto, -a   respetuoso, -a

* *Convenir* follows the pattern of *venir*.

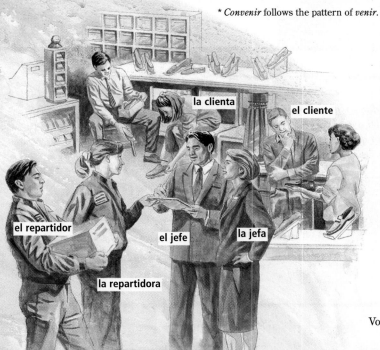

la clienta
el cliente
el repartidor
el jefe
la jefa
la repartidora

¡NO OLVIDES!

Remember these words:
el abogado, la abogada
el / la dentista
el enfermero, la enfermera
el hombre de negocios, la mujer
de negocios
el mecánico, la mecánica
el médico, la médica
el músico, la música
el pintor, la pintora
el / la policía
el técnico, la técnica (de
computadoras)
el veterinario, la veterinaria

Vocabulario para comunicarse   295

Class Starter Review
On the day following the presentation of vocabulary, you might begin the class with this activity: Give sentences in Spanish defining the vocabulary words. Have students guess which words you are defining. For example:
Si llego siempre a tiempo, soy muy ____. (puntual)

www **Internet Activities**
Juegos

Extended Written Practice/Homework
1. Choose three types of work from pp. 294–295 and write sentences saying whether or not they suit you and why.
2. Write three sentences describing the work of different people you know: *Mi tía es . . . Se encarga de . . .*
3. Choose three types of work and write sentences naming qualities or abilities one should have for these jobs.
4. Write three commands telling a person what to do to get a job.

Multiple Intelligences
Intrapersonal/Introspective and Bodily/Kinesthetic
Have students make a collage showing their own possible career plans.
Logical/Mathematical
Have students interview their classmates and make a graph or chart showing their parents' or guardians' professions.

Verbal/Linguistic
See Vocabulary Tape 9-1 and Class Starter Review.
Visual/Spatial
See Overheads 27–28 and the Vocabulary Art BLMs/CD-ROM.

Standards 1.1; 1.2; 4.1; 5.1   **295**

Practice

Re-enter / Recycle

Exs. 2–4: present perfect from Chap. 4

Answers: Empecemos a conversar

1 ESTUDIANTE A
a. ¿Qué se necesita para ser vendedor?
b. ... gerente?
c. ... mujer de negocios?
d. ... médico?
e. ... diplomática?
f. ... abogado?
g. Questions will vary.

ESTUDIANTE B
a.–g. Answers will vary, but should begin *Lo más importante es ser* + adj. *y* adj. Look for correct agreement of adjectives.

2 ESTUDIANTE A
a. ¿Has llenado la solicitud?
b. ... pedido una entrevista?
c. ... hecho una cita?
d. ... hablado con el jefe / la jefa?
e. ... llevado cartas de recomendación?
f. Questions will vary.

ESTUDIANTE B
a.–f. Answers will vary.

Empecemos a conversar

Túrnate con un(a) compañero(a) para ser *Estudiante A* y *Estudiante B*. Reemplacen las palabras subrayadas con palabras representadas o escritas en los recuadros. 💡 quiere decir que puedes escoger tu propia respuesta.

¡NO OLVIDES!
Remember these adjectives:
comprensivo, -a
considerado, -a
inteligente
leal
ordenado, -a
prudente
sociable
trabajador, -a

1
A — ¿Qué se necesita para ser *recepcionista*?
B — *Lo más importante es ser amable y respetuoso(a).*

Estudiante A

a. b. c. d. e. f. g.

Estudiante B

honesto, -a
productivo, -a
responsable
puntual
maduro, -a
capaz
ambicioso, -a
cuidadoso, -a

2   leer los anuncios clasificados

A — ¿Has *leído los anuncios clasificados*?
B — *Sí, los leí ayer. Quiero conseguir un trabajo pronto.*
o: *¿Para qué? Ya tengo trabajo.*

Estudiante A

a. llenar la solicitud
b. pedir una entrevista
c. hacer una cita
d. hablar con el jefe / la jefa
e. llevar cartas de recomendación
f.

Estudiante B

la semana pasada
la semana próxima
ayer
mañana
todavía no

Options

Strategies for Reaching All Students

Spanish-Speaking Students
Exs. 1–4: Pair bilingual and non-bilingual students, if possible.

Students Needing Extra Help
¡No olvides!: Review the meanings of the given words.
Ex. 2: Brainstorm phrases that will complete the *Estudiante B* responses. Review the present perfect for use with the *Estudiante A* statements. Do a model using *mañana* and *la semana próxima*. Point out that students'

answers do not always have to be in the past tense.
Ex. 3: Brainstorm other possibilities for the *Estudiante B* response.
Ex. 4: Brainstorm *Estudiante B* responses. Refer to the list in Ex. 1. Discuss the qualifications a person would need to have in order to perform these duties.

3

A —¡*Mira! Aquí dice que necesitan un(a) cocinero(a).*

B —¡*Qué bien! Voy a llamar en seguida.*

    o: *Pero yo no tengo experiencia. Nunca he trabajado como cocinero(a) antes.*

Estudiante A   Estudiante B

a.
b.
c.
d.
e.
f.

También se dice

Para *sueldo* también se dice: **salario**

Para *(de) tiempo completo* también se dice: **jornada completa**

Para *(de) tiempo parcial* también se dice: **media jornada**

4   **tenga experiencia**

A —*Necesitamos una persona que tenga experiencia.*

B —*Bueno, yo ya he trabajado antes.*

    o: *Bueno, yo no tengo mucha experiencia pero . . .*

A —*Si no has trabajado antes . . .*

    o: *Si no tienes experiencia . . .*

Estudiante A   Estudiante B

a. trate bien a los clientes

b. sepa administrar el negocio

c. se encargue de los teléfonos

d. tenga buenos modales

e. cumpla bien con sus tareas

f. realice un buen trabajo

g.

---

3 ESTUDIANTE A

a. ¡Mira! Aquí dice que necesitan un intérprete.

b. . . . una vendedor(a).

c. . . . una salvavidas.

d. . . . una pintor(a).

e. . . . un repartidor(a).

f. Statements will vary.

ESTUDIANTE B

a.–f. Statements will vary.

4 ESTUDIANTE A

The use of subjunctive in adjective clauses is previewed lexically in this exercise. The explanation appears in the grammar section on p. 311.

a. Necesitamos una persona que trate bien a los clientes.

b. . . . sepa administrar el negocio.

c. . . . se encargue de los teléfonos.

d. . . . tenga buenos modales.

e. . . . cumpla bien con sus tareas.

f. . . . realice un buen trabajo.

g. Statements will vary.

ESTUDIANTE B

a.–g. Statements will vary.

ESTUDIANTE A

a.–g. Si no has trabajado antes . . . (Si no tienes experiencia . . .) *Statements will vary.*

Enrichment

Ex. 1: As homework, ask students to name the occupation for which they feel they are best suited and to describe the personal traits that make them good candidates for that occupation.

Ex. 3: To extend this dialogue, *Estudiante A* and *Estudiante B* can role play the call to the company advertising a job.

Cooperative Learning

In groups of four, have students review the adjectives listed in the *¡No olvides!* section and in Ex. 1. Have them select what they consider to be the four most important elements for success in life. Have them prioritize their list and share their results by constructing a pie chart. One student should make a statement: *Es importante ser sociable,* for example. Another might say: *Hay que tener muchos amigos.* Each student

should be responsible for summarizing his or her own opinion. Post the charts and discuss.

Multiple Intelligences

Interpersonal/Social, Visual/Spatial, and Logical/Mathematical

See Cooperative Learning.

Verbal/Linguistic

See Exs. 1–4.

Practice & Apply

Answers: ¿Y qué piensas tú?

5–9 Answers will vary.

Cómo tener éxito en el mundo del trabajo

¿Y qué piensas tú?

Aquí tienes otra oportunidad para usar el vocabulario de este capítulo.

5 ¿Qué trabajo te gustaría tener? ¿En qué has trabajado antes? ¿Cuáles de los trabajos que aparecen en la página 292 te parecen mejores para los jóvenes? ¿Por qué?

6 Durante el verano, ¿qué clase de trabajo te conviene más: uno de tiempo parcial o uno de tiempo completo? ¿Por qué?

7 ¿Conoces a alguien que tenga uno de los trabajos de la página 292? ¿Quién es? ¿Qué responsabilidades tiene? ¿Qué habilidades se necesitan para realizar ese trabajo?

8 Haz un diagrama de Venn como el de abajo. En el círculo de la izquierda escribe tu nombre y tus cualidades y habilidades. En el de la derecha escribe el trabajo que te gustaría tener y las cualidades y habilidades necesarias para hacer ese trabajo.

Compara tu diagrama con el de otros(as) compañeros(as).

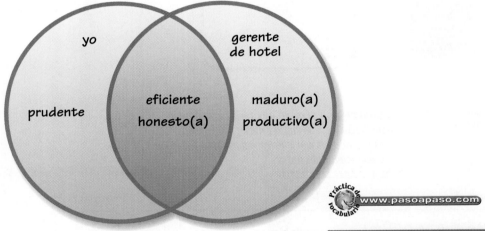

www.pasoapaso.com

MÁS PRÁCTICA

Más práctica y tarea, p. 571
Practice Workbook 9–1, 9–2

298 Capítulo 9

Options

Strategies for Reaching All Students

Spanish-Speaking Students
Ex. 7: Additional questions: *¿Gana un buen sueldo? ¿Cuánta educación tiene? ¿Qué experiencia tuvo antes de conseguir el trabajo?*

Students Needing Extra Help
Ex. 7: Discuss what skills are necessary for certain jobs.
Ex. 8: Model this activity using yourself and your qualities and skills.

Ex. 9: Have some classified ads available so that students have a model. Do one ad as a class.

Enrichment
Exs. 5–8: Additional questions: *¿A qué edad crees tú que deben empezar los jóvenes a trabajar? ¿Por qué a esa edad? Para un(a) estudiante, ¿cuáles son algunas ventajas de tener un trabajo? ¿Cuáles son algunas desventajas?*

Multiple Intelligences
Intrapersonal/Introspective
See Exs. 5–8.
Verbal/Linguistic
See Audio Activity 9.1.
Visual/Spatial
See Practice Wkbk. 9-1 and 9-2 and Writing Activity 9-A.

298 Standards 1.1; 3.1

9 Imagínate que eres gerente de un negocio y necesitas ayuda. Escribe un anuncio clasificado. Describe:

- el nombre del trabajo
- el entrenamiento necesario para realizar el trabajo
- las habilidades y cualidades que se deben tener
- el sueldo y el horario (tiempo completo o parcial)

Pon tu anuncio con los de tus compañeros para hacer una página de anuncios clasificados.

Practice Wkbk. 9-1, 9-2

Audio Activity 9.1

Writing Activity 9-A

Pruebas 9-1, 9-2

Arquitecta Marcela Abadi delante de la sede *(headquarters)* de Univisión en Dallas, un edificio que fue diseñado por ella

En una fábrica de piezas para coches en Querétaro, México

Vocabulario para comunicarse   299

Cultural Notes

(p. 299, top photo)
Dallas-based Marcela Abadi is one of the few women to have established herself in the historically male-dominated profession of architecture. After years of struggling with discrimination and disparagement, Abadi got her big break in 1996, when she was named project architect for Univisión's Dallas headquarters and received the American Institute of Architect's Intern Architect of the Year Award.

(p. 299, bottom photo)
Automotive industry worker in Querétaro, one of Mexico's leading industrial cities. Querétaro lies on the nation's busiest highway, between Mexico City and Guadalajara. Many foreign companies have offices there, including Kellogg's, Campbell's, Nestlé, Siemens, and the Rockwell Corporation. Tremec, a domestic producer of automotive transmissions, is also based there. Its annual sales are nearly $150 million, with exports to U.S. companies such as Ford and Chrysler, as well as to Europe, Brazil, and Japan.

Present

Chapter Theme
Preparing for the job market

Communicative Objectives
- *Describir las cualidades necesarias para un trabajo*
- *Explicar los requisitos de un trabajo*
- *Buscar y conseguir trabajo*

 Vocabulary Tape 9-2

Grammar Preview
Use of the subjunctive in adjective clauses is previewed lexically. The explanation appears in the grammar section on p. 311.

Teaching Suggestions
Getting ready to speak:
Remind students of the reading strategies that they learned (getting meaning from context and coping with unknown words) to help them understand the *Tema para investigar.* For further details and some sample activities, see pp. T24–T25.

Answers: Tema para investigar
Answers may vary:
Están mirando los anuncios clasificados. / Están en la escuela.

Tema para investigar

Aquí tienes más palabras e ideas para hablar sobre cómo tener éxito en el mundo del trabajo. Mira la ilustración y las fotos de esta página. ¿Qué están haciendo estos jóvenes? ¿Dónde están?

ANUNCIOS CLASIFICADOS

Options

Strategies for Reaching All Students

Spanish-Speaking Students
Imagina que quieres hablar con tu jefe(a) para pedirle un aumento de sueldo. ¿Qué le vas a decir? Piensa en las razones que puedes darle para que esté más dispuesto(a) a darte el aumento. Haz una lista de ellas.

Students Needing Extra Help
Distinguish between *meter un gol* (the goal that is scored in a game) and *la meta* (your goal in life). Write a complete paradigm for *merecer.*
Emphasize that *cortés* is not associated with the verb *cortar,* but has an English cognate, "courteous."

Multiple Intelligences
Verbal/Linguistic
See Vocabulary Tape 9-2 and Class Starter Review.

¿Cómo te estás preparando?

¿Vas a buscar un trabajo cuando termines las clases o ya tienes uno? ¿Trabajarás durante las vacaciones o no quieres trabajar antes de graduarte? Piensa en tu futuro. ¿Cómo te puede ayudar **cualquier** trabajo que hagas ahora para **alcanzar** tus **metas**?

Se necesitan cualidades y habilidades para hacer cualquier trabajo. Si eres cajero o cajera en un supermercado, por ejemplo, tienes que ser eficiente, tener habilidad con los números y ser **cortés** y amable con los clientes.

Si tienes un trabajo de tiempo parcial en una oficina, es probable que sepas usar una computadora, una máquina de fotocopias y posiblemente un fax. También es posible que hayas aprendido a usar y mantener **los archivos**. Esa experiencia te servirá en un futuro **no sólo** para realizar cualquier trabajo de oficina **sino también** para calcular el tiempo que toma hacer un trabajo, **distribuir** las tareas a otros empleados y poder dedicarte a tareas **administrativas**.

Antes de ahora hemos considerado el entrenamiento para el futuro desde el punto de vista de **las destrezas** que se pueden adquirir. Pero, ¿cuáles son las cualidades personales que se desarrollan cuando se hace un buen trabajo? **La puntualidad** y la responsabilidad son muy importantes. Si tienes un trabajo debes llegar a una hora **fija** y ser responsable de ciertas tareas. Recibir un sueldo te obliga también a ser responsable de tu propio dinero. ¿En qué y cómo gastarlo? ¿Cuánto y para qué ahorrar?

Todavía queda algo más: **la paciencia**. **Cuando creas** que **mereces** un **aumento** de sueldo o un **ascenso**, debes aprender a esperar el momento **oportuno** para hablar con tu jefe o con la persona **adecuada** para pedírselo.

Después de leer todo esto, ¿vas a buscar un trabajo **ahora mismo** o te parece que tienes razones suficientes para esperar un poco?

cualquier	*any*	Cuando creas	*When you*
alcanzar *(z → c)**	*to reach, to achieve*	(*from*: creer)	*think*
la meta	*goal*	merecer *(c → zc)*†	*to deserve*
cortés, *pl.* corteses	*courteous, polite*	el aumento (de sueldo)	*raise*
el archivo	*office file*	el ascenso	*promotion*
no sólo ... sino también**	*not only ... but also*	adecuado, -a	*appropriate*
la destreza	*skill*	ahora mismo	*right now*
fijo, -a	*fixed*		

¿Y qué quiere decir ... ?

distribuir *(i → y)*	la paciencia
administrativo, -a	oportuno, -a
la puntualidad	

*Alcanzar follows the pattern of *cruzar.*
After a negative, we use *sino* (not** *pero*) to mean "but": *Tengo un trabajo, pero no me gusta. / El trabajo no es de tiempo completo sino de tiempo parcial.*
† *Merecer* follows the pattern of *conocer.*

Tema para investigar 301

Cultural Notes ☼

(p. 300, top left photo)
The lack of medical insurance is a major concern for many people in the U.S., particularly Hispanics. In 1989, 31.5 percent of working Hispanic Americans did not have adequate health coverage. Hispanics also had the highest number of uninsured people below the poverty line, nearly 41 percent.

(p. 300, top right photo)
These Hispanic students at the University of Texas at Austin are part of a growing number of Hispanic Americans attending college. Although only 18 percent of college-age Hispanics were enrolled in four-year universities in 1990, this is a 15 percent increase over 1985.

(p. 300, bottom photo)
In the U.S., Hispanic American women are increasingly entering professions traditionally dominated by men and now hold significant positions in many top U.S. corporations and in the government. In 1995, the FBI employed 56 Hispanic female special agents.

Practice & Apply

Re-enter / Recycle
Ex. 4: present perfect subjunctive from Chap. 8

Answers: ¿Comprendiste?
1 Las ideas incluidas son: b, c, d.

2 Answers will vary.

Answers: ¿Y qué piensas tú?
3–7 Answers will vary.

¿Comprendiste?

1 ¿Cuáles de estas ideas están incluidas en el tema y cuáles no?

   a. Todos los estudiantes necesitan trabajar antes de entrar en la universidad.

   b. Trabajar en una oficina es práctico para aprender tareas administrativas.

   c. Las destrezas que adquieren los jóvenes en un trabajo son un entrenamiento para el futuro.

   d. La responsabilidad, la puntualidad y la paciencia son cualidades necesarias en cualquier trabajo.

   e. Si una persona piensa que merece un ascenso, debe hablar con su jefe(a) inmediatamente.

2 ¿Cuáles piensas que son las tres ideas más importantes de la lectura? Discútelas con un(a) compañero(a).

¿Y qué piensas tú?

3 Escribe cinco consejos que le darías a alguien que busca trabajo. Discútelos con un(a) compañero(a). Puedes compartirlos con otros estudiantes.

4 Haz una lista de cualidades y destrezas que hayas adquirido en algún trabajo. Luego, compara tu lista con la de un(a) compañero(a).

5 ¿Qué preguntas son las más frecuentes en una entrevista de trabajo? Y, ¿qué preguntas debe hacer la persona que busca trabajo? Con un(a) compañero(a) haz una lista de cuatro o cinco preguntas para hacer en una entrevista de trabajo.

6 Ahora, haz una entrevista de trabajo con tu compañero(a). Túrnense para ser la persona que busca trabajo y la persona que entrevista. Hablen de:

   • las cualidades y habilidades del (de la) candidato(a)
   • la experiencia necesaria
   • la educación o el entrenamiento
   • las metas
   • el sueldo

7 Piensa en algún trabajo o en una profesión que te interese. Descríbele a tu compañero(a) los requisitos del trabajo y las cualidades y las habilidades que se necesitan. Tu compañero(a) va a tratar de adivinar qué trabajo

MÁS PRÁCTICA

   Más práctica y tarea, p. 572
   Practice Workbook 9–3, 9–4

302   Capítulo 9

Options

Strategies for Reaching All Students

Spanish-Speaking Students
Ex. 3: After this exercise, ask students: *¿Cuáles son los consejos más comunes entre tus compañeros? ¿Crees que son buenos consejos? ¿Por qué?*

Students Needing Extra Help
Ex. 4: Brainstorm the vocabulary necessary to express students' answers regarding the skills and qualities they need on their job.
Ex. 5: Before beginning this exercise, discuss the difficulty asking questions in a job interview because of nervousness, or because of lack of information about the

company. Emphasize that nervousness is natural. Agressiveness and bravado are rarely productive in a job interview.
Ex. 6: Discuss the goals people have when applying for a job.
Ex. 7: Model for the class.
¿Qué sabes ahora?: Have students write this so they can record their progress.

Answers: ¿Qué sabes ahora?
• All answers will vary.

 Practice Wkbk. 9-3, 9-4

 Audio Activity 9.2

 Writing Activities 9-B, 9-C

 Pruebas 9-3, 9-4

 Comm. Act. BLM 9-1

¿Qué sabes ahora?

¿Puedes:

■ nombrar algunas profesiones que consideras para el futuro?

—En el futuro, me gustaría ser ___ o ___ porque ___.

■ describir las habilidades y las cualidades necesarias para un trabajo o una profesión?

—Para ser ___, uno necesita ser ___, ___ y ___.

■ hablar de lo que es necesario hacer en un trabajo?

—Un(a) ___ tiene que ___, ___ y ___.

■ hablar de los pasos que se deben seguir para buscar y encontrar un trabajo?

—Para encontrar un trabajo, hay que ___, ___ y ___.

Enrichment
Ex 5: Additional questions: *¿Qué preguntas no debes hacer en una entrevista de trabajo? ¿Qué preguntas no te deben hacer en una entrevista de trabajo porque son ilegales?*
Ex 7: Additional questions: *¿Cuáles son algunos trabajos de los que existen ahora que no existían hace veinticinco años? ¿Cómo han cambiado los trabajos desde que tú naciste? ¿Te gustaría trabajar en casa? ¿Porqué sí o no?*

Extended Written Practice/Homework
1. Write three sentences saying what is necessary to accomplish the following: *alcanzar las metas, merecer un aumento, recibir un ascenso.*
2. Write three sentences naming jobs in which the following are important: *la paciencia, ser cortés, la puntualidad.*
3. Write three sentences indicating if you have done the following: *mantener los archivos, distribuir tareas a otros empleados, cumplir tareas administrativas.*

Multiple Intelligences
Verbal/Linguistic
See Audio Activity 9.2.
Verbal/Linguistic and Bodily/Kinesthetic
Have groups of students write two dialogues representing job interviews, one well done and the other poorly done, and present them to the class.
Visual/Spatial
See Practice Wkbk. 9-3 and 9-4, Writing Activities 9-B and 9-C, and Comm. Act. BLM 9-1.

Standards 1.1; 1.2; 3.1   303

Present & Apply

Cultural Objective
• *Hablar sobre cómo ha cambiado el mundo del trabajo en los países de habla hispana*

Answers
Answers will vary.

Using Realia
Using reading strategies that students have learned, ask them to skim the text on p. 304 to discover the gist of the two articles.

ÁLBUM CULTURAL

Para encontrar un buen trabajo es necesario saber qué clase de trabajo nos interesa y qué preparación se necesita para hacerlo. ¿Qué trabajo te gustaría hacer? ¿Cómo piensas prepararte para ese trabajo?

EL MACHISMO

SIGLO XXI. La mujer ya habrá roto en Occidente el *techo de cristal* que le impide acceder a los centros de poder y de decisión. La discriminación sexual será difícil de defender en un mundo donde la educación se extiende. La mujer aportará a las empresas los valores que ha aprendido en siglos de arrinconamiento: la sensibilidad y la capacidad de negociación y de trabajo en equipo. Para el año 2025 habrá más de 4.000 millones de mujeres en el mundo, ahora son 2.800. En España en el 2000 trabajará el 70 por ciento de las mujeres en edad de hacerlo, frente al 48 por ciento de 1989. En Francia la previsión para el siglo XXI es que trabaje el 91,5 por ciento.

En el tercer mundo, la mujer seguirá llevando el peso de la agricultura. El peligro para la mujer son los fundamentalismos que le impiden acceder a la educación. Pero sus hijas difícilmente aceptarán esas condiciones de vida y de pobreza al difundirse por los medios de comunicación cómo se vive en otras partes del planeta.

El mundo del trabajo ha cambiado mucho en los últimos años. Cada día es mayor el número de mujeres que han recibido educación superior y que ahora trabajan fuera de casa. También muchos hombres han escogido quedarse en casa y cuidar a sus hijos. Estos cambios también afectan a los países hispanos.

EL HOMBRE EN CASA

Ahora que las mujeres se están adentrando en todas las profesiones reservadas hasta hace poco a los hombres, ellos han irrumpido triunfalmente en el último gueto de poder femenino: las labores domésticas. Cada vez con más frecuencia la mujer profesional gana más dinero que su cónyuge, y cuando un hijo llega es él quien debe quedarse en casa.

Algunas características masculinas, como la falta de obsesión por el detalle, les facilitan inmensamente las labores domésticas. El hombre que se queda en casa ya no es un hippy desempleado que no tiene nada mejor que hacer. Los nuevos hombres de hogar son tan profesionales como sus mujeres y son felices por poder ser testigos diarios del desarrollo de sus hijos.

Algunos padres se quejan del rechazo que sufren por parte de muchas madres, que todavía no se acostumbran a su presencia como amos de casa. Se ha abierto un nuevo frente en la batalla de los sexos.

304   Capítulo 9

Options

Strategies for Reaching All Students

Spanish-Speaking Students
Ask: *¿Estás de acuerdo con lo que dice el autor del artículo "El hombre en casa"? Explica tu respuesta.*

Multiple Intelligences
Visual/Spatial
If Spanish-language job applications are available from local businesses, have students practice filling them out.

In many rural areas of Latin America, children participate in the harvest of crops, such as picking coffee beans. In many places, the children will also help with more hazardous work, such as spraying pesticides on crops. Having the opportunity to continue on to high school could mean that a young person would have to move away from his or her immediate family and live with a relative in a town that has a high school. Young girls sometimes work as domestics for other families in order to have room and board and be able to attend high school.

El desarrollo de las comunicaciones ha contribuido a crear nuevos trabajos, como el de esta operadora de Telefónica Mexicana. Aunque la mayoría de las llamadas telefónicas pueden hacerse directamente, los operadores siempre están preparados para ayudar al público.

La agricultura siempre ha atraído a muchos trabajadores. Durante un tiempo, los jóvenes abandonaron el campo y disminuyó *(decreased)* el número de agricultores. Pero hoy en día muchos han vuelto para escaparse de las presiones de la vida en la ciudad.

Álbum cultural 305

(p. 305, top photo)
One of Mexico's most powerful labor unions, the Sindicato de Trabajadores de Teléfonos de la República Mexicana, is described as "modernizing." This means it has more democratic tendencies than do the old guard "corporatist" unions, whose leaders work closely with the government. Yet the telephone workers' union is still an "official" union and never entirely or acrimoniously defies the government, as is sometimes the case with independent unions including that of university workers.

(p. 305, bottom photo)
This pimento farmer is working in Almería, a province on Spain's southern coast. Agricultural labor continues to be less expensive in Spain than in other European countries. Frequently, entire families work in the fields, getting paid as a unit, not individually. Spain's agricultural workers are often unavailable or unwilling to work on large properties. As a result, many foreign workers take the jobs at significantly less pay than would be offered to a Spaniard.

Present & Apply

Critical Thinking: Formulating Appropriate Questions

Have students role play the part of interviewees for one of the jobs in the ads presented here. Tell them to write three questions they would ask the company before accepting a job offer.

EN MEXICO SE NECESITA...

-Vendedor de comercio
-Mesero
-Representante de ventas
-Técnicos en mercadotecnia
-Jefes de piso
-Seguridad pública y privada
-Bibliotecario
-Manipulador de comida rápida
-Cocinero de comida rápida
-Analistas de sistemas infor-

máticos
-Auxiliar administrativo
-Secretaria ejecutiva bilingüe
-Publirrelacionista
-Contador público y privado
-Técnicos agrarios
-Redactores
-Zootecnista
-Médicos, en los estados
-Dentistas, en los estados

LOS 40 PRINCIPALES

Se ha publicado recientemente la lista de trabajos con más demanda en el mundo, según un estudio de la Revista Mensual de Empleo de los EE. UU. Pocos precisan títulos medios o superiores.

-Portero de finca urbana
-Cajero
-Secretaria
-Oficinista
-Vendedor
-Enfermera
-Mesero
-Maestro
-Chofer de camión
-Personal sanitario auxiliar
-Representante de ventas
-Contable y auditor
-Mecánico del automóvil
-Capataz
-Garrotero
-Guardia y velador
-Manipulador de comida rápida
-Jefe de almacén
-Carpintero
-Técnico de electricidad y electrónica
-Enfermera obstetra
-Analista de sistemas informáticos
-Ingeniero electrónico
-Programador informático
-Operario de servicios generales
-Ayudante de comercio
-Recepcionista
-Electricista
-Médico
-Jefe de administración
-Operador de computadora
-Representante de ventas, no cualificado
-Abogado
-Controlador de existencias de almacenes y depósitos
-Mecanógrafa
-Mensajero
-Bibliotecario
-Cocinero de restaurante
-Cajero bancario
-Cocinero de comida rápida

El tipo de trabajo a que podrás dedicarte puede depender de las necesidades de la comunidad. Estas tablas, publicadas en una revista mexicana, indican los tipos de trabajos para los que hay más oportunidades en México.

Options

Strategies for Reaching All Students

Spanish-Speaking Students
Ask: *¿Cuál(es) de estos trabajos te gustaría(n)? ¿Por qué?*

Students Needing Extra Help
Reacción personal: In the first question, students may not be aware that there was once a time when many job opportunities were not open to women. Give them some background information.
Help with the *¿Por qué?* question as needed.

Multiple Intelligences
Verbal/Linguistic and Visual/Spatial
See Critical Thinking.

...desempleados

Un sondeo realizado por una organización a nivel internacional sobre una muestra del 2 por 100 de la población activa de varios países en desarrollo arrojó los datos de desempleo universitario que se reflejan en esta gráfica. Los que peor la llevan son los licenciados en filosofía y letras (con un 29.96 por 100 de desempleados). Las carreras con valores negativos presentan más puestos de trabajo que licenciados existentes.

Esta tabla preparada por una organización internacional indica en qué profesiones o trabajos hay mayor número de desempleados. Esta información se puede usar para decidir qué trabajos ofrecen mejores oportunidades para el futuro.

Reacción personal

Contesta las siguientes preguntas en una hoja de papel.

1 ¿Crees que las mujeres tienen más oportunidades de trabajo hoy en día? ¿Por qué? ¿Qué clase de trabajo pueden hacer?

2 ¿Te parece bien que los hombres se queden en casa a cuidar a sus hijos? ¿Por qué o por qué no?

3 ¿Qué trabajos crees que ofrecerán más oportunidades en tu comunidad en el futuro? ¿Cuál te gustaría hacer a ti? ¿Cómo deberás prepararte para ese trabajo?

www.pasoapaso.com

Álbum cultural 307

Cultural Notes

(p. 306, photo)
Steady jobs with adequate pay are difficult to find in Mexico. Although the government calculates the urban unemployment rate at about three percent, excluded from that figure is anyone who works outside the home even one hour per week. Mexico's minimum wage is low, at an average of 28 *nuevos pesos,* or slightly more than three U.S. dollars per day.

Preview

Overhead 29

Teaching Suggestions

A If students have difficulty identifying the subjunctive form used in negative commands, ask them when they have used *"-e"* endings on *-ar* verbs and *"-a"* endings on *-er / -ir* verbs.

B–C Tell students to use their prior knowledge of the use of subjunctive and indicative to help answer the questions.

Answers

Answers will vary.

A *usa, mira, escoge /* The affirmative commands all use the *Ud. / él / ella* present indicative form. The negative commands all use the *tú* present subjunctive form.

B *Las cosas que ya tienes. /* In *ropa de colores y estilos que vayan bien,* an item of clothing is referred to that the person does not yet own. / *Tienes* is in the present indicative because it refers to items we are sure the person has. *Vayan* is in the present subjunctive because we are not sure the items exist.

C The actions may or may not take place. / subjunctive / In the first sentence, the interview will definitely take place. In the second, the person may or may not have an interview.

Gramática en contexto

¿Has pensado alguna vez en la ropa que se debe usar en el trabajo? Este artículo te puede ayudar a contestar esa pregunta.

A Look at the magazine article for examples of affirmative commands. Make a list of them. What form of the verb do all these commands use? Many negative commands are also used: *nunca lleves, no te vistas, no te pongas . . . ni uses.* What form of the verb do these commands use?

B In the article, the following constructions are used: *ropa de colores y estilos que vayan bien* and *las cosas que ya tienes.* Which refers to clothing that the person already has? In which construction is clothing referred to that the person does not yet own? Are the verbs used in these descriptions in the indicative or the subjunctive? Can you explain why?

C Find the sentences in which the following phrases are used: *cuando consigas,* and *cuando vayas.* Will the actions in these expressions definitely take place? Is the indicative or the subjunctive used? Explain to a partner the difference in meaning between these two sentences: *¿Cuándo tienes tu primera entrevista?* and *Cuando tengas tu primera entrevista . . .*

¿Qué ropa debes usar en el trabajo?

Nunca lleves jeans o camisetas para la primera entrevista. Usa ropa que muestre una actitud seria. No te vistas demasiado informal.

Cuando consigas un trabajo, mira lo que llevan los otros empleados.

Después, cuando vayas a comprar la ropa que llevarás en tu trabajo, escoge ropa de colores y estilos que vayan bien con las cosas que ya tienes. No te pongas adornos exagerados ni uses perfumes fuertes.

MÁS PRÁCTICA

Más práctica y tarea, pp. 572–573
Practice Workbook 9–5, 9–9

308 Capítulo 9

Options

Strategies for Reaching All Students

Students Needing Extra Help
Begin the grammar section of the Organizer. Discuss the idea of dressing for an interview or the theater.
A: If available, refer to the grammar section of the Book 2, Chaps. 12 and 13 Organizers. Review affirmative commands. Present additional examples to help students discover the pattern.

Repaso: Mandatos afirmativos y negativos con tú: Give further examples. Make a three-column chart on the chalkboard where you list the infinitive and then the command words under the heading *Mandatos afirmativos* or *Mandatos negativos.* Add to this chart as you move through the chapter. Give additional examples of commands using object and reflexive pronouns. Add them to the list.

Enrichment
As homework, ask students to write a list of negative commands for an employee manual at any of the following workplaces: public library, hospital, childcare center, restaurant, museum, movie theater.

Repaso: Mandatos afirmativos y negativos con *tú*

You know that when we give an affirmative command to someone we address as *tú*, we usually use the present indicative *Ud. / él / ella* form. When we give negative commands in the *tú* form, we use present subjunctive forms. Compare the following commands:

Llena la solicitud con cuidado.	**No llenes** la solicitud sin leerla primero.
Escribe con bolígrafo.	**No escribas** con lápiz.
Incluye una carta de recomendación.	**No incluyas** fotos.

- Here are the affirmative and negative *tú* commands for *llamar, traer, pedir,* and *venir.*

Llamar	**Llama**	**No llames**
Traer	**Trae**	**No traigas**
Pedir	**Pide**	**No pidas**
Venir	**Ven**	**No vengas**

- Verbs that have irregular or stem-changing forms in the present subjunctive have those same forms in the negative *tú* commands.

> **No seas** impaciente. El gerente llegará pronto.
> **No cuelgues** el teléfono. Necesito hablarte.
> **No tengas** miedo. Tu nueva jefa es muy amable.

- Remember that object and reflexive pronouns are attached to affirmative commands. However, these pronouns go before negative commands.

> **Llámalo** por teléfono si no puedes ir a trabajar.
> **Despiértate** temprano para no llegar tarde.
> **No te preocupes** por ganar más sino por trabajar bien.

Buscando trabajo en los anuncios clasificados

Gramática en contexto   309

Present

Class Starter Review
On the day following the review of *tú* commands, you might begin the class with this activity:
Give an affirmative command to one of the students. (Ask the class for the equivalent negative command.) After he or she carries out your command, have him or her give another command to another student, and so on. Continue until all students have had a turn.
As an alternate way to respond, have the whole class react to the commands.

Extended Written Practice/Homework
1. Write three commands telling a classmate what to do or what not to do in order to succeed in your Spanish class.
2. Read the magazine article on p. 308. Write three additional commands telling a person what to do or what not to do in applying for a job.

3. Refer to p. 57 and write four commands telling a person what to do or what not to do to maintain relationships.
4. Write three commands telling a friend what to do or what not to do with respect to TV, videos, and movies.

Multiple Intelligences
Verbal/Linguistic
See Enrichment.
Verbal/Linguistic and Bodily/Kinesthetic
See Class Starter Review.
Visual/Spatial
See Exs. A–C.

Present & Practice

Answers

1 ESTUDIANTE A

Questions will vary, but may follow this pattern:

a. Voy a trabajar de intérprete, ¿qué uso?

b. ...de salvavidas, ¿qué llevo?

c. ...de mecánico(a), ¿qué compro?

d. ...de veterinario(a), ¿qué uso?

e. ...de cajero(a), ¿cómo me visto?

f. ...de pintor(a), ¿qué me pongo?

g. Questions will vary.

ESTUDIANTE B

a.–g. Answers will vary.

2 ESTUDIANTE A

(Students may choose the following endings: *la recepcionista, el cartero, la enfermera, el abogado, el secretario, la jefa.*)

a. ¿Debo explicarle lo que me pasa al (a la) ___?

b. ¿Debo decirle mi nombre ...

c. ¿Debo mostrarle mi solicitud ...

d. ¿Debo preguntarle sobre el sueldo ...

e. Questions will vary.

---

1 Tu compañero(a) tiene un trabajo nuevo y no está seguro(a) de la ropa que debe llevar. Aconséjale usando: *ponerse, usar, vestirse (con), llevar y comprar.*

A —*Voy a trabajar de repartidor. ¿Qué me pongo?*

B —*Lleva jeans y camiseta. No te pongas corbata.*

Estudiante A   Estudiante B

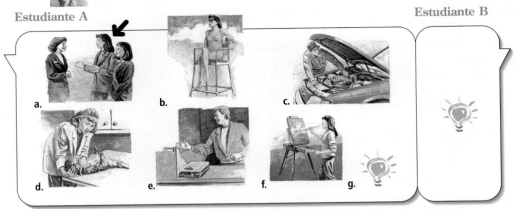

a.   b.   c.

d.   e.   f.   g.

2 Tu compañero(a) te pide consejos usando elementos de los dos recuadros. Contéstale con mandatos negativos y afirmativos.

A —*¿Debo pedirle una carta de recomendación al profesor?*

B —*Sí, pídele una carta de recomendación.*

o: *No, no se la pidas a él. Pídesela al (a la) director(a).*

pedirle una carta de recomendación

a. explicarle lo que me pasa

b. decirle mi nombre

c. mostrarle mi solicitud

d. preguntarle sobre el sueldo

e.

310   Capítulo 9

Options

Strategies for Reaching All Students

Students Needing Extra Help

Ex. 1: Give students time to compile a list of the affirmative and negative commands. Model how the other verbs *(usar, vestirse con,* etc.) can be used. Brainstorm different clothing words. Write them on the chalkboard to help students stay focused on the commands.

Ex. 2: As a class, match the columns. Point out the change from *pedirle* to *pídele* to *no se la pidas.* Give students time to form the commands before combining all the elements of the dialogue. Practice once using the affirmative commands and again using the negative commands.

El subjuntivo en cláusulas adjetivas: Have students add the rules that come up in this chapter to the list they have been creating. Help students understand the meaning of the opening statement. Before proceeding, give models that demonstrate a clause serving as an adjective. Examples may have to be in English. Give additional examples, emphasizing which words make the sentence specific and which show that we are unsure that the situation exists.

El subjuntivo en cláusulas adjetivas

Sometimes we use an entire clause to describe a noun. We call it an adjective clause.

• When we have a specific person or thing in mind, we use the indicative:

Ese restaurante tiene un cocinero **que sabe preparar paella.**

• If we do not have a specific person or thing in mind, or if we are not sure the person or thing exists, we use the subjunctive:

El restaurante busca un cocinero **que sepa preparar paella.**

• We also use the subjunctive in an adjective clause when it describes a negative word such as *nadie, nada,* or *ninguno(a).*

No hay **ningún puesto** en los anuncios clasificados **que me guste.**
No hay **nadie que tenga** la experiencia necesaria.

3 Imagina que se necesitan personas para hacer diferentes trabajos. Con un(a) compañero(a), forma frases con elementos de los dos recuadros.

A —*Se necesita un cocinero que sepa preparar hamburguesas.*
B —*Entonces, Miguel debe solicitar ese trabajo porque siempre cocina hamburguesas.*
o: Debo solicitar ese trabajo porque me gusta mucho cocinar.

a.   b.   c.

d.   e.   f.

saber nadar

hablar idiomas

saber preparar
   hamburguesas

ser honesto

acompañar al (a la)
   diplomático(a)

tener buenos modales

Gramática en contexto   311

El subjuntivo en cláusulas adjetivas: Tell students that we usually omit the *a personal* if the person is indefinite: *Buscamos un secretario que sepa español.*

Extended Written Practice/Homework
1. Write three sentences describing the kind of school or college you would like to attend: *Me gustaría asistir a una universidad que esté cerca de la playa.*
2. Write three sentences describing the ideal boyfriend or girlfriend: *Quiero conocer a un(a) muchacho(a) que tenga los mismos intereses que yo.*

Multiple Intelligences
Verbal/Linguistic
See Exs. 1–3.
Visual/Spatial
See Practice Wkbk. 9-5 and 9-6, Writing Activity 9-D, and Comm. Act. BLM 9-2.

Present & Practice

Teaching Suggestions

Ex.4: Remind students that the subjunctive is used if we do not have a specific person or thing in mind, or if we are unsure if that person or thing actually exists. Ask students to identify what it is in these exercises that is uncertain.

Answers

4 Statements will vary, but students should use the subjunctive in the adjective clauses.

Strategies for Reaching All Students

MULTIPLE INTELLIGENCES
Verbal/Linguistic
See Enrichment and Audio Activities 9.3, 9.4, and 9.5.
Visual/Spatial
See Practice Wkbk. 9-7, 9-8, and 9-9; Writing Activities 9-E and 9-F; and Comm. Act. BLM 9-3.

 Practice Wkbk. 9-7, 9-8

 Writing Activity 9-E

 Prueba 9-6

4 ¿Cuáles piensas que son los aspectos más importantes de un trabajo? Habla con un(a) compañero(a) y completa cada frase de varias maneras.

> *Me conviene trabajar en un lugar que sea callado (que quede cerca de mi casa).*

a. Quiero conseguir un trabajo que . . .
b. Me gustaría trabajar para un jefe (una jefa) que . . .
c. Prefiero trabajar con otros empleados que . . .
d. Quisiera tener un horario de trabajo que . . .
e. Necesito una persona que . . .
f. Me gustaría tener un sueldo que . . .
g. 💡

Analizando información médica en una computadora

El subjuntivo con *cuando*

We use the subjunctive after *cuando* to discuss something that has not yet occurred or that may or may not happen in the future.

> Voy a trabajar en una oficina de turismo **cuando aprenda** a hablar francés.

• We use the indicative when an event will definitely take place or if it occurs regularly. Compare:

> Los domingos, **cuando tengo tiempo,** siempre les escribo a mis abuelos.
> Les escribiré a mis abuelos **cuando tenga tiempo.**

312   Capítulo 9

Options

Strategies for Reaching All Students

Students Needing Extra Help
Ex. 4: Help brainstorm some endings to the statements.
El subjuntivo con cuando: Have students add these rules to their list. Explain that the model sentence sounds as if the verb should be in the future, but that it really shows uncertainty. Present several additional examples, emphasizing why one uses the subjunctive, while the other uses the indicative.

Ex. 5: Review the possible choices to complete the *Estudiante A* statements. Help students see when they will respond with a *yo* form and when they have to respond with the *Ud. / él / ella* form.
Ahora lo sabes: Have students write this so that they can record their progress.

Enrichment
El subjuntivo con cuando: In groups of four or five, have students ask one another the one thing each person is putting off doing

and when or under what conditions he or she plans to do it. Each group can then report to the class on these things, and the class can give its opinion as to whether the person is only procrastinating or has put off doing the thing for valid reasons. Class members may also give advice using affirmative and negative commands with *tú* on how best to overcome the habit of procrastination.

312

5 Tu compañero(a) quiere saber cuándo piensas hacer algo pero tú no estás seguro(a). Explícale de qué depende la situación.

hablar
con la jefa

A — ¿Cuándo vas a hablar con la jefa?
B — Cuando ella regrese a la oficina.

Estudiante A

a. leer los anuncios clasificados
b. buscar un trabajo . . .
c. seguir un entrenamiento . . .
d. visitar al (a la) gerente
e. recibir un aumento de sueldo . . .
f. hacer una llamada . . .
g. hacer una presentación sobre . . .
h.

Estudiante B

entregar el trabajo
comprar el periódico
recordar su número
conseguir más información
tener tiempo
tener más experiencia
hacer una cita con él (ella)

Ahora lo sabes

¿Puedes:

- dar un consejo a un(a) amigo(a)?
  —Si necesitas trabajo, ____ un trabajo de tiempo parcial. No ____ un trabajo de tiempo completo.

- describir a una persona o una cosa que no sabes si existe o no?
  —Buscan una recepcionista que ____ español y francés.

- hablar sobre hechos que pueden ocurrir en el futuro?
  —No sé qué estudiaré cuando ____ a la universidad.

MÁS PRÁCTICA

- Más práctica y tarea, pp. 572–573
  Practice Workbook 9–5, 9–9

Un científico en un laboratorio de biología molecular

Gramática en contexto   313

5 **ESTUDIANTE A**
a. ¿Cuándo vas a leer los anuncios clasificados?
b. . . . buscar un trabajo ___?
c. . . . seguir un entrenamiento ___?
d. . . . visitar al (a la) gerente?
e. . . . recibir un aumento de sueldo ___?
f. . . . hacer una llamada ___?
g. . . . hacer una presentación sobre ___?
h. Questions will vary.
ESTUDIANTE B
a.–h. Answers will vary, but students should use the subjunctive.

Answers: Ahora lo sabes
- busca / busques
- hable (sepa)
- vaya

 Practice Wkbk. 9-9

 Audio Activities 9.3, 9.4, 9.5

 Writing Activity 9-F

 Prueba 9-7

 Comm. Act. BLM 9-3

Cultural Notes

Extended Written Practice/Homework
1. Write a sentence for each expression telling what you will do when these happen: *graduarse de la escuela secundaria, tener 25 años, salir de la casa de tus padres, conseguir un trabajo de tiempo completo. Cuando tenga 25 años, iré a Europa.*
2. Write three sentences telling when you will do different work-related tasks: *Llenaré una solicitud para el trabajo en el restaurante cuando mi amigo me la traiga.*

(p. 312, photo)
In general, medical care and research are not as advanced in Mexico as in wealthier countries. In the field of cardiovascular surgery, however, Mexico City's Centro Médico de la Raza ranks among the finest institutions in the world. Patients need pay only a fraction of what the surgery would cost in the U.S. because of Mexico's socialized medical program.

(p. 313, photo)
A need exists in the U.S. for additional Hispanic medical scientists and personnel, such as this molecular biologist. Although Hispanics made up nearly 10 percent of the U.S. population in 1990, they accounted for only 4.5 percent of physicians. This scarcity of Hispanic medical professionals compounds specific critical health issues such as AIDS, diabetes, and infant mortality.

Point out the key chapter question. Tell students that completing these activities will help them answer this key question. You may select one, two, or all three of these activities, as time permits.

Answers: Sopa de actividades

1–3 Responses will vary.

Cómo tener éxito en el mundo del trabajo

Esta sección te ofrece la oportunidad de combinar lo que aprendiste en este capítulo con lo que ya sabes para responder a la pregunta clave.

Para decir más

Aquí tienes vocabulario adicional que te puede ayudar para hacer las actividades de esta sección.

contratar
here: *to hire*

despedir
to fire

el trabajo en equipo
teamwork

la informática
computer science

programador, -a
computer programmer

redactor, -a
editor

ingeniero, -a
engineer

diseñador, -a
designer

sicólogo, -a
psychologist

el / la asistente, -a social
social worker

314   Capítulo 9

Sopa de actividades

1 En parejas, preparen una conversación entre un(a) estudiante que quiere buscar trabajo y un(a) consejero(a) que le ayuda. Deben incluir la siguiente información:

- los intereses del (de la) estudiante
- sus habilidades, cualidades y experiencia
- qué tipo de trabajo quiere
- cuándo puede trabajar
- qué debe hacer para saber qué trabajos hay
- los requisitos de los trabajos
- qué debe hacer para llenar la solicitud
- cómo debe prepararse para la entrevista

Presenten la conversación a la clase. Los demás estudiantes pueden hacer sugerencias.

Si quieres trabajar de___, ve a ___. Están buscando un(a) ___ que ___ .

Trabajando con una computadora en la tienda de la escuela

Options

Strategies for Reaching All Students

Spanish-Speaking Students
Ex. 2: Add the following to this exercise: *Piensen en cómo los estudios que siguen ahora pueden prepararlos para las carreras que han escogido. ¿Qué materias pueden ayudarles más en las tres profesiones o carreras más populares? ¿Por qué creen que les ayudarán o les serán útiles?*

Students Needing Extra Help
Sopa de actividades: If time is a factor, do only one of the first two activities.
Ex. 1: Allow students to use the vocabulary and grammar sections of the Organizer. Brainstorm phrases that help the conversation flow and move forward. Model a conversation with a complete suggestion.
Ex. 3: Point out that students need to choose only one situation. Allow them to give five or six pieces of advice. Review commands.

Cooperative Learning
Divide the class into groups of three and assign each an occupation. One student should list the qualifications, one the duties, and one the salary and benefits. Encourage creativity and use of new vocabulary and grammar. After all the groups have presented their occupations, have the class vote on the best one.

2 En grupos de tres o cuatro, van a averiguar cuáles serán las profesiones que van a seguir más estudiantes de la clase.

- Hagan una tabla con una lista de los nombres y las profesiones que va a seguir cada miembro del grupo.
- Den la lista a otro grupo. ¿Qué profesiones tienen las listas en común? Trabajen con el otro grupo para hacer una lista que las incluya todas.
- Compartan esta lista con la clase. Hagan una tabla con todas las profesiones escogidas.
- Decidan cuáles son las tres profesiones más populares de toda la clase. Expliquen por qué son las más populares.

3 Trabajen en grupos de tres para darle consejos a un(a) estudiante sobre una situación que le interese. Pueden darle consejos sobre cómo:

- conseguir un trabajo
- tener buena salud
- preparar algún plato que le guste
- practicar algún deporte o pasatiempo
- ser un(a) buen(a) estudiante, deportista, músico(a), artista, etc.

Piensen de cuatro a seis consejos que quieren darle usando mandatos afirmativos y negativos. Para presentar cada situación, pueden hacer un cartel, grabar una canción "rap" o hacer una dramatización.

Sopa de actividades   315

Video Activity A

Video, Capítulo 9

Chapter 9: Play

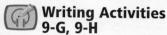
Step

Video Activities B–C

Writing Activities 9-G, 9-H

Comm. Act. BLMs 9-4, 9-5

Cultural Notes ☀

Multiple Intelligences
Interpersonal/Social and Verbal/Linguistic
See Exs. 1 and 3 and Cooperative Learning.
Interpersonal/Social, Verbal/Linguistic, and Logical/Mathematical
See Ex. 2.
Visual/Spatial
See Writing Activities 9-G and 9-H and Comm. Act. BLMs 9-4 and 9-5.

(p. 314, photo)
Student at La Escuela Regional Preparatoria de la Universidad de Guadalajara in Puerto Vallarta. Only four out of ten university students in Mexico are women, in spite of the fact that females make up more than half of the student population at lower educational levels. This figure is expected to rise, however, as the growing feminist movement focuses attention on changing the attitudes and economic conditions that make it more difficult for women to pursue a higher education.

Apply

Teaching Suggestions

Remind students that working through the *Para leer* section will help them answer the key chapter question.

Encourage students to use the strategies given in the text to help them understand the reading. Remind them that they do not need to understand every word.

Process Reading

For a description of process reading, see p. 52.

Answers
Antes de leer

Answers will vary, but students may mention:
Por lo general, hacen preguntas sobre lo que te gusta, los pasatiempos, las cosas que haces, etc. / Número 3 no aparecerá en una prueba de personalidad.

Mira la lectura

Para tomar la prueba, hay que leer las explicaciones de las categorías, darle puntaje a varias actividades y sumar los puntos. (Número 1)

Para leer

Antes de leer

STRATEGY ➤ Using prior knowledge

A mucha gente le gusta tomar pruebas de personalidad que salen en revistas. Por lo general, ¿sobre qué cosas hacen preguntas? ¿Cuál de estas preguntas crees que no aparecerá en una prueba de personalidad?

1. Tus amigos empiezan a cantar. Tú (a) también cantas, (b) te vas en seguida, (c) mueves los labios sin cantar.

2. Si estás trabajando en grupo en la clase y alguien no quiere cooperar, tú (a) tratas de convencerle de que coopere, (b) apoyas su decisión, (c) te quejas al (a la) profesor(a).

3. Si una blusa vale $17.95 y tiene un descuento del 25%, ¿cuánto tienes que pagar por ella?

4. Puedes imitar bien un paso de baile. ¿Sí o no?

Mira la lectura

STRATEGY ➤ Skimming

Lee este artículo rápidamente sólo para ver su organización. Para tomar la prueba, ¿qué pasos hay que seguir?

1. a. leer las explicaciones de las categorías
   b. darle puntaje a varias actividades
   c. sumar los puntos

2. a. darle puntaje a varias actividades
   b. sumar los puntos
   c. leer las explicaciones de las categorías

3. a. sumar los puntos
   b. darle puntaje a varias actividades
   c. leer las explicaciones de las categorías

¿Qué TIPO de *inteligencia* tienes?

El intelecto es muy importante, pero aún más esencial es saber aprovecharlo al máximo. Y eso sólo puedes lograrlo si sabes qué clase de inteligencia tienes. Sí, porque muchas personas desaprovechan su potencial y no logran alcanzar sus metas. ¡Tú no quieres cometer ese fallo! Descubre ahora mismo tu área fuerte en materia gris ... ¡Adelante!

Piensa lo buena que eres o serías en cada una de estas actividades, en comparación con tus amigas. Si te sientes tan buena como ellas, date un 0. Pero si piensas que lo harías un poco mejor, apúntate un 1. Si crees que las dejarías enanas, anótate un grandioso 2.

___ 1 Encontrar una dirección en un mapa.

___ 2 Reconocer que estás de mal humor y salir de él.

___ 3 Tocar, de oído, una canción que te gusta.

___ 4 Cargar una enorme cantidad de libros.

___ 5 Conversar con los amigos de tus padres.

___ 6 Empacar una maleta, con todo bien acomodado.

___ 7 Recordar la letra de una canción.

___ 8 Jugar damas.

___ 9 Reconocer la guitarra, bajo, etc., en tu canción favorita.

___ 10 Aprender suficiente francés como para "defenderte" una semana en Francia.

___ 11 Lograr que tus amigos se pongan de acuerdo sobre qué película van a ver.

316   Capítulo 9

Options

Strategies for Reaching All Students

Students Needing Extra Help
Mira la lectura: Point out to students that they are not taking the quiz until they finish the *Infórmate* section. At this point, they should be skimming and deciding the order of the steps they need to follow.

Multiple Intelligences
Logical/Mathematical and Verbal/Linguistic
See *Para leer.*

316 Standards 1.2; 3.1; 5.1; 5.2

PUNTUACIÓN

Mira qué número pusiste para cada pregunta y suma cada categoría. El máximo puntaje que puedes obtener de cada categoría es 8. En las que adquieres el puntaje más alto son tus áreas más fuertes en esto de la materia gris.

— **1** espacio
— **2** relaciones
— **3** música
— **4** cuerpo
— **5** _____
— **6** espacio
— **7** capacidad oral
— **8** espacio
— **9** música
— **10** capacidad oral
— **11** relaciones
— **12** capacidad oral
— **13** _____
— **14** cuerpo
— **15** espacio
— **16** lógica/matemáticas
— **17** cuerpo
— **18** _____
— **19** lógica/matemáticas
— **20** relaciones
— **21** cuerpo
— **22** lógica/matemáticas
— **23** capacidad oral
— **24** música

¿Quieres saber más?
Pues sigue leyendo…

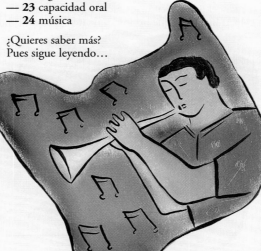

___ **12** Hacer un crucigrama.

___ **13** Llevar una cuenta—en tu cabeza—de cuánto dinero has gastado durante el día.

___ **14** Imitar los manerismos de tu maestra.

___ **15** Armar la batidora que se desarmó.

___ **16** Sacar la cuenta para saber cuándo tu cumpleaños caerá un sábado.

___ **17** Aplicar esmalte de uñas, que te las cubra todas (no las cutículas ni tus jeans favoritos).

___ **18** Identificar una canción instantáneamente.

___ **19** Crear un programa de computadora.

___ **20** Intuir cuándo debes actuar.

___ **21** Hacer un acto de malabarismo.

___ **22** Jugar barajas.

___ **23** Hacer chistes… y que sean graciosos.

___ **24** Distinguir cuándo cantan fuera de tono.

Para leer   317

Apply

Para leer

¿CÓMO ERES?

Ahora vamos a explicarte a qué nos referimos con inteligencia del cuerpo, espacio, etc. Pon mucho ojo, chica...

ESPACIO: Esto se refiere a tu capacidad de percibir el mundo físico y de "verlo" en tu mente e incluso "jugar" con esos elementos en tu imaginación. Es la cualidad que "hace" a un buen artista, ingeniero, arquitecto, diseñador, inventor, etc.

CAPACIDAD ORAL: Se relaciona con tu forma de hablar, tu amor por las palabras, la sutileza de una frase, la cadencia de tal oración. Es la cualidad de los escritores, abogados, políticos, historiadores, editores, personas de relaciones públicas, etc.

RELACIONES: Esta área de tu inteligencia tiene que ver con el arte de conocerte y de saber "leer" a los demás. También, con tu sensibilidad, intuición, compasión... Es la parte fuerte de los maestros, sicólogos, políticos, trabajadores sociales, ministros, etc.

LÓGICA/MATEMÁTICAS: Esta clase de inteligencia es rápida para los números y buenísima para el pensamiento abstracto (ver conexiones, patrones, etc., que no son evidentes o concretos). Si

318

ésta es tu área fuerte, quizás te "hala" la matemática, la contabilidad, la ciencia, las computadoras... Tienes un amplio campo para escoger.

CUERPO: Concierne a la habilidad de coordinar tu cuerpo; de moverte en forma grácil, según la ocasión. Ésta es la capacidad básica de los bailarines, deportistas, actores, músicos e incluso los cirujanos que necesitan total control de sus manos.

MÚSICA: Este aspecto de la inteligencia tiene que ver con la capacidad de percibir y apreciar los ritmos y las melodías... y de reproducirlos. Apostamos a que te pasas el día oyendo música y que muchos amigos te dicen que deberías ser cantante. Entre las profesiones que podrían "llamarte" se encuentran: músico, maestro de música, locutor de radio, ingeniero de sonido, etc.

Bueno, ya conoces cuáles son tus áreas fuertes y qué trabajos se adaptan a tu tipo de inteligencia. No creas que te conviene saberlo por simple curiosidad... "Armada" con esta información, podrás tomar una decisión astuta, precisamente, sobre tu futuro: la carrera para la que tienes aptitud, la que más te gusta de ellas y todo ese rollo universitario. Sácale provecho...

Options

Strategies for Reaching All Students

Infórmate

STRATEGY ➤ Coping with unknown words

Recuerda que puedes seguir tres pasos cuando encuentras una palabra que no conoces. Primero, pregúntate ¿es importante saber esta palabra para entender la selección? Si es así, la segunda pregunta es ¿qué me dice el contexto sobre la palabra? Si todavía no sabes su significado, pregúntate ¿quién o qué cosa me puede ayudar? Por ejemplo, puedes preguntarle a un(a) compañero(a), o puedes buscar la palabra en un diccionario.

1. Mira la frase número 9 que empieza *Reconocer la guitarra, bajo, etc.*,... Si no conoces la palabra *bajo,* en realidad no es muy importante, pero vale la pena usar el contexto como ayuda. Como la palabra *bajo* sigue a la palabra *guitarra,* es probable que también sea un instrumento musical. ¿Qué instrumento musical tiene un tono muy bajo? Adivina *(guess),* luego busca la palabra en un diccionario.

2. En la sección **Puntuación** faltan los números 5, 13 y 18. Léelos de nuevo y decide a qué categoría pertenecen. En una hoja de papel, escribe las categorías y los números correspondientes.

3. Ahora toma la prueba. Usa la estrategia que acabamos de practicar como ayuda.

Aplicación

¿Qué categorías les hacen falta a los que siguen estas profesiones? Decide con un(a) compañero(a). Pueden asignar más de una categoría a cada una.

- profesor(a) universitario(a)
- enfermero(a)
- piloto
- abogado(a)

Para leer   319

Apply

Teaching Suggestions
Remind students that working through the *Para escribir* section will help them answer the key chapter question.

Process Writing
For information regarding writing portfolios, see p. 54.

Answers
Résumés will vary.

Multicultural Perspectives
Since the job market is generally tighter than in the U.S., a Latin American would almost never send out mass mailings of an unsolicited *curriculum vitae,* or résumé. Instead, hopeful candidates responding to a classified ad will hand-deliver their *curricula* to the company to which they are applying. For extra credit, have students critique each other's résumés from this section's activity.

Para escribir

Antes de graduarse de la secundaria, muchos jóvenes ya están pensando en el trabajo que van a tener o en la profesión que van a seguir. ¿Has pensado tú en esto? Para poder escoger lo que te conviene tienes que analizar tus intereses, tus habilidades y tu experiencia. Vas a preparar un resumen que te ayudará a decidir cómo puedes tener éxito en el mundo del trabajo.

1 Primero, considera estas preguntas.

- ¿Cómo eres? ¿Cuáles son tus características?
- ¿Cuáles son tus habilidades?
- ¿Qué sabes de diferentes trabajos o profesiones? ¿Qué experiencias de trabajo has tenido?
- ¿Cuáles son tus intereses principales?

En una hoja de papel haz cuatro columnas. Escribe tus respuestas para cada categoría.

2 Ahora, piensa en un trabajo o una profesión que te interesa.

- ¿Cuál es? ¿Por qué te atrae?
- ¿Cuáles son los requisitos para el trabajo?
- ¿Qué necesitas saber? ¿Qué tipo de educación debes tener?
- ¿Qué experiencia necesitas?

Responde brevemente a estas preguntas. Luego, revisa la tabla que has hecho y compara tus habilidades, características, experiencia e intereses con los que se necesitan para el trabajo que has escogido. Escribe un breve análisis y preséntalo a la clase.

320   Capítulo 9

Options

Strategies for Reaching All Students

Students Needing Extra Help
Assign this activity ahead of time so that students can check with their guidance counselor or someone they know in the field. Discuss with students the differences between their charts and the reality of the career. Review the meanings of the expressions in Step 2.

Recuerda que debes revisar tu análisis con un(a) compañero(a) y seguir los pasos del proceso de escribir.

Aquí tienes algunas palabras y expresiones que te pueden ayudar.

además	hasta ahora	por un lado / por otro lado
de la misma manera	por esto	sin embargo
desde que		

 Para compartir tu trabajo puedes:

- exhibirlo en la sala de clases
- hacer una "Feria de trabajo" para ayudar a otros estudiantes a preparar su propio autoanálisis y darles información sobre trabajos y profesiones
- juntar las descripciones de los diferentes trabajos en una colección llamada *Trabajos y profesiones para nuestro futuro*
- poner tu trabajo en tu portafolio

Para escribir   321

Assess & Summarize

Test Preparation
You may want to assign parts of this section as written homework or as an in-class writing activity prior to administering the *Examen de habilidades.*

Answers
Listening
—*Quisiera conseguir un trabajo. He leído los anuncios clasificados pero no veo ninguno que acepte a alguien sin experiencia.*
—*¿Buscas de tiempo completo o de tiempo parcial?*
—*Me conviene más de tiempo parcial.*
—*¿En qué has trabajado antes? ¿Tienes habilidad en algo?*
—*Bueno, no tengo ningún entrenamiento, pero tengo buenos modales, y soy capaz y honesto.*
—*Son cualidades muy importantes, pero sin destreza, no puedo ofrecerte mucho. A ver, aquí hay dos. ¿Qué te parece éste como repartidor, o ése trabajando en el archivo en una oficina?*
Answers will vary, but students may mention:
Ha sido difícil para la persona encontrar trabajo porque no tiene ninguna experiencia. Esta persona es capaz y honesta. Le han ofrecido un trabajo como repartidor, o un trabajo en los archivos de una oficina.

Esta sección te ayudará a preparate para el examen de habilidades, donde tendrás que hacer tareas semejantes.

Listening
¿Puedes entender una conversación sobre trabajos? Escucha mientras el(la) profesor(a) lee un ejemplo semejante al que vas a oír en el examen. ¿Por qué ha sido difícil para esta persona encontrar trabajo? ¿Qué cualidades personales tiene? ¿Cuáles son los trabajos que le han ofrecido?

Reading
¿Puedes leer este anuncio que salió en un periódico y usar lo que sabes sobre los cognados, el contexto y las familias de palabras para saber de qué se trata?

Writing
¿Puedes escribir una carta como la que Agustín le escribió a su hermano?

Querido Jaime:

Quisiera conseguir un trabajo de tiempo completo para las vacaciones. Aunque tengo poca experiencia, soy honesto y respetuoso y tengo buenas recomendaciones. He leído los anuncios clasificados y he visto algo que me conviene. Presenté una solicitud en una tienda que vende computadoras. ¿Podrías prepararme para la entrevista? Escríbeme cuando puedas.

Saludos,

Agustín

Culture
¿Cuáles son algunos de los trabajos más populares en México hoy? ¿Y en los Estados Unidos?

Speaking
¿Puedes hablar con el/la gerente de un restaurante sobre un trabajo?

A —*Buenas tardes. Leí su anuncio en la puerta y me gustaría trabajar en su restaurante. ¿Qué necesito hacer?*

B —*Primero, llena esta solicitud. Escribe con bolígrafo, por favor. ¿Tienes alguna experiencia?*

A —*Bueno, he trabajado antes en un restaurante, soy puntual y honesto y tengo mucha paciencia.*

B —*¿Tienes entrenamiento como cocinero(a)? Necesitamos a una persona con experiencia.*

A —*Pues, nunca he trabajado como cocinero(a), pero . . .*

www.pasoapaso.com

¿Qué tienen estas dos personas en común?

Las dos recibieron entrenamiento en el Instituto Global de Carreras mientras mantenían sus trabajos de tiempo completo.

Ud. también podrá conseguir un ascenso o aumento de sueldo si desarrolla sus habilidades y adquiere nuevas destrezas. Llene su solicitud en cuanto pueda y el Instituto Global de Carreras le ayudará a alcanzar su meta.

322 Capítulo 9

Options

Strategies for Reaching All Students

Students Needing Extra Help
Have students write this exercise so that they can check off what they have mastered. Remind them that this is just a sample of what the test will be like.
Listening: Read more than once. Brainstorm the vocabulary that students should be listening for.
Reading: Remind students that they do not need to know every word in the text. Point out that this exercise is asking them what the ad is about.

Writing: Have students use the Organizer and write a sample letter as practice. Have them review what they wrote in the *Para escribir* section.
Culture: Have students review the notes they took from the *Álbum cultural.*
Speaking: Use the vocabulary section of the Organizer. Complete the model and limit the number of lines of dialogue.
Have students review Ex. 6 on p. 302 for further practice.

Resumen del vocabulario

Usa el vocabulario de este capítulo para:

- responder a la pregunta clave: Cómo tener éxito en el mundo del trabajo
- hablar de diferentes tipos de trabajo
- describir las cualidades y habilidades que se necesitan para realizar un trabajo
- explicar los pasos necesarios para buscar y conseguir trabajo

para hablar de distintos trabajos
el cliente, la clienta
el diplomático, la diplomática
el /la gerente
el /la intérprete
el jefe, la jefa
el /la recepcionista
el repartidor, la repartidora
el /la salvavidas
(de) tiempo completo
(de) tiempo parcial

para describir las cualidades necesarias para un trabajo
adecuado, -a
ambicioso, -a
capaz, *pl.* capaces
cortés, *pl.* corteses
la cualidad
cuidadoso, -a
la destreza
la habilidad
honesto, -a
maduro, -a
los modales, *pl.*
la paciencia
productivo, -a
puntual
la puntualidad
respetuoso, -a

para explicar los requisitos de un trabajo
administrar
administrativo, -a
el archivo
atender *(e → ie)* (a)
cualquier
cumplir con
distribuir *(i → y)*
encargarse *(g → gu)* (de)
el entrenamiento
la experiencia
merecer *(c → zc)*
oportuno, -a
realizar *(z → c)*
la recomendación, *pl.* las recomendaciones
el requisito
la tarea
tratar (bien /mal)

para buscar y conseguir trabajo
alcanzar *(z → c)*
los anuncios clasificados
el ascenso
el aumento (de sueldo)
la cita
fijo, -a
la meta
la solicitud
el sueldo

otras palabras y expresiones útiles
ahora mismo
convenir *(e → ie):*
    me conviene
cuando creas (from: *creer*)
no sólo . . . sino también

Resumen 323

Reading
Answers will vary, but students may mention:
El anuncio se trata del entrenamiento de carreras en el Instituto Global de Carreras.

Writing
Letters will vary.

Culture
Answers will vary, but students may refer to the list on p. 306.

Speaking
Dialogues will vary.

Assessment

 Prueba cumulativa

 Examen de habilidades

 Test Generator

Additional Assessment Options

 Comm. Act. BLMs

Small Group Activities
Situation Cards

 ¿Lo sabes bien? Video Quiz

Internet Activities
Self-Test

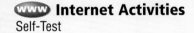

CAPÍTULO 10

THEME: CONTROLLING VIOLENCE

SCOPE AND SEQUENCE Pages 324–361

COMMUNICATION

Topics

Types of crime

Trial participants

Types of punishment

Objectives

Dar ejemplos del control de la violencia en los países de habla hispana y en los Estados Unidos

Describir un hecho de violencia

Hablar sobre el control de la violencia

Describir los efectos de la violencia

Hablar de soluciones a la violencia

CULTURE

El control de la violencia en los países hispanos

GRAMMAR

Mandatos afirmativos y negativos con Ud. *y* Uds.

El subjuntivo con expresiones de emoción

Ancillaries available for use with Chapter 10

Multisensory/Technology

Overheads, 30–32

Audio Tapes and CDs

Vocabulary Art Blackline Masters for Hands-On Learning, pp. 46–49/CD-ROM

Classroom Crossword

Video

Internet Activities
www.pasoapaso.com

Print

Practice Workbook, pp. 101–109

Writing, Audio & Video Activities, pp. 59–64, 120–122, 151–152

Communicative Activity Blackline Masters

Pair and Small Group Activities, pp. 64–69

Situation Cards, p. 70

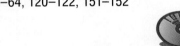

RESOURCE PRO®

Planning Express, Teaching Resources Library, and Clip Art Library

Assessment

Assessment Program

Pruebas, pp. 139–148

Examen de habilidades, pp. 149–152

Test Generator

¿Lo sabes bien? Video Quiz

Video, Chap. 10

Violence in Latin America

Violence is one of the consuming issues of our time. In the U.S. and throughout Latin America, the daily news is filled with accounts of attacks on individuals. Spain is not spared the problem, although its violent crime rate is not as high as in many parts of the Americas.

The U.S. has long been viewed internationally as a violent society. Today our high-profile trials are broadcast around the world, while some popular television shows and films produced in the U.S. graphically depict instances of violence.

While politically inspired attacks are rare in the U.S., violence in Latin American nations has frequently had political overtones. During the 1980s, civil wars and guerrilla fighting consumed the nations of El Salvador, Guatemala, Peru, and Nicaragua. The victims of these conflicts included many civic leaders, such as mayors, jurists, priests, and important businesspeople. The fighting prompted many people to seek shelter in the U.S. And Colombia's often futile attempts to control its drug lords are well known.

Many acts of violence often have a seemingly random nature in the U.S. This contrasts with the events that transpired during the so-called *guerra sucia,* or "dirty war," in Argentina in the 1970s, where a systematic government campaign of kidnapping and murder was conducted against the intellectual and university student population.

Preoccupation with personal safety can be observed everywhere in Latin America and in Spain. Tourists are often surprised to note the number of bank guards, local police, and other security professionals who carry machine guns. Some people employ armed escorts. Security cameras are mounted on the homes of the upper class, focused on the entrance to record the presence of an intruder. Violence may take on different characteristics in Latin America as compared to the U.S., but it is a problem that both must learn to solve.

Introduce

Re-entry of Concepts

The following list represents words, expressions, and grammar topics re-entered from Books 1, 2, and 3 (Chaps. 3–8):

Book 1
direct and indirect object pronouns, preterite

Book 2
imperfect, impersonal *se,* subjunctive

Chapter 3
imperfect progressive

Chapter 4
present perfect

Chapter 7
subjunctive with verbs of persuasion

Chapter 8
present perfect subjunctive

Planning

Cross-Curricular Connections

Math Connection *(pp. 334–335)*
Have students conduct a survey of other students in their school to find out if they personally have been the victim of a crime, or if someone in their family or someone they know has been the victim of a crime. Tabulate the results and calculate the percentages in each category. For example: 8 out of 25 people interviewed said they were the victim of a robbery = 32 percent.

Civics Connection *(pp. 352–353)*
Have groups of five students create a proposal for changes in our judicial system, including prisons, which would truly and fairly deal with violent criminals. Tell them to describe what sentencing law and incarceration would be like under their system.

Spanish in Your Community
Have students obtain crime prevention material in Spanish from the local police department. Have them study this material and develop a bulletin board using it. If such material is not available, tell the class to develop a crime-prevention flyer focused at younger Spanish-speaking students. Make it available at middle or junior high schools and at local community agencies that serve a Spanish-speaking population.

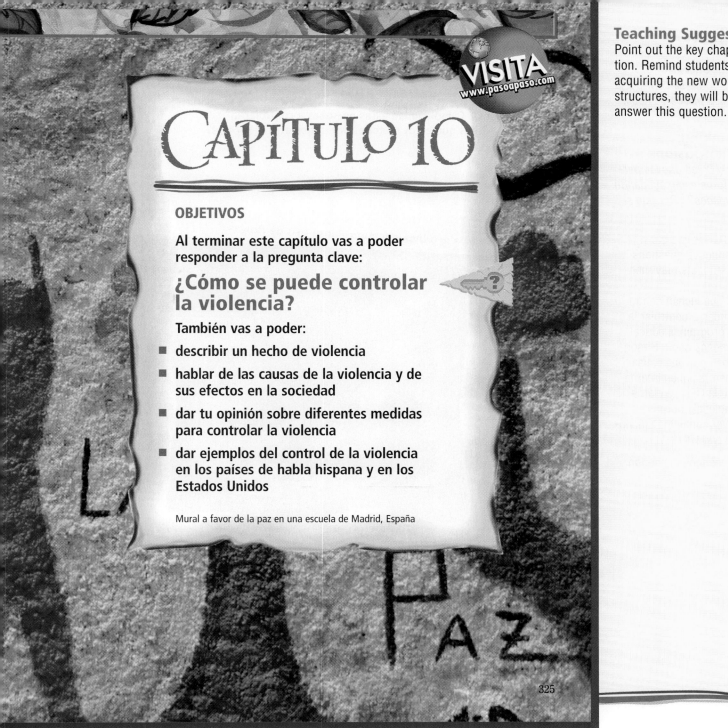

CAPÍTULO 10

OBJETIVOS

Al terminar este capítulo vas a poder responder a la pregunta clave:

¿Cómo se puede controlar la violencia?

También vas a poder:

- describir un hecho de violencia
- hablar de las causas de la violencia y de sus efectos en la sociedad
- dar tu opinión sobre diferentes medidas para controlar la violencia
- dar ejemplos del control de la violencia en los países de habla hispana y en los Estados Unidos

Mural a favor de la paz en una escuela de Madrid, España

325

VISITA www.pasoapaso.com

Cultural Notes

Cultural Objective
• *Hablar sobre cómo se controla la violencia en los países de habla hispana*

Critical Thinking: Drawing Conclusions
Ask students: *¿Crees que las personas en las fotos están ayudando a sus comunidades? ¿Por qué sí o no?*

Answers: Anticipación
Answers to inductive questions will vary, but students may mention:
Las personas que luchan contra las drogas ayudan a controlar la violencia con programas educativos. Las personas como Simón Bolívar luchaban por una causa justa. Las organizaciones internacionales como la OEA ayudan a controlar la violencia porque quieren resolver conflictos sin violencia. / *Answers will vary.*

Answers to questions in caption text will vary.

Anticipación

Mira las fotos. ¿Cómo ayudan estas personas a controlar la violencia? ¿Crees que estos métodos son suficientes? ¿Por qué?

"Educando a otros ayudamos a controlar el uso de drogas."

Muchos jóvenes en todo el mundo luchan contra la violencia y las drogas a través de campañas educativas como ésta, en Madrid, España. ¿Por qué es efectiva la educación para reducir el uso de drogas?

326   Capítulo 10

Options

Strategies for Reaching All Students

Spanish-Speaking Students
Ask: *¿Cuáles son algunas actividades que contribuyen a disminuir la violencia? ¿Dónde hay que empezar a controlar la violencia, en casa o en la escuela? ¿Por qué?*

Students Needing Extra Help
Use cognates and word families to help students understand words such as *pacíficamente* and *fines*.
Brainstorm other international organizations. Explain that elections in other countries may tend to sometimes bring about violent situations.

Multiple Intelligences
Visual/Spatial and Bodily/Kinesthetic
Have students create posters that give messages about stopping violence and saying *no* to drugs.

A veces la violencia y la lucha son inevitables. Durante la guerra de independencia, las personas se unían para luchar por una causa justa. Esta estatua en Caracas, Venezuela, está dedicada al Libertador Simón Bolívar, líder de la lucha por la independencia de su país. ¿En qué casos crees que la violencia es inevitable?

Algunas organizaciones internacionales como la Organización de los Estados Americanos (OEA), ayudan a resolver conflictos pacíficamente. En Nicaragua en 1990 y de nuevo en 1996, los representantes de la OEA ayudaron a supervisar las elecciones para garantizar que fueran libres y seguras. ¿Qué otras organizaciones internacionales conoces? ¿Trabajan por la paz o tienen otros fines?

Visita estos países

327

Cultural Notes ☀

(p. 326, photo)
As in any major world city, drugs are a problem in Madrid. The location of this display is not far from the Gran Vía, one of Madrid's most elegant thoroughfares, but also now the center of the city's drug trade.

(p. 327, top photo)
The memory of Simón Bolívar, South America's *Libertador,* is revered in Caracas, his birthplace. Statues, streets, plazas, and buildings bear his name. Born in 1783, Bolívar led the fight for freedom from Spanish rule in the area that would become Venezuela, Colombia, Ecuador, Bolivia, and Peru. He died in 1830, disillusioned by the factionalism of the people whose lands he had liberated and convinced that whoever worked for a revolution was "plowing the sea."

(p. 327, bottom photo)
Until 1990, Nicaragua's leftist government was run by the Sandinista political party, named for the rebel leader Augusto César Sandino. Since 1983, they had been challenged by anti-Sandinistas, or *contras,* who invaded the country. Fighting ended in April 1990 with a cease-fire agreement negotiated by the United Nations. This photo shows the Organization of American States peacekeeping forces in El Almendro during the disarmament of the *contras* in June 1990.

Present

Chapter Theme
Violent crime

Communicative Objectives
- *Describir un hecho de violencia*
- *Hablar sobre el control de la violencia*
- *Describir los efectos de la violencia*
- *Hablar de soluciones a la violencia*

 Overheads 30–31

 Vocabulary Art BLMs/CD-ROM

 Vocabulary Tape 10-1

Teaching Suggestions
Preparing students to speak: Use one or two options from each of the categories of Comprehensible Input or Limited Verbal Response. For a complete explanation of these categories and some sample activities, see pp. T20–T21.

Class Starter Review
On the day following the presentation of vocabulary, you may want to begin the class with this activity:
Using the Overhead for this vocabulary section, ask students to describe the crime scene. In addition, have them describe what was taking place ten minutes

Options

Vocabulario para comunicarse

La violencia en nuestra vida
Aquí tienes palabras y expresiones necesarias para hablar sobre la violencia. Léelas varias veces y practícalas con un(a) compañero(a) en las páginas siguientes.

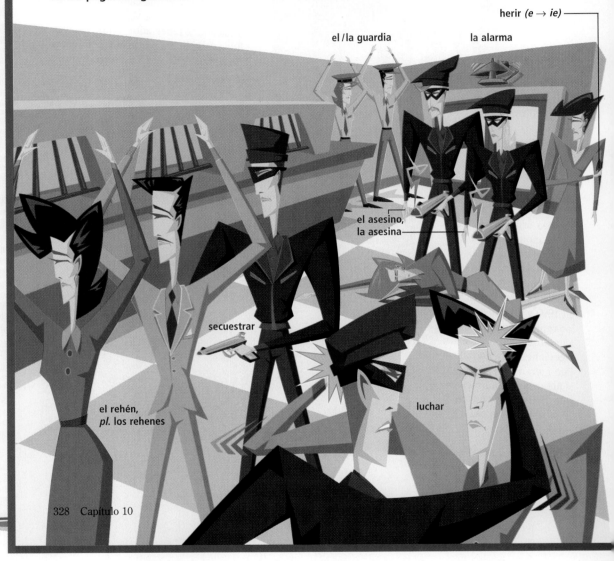

herir *(e → ie)*

el /la guardia

la alarma

el asesino, la asesina

secuestrar

el rehén, *pl.* los rehenes

luchar

328   Capítulo 10

Strategies for Reaching All Students

Spanish-Speaking Students
Have students write: *Escribe una descripción de cada dibujo usando el pasado. Explica lo que crees que ha ocurrido. Usa el vocabulario de esta lista en tu descripción.*

Students Needing Extra Help
Have students begin the vocabulary section of the Organizer. Explain why *herir* is rarely used in the present tense.
Point out the relationship between *secuestrar* and *el secuestro*.
Point out that there is no written accent on *rehenes*. Present *el asesino* and *el asesinato* together. Show that *testigo* is invariable: *el testigo, la testigo*.

También necesitas . . . : Write out the complete verb paradigm for *castigar* in the preterite. Point out the relationship between *culpable* and *tener la culpa (de)*. Explain the meaning of *vigilar*. Point out that *temer* and *tener miedo (de)* are synonyms. If available, refer to the vocabulary section of the Book 2, Chap. 10 Organizer.

También necesitas . . .

el asesinato	*murder*	el sospechoso,	*suspect*
la autodefensa	*self-defense*	la sospechosa	
castigar *(g → gu)*	*to punish*	tener la culpa (de)	*to be guilty, to be at*
culpable	*guilty*		*fault*
el lugar de los hechos	*scene of the crime*	el tiroteo	*shooting*
la medida	*measure*	asombrar	*to astonish*
meter en (la cárcel)	*to put (in jail)*	preocupar(se)	*to worry*
la muerte	*death*	sorprender(se)	*to surprise*
el narcotráfico	*drug trafficking*	temer (a)	*to fear, to be afraid (of)*
la pena	*penalty*	tener miedo (de)	*to be afraid (of)*
el secuestro	*kidnapping, hijacking*	vigilar	*to guard, to watch*

¿Y qué quiere decir . . . ?
defender(se) *(e → ie)*   la droga
el / la delincuente   inocente

el jurado

la cárcel

el acusado,
la acusada

el / la testigo

329

¡NO OLVIDES!
You can also use these words:

arrestar	matar
el crimen	ocurrir
el / la criminal	la policía
la escena	robar
el hecho	la víctima
investigar	la violencia
el ladrón, la ladrona	violento, -a
pl. los ladrones	

before the crime, and what will take place later after the trial *(el juicio).*

Multicultural Perspectives
During the 1980s, the violence of a civil war in El Salvador and military regimes in Argentina and other South American countries added new words to the dictionary. The term *los desplazados* has come to name those who had been displaced from their homes because of the civil war in El Salvador. In Argentina, a group known as Las Madres de la Plaza de Mayo gathered daily to protest *los desaparecidos*—the disappeared ones. These women carried pictures of their sons, daughters, and husbands to show the world those who had disappeared. Other words that have become commonplace on television and in the newspaper are *guerrilla, guerrilleros, cartel,* and *comandantes.* Help students brainstorm the meanings of these words, if they are not already familiar with them.

www **Internet Activities**
Juegos

Extended Written Practice/Homework
1. Imagine that you arrived after the scene on p. 328 occurred. Write three sentences describing what had happened: *Los criminales habían herido a una empleada.*
2. Write three sentences telling what the people pictured on p. 329 should do.

3. Choose three crimes and write sentences saying if they are a serious problem in your community and why: *Los tiroteos son un problema grave porque muchas personas inocentes se mueren.*

Multiple Intelligences
Verbal/Linguistic
See Vocabulary Tape 10-1.
Visual/Spatial
1) Have students write a brief story about what is taking place in the pictures on pp. 328–329.
2) See Overheads 30–31 and the Vocabulary Art BLMs/CD-ROM.
Visual/Spatial and Verbal/Linguistic
See Class Starter Review.

Practice

Re-enter / Recycle
Ex. 3: imperfect progressive from Chap. 3

Answers: Empecemos a conversar

1 ESTUDIANTE A
a. ¿Sabes qué es un ladrón?
b. ...un rehén?
c. ...una guardia?
d. ...una abogada?
e. ...un acusado?
f. ...un jurado?
g. Questions will vary.

ESTUDIANTE B
a. Sí, una persona que roba.
b. ...que es secuestrada.
c. ...que vigila los edificios.
d. ...que defiende al acusado.
e. ...que es acusada del crimen.
f. ...unas personas que deciden quién tiene la culpa.
g. Answers will vary.

2 ESTUDIANTE A
a. En el lugar de los hechos arresté a dos sospechosos.
b. ¡No hay suficientes pruebas! El acusado es inocente.
c. Yo estaba vigilando el museo esa noche cuando oí la alarma.
d. Vi a dos hombres salir del museo corriendo.
e. Hemos decidido que es culpable.
f. ¡A la cárcel por quince años!
g. ¡Soy inocente! ¡Tienen que creerme!

Empecemos a conversar

Túrnate con un(a) compañero(a) para ser *Estudiante A* y *Estudiante B*. Reemplacen las palabras subrayadas con palabras representadas o escritas en los recuadros. 💡 quiere decir que puedes escoger tu propia respuesta.

1
    A — ¿Sabes qué es *un asesino*?
    B — *Sí, una persona que mata a otra*.

Estudiante A

Estudiante B

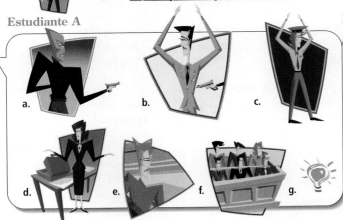

a.   b.   c.

d.   e.   f.   g.

Estudiante B
ser secuestrado(a)
ser acusado(a) del crimen
defender al (a la) acusado(a)
vigilar los edificios
decidir quién tiene la culpa
robar

¿Quién lo dice?

2   A — *Pero, no pude herir a nadie porque yo no tenía pistola*.
    B — *Eso es lo que dice el acusado*.

Estudiante A

Estudiante B

a. En el lugar de los hechos arresté a dos sospechosos.
b. ¡No hay suficientes pruebas! El acusado es inocente.
c. Yo estaba vigilando el museo esa noche cuando oí la alarma.
d. Vi a dos hombres salir del museo corriendo.
e. Hemos decidido que es culpable.
f. ¡A la cárcel por quince años!
g. ¡Soy inocente! ¡Tienen que creerme!

Options

Strategies for Reaching All Students

Spanish-Speaking Students
Ex. 1: Pair Spanish-speaking students for this exercise, if possible.
Exs. 2–3: Pair bilingual with non-bilingual students, if possible.

Students Needing Extra Help
Ex. 1: Students may not recognize *ser secuestrado(a)* and *ser acusado(a)*. Explain that the past participle will agree with *persona* in these two sentences.
Ex. 3: Decide what verbs are needed in order to describe the pictures.
Review the imperfect progressive.

Enrichment
Ex. 1: To extend this exercise, divide students into groups of three or four, giving each group an index card with one of the following words or phrases on it: *la autodefensa, el lugar de los hechos, el narcotráfico, el secuestro, el tiroteo*. Tell students that they are to plan dialogue and actions for a scene in a movie about the word or phrase on their index card without actually saying

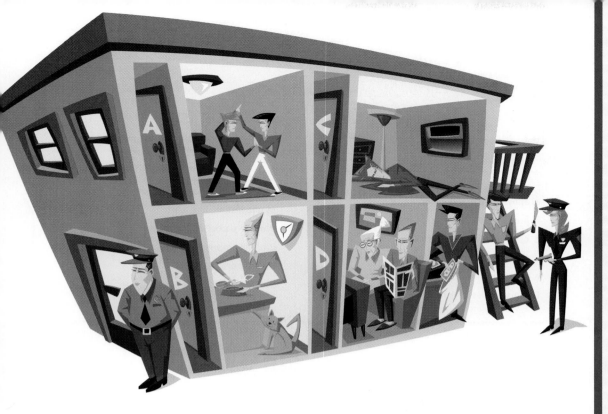

Para este ejercicio, mira el dibujo de arriba.

3 **A** —*¿Qué <u>estaba</u> haciendo <u>el guardia</u> cuando ocurrió el asesinato?*
B —*Dice que <u>estaba vigilando el edificio</u>.*
A —*¿Crees que tiene la culpa?*
B —*No, porque . . .*
    o: *Sí, porque . . .*

Estudiante A

a. los niños del apartamento A

b. el hombre del apartamento B

c. la policía

d. la señora del apartamento D

e. el ladrón

f. el hombre de la camisa azul

Estudiante B

Practice & Apply

Re-enter / Recycle
Ex. 4: subjunctive from Chap. 7
Ex. 8: present perfect from Chap. 4

Teaching Suggestions
Ex. 4: Point out that *Estudiante B*'s answers require the subjunctive. Encourage students to express their own opinions in their answers.

4 ESTUDIANTE A
a. ¿Crees que debemos apoyar la pena de muerte?
b. ...proteger los derechos de las víctimas?
c. ...castigar a los delincuentes?
d. ...terminar el terrorismo?
e. ...construir más cárceles?
f. ...tomar clases de autodefensa?

ESTUDIANTE B
a.–f. Answers will vary, but should contain the correct *nosotros* forms of the present subjunctive.

4 meter a los criminales en la cárcel

A — ¿Crees que debemos <u>meter a los criminales en la cárcel</u>?

B — ¡Claro! Me parece bien que los metamos en la cárcel porque . . .
o: No. Es una lástima que los metamos en la cárcel porque . . .

¡NO OLVIDES!
Remember that verbs ending in *-gar* change *g* to *gu* in the *yo* form of the preterite and all forms of the present subjunctive. *Castigar* follows this pattern.

Estudiante A

a. apoyar la pena de muerte
b. proteger los derechos de las víctimas
c. castigar a los delincuentes
d. terminar con el terrorismo
e. construir más cárceles
f. tomar clases de autodefensa

Estudiante B

Es una lástima que . . .
(No) Me parece bien que . . .
(No) Me sorprende que . . .
(No) Me preocupa que . . .
(No) Me molesta que . . .

5 la violencia en la televisión o la censura

A — ¿Qué te preocupa más, <u>la violencia en la televisión o la censura</u>?

B — <u>La censura, porque nadie tiene derecho a decidir qué debo ver</u>.
o: Las dos porque . . .

Estudiante A

a. el narcotráfico o la guerra contra las drogas
b. las pistolas o las leyes para controlarlas
c. los secuestros de aviones o las medidas de seguridad en los aeropuertos
d. los derechos de los acusados o los de las víctimas
e. el gran número de asesinatos o la pena de muerte

Estudiante B

Options

Strategies for Reaching All Students

Spanish-Speaking Students
Exs. 4–5: Pair Spanish-speaking students for these exercises, if possible.
Ex. 7: Additional question: *¿Qué puedes hacer para evitar ser víctima de un crimen?*

Students Needing Extra Help
Ex. 4: Review the present subjunctive. Brainstorm possible endings to the *porque* phrase.
Ex. 5: Brainstorm the *Estudiante B* responses. Some of these issues may need to be explained before students can discuss them.

Enrichment
Ex. 4: To extend this dialogue, students can ask each other these questions: *¿Crees que debemos castigar a los niños criminales? ¿Crees que debe haber programas de gimnasia y escuela para los criminales en la cárcel?*
Ex. 9: Additional questions: *¿Por qué crees que a la gente le gustan los programas de televisión violentos? ¿Puedes nombrar algunos deportes que te parecen demasiado*

¿Y qué piensas tú?

Aquí tienes otra oportunidad para usar el vocabulario de este capítulo.

6 ¿A qué temes más? ¿A qué temías más de pequeño(a)? ¿Todavía tienes miedo?

7 ¿Qué clase de crímenes ocurren con más frecuencia en tu ciudad o pueblo? ¿Crees que es peligroso o no el lugar donde vives? ¿Cómo se puede hacer menos peligroso el mundo en que vivimos?

8 ¿Qué haces para defenderte contra la violencia? ¿Crees que es una buena idea aprender a defenderse? ¿Por qué? ¿Tomas o has tomado clases de autodefensa? ¿Te interesa tomar alguna? ¿Por qué?

9 Trae periódicos recientes a la clase. Trabaja con un(a) compañero(a). Hagan una lista de los hechos de violencia que vean en los periódicos. Luego hagan una tabla y numeren estos actos de 0 a 5 en orden de importancia. Comparen su tabla con la de otros compañeros. Después, pueden hacer una tabla general de toda la clase.

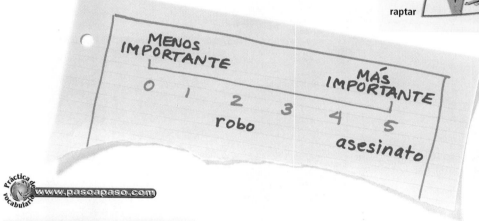

También se dice

el guardián, la guardiana
el / la vigilante

la prisión, *pl.* las prisiones

raptar

www.pasoapaso.com

MÁS PRÁCTICA

- Más práctica y tarea, p. 574
- Practice Workbook 10–1, 10–2

Vocabulario para comunicarse 333

---

violentos? ¿Cómo se puede controlar la violencia que a veces ocurre durante algún partido—por ejemplo, peleas entre los jugadores o entre los espectadores? ¿Puedes nombrar algún incidente reciente de este tipo de violencia durante un partido? ¿Puedes nombrar y describir algún incidente reciente de violencia en un lugar público, como en una oficina de correos, un restaurante o en el metro?

Cooperative Learning
Assign each student a letter a–e from Ex. 5. Have students interview, in Spanish, the others who were assigned their letter, and choose one person who shares their opinion on the given topic. Tell pairs to combine their answers for that portion of the exercise, putting their reasons in priority order. Have each pair share their reasons with the class and be prepared to explain them.

Multiple Intelligences
Interpersonal/Social and Verbal/Linguistic
See Cooperative Learning.
Intrapersonal/Introspective
See Exs. 6–8.
Verbal/Linguistic
See Exs. 4–5 and Audio Activity 10.1.
Visual/Spatial
See Practice Wkbk. 10-1 and 10-2 and Writing Activity 10-A.

Present

Chapter Theme
Solutions to violence

Communicative Objectives
- *Describir un hecho de violencia*
- *Hablar sobre el control de la violencia*
- *Describir los efectos de la violencia*
- *Hablar de soluciones a la violencia*

 Vocabulary Tape 10-2

Grammar Preview
Use of subjunctive with expressions of emotion is previewed lexically. The grammar explanation appears on p. 346.

Teaching Suggestions
Getting ready to speak:
Remind students of the reading strategies that they learned (getting meaning from context and coping with unknown words) to help them understand the *Tema para investigar.* For further details and some sample activities, see pp. T24–T25.

Answers: Tema para investigar
En la pintura de Orozco vemos los efectos violentos de la guerra, y en la de Goya el asesinato de algunos hombres. / *Answers will vary.*

Tema para investigar

Aquí tienes más palabras e ideas para hablar sobre la violencia. Mira las pinturas de esta página. ¿Qué ejemplos de violencia ves aquí? ¿Qué soluciones se podrían proponer para controlarla?

Panel # 16 del *Fresco de Hispanoamérica* (1932-34), José Clemente Orozco

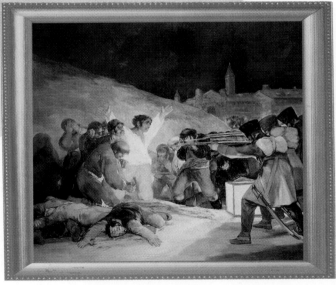

Los fusilamientos del 3 de mayo de 1808 (1815), Francisco de Goya

334   Capítulo 10

Options

Strategies for Reaching All Students

Spanish-Speaking Students
Tell students: *Usa diez de las palabras de la lista en oraciones originales.*

Students Needing Extra Help
Keep students focused on the two questions by making a chart with two columns, headed *Los ejemplos de violencia* and *Las soluciones para controlar la violencia.* Relate *el castigo* to *castigar* and *el temor* to *temer.*

Drill *acabar con.* Students have been using *acabar* with different meanings. Explain *el arma* versus *las armas*: We use *el* before feminine singular nouns that begin with stressed *a* or *ha.*
¿Y qué quiere decir…?: Corporal may be a word whose English meaning is unfamiliar to students. Explain if necessary.

Extended Written Practice/Homework
1. Write three sentences naming ways in which people try to guarantee safety in the following places: *un aeropuerto, una tienda, una escuela, una casa, un banco.*
2. Using the vocabulary on p. 335, write three sentences describing crimes that have taken place recently.
3. Write three sentences saying what should happen to the suspects or convicted criminals involved in the crimes you mentioned in Ex. 2.

La violencia y la justicia

Hoy en día hay tanta violencia que casi todos vivimos con **inseguridad.** En algunas partes de nuestras ciudades la gente **arriesga** su vida sólo saliendo a la calle. No nos sorprende que haya tantos **ataques a mano armada** todos los días. Hoy por la mañana intentaron secuestrar un coche en esta calle; en otra ciudad hubo un **atentado. El terrorismo** continúa con sus actos de violencia en todo el mundo. Ayer por la noche un grupo terrorista internacional se confesó autor de una **explosión.** Otro pidió millones de dólares como **rescate** para **poner en libertad** a los rehenes.

Hay personas que afirman que la causa de todo esto es que los jóvenes ven demasiada violencia en la televisión y en los videojuegos, y que algunas canciones que escuchan son demasiado violentas también. Otros creen que lo que llaman la "desintegración de la familia" tiene la culpa, y que debemos volver a los "valores tradicionales." Para ellos la solución es castigar a los criminales, **contratar** más policías, construir más cárceles e

imponer penas más **severas.** Dicen que no se puede poner en libertad a los culpables, que los criminales deben quedarse en la cárcel hasta que terminen su **sentencia** y que, en algunos casos, los jóvenes deben recibir el mismo **castigo** que los adultos. También recomiendan el castigo **corporal** y creen que se debe imponer la pena de muerte porque, según ellos, **el temor** a la pena servirá para **acabar con** el crimen.

Otros creen que lo que hay que hacer es **evitar** que el crimen ocurra. Dicen que cualquiera puede comprar una pistola en este país, que lo más importante es controlar **las armas,** no los programas de televisión. En todas las escuelas se debe enseñar a resolver conflictos sin **recurrir a** la violencia. También se necesitan campañas de **seguridad** pública para que la gente aprenda a protegerse.

Es importante que todos tengamos seguridad en nuestras casas y en nuestras ciudades. ¿Qué piensas tú?

arriesgar *(g → gu)*	*to risk*	el temor	*fear*
a mano armada	*armed*	acabar (con)	*to put an end to*
el atentado	*assault, attempted murder*	evitar	*to avoid*
el rescate	*ransom*	el arma, *pl.* las armas	*weapon*
poner en libertad	*set free*	recurrir (a)	*to resort (to)*
contratar	*to hire*	la seguridad	*here: safety*
imponer*	*to impose*		

¿Y qué quiere decir ... ?

la inseguridad	severo, -a
el ataque	la sentencia
el terrorismo	el castigo
la explosión, *pl.* las explosiones	corporal

* *Imponer* follows the pattern of *poner.*

Class Starter Review
On the day following the presentation of the *Tema para investigar,* you may want to begin the class with this activity:
Using chapter vocabulary, prepare a brief commentary in which you express an opinion about a crime or violence-related issue. Generate a brief class discussion by asking students their opinions.

Multicultural Perspectives

The most common definition of violence is the use of force to injure or damage someone or something. However, some consider hunger, homelessness, disease, and repression to be forms of violence as well. They believe that in order for peace to exist, these and other conditions must be eradicated. International organizations, such as the United Nations, sponsor worldwide programs designed to eliminate these aspects of conflict. UNICEF's program, called Zones of Peace, Days of Tranquility, tries to aid children in war zones. Representatives attempt to negotiate cease-fire agreements so that supplies can be safely distributed to children. As a class, discuss which countries in the world today could most benefit from the UNICEF program.

www **Internet Activities**
Juegos

Cultural Notes

(p. 334, top photo)
This fresco is part of a series of murals created by Mexican artist José Clemente Orozco (1883–1949) at Dartmouth College's Baker Library between 1932 and 1934. The series, entitled *The Epic of Civilization,* presents Orozco's decidedly pessimistic view of the course of history on the North American continent.

(p. 334, bottom photo)
One of the most riveting depictions of the horrors of war, Francisco Goya's *Los fusilamientos del tres de mayo de 1808* is said to have been inspired by personal experience. According to legend, Goya was deeply moved and angered after witnessing from his window the execution of rebel *madrileños* by Napoleon's army. He is said to have rushed to the execution site immediately afterward, and to have sketched the horrific scene by lantern light.

Ask students: Have you ever had an experience so powerful that you felt that you had to write about it, draw it, or tell someone about it immediately? Tell the class about your experience.

Practice & Apply

Answers: ¿Comprendiste?

1 Causas: La influencia que tiene la violencia de la televisión, los videojuegos y la música; y la "desintegración de la familia." Maneras de controlarla: Castigar más a los criminales, contratar más policías, construir más cárceles e imponer penas más severas.

2 Answers will vary.

Answers: ¿Y qué piensas tú?

3–7 Answers will vary.

Strategies for Reaching All Students

MULTIPLE INTELLIGENCES

Interpersonal/Social and Logical/Mathematical
Have students conduct a survey to determine what their classmates feel are factors (television, violent movies, poverty, few after-school programs for youth, and so on) contributing to violence and crime. Display the results in a chart or graph.

Verbal/Linguistic
See Enrichment Ex. 6 and Audio Activity 10.2.

Visual/Spatial
See Enrichment (paragraph 1), Practice Wkbk. 10-3 and 10-4, Writing Activities 10-B and 10-C, and Comm. Act. BLM 10-1.

¿Comprendiste?

1 ¿Cuáles son dos de las causas de la violencia según el tema? ¿Y dos maneras de controlarla?

2 Haz una lista de otras causas de la violencia o de maneras de controlarla que no están en el tema. Luego, con un(a) compañero(a), pónganlas en orden de importancia.

¿Y qué piensas tú?

3 ¿Cuáles son algunas maneras de resolver un conflicto? ¿Cuáles usas tú? ¿Cuál es la más efectiva para ti? ¿Por qué?

4 ¿Qué medidas de seguridad hay en tu escuela? ¿Cómo se resuelven conflictos en tu escuela? ¿Es efectivo ese método? Si no, ¿qué método sugieres tú?

5 ¿Cuáles son las penas por no obedecer las reglas de tu escuela? ¿Crees que son justas? ¿Por qué sí o no? Si no, ¿qué cambios sugieres tú?

6 ¿Conoces algún hecho histórico con resultados positivos pero que fue considerado como un acto de violencia en su época? Piensa, por ejemplo, en el *Boston Tea Party*. Explica tu respuesta.

7 ¿De acuerdo o no? Formen dos grupos. Los miembros de un grupo van a afirmar que la violencia que presentan la televisión, el cine y los videojuegos es una causa de la violencia que ocurre en la vida real. El otro grupo no va a estar de acuerdo con esta idea.

Organicen un debate entre los dos grupos. Van a discutir:

- ¿Imita la gente los crímenes que ve en la televisión y en el cine?
- Si la respuesta es sí, ¿qué tipo de crímenes imita?
- ¿Quiénes los imitan generalmente: los niños, los adolescentes, los adultos?
- ¿Por qué crees que los imitan?
- ¿Se debe permitir la censura de programas de televisión, de películas y de videojuegos? ¿Por qué?
- Si la respuesta es sí, ¿en qué tipo de programas debe haber censura?
- ¿Quién(es) debe(n) participar en esa censura?

Práctica de vocabulario www.pasoapaso.com

MÁS PRÁCTICA

- Más práctica y tarea, p. 575
- Practice Workbook 10–3, 10–4

336 Capítulo 10

Options

Strategies for Reaching All Students

Spanish-Speaking Students
Ex. 6: After or instead of this exercise, ask students: *¿Crees que hay ocasiones en que se pueden justificar los actos de violencia? Explica.*

Students Needing Extra Help
Ex. 1: Refer to the charts that students completed at the beginning of the *Tema.*
Ex. 2: Add to the chart that students started earlier.
Ex. 3: Use the vocabulary section of the Chap. 1 Organizer. Point out that the topic changes from violence to conflict.
Ex. 4: Students may need more vocabulary depending on the environment in their

school: are there security checks before entering the building, weapon scanners, etc.? Remind students to use the subjunctive in their suggestions.
Ex. 5: Brainstorm the vocabulary for terms such as detention *(el castigo),* skipping classes *(hacer novillos, ponerse la leva),* suspension *(la suspensión),* and expulsion *(la expulsión).*
Ex. 6: Explain why the Boston Tea Party is

Guernica (1937), Pablo Picasso

¿Qué sabes ahora?

¿Puedes:

- describir un hecho de violencia?

  —Hubo un ___ en ___. Alguien ___.

- hablar de las causas de la violencia y de sus efectos?

  —Pienso que la causa de la violencia puede ser ___. La violencia me ___ porque ___.

- mencionar algunas medidas para controlar la violencia?

  —Para acabar con la violencia se debe ___ y ___.

Using Photos
Ask students to look at Picasso's *Guernica* on this page, and then compare it to *El eco de una queja* by Siqueiros (p. 349). Have them explain what they think the artists were trying to say about violence. How are these works different or similar? Accept any logical statements.

 Practice Wkbk. 10-3, 10-4

 Audio Activity 10.2

 Writing Activities 10-B, 10-C

 Pruebas 10-3, 10-4

 Comm. Act. BLM 10-1

---

used as the example. Direct the discussion to events such as protests surrounding the issues of gun control, foreign policy, or budget cuts.
Ex. 7: Discuss censorship before answering the question that asks if censorship should be allowed.
¿Qué sabes ahora?: Have students write this so that they can record their progress.

Enrichment
Have students research and write a brief report to present to the class on advocates of non-violence such as Mahatma Gandhi, César Chávez, and Martin Luther King, Jr. Students may also want to do research on winners of the Nobel Peace Prize.
Ex. 6: In connection with this question, conduct a class discussion on positive effects that may have resulted from public awareness of "secret" acts of violence, such as child or spousal abuse.

Cultural Notes ☀

(p. 337, photo)
Guernica (1937) is a powerful expression of Picasso's revulsion at one of the major episodes of the Spanish Civil War, the attack on the Basque town of Guernica by German aircraft on April 27, 1937. The Nazi "Condor Legion," with the approval of Spanish Fascist forces, dropped 100,000 pounds of bombs on Guernica over a three-hour period, killing a third of the civilian population and destroying the town.

Present & Apply

Cultural Objective

• *Dar ejemplos del control de la violencia en los países de habla hispana y en los Estados Unidos*

Critical Thinking: Making Comparisons

Ask students: *Mira las fotos en la página 339. Compara esta manifestación con las que tenemos en los Estados Unidos. ¿Cómo son diferentes?*

Answers

Answers will vary.

Hoy en día la violencia afecta a toda la sociedad. Muchos grupos participan en manifestaciones pacíficas para protestar contra la violencia, el narcotráfico y otros problemas. ¿Crees que las protestas pacíficas ayudan a controlar la violencia? ¿Por qué?

El uso de murales como medio para expresar ideas se ha extendido mucho gracias a la obra de grandes artistas como Rivera y Orozco. Muchas comunidades expresan su intención de controlar la violencia por medio de murales como éste en Oaxaca, México. Tradicionalmente, la paloma *(dove)* es el símbolo de la paz. Trabajando juntos, los miembros de la comunidad pueden ayudar a que se reduzcan el crimen y la violencia.

338   Capítulo 10

Options

Strategies for Reaching All Students

Students Needing Extra Help

Have students take notes for use later in the *¿Lo sabes bien?* section. Students may not be aware of the military dictatorship that once existed in Argentina. Explain if necessary.

Multiple Intelligences
Logical/Mathematical
See Critical Thinking.

Las Madres de la Plaza de Mayo se reúnen semanalmente en Buenos Aires, Argentina, en una manifestación pacífica. Su objetivo es conseguir información sobre sus hijos y familiares que fueron secuestrados y desaparecieron durante la dictadura militar entre 1976 y 1982.

Álbum cultural 339

Cultural Notes

(p. 338, photo)
This peace mural adorns a building in the mixed Indian and colonial city of Oaxaca, the majority of whose population is Zapotec and Mixtec Indian, more than a fifth of whom speak no Spanish. This, combined with the harsh poverty of the region, make it difficult for peace to prevail. In 1994 indigenous rebels in nearby Chiapas had many sympathizers among the *oaxaqueños.*

(p. 339, photos)
The group of women shown here marching in Buenos Aires' Plaza de Mayo gathers every Thursday afternoon in remembrance of their children and other loved ones. These missing relatives came to be known as the *desaparecidos.* They were taken by the military government that ruled Argentina from 1976 to 1983. Officially, about 9,000 people disappeared during the *guerra sucia;* however, human rights organizations believe the true total to be at least twice that number.

Present & Apply

Multicultural Perspectives

The effects of violence and political oppression are often expressed through the arts. Jacobo Timerman's *Preso sin nombre, celda sin número* vividly describes his experience as a political prisoner in Argentina. Mercedes Sosa and other members of La Nueva Canción sang about social justice and, through their music, educated people all over the world about human rights violations. Manual Puig's *El beso de la mujer araña* became a musical production and a major motion picture. This powerful film about two prisoners sharing a jail cell explores how a society can imprison people for political and social reasons.

EL 0,7%

BART SIMPSON

Keanu Reeves

LOS DELFINES

LOS TEBEOS

Mi amiga

EL AÑO 2000

El campo

MI PERRO

Mis vaqueros viejos

Las gominolas

EL PING PONG

Hablar por teléfono

HAY UN MONTÓN DE RAZONES PARA DECIR

NO.

FUNDACIÓN DE AYUDA CONTRA LA DROGADICCIÓN

340   Capítulo 10

Options

Strategies for Reaching All Students

Students Needing Extra Help
Explain the expression *se lleva a cabo* if students have difficulty with this section of the text.
Reacción personal: In the first question, students may have a different sense of the term community (a church, self-help group, etc.), depending on your location.

Enrichment
Additional question: *¿Qué ciudad en los Estados Unidos te parece la más violenta o peligrosa? ¿Por qué?*

Multiple Intelligences
Intrapersonal/Introspective
See Exs. 1–3.

La oposición al narcotráfico y al uso de drogas se extiende por todo el mundo. En España, el Fondo de Ayuda contra la Drogadicción usa anuncios, como el que aparece a la izquierda, para animar a los jóvenes a decir no a las drogas. En Austin, Texas, se lleva a cabo una marcha con el mismo fin.

Reacción personal

Contesta las siguientes preguntas en una hoja de papel.

1 ¿Qué puede hacer una comunidad para controlar el crimen y la violencia?

2 Menciona algunas cosas que puedes hacer para evitar ser víctima de un crimen.

3 ¿Te parecen efectivas las campañas pacíficas en contra de la violencia y el narcotráfico? ¿Por qué?

Actividad cultural
www.pasoapaso.com

Answers: Reacción personal
1–3 Answers will vary.

www Internet Activities
Álbum cultural

Cultural Notes ☼

(p. 340, realia)
This ad from Spain's *Fundación de ayuda contra la drogadicción* appeals to young people as it lists the reasons *(un montón)* to say *no* to drugs. The list itself is a fascinating mix of elements traditionally cherished by all young Spaniards *(Mi amiga, Mi perro, El campo)* and elements from contemporary, international youth culture *(Bart Simpson, Mis vaqueros viejos).*

Ask students: If you were creating this ad, what would be your personal list of reasons for affirming life and saying *no* to drugs?

(p. 341, photo)
Thanks in part to "Just say no" anti-drug campaigns such as this one in Austin, Texas, illegal drug use in the U.S. is declining. From 1988 to 1991, the number of adolescents who regularly used drugs fell by approximately 27 percent.

Preview

Overhead 32

Teaching Suggestions

A If students cannot easily identify the subjunctive forms used in the commands, point out the infinitives. Ask when they have used the ending *-en* with *-ar* verbs, and *-an* with *-er* / *-ir* verbs. See if they remember some of the more common *Uds.* commands heard in class: *abran, cierren, pongan, repitan,* etc.

B Following their explanation to a partner, give students additional examples of when to use the indicative or subjunctive with expressions of emotion.

Answers

Answers to inductive question will vary.

A The *Uds. / ellos / ellas* form of the present subjunctive / *Encuentren, tengan, No arriesguen* / There is no difference. / Use the *Uds. / ellos / ellas* form of the present subjunctive.

B *Tememos que hieran* expresses an emotion. / subjunctive / Yes, it expresses an emotion. / subjunctive / *Estoy contento de que* and *Es trágico que* will be followed by a verb in the subjunctive. *Yo sé que* will be followed by a verb in the indicative.

Gramática en contexto

¿Qué piensas encontrar en una novela o en una tira cómica *(comic strip)* donde secuestran a alguien? Mira las ilustraciones y lee el texto para averiguarlo.

A In the first scene of the comic strip, the *Uds.* command *metan* is used. What form that you know is it similar to? In the last scene, three *Uds.* commands are given. What are they? Two of these are affirmative commands and one is negative. Is there any difference between them? Explain to another student how to give a command using the *Uds.* form.

B In the second scene, it says, *sabemos que los criminales piden* and *tememos que hieran.* Which of these expresses an emotion? Is the verb that follows *que* in this sentence in the indicative or the subjunctive? In the third scene, it says, *sentimos mucho que estos hombres hayan secuestrado.* Does this statement express an emotion? Is *que* followed by the indicative or the subjunctive? Explain to a partner whether you would use the indicative or the subjunctive after the following expressions: *Estoy contento de que . . . Yo sé que . . . Es trágico que . . .*

342   Capítulo 10

Options

Strategies for Reaching All Students

Students Needing Extra Help
Have students begin the grammar section of the Organizer.
Mandatos afirmativos y negativos con Ud. y Uds: Explain the chart. Emphasize that these are verbs with spelling changes that remain the same when the negative command is

used. Brainstorm other verbs that follow these patterns. If available, refer to the grammar sections of the Organizers for Book 2, Chaps. 12 and 13.
Give additional examples of the different positions of the pronouns. Refer to the grammar section of the Chap. 9 Organizer.

Extended Written Practice/Homework
1. Write three commands telling a visitor to your city what to do or not to do: *No salga solo(a) por la noche en el centro.*
2. Write three commands that you would like to give your Spanish teacher: *Denos menos tarea los fines de semana.*
3. Write three commands that you might give a politician in your state or community to improve society: *No permita que construyan más fábricas en nuestra comunidad.*

Mandatos afirmativos y negativos con *Ud.* y *Uds.*

The forms we use to give affirmative and negative commands to more than one person and to people we address as *Ud.*, are the same as those used in the present subjunctive.

> **Escriba** un informe sobre la seguridad pública.
> **Lean** esta noticia en el periódico.

- Here are the affirmative and negative *Ud.* and *Uds.* commands of *explicar, obedecer,* and *decir.*

	Ud.		Uds.	
explicar	explique	no explique	expliquen	no expliquen
obedecer	obedezca	no obedezca	obedezcan	no obedezcan
decir	diga	no diga	digan	no digan

> Señor, **explique** su situación al abogado, **diga** la verdad al jurado y **obedezca** al juez.
> **Obedezcan** las órdenes del policía, **expliquen** lo que vieron pero no **digan** el nombre del testigo.

- As with the negative *tú* commands, verbs that have irregular forms in the present subjunctive have the same irregular forms in the *Ud.* and *Uds.* commands.

> **No vaya Ud.** solo por esa calle por la noche. Es bastante peligrosa.
> **No vengan** al lugar de los hechos. Puede ser peligroso.

- Like the *tú* commands, object and reflexive pronouns are attached to the end of affirmative commands but go before negative commands.

> **Quédese** aquí un momento, señor.
> **Explíqueme** por qué cree que el castigo es justo.
> Ese periódico no es muy objetivo. **No lo compre**, señora.

Manifestación contra las drogas durante el desfile del Día Dominicano en Nueva York

Gramática en contexto   343

Present
Teaching Suggestions
You may also wish to review all the irregular affirmative *tú* commands after this presentation.

Multiple Intelligences
Visual/Spatial
See Overhead 32.

Cultural Notes

(p. 343, photo)
Hispanic parades in the U.S. often include groups representing community concerns. These anti-crack marchers in the Dominican Day Parade in New York City have a large audience for their message, as 77 percent of Dominicans in the U.S. are concentrated there.

Practice

Teaching Suggestions

Ex. 1: Encourage your more able students to complete the sentences using chapter vocabulary: *Digan al testigo que explique lo que vio.*

Answers

1 Answers will vary, but may include:

a. Lleven a la víctima (al rehén) a ___.

b. Vigilen a la testigo.

c. Busquen la pistola.

d. Pongan en libertad a la guardia.

e. Metan en la cárcel a la asesina.

f. Statements will vary.

2 ESTUDIANTE A

a. Si son testigos de un robo . . .

b. Si encuentran una pistola…

c. Si ven a un sospechoso…

d. Si se encuentran en un tiroteo . . .

e. Si sospechan de alguien . . . .

f. Si suena la alarma . . . .

ESTUDIANTE B

a. Digan a la policía todo lo que saben.

b. No la toquen.

c. Obsérvenlo desde lejos.

d. Busquen un lugar para esconderse.

e. Informen a la policía dónde ___.

f. Obedezcan las instrucciones.

---

1 Túrnate con un(a) compañero(a) para imaginar que son jefes de policía que van al lugar de los hechos. Usen expresiones de los dos recuadros para dar órdenes a otros policías.

Llamen a la ambulancia.

a. llevar

b. vigilar

c. buscar

d. poner en libertad

e. meter en la cárcel

f.

2 Trabaja con un(a) compañero(a) para dar consejos a un grupo de estudiantes que van a visitar un área peligrosa.

oír una explosión / no moverse

A —*Si oyen una explosión* . . .
B —*No se muevan.*

Estudiante A

a. ser testigos de un robo

b. encontrar una pistola

c. ver a un sospechoso

d. encontrarse en un tiroteo

e. sospechar de alguien

f. sonar la alarma

Estudiante B

observarlo desde lejos

buscar un lugar para esconderse

obedecer las instrucciones

informar a la policía dónde . . .

no tocarla

decir a la policía todo lo que saben

344　Capítulo 10

Options

Strategies for Reaching All Students

Students Needing Extra Help

Ex. 1: Remind students that this exercise contains regular verbs and verbs that have spelling changes.

Ex. 2: Do two more examples with the class, one affirmative and one that contains an object pronoun. Review the placement of pronouns with commands. Complete the phrase that begins with *informar,* reminding students that with some of the possibilities they will have to use other tenses.

Ex. 3: Some of the verbs will need a phrase added to them in order for them to make sense. Brainstorm possibilities. Remind students that there are verbs with spelling changes in this list and that *prohibir* will require *que* + the subjunctive.

Enrichment

Ex. 2: As homework, ask students to list advice they would give to children or to older people regarding their safety at and away from home.

3 Imagina que tu compañero(a) y tú van a preparar carteles que van a usar en una manifestación. Trabajen juntos para formar las frases que van a escribir.

Metan a los criminales en la cárcel.

a. proteger
b. castigar
c. ayudar
d. leer
e. poner en libertad
f. preguntar
g. arrestar
h. prohibir

¡Metan a los criminales en la cárcel!

LA PRENSA DE LA MAÑANA

Gramática en contexto   345

Teaching Suggestions
Ex. 3 You may want to expand this exercise by having students work in pairs to create their own signs that could be used in a demonstration. When they have finished, display the signs in the classroom and use them for discussion of the *Pregunta clave.*

3 Answers will vary, but students may mention:
a. Protejan al jurado.
b. Castiguen a los asesinos.
c. Ayuden a las víctimas.
d. Lean el periódico cada día.
e. Pongan en libertad a los rehenes.
f. Pregunten al testigo lo que vio.
g. Arresten a los ladrones.
h. Prohiban que los jueces hablen con los reporteros.

 Practice Wkbk. 10-5, 10-6

 Writing Activity 10-D

 Pruebas 10-5, 10-6

 Comm. Act. BLM 10-2

Extended Written Practice/Homework
1. Write three commands that you could give different groups of people in your school: *A los músicos de la banda: Sigan tocando canciones populares durante los partidos de básquetbol.*
2. Write three commands that could be sent to a TV station or movie producer: *No den programas que tratan de manipular las ideas de las personas.*

3. Write three commands to your fellow citizens telling them what to do or not to do to help your community.

Multiple Intelligences
Bodily/Kinesthetic and Visual/Spatial
See Teaching Suggestions (p. 345).
Verbal/Linguistic
See Exs. 1–3.

Visual/Spatial
1) Have students create a videotape or photo album showing successful programs or activities that combat violence.
2) See Enrichment, Practice Wkbk. 10-5 and 10-6, Writing Activity 10-D, and Comm. Act. BLM 10-2.

Present & Practice

Re-enter / Recycle
Ex. 4: present perfect subjunctive from Chap. 8

Answers
4 Statements will vary, but students should use the indicative in items b. and d., and the subjunctive in all others:
a. Me sorprende que el asesinato haya ocurrido cerca de mi casa.
b. Es cierto que el sospechoso dice que es inocente.
c. Me preocupa que la abogada quiera poner en libertad al sospechoso.
d. Es evidente que el sospechoso está en la cárcel.
e. Me molesta que la policía no tenga testigos.
f. Es una lástima que el juez no permita al jurado leer los periódicos.
g. Es triste que el guardia no sepa el nombre de la víctima.
h. Temo que haya muchos crímenes en la ciudad.
i. Siento que el sospechoso sea tan joven.

El subjuntivo con expresiones de emoción

You know that we use the subjunctive to say what one person asks, hopes, tells, insists, or requires someone else to do.

• We also use the subjunctive after verbs and expressions that indicate emotions.

Tememos que los jueces **no castiguen** a los criminales.
Me preocupa que **haya** tanta violencia en las ciudades.
Es una lástima que no **puedan** encontrar al asesino.

• You have already learned many expressions of emotion such as *alegrarse de, sentir, temer,* and *tener miedo.* These are followed by the subjunctive when there are two different subjects in the sentence.

Sentimos que la víctima del accidente **esté** todavía en el hospital.
Me sorprende que los médicos no la **puedan** ayudar.

4 Imagina que ha ocurrido un asesinato en tu ciudad. Mira las expresiones en la primera columna. ¿Cuáles requieren el subjuntivo? ¿Cuáles requieren el indicativo? Ahora con un(a) compañero(a) expresen sus reacciones.

Me asombra que ...   *Me asombra que el asesinato haya ocurrido cerca de mi casa.*

a. Me sorprende que ...   la policía no (tener) testigos
b. Es cierto que ...   el guardia no (saber) el nombre de la víctima
c. Me preocupa que ...   el sospechoso (estar) en la cárcel
d. Es evidente que ...   la abogada (querer) poner en libertad al sospechoso
e. Me molesta que ...   el sospechoso (ser) tan joven
f. Es una lástima que ...   el juez no (permitir) al jurado leer los periódicos
g. Es triste que ...   el asesinato (haber) ocurrido cerca de mi casa
h. Temo que ...   el sospechoso (decir) que es inocente
i. Siento que ...   (haber) muchos crímenes en la ciudad

346   Capítulo 10

Options

Strategies for Reaching All Students

Students Needing Extra Help
El subjuntivo con expresiones de emoción: Give additional examples using expressions of emotion. Have students add these to the list they began when the subjunctive was first introduced.

Ex. 4: Have students review their list. Have them identify the phrases in the left column that express emotion before they begin putting the verbs into the subjunctive or the indicative.
Ex. 5: Brainstorm the possible phrases needed to complete the sentences.

Extended Written Practice/Homework
1. Consider the crimes that have been discussed in this chapter and write four sentences telling your feelings about them: *Temo que el terrorismo sea uno de los problemas internacionales más severos.*
2. Write three sentences describing positive feelings that you have about things going on in our society. Use: *alegrarse de, estar contento(a) de, es bueno.*

5 Trabaja con un(a) compañero(a) para expresar lo que sientes cuando piensas en ciertos aspectos de la sociedad en que vivimos. Forma frases usando elementos de los dos recuadros.

No nos gusta que roben a la gente que camina por la calle.

a. (no) Nos asombra
b. (no) Nos alegramos de
c. (no) Nos gusta
d. (no) Estamos contentos(as) de
e. (no) Nos da miedo
f. (no) Nos impresiona
g. (no) Nos molesta
h. (no) Nos preocupa

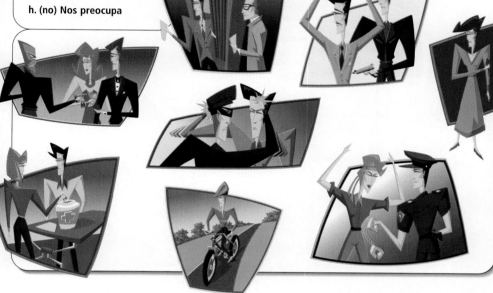

3. Write three sentences expressing your feelings about TV programming and the content of the shows you watch.

Practice

Re-enter / Recycle
Ex. 6: present perfect from
Chap. 4, present perfect subjunctive from Chap. 8.

Answers
6 Answers will vary, but students should use the indicative in the first statements and the subjunctive when expressing their reactions to those statements.

6 Con un(a) compañero(a) escriban cinco frases contando algo que ha pasado en la escuela recientemente. Traten de incluir buenas y malas noticias en sus frases.

El equipo de básquetbol ha ganado el campeonato.
Alguien ha roto una ventana.

Ahora lean sus frases a otra pareja. Cuando escuchen las noticias, deben expresar su reacción usando la expresión apropiada.

Estamos muy contentos de que el equipo de básquetbol haya ganado el campeonato.
Es una lástima que alguien haya roto una ventana.

348　Capítulo 10

Options

Strategies for Reaching All Students

Students Needing Extra Help
Ex. 6: Review the present perfect subjunctive.
Ahora lo sabes: Have students write this so that they can record their progress.

Enrichment
Ex. 6: As homework, students can write five phrases about some local, national, or international event, giving their own opinions about them using an expression of emotion.

Extended Written Practice/Homework
Write five sentences telling how you feel about different things that have taken place in your community. You might write about help given to people, environmental concerns, crimes, community and individual achievements, and so on: *Siento mucho que hayan secuestrado a la hija de una familia en mi comunidad.*

El eco de una queja (1937),
David Alfaro Siqueiros

Ahora lo sabes

¿Puedes:

- dar órdenes a una persona o a un grupo de personas?

  —Señora, ___ al jurado qué estaba haciendo Ud. la noche del 16.

  —Por favor, ___ Uds. en la campaña de seguridad pública.

- expresar cómo te sientes respecto a una situación o a algo que hace otra persona?

  —Es una lástima que ___ tantos crímenes en esta ciudad.

  —Me alegro de que el sospechoso ___ en la cárcel.

MÁS PRÁCTICA

- Más práctica y tarea, pp. 575–576
- Practice Workbook 10–5, 10–8

Answers: Ahora lo sabes
- diga (explique)
  participen
- haya
  esté

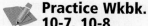 **Practice Wkbk. 10-7, 10-8**

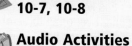 **Audio Activities 10.3, 10.4, 10.5**

 **Writing Activity 10-E**

 **Prueba 10-7**

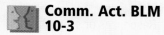 **Comm. Act. BLM 10-3**

Cultural Notes

Multiple Intelligences
Intrapersonal/Introspective
See Enrichment.
Verbal/Linguistic
See Audio Activities 10.3, 10.4, and 10.5.
Visual/Spatial
See Practice Wkbk. 10-7 and 10-8, Writing Activity 10-E, and Comm. Act. BLM 10-3.

(p. 349, photo)
Mexican muralist and sculptor David Alfaro Siqueiros (1896–1974) vividly conveys the tragedy of the suffering of children in war in his nightmarish *El eco de una queja* (1937). Of the three great Mexican muralists of the twentieth century (Rivera and Orozco being the others), Siqueiros was the most experimental in his techniques. Among the new methods and materials he brought to the art were synthetic paints and the spray gun.

Apply

Point out the key chapter question. Tell students that completing these activities will help them answer this key question. You may select one, two, or all three of these activities, as time permits.

Ex. 3: Students could also present their advice through posters, a bulletin-board display, a video presentation, or a presentation for other Spanish classes.

Answers: Sopa de actividades

1–3 Responses or presentations will vary, but should include a wide variety of chapter vocabulary and correct use of *Uds.* commands and subjunctive where appropriate.

¿Cómo se puede controlar la violencia?

Esta sección te ofrece la oportunidad de combinar lo que aprendiste en este capítulo con lo que ya sabes para responder a la pregunta clave.

Para decir más

Aquí tienes vocabulario adicional que te puede ayudar para hacer las actividades de esta sección.

amenazar *(z → c)*
to threaten

el drogadicto, la drogadicta
drug addict

la pandilla, la banda
gang

superar
to overcome

reformar(se)
to reform

el acuerdo
agreement

la negociación
negotiation

la regla
rule

la norma
norm

legal / ilegal
legal / illegal

Sopa de actividades

1 Van a hacer un cartel con cada una de estas palabras. Después pongan los carteles en seis lugares diferentes de la sala de clases.

- el narcotráfico
- la violencia doméstica
- los tiroteos
- el terrorismo
- los secuestros
- los asesinatos

Considera los problemas representados por estas palabras y decide cuál te preocupa más. Ve al lugar donde está el cartel y forma un grupo con los otros estudiantes que estén allí. Cada grupo va a preparar una presentación oral para:

- describir el problema y explicar a quiénes afecta más
- expresar lo que sienten sobre el problema y por qué
- sugerir ideas para mejorar la situación

Hagan la presentación a la clase.

350 Capítulo 10

Options

Strategies for Reaching All Students

Spanish-Speaking Students
Ex. 1: Instead of this exercise, present the following situation: *Eres un(a) reportero(a) para un periódico en español. Escucha a cada grupo y toma apuntes de lo que dicen los participantes. Luego, escribe un artículo sobre las presentaciones de los diferentes grupos. Incluye lo que dicen acerca de* cuáles son los problemas, cómo ha reaccionado la comunidad y qué sugieren para mejorar la situación. Revisa tu artículo con un(a) compañero(a) y el (la) profesor(a). Envíalo a tu periódico escolar, a un periódico o a una revista para jóvenes que hablen español.*

Students Needing Extra Help
If time is a factor, Exs. 1 and 2 are more concrete and therefore easier for students to complete. Ex. 3 uses commands.
Ex. 1: Use the vocabulary section of the Organizer. Students may need some help with the vocabulary. Have them reread the *Tema para investigar* to find phrases that will help them express themselves and / or spark some ideas. Make the groups fairly equal in size. Brainstorm possible ways to improve the situation. Use the vocabulary

2 En grupos de tres, piensen en un acto de violencia donde una o varias personas ayudaron a la víctima. Digan:

- qué acto de violencia fue
- cuándo y dónde ocurrió
- qué le pasó a la víctima
- qué hizo (hicieron) la(s) persona(s) para ayudarla

Hagan una presentación oral para la clase. Después discutan cuáles son las mejores ideas para ayudar a personas que lo necesitan.

3 En grupos, preparen una lista de consejos sobre qué se debe y qué no se debe hacer para defenderse de la violencia. Van a dar sus consejos a otros estudiantes. Pueden decirles cómo:

- ir a la escuela y volver a sus casas con seguridad
- vestirse para evitar que les roben
- reaccionar si ven un crimen
- protegerse si alguien trata de herirlos
- practicar la autodefensa
- ayudar para que no haya armas en la escuela

Sopa de actividades   351

 Video Activity A

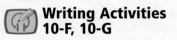 **Video, Capítulo 10**

Chapter 10: Play

Step

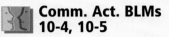 **Video Activities B–C**

Writing Activities 10-F, 10-G

Comm. Act. BLMs 10-4, 10-5

section of the Chap. 7 Organizer, which discussed community services.

Ex. 2: If students are not creative, have them watch the television or read the newspapers for incidents where the victim was aided.

Brainstorm the vocabulary that will be necessary to present this scenario.

Ex. 3: Review commands. Brainstorm the vocabulary that will be necessary for giving advice.

Cooperative Learning

In groups of three, have students brainstorm one security problem in their school. Then each student will assume the role of either the principal, a teacher, or the president of the student council, and list three ways that they can help eliminate this problem. Have groups combine their lists and present them to the class.

Multiple Intelligences
Interpersonal/Social
See Exs. 2–3.
Interpersonal/Social and Logical/Mathematical
See Cooperative Learning.
Visual/Spatial
See Writing Activities 10-F and 10-G and Comm. Act. BLMs 10-4 and 10-5.
Visual/Spatial and Bodily/Kinesthetic
See Ex. 1.

Apply

Process Reading
For a description of process reading, see p. 52.

Teaching Suggestions
Point out the key chapter question. Remind students that working through the *Para leer* section will help them answer it.

Encourage students to use the strategies given to them in the text to help them understand the reading. Remind them that they do not need to understand every word.

Answers
Antes de leer
Answers will vary, but students may mention:
Cuando alguien desaparece en una historia de detectives, los parientes o los amigos del (de la) desaparecido(a) hablan con la policía o un(a) detective. El (la) detective les hace preguntas a los sospechosos. Un(a) amigo(a) dice lo que le pasó al (a la) desaparecido(a).

Mira la lectura
Responses will vary.

Para leer

Antes de leer
STRATEGY ➤ Using prior knowledge

¿Qué ocurre en una historia de detectives cuando alguien desaparece? Haz una lista de tres cosas que pueden pasar.

Mira la lectura
STRATEGY ➤ Skimming

Lee la historia rápidamente, sólo para familiarizarte con los hechos.

> **HASTA ACLARAR** *el misterio*

Ola Thune alzó la vista del rimero de papeles que tenía sobre el escritorio de su oficina en Oslo, y vio entrar a un anciano. A los 63 años, Johan Jensen tenía los hombros encorvados y la mirada de cansancio de un hombre prematuramente envejecido.

Hacía 18 meses que Marit, la esposa de Jensen, se había llevado a la única hija de ambos, Anne Kristin, a pasar unas vacaciones en la isla de Fuerteventura, una de las Canarias. La noche anterior a su regreso, la joven estudiante de 22 años había desaparecido sin dejar rastro.

Los Jensen se habían dedicado durante un año y medio a buscarla. Tanto la policía noruega como la española se habían lavado las manos. "Es cosa de todos los días que desaparezcan muchachas," dijo un policía encogiéndose de hombros. Desde entonces, Johan y Marit habían gastado todos sus ahorros en investigadores privados—y habían recurrido incluso a videntes—para encontrar a su hija.

"Usted es nuestra última esperanza," le dijo Jensen a Ola, miembro del KRIPOS, el eficiente escuadrón de detectives al que a menudo se daba el nombre de Scotland Yard noruego. "Ya no tenemos dinero, pero nos queda la casa. Tómela, señor Thune... y encuentre a nuestra Anne Kristin."

Ola ya se había interesado en el caso. Por casualidad, él también había estado de vacaciones en Fuerteventura los mismos días que Anne y Marit, en febrero de 1990.

En esos momentos tenía frente a sí al padre de Anne Kristin, cuya angustia había crecido a causa del muro de indiferencia oficial con el que se había topado. *No puedo inmiscuirme en esto sin permiso,* pensó Ola. Había trabajado mucho para llegar a ser uno de los cuatro principales inspectores de su departamento; aún no tenía 40 años, y podía aspirar a una larga y satisfactoria carrera. Luego miró los cansados ojos de Jensen. Era su deber ayudarle, aunque la búsqueda resultara infructuosa.

Ola tomó la decisión de por lo menos revisar los archivos. Tardó varias semanas en dar cuenta de ese montón de papeles: los informes de la policía española, los de la policía noruega y los recortes de periódico.

Options

Strategies for Reaching All Students

Students Needing Extra Help
Antes de leer: If students have difficulty answering the question, ask them for a brief synopsis of a mystery or detective story with which they are all familiar. From this reference, they can more easily list the three items.

Mira la lectura: Prepare students for a story that involves many people and places. Provide help as needed with unfamiliar vocabulary and expressions. You may wish to prepare a list of these words beforehand and go over them with the class.

Lo primero que llamó su atención fue que menos de diez por ciento de los informes oficiales tenían que ver con los hechos. En el resto sólo se explicaba por qué era imposible avanzar más en la investigación. Los hechos eran relativamente simples. Marit Jensen se retiró a dormir temprano a su cuarto del hotel Alameda, la noche anterior a su vuelo de regreso a Oslo. Anne Kristin quería despedirse de sus amigos que había hecho en una discoteca cerca de allí, el bar Graffiti. Muchos testigos dijeron haberla visto platicando y bromeando con unas muchachas noruegas, y bailando con unos chicos alemanes.

Cuando el bar cerró, en las primeras horas de la madrugada, el popular cantinero de 18 años, Alejandro González, a quien llamaban Alexis, invitó a Anne Kristin a la discoteca de Ángel, cercana al bar. Los últimos parroquianos vieron a Anne Kristin subirse como pasajera en la motocicleta de González. Desde entonces nadie la había visto.

Para la policía, el sospechoso más obvio era Alexis. El chico confesó que, en lugar de llevar a Anne Kristin a la discoteca, la llevó a la playa, donde trató de besarla pero fue rechazado. Según él, cuando la vio por última vez estaba junto al bar donde se habían despedido.

No era una historia muy convincente, pero la policía no encontró motivos para arrestarlo. Después de todo, no había cadáver, ni sangre. Además, la policía, como todos en la isla, no tomaba muy en serio al joven de liso y brillante cabello negro y arete de oro en la oreja izquierda. Pia, una chica sueca que era novia de Alexis, atestiguó que cuando regresó a su casa de la discoteca, lo encontró durmiendo plácidamente. Cuando Alexis se topó con Marit Jensen en la jefatura de policía, la abrazó amigablemente. El mismo Ola había mirado de arriba abajo a Alexis cuando acudió al Graffiti la noche antes del regreso a Noruega. Vio al chico "tan despreocupado y alegre como siempre."

Para leer   353

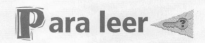

Para leer

El primer paso que dio Ola para reconstruir los sucesos de aquella fatídica noche fue ir a Alemania, donde buscó a tres muchachos que estuvieron en el Graffiti en esa ocasión. Ellos se acordaban de casi todas las personas que habían hablado con Anne Kristin. Uno recordó incluso que, después de que cerraron la discoteca, se topó con otro cliente que estaba buscando su motocicleta... la misma que Alexis tomó prestada para llevar a Anne Kristin a dar su último paseo.

Con esta información, Ola estaba listo para visitar Fuerteventura de nuevo; esta vez de incógnito para que nadie supiera que era investigador. Necesitaba un asistente que hablara español con fluidez. Por un golpe de suerte, le presentaron a una mujer que acababa de regresar a Oslo después de pasar más de 20 años en Mallorca. Liten Winther era brillante e ingeniosa, le atraía la aventura, hablaba español como si fuera su lengua, y hasta tenía el aspecto físico de una española. No le sería difícil mezclarse con la gente del lugar. Y Ola, que dominaba el alemán y no aparentaba los 39 años que tenía, podía pasar fácilmente por un muchacho hamburgués dispuesto a prestar diversos servicios en las playas.

Fue fácil eliminar los rumores. Un hombre dijo a investigadores anteriores que González había presumido de vender a Anne Kristin a una banda de narcotraficantes. Cuando lo presionaron para que fuera más explícito, se desdijo. Si Anne Kristin no había sido secuestrada, tampoco se había ido a correr

una aventura romántica. Todo lo que Ola y Liten escucharon en la isla confirmó que, tal como aseguraban los amigos noruegos de la chica desaparecida, ella no era el tipo de persona que hace cosas estúpidas, o que es capaz de jugarle una mala pasada a su madre.

Sólo quedaba una posibilidad: algo terrible se había cruzado en el camino de Anne Kristin. Ola y Liten escucharon las reminiscencias de la gente que había estado en la discoteca esa noche, y anotaron meticulosamente sus relatos. No había incongruencias. Uno por uno, todos pudieron ser eliminados de la investigación... todos menos Alexis.

Éste estaba dispuesto a hablar, especialmente con una acompañante tan atractiva como Liten. La agasajó con historias de hazañas imaginarias realizadas para los "grandes" del narcotráfico.

Una noche en que González llevaba a Liten a su hotel, ésta advirtió que el muchacho tomaba por una calle desconocida.

—Es un atajo— le dijo él para tranquilizarla.

Options

Strategies for Reaching All Students

Students Needing Extra Help
If students seem overwhelmed by the amount of text, divide the reading so that you cover it over a period of several days.

En ese momento ella se dio cuenta de que se dirigían a la playa adonde él había llevado a Anne Kristin. Pensando rápido, Liten empezó a hablarle de unos supuestos planes que tenía ella de abrir una discoteca elegante en Ibiza, donde necesitaría un cantinero bien parecido y con experiencia. Tal como lo previó, la perspectiva de un empleo atractivo en las Baleares adquirió más importancia que cualquier otra cosa que Alexis hubiera tenido en mente. Platicando animadamente, Liten consiguió que el joven la llevara de regreso a su hotel.

A estas alturas ya era obvio que González era un mentiroso sin escrúpulos, y que las pruebas circunstanciales contra él eran abrumadoras. Pero, ¿cómo puede acusarse a alguien de asesinato cuando no hay cadáver, no hay pruebas tangibles y no hay testigos?

Tal vez la respuesta la tuviera Pia, la novia de González. La muchacha había terminado repentinamente su relación con él, unas semanas después de la desaparición de Anne Kristin, y había regresado a Estocolmo. Establecer contacto con ella sería difícil. Cuando los investigadores privados de los Jensen trataron de interrogarla, ella sumamente indignada, le envió al matrimonio una carta amenazándolos con emprender acciones legales en su contra si no dejaban de acosarla.

Ola le siguió la pista a Pia hasta una guardería de Estocolmo, donde trabajaba la chica. Entró al lugar y la abordó en el momento en que ella cambiaba unos pañales; en seguida se presentó. Ola le pidió su ayuda encarecidamente...no por él, sino por los padres de Anne Kristin. Insinuándole que sabía lo que había pasado, logró despertar su curiosidad. Después de un largo silencio, ella dijo:

—Nos vemos en el café de al lado cuando salga yo de trabajar.

Bebiendo café tras café, hablaron y hablaron de la vida en Fuerteventura, y de Alexis. Detrás de su cara bonita y de sus ojos brillantes e inteligentes, Ola percibió un velo de tristeza. *Tiene buen corazón, pero está asustada,* pensó.

La conversación duró más de tres horas. Pia estaba cada vez más nerviosa y agitada. Por fin, llorando abiertamente, se inclinó hacia adelante y dijo:

Apply

Teaching Suggestions

You may wish to present the radio play that students have prepared in Ex. 2 of the *Aplicación* section. If so, edit or ask advanced students to help edit the script. Have students practice before presenting their plays. Record the presentations if possible.

Infórmate

1 Responses will vary, but students may mention:
Lugares: Oslo, Noruega / Fuerteventura (una de las Canarias)
Personajes: El detective, la víctima, el asesino y su novia
Nombres y características: La víctima se llama Anne Kristin. Es una estudiante noruega de 22 años. El detective se llama Ola Thune. Él tiene 39 años pero parece más joven, y es muy inteligente. El asesino se llama Alejandro González. Es un cantinero guapo y popular que no se preocupa por nada. Su novia se llama Pia. Es una chica sueca, muy bonita pero está bastante asustada.

Para leer

—¿Le sorprendería mucho saber que yo conozco la suerte que corrió Anne Kristin?

Era el momento que Ola había estado aguardando. Para no asustarla y obligarla a callar, siguió hablando sin demostrar excesivo interés, y poco a poco ella reveló los detalles de su terrible secreto.

Pia aseguró que había dicho la verdad cuando la policía la interrogó al día siguiente de la desaparición. Pero unos días después, Alexis admitió que había estado con Anne Kristin esa noche. Poco a poco agregó que la llevó a la playa, que ella trató de rechazarlo y que él le puso un cinturón alrededor del cuello y la estranguló con él.

Tardó un rato en darse cuenta de que estaba muerta. Desesperadamente, hizo un hoyo en la arena y la enterró. Al día siguiente le contó todo a su padre, quien acudió a la playa por la noche, desenterró el cadáver, lo puso en su barco de pesca y navegó mar adentro. Llegó a un lugar, que él conocía bien, donde las aguas eran profundas y había una fuerte corriente que iba en dirección a África. Ahí arrojó el cuerpo lastrado al mar.

Con la declaración de Pia en la mano, Ola vislumbraba ya el final de su largo viaje. Pero existía el peligro de que un abogado astuto tergiversara las palabras de Pia para que se interpretaran como la amarga venganza de una mujer burlada. Por tanto, en mayo de 1992 Ola y Liten regresaron a Fuerteventura para reunir más pruebas. El 15 de junio de 1992, Ola presentó un imponente cúmulo de pruebas contra Alejandro González ante el procurador general de Noruega. Después de una audiencia pública en Oslo, en la que Pia testificó, los documentos se trasmitieron a España.

De la noche a la mañana, después de más de dos años de apatía burocrática, las cosas empezaron a moverse con celeridad. Gracias a las nuevas pruebas, la policía arrestó a Alexis. Seguía siendo el mismo fanfarrón. Pero antes de que trascurriera una hora, tiempo que tardó la policía en leerle un detalle incriminatorio tras otro, agachó la cabeza. Por fin, tartamudeando, contó toda la historia. Su padre también fue arrestado, y también confesó.

Options

Strategies for Reaching All Students

Students Needing Extra Help
Infórmate: Allow students to create their own organizer or web if the one provided in the text does not suit their learning style.
Aplicación: As a class, brainstorm the story, TV show, or movie that students will use as a comparison to answer the first question. For the second activity, help students with writing dialogues and narration as needed. Tell them to make sure the scenes help move the story along.

Multiple Intelligences
Interpersonal/Social
See *Infórmate* Ex. 2.
Interpersonal/Social and Bodily/Kinesthetic
See *Aplicación* Ex. 2.

Infórmate

STRATEGY ▸ Using prior knowledge to structure understanding

1 La red narrativa, dibujada más abajo, te puede ayudar a entender la historia. Según vayas comprendiendo el argumento, rellena los distintos óvalos (*ovals*) de la red.

2 En grupos, escojan otro título para esta historia.

Aplicación

1 ¿Se parece esta historia a una historia que hayas leído o que hayas visto en la televisión o en el cine? Compáralas. Haz una lista de tres semejanzas y tres diferencias.

2 En grupos, escriban una adaptación de esta historia para la radio. Divídanla en varias escenas, y asignen una escena a cada grupo. Combinen las escenas para hacer un guión de la obra completa.

Argumento: Los padres de Anne Kristin piden al detective que investiguen lo que pasó a su hija cuando estaba de vacaciones con su madre en Fuerteventura. El Sr. Thune y su ayudante van a Fuerteventura y hablan con los jóvenes que la vieron por última vez. Les dijeron que Anne Kristin estaba con Alejandro cuando la vieron. Después de que su ayudante tuvo una cita con Alejandro, estaba muy nerviosa, y el detective entrevistó a la novia del cantinero. Ella le dijo que Alejandro mató a Anne Kristin en la playa.

2 Titles will vary.

Aplicación
1–2 Lists and scripts will vary.

Fondo literario
Espuma y nada más
(pp. 482–487)

www **Internet Activities**

Apply

Process Writing
For information regarding writing
portfolios, see p. 54.

Teaching Suggestions
Tell students that working through
the *Para escribir* section will help
them answer the key chapter
question.

Answers
Responses will vary.

Para escribir

A veces parece que la violencia se encuentra por todas partes,
pero no podemos, ni debemos, poner el control de nuestra
comunidad, seguridad e independencia en sus manos. Es
importante luchar contra la violencia. El problema es cómo
hacerlo de una forma no violenta.

1 Primero, piensa en estas preguntas:

- ¿Cuáles son las formas o los tipos de violencia?
- ¿Cómo nos afectan?
- ¿Qué podemos hacer para protegernos y para que haya
  más seguridad en nuestra comunidad?

Haz una tabla como la de abajo. Escribe algunas
recomendaciones para tratar de evitar la violencia.

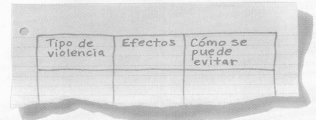

Tipo de violencia	Efectos	Cómo se puede evitar

2 Ahora, piensa en estas preguntas y escribe tus ideas:

- ¿Cuáles son las causas más frecuentes de violencia
  en tu comunidad?
- ¿Qué programas o actividades se pueden sugerir para
  educar a las personas sobre la violencia y para tratar
  de evitarla?

Usa la información en tu tabla y lo que has aprendido en las
actividades de este capítulo para escribir un programa de
prevención o control de la violencia.

Explica tu programa y di cómo se puede hacer. Incluye ejemplos
de hechos violentos en tu comunidad. Da tu opinión sobre las
causas y los efectos de la violencia. Habla de las actividades y los
programas que se pueden hacer para educar a la comunidad en
general, especialmente a los niños y a los jóvenes. Sé específico(a).

358   Capítulo 10

Options

Strategies for Reaching All Students

Students Needing Extra Help
You may want to have students complete
only Steps 1 and 2. Either omit Step 3, or
have students choose just one or two of the
ideas required.

Multiple Intelligences
Interpersonal/Social and Visual/Spatial
See step 3.

3 Recuerda que debes revisar tu trabajo con un(a) compañero(a) y seguir los pasos del proceso de escribir.

Puedes usar estas palabras y expresiones u otras.

aunque	crear	hacer daño	preocupar(se)
cada vez más	en contra	imponer	sin embargo
contribuir	entonces	justo, -a	

Para compartir tu trabajo, puedes:

- exhibirlo en la sala de clases
- enviarlo al Consejo para los jóvenes de tu comunidad
- hacer una presentación en tu comunidad para hablar sobre la violencia
- incluirlo en tu portafolio

Para escribir   359

Assess & Summarize

Test Preparation

You may want to assign parts of this section as written homework or as an in-class writing activity prior to administering the *Examen de habilidades*.

Answers

Listening

—*Cuando el asesinato ocurrió, el guardia estaba en otra parte del edificio. En cuanto oyó el ruido de una pistola, corrió al lugar de los hechos donde sorprendió al acusado, que en ese momento robaba a la víctima. En la lucha que siguió, el acusado se escapó, hiriendo al guardia en el brazo. Gracias a la descripción que el guardia le dio a la policía, el sospechoso fue arrestado cerca de la escena del crimen unos pocos minutos después. Señores y señoras del jurado, es evidente que el acusado es culpable del asesinato.*

Ocurrió en un edificio, Hay un criminal en la descripción, La persona que describe el hecho es un abogado.

Repaso ¿Lo sabes bien?

Esta sección te ayudará a prepararte para el examen de habilidades, donde tendrás que hacer tareas semejantes.

Listening

¿Puedes entender la descripción de un hecho de violencia? Escucha mientras el (la) profesor(a) lee un ejemplo semejante al que vas a oír en el examen. ¿Dónde ocurrió el crimen? ¿Hay sólo un criminal en esta descripción? ¿Quién describe el hecho?

Reading

¿Puedes leer un folleto que publicó un grupo de la comunidad? Según la información del folleto, ¿qué ofrece este grupo? ¿Piensas que ellos pueden tener más éxito en ayudar a los jóvenes que otros grupos? ¿Por qué?

Nuestro club existe para apoyar a los jóvenes de nuestra comunidad. Somos miembros de un grupo contra la violencia y nuestro propósito es comunicarnos con ustedes. No queremos que se arriesguen más ni que recurran a la falsa seguridad que ofrecen las armas y las drogas. Nos preocupa la muerte de las personas jóvenes e inocentes. Sabemos que ustedes pueden superar estos problemas y queremos ayudarles. Pueden llamarnos al 4–CRISIS.

Writing

¿Puedes escribir un mensaje como el que escribió Rosario por el *Internet*?

Nos gustaría ponernos en contacto con otros estudiantes interesados en acabar con la violencia en la escuela y la comunidad. Nos preocupa que tantos jóvenes tengan armas y que haya cada vez más muertes a causa de las drogas. Sabemos que no podremos influir sobre crímenes como los secuestros y el terrorismo internacional. Sin embargo, si no hacemos algo para ayudarnos seguiremos teniendo miedo. Si tienen experiencias o sugerencias para E.C.V., (Estudiantes Contra la Violencia) por favor pónganse en contacto con nosotros. Pueden escribirnos por el *Internet* a rosario@ecv

Culture

¿Puedes dar un ejemplo de lo que ha hecho la gente en algún país de habla hispana para tratar de controlar la violencia en su país?

El futuro está en tus manos

Speaking

¿Puedes hablar con un(a) compañero(a) sobre un hecho de violencia?

A —*Leí en un periódico que un joven de doce años mató a otro con la pistola que sus padres tenían en casa.*

B —*¡Qué lástima! ¿Fue un accidente?*

A —*¡Qué va, ni fue un acto de autodefensa! Sólo quería robarle. Por eso me parece bien que lo castiguen.*

B —*Pero es un menor de edad. Yo creo que . . .*

www.pasoapaso.com

Options

Strategies for Reaching All Students

Students Needing Extra Help
Remind students that this is just a sample of what the real test will be like.
Listening: Read more than once. Write the three questions on the chalkboard. Remind students that they need to listen for only certain pieces of information.
Reading: Remind students that they don't need to know every word. Review strategies for finding cognates, context clues, and word families. Remind them that they are looking for only certain pieces of information. Be sure they read the questions before starting to read. You may want to list the questions on the chalkboard or overhead.
Writing: Have students use the Organizer and write a sample paragraph before the test as practice. Brainstorm other reasons why students might form support groups: Students Against Drunk Driving, Peer Mediation, Random Acts of Kindness, etc.

Culture: Have students review the notes they took in the *Álbum cultural*.
Speaking: Use the vocabulary section of the Organizer. Limit the number of lines of dialogue. Finish the model so that students know how to end the conversation. Brainstorm other methods of punishment and other less violent crimes, e.g., breaking into a locker, breaking a window, writing graffiti on walls, etc.

Resumen del vocabulario

Usa el vocabulario de este capítulo para:

- responder a la pregunta clave: ¿Cómo se puede controlar la violencia?
- describir un hecho de violencia
- hablar de las causas de la violencia y de sus efectos en la sociedad
- dar tu opinión sobre diferentes medidas para controlar la violencia

para describir un hecho de violencia
a mano armada
el arma, pl. las armas
el asesinato
el asesino, la asesina
el ataque
el atentado
el / la delincuente
la droga
la explosión,
   pl. las explosiones
herir (e → ie)
luchar
el lugar de los hechos
el narcotráfico
el rehén, pl. los rehenes
el rescate
secuestrar
el secuestro
el terrorismo
el tiroteo

para hablar sobre el control de la violencia
la alarma
castigar (g → gu)
el castigo
contratar
corporal
el / la guardia
la seguridad
vigilar

para describir los efectos de la violencia
arriesgar (g → gu)
asombrar
la inseguridad
la muerte
preocupar(se)
sorprender(se)
temer (a)
el temor
tener la culpa (de)
tener miedo (de)

para hablar de soluciones a la violencia
acabar (con)
el acusado, la acusada
la autodefensa
la cárcel
culpable
defender(se) (e → ie)
evitar
imponer
inocente
el jurado
la medida
meter en
   (la cárcel)
la pena
poner en libertad
recurrir (a)
la sentencia
severo, -a
el sospechoso, la sospechosa
el / la testigo

Resumen **361**

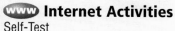

CAPÍTULO 11
THEME: MULTICULTURALISM

SCOPE AND SEQUENCE Pages 362–395

COMMUNICATION

Topics

Christians, Jews, and Muslims in Spain

Cultural influences in Latin America

Objectives

Describir la interacción entre las culturas en España y en América Latina

Describir cómo interactúan dos o más culturas

Hablar de la fusión de culturas en España antes de 1492

Hablar de la fusión de las culturas después que los españoles llegaron a las Américas

CULTURE

La interacción entre las culturas en España y en América Latina

GRAMMAR

El imperfecto del subjuntivo

El imperfecto del subjuntivo: Los verbos irregulares

El subjuntivo en frases con para que

Ancillaries available for use with Chapter 11

Multisensory/Technology	Print	Assessment

 Overheads, 33–35

 Audio Tapes and CDs

 Vocabulary Art Blackline Masters for Hands-On Learning, pp. 50–56/CD-ROM

 Classroom Crossword

 Video

 Internet Activities
www.pasoapaso.com

 Practice Workbook, pp. 110–120

 Writing, Audio & Video Activities, pp. 65–70, 123–125, 153–154

 Communicative Activity Blackline Masters
  Pair and Small Group Activities, pp. 71–76
  Situation Cards, p. 77

RESOURCE PRO®

Planning Express, Teaching Resources Library, and Clip Art Library

 Assessment Program
  Pruebas, pp. 153–162
  Examen de habilidades, pp. 163–166

 Test Generator

 ¿Lo sabes bien? Video Quiz

Video, Chap. 11

Cultural Diversity in Latin America

Even though the Americas have experienced unprecedented immigration, it is easy to overlook the variety of ethnicities that have arrived. The interaction between these distinct cultures continues even today.

Many people do not realize that sizable populations of Middle Eastern immigrants inhabit cities in Colombia and Argentina and the Yucatán Peninsula of Mexico. Descendants of German immigrants populate much of modern Paraguay. Persons of Japanese descent may be found in Peru, Panama, and especially in Brazil.

Descendants of African slaves form a large percentage of the population of Puerto Rico, the Dominican Republic, and Cuba. Their influence on those cultures has been profound. Due to African assimilation into the island cultures, most Caribbean societies contain a broad continuum of racial types, including persons with varying degrees of either European or African heritage.

The extent to which native populations in Latin America outside of the Caribbean have intermixed with other groups has often been determined by the type of native population. In some countries, many people with indigenous ancestry can be found, while in others virtually no Native American communities survive today. In the Southern Cone countries of Argentina and Chile, for example, the indigenous populations at the time of initial European settlement were relatively sparse. The subsequent massive European immigration overwhelmed them. As a result, few of today's Chileans or Argentines have indigenous ancestry.

Elsewhere in Latin America the indigenous populations were larger and lived in more firmly established societies. The Aztecs and Incas, for example, had large, highly developed societies. These groups were treated as a resource by their conquerors, a fact that to some extent prevented their destruction. Thus, the modern nations of Mexico and Peru include large numbers of both indigenous people and *mestizos,* whose ancestry is both European and Native American.

The interaction and combination of cultures is not a thing of the past, but continues unabated in the Americas today. Even in Spain, the European Common Market is fostering increasing cultural exchange and transformation between Spain and the other European states.

In the U.S., cultural interaction is ongoing. It includes communities with long-established roots, such as sixth-generation European and African descendants, as well as recently established Asian and Hispanic communities. Issues such as bilingual education and affirmative action are testimonies to our continuing struggle to determine how best to handle the interaction of the various groups within one nation.

Introduce

Re-entry of Concepts
The following list represents words, expressions, and grammar topics re-entered from Books 1, 2, and 3 (Chaps. 2–4):

Book 1
direction words, preterite

Book 2
imperfect, direction words

Chapter 2
past participles

Chapter 4
present perfect

Planning

Cross-Curricular Connections

World History Connection *(pp. 370–371)*
Have each student interview an older relative, neighbor, or friend to learn more about their ethnic, cultural, or religious heritage. Students should also ask what important historical events affected their ancestral countries, and how the lives and customs of the people of that era were changed by them. Compare those events with the current world situation.

Sociology Connection *(pp. 380–381)*
Tell students to imagine that they are grandparents and are telling their teenage grandchildren about today's events and times. Have them explain what it was like to live in this time period, giving details about the culture and people.

Spanish in Your Community
Have students cite specific influences of Hispanic cultures in their community. If they aren't a factor in your community, students may include non-Hispanic cultures that are strongly represented. Have students share their findings with the entire class.

CAPÍTULO 11

OBJETIVOS

Al terminar este capítulo vas a poder responder a la pregunta clave:

¿Cómo se mezclan culturas diferentes?

También vas a poder:

- describir cómo interactúan dos o más culturas

- hablar de la fusión de culturas en España antes de 1492

- explicar la fusión de culturas que tuvo lugar cuando los españoles llegaron a las Américas

- describir el impacto de diferentes culturas hispanas en los Estados Unidos hoy en día

Baile de la Conquista en Chichicastenango, Guatemala

363

Teaching Suggestions
Point out the key chapter question. Tell students that by acquiring the new words and structures, they will be able to answer this question.

Cultural Notes

(pp. 362–363, photo)
Traditions, whether Mayan, Spanish, or a blend of both, are important to Guatemala's Quiché Mayan Indians. In the remote highland town of Chichicastenango, an ancient center of the Quiché, major Catholic holidays are observed with solemn religious processions through the streets. In addition, there are performances by splendidly costumed dancers, such as those shown here, who act out ancient Mayan legends and events of the Spanish conquest.

Preview

Cultural Objective

• *Hablar de la influencia de diferentes culturas en España*

Multicultural Perspectives

The Arabs conquered Egypt and Northern Africa before reaching Spain in A.D. 711. They occupied Spain until 1492, when the *Reconquista* was completed. During the more than 700 years of occupation, three major religions simultaneously existed in Spain: Christianity, Islam, and Judaism. The influence of these cultures is still recognizable in the language, food, and music of Spain and Latin America. Spanish words with Arabic origins are common (for example: *el álgebra, el alcázar, el cénit*). The root of the Spanish name Carmen is Arabic. In Granada, *carmens* were small interior gardens not visible from the street. Arabic spices such as *comino* and *azafrán* are used to flavor Latin American dishes.

Critical Thinking: Synthesizing

As a class, brainstorm descriptive adjectives for the photo content. Later, have students write one or two sentences about each photo.

Anticipación

Mira las fotos. ¿Piensas que representan una misma cultura o culturas diferentes? ¿Cómo lo sabes?

La iglesia de la Sagrada Familia en Barcelona es obra del arquitecto Antoni Gaudí. Aunque quedó sin terminar cuando Gaudí murió en 1926, hoy se trata de terminarla siguiendo su modelo. ¿Dónde has visto una iglesia parecida a ésta?

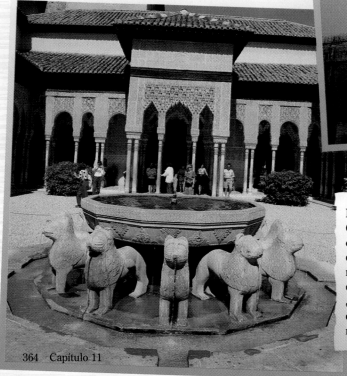

El palacio de la Alhambra en Granada, España, fue construido entre los siglos IX y XIV. El patio de los Leones, uno de sus lugares más conocidos, recibe su nombre de la fuente que tiene en el centro. ¿Se parece esta fuente a alguna que tú conoces? ¿Qué es lo que más te gusta de ella?

364   Capítulo 11

Options

Strategies for Reaching All Students

Spanish-Speaking Students
Ask: *¿Cómo se manifiestan otras culturas? ¿Has visto o has participado alguna vez en actos para conmemorar las aportaciones de alguna cultura específica? ¿Cómo eran?*

Students Needing Extra Help
Assist students as needed with the questions on these pages.

Multiple Intelligences
Visual/Spatial
See Critical Thinking.

Cultural Notes

(p. 364, top photo)
This vast, fantastic church, the Templo Expiatori de la Sagrada Família in Barcelona, is the unfinished masterpiece of Spanish architect Antoni Gaudí i Cornet (1852–1926). Construction of the church, which had begun in 1882, was taken over in 1884 by Gaudí, who brought his own famously odd features (cigar-shaped towers, undulating, richly textured stonework, sculptures of snails and tortoises) to the structure's initial neo-Gothic design.

La gran mezquita de Córdoba es la mayor del mundo musulmán después de La Meca. Su construcción empezó alrededor del año 788 en el lugar donde antes había una iglesia. ¿Dónde podrías ver mezquitas como ésta?

La sinagoga del barrio de la Judería en Córdoba, España, fue construida alrededor del siglo XIV. Su interior combina diseños mozárabes con inscripciones hebreas *(Hebrew)*. ¿Has estado alguna vez en una sinagoga? ¿Se parecía a ésta? ¿Cómo era?

Exploración cultural www.pasoapaso.com
Visita estos países

365

(p. 364, bottom photo)
Granada's *patio de los Leones* in the medieval Moorish palace-fortress la Alhambra. This lavish, quintessentially Arabic courtyard was the heart of the Moorish rulers' domestic life. It measures 90 by 50 feet and is adorned with elegant horseshoe arches and white marble columns on its borders. The fountain at its center is supported by 12 marble lions.

(p. 365, top photo)
Originally 1,000 of these columns stood inside Córdoba's Mezquita, supporting the two tiers of red and white striped arches seen here. In 1523, when construction of the cathedral within the mosque began, 150 columns were removed. Legend has it that upon seeing this architectural and artistic mutilation, Charles V told the builders: "You have built here what you or anyone might have built anywhere, but you have destroyed what was unique in the world."

(p. 365, bottom photo)
During Spain's Golden Age, when Córdoba was one of the largest, wealthiest, and most cosmopolitan cities in western Europe, the city's Jews were not only welcome there but were also highly esteemed by the caliphs for their learning and culture. They lived in the labyrinthine *barrio de la Judería,* the location of the fourteenth-century synagogue, whose interior decorated with Mozarabic patterns and Hebrew inscriptions from the psalms, is shown here.

Present

Chapter Theme
Multiculturalism in fifteenth-century Spain

Communicative Objectives
- *Describir cómo interactúan dos o más culturas*
- *Hablar de la fusión de culturas en España antes de 1492*
- *Hablar de la fusión de las culturas después que los españoles llegaron a las Américas*

 Overheads 33–34

 Vocabulary Art BLMs/CD-ROM

 Vocabulary Tape 11-1

Grammar Preview
Irregular imperfect subjunctive is previewed here lexically. The explanation appears on pp. 382–383.

Teaching Suggestions
Preparing students to speak: Use one or two options from each of the categories of Comprehensible Input or Limited Verbal Response. For a complete explanation of these categories and some sample activities, see pp. T20–T21.

Vocabulario para comunicarse

Musulmanes, judíos y cristianos en España

Aquí tienes palabras y expresiones necesarias para hablar sobre la integración de diferentes culturas. Léelas varias veces y practícalas con un(a) compañero(a) en las páginas siguientes.

la torre

el castillo

el alcázar, *pl.* los alcázares

el rey
la reina
pl. los reyes

la reja

el balcón, *pl.* los balcones

366   Capítulo 11

Options

Strategies for Reaching All Students

Spanish-Speaking Students
Imagina que eres el pintor del cuadro que ilustra el nuevo vocabulario. Descríbelo y explica por qué has incluido cada elemento en él. Usa el vocabulario de la lección en tu descripción.

Students Needing Extra Help
Begin the vocabulary section of the Organizer. Make the distinction between *el alcázar* and *el castillo*. Emphasize that while the plural of *el alcázar* retains the accent, the plural of *el balcón* does not. Explain what a mosque is.
También necesitas . . . : Explain *el rasgo* as used in this chapter.

Extended Written Practice/Homework
1. Refer to pp. 366–367 and write four sentences describing this scene about Spanish history: *Había un castillo que tenía una torre muy alta.*
2. Write three sentences naming places in the U.S. where there has been a mixture of cultures. Use: *influencia, diversidad cultural, mezclar, región.*

También necesitas . . .

la batalla	*battle*	el musulmán, la musulmana	*Muslim*
conquistar	*to conquer*	la poesía	*poetry*
fundar	*to found*	el pueblo	here: *people*
el /la hispanohablante	*Spanish speaker*	el rasgo	*feature*
el judío, la judía	*Jew*	(que nosotros)	*that we made / did*
mezclar	*to mix*	hiciéramos	
el mundo	*world*	(from: *hacer*)	

¿Y qué quiere decir . . . ?
el continente
el cristiano, la cristiana
cultural
la diversidad

la influencia
reconquistar
la región, *pl.* las regiones

—la sinagoga

la mezquita

el techo

la fuente

el azulejo

Vocabulario para comunicarse 367

3. Refer to pp. 364–365 and write three sentences saying what interests you or what you would like to see in Spain: *Me interesa la influencia musulmana en los edificios.*

Multiple Intelligences
Verbal/Linguistic
See Vocabulary Tape 11-1.
Visual/Spatial
See Overheads 33–34 and the Vocabulary Art BLMs/CD-ROM.
Visual/Spatial and Bodily/Kinesthetic
See Class Starter Review.

Practice

Answers: Empecemos a conversar

1 ESTUDIANTE A

a. Dime, ¿se ven balcones en estas fotos de la Alhambra?

b. ... azulejos ...

c. ... rejas ...

d. ... árboles ...

e. ... fuentes ...

f. Questions will vary.

ESTUDIANTE B

Answers will vary, but may include:

a. Sí, hay un balcón en una de las fotos.

b. Sí, hay azulejos en una de las fotos.

c. No, no veo ninguna reja.

d. Sí, hay árboles en las fotos.

e. Sí, hay una fuente en una de las fotos.

f. Answers will vary.

Empecemos a conversar

Túrnate con un(a) compañero(a) para ser *Estudiante A* y *Estudiante B*. Reemplacen las palabras subrayadas con palabras representadas o escritas en los recuadros. 💡 quiere decir que puedes escoger tu propia respuesta.

Para el Ejercicio 1, mira las fotos de abajo.

1
A — *Dime, ¿se ven <u>techos</u> en estas fotos de la Alhambra?*
B — *Sí, hay <u>techos</u> en las dos fotos.*

Estudiante A   Estudiante B

a.   b.   c.   d.   e.   f.

Vistas de la Alhambra

368   Capítulo 11

Options

Strategies for Reaching All Students

Spanish-Speaking Students
Exs. 1–2: Pair bilingual and non-bilingual students, if possible.

Students Needing Extra Help
Exs. 1–2: Point out the *¡No olvides!* section containing location words students have previously learned.

Enrichment
Ex. 2: As homework, have students look for a photo of a building in this book and describe what they see, using as much of the new vocabulary as possible. Remind them to give page references for the photos they choose.

368   Standards 1.1; 3.2

Para el Ejercicio 2, mira el mapa de arriba.

2

A —En la ciudad, ¿dónde estaba la catedral?
B —*La catedral estaba detrás de la mezquita.*

¡NO OLVIDES!

Do you remember these expressions that indicate location: *al fondo de, a la derecha, a la izquierda, cerca de, junto a, al lado de, debajo de, detrás de, delante de, entre, lejos de?*

Estudiante A   **Estudiante B**

a.
b.
c.
d.
e.
f.
g.

Reteach / Review: Vocabulary

Ex. 2: To prepare students for this exercise, first review the expressions in the *¡No olvides!* box that indicate location. Call on students to create a riddle about a place inside or outside of school, using at least one of the expressions in their clues. Have the class try to answer the riddles.

2 ESTUDIANTE A

a. En la ciudad, ¿dónde estaba el castillo?
b. ...estaba la mezquita?
c. ...estaba la fuente?
d. ...estaba el puente?
e. ...estaba el sendero?
f. ...estaban los árboles?
g. Questions will vary.

ESTUDIANTE B

Answers will vary, but may include:

a. El castillo estaba detrás de los árboles.
b. La mezquita estaba delante de la catedral.
c. La fuente estaba cerca de la casa.
d. El puente estaba lejos de la mezquita.
e. El sendero estaba delante del castillo.
f. Los árboles estaban a la izquierda del sendero.
g. Answers will vary.

Cultural Notes ☀

Multiple Intelligences
Verbal/Linguistic
See Exs. 1–2.
Visual/Spatial and Verbal/Linguistic
See Enrichment.

(p. 368, left photo)
The Alhambra's name is derived from the Moorish *Al Qual'a al-Hambra,* which means "the red (one)." It refers to the color of the clay of the hill upon which the Alhambra stands, and which was used to build it. Considered to be the most beautiful example of medieval Arabic architecture anywhere, the Alhambra was the last outpost of the Moors in Spain. In 1492, it fell to the *Reconquista* forces led by the Catholic monarchs Fernando and Isabel.

(p. 368, right photo)
This view of the *patio de los Leones* is from one of the many richly ornamented rooms that radiate out from it. The part of the Alhambra that includes this courtyard is known as the Alcázar, and was built in the fourteenth century as the royal residence of the Moorish rulers. The oldest part of the Alhambra, the Alcazaba, was a military fortress built between 1238 and 1358.

Practice & Apply

Re-enter / Recycle

Ex. 5: past participles from Chap. 2

Ex. 7: present perfect from Chap. 4

Answers: Empecemos a conversar

3 **ESTUDIANTE A**

a. ¿Y en el siglo diez, qué pasó?

b. ... once, ...

c. ... doce, ...

d. ... trece, ...

e. ... quince, ...

ESTUDIANTE B

a. En el siglo diez los musulmanes construyeron la ciudad de Medina Azahara.

b. ... once los cristianos reconquistaron la ciudad de Toledo.

c. ... doce los judíos construyeron la sinagoga de Toledo.

d. ... trece los cristianos empezaron a construir la catedral de Toledo.

e. ... quince los cristianos destruyeron la mezquita de Sevilla.

3 siglo VIII

A —¿Y en el _siglo ocho_, qué pasó?

B — _En el siglo ocho los musulmanes conquistaron la ciudad de Córdoba._

SIGLO

VIII

siglo VIII
musulmanes
conquistar
ciudad de Córdoba

siglo X
musulmanes
construir
ciudad de Medina
Azahara

X

XI

siglo XII
judíos
construir
sinagoga de Toledo

siglo XI
cristianos
reconquistar
ciudad de Toledo

XII

XIII

siglo XIII
cristianos
empezar a construir
catedral de Toledo

siglo XV
cristianos
destruir
mezquita de Sevilla

XV

Estudiante A

a. siglo X   d. siglo XIII

b. siglo XI   e. siglo XV

c. siglo XII

Estudiante B

Options

Strategies for Reaching All Students

Spanish-Speaking Students

Exs. 3–4: Pair bilingual and non-bilingual students, if possible.

Ex. 8: After this exercise, ask: ¿Qué es lo que más te impresiona de las culturas representadas en tu comunidad o región? ¿Hay alguna característica de esas culturas que les llame la atención a otros miembros de la comunidad? ¿Cuál es?

Students Needing Extra Help

Ex. 3: Review Roman numerals. Remind students that *construir* and *destruir* have a spelling change.

Cooperative Learning

As a class, discuss students' responses to Ex. 6. Write the names of represented cultures on the chalkboard. Have students form groups of four, if possible, based on the culture with which they most identify. Tell each student to write a contribution that

their culture has made to the U.S. When lists are completed, have groups share them with the class.

Multiple Intelligences

Verbal/Linguistic
See Audio Activity 11.1.

Visual/Spatial
See Practice Wkbk. 11-1 and 11-2 and Writing Activities 11-A and 11-B.

Visual/Spatial and Interpersonal/Social
See Cooperative Learning.

4 español
A —*¿Qué nos pidió el (la) profesor(a) de <u>español</u> que hiciéramos?*
B —*Nos pidió que hiciéramos <u>un trabajo sobre las diferentes culturas en España</u>.*

Estudiante A

a. geografía
b. arte
c. inglés
d. matemáticas
e. historia
f.

Estudiante B

un informe sobre la poesía moderna
un mapa de las regiones de España
tres problemas de álgebra
un estudio sobre los reyes de España
un dibujo del alcázar

¿Y qué piensas tú?

Aquí tienes otra oportunidad para usar el vocabulario de este capítulo.

5 ¿Qué culturas están representadas en tu comunidad? ¿Cuál es la que tiene más influencia? ¿Hay hispanohablantes en tu comunidad? ¿De qué país o países son? ¿Cómo se ve la diversidad cultural en tu comunidad?

6 ¿Qué cultura(s) representas tú? ¿De dónde eran tus abuelos? ¿Qué idioma(s) hablaban? ¿Lo(s) sigue(n) hablando? ¿Por qué?

7 ¿Cuáles son algunas de las culturas que han contribuido a la cultura de los Estados Unidos? ¿Cuáles son algunos rasgos culturales que otras culturas han traído a nuestro país?

8 Imagínate que te mudas a un país con una cultura diferente. Piensa en las características de tu propia cultura y escribe cinco contribuciones que podrías hacer.

MÁS PRÁCTICA

Más práctica y tarea, pp. 577–578
Practice Workbook 11–1, 11–2

4 ESTUDIANTE A
a. ¿Qué nos pidió el (la) profesor(a) de geografía que hiciéramos?
b. . . . arte . . .
c. . . . inglés . . .
d. . . . matemáticas . . .
e. . . . historia . . .
f. Questions will vary.
ESTUDIANTE B
a. Nos pidió que hiciéramos un mapa de las regiones de España.
b. . . . un dibujo del alcázar.
c. . . . un informe sobre la poesía moderna.
d. . . . tres problemas de álgebra.
e. . . . un estudio sobre los reyes de España.
f. Answers will vary.

Answers: ¿Y qué piensas tú?
5–8 Answers will vary.

 Practice Wkbk. 11-1, 11-2

 Audio Activity 11.1

 Writing Activities 11-A, 11-B

 Pruebas 11-1, 11-2

Cultural Notes

(p. 370, bottom left photo)
Symbol of Sevilla and the city's most photographed monument, the Giralda tower was formerly the minaret to a mosque that was razed in 1401 so that the city's grand cathedral (the largest Gothic cathedral in the world) could be built on that site. The tower, which rises some 300 feet alongside the cathedral, was built between 1184 and 1196. In 1565 a Renaissance belfry was added to its top, with arches and a set of 25 bells.

(p. 370, top right photo)
Construction of Córdoba's *mezquita* began in 785 and ended two centuries later. The mosque covers an area 570 by 450 feet, which makes it only somewhat smaller than St. Peter's Basilica in Rome. A 180-foot-long lavishly decorated cathedral was built in the sixteenth century within the mosque.

Ask students: Think of the vast number of events that have occurred in and around these buildings across the centuries. When was the oldest building in your community constructed? What types of events has it witnessed?

Present

Chapter Theme
Cultural contributions to Latin America

Communicative Objectives
- *Describir cómo interactúan dos o más culturas*
- *Hablar de la fusión de las culturas después que los españoles llegaron a las Américas*

 Vocabulary Tape 11-2

Teaching Suggestions
Getting ready to speak:
Remind students of the reading strategies that they learned (getting meaning from context and coping with unknown words) to help them understand the *Tema para investigar.* For further details and some sample activities, see pp. T24–T25.

Answers: Tema para investigar
Answers will vary.

Class Starter Review
On the day following the presentation of the *Tema para investigar,* you may want to begin the class with the following activity:

Tema para investigar

Aquí tienes más palabras e ideas para hablar sobre la integración de diferentes culturas. Mira la ilustración de esta página. ¿Qué crees que representa?

La civilización totonaca (1950), Diego Rivera

¿Una cultura española, africana o indígena?

Hernán Cortés y **los conquistadores** españoles invadieron y conquistaron México en el año 1519. Fueron responsables de **la creación** de una nación y una cultura nueva. De España **trajeron** su arquitectura, su religión, su sistema legal y, por supuesto, **la lengua** española. **Establecieron colonias** y fundaron ciudades. **A través de** los años, **las razas** y culturas **europeas** e indígenas se mezclaron, y de esta **mezcla** resultó la raza **mestiza.**

El idioma español **adoptó** palabras de las lenguas indígenas, como "huracán" y "canoa" por ejemplo. Hay palabras que se refieren a **productos** nativos que los españoles no conocían antes: tomate y chocolate, entre otras. Más que el oro y la plata que los conquistadores llevaron a España, la importancia **duradera** de su invasión fue la extensión por todo el mundo de plantas nativas de las Américas, como la papa y el maíz.

372   Capítulo 11

Options

Strategies for Reaching All Students

Spanish-Speaking Students
Have students write a response to the following: *Escoge uno de los elementos culturales (religión, comida, esclavitud, lengua, arte) mencionados en esta lectura. ¿Cómo ha influido en cómo se perciben a sí mismos los hispanos y en su vida de hoy?*

Students Needing Extra Help
Emphasize the word families of the following: *el conquistador, esclavizar, el encuentro,* etc.
Point out the footnotes for the mentioned verbs on p. 373.

Enrichment
As an extra-credit assignment, have students work in groups to research and report to the class on the colonial history of a particular Latin American country, focusing on ways in which ethnic groups mixed. Have them give the ethnic breakdown of the country they researched. Some countries to consider include: Guatemala, Argentina, Paraguay, Venezuela, and Costa Rica. Ask students to also research the early history of Louisiana and New Mexico.

Los **indígenas** también influyeron en las prácticas religiosas cristianas. En la celebración del **Día de los Muertos**, que tiene lugar el dos de noviembre para recordar a los familiares que **han muerto, se combinan** elementos de las religiones católica e indígenas.

Los españoles **esclavizaron** a los indígenas hasta que el Padre Bartolomé de las Casas **propuso** importar a **africanos** como **esclavos.** Aunque esta "solución" dio fin a una **injusticia,** sólo sirvió para crear otra. Como **resultado** de la opresión, algunos de ellos empezaron a **rebelarse.** Los que pudieron escaparse formaron sus propias comunidades. Todavía existen pueblos en los que **la mayoría** de la población es de **descendencia** africana.

El resultado de esta **fusión** de **diversas** culturas se ve hoy en día especialmente en la región del Caribe. En la música—en la salsa y la rumba, por ejemplo—se encuentran **ritmos** de la música africana. Los africanos también contribuyeron mucho a las prácticas religiosas en los países del Caribe. Por ejemplo, la santería, que contiene elementos de la religión católica y las religiones tradicionales de África, es resultado del **encuentro** de varias culturas.

Hoy en día, se ve la mezcla de muchas culturas diferentes por todo el mundo hispanohablante. La población de las Américas **se compone de** gente de muchas culturas diferentes. Aunque todos estos grupos adoptaron el estilo europeo de vida, todavía conservan muchas tradiciones de sus propias culturas.

trajeron *(from* traer)*	*they brought*	el/la indígena	*Native American*
la lengua	*language*	el Día de los Muertos	*Day of the Dead,*
establecer *(c → zc)*	*to establish*		*All Souls Day*
a través de	*through*	morir(se) *(o → ue)*	*to die*
la raza	*race*	esclavizar *(z → c)*	*to enslave*
mestizo, -a	*mestizo (Native*	proponer†	*to propose*
	American and	la mayoría	*majority*
	European)	el encuentro	*encounter, meeting*
duradero, -a	*long-lasting, enduring*	componer(se) de†	*to be composed of*

¿Y qué quiere decir . . . ?

el conquistador	el producto	la descendencia
la creación, *pl.* las	combinar(se)	la fusión, *pl.* las
creaciones	africano, -a	fusiones
la colonia	el esclavo, la esclava	diverso, -a
europeo, -a	la injusticia	el ritmo
la mezcla	el resultado	
adoptar	rebelarse	

* *Traer* follows the pattern of *decir* in the preterite.
† *Proponer* and *componer* follow the pattern of *poner.*

Tema para investigar   373

Multicultural Perspectives

Sincretismo is the combination of different religions or philosophies. This term is often used to describe what occurred in Latin America when Catholicism encountered the indigenous belief system and the African religions brought in by slaves. In countries such as Cuba, combinations of Catholicism and African religions are sometimes known as *macumba, santería,* and *vudú.* The slaves brought to Cuba and other Latin American countries were not permitted to practice their native religions. By giving African deities the names of Catholic saints, they could practice their religions without arousing the suspicion of their masters. So La Virgen de la Caridad del Cobre, the patron saint of Cuba, was used to worship Ochum, the female deity of love and fresh water.

www Internet Activities
Juegos

Cultural Notes ☼

(p. 372, photo)
La civilización totonaca (1950), mural by Diego Rivera (1886–1957) at Mexico City's Palacio Nacional. At the time of Cortés's arrival at Mexico's Veracruz coast, the Totonacs, an ancient Indian people of the area, were under the domination of the Aztec emperor, Moctezuma, and had to pay him goods as tribute as well as give him people to serve as slaves or sacrificial victims. The Totonacs were the first of several Indian tribes subjugated by the Aztecs who allied themselves with Cortés to bring down the Aztec empire.

Practice & Apply

Answers: ¿Comprendiste?

1 La española, la indígena americana y la africana.

Answers will vary, but students may mention: La influencia de los españoles se nota en la lengua, la religión, la arquitectura y el sistema legal. La influencia de los indígenas se nota en el arte, la arquitectura, el vocabulario y la alimentación. La influencia africana se nota en la música y la religión.

2 Lists will vary.

Answers: ¿Y qué piensas tú?

3–7 Answers will vary.

¿Comprendiste?

1 ¿Cuáles fueron las tres culturas más importantes que se combinaron en Hispanoamérica? ¿En qué se nota su influencia?

2 Haz una lista de las tres o cuatro ideas principales del tema. Compara tu lista con la de un(a) compañero(a).

¿Y qué piensas tú?

3 En tu opinión, ¿cuál de las contribuciones de las tres culturas principales que menciona el tema es la más interesante? ¿Por qué?

4 ¿Qué te gustaría preguntarle a Hernán Cortés? Escribe tres o cuatro preguntas. Compara tus preguntas con las de un(a) compañero(a).

5 Piensa en la llegada de los primeros europeos a lo que hoy es Estados Unidos. ¿Cómo se compara con la llegada de los españoles a México? ¿Cómo se comparan los resultados de los dos encuentros?

6 Imagínate que eres uno de los escritores que viajó con Cortés al nuevo mundo. Con un(a) compañero(a) describan lo que vieron al llegar allí. ¿Qué aprendieron Uds. de los indígenas? ¿Y los indígenas de Uds.?

7 ¿Por qué te parece importante que haya diversidad cultural? ¿Qué pasa cuando no se respetan las diferentes culturas que están representadas en nuestra sociedad?

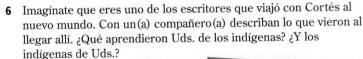

MÁS PRÁCTICA

- Más práctica y tarea, p. 578
- Practice Workbook 11–3, 11–4

Adorno de cabeza con leopardo usado en Camerún

374 Capítulo 11

Options

Strategies for Reaching All Students

Spanish-Speaking Students
Ex. 7: Additional questions: *¿Ha habido algún incidente en tu comunidad que demuestre la importancia de conocerse y respetarse unos a otros? Explica lo que pasó.*

Students Needing Extra Help
Ex. 1: Emphasize that you are looking for cultural influences, not historical events.
Ex. 4: Brainstorm possible questions as a class.
¿Qué sabes ahora?: Have students write this so that they can record their progress.

Extended Written Practice/Homework
1. Write three sentences naming ways in which the Spaniards influenced the Native American civilizations: *Los españoles fundaron ciudades en muchas regiones de las Américas.*
2. Write three sentences naming ways in which Native Americans and Africans influenced Spain and the Spanish colonies.
3. Write three sentences describing the encounter of two different cultures in different parts of the U.S. or the world.

COSTA RICA
LIMO
El Exótico Contraste del Caribe

MAR CARIBE
LIMON
SAN JOSE
OCEANO PACIFICO
PROVINCIA DE LIMON

TELEFONOS (506) 23-1733 EXT. 277 / (506) 22-1090
FAX (506) 23-5452 TEL. USA 1-800-327-7033
APARTADO POSTAL 777 - 1000
SAN JOSE COSTA RICA

¿Qué sabes ahora?

¿Puedes:

■ describir las culturas representadas en tu comunidad?
—En la comunidad donde vivo hay ___ .
■ hablar de la influencia de los musulmanes en España?
—En España los musulmanes ___ ciudades y construyeron ___ y ___ .
■ explicar la fusión de diferentes culturas en Hispanoamérica?
—En las culturas de Hispanoamérica se combinan elementos ___ , ___ y ___ .

Tema para investigar 375

Answers: ¿Qué sabes ahora?
• Answers will vary.
• Answers will vary.
• indígenas / europeos / africanos

 Practice Wkbk. 11-3, 11-4

 Audio Activity 11.2

 Writing Activity 11-C

 Pruebas 11-3, 11-4

 Comm. Act. BLM 11-1

Cultural Notes

Multiple Intelligences
Verbal/Linguistic
1) In pairs, have students play *Password*. One student is given a vocabulary word and gives one-word clues (Spanish only) to help his or her partner guess the word.
2) See Audio Activity 11.2.
Visual/Spatial
See Practice Wkbk. 11-3 and 11-4, Writing Activity 11-C, and Comm. Act. BLM 11-1.

(p. 374, photo)
Because Africans slaves were brought over very early in the Spanish colonization of the Americas, African culture is a very old, deep, and vital part of many Latin American cultures. In Cuba, the African influence is especially strong, as slavery was practiced there for more than 300 years. Much traditional Cuban music and the *santería* religion are a result of the unique, thorough mix of Hispanic and African cultures on the island.

Present & Apply

Cultural Objective
• *Describir la interacción entre las culturas en España y en América Latina*

Critical Thinking: Making Comparisons
In groups of four, have students choose a photo in the *Álbum cultural* and list as many similarities and differences between what they see in the photo and what happens at celebrations in their own community (Fourth of July parades, St. Patrick's Day, etc.). Have groups share their lists with the class.

Answers
Answers to inductive question will vary.

Los países hispanos, y también los grupos hispanos en Estados Unidos celebran la fusión de culturas con varios festivales durante el año. ¿Qué festivales celebran en tu comunidad?

La fiesta del Día del Descubrimiento de Puerto Rico se celebra cada año en noviembre. Este grupo de jóvenes presenta un Baile de Época como parte de la celebración en el Viejo San Juan.

376   Capítulo 11

Options

Strategies for Reaching All Students

Students Needing Extra Help
Have students take notes for use later in the *¿Lo sabes bien?* section.
Brainstorm the festivals celebrated in your school's community.

Multiple Intelligences
Interpersonal/Social
See Critical Thinking.

Las personas de descendencia mexicana que viven en los Estados Unidos celebran el Día de la Independencia, el 16 de septiembre, con desfiles como éste en Chicago. Estas fiestas les dan la oportunidad de afirmar su cultura y celebrar las contribuciones hechas por los mexicanos a la cultura de la comunidad.

La fiesta del Corpus Christi, nueve semanas después de Pascua, se celebra en varias ciudades de España con procesiones, grupos folklóricos y flores en las calles. Las figuras conocidas como Gigantes y Cabezudos, como éstas en Valencia, son una tradición en esta fiesta.

377

Cultural Notes

Present & Apply

Answers: Reacción personal
1–3 Answers will vary.

www **Internet Activities**
Álbum cultural

Para celebrar el centenario *(centennial)* de Pasto, Colombia, los habitantes de la ciudad prepararon un desfile de carrozas *(floats)*. Además de la imaginación de quienes las construyeron, muchas de ellas muestran elementos del folklore colombiano.

378   Capítulo 11

Options

Strategies for Reaching All Students

Students Needing Extra Help
Reacción personal: For Ex. 2, ask someone from your music department to help provide this information.
In Ex. 3, have materials available about the American Indian groups native to your area.

Multiple Intelligences
Intrapersonal/Introspective
See Exs. 1–3.

La zona conocida como la Pequeña Habana en Miami, Florida, celebra varios festivales durante el año en la Calle Ocho. Este festival, parecido al Mardi Gras de Nueva Orleans, lo celebran los cubanos y otros hispanohablantes de Miami. Hay música, comida y bailes típicos, y algunas personas se visten con disfraces.

Reacción personal

Contesta las siguientes preguntas en una hoja de papel.

1 ¿Qué celebraciones interculturales hay en tu comunidad o en la región donde vives? ¿Cómo son? ¿Quiénes pueden participar?

2 ¿Cuáles son las culturas que han influido en la música que más te gusta? ¿En qué se nota esa influencia? ¿En el ritmo, los temas, los instrumentos…?

3 ¿Hay influencias indígenas en el lugar donde vives? ¿En qué se ven?

Actividad cultural www.pasoapaso.com

Álbum cultural 379

Cultural Notes ☀

(p. 378, photo)
The colonial city of Pasto is located in southwestern Colombia, and has a population of 300,000. Pasto is known for its celebrations, particularly to mark the beginning and end of the year. On December 31, gigantic dolls representing the old year are burned. On January 5, *El día de los negros,* people smear each others' faces with black grease, and the next day on *El día de los blancos,* they do the same with talcum powder or flour.

(p. 379, photo)
The *Festival de la calle Ocho,* held each year since 1977 in Miami's Little Havana district, is considered the largest Hispanic festival in the U.S. Originally a Cuban event, the festival has become extremely diverse: the Mexican, Puerto Rican, Nicaraguan, Dominican, and Colombian populations are also well represented. This mirrors the change in the South Florida Hispanic population, which has shifted from almost entirely Cuban to only 80 percent Cuban.

Preview

Overhead 35

Teaching Suggestions

A Encourage students to use their knowledge of preterite forms to help answer the question.

B Ask students whether the forms are present, past, or future.

C Have students list when we use the subjunctive: emotion, doubt, uncertainty, etc. Ask them to apply this information to their answer.

Answers

Son los lugares donde los misioneros enseñaban a los indígenas.

A The preterite indicative ending is -*ron,* and the imperfect subjunctive is -*ran.* / *vivieran, hicieran, mostraran, se convirtieran, tuvieran* / *vivieron, hicieron, mostraron, se convirtieron, tuvieron* / The imperfect subjunctive uses the *Uds. / ellos / ellas* preterite form, changing the ending to -*ran.*

B Imperfect indicative. When the first verb is in the present indicative the verb that follows *que* is in the present subjunctive. When the first verb is in either the imperfect or the preterite indicative the second verb is in the imperfect subjunctive.

C The subjunctive is used following *para que* because it wasn't certain that the action would have taken place.

Gramática en contexto

¿Qué son las misiones de California? Mira las ilustraciones y lee el texto para averiguarlo.

LAS MISIONES DE CALIFORNIA

¿Lo sabías?

La vida de los indígenas del suroeste de California cambió cuando llegaron los españoles en el siglo XVIII. Los misioneros querían que los indígenas vivieran en misiones.

A los misioneros les impresionaba que los jóvenes hicieran tan bien su trabajo y que mostraran tanto talento artístico.

Los misioneros les daban clases de religión a los indígenas para que se convirtieran al cristianismo. Insistían en que aprendieran a hablar español.

Generalmente les pedían que cambiaran sus nombres indígenas para que tuvieran nombres cristianos.

86

87

A In the last caption, it says, *insistían en que aprendieran* and *les pedían que cambiaran. Aprendieran* and *cambiaran* are forms of the imperfect subjunctive. They are similar to the preterite *Uds. / ellos / ellas* forms. How are they different? What other imperfect subjunctive forms are used? Identify the preterite *Uds. / ellos / ellas* forms of these verbs. What pattern do you see?

B Note the following expressions used in the captions: *querían que . . . , les impresionaba que . . . . insistían en que . . . , les pedían que . . . .* What tense are these verbs in? Explain to a partner when to use an imperfect subjunctive form and when to use a present subjunctive form.

C Think about the expression *para que se convirtieran al cristianismo.* Based on what you know about the subjunctive, why do you think it is used here?

380 Capítulo 11

Options

Strategies for Reaching All Students

Students Needing Extra Help
Begin the grammar section of the Organizer. A–C: Tell students to refer to the captions so that they can see the phrases in context. *El imperfecto del subjuntivo:* Remind students of the accent on the *nosotros* form. Give further examples if necessary.

Extended Written Practice/Homework
1. Write four sentences saying what your parents used to want or insist that you and your siblings or friends do. Use: *comer, llevar, ver, arreglar, dormir, respetar. Mis padres siempre querían que durmiéramos tarde los fines de semana.*

2. Write four sentences saying what the teachers and principals of your elementary school used to recommend or demand. Use: *estudiar, usar, aprender, vestirse, leer, obedecer, seguir. La directora exigía que obedeciéramos a los maestros.*

El imperfecto del subjuntivo

We use the subjunctive to say what one person asks, hopes, tells, insists, or requires someone else to do. If the main verb is in the present tense, we use the present subjunctive. If the main verb is in the preterite or imperfect, we use the imperfect subjunctive.

El rey **quiere** que los indígenas **aprendan** a hablar español.
El rey **quiso** que los indígenas **aprendieran** a hablar español.

Los indígenas **dudan** que el ejército **luche** con caballos.
Los indígenas **dudaban** que el ejército **luchara** con caballos.

Es injusto que muchos pobres **vivan** en condiciones tan malas.
Era injusto que muchos pobres **vivieran** en condiciones tan malas.

- To form the imperfect subjunctive, we take the *Uds./ellos/ellas* form of the preterite and replace the ending *-ron* with the imperfect subjunctive endings. Here are the forms of the imperfect subjunctive for *luchar, aprender,* and *vivir*.

luchar		**aprender**		**vivir**	
que luch**ara**	luch**áramos**	que aprendi**era**	aprendi**éramos**	que vivi**era**	vivi**éramos**
que luch**aras**	luch**arais**	que aprendi**eras**	aprendi**erais**	que vivi**eras**	vivi**erais**
que luch**ara**	luch**aran**	que aprendi**era**	aprendi**eran**	que vivi**era**	vivi**eran**

- Since we use the stem of the *Uds./ellos/ellas* form of the preterite, *-ir* stem-changing verbs and $i \rightarrow y$ spelling-changing verbs keep their same spelling changes.

  Insistió en que **siguieran** sus instrucciones.
  El rey **quería** que le **construyeran** un castillo.
  Era necesario que todos **contribuyeran** con su trabajo.

Basílica de la misión de Alcalá, fundada por
el padre Serra en San Diego, California

381

Cultural Notes ☼

Multiple Intelligences
Visual/Spatial
See Overhead 35

(p. 381, photo)
The church at the Misión San Diego de Alcalá, in San Diego, California, was the first of nine missions founded by Fray Junípero de Serra along the west coast between 1769 and 1784. The mission was originally quite extensive, with shops, living quarters, and storage rooms built along a spacious quadrangle. Today, only the partly restored church and a portion of the monastery remain.

Present & Practice

Teaching Suggestions

Ex. 1: Emphasize that this exercise not only gives students the opportunity to practice the imperfect subjunctive but also to process information they have learned. Accept only sentences that are correct based on studies done in this and other classes.

Answers

1 Answers will vary, but the second-column verbs should be in the imperfect indicative *(querían, pedían, esperaban, exigían, preferían)*, and the fourth-column verbs should be in the imperfect subjunctive *(hablaran, comieran, aceptaran, sirvieran, aprendieran, contribuyeran, se vistieran, construyeran, adoptaran).*

 Practice Wkbk. 11-6

 Writing Activity 11-D

 Prueba 11-5

---

1 Trabaja con un(a) compañero(a) para describir cómo estos grupos trataban de influirse entre sí. Usen lo que han aprendido para formar frases correctas. Deben usar elementos de las cuatro columnas en sus frases.

Los misioneros querían que los indígenas aprendieran a hablar español.

los musulmanes	querer	los musulmanes	hablar
los judíos	pedir	los cristianos	comer
los cristianos	esperar	los judíos	aceptar
los indios	exigir	los españoles	servir
los españoles	preferir	los indígenas	aprender
los misioneros		los esclavos	contribuir
			vestirse
			construir
			adoptar

¡NO OLVIDES!

Remember that these verbs follow the pattern of *influir*:
contribuir → contribuyeron → contribuyera; construir → construyeron → construyera.

El imperfecto del subjuntivo: Los verbos irregulares

You know that we form the imperfect subjunctive by taking the *Uds./ellos/ellas* form of the preterite and replacing the ending -*ron* with the imperfect subjunctive endings. Irregular verbs also follow this rule. Here are all the imperfect subjunctive forms of *ir* and *ser*.

ir / ser

que fue**ra**	que fué**ramos**
que fue**ras**	que fue**rais**
que fue**ra**	que fue**ran**

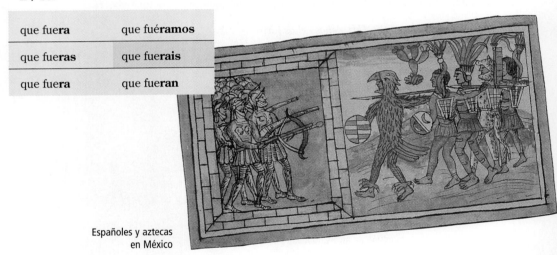

Españoles y aztecas en México

382   Capítulo 11

Options

Strategies for Reaching All Students

Students Needing Extra Help
Ex. 1: Brainstorm possible phrases to complete the sentences.
Ex. 2: Emphasize that this exercise practices when to use the subjunctive.

Enrichment
Ex. 1: As homework, ask students to write five false phrases about what the groups tried to influence each other to do. Before collecting the homework, call on students to read their phrases, and ask the class how the phrase could be changed to be made true.

Extended Written Practice/Homework
1. Write three sentences saying what you hoped or feared might happen when you were a child: *Siempre temía que hubiera un monstruo debajo de mi cama.*
2. Refer to p. 373 and, using what you know about slavery in different parts of the world, write three sentences saying what slave owners used to require their slaves to do: *En el sur de los Estados Unidos, exigían que los esclavos hicieran todo el trabajo manual en los campos.*

Multiple Intelligences
Verbal/Linguistic
See Ex. 1 and Enrichment.
Visual/Spatial
See Practice Wkbk. 11-6 and Writing Activity 11-D.

- Here are other irregular preterites and their corresponding imperfect subjunctive forms.

infinitivo	pretérito	imperfecto del subjuntivo
estar	estuvieron	que estuvie**ra**
haber	hubieron	que hubie**ra**
poder	pudieron	que pudie**ra**
poner	pusieron	que pusie**ra**
tener	tuvieron	que tuvie**ra**
hacer	hicieron	que hicie**ra**
querer	quisieron	que quisie**ra**
decir	dijeron	que dije**ra**
dar	dieron	que die**ra**
saber	supieron	que supie**ra**
traer	trajeron	que traje**ra**
venir	vinieron	que vinie**ra**

¡NO OLVIDES!

Remember that these verbs follow the pattern of *tener: entretener, mantener, obtener*; these follow the pattern of *poner: componer, imponer, proponer, suponer.*

2 a. el indicativo, era
b. el subjuntivo, estuviera
c. el subjuntivo, tuvieran
d. el subjuntivo, fuera
e. el indicativo, había
f. el subjuntivo, pudiera
g. el subjuntivo, supieran
h. el subjuntivo, fuera

2 Bernal Díaz del Castillo (1492-1581), un soldado de Hernán Cortés, escribió un libro sobre los hechos de la conquista de México. Con un(a) compañero(a) decidan cuáles de las frases requieren el subjuntivo y cuáles requieren el indicativo. Luego escojan los verbos apropiados.

a. Vimos que la capital de los aztecas (era / fuera) enorme.
b. Era impresionante que la ciudad (estaba / estuviera) construida sobre un lago.
c. Era increíble que los edificios de la ciudad (tenían / tuviera torres tan altas y grandes.
d. Dudábamos que lo que veíamos (era / fuera) verdad. Parecía un sueño.
e. Era evidente que (había / hubiera) muchos árboles y flores en los jardines que no conocíamos.
f. No podíamos creer que la gente (podía / pudiera) pasear por la ciudad en canoa.
g. Parecía imposible que los indígenas (sabían / supieran) cultivar el maíz en un lago enorme.
h. Era increíble que esta civilización (era / fuera) tan avanzada.

Gramática en contexto 383

Cultural Notes

(p. 382, photo)
This drawing of battle between Aztecs and Spaniards depicts the conquest of Tenochtitlán. Although only 500 in number, the Spaniards came to the fight against the Aztecs with superior equipment such as the harquebuses and crossbow shown here, cannon, armor, and horses. Most critical to their victory, however, was the support they had from thousands of allied Indian warriors who bitterly hated the Aztecs.

(p. 383, realia)
In *Historia verdadera de la conquista de la Nueva España,* Bernal Díaz del Castillo (1492–1584) recounts the events he witnessed and in which he participated as a soldier in Cortés's army from 1519 to 1521. Díaz del Castillo devotes special attention to the last two years of this period, during which the Spaniards conquered Mexico, giving invaluable, detailed information about the everyday life of the Aztecs as well as about the dramatic battles of the conquest.

Ask students: Imagine yourself as a member of Cortés's expedition. What would it feel like to encounter a civilization that you had not known existed? Would you like to visit a place that is totally unknown and unexplored? Why or why not?

Present & Practice

Answers

3 ESTUDIANTE A

a. ¿Quería el rey azulejos?
b. ... una torre?
c. ... un balcón?
d. ... una fuente?
e. ... un puente?
f. ... un techo?
g. ... unas rejas?
h. ... un mar?
i. Questions will vary.

ESTUDIANTE B

a.–i. Answers will vary, but verbs following *Sí, quería que ...* should be in the imperfect subjunctive.

 Practice Wkbk.
11-7, 11-8

 Writing Activity
11-E

 Prueba 11-6

 Comm. Act. BLM
11-2

Teaching Suggestions

El subjuntivo en frases con para que: Point out that *para que* can also be used with the present subjunctive. Write the following example sentence on the chalkboard, underlining the present subjunctive: *La escuela presenta programas para que los estudiantes aprendan más sobre la cultura.*

¿Cómo se mezclan culturas diferentes?

3 Imagina que un rey de España quería que le construyeran un castillo. Dibuja el castillo que tú le construirás con los elementos que ves abajo. Luego contesta las preguntas de tu compañero(a). Después comparen los dibujos.

A — *¿Quería el rey un castillo grande?*
B — *Sí, quería que construyeran un castillo con tres pisos.*
    o: Sí, quería que el castillo fuera muy grande y que tuviera tres pisos.

a.
b.
c.
d.
e.
f.
g.
h.
i.

poner
usar
construir
traer
hacer
ser
estar
tener
haber

El subjuntivo en frases con *para que*

We always use the subjunctive after *para que* to explain why someone did something.

Escondieron sus objetos de oro **para que** los soldados no **pudieran** encontrarlos.

Construyeron misiones **para que** los indígenas **vivieran** allí.

384   Capítulo 11

Options

Strategies for Reaching All Students

Students Needing Extra Help
Ex. 3: Brainstorm phrases that will complete the sentences. Have pictures of castles available. Present a model.
El subjuntivo en frases con para que: Present additional examples using *para* and *para que.*

Enrichment
As homework, ask students to write about a situation in which they tried to influence someone else's actions by changing their usual behavior, giving something up, or doing something that was difficult for them.

Extended Written Practice/Homework
1. Think about the architecture used by the Spaniards in Spain and the Americas and write three sentences explaining why they used different features: *Frecuentemente pintaban las casas de blanco para que no tuvieran mucho calor en el verano.*
2. Write three sentences explaining why your grandparents or other relatives did certain things in the past: *Mis bisabuelos no hablaban alemán en casa para que sus hijos aprendieran a hablar inglés.*

Standards 1.2

4 Imagina que eras un profesor de una escuela española en el siglo XIV. En la escuela había programas para que los estudiantes apreciaran más la diversidad cultural. Trabaja con un(a) compañero(a) para explicar qué quería conseguir la escuela con estos programas. Usen elementos de las tres columnas en sus frases.

Se celebraban estas fechas para que los estudiantes comprendieran otras culturas.

Dar clases sobre arquitectura musulmana	conocer	otras culturas
Celebrar varios días festivos	comprender	su influencia en la arquitectura española
Ofrecer clases de idiomas extranjeros	identificar	la contribución de diferentes grupos a la música
Estudiar la diversidad cultural	entender	el valor de la fusión de diversas culturas
Tocar música de otras regiones	expresar(se)	un punto de vista diferente sobre la vida
	aprender	sus costumbres
	ver	

Ahora lo sabes

¿Puedes:

- decir lo que una persona le pidió a otra o cómo te sentías respecto a una situación?
  —El rey les pidió que ___ un palacio con muchas fuentes.
  —Era importante que los indígenas ___ sus tradiciones.
- expresar dudas sobre una situación en el pasado?
  —Dudaban que ___ encontrar la ciudad que buscaban.
- expresar con qué intención hizo una persona algo?
  —Los españoles establecieron misiones en el suroeste para
  que otros países no ___ colonias allí.

MÁS PRÁCTICA

Más práctica y tarea, p. 579
Practice Workbook 11–5, 11–10

Gramática en contexto   385

4 Answers will vary, but the verb following *para que* should be in the imperfect subjunctive.

Remind students that the imperfect subjunctive follows any verb in the past tense, whether preterite or imperfect. For example: *Los españoles crearon universidades en América para que hubiera un intercambio cultural. También querían que los indígenas aprendieran español.*

Answers: Ahora lo sabes
- construyeran
  conservaran
- pudieran
- fundaran (establecieran)

 Practice Wkbk. 11-9, 11-10

 Audio Activities 11.3, 11.4, 11.5

 Writing Activity 11-F

 Prueba 11-7

 Comm. Act. BLM 11-3

Multiple Intelligences
Verbal/Linguistic
See Audio Activities 11.3, 11.4, and 11.5.
Visual/Spatial
See Enrichment; Practice Wkbk. 11-7, 11-8, 11-9, and 11-10; Writing Activities 11-E and 11-F; and Comm Act. BLMs 11-2 and 11-3.

Apply

Teaching Suggestions
Point out the key chapter question. Remind students that completing these activities will help them answer it. You may select one, two, or all three of these activities, as time permits.

Answers: Sopa de actividades
1–3 Reponses will vary.

Using Photos
Ask: *¿Hay tiendas como éstas en tu comunidad? Si hay, ¿cómo son? / ¿Has comido alguna vez en un restaurante chino-cubano? ¿Cuáles son los restaurantes más populares de tu comunidad?*

Tiendas en El Barrio, Nueva York

Puntos de Vista

¿Cómo se mezclan culturas diferentes?

Esta sección te ofrece la oportunidad de combinar lo que aprendiste en este capítulo con lo que ya sabes para responder a la pregunta clave.

Sopa de actividades

1 Trabaja con tus compañeros de clase para identificar diferentes culturas en tu comunidad o en una comunidad que esté cerca. Cuando tengan una lista de diferentes culturas, divídanse en grupos para estudiar y explicar cómo están representadas estas culturas. Pueden usar la siguiente lista o sus propias ideas.

- restaurantes
- tiendas y mercados
- anuncios
- radio y televisión
- publicaciones
- música
- manera de vestirse
- arte

Cada grupo debe describir la cultura y decir cómo se relaciona con otras culturas. Necesitan decidir cómo van a presentar su información a los otros miembros de la clase. Si es posible, usen dibujos, fotos, materiales auténticos: comida, música, etc. para hacer más interesante su presentación.

Un restaurante chino-cubano en Nueva York

386 Capítulo 11

Options

Strategies for Reaching All Students

Spanish-Speaking Students
Ex. 1: After this exercise, tell students: *Escribe una carta al (a la) editor(a) de un periódico publicado en español. En tu carta, debes hacer un resumen de las presentaciones hechas en clase sobre las diferentes culturas en tu comunidad. Explica cómo les ayudan a los estudiantes a comprender mejor la comunidad donde viven. Revisa la carta con cuidado, haz una copia en limpio y envíala al periódico.*

Students Needing Extra Help
If time is a factor, Exs. 1 and 2 are similar.
Ex. 1: Use the vocabulary section of the Organizer. Remind students that the list is there for suggestions and that they don't need to use every item. Brainstorm ways for students to present their information.
Ex. 2: Use the vocabulary section of the Organizer. Model using the meeting of the Pilgrims and Native Americans. Have materials available. Brainstorm some possible encounters of the cultures.

Cooperative Learning
Bring Spanish versions of common fairy tales to class. Allow groups of three to choose one. Set a time limit for them to read their stories, pointing out that the Spanish versions are not always exact translations of the English. Tell each student to choose a character in their story, change that character's actions, and invent a different ending. Have them combine all the changes to reflect a new ending created by

2 Con tus compañeros de clase vas a describir un encuentro de dos culturas del pasado. Pueden escoger situaciones que han visto en este capítulo o en sus clases de ciencias sociales. Divídanse en grupos para describir el encuentro. Pueden incluir las siguientes ideas en su presentación:

- ¿qué culturas se encontraron?
- ¿cuándo y dónde fue el encuentro?
- ¿cómo fue el encuentro?
- ¿exigía un grupo que el otro hiciera algo en especial?
- ¿cambió un grupo más que el otro?
- ¿cuál fue el resultado del encuentro?

Pueden visualizar este encuentro por medio de una dramatización, un cartel, un video, etc.

3 En grupos de tres, describan e ilustren un plato típico de alguna cultura representada en su comunidad. Pueden preguntarle a una persona de esa cultura o pedir información en la biblioteca. Muestren sus trabajos a la clase. Luego voten para ver cuáles les parecen los mejores.

Video Activity A

Video, Capítulo 11

Chapter 11: Play

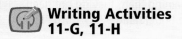
Step

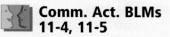
Video Activities B–C

Writing Activities 11-G, 11-H

Comm. Act. BLMs 11-4, 11-5

the group. Encourage creativity and use of chapter grammar. When completed, call on students to read original and group endings to the class.

Multiple Intelligences
Bodily/Kinesthetic and Verbal/Linguistic
Have students prepare and bring in dishes from various ethnic backgrounds. Have them present the recipes to the class.

Interpersonal/Social and Verbal/Linguistic
See Cooperative Learning and Exs. 1–3.
Visual/Spatial
1) Have students write a review of a local ethnic restaurant.
2) See Writing Activities 11-G and 11-H and Comm. Act. BLMs 11-4 and 11-5.

Cultural Notes

(p. 386, photos)
These signs bear witness to New York City's large and diverse Hispanic population. Approximately 44 percent of the Puerto Ricans living in the continental U.S. reside there, as do 70 percent of Dominicans and 60 percent of Ecuadorians. Other groups combine with them to make New York City home to 12 percent of all Hispanics living in the U.S.

Apply

Process Reading
For a description of process reading, see p. 52.

Teaching Suggestions
Point out the key chapter question. Working through the *Para leer* section will help students answer this question. Encourage students to use the strategies given to them in the text to help them understand the reading. Remind them they do not need to understand every word.

Answers
Antes de leer
Answers will vary, but students may mention:
Las raíces de un país son las culturas de la gente. Las dos raíces de México pueden ser la cultura española y la cultura indígena. La tercera puede ser la cultura africana.

Mira la lectura
Responses will vary.

Para leer

Antes de leer
STRATEGY Using prior knowledge

Cuando hablamos de las raíces de un país, ¿a qué nos referimos? ¿Cuáles pueden ser las dos raíces de México? ¿Y la tercera?

Mira la lectura
STRATEGY Skimming

Lee la selección rápidamente, sólo para familiarizarte con las ideas principales.

La tercera raíz de México

Donde quiera que la gente se reúne en las empobrecidas villas pesqueras de Costa Chica, en la costa suroeste de México—en sus casas, en las calles, en las plazas durante los festivales—es probable que alguien se adelante y comience a cantar. Estos cantantes improvisadores agasajan a su audiencia con canciones de romance, tragedia, comedia y protesta social, todas inspiradas por eventos y personajes locales. En estas canciones, llamadas "corridos," hay un sentido de dignidad humana y un deseo de libertad arraigados en las vidas e historia de las gentes de Costa Chica, muchos de los cuales son descendientes de esclavos fugitivos.

Los corridos reflejan la tradición oral de África. La letra se improvisa, y un corrido que tenga éxito se aprende de memoria y se canta una y otra vez como una crónica oral de la vida del pueblo. La letra es rica en símbolos, tradición que probablemente comenzó cuando los cantantes inventaron "palabras en clave" para protestar contra las crueldades de sus amos.

La huella africana en Costa Chica no se limita a la música. En el "Baile de los Diablos,"

celebrado durante la Semana Santa en las calles de Collantes, Oaxaca, los bailarines usan máscaras que reflejan la clara influencia de África. Y en los muelles, los pescadores emplean técnicas de trabajo que posiblemente se trajeron desde la costa oeste africana hace siglos.

Los colonizadores españoles aprovecharon la tecnología que los africanos habían desarrollado en los trópicos y que los negros adaptaron y mejoraron en el Nuevo Mundo. Pero aún hoy en México, muchas de las contribuciones africanas a las técnicas de la pesca, la agricultura, la ganadería y los textiles no se aprecian debidamente.

Aunque es más fuerte en los enclaves negros como Costa Chica, la presencia africana se esparce por la cultura mexicana. En cuentos y leyendas, en la música y el baile, en refranes y canciones—el legado de África está presente en la vida de cada mexicano.

Sin embargo, es difícil distinguir una influencia como "puramente" africana. Desde luego, la presencia africana en México nunca ha sido monolítica. Aunque la mayoría de los esclavos

388   Capítulo 11

Options

Strategies for Reaching All Students

Students Needing Extra Help
Antes de leer: If students have difficulty answering the questions, refer them to the *Tema para investigar.*
Mira la lectura: Because of the length of the reading, have students write the main ideas as they skim. Ask them to leave several line spaces on their paper after each notation so that they can complete the activity in the *Infórmate* section.

fueron traídos de la costa oeste de África, éstos representaron muchos grupos étnicos— los Cafí, los Arara, los Carabalí, los Wolof y los Mandinga, para mencionar unos cuantos—cada uno con una cultura y cosmovisión diferente. Hoy, después de 500 años de mezcla con las tradiciones de los indígenas y de los europeos, resulta casi imposible señalar las contribuciones específicas de algunos de estos grupos.

Además, es un hecho que los elementos africanos en la cultura de México no se reconocen como en otros países de las Américas. De hecho, *el mestizaje*—la ideología oficial que define la cultura de México como una mezcla de influencias europeas e indígenas—ignora completamente las contribuciones de la "tercera raíz" de nuestra nación. Los africanos y sus descendientes, casi invisibles en las crónicas españolas del período colonial, continúan recibiendo poca atención en la "historia oficial" de México. Así que no es sorprendente que los negros, que viven principalmente en áreas rurales pobres, donde el nivel de educación es muy bajo, carezcan de una clara conciencia de su herencia africana.

Apply

Teaching Suggestions

You may want students to use the comparison made in the *Aplicación* section as the basis for a composition. A related project would be to identify the African roots of Mexico or another Latin American culture.

Answers
Infórmate

1 Responses will vary.

2 Answers will vary, but may include:
1. Los corridos reflejan un deseo de libertad, porque muchas personas en Costa Chica son descendientes de esclavos fugitivos.
2. La letra de los corridos refleja la tradición oral de África. La letra se improvisa y es rica en símbolos.
3. Otras huellas africanas incluyen el "Baile de los Diablos" y algunas técnicas de trabajo usadas por los pescadores.
4. Las muchas contribuciones africanas fueron aprovechadas por los españoles, pero hoy no se aprecian debidamente en México.
5. La presencia africana se esparce por todo México en cuentos, bailes, música y refranes.
6. Es difícil distinguir entre las contribuciones de los distintos grupos africanos. Cada uno tiene su propia cultura y contribución.

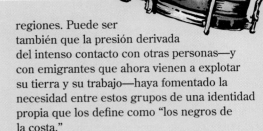

Puntos de Vista

Para leer

Hasta cierto punto, la geografía ha determinado la herencia de las comunidades negras de México. El aislamiento de la costa oeste y las montañas, que ofrecieron santuario a los esclavos fugitivos, ha preservado muchos elementos de la tradición africana. Por otro lado, la región de la costa del Golfo—especialmente el puerto de Veracruz—ha sido una encrucijada donde la cultura indígena de México se mezcló con innumerables influencias de África, Europa, América del Sur y, en especial, del Caribe. En esta variada mezcla, es a veces difícil aislar, como tal, la presencia africana.

Como en el pasado, los negros en la costa del Golfo tienden más a trazar el origen de su linaje al Caribe. Sin embargo, la gente en la costa oeste y en las montañas ha comenzado a reconocer recientemente sus vínculos con África y con su pasado esclavo. En parte, esto es el resultado de recientes estudios etnográficos, folklorísticos e históricos, como también de las frecuentes visitas de estudiosos a estas

regiones. Puede ser también que la presión derivada del intenso contacto con otras personas—y con emigrantes que ahora vienen a explotar su tierra y su trabajo—haya fomentado la necesidad entre estos grupos de una identidad propia que los define como "los negros de la costa."

Es un hecho que las presiones económicas obligan a los grupos étnicos en contacto súbito con gente de afuera, a reforzar sus tradiciones o a ceder ante los atractivos que la homogenización cultural puede ofrecer. Así es como los grupos culturales se despersonalizan y sus valores tradicionales se pierden. Es de desear que los negros de Costa Chica—y de otras partes de México—lleguen a encontrar un nuevo significado en las tradiciones que los han mantenido por siglos. México será mucho más rico gracias a ello.

390

Options

Strategies for Reaching All Students

Students Needing Extra Help
Infórmate: Using the example given *(los corridos),* return to the section in the reading so that students can see how this information was obtained.
Aplicación: As a class, brainstorm some possible countries that meet this criterion.

Multiple Intelligences
Musical/Rhythmic
For extra credit, have students make presentations that include taped samples of music from various Hispanic cultures. Have them stress the geographic origins and ethnic influences of the music.

Infórmate

STRATEGIES► Monitoring understanding

Identifying the main idea

Identifying supporting details

1 Ahora lee la selección con cuidado. Haz una pausa después de cada párrafo y trata de expresar la idea principal de ese párrafo. Usa oraciones que comiencen con estas palabras. No escribas las oraciones todavía, sólo piénsalas.

1. Los corridos . . .
2. La letra de los corridos . . .
3. Otras huellas africanas . . .
4. Las muchas contribuciones africanas . . .
5. La presencia africana . . .
6. Es difícil distinguir . . .
7. La historia oficial de México . . .
8. La geografía . . .
9. Es importante que . . .

2 Ahora lee la selección por tercera vez. En una hoja de papel, escribe la idea principal de cada párrafo y apunta algunos detalles que apoyen esta idea. Por ejemplo:

Los corridos del área de Costa Chica reflejan la cultura de los habitantes de aquella zona.

- *Los corridos están inspirados en eventos y personajes locales.*
- *La cultura de Costa Chica tiene raíces africanas.*

Compara tu esquema con el de un(a) compañero(a).

3 Con tu compañero(a), identifica tres rasgos de la cultura africana en México. Identifica también tres motivos por los cuales no se reconoce debidamente la contribución africana a la cultura mexicana.

Aplicación

Piensa en otro país donde hay una mezcla de culturas y donde una de ellas no se reconozca. Haz una lista de tres semejanzas y tres diferencias con la situación en México.

7. La historia oficial de México se llama *mestizaje.* Reconoce las culturas indígenas y la española, pero no reconoce las contribuciones africanas.
8. La geografía ha influido en la situación de los descendientes africanos. La cultura africana en lugares como Veracruz se ha mezclado tanto con las culturas indígenas que no se puede distinguir una pura presencia africana.
9. Es importante que la gente de Costa Chica mantenga sus tradiciones para que México sea más rico.

3 Answers will vary.

Aplicación
Responses will vary.

Fondo literario
Balada de los dos abuelos
(pp. 488–491)

www **Internet Activities**

Cultural Notes ☀

(p. 391, realia)
Latin American music is a rich variety and blend of Indian, African, and European influences. This CD by vocalist Tania Libertad explores African influences. These elements are noticed most strongly in the Caribbean region, but Africa has influenced the development of music throughout Latin America. Libertad is known for her interpretations of the Afro-Peruvian music from the Pacific coastal region of her native Peru.

Apply

Process Writing
For information regarding writing portfolios, see p. 54.

Teaching Suggestions
Tell students that working through the *Para escribir* section will help them answer the key chapter question.

Answers
Paragraphs will vary.

Para escribir

Para analizar una cultura debemos conocer sus características sociales, religiosas, artísticas e intelectuales. Cuando no son como las nuestras, a veces no sabemos cómo reaccionar. Cada cultura tiene características que dependen de su lugar de origen.

1 Piensa en tu propia cultura. Haz una lista con algunas de las características sociales, religiosas y artísticas de esta cultura. Ahora piensa en otra cultura que conozcas de tu misma comunidad o de otro lugar, y haz una lista de sus características sociales, religiosas y artísticas. Si puedes, pregúntale a alguien de esa cultura. También puedes hablar con tus profesores o hacer una investigación en la biblioteca. Compara las dos listas.

2 Ahora piensa en lo que ocurre cuando dos o más culturas se mezclan. Usa tus notas y lo que has aprendido en este capítulo para escribir un trabajo sobre este tema. Considera las siguientes preguntas para organizar mejor tus ideas:

- ¿Qué culturas has escogido?
- ¿Cómo influye cada cultura en la(s) otra(s)? ¿Qué cambios ocurren en cada una? ¿Cómo se sienten o notan los cambios?
- ¿Cómo se beneficia cada grupo?
- ¿Qué problemas hay? ¿Cómo se solucionan?
- ¿Hay algo que sabes o que puedes hacer gracias a la otra cultura?
- ¿Cuáles son los resultados de este encuentro?

Options

Strategies for Reaching All Students

Students Needing Extra Help
You may want to rephrase questions to elicit additional student responses. Provide background material. Discuss this activity with the social studies department, and see what help they may be able to offer. Invite a local college professor or historian to come in and talk about this topic.

Step 1: You may want to narrow this assignment by focusing only on traditions. Have students compare their own family or cultural traditions with those of other students.
Step 2: Use the vocabulary section of the Organizer. Refer students to the *Tema para investigar* and Ex. 2 in the *Sopa de actividades.*

3 Recuerda que debes revisar tu escrito con un(a) compañero(a) y seguir los pasos del proceso de escribir.

Aquí tienes una lista de palabras y expresiones que te pueden ayudar.

aceptar	conocer	integrarse
adaptar	conveniente	lo más (menos) importante
adoptar	desconocido	proponer
adquirir	igual	resultado
beneficiar(se)		

Para compartir tu trabajo, puedes:

- exhibirlo en la sala de clases
- incluirlo en una colección llamada *Encuentros*
- enviarlo a un periódico o a una revista en español
- ponerlo en tu portafolio

Para escribir   393

Assess & Summarize

Test Preparation
You may want to assign parts of this section as written homework or as an in-class writing activity prior to administering the *Examen de habilidades*.

Answers
Listening
—*El profesor de español me pidió que les hablara sobre la ciudad donde vivo en España. La ciudad de Toledo es una mezcla de culturas y civilizaciones. En el siglo ocho, los árabes conquistaron la ciudad y construyeron varias mezquitas. Los cristianos la reconquistaron en el siglo once, y dos siglos más tarde empezaron la impresionante catedral que se ve a la derecha en esa foto. También había varias sinagogas judías, como ésta del siglo doce. Toledo es como un museo en el cual se encuentran los rasgos que distinguen a España de otros países europeos. Cuando vine a los Estados Unidos, me sorprendió ver la influencia española en la arquitectura, por ejemplo las casas con balcones con rejas y fuentes en el patio.*

Answers will vary:
Las diferentes culturas contribuyeron con mezquitas, catedrales y sinagogas. El / la estudiante ve la influencia española en la arquitectura de los Estados Unidos.

Esta sección te ayudará a prepararte para el examen de habilidades, donde tendrás que hacer tareas semejantes.

Listening
¿Puedes entender una descripción sobre las culturas que existían en España? Escucha mientras el (la) profesor(a) lee un ejemplo semejante al que vas a oír en el examen. Según la descripción, ¿qué contribuyeron las diferentes culturas a la ciudad de Toledo? ¿Dónde encuentra este(a) estudiante la influencia española en los Estados Unidos?

Reading
¿Puedes leer este artículo de un periódico hispano y decir de qué habla? ¿Qué otro título podría tener?

Variedad étnica
La población de habla española comparte rasgos de tres principales grupos étnicos. A través de los años, la mezcla de europeos, indígenas y africanos, y la integración de sus rasgos culturales ha formado un mosaico fascinante. Un ejemplo de esta contribución es el jazz afro-cubano, que en parte se compone de ritmos e instrumentos africanos, y las canciones y bailes mexicanos, que mezclan la guitarra española con la marimba indígena.

www.pasoapaso.com

394   Capítulo 11

Writing
¿Puedes escribir un comentario editorial breve como el que escribió Mateo para el periódico escolar esta semana?

Durante la celebración de la Semana Internacional, empecé a pensar en mi propia cultura. ¿Quiénes somos nosotros, los que formamos los Estados Unidos? Entre mis amigos está Olga. Sus padres vinieron a este país para escapar de la opresión. A su lado estaba Sam. Aunque su familia es del Japón, él prefiere la pizza al sushi. Pensé en Josh, que no pudo salir conmigo ayer porque iba a la sinagoga; y en Maya, que a veces me muestra las poesías que escribe sobre su descendencia africana. Los Estados Unidos son una fusión de las diversas culturas y razas que ellos y yo representamos.

Culture
¿Puedes explicar cómo las diversas culturas contribuyen a nuestro país? ¿Cuál es el impacto que tienen las diferentes culturas hispanas en los Estados Unidos?

Festival de Moros y Cristianos en Villajoyosa, cerca de Alicante, España

Speaking
¿Puedes hablar con un(a) compañero(a) sobre la fusión de culturas que tuvo lugar cuando los españoles llegaron a las Américas?

A —*En la clase de historia leímos sobre las misiones de California.*

B —*¿Por qué querían que los indígenas vivieran en misiones?*

A —*Querían que aprendieran a hablar español, y también querían convertirles al cristianismo.*

B —*No me gusta que una cultura se imponga sobre otra.*

A —*Pero la mezcla de culturas…*

Options

Strategies for Reaching All Students

Students Needing Extra Help
Have students write this exercise so that they can check off what they have mastered. Remind them that this is just a sample of what the test will be like.
Listening: Read more than once. If necessary, write the questions on the chalkboard. Tell students how many contributions they should list to answer the first question.

Reading: Remind students that they don't need to know every word in the text. Review strategies for finding cognates, context clues, and word families.
Read the questions before students start the reading. You may wish to write them on the chalkboard or overhead.

Writing: Have students use the Organizer and write a sample commentary before the test.
If they wish to write about their classmates as in the model, allow them appropriate time to gather information.
Have students refer to Exs. 6 and 8 in *¿Qué piensas tú?* (p. 371) and Ex. 1 in the *Sopa de actividades.*

Resumen del vocabulario

Usa el vocabulario de este capítulo para:

- responder a la pregunta clave: ¿Cómo se mezclan culturas diferentes?
- describir cómo interactúan dos o más culturas
- hablar de la fusión de culturas en España antes de 1492
- explicar la fusión de culturas que tuvo lugar cuando los españoles llegaron a las Américas

para describir cómo interactúan dos o más culturas
adoptar
combinar(se)
componer(se) de
la creación, *pl.* las creaciones
cultural
la descendencia
la diversidad
diverso, -a
duradero, -a
el encuentro
la fusión, *pl.* las fusiones
la influencia
la lengua
la mezcla
mezclar
el mundo
proponer
el pueblo
el rasgo
la región, *pl.* las regiones
el resultado

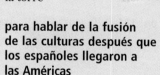

para hablar de la fusión de culturas en España antes de 1492
el alcázar, *pl.* los alcázares
el azulejo
el balcón, *pl.* los balcones
el castillo
el cristiano, la cristiana
la fuente
el judío, la judía
la mezquita
el musulmán, la musulmana
la poesía
reconquistar
la reja
el rey, la reina, *pl.* los reyes
la sinagoga
el techo
la torre

para hablar de la fusión de las culturas después que los españoles llegaron a las Américas
africano, -a
la batalla
la colonia
el conquistador
conquistar

el continente
el Día de los Muertos
esclavizar (*z → c*)
el esclavo, la esclava
establecer (*c → zc*)
europeo, -a
fundar
el / la hispanohablante
el / la indígena
la injusticia
mestizo, -a
morir(se) (*o → ue*)
el producto
la raza
rebelarse
el ritmo
trajeron (*from:* traer)

otras palabras y expresiones útiles
a través de
la mayoría
(que nosotros) hiciéramos
    (*from:* hacer)

Resumen 395

Reading
Los europeos, los indígenas y los africanos contribuyen a las culturas de habla español. / *Answers will vary.*

Writing
Paragraphs will vary.

Culture
Answers will vary, but students may mention:
Contribuyen a nuestro país con su música, su idioma, su arquitectura, etc. / Las diferentes culturas hispanas han contribuido con festivales, tradiciones, su música, su comida, el idioma, etc.

Speaking
Dialogues will vary.

Assessment

 Prueba cumulativa

 Examen de habilidades

 Test Generator

Additional Assessment Options

 Comm. Act. BLMs
Small Group Activities
Situation Cards

 ¿Lo sabes bien? Video Quiz

 Internet Activities
Self-Test

Cultural Notes ☼

Culture: Have students review the notes they took from the *Álbum cultural.*
Again, have them refer to Exs. 6 and 8 in *¿Qué piensas tú?* (p. 371) and Ex. 1 in the *Sopa de actividades* for ideas.
Speaking: Have students use the vocabulary section of the Organizer. Finish the model so that they know how to end the conversation. Limit the number of lines of dialogue. Have them refer to the *Tema para investigar.*

(p. 394, photo)
Every year during the last week of July the small Spanish resort town of Villajoyosa celebrates the *Fiesta de los moros y cristianos.* Located on the Mediterranean coast between Valencia and Alicante, Villajoyosa is one of several towns in the area that stages annual reenactments of battles between Muslims and Christians. The festival at Villajoyosa includes cannonades and parades and recreates a sixteenth-century naval victory over Algerian pirates.

CAPÍTULO 12

THEME: LEARNING A SECOND LANGUAGE

SCOPE AND SEQUENCE   Pages 396–427

COMMUNICATION

Topics

Professions

Advantages of being multilingual

Objectives

Comparar el aprendizaje de otros idiomas en los países de habla hispana y en los Estados Unidos

Explicar la importancia de saber una lengua extranjera

Describir una situación donde se usa una lengua extranjera

Hablar de cómo puedes expresarte en otra lengua

Decir qué carrera quieres seguir

CULTURE

El aprendizaje de otros idiomas en los países de habla hispana

GRAMMAR

El condicional

El imperfecto del subjuntivo con si

Ancillaries available for use with Chapter 12

Multisensory/Technology

Overheads, 36–38

Audio Tapes and CDs

Vocabulary Art Blackline Masters for Hands-On Learning, pp. 57–58/CD-ROM

Classroom Crossword

Video

Internet Activities
www.pasoapaso.com

Print

Practice Workbook, pp. 121–129

Writing, Audio & Video Activities, pp. 71–76, 126–128, 155–156

Communicative Activity Blackline Masters
  Pair and Small Group Activities, pp. 78–83
  Situation Cards, p. 84

RESOURCE PRO®

Planning Express, Teaching Resources Library, and Clip Art Library

Assessment

Assessment Program
  Pruebas, pp. 167–176
  Examen de habilidades, pp. 177–180

Test Generator

¿Lo sabes bien? Video Quiz

Video, Chap. 12

Learning Another Language

For countless people around the world, bilingualism or even multilingualism is an everyday fact of life. Throughout Europe, Africa, and Asia, people may conduct commerce, complete a formal education, or simply talk to neighbors in several languages. The relatively small size of many nations puts their residents into regular contact with speakers of other languages. In some places, "hybrid" or pidgin languages evolve, formed of two or more languages meshed together to enable communication.

Although the value of knowing more than one language is considered an obvious asset in other societies, there are frequent debates in the U.S. about the value of language study. Teachers of foreign languages are often obligated to defend the utility of knowing Spanish, French, or another language. Many secondary schools in the U.S. do not require students to study languages, and at the university level, only the liberal arts programs may have a minimal foreign language requirement.

Students concerned with doing well in school might look to language study to improve their overall academic performance. Researchers have found that students who have taken a foreign language in high school have relatively higher grade point averages. These same students also do academically better in their freshman English classes in college.

Another investigation showed that the SAT scores of students increased steadily with years of foreign language study. Students with five or more years of language study achieved an average score of 504 on the verbal portion of the SAT and an average score of 534 on the math portion.

Bilingual or multilingual abilities often give a job seeker an edge during interviews with employers. Once on the job, second-language abilities can lead to promotions or more engaging work assignments. Learning another language enhances an individual's English vocabulary and conceptual abilities, leading to improved communication skills that are invaluable in the work world. One of the most compelling reasons for students to study second languages, then, may be to improve their economic opportunities.

Many of the responses to the question "Why learn another language?" deal with the fact that people have greater employment opportunities when they are bilingual. But aside from economic considerations, the decision to learn a second language is a question of intellectual empowerment. Being monolingual limits people to knowing only their own culture and to experiencing other cultures in a translated, interpreted, often erroneous form. Understanding Spanish, for example, gives first-hand, unfiltered access to the cultures, thought, and histories of the millions of people around the world who speak it.

Introduce

Re-entry of Concepts

The following list represents words, expressions, and grammar topics re-entered from Books 1, 2, and 3 (Chaps. 4–11):

Book 1
school subjects, preterite

Book 2
school subjects, preterite, imperfect, impersonal *se,* professions

Chapter 4
present perfect

Chapter 5
seguir + present progressive

Chapter 7
present subjunctive

Chapter 11
imperfect subjunctive

Planning

Cross-Curricular Connections

Sociology Connection *(pp. 420–421)*
In small groups or pairs, have students present a plan for improved second-language teaching to English speakers. Some questions to consider could include: What kinds of classes and methods would be most beneficial? At what age would these students begin classes? What sources could be used to finance the classes? Students can present their plans with speeches, posters, charts, or videos.

Civics / Political Science Connection *(pp. 424–425)*
In groups or pairs, have students create a script for a television or radio commercial that deals with the topic of English-only laws in the U.S. Tell them to include examples of why it is important to know other languages. You may wish to tape their presentations.

Spanish in Your Community
Have students call various businesses in the community and speak to someone in the Human Resources Office regarding the company's needs for employees who speak other languages. Students should ask about Spanish in particular. Have students compile their findings and write an article for the local newspaper, highlighting the needs for bilingual employees in their community.

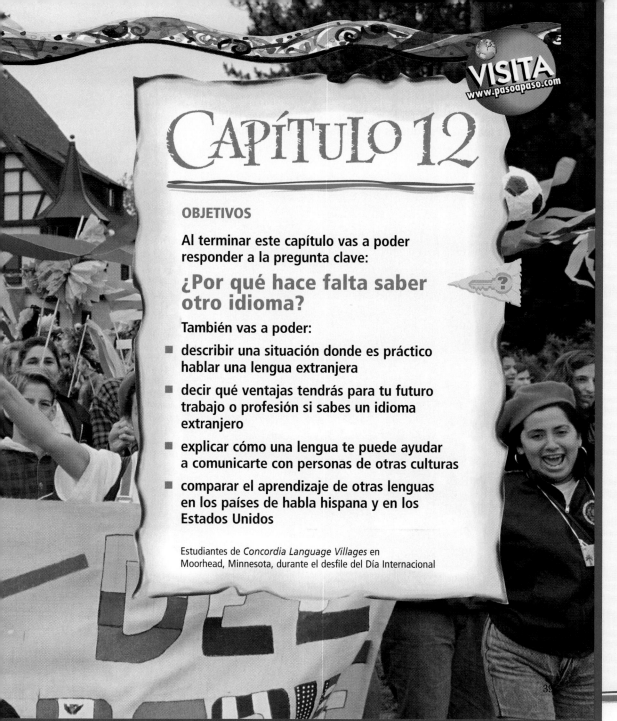

CAPÍTULO 12

VISITA
www.pasoapaso.com

OBJETIVOS

Al terminar este capítulo vas a poder responder a la pregunta clave:

¿Por qué hace falta saber otro idioma?

También vas a poder:

- describir una situación donde es práctico hablar una lengua extranjera
- decir qué ventajas tendrás para tu futuro trabajo o profesión si sabes un idioma extranjero
- explicar cómo una lengua te puede ayudar a comunicarte con personas de otras culturas
- comparar el aprendizaje de otras lenguas en los países de habla hispana y en los Estados Unidos

Estudiantes de *Concordia Language Villages* en Moorhead, Minnesota, durante el desfile del Día Internacional

Teaching Suggestions
Point out the key chapter question. Remind students that by acquiring the new words and structures, they will be able to answer this question.

Cultural Notes

(pp. 396–397, photo)
These high-school students, bearing the banner of their Spanish "village," Lago del Bosque, are among the 9,000 who come to Concordia College Language Villages in Moorehead, Minnesota, every year. They participate in total language immersion programs lasting one to four weeks. As part of their study experience, these students have been issued a Spanish passport, currency, and, of course, must speak only Spanish during their stay.

Preview

Cultural Objective
- *Discutir por qué es útil saber dos o más lenguas*

Critical Thinking: Summarizing Information
Have students study the photos on these two pages. Ask: *¿Qué tienen en común estas fotos? (Hablan una lengua extranjera, Están comunicándose en una lengua extranjera, etc.)* Keep a list on the chalkboard of their responses. As a class, brainstorm a list of jobs requiring foreign language skills.

Answers: Anticipación
Answers will vary, but students may mention:
Todas estas personas hablan más de un idioma. / Es útil porque se puede comunicar con mucha gente diferente, y es necesario para algunos trabajos.

Answers will vary for questions in caption text.

Anticipación

Mira las fotos. ¿Cuáles de estas personas crees que saben hablar más de una lengua? ¿Por qué es útil hablar más de un idioma?

La Organización de las Naciones Unidas (ONU) trabaja para mantener la paz en todo el mundo. Tiene más de cien países miembros, y sus diplomáticos hablan varios idiomas. Para ser intérprete de la ONU, se necesita saber tres lenguas por lo menos. ¿En qué otros trabajos es necesario hablar más de un idioma?

398　Capítulo 12

Options

Strategies for Reaching All Students

Spanish-Speaking Students
Ask: *¿Se encuentran periódicos y revistas en español en tu comunidad? ¿Cuáles son? Además de para ser intérprete, ¿para qué otras profesiones de las ilustradas aquí es necesario o aconsejable saber otro idioma?*

Students Needing Extra Help
For the top photo caption text, have foreign language magazines and newspapers available beforehand.

Multiple Intelligences
Bodily/Kinesthetic, Verbal/Linguistic, and Visual/Spatial
Have the class stage a mock United Nations session with individuals representing Spanish-speaking countries. Select an issue and give each representative three minutes to state his or her country's position.

Possible issues might include: *Qué deben hacer las Naciones Unidas 1) cuando los derechos humanos no se respetan en un país, 2) cuando la destrucción de la naturaleza es importante para la cultura o la economía de un país,* or *3) cuando dos países están en guerra.*

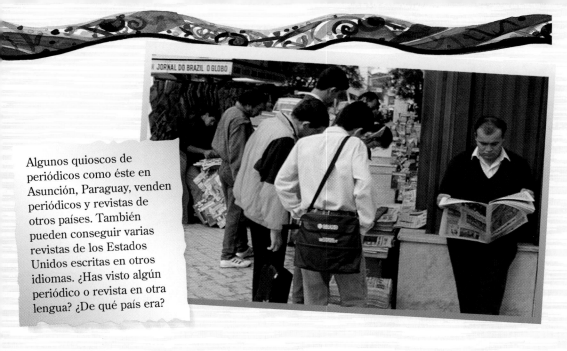

Algunos quioscos de periódicos como éste en Asunción, Paraguay, venden periódicos y revistas de otros países. También pueden conseguir varias revistas de los Estados Unidos escritas en otros idiomas. ¿Has visto algún periódico o revista en otra lengua? ¿De qué país era?

Each individual views the world differently, regardless of the language they speak. Among the many countries of Central and South America, each country has developed a unique perspective. Values, socioeconomic status, history, religion, and education all influence the perspective developed by people of a particular country. For example: the word *arroz.* The correct translation is rice, yet there is also a much deeper meaning. The simple dish of rice and beans common to many Spanish-speaking countries becomes a historical, linguistic, and cultural lesson. In Cuba, it is called *congrí* or *moros y cristianos.* In Costa Rica it is known as *gallo pinto.* And in other countries it is referred to as *romeo y julieta.* All describe a similar combination of rice and beans cooked together with other ingredients. Yet each name also describes a particular history or social situation.

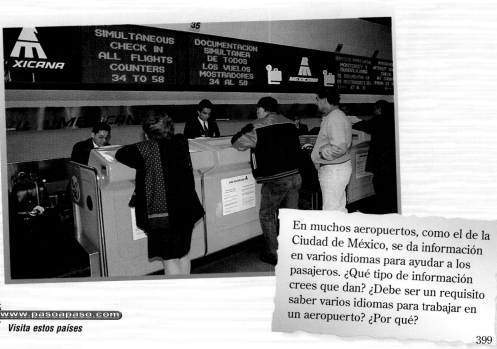

En muchos aeropuertos, como el de la Ciudad de México, se da información en varios idiomas para ayudar a los pasajeros. ¿Qué tipo de información crees que dan? ¿Debe ser un requisito saber varios idiomas para trabajar en un aeropuerto? ¿Por qué?

Exploración cultural **www.pasoapaso.com**
Visita estos países

399

Cultural Notes

(p. 398, photo)
Every speech given at the United Nations must be in one of the following official languages: Arabic, Chinese, French, English, Russian, or Spanish. As it is being delivered, the speech is translated into the other languages by highly skilled simultaneous interpreters. In order to interpret for the U.N., one must be fluent in at least three of its six official languages.

(p. 399, top photo)
In Paraguay, books, newspapers, and magazines are published in the country's two official languages, Spanish and Guaraní. The latter is the language of the indigenous people who had been living in what is now Paraguay for centuries before the arrival of the first Spanish and Portuguese explorers in the early 1500s. While Spanish is used in government, business, and education, Guaraní is in more common use in everyday conversation.

(p. 399, bottom photo)
At the Mexicana Airlines terminal at Mexico City's Benito Juárez airport, international travelers find many conveniences, including 161 check-in counters, a hotel, an international business center, facilities for the handicapped, and a 1,300-car parking lot.

Present

Chapter Theme
Professions

Communicative Objectives
- *Explicar la importancia de saber una lengua extranjera*
- *Describir una situación donde se usa una lengua extranjera*
- *Hablar de cómo puedes expresarte en otra lengua*
- *Decir qué carrera quieres seguir*

 Overheads 36–37

 Vocabulary Art BLMs/CD-ROM

 Vocabulary Tape 12-1

Grammar Preview
The conditional is presented here lexically. The grammar explanation is on p. 415.

Teaching Suggestions
Preparing students to speak: Use one or two options from each of the categories of Comprehensible Input or Limited Verbal Response. For a complete explanation of these categories and some sample activities, see pp. T20–T21.

Vocabulario para comunicarse

¿Por qué hace falta saber una lengua extranjera?

Aquí tienes palabras y expresiones necesarias para hablar sobre las ventajas de saber una lengua extranjera. Léelas varias veces y practícalas con un(a) compañero(a) en las páginas siguientes.

el bibliotecario

la bibliotecaria

la redactora

la banquera, el banquero

la redactora

el redactor

el contador, la contadora

el /la periodista

400　Capítulo 12

Options

Strategies for Reaching All Students

Spanish-Speaking Students
Have students write: *Escoge cinco de las profesiones mencionadas aquí. Investiga y escribe un párrafo sobre lo que hace una persona en cada uno de esos trabajos.*

Students Needing Extra Help
Have students begin the vocabulary section of the Organizer.
También necesitas . . . : Emphasize the spelling of *corresponsal* and the meanings of *defenderse, dominar,* and *hacer falta.* Their spellings closely resemble English words with different meanings.

Enrichment
To present and review vocabulary for professions, list them on the chalkboard. Remember to include more unusual professions, such as *detective, científico(a), arqueólogo(a), antropólogo(a),* and *astrónomo(a).* Ask students to raise their hands when you call out the profession(s) that interest them. Record the number of students interested in each profession, and conduct a class discussion on why some jobs were more appealing than others.

También necesitas . . .

el /la agente de ventas	sales agent	el /la estudiante de intercambio	exchange student
el /la asistente social	social worker		
la carrera	career	hacer falta	to be necessary
cometer	to commit	la lengua extranjera	foreign language
confundirse	to be confused	seguir *(e → i)*	here: *to pursue*
el /la corresponsal	correspondent	sería *(from: ser)*	*it would be*
defenderse *(e → ie)* (en)	here: *to get along, to not do badly*	soñar *(o → ue)* (con)	*to dream (about)*
		sordo, -a	deaf
dominar	*to have a good knowledge of, to master*	tener facilidad para	*to be good at*
		tendría que, tendrías que *(from:* tener que)	*I would have to, you would have to*
		viajar	*to travel*

¿Y qué quiere decir . . . ?
bilingüe†
la dificultad
el error

la traducción,
 pl. las traducciones

el traductor, la traductora

el lenguaje por señas

traducir *(c → zc)**

hablar por señas

* In the preterite and in the imperfect subjunctive, *traducir* follows the pattern of *decir: traduje → tradujera.*
† In Spanish the two dots over the *u*, called a *diéresis*, indicate that the *u* is pronounced [u].

¡NO OLVIDES!
Do you remember these words for professions?
el aduanero, la aduanera
el / la agente de viajes
el / la auxiliar de vuelo
el diplomático, la diplomática
el / la gerente
el / la intérprete
el / la recepcionista
el vendedor, la vendedora

Extended Written Practice/Homework
1. Write three sentences saying what you would have to be good at in order to work in different professions: *Para ser periodista, tendrías que tener facilidad para escribir.*
2. Write three pairs of sentences naming people whom you know in different professions and describing their work.

3. Write three sentences saying why you would or would not like to: *hablar por señas, ser estudiante de intercambio, hacer traducciones profesionalmente.*

Class Starter Review
On the day following the presentation of vocabulary, you might begin the class with this activity: Describe in Spanish the qualifications necessary for several of the professions listed in this chapter. Have students name the profession you are describing. For example: *En esta profesión, uno tiene que saber muchas matemáticas. ¿Qué es? [un(a) contador(a)]*

www Internet Activities
Juegos

Multiple Intelligences
Bodily/Kinesthetic and Verbal/Linguistic
Have students bring in items that are associated with a particular profession and describe the importance each item has to that profession.
Verbal/Linguistic
See Vocabulary Tape 12-1 and Class Starter Review.
Visual/Spatial
See Overheads 36–37 and Enrichment.

Practice

Answers: Empecemos a conversar

1 ESTUDIANTE A

a. ¿Qué tendría que estudiar para ser contador(a)?

b. ... hombre / mujer de negocios?

c. ... redactor(a)?

d. ... traductor(a)?

e. ... astronauta?

f. ... guía?

g. Questions will vary.

ESTUDIANTE B

a. Tendrías que estudiar matemáticas. (No sé, me parece que tendrías que estudiar ___.)

b. ... negocios.

c. ... inglés.

d. ... traducción.

e. ... ciencias.

f. ... lenguas extranjeras.

g. Answers will vary.

Empecemos a conversar

Túrnate con un(a) compañero(a) para ser *Estudiante A* y *Estudiante B*. Reemplacen las palabras subrayadas con palabras representadas o escritas en los recuadros. 💡 quiere decir que puedes escoger tu propia respuesta.

1

A — ¿Qué tendría (yo) que estudiar para ser *banquero(a)*?

B — *Tendrías que estudiar matemáticas.*

   o: *No sé, me parece que tendrías que estudiar ___.*

Estudiante A

Estudiante B

a.   b.   c.

d.   e.   f.   g.

traducción

ciencias

matemáticas

inglés

lenguas extranjeras

negocios

402   Capítulo 12

Options

Strategies for Reaching All Students

Students Needing Extra Help
Exs. 2–3: Brainstorm the *Estudiante B* responses.

Enrichment
Ex. 2: As a homework assignment, have students choose a profession and write at least three of its advantages and disadvantages.

Extended Written Practice/Homework
1. Write three sentences saying what is necessary to be able to do the following: *defenderse en una lengua extranjera, dominar una lengua, ser bilingüe. Para dominar una lengua, hace falta ...*
2. Write three sentences saying what is necessary in order to pursue different careers: *Para seguir la carrera de ..., hay que ...*

2

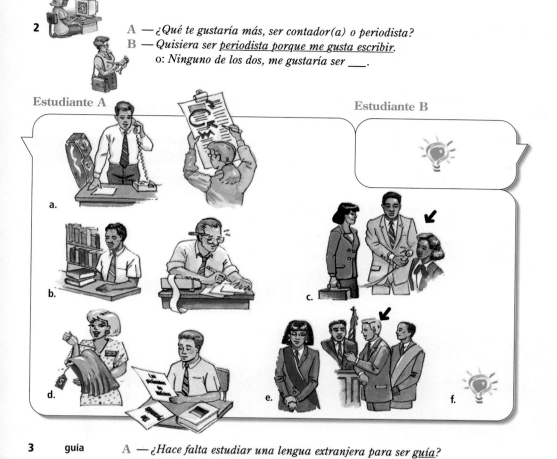

A — ¿Qué te gustaría más, ser contador(a) o periodista?
B — Quisiera ser _periodista porque me gusta escribir_.
   o: Ninguno de los dos, me gustaría ser ___.

Estudiante A

a.

b.

c.

d.

e.

f.

Estudiante B

3   guía

A — ¿Hace falta estudiar una lengua extranjera para ser _guía_?
B — No, no es necesario, pero sería una gran ventaja porque . . .
   o: Sí, es necesario porque . . .

Estudiante A

a. corresponsal

b. banquero, -a internacional

c. bibliotecario, -a

d. agente de ventas

e. asistente social

f. redactor, -a

g. diplomático, -a

h. aduanero, -a

i. intérprete

j.

Estudiante B

Vocabulario para comunicarse   403

2 ESTUDIANTE A
a. ¿Qué te gustaría más, ser hombre (mujer) de negocios o redactor(a)?
b. . . . bibliotecario(a) o contador(a)?
c. . . . banquero(a) o periodista ?
d. . . . vendedor(a) o traductor(a)?
e. . . . diplomático(a) o intérprete?
f. Questions will vary.
ESTUDIANTE B
a.–f. Answers will vary, but should be logical.

3 ESTUDIANTE A
a. ¿Hace falta estudiar una lengua extranjera para ser corresponsal?
b. . . . banquero(a) internacional?
c. . . . bibliotecario(a)?
d. . . . agente de ventas?
e. . . . asistente social?
f. . . . redactor(a)?
g. . . . diplomático(a)?
h. . . . aduanero(a)?
i. . . . intérprete?
j. Questions will vary.
ESTUDIANTE B
a.–j. Answers will vary, but should be logical.

Multiple Intelligences

Bodily/Kinesthetic and Visual/Spatial
Have students combine photos of themselves with magazine cut-outs or original drawings to make a poster entitled: _Mi futura carrera con la lengua española._ On these posters, students can be shown using Spanish as teachers, mail carriers, physicians, and so on.

Intrapersonal/Introspective
Have students write a journal entry in which they reflect on the advantages of knowing another language.

Verbal/Linguistic
See Exs. 1–3.

Visual/Spatial
See Enrichment.

Practice & Apply

Re-enter / Recycle
Exs. 7–8: present perfect from Chap. 4.

Answers: ¿Y qué piensas tú?
4–9 Answers will vary.

¿Y qué piensas tú?

Aquí tienes otra oportunidad para usar el vocabulario de este capítulo.

4 ¿Qué lengua(s) dominas? ¿En cuáles puedes defenderte? ¿Qué lengua(s) hablan tus padres? ¿Son tus padres bilingües? ¿Y tú?

5 Cuando hablas en español, ¿en qué idioma piensas? Cuando escribes en español, ¿todavía traduces del inglés, o empiezas a escribir en español directamente? ¿En qué idioma sueñas? ¿Te gustaría soñar en otro idioma? ¿Por qué?

6 Imagínate que eres un estudiante de intercambio, ¿a qué país te gustaría viajar? ¿Por qué?

7 ¿Cuándo hace falta aprender a hablar por señas? ¿Sabes hablar por señas? ¿Por qué o por qué no has aprendido?

www.pasoapaso.com

MÁS PRÁCTICA

- Más práctica y tarea, p. 580
- Practice Workbook 12–1, 12–2

404 Capítulo 12

Options

Strategies for Reaching All Students

Spanish-Speaking Students
Ex. 6: Additional questions: *¿Qué sería lo más difícil de ser un(a) estudiante de intercambio? ¿Y de tener un(a) estudiante de intercambio en tu casa? Además de aprender bien el idioma, ¿qué otros beneficios hay en ser un(a) estudiante de intercambio?*

Students Needing Extra Help
Ex. 5: If possible, have a native speaker work with the class on occasion.
Ex. 8: Students may need some help with the vocabulary for words or expressions such as "spelling" *(la ortografía)*.
Ex. 9: Complete the model. Students may have difficulty with the vocabulary necessary to describe what people in certain occupations do. Assist as needed.

Enrichment
Additional questions: *¿Conoces a alguien fuera de tu familia que sea bilingüe? ¿Qué lenguas habla esa persona? ¿Desde cuándo las habla? ¿Cómo y cuándo las aprendió? ¿Cuándo fue la última vez que viste a alguien hablar por señas?*

8 ¿Cuáles son algunas de las dificultades que has tenido para aprender a hablar español? ¿Con qué te confundes más, con los verbos o con el masculino y el femenino? ¿Cuáles son algunos de los errores que cometen los estudiantes de tu clase de español?

- Ahora con un(a) compañero(a), haz una tabla como la de la derecha ¿Cuáles son sus errores más frecuentes? ¿Y los menos frecuente

- Compartan su gráfica con la clase.

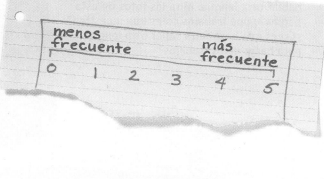

menos frecuente — más frecuente

0 1 2 3 4 5

9 Conversa con un(a) compañero(a) sobre qué carrera quieres seguir y cómo saber español podría ayuda Sigue el modelo.

A —*Después de graduarte, ¿qué ___?*
B —*Me gustaría ___.*
A —*¿Qué hace un(a) ___?*
B —*Pues, ___.*
A —*Para ser ___, ¿hace falta ___?*
B —*. . .*

 Practice Wkbk. 12-1, 12-2

 Audio Activity 12.1

 Writing Activities 12-A, 12-B

 Pruebas 12-1, 12-2

Comm. Act. BLM 12-1

Cooperative Learning
Have students form groups based on the country they chose in Ex. 6. Tell them to design an itinerary that would maximize exposure to the language and culture of their chosen location. Each student should plan one day of the group's stay, writing a paragraph about specific places they would go and how they would interact with the local people. After the group has discussed the entire itinerary, have pairs of students present it to the class.

Multiple Intelligences
Interpersonal/Social, Verbal/Linguistic, and Visual/Spatial
See Cooperative Learning.
Logical/Mathematical
See Ex. 8.
Verbal/Linguistic
See Audio Activity 12.1.

Visual/Spatial
1) Have students write a "Dear Abby" letter in which they voice their opinion on laws requiring that English be the only language spoken in the public schools.
2) See Practice Wkbk. 12-1 and 12-2, Writing Activities 12-A and 12-B, and Comm. Act. BLM 12-1.

Present

Chapter Theme
Reasons for learning a second language

Communicative Objectives
- *Explicar la importancia de saber una lengua extranjera*
- *Describir una situación donde se usa una lengua extranjera*
- *Hablar de cómo puedes expresarte en otra lengua*

 Vocabulary Tape 12-2

Teaching Suggestions
Getting ready to speak:
Remind students of the reading strategies that they learned (getting meaning from context and coping with unknown words) to help them understand the *Tema para investigar*. For further details and some sample activities, see pp. T24–T25.

Answers: Tema para investigar
Answers will vary, but students may mention:
recepcionista, diplomático, intérprete / *Answers will vary.*

Tema para investigar

Aquí tienes más palabras e ideas que te ayudarán a hablar sobre la necesidad de hablar otra lengua. Mira las fotos de esta página. ¿Qué trabajos crees que muestran? ¿Crees que hace falta saber otra lengua para hacer estos trabajos?

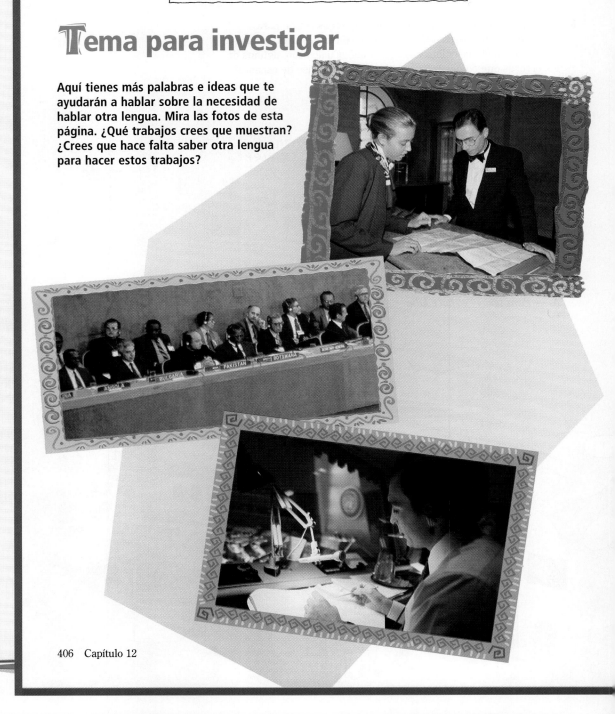

406   Capítulo 12

Options

Strategies for Reaching All Students

Spanish-Speaking Students
Have students write: *Este artículo dice que, para ser verdaderamente bilingüe, es necesario saber la lengua y también conocer a la gente y su cultura. ¿Qué aspectos de tu cultura crees que otras personas deberían conocer y apreciar? Explica tu respuesta.*

Students Needing Extra Help
Explain the English word "idiom." Use the synonym "expression" if students are having difficulty with the concept.
¿Y qué quiere decir . . . ?: Emphasize the spelling of *inmigrante* and *inmigración*.

Extended Written Practice/Homework
1. Write three sentences saying in what situations or locations it is useful to know another language: *Para hacer el trabajo voluntario es útil hablar otra lengua.*
2. Write three sentences naming skills that help people of different languages and cultures live together.
3. Write your top three reasons for studying and learning another language.

¿Para qué sirve hablar una lengua extranjera?

Es posible que te hayan preguntado: ¿por qué estudias español?, o te hayan dicho que, **en realidad**, no es necesario saber otra lengua si tu **lengua materna** es el inglés. Sin embargo, aprender otra lengua nos beneficia a todos. Cada día **aumentan** las oportunidades de aprender otra lengua en la escuela primaria. Conocemos **los beneficios** de esto desde un punto de vista **académico.** Por ejemplo, los estudiantes de la escuela secundaria que han estudiado otra lengua obtienen resultados más altos en el examen de S.A.T. En muchas universidades, saber otra lengua es un requisito para graduarse.

Por otro lado, si vives en una ciudad grande, como Nueva York o Los Ángeles, vives en un mundo **multicultural**. Pero también en un pueblo puedes estar en **contacto** con otras culturas. En los Estados Unidos hay cada vez más **inmigrantes**. Esa **inmigración** nos hace ver que debemos hablar otras lenguas para poder comunicarnos mejor. Nuestra sociedad **se diversifica** y es **útil** que las personas puedan comunicarse, **convivir** y trabajar en **armonía** con personas de otras culturas.

Además, para poder participar **activamente** en el mundo de hoy hace falta saber otras lenguas. Muchos creen que lo único que se puede hacer con una lengua extranjera es **interpretar**, traducir o seguir una carrera en relaciones internacionales. Pero hay muchas más posibilidades: hay cada vez más compañías que necesitan empleados que conozcan la cultura y la lengua de otros países. En las escuelas de muchos países los estudiantes aprenden a comunicarse por lo menos en dos idiomas. En el mercado **mundial** los europeos y los japoneses, por ejemplo, se comunican sin problemas. Gracias a los nuevos medios de comunicación, podemos decir que vivimos en un mundo sin **fronteras**.

Hay muchas oportunidades para las personas que pueden **expresarse** en otra lengua. Para ser **completamente** bilingüe es necesario saber más que la lengua **oficial** y sus **modismos**; hace falta conocer bien a la gente y **apreciar** su cultura. ¿Qué piensas tú sobre **el aprendizaje** de otras lenguas? ¿Vale la pena?

en realidad	*really*	mundial	*world, world-wide*
aumentar	*to increase*	la frontera	*border*
útil	*useful*	el modismo	*idiom*
convivir	*to live together*	el aprendizaje	*learning*

¿Y qué quiere decir . . . ?

la lengua materna	el /la inmigrante	interpretar
el beneficio	la inmigración	expresar(se)
académico, -a	diversificar(se) *(c → qu)*	completamente
multicultural	la armonía	oficial
el contacto	activamente	apreciar

Tema para investigar 407

Class Starter Review

On the day following the presentation of the *Tema para investigar,* you might begin the class with this activity:
Generate a class discussion in which students take turns paraphrasing the main ideas in the *Tema*. As students state their suggestions, write them on the chalkboard until all main points have been discussed.

www Internet Activities
Juegos

Multiple Intelligences
Verbal/Linguistic
See Vocabulary Tape 12-2 and Class Starter Review.

Practice & Apply

Re-enter / Recycle
Ex. 3: present perfect from Chap. 4
Ex. 7: present subjunctive from Chap. 7
Ex. 9: *seguir* + present participle from Chap. 5

Answers: ¿Comprendiste?
1 Ideas incluidas: c, d, e, f.
Ideas no incluidas: a, b, g.

2 Answers will vary, but may include: *conocer mejor otra cultura, recibir mejores notas en todas las clases, tener más oportunidades de trabajo.*

Answers: ¿Y qué piensas tú?
3–9 Answers will vary.

Strategies for Reaching All Students
MULTIPLE INTELLIGENCES
Interpersonal/Social
See Exs. 8–9.
Interpersonal/Social and Verbal/Linguistic
See Cooperative Learning.
Intrapersonal/Introspective
See Exs. 3–7.
Verbal/Linguistic
See Audio Activity 12-2.
Visual/Spatial
See Using Realia, Practice Wkbk. 12-3, and Writing Activity 12-C.

¿Comprendiste?

1 ¿Cuáles de estas ideas están incluidas en el tema y cuáles no?
   a. En todas partes del mundo hay personas que hablan inglés.
   b. Si tu lengua materna es el español, podrás comunicarte fácilmente en cualquier lugar del mundo.
   c. Los estudiantes que saben otra lengua obtienen mejores resultados en otras materias.
   d. Vivimos en un mundo sin fronteras.
   e. Es importante aprender una lengua extranjera antes de entrar en la universidad.
   f. Es importante saber otras lenguas para poder apreciar la cultura de otros países.
   g. Lo único que hace falta para ser bilingüe es aprender los modismos de un idioma.

2 Da tres ejemplos de por qué es importante aprender otra lengua.

¿Y qué piensas tú?

3 ¿Has estado en otro país o países? ¿En cuál(es)? ¿Hablaban allí tu misma lengua? Si no, ¿cómo te comunicaste?

4 Cuando hablas español fuera de la sala de clases, ¿qué ocurre? ¿Cómo te sientes?

5 ¿Es multicultural tu ciudad o pueblo? ¿En qué se ve? ¿Hay inmigrantes de otros países? ¿De dónde son?

6 ¿Hay mucha gente bilingüe en tu comunidad? Haz una lista de los lugares donde se puede escuchar una lengua extranjera en tu comunidad. Compárala con la de un(a) compañero(a).

7 Hay algunos políticos que quieren que el inglés sea la lengua oficial de los Estados Unidos. ¿Estás de acuerdo con ellos? ¿Por qué?

Joven hispana en una entrevista de trabajo

www.pasoapaso.com
Práctica de vocabulario

MÁS PRÁCTICA

Más práctica y tarea, p. 581
Practice Workbook 12–3, 12–4

408   Capítulo 12

Options

Strategies for Reaching All Students

Spanish-Speaking Students
Ex. 9: After this exercise, ask students: *¿Conoces el refrán en español que dice que "él que sabe dos lenguas vale por dos"? ¿Crees que es cierto lo que dice el refrán? ¿Qué quiere decir "vale por dos"? ¿Cuáles son los beneficios personales de saber dos lenguas?*

Students Needing Extra Help
Ex. 1: Remind students that their answers are based on the information they gleaned from the *Tema,* and not from their general knowledge or opinions.
Ex. 4: Students may confuse *fuera* with the imperfect subjunctive form.
Ex. 6: Use the ESL teacher or department as a resource.
Ex. 7: Students may have difficulty expressing the significance of making English the

official language and expressing their reasons. Help them as needed.
Ex. 8: Point out that the applicants may need to know English or languages other than Spanish.
Ex. 9: Assign this a few days prior to the lesson so that students can discuss ancestry with their families.
¿Qué sabes ahora?: Have students write this so that they can record their progress.

8 En grupos de tres o cuatro decidan:

- para qué trabajos hace falta saber otra lengua
- para cuáles se necesita tener facilidad para una lengua
- para cuáles no se necesita una lengua extranjera
- para cuáles sería una ventaja saber otra lengua

Expliquen sus decisiones.

9 Los Estados Unidos es un país de inmigrantes.
Entrevista a cinco o seis amigos(as) o compañeros(as)
para averiguar de qué país son sus abuelos y qué
lengua(s) hablaban. Luego prepara una tabla como
la de abajo.

Haz estas preguntas:

- ¿De dónde son tus abuelos?
- ¿Qué lengua(s) hablaban?
- ¿Siguen hablando esa(s) lengua(s)?
- ¿Por qué siguen o no siguen hablándola(s)?

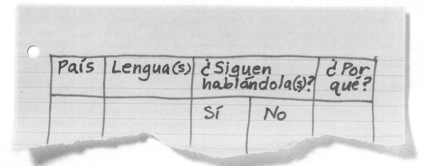

¿Qué sabes ahora?

¿Puedes:

■ describir una situación donde puedes usar otra lengua?

—Es útil saber otra lengua para ___ y para ___ .

■ explicar en qué te puede ayudar saber otra lengua?

—Si ___ otra lengua, puedes ___ mejor a personas de otros países y ___ su cultura.

■ decir cómo el aprendizaje de una lengua extranjera te puede ayudar en una carrera o profesión?

—En muchas carreras, como por ejemplo ___ y ___ , es ___ saber otra ___ .

Tema para investigar   409

Answers: ¿Qué sabes ahora?
- Answers will vary.
- Answers will vary but may include the following: *dominas (conoces, sabes) / entender / apreciar (entender)*.
- Answers will vary.

Using Realia
Ask students to scan the ad on this page and see if they can determine for which type of job this company is advertising (computer science specialist). What are some of the requirements? (college graduate in the last four years, minimum experience of two years in a similar job, knowledge of certain computer skills / programming, command of spoken and written English, previous military service)

 Practice Wkbk. 12-3

 Audio Activity 12.2

 Writing Activity 12-C

 Pruebas 12-3, 12-4

Enrichment
Additional questions: *¿Te gustaría enseñar el inglés en un país extranjero? ¿Qué otras lenguas, además del español, has estudiado? ¿Cuánto tiempo hace que las estudias? Esas lenguas, ¿son más fáciles o más difíciles que el español? ¿Por qué?*
Ex. 9: You may want to model this interview by bringing in someone you know well and asking them these questions in front of the class.

Cooperative Learning
In groups of four, have students brainstorm a real or fictional situation in which they would have to speak Spanish outside of the classroom. Tell them to create a one-minute scene for the class, re-enacting this situation. One student should act as a narrator, one as a native Spanish-speaker, and the other two as themselves. Encourage creativity.

Cultural Notes

(p. 408, photo)
It is estimated that by the year 2050, one in five Americans will be of Hispanic descent. As the Hispanic population in the U.S. continues to grow, so does the value of being bilingual. More and more jobs are being created not only to serve the Hispanic American community, but to tap into its buying power. Hispanic American professionals and others with fluency in both Spanish and English can look forward to increasing career opportunities.

Standards 1.1; 1.2; 1.3; 3.1   **409**

Present & Apply

Cultural Objective

• *Comparar el aprendizaje de otros idiomas en los países hispanos y en los Estados Unidos*

Critical Thinking: Formulating Appropriate Questions

After reviewing the photos and captions, have students write three questions pertaining to foreign language study that they might ask their classmates.

Answers

Answers to inductive question will vary.

Gracias a los adelantos en el transporte y las comunicaciones, el mundo es cada vez más pequeño. Para que podamos entendernos mejor, es necesario aprender otros idiomas que nos ayuden a comunicarnos con más facilidad. ¿Puedes dar otras razones para aprender un segundo idioma?

Estos estudiantes participan en cursos intensivos de idiomas ofrecidos por *Concordia Language Villages* en Minnesota. Además de escoger la lengua que estudiará, cada estudiante decide a qué nivel empezará su aprendizaje. Otro aspecto importante del programa es el uso de las canciones populares de un país en el aprendizaje del idioma. En 1994, un total de 975 estudiantes participaron en este programa.

Options

Strategies for Reaching All Students

Students Needing Extra Help

Have students take notes for use later in the *¿Lo sabes bien?* section.

Lucía (1968), Raúl Martínez

Quinto Festival de Teatro (1962), Lorenzo Homar

Una de las ventajas de hablar otra lengua es la de entender sin necesidad de intérprete. Podemos ver películas como esta película cubana en versión original y sin subtítulos. También se puede asistir a festivales de teatro como éste en el que participa el Instituto de Cultura Puertorriqueña, y apreciar cada obra en el idioma original en lugar de oír una traducción.

Álbum cultural 411

Cultural Notes

(p. 410, photos)
In order to enroll at Concordia College's Language Villages, students must be 7 to 18 years of age and have a good academic record. They may choose from ten languages for immersion: Chinese, Danish, Finnish, French, German, Japanese, Norwegian, Russian, Spanish, and Swedish. The atmosphere at Concordia is relaxed, yet purposeful, with music playing an important role in the teaching.

(p. 411, photos)
Like many recent Latin American films, the classic Cuban film *Lucía* deals with issues of identity and social and political history. As the poster suggests, *Lucía* tells the story of three women bearing that name, each living in a different period of Cuban history. These provocative issues are also frequently addressed in plays and performance art produced in Latin American countries and by Hispanics in the U.S.

Present & Apply

www **Internet Activities**
Álbum cultural

En España e Hispanoamérica se da mucha importancia al aprendizaje de otra lengua, no sólo para las relaciones personales, sino también como una ventaja en el mundo del trabajo. Cada día son más los estudiantes que aprenden inglés como segundo idioma, como éstos en una escuela secundaria en Málaga, España.

412   Capítulo 12

Options

Strategies for Reaching All Students

Students Needing Extra Help
Share with students any personal knowledge you have regarding the importance given to the study of other languages.
Ex. 1: Discuss how the location of a country makes a difference in the people's opportunities to learn and speak other languages.

Multiple Intelligences
Interpersonal/Social and Verbal/Linguistic
Have students stage a debate to discuss the pros and cons of requiring second-language study starting in kindergarten in all U.S. public schools.

Intrapersonal/Introspective
See Exs. 1–3.
Visual/Spatial
Have students use the Internet to contact key pals in Spanish-speaking countries and ask them whether they think it is important to know more than one language and why.

Los adelantos de la tecnología también pueden usarse en la sala de clases. Estos estudiantes de Monterrey, México, usan las grabadoras y audífonos *(earphones)* del laboratorio de idiomas para practicar su pronunciación y mejorar su capacidad de comprensión *(understanding)*.

Reacción personal

Contesta las siguientes preguntas en una hoja de papel.

1 ¿Te gustaría hablar varios idiomas? ¿Por qué? ¿Qué ventajas tiene poder hablar varios idiomas?

2 ¿Cómo ayuda la tecnología a aprender otras lenguas? ¿Usas el laboratorio de idiomas con frecuencia? ¿Por qué?

3 Además de ver películas y obras de teatro en el idioma original, ¿qué otras cosas estarían a tu alcance si hablaras una segunda lengua?

www.pasoapaso.com

Álbum cultural 413

Cultural Notes

Preview

Overhead 38

Teaching Suggestions

A Review the meanings of *sería* and *tendría*. Point out that these are examples of the conditional. Ask what other verb endings were attached to the infinitive (future).

B Since *poder* and *tener* use the same endings in the conditional as in the future, ask students to predict what other verbs will have irregular conditional forms.

C If students need help in discerning the meaning of the past subjunctive form, begin with the clause containing the conditional. Ask them to give the logical meaning of the verb in the *si* clause.

Answers

Les ofrecen mejores trabajos y la oportunidad de viajar.

A The subject is *yo*. / I would go, I would work. / *viajaríamos* / The endings have been added to the infinitive form. / The endings are the same. / Use the infinitive and add the endings: *-ía, -ías, -ía; -íamos, -íais, -ían.*

B *Poder* and *tener*. / They don't use the infinitive form. They have the same stem as future irregular verbs. / *decir (diría), poner (pondría)*

C If I knew (were to know), if I spoke (were to speak) / *trabajara*

Gramática en contexto

Mira este anuncio de una escuela de idiomas. ¿Qué les ofrece a las personas que sigan sus cursos?

A You already know the meaning of *sería* and *tendría*. In the ads, find the verbs *iría* and *trabajaría*. What is the subject of these verbs? What do you think they mean? Now find the example of the conditional form for *nosotros*. To what form of the verb have the endings been added? Are the endings the same or different for *-ar, -er,* and *-ir* verbs? Explain to a classmate how to form the conditional tense of a regular *-ar, -er,* or *-ir* verb.

B *Podría* and *tendría* are also used here. What are the infinitives of these verbs? How are they irregular in the conditional? Which of the following verbs do you think will have irregular conditional forms: *estar, decir, poner, dar?*

C The two captions begin with *si yo supiera* ... and *si yo hablara* .... What do you think they mean? Do you think these are subjunctive or indicative forms? What do you think the form of *trabajar* would be in this sentence: *Si yo ___ en México, hablaría español todo el tiempo.*

Si yo supiera bien español, iría a la Organización de las Naciones Unidas y trabajaría como intérprete.

Si yo hablara otro idioma, podría conseguir un trabajo como agente de viajes y no tendría que trabajar por la noche. Mi familia y yo viajaríamos por todo el mundo sin problemas.

Escuela Mundo Sin Fronteras
Donde sus sueños están al alcance de la mano
Clases de todos los niveles
Calle Cea Bermúdez 1213 • Teléfono 555–7777

414   Capítulo 12

Options

Strategies for Reaching All Students

Students Needing Extra Help
Have students begin the grammar section of the Organizer.
B: Have students refer to the list on the following page to check their answers.
El condicional: Emphasize that the conditional form has an accent. Downplay the similarities with the future tense.

Enrichment
El condicional: Do a quick oral drill to review verbs with irregular future / conditional stems by giving the infinitive and calling on students to give you the future and conditional forms.

Extended Written Practice/Homework
1. Write three sentences saying what you would do if you were an exchange student: *Trataría de entender las costumbres del lugar donde viviría.*
2. Write three sentences saying what would be necessary in order to improve situations in our society: *Para controlar la violencia, sería necesario …*

El condicional

We use the conditional in Spanish to express what we *would do* or what a situation *would be* like.

Me **gustaría** estudiar otro idioma.
Yo le **pediría** ese libro al bibliotecario.

- As with the future tense, we form the conditional by adding the endings to the infinitive. The conditional endings are the same for all verbs.
- Here are the conditional forms of *hablar, ser,* and *ir.*

¡NO OLVIDES!

Remember that you already know two conditional forms. *¿Te **gustaría** ir al cine hoy? ¿**Podrías** abrir la ventana?*

hablar		ser		ir	
hablaría	hablaríamos	sería	seríamos	iría	iríamos
hablarías	hablaríais	serías	seríais	irías	iríais
hablaría	hablarían	sería	serían	iría	irían

- All verbs that are irregular in the future tense have the same irregular stems in the conditional. Here, for example, are the conditional forms of *tener.*

tener

tendría	tendríamos
tendrías	tendríais
tendría	tendrían

- Here are the future and conditional stems of other irregular verbs:

decir	**dir-**	querer	**querr-**
haber	**habr-**	saber	**sabr-**
hacer	**har-**	salir	**saldr-**
poder	**podr-**	venir	**vendr-**
poner	**pondr-**		

Gramática en contexto   415

Present

Multicultural Perspectives
(See previous page.)
Language is the expression of culture, values, and identity. What is an official language of a country? How and by whom is that language chosen? These questions and others guide researchers in a relatively new field of linguistic human rights. Language is essential for political representation, to be able to stand trial, to receive an education and to have access to information. Many ethnic groups believe in maintaining their "mother tongue," but there have been cases where languages other than English were prohibited. In the U.S. in 1898, the Curtis Act eliminated schools created by Native Americans to teach in their own languages. During the Spanish dictatorship of Francisco Franco from 1938 to 1975, regional Spanish languages such as *catalán* and *vasco* were banned. Ask students to discuss the reasons why a country might have an official language.

Multiple Intelligences
Verbal/Linguistic
See Enrichment.
Visual/Spatial
See Exs. A–C.

Standards 2.1; 4.2   **415**

Present & Practice

Re-enter / Recycle
Ex. 3: imperfect subjunctive from Chap. 11

Answers

1 Statement endings will vary:
a. Para ser banquero(a), sería . . .
b. Para ser profesor(a), . . .
c. Para ser guía, . . .
d. Para ser periodista, . . .
e. Para ser contador(a), . . .
f. Para ser redactor(a), . . .
g. Para ser médico(a), . . .
h. Statements will vary.

2 Answers will vary, but students may mention:
a. Podría pedir otro pasaporte.
b. Tendría que ir al supermercado.
c. Me pondría un abrigo.
d. Querría ir a la biblioteca.
e. Saldría con ellos.
f. Haría una llamada de larga distancia.

 Practice Wkbk.
12-5, 12-6

 Writing Activities
12-D, 12-E

 Prueba 12-5

 Comm. Act. BLM
12-2

¿Por qué hace falta saber otro idioma?

1 ¿Qué le aconsejarías a alguien que va a seguir una de estas carreras? Habla con un(a) compañero(a) sobre lo que sería importante para esta persona. Usa elementos de los dos recuadros.

 Para ser aduanero, sería útil hablar dos o más idiomas.

una buena idea	conocer
necesario	dominar
importante	hablar
útil	usar
una ventaja	defenderse
práctico	leer
mejor	estudiar

2 Imagina que eres un estudiante de intercambio en otro país. ¿Qué harías en las situaciones siguientes? Usa elementos de las dos columnas.

Alguien te ha robado la cartera.   decirle al (a la) policía …
Le diría a un (a una) policía que alguien me robó la cartera.

a. Perdiste tu pasaporte.
b. Tienes hambre.
c. Hace mucho frío.
d. Para las clases, necesitas hacer un trabajo.
e. Unos amigos te invitaron a ver una película.
f. Quieres hablar con tus hermanos que están en otro país.

poder pedir . . .
querer ir . . .
ponerme un . . .
tener que ir . . .
salir con . . .
hacer una llamada . . .

416   Capítulo 12

Options

Strategies for Reaching All Students

Students Needing Extra Help
Exs. 1–2: Brainstorm ways to complete the phrases in the second column.
El imperfecto del subjuntivo con si: Give additional examples, putting the *si* clause at the beginning and at the end. Emphasize that the phrase can appear in either location. Repeat the same three phrases, reversing the order of the *si* clause.

Enrichment
Ex. 1: You may want to expand this exercise for more able students and have them explain the reason for their choice: *. . . sería útil hablar dos o más idiomas porque necesito hacer preguntas a los turistas.*
Ex. 2: As homework, ask students to tell what would be the most useful thing they could do to prepare for a trip as an exchange student.

El imperfecto del subjuntivo con si: As homework, have students write five sentences using the imperfect subjunctive of a verb following *si* and the conditional form of another verb. Encourage humor and creativity.

416   Standards 1.1

El imperfecto del subjuntivo con *si*

We use the imperfect subjunctive after *si* when a situation is unlikely, impossible, or not true.

> **Si hablaras** japonés, podrías trabajar para esa compañía.
> **Si yo fuera** el jefe, buscaría una persona que supiera inglés y español.
> Iríamos a otro país por un año **si tuviéramos** suficiente dinero.

- After *si* we use an imperfect subjunctive form. In the other part of the sentence, we use the conditional.

3 Habla con tu compañero(a) sobre qué harías si tuvieras estos trabajos.

> A — *¿Qué harías si fueras guía?*
> B — *Si fuera guía, llevaría a los turistas a todos los lugares históricos de la ciudad.*

Estudiante A

a.   b.   c.   d.   e.   f.   g.   h.

Estudiante B

- prometer calles menos peligrosas
- vigilar el edificio para evitar los robos
- entregar el correo a los demás todos los días
- pedir nuevos libros y revistas
- poder hablar por teléfono con todos los países del mundo
- descubrir más cosas sobre las civilizaciones antiguas
- querer participar en conferencias internacionales

> **¡NO OLVIDES!**
>
> All imperfect subjunctive forms are based on the preterite *Uds. / ellos / ellas* form of the verb:
> hablar → hablaron → hablara;
> ser → fueron → fuera;
> tener → tuvieron → tuviera.

Gramática en contexto   417

Practice

Answers

4 ESTUDIANTE A

a.–g. Questions will vary, but should begin with *¿Podrías* + inf.

ESTUDIANTE B

a. Te daría . . .

b. Te diría . . .

c. Trabajaría contigo . . .

d. Iría contigo . . .

e. Te prestaría . . .

f. Te explicaría . . .

g. Answers will vary.

Estudiante B should complete the answers with the imperfect subjunctive: *estuviera, tuviera, entendiera, supiera, pudiera.*

5 ESTUDIANTE A

a. ¿Qué harías si tuvieras mucho tiempo libre?

b. . . . si dominaras tres idiomas?

c. . . . si ganaras la lotería?

d. . . . si fueras el (la) presidente(a)?

e. . . . si jugaras bien tenis?

f. Questions will vary.

ESTUDIANTE B

a.–f. Answers will vary, but should include verbs in the conditional.

Encourage creativity for the final statement for *Estudiante A.*

---

4 Pídele a un(a) compañero(a) que haga algo por ti. Tu compañero(a) va a decirte por qué no puede hacerlo.

ayudarme . . .   A —¿Podrías ayudarme con la tarea de química?
 B —Te ayudaría si no estuviera tan ocupado(a).
  o: Te ayudaría si supiera más.

Estudiante A   Estudiante B

a. darme . . .

b. decirme . . .

c. trabajar conmigo . . .

d. ir conmigo . . .

e. prestarme . . .

f. explicarme . . .

g.

estar . . .

tener . . .

entender . . .

saber . . .

poder . . .

5 Con un(a) compañero(a), habla de qué harías en estas situaciones.

ser director(a) de tu colegio   A —¿Qué harías si fueras director(a) del colegio?
 B —Si fuera director(a), les permitiría a los estudiantes comer en clase. ¿Y tú?
 A —Yo compraría más computadoras para el colegio.

Estudiante A   Estudiante B

a. tener mucho tiempo libre

b. dominar tres idiomas

c. ganar la lotería

d. ser el (la) presidente(a)

e. jugar bien tenis

f.

Options

Strategies for Reaching All Students

Students Needing Extra Help

Ex. 4: Remind students that all of the verbs except *entender* are irregular.

Ex. 5: Brainstorm the *Estudiante B* and the second *Estudiante A* responses.

Ahora lo sabes: Have students write this so that they can record their progress.

Enrichment

Ex. 5: You may want to have students work in pairs to name other things they would do if they were in the professions named.

Multiple Intelligences

Interpersonal/Social and Verbal/Linguistic
See Enrichment.

Verbal/Linguistic
See Exs. 4–5 and Audio Activities 12.3, 12.4, and 12.5.

Visual/Spatial
See Practice Wkbk. 12-7 and 12-8, Writing Activity 12-F, and Comm. Act. BLM 12-3.

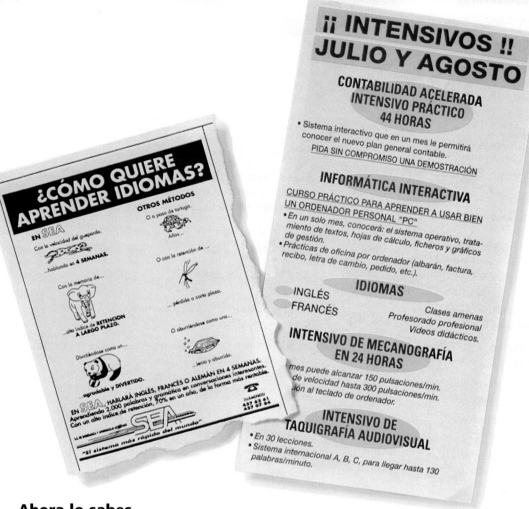

¿CÓMO QUIERE APRENDER IDIOMAS?

¡¡ INTENSIVOS !! JULIO Y AGOSTO

CONTABILIDAD ACELERADA INTENSIVO PRÁCTICO 44 HORAS

• Sistema interactivo que en un mes le permitirá conocer el nuevo plan general contable.
PIDA SIN COMPROMISO UNA DEMOSTRACIÓN

INFORMÁTICA INTERACTIVA

CURSO PRÁCTICO PARA APRENDER A USAR BIEN UN ORDENADOR PERSONAL "PC"

• En un solo mes, conocerá: el sistema operativo, tratamiento de textos, hojas de cálculo, ficheros y gráficos de gestión.
• Prácticas de oficina por ordenador (albarán, factura, recibo, letra de cambio, pedido, etc.).

IDIOMAS

INGLÉS
FRANCÉS

Clases amenas
Profesorado profesional
Videos didácticos.

INTENSIVO DE MECANOGRAFÍA EN 24 HORAS

mes puede alcanzar 150 pulsaciones/min.
de velocidad hasta 300 pulsaciones/min.
ión al teclado de ordenador.

INTENSIVO DE TAQUIGRAFÍA AUDIOVISUAL

• En 30 lecciones.
• Sistema internacional A, B, C, para llegar hasta 130 palabras/minuto.

Ahora lo sabes

¿Puedes:

■ decir qué haría alguien en una situación?
  —Mi abuela nunca ___ a una tienda sola.
■ explicar qué dijo una persona que haría?
  —Tomás dijo que ___ la carta del inglés al español.
■ decir qué haría una persona si estuviera en otra situación?
  —Si yo hablara ruso, ___ a Moscú.
  —Antonio estudiaría negocios internacionales, si ___ ir a la universidad.

MÁS PRÁCTICA

Más práctica y tarea, pp. 581–582
Practice Workbook 12–5, 12–8

Gramática en contexto   419

Cultural Notes

(p. 419, realia)
Advertisements from Spain for intensive courses in languages and other fields teaching skills for the modern workplace. Knowledge of foreign languages and skill at using high-tech tools are important to Spain's students and professionals. Spain depends heavily on highly industrialized foreign countries for its modernization (with their technology) and prosperity. Between 1988 and 1991 annual foreign investment in Spain tripled to 34 billion dollars.

Apply

Teaching Suggestions

Point out the key chapter question. Remind students that completing these activities will help them answer it. You may select one, two, or all three of these activities, as time permits.

Ex. 2: You might want to videotape students' oral presentations. As a class, brainstorm how the information from this tape could be shared with others.

Ex. 3: Have students take notes and discuss the issues brought up in the presentations so that they can use the information as they respond to the *Pregunta clave*.

Answers: Sopa de actividades

1–3 Responses will vary.

Para decir más

Aquí tienes vocabulario adicional que te puede ayudar para hacer las actividades de esta sección.

acostumbrarse (a)
to get used to

averiguar
to find out

la comprensión
understanding

el entendimiento
understanding

los trámites, *pl.*
arrangements

el árabe
Arabic

el chino
Chinese

el italiano
Italian

el japonés
Japanese

el ruso
Russian

420   Capítulo 12

¿Por qué hace falta saber otro idioma?

Esta sección te ofrece la oportunidad de combinar lo que aprendiste en este capítulo con lo que ya sabes para responder a la pregunta clave.

Sopa de actividades

1. En grupos de tres o cuatro, escojan dos o tres de las frases siguientes:

> Si el estudio de español empezara en primer grado . . .
> Si todos fuéramos bilingües . . .
> Si yo fuera trilingüe . . .
> Si tuviera que vivir en un país donde no hablan inglés . . .
> Si tuviera que estudiar matemáticas en alemán . . .
> Si hubiera vida en la Luna . . .

- Completen las frases escogidas con la mayor variedad de posibilidades que puedan imaginar.
- Escojan las frases más originales de cada grupo. Compártanlas con toda la clase.

Options

Strategies for Reaching All Students

Spanish-Speaking Students
Ex. 2: In addition to this exercise, tell students: *Toma apuntes de las presentaciones y escribe un resumen de lo que dicen los estudiantes acerca de la importancia de saber otro idioma en las distintas profesiones. Luego, pon las profesiones mencionadas en orden, según la importancia que tiene el saber otro idioma. Explica por qué has decidido en tal orden.*

Students Needing Extra Help
If time is a factor, omit Ex. 3.
Ex. 1: Choose one of the phrases and brainstorm possible endings as a class so that students have a model.
Ex. 2: Brainstorm possible endings for the model and use this as an example.
Ex. 3: Set aside some time for students to discuss and / or research the responsibilities basic to certain professions. Remind them that they need to know enough about their own profession to answer questions,

and enough to be able to ask another person questions about their profession. Keep students focused on the key question.

Multiple Intelligences
Interpersonal/Social
See Exs. 1–3.
Interpersonal/Social and Visual/Spatial
See Cooperative Learning.
Visual/Spatial
See Writing Activities 12-G and 12-H and Comm. Act. BLMs 12-4 and 12-5.

420   Standards 1.1; 1.2; 1.3

2 Formen grupos de tres o cuatro. Cada grupo debe escoger un grupo de personas y sugerir cómo cambiaría nuestro mundo si todos ellos supieran hablar otro idioma. Deben pensar en diferentes cambios que podrían ocurrir. Preparen una presentación oral para su clase. Pueden escoger uno de estos grupos:

- los políticos
- los vendedores
- los enfermeros y los médicos
- los asistentes sociales
- los jefes y gerentes
- los salvavidas
- los diplomáticos
- los profesores

Si los políticos supieran hablar otro idioma, podrían ___ .

3 Formen grupos de tres o cuatro.

- Escojan grupos de personas que representen diferentes profesiones.
- Preparen cuatro o cinco preguntas para hacerles a estas personas sobre su profesión, y la ventaja o necesidad de saber otras lenguas.
- Con estas preguntas hagan una entrevista a una o más personas del grupo que hayan escogido.
- Preparen una presentación oral con la información que reciban en sus entrevistas.

Bill Richardson de Nuevo México, secretario de energía de los Estados Unidos, es bilingüe en inglés y español, y también habla francés.

421

Video Activity A

Video, Capítulo 12

Chapter 12: Play

Step

Video Activities B–C

Writing Activities 12-G, 12-H

Comm. Act. BLMs 12-4, 12-5

Cultural Notes

Cooperative Learning
Tell groups of three students to plan a language school. Have each student write one paragraph: one about the three languages that would be taught there, and why he or she feels it is important to know those three languages; one about the types of students he or she would recruit and how this program would improve their lives; and one about the types of teachers who would work there, and how classes would be conducted. The three should then work together to reconcile any differences in their planning. Encourage creativity and use of the conditional. Have each group create a prospectus based on soliciting funds for the establishment of the school.

(p. 421, photo)
The first Hispanic to serve in a cabinet-level foreign policy position, Bill Richardson was named U.S. ambassador to the United Nations in 1996 after being reelected seven times to New Mexico's 3rd Congressional District. He also served as President Clinton's special envoy to trouble spots throughout the world. For his work as a mediator, Richardson was nominated for the Nobel Peace Prize in 1995 and again in 1997.

Apply

Teaching Suggestions

Point out the key chapter question. Tell students that working through the *Para leer* section will help them answer it.

Encourage students to use the strategies given to them in the text to help them understand the reading. Remind them they do not need to understand every word.

Process Reading

For a description of process reading, see p. 52.

Answers
Antes de leer

You may wish to assign this section in advance. If students ask, tell them the following translations: *la crisis de los misiles en Cuba* (Cuban Missile Crisis), *la bomba nuclear* (nuclear bomb), *el polvo radiactivo* (radioactive fallout), *el refugio* (bomb shelter). / Sentences will vary.

Mira la lectura

(Answers will vary.) Se trata de una muchacha (Yolanda) y de su primer año en Nueva York.

Para leer

Antes de leer

STRATEGY > Using prior knowledge

Pregúntale a una persona mayor qué significan estos términos que se usaban mucho durante la guerra fría: *Cuban missile crisis, nuclear bomb, radioactive fallout, bomb shelter.* Escribe una frase en español para cada uno. Luego, formen grupos y comparen su información.

Mira la lectura

STRATEGY > Skimming

Lee esta selección de Julia Álvarez, sólo para averiguar de qué se trata.

Nieve

Durante nuestro primer año en Nueva York alquilamos un pequeño apartamento con una escuela católica en las cercanías, regida por las Hermanas de la Caridad, fornidas mujeres de largos hábitos negros y unas tocas que les daban un aspecto peculiar, como de muñecas vestidas de luto. A mí me gustaban mucho, especialmente mi profesora de cuarto curso, la hermana Zoe, que tenía vocación de abuela. Mi nombre era adorable, decía, e hizo que yo enseñara a toda la clase cómo pronunciarlo: *Yo-lan-da.* Por ser la única inmigrante en la clase, se me adjudicó un sitio especial, en primera fila y junto a la ventana, apartada de las otras niñas para que la hermana Zoe pudiera darme lecciones especiales sin estorbar a las demás. Esta enunciaba despacio las palabras nuevas que yo debía repetir: *Laundromat, corn flakes, subway, snow.*

Pronto entendí suficiente inglés como para percatarme de que el holocausto estaba en el aire. La hermana Zoe explicó a una clase entera de ojos muy abiertos lo que ocurría en Cuba: se estaban instalando allí misiles rusos, supuestamente apuntando a Nueva York. El presidente Kennedy, con aspecto preocupado él también, apareció en la televisión de nuestra casa, explicando que tendríamos que ir a la guerra contra los comunistas. En la escuela hacíamos prácticas de alarma aérea: sonaba una ominosa campana y formábamos en fila en el pasillo, nos echábamos al suelo, nos cubríamos las cabezas con los abrigos, e imaginábamos que se nos caía el cabello y se nos ablandaban los huesos de los brazos. En casa, Mami, mis hermanas y yo rezábamos el rosario por la paz del mundo. Yo adquirí un nuevo vocabulario: *nuclear bomb, radioactive fallout, bomb shelter.* La

Options

Strategies for Reaching All Students

Students Needing Extra Help

Antes de leer: If necessary, briefly familiarize students with the Cold War and Cuban Missile Crisis. You may want to speak to someone in your Social Studies department to obtain information.
Mira la lectura: You may wish to give some pertinent background information regarding parochial schools to help set the opening scene.

Infórmate: In the first section, do one of the letters as a model, showing students how to find the evidence in the text.
Aplicación: In Ex. 1, point out that the exercise is designed to reinforce reading strategies.
In Ex. 2, have examples ready beforehand of when someone might misunderstand an event or situation, such as in the case of Yolanda mistaking snowflakes for radioactive fallout.

Multiple Intelligences
Logical/Mathematical
See *Infórmate* Ex. 1.
Visual/Spatial
See *Aplicación* Ex. 1.

Infórmate

STRATEGIES Coping with unknown words

Reading for details

Recuerda que ya sabes varias maneras de averiguar el significado de una palabra nueva:

- reconocer un cognado
- reconocer una familia de palabras
- usar el contexto

1 Copia esta escala en una hoja de papel. Luego coloca la letra de la expresión apropiada en el lugar correspondiente según lo que siente Yolanda.

⊢--⊢--⊢--⊢--⊢--⊢--⊢--⊣
NO LE GUSTA NADA.   **LE GUSTA MUCHO.**

a. el frío
b. la hermana Zoe

c. los misiles rusos
d. la nieve

2 Ahora compara tu escala con la de un(a) compañero(a). Discutan las diferencias. Usen el texto para explicar sus decisiones.

Aplicación

1 Busca una forma de los infinitivos de la lista para sustituir las palabras subrayadas. Luego, dile las frases a un(a) compañero(a).

1. El jugador de béisbol <u>tiró</u> la pelota.
2. "No <u>señales</u> con el dedo. Es una falta de educación."
3. Despidieron al empleado y no lo <u>sustituyeron</u>.

adjudicarse	lanzar
apuntar	reemplazar
chillar	

2 Piensa en lo que siente Yolanda en esta historia. ¿Has sentido una emoción semejante alguna vez? Escribe un párrafo breve explicando la emoción y por qué la sentiste.

Infórmate

1 Responses will vary, but students may indicate somewhere on the scale (from left to right) the following order:
c. los misiles rusos, a. el frío, d. la nieve, b. la hermana Zoe

2 Responses will vary.

Aplicación
1 1. lanzó
2. apuntes
3. reemplazaron

2 Responses will vary.

Fondo literario
Las salamandras (pp. 492–497)

 Internet Activities

---

hermana Zoe explicaba cómo ocurriría. Dibujó una seta en la pizarra y punteó con tiza una lluvia que significaba la precipitación de polvo radiactivo que nos mataría a todos.

Los meses trajeron más frío, noviembre, diciembre. Todavía estaba oscuro cuando me levantaba por la mañana; helaba cuando caminaba en pos de mi aliento hacia la escuela. Una mañana, estaba sentada ante mi pupitre, mirando por la ventana y soñando despierta, cuando vi en el aire exterior unos puntos iguales a los que la hermana Zoe había dibujado; dispersos al principio, luego cada vez más densos, cada vez en mayor número. Lancé un chillido:

— ¡La bomba! ¡La bomba!

La hermana Zoe acudió convulsionada, su larga

falda negra se hinchó como un globo al correr hacia mí. Unas pocas chicas empezaron a llorar.

Pero al instante desapareció del rostro de la hermana Zoe la expresión de sobresalto.

— ¡Vamos, Yolanda, querida, eso es nieve!
— Se echó a reír —. ¡Nieve!
— Nieve — repetí.

Miré cautelosamente por la ventana. Toda mi vida había oído hablar de los cristales blancos que en invierno caían de los cielos de Norteamérica. Desde mi pupitre presencié cómo el fino polvo cubría la acera y los coches aparcados en las inmediaciones de la escuela. Cada copo era diferente había dicho la hermana Zoe, como lo era una persona, irreemplazable y bello.

Para leer   423

Apply

Process Writing
For information regarding writing portfolios, see p. 54.

Teaching Suggestions
Tell students that working through the *Para escribir* section will help them answer the key chapter question.

Answers
Student brochures will vary.

Puntos de Vista

Para escribir

Actualmente, con unos medios de transporte y una tecnología tan avanzados, podemos decir que vivimos en un mundo sin fronteras. Las oportunidades para estudiar, aprender, hacer negocios, ver lugares nuevos y conocer a otras personas se presentan todos los días. Saber otro idioma es un requisito de la sociedad moderna.

1 Primero, haz una lista de trabajos y profesiones donde sería útil hablar una lengua extranjera. Luego piensa en estas preguntas y escribe tus ideas:

- De los trabajos de la lista, ¿cuáles son los que más te atraen?
- ¿Qué habilidades necesitas? ¿Cómo te prepararías?
- Si tuvieras esas habilidades, ¿dónde y con quién(es) podrías trabajar?

Prepara una tabla como la siguiente para organizar tus ideas.

Carrera/ profesión	Habilidades necesarias	Preparación	Dónde podrías trabajar	Con quién(es)

2 Ahora, habla con tu profesor(a), tu consejero(a), tu familia y, si es posible, con personas que hayan tenido éxito en esos trabajos o profesiones. Pregúntales qué oportunidades habría en esos trabajos si se hablara más de un idioma. Escribe lo que te digan.

424   Capítulo 12

Options

Strategies for Reaching All Students

Students Needing Extra Help
Step 2: Remind students that they can interview in English. Be sure they understand that the questions should deal with job opportunities if one speaks more than one language.
Step 3: Each student is going to have the information obtained from the interview. Divide the classroom into four areas where students can write their information, with headings specified by the four bullets in this section.

Multiple Intelligences
Bodily/Kinesthetic and Visual/Spatial
See step 3.
Logical/Mathematical and Visual/Spatial
See step 1.
Verbal/Linguistic and Visual/Spatial
See step 2.

424   Standards 1.3; 3.1; 5.1

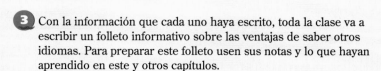

3 Con la información que cada uno haya escrito, toda la clase va a escribir un folleto informativo sobre las ventajas de saber otros idiomas. Para preparar este folleto usen sus notas y lo que hayan aprendido en este y otros capítulos.

En el folleto deben incluir:
- qué trabajos y profesiones exigirían saber otra(s) lengua(s).
- en cuáles se recomendaría tener conocimientos de otra(s) lengua(s).
- cómo se podrían adquirir estos conocimientos y cuánta preparación se necesitaría (clases, intercambios, organizaciones culturales, etc.)
- cuáles serían las ventajas de poder hablar otras lenguas (puestos de mayor responsabilidad, oportunidades para viajar, mejores sueldos, etc.)

Aquí tienen algunas palabras que les pueden ser útiles.

además	la oportunidad	por eso
a través de	no sólo...sino también	proteger
formar parte de	permitir	usar
igualmente		

Cuando terminen el texto para el folleto, revísenlo y sigan los pasos del proceso de escribir.

Luego, añadan fotos y/o dibujos y decidan un título entre todos.

Para compartir su trabajo pueden:
- hacer fotocopias para sus consejeros
- ponerlo en sus portafolios
- enviarlo a la biblioteca de la escuela
- ofrecerlo a la biblioteca de su comunidad
- compartirlo con otros estudiantes de español de su escuela

Para escribir 425

Assess & Summarize

Test Preparation
You may want to assign parts of this section as written homework or as an in-class writing activity prior to administering the *Examen de habilidades.*

Answers
Listening
—*Mucha gente sueña con seguir una carrera que pague bien y que tenga buenos beneficios. Si hablaran y escribieran otro idioma, nuestra agencia podría ofrecerles más oportunidades. Vivimos en un mundo sin fronteras gracias a los medios de comunicación, y por eso el número de trabajos aumenta cada día más. Sin embargo, muchas compañías que usan nuestro servicio piden como requisito que el empleado sea bilingüe. Por eso les recomiendo a todos que dominen una lengua extranjera antes de que se gradúen de la secundaria. Tendrían así grandes oportunidades en el mundo del trabajo.*
La ventaja de hablar otra lengua es: Hay más oportunidades de tener un mejor trabajo.

Repaso ¿Lo sabes bien?

Esta sección te ayudará a prepararte para el examen de habilidades, donde tendrás que hacer tareas semejantes.

Listening
¿Puedes entender a alguien que habla sobre las ventajas de saber otro idioma? Escucha mientras el (la) profesor(a) lee un ejemplo semejante al que vas a oír en el examen. Según la descripción, ¿cuál es la ventaja de hablar otra lengua?

Reading
¿Puedes leer estos anuncios de una agencia de empleos y decir qué requisito tienen todos en común? ¿Para qué trabajo sólo sería necesario leer el idioma? ¿Para qué trabajos sería necesario saber comunicarse con gente que no pueda oír?

EMPLEOS COMERCIALES S.A.

- Agente de viajes que sepa hablar bien inglés, español y japonés. Beneficios excelentes.
- Asistente social con experiencia. Bilingüe en chino e inglés. Necesita saber hablar por señas.
- Bibliotecarias con experiencia. Deben leer bien español y ruso.

426   Capítulo 12

Writing
¿Puedes escribir una breve carta como la que escribió Angélica a su amigo?

Querido Ernesto:

Como no tengo bastante dinero para asistir a la universidad el año que viene, quiero tomar clases por la noche y trabajar durante el día. Tal vez podría trabajar como recepcionista o camarera, pero sería mejor encontrar algo que me ayudara para el futuro. Podría usar mis habilidades en español y en computadoras y más tarde, cuando tenga más experiencia y la preparación necesaria, podría seguir la carrera de corresponsal internacional. Eso sí me gustaría, pero no sé todavía qué hacer. ¿Qué me sugieres?

Saludos,

 Angélica

Una clase de inglés en España

Culture
¿Puedes comparar el aprendizaje de otras lenguas en los países de habla hispana y en los Estados Unidos? Explica.

Speaking
Con un(a) compañero(a) habla sobre las ventajas de hablar una lengua extranjera.

A —*¿Escribiste ya el informe para la clase de sociología?*
B —*Sí. Escribí sobre los beneficios de vivir en un lugar multicultural y sobre las ventajas de saber otro idioma. ¿Y tú?*
A —*Escribí sobre las ventajas de insistir en que el inglés sea la lengua oficial de los Estados Unidos.*
B —*¿Cómo puedes decir eso? Es importante que . . .*

www.pasoapaso.com

MÁS PRÁCTICA

Más práctica y tarea, pp. 583–587

Options

Strategies for Reaching All Students

Students Needing Extra Help
Have students write this so that they can check off what they have mastered. Remind them that this is just a sample of what the test will be like.
Listening: Read more than once.
Reading: Remind students that they don't need to know every word. Review strategies for finding cognates, context clues, and word families.

Writing: Have students use the Organizer and write a sample letter as practice before the test. Remind them that the focus of the assignment is looking for a job that incorporates foreign language skills. Refer students to previous sections in the chapter for ideas: Ex. 9 on p. 405 and Step 1 in *Para escribir.*

Culture: Have students review the notes they took when they read the *Álbum cultural.*
Speaking: Use the vocabulary section of the Organizer. Finish the model so that students know how to end the conversation. Limit the number of lines of dialogue. Refer students to the *Tema para investigar* for ideas.

Resumen del vocabulario

Usa el vocabulario de este capítulo para:

- responder a la pregunta clave: ¿Por qué hace falta saber otro idioma?
- describir una situación donde es práctico hablar una lengua extranjera
- decir qué ventajas tendrás para tu futuro trabajo o profesión si sabes un idioma extranjero
- explicar cómo una lengua te puede ayudar a comunicarte con personas de otras culturas

para explicar la importancia de saber una lengua extranjera
académico, -a
activamente
apreciar
el aprendizaje
la armonía
aumentar
el beneficio
el contacto
convivir
diversificar(se) *(c → qu)*
el / la estudiante de intercambio
expresar(se)
la frontera
la lengua extranjera
la lengua materna
el modismo
multicultural
oficial
útil
viajar

para describir una situación donde se usa una lengua extranjera
hacer falta
la inmigración
el / la inmigrante
mundial
la traducción, *pl.* las traducciones

para hablar de cómo puedes expresarte en otra lengua
bilingüe
cometer
confundirse
defenderse *(e → ie)* (en)
la dificultad
dominar
el error
tener facilidad para
hablar por señas
interpretar
el lenguaje por señas
sordo, -a
traducir *(c → zc)*

para decir qué carrera quieres seguir
el / la agente de ventas
el / la asistente social
el banquero, la banquera
el bibliotecario, la bibliotecaria
la carrera
el contador, la contadora
el / la corresponsal
el / la periodista
el redactor, la redactora
seguir *(e → i)*
el traductor, la traductora

otras palabras y expresiones útiles
completamente
en realidad
sería *(from: ser)*
soñar *(o → ue)* (con)
tendría que *(from: tener)*
tendrías que *(from: tener)*

Resumen 427

Cultural Notes ☀

(p. 426, photo)
The tourism industry is crucial to Spain's economy, earning approximately 18.5 billion dollars a year, or 10 percent of the country's income. Although most of Spain's more than 55 million annual tourists come from non-English speaking countries, with France, Portugal, and Germany being the top three, English, because of its importance in commerce, remains one of the most valuable languages to know for professionals in the tourism industry.

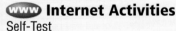

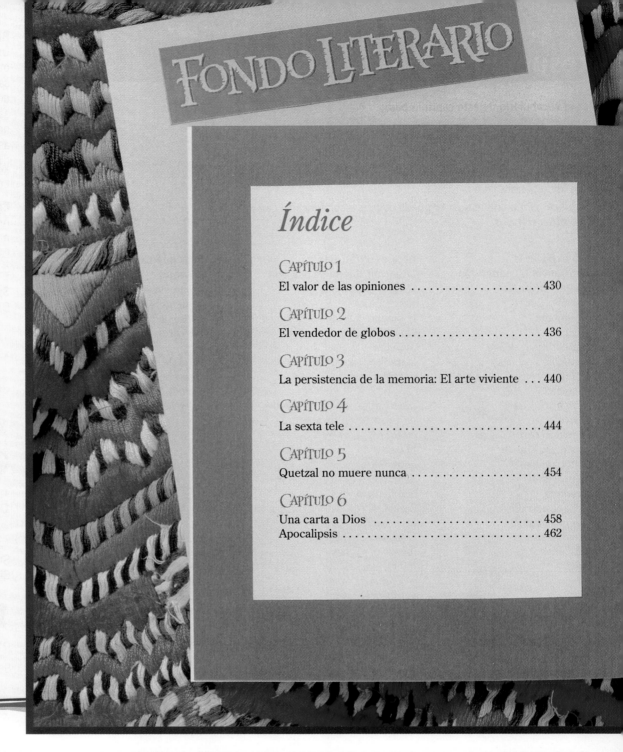

FONDO LITERARIO

Índice

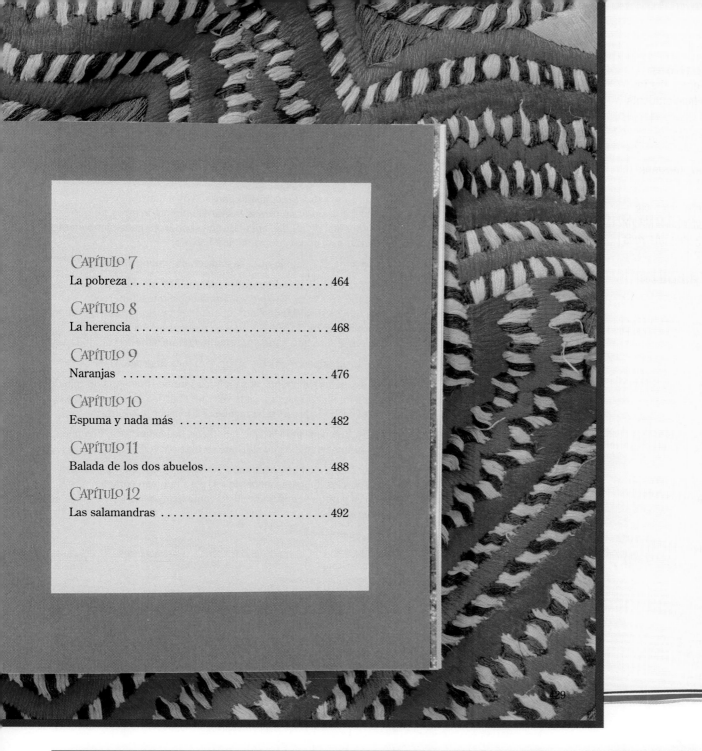

Apply

Teaching Suggestions

You may want to suggest the following strategies to help students with this reading:

- Using the title and illustrations for meaning
- Recognizing time expressions

Antes de leer
Ask students: *¿Cuánto valen las opiniones de tu familia para ti? ¿Y las de tus amigos? ¿Vale una más que otra? ¿Por qué?*

Answers: Para empezar
Answers will vary.

El valor de las opiniones

Don Juan Manuel (1282 - 1348?) es conocido por su colección de historias *El conde Lucanor*. Sus observaciones sobre la naturaleza humana son tan válidas hoy como hace 700 años.

PARA EMPEZAR

Generalmente, ¿pides consejos? ¿A quién o a quiénes se los pides?

El conde[1] Lucanor tenía como consejero a un hombre sabio y prudente que se llamaba Patronio. Éste era conocido por su buen sentido para juzgar a los hombres y para tomar decisiones juiciosas.[2] Era su costumbre no contestar directamente sino después de contar una anécdota. En una ocasión le dijo el conde:

—Patronio: estoy preocupado porque voy a hacer algo muy particular y, como no pienso seguir la opinión de otros, sé que hablarán mal de mí. Sé, además, que si no hago nada, también me juzgarán mal, con o sin razón para hacerlo.

En seguida, le contó lo que iba a hacer, pidiéndole una opinión.

—Señor conde—dijo Patronio—, sé que hay muchos que podrían darle mejores consejos que yo. También sé que su merced[3] tiene clara inteligencia. Me inclino[4] a pensar que mis palabras no van a tener ningún efecto. Pero, como su merced me ha pedido una opinión, le diré qué haría yo, estando en una situación como la suya.

—Te lo agradeceré mucho. Habla con toda libertad.[5]

—Pues, señor, había una vez un buen hombre que tenía un hijo de mucha inteligencia, pero, cada vez que el padre decidía hacer algo, el muchacho le presentaba razones para hacer lo contrario.

"Padre, ¿ha pensado Ud. que todo tiene dos lados?" "Sí, hijo mío, pero lo importante es decidir qué es más conveniente."

Es cosa bien sabida—continuó Patronio—que los jóvenes tienen gran percepción para ciertas cosas, pero también cometen grandes errores porque ven claramente el comienzo y no la terminación de lo que proponen.

—Y ¿qué ocurrió?

---

[1] el conde *count*
[2] juiciosas *judicious, wise*
[3] su merced *your Grace*
[4] me inclino *I am inclined*
[5] la libertad *freedom*

Planning

Strategies for Reaching All Students

Spanish-Speaking Students
Students can respond orally to the following questions during class discussions or in writing following the discussions.
El valor de las opiniones: ¿Cuál es la moraleja de este cuento? ¿Crees que todavía es premiada la honradez? ¿Qué otras características personales se valoran en nuestra sociedad?

Students Needing Extra Help
These readings may be teacher directed or gone over in small groups.
Make vocabulary lists ahead of time.
Present reading strategies similar to those found in *Para leer*. Or, have students read this after each *Para leer* so that the strategies are still fresh in their minds.
If the reading is going to take more than one period, have students take notes, make an outline, etc. that they can use to review for the next day.

Students may not be familiar with the use of footnotes. Be sure they understand their purpose and their location. If they have difficulty going from the footnote back to the reading, review the list beforehand.
Review grammar points that students had difficulty with in the chapter.
Discuss the themes of the readings.
After each paragraph, summarize or ask comprehension questions. Write key ideas on the chalkboard so that students have a visual to help them focus. Bring in related

—Pues, señor, ese hijo hablaba de cómo se debían hacer muchas cosas, pero, cuando era necesario hacerlas, nunca lo hacía bien. Y con esto creaba a su padre muchos problemas, pues no lo dejaba hacer lo que era necesario para el bien de todos.

—Así ocurre muchas veces.

—Como el padre tenía que vivir oyendo las opiniones de su hijo, decidió darle una lección, no para castigarlo,[6] sino para obligarlo a pensar seriamente.

El buen hombre y su hijo eran labradores[7]—continuó Patronio—, y vivían cerca de una aldea.[8] Un día, necesitando comprar algunas cosas en el mercado, decidieron ir con una mula[9] para traer, en el viaje de vuelta, lo que iban a comprar. Salieron de casa y caminaron alegremente, sin poner ninguna carga[10] sobre el animal. Muy pronto vieron a varios hombres que venían en dirección opuesta.[11] Se detuvieron[12] un momento para charlar con ellos. Hablando del animal, dijo uno de los hombres:

"No entiendo por qué va este muchacho a pie teniendo Uds. una mula que nada lleva encima."

---

[6] castigarlo *punish him*
[7] los labradores *farmers*
[8] la aldea *village*
[9] la mula *mule*
[10] la carga *cargo, burden*
[11] opuesta *opposite*
[12] se detuvieron *they stopped*

El valor de las opiniones   Fondo literario   431

Teaching Suggestions
You may want to tell students that don Juan Manuel was among the first Spaniards to write prose fiction. He was the grandson of King Fernando III and a statesman and warrior as well as a writer, exemplifying the Spanish ideal of an *hombre de armas y letras.*
El libro de los exemplos del conde Lucanor et de Patronio, from which this story is taken, is his best-known and most important work. Finished in 1335, it consists of 50 tales strung together by a framing device: Count Lucanor, a nobleman, asks his counselor Patronio for advice. Each problem reminds Patronio of a story which he tells and then sums up with a moral. The stories are not original, as was common in the Middle Ages, but Juan Manuel's retelling of them is. The book consists of animal stories, many from Aesop's fables, medieval legends, folk tales, and anecdotes about contemporary people.

artwork to aid comprehension.
El valor de las opiniones: Have students create a visual representation of the story, either in art or theater, to check their comprehension.

Enrichment
Discuss this tale with students, asking them to think of other stories with a moral (Aesop's fables, etc.). Ask students whether they think the moral of this story is applicable today.

Cuando los hombres ya no estaban presentes, le pidió el padre una opinión a su hijo y éste contestó que tenían razón. Entonces dijo el padre: "Puedes ir en la mula; así vas a descansar."

Poco después vino otro grupo de caminantes y uno dijo: "No entiendo por qué va el viejo a pie y el muchacho montado en el animal: un joven siempre sufre menos, precisamente porque es joven, ¿verdad?"

432   Fondo literario   *El valor de las opiniones*

Poco después preguntó el padre: "¿Qué piensas tú ahora?" El muchacho contestó inmediatamente: "Tienen razón." Bajó del animal, y el padre ocupó su lugar.

Poco más tarde, encontraron un tercer grupo de vecinos, y varios dijeron que no era justo obligar a un muchacho a caminar, no siendo todavía muy fuerte. Cuando estuvieron solos, preguntó el padre: "Y ¿qué dices tú ahora?" "Digo que tienen razón." Decidieron entonces subir los dos sobre el animal para evitar nuevos comentarios.

433

Viajaban en esta forma, cuando un campesino se detuvo para preguntarles: "¿Cómo pueden Uds. poner tanto peso sobre un pobre animal tan flaco[13] y tan pequeño? Es seguro que lo van a matar."

El muchacho dijo que ambos hacían mal y comenzaron otra vez a viajar a pie. "¿Ves?" dijo el padre, "primero diste una opinión, después otra, y después, otra, sin pensar antes de hablar. Ahora quiero oír tu opinión una vez más." El hijo no sabía qué contestar. "Hijo mío, en este mundo casi nunca es posible dar opiniones y agradar[14] a todo el mundo. Lo que es bueno para unos, es malo para otros. Por esta razón, siempre debemos hacer lo que uno cree mejor, pero sin hacer mal a nadie. Hay muchos que dan opiniones sólo para expresar su voluntad,[15] sin pensar en las personas a quienes dan consejos. Entre ésos estás tú."

—Ahora bien, señor conde, su merced me pregunta qué debe hacer para que otros no hablen mal. Mi consejo es éste: antes de hacer nada, debe pensar en el bien y el mal que puede resultar de lo que va a hacer. Lo importante es usar la razón. Su merced debe escuchar a otros sólo cuando los que dan una opinión son personas leales[16] y de mucho conocimiento.

—Te agradezco tu consejo, buen Patronio. Así lo haré.

—Pero, si no encuentra su merced a tales consejeros, debe esperar un día y una noche. Y, si halla[17] que lo que piensa hacer es para su bien, y no para el mal de otros, su merced debe hacerlo, sin pensar en la opinión de los demás.

---

[13]flaco *thin, skinny*
[14]agradar *to please*
[15]la voluntad *will*
[16]leales *loyal*
[17]si halla *if you find*

El conde Lucanor comprendió que había recibido muy buen consejo y, para no olvidarlo, escribió estos versos:

> Sigue la opinión de otros,
> si no es para tu mal;
> piensa en lo que es bueno,
> siendo siempre prudencial.[18]

---

[18]prudencial *sensible, reasonable*

Opinión personal
1. Patronio dice que "los jóvenes tienen gran percepción para ciertas cosas, pero también cometen grandes errores porque ven claramente el comienzo y no la terminación de lo que proponen." ¿Estás de acuerdo con él? ¿Por qué?
2. ¿Crees que el hijo aprendió la lección que el padre trató de *(tried to)* enseñarle? Explica tu respuesta.

 Writing Activity FL-A

DESPUÉS DE LEER

1. ¿Crees que el consejo que Patronio le dio al conde es bueno? ¿Por qué?
2. Por lo general, ¿te gusta dar consejos a tus amigos? ¿Por qué?
3. ¿Puedes explicar el mensaje del cuento?

El valor de las opiniones Fondo literario 435

Apply

Teaching Suggestions

You may want to suggest the following strategies to help students with this reading:

• Skimming
• Identifying the setting
• Making predictions

Explain that *globos* in the story refers to "balloons," not "globes."

Point out to students that IBBY stands for the International Board on Books for Young People, an organization now located in 65 countries, whose goal is to increase international understanding and good will between all people through children's literature.

Antes de leer

Ask students to brainstorm some adults outside of the family whom they interacted with as children: the ice cream man, a favorite teacher, etc. Call on volunteers to describe their memory of that person.

Answers: Para empezar

Answers will vary, but students may mention: *la niñez, la libertad, el vuelo,* etc.

Eduardo Robles Boza (Tío Patota) nació en México D.F. el 7 de junio de 1941. Es licenciado en periodismo por la universidad de Venezuela. Presenta el programa de televisión *El círculo de la imaginación.* Es también fundador de IBBY en México y presidente de la Asociación nacional de narradores de cuento. En 1980, recibió el premio nacional Juan Pablos de literatura infantil con el libro *Los cuentos del Tío Patota.*

PARA EMPEZAR

¿Te gustan los globos?
¿Qué pueden simbolizar los globos?

El vendedor de globos

El pueblo de Tapatán es un pueblo pequeño porque tiene pocos habitantes. La mayoría trabaja en la tierra y unos pocos son comerciantes[1] que venden alimentos y ropa a los campesinos. Los niños y los jóvenes estudian en la escuelita del maestro Gabriel y, en el tiempo que les queda libre, ayudan a sus papás en el campo. También trabajan.

Están ocupados de lunes a sábado, porque en el pueblo hay muchas cosas que hacer. Pero cuando llega el domingo, los niños y los adultos se olvidan del trabajo y los estudios y saben divertirse. ¡Es la gente más alegre que uno pueda imaginarse! La plaza del pueblo es, como en todos los pueblos pequeños, el lugar de reunión preferido de sus habitantes. Y es que alrededor de esa plaza está la tienda de don Gaspar, el lugar donde venden periódicos y revistas, la oficina de correos, donde se compran timbres[2] para las cartas y, por supuesto, la casa del gobierno y la iglesia. Como verán, hay de todo.

Ese día, los muchachos inventan juegos, competencias deportivas[3] y bailes muy divertidos. La orquesta del pueblo sabe tocar bonitas canciones y cada domingo se luce[4] con el tambor, el trombón y la trompeta, que hacen mucho ruido en las fiestas.

Pero lo que más les gusta a los niños y a los jóvenes son los globos, esas pelotas redondas que don Nacho, el globero, vende cada domingo en la plaza del pueblo.

---

[1] los comerciantes *merchants*
[2] los timbres = sellos
[3] las competencias deportivas *sports contests*
[4] se luce *(it) shows off*

Options

Strategies for Reaching All Students

Spanish-Speaking Students
Ask: *¿Qué tradición observa el pueblo los domingos? ¿En tu familia o comunidad se observa una tradición más o menos semejante? Descríbela. ¿Por qué son importantes estas tradiciones?*

Students Needing Extra Help
This story lends itself to artwork and / or skits as a way of checking comprehension.

Amarrados a un cordón[5] para no escaparse ni volar al cielo, don Nacho los va ofreciendo a niños y a adultos:

—¡Globos, globos, de todos los tamaños y todos los colores! ¡Lleve uno o lleve dos!

Y de repente los muchachos corren hasta donde se encuentra el globero para escoger el mejor. Algunos globos son rojos, otros verdes o amarillos, pero también los hay de muchos colores, que son los que más lucen.

—¡Yo quiero uno verde!

—¡Y yo el azul!

—¡Yo prefiero de todos los colores, don Nacho!

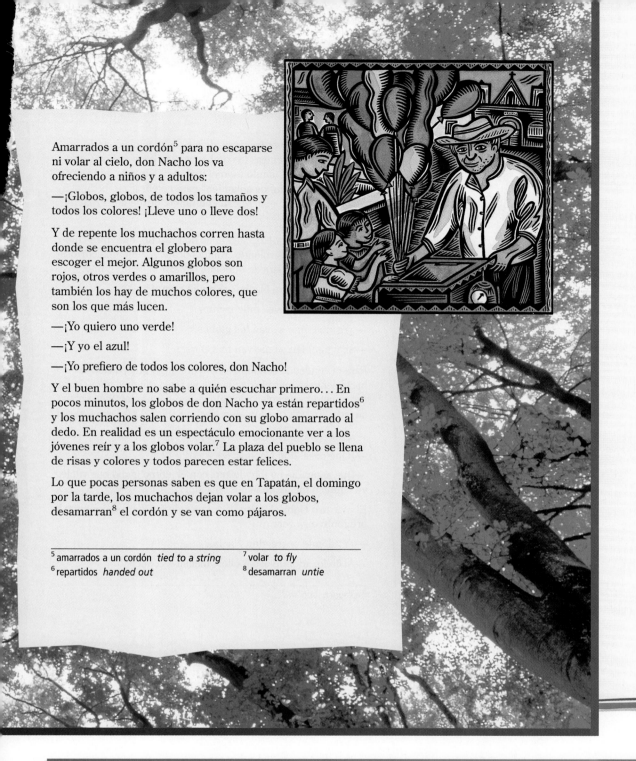

Y el buen hombre no sabe a quién escuchar primero... En pocos minutos, los globos de don Nacho ya están repartidos[6] y los muchachos salen corriendo con su globo amarrado al dedo. En realidad es un espectáculo emocionante ver a los jóvenes reír y a los globos volar.[7] La plaza del pueblo se llena de risas y colores y todos parecen estar felices.

Lo que pocas personas saben es que en Tapatán, el domingo por la tarde, los muchachos dejan volar a los globos, desamarran[8] el cordón y se van como pájaros.

---

[5] amarrados a un cordón *tied to a string*
[6] repartidos *handed out*
[7] volar *to fly*
[8] desamarran *untie*

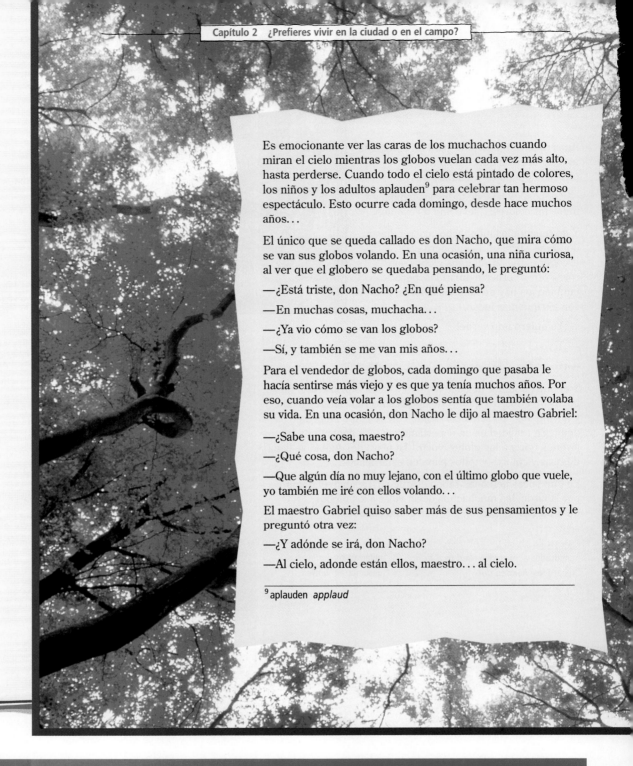

Es emocionante ver las caras de los muchachos cuando miran el cielo mientras los globos vuelan cada vez más alto, hasta perderse. Cuando todo el cielo está pintado de colores, los niños y los adultos aplauden[9] para celebrar tan hermoso espectáculo. Esto ocurre cada domingo, desde hace muchos años...

El único que se queda callado es don Nacho, que mira cómo se van sus globos volando. En una ocasión, una niña curiosa, al ver que el globero se quedaba pensando, le preguntó:

—¿Está triste, don Nacho? ¿En qué piensa?

—En muchas cosas, muchacha...

—¿Ya vio cómo se van los globos?

—Sí, y también se me van mis años...

Para el vendedor de globos, cada domingo que pasaba le hacía sentirse más viejo y es que ya tenía muchos años. Por eso, cuando veía volar a los globos sentía que también volaba su vida. En una ocasión, don Nacho le dijo al maestro Gabriel:

—¿Sabe una cosa, maestro?

—¿Qué cosa, don Nacho?

—Que algún día no muy lejano, con el último globo que vuele, yo también me iré con ellos volando...

El maestro Gabriel quiso saber más de sus pensamientos y le preguntó otra vez:

—¿Y adónde se irá, don Nacho?

—Al cielo, adonde están ellos, maestro... al cielo.

---

[9] aplauden *applaud*

Options

Strategies for Reaching All Students

Spanish-Speaking Students
Ask: *¿Por qué usa el autor el color blanco para el último globo? ¿Hay otro color que representa lo mismo? ¿Cuál es?*

Students Needing Extra Help
Ex. 1: Have students review the story to help them with the description.
Ex. 2: Students may have some difficulty with the symbolic meaning of the balloons and with putting that meaning into Spanish. Assist as needed.

Enrichment
As a homework assignment, have students write a paragraph about one of the following topics: symbols used in the story (balloons, flight, colors), the character of don Nacho (can students think of someone similar in literature or in their own lives who brings pleasure to everyone but is somehow apart or private?), or the contrast between tension and release throughout the story.

Y así pasó el tiempo y con el tiempo los años, pero don Nacho no dejaba de[10] vender sus globos ni los muchachos se olvidaban de comprarlos. Uno de esos domingos se encontraba el globero repartiendo sus globos, cuando de repente descubrió que sólo le quedaba uno por vender y era de color blanco. Llegó una muchacha y le preguntó:

—¿Ya no le queda ningún rojo, don Nacho?

—¿No te gusta el blanco? Es el último que me queda.

—Es que los rojos vuelan más alto.

—Ni te fijes en eso, muchacha. El color no es lo que los hace volar. Es lo que llevan adentro. ¡Toma, te lo regalo!

La muchacha, emocionada, lo tomó y antes de salir corriendo con su regalo, le dio un beso a don Nacho.

El globero terminó su venta, pero esa tarde, más que ninguna otra, se sentía realmente cansado, muy cansado. Lejos del resto de la gente, dejó que los muchachos lanzaran[11] sus globos al aire. Escuchó las risas y los aplausos:

—¡Bravo, bravo!

Y esperó la noche y el silencio de la plaza vacía. Entonces, como lo prometió, se quitó el sombrero, que nunca antes abandonaba, miró al cielo. . . y voló.

_____

[10]no dejaba de *didn't stop*
[11]lanzaran *launch, let go*

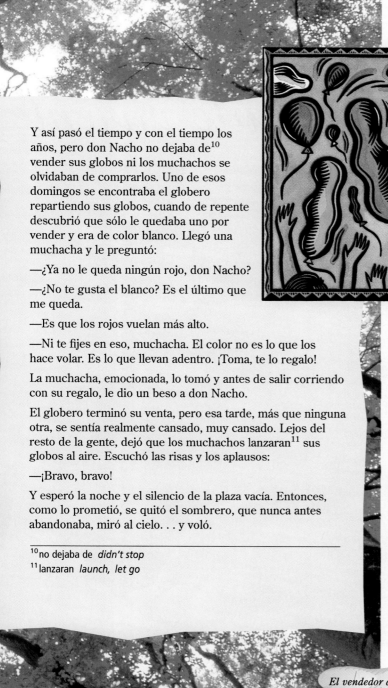

DESPUÉS DE LEER

1 ¿Dónde tiene lugar este cuento? Describe el lugar.

2 Para don Nacho, ¿qué representan los globos? ¿Y para los niños del pueblo? ¿Cómo lo sabes?

El vendedor de globos Fondo literario 439

Apply

Answers: Después de leer

1 En el pueblo de Tapatán. *Answers will vary, but may include:* Es un pueblo pequeño con pocos habitantes. La plaza es el centro de reunión. Alrededor están la tienda de don Gaspar, la oficina de correos, la casa del gobierno y la iglesia.

2 Para don Nacho, los globos representan su vida. Para los niños, representan juguetes; parecen pájaros de colores. Lo sabemos porque los niños siempre piden ciertos colores. Piensan que vuelan mejor.

Opinión personal

1. Don Nacho dice que el color de un globo no es lo que lo hace volar, sino lo que lleva adentro. ¿Qué piensas que quiere decir? ¿Estás de acuerdo?
2. ¿Por qué crees que don Nacho se quitó el sombrero que siempre llevaba cuando sabía que iba a morirse?
3. ¿Crees que don Nacho realmente voló al cielo como los globos?

 Writing Activity FL-B

Apply

Teaching Suggestions

You may want to suggest the following strategies to help students with this reading:

- Activating prior knowledge of magazine articles
- Scanning for information about art movements
- Using cognates and context to get meaning

Antes de leer

Ask: *¿Has podido ver obras de arte popular?*

Answers: Para empezar

Answers will vary, but may include: *Conservando el arte popular tradicional. Haciendo que los niños (jóvenes) participen en estas exposiciones de arte.*

En este artículo de la revista *Américas* de Patricia Harris y David Lyon se nos habla sobre el arte tradicional hispano de Nuevo México y del papel de los jóvenes en la continuación del arte popular.

La persistencia de la memoria:
El arte viviente

PARA EMPEZAR

¿Cómo se pueden conservar las tradiciones de una cultura?

440 Fondo literario *La persistencia de la memoria: El arte viviente*

Options

Strategies for Reaching All Students

Spanish-Speaking Students
¿Cuáles son las artes tradicionales de tu comunidad? ¿Por qué es importante que sobrevivan estas artes? ¿Cómo se puede asegurar su continuación y supervivencia? ¿Practica alguien en tu familia o alguien que conoces una de las artes tradicionales?

Students Needing Extra Help
Have pictures of traditional art available so that students can have a visual reference as they read. Give them an overview of what the reading is about. Have them write a brief summary after each paragraph or create a graphic organizer (webs, maps, etc.) to help them organize their thoughts.

Enrichment
As a class, discuss traditional arts and crafts, asking the following questions: *¿Hay algún arte tradicional (en la cultura norteamericana, hispana o alguna otra) que te gustaría aprender? ¿Por qué sí o no? ¿Hay algún arte o algún trabajo en tu familia o comunidad que se haya hecho desde hace muchos años? ¿Sabes hacerlo(la) tú? ¿Quién te enseñó? ¿Qué arte o trabajo tradicional te gustaría enseñar a tus hijos?*

Santa Fe, en Nuevo México, exhibe sus raíces españolas en el corazón de la ciudad, donde la plaza tradicional se extiende al pie[1] del Palacio de los Gobernadores. El edificio, construido en 1610, estableció a Santa Fe como sede de gobierno.[2] La ciudad pasó al poder de México en 1821 y a manos de los Estados Unidos en 1848. Ambos—el palacio y la plaza—sobrevivieron las distintas dominaciones.

El *Traditional Spanish Market* (Mercado Español Tradicional) que tiene lugar el último fin de semana del mes de julio, demuestra que las artes del período colonial español siguen vivas en los Estados Unidos del siglo XX. Parece increíble que estas artes domésticas y religiosas tengan tanta aceptación: *bultos* (imágenes de santos talladas[3]), *retablos* (imágenes de santos pintadas), trabajos en hojalata,[4] cruces de paja,[5] muebles de pino y cedro locales y finos tejidos[6] hechos en telares[7] españoles de pie. Pero esta muestra pública constituye una manifestación de orgullo individual e identidad cultural. El hecho de tallar la imagen de un santo tal como lo hacía el abuelo, de tejer alfombras como las que han estado en la familia durante un siglo o de seguir la meditación devota que produce una cruz adornada con paja brillante, son formas de honrar la tradición, y esto significa mantener vivas la memoria y la identidad.

Resulta difícil creer que estas artes llegaron al borde de[8] la extinción hace muy pocas generaciones. Hacia 1920 era posible contar con los dedos de una mano a los *santeros,* creadores de imágenes de santos, que había en Nuevo México. Los maestros de estas manifestaciones artísticas disminuían,[9] en parte, debido a la baja en la demanda de sus obras.

---

[1] al pie *at the foot*

[2] la sede de gobierno *seat of government*

[3] talladas *carved*

[4] la hojalata *tin*

[5] la paja *straw*

[6] los tejidos *woven cloth*

[7] los telares *looms*

[8] al borde de *on the verge of*

[9] disminuían *diminished*

La persistencia de la memoria: El arte viviente   Fondo literario   441

Cultural Notes

(pp. 440–441, photos)
The Spanish market in Santa Fe, New Mexico, takes place every year on the last full weekend in July, where works such as these are exhibited by traditionally trained artists and craftspeople. Especially popular are the religiously inspired works of *santeros* and *santeras,* men and women who carve and paint *bultos* (statues), *reredos* (altar screens), and *retablos* (paintings on wood that recount miracles brought about by the intervention of a particular saint). They may also be made of tin, copper, or canvas. Markets such as this featuring the beauty and variety of Hispanic art continue to thrive in the Santa Fe area.

441

Apply

Answers: Después de leer

1 Los requisitos para participar en el *Traditional Spanish Market* son: ser de ascendencia hispana; provenir de las comunidades del norte de Nuevo México y de Colorado; que las obras sean hechas a mano, usando materiales y técnicas tradicionales; y que cada obra sea única.

2 Es importante que ellos participen porque los artistas jóvenes representan el futuro para las artes tradicionales.

En 1925 se fundó la *Spanish Colonial Arts Society (SCAS)* (Sociedad de Artes Coloniales Españolas). Sus metas[10] eran proteger y documentar las artes tradicionales del Nuevo México colonial y encontrar las vías[11] para perpetuar[12] la tradición. Además, los miembros de la *SCAS* deseaban alertar a los artistas de hoy educando a la gente sobre su trabajo y creando un mercado para las artes de acuerdo con la tradición colonial. Uno de los primeros pasos fue el establecimiento del *Traditional Spanish Market*.

Para participar en el *Traditional Spanish Market,* los artistas deben satisfacer una serie de requisitos culturales y artísticos. La *SCAS* dice que los artistas deben de ser de ascendencia[13] hispana y provenir de las comunidades del norte de Nuevo México y de Colorado, y que sus obras deben haber sido hechas a mano, usando materiales y técnicas tradicionales. Asimismo, cada obra debe ser única, eliminando de esta forma las innovaciones "modernas," como la litografía.

Una de las características más notables del *Spanish Market* es la inclusión de los "expositores[14] jóvenes," que sumaron 59 en el mercado de 1993. Estos artistas, de edades entre cinco y dieciocho años, exponen, a veces, junto con sus familias, pero muchos de ellos instalan su propia mesa en las sendas diagonales que atraviesan la plaza. En la mayoría de los casos están aún en el período de aprendizaje, pero sus obras tienden a ser sumamente refinadas y hermosas.

[10]las metas *objectives*
[11]las vías *ways*
[12]perpetuar *to perpetuate, to carry on*
[13]la ascendencia *ancestry*
[14]los expositores *exhibitors*

442   Fondo literario   *La persistencia de la memoria: El arte viviente*

"Los expositores jóvenes son los favoritos del mercado y constituyen una de las adiciones más importantes que se haya hecho al acontecimiento[15] en muchos años," dice Bud Redding, director ejecutivo de la *SCAS*. "Los chicos[16] muestran sus obras, comparten sus conocimientos y practican su talento como vendedores. Sus obras son admiradas por muchos coleccionistas."

La *SCAS* da premios a los jóvenes artistas según su edad. Los artistas adultos y los organizadores de la *SCAS* consideran que es fundamental fomentar el interés de los artistas jóvenes, porque éstos representan un futuro para las artes tradicionales.

Los niños y jóvenes que solicitan participar en el mercado deben contar con[17] el patrocinio[18] de un artista adulto, no necesariamente miembro de su familia. En muchos casos el patrocinador es un padre o abuelo, un tío o una tía. En otros puede ser el maestro[19] de esa rama artesanal[20] en su comunidad o ciudad, alguien que haya encontrado una nueva generación que siga adelante.

La *Spanish Colonial Arts Society* amplía todos los años su colección mediante compras directas en el *Spanish Market*. Coleccionistas privados y museos, como el *Museum of International Folk Art* en Santa Fe, también hacen adquisiciones. Y, por supuesto, muchas otras personas no coleccionistas muestran su interés en este arte comprando piezas[21] que para ellas tienen un encanto[22] especial.

---

[15] el acontecimiento *event*

[16] los chicos = los niños

[17] contar con *to count on*

[18] el patrocinio *the sponsorship*

[19] el maestro *master*

[20] artesanal *pertaining to craftspeople*

[21] las piezas *pieces*

[22] el encanto *charm*

DESPUÉS DE LEER

1 **¿Cuáles son algunos de los requisitos necesarios para participar en el *Traditional Spanish Market*?**

2 **¿Por qué es tan importante que artistas jóvenes participen en ésta u otras exposiciones?**

Opinión personal

1. Imagina que eres un(a) joven artista del norte de Nuevo México. Describe la importancia del arte tradicional en tu familia, lo que haces tú y cómo aprendes a hacer tu oficio. Después habla de tus experiencias durante los días del Mercado. ¿Ganarás un trofeo? ¿Competirás con tus hermanos? Lee tu párrafo a un(a) compañero(a).

2. ¿Hay arte tradicional en tu región del país? ¿Representa a un grupo étnico? Si hay, trae ejemplos de este arte o fotos a la clase. Describe el objeto de arte. ¿De qué está hecho? ¿Qué representa? ¿Es sencilla la forma? ¿Por qué te gusta o no te gusta?

3. ¿Cómo se explica que una obra de arte bella es una expresión individual y colectiva a la vez?

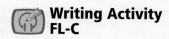 **Writing Activity FL-C**

La persistencia de la memoria: El arte viviente   Fondo literario   443

Apply

Teaching Suggestions

You may want to suggest the following strategies to help students with this reading:

- Using a word web around the term *TV sets*
- Using pictures to predict
- Identifying the author's attitude

Antes de leer

Ask: *¿Hay una tele para cada miembro de tu familia?*

Answers: Para empezar

Answers will vary.

La sexta tele

Alfredo Gómez Cerdá es un escritor madrileño que ha escrito varios libros para lectores jóvenes. Se caracteriza por un estilo directo e irónico, pero al mismo tiempo nos hace reflexionar sobre temas importantes.

PARA EMPEZAR

¿Cuántos televisores hay en tu casa? ¿Qué pasa cuando todos quieren ver programas diferentes?

Rebeca Revuelta Revuelta decidió escribir unas cartas al director de la revista *A ver si te enteras* para que se comentaran los problemas que tuvo su familia con la televisión.

Cada vez que se emitía[1] otro canal de televisión en Urbecualquiera la familia de Rebeca buscaba una excusa para comprar otra tele. Fue poco después de nacer ella cuando compraron la segunda tele, ya que[2] la madre quería ver un partido de fútbol y el padre un concurso que daban a la misma hora. Un día el abuelo, que andaba en danza con su vieja silla de madera del salón a la habitación de los padres, quiso ver su programa—"El asilo ataca" que daban en el canal tres. Resultó que le compraron la tercera tele. La puso en el cuarto de estar o lo que era lo mismo, el dormitorio del abuelo Jeremías. La compra de la tercera tele les hizo felices a todos.

Unos años más tarde se enteraron de que[3] el cuarto canal se emitiría. En éste el hijo Jeremías podría ver partidos de ping-pong (Él era un buen jugador de ping-pong.). Cuando se perdió[4] la final del campeonato mundial[5] porque los otros miraban sus programas, decidieron comprar la cuarta tele. Entonces dejó de[6] jugar porque le pareció más divertido ser espectador. Ahora ya todos estaban contentos menos la hija, Rebeca, que tenía que andar de un lado para otro para ver el programa que deseaba. Cuando comenzaron a emitir el quinto canal, fue ella la que dio la noticia en casa. La compraron y la instalaron en su cuarto.

Entonces todos dedicaban sus horas libres a ver la tele. No tenían tiempo para nada más. No sentían necesidad de verse porque no tenían cosas importantes que decirse. Eran felices y no tenían problemas.

Pero todavía les quedaba el problema de hacer la comida, primero, y de recoger la mesa y fregar los platos después. Y no porque no les gustara este trabajo. Todos lo hacían de buen grado. El problema estaba en que durante el tiempo que empleaban[7] en esa actividad, no podían ver la tele y, a veces, se perdían programas muy divertidos.

---

[1] se emitía *broadcast*
[2] ya que *since*
[3] se enteraron de que *they found out that*
[4] se perdió = no pudo ver
[5] el campeonato mundial *world championship*
[6] dejó de *stopped*
[7] empleaban *spent*

444   Fondo literario   *La sexta tele*

Options

Strategies for Reaching All Students

Spanish-Speaking Students
Ask: *Según este cuento, ¿cómo puede la televisión influir en la vida, especialmente la vida en familia? ¿Qué puede o debe hacer una familia para mantener el equilibrio y, a la misma vez, disfrutar de lo que se ofrece en la tele?*

Students Needing Extra Help
Have students make a list of unfamiliar words and phrases before reading the story. Divide the reading into sections.
Discuss the fantasy aspect of the reading. Have students draw their own conclusions about the story. After each episode, have them make a visual to keep them focused.

Enrichment
Have students work in small groups to create and perform skits about the influence of television in their lives. Students may also wish to present scenes from this story. After the skits are presented, ask the following questions: *¿Cuántos televisores hay en tu casa? ¿En qué cuartos están? ¿Cuándo ves la televisión? ¿De qué maneras nos ayuda la televisión? ¿De qué maneras nos hace daño?*

Elevando el volumen de la tele del salón, podían oír algo desde la cocina. Pero no era lo mismo. La televisión se inventó para ser vista, no para ser oída. Para ser oída ya estaba la radio.

Entonces se le ocurrió una brillante idea al padre. Se lo explicó en el salón, donde la madre, el abuelo y el hijo estaban viendo "La digestión con *Jota* Hormiga,"[8] un programa que a todos les gustaba.

—¿Qué tal está hoy el programa? —preguntó el padre.

—¡Qué ocurrencias tiene este *Jota* Hormiga! —exclamó el abuelo.

—Rebeca y yo no hemos podido verlo porque nos tocaba fregar los cacharros —añadió el padre.

---

[8] La digestión con *Jota* Hormiga = Después de la comida (en España se come desde las 2 hasta las 4) se habla de hacer la digestión. Hay programas de televisión desde las 3 hasta las 5 que son ligeros para ayudar a hacer la digestión. *Jota* Hormiga está basado en el típico presentador popular.

La sexta tele Fondo literario 445

Teaching Suggestions
These fragments come from the book *La sexta tele* by Alfredo Gómez Cerdá. An amusing parody, it entertains both young and older people by satirizing TV programs and by the absurd situation that results from being so addicted to television. Tell students to think about the meaning behind the names of people, magazines, and TV programs in the story as they read.

La madre, sin duda sorprendida por las palabras del padre, volvió la cabeza y les clavó su mirada.

—Claro—dijo al fin—. Y mañana Jeremías y yo nos quedaremos sin verlo porque tendremos que fregar los cacharros.

—A no ser que. . .—el padre repitió esa enigmática frase, que volvió a dejar sin terminar.

Todos miraban al padre. Tal vez hasta *Jota* Hormiga le miraba.

—A no ser. . . ¿qué? —preguntó la madre al cabo de un rato.

—A no ser que compremos la sexta tele.

Y la compraron.

El primer síntoma de que algo estaba pasando se produjo dos días después de la llegada de la sexta tele, a la hora de comer. Daban un reportaje sobre el circo. Salieron primero unos trapecistas muy buenos, luego unos payasos[9] y finalmente un domador[10] con varios tigres. En ese instante, oímos en el salón un rugido de tigre. Aquel rugido resonó en el salón de la casa como si el tigre estuviese[11] debajo de la mesa.

Se asustaron mucho. La madre tiró incluso un vaso de agua que iba a coger en esos momentos. Al hermano Jeremías se le abrió la boca de par en par y Rebeca se abrazó a su padre.

El único que no se asustó fue el abuelo Jeremías, porque él, en su juventud, fue domador de fieras y durante algunos años trabajó en un circo.

Al cabo de un rato,[12] un olor[13] extraño comenzó a invadir el salón. Era un olor sencillamente repugnante.

El padre miró con extrañeza la fuente de pescado que estaba en el centro de la mesa.

—¿Dónde has comprado este pescado? —le preguntó el padre al abuelo.

---

[9] los payasos *clowns*
[10] el domador *trainer*
[11] estuviese *were*
[12] al cabo de un rato *after a while*
[13] el olor *smell*

446   Fondo literario   *La sexta tele*

—Hijo, no entiendes nada de olores —respondió el abuelo.

—¡Ah, no! ¡Este pescado está podrido![14]

—¡No huele a pescado! ¡Huele a tigre! —se enfadó un poco el abuelo.

De la pantalla emanaba un olor difícilmente soportable, sobre todo a la hora de comer.

—¡Es verdad! —gritó el hermano Jeremías—. ¡Huele a tigre!

Todo esto le había escrito Rebeca al director de la revista *A ver si te enteras* en sus cuatro cartas anteriores. Entonces decidió escribirle la QUINTA CARTA.

---

[14] podrido *spoiled*

Urbecualquiera, martes 17 de abril

Sr. Director de "A ver si te enteras"

Muy Sr. mío:

Pues bien, después de lo del olor a tigre, que le aseguro salía de la mismísima pantalla del televisor del salón, sucedió otra cosa extraña al día siguiente, poco más o menos a la misma hora, ya que todos estábamos en el salón terminando de comer. Después de las noticias y del reportaje correspondiente, comenzó "La digestión con *Jota* Hormiga."

A mi hermano y a mi madre les tocaba ese día fregar los cacharros, así que, una vez acabado el postre, me senté en el sofá con ánimo de disfrutar del programa hasta la hora del colegio.

Mi abuelo se levantó tras de mí y se dispuso a colocar su silla junto al sofá. En ese preciso instante, Jota Hormiga, con su gesto característico, decía aquello de...

—"Señorasssssss, señoressssss, buenasssss tardesssss."

Mi abuelo, que en ese instante pasaba frente al televisor, se detuvo en seco[15] y, llevándose una mano a la frente, exclamó:

—¡Caramba!—

—¡Pero qué te pasa! —insistió mi padre.

---

[15] se detuvo en seco *he stopped dead*

—¿Es que no le habéis visto? Con esa manía que tiene de arrastrar las eses, se le ha escapado de la boca una salivilla, que me ha caído en la mismísima frente.

El abuelo se enfadó mucho con *Jota Hormiga*. Estaba indignadísimo.

—¡No volveré a ver jamás "La digestión con *Jota Hormiga*"! ¡En la vida!

Pues bien, señor director de "A ver si te enteras," ya conoce usted los dos primeros síntomas de lo que se avecinaba: primero, el olor a tigre; después las salivillas de *Jota Hormiga*. Tal vez ninguno de los dos sucesos le parezca realmente importante y significativo, pero estoy segura de que lo que sucedió después le despejará[16] cualquier duda.

Y lo que sucedió después, ocurrió aquella misma noche.

Mi madre veía la tele en el salón, mi padre en su dormitorio, mi abuelo en su cuarto, mi hermano en el suyo y yo en el mío. Todos estábamos tranquilos y felices, disfrutando de nuestros programas favoritos, hasta que de pronto un grito angustioso resonó en toda la casa.

¡¡¡Aaaaahhhhh!!!

Era mi padre.

Iniciamos todos a la vez una carrera hacia el dormitorio, donde se suponía que estaba mi padre, pero al instante nos detuvimos en seco, pues él ya salía también al pasillo.

---

[16] despejará *will clear up*

Mi padre se acercó al grupo. Estaba pálido, con los ojos ausentes y andaba como si fuese un zombi. Con una de sus manos se tapaba la boca.

Entonces se quitó la mano de la boca y todos pudimos verlo. Su bigote había desaparecido. En su lugar quedaba únicamente una especie de rasguño,[17] en perfecta línea recta, sobre su labio superior.

—¿Quién te lo ha afeitado? —preguntó mi abuelo.

—¡Ha sido Toro Sentado! —dijo mi padre, señalando hacia el interior de su dormitorio.

Entramos todos en el dormitorio y lo primero que nos llamó la atención fue la pantalla de la tele, encendida, en la que un grupo de indios, en pie de guerra,[18] cabalgaba al galope[19] por una pradera, enarbolando[20] arcos y lanzas con ademanes[21] claramente amenazantes.[22]

—¡Ha sido Toro Sentado! —repitió mi padre—. ¡Ha sido él!

Todos creímos a mi padre. No porque nos pareciese verosímil lo que decía, sino porque, clavada en una de las puertas del armario,[23] con restos de su bigote, había una flecha.[24]

—¿Tú crees que se trata de una flecha envenenada?[25] —le preguntó mi hermano a mi abuelo, en voz baja, para que mi padre no se inquietase.

—No lo creo.

—¡Menos mal!

En esto mi hermano gritó—. ¡Mis pies han desaparecido!

[17] el rasguño *scratch*
[18] en pie de guerra *on the war path*
[19] cabalgaba al galope *riding at full gallop*
[20] enarbolando *raising up*
[21] los ademanes *gestures*
[22] amenazantes *threatening*
[23] el armario *closet*
[24] la flecha *arrow*
[25] envenenada *poisonous*

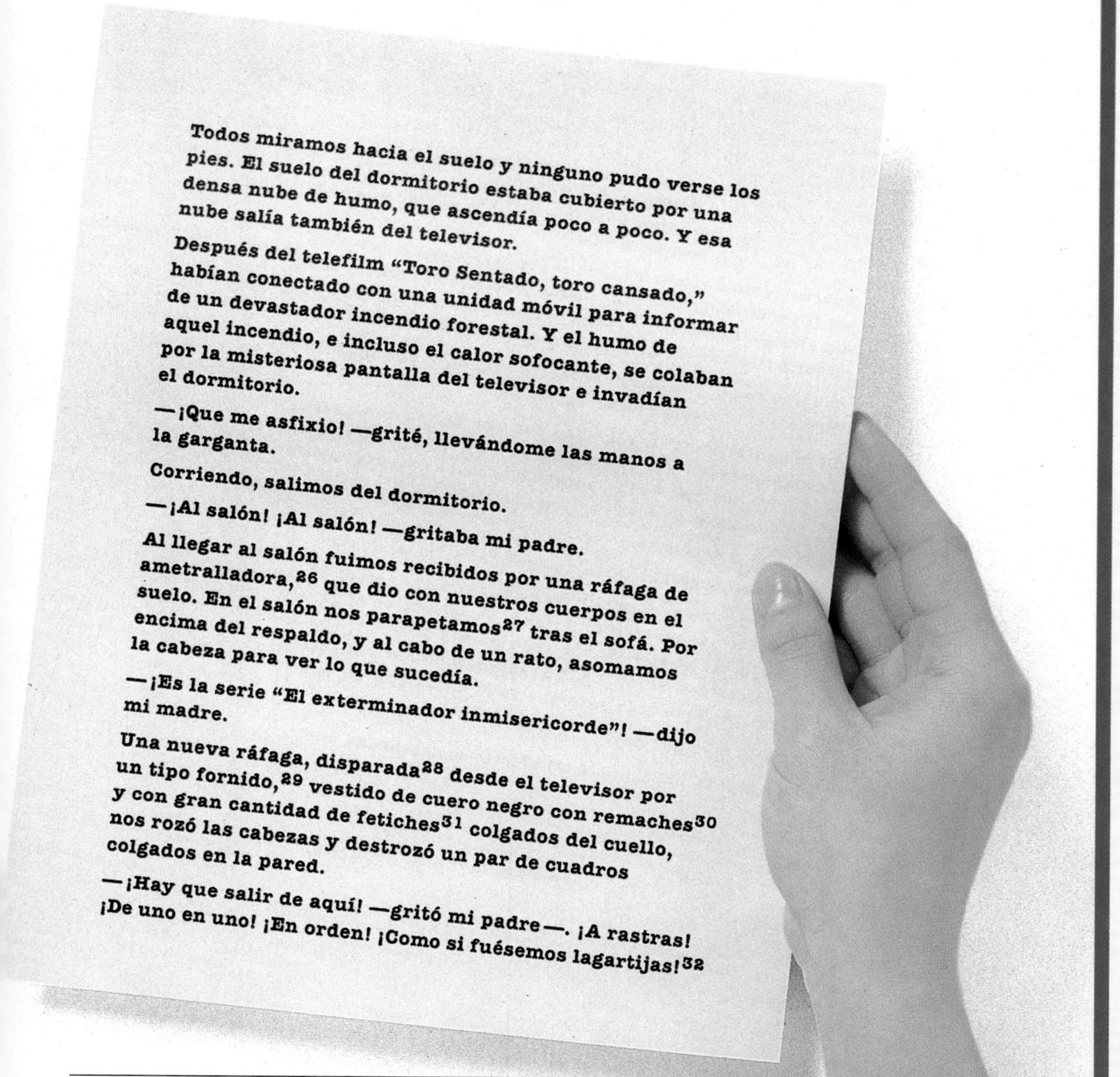

Todos miramos hacia el suelo y ninguno pudo verse los pies. El suelo del dormitorio estaba cubierto por una densa nube de humo, que ascendía poco a poco. Y esa nube salía también del televisor.

Después del telefilm "Toro Sentado, toro cansado," habían conectado con una unidad móvil para informar de un devastador incendio forestal. Y el humo de aquel incendio, e incluso el calor sofocante, se colaban por la misteriosa pantalla del televisor e invadían el dormitorio.

—¡Que me asfixio! —grité, llevándome las manos a la garganta.

Corriendo, salimos del dormitorio.

—¡Al salón! ¡Al salón! —gritaba mi padre.

Al llegar al salón fuimos recibidos por una ráfaga de ametralladora,[26] que dio con nuestros cuerpos en el suelo. En el salón nos parapetamos[27] tras el sofá. Por encima del respaldo, y al cabo de un rato, asomamos la cabeza para ver lo que sucedía.

—¡Es la serie "El exterminador inmisericorde"! —dijo mi madre.

Una nueva ráfaga, disparada[28] desde el televisor por un tipo fornido,[29] vestido de cuero negro con remaches[30] y con gran cantidad de fetiches[31] colgados del cuello, nos rozó las cabezas y destrozó un par de cuadros colgados en la pared.

—¡Hay que salir de aquí! —gritó mi padre—. ¡A rastras! ¡De uno en uno! ¡En orden! ¡Como si fuésemos lagartijas![32]

---

[26] una ráfaga de ametralladora
burst of gunfire from a machine gun
[27] nos parapetamos *hid*
[28] disparada *shot*

[29] fornido *robust*
[30] con remaches *riveted*
[31] los fetiches *fetishes*
[32] las lagartijas *small lizards*

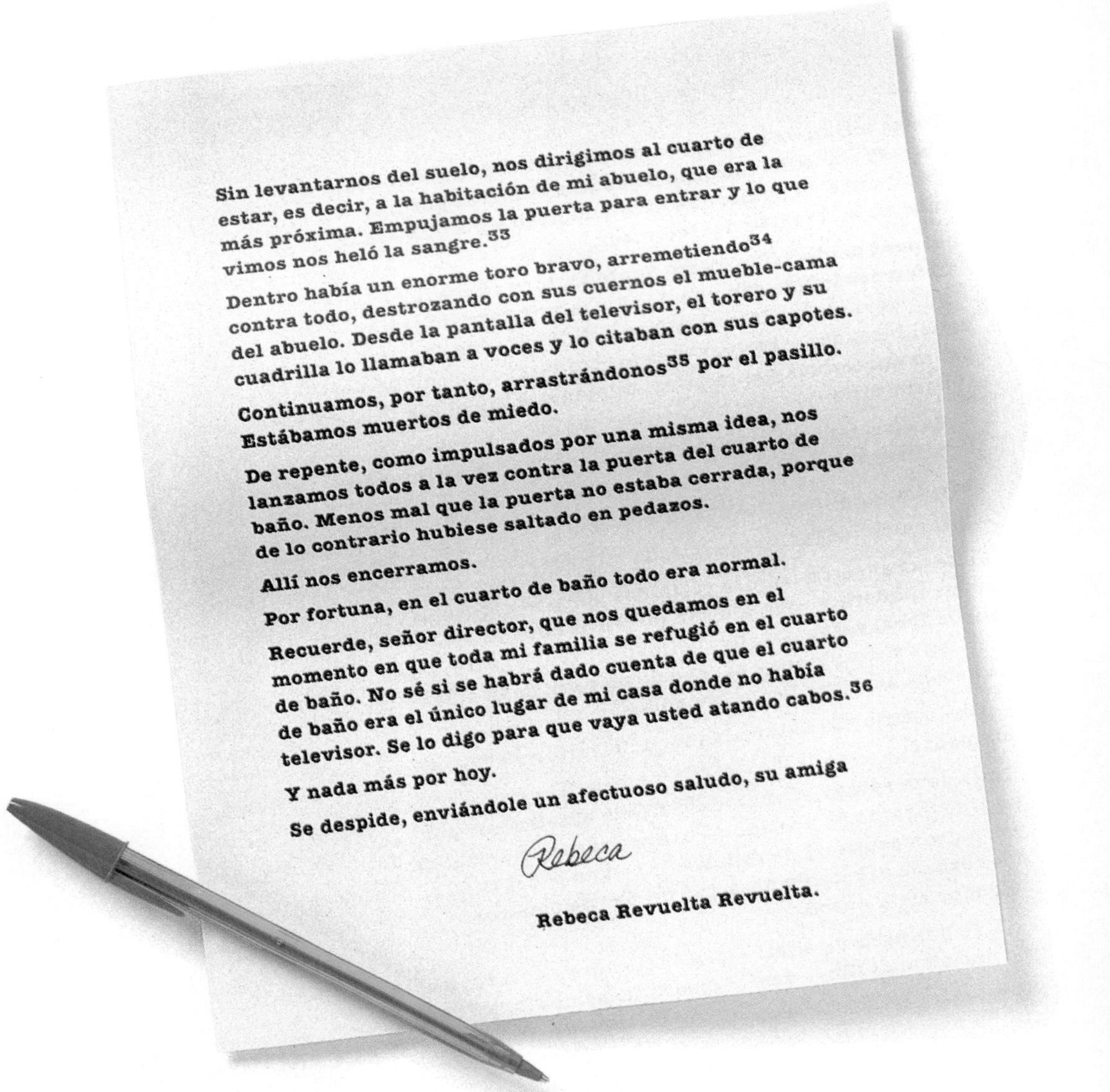

Sin levantarnos del suelo, nos dirigimos al cuarto de estar, es decir, a la habitación de mi abuelo, que era la más próxima. Empujamos la puerta para entrar y lo que vimos nos heló la sangre.[33]

Dentro había un enorme toro bravo, arremetiendo[34] contra todo, destrozando con sus cuernos el mueble-cama del abuelo. Desde la pantalla del televisor, el torero y su cuadrilla lo llamaban a voces y lo citaban con sus capotes.

Continuamos, por tanto, arrastrándonos[35] por el pasillo. Estábamos muertos de miedo.

De repente, como impulsados por una misma idea, nos lanzamos todos a la vez contra la puerta del cuarto de baño. Menos mal que la puerta no estaba cerrada, porque de lo contrario hubiese saltado en pedazos.

Allí nos encerramos.

Por fortuna, en el cuarto de baño todo era normal.

Recuerde, señor director, que nos quedamos en el momento en que toda mi familia se refugió en el cuarto de baño. No sé si se habrá dado cuenta de que el cuarto de baño era el único lugar de mi casa donde no había televisor. Se lo digo para que vaya usted atando cabos.[36]

Y nada más por hoy.

Se despide, enviándole un afectuoso saludo, su amiga

Rebeca

Rebeca Revuelta Revuelta.

---

[33] nos heló la sangre *froze our blood*
[34] arremetiendo = atacando
[35] arrastrándonos *crawling*
[36] atando cabos *putting two and two together*

452   Fondo literario   *La sexta tele*

¿Y cómo termina esta extraña historia? En su sexta y última carta, Rebeca le contó al director de la revista *A ver si te enteras* cómo había terminado todo.

Decidieron que la causa de estos problemas era la sexta tele. Después de unos días difíciles en que todos se quedaron en el cuarto de baño, Jeremías hijo escapó por el ventanuco[37] y se deslizó[38] al suelo usando toallas y pantalones, que, anudados, le hicieron una cuerda. Al llegar al suelo se dirigió al cuarto donde estaban los contadores de luz.[39] Cogió un pico y se lió a golpes con los contadores.[40] Al irse la luz, se acabaron los problemas. Una vez fuera del baño y sin decir más, el padre cogió la sexta tele, la de la cocina, y la devolvió a la tienda.

Después la familia Revuelta podía ver la tele sin problemas, cada uno su tele, en su cuarto, tranquilamente. Rebeca quería que el señor director avisara a todo el mundo a través de su prestigiosa revista de las cosas que podrían pasar al comprar una sexta tele. Sólo a ella le quedaba una duda: Si los problemas surgieron al comprar la sexta tele o al comprar una tele de más.

---

[37] el ventanuco *small window*
[38] se deslizó *he slid down*
[39] los contadores de luz *circuit breakers*

[40] Cogió un pico y se lió a golpes con los contadores. *He took a pickaxe and started to hit the circuit breakers.*

La sexta tele   Fondo literario   453

DESPUÉS DE LEER

1 ¿Qué trata de decirnos el autor en esta obra? ¿Estás de acuerdo con él? ¿Por qué?

2 ¿En qué aspectos crees que nos influye más la televisión? Explica tu respuesta.

Apply

Answers: Después de leer

1 Answers will vary, but may include: *La televisión tiene demasiada influencia en nuestras vidas. No es necesario tener tantos televisores. No debemos ver demasiada televisión.*

2 Answers will vary.

Opinión personal

1. Según este cuento, ¿qué programas de televisión son populares en España? Con un(a) compañero(a), haz una lista de estos programas. Al lado de cada programa indica quién crees que verá este programa. Ejemplo: El asilo ataca—los ancianos.
2. Imagina que en tu casa pasa la misma cosa. ¿Qué programas de televisión pueden invadir tu casa? ¿Qué les puede pasar a Uds.? Escribe un párrafo y después compáralo con el de un(a) compañero(a).

 **Writing Activity
FL-D**

Apply

Teaching Suggestions

You may want to suggest the following strategies to help students with this reading:

- Activating prior knowledge about legends
- Identifying main characters
- Distinguishing essential from non-essential words

Antes de leer

Have students respond to the following either orally or in writing: *Usa lo que sabes de los lugares de los mayas para describir la escena del cuento.*

Answers: Para empezar

Answers will vary.

PARA EMPEZAR

¿Qué leyenda(s) te ha contado o leído alguien de tu familia? ¿De qué se trata(n)?

Quetzal
no muere nunca

Quetzal era un valiente muchacho, hijo del poderoso cacique[1] de una tribu quiché. Era admirado y querido por todos. Esperaban de él grandes hazañas,[2] pues desde el día de su nacimiento habían notado en Quetzal muchas señales de predestinación.[3]

Cuando el joven llegó a la mayoría de edad y pudo participar en todos los asuntos de los guerreros[4] quichés, se reunió la tribu en un gran claro del bosque para celebrar la ocasión. Primero, los músicos tocaron los tambores, después las flautas y más tarde la marimba. Entonces llegó el momento tan esperado cuando se daría a conocer el destino de Quetzal.

En medio de un silencio expectante, el adivino más anciano se levantó de su asiento bajo el árbol de color coral. Lentamente y con dignidad, arrojó a su alrededor con sabia mano los granos coralinos.[5] Los estudió por unos momentos, algo perplejo[6] y lleno de admiración. Al fin anunció claro y firme:

—Tu destino está decidido, Quetzal. No has de morir nunca. Vivirás eternamente a través de generaciones de quichés.

Todas las personas reunidas se quedaron perplejas ante aquella profecía, y la admiración y el entusiasmo que tenían por Quetzal aumentaron.

---

[1] el cacique *indigenous chief*
[2] las hazañas *feats*
[3] la predestinación *predestination or sign of a good future*

[4] los guerreros *warriors*
[5] los granos coralinos *seeds from a coral tree*
[6] perplejo *perplexed, confused*

454   Fondo literario   *Quetzal no muere nunca*

Options

Strategies for Reaching All Students

Spanish-Speaking Students
Ask: *¿Cómo aprenden los niños hoy de nuestras costumbres y leyendas? ¿Quién se las cuenta?*

Students Needing Extra Help
Be sure that students understand the characteristics that make up mythical stories. Explain how animals are often portrayed in myths as wise helpmates to humans. Give further examples.

Enrichment
In pairs, have students write a paragraph about what happens to Chiruma after the death of Quetzal. Ask them to share their paragraphs with the class.

Pero no toda la tribu amaba al muchacho. Había una persona a quien los éxitos de Quetzal le molestaban. Era Chiruma, el hermano del cacique.

Chiruma era casi tan joven como Quetzal y había soñado[7] toda su vida con ser cacique. Pero ahora, después de escuchar la profecía del adivino, ¿cómo podría él realizar su ambición? Era indudable que Quetzal, admirado por todos y considerado casi un dios, sería el jefe de la tribu al morir su padre.

Poco después de la ceremonia en honor de Quetzal, él y los otros jóvenes de su edad participaron en una lucha contra un enemigo del sur. Chiruma aprovechó esta ocasión para no perder de vista a Quetzal. Estaba perplejo al notar que las flechas que rodeaban al joven nunca lo herían.[8] ¿Sería cierta la profecía que el adivino había hecho? Pero no, ¡aquello era imposible! ¿Cómo iba a vivir Quetzal a través de generaciones?

De pronto, Chiruma tuvo una idea.

—Ya sé —pensó. —Ya sé por qué la muerte respeta a Quetzal. Tiene algún amuleto[9] poderoso que lo protege y yo voy a robárselo cuando esté durmiendo.

---

[7] había soñado...con *had dreamed of*
[8] herían *wounded*
[9] el amuleto *amulet, good luck charm*

Esa misma noche cuando Quetzal dormía profundamente sobre su estera,[10] Chiruma se acercó a él con paso silencioso. Miró sobre su pecho. El amuleto no estaba allí. Iba ya a irse cuando vio a la cabeza de la estera donde dormía el joven una pluma de colibrí.[11] Chiruma no dudó ni por un momento de que aquello era lo que buscaba. Con todo el cuidado posible sacó la brillante pluma mientras sonreía de felicidad.

Entonces recordó lo que había dicho el adivino cuando nació Quetzal: que el colibrí era el símbolo de la buena suerte del niño.

Pasó algún tiempo y murió el cacique. Inmediatamente los ancianos[12] eligieron a Quetzal para ser el nuevo jefe.

Chiruma, por supuesto, no dio ninguna seña de su enojo. Estaba seguro de que muy pronto el nuevo cacique sin su amuleto poderoso podría ser vencido.

Cierta tarde, Quetzal, el nuevo cacique, paseaba por el bosque, solitario, armado de su arco y sus flechas. De súbito[13] un colibrí hermoso descendió de un árbol y sin miedo se posó sobre su hombro.

—Escúchame, Quetzal. Soy tu protector y vengo a prevenirte de que la muerte te persigue. Guárdate de cierto hombre.

---

[10] la estera *sleeping mat*
[11] el colibrí *hummingbird*
[12] los ancianos *elders*
[13] de súbito *suddenly*

—¿De cuál hombre he de guardarme, hermoso colibrí? —preguntó el joven.

Pero el pájaro no pronunció ni una palabra más. Después de mirar unos instantes a Quetzal, emprendió el vuelo y desapareció.

El joven, con una seña de incomprensión continuó su camino. De pronto un agudo silbido llegó hasta él y una flecha quedó clavada en su pecho. Cayó sobre la hierba verde y cerró los ojos dispuesto a morir.

Pero los dioses habían predicho[14] su inmortalidad y Quetzal quedó convertido en un hermoso pájaro. Su cuerpo tomó el color verde de la hierba sobre la que había caído y su pecho conservó el color de la sangre. El sol dorado de la tarde puso en su larga cola una gran variedad de colores.

Por muchos siglos se ha considerado al Quetzal como pájaro sagrado que hasta hoy día no se permite cazarlo. Guatemala ha honrado a este pájaro bello, colocando su imagen en el escudo nacional de armas. También la moneda de este país se llama quetzal.

Así como lo predijo el adivino, y como lo quisieron los dioses, el joven y valiente cacique vive y vivirá para siempre en el país de los maya-quiché.

---

[14]habían predicho *had predicted*

DESPUÉS DE LEER

1 Según la lectura, ¿cuáles son algunas de las características de Quetzal?

2 ¿Conoces algún otro símbolo que represente los valores de otro país? Descríbelo.

Apply

Answers: Después de leer

1 Quetzal era valiente, hijo del cacique, admirado y querido por todos. Esperaban de él grandes hazañas.

2 Answers will vary.

Opinión personal

1. Con un(a) compañero(a), discute el valor de las creencias *(beliefs)* en la cultura maya. Compáralas con las creencias en nuestra sociedad de hoy. Escribe un párrafo que comienza: En la cultura maya las creencias . . . .

2. En esta lectura, ¿qué indica que este período fue uno de gran esplendor de la cultura maya?

Writing Activity FL-E

Apply

Teaching Suggestions

You may want to suggest the following strategies to help students with this reading:

- Skimming
- Using context to get meaning
- Making predictions

Antes de leer

Ask: *Imagina que vas a escribir una carta para pedir algo a alguien. ¿Qué vas a pedir?*

Answers: Para empezar

Answers will vary.

Gregorio López y Fuentes, (1897-1966) es un escritor y novelista mexicano, y uno de los mejores intérpretes de la gente común, los campesinos. López y Fuentes formó parte de un grupo de hombres y mujeres interesados en la reconstrucción nacional en el período que siguió a la revolución.

PARA EMPEZAR

¿Qué haces cuando tienes algún problema? ¿Pides ayuda a alguien? ¿A quién(es)?

Una carta a Dios

La casa está en lo alto de una colina. Desde allí se ven el río y, junto al corral,[1] el campo de maíz maduro. El aire está fresco y dulce. Pero de pronto[2] comienza a soplar[3] un fuerte viento y, con la lluvia, comienzan a caer granizos[4] muy grandes.

—¡Qué malo!—exclama mortificado[5] el hombre— ¡Ojalá que pase pronto!

No pasa pronto. Durante una hora cae el granizo sobre la casa, el maíz y todo el valle. El campo está blanco, como cubierto de sal. Los árboles están sin una hoja. El jardín, sin una flor. El maíz, destruido. Y Lencho, con el alma[6] llena de tristeza. La noche es de lamentaciones:[7]

—Todo nuestro trabajo, ¡perdido!

—¡Y nadie para ayudarnos!

—Este año pasaremos hambre…[8]

---

[1] el corral *barnyard*

[2] de pronto *suddenly*

[3] soplar *to blow*

[4] los granizos *hail*

[5] mortificado = triste

[6] el alma *soul*

[7] las lamentaciones *mournings*

[8] pasaremos hambre = tendremos hambre

458 Fondo literario *Una carta a Dios*

Options

Strategies for Reaching All Students

Spanish-Speaking Students

Have students respond in writing to the following: *Estos dos cuentos tienen que ver con la comunicación; uno, a un nivel muy sencillo y directo, y el otro, por medio de la tecnología superavanzada. ¿Cuáles son las ventajas y desventajas de cada tipo de comunicación?*

Students Needing Extra Help

Una carta a Dios: Give some background information regarding the reconstruction period and the Mexican Revolution.
Be sure the students know the meaning of *esperar.*
Discuss irony so that students can have more to say about the ending of the story.

Enrichment

Una carta a Dios: As homework, have students answer the following questions. *¿Qué crees que hizo el jefe de correos después de leer la segunda carta de Lencho? ¿Cómo crees que se sintió? ¿Crees que tuvo razón en mandarle el dinero a Lencho en primer lugar? ¿Por qué sí o no? ¿Qué clase de persona es el jefe de correos? ¿Qué clase de persona es Lencho?*

Pero en el corazón de todos hay una esperanza: la ayuda de Dios. Y, durante la noche, Lencho piensa en esta sola esperanza: Dios, cuyos ojos lo miran todo hasta lo que está en el fondo de las conciencias.[9]

Lencho es un hombre rudo,[10] pero sin embargo sabe escribir. Al día siguiente, después de haberse fortificado[11] en la idea de que hay alguien que nos protege, escribe una carta que él mismo lleva al pueblo para echarla al correo.

No es nada menos que una carta a Dios.

Aquella misma tarde, un empleado de la oficina de correos llega riéndose mucho ante su jefe, y le muestra la carta que está dirigida a Dios. El jefe—gordo y amable—también empieza a reírse, pero muy pronto se pone serio.

—¡La fe!—comenta, dando golpecitos[12] en la mesa con la carta—.

¡Qué estupendo, creer como cree aquel hombre! ¡Esperar con la confianza con que él sabe esperar!

---

[9] las conciencias *conscience*

[10] rudo *having few years of school instruction*

[11] después de haberse fortificado *after having strengthened himself*

[12] los golpecitos *little taps*

Y, para no desilusionar aquel tesoro de fe, el jefe decide contestar la carta. Pero al leerla, descubre que no va a ser fácil. Lencho ha pedido cien pesos para poder mantener a su familia hasta la próxima cosecha. Sin embargo, el jefe sigue con su determinación. Y, aunque no puede reunir[13] todo el dinero, logra enviar un poco más de la mitad.

Al siguiente domingo, Lencho vuelve a la oficina de correos para preguntar si hay una carta para él. El mismo empleado le entrega el sobre mientras que el jefe, con la alegría de un hombre que ha hecho una buena acción, mira desde su oficina.

Lencho no muestra la menor sorpresa al ver los billetes—tan seguro está de recibirlos—pero se enfada al contar el dinero… ¡Dios no puede equivocarse, ni negar[14] lo que Lencho le ha pedido!

[13] reunir *here: to gather*
[14] negar *to deny*

460   Fondo literario   *Una carta a Dios*

Inmediatamente, se acerca a la ventanilla para pedir papel y tinta. En la mesa para el público, escribe otra carta, arrugando la frente[15] a causa del trabajo que le da expresar sus ideas.

Tan pronto como la carta cae al buzón, el jefe de correos corre a abrirla. Dice:

Dios: Del dinero que te pedí sólo llegaron a mis manos setenta pesos. Mándame[15] el resto, pero no me lo mandes por la oficina de correos, porque los empleados son muy ladrones — Lencho.

---

[15] arrugando la frente *wrinkling his forehead*

[16] mándame = envíame

DESPUÉS DE LEER

1 ¿Por qué Lencho no mostró ninguna sorpresa al ver el dinero?

2 Imagínate que eres el jefe de correos. ¿Cómo vas a contestar la segunda carta?

Apply

Answers: Después de leer

1 Él no mostró ninguna sorpresa porque estaba seguro de recibirlo.

2 Answers will vary.

Opinión personal

1. ¿Crees que al final Lencho tiene todavía tanta fe *(faith)* en Dios como antes? Explica tu respuesta.

2. En la segunda carta, ¿crees que el jefe debe decirle la verdad a Lencho o no? ¿Por qué?

 **Writing Activity
FL-F**

461

Apply

Teaching Suggestions

You may want to suggest the following strategies to help students with this reading:

- Activating prior knowledge about science fiction
- Using the title and illustrations as context clues
- Identifying the author's attitude

Antes de leer

Brainstorm with students other science fiction stories, with both positive and negative outlooks for the future. Ask: *¿Crees que este cuento va a tener un final positivo o negativo? ¿Por qué?*

Answers: Para empezar

Answers will vary.

Marco Denevi, escritor argentino, nacido en 1922, es autor de relatos y de obras de teatro. *Apocalipsis* es un cuento de ciencia ficción que trata de la extinción de la raza humana.

PARA EMPEZAR

¿En qué piensas cuando oyes la palabra "futuro"? ¿Cómo crees que será?

La extinción de la raza de los hombres se sitúa aproximadamente a fines del siglo XXXII. La cosa ocurrió así: las máquinas habían alcanzado tal[1] perfección que los hombres ya no necesitaban comer, ni dormir, ni leer, ni hablar, ni escribir, ni siquiera[2] pensar. Les bastaba[3] apretar botones[4] y las máquinas lo hacían todo por ellos. Gradualmente fueron desapareciendo las biblias, los Leonardo da Vinci,[5] las mesas y los sillones, las rosas, los discos con las nueve sinfonías de Beethoven, las tiendas de antigüedades, el vino de Burdeos, las oropéndolas,[6] los tapices flamencos,[7] todo Verdi, las azaleas, el palacio de Versalles. Sólo había máquinas. Después los hombres empezaron a notar que ellos mismos iban desapareciendo[8] gradualmente, y que en cambio[9] las máquinas se multiplicaban. Bastó poco tiempo para que el número de los hombres quedase reducido[10] a la mitad y el de las máquinas aumentase al doble.[11] Las máquinas terminaron por ocupar todo el espacio disponible.[12] Nadie podía moverse sin tropezar con[13] una de ellas. Finalmente los hombres desaparecieron. Como el último se olvidó de desconectar las máquinas, desde entonces seguimos funcionando.

DESPUÉS DE LEER

1 ¿Qué crees que piensa el autor sobre la tecnología?

2 Cambia las dos últimas frases de este cuento para que tenga un final diferente.

[1] tal *such*

[2] ni siquiera *or even*

[3] bastaba *it was sufficient; it was enough*

[4] apretar botones *to press buttons*

[5] los Leonardo da Vinci *here: the works of da Vinci*

[6] las oropéndolas *golden orioles*

[7] los tapices flamencos *Flemish tapestries*

[8] iban desapareciendo = comenzaban a desaparecer

[9] en cambio = al contrario

[10] quedase reducido *was reduced*

[11] aumentase al doble *doubled*

[12] disponible *available*

[13] tropezar con *bumping into*

462   Fondo literario   *Apocalipsis*

Options

Strategies for Reaching All Students

Students Needing Extra Help

Review Roman numerals. Help students to understand the unusual time perspective here: the characters are looking back at an event that in reality is in the future.

Help them understand the cultural images so that they are not prevented from understanding the story.

Relate the reading to *Star Trek, Brave New World,* etc.

Enrichment

As homework, have students answer the following questions: *¿Qué cosas hace mejor una persona que una máquina? ¿Qué cosas hace mejor una máquina? ¿Crees que puede llegar un momento en que las máquinas tomen el lugar de las personas? ¿Por qué sí o no?*

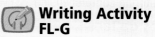

Writing Activity
FL-G

Apply

Teaching Suggestions

You may want to suggest the following strategies to help students with this reading:

- Using context clues
- Identifying main characters
- Monitoring comprehension

Antes de leer

Ask: *¿Qué haces cuando te dicen que hagas algo que tú no quieres hacer en ese momento? Si no lo haces, ¿qué tipo de excusas das?*

Answers: Para empezar

Answers will vary.

LA POBREZA

María Luisa Góngora Pacheco se ha dedicado a conservar las narraciones orales de los pueblos mayas de Yucatán. También ha trabajado para promover la artesanía, la cocina y el teatro popular en la lengua maya.

PARA EMPEZAR

Cuando eras pequeño(a), ¿te gustaban los cuentos? ¿Cuáles eran los que más te gustaban?

El señor Aurelio Zumárraga cuenta que hubo una vez cierta viejita cuyo nombre era Pobreza y que vivía en las afueras de la población. En la puerta de su casa había sembrado[1] una mata de huaya[2] y ésta le daba frutos todo el año. Lo que le molestaba a la viejita es que a aquél que veía el fruto le daban ganas de[3] comérselo y sin pedirle permiso se subía a la mata y se anolaba[4] las huayas.

Un día, cuando la viejita llegó al centro del poblado,[5] vio que un viejito pedía limosna, pedía aunque sea le dieran algo para comer en vez de unas monedas, pero nadie lo tomaba en cuenta.

---

[1]había sembrado *had planted*
[2]una mata de huaya *guava tree*
[3]le daban ganas de = tenía ganas de
[4]se anolaba = se comía
[5]el poblado = el pueblo

464   Fondo literario   *La pobreza*

Options

Strategies for Reaching All Students

Spanish-Speaking Students
Ask: *¿Qué adjetivos usarías para describir a Pobreza?*

Students Needing Extra Help
Before beginning this reading, make a vocabulary list of words and phrases with which students are unfamiliar: *limosna, ¡Que se cumpla lo que pides!,* etc. Make sure they understand the meaning of the woman's wish. This is the key point in the story. Remind students to use the artwork to assist in comprehension.

Enrichment
You may want to ask students to bring in other folk tales or myths from the library about cheating death. Students may also want to invent their own stories. You may wish to use this story as a point of departure for a class discussion about Hispanic attitudes toward death and poverty.

A la viejita le dio pena verlo en ese estado tan lastimoso y se lo llevó a su casa para darle de almorzar. Cuando el hombrecito terminó de comer, le dijo a la viejita:

—Ahora que ya comí lo que me diste, pídeme lo que quieras, que yo puedo concedértelo.[6]

—Buen hombre, —dijo la viejita—, lo único que quiero es que le digas a la huaya que no deje bajar al que se suba a sus ramas,[7] hasta que yo se lo mande.

—¡Que se cumpla lo que pides! —contestó el viejito y se fue satisfecho.

La viejita se quedó muy complacida[8] al ver que se cumplía lo prometido por el viejito.

Pasaron muchos años, y un día llegó con la viejita el señor de la Muerte quien le ordenó:

—Ya es tiempo de que vengas conmigo vieja Pobreza, por eso te vine a buscar.

Ella pensó rápidamente la forma de deshacerse[9] de la Muerte y le dijo: —Me voy contigo, pero primero quiero que bajes unas huayas para que yo anole.

—Bien, en seguida lo haré, —contestó la Muerte.

Se dirigieron al árbol y ya debajo, la viejita le dijo a la Muerte:

—Sube hasta allá en lo más alto, ahí se encuentran las más grandes y hermosas huayas, de ésas quiero.

La Muerte, muy segura de sí misma, trepó[10] a la mata, pero no pudo bajarse.

La Pobreza al ver lo que sucedía, se metió a su casa y se desajenó[11] de todo.

---

[6] concedértelo = dártelo
[7] las ramas *branches*
[8] complacida = contenta

[9] deshacerse *to get rid of*
[10] trepó *climbed*
[11] se desajenó *washed her hands off*

Así pasaron muchos años y la Muerte no llegaba a nadie, aunque se enfermara la persona. Los doctores veían con asombro que la viejita Pobreza no moría aún buscando alguna manera para hacerlo.

Un día, uno de los doctores fue a casa de la viejita y lo primero que vio fue la mata llena de frutos, dándole tantas ganas de comer algunos se subió y no pudo bajar. En las ramas encontró al señor de la Muerte y le preguntó:

—¿Qué haces aquí?, todos te andan buscando, pues ya quieren morirse y tú no llegas para llevártelos.

—Mira, lo que pasó fue que esa mentecata[12] de viejita de la casa, me fregó;[13] pues vine a buscarla y la muy taimada[14] me dijo que se iría conmigo, pero antes le bajara unas cuantas huayas. Al subir no pude bajarme y aquí me tienes, y todo aquel que se sube, se queda y hasta tú te quedarás— contestó la Muerte.

—Entonces, a eso se debe que no mueran las personas, —dijo el doctor.— Lo que debemos hacer es bajar, —y empezó a gritar: ¡vengan aquí, vengan aquí, la Muerte está en mi poder, vengan a verla!

---

[12]mentecata *silly, stupid*
[13]me fregó *ruined my plans*
[14]taimada *sly, crafty*

466   Fondo literario   *La pobreza*

Options

Strategies for Reaching All Students

Spanish-Speaking Students
Tell students to respond to the following in writing: *Si es verdad que siempre habrá pobres, ¿qué podemos hacer para ayudarles y aliviar su pena? ¿Crees que tenemos esta responsabilidad? ¿Por qué?*

Fue tanto lo que gritó y tan fuerte, que la gente de la población[15] se reunió debajo del árbol.

—Bajen, —les decían.

—No podemos, todo el que se sube, se queda aquí, —contestó el doctor.

Entonces la gente acordó[16] cortar el árbol para que bajaran el doctor y la Muerte. Al momento que lo iban a comenzar a cortar, se asomó[17] la viejita Pobreza.

—¿Qué pretenden hacer, si quieren bajar a los que están en la mata de huaya, por qué no me lo dicen?

—Discúlpenos,[18] —dijeron los allí reunidos.

La vieja Pobreza se volvió hacia el árbol y le dijo:

—¡Deja que todos bajen!

Cuando todos bajaron, el señor de la Muerte le dijo:

—Vieja Pobreza, por dejarme bajar del árbol, ahora tengo mucho trabajo y no te puedo llevar, otro día será.

Se fue el señor de la Muerte y la Pobreza se quedó en la tierra. Por eso hasta ahora la tenemos con nosotros.

---

[15] la población = el pueblo
[16] acordó = decidió
[17] se asomó *she appeared*
[18] discúlpenos *excuse us*

DESPUÉS DE LEER

1 ¿Qué tipo de persona es la viejita Pobreza? ¿Cómo lo sabes?
2 ¿Cómo termina la historia? ¿Tiene un final feliz?

La pobreza Fondo literario 467

Apply

Answers: Después de leer

1 Answers will vary, but students may mention: *Era una persona generosa, porque llevó al viejito a su casa para darle de almorzar. Ella es taimada también, porque le engañó a la Muerte para subirse a la mata de huaya.*

2 *Se fue el señor de la Muerte y la Pobreza se quedó en la Tierra.* Answers will vary, but students may mention: *Sí, porque la viejita no se murió.* or: *No, porque todavía tenemos pobreza con nosotros.*

Opinión personal

1. ¿Por qué crees que la vieja Pobreza se metió en su casa cuando vio que la Muerte no podía bajarse del árbol?
2. ¿Qué es más importante para la vieja Pobreza, la mata de huaya o la Muerte? ¿Cómo lo sabes?
3. ¿Cuáles son algunas características de la Muerte? ¿Esperabas un final así? ¿Por qué?

Writing Activity FL-H

Apply

Teaching Suggestions
You may want to suggest the following strategies to help students with this reading:

- Activating prior knowledge about legends.
- Using the title and illustrations as context clues
- Identifying sequence of events
- Reading for detail

Antes de leer
Have students respond either orally or in writing to the following:
¿Qué tipo de historias inexplicables conoces? ¿Por qué son inexplicables? ¿De qué se tratan? (or: *¿Cuáles son sus temas?*)
¿Quiénes son los personajes?

Answers: Para empezar
Answers will vary.

LA HERENCIA

PARA EMPEZAR

¿Crees en los espíritus?
¿Por qué?

Eran las doce de la noche y la campanilla[1] del convento de San Francisco en la capital de México tocaba a maitines.[2] Los frailes[3] fueron saliendo de sus celdas[4] y silenciosamente entraron en la capilla[5] iluminada por la temblorosa luz de las velas que estaban encendidas en el altar, luz que proyectaba extrañas sombras en las paredes, creando un mundo fantasmagórico.[6] El padre guardián, fray Lucas, permaneció junto a la puerta hasta que todos estuvieron en sus sitios. Entonces se colocó en el suyo.

---

[1] la campanilla *small bell*
[2] tocaba a maitines *rang matins (one of the hours of prayer observed by monks)*
[3] los frailes *friars, monks*
[4] las celdas *cells*
[5] la capilla *chapel*
[6] fantasmagórico *ghostly*

468   Fondo literario   *La herencia*

Options

Strategies for Reaching All Students

Spanish-Speaking Students
Students can respond orally to the following questions during class discussions or in writing following the discussions:
¿Cuáles son los elementos fantásticos de este cuento? ¿Y los verdaderos? ¿Por qué crees que leyendas tales como ésta surgen o aparecen en muchas culturas? ¿Has oído contar alguna otra leyenda fantástica? ¿Cómo es?

Students Needing Extra Help
This reading may need a vocabulary list (to review ahead of time) and an organizer to aid in comprehension.
Discuss legends in general.
Keep students focused by reminding them of the progression of the action.

Enrichment
Ask students to share any supernatural tales they may know from childhood.

El rezo sagrado comenzó con la salmodia[7] eterna. De pronto, se abrió la puerta y entró un hermano desconocido con la capucha[8] puntiaguda calada sobre el rostro.[9] Avanzó hasta el centro de la capilla, se arrodilló[10] y allí quedó rezando hasta que todos los frailes, terminadas sus oraciones, volvieron a sus celdas, excepto fray Lucas.

Por fin el desconocido se levantó. Con la cabeza inclinada y las manos cruzadas sobre el pecho y ocultas[11] bajo las anchas mangas, se dirigió lentamente hacia la puerta, donde se encontró con fray Lucas, el padre guardián.

---

[7] la salmodia = música con que se acompañan los salmos

[8] la capucha *hood*

[9] el rostro *face*

[10] se arrodilló *he knelt down*

[11] ocultas *hidden*

—Bienvenido, hermano. ¿De qué provincia vienes? ¿De Jalisco o de Oaxaca? —preguntó fray Lucas.

El desconocido se detuvo y permaneció silencioso.

Fray Lucas repitió la pregunta y al mismo tiempo levantó la vela que sostenía en la mano hacia la cara del nuevo fraile. Pero sus ojos se quedaron abiertos de estupor[12] mientras sentía flaquear[13] sus piernas—¡la temblorosa llama iluminaba débilmente una calavera[14] amarilla!

Tras unos momentos, que a fray Lucas le parecían eternos, se oyó una voz grave que dijo:

—No tengas miedo, fray Lucas. Has de saber que yo fui en este mundo fray Bernardino de Ypes, también guardián como tú, de este convento.

—Ah, sí, hermano—respondió fray Lucas, algo más tranquilo. —He visto tu nombre varias veces en la crónica del convento.

La calavera continuó:

—Cierta vez, siendo yo guardián de este convento, llegó aquí un señor que vivía en San Luis Potosí. Se llamaba don Francisco Balandrano. Había venido a la capital para recoger una gran herencia que le había dejado un pariente rico. Pero, a causa de una rebelión india en la proximidad de su casa, temía llevar consigo esa fortuna.

—Es natural—observó fray Lucas.

—Me pidió que, por favor, le guardara en el convento aquel tesoro hasta que hubiera paz en su región. Entonces él volvería, o mandaría a alguna persona de su confianza, para recoger sus bienes.

—¿Y qué hiciste, hermano? —preguntó fray Lucas, que ya se había olvidado que hablaba con un aparecido.[15]

---

[12] el estupor *amazement*

[13] flaquear to *weaken*

[14] la calavera *skull*

[15] el aparecido *ghost*

470   Fondo literario   *La herencia*

La herencia Fondo literario 471

—Yo le di permiso para dejar aquí su herencia, y aquella misma tarde, antes de salir para su casa, la trajo. Había gran cantidad de talegas[16] llenas de oro y plata. Nadie en el convento, excepto el padre prior, supo esto.

—¿Qué hicieron con el tesoro, fray Bernardino?

—Pues —continuó el aparecido— llevamos las talegas a nuestra pequeña biblioteca. Allí, debajo del gran cuadro de la Virgen, levantamos las losas[17] del suelo, cavamos un agujero[18] y enterramos el tesoro. Pasó el tiempo y al morir el padre y yo, el secreto se fue con nosotros a la tumba.

—Entonces —preguntó fray Lucas— ¿la herencia continúa escondida?

—Así es, pero ha llegado el momento de sacarla a la luz del día, y tú, fray Lucas, vas a ser el encargado de hacerlo.

—Sí, sí, la sacaré, pero ¿qué voy a hacer con ella? ¿La repartiré entre los pobres? Pues bien sabes nuestro voto de pobreza.[19]

—Ten paciencia y te explicaré lo que debes hacer. En la cárcel de México está Juan Balandrano, hijo honrado y bueno de don Francisco. Es el heredero[20] legítimo de la herencia enterrada aquí. Hazme el favor de entregársela.

Fray Lucas estaba perplejo, dudoso. Tenía ganas de enterarse más en esos sucesos misteriosos, pero notando que el aparecido estaba para salir, respondió:

—Sí, fray Bernardino, mañana llevaré a cabo tus deseos.

Una vez dicho esto, el alto esqueleto cruzó de nuevo sus huesudas[21] manos, inclinó la encapuchada calavera y caminando lentamente, cruzó la puerta de la capilla hasta perderse entre las sombras del claustro.[22]

A la mañana siguiente, fray Lucas se apresuró[23] a contar al padre prior todo lo que había sucedido en la capilla.

---

[16] las talegas *sacks*

[17] las losas *slabs*

[18] cavamos un agujero *dug a hole*

[19] el voto de pobreza *vow of poverty*

[20] el heredero *heir*

[21] huesudas *bony*

[22] el claustro *cloister*

[23] se apresuró = corrió

472 Fondo literario *La herencia*

La herencia   Fondo literario   473

—De veras, parece un milagro, pero vamos a la biblioteca para sacar el tesoro.

Dicho y hecho. En el lugar indicado por el aparecido encontraron las talegas.

Inmediatamente fray Lucas, llevando una talega llena de oro, se encaminó a la cárcel para llevar a cabo la promesa hecha a fray Bernardino. Pero ¿cómo sabía éste que don Juan estaba en la cárcel, o que era el heredero legítimo? ¡Era un gran misterio!

Al llegar a su destino, fray Lucas fue llevado a una pequeña sala de espera. A los pocos minutos el sonido de pasos en los silenciosos y oscuros corredores[24] anunció la llegada de un joven acompañado del carcelero.[25] Los dos se sentaron al lado del fraile.

—¿Es usted don Juan Balandrano, hijo de don Francisco?

—Sí, padre, yo soy —respondió el joven, perplejo.

—No tema usted. Soy fray Lucas, del convento franciscano.

—¿Usted fue amigo de mi padre?, ¡que en paz descanse!

—No, no lo conocí, pero tengo para usted una herencia que él dejó en el convento la última vez que estuvo aquí en la capital.

Don Juan no salía de su asombro; las últimas palabras del fraile trajeron a su memoria lo que tantas veces había oído. Su padre regresaba a casa cuando los indios le dieron muerte y así él quedó huérfano[26] a la edad de dos años.

Durante los dieciocho años siguientes sus tutores deshonestos habían malgastado[27] su fortuna; y ahora, agobiado[28] por deudas que no podía pagar, sus acreedores[29] lo habían puesto en prisión. Todo había salido en contra de él, y ahora no podía creer que aquel fraile viniera en su ayuda.

—¡Oh, padre, explíqueme todo, por favor! —sollozó[30] el joven, lleno de gratitud.

---

[24]los corredores *corridors*

[25]el carcelero *warden, jailer*

[26]huérfano *orphan*

[27]habían malgastado *had wasted*

[28]agobiado *burdened*

[29]los acreedores *creditors*

[30]sollozó = lloró

474   Fondo literario   *La herencia*

—Es una larga historia que le contaré más tarde —contestó el padre, poniendo una mano benévola[31] sobre el hombro del joven. —Lo importante en este momento es que usted use esta talega de oro para pagar a sus acreedores. Luego, salga de aquí y vaya al convento para recoger el resto del tesoro. Adiós, Juan.

—Hasta la vista, padre. ¡Que Dios lo bendiga!

En cuanto don Juan se vio libre, se apresuró a visitar el convento de los franciscanos. Cuando supo todo lo sucedido, dio gracias a Dios y a los frailes que habían cumplido el deseo de fray Bernardino. Después de rezar en la capilla, abandonó el convento y se dirigió a San Luis Potosí. Y en los meses que siguieron, repartió entre los pobres de su región una buena parte de aquella herencia que tan maravillosamente había llegado a sus manos.

Desde entonces, el joven visitó el convento cada año en el aniversario de la milagrosa aparición de fray Bernardino, el buen franciscano que regresó a este mundo para cumplir con su obligación de dar la herencia a la familia Balandrano.

---

[31] benévola *benevolent, kind*

Apply

Answers: Después de leer

1 Answers will vary, but students may mention: *Al principio, tuvo miedo. Después de hablar con el aparecido, Fray Lucas estaba muy emocionado y un poco perplejo porque vio un milagro.*

2 Answers will vary, but students may mention: *Don Juan dio parte de su herencia a los pobres para compartir su buena suerte, y para dar gracias a Dios.*

Opinión personal

1. En esta leyenda hay varios hechos inexplicables. ¿Cuáles son? ¿Por qué crees que son inexplicables?
2. ¿Qué tipo de persona es don Juan Balandrano? ¿Cómo lo sabes? ¿Cuándo y por qué visitó después el convento?

 Writing Activity FL-I

DESPUÉS DE LEER

1 ¿Qué crees que sintió fray Lucas después de hablar con el aparecido?

2 ¿Por qué crees que don Juan repartió parte de su herencia entre los pobres?

La herencia Fondo literario 475

Apply

Teaching Suggestions

You may want to suggest the following strategies to help students with this reading:

- Using the title and context clues for meaning
- Predicting the outcome

Antes de leer

Ask: *¿Cuál es el sueño de tu vida? ¿Qué trabajo buscarás para realizar tu sueño?*

Answers: Para empezar

Answers will vary, but students may mention: *La gente cambia de trabajo para obtener una vida mejor. Se muda a otra ciudad u otro país para conseguir un trabajo mejor.*

Ángela McEwan-Alvarado nació en Los Ángeles. Estudió en México donde se casó. Viajó y trabajó en Nicaragua. Es intérprete de español en los tribunales estatales y federales de Los Ángeles, y hace traducciones legales y de literatura.

PARA EMPEZAR

¿Por qué crees que las personas cambian de trabajo? ¿Por qué se mudan a otra ciudad o a otro país?

NARANJAS

Desde que me acuerdo, las cajas de naranjas eran parte de mi vida. Mi papá trabajaba cortando naranjas y mi mamá tenía un empleo en la empacadora, donde esos globos dorados rodaban sobre bandas para ser colocados en cajas de madera. En casa, esas mismas cajas burdas[1] nos servían de cómoda, bancos y hasta lavamanos, sosteniendo una palangana y un cántaro de esmalte descascarado.[2] Una caja con cortina se usaba para guardar las ollas.

Cada caja tenía su etiqueta[3] con dibujos distintos. Esas etiquetas eran casi los únicos adornos que había en la habitación pequeña que nos servía de sala, dormitorio y cocina. Me gustaba trazar con el dedo los diseños coloridos—tantos diseños—me acuerdo que varios eran de flores—azahares,[4] por supuesto—y amapolas y orquídeas, pero también había un gato negro y una calavera.[5] El único inconveniente eran las astillas. De vez en cuando se me metía una en la mano. Pero como dicen, "A caballo regalado, no se le miran los dientes."[6]

Mis papás llegaron de México siguiendo su propio sueño de El Dorado.[7] Pero lo único dorado que encontramos eran las naranjas colgadas entre abanicos de hojas en hectáreas y hectáreas de árboles verdes y perfumados. Ganábamos apenas lo suficiente para ajustar, y cuando yo nací el dinero era más escaso aún, pero lograron seguir comiendo y yo pude ir a la escuela. Iba descalzo, con una camisa remendada y un pantalón recortado de uno viejo de mi papá. El sol había acentuado el color de mi piel y los otros muchachos se reían de mí. Quería dejar de asistir, pero mi mamá me decía —Estudia, hijo, para que consigas un buen empleo, y no tengas que trabajar duro como tus papás—. Por eso, iba todos los días a luchar con el sueño y el aburrimiento mientras la maestra seguía su zumbido monótono.

---

[1] burdas *rough, sturdy*
[2] una palangana y un cántaro de esmalte descascarado *a washbasin and a chipped enamel pitcher*
[3] la etiqueta = papel que describe el producto
[4] los azahares = flores de naranjos
[5] la calavera *skull*
[6] "A caballo regalado, no se le miran los dientes." *"Don't look a gift horse in the mouth."*
[7] El Dorado *a fabulous place where one would find large amounts of gold*

476   Fondo literario   *Naranjas*

Options

Strategies for Reaching All Students

Spanish-Speaking Students

Este cuento presenta la vida difícil de un trabajador migratorio y promueve la educación como vía de escape. ¿Crees que tiene razón la autora? ¿Qué se puede ganar o perder con la educación?

Students Needing Extra Help

Explain the expression "Don't look a gift horse in the mouth."
Define *overoles.*
Discuss migrant workers.
Make a vocabulary list for students to review ahead of time. Help students by summarizing as they read through the text. This gives them a sense of progress.

Enrichment

As a homework assignment, have students write about an incident or object from their childhood that they remember vividly, and identify the senses that are involved in this remembrance. Ask for volunteers to share and discuss their writing with the class. You may also want to conduct a class discussion on the view of work, education, and family presented in this story.

Apply

Teaching Suggestions
Tell students that Our Lady of Zapopan, also known as *La Zapopanita,* is venerated as the source of many miracles in and around the city of Guadalajara.

En los veranos acompañaba a mi papá a trabajar en los naranjales. Eso me parecía más interesante que ir a la escuela. Ganaba quince centavos por cada caja que llenaba. Iba con una enorme bolsa de lona colgada de una banda ancha para tener las manos libres, y subía por una escalerilla angosta y tan alta que podía imaginarme pájaro. Todos usábamos sombreros de paja de ala ancha para protegernos del sol, y llevábamos un pañuelo para limpiar el sudor que salía como rocío[8] salado en la frente. Al cortar las naranjas se llenaba el aire del olor punzante del zumo,[9] porque había que cortarlas justo a la fruta sin dejar tallo.[10] Una vez nos tomaron una foto al lado de las naranjas recogidas. Eso fue un gran evento para mí. Me puse al lado de mi papá, inflándome los pulmones y echando los hombros para atrás, con la esperanza de aparecer tan recio[11] como él, y di una sonrisa tiesa a la cámara. Al regresar del trabajo, mi papa solía sentarme sobre sus hombros, y así caminaba a la casa riéndose y cantando.

Mi mamá era delicada. Llegaba a casa de la empacadora, cansada y pálida, a preparar las tortillas y recalentar los frijoles; y todas las noches, recogiéndose en un abrigo de fe, rezaba el rosario ante un cuadro de la Virgen de Zapopan.

Yo tenía ocho años cuando nació mi hermana Ermenegilda. Pero ella sólo vivió año y medio. Dicen que se enfermó por una leche mala que le dieron cuando le quitaron el pecho. Yo no sé, pero me acuerdo que estuvo enferma un día nada más, y al día siguiente se murió.

Nuestras vidas hubieran seguido de la misma forma de siempre, pero vino un golpe inesperado. El dueño de la compañía vendió parte

---

[8] el rocío = gotas de agua en las plantas en la madrugada
[9] el zumo *zest*

[10] el tallo *stem*
[11] recio = fuerte

478   Fondo literario   *Naranjas*

de los terrenos para un reparto de casas, y por eso pensaba despedir a varios empleados. Todas las familias que habíamos vivido de las naranjas sufríamos, pero no había remedio. Mi mamá rezaba más y se puso más pálida, y mi papá dejó de cantar. Caminaba cabizbajo y no me subía a los hombros.

—Ay, si fuera carpintero podría conseguir trabajo en la construcción de esas casas—decía. Al fin se decidió a ir a Los Ángeles donde tenía un primo, para ver si conseguía un trabajo. Mi mamá sabía coser y tal vez ella podría trabajar en una fábrica. Como no había dinero para comprarle un pasaje en el tren, mi papá decidió meterse a escondidas en el tren de la madrugada. Una vez en Los Ángeles, seguramente conseguiría un empleo bien pagado. Entonces nos mandaría el pasaje para trasladarnos.[12]

La mañana que se fue hubo mucha neblina.[13] Nos dijo que no fuéramos a despedirle al tren para no atraer la atención. Metió un pedazo de pan en la camisa y se puso un gorro. Después de besarnos a mi mamá y a mí, se fue caminando rápidamente y desapareció en la neblina.

Mi mamá y yo nos quedamos sentados juntos en la oscuridad, temblando de frío y de los nervios, y tensos por el esfuerzo de escuchar el primer silbido del tren. Cuando al fin oímos que el tren salía, mi mamá dijo: —Bueno, ya se fue. Que vaya con Dios—.

No pudimos volver a dormir. Por primera vez me alisté[14] temprano para ir a la escuela.

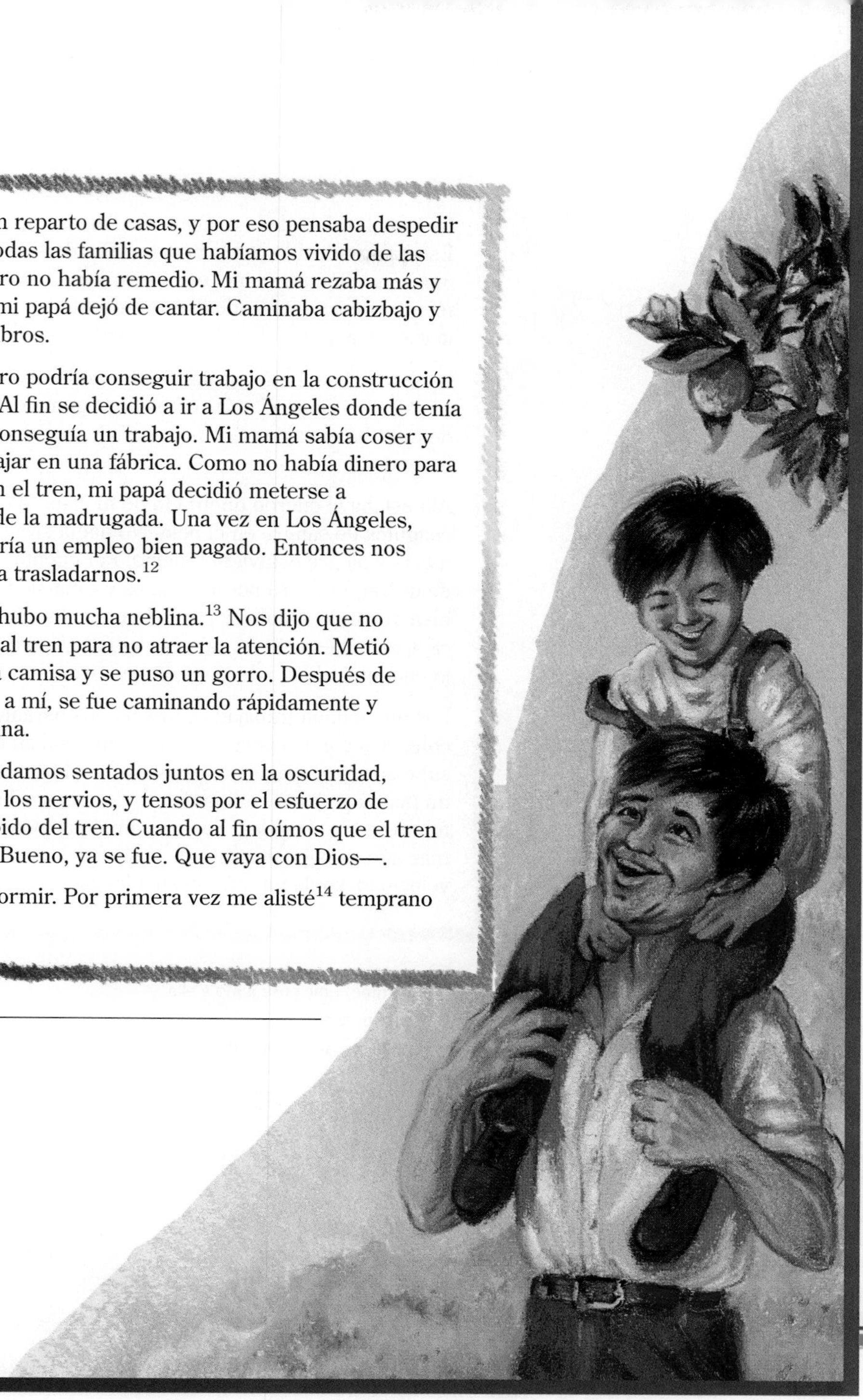

---

[12] trasladarnos = mudarnos
[13] la neblina *fog*
[14] me alisté = me vestí

Como a las diez de la mañana me llamaron para que fuera a mi casa. Estaba agradecido por la oportunidad de salir de la clase, pero tenía una sensación rara en el estómago y me bañaba un sudor helado mientras corría. Cuando llegué jadeante, estaban varias vecinas en la casa y mi mamá lloraba sin cesar.

—Se mató, se mató—gritaba entre sollozos. Me arrimé[15] a ella mientras el cuarto[16] y las caras de la gente daban vueltas alrededor de mí. Ella me agarró como un náufrago[17] a una madera, pero siguió llorando.

Allí estaba el cuerpo quebrado de mi papá. Tenía la cara morada y coágulos de sangre en el pelo. No podía creer que ese hombre tan fuerte y alegre estuviera muerto. Por cuenta había tratado de cruzar de un vagón a otro por los techos y a causa de la neblina no pudo ver bien el paraje. O tal vez por la humedad se deslizó. La cosa es que se cayó poco después de haberse subido. Un vecino que iba al trabajo lo encontró al lado de la vía, ya muerto.

Los que habían trabajado con él en los naranjales hicieron una colecta, y con los pocos centavos que podían dar reunieron lo suficiente para pagarnos el pasaje en el tren. Después del entierro, mi mamá empacó en dos bultos los escasos bienes que teníamos y fuimos a Los Ángeles. Fue un cambio decisivo en nuestras vidas, más aún, porque íbamos solos, sin mi papá. Mientras el tren ganaba velocidad, soplé un adiós final a los naranjos.

---

[15] me arrimé = me puse junto a ella
[16] el cuarto *room*
[17] el náufrago *shipwrecked person*

El primo de mi papá nos ayudó y mi mamá consiguió trabajo cosiendo en una fábrica de overoles.[18] Yo empecé a vender periódicos después de la escuela. Hubiera dejado de ir del todo a la escuela para poder trabajar más horas, pero mi mamá insistió en que terminara la secundaria.

Eso pasó hace muchos años. Los naranjales de mi niñez han desaparecido. En el lugar donde alzaban sus ramas perfumadas hay casas, calles, tiendas y el constante vaivén de la ciudad. Mi mamá se jubiló con una pensión pequeña, y yo trabajo en una oficina del estado. Ya tengo familia y gano lo suficiente para mantenerla. Tenemos muebles en vez de cajas, y mi mamá tiene una mecedora donde sentarse a descansar. Ya ni existen aquellas cajas de madera, y las etiquetas que las adornaban se coleccionan ahora como una novedad.

Pero cuando veo las pirámides de naranjas en el mercado, hay veces que veo esas cajas de antaño y detrás de ellas está mi papá, sudado y sonriendo, estirándome los brazos para subirme a sus hombros.

---

[18] los overoles *overalls*

DESPUÉS DE LEER

1 **¿Cómo crees que la vida de los hijos del autor será diferente a la suya?**

2 **El hijo dice que cuando ve las naranjas en el mercado le parece ver a su papá detrás de ellas. ¿Hay algo que te recuerda a una persona que conoces? Explica.**

Apply

Answers: Después de leer
1–2 Answers will vary.

Opinión personal

1. ¿Cuál fue el sueño de esta familia? Apunta los problemas que tuvieron ellos tratando de realizar su sueño. ¿Cómo llegó a realizarse al final? Compara tus ideas con las de un(a) compañero(a).

2. La foto del niño con su papá nos dice mucho de su trabajo en los naranjales y de su relación con su papá. Busca una foto tuya que evoque un momento especial de tu niñez. (Si no tienes, haz un dibujo de una ocasión que recuerdas con ilusión.) Describe ese momento en una corta composición.

 Writing Activity FL-J

Apply

Standards 1.1; 1.2; 1.3; 3.1; 3.2; 5.2

Teaching Suggestions
You may want to suggest the following strategies to help students with this reading:

- Identifying the writer's attitude
- Identifying supporting details
- Making predictions

This story, by Colombian author Hernando Téllez, explores the personal and political conflict of a small-town barber who is given a chance to kill one of his enemies.

Antes de leer

Ask: *¿Crees que es difícil matar a una persona? ¿Aun si esta persona mata a los tuyos?*

Answers: Para empezar

Answers will vary.

Espuma y nada más

Hernando Téllez (1908-1966), cuentista y ensayista colombiano. Es un maestro del lenguaje. En *Espuma y nada más* usa las palabras para describir física y sicológicamente a los personajes.

PARA EMPEZAR

¿Qué debes hacer cuando tienes que tomar una decisión importante?

No saludó al entrar. Yo estaba repasando sobre una badana[1] la mejor de mis navajas.[2] Y cuando lo reconocí me puse a temblar. Pero él no se dio cuenta. Para disimular continué repasando la hoja. La probé luego sobre la yema del dedo gordo y volví a mirarla contra la luz. En este instante se quitaba el cinturón ribeteado de balas[3] de donde pendía[4] la funda de la pistola. Lo colgó de uno de los clavos del ropero y encima colocó el kepis.[5] Volvió completamente el cuerpo para hablarme y deshaciendo el nudo de la corbata, me dijo: "Hace un calor de todos los demonios. Aféiteme." Y se sentó en la silla. Le calculé cuatro días de barba. Los cuatro días de la última excursión[6] en busca de los nuestros. El rostro aparecía quemado, curtido por el sol. Me puse a preparar minuciosamente el jabón. Corté unas rebanadas de la pasta, dejándolas caer en el recipiente, mezclé un poco de agua tibia y con la brocha empecé a revolver. Pronto subió la espuma. "Los muchachos de la tropa deben tener tanta barba como yo." Seguí batiendo la espuma. "Pero nos fue bien, ¿sabe? Pescamos[7] a los principales. Unos vienen muertos y otros todavía viven. Pero pronto estarán todos muertos." "¿Cuántos cogieron?" pregunté. "Catorce. Tuvimos que internarnos bastante para dar con[8] ellos. Pero ya la están pagando. Y no se salvará ni uno." Se echó para atrás en la silla al verme con la brocha en la mano, rebosante de espuma. Faltaba ponerle la sábana. Ciertamente yo estaba aturdido. Extraje del cajón una sábana y la anudé al cuello de mi cliente. Él no cesaba de hablar. Suponía que yo era uno de los partidarios del orden. "El pueblo habrá escarmentado[9] con lo del otro día," dijo. "Sí," repuse mientras concluía de hacer el nudo sobre la oscura nuca,[10] olorosa a sudor. "¿Estuvo bueno, verdad?" "Muy bueno," contesté mientras regresaba a la brocha. El hombre cerró los ojos con un gesto de fatiga y esperó así la fresca caricia del jabón. Jamás lo había tenido tan cerca de mí.

---

[1] la badana *razor strop*
[2] las navajas *razors*
[3] las balas *bullets*
[4] pendía *was hanging*
[5] el kepis = gorra militar
[6] la excursión *raid*
[7] Pescamos *caught*
[8] dar con *to find*
[9] habrá escarmentado *will have learned by example*
[10] la nuca *nape*

482 Fondo literario *Espuma y nada más*

Options

Strategies for Reaching All Students

Spanish-Speaking Students
El barbero de este cuento tiene un conflicto interno. ¿Cuál es? ¿Crees que es cobarde, valiente u honesto? Explica tu respuesta.

Students Needing Extra Help
Discuss the term *revolution* in general, and this revolution in particular.
Discuss the custom of going to the barbershop for a shave. Explain about the equipment used: the strop, the lather, etc.
Discuss the concept of taking pride in one's work.

Enrichment
As a class, discuss the following questions: *¿Qué es lo que hace que este cuento esté lleno de suspense? ¿Qué piensas del final del cuento? ¿Qué clase de hombre dice el barbero que Torres es? ¿Qué clase de hombre es el barbero, según lo que él mismo dice? ¿Crees que hay momentos cuando está justificado matar a alguien? ¿Cuándo? Si crees que nunca se puede justificar matar a nadie, explica por qué.*

El día en que ordenó que el pueblo desfilara por el patio de la Escuela para ver a los cuatro rebeldes allí colgados, me crucé con él un instante. Pero el espectáculo de los cuerpos mutilados me impedía fijarme[11] en el rostro del hombre que lo dirigía todo y que ahora iba a tomar en mis manos. No era un rostro desagradable, ciertamente. Y la barba, envejeciéndolo un poco, no le caía mal. Se llamaba Torres. El capitán Torres. Un hombre con imaginación, porque ¿a quién se le había ocurrido antes colgar a los rebeldes desnudos y luego ensayar sobre determinados sitios del cuerpo una mutilación a bala? Empecé a extender la primera capa de jabón. Él seguía con los ojos cerrados. "De buena gana me iría a dormir un poco,"[12] dijo, "pero esta tarde hay mucho que hacer." Retiré la brocha y pregunté con aire falsamente desinteresado: "¿Fusilamiento?"[13] "Algo por el estilo, pero más lento," respondió. "¿Todos?" "No. Unos cuantos apenas." Reanudé de nuevo la tarea de enjabonarle la barba. Otra vez me temblaron las manos. El hombre no podía darse cuenta de ello y ésa era mi ventaja. Pero yo hubiera querido que él no viniera. Probablemente muchos de los nuestros lo habrían visto entrar. Y el enemigo en la casa impone condiciones. Yo tendría que afeitar esa barba como cualquiera otra, con cuidado, con esmero,[14] como la de un buen parroquiano,[15] cuidando de que ni por un solo poro fuese a brotar una gota de sangre. Cuidando de que en los pequeños remolinos no se desviara la hoja.

Cuidando de que la piel quedara limpia, templada, pulida, y de que al pasar el dorso de mi mano por ella, sintiera la superficie sin un pelo. Sí. Yo era un revolucionario clandestino, pero era también un barbero de conciencia, orgulloso de la pulcritud[16] en su oficio. Y esa barba de cuatro días se prestaba para una buena faena.[17]

---

[11] me impedía fijarme *prevented me from looking*

[12] "De buena gana me iría a dormir un poco" *"I would really like to get some sleep"*

[13] el fusilamiento *execution by firing squad*

[14] el esmero *painstaking care*

[15] el parroquiano *client, customer*

[16] la pulcritud *ethical conduct*

[17] la faena = el trabajo

Tomé la navaja, levanté en ángulo oblicuo las dos cachas,[18] dejé libre la hoja y empecé la tarea, de una de las patillas[19] hacia abajo. La hoja respondía a la perfección. Hice una pausa para limpiarla, tomé la badana de nuevo y me puse a asentar el acero, porque yo soy un barbero que hace bien sus cosas. El hombre había mantenido los ojos cerrados, los abrió, sacó una de las manos por encima de la sábana, se palpó[20] la zona del rostro que empezaba a quedar libre de jabón, y me dijo: "Venga usted a las seis, esta tarde a la Escuela." "¿Lo mismo del otro día?" le pregunté horrorizado. "Puede que resulte mejor," respondió. "¿Qué piensa usted hacer?" "No sé todavía. Pero nos divertiremos." Otra vez se echó hacia atrás y cerró los ojos. Yo me acerqué con la navaja en alto. "¿Piensa castigarlos a todos?" aventuré[21] tímidamente. "A todos." El jabón se secaba sobre la cara. Debía apresurarme. Ahora de la otra patilla hacia abajo. Le quedaría bien. Muchos no lo reconocerían. Y mejor para él, pensé, mientras trataba de pulir suavemente todo el sector del cuello. Porque allí sí que debía manejar con habilidad la hoja. Los poros podían abrirse,[22] diminutos, y soltar su perla de sangre.[23] Un buen barbero como yo finca su orgullo en[24] que eso no ocurra a ningún cliente. Y éste era un cliente de calidad.

¿A cuántos de los nuestros había ordenado matar? ¿A cuántos de los nuestros había ordenado que los mutilaran?... Mejor no pensarlo. Torres no sabía que yo era su enemigo. No lo sabía él ni lo sabían los demás. Se trataba de un secreto entre muy pocos, precisamente para que yo pudiese informar a los revolucionarios de lo que Torres estaba haciendo en el pueblo y de lo que proyectaba hacer cada vez que emprendía una excursión para cazar revolucionarios. Iba a ser, pues, muy difícil explicar que yo lo tuve entre mis manos y lo dejé ir tranquilamente, vivo y afeitado.

---

[18] las cachas *handgrips*   [22] Los poros podían abrirse *The pores might open*

[19] las patillas *sideburns*   [23] su perla de sangre *a pearl of blood*

[20] se palpó *he touched*   [24] finca su orgullo en *takes pride in*

[21] aventuré *I ventured to say*

484   Fondo literario   *Espuma y nada más*

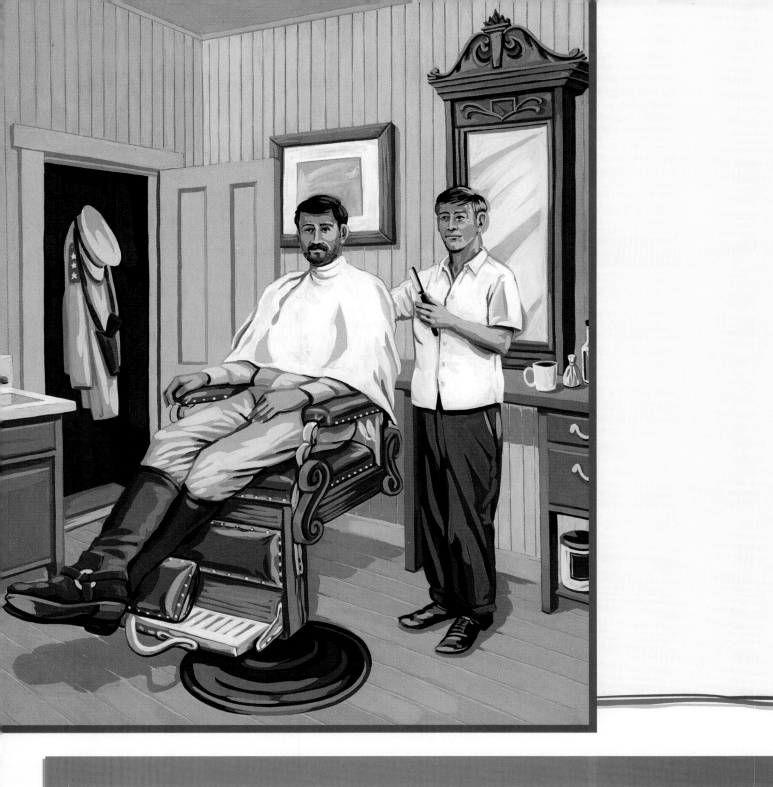

La barba le había desaparecido casi completamente. Parecía más joven, con menos años de los que llevaba a cuestas cuando entró.[25] Yo supongo que eso ocurre siempre con los hombres que entran y salen de las peluquerías. Bajo el golpe de mi navaja[26] Torres rejuvenecía, sí, porque yo soy un buen barbero, el mejor de este pueblo, lo digo sin vanidad. Un poco más de jabón, aquí, bajo la barbilla, sobre la manzana,[27] sobre esta gran vena. ¡Qué calor! Torres debe estar sudando como yo. Pero él no tiene miedo. Es un hombre sereno que ni siquiera piensa en lo que ha de hacer esta tarde con los prisioneros. En cambio yo, con esta navaja entre las manos, puliendo y puliendo esta piel, evitando que brote sangre de estos poros, cuidando todo golpe, no puedo pensar serenamente. Maldita la hora en que vino, porque yo soy un revolucionario pero no un asesino. Y tan fácil como resultaría matarlo. Y lo merece.[28] ¿Lo merece? No, ¡qué diablos! Nadie merece que los demás hagan el sacrificio de convertirse en asesinos. ¿Qué se gana con ello? Pues nada. Vienen otros y otros y los primeros matan a los segundos y éstos a los terceros y siguen y siguen hasta que todo es un mar de sangre. Yo podría cortar este cuello, así, ¡zas!, ¡zas! No le daría tiempo de quejarse y como tiene los ojos cerrados no vería ni el brillo de la navaja ni el brillo de mis ojos. Pero estoy temblando como un verdadero asesino. De ese cuello brotaría un chorro de sangre sobre la sábana, sobre la silla, sobre mis manos, sobre el suelo. Tendría que cerrar la puerta.

Y la sangre seguiría corriendo por el piso, tibia, imborrable, incontenible, hasta la calle, como un pequeño arroyo escarlata.[29] Estoy seguro de que un golpe fuerte, una honda incisión, le evitaría todo dolor. No sufriría. ¿Y qué hacer con el cuerpo? ¿Dónde ocultarlo? Yo tendría que huir, dejar estas cosas, refugiarme lejos, bien lejos.

---

[25] con menos años de los que llevaba a cuestas cuando entró *younger than he seemed when he entered*

[26] Bajo el golpe de mi navaja *At the stroke of the razor*

[27] la manzana *Adam's apple*

[28] Y lo merece. *And he deserves it.*

[29] como un pequeño arroyo escarlata *like a small crimson stream*

486   Fondo literario   *Espuma y nada más*

Pero me perseguirían hasta dar conmigo. "El asesino del Capitán Torres. Lo degolló[30] mientras le afeitaba la barba. Una cobardía."[31] Y por otro lado: "El vengador[32] de los nuestros. Un nombre para recordar (aquí mi nombre). Era el barbero del pueblo. Nadie sabía que él defendía nuestra causa..." ¿Y qué? ¿Asesino o héroe? Del filo de esta navaja depende mi destino. Puedo inclinar más la mano, apoyar un poco más la hoja, y hundirla. La piel cederá[33] como la seda, como el caucho, como la badana. No hay nada más tierno que la piel del hombre, y la sangre siempre está ahí, lista a brotar. Una navaja como ésta no traiciona. Es la mejor de mis navajas. Pero yo no quiero ser un asesino, no señor. Usted vino para que yo lo afeitara. Y yo cumplo honradamente con mi trabajo. No quiero mancharme de sangre. De espuma y nada más. Usted es un verdugo[34] y yo no soy más que un barbero. Y cada cual en su puesto.[35] Eso es. Cada cual en su puesto.

La barba había quedado limpia, pulida y templada. El hombre se incorporó para mirarse en el espejo. Se pasó las manos por la piel y la sintió fresca y nuevecita.

"Gracias," dijo. Se dirigió al ropero en busca del cinturón, de la pistola y del kepis. Yo debía estar muy pálido y sentía la camisa empapada.[36] Torres concluyó de ajustar la hebilla,[37] rectificó la posición de la pistola en la funda y luego de alisarse maquinalmente los cabellos, se puso el kepis. Del bolsillo del pantalón extrajo[38] unas monedas para pagarme el importe del servicio. Y empezó a caminar hacia la puerta. En el umbral[39] se detuvo un segundo y volviéndose me dijo:

"Me habían dicho que usted me mataría. Vine para comprobarlo. Pero matar no es fácil. Yo sé por qué se lo digo." Y siguió calle abajo.

---

[30] degolló *decapitated*	[35] Y cada cual en su puesto. *And to each his own.*
[31] la cobardía *cowardly deed*	[36] empapada *soaked*
[32] El vengador *avenger*	[37] la hebilla *buckle*
[33] cederá *will give in*	[38] extrajo *took out*
[34] el verdugo *executioner*	[39] el umbral *threshold*

DESPUÉS DE LEER

1 ¿Cuál es el secreto del barbero? ¿Por qué no quiere que nadie lo sepa?

2 ¿Por qué crees que el barbero no mató al capitán? ¿Cómo hubieras reaccionado *(would have reacted)* tú?

Espuma y nada más   Fondo literario   487

Apply

Answers: Después de leer

1 El secreto es que el barbero es un revolucionario. Él no quiere que nadie sepa su secreto para poder informar a los otros revolucionarios de lo que están haciendo sus enemigos.

2 Answers will vary.

Opinión personal

1. Escribe un párrafo en el cual el barbero tiene que defenderse ante sus amigos. Escríbelo en la primera persona.
2. Escribe otro párrafo, también en la primera persona, en el cual exploras las reacciones del capitán cuando está en la peluquería.

Writing Activity FL-K

Apply

Teaching Suggestions

You may want to suggest the following strategies to help students with this reading:

- Using the title and illustrations to predict
- Reading aloud to recognize rhythm
- Using context to get meaning

Refer students to the maps on pp. XVIII–XIX to show the African presence in Latin America.

If available, bring in a recording of Guillén reading his own poetry.

Antes de leer

Ask : *¿Por qué piensas que el autor escribió la historia de su familia en un poema y no en un cuento?*

Answers: Para empezar

Answers will vary.

Nicolás Guillén (1902 - 89) es uno de los poetas afrocubanos más conocidos. Muchas de sus obras tratan del folklore africano y de las tradiciones de los cubanos. Guillén ha escrito también poesía de protesta social, y ha creado una nueva forma poética, el son, basada en un baile popular cubano.

PARA EMPEZAR

Mira el título y las ilustraciones. ¿De qué crees que se va a hablar en este poema?

---

[1] las sombras *shadows*
[2] escoltan *escort*
[3] la lanza *spear*
[4] el tambor *drum*
[5] la gorguera *an armor piece for the neck and throat*
[6] la armadura *armor*
[7] los gongos *gongs, metal musical instruments*
[8] aguaprieta de caimanes *murky, thick waters with alligators*
[9] los cocos *coconut palms*
[10] el galeón *galleon (large ship with three or four decks, used especially in the 1500s.)*
[11] engañadas de abalorios *deceived by glass beads*

488   Fondo literario   *Balada de los dos abuelos*

Balada de los dos abuelos

Sombras[1] que sólo yo veo,
me escoltan[2] mis dos abuelos.

Lanza[3] con punta de hueso,
tambor[4] de cuero y madera:
mi abuelo negro.
Gorguera[5] en el cuello ancho,
gris armadura[6] guerrera:
mi abuelo blanco.

África de selvas húmedas
y de gordos gongos[7] sordos.
—¡Me muero!
(Dice mi abuelo negro.)
Aguaprieta de caimanes[8]
verdes mañanas de cocos[9]…
—¡Me canso!
(Dice mi abuelo blanco.)
Oh velas de amargo viento,
galeón[10] ardiendo en oro…
—¡Me muero!
(Dice mi abuelo negro.)
¡Oh costas de cuello virgen
engañadas de abalorios[11]…
—¡Me canso!
(Dice mi abuelo blanco.)

Options

Strategies for Reaching All Students

Spanish-Speaking Students
Ask: *¿Qué o quién une a las dos razas en este poema? ¿Por qué tiene este poder de unirlas? ¿Ves esta unión reflejada en tu comunidad? ¿Qué puedes hacer para fomentarla y apoyarla?*

Students Needing Extra Help
Define *galleons.*
This reading lends itself to artwork.
Discuss the impact of the slave trade on ethnicity in Latin America.
Be sure that students understand the image of death making all things equal.

Enrichment
Discuss the various ways Guillén contrasts and then joins his grandfathers *("Yo los junto.")* and why he wants to do this. In addition, bring other Guillén poems to class, and have the entire class or individuals read them aloud to appreciate the power of their rhythm and repetition.

¡Oh puro sol repujado,[12]
preso en al aro[13] del trópico;
oh luna redonda y limpia
sobre el sueño de los monos!

¡Qué de barcos, qué de barcos![14]
¡Qué de negros, qué de negros!
¡Qué largo fulgor de cañas![15]
¡Qué látigo[16] el del negrero![17]
Piedra de llanto[18] y de sangre,
venas y ojos entreabiertos,[19]
y madrugadas vacías,
y atardeceres de ingenio,[20]
y una gran voz, fuerte voz
despedazando[21] el silencio.
¡Qué de barcos, qué de barcos,
qué de negros!

Sombras que sólo yo veo,
me escoltan mis dos abuelos.

Don[22] Federico me grita,
y Taita[23] Facundo calla:
los dos en la noche sueñan,
y andan, andan.
Yo los junto.

¹²repujado *embossed*
¹³preso en el aro *caught in the arc*
¹⁴¡Qué de barcos, qué de barcos! *How many ships,
  how many ships!*
¹⁵el fulgor de cañas *splendor of sugar cane*
¹⁶el látigo *whip*
¹⁷el negrero *slave trader*
¹⁸el llanto *lamentation*
¹⁹entreabiertos *half-open*
²⁰el ingenio *sugar mill*
²¹despedazando *breaking*
²²Don *title of respect used before
  a male person's first name*
²³Taita *name used respectfully
  for an elderly black man*

Balada de los dos abuelos   Fondo literario   489

Apply

Answers: Después de leer

1 Answers will vary, but may include: *Describe a sus abuelos como: el abuelo negro que tiene una lanza y el abuelo blanco que tiene una armadura gris. El abuelo negro es de África, y el abuelo blanco es de España.*

2 Answers will vary.

3 *Son grupos africanos, europeos e indígenas. / En la música, la poesía, la comida, etc.*

Opinión personal

1. Mira la estrofa *(stanza)* que comienza "Lanza con punta de hueso." Para ver la técnica poética que usa Guillén para unir los mundos de los dos abuelos, busca las palabras en las cuales los vocales finales riman en: e-o, e-a, a-o.
2. ¿Cuál es el efecto de la repetición de la frase "¡Qué de barcos, qué de negros!"?
3. Con un(a) compañero(a), busca unas imágenes visuales. Por ejemplo: "Oh puro sol repujado."

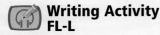

**Writing Activity
FL-L**

Capítulo 11   ¿Cómo se mezclan culturas diferentes?

—¡Federico!
¡Facundo! Los dos se abrazan.
Los dos suspiran. Los dos
las fuertes cabezas alzan;[24]
los dos del mismo tamaño,
bajo las estrellas altas;
los dos del mismo tamaño,
ansia[25] negra y ansia blanca;
los dos del mismo tamaño,
gritan, sueñan, lloran, cantan.
Sueñan, lloran, cantan.
Lloran, cantan.
¡Cantan!

DESPUÉS DE LEER

1 ¿Cómo describe el autor a los dos abuelos? ¿De dónde crees que viene cada uno?
2 El autor llama a los dos abuelos "sombras que sólo yo veo." ¿Qué crees que quiere decir?
3 ¿Qué grupos étnicos viven en Cuba? ¿Dónde se ve su influencia?

---

[24]alzan *lift up*
[25]el ansia *yearning*

490   Fondo literario   *Balada de los dos abuelos*

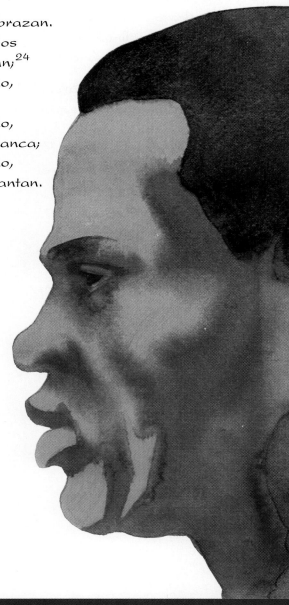

490   **Standards** 1.1; 1.2; 1.3; 2.2; 3.1; 3.2; 5.2

Balada de los dos abuelos   Fondo literario   491

Apply

Teaching Suggestions

You may want to suggest the following strategies to help students with this reading:

- Activating prior knowledge to structure understanding
- Identifying main characters and their feelings
- Monitoring understanding

After student have read the story, have them compare it with *Naranjas* from Chap. 9, which also deals with the experiences of migrant workers.

Answers: Para empezar
Answers will vary.

Tomás Rivera (1935 - 1984) es uno de los principales escritores chicanos. Nació en Crystal City, Texas. Cursó estudios universitarios y recibió el doctorado en Literatura Española. En sus obras, Rivera quería retratar la vida chicana, sobre todo las experiencias de los obreros migratorios, como las que él había vivido en su juventud. Incluso escribe su narrativa como hablan los chicanos del cuento.

PARA EMPEZAR

Imagínate que te discriminan *(discriminated against)* por no hablar el idioma o por otra razón. ¿Cómo te sentirías?

Las salamandras

Lo que más recuerdo de aquella noche es lo oscuro de la noche, el lodo[1] y lo resbaloso[2] de las salamandras. Pero tengo que empezar desde el principio para que puedan comprender todo esto que sentí y también de que, al sentirlo, comprendí algo que traigo todavía conmigo. Y no lo traigo como recuerdo solamente, sino también como algo que siento aún.

Todo empezó porque había estado lloviendo por tres semanas y no teníamos trabajo. Se levantó el campamento, digo campamento porque eso parecíamos. Con ese ranchero[3] de Minesora[4] habíamos estado esperando ya por tres semanas que se parara el agua, y nada. Luego vino y nos dijo que mejor nos fuéramos de sus gallineros[5] porque ya se le había echado a perder[6] el betabel.[7] Luego comprendimos yo y mi 'apá[8] que lo que tenía era miedo de nosotros, de que le fuéramos a robar algo o de que alguien se le enfermara y entonces tendría él que hacerse el responsable. Le dijimos que no teníamos dinero, ni qué comer, y ni cómo regresarnos a Texas; apenas tendríamos con qué comprar gasolina para llegarle a Oklahoma. Y él nomás nos dijo que lo sentía pero quería que nos fuéramos, y nos fuimos. Ya para salir se le ablandó el corazón[9] y nos dio dos carpas[10] llenas de telarañas que tenía en la bodega y una lámpara y kerosín. También le dijo a 'apá que, si nos íbamos rumbo a Crystal Lake en Iowa, a lo mejor encontrábamos trabajo en la ranchería que estaba por allí, y que a lo mejor no se les había echado a perder el betabel. Y nos fuimos.

---

[1] el lodo *mud*
[2] resbaloso *slipperiness*
[3] el ranchero *farmer* (rancho-*farm*)
[4] Minesora *Minnesota*
[5] los gallineros *chicken coops*

[6] echado a perder *was ruined*
[7] el betabel *beet crop*
[8] 'apá = papá
[9] se le ablandó el corazón *he was moved*
[10] las carpas *tents*

492   Fondo literario   *Las salamandras*

Options

Strategies for Reaching All Students

Spanish-Speaking Students
¿Cómo se relaciona este cuento con el tema del capítulo? ¿Qué valor tiene saber otro idioma para familias como ésta o para cualquier familia?

Students Needing Extra Help
Be sure students understand that the story is told from a specific point of view. Discuss why the narrator wanted to kill all the salamanders rather than just go back inside the car.

Enrichment
Bring books and articles to class concerning the conditions under which migrant workers live and work in the U.S. Have students use them to research migrant conditions and resources throughout the U.S., as well as in their particular region or community. Call on individuals to present their information to the class.

En los ojos de 'apá y 'amá[11] se veía algo original y puro que nunca les había notado. Era como cariño triste. Casi ni hablábamos al ir corriendo los caminos de grava.[12] La lluvia hablaba por nosotros. Ya al faltar algunas cuantas millas de llegar a Crystal Lake, nos entró el remordimiento.[13] La lluvia que seguía cayendo nos continuaba avisando que seguramente no podríamos hallar trabajo, y así fue. En cada rancho que llegamos, nomás nos movían la cabeza desde adentro de la casa, ni nos abrían la puerta para decirnos que no. Entonces me sentía que no era parte ni de 'apá ni de 'amá, y lo único que sentía que existía era el siguiente rancho.

El primer día que estuvimos en el pueblito de Crystal Lake nos fue mal. En un charco se le mojó el alambrado al carro y papá le gastó la batería al carro. Por fin un garaje nos hizo el favor de cargarla. Pedimos trabajo en varias partes del pueblito pero luego nos echó la chota.[14] Papá le explicó que sólo andábamos buscando trabajo pero él nos dijo que no quería húngaros[15] en el pueblo y que nos saliéramos. El dinero ya casi se nos había acabado, y nos fuimos. Nos fuimos al oscurecer y paramos el carro a unas tres millas del pueblo, y allí vimos el anochecer.

---

[11] 'amá = mamá
[12] la grava *gravel*
[13] el remordimiento *hopelessness*
[14] la chota = la policía
[15] húngaros *gypsies*

La lluvia se venía de vez en cuando. Sentados todos en el carro a la orilla del camino, hablábamos un poco. Estábamos cansados. Estábamos solos. En los ojos de 'apá y 'amá veía algo original. Ese día no habíamos comido casi nada para dejar dinero para el siguiente día. Ya 'apá se veía más triste, agüitado.[16] Creía que no íbamos a encontrar trabajo. Y nos quedamos dormidos sentados en el carro esperando el siguiente día. Casi ni pasaron carros por ese camino de grava durante la noche.

En la madrugada desperté y todos estaban dormidos, y podía verles los cuerpos y las caras a mi 'apá, a mi 'amá y a mis hermanos, y no hacían ruido. Eran caras y cuerpos de cera.[17] Me recordaron a la cara de 'buelito[18] el día que lo sepultamos.[19] Pero no me entró miedo como cuando lo encontré muerto a él en la troca.[20] Yo creo porque sabía que estaban vivos. Y por fin amaneció completamente.

Ese día buscamos trabajo todo el día, y nada. Dormimos en la orilla del camino y volví a despertar en la madrugada y volví a ver a mi gente dormida. Y esa madrugada, la tercera, me dieron ganas de dejarlos a todos porque ya no me sentía que era de ellos.

A mediodía paró de llover y nos entró ánimo. Dos horas más tarde encontramos a un ranchero que tenía betabel y a quien, según creía él, no se le había echado a perder la cosecha. Pero no tenía casas ni nada.

---

[16]agüitado *depressed*
[17]la cera *wax*
[18]'buelito = abuelo
[19]lo sepultamos *we buried him*
[20]la troca *pick-up truck*

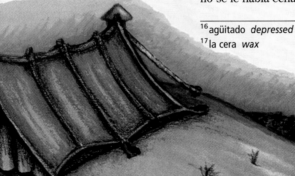

494   Fondo literario   *Las salamandras*

Nos enseñó los acres de betabel que tenía y todo estaba por debajo del agua, todo enlagunado.[21] Nos dijo que, si nos esperábamos hasta que se bajara el agua para ver si no estaba echado a perder, y si estaba bien el betabel, nos pagaría bonos por cada acre que le preparáramos. Pero no tenía casas ni nada. Nosotros le dijimos que teníamos unas carpas que, si nos dejaba, podríamos sentarlas en su yarda. Pero no quiso. Nos tenía miedo. Nosotros lo que queríamos era estar cerca del agua de beber que era lo necesario, y también ya estábamos cansados de dormir sentados, todos entullidos,[22] y claro que queríamos estar debajo de la luz que tenía en la yarda. Pero no quiso, y nos dijo que, si queríamos trabajar allí, que pusiéramos las carpas al pie de la labor[23] de betabel y que esperáramos allí hasta que se bajara el agua. Y pusimos las carpas al pie de la labor de betabel, y nos pusimos a esperar.

---

[21] enlagunado *flooded*   [23] la labor *plowed field*
[22] entullidos *paralyzed*

Al oscurecer prendimos la lámpara de kerosín en una de las carpas y luego decidimos dormir todos en una sola carpa. Recuerdo que todos nos sentíamos a gusto al poder estirar las piernas,[24] y el dormirnos fue fácil. Luego lo primero que recuerdo de esa noche y lo que me despertó fue el sentir lo que yo creía que era la mano de uno de mis hermanos, y mis propios gritos. Me quité la mano de encima y luego vi que lo que tenía en la mano yo era una salamandra. Estábamos cubiertos de salamandras que habían salido de lo húmedo de las labores, y seguimos gritando y quitándonos las salamandras del cuerpo. Con la ayuda de la luz de kerosín, empezamos a matar las salamandras. De primero nos daba asco[25] porque al aplastarlas[26] les salía como leche del cuerpo, y el piso de la carpa se empezó a ver negro y blanco. Se habían metido en todo, dentro de los zapatos, en las colchas… Al ver fuera de la carpa con la ayuda de la lámpara, se veía todo negro el suelo. Yo realmente sólo las veía como bultitos[27] negros que al aplastarlos les salía leche.

---

[24] estirar las piernas *to stretch our legs*   [26] al aplastarlas *upon crushing them*
[25] nos daba asco *we were disgusted*   [27] los bultitos *little bundles*

Luego parecía que nos estaban invadiendo la carpa, como que querían reclamar el pie de la labor. No sé por qué matamos tantas salamandras esa noche. Lo fácil hubiera sido subirnos al carro. Ahora que recuerdo, creo que sentíamos nosotros también el deseo de recobrar[28] el pie de la labor, no sé. Sí recuerdo que hasta empezamos a buscar más salamandras, para matarlas. Queríamos encontrar más para matar más. Y luego recuerdo que me gustaba aluzar[29] con la lámpara y matar despacio a cada una. Sería que les tenía coraje[30] por el susto. Sí, me empecé a sentir como que volvía a ser parte de mi 'apá y de mi 'amá y de mis hermanos.

Lo que más recuerdo de aquella noche fue lo oscuro de la noche, el zoquete,[31] lo resbaloso de las salamandras y lo duro que a veces se ponían antes de que las aplastara. Lo que traigo conmigo todavía es lo que vi y sentí al matar la última. Y yo creo que por eso recuerdo esa noche de las salamandras. Pesqué a una y la examiné bien con la lámpara, luego le estuve viendo los ojos antes de matarla. Lo que vi y sentí es algo que traigo todavía conmigo, algo puro — la muerte original.

---

[28]recobrar *to reclaim*
[29]aluzar *to shine the light on them*
[30]tenía coraje *I was angry at them*
[31]el zoquete *mud*

DESPUÉS DE LEER

1 El narrador piensa que los rancheros tenían miedo de él y su familia. ¿Estás de acuerdo? ¿Por qué?

2 ¿Por qué crees que el autor y su familia querían matar a las salamandras?

Apply

Answers: Después de leer
1–2 Answers will vary.

Opinión personal
1. Busca en el cuento las dos veces que el narrador menciona que no se siente parte de su familia. ¿Cuándo volvió a sentirse parte de ella otra vez?
2. Escribe una composición en la cual describes la vida migratoria de estos trabajadores. ¿Cómo les trata la sociedad?

 **Writing Activity
FL-M**

Las salamandras Fondo literario 497

Verbos

Regular Verbs

estudiar

PRESENT	estudio		PRESENT PERFECT	he estudiado
PRESENT SUBJUNCTIVE	estudie		PRESENT PERFECT SUBJUNCTIVE	haya estudiado
PRETERITE	estudié		PLUPERFECT	había estudiado
IMPERFECT	estudiaba		TÚ/UD./UDS. COMMANDS	estudia, no estudies / (no)
IMPERFECT SUBJUNCTIVE	estudiara			estudie / (no) estudien
FUTURE/CONDITIONAL	estudiaré / estudiaría		PARTICIPLES	estudiando, estudiado

comer

PRESENT	como		PRESENT PERFECT	he comido
PRESENT SUBJUNCTIVE	coma		PRESENT PERFECT SUBJUNCTIVE	haya comido
PRETERITE	comí		PLUPERFECT	había comido
IMPERFECT	comía		TÚ/UD./UDS. COMMANDS	come, no comas / (no) coma /
IMPERFECT SUBJUNCTIVE	comiera			(no) coman
FUTURE/CONDITIONAL	comeré / comería		PARTICIPLES	comiendo, comido

vivir

PRESENT	vivo		PRESENT PERFECT	he vivido
PRESENT SUBJUNCTIVE	viva		PRESENT PERFECT SUBJUNCTIVE	haya vivido
PRETERITE	viví		PLUPERFECT	había vivido
IMPERFECT	vivía		TÚ/UD./UDS. COMMANDS	vive, no vivas / (no) viva / (no)
IMPERFECT SUBJUNCTIVE	viviera			vivan
FUTURE/CONDITIONAL	viviré / viviría		PARTICIPLES	viviendo, vivido

Reflexive Verbs

lavarse

PRESENT	me lavo		PRESENT PERFECT	me he lavado
PRESENT SUBJUNCTIVE	me lave		PRESENT PERFECT SUBJUNCTIVE	me haya lavado
PRETERITE	me lavé		PLUPERFECT	me había lavado
IMPERFECT	me lavaba		TÚ/UD./UDS. COMMANDS	lávate, no te laves / lávese,
IMPERFECT SUBJUNCTIVE	me lavara			no se lave / lávense, no se laven
FUTURE/CONDITIONAL	me lavaré / me lavaría		PARTICIPLES	lavándose, lavado

Stem-Changing Verbs

adquirir (i → ie)

PRESENT	adquiero, adquieres, adquiere; adquirimos, adquirís, adquieren		PRESENT SUBJUNCTIVE	adquiera, adquieras, adquiera; adquiramos, adquiráis, adquieran
			PRETERITE	adquirí

For all other forms, see **preferir.**

cerrar (e → ie)

PRESENT	cierro, cierras, cierra; cerramos, cerráis, cierran		FUTURE/CONDITIONAL	cerraré / cerraría
			PRESENT PERFECT	he cerrado
PRESENT SUBJUNCTIVE	cierre, cierres, cierre; cerremos, cerréis, cierren		PRESENT PERFECT SUBJUNCTIVE	haya cerrado
			PLUPERFECT	había cerrado
PRETERITE	cerré		TÚ/UD./UDS. COMMANDS	cierra, no cierres / (no) cierre /
IMPERFECT	cerraba			(no) cierren
IMPERFECT SUBJUNCTIVE	cerrara		PARTICIPLES	cerrando, cerrado

Verbs like **cerrar: despertarse, gobernar, pensar,** *and* **recomendar.**

dormir (o → ue)

PRESENT	duermo, duermes, duerme; dormimos, dormís, duermen		IMPERFECT SUBJUNCTIVE	durmiera
			FUTURE/CONDITIONAL	dormiré / dormiría
PRESENT SUBJUNCTIVE	duerma, duermas, duerma; durmamos, durmáis, duerman		PRESENT PERFECT	he dormido
			PRESENT PERFECT SUBJUNCTIVE	haya dormido
PRETERITE	dormí, dormiste, durmió; dormimos, dormisteis, durmieron		PLUPERFECT	había dormido
			TÚ/UD./UDS. COMMANDS	duerme, no duermas / (no) duerma / (no) duerman
IMPERFECT	dormía		PARTICIPLES	durmiendo, dormido

Verbs like **dormir: morir(se).**

empezar (e → ie), (z → c)   PRETERITE   empecé, empezaste, empezó; empezamos, empezasteis, empezaron   PRESENT SUBJUNCTIVE   empiece, empieces, empiece; empecemos, empecéis, empiecen

For all other forms, see **cerrar.**

---

jugar (u → ue)		
PRESENT	juego, juegas, juega; jugamos, jugáis, juegan	FUTURE/CONDITIONAL jugaré / jugaría
PRESENT SUBJUNCTIVE	juegue, juegues, juegue; juguemos, juguéis, jueguen	PRESENT PERFECT he jugado PRESENT PERFECT SUBJUNCTIVE haya jugado PLUPERFECT había jugado
PRETERITE	jugué, jugaste, jugó; jugamos, jugasteis, jugaron	TÚ/UD./UDS. COMMANDS juega, no juegues / (no) juegue / (no) jueguen
IMPERFECT	jugaba	
IMPERFECT SUBJUNCTIVE	jugara	PARTICIPLES jugando, jugado

---

llover (o → ue)		
PRESENT	llueve	FUTURE/CONDITIONAL lloverá / llovería
PRESENT SUBJUNCTIVE	llueva	PRESENT PERFECT ha llovido
PRETERITE	llovió	PRESENT PERFECT SUBJUNCTIVE haya llovido
IMPERFECT	llovía	PLUPERFECT había llovido
IMPERFECT SUBJUNCTIVE	lloviera	PARTICIPLES lloviendo, llovido

---

mover (o → ue)		
PRESENT	muevo, mueves, mueve; movemos, movéis, mueven	FUTURE/CONDITIONAL moveré / movería PRESENT PERFECT he movido
PRESENT SUBJUNCTIVE	mueva, muevas, mueva; movamos, mováis, muevan	PRESENT PERFECT SUBJUNCTIVE haya movido PLUPERFECT había movido
PRETERITE	moví	TÚ/UD./UDS. COMMANDS mueve, no muevas / (no) mueva / (no) muevan
IMPERFECT	movía	
IMPERFECT SUBJUNCTIVE	moviera	PARTICIPLES moviendo, movido

Verbs like **mover: doler.**

---

nevar (e → ie)		
PRESENT	nieva	FUTURE/CONDITIONAL nevará / nevaría
PRESENT SUBJUNCTIVE	nieve	PRESENT PERFECT ha nevado
PRETERITE	nevó	PRESENT PERFECT SUBJUNCTIVE haya nevado
IMPERFECT	nevaba	PLUPERFECT había nevado
IMPERFECT SUBJUNCTIVE	nevara	PARTICIPLES nevando, nevado

---

pedir (e → i)		
PRESENT	pido, pides, pide; pedimos, pedís, piden	FUTURE/CONDITIONAL pediré / pediría PRESENT PERFECT he pedido
PRESENT SUBJUNCTIVE	pida, pidas, pida; pidamos, pidáis, pidan	PRESENT PERFECT SUBJUNCTIVE haya pedido PLUPERFECT había pedido
PRETERITE	pedí, pediste, pidió; pedimos, pedisteis, pidieron	TÚ/UD./UDS. COMMANDS pide, no pidas / (no) pida / (no) pidan
IMPERFECT	pedía	PARTICIPLES pidiendo, pedido
IMPERFECT SUBJUNCTIVE	pidiera	

Verbs like **pedir: conseguir, despedirse, medir, seguir, servir,** *and* **vestirse.**

---

perder (e → ie)		
PRESENT	pierdo, pierdes, pierde; perdemos, perdéis, pierden	FUTURE/CONDITIONAL perderé / perdería PRESENT PERFECT he perdido
PRESENT SUBJUNCTIVE	pierda, pierdas, pierda; perdamos, perdáis, pierdan	PRESENT PERFECT SUBJUNCTIVE haya perdido PLUPERFECT había perdido
PRETERITE	perdí	TÚ/UD./UDS. COMMANDS pierde, no pierdas / (no) pierda / (no) pierdan
IMPERFECT	perdía	
IMPERFECT SUBJUNCTIVE	perdiera	PARTICIPLES perdiendo, perdido

Verbs like **perder: atender, defender(se), encender,** *and* **entender(se).**

preferir (e → ie)

PRESENT	prefiero, prefieres, prefiere; prefermos, preferís, prefieren	IMPERFECT SUBJUNCTIVE	prefiriera
PRESENT SUBJUNCTIVE	prefiera, prefieras, prefiera; prefiramos, prefiráis, prefieran	FUTURE/CONDITIONAL	preferiré / preferiría
		PRESENT PERFECT	he preferido
		PRESENT PERFECT SUBJUNCTIVE	haya preferido
PRETERITE	preferí, preferiste, prefirió; preferimos, preferisteis, prefirieron	PLUPERFECT	había preferido
		TÚ/UD./UDS. COMMANDS	prefiere, no prefieras / (no) prefiera / (no) prefieran
IMPERFECT	prefería	PARTICIPLES	prefiriendo, preferido

Verbs like **preferir**: **divertirse, herir, hervir, mentir, sentirse,** *and* **sugerir.**

---

probar (o → ue)

PRESENT	pruebo, pruebas, prueba; probamos, probáis, prueban	PRETERITE	probé
PRESENT SUBJUNCTIVE	pruebe, pruebes, pruebe; probemos, probéis, prueben	TÚ/UD./UDS. COMMANDS	prueba, no pruebes / (no) pruebe / (no) prueben
		PARTICIPLES	probando, probado

For all other forms see **estudiar.**

Verbs like **probar**: **acostarse.**

---

resolver (o → ue)

PRESENT	resuelvo, resuelves, resuelve; resolvemos, resolvéis, resuelven	PRESENT SUBJUNCTIVE	resuelva, resuelvas, resuelva; resolvamos, resolváis, resuelvan
PARTICIPLES	resolviendo, resuelto		

For all other forms, see **mover.**

Verbs like **resolver**: **devolver, envolver, revolver,** *and* **volver.**

---

soler (o → ue)

PRESENT	suelo, sueles, suele; solemos, soléis, suelen	IMPERFECT	solía
		PAST PARTICIPLE	solido

Verbs with Spelling Changes

actuar (u → ú)

PRESENT	actúo, actúas, actúa; actuamos, actuáis, actúan	TÚ/UD./UDS. COMMANDS	actúa, no actúes / (no) actúe / (no) actúen
PRESENT SUBJUNCTIVE	actúe, actúes, actúe; actuemos, actuéis, actúen	PARTICIPLES	actuando, actuado

For all other forms, see **estudiar.**

Verbs like **actuar**: **evaluar, graduarse.**

---

apagar (g → gu)

PRESENT	apago, apagas, apaga; apagamos, apagáis, apagan	PRESENT SUBJUNCTIVE	apague, apagues, apague; apaguemos, apaguéis, apaguen

For all other forms, see **jugar.**

Verbs like **apagar**: **arriesgar, castigar, colgar, descolgar, despegar, encargarse, entregar, investigar, llegar, navegar,** *and* **pagar.**

---

buscar (c → qu)

PRESENT	busco, buscas, busca; buscamos, buscáis, buscan	PRETERITE	busqué, buscaste, buscó; buscamos, buscasteis, buscaron
PRESENT SUBJUNCTIVE	busque, busques, busque; busquemos, busquéis, busquen	TÚ/UD./UDS. COMMANDS	busca, no busques / (no) busque / (no) busquen

For all other forms, see **estudiar.**

Verbs like **buscar**: **clasificar, comunicar(se), criticar, dedicarse, diversificar(se), equivocarse, explicar, fabricar, indicar, marcar, picar, practicar, sacar, secar(se),** *and* **tocar.**

---

conocer (c → zc)

PRESENT	conozco, conoces, conoce; conocemos, conocéis, conocen	TÚ/UD./UDS. COMMANDS	conoce, no conozcas / (no) conozca / (no) conozcan
PRESENT SUBJUNCTIVE	conozca, conozcas, conozca; conozcamos, conozcáis, conozcan		

For all other forms, see **comer.**

Verbs like **conocer**: **aparecer, desobedecer, establecer, merecer, nacer, obedecer, ofrecer, parecer,** *and* **pertenecer.**

500 Verbos

creer (i → y)

	PRESENT	creo	PRESENT PERFECT	he creído
	PRESENT SUBJUNCTIVE	crea	PRESENT PERFECT SUBJUNCTIVE	haya creído
	PRETERITE	creí, creíste, creyó; creímos, creísteis, creyeron	PLUPERFECT	había creído
			TÚ/UD./UDS. COMMANDS	cree, no creas / (no) crea / (no) crean
	IMPERFECT	creía		
	IMPERFECT SUBJUNCTIVE	creyera	PARTICIPLES	creyendo, creído
	FUTURE/CONDITIONAL	creeré / creería		

Verbs like **creer: leer.**

---

cruzar (z → c)

	PRESENT	cruzo	FUTURE/CONDITIONAL	cruzaré / cruzaría
	PRESENT SUBJUNCTIVE	cruce, cruces, cruce; crucemos, crucéis, crucen	PRESENT PERFECT	he cruzado
			PRESENT PERFECT SUBJUNCTIVE	haya cruzado
	PRETERITE	crucé, cruzaste, cruzó; cruzamos, cruzasteis, cruzaron	PLUPERFECT	había cruzado
			TÚ/UD./UDS. COMMANDS	cruza, no cruces / (no) cruce / (no) crucen
	IMPERFECT	cruzaba	PARTICIPLES	cruzando, cruzado
	IMPERFECT SUBJUNCTIVE	cruzara		

Verbs like **cruzar: abrazarse, alcanzar, analizar, aterrizar, bostezar, esclavizar, garantizar, lanzar, realizar,** *and* **trazar.**

---

dirigir (g → j) PRESENT dirijo, diriges, dirige; dirigimos, dirigís, dirigen

For all other forms, see **escoger.**

Verbs like **dirigir: exigir.**

---

empezar (z → c) See Stem-Changing Verbs.

---

enviar (i → í)

	PRESENT	envío, envías, envía; enviamos, enviáis, envían	FUTURE/CONDITIONAL	enviaré / enviaría
			PRESENT PERFECT	he enviado
	PRESENT SUBJUNCTIVE	envíe, envíes, envíe; enviemos, enviéis, envíen	PRESENT PERFECT SUBJUNCTIVE	haya enviado
			PLUPERFECT	había enviado
	PRETERITE	envié	TÚ/UD./UDS. COMMANDS	envía, no envíes / (no) envíe / (no) envíen
	IMPERFECT	enviaba		
	IMPERFECT SUBJUNCTIVE	enviara	PARTICIPLES	enviando, enviado

Verbs like **enviar: esquiar**.

---

escoger (g → j)

	PRESENT	escojo, escoges, escoge; escogemos, escogéis, escogen	FUTURE/CONDITIONAL	escogeré / escogería
			PRESENT PERFECT	he escogido
	PRESENT SUBJUNCTIVE	escoja, escojas, escoja; escojamos, escojáis, escojan	PRESENT PERFECT SUBJUNCTIVE	haya escogido
			PLUPERFECT	había escogido
	PRETERITE	escogí	TÚ/UD./UDS. COMMANDS	escoge, no escojas / (no) escoja / (no) escojan
	IMPERFECT	escogía		
	IMPERFECT SUBJUNCTIVE	escogiera	PARTICIPLES	escogiendo, escogido

Verbs like **escoger: proteger(se)** *and* **recoger.**

---

incluir (i → y)

	PRESENT	incluyo, incluyes, incluye; incluimos, incluís, incluyen	IMPERFECT SUBJUNCTIVE	incluyera
			FUTURE/CONDITIONAL	incluiré / incluiría
	PRESENT SUBJUNCTIVE	incluya, incluyas, incluya; incluyamos, incluyáis, incluyan	PRESENT PERFECT	he incluido
			PRESENT PERFECT SUBJUNCTIVE	haya incluido
	PRETERITE	incluí, incluiste, incluyó; incluimos, incluisteis, incluyeron	PLUPERFECT	había incluido
			TÚ/UD./UDS. COMMANDS	incluye, no incluyas / (no) incluya / (no) incluyan
	IMPERFECT	incluía	PARTICIPLES	incluyendo, incluido

Verbs like **incluir: construir, contribuir, destruir, distribuir,** *and* **influir.**

---

jugar (g → gu) See Stem-Changing Verbs.

Verbos   501

Irregular Verbs

caerse

PRESENT	me caigo, te caes, se cae; nos caemos, os caéis, se caen	IMPERFECT SUBJUNCTIVE	me cayera
		FUTURE/CONDITIONAL	me caeré / me caería
PRESENT SUBJUNCTIVE	me caiga, te caigas, se caiga; nos caigamos, os caigáis, se caigan	PRESENT PERFECT	me he caído
		PRESENT PERFECT SUBJUNCTIVE	me haya caído
		PLUPERFECT	me había caído
PRETERITE	me caí, te caíste, se cayó; nos caímos, os caísteis, se cayeron	TÚ/UD./UDS. COMMANDS	cáete, no te caigas / cáigase, no se caiga / cáiganse, no se caigan
IMPERFECT	me caía	PARTICIPLES	cayéndose, caído

dar

PRESENT	doy, das, da; damos, dais, dan	PRESENT PERFECT	he dado
PRESENT SUBJUNCTIVE	dé, des, dé; demos, deis, den	PRESENT PERFECT SUBJUNCTIVE	haya dado
PRETERITE	di, diste, dio; dimos, disteis, dieron	PLUPERFECT	había dado
		TÚ/UD./UDS. COMMANDS	da, no des / (no) dé / (no) den
IMPERFECT	daba		
IMPERFECT SUBJUNCTIVE	diera	PARTICIPLES	dando, dado
FUTURE/CONDITIONAL	daré / daría		

decir

PRESENT	digo, dices, dice; decimos, decís, dicen	FUTURE/CONDITIONAL	diré / diría
		PRESENT PERFECT	he dicho
PRESENT SUBJUNCTIVE	diga, digas, diga; digamos, digáis, digan	PRESENT PERFECT SUBJUNCTIVE	haya dicho
		PLUPERFECT	había dicho
PRETERITE	dije, dijiste, dijo; dijimos, dijisteis, dijeron	TÚ/UD./UDS. COMMANDS	di, no digas / (no) diga / (no) digan
IMPERFECT	decía	PARTICIPLES	diciendo, dicho
IMPERFECT SUBJUNCTIVE	dijera		

estar

PRESENT	estoy, estás, está; estamos, estáis, están	IMPERFECT SUBJUNCTIVE	estuviera
		FUTURE/CONDITIONAL	estaré / estaría
PRESENT SUBJUNCTIVE	esté, estés, esté; estemos, estéis, estén	PRESENT PERFECT	he estado
		PRESENT PERFECT SUBJUNCTIVE	haya estado
PRETERITE	estuve, estuviste, estuvo; estuvimos, estuvisteis, estuvieron	PLUPERFECT	había estado
		TÚ/UD./UDS. COMMANDS	está, no estés / (no) esté / (no) estén
IMPERFECT	estaba	PARTICIPLES	estando, estado

haber

PRESENT	hay	IMPERFECT	había
PRESENT SUBJUNCTIVE	haya	IMPERFECT SUBJUNCTIVE	hubiera
PRETERITE	hubo	FUTURE/CONDITIONAL	habrá / habría

hacer

PRESENT	hago, haces, hace; hacemos, hacéis, hacen	FUTURE/CONDITIONAL	haré / haría
		PRESENT PERFECT	he hecho
PRESENT SUBJUNCTIVE	haga, hagas, haga; hagamos, hagáis, hagan	PRESENT PERFECT SUBJUNCTIVE	haya hecho
		PLUPERFECT	había hecho
PRETERITE	hice, hiciste, hizo; hicimos, hicisteis, hicieron	TÚ/UD./UDS. COMMANDS	haz, no hagas / (no) haga / (no) hagan
IMPERFECT	hacía	PARTICIPLES	haciendo, hecho
IMPERFECT SUBJUNCTIVE	hiciera		

ir

PRESENT	voy, vas, va; vamos, vais, van	FUTURE/CONDITIONAL	iré / iría
PRESENT SUBJUNCTIVE	vaya, vayas, vaya; vayamos, vayáis, vayan	PRESENT PERFECT	he ido
		PRESENT PERFECT SUBJUNCTIVE	haya ido
PRETERITE	fui, fuiste, fue; fuimos, fuisteis, fueron	PLUPERFECT	había ido
		TÚ/UD./UDS. COMMANDS	ve, no vayas / (no) vaya / (no) vayan
IMPERFECT	iba, ibas, iba; íbamos, ibais, iban	PARTICIPLES	yendo, ido
IMPERFECT SUBJUNCTIVE	fuera		

oír	PRESENT	oigo, oyes, oye; oímos, oís, oyen	FUTURE/CONDITIONAL	oiré / oiría	
	PRESENT SUBJUNCTIVE	oiga, oigas, oiga; oigamos, oigáis, oigan	PRESENT PERFECT	he oído	
			PRESENT PERFECT SUBJUNCTIVE	haya oído	
			PLUPERFECT	había oído	
	PRETERITE	oí, oíste, oyó; oímos, oísteis, oyeron	TÚ/UD./UDS. COMMANDS	oye, no oigas / (no) oiga / (no) oigan	
	IMPERFECT	oía	PARTICIPLES	oyendo, oído	
	IMPERFECT SUBJUNCTIVE	oyera			

poder	PRESENT	puedo, puedes, puede; podemos, podéis, pueden	FUTURE/CONDITIONAL	podré / podría
	PRESENT SUBJUNCTIVE	pueda, puedas, pueda; podamos, podáis, puedan	PRESENT PERFECT	he podido
			PRESENT PERFECT SUBJUNCTIVE	haya podido
			PLUPERFECT	había podido
	PRETERITE	pude, pudiste, pudo; pudimos, pudisteis, pudieron	TÚ/UD./UDS. COMMANDS	puede, no puedas / (no) pueda / (no) puedan
	IMPERFECT	podía	PARTICIPLES	pudiendo, podido
	IMPERFECT SUBJUNCTIVE	pudiera		

poner	PRESENT	pongo, pones, pone; ponemos, ponéis, ponen	FUTURE/CONDITIONAL	pondré / pondría
	PRESENT SUBJUNCTIVE	ponga, pongas, ponga; pongamos, pongáis, pongan	PRESENT PERFECT	he puesto
			PRESENT PERFECT SUBJUNCTIVE	haya puesto
			PLUPERFECT	había puesto
	PRETERITE	puse, pusiste, puso; pusimos, pusisteis, pusieron	TÚ/UD./UDS. COMMANDS	pon, no pongas / (no) ponga / (no) pongan
	IMPERFECT	ponía	PARTICIPLES	poniendo, puesto
	IMPERFECT SUBJUNCTIVE	pusiera		

Verbs like **poner:** **componer, imponer, proponer,** *and* **suponer.**

querer	PRESENT	quiero, quieres, quiere; queremos, queréis, quieren	IMPERFECT SUBJUNCTIVE	quisiera
			FUTURE/CONDITIONAL	querré / querría
	PRESENT SUBJUNCTIVE	quiera, quieras, quiera; queramos, queráis, quieran	PRESENT PERFECT	he querido
			PRESENT PERFECT SUBJUNCTIVE	haya querido
	PRETERITE	quise, quisiste, quiso; quisimos, quisisteis, quisieron	PLUPERFECT	había querido
			TÚ/UD./UDS. COMMANDS	quiere, no quieras / (no) quiera / (no) quieran
	IMPERFECT	quería	PARTICIPLES	queriendo, querido

reírse	PRESENT	me río, te ríes, se ríe; nos reímos, os reís, se ríen	FUTURE/CONDITIONAL	me reiré / me reiría
			PRESENT PERFECT	me he reído
	PRESENT SUBJUNCTIVE	me ría, te rías, se ría; nos riamos, os riáis, se rían	PRESENT PERFECT SUBJUNCTIVE	me haya reído
			PLUPERFECT	me había reído
	PRETERITE	me reí, te reíste, se rio; nos reímos, os reísteis, se rieron	TÚ/UD./UDS. COMMANDS	ríete; no te rías / ríase, no se ría / ríanse, no se rían
	IMPERFECT	me reía	PARTICIPLES	riéndose, reído
	IMPERFECT SUBJUNCTIVE	me riera		

saber	PRESENT	sé, sabes, sabe; sabemos, sabéis, saben	FUTURE/CONDITIONAL	sabré / sabría
			PRESENT PERFECT	he sabido
	PRESENT SUBJUNCTIVE	sepa, sepas, sepa; sepamos, sepáis, sepan	PRESENT PERFECT SUBJUNCTIVE	haya sabido
			PLUPERFECT	había sabido
	PRETERITE	supe, supiste, supo; supimos, supisteis, supieron	TÚ/UD./UDS. COMMANDS	sabe, no sepas / (no) sepa / (no) sepan
	IMPERFECT	sabía	PARTICIPLES	sabiendo, sabido
	IMPERFECT SUBJUNCTIVE	supiera		

salir	PRESENT	salgo, sales, sale; salimos, salís, salen	FUTURE/CONDITIONAL	saldré / saldría
			PRESENT PERFECT	he salido
	PRESENT SUBJUNCTIVE	salga, salgas, salga; salgamos, salgáis, salgan	PRESENT PERFECT SUBJUNCTIVE	haya salido
			PLUPERFECT	había salido
	PRETERITE	salí	TÚ/UD./UDS. COMMANDS	sal, no salgas / (no) salga / (no) salgan
	IMPERFECT	salía	PARTICIPLES	saliendo, salido
	IMPERFECT SUBJUNCTIVE	saliera		

Verbos   503

ser	PRESENT	soy, eres, es; somos, sois, son	FUTURE/CONDITIONAL	seré / sería
	PRESENT SUBJUNCTIVE	sea, seas, sea; seamos, seáis, sean	PRESENT PERFECT	he sido
			PRESENT PERFECT SUBJUNCTIVE	haya sido
	PRETERITE	fui, fuiste, fue; fuimos, fuisteis, fueron	PLUPERFECT	había sido
			TÚ/UD./UDS. COMMANDS	sé, no seas / (no) sea / (no) sean
	IMPERFECT	era, eras, era; éramos, erais, eran	PARTICIPLES	siendo, sido
	IMPERFECT SUBJUNCTIVE	fuera		

tener	PRESENT	tengo, tienes, tiene; tenemos, tenéis, tienen	FUTURE/CONDITIONAL	tendré / tendría
			PRESENT PERFECT	he tenido
	PRESENT SUBJUNCTIVE	tenga, tengas, tenga; tengamos, tengáis, tengan	PRESENT PERFECT SUBJUNCTIVE	haya tenido
			PLUPERFECT	había tenido
	PRETERITE	tuve, tuviste, tuvo; tuvimos, tuvisteis, tuvieron	TÚ/UD./UDS. COMMANDS	ten, no tengas / (no) tenga / (no) tengan
	IMPERFECT	tenía	PARTICIPLES	teniendo, tenido
	IMPERFECT SUBJUNCTIVE	tuviera		

Verbs like **tener: entretener(se), mantener(se),** *and* **obtener.**

traducir	PRESENT	traduzco, traduces, traduce; traducimos, traducís, traducen	IMPERFECT SUBJUNCTIVE	tradujera
			FUTURE/CONDITIONAL	traduciré / traduciría
	PRESENT SUBJUNCTIVE	traduzca, traduzcas, traduzca; traduzcamos, traduzcáis, traduzcan	PRESENT PERFECT	he traducido
			PRESENT PERFECT SUBJUNCTIVE	haya traducido
			PLUPERFECT	había traducido
	PRETERITE	traduje, tradujiste, tradujo; tradujimos, tradujisteis, tradujeron	TÚ/UD./UDS. COMMANDS	traduce, no traduzcas / (no) traduzca / (no) traduzcan
	IMPERFECT	traducía	PARTICIPLES	traduciendo, traducido

Verbs like **traducir: reducir.**

traer	PRESENT	traigo, traes, trae; traemos, traéis, traen	FUTURE/CONDITIONAL	traeré / traería
			PRESENT PERFECT	he traído
	PRESENT SUBJUNCTIVE	traiga, traigas, traiga; traigamos, traigáis, traigan	PRESENT PERFECT SUBJUNCTIVE	haya traído
			PLUPERFECT	había traído
	PRETERITE	traje, trajiste, trajo; trajimos, trajisteis, trajeron	TÚ/UD./UDS. COMMANDS	trae, no traigas / (no) traiga / (no) traigan
	IMPERFECT	traía	PARTICIPLES	trayendo, traído
	IMPERFECT SUBJUNCTIVE	trajera		

Verbs like **traer: atraer.**

venir	PRESENT	vengo, vienes, viene; venimos, venís, vienen	FUTURE/CONDITIONAL	vendré / vendría
			PRESENT PERFECT	he venido
	PRESENT SUBJUNCTIVE	venga, vengas, venga; vengamos, vengáis, vengan	PRESENT PERFECT SUBJUNCTIVE	haya venido
			PLUPERFECT	había venido
	PRETERITE	vine, viniste, vino; vinimos, vinisteis, vinieron	TÚ/UD./UDS. COMMANDS	ven, no vengas / (no) venga / (no) vengan
	IMPERFECT	venía	PARTICIPLES	viniendo, venido
	IMPERFECT SUBJUNCTIVE	viniera		

Verbs like **venir: convenir.**

ver	PRESENT	veo, ves, ve; vemos, veis, ven	FUTURE/CONDITIONAL	veré / vería
	PRESENT SUBJUNCTIVE	vea, veas, vea; veamos, veáis, vean	PRESENT PERFECT	he visto
			PRESENT PERFECT SUBJUNCTIVE	haya visto
	PRETERITE	vi, viste, vio; vimos, visteis, vieron	PLUPERFECT	había visto
			TÚ/UD./UDS. COMMANDS	ve, no veas / (no) vea / (no) vean
	IMPERFECT	veía, veías, veía; veíamos, veíais, veían	PARTICIPLES	viendo, visto
	IMPERFECT SUBJUNCTIVE	viera		

504   Verbos

VOCABULARIO ESPAÑOL-INGLÉS

This *Vocabulario* contains all active vocabulary from PASO A PASO 1, 2, and 3.

A dash (—) represents the main entry word. For example, **la — extranjera** after **la lengua** means **la lengua extranjera.**

The number following each entry indicates the chapter in which the word or expression is presented. A Roman numeral (I) indicates that the word was presented in PASO A PASO 1; a Roman numeral (II), that it was presented in PASO A PASO 2.

The following abbreviations are used: *adj.* (adjective), *dir. obj.* (direct object), *f.* (feminine), *fam.* (familiar), *ind. obj.* (indirect object), *inf.* (infinitive), *m.* (masculine), *pl.* (plural), *prep.* (preposition), *pron.* (pronoun), *sing.* (singular).

a, al (a + el) at; to (I)
abajo below (3)
la **abeja** bee (II)
el **abogado, la abogada** lawyer (II)
abrazarse *(z → c)* to hug, to embrace (II)
el **abrelatas** can opener (II)
el **abrigo** coat (I)
abril April (I)
abrir to open (I)
abrocharse to fasten (II)
abstracto, -a abstract (3)
el **abuelo, la abuela** grandfather, grandmother (I)
los **abuelos** grandparents (I)
abundante abundant, generous (2)
aburrido, -a boring (I)
aburrir to bore (I)
　　—se to be bored (II)
acabar (con) to put an end (to) (10)
académico, -a academic (12)
acampar: la tienda de — tent (II)
el **accidente** accident (II)
la **acción: la película de —** action film (II)
el **aceite** oil (II)
aceptar to accept (5)
la **acera** sidewalk (2)
acondicionado *see* **aire**
acostarse *(o → ue)* to go to bed (II)
activamente actively (12)
la **actividad** activity (II)
el **actor, la actriz** actor, actress (I)
la **actuación** acting (II)
actual present-day (5)
actualmente at present (7)
actuar *(u → ú)* to act (II)
acuático, -a *see* **esquí, moto**
acuerdo: estar de — to agree (I)
el **acusado, la acusada** accused *(person)* (10)
adecuado, -a appropriate (9)
además in addition, besides (II)
adiós good-by (I)
administrar to manage *(a business)* (9)
administrativo, -a administrative (9)
admirar to admire (1)
¿adónde? (to) where? (I)

adoptar to adopt (11)
adquirir *(i → ie)* to acquire, to become (1)
la **aduana** customs (II)
el **aduanero, la aduanera** customs agent (II)
aérea: la línea — airline (II)
el **aeropuerto** airport (II)
afeitar:
　　—se to shave (II)
　　la **crema de —** shaving cream (II)
　　la **máquina de —** razor (II)
el **aficionado, la aficionada** enthusiast, fan (1)
la **afirmación** affirmation, statement (8)
afirmar to affirm, to state (8)
africano, -a African (11)
las **afueras** *pl.* outskirts, suburbs (2)
la **agencia de viajes** travel agency (II)
agente:
　　el/la — (de ventas) (sales) agent (12)
　　el/la — (de viajes) (travel) agent (II)
agosto August (I)
la **agricultura** agriculture (5)
agrio, -a sour (5)
el **agua** *f.* water (I)
el **aguacate** avocado (I)
ahora now (I)
　　— mismo right now (9)
ahorrar to save (II)
el **aire** air (I)
　　al — libre outdoors (II)
　　el — acondicionado air conditioning (II)
aislado, -a isolated (2)
el **ajedrez** chess (II)
el **ajo** garlic (II)
la **alarma** alarm (10)
alcance: al — de la mano within reach (2)
alcanzar *(z → c)* to reach, to achieve (9)
el **alcázar,** *pl.* **los alcázares** fortress (11)
alegre happy, festive (II)
el **alemán** German *(language)* (II)
la **alergia** allergy (II)
alérgico, -a (a) allergic (to) (II)

el **álgebra** *f.* algebra (II)
algo something (I)
　　— más something else (I)
el **algodón** cotton (II)
alguien someone, somebody (I, II)
alguno (algún), -a some (I, II)
　　—a vez ever (I)
la **alimentación** nourishment, food (II)
allí there (I)
　　— está there it is (I)
el **almacén** department store (I)
el **almuerzo** lunch (I)
　　en el — for lunch (I)
¡Aló! hello! *(on the telephone)* (6)
alquilar to rent (4)
alto, -a tall (I)
el **alto** height (8)
　　la **señal de —** stop sign (II)
el **aluminio** aluminum (I)
amable kind, nice (I)
el **amanecer** dawn, sunrise (II)
amargo, -a bitter (II)
amarillo, -a yellow (I)
ambicioso, -a ambitious (9)
el **ambiente** atmosphere (I)
　　el medio — environment (I, II)
la **ambulancia** ambulance (II)
la **amenaza** threat (I)
el **amigo, la amiga** friend (I)
la **amistad,** *pl.* **las amistades** friendship (1)
el **análisis** medical test (II)
analizar *(z → c)* to analyze, to judge (4)
anaranjado, -a orange *(color)* (I)
el **ancho** width (8)
el **anciano, la anciana** older person (7)
el **anillo** ring (II)
animado, -a lively (2)
el **animal** animal (I, II)
　　el — de peluche stuffed animal (II)
el **aniversario (de boda)** (wedding) anniversary (II)
anoche last night (I)
la **antena parabólica** satellite dish (4)
los **anteojos (de sol)** (sun)glasses (I, II)
los **antepasados** ancestors (5)
antes de + *verb* before + *verb* + -ing (II)

antialérgico, -a non-allergenic (II)

el **antibiótico** antibiotic (II)

antiguo, -a old, traditional (I)

antipático, -a unfriendly, unpleasant (I)

el **antropólogo, la antropóloga** anthropologist (5)

el **anuario** yearbook (II)

el **anuncio** ad, commercial (I)

los —**s clasificados** classified ads (9)

el **año** year (I)

a los . . . —s at the age of . . . (II)

el — **Nuevo** New Year's Day (II)

¿**cuántos — tienes?** how old are you? (I)

cumplir —s to have a birthday (II)

la fiesta de fin de — New Year's Eve party (I)

el fin de — New Year's Eve (II)

tener . . . —s to be . . . years old (I)

apagado, -a dull (3)

apagar *(g → gu)* to turn off (I, II); to blow out *(candles)* (II)

el **aparato** appliance, device (II)

aparecer *(c → zc)* to appear (8)

el **apartado postal** post office box (6)

el **apartamento** apartment (I)

apoyar(se) to support (each other) (1)

apreciar to value, to appreciate (12)

aprender to learn (I)

el **aprendizaje** learning (12)

apretado, -a tight *(clothing)* (II)

aproximadamente approximately (6)

apta: — para toda la familia suitable for the whole family (4)

aquel, aquella; aquellos, -as *adj.* that (over there); those (over there) (II)

aquél, aquélla; aquéllos, -as *pron.* that one (over there); those (over there) (II)

aquí here (I)

—**está** here it is (I)

por — around here (I)

la **araña** spider (II)

el **árbol** tree (I, II)

el **archivo** file (9)

la **ardilla** squirrel (II)

el **arete** earring (I, II)

el **argumento** plot (II)

el **arma,** *pl.* **las armas** weapon (10)

el **armario** locker (II)

la **armonía** harmony (12)

el **arqueólogo, la arqueóloga** archaeologist (5)

el **arquitecto, la arquitecta** architect (5)

arreglar to clean up (I)

arrestar to arrest (II)

arriba on top (3)

arriesgar *(g → gu)* to risk (10)

el **arroz** rice (I)

el **arte** art (I, II)

las —**s marciales** martial arts (II)

la **artesanía** handicrafts (II)

el/la **artista** artist (3)

artístico, -a artistic (I)

asado, -a roasted (II)

el **ascenso** promotion (9)

el **ascensor** elevator (II)

asco: ¡qué —! yuck! that's disgusting! (I)

el **asesinato** murder (10)

el **asesino, la asesina** murderer (10)

así, así so-so, fair (I)

el **asiento** seat (II)

el **asilo** nursing home (1)

el/la **asistente social** social worker (12)

asombrar to astonish (10)

la **aspiradora** vacuum cleaner (I)

pasar la — to vacuum (I)

el/la **astronauta** astronaut (II)

el **astrónomo, la astrónoma** astronomer (5)

el **ataque** attack (10)

el **atardecer** sunset (II)

el **atasco** traffic jam (2)

atender *(e → ie)* **(a)** to attend to (9)

atentado assault, attempted murder (10)

aterrizar *(z → c)* to land (II)

atractivo, -a attractive (I)

atraer to attract (3)

atrevido, -a bold, daring (I)

el **auditorio** auditorium (II)

aumentar to increase (12)

el **aumento (de sueldo)** raise (in salary) (9)

aunque although (1)

el **autobús** bus (I)

la parada del — bus stop (I)

la **autodefensa** self-defense (10)

automático, -a automatic (II)

la **autopista** highway (2)

el **autorretrato** self-portrait (3)

el/la **auxiliar de vuelo** flight attendant (II)

avanzado, -a advanced (5)

la **avenida** avenue (I)

aventura: la película de —s adventure film (I)

el **avión** airplane (II)

¡**ay!** ouch! (I)

ayer yesterday (I)

la **ayuda** help, assistance (II)

el/la **ayudante** aide, assistant (1)

ayudar to help (I)

el **azúcar** sugar (I)

azul, *pl.* **azules** blue (I)

el **azulejo** tile (11)

bailar to dance (I, II)

el **bailarín, la bailarina** dancer (II)

el **baile** dance (I, II)

baja: el sube y — seesaw (II)

bajo, -a short *(height)* (I)

el **balcón,** *pl.* **los balcones** balcony (11)

la **ballena** whale (I, II)

el **balón** *(inflated)* ball (II)

la **balsa** raft (II)

navegar *(g → gu)* **en —** to go river rafting (II)

el **banco** bank (I)

la **banda** band (II)

la **bandera** flag (II)

el **banquero, la banquera** banker (12)

bañarse to take a bath (II)

el **baño** bathroom (I)

el traje de — bathing suit (I)

barato, -a cheap, inexpensive (I)

la **barbacoa** barbecue (II)

hacer una — to have a barbecue (II)

basado, -a (en) based (on) (II)

básquetbol: jugar — to play basketball (I)

bastante rather, quite (I, II)

la **basura** garbage (I)

la **batalla** battle (11)

el **bate** (baseball) bat (II)

beber to drink (I)

la **bebida** beverage (I)

béisbol: jugar — to play baseball (I)

bello, -a beautiful (2)

beneficiar(se) to benefit (7)

el **beneficio** benefit (12)

besarse to kiss (II)

la **biblioteca** library (I)

el **bibliotecario, la bibliotecaria** librarian (12)

la **bicicleta** bicycle (I, II)

montar en — to ride a bike (II)

bien well (I)

bilingüe bilingual (12)

la **biología** biology (II)

el **bisabuelo, la bisabuela** great-grandfather, great-grandmother (II)

el **bistec** steak (I)

blanco, -a white (I)

el **bloque** block *(toy)* (II)

la **blusa** blouse (I)

la **boca** mouth (I)

el **bocadillo** Spanish-style sandwich (II)

la **boda** wedding (II)

el **boleto (de ida y vuelta)** (round-trip) ticket (II)

el **bolígrafo** pen (I)

los **bolos** bowling (II)

el **bolsillo** pocket (II)

el **bolso** gym bag, book bag (II); purse (II)

el **bombero, la bombera** firefighter (II)

la estación de —s fire station (II)

el **bombillo** light bulb (II)

bonito, -a pretty (I)

el **bosque** woods (II)
bostezar *(z → c)* to yawn (4)
la **bota** boot (I)
el **bote** rowboat (I)
pasear en — to row (I)
la **botella** bottle (I, II)
el **botín** half boot (II)
el **botón** button (II)
el **brazo** arm (I)
el **bronceador** suntan lotion (I)
bucear to skin-dive (I)
bueno (buen), -a good (I)
bueno OK, fine, all right (I)
la **bufanda** muffler, scarf (I)
el **bufet de ensaladas** salad bar (II)
el **búho** owl (II)
el **burrito** burrito (I)
buscar *(c → qu)* to look for (I)
el **buzón** mailbox (II)

el **caballero: la ropa para —s** men's wear (II)
el **caballo** horse (II)
montar a — to ride a horse (II)
la **cabeza** head (I)
tener dolor de — to have a headache (I)
cable: la televisión por — cable television (4)
el **cacto** cactus (II)
la **cadena** chain (II)
caerse to fall down (II)
el **café** coffee (I)
la **cafetería** cafeteria (II)
la **caja** cashier's station (II)
el **cajero, la cajera** cashier (II)
el **cajón de arena** sandbox (II)
la **calabaza** pumpkin (II)
la **calamina** calamine lotion (II)
el **calcetín** sock (I)
la **calculadora** calculator (I)
calcular to calculate (8)
la **calefacción** heating (II)
el **calendario** calendar (5)
el **calentador** heater (II)
caliente: el perro — hot dog (II)
callado, -a quiet (I)
la **calle** street (I)
calor:
hace — it's hot (out) (I)
tener — to be hot *(person)* (I)
la **caloría** calorie (II)
la **cama** bed (I)
la **cámara** camera (I)
el **camarero, la camarera** waiter, waitress (I)
el **camarón** shrimp (II)
cambiar to change (II); to cash (II)
— de canal to change channels (4)

el **cambio** change (II)
la casa de — currency exchange (II)
caminar to walk (I, II)
caminata: dar una — to go hiking (II)
el **camino** road (2)
el **camión** truck (II)
la **camisa** shirt (I)
la **camiseta** T-shirt (I)
el **campamento** campground (II)
la **campaña** campaign (1)
— electoral electoral campaign (7)
el **campeón, la campeona** champion (II)
el **campeonato** championship (II)
camping: ir de — to go camping (II)
el **campo** countryside (I); field, area (5)
el **canal** (TV) channel (I)
la **canción** song (II)
el **candidato, la candidata** candidate (7)
la **canoa** canoe (II)
navegar *(g → gu)* **en —** to go canoeing (II)
canoso: pelo — gray hair (I)
cansado, -a tired (I)
el/la **cantante** singer (II)
cantar to sing (I, II)
capaz, *pl.* **capaces** capable (9)
el **capítulo** chapter (II)
la **cara** face (II)
la **cárcel** jail (10)
el **carbohidrato** carbohydrate (II)
Cariños *pl.* Love *(as a closing in a letter)* (6)
cariñoso, -a affectionate, loving (I)
la **carne (de res)** beef (I)
el **carnet de identidad** ID card (II)
la **carnicería** butcher shop (II)
caro, -a expensive (I)
la **carpeta** pocket folder (I)
la — de argollas three-ring binder (I)
la **carrera** career (12)
la **carretera** highway (II)
el **carrusel** merry-go-round (II)
la **carta** letter (I)
a la — a la carte (I)
el **cartel** poster (I)
la **cartera** wallet (II)
el **cartero, la cartera** mail carrier (6)
el **cartón** cardboard (I, II)
la **casa** house (I)
la — de cambio currency exchange (II)
en — at home (I)
la especialidad de la — house specialty (I)
casado, -a (con) married (to) (II)
casarse (con) to marry, to get married (to) (I)
el **casco** helmet (II)
el **casete** cassette (II)

casi almost (I)
caso: en — de in case of (II)
castaño: pelo — brown (chestnut) hair (I)
castigar *(g → gu)* to punish (10)
el **castigo** punishment (10)
el **castillo** castle (11)
el **catálogo** catalog (II)
las **cataratas** waterfall (I)
la **catedral** cathedral (I)
catorce fourteen (I)
la **causa** cause (7)
la **cebolla** onion (I)
la **celebración** celebration (II)
celebrar to celebrate (II)
la **cena** dinner (I)
la **censura** censorship (4)
el **centímetro** centimeter (8)
central central (II)
el **centro** center (I); downtown (II); center *(middle)* (3)
el — comercial mall (I)
el — de la comunidad community center (7)
el — de reciclaje recycling center (I)
el — de rehabilitación rehabilitation center (7)
el — recreativo recreation center (7)
cepillarse (los dientes) to brush (one's teeth) (II)
el **cepillo** brush (II)
el — de dientes toothbrush (II)
cerca (de) near (I)
la **cerca** fence (2)
el **cerdo** pork (II)
el **cereal** cereal (I)
la **ceremonia** ceremony (5)
la **cereza** cherry (II)
cero zero (I)
cerrar *(e → ie)* to close (I)
el **césped** lawn (I)
el **cesto de la ropa sucia** laundry hamper (II)
el **chaleco** vest (II)
el **champiñón** mushroom (II)
el **champú** shampoo (I)
el **chandal** sweatsuit (II)
la **chaqueta** jacket (I)
el **chaquetón** car coat (II)
charlar to chat (II)
el **cheque** check (II)
el — de viajero traveler's check (II)
el **chile** chili pepper (I)
el — con carne beef with beans (I)
el — relleno stuffed pepper (I)
el **chocolate** hot chocolate (I)
el **chorizo** sausage (II)
la **choza** hut, shack (5)
el **churro** churro (I)

el/la **ciclista** cyclist (2)
cien one hundred (I)
la **ciencia ficción** science fiction (I)
las **ciencias** science (I)
  — de la salud health (science) (I)
  — sociales social studies (I)
el **científico, la científica** scientist (II)
ciento uno, -a; ciento dos; etc. 101, 102, etc. (I)
cierto, -a true, certain (8)
cinco five (I)
cincuenta fifty (I)
el **cine** movies, movie theater (I)
el **cinturón** belt (II)
  el — de seguridad seatbelt (II)
la **cita** appointment (9)
la **ciudad** city (I)
la **ciudadanía** citizenship (7)
el **ciudadano, la ciudadana** citizen (7)
la **civilización** civilization (5)
el **clarinete** clarinet (II)
claro: ¡— que sí(no)! of course (not) (I)
claro, -a light *(color)* (II)
la **clase (de)** class; kind, type (I)
después de las —s after school (I)
la sala de —s classroom (I)
clásico, -a classical (II)
clasificar *(c → qu)* to classify (4)
el **cliente, la clienta** client, customer (9)
la **clínica** clinic (I)
el **club** club (II)
el **coche** car (I)
cocido, -a cooked (II)
la **cocina** kitchen (I)
cocinar to cook (I)
el **cocinero, la cocinera** cook (II)
el **codo** elbow (II)
colaborar (con) to collaborate (7)
la **colección** collection (II)
coleccionar to collect (II)
colgar *(o → ue)* *(g → gu)* to hang (II); to hang up *(the telephone)* (6)
la **colina** hill (II)
el **collar** necklace (I, II)
la **colonia** colony (11)
el **color** color (I)
¿de qué —? what color? (I)
en —es in color (I)
el **columpio** swing (II)
combinar(se) to combine (11)
la **comedia** comedy, sitcom (I)
el **comedor** dining room (I)
  el — de beneficencia soup kitchen (7)
el **comentario (sobre)** review (of) (II); commentary (4)
comer to eat (I)
los **comestibles** groceries (I)
cometer to commit (12)

cómico, -a comical (I)
la **comida** meal, food (I)
como like, as (I)
  tan + *adj.* + **—** as + *adj.* + as (II)
  tanto(s), -a(s) + noun + **—** as much (many) + *noun* + as (II)
¿cómo? how? (I)
  ¿— eres? what are you like? (I)
  ¿— estás/está Ud.? how are you? (I)
  ¡— no! certainly! (I)
  ¿— se dice . . . ? how do you say . . . ? (I)
  ¿— se llama(n)? what is his/her/their name? (I)
  ¿— te llamas? what's your name? (I)
la **cómoda** dresser (I)
cómodo, -a comfortable (I)
el **compañero, la compañera** classmate (I)
compartir to share (1)
completamente completely (12)
completar to complete (7)
componer(se) de to be composed of (11)
la **composición** composition (II)
comprar to buy (I)
compras:
  hacer las — to shop (II)
  ir de — to go shopping (I)
  el programa de — home shopping show (II)
comprensivo, -a understanding (1)
comprobar *(o → ue)* to prove (4)
la **computadora** computer (II)
común: tener en — to have in common (1)
comunicar(se) *(c → qu)* to communicate (6)
la **comunidad** community (I)
con with (I)
el **concierto** concert (I)
concursos: el programa de — game show (II)
la **conferencia por video** video conference (6)
el **conflicto** conflict (1)
confundirse to be confused (12)
congelado, -a frozen (II)
conmigo with me (I)
conocer *(c → zc)* to know, to be acquainted with (I, II)
el **conquistador** conqueror (11)
conquistar to conquer (11)
conseguir *(e → i)* to get, to obtain (II)
el **consejero, la consejera** counselor (II)
el **consejo** piece of advice; *pl.* advice (1)
  dar un — to give advice (1)
el **consejo estudiantil** student council (II)

consentido, -a spoiled *(child)* (II)
conservar to conserve, to save (I, II)
considerado, -a considerate (1)
construir *(i → y)* to build, to construct (5)
el **contacto** contact (12)
el **contador, la contadora** accountant (12)
la **contaminación** pollution (2)
contaminado, -a contaminated, polluted (I, II)
contaminar to pollute (II)
el **contestador automático** answering machine (6)
contestar to answer (II)
contigo with you (I)
el **continente** continent (11)
contra: en — de against (7)
el **contrabajo** bass (II)
contratar to hire (10)
la **contribución** contribution (5)
contribuir *(i → y)* to contribute (2)
el **control remoto** remote control (II)
controlar to control (4)
conveniente convenient (2)
convenir *(e → ie)*: **me conviene** to be convenient; to suit: it suits me (9)
convivir to live together (12)
la **corbata** necktie (I, II)
el **coro** chorus, choir (II)
corporal corporal (10)
el **correo** post office (I)
  el — electrónico electronic mail (6)
  por — urgente by special delivery (6)
correr to run, to jog (II)
la **correspondencia** correspondence (6)
el/la **corresponsal** correspondent (12)
cortar to cut (I, II)
  —se to cut oneself (II)
cortés, *pl.* **corteses** courteous (9)
corto, -a short *(length)* (I)
la **cosa** thing (I)
la **cosecha** harvest (5)
coser to sew (II)
costar *(o → ue)* to cost (I)
la **costumbre** custom (5)
el **coyote** coyote (II)
la **creación** creation (11)
el **creador, la creadora** creator (8)
crear to create (6)
creará *see* **crear**
crédito: la tarjeta de — credit card (II)
creer to think, to believe (I)
  creo que sí (no) I (don't) think so (I)
la **cremallera** zipper (II)
el **crimen** crime (II)
el/la **criminal** criminal (II)
el **cristiano, la cristiana** Christian (11)

criticar *(c → qu)* to critique (3)
crítico, -a critical (4)
el cruce intersection (II)
el crucigrama crossword puzzle (II)
la Cruz Roja Red Cross (7)
cruzar *(z → c)* to cross (II)
el cuaderno spiral notebook (I)
la cuadra block (I)
cuadrado, -a square (I)
el cuadro picture (I)
cuadros: a — plaid, checked (II)
¿cuál(es)? what? which? which one(s)? (I)
la cualidad quality (9)
cualquier any (9)
cualquiera anybody (6)
cuando, ¿cuándo? when (I)
de vez en — sometimes (II)
¿cuánto? how much? (I)
¿— (tiempo) hace que . . . ? how long has it been since . . . ? (I)
¿cuántos, -as? how many? (I)
¿— años tiene . . . ? how old is . . . ? (I)
cuarenta forty (I)
cuarto, -a quarter; fourth (I)
y — *(time)* quarter after, quarter past (I)
el cuarto room (I)
cuatro four (I)
cuatrocientos four hundred (I)
el cubismo cubism (3)
la cucaracha cockroach (II)
la cuchara spoon (I)
el cuchillo knife (I)
el cuello neck (I)
el suéter de — alto turtleneck (II)
el cuenco *(earthenware)* bowl (5)
la cuenta bill *(restaurant)* (I)
la cuerda rope (II)
saltar a la — to jump rope (II)
el cuero leather (I)
de — (made of) leather (I)
el cuerpo body (I)
cuidado: tener — (con) to be careful (with / of) (II)
cuidadoso, -a careful (9)
cuidar niños to babysit (II)
culpa: tener la — (de) to be guilty (of), to be at fault (10)
culpable guilty (10)
cultivar to cultivate, to grow *(crops)* (2)
la cultura culture (5)
cultural cultural (11)
el cumpleaños birthday (I, II)
¡feliz —! happy birthday! (I)
la fiesta de — birthday party (I)
la tarjeta de — birthday card (I)
cumplir:
— años to have a birthday (II)
— con to fulfill (9)
el cuñado, la cuñada brother-in-law, sister-in-law (II)

damas: la ropa para — ladies' wear (II)
las damas checkers (II)
dañar to damage (II)
daño:
hacer — to be harmful (4)
hacer — a to make ill, not to agree with *(food)* (II)
dar to give (I)
— + *movie or TV program* to show (I)
— una caminata to go hiking (II)
— clases particulares to give private lessons, to tutor (1)
— un consejo to give advice (1)
— miedo a to scare (I)
— saltos to dive (II)
—se la mano to shake hands (II)
(me) da igual it's all the same (to me) (II)
los datos data, information (8)
de, del *(de + el)* from; of; —'s, —s' (I)
— + *material* made of (I)
— nada you're welcome (I)
— pie standing (3)
— postre for dessert (I)
¿— veras? really? (I)
debajo de under(neath) (I)
deber ought to, should (I)
decidir to decide (2)
decir to say, to tell (I)
¿cómo se dice . . . ? how do you say . . . ? (I)
—se "¡Hola!" to say hello (II)
¡no me digas! really?, you don't say! (I)
¿qué quiere — . . . ? what does . . . mean? (I)
se dice . . . it is said (I)
la decoración decoration (I)
decorar to decorate (I)
dedicarse *(c → qu)* (a) to be involved in; to devote oneself (to) (II)
el dedo finger (I)
el — del pie toe (I)
defender(se) *(e → ie)* to defend (oneself) (10)
— en + *language* to get along, to not do badly *(in a language)* (12)
dejar to leave *(a message)* (6)
delante de in front of (I)
el/la delincuente delinquent (10)
los demás the others (1)
demasiado *adv.* too (I); *adj.* too many (4)
dental: la seda — dental floss (II)
el/la dentista dentist (I)
depender (de) to depend (on) (I, II)
los deportes sports (I)
deportista athletic (I)
el/la deportista athlete (II)

deportivo, -a *adj.* sports (I)
depositar to deposit (I)
derecha: a la — (de) to the right (of) (I)
derecho, -a right (I)
el derecho right (4)
el derrumbe landslide (II)
desabrocharse to unfasten (II)
desaparecido, -a disappeared (5)
desarrollar to develop (5)
el desastre disaster (II)
desayunar to have breakfast (II)
el desayuno breakfast (I)
descansar to rest (I)
la descendencia descent, ancestry (11)
descolgar *(o → ue) (g → gu)* to pick up *(telephone)* (6)
desconocido, -a unknown (8)
descubierto, -a exposed, open (5)
el descubrimiento discovery (5)
descubrir to discover (5)
el descuento: la tienda de —s discount store (I)
desde (que + *verb*) since, from (II)
desear: ¿qué desea Ud? may I help you? (I)
el desfile parade (II)
el desierto desert (II, 8)
desobedecer *(c → zc)* to disobey (II)
desobediente disobedient (II)
el desodorante deodorant (II)
desordenado, -a messy (I)
despedirse *(e → i)* (de) to say good-by (to) (II)
despegar *(g → gu) (plane)* to take off (II)
el despertador alarm clock (II)
despertarse *(e → ie)* to wake up (II)
después de + *inf.* after + *verb* + -ing (I, II)
el destinatario, la destinataria addressee (6)
destino: con — a going to (II)
la destreza skill (9)
destruir *(i → y)* to destroy (II)
la desventaja disadvantage (II)
el/la detective detective (II)
el programa de —s detective show (I)
el detector de humo smoke detector (II)
detrás (de) behind (I)
devolver *(o → ue)* to return *(something)* (I)
el día day (I)
buenos —s good morning (I)
el — de fiesta holiday (II)
el plato del — daily special (I)
¿qué — es hoy? what day is it? (I)
todos los —s every day (I)

el **Día de (Acción de) Gracias** Thanksgiving (II)

el **Día de los Enamorados** Valentine's Day (II)

el **Día de la Independencia** Independence Day (II)

el **Día de la Madre** Mother's Day (II)

el **Día de los Muertos** Day of the Dead/All Souls' Day (11)

el **Día del Padre** Father's Day (II)

el **Día de la Raza** Columbus Day (II)

el **diámetro** diameter (8)

la **diapositiva** slide (II)

diario, -a daily (2)

dibujar to draw (I)

el **dibujo** drawing (I)

    los **—s animados** cartoons (I)

el **diccionario** dictionary (I)

diciembre December (I)

diecinueve nineteen (I)

dieciocho eighteen (I)

dieciséis sixteen (I)

diecisiete seventeen (I)

los **dientes** teeth (II)

    el **cepillo de —** toothbrush (II)

dieron *see* **dar**

diez ten (I)

diferente different (2)

difícil difficult, hard (I)

la **dificultad** difficulty (12)

digas *see* **decir**

el **dinero** money (I)

el **dinosaurio** dinosaur (II)

el **dios**, *pl.* **los dioses** god (5)

el **diplomático, la diplomática** diplomat (9)

la **dirección** address (II); direction (II)

el **director, la directora** *(school)* principal (II); *(film)* director (II)

dirigir *(g → j)* to direct (II)

el **disco** disk (II)

    el **— compacto** compact disk (II)

    el **— (de hockey)** (hockey) puck (II)

discreción: se recomienda — parental guidance suggested (4)

la **discusión** discussion (I)

discutir to argue, to discuss (1)

el **diseño** design (8)

disfraces: la fiesta de — costume party (I, II)

disfrutar de to enjoy (II)

la **distancia** distance (II)

distribuir *(i → y)* to distribute (9)

la **diversidad** diversity (11)

diversificar(se) *(c → qu)* to diversify (12)

la **diversión** fun, entertainment (II)

    el **parque de —es** amusement park (I)

diverso, -a diverse (11)

divertido, -a amusing, funny (I)

divertirse *(e → ie)* to have fun (I, II)

divorciado, -a (de) divorced (from) (II)

doblar to turn (II)

doble double (II)

doce twelve (I)

el **documental** documentary (I)

el **dólar** dollar (I)

doler *(o → ue)* to hurt, to ache (I)

dolor: tener — de . . . to have a . . . ache (I)

doméstico, -a domestic (II)

dominar + *language* to master, to have a good knowledge of *(a language)* (12)

domingo Sunday (I)

    el **—** on Sunday (I)

donar to donate (7)

donde, ¿dónde? where (I)

dormir *(o → ue)* to sleep (I)

    el **saco de —** sleeping bag (II)

el **dormitorio** bedroom (I)

dos two (I)

doscientos two hundred (I)

la **droga** drug (10)

ducharse to take a shower (II)

la **duda** doubt (8)

dudar to doubt (8)

dulce sweet (II)

el **dulce** candy (II)

duradero, -a long-lasting, enduring (11)

durar to last (I)

el **durazno** peach (II)

duro: el huevo — hard-boiled egg (II)

echar to throw out, to dump (II)

económico, -a economical (II)

la **edad: ¿a qué —?** at what age? (II)

el **edificio** building (II)

la **educación** education (II)

    la **— física** physical education (I)

educado, -a polite, well-mannered (II)

educativo, -a educational (I)

efectivo: (el dinero) en — cash (II)

los **efectos especiales** special effects (II)

eficiente efficient (II)

el **ejercicio** exercise (I)

    hacer — to exercise (I)

el **ejército** army (7)

el the *m. sing.* (I)

él he; him *after prep.* (I)

la **elección** election (7)

la **electricidad** electricity (II)

eléctrico, -a electric (II)

el **elefante** elephant (I, II)

elegante elegant (I, II)

ella she; her *after prep.* (I)

ellos, ellas they; them *after prep.* (I)

el **embarque: la tarjeta de —** boarding pass (II)

la **emergencia** emergency (II)

    en caso de — in case of emergency (II)

    la **sala de —** emergency room (II)

emocionante exciting, touching (I)

emocionarse to be moved, touched (4)

la **empanada** turnover (II)

empatar to tie *(in scoring)* (II)

empezar *(e → ie) (z → c)* to begin, to start (I)

el **empleado, la empleada** employee (II)

en in, at, on (I)

    — + *vehicle* by (I)

enamorarse (de) to fall in love (with) (II)

encantado, -a delighted (I); haunted (8)

encantar to love (I)

encargarse *(g → gu)* **(de)** to take charge (of) (9)

encender *(e → ie)* to light (II); to turn on (II)

la **enchilada** enchilada (I)

encima (de) on (top of) (I)

encontrar *(o → ue)* to find (II)

    —se *(o → ue)* to meet (II)

el **encuentro** encounter (11)

la **energía** energy (I, II)

enero January (I)

la **enfermedad** illness (II)

la **enfermería** nurse's office (I)

el **enfermero, la enfermera** nurse (II)

enfermo, -a ill, sick (I)

enfrente (de) facing, opposite, in front of (I)

enlatado, -a canned (II)

enojarse to get angry (1)

enorme enormous (8)

la **ensalada** salad (I)

    el **bufet de —s** salad bar (II)

    la **— de frutas** fruit salad (II)

enseñar to teach (I)

entender(se) *(e → ie)* to understand (each other) (1)

enterrado, -a buried (5)

entonces then (6)

la **entrada** ticket (I); entrance (II)

entre between, among (I)

entregar *(g → gu)* to deliver (I); to hand in (I)

el **entrenador, la entrenadora** coach (II)

el **entrenamiento** training (9)

entretener(se) *(e → ie)* to amuse (oneself) (4)

la **entrevista** interview (II)

    el **programa de —s** talk show (I)

enviar *(i → i)* to send, to mail (I)

envolver *(o → ue)* to wrap (6)

la **época** time, age (3)

el **equipaje** baggage (II)

    la **terminal de —** baggage claim (II)

el **equipo** team (II)
    el **— de sonido** stereo (I)
equivocado, -a wrong (6)
equivocarse *(c → qu)* to make a mistake, to be mistaken (6)
el **error** error (12)
la **erupción** eruption (II)
la **escala** stopover (II)
    sin — nonstop (II)
escalar montañas to go mountain climbing (II)
la **escalera** stairs (II)
    la **— mecánica** escalator (II)
escaparse to escape, to get away (2)
la **escena** scene (II)
el **escenario** stage (II)
esclavizar *(z → c)* to enslave (11)
el **esclavo, la esclava** slave (11)
escoger *(g → j)* to choose (I, II)
escolar *adj.* school (II)
esconder to hide *(something)* (II)
    —se to hide (II)
escribir to write (I, II)
    ¿cómo se escribe . . . ? how do you spell . . . ? (I)
    —se to write each other (II)
el **escritor, la escritora** writer (II)
el **escritorio** desk (I)
la **escritura** writing (5)
escuchar to listen (to) (I)
la **escuela** school (I)
la **escultura** sculpture (5)
ese, -a; -os, -as *adj.* that; those (I, II)
ése, -a; -os, -as *pron.* that one; those (I, II)
la **esgrima** fencing (1)
el **esmalte de uñas** nail polish (II)
eso: por — that's why (I)
el **espacio** outer space (II); space (2)
la **espalda** back (I)
el **español** Spanish *(language)* (I)
el **espárrago** asparagus (II)
especial special (II)
la **especialidad de la casa** house specialty (I)
el **espejo** mirror (I)
esperar to wait (for) (6); to hope (7)
la **espina** thorn, spine (II)
las **espinacas** spinach (II)
el **esplendor** splendor (5)
el **esposo, la esposa** husband, wife (II)
el **esquí** ski (II)
    el **— acuático** water skiing (II)
    hacer — acuático to water ski (II)
esquiar *(i → í)* to ski (I)
la **esquina** corner (I)
establecer *(c → zc)* to establish (11)
la **estación** season; station (I)
el **estadio** stadium (I)

el **estante** shelf (II)
estar to be (I)
    ¿cómo estás/está Ud.? how are you? (I)
    la **sala de —** family room (I)
la **estatua** statue (5)
este, -a; -os, -as *adj.* this; these (I, II)
éste, -a; -os, -as *pron.* this one; these (II)
el **estilo** style (3)
el **estómago** stomach (I)
    tener dolor de — to have a stomachache (I)
estornudar to sneeze (II)
la **estrella** star (5)
el/la **estudiante** student (I)
    el/la **— de intercambio** exchange student (12)
estudiantil *adj.* student (II)
estudiar to study (I)
la **estufa** stove (I)
la **etapa** stage *(in a process)* (3)
europeo, -a European (11)
evaluar *(u → ú)* to evaluate (4)
la **evidencia** evidence (8)
evitar to avoid (10)
exagerado, -a exaggerated (II)
el **examen** exam, test (II)
excavar to excavate (5)
excelente excellent (II)
la **excursión** excursion, short trip (II)
    hacer una — to take an excursion (II)
exigir *(g → j)* to demand (7)
existir to exist (5)
éxito: tener — to be successful (II)
la **experiencia** experience (9)
explicar *(c → qu)* to explain (II)
explorar to explore (I, II)
la **explosión** explosion (10)
la **exposición (de arte)** (art) exhibit (II)
expresar(se) to express (oneself) (12)
la **extinción: en peligro de —** endangered (I, II)
extracurricular extracurricular (II)
extraño, -a strange (8)
extraordinario, -a extraordinary (8)
el/la **extraterrestre** alien (II)

la **fábrica** factory (I)
fabricar *(c → qu)* to manufacture (6)
fácil easy (I)
facilidad: tener — para to be good at (12)
fácilmente easily (II)
facturar to check *(baggage)* (II)
la **falda** skirt (I)
falso, -a false (8)
faltar to be lacking, to be missing (I)
la **familia** family (I)
familiar *adj.* family (II)
el **fantasma** ghost (8)

fantástico, -a fantastic (I)
la **farmacia** drugstore (I)
fascinante fascinating (I)
fascinar to fascinate (I)
favor: a — (de) in favor (of) (7)
el **fax** fax (6)
febrero February (I)
la **fecha** date (I)
¡felicidades! congratulations! (II)
felicitar to congratulate (II)
¡feliz cumpleaños! happy birthday! (I)
el **fenómeno** phenomenon (8)
feo, -a ugly (I)
la **ficha** token (6)
la **fiebre** fever (I)
    tener — to have a fever (I)
la **fiesta** party (I, II)
    el **día de —** holiday (II)
    la **— de cumpleaños** birthday party (I, II)
    la **— de disfraces** costume party (I, II)
    la **— de fin de año** New Year's Eve party (I, II)
    la **— de sorpresa** surprise party (I, II)
la **figura** form, shape (3)
fijarse (en) to pay attention (to) (3)
fijo, -a fixed (9)
fila: hacer — to line up, to stand in line (II)
el **fin:**
    el **— de año** New Year's Eve (II)
    el **— de semana** on the weekend (I)
financiero, -a financial (7)
física: la educación — physical education (I)
el **flan** flan (I)
la **flauta** flute (II)
flojo, -a loose *(clothing)* (II)
la **flor** flower (I, II)
floreado, -a flowered (II)
la **floristería** flower shop (II)
el **fondo** background (3)
    al — in the back (II)
la **forma** form (3)
    formar parte de to be a part of (I)
el **formulario** form (6)
el **fósforo** match (II)
el **fósil** fossil (II)
la **foto** photo (I)
    sacar —s to take pictures (I)
la **fotografía** photography (II)
el **fracaso** failure (I)
el **francés** French *(language)* (II)
frecuentemente frequently (1)
el **fregadero** sink (II)
los **frenillos** braces (II)
la **fresa** strawberry (II)

fresco, -a fresh (II)
fresco: hace — it's cool outside (I)
el **frijol** bean (I)
   los **—es refritos** refried beans (I)
frío:
   hace — it's cold outside (I)
   tener — to be cold *(person)* (I)
frito, -a fried (II)
la **frontera** border (12)
la **fruta** fruit (I)
la **frutería** fruit store (II)
fue *see* **ser**
el **fuego** fire (II)
   los **—s artificiales** fireworks (II)
la **fuente** fountain (11)
fuerte strong (II)
fui, fuiste *see* **ir, ser**
funcionar to work, to function (II)
fundar to found (11)
la **fusión** fusion (11)
el **fútbol** soccer (I)
   el **— americano** football (I)
el **futuro** future (II)

el **galán** *(film)* hero (II)
la **galería** gallery (3)
ganar to earn money (II); to win (II)
   —se la vida to earn a living (II)
la **ganga** bargain (I)
el **garaje** garage (I)
garantizar *(z → c)* to guarantee (7)
la **garganta** throat (I)
   las **pastillas para la —** throat
      lozenges (I)
   tener dolor de — to have a sore
      throat (I)
gastar to spend (II); to waste (II)
el **gato** cat (I)
el **gazpacho** gazpacho (I, II)
el **gemelo, la gemela** twin (I)
generalmente usually, generally (I)
generoso, -a generous (I)
¡genial! great! wonderful! (I)
la **gente** people (I)
   la **— sin hogar** the homeless (7)
la **geografía** geography (II)
el **geólogo, la geóloga** geologist (8)
la **geometría** geometry (II)
geométrico, -a geometric (8)
el/la **gerente** hotel manager (9)
gigante: la pantalla — big screen TV (II)
gigantesco, -a gigantic (8)
el **gimnasio** gymnasium (I)
gobernar *(e → ie)* to govern (7)
el **gobierno** government (7)
el **gol** goal (II)
el **golf** golf (II)
el **gorila** gorilla (I, II)
la **gorra** cap (II)

el **gorro** ski cap (I)
las **gotas (para los ojos)** (eye)drops (II)
la **grabadora** tape recorder (I)
grabar to record (4)
gracias thank you (I)
   — a thanks to (5)
gracioso, -a funny (I)
la **graduación** graduation (II)
graduarse *(u → ú)* to graduate (II)
grande big, large (I, II)
la **granja** farm (2)
la **grapadora** stapler (II)
grasoso, -a greasy (II)
la **gripe** flu (I)
   tener — to have the flu (I)
gris gray (I)
el **guacamole** avocado dip (I)
el **guante** glove (I)
guapo, -a handsome, good-looking (I)
guardar to put away, to keep (II)
el **guardarropa** closet (I)
la **guardería infantil** day-care center (II)
el/la **guardia** security guard (10)
la **guerra** war (II)
el/la **guía** guide (II)
   la **—** guidebook (II)
   la **— telefónica** phone book (I)
el **guión** script (II)
guisado, -a stewed (II)
el **guisante** pea (I)
la **guitarra** guitar (I)
gustar to like (I)
   me (te) gustaría I'd (you'd)
      like . . . (I)

haber:
   había there was / were (II)
   hay there is / are (I)
   hubo there was / were (II)
la **habilidad** skill (9)
la **habitación** hotel room (II)
el/la **habitante** inhabitant (8)
hablar to talk, to speak (I)
   — por señas to speak in sign
      language (12)
   —se to talk to each other (II)
   se habla is spoken (II)
hacer to do, to make (I)
   hace + *(time)* . . . ago (I)
   hace + *(time)* **+ que** it's been *(time)*
      since (I)
   — caso a to pay attention to (1)
   — ejercicio to exercise (I)
   — falta to be necessary (12)
   — el servicio militar to serve in
      the armed forces (7)
   se hace(n) con . . . it's (they're)
      made with . . . (I)
hagan *see* **hacer**

he visto *see* **ver**
has visto *see* **ver**
hambre: tener — to be hungry (I)
la **hamburguesa** hamburger (I)
la **harina** flour (I)
hasta until (I)
   — luego see you later (I)
hay there is /are (I)
   — que + *inf.* it's necessary to (I, II)
haya resuelto *see* **resolver**
hecho, -a (de) made (of) (I, II)
el **hecho** fact (I, II)
la **heladería** ice cream shop (II)
helado: el té — iced tea (I)
el **helado** ice cream (I)
heredar to inherit (5)
herir *(e → ie)* to injure (10)
el **hermano, la hermana** brother,
   sister (I)
los **hermanos** brothers; brother(s) and
   sister(s) (I)
la **heroína** heroine (II)
hervir *(e → ie)* to boil (II)
hice, hiciste *see* **hacer**
hiciéramos *see* **hacer**
el **hielo** ice (II)
la **higiene** hygiene (1)
el **hijo, la hija** son, daughter (I)
los **hijos** sons; children (I)
el/la **hispanohablante** Spanish speaker (11)
la **historia** history (II)
histórico, -a historic(al) (II)
el **hockey** hockey (II)
la **hoja** leaf (II)
   la **— de papel** sheet of paper (I)
¡hola! hi!, hello! (I)
el **hombre** man (I)
   el **— de negocios** businessman (II)
honesto, -a honest (9)
la **hora** period; time (I)
   ¿a qué —? at what time? (I)
   ¿qué — es? what time is it? (I)
el **horario** schedule (I)
la **hormiga** ant (II)
el **horno** oven (II)
   al — baked (II)
horrible horrible (I)
el **horror** horror (II)
el **hospital** hospital (I)
el **hotel** hotel (I)
hoy today (I)
   — en día nowadays (6)
   — no not today (I)
hubo *see* **haber**
la **huella** footprint (II, 8)
el **hueso** bone (II)
el **huevo** egg (I)
   el **— duro** hard-boiled egg (II)
humano, -a human (II)

humo: el detector de — smoke detector (II)

humor: de buen / mal — in a good / bad mood (II)

el **huracán** hurricane (II)

ida *see* **boleto**

sólo de — one way (II)

idealizado, -a idealized (2)

la **identidad: el carnet de —** ID card (II)

la **identificación** identification (II)

el **idioma** language (II)

la **iglesia** church (I)

igual: (me) da — it's all the same (to me) (II)

igualmente likewise (I)

la **imagen,** *pl.* **las imágenes** image (3)

la **imaginación** imagination (3)

impaciente impatient (I)

el **impermeable** raincoat (I)

imponer to impose (10)

imposible impossible (8)

impresionista impressionist (3)

improbable improbable (8)

los **impuestos** taxes (2)

el **incapacitado, la incapacitada** person with a physical disability (7)

el **incendio** fire (II)

el extinguidor de —s fire extinguisher (II)

incluir *(i → y)* to include (II)

incómodo, -a uncomfortable (I)

incomprensivo, -a insensitive (1)

increíble unbelievable (8)

indicar *(c → qu)* to indicate, to show, to point out (II)

indígena indigenous, native, *adj.* (II)

el/la **indígena** Native American (11)

individual: la habitación — single room (II)

inexplicable inexplicable (8)

infantil *see* **guardería**

la **infección** infection (II)

la **influencia** influence (11)

influir *(i → y)* **(en / sobre)** to influence (1)

la **información** information (II)

informativo, -a informative (4)

el **informe** report (II)

el **inglés** English *(language)* (I)

el **ingrediente** ingredient (I, II)

la **injusticia** injustice (11)

injusto, -a unjust (7)

la **inmigración** immigration (12)

el/la **inmigrante** immigrant (12)

inocente innocent (10)

inscribirse to enroll, to sign up (1)

el **insecticida** insecticide (II)

la **inseguridad** insecurity (10)

la **inspiración** inspiration (3)

el **instrumento** instrument (II)

inteligente intelligent (I)

interactivo, -a interactive (6)

el **interés** interest (I)

interesante interesting (I)

interesar to interest (I)

internacional international (II)

interpretar to interpret (3, 12)

el/la **intérprete** interpreter (9)

íntimo, -a close (1)

la **inundación** flood (II)

inventar to invent (6)

el **invento** invention (6)

investigar *(g → gu)* to investigate (II)

el **invierno** winter (I)

la **invitación** invitation (I, II)

el **invitado, la invitada** guest (I)

invitar to invite (I, II)

la **inyección** injection, shot (II)

poner una — to give an injection (II)

ir to go (I)

— a + *inf.* to be going to + *verb* (I)

izquierda: a la — (de) to the left (of) (I)

izquierdo, -a left (I)

el **jabón** soap (I)

el **jade** jade (5)

el **jaguar** jaguar (I)

el **jamón** ham (I)

el **jarabe (para la tos)** cough syrup (II)

el **jardín,** *pl.* **los jardines** garden (2)

los **jeans** jeans (I)

el **jefe, la jefa** boss (9)

los **jeroglíficos** hieroglyphics (5)

joven *adj.* young (I)

el/la **joven** young man, young woman (I)

los **jóvenes** young people (I)

las **joyas** jewelry (I)

las **judías verdes** green beans (I)

el **judío, la judía** Jew (11)

jueves Thursday (I)

el — on Thursday (I)

el/la **juez** judge (II)

el **jugador, la jugadora** player (II)

jugar *(u → ue) (g → gu)* to play (I)

el **juguete** toy (II)

de — *adj.* toy (II)

el **jugo** juice (I)

julio July (I)

junio June (I)

juntar fondos to raise funds (7)

junto a next to (3)

el **jurado** jury (10)

justo, -a just, fair (7)

el **kilómetro** kilometer (II)

el **kindergarten** kindergarten (II)

la the *f. sing.;* her, it *dir. obj. pron.* (I)

los **labios** lips (II)

el lápiz de — lipstick (II)

el **laboratorio** laboratory (II)

lado:

al — de next to, beside (I)

por otro — on the other hand (2)

por un — on the one hand (2)

el **ladrón, la ladrona** thief (II)

el **lago** lake (I)

la **lámpara** lamp (I)

la **lana** wool (II)

lanzar *(z → c)* to shoot (II)

el **lápiz** pencil (I)

el — de labios lipstick (II)

largo, -a long (I)

el **largo** length (8)

las the *f. pl.;* them *dir. obj. pron.* (I)

lástima: ¡qué —! that's too bad! what a shame! (I)

lastimar to hurt (I)

la **lata** can (I, II)

el **lavadero** laundry room (I)

la **lavadora** (clothes) washer (II)

el **lavaplatos** dishwasher (II)

lavar to wash (I)

—se (la cara, etc.) to wash (one's face, etc.) (II)

le *ind. obj. pron.* (to) him, her, it, you (I)

la **lección** lesson (II)

la **leche** milk (I)

la **lechuga** lettuce (I)

leer to read (I)

el **legado** legacy (5)

lejos (de) far (from) (I)

la **lengua** language (11)

la — extranjera foreign language (12)

la — materna mother tongue (12)

el **lenguaje por señas** sign language (12)

los **lentes de contacto** contact lenses (II)

lento, -a slow (6)

la **leña** firewood (II)

les *ind. obj. pron.* (to) them (I)

levantar to lift (II)

—se to get up (II)

leve light, minor (II)

la **ley,** *pl.* **las leyes** law (7)

la **leyenda** legend (8)

libertad: poner en — to set free (10)

libre: al aire — outdoors (II)

la **librería** bookstore (I)

el **libro** book (I)

el/la **líder** leader (5)

la **liga** league (II)

ligero, -a light *(weight)* (II)

el **limón** lemon, lime (II)

la limonada lemonade (I)
limpiar to clean (I)
limpio, -a clean (I)
la línea line (6)
  la — aérea airline (II)
la linterna flashlight (II)
la liquidación sale (II)
  estar en — to be on sale (II)
liso, -a plain (II)
literario, -a literary (II)
la literatura literature (II)
la llamada phone call (6)
  hacer una — to make a phone call (6)
  hacer una — a cobro revertido to
    make a collect call (6)
  hacer una — de larga distancia to
    make a long-distance call (6)
llamar to call (I)
  —se to be named (I, II)
la llave key (II)
el llavero keychain (II)
llegar *(g → gu)* to arrive (I)
llenar un formulario to fill out a form
  (6)
lleno, -a de gente crowded (2)
llevar to wear; to take, to carry along (1)
  —se (bien / mal) to get along
    (well / badly) (1)
llorar to cry (II)
llover *(o → ue)* to rain (I)
llueve it rains, it's raining (I)
la lluvia rain (I)
lo *dir. obj. pron.* him, it (I)
  — que what (II)
  — siento I'm sorry (I)
el lobo, la loba wolf (I, II)
local local (II)
el locutor, la locutora announcer (II)
la lona canvas (II)
los the *m. pl.; dir. obj. pron.* them (I)
  — + *day of week* on (I)
luchar to struggle, to fight (10)
lucro: sin fines de — non-profit (7)
luego then, afterward, later (I)
el lugar place (I)
  el — de los hechos scene of the
    crime (10)
el lujo luxury (II)
la Luna moon (II)
lunes Monday (I)
  el — on Monday (I)
la luz light (I)

la madera wood (I)
  de — (made of) wood (I)
la madre mother (I)
maduro, -a mature (9)
el maíz corn (I)

mal badly (I)
  menos — que . . . it's a good thing
    that . . . (I)
  me siento — I feel ill (I)
maleducado, -a rude, impolite (II)
la maleta suitcase (I, II)
  (des)hacer la — to (un)pack (II)
malo, -a bad (I)
mandar to send (6)
manera: de ninguna — not at all (I)
la manga sleeve (I)
la manifestación demonstration (7)
manipular to manipulate (4)
la mano hand (I)
  a — armada armed (10)
  a — by hand (II)
  darse la — to shake hands (II)
  hecho, -a a — handmade (I)
el mantel tablecloth (I)
mantener *(e → ie)* to maintain (1)
  —se sano, -a to stay healthy (II)
la mantequilla butter (I)
la manzana apple (I)
mañana tomorrow (I)
la mañana morning (I)
  de/por la — in the morning (I)
el mapa map (II)
el maquillaje make-up (II)
maquillarse to put on makeup (II)
el mar sea (I)
  maravilla: ¡una —! wonderful! (2)
el marcador marker (I)
marcar *(c → qu)* to dial *(a telephone*
  number) (6)
la marcha walk; hike (7)
la mariposa butterfly (II)
los mariscos seafood (II)
marrón brown (I)
martes Tuesday (I)
  el — on Tuesday (I)
marzo March (I)
más more, *adj.* + -er (I)
  el / la / los / las — + *adj.* the most
    + *adj.*, the *adj.* + -est (I, II)
  lo — + *adj.* (thing) (1)
la masa dough (I)
matar to kill (II)
las matemáticas mathematics (I)
la materia school subject (II)
los mayas Mayas (5)
mayo May (I)
la mayonesa mayonnaise (II)
mayor older (I)
  el — the oldest (I)
mayores: sólo para — adults only (4)
la mayoría majority (11)
me *obj. pron.* me (I)
mecánica: la escalera — escalator (II)
el mecánico, la mecánica mechanic (II)

media:
  una hora y — an hour and a half (I)
  — hora *f.* half an hour (I)
  y — half-past (I)
mediano, -a medium *(in sizes)* (II)
la medianoche midnight (I)
la medicina medicine (II)
el médico, la médica doctor (I)
la medida measure (10)
  medio: *(número)* **y —** and a half *(in*
    sizes) (I)
el medio ambiente environment (I, II)
el medio de comunicación means of
  communication (6)
el mediodía noon (I)
medir *(e → i)* to measure (8)
  — . . . de alto to be/measure . . .
    high (8)
  — . . . de ancho to be/measure . . .
    wide (8)
  — . . . de diámetro to be/measure
    . . . in diameter (8)
  — . . . de largo to be/measure . . .
    long (8)
mejor better (I)
  el / la / (los / las) —(es) the best
    (I)
  lo — the best (thing) (1)
el melón cantaloupe (II)
menor younger (I)
menos:
  el / la /los / las — + *adj.* the least
    + *adj.* (I, II)
  lo — + *adj.* the least + *adj.* (thing) (1)
  — mal que . . . it's a good thing
    that . . . (I)
  por lo — at least (II)
el mensaje message (3)
mentir *(e → ie)* to lie (II)
el menú menu (I)
menudo: a — often (I)
el mercado market (II)
merecer *(c → zc)* to deserve (9)
la merienda afternoon snack (I)
  de — for a snack (I)
el mes month (I)
la mesa table (I)
  la — de noche night table (II)
mestizo, -a (Native American and
  European) mestizo (11)
la meta goal (9)
  metal: de — (made of) metal (I)
meter en (la carcel) to put (in jail) (10)
  — un gol to score a goal (II)
el metro subway (I); meter
  (measurement) (II)
la mezcla mixing, mixture (11)
mezclar to mix (II, 11)
la mezquita mosque (11)

mi, mis my (I)

mí me *after prep.* (I)

el **microondas** microwave (oven) (II)

miedo: tener — (de) to be afraid (of) (10)

el **miembro** member (II)

ser — de to be a member of (II)

mientras while (II)

miércoles Wednesday (I)

el **—** on Wednesday (I)

mil one thousand (I)

la **milla** mile (II)

el **minuto** minute (I)

mío, -a my, (of) mine (II)

el **mío, la mía** mine (II)

mismo, -a same (II)

lo — the same thing (I)

(yo) — myself (II)

el **misterio** mystery (8)

misterioso, -a mysterious (8)

el **mito** myth (8)

el **mocasín** loafer (II)

la **mochila** backpack (I)

la **moda** fashion (II)

estar de — to be fashionable (II)

los **modales** manners (9)

moderno, -a modern (I)

modesto, -a modest (1)

el **modismo** idiom (12)

mojado, -a wet (II)

molestar to bother, to annoy (II)

la **moneda** coin (II)

el **mono** monkey (8)

el **monstruo** monster (II)

la **montaña** mountain (I)

montar:

— a caballo to ride horseback (II)

— en bicicleta to ride a bike (I, II)

el **monumento** monument (I)

morado, -a purple (I)

morir(se) *(o → ue)* to die (11)

la **mosca** fly (II)

el **mosquito** mosquito (II)

la **mostaza** mustard (II)

el **mostrador** counter (II)

mostrar *(o → ue)* to show (II)

la **moto acuática** jet skiing (II)

hacer — to jet ski (II)

mover *(o → ue)* to move (8)

el **movimiento** movement, school (3)

el **muchacho, la muchacha** boy, girl (I)

mucho, -a a lot of, much (I)

— gusto pleased / nice to meet you (I)

—as veces many times (I)

mudarse to move *(residence)* (1)

los **muebles** furniture (I)

las **muelas: tener dolor de —** to have a toothache (I)

la **muerte** death (10)

muerto, -a dead (II)

la **mujer** woman (I)

la **— de negocios** businesswoman (II)

las **muletas** crutches (II)

la **multa** fine (4)

multicultural multicultural (12)

mundial world, world-wide (12)

el **mundo** world (11)

la **muñeca** doll (II); wrist (II)

el **muñeco** action figure (II)

el **mural** mural (3)

el **músculo** muscle (II)

el **museo** museum (I)

la **música** music (I)

musical *adj.* musical (I, II)

el video — music video (II)

el **músico, la música** musician (II)

el **musulmán, la musulmana** Muslim (11)

muy very (I)

nacer *(c → zc)* to be born (II)

nacional national (II)

nada nothing, not at all (I)

de — you're welcome (I)

nadar to swim (I)

nadie no one (I)

la **naranja** orange (I)

el **narcotráfico** drug trafficking (10)

la **nariz** nose (I)

la **naturaleza** nature (II)

la **— muerta** still life (3)

la **nave espacial** spaceship (8)

navegar *see* **balsa, canoa**

la **Navidad** Christmas (II)

necesario, -a necessary (II)

la **necesidad** necessity (II)

necesitar to need (I)

negativo, -a negative (4)

los **negocios** business (II)

el hombre / la mujer de — businessman, businesswoman (II)

negro, -a black (I)

en blanco y — in black and white (I)

nervioso, -a nervous (1)

nevar: nieva it snows, it's snowing (I)

ni . . . ni neither . . . nor, not . . . or (I)

el **nieto, la nieta** grandson, granddaughter (II)

la **nieve** snow (I)

el **nilón** nylon (II)

ninguno (ningún), -a no, not any (I, II)

—a parte nowhere, not anywhere (I)

el **niño, la niña** boy, girl (II)

cuidar niños to baby-sit (II)

los niños children (II)

no no, not (I)

¿no? don't you?, aren't I?, etc. (I)

la **noche** evening (I)

buenas —s good evening, good night (I)

de la — at night (I)

por la — in the evening (I)

la **Nochebuena** Christmas Eve (II)

el **nombre** name (I)

nos *obj. pron.* us (I)

nosotros, -as we (I); us *after prep.* (I)

la **nota** grade (II)

notar to notice (11)

las **noticias** news (I)

el **noticiero** newscast (4)

novecientos nine hundred (I)

la **novela** novel (II)

noventa ninety (I)

noviembre November (I)

el **novio, la novia** boyfriend, girlfriend (I)

nuestro, -a our (I); (of) ours (II)

el **nuestro, la nuestra** ours (II)

nueve nine (I)

nuevo, -a new (I)

de — again (II)

el **número** number (I); (shoe) size (II)

nunca never (I)

o or (I)

obedecer *(c → zc)* to obey (II)

obediente obedient (II)

objetivo, -a objective (4)

el **objeto** object, thing (5)

obligatorio, -a obligatory (7)

la **obra (de arte)** work (of art) (3)

la **— de teatro** play (II)

el **obrero, la obrera** laborer (II)

el **observatorio** observatory (5)

obtener *(e → ie)* to obtain (7)

el **océano** ocean (I, II)

ochenta eighty (I)

ocho eight (I)

ochocientos eight hundred (I)

octavo, -a eighth (I)

octubre October (I)

ocupado, -a busy (I)

ocurrir to occur, to happen (II)

el **oeste: la película del —** western (I)

oficial official (12)

la **oficina** office (II)

ofrecer *(c → zc)* to offer (2)

el **oído** ear (I)

tener dolor de — to have an earache (I)

oír to hear (2)

el **ojo** eye (I)

las **olimpiadas de minusválidos** Special Olympics (games for people with disabilities) (7)

la **olla** pot (II)

once eleven (I)

la **operación** operation (II)

el **operador, la operadora** operator (6)
la **opinión** opinion (4)
la **oportunidad** chance, opportunity (2)
oportuno, -a opportune, appropriate (9)
ordenado, -a neat, tidy (I)
el **orfanato** orphanage (1)
la **organización** organization (7)
el **origen,** *pl.* **los orígenes** origin (5)
el **oro** gold (II)
   de — (made of) gold (II)
la **orquesta** orchestra (II)
oscuro, -a dark *(color)* (II)
el **oso** bear (I, II)
el **otoño** fall, autumn (I)
otro, -a another, other (I)
ovalado, -a oval (8)
el **oxígeno** oxygen (II)

la **paciencia** patience (9)
paciente *adj.* patient (I)
el **padre** father (I)
   los —s parents (I)
la **paella** paella (II)
pagar *(g → gu)* to pay (I)
la **página** page (II)
el **país** country (I)
el **paisaje** landscape (2)
el **pájaro** bird (I, II)
el **palacio** palace (II)
la **paleta** palette (3)
el **palito** twig; *pl.* kindling (II)
el **palo (de golf, de hockey)** golf club,
   hockey stick (II)
el **pan** bread (I)
   el — tostado toast (I)
la **panadería** bakery (II)
la **pantalla** screen (II)
los **pantalones** pants (I)
las **pantimedias** pantyhose (I)
el **pañuelo** scarf (II)
la **papa** potato (I)
   la — frita French fry (I)
el **papel** paper (I); part, role (II)
   hacer el — (de) to play the part (of)
   (II)
   la hoja de — sheet of paper (I)
el **paquete** package, parcel (6)
para for, in order to (I)
la **parada del autobús** bus stop (I)
el **paraguas** umbrella (I)
parecer *(c → zc)* to appear, to seem (II)
la **pared** wall (II)
el **pariente, la parienta** relative (I, II)
el **parque** park (I)
   el — de diversiones amusement
   park (I)
la **parrilla: a la —** grilled (II)
parte:
   ¿de — de quién? who's calling? (6)
   por todas —s all over, everywhere (II)

participar (en) to participate (in) (II)
el **partido** match, game (I, II)
   el — político political party (7)
pasado, -a last, past (I)
el **pasado** past (5)
el **pasajero, la pasajera** passenger (II)
el **pasaporte** passport (I)
pasar to pass; to happen (I)
   — la aspiradora to vacuum (I)
   —lo bien / mal to have a good /
   bad time (I, II)
   ¿qué pasa? what's the matter? (I)
el **pasatiempo** pastime, hobby (I)
pasear:
   ir a — to take a walk (I)
   — en bote to row (I)
el **pasillo** aisle (II)
la **pasta dentífrica** toothpaste (I)
pastel pastel *(color)* (3)
el **pastel** cake (I, II)
la **pastilla** pill (I, II)
el **patín** skate (II)
patinar to skate (I)
   — sobre hielo to ice skate (II)
el **patio de recreo** playground (II)
el **pavo** turkey (II)
la **paz** peace (II)
el **peaje** toll booth (2)
el **peatón,** *pl.* **los peatones** pedestrian (2)
pedir *(e → i)* to ask for, to order (I)
   — prestado, -a (a) to borrow
   (from) (II)
peinarse to comb one's hair (II)
el **peine** comb (II)
pelearse to fight (II)
la **película** film, movie (I)
el **peligro** danger (I, II)
   en — de extinción endangered (I, II)
peligroso, -a dangerous (II, 2)
pelirrojo, -a red-haired (I)
el **pelo** hair (I, II)
   el secador de — hair dryer (II)
la **pelota** ball (II)
peluche:
   el animal de — stuffed animal (II)
   el oso de — teddy bear (II)
la **pena** penalty (10)
pensar *(e → ie)* to think (I)
   — + *inf.* to plan (I)
la **pensión** inexpensive lodging (II)
peor worse (I)
   el / la (los / las) —(es) the worst (I)
   lo — the worst (thing) (1)
el **pepino** cucumber (II)
pequeño, -a small (I, II)
   de — as a child (II)
la **percepción** perception (4)
perder *(e → ie)* to lose (II)
perdón excuse me (I)

perdonar to excuse, to pardon (II)
   perdone (Ud.) excuse me, pardon
   me (II)
perezoso, -a lazy (I)
el **perfil** profile (3)
el **perfume** perfume (II)
el **periódico** newspaper (I, II)
el/la **periodista** journalist (12)
permitir to permit, to allow (II)
   se permite it's allowed (II)
pero but (I)
el **perro** dog (I)
   el — caliente hot dog (II)
la **persona** person (I)
el **personaje** character (II)
personal personal (I)
pertenecer *(c → zc)* to belong (8)
pesado, -a heavy (II)
pesar: a — de (que) in spite of
   (the fact that) (8)
pesar to weigh (8)
las **pesas** weights (II)
pesca: ir de — to go fishing (I)
la **pescadería** fish store (II)
el **pescado** fish *(cooked)* (I)
el **peso** weight (8)
el **pez,** *pl.* **los peces** fish *(live)* (II)
el **piano** piano (II)
la **picadura (de insecto)** insect bite,
   sting (II)
picante spicy, peppery, hot *(flavor)* (I)
   no — mild *(flavor)* (I)
picar *(c → qu)* to sting (II); to chop (II)
el **picnic** picnic (II)
   hacer un — to have a — picnic (II)
el **pie** foot (I)
   a — walking, on foot (I)
   de — standing (3)
   el dedo del — toe (I)
la **piedra** rock, stone (II, 8)
la **piel** fur (I)
la **pierna** leg (I)
la **pila** battery (II)
el/la **piloto** pilot (II)
la **pimienta** pepper *(seasoning)* (I)
el **pimiento verde** green pepper (II)
el **pincel** paintbrush (3)
el **pintor, la pintora** painter (II)
pintoresco, -a picturesque (II)
la **pintura** painting (3)
la **piña** pineapple (II)
la **pirámide** pyramid (I)
la **piscina** pool (I)
el **piso** story, floor (I)
la **pistola (de agua)** (water) pistol (II)
la **pizarra** chalkboard (I)
planear to plan (II)
el **planeta** planet (II)
   plano: el primer — foreground (3)

la planta plant (I, II)
el plástico plastic (I, II)
   de — (made of) plastic (I)
la plata silver (II)
   de — (made of) silver (II)
el plátano banana (I)
el platillo saucer (I)
el plato dish, plate (I)
   el — del día daily special (I)
la playa beach (I)
la plaza town square (I)
la pluma feather (II)
la población population (2)
los pobres poor people (7)
poco: un — (de) a little (I)
poder *(o → ue)* can, to be able (I)
   ¿podría(s)? could you? (II)
la poesía poetry (11)
el polen pollen (II)
el/la policía police officer (II)
   la — the police (I)
la política politics (II)
el político, la política politician (II)
el pollo chicken (I)
el polvo dust (II)
poner to put, to place (I)
   — la mesa to set the table (I)
   — una tienda to pitch a tent (II)
   —se to put on *(clothing, make-up, etc.)* (II); to become (3)
por for (I, II); *(+ place)* by, through, at (II); on behalf of; *(agent)* by (7)
   — aquí around here (I)
   — eso that's why, therefore (I)
   — la mañana / la tarde / la noche in the morning / afternoon / evening (I)
   — lo menos at least (II)
   — otro lado on the other hand (2)
   ¿— qué? why? (I)
   — supuesto of course (I, II)
   — todas partes all over, everywhere (II)
   — un lado on the one hand (2)
porque because (I)
portarse (bien / mal) to behave (well / badly) (II)
la posdata postscript (6)
la posesión possession (II)
posible possible (8)
positivo, -a positive (4)
el postre dessert (I)
   de — for dessert (I)
practicar *(c → qu)* to practice (I)
práctico, -a practical (I)
precolombino, -a pre-Columbian (5)
preferir *(e → ie)* to prefer (I)
la pregunta question (II)
   hacer una — to ask a question (II)

preguntar to ask (II)
preocupar(se) to worry (10)
preparar to prepare (I)
presentar to introduce (I)
   —(se) to join *(army)* (7)
   te presento a . . . I'd like you to meet . . . (I)
el presente present (5)
la presión pressure, stress (2)
prestado, -a: pedir — (a) to borrow (from) (I)
prestar to lend (II)
primaria: la escuela — elementary school (II)
la primavera spring (I)
primero (primer), -a first (I)
el primo, la prima cousin (I)
principal *adj.* main, principal (II)
privado, -a private (6)
probable probable (8)
probar *(o → ue)* to try, to taste (I)
   —se to try on (II)
el problema problem (II)
procedente de arriving from (II)
productivo, -a productive (9)
el producto product (11)
la profesión profession (II)
el profesor, la profesora teacher (I)
el programa program (I)
prohibida: — para menores under 17 not admitted without an adult (4)
prohibir to prohibit (II)
   se prohíbe it's prohibited (II)
prometer to promise (7)
el pronóstico del tiempo weather forecast (I)
propio, -a own (II)
proponer to propose (11)
proteger(se) *(g → j)* to protect (oneself) (I, II)
la proteína protein (II)
protestar to protest (7)
próximo, -a next (II)
el proyector projector (II)
prudente cautious (II)
la prueba quiz (II); proof (8)
público, -a public (II)
el público viewers, public (4)
pude, pudiste *see* **poder**
el pueblo town (II); people (11)
el puente bridge (2)
la puerta door (I); gate (II)
pues well *(to indicate pause)* (I)
la pulsera bracelet (I, II)
   el reloj — wristwatch (I, II)
las puntadas stitches (II)
   hacer — to stitch *(surgically)* (II)
punto:
   el — de vista point of view (3)
   en — sharp, on the dot (I)

puntual punctual (9)
la puntualidad punctuality (9)
puntualmente on time (I)
el pupitre student desk (I)
puro, -a pure, clean (I)
puse, pusiste *see* **poner**

que that, who (I)
   lo — what (II)
¿qué? what? (I)
   ¿de — es...? what's it made of? (II)
   ¡— + *adj.*! how + *adj.!* (I)
   ¿— tal? how's it going? (I)
   ¿— tal es . . . ? how is . . . ? (II)
   ¡— va! not at all! (1)
quedar to fit; to be located (I)
   —se (en la cama) to stay (in bed) (I)
el quehacer (de la casa) household chore (I)
quejarse (de) to complain (about) (1)
quemar(se) to burn (oneself) (II)
querer *(e → ie)* to want (I)
   ¿qué quiere decir . . . ? what does . . . mean? (I)
   quisiera(s) I'd / you'd like (I, II)
querido, -a dear (6)
querremos, *see* **querer**
la quesadilla quesadilla (I)
el queso cheese (I)
el quiché Quiche (a Mayan language) (5)
¿quién(es)? who? whom? (I)
la química chemistry (II)
quince fifteen (I)
quinientos five hundred (I)
quinto, -a fifth (I)
el quiosco (de periódicos) newsstand (II)
quisiera *see* **querer**
quisieron *see* **querer**
quitar la mesa to clear the table (I)
quitarse to take off *(clothing, make-up, etc.)* (II)

el radio radio (set) (II)
la radiografía X-ray (II)
   sacar una — to take an X-ray (II)
la rana frog (II)
la rapidez speed (6)
rápido, -a fast (2)
la raqueta (de tenis) (tennis) racket (II)
el rascacielos, *pl.* **los rascacielos** skyscraper (2)
el rasgo feature (11)
rayas: a — striped (II)
la raza race (11)
la Raza *see* **Día**
razón: (no) tener — to be right (wrong) (I)
la reacción reaction (II)
real real (I)

realidad: en — really (12)
el **realismo** realism (3)
realista realistic (I)
realizar *(z → c)* to perform (9)
rebelarse to revolt (11)
el **recado** message (6)
el/la **recepcionista** receptionist (9)
la **receta** prescription (II); recipe (II)
recetar to prescribe (II)
recibir to receive (I)
el **reciclaje: el centro de —** recycling
    center (I)
reciclar to recycle (I, II)
recientemente recently (4)
recoger *(g → j)* to gather, to pick up
    (I, II)
la **recomendación** recommendation (9)
recomendar *(e → ie)* to recommend (II)
reconquistar to reconquer (11)
recordar *(o → ue)* to remember (II)
recreo: el patio de — playground (II)
el **recuerdo** souvenir (I)
recurrir (a) to resort (to) (10)
la **redacción** editing (1)
el **redactor, la redactora** editor (12)
redondo, -a round (I)
reducir *(c → zc)* to reduce (I, II)
reflejado, -a reflected (3)
el **refresco** soft drink (I)
el **refrigerador** refrigerator (I)
el **refugio** shelter (7)
regalar to give a gift (I, II)
el **regalo** gift (I)
    la tienda de —s gift shop (I)
regatear to bargain (II)
la **región** region (11)
registrar to inspect, to search (II)
la **regla** ruler (I)
regresar to come back, to return (I)
regular so-so, fair (I)
el **rehén,** *pl.* **los rehenes** hostage (10)
la **reina** queen (11)
reírse *(e → i)* to laugh (4)
la **reja** grating (11)
relacionarse con to relate to (1)
la **religión** religion (5)
el **relleno** filling (II)
el **reloj** clock (II)
el/la **remitente** sender (6)
reparar to repair, to fix (II)
el **repartidor, la repartidora** delivery
    person (9)
repartir to deliver (II)
repasar to review (II)
el **repelente** insect repellent (II)
el **reportaje** report (4)
el **requisito** requirement (9)
el **rescate** ransom (10)
la **reservación** reservation (II)

el **resfriado** cold (I)
resolver *(o → ue)* to solve (1)
respetar to respect (1)
respetuoso, -a respectful (9)
la **responsabilidad** responsibility (7)
responsable responsible (1)
la **respuesta** answer (II)
el **restaurante** restaurant (I)
el **resultado** result (11)
el **retraso** delay (II)
el **retrato** portrait (3)
la **reunión** gathering, get-together (I, II)
la **revista** magazine (I, II)
revolver *(o → ue)* to stir (II)
el **rey,** *pl.* **los reyes** king (11)
rico, -a rich (5)
el **río** river (II)
el **ritmo** rhythm (11)
robar to rob (II)
el **robot** robot (II)
rock: la música — rock music (II)
la **rodilla** knee (II)
rojo, -a red (I)
romántico, -a romantic (I)
el **rompecabezas** jigsaw puzzle (II)
romperse to break *(a bone)* (II)
la **ropa** clothes (I)
    la — para caballeros men's wear (II)
    la — para damas ladies' wear (II)
    la — para niños children's wear (II)
rosado, -a pink (I)
roto, -a broken (II); torn (II)
rubio, -a blonde (I)
la **rueda** wheel (8)
    la silla de —s wheelchair (II)
el **ruido** noise (2)
las **ruinas** ruins (I)
rural rural (2)

sábado Saturday (I)
    el — on Saturday (I)
saber to know (how) (I, II)
    (yo) no lo sabía I didn't know that (I)
sabroso, -a delicious, tasty (I)
el **sacapuntas** pencil sharpener (II)
sacar *(c → qu)* to take; to take out (I)
    — dinero to withdraw money (I)
    — fotos to take pictures (I)
    — una buena / mala nota to get a
    good / bad grade (II)
    — un libro to check out a book (I)
el **saco de dormir** sleeping bag (II)
sacudir to dust (I)
sagrado, -a sacred (5)
la **sal** salt (I)
la **sala** living room (I)
    la — de clases classroom (I)
    la — de emergencia emergency
    room (II)
    la — de estar family room (I)

salado, -a salty (II)
la **salida** exit (II)
salir to go out, to leave (I)
la **salsa** sauce, dressing (I, II)
saltar (a la cuerda) to jump (rope) (II)
saltos: dar — to dive (II)
la **salud** health (I)
saludar to greet (II)
    saludos a todos greetings to
    everyone (6)
salvaje wild *(animals)* (II)
el/la **salvavidas** lifeguard (9)
la **sandía** watermelon (II)
el **sandwich** sandwich (I)
la **sangre** blood (II)
sano, -a healthy (II, 2)
satélite: la televisión por — satellite
    television (4)
el **saxofón** saxophone (II)
se ha dicho *see* **decir**
el **secador de pelo** hair dryer (II)
la **secadora** (clothes) dryer (II)
secar *(c → qu)* to dry (II)
    —se (el pelo) to dry (one's hair) (II)
la **sección** section (II)
seco, -a dry (II)
el **secretario, la secretaria** secretary (II)
secuestrar to kidnap (10)
el **secuestro** kidnapping, hijacking (10)
sed: tener — to be thirsty (I)
la **seda dental** dental floss (II)
seguida: en — right away (I)
seguir *(e → i)* to follow; to continue
    (II); to pursue (12)
    — + *present participle* to continue +
    verb + -ing (5)
según according to (II)
segundo, -a second (I)
la **seguridad** safety (10)
    el cinturón de — seatbelt (II)
    el sistema de — security system (II)
seguro, -a safe (2)
    estar — to be sure (8)
seis six (I)
seiscientos six hundred (I)
el **sello** stamp (I)
la **selva** forest (I)
    la — tropical rain forest (I)
el **semáforo** traffic light (II)
la **semana** week (I)
    el fin de — on the weekend (I)
el **semestre** semester (I)
sencillo, -a simple (II)
el **sendero** path (II, 2)
sensacionalista sensationalistic (II)
sentado, -a seated (3)
la **sentencia** sentence (10)
sentido: el — del humor sense of
    humor (1)

sentir:
   lo siento I'm sorry (I)
   —se *(e → ie)* to feel (II)
la **señal de alto** stop sign (II)
  señor Mr.; sir (I)
  señora Mrs.; ma'am (I)
  señorita Miss; miss (I)
  separado, -a (de) separated (from) (II)
  separar to separate; to sort (I, II)
  septiembre September (I)
  séptimo, -a seventh (I)
  ser to be (I)
el **ser humano** human being (II)
  sería *see* ser
  serio, -a serious (I)
la **serpiente** snake (I, II)
el **servicio:**
   la estación de — gas station (I)
   el — social social service (7)
los **servicios** restroom (II)
la **servilleta** napkin (I)
  servir *(e → i)* to serve (I)
   — para to be used for (8)
   ¿para qué sirve? what's it used for? (8)
  sesenta sixty (I)
  setecientos seven hundred (I)
  setenta seventy (I)
  severo, -a severe (10)
  sexto, -a sixth (I)
  si if, whether (I)
  sí yes; do + *verb (emphatic)* (I)
la **siembra** planting, sowing (5)
  siempre always (I)
  siete seven (I)
el **siglo** century (3)
el **significado** meaning (5)
la **sílaba** syllable (5)
la **silla** chair (I)
   la — de ruedas wheelchair (II)
el **sillón** armchair (I)
  silvestre wild *(plants)* (II)
el **símbolo** symbol (5)
  simpático, -a nice, friendly (I)
  sin without (II)
   — embargo nevertheless (2)
la **sinagoga** synagogue (11)
  sincero, -a sincere (1)
  sino but *(after negative)* (7)
   no sólo . . . — también not only . . . but also (9)
  sintético, -a synthetic (II)
el **síntoma** symptom (II)
el **sistema de seguridad** security system (II)
  situado, -a situated, placed (2)
  sobre about; on (I)
   patinar — hielo to ice skate (II)
el **sobre** envelope (6)

el **sobrino, la sobrina** nephew, niece (II)
  sociable outgoing (I)
la **sociedad** society (7)
el **sofá** sofa (I)
el **sol** sun (I)
   los anteojos de — sunglasses (I)
   hace — it's sunny (I)
   tomar el — to sunbathe (I)
  solar solar (II)
  soler *(o → ue) + inf.* to be in the habit of (I, II)
  solicitar to solicit *(donations)* (7)
la **solicitud** application (9)
  solo, -a alone (I)
  sólo only (I)
   no — . . . sino también not only . . . but also (9)
  soltero, -a single, unmarried (II)
la **sombra** shade (II); shadow (3)
  sonar *(o → ue)* to ring (6)
  sonido: el equipo de — stereo (I)
  soñar *(o → ue)* **(con)** to dream (about) (12)
la **sopa** soup (I)
  soportar to tolerate, to stand (II)
  sordo, -a deaf (12)
  sorprender(se) to surprise (10)
la **sorpresa: la fiesta de —** surprise party (I, II)
  soso, -a tasteless (II)
el **sospechoso, la sospechosa** suspect (10)
el **sótano** basement (I)
  su, sus his, her; your *formal,* their (I)
el **subconsciente** subconscious (3)
el **sube y baja** seesaw (II)
  subir to climb (I)
  subjetivo, -a subjective (4)
  sucio, -a dirty (I)
la **sudadera** sweatshirt (I)
el **sueldo** salary (9)
el **suelo** floor (II)
  sueño: tener — to be sleepy (I)
el **sueño** dream (3)
  suerte: por — luckily (II)
el **suéter** sweater (I)
   el — de cuello alto turtleneck (II)
  suficiente sufficient, enough (II)
  sugerir *(e → ie)* to suggest (II)
el **sujetapapeles** paper clip (II)
el **supermercado** supermarket (I)
  suponer to suppose (8)
  supuesto: por — of course (I, II)
  surf:
   hacer — to surf (II)
   hacer — de vela to windsurf (II)
   la tabla de — surfboard (II)
el **surrealismo** surrealism (3)

  suyo, -a (of) his, her (of hers), your (of yours), their (of theirs) (II)
el **suyo, la suya** yours, his, hers, theirs (II)

la **tabla (de surf)** surfboard (II)
  tacaño, -a stingy (I)
el **taco** taco (I)
el **tacón** heel (I, II)
  tal:
   ¿qué —? how's it going? (I)
   ¿qué — es . . . ? how is . . . ? (II)
   — como such as (4)
la **talla** clothing size (II)
el **tamaño** size (II)
  también also, too (I)
el **tambor** drum (II)
  tampoco either, neither, not either (I)
  tan + *adj.* + **como** as + *adj.* + as (II)
  tanto(s), -a(s) + *noun* + **como** as much / many + *noun* + as (II)
las **tapas** Spanish-style appetizers (II)
  tardar (en) to take time (to) (2)
  tarde late (I)
la **tarde** afternoon (I)
   buenas —s good afternoon, good evening (I)
   de/por la — in the afternoon (I)
la **tarea** homework (I); task (9)
la **tarjeta** card (I)
   la — de crédito credit card (II)
   la — de embarque boarding pass (II)
   la — postal post card (I)
la **tarta** pie (II)
el **taxi** taxi (I)
la **taza** cup (I)
el **tazón** bowl (I)
  te *fam. obj. pron.* you (I)
el **té** tea (I)
   el — helado iced tea (I)
el **teatro** theater (I)
   la obra de — play (II)
el **techo** roof (11)
el **técnico, la técnica (de computadoras)** (computer) technician (II)
la **tecnología** technology (II)
la **tela** fabric, cloth (II)
  telefónica: la oficina — telephone office (II)
el **teléfono** telephone (I)
   el número de — phone number (I)
   por — on the telephone (I)
   el — celular cellular phone (6)
   el — con video video telephone (II)
   el — inalámbrico cordless phone (6)
   el — público public (pay) phone (II)
el **telegrama** telegram (6)
la **telenovela** soap opera (I)

Vocabulario español-inglés 519

la **tele(visión)** television (I)
    la **— por cable** cable television (4)
    la **— por satélite** satellite television (4)
el **televisor** TV set (II)
el **tema** subject (3)
temer (a) to fear (10)
el **temor** fear (10)
el **templo** temple (I, 5)
temprano early (I)
el **tenedor** fork (I)
tener to have (I)
    ¿qué tienes? what's wrong? (I)
    — que + *inf.* to have to (I)
    — en común to have in common (1)
(yo) tendría que *see* **tener**
(tú) tendrías que *see* **tener**
el **tenis** tennis (I)
los **tenis** sneakers (I)
la **teoría** theory (8)
tercer, -a third (I)
la **terminal de equipaje** baggage claim (II)
terminar to end (I)
el **terremoto** earthquake (II)
terrible terrible (I)
terror: la película de — horror film (I)
el **terrorismo** terrorism (10)
el/la **testigo** witness (10)
ti you *fam. after prep.* (I)
el **tiempo** time; weather (I)
    (de) — completo full-time (9)
    (de) — parcial part-time (9)
    hace buen/mal — the weather is nice/bad (I)
    el pronóstico del — weather forecast (I)
    ¿qué — hace? what's the weather like? (I)
tener — de + *inf.* to have time + *inf.* (II)
la **tienda** store (I)
    poner una — to pitch a tent (II)
    la — (de acampar) tent (II)
la **Tierra** Earth (I, II)
el **tigre** tiger (I)
tímido, -a shy (II)
el **tío, la tía** uncle, aunt (I)
    los tíos uncles; aunts and uncles (I)
típico, -a typical (I, II)
el **tiroteo** shooting (10)
el **tobillo** ankle (II)
el **tobogán** slide (II)
el **tocacintas** tape player (II)
tocar *(c → qu)* to play (I)
todavía still (I)
    — no not yet (I)
todos, -as all; everyone (I)
    — los días every day (I)
tomar to take (I)
    — el sol to sunbathe (I)

el **tomate** tomato (I)
la **tonelada** ton (8)
el **tono** tone *(in a painting)* (3); dial tone (6)
tonto, -a silly, dumb (I)
la **tormenta** storm (II)
la **torre** tower (11)
la **tortilla** tortilla (I)
    la — española potato and onion omelet (II)
la **tortuga** turtle (II)
la **tos** cough (II)
    el jarabe (para la —) cough syrup (II)
toser to cough (II)
tostado: el pan — toast (I)
el **tostador** toaster (II)
trabajador, -a hardworking (I)
trabajar to work (I)
el **trabajo** work (7)
la **tradición** tradition (5)
la **traducción** translation (12)
traducir *(c → zc)* to translate (12)
el **traductor, la traductora** translator (12)
traer to bring (I)
el **tráfico** traffic (II)
el **traje** suit (I, II)
    el — de baño bathing suit (I)
trajeron *see* **traer**
el **trampolín** diving board (II)
tranquilo, -a still, calm (1)
transformar(se) to transform (3)
el **transporte** transportation (II)
tratar (bien/mal) to treat (well/badly) (9)
    — de to try to (3)
    —se de to be about (II)
través: a — de through (11)
travieso, -a mischievous, naughty (II)
trazar *(z → c)* to draw (8)
trece thirteen (I)
treinta thirty (I)
el **tren** train (I)
tres three (I)
trescientos three hundred (I)
el **triciclo** tricycle (II)
    montar en — to ride a tricycle (II)
triste sad (I)
la **trompeta** trumpet (II)
tu, tus your *fam.* (I)
tú you *fam.* (I)
la **tumba** tomb (5)
el **turismo: la oficina de —** tourist office (II)
el/la **turista** tourist (II)
el **tutor, la tutora** tutor (II)
tuve, tuviste *see* **tener**
tuyo, -a your, (of) yours (II)
el **tuyo, la tuya** yours (II)

último, -a last (II)
la **uña** fingernail (II)
    el esmalte de —s nail polish (II)
único, -a only (I)
unir to unite (7)
la **universidad** university (II)
uno (un), una a, an, one (I)
    es la una it's one o'clock (I)
    — one, a person (II)
unos, -as a few, some (I)
usar to use (I, II); to wear (II)
usted (Ud.) you *formal sing.* (I)
ustedes (Uds.) you *formal pl.* (I)
útil useful (12)
la **uva** grape (I)

la **vaca** cow (I)
las **vacaciones** vacation (I)
    ir de — to go on vacation (I)
valer: (no) vale la pena it's (not) worthwhile (I)
el **valle** valley (II)
el **valor** value (3)
vanidoso, -a vain (1)
el **vaquero, la vaquera** cowboy, cowgirl (II)
la **vasija** jar (5)
el **vaso** glass (I)
    ¡vaya! my goodness! gee! wow! (I)
el **vecino, la vecina** neighbor (II)
veinte twenty (I)
veintiuno (veintiún) twenty-one (I)
la **vela** candle (II); sail (II)
el **venado** deer (II)
la **venda** bandage (II)
el **vendedor, la vendedora** salesperson (II)
vender to sell (I)
    —se to be sold (II)
venenoso, -a poisonous (II)
venir *(e → ie)* to come (2)
venta: el / la agente de —s (sales) agent (12)
la **ventaja** advantage (II)
la **ventana** window (I)
la **ventanilla** *(plane)* window (II)
el **ventilador** electric fan (II)
ver to see, to watch (I)
    a — let's see (I)
    —se to see each other (II)
el **verano** summer (I)
veras: ¿de —? really? (I)
la **verdad** truth (I)
    ¿—? isn't that so?, right? (I)
verde green (I)
la **verdulería** greengrocer (II)
las **verduras** vegetables (I)
el **vestido** dress (I)
vestirse *(e → i)* to get dressed (II)
el **veterinario, la veterinaria** veterinarian (II)

la **vez,** *pl.* **las veces** time (I)
   a la — at the same time (I)
   a veces at times, sometimes (I)
   alguna — ever (I)
   cada — más more and more (6)
   de — en cuando sometimes (II)
   dos veces twice (I)
   muchas veces many times (I)
   una — one time, once (I)
  vía: por — aérea by air mail (6)
  viajar to travel (12)
el **viaje** trip, voyage (II)
   la agencia de —s travel agency (II)
   el / la agente de —s travel agent (II)
el **viajero, la viajera** traveler (II)
   el cheque de — traveler's check (II)
la **víctima** victim (II)
la **vida** life (I)
   ganarse la — to earn a living (II)
   el programa de hechos de la —
     real fact-based program (I)
el **video** video (II)
la **videocasetera** VCR (I)
el **videojuego** video game (I)

el **vidrio** glass (I, II)
   de — (made of) glass (I)
  viejo, -a old (I)
el **viento** wind (I)
   hace — it's windy (I)
  viernes Friday (I)
   el — on Friday (I)
  vigilar to guard (10)
el **vinagre** vinegar (II)
la **violencia** violence (II)
  violento, -a violent (II)
el **violín** violin (II)
el **virus** virus
  visitar to visit (I)
la **vitamina** vitamin (II)
  vivir to live (I)
  vivo, -a bright (3)
  volar *(o → ue)* to fly (8)
el **vóleibol** volleyball (I)
  voluntario(a): trabajar como — to
   volunteer (II)
  volver *(o → ue)* **a** + *inf.* to do
   (something) again (6)
  vomitar to vomit (II)

  vosotros, -as you *pl.* (I)
  votar to vote (7)
  voz: en — alta/baja in a loud/soft
   voice (6)
el **vuelo** flight (II)
   el / la auxiliar de — flight
    attendant (II)
  vuelta *see* **boleto**

  y and (I)
  ya already (I)
   — no no longer, not anymore (I)
el **yeso** cast (II)
el **Yeti** the abominable snowman (8)
  yo I (I)

la **zanahoria** carrot (I)
la **zapatería** shoe store (I)
el **zapato** shoe (I)
   los —s de tacón alto high-heeled
    shoes (I, II)
el **zoológico** zoo (I)

ENGLISH-SPANISH VOCABULARY

This *Vocabulary* contains all active vocabulary from PASO A PASO 1, 2, and 3.

A dash (—) represents the main entry word. For example, **to make a phone —** following **call** means **to make a phone call.**

The number following each entry indicates the chapter in which the word or expression is presented. A Roman numeral (I) indicates that the word was presented in PASO A PASO 1; a Roman numeral (II), that it was presented in PASO A PASO 2.

The following abbreviations are used: *adj.* (adjective), *dir. obj.* (direct object). *f.* (feminine), *fam.* (familiar), *ind. obj.* (indirect object), *inf.* (infinitive), *m.* (masculine), *pl.* (plural), *prep.* (preposition), *pron.* (pronoun), *sing.* (singular).

a, an un, una (I)
able: to be — poder *(o → ue)* (I)
abominable snowman el Yeti (8)
about sobre (I)
  to be — tratarse de (II)
abstract abstracto, -a (3)
abundant abundante (2)
academic académico, -a (12)
to **accept** aceptar (5)
accident el accidente (II)
according to según (II)
accountant el contador, la contadora (12)
accused (person) el acusado, la acusada (10)
ache el dolor (I)
to **achieve** alcanzar *(z → c)* (9)
acquainted: to be — with conocer *(c → zc)* (I, II)
to **acquire** adquirir *(i → ie)* (1)
to **act** actuar *(u → ú)* (II)
acting la actuación (II)
action:
  — figure el muñeco (II)
  — film la película de acción (II)
actively activamente (12)
activity la actividad (II)
actor, actress el actor, la actriz (I)
ad el anuncio (I)
addition: in — además (II)
address la dirección, *pl.* las direcciones (II)
addressee el destinatario, la destinataria (6)
administrative administrativo, -a (9)
to **admire** admirar (1)
to **adopt** adoptar (11)
adults only sólo para mayores (4)
advanced avanzado, -a (5)
advantage la ventaja (II)
adventure film la película de aventuras (I)
advice el consejo (1)
  to give a piece of — dar un consejo (1)
affectionate cariñoso, -a (I)
to **affirm** afirmar (8)
affirmation la afirmación (8)

afraid: to be — (of) tener miedo (de) (10)
African africano, -a (11)
after después (de) (I)
  — + *verb* después de + *inf.* (II)
  — school después de las clases (I)
afternoon la tarde (I)
  — snack la merienda (I)
  good — buenas tardes (I)
  in the — por la tarde (I)
afterward luego (I)
again de nuevo (II)
  to do something — volver a + *inf.* (6)
against en contra (de) (7)
age la época (3)
  at the age of ... a los ... años (II)
  at what —? ¿a qué edad? (II)
agency: travel — la agencia de viajes (II)
agent:
  sales — el / la agente de ventas (12)
  travel — el / la agente de viajes (II)
ago hace + *(time)* ... (I)
to **agree** estar de acuerdo (I)
  not to — with *(food)* hacer daño a (II)
agriculture la agricultura (5)
aide el / la ayudante (1)
air el aire (I)
  — conditioning el aire acondicionado (II)
  by —mail por vía aérea (6)
airline la línea aérea (II)
airplane el avión, *pl.* los aviones (II)
airport el aeropuerto (II)
aisle el pasillo (II)
alarm la alarma (10)
  — clock el despertador (II)
algebra el álgebra *f.* (II)
alien el / la extraterrestre (II)
all todo, -a (I)
  — over por todas partes (II)
  — right bueno (I)
  — the same (to me) (me) da igual (II)
All Souls' Day el Día de los Muertos (11)
allergic (to) alérgico, -a (a) (II)
allergy la alergia (II)
to **allow** permitir (II)
  it's —ed se permite (II)
almost casi (I)

alone solo, -a (I)
already ya (I)
also también (I)
although aunque (1)
aluminum el aluminio (I)
always siempre (I)
ambitious ambicioso, -a (9)
ambulance la ambulancia (II)
among entre (I)
to **amuse (oneself)** entretener(se) *(e → ie)* (4)
amusement park el parque de diversiones (I)
amusing divertido, -a (I)
to **analyze** analizar *(z → c)* (4)
ancestors los antepasados (5)
ancestry la descendencia (11)
and y (I)
angry: to get — enojarse (1)
animal el animal, *pl.* los animales (I, II)
  stuffed — el animal de peluche (II)
  wild — el animal salvaje (II)
ankle el tobillo (II)
anniversary el aniversario (II)
announcer el locutor, la locutora (II)
to **annoy** molestar (II)
another otro, -a (I)
answer la respuesta (II)
to **answer** contestar (I)
answering machine el contestador automático (6)
ant la hormiga (II)
anthropologist el antropólogo, la antropóloga (5)
antibiotic el antibiótico (II)
any cualquier (9)
  not — ninguno (ningún), -a (I, II)
anybody cualquiera (6)
anything else algo más (I)
anywhere: not — ninguna parte (I)
apartment el apartamento (I)
to **appear** aparecer *(c → zc)* (8)
appetizers *(Spanish-style)* las tapas (II)
apple la manzana (I)
appliance el aparato (II)
application la solicitud (9)
appointment la cita (9)

appropriate adecuado, -a; oportuno, -a (9)

approximately aproximadamente (6)

April abril (I)

archaeologist el arqueólogo, la arqueóloga (5)

architect el arquitecto, la arquitecta (5)

area el campo (5)

to **argue** discutir (1)

arm el brazo (I)

armchair el sillón, *pl.* los sillones (I)

armed a mano armada (10)

army el ejército (7)

around here por aquí (I)

to **arrest** arrestar (II)

to **arrive** llegar *(g → gu)* (I)

arriving from procedente de (II)

art el arte (I, II)

    — exhibit la exposición *(pl.* las exposiciones) de arte (II)

artist el / la artista (3)

artistic artístico, -a (I)

as:

    — + *adj.* **—** tan + *adj.* + como (II)

    — much (many) + *noun* **+ —** tanto, -a (tantos, -as) + *noun* + como (II)

    such — tal como (4)

to **ask** preguntar (II)

    to — a question hacer una pregunta (II)

    to — for pedir *(e → i)* (I)

asparagus el espárrago (II)

assault el atentado (10)

assistance la ayuda (II)

assistant el / la ayudante (1)

to **astonish** asombrar (10)

astronaut el / la astronauta (II)

astronomer el astrónomo, la astrónoma (5)

at en; a (I); por (II)

athlete el / la deportista (II)

athletic deportista (I)

atmosphere el ambiente (I)

attack el ataque (10)

to **attend to** atender *(e → ie)* (a) (9)

attention: to pay — to hacer caso a (1); fijarse (en) (3)

to **attract** atraer (3)

attractive atractivo, -a (I)

auditorium el auditorio (II)

August agosto (I)

aunt la tía (I)

    — s and uncles los tíos (I)

automatic automático, -a (II)

autumn el otoño (I)

avenue la avenida (I)

avocado el aguacate (I)

    — dip el guacamole (I)

to **avoid** evitar (10)

to **baby-sit** cuidar niños (II)

back la espalda (I)

    in the — al fondo (II)

background el fondo (3)

backpack la mochila (I)

bad malo, -a (I)

    to have a — time pasarlo mal (I, II)

    That's too —! ¡Qué lástima! (I)

badly mal (1)

baggage el equipaje (II)

    — claim la terminal de equipaje (II)

baked *adj.* al horno (II)

bakery la panadería (II)

balcony el balcón, *pl.* los balcones (11)

ball la pelota (II); *(inflated)* el balón, *pl.* los balones (II)

banana el plátano (I)

band la banda (II)

bandage la venda (II)

bank el banco (I)

banker el banquero, la banquera (12)

barbecue la barbacoa (II)

    to have a — hacer una barbacoa (II)

bargain la ganga (I)

to **bargain** regatear (II)

baseball el béisbol (I)

based (on) basado, -a (en) (II)

basement el sótano (I)

basketball el básquetbol (I)

bass el contrabajo (II)

bat *(baseball)* el bate (de béisbol) (II)

bath: to take a — bañarse (II)

bathing suit el traje de baño (I)

bathroom el baño (I)

battery la pila (II)

battle la batalla (11)

to **be** estar; ser (I)

    to — a part (of) formar parte (de) (11)

    to — about tratarse de (II)

    to — (used) for servir *(e → i)* para (8)

beach la playa (I)

bean el frijol (I)

    green —s las judías verdes (I)

    refried —s los frijoles refritos (I)

bear el oso (I)

beautiful bello, -a (2)

because porque (I)

to **become** adquirir *(i → ie)* (1)

bed la cama (I)

    to go to — acostarse *(o → ue)* (II)

bedroom el dormitorio (I)

bee la abeja (II)

beef la carne (de res) (I)

before + *verb* antes de + *inf.* (II)

to **begin** empezar *(e → ie) (z → c)* (I)

behalf: on — of por (7)

to **behave (well / badly)** portarse (bien / mal) (II)

behind detrás (de) (I)

to **believe** creer (I)

to **belong** pertenecer *(c → zc)* (8)

below abajo (3)

belt el cinturón, *pl.* los cinturones (II)

benefit el beneficio (12)

to **benefit** beneficiar(se) (7)

beside al lado de (I)

besides además (II)

best el / la (los / las) mejor(es) (I)

    the — (thing) lo mejor (1)

better mejor (I)

between entre (I)

beverage la bebida (I)

bicycle la bicicleta (I, II)

    to ride a — montar en bicicleta (I, II)

big grande (I)

    — screen TV la pantalla gigante (II)

bike *see* **bicycle**

bilingual bilingüe (12)

bill *(restaurant)* la cuenta (I)

binder (3-ring) la carpeta de argollas (I)

biology la biología (II)

bird el pájaro (I, II)

birthday el cumpleaños (I)

    — card la tarjeta de cumpleaños (I)

    — party la fiesta de cumpleaños (I, II)

    happy —! ¡feliz cumpleaños! (I)

    to have a — cumplir años (II)

bite *(insect)* la picadura (II)

to **bite** *(insect)* picar *(c → qu)* (II)

bitter amargo, -a (II)

black negro, -a (I)

    in — and white en blanco y negro (I)

block la cuadra (I); *(toy)* el bloque (II)

    how many —s (from . . .)? ¿a cuántas cuadras (de . . .)? (I)

blond rubio, -a (I)

blood la sangre (II)

blouse la blusa (I)

to **blow out** *(candles)* apagar *(g → gu)* (II)

blue azul (I)

boarding pass la tarjeta de embarque (II)

body el cuerpo (I)

to **boil** hervir *(e → ie)* (II)

bold atrevido, -a (I)

bone el hueso (II)

    to break a — romperse (II)

book el libro (I)

    — bag el bolso (II)

bookstore la librería (I)

boot la bota (I)

    half — el botín, *pl.* los botines (II)

English-Spanish Vocabulary   523

border la frontera (12)
to **bore** aburrir (I)
bored: to be — aburrirse (II)
boring aburrido, -a (I)
born: to be — nacer (II)
to **borrow (from)** pedir *(e → i)* prestado, -a (a) (II)
boss el jefe, la jefa (9)
to **bother** molestar (II)
bottle la botella (I, II)
bowl el tazón, *pl.* los tazones (I); *(earthenware)* el cuenco (5)
bowling los bolos (II)
boy el muchacho (I); el niño (II)
boyfriend el novio (I)
bracelet la pulsera (I, II)
braces los frenillos (II)
bread el pan (I)
to **break** *(a bone)* romperse (II)
breakfast el desayuno (I)
for — en el desayuno (I)
to have — desayunar (II)
bridge el puente (2)
bright vivo, -a (3)
to **bring** traer (I)
they brought trajeron (11)
broken roto, -a (II)
brother el hermano (I)
—s and sisters los hermanos (I)
—-in-law el cuñado (II)
brown marrón, *pl.* marrones (I); *(hair)* castaño (I)
to **brush** *(one's teeth, hair, etc.)* cepillarse (los dientes, el pelo, etc.) (II)
to **build** construir *(i → y)* (5)
building el edificio (II)
buried enterrado, -a (5)
to **burn** quemar (II)
to — oneself quemarse (II)
burrito el burrito (I)
bus el autobús, *pl.* los autobuses (I)
— stop la parada del autobús (I)
business los negocios (II)
—man, —woman el hombre / la mujer de negocios (II)
busy ocupado, -a (I)
but pero (I); *(after negative)* sino (7)
butcher shop la carnicería (II)
butter la mantequilla (I)
butterfly la mariposa (II)
button el botón, *pl.* los botones (II)
to **buy** comprar (I)
by por (I); + *vehicle* en (I)

cable television la televisión por cable (4)
cactus el cacto (I, II)
cafeteria la cafetería (II)
cake el pastel (I, II)

calamine lotion la calamina (II)
to **calculate** calcular (8)
calculator la calculadora (I)
calendar el calendario (5)
call la llamada (6)
to make a — hacer una llamada (6)
to make a collect — hacer una llamada a cobro revertido (6)
to make a long-distance — hacer una llamada de larga distancia (6)
to **call** llamar (I)
calm tranquilo, -a (1)
calorie la caloría (II)
camera la cámara (I)
campaign la campaña (1)
electoral — la campaña electoral (7)
campground el campamento (II)
camping: to go — ir de camping (II)
can poder *(o → ue)* (I); la lata (I, II)
— opener el abrelatas (II)
candidate el candidato, la candidata (7)
candle la vela (II)
candy el dulce (II)
canned enlatado, -a (II)
canoe la canoa (II)
to go —ing navegar *(g → gu)* en canoa (II)
cantaloupe el melón, *pl.* los melones (II)
canvas la lona (II)
cap la gorra (II)
ski — el gorro (I)
capable capaz, *pl.* capaces (9)
car el coche (I)
— coat el chaquetón, *pl.* los chaquetones (II)
carbohydrate el carbohidrato (II)
card la tarjeta (I)
ID — el carnet de identidad (II)
cardboard el cartón (I, II)
career la carrera (12)
careful cuidadoso, -a (9)
to be — (of / with) tener cuidado (con) (II)
carousel el carrusel (II)
carrot la zanahoria (I)
carte: a la — a la carta (I)
cartoons los dibujos animados (I)
case: in — of en caso de (II)
cash (el dinero) en efectivo (II)
to **cash** cambiar (II)
cashier el cajero, la cajera (II)
—'s station la caja (II)
cassette el casete (II)
cast el yeso (II)
castle el castillo (11)
cat el gato (I)
catalog el catálogo (II)
cathedral la catedral (I)
cause la causa (7)

cautious prudente (I)
CD el disco compacto (II)
to **celebrate** celebrar (II)
celebration la celebración, *pl.* las celebraciones (II)
censorship la censura (4)
center el centro (I); *(middle)* el centro (3)
community — el centro de la comunidad (7)
day-care — la guardería infantil (II)
recreation — el centro recreativo (7)
recycling — el centro de reciclaje (I)
rehabilitation — el centro de rehabilitación (7)
shopping — el centro comercial (I)
centimeter el centímetro (8)
central central (II)
century el siglo (3)
cereal el cereal (I)
ceremony la ceremonia (5)
certain cierto, -a (8)
chain la cadena (II)
key — el llavero (II)
chair la silla (I)
chalkboard la pizarra (I)
champion el campeón, *pl.* los campeones; la campeona (II)
championship el campeonato (II)
chance la oportunidad (2)
change el cambio (II)
to **change** cambiar (II)
to — channels cambiar de canal (4)
channel el canal (I)
chapter el capítulo (II)
character el personaje (II)
charge: to take — of encargarse *(g → gu)* (de) (9)
to **chat** charlar (II)
cheap barato, -a (I)
check el cheque (II)
to **check** *(baggage)* facturar (II)
to — out a book sacar un libro (I)
checked *(design)* a cuadros (II)
checkers las damas (II)
cheese el queso (I)
chemistry la química (II)
cherry la cereza (II)
chess el ajedrez (II)
chestnut(-colored) castaño, -a (I)
chicken el pollo (I)
— soup la sopa de pollo (I)
child el niño, la niña (II)
as a — de pequeño, -a (II)
only — el hijo único, la hija única (I)
children los niños (II)
—'s wear la ropa para niños (II)
chili pepper el chile (I)
chocolate: hot — el chocolate (I)
choir el coro (II)

to choose escoger *(g → j)* (I, II)
to chop picar *(c → qu)* (II)
   chore el quehacer (I)
      household — el quehacer de la casa (I)
   chorus el coro (II)
   Christian el cristiano, la cristiana (11)
   Christmas la Navidad (II)
      — Eve la Nochebuena (II)
   church la iglesia (I)
   churro el churro (I)
   citizen el ciudadano, la ciudadana (7)
   citizenship la ciudadanía (7)
   city la ciudad (I)
   civilization la civilización, *pl.* las civilizaciones (5)
   clarinet el clarinete (II)
   class la clase (de) (I)
   classical clásico, -a (II)
   classified ads los anuncios clasificados (9)
to classify clasificar *(c → qu)* (4)
   classmate el compañero, la compañera (I)
   classroom la sala de clases (I)
   clean limpio, -a; puro, -a (I)
to clean limpiar (I)
      to — up arreglar (I)
to clear the table quitar la mesa (I)
   client el cliente, la clienta (9)
to climb subir (I)
   clinic la clínica (I)
   clock el reloj (II)
      alarm — el despertador (II)
   close íntimo, -a (1)
to close cerrar *(e → ie)* (I)
   closet el guardarropa (I)
   cloth la tela (II)
   clothes la ropa (I)
   club el club, *pl.* los clubes (II)
   coach el entrenador, la entrenadora (II)
   coat el abrigo (I)
      car — el chaquetón, *pl.* los chaquetones (II)
   cockroach la cucaracha (II)
   coffee el café (I)
   coin la moneda (II)
   cold frío, -a (I)
      to be (very) — tener (mucho) frío (I)
      to have a — tener (un) resfriado (I)
      it's — out hace frío (I)
to collaborate colaborar (con) (7)
to collect coleccionar (II)
   collect call la llamada a cobro revertido (6)
   collection la colección, *pl.* las colecciones (II)
   colony la colonia (11)
   color el color (I)
      in — en colores (I)
      what —? ¿de qué color? (I)

Columbus Day el Día de la Raza (II)
   comb el peine (II)
to comb one's hair peinarse (II)
to combine combinar(se) (11)
to come venir *(e → ie)* (2)
   comedy la comedia (I)
   comfortable cómodo, -a (I)
   comical cómico -a (I)
   commentary el comentario (4)
   commercial el anuncio (de televisión) (I)
to commit cometer (12)
   common: to have in — tener en común (1)
to communicate comunicar(se) *(c → qu)* (6)
   community la comunidad (I)
   compact disc el disco compacto (II)
to complain (about) quejarse (de) (1)
to complete completar (7)
   completely completamente (12)
   composed: to be — of componer(se) de (11)
   composition la composición (II)
   computer la computadora (II)
      — technician el técnico, la técnica de computadoras (II)
   concert el concierto (I)
   conflict el conflicto (1)
   confused: to be — confundirse (12)
to congratulate felicitar (II)
   congratulations! ¡felicidades! (II)
to conquer conquistar (11)
   conqueror el conquistador (11)
to conserve conservar (I, II)
   considerate considerado, -a (1)
   consist: to — of componer(se) de (11)
to construct construir *(i → y)* (5)
   contact el contacto (12)
   contact lenses los lentes de contacto (II)
to contaminate contaminar (II)
   contaminated contaminado, -a (I, II)
   continent el continente (11)
to continue + *verb* + *-ing* seguir *(e → i)* + *present participle* (5)
to contribute contribuir *(i → y)* (2)
   contribution la contribución, *pl.* las contribuciones (5)
to control controlar (4)
   convenient conveniente (2)
      to be — convenir *(e → ie)* (9)
   cook el cocinero, la cocinera (II)
to cook cocinar (I)
   cooked cocido, -a (II)
   cool: it's — out hace fresco (I)
   corn el maíz (I)
      — tortilla la tortilla de maíz (I)
   corner la esquina (I)
   corporal corporal (10)

   correspondence la correspondencia (6)
   correspondent el / la corresponsal (12)
to cost costar *(o → ue)* (I)
   cotton el algodón (II)
   cough la tos (II)
      — syrup el jarabe (para la tos) (II)
to cough toser (II)
   could you . . . ? ¿podría (Ud.) / podrías (tú) + *inf.?* (II)
   counselor el consejero, la consejera (II)
   counter el mostrador (II)
   country el país (I)
   countryside el campo (I)
   course:
      of — claro que sí (I); por supuesto (I, II)
      of — not ¡claro que no! (I)
   courteous cortés, *pl.* corteses (9)
   cousin el primo, la prima (I)
   cow la vaca (I)
   cowboy, cowgirl el vaquero, la vaquera (II)
   coyote el coyote (II)
to create crear (6)
   it will create creará (6)
   creation la creación, *pl.* las creaciones (11)
   creator el creador, la creadora (8)
   credit card la tarjeta de crédito (II)
   crime el crimen (II)
   criminal el / la criminal (II)
   critical crítico, -a (4)
to critique criticar *(c → qu)* (3)
to cross cruzar *(z → c)* (II)
   crossword puzzle el crucigrama (II)
   crowded lleno, -a de gente (2)
   crutches las muletas (II)
to cry llorar (II)
   cubism el cubismo (3)
   cucumber el pepino (II)
to cultivate cultivar (2)
   cultural cultural (11)
   culture la cultura (5)
   cup la taza (I)
   currency exchange la casa de cambio (II)
   custom la costumbre (5)
   customer el cliente, la clienta (8)
   customs la aduana (II)
      — agent el aduanero, la aduanera (II)
to cut cortar (I)
      to — oneself cortarse (II)
   cyclist el / la ciclista (2)

   daily diario, -a (2)
   daily special el plato del día (I)
to damage dañar (II)
   dance el baile (I, II)
to dance bailar (I, II)
   dancer el bailarín, la bailarina (II)
   danger el peligro (I, II)

dangerous peligroso, -a (II, 2)
daring atrevido, -a (I)
dark *(color)* oscuro, -a (II)
data los datos (8)
date la fecha (I)
  what's today's —? ¿cuál es la fecha de hoy? (I)
daughter la hija (I)
dawn el amanecer (II)
day el día (I)
  every — todos los días (I)
Day of the Dead el Día de los Muertos (11)
dead muerto, -a (II)
deaf sordo, -a (12)
dear querido, -a (6)
death la muerte (10)
December diciembre (I)
to **decide** decidir (2)
to **decorate** decorar (I)
decoration la decoración, *pl.* las decoraciones (I)
deer el venado (II)
to **defend (oneself)** defender(se) *(e → ie)* (10)
delay el retraso (II); tardar (en) (2)
delicious sabroso, -a (I)
delighted encantado, -a (I)
delinquent el / la delincuente (10)
to **deliver** repartir (II)
delivery: by special — por correo urgente (6)
delivery person el repartidor, la repartidora (9)
to **demand** exigir *(g → j)* (7)
  I demand, you demand (yo) exijo, (tú) exiges (7)
demonstration la manifestación, *pl.* las manifestaciones (7)
dental floss la seda dental (II)
dentist el / la dentista (I)
deodorant el desodorante (II)
to **depend (on)** depender (de) (I, II)
to **deposit** depositar (I)
descent la descendencia (11)
desert el desierto (II, 8)
to **deserve** merecer *(c → zc)* (9)
design el diseño (8)
desk el escritorio; *(student)* el pupitre (I)
dessert el postre
  for — de postre (I)
to **destroy** destruir *(i → y)* (II)
detective el / la detective (II)
  — show el programa de detectives (I)
to **develop** desarrollar (5)
device el aparato (II)
to **devote oneself (to)** dedicarse

(c → qu) (a) (II)
to **dial** *(a telephone number)* marcar *(c → qu)* (6)
dial tone el tono (6)
diameter el diámetro (8)
dictionary el diccionario (I)
to **die** morir(se) *(o → ue)* (11)
different diferente (2)
difficult difícil (I)
difficulty la dificultad (12)
dining room el comedor (I)
dinner la cena (I)
  for — en la cena (I)
dinosaur el dinosaurio (II)
diplomat el diplomático, la diplomática (9)
to **direct** dirigir *(g → j)* (II)
direction la dirección, *pl.* las direcciones (II)
director *(film)* el director, la directora (II)
dirty sucio, -a (I)
disability: person with a physical — el incapacitado, la incapacitada (7)
disadvantage la desventaja (II)
to **disagree** no estar de acuerdo (I)
disappeared desaparecido, -a (5)
disaster el desastre (II)
to **discover** descubrir (5)
discovery el descubrimiento (5)
to **discuss** discutir (1)
discussion la discusión, *pl.* las discusiones (1)
disgusting: that's —! ¡qué asco! (I)
dish el plato (I)
  main — el plato principal (I)
dishwasher el lavaplatos (II)
disk el disco (II)
disobedient desobediente (II)
to **disobey** desobedecer *(c → zc)* (II)
distance la distancia (II)
to **distribute** distribuir *(i → y)* (9)
to **dive** dar saltos (II)
diverse diverso, -a (11)
to **diversify** diversificar(se) *(c → qu)* (12)
diversity la diversidad (11)
diversion la diversión, *pl.* las diversiones (II)
diving board el trampolín, *pl.* los trampolines (II)
divorced (from) divorciado, -a (de) (II)
to **do** hacer (I)
  that we did (que nosotros) hiciéramos (11)
  to — (something) again volver *(o → ue)* a + *inf.* (6)
  to not — badly *(in a language)* defenderse *(e → ie)* en + *language* (12)

doctor el médico, la médica (I)
documentary el documental (I)
dog el perro (I)
doll la muñeca (II)
dollar el dólar (I)
domestic doméstico, -a (II)
to **donate** donar (7)
door la puerta (I)
dot: on the — en punto (I)
double doble (I)
doubt la duda (8)
to **doubt** dudar (8)
dough la masa (II)
downtown el centro (II)
to **draw** dibujar (I); trazar *(z → c)* (8)
drawing el dibujo (I)
dream el sueño (3)
to **dream (about)** soñar *(o → ue)* (con) (12)
dress el vestido (I)
  party — el vestido de fiesta (I)
dressed: to get — vestirse *(e → i)* (II)
dresser la cómoda (I)
to **drink** beber (I)
drops las gotas (II)
drug la droga (10)
  — store la farmacia (I)
  — trafficking el narcotráfico (10)
drum el tambor (II)
dry seco, -a (II)
to **dry** secar *(c → qu)* (II)
  to — one's hair secarse el pelo (II)
dryer:
  clothes — la secadora (II)
  hair — el secador de pelo (II)
dull apagado, -a (3)
dumb tonto, -a (I)
to **dump** echar (II)
dust el polvo (II)
to **dust** sacudir (I)

ear el oído (I)
  —ache el dolor de oído (I)
early temprano (I)
to **earn** ganar (I)
  to — a living ganarse la vida (II)
earring el arete (I, II)
Earth la Tierra (I, II)
earthquake el terremoto (II)
easily fácilmente (II)
easy fácil (I)
to **eat** comer (I)
economical económico, -a (II)
editing la redacción (1)
editor el redactor, la redactora (12)
education la educación (II)
educational educativo, -a (I)
efficient eficiente (II)

egg el huevo (I)

   hard-boiled — el huevo duro (II)

eight ocho (I)

   — hundred ochocientos (I)

eighteen dieciocho (I)

eighth octavo, -a (I)

eighty ochenta (I)

either: not — no . . . tampoco (I)

elbow el codo (II)

election la elección, *pl.* las elecciones (7)

electric eléctrico, -a (II)

electricity la electricidad (II)

elegant elegante (I, II)

elementary school la escuela primaria (II)

elephant el elefante (I, II)

elevator el ascensor (II)

eleven once (I)

else: anything — algo más (I)

to **embrace** abrazarse *(z → c)* (II)

emergency la emergencia (II)

   — room la sala de emergencia (II)

   in case of — en caso de emergencia (II)

employee el empleado, la empleada (II)

enchilada la enchilada (I)

encounter el encuentro (11)

to **end** terminar (I)

endangered en peligro de extinción (I, II)

enduring duradero, -a (11)

energy la energía (I, II)

English *(language)* el inglés (I)

to **enjoy** disfrutar de (II)

enormous enorme (8)

enough suficiente (II)

to **enroll** inscribirse (1)

to **enslave** esclavizar *(z → c)* (11)

entertainment la diversión, *pl.* las diversiones (II)

enthusiast el aficionado, la aficionada (1)

entrance la entrada (II)

envelope el sobre (6)

environment el medio ambiente (I, II)

error el error (12)

eruption la erupción, *pl.* las erupciones (II)

escalator la escalera mecánica (II)

to **escape** escaparse (2)

to **establish** establecer *(c → zc)* (11)

European europeo, -a (11)

to **evaluate** evaluar *(u → ú)* (4)

evening la noche (I)

   good — buenas noches / tardes (I)

   in the — por la noche / tarde (I)

ever alguna vez (I)

every day todos los días (I)

everyone todos, -as (I)

everywhere por todas partes (II)

evidence la evidencia (8)

exaggerated exagerado, -a (II)

exam el examen, *pl.* los exámenes (II)

to **excavate** excavar (5)

excellent excelente (II)

exchange intercambio (12)

   — student el / la estudiante de intercambio (12)

exciting emocionante (I)

excursion la excursión, *pl.* las excursiones (II)

   to take an — hacer una excursión (II)

to **excuse** perdonar (II)

   — me perdón (I); perdone (Ud.) (II)

exercise el ejercicio (II)

to **exercise** hacer ejercicio (I)

exhibit *(art)* la exposición, *pl.* las exposiciones (de arte) (II)

to **exist** existir (5)

exit la salida (II)

expensive caro, -a (I)

experience la experiencia (9)

to **explain** explicar *(c → qu)* (II)

to **explore** explorar (I)

explosion la explosión (10)

exposed descubierto, -a (5)

to **express (oneself)** expresar(se) (12)

extracurricular extracurricular (II)

extraordinary extraordinario, -a (8)

eye el ojo (I)

   — drops las gotas para los ojos (II)

fabric la tela (II)

face la cara (II)

facing enfrente (de) (I)

fact el hecho (I, II)

   —-based program el programa de hechos de la vida real (I)

factory la fábrica (I)

failure el fracaso (II)

fair regular; así, así (I); justo, -a (7)

fall el otoño (I)

to **fall (down)** caerse (II)

   to — in love (with) enamorarse (de) (II)

false falso, -a (8)

family la familia (I); *adj.* familiar (II)

   — room la sala de estar (I)

fan *(electric)* el ventilador (II); el aficionado, la aficionada (1)

fantastic fantástico, -a (I)

far (from) lejos (de) (I)

farm la granja (2)

to **fascinate** fascinar (I)

fascinating fascinante (I)

fashion la moda (II)

fashionable: to be — estar de moda (II)

fast rápido, -a (2)

to **fasten** abrocharse (II)

father el padre (I)

   —'s Day el Día del Padre (II)

fault: to be at — tener la culpa (de) (10)

favor: in — (of) a favor (de) (7)

fax el fax (6)

fear el temor (a) (10)

to **fear** temer (a) (10)

feather la pluma (II)

feature el rasgo (11)

February febrero (I)

to **feel** sentirse *(e → ie)* (II)

   how do you —? ¿cómo te sientes? (I)

fence la cerca (2)

fencing la esgrima (1)

festive alegre (II)

fever la fiebre (I)

   to have a — tener fiebre (I)

few: a — unos, unas (I)

field campo (5)

fifteen quince (I)

fifth quinto, -a (I)

fifty cincuenta (I)

to **fight** pelearse (II); luchar (10)

file el archivo (9)

to **fill out a form** llenar un formulario (6)

filling el relleno (II)

film la película (I)

financial financiero, -a (7)

to **find** encontrar *(o → ue)* (II)

fine la multa (4)

finger el dedo (I)

fingernail la uña (II)

   — polish el esmalte de uñas (II)

fire el incendio (II); el fuego (II)

   — extinguisher el extinguidor de incendios (II)

   — station la estación de bomberos (II)

firefighter el bombero, la bombera (II)

firewood la leña (II)

fireworks los fuegos artificiales (II)

   to shoot — lanzar *(z → c)* fuegos artificiales (II)

first primero (primer), -a (I)

fish *(cooked)* el pescado (I); *(live)* el pez, *pl.* los peces (II)

   — store la pescadería (II)

   to go —ing ir de pesca (I)

to **fit** quedar (I)

five cinco (I)

   — hundred quinientos (I)

to **fix** reparar (II)

fixed fijo, -a (9)

flag la bandera (II)

flan el flan (I)

flashlight la linterna (II)

flight el vuelo (II)

   — attendant el / la auxiliar de vuelo (II)

flood la inundación, *pl.* las inundaciones (II)

floor *(story)* el piso (I); el suelo (II)
floss: dental — la seda dental (II)
flour la harina (I)
  — tortilla la tortilla de harina (I)
flower la flor (I, II)
  — shop la floristería (II)
flowered floreado, -a (II)
flu la gripe (I)
  to have the — tener gripe (I)
flute la flauta (II)
fly la mosca (II)
to **fly** volar *(o → ue)* (8)
folder la carpeta (I)
to **follow** seguir *(e → i)* (II)
food la comida (I); la alimentación (II)
foot el pie (I)
football el fútbol americano (I)
footprint la huella (II, 8)
for para (I, II); por (I)
  — + *time expression* por (II)
foreground el primer plano (3)
forest la selva (I)
  rain — la selva tropical (I)
fork el tenedor (I)
form *(shape)* la figura, la forma (3); el formulario (6)
  to fill out a — llenar un formulario (6)
fortress el alcázar, *pl.* los alcázares (11)
forty cuarenta (I)
fossil el fósil (II)
to **found** fundar (11)
fountain la fuente (11)
four cuatro (I)
  — hundred cuatrocientos (I)
fourteen catorce (I)
fourth cuarto, -a (I)
free: to set — poner en libertad (10)
French *(language)* el francés (II)
  — fries las papas fritas (I)
frequently frecuentemente (1)
fresh fresco, -a (II)
Friday viernes (I)
  on — el viernes (I)
fried frito, -a (II)
friend el amigo, la amiga (I)
friendly simpático, -a (I)
friendship la amistad, *pl.* las amistades (1)
frog la rana (II)
from de (I); desde (II)
front: in — of enfrente de; delante de (I)
frozen congelado, -a (II)
fruit la fruta (I)
  — salad la ensalada de frutas (II)
  — shop la frutería (II)
to **fulfill** cumplir con (9)
full-time (de) tiempo completo (9)
fun: to have — divertirse *(e → ie)* (II)

to **function** funcionar (II)
funny gracioso, -a; divertido, -a (I)
fur la piel (I)
furniture los muebles (I)
fusion la fusión, *pl.* las fusiones (11)
future el futuro (II)

gallery la galería (3)
game el partido (I, II)
  — show el programa de concursos (II)
garage el garaje (I)
garbage la basura (I)
garden el jardín, *pl.* los jardines (2)
garlic el ajo (II)
gas station la estación de servicio (I)
gate la puerta (II)
to **gather** recoger *(g → j)* (II)
gathering la reunión, *pl.* las reuniones (I, II)
gazpacho el gazpacho (II)
gee! ¡vaya! (I)
generally generalmente (I)
generous generoso, -a (I); abundante (2)
geography la geografía (II)
geologist el geólogo, la geóloga (8)
geometric geométrico, -a (8)
geometry la geometría (II)
German *(language)* el alemán (II)
to **get** conseguir *(e → i)* (II)
  to — along *(in a language)* defenderse *(e → ie)* en + *language* (12)
  to — along (well / badly) llevarse (bien / mal) (1)
  to — angry enojarse (2)
  to — away escaparse (2)
  to — up levantarse (II)
get-together la reunión, *pl.* las reuniones (I, II)
ghost el fantasma (8)
gift el regalo (I)
  — shop la tienda de regalos (I)
  to give a — regalar (I, II)
gigantic gigantesco, -a (8)
girl la muchacha (I); la niña (II)
girlfriend la novia (I)
to **give** dar (I)
  they gave dieron (4)
  to — a gift regalar (I, II)
  to — an injection poner una inyección (II)
  to — private lessons dar clases particulares (1)
glass el vaso (I); *(material)* el vidrio (I, II)
  (made of) — de vidrio (I)
glasses los anteojos (I, II)
glove el guante (I)
  baseball — el guante de béisbol (II)

to **go** ir (I)
  to be —ing to + *verb* ir a + *inf.* (I)
  to — fishing ir de pesca (I)
  — on! ¡vaya! (I)
  to — on a trip hacer una excursión (II)
  to — on vacation ir de vacaciones (I)
  to — shopping ir de compras (I)
  to — to bed acostarse *(o → ue)* (II)
  to — to school ir a la escuela (I)
goal el gol (II); la meta (9)
god el dios *pl.* los dioses (5)
going to con destino a (II)
gold el oro (II)
  (made of) — de oro (II)
golf el golf (II)
  — club el palo (de golf) (II)
good bueno (buen), -a (I)
  — afternoon buenas tardes (I)
  — evening buenas noches (I)
  — morning buenos días (I)
  — night buenas noches (I)
  it's a — thing that . . . menos mal que . . . (I)
  to be — at tener facilidad para (12)
  to have a — time pasarlo bien (I, II)
good-by adiós (I)
  to say — (to) despedirse *(e → i)* (de) (II)
good-looking guapo, -a (I)
goodness: my —! ¡vaya! (I)
gorilla el gorila (I, II)
to **govern** gobernar *(e → ie)* (7)
government el gobierno (7)
grade la nota (II)
  to get a good / bad — sacar una buena / mala nota (II)
to **graduate** graduarse *(u → ú)* (II)
graduation la graduación, *pl.* las graduaciones (II)
granddaughter la nieta (II)
grandfather el abuelo (I)
grandmother la abuela (I)
grandparents los abuelos (I)
grandson el nieto (II)
grape la uva (I)
grating la reja (11)
gray gris, *pl.* grises (I)
  — hair pelo canoso (I)
greasy grasoso, -a (II)
great! ¡genial! (I); ¡una maravilla! (2)
great-grandfather / grandmother el bisabuelo, la bisabuela (II)
green verde (I)
  — beans las judías verdes (I)
  — pepper el pimiento verde (II)
greengrocer la verdulería (II)
to **greet** saludar (II)
greetings to everyone saludos a todos (6)

grilled a la parrilla (II)
groceries los comestibles (I)
to **grow** *(crops)* cultivar (2)
to **guarantee** garantizar *(z → c)* (7)
to **guard** vigilar (10)
guest el invitado, la invitada (I)
guide el / la guía (II)
guidebook la guía (II)
guilty culpable (10)
   to be — *(of)* tener la culpa (de) (10)
guitar la guitarra (I)
gun la pistola (II)
gym el gimnasio (I)
   — bag el bolso (II)

habit: to be in the — of soler *(o → ue)* + *inf.* (I, II)
hair el pelo (I)
   to comb one's — peinarse (II)
   — dryer el secador de pelo (II)
half:
   and a — *(in sizes)* y medio (II)
   — an hour media hora (I)
   — boots el botín, *pl.* los botines (II)
   —-past y media (I)
ham el jamón (I)
hamburger la hamburguesa (I)
hamper: laundry — el cesto de la ropa sucia (II)
hand la mano (I)
   by — a mano (II)
   — made hecho, -a a mano (I)
   on the one — por un lado (2)
   on the other — por otro lado (2)
   to shake —s darse la mano (II)
to **hand in** entregar *(g → gu)* (II)
handicrafts la artesanía (II)
handsome guapo, -a (I)
to **hang** colgar *(o → ue)* *(g → gu)* (II)
to **hang up** *(the telephone)* colgar *(o → ue)* *(g → gu)* (6)
to **happen** pasar (I); ocurrir (II)
   what —ed to you? ¿qué te pasó? (II)
happy alegre (II)
hard difícil (I)
hard-boiled egg el huevo duro (II)
hard-working trabajador, -a (I)
harmful: to be — hacer daño (4)
harmony la armonía (12)
harvest la cosecha (5)
haunted encantado, -a (8)
to **have** tener *(e → ie)* (I)
   to — fun divertirse *(e → ie)* (II)
   to — a good / bad time pasarlo bien / mal (I, II)
   to — time + *inf.* tener tiempo de + *inf.* (II)
   to — to tener que + *inf.* (I)

I would have to (yo) tendría que (12)
you would have to (tú) tendrías que (12)
he él (I)
head la cabeza (I)
   —ache el dolor de cabeza (I)
health la salud (I); *(class)* las ciencias de la salud (I)
healthy sano, -a (II, 2)
   to stay — mantenerse *(e → ie)* sano, -a (II)
to **hear** oír (2)
heater el calentador (II)
heating la calefacción (II)
heavy pesado, -a (II)
height el alto (8)
hello! ¡hola! (I); *(on the telephone)* ¡aló! (6)
helmet el casco (II)
help la ayuda (II)
to **help** ayudar (I)
   may I — you? ¿qué desea (Ud.)? (I)
her *adj.* su, sus (I); suyo, -a (II); *dir. obj. pron.* la; *ind. obj. pron.* le (I)
here aquí (I)
   around — por aquí (I)
   — it is aquí está (I)
hero *(film)* el galán, *pl.* los galanes (II)
heroine la heroína (II)
hers el suyo, la suya, los suyos, las suyas (II)
hi! ¡hola! (I)
to **hide** esconder(se) (II)
hieroglyphics los jeroglíficos (5)
high-heeled shoes los zapatos de tacón alto (I, II)
highway la carretera (II); la autopista (2)
hijacking el secuestro (10)
hike la marcha (7)
hiking: to go — dar una caminata (II)
hill la colina (II)
him *dir. obj. pron.* lo; *ind. obj. pron.* le (I)
to **hire** contratar (10)
his *adj.* su, sus (I); suyo, -a (II); *pron.* el suyo, la suya, los suyos, las suyas (II)
historic(al) histórico, -a (II)
history la historia (II)
hobby el pasatiempo (I)
hockey el hockey (II)
   — puck el disco (de hockey) (II)
   — stick el palo (de hockey) (II)
holiday el día de fiesta (II)
home:
   at — en casa (I)
   — shopping show el programa de compras (II)
homeless la gente sin hogar (7)
homework la tarea (I)

honest honesto, -a (9)
to **hope** esperar (7)
horrible horrible (I)
horror el horror (II)
   — movie la película de terror (I)
horse el caballo (I, II)
   to ride —back montar a caballo (II)
hospital el hospital (I)
hostage el rehén, *pl.* los rehenes (10)
hot *(flavor)* picante (I)
   to be — *(person)* tener calor (I)
   it's — out hace calor (I)
hot dog el perro caliente (II)
hotel el hotel (I)
   — room la habitación, *pl.* las habitaciones (II)
   — manager el / la gerente (9)
house la casa (I)
   — specialty la especialidad de la casa (I)
household chore el quehacer de la casa (I)
how + *adj.* ¡qué + *adj.*! (I)
how? ¿cómo? (I)
   — are you? ¿cómo estás /está (Ud.)? (I)
   — long has it been since …? ¿cuánto (tiempo) hace que …? (I)
   — many? ¿cuántos, -as? (I)
   — much? ¿cuánto? (I)
   — old is …? ¿cuántos años tiene …? (I)
   — is …? ¿qué tal es …? (II)
   —'s it going? ¿qué tal? (I)
to **hug** abrazarse *(z → c)* (II)
human being el ser humano (II)
humor: sense of — el sentido del humor (1)
hundred cien; ciento (I)
hungry: to be — tener hambre (I)
hurricane el huracán, *pl.* los huracanes (II)
to **hurt** doler *(o → ue)* (I)*;* lastimarse + *part of body* (I)
husband el esposo (II)
hut la choza (5)
hygiene la higiene (1)

I yo (I)
ice el hielo (II)
   to — skate patinar sobre hielo (II)
ice cream el helado (I)
   — shop la heladería (II)
iced tea el té helado (I)
idealized idealizado, -a (2)
identification la identificación (II)
   — card el carnet de identidad (II)
idiom el modismo (12)
if si (I)

ill enfermo, -a (I)
    to feel — sentirse *(e → ie)* mal (I)
    to make — hacer daño a (II)
illness la enfermedad (II)
image la imagen, *pl.* las imágenes (3)
imagination la imaginación (3)
immigrant el / la inmigrante (12)
immigration la inmigración (12)
impatient impaciente (I)
impolite maleducado, -a (II)
to **impose** imponer (10)
impossible imposible (8)
impressionist impresionista (3)
improbable improbable (8)
in en (I)
    — order to para + *inf.* (I)
to **include** incluir *(i → y)* (II)
to **increase** aumentar (12)
Independence Day el Día de la
    Independencia (II)
to **indicate** indicar *(c → qu)* (II)
indigenous indígena (II)
inexpensive barato, -a (I)
    — lodging la pensión, *pl.* las
    pensiones (II)
inexplicable inexplicable (8)
infection la infección, *pl.* las infecciones
    (II)
influence la influencia (11)
    to — influir *(i → y)* (en / sobre) (1)
information la información (II); los
    datos (8)
informative informativo, -a (4)
ingredient el ingrediente (I, II)
inhabitant el / la habitante (8)
to **inherit** heredar (5)
injection la inyección, *pl.* las
    inyecciones (II)
    to give an — poner una inyección (II)
to **injure** herir *(e → ie)* (10)
injustice la injusticia (11)
innocent inocente (10)
insect el insecto (II)
    — bite la picadura (de insecto) (II)
    — repellent el repelente (II)
insecticide el insecticida (II)
insecurity la inseguridad (10)
insensitive incomprensivo, -a (1)
to **inspect** registrar (II)
inspiration la inspiración (3)
instrument el instrumento (II)
intelligent inteligente (I)
interactive interactivo, -a (6)
interest: place of — el lugar de interés
    (I)
to **interest** interesar (I)
interesting interesante (I)
international internacional (II)
to **interpret** interpretar (3, 12)

interpreter el / la intérprete (9)
intersection el cruce (II)
interview la entrevista (II)
to **introduce** presentar (I)
to **invent** inventar (6)
invention el invento (6)
to **investigate** investigar *(g → gu)* (II)
invitation la invitación, *pl.* las invitaciones
    (I, II)
to **invite** invitar (I, II)
involved: to be — in dedicarse
    (c → qu) (a) (II)
isolated aislado, -a (2)
it *dir. obj.* lo (I)

jacket la chaqueta (I)
jade el jade (5)
jaguar el jaguar (I)
jail la cárcel (10)
January enero (I)
jar la vasija (5)
jeans los jeans (I)
to **jet ski** hacer moto acuática (II)
jet skiing la moto acuática (II)
Jew el judío, la judía (11)
jewelry las joyas (I)
jigsaw puzzle el rompecabezas (II)
to **jog** correr (II)
to **join** *(army)* presentar(se) (7)
journalist el / la periodista (12)
judge el / la juez, *pl.* los / las jueces (II)
to **judge** analizar *(z → c)* (4)
juice el jugo (I)
    orange — el jugo de naranja (I)
July julio (I)
to **jump (rope)** saltar (a la cuerda) (II)
    — rope la cuerda (II)
June junio (I)
jury el jurado (10)
just justo, -a (7)

to **keep** guardar (II)
key la llave (II)
    — chain el llavero (II)
to **kidnap** secuestrar (10)
kidnapping el secuestro (10)
to **kill** matar (II)
kilometer el kilómetro (II)
kind *adj.* amable; la clase (I)
kindergarten el kindergarten (II)
kindling los palitos (II)
king el rey, *pl.* los reyes (11)
to **kiss** besarse (II)
kitchen la cocina (I)
knee la rodilla (II)
knife el cuchillo (I)
to **know** conocer *(c → zc)*; saber (I, II)
    to — how saber (I, II)
knowledge: to have a good
    — of *(a language)* dominar + *(language)*
    (12)

laboratory el laboratorio (II)
laborer el obrero, la obrera (II)
lacking: to be — faltar a (I)
ladies' wear la ropa para damas (II)
lake el lago (I)
lamp la lámpara (I)
to **land** aterrizar *(z → c)* (II)
landscape el paisaje (2)
landslide el derrumbe (II)
language el idioma (II); la lengua (11)
    foreign — la lengua extranjera (12)
    sign — el lenguaje por señas (12)
large grande (I, II)
last pasado, -a (I); último, -a (II)
    — night anoche (I)
to **last** durar (I)
late tarde (I)
later luego (I)
    see you — hasta luego (I)
to **laugh** reírse *(e → i)* (4)
laundry hamper el cesto de la ropa
    sucia (II)
laundry room el lavadero (I)
law la ley, *pl.* las leyes (7)
lawn el césped (I)
    to mow the — cortar el césped (I)
lawyer el abogado, la abogada (II)
lazy perezoso, -a (I)
leader el / la líder (5)
leaf hoja (II)
league la liga (II)
to **learn** aprender (I)
learning el aprendizaje (12)
least el / la / los / las menos + *adj.* (I)
    at — por lo menos (II)
    the — + *adj.* thing lo menos + *adj.*
    (1)
leather el cuero (I)
    (made of) — de cuero (I)
to **leave** salir (I, II); *(a message)* dejar (6)
left izquierdo, -a (I)
    to the — (of) a la izquierda (de) (I)
leg la pierna (I)
legacy el legado (5)
legend la leyenda (8)
lemon el limón, *pl.* los limones (II)
lemonade la limonada (I)
to **lend** prestar (II)
length el largo (8)
lenses: contact — los lentes de
    contacto (II)
less menos (I)
lesson la lección, *pl.* las lecciones (II)
letter la carta (I)
lettuce la lechuga (I)
librarian el bibliotecario, la
    bibliotecaria (12)
library la biblioteca (I)
to **lie** mentir *(e → ie)* (II)
life la vida (I)
    —guard el / la salvavidas (9)

to lift levantar (II)
light *(color)* claro, -a (II); *(minor)* leve (II); *(weight)* ligero, -a (II)
light la luz, *pl.* las luces (I)
— **bulb** el bombillo (II)
traffic — el semáforo (II)
to light encender *(e → ie)* (II)
to like gustar (I)
I'd (you'd) — quisiera(s); me (te) gustaría (I)
likewise igualmente (I)
lime el limón, *pl.* los limones (I)
line la línea (6)
to — **up** hacer fila (II)
lips los labios (II)
lipstick el lápiz *(pl.* los lápices) de labios (II)
to listen (to) escuchar (I)
literary literario, -a (II)
lit(erature) la literatura (II)
little pequeño, -a (I)
a — un poco (de) (I)
to live vivir (I)
to live together convivir (12)
lively animado, -a (2)
living: to earn a — ganarse la vida (II)
living room la sala (I)
loafer el mocasín, *pl.* los mocasines (II)
local local (II)
located: to be — quedar (I)
locker el armario (II)
lodging: inexpensive — la pensión, *pl.* las pensiones (II)
long largo, -a (I); el largo (8)
—**-lasting** duradero, -a (11)
to look (at) mirar (I)
to — **for** buscar *(c → qu)* (I)
loose *(clothing)* flojo, -a (II)
to lose perder *(e → ie)* (II)
lot: a — **of** mucho, -a (I)
Love *(as a closing in a letter)* Cariños *pl.* (6)
love: to fall in — **(with)** enamorarse (de) (II)
to love encantar (I)
loving cariñoso, -a (I)
luckily por suerte (II)
lunch el almuerzo (I)
for — en el almuerzo (I)
luxury el lujo (II)

ma'am señora (I)
made hecho, -a (I, II)
it's — **of . . .** es de . . . (II)
— **of** de + *material* (I)
what's (it) — **of ?** de qué es . . .? (II)
magazine la revista (I)
to mail enviar *(i → i)* (I)
by air — por vía aérea (6)

electronic — el correo electrónico (6)
— **carrier** el cartero, la cartera (6)
mailbox el buzón, *pl.* los buzones (II)
main principal (II)
to maintain mantener *(e → ie)* (1)
majority la mayoría (11)
to make hacer (I)
that we made (que nosotros) hiciéramos (11)
make-up el maquillaje (II)
to put on — maquillarse (II)
mall el centro comercial (I)
man el hombre (I)
to manage (a business) administrar (9)
to manipulate manipular (4)
manners los modales (9)
to manufacture fabricar *(c → qu)* (6)
many muchos, -as (I)
as — **as** tantos, -as + *noun* + como (II)
map el mapa (II)
March marzo (I)
market el mercado (II)
marker el marcador (I)
married (to) casado, -a (con) (II)
to get — **(to)** casarse (con) (II)
to marry casarse (con) (II)
martial arts las artes marciales (II)
to master *(a language)* dominar + *language* (12)
match *(game)* el partido (I); el fósforo (II)
mathematics las matemáticas (I)
matter: what's the —? ¿qué pasa? (I)
mature maduro, -a (9)
May mayo (I)
Mayas los mayas (5)
mayonnaise la mayonesa (II)
me *obj. pron.* me; *after prep.* mí (I)
meal la comida (I)
meaning el significado (5)
means of communication el medio de comunicación (6)
measure la medida (10)
to measure medir *(e → i)* (8)
to be/— **. . . high** medir . . . de alto (8)
to be/— **. . . in diameter** medir . . . de diámetro (8)
to be/— **. . . long** medir . . . de largo (8)
to be/— **. . . wide** medir . . . de ancho (8)
mechanic el mecánico, la mecánica (II)
medical test el análisis, *pl.* los análisis (II)
medicine la medicina (II)
medium *(in sizes)* mediano, -a (II)
to meet encontrarse *(o → ue)* (II)
I'd like you to — **. . .** te presento a . . . (I)
pleased to — **you** mucho gusto; encantado, -a (I)
member el miembro (II)
to be a — **of** ser miembro de (II)

men's wear la ropa para caballeros (II)
menu el menú (I)
merry-go-round el carrusel (II)
message el mensaje (3); *(phone)* el recado (6)
messy desordenado, -a (I)
mestizo (Native American and European) mestizo, -a (11)
metal el metal (I)
(made of) — de metal (I)
meter *(measurement)* el metro (II)
microwave oven el microondas (II)
midnight la medianoche (II)
mild *(flavor)* no picante (I)
mile la milla (II)
military el ejército (7)
milk la leche (I)
mine el mío, la mía, los míos, las mías (II)
minor leve (II)
minute el minuto (I)
mirror el espejo (I)
mischievous travieso, -a (II)
miss (la) señorita (I)
miss: to be —**ing** faltar (I)
mistake: to make a — equivocarse *(c → qu)* (6)
mistaken: to be — equivocarse *(c → qu)* (6)
to mix mezclar (II, 11)
mixing la mezcla (11)
mixture la mezcla (11)
modern moderno, -a (I)
modest modesto, -a (1)
Monday lunes (I)
on — el lunes (I)
money el dinero (I)
monkey el mono (8)
monster el monstruo (II)
month el mes (I)
monument el monumento (I)
mood: in a good / bad — de buen / mal humor (II)
moon la Luna (II)
more más (I)
— **and** — cada vez más (6)
— **or less** más o menos (I)
morning la mañana (I)
good — buenos días (I)
in the — por la mañana (I)
mosque la mezquita (11)
mosquito el mosquito (II)
most: the — + *adj.* el / la / los / las más + *adj.* (I, II)
the — *(adj.)* **thing** lo más + *adj.* (1)
mother la madre (I)
— **tongue** la lengua materna (12)
—**'s Day** el Día de la Madre (II)
mountain la montaña (I)
to go — **climbing** escalar montañas (II)

English-Spanish Vocabulary   531

mouth la boca (I)

to **move** mudarse *(residence)* (1); mover
     (*o → ue*) (8)

moved: to be — emocionarse (4)

movement el movimiento (3)

movie la película (I)
     — theater el cine (I)
     —s el cine (I)
     to show a — dar una película (I)

to **mow the lawn** cortar el césped (I)

Mr. (el) señor (I)

Mrs. (la) señora (I)

much mucho, -a (I)
     as — as tanto, -a + *noun* + como (II)
     how —? ¿cuánto? (I)

muffler la bufanda (I)

multicultural multicultural (12)

mural el mural (3)

murder el asesinato (10)
     attempted — el atentado (10)

to **murder** matar (II)

murderer el asesino, la asesina (10)

muscle el músculo (II)

museum el museo (I)

mushroom el champiñón, *pl.* los
     champiñones (II)

music la música (I)
     — program el programa musical (I)
     — video el video musical (II)

musical musical (I)

musician el músico, la música (II)

Muslim el musulmán, la musulmana (11)

mustard la mostaza (II)

my mi, mis (I); mío, -a (II)

myself (yo) mismo, -a (II)

mysterious misterioso, -a (8)

mystery el misterio (8)

myth el mito (8)

nail *see* **fingernail**

name el nombre (I)
     my — is me llamo (I)
     what's your —? ¿cómo te llamas? (I)

named: to be — llamarse (I, II)

napkin la servilleta (I)

national nacional (II)

native *adj.* indígena (II)

Native American el / la indígena (11)

nature la naturaleza (II)

naughty travieso, -a (II)

near cerca (de) (I)

neat ordenado, -a (I)

necessary necesario (II)
     it's — to hay que + *inf.* (I, II); es
     necesario (II)
     to be — hacer falta (12)

necessity la necesidad (II)

neck el cuello (I)

necklace el collar (I, II)

necktie la corbata (I, II)

to **need** necesitar (I)

negative negativo, -a (4)

neighbor el vecino, la vecina (II)

neither tampoco (I)

neither . . . nor ni . . . ni (I)

nephew el sobrino (II)

nervous nervioso, -a (1)

never nunca (I)

nevertheless sin embargo (2)

new nuevo, -a (I)
     — Year's Day el Año Nuevo (II)
     — Year's Eve el fin de año (II)
     — Year's Eve party la fiesta de fin
     de año (I)

news las noticias (I)

newscast el noticiero (4)

newspaper el periódico (I, II)

newsstand el quiosco (de periódicos) (II)

next próximo, -a (II)
     — to al lado (de) (I); junto a (3)

nice amable; simpático, -a (I)

niece la sobrina (II)

night la noche (I)
     at — de la noche (I)
     good — buenas noches (I)
     last — anoche (I)
     — table la mesa de noche (II)

nine nueve (I)
     — hundred novecientos (I)

nineteen diecinueve (I)

ninety noventa (I)

no no (I)
     — longer ya no (I)

nobody, no one nadie (I)

noise el ruido (2)

nonallergenic antialérgico, -a (II)

nonprofit sin fines de lucro (7)

nonstop sin escala (II)

noon el mediodía (I)

nor: neither . . . — ni . . . ni (I)

nose la nariz (I)

not no (I)
     — anymore ya no (I)
     — at all nada (I); de ninguna manera
     (I)
     — at all! ¡qué va! (1)
     — only . . . but also no sólo . . . sino
     también (9)
     — yet todavía no (I)

notebook el cuaderno (I)

nothing nada (I)

to **notice** notar (11)

nourishment la alimentación (II)

novel la novela (II)

November noviembre (I)

now ahora (I)
     right — ahora mismo (9)

nowadays hoy en día (6)

nowhere ninguna parte (I)

number el número (I)
     phone — el número de teléfono (I)

nurse el enfermero, la enfermera (II)
     —'s office la enfermería (I)

nursing home el asilo (1)

nylon el nilón (II)

obedient obediente (II)

to **obey** obedecer (*c → zc*) (II)

object el objeto (5)

objective objetivo, -a (4)

obligatory obligatorio, -a (7)

observatory el observatorio (5)

to **obtain** conseguir (*e → i*) (II); obtener
     (*e → ie*) (7)

to **occur** ocurrir (II)

ocean el océano (I, II)

October octubre (I)

of de (I)
     — course claro que sí (I); por
     supuesto (I, II)
     — course not ¡Claro que no! (I)

to **offer** ofrecer (*c → zc*) (2)

office la oficina (II)
     telephone — la oficina telefónica (II)
     tourist — la oficina de turismo (II)

official oficial (12)

often a menudo (I)

oil el aceite (II)

OK bueno (I)

old viejo -a; antiguo, -a (I)
     how — is . . . ? ¿cuántos años tiene
     . . . ? (I)

older mayor (I)

older person el anciano, la anciana (7)

**olympic games for people with
     disabilities** las olimpiadas de
     minusválidos (7)

omelet: Spanish — la tortilla española
     (II)

on en; sobre (I)
     — behalf of por (7)
     — the dot en punto (I)
     — the one hand por un lado (2)
     — the other hand por otro lado (2)
     — time puntualmente (I)
     — top arriba (3)
     — top (of) encima (de) (I)

once una vez (I)

one uno (un), una (I); *(a person)* uno
     (II)
     it's — o'clock es la una (I)
     —-way sólo de ida (II)

onion la cebolla (I)

only sólo (I)
     — child el hijo único, la hija única
     (I)

open descubierto, -a (5)

to **open** abrir (I)

operation la operación, *pl.* las
     operaciones (II)

operator el operador, la operadora (6)
opinion la opinión, *pl.* las opiniones (4)
opportune oportuno, -a (9)
opportunity la oportunidad (2)
opposite enfrente (de) (I)
or o (I)
    not . . . — ni . . . ni (I)
orange *adj.* anaranjado, -a; la naranja (I)
    — juice el jugo de naranja (I)
orchestra la orquesta (II)
order: in — to para + *inf.* (I)
to **order** pedir *(e → i)* (I)
organization la organización, *pl.* las organizaciones (7)
origin el origen, *pl.* los orígenes (5)
orphanage el orfanato (1)
other otro, -a (I)
others los demás (1)
ouch! ¡ay! (I)
ought to deber (I)
our nuestro, -a (I)
ours el nuestro, la nuestra, los nuestros, las nuestras (II)
outdoors al aire libre (II)
outgoing sociable (I)
outskirts las afueras (2)
oval ovalado, -a (8)
oven el horno (II)
over: all — por todas partes (II)
owl el búho (II)
own propio, -a (II)
oxygen el oxígeno (II)

to **pack** hacer la maleta (II)
package el paquete (6)
paella la paella (II)
page la página (II)
paintbrush el pincel (3)
painter el pintor, la pintora (II)
painting la pintura (3)
palace el palacio (II)
palette la paleta (3)
pants los pantalones (I)
pantyhose las pantimedias (I)
paper el papel (I)
    — clip el sujetapapeles, *pl.* los sujetapapeles (II)
    sheet of — la hoja de papel (I)
parade el desfile (II)
parcel el paquete (6)
to **pardon** perdonar (II)
    — me perdone (Ud.) (II)
parental guidance suggested se recomienda discreción (4)
parents los padres (I)
park el parque (I)
    amusement — el parque de diversiones (I)
part: to be a — of formar parte de (I)

part *(film, play)* el papel (II)
    to play the — (of) hacer el papel (de) (II)
part-time (de) tiempo parcial (9)
to **participate (in)** participar (en) (II)
party la fiesta (I)
    birthday — la fiesta de cumpleaños (I, II)
    costume — la fiesta de disfraces (I, II)
    New Year's Eve — la fiesta de fin de año (I, II)
    surprise — la fiesta de sorpresa (I, II)
to **pass** pasar (I)
passenger el pasajero, la pasajera (II)
passport el pasaporte (I)
past el pasado (I, 5); pasado, -a (I)
    half- — y media (I)
    quarter — y cuarto (I)
pastel *(color)* pastel (3)
pastime el pasatiempo (I)
pastry el pastel (I)
path el sendero (II, 2)
patience la paciencia (9)
patient *adj.* paciente (I)
to **pay** pagar *(g → gu)* (I)
    — attention (to) hacer caso a (1); fijarse (en) (3)
pedestrian el peatón, *pl.* los peatones (2)
pea el guisante (I)
peace la paz (II)
peach el durazno (II)
pen el bolígrafo (I)
penalty la pena (10)
pencil el lápiz, *pl.* los lápices (I)
    — sharpener el sacapuntas, *pl.* los sacapuntas (II)
people la gente (I); el pueblo (11)
pepper la pimienta (I)
    green — el pimiento verde (II)
    stuffed — el chile relleno (I)
peppery picante (I)
perception la percepción (4)
to **perform** *(volunteer work)* hacer (7); realizar *(z → c)* (9)
perfume el perfume (II)
period la hora (I); *(time)* la época (3)
to **permit** permitir (II)
    it's —ted se permite (II)
person la persona (I)
    a — uno (II)
personal personal (I)
phenomenon el fenómeno (8)
phone el teléfono (I)
    cellular — el teléfono celular (6)
    cordless — el teléfono inalámbrico (6)
    on the — por teléfono (I)
    pay — el teléfono público (II)
    — book la guía telefónica (I)
    — number el número de teléfono (I)

photo la foto (I)
photography la fotografía (II)
physical education la educación física (I)
physician el médico, la médica (I)
piano el piano (II)
to **pick up** recoger *(g → j)* (I, II); *(the telephone)* descolgar *(o → ue)* *(g → gu)* (6)
picnic el picnic (II)
    to have a — hacer un picnic (II)
picture el cuadro (I)
picturesque pintoresco, -a (II)
pie la tarta (II)
pill la pastilla (II)
pilot el / la piloto (II)
pineapple la piña (II)
pink rosado, -a (I)
pistol la pistola (II)
to **pitch a tent** poner una tienda (II)
place el lugar (I)
    — of interest el lugar de interés (I)
to **place** poner (I)
placed situado, -a (2)
plaid a cuadros (II)
plain liso, -a (II)
to **plan** pensar *(e → ie)* + *inf.* (I); planear (II)
plane el avión, *pl.* los aviones (I)
planet el planeta (II)
plant la planta (I, II)
planting la siembra (5)
plastic el plástico (I, II)
    (made of) — de plástico (I)
plate el plato (I)
play la obra de teatro (II)
to **play** jugar *(u → ue)* *(g → gu)* (I); *(a musical instrument)* tocar *(c → qu)* (I)
    to — the part (of) hacer el papel (de) (II)
player el jugador, la jugadora (II)
playground el patio de recreo (II)
pleased to meet you mucho gusto; encantado, -a (I)
plot el argumento (II)
pocket el bolsillo (II)
    — folder la carpeta (II)
poetry la poesía (11)
point of view el punto de vista (3)
to **point out** indicar *(c → qu)* (II)
poisonous venenoso, -a (II)
police la policía (I)
    — officer el / la policía (II)
    — station la estación de policía (I)
polish: nail — el esmalte de uñas (II)
polite (bien) educado, -a (II); cortés (9)
political party el partido político (7)
politician el político, la política (II)
politics la política (II)

pollen el polen (II)
to **pollute** contaminar (II)
polluted contaminado, -a (I, II)
pollution la contaminación (2)
pool la piscina (I)
poor people los pobres (7)
population la población (2)
pork el cerdo (II)
portrait el retrato (3)
positive positivo, -a (4)
possession la posesión, *pl.* las posesiones (II)
possible posible (8)
post card la tarjeta postal (I)
post office el correo (I)
post office box el apartado postal (6)
poster el cartel (I)
postscript la posdata (6)
pot la olla (II)
potato la papa (I)
  baked — la papa al horno (I)
  French-fried — la papa frita (I)
practical práctico, -a (I)
to **practice** practicar *(c → qu)* (I)
pre-Columbian precolombino, -a (5)
to **prefer** preferir *(e → ie);* gustar más (I)
to **prepare** preparar (I)
to **prescribe** recetar (II)
prescription la receta (II)
present el presente (5)
  at — actualmente (7)
present-day actual (5)
pressure la presión, *pl.* las presiones (2)
pretty bonito, -a (I)
principal *(school)* el director, la directora (II); *adj.* principal (II)
private privado, -a (6)
probable probable (8)
problem el problema (II)
  to solve a — resolver *(o → ue)* un problema (1)
product el producto (11)
productive productivo, -a (9)
profession la profesión, *pl.* las profesiones (II)
profile el perfil (3)
program el programa (I)
to **prohibit** prohibir (I)
  it's —ed se prohíbe (II)
projector el proyector (II)
to **promise** prometer (7)
promotion el ascenso (9)
proof la prueba (8)
to **propose** proponer (11)
to **protect (oneself)** proteger(se) *(g → j)* (I, II)
protein la proteína (II)
to **protest** protestar (7)
to **prove** comprobar *(o → ue)* (4)

public público, -a (II, 4)
puck el disco (de hockey) (II)
pumpkin la calabaza (II)
punctual puntual (9)
punctuality la puntualidad (9)
to **punish** castigar *(g → gu)* (10)
punishment el castigo (10)
pure puro, -a (I)
purple morado, -a (I)
purse el bolso (II)
to **pursue** seguir *(e → i)* (12)
to **put** poner (I)
  to — an end (to) acabar (con) (10)
  to — away guardar (II)
  to — (in jail) meter en (la cárcel) (10)
  to — on *(clothes)* ponerse (II); *(make-up)* maquillarse (II)
pyramid la pirámide (I)

quality la cualidad (9)
quarter cuarto, -a (I)
  — past y cuarto (I)
queen la reina (11)
quesadilla la quesadilla (I)
question la pregunta (II)
  to ask a — hacer una pregunta (II)
Quiche *(a Mayan language)* el quiché (6)
quiet callado, -a (I)
quite bastante (II)
quiz la prueba (II)

race la raza (11)
racket: tennis — la raqueta de tenis (II)
radio *(set)* el radio (II)
raft la balsa (II)
  to go —ing navegar *(g → gu)* en balsa (II)
rain la lluvia (I)
to **rain** llover *(o → ue)* (I)
  it's —ing llueve (I)
raincoat el impermeable (I)
rain forest la selva tropical (I)
raise (salary) el aumento (de sueldo) (9)
to **raise funds** juntar fondos (7)
ransom el rescate (10)
rather bastante (I)
razor la máquina de afeitar (II)
to **reach** alcanzar *(z → c)* (9)
  within — al alcance de la mano (2)
reaction la reacción, *pl.* las reacciones (II)
to **read** leer (I)
real real (I)
realism el realismo (3)
realistic realista (I)
really en realidad (12)
really? ¿de veras?; ¡no me digas! (I)
to **receive** recibir (I)
recently recientemente (4)

receptionist el / la recepcionista (9)
recipe la receta (II)
to **recommend** recomendar *(e → ie)* (II)
recommendation la recomendación, *pl.* las recomendaciones (9)
to **reconquer** reconquistar (11)
to **record** grabar (4)
to **recycle** reciclar (I, II)
red rojo, -a (I)
  —-haired pelirrojo, -a (I)
Red Cross la Cruz Roja (7)
to **reduce** reducir *(c → zc)* (I, II)
reflected reflejado, -a (3)
refrigerator el refrigerador (I)
region la región, *pl.* las regiones (11)
to **relate to** relacionarse con (1)
relative el pariente, la parienta (I, II)
religion la religión, *pl.* las religiones (5)
to **remember** recordar *(o → ue)* (II)
remote control el control remoto (II)
to **rent** alquilar (4)
to **repair** reparar (I)
repellent el repelente (II)
report el informe (II); el reportaje (4)
requirement el requisito (9)
reservation la reservación, *pl.* las reservaciones (II)
to **resort (to)** recurrir (a) (10)
to **respect** respetar (1)
respectful respetuoso, -a (9)
responsibility la responsabilidad (7)
responsible responsable (1)
to **rest** descansar (I)
restaurant el restaurante (I)
restroom los servicios (II)
result el resultado (11)
to **return** regresar; devolver *(o → ue)* (I)
review (of) el comentario (sobre) (II)
to **review** repasar (II)
to **revolt** rebelarse (11)
rhythm el ritmo (11)
rice el arroz (I)
rich rico, -a (5)
to **ride:**
  to — a bike montar en bicicleta (II)
  to — horseback montar a caballo (II)
right derecho, -a (I)
  to be — tener razón (I)
  —? ¿verdad? (I)
  — away en seguida (I)
  — now ahora mismo (9)
  to the — (of) a la derecha (de) (I)
right el derecho (4)
ring el anillo (II)
to **ring** sonar *(o → ue)* (6)
to **risk** arriesgar *(g → gu)* (10)
river el río (II)
road el camino (2)
roasted asado, -a (II)

to rob robar (II)
robot el robot, *pl.* los robots (II)
rock la piedra (II, 8); *(music)* la música
rock (II)
role el papel (II)
  to play the — (of) hacer el papel (de)
(II)
romantic movie la película romántica (I)
roof el techo (11)
room el cuarto (I); *(hotel)* la habitación,
pl. las habitaciones (II)
rope la cuerda (II)
  to jump — saltar a la cuerda (II)
round redondo, -a (I)
  —-trip ticket el boleto de ida y vuelta
(II)
to row pasear en bote (I)
rowboat el bote (I)
rude maleducado, -a (II)
ruins las ruinas (I)
ruler la regla (I)
to run correr (II)
rural rural (2)

sacred sagrado, -a (5)
sad triste (I)
safe seguro, -a (2)
safety la seguridad (10)
sail la vela (II)
salad la ensalada (I)
  fruit — la ensalada de frutas (II)
  — bar el bufet de ensaladas (II)
  — dressing la salsa (II)
salary el sueldo (9)
sale la liquidación, *pl.* las liquidaciones (II)
  to be for — se vende (II)
  to be on — estar en liquidación (II)
sales agent el / la agente de ventas (12)
salesperson el vendedor, la vendedora
(II)
salt la sal (I)
salty salado, -a (II)
same mismo, -a (II)
  it's all the — (to me) (me) da igual
(II)
  the — thing lo mismo (I)
sandbox el cajón *(pl.* los cajones) de
arena (II)
sandwich el sandwich (I); *(Spanish-
style)* el bocadillo (II)
satellite:
  — dish la antena parabólica (4)
  — television la televisión por satélite
(4)
Saturday sábado (I)
  on — el sábado (I)
sauce la salsa (I)
saucer el platillo (I)
sausage el chorizo (II)

to save conservar (I, II); ahorrar (II)
sax(ophone) el saxofón, *pl.* los
saxofones (II)
to say decir (I)
  how do you — . . . ? ¿cómo se dice
. . . ? (I)
  it has been said se ha dicho (4)
  it is said . . . se dice . . . (I)
  to — good-by (to) despedirse
(e → i) (de) (II)
  to — hello decirse "¡Hola!" (II)
  you don't —! ¡no me digas! (I)
to scare dar miedo a (I)
scarf el pañuelo (II)
  winter — la bufanda (I)
scene la escena (II)
  — of the crime el lugar de los
hechos (10)
schedule el horario (I)
school la escuela (I); *adj.* escolar (II); el
movimiento (3)
  after — después de las clases (I)
  elementary — la escuela primaria (II)
school (of thought) el movimiento (3)
science las ciencias (I)
  — fiction la ciencia ficción (I)
scientist el científico, la científica (II)
to score (a goal) meter (un gol) (II)
screen la pantalla (II)
  big — TV la pantalla gigante (II)
script el guión, *pl.* los guiones (II)
sculpture la escultura (5)
sea el mar (I)
seafood los mariscos (II)
to search *(baggage)* registrar (II)
season la estación, *pl.* las estaciones (I)
seat el asiento (II)
seatbelt el cinturón *(pl.* los cinturones)
de seguridad (II)
seated sentado, -a (3)
second segundo, -a (I)
secretary el secretario, la secretaria (II)
section la sección, *pl.* las secciones (II)
security guard el / la guardia (10)
security system el sistema de seguridad
(II)
to see ver (I)
  I have seen, you have seen (yo) he
visto, (tú) has visto (4)
  let's — a ver (I)
  to — each other verse (II)
seesaw el sube y baja (II)
self-defense la autodefensa (10)
self-portrait el autorretrato (3)
to sell vender (I)
semester el semestre (I)
to send enviar *(i → i)* (I); mandar (6)
sender el / la remitente (6)
sensationalistic sensacionalista (II)

sense of humor el sentido del humor (I)
sentence la sentencia (10)
to separate separar (I, II)
separated (from) separado, -a (de) (II)
September septiembre (I)
serious serio, -a (I)
to serve servir *(e → i)* (I)
  to — in the armed forces hacer el
servicio militar (7)
to set poner (I)
  — the table poner la mesa (I)
seven siete (I)
  — hundred setecientos (I)
seventeen diecisiete (I)
seventh séptimo, -a (I)
seventy setenta (I)
severe severo, -a (10)
to sew coser (II)
shack la choza (5)
shade la sombra (II)
shadow la sombra (3)
to shake hands darse la mano (II)
shame: that's a —! ¡qué lástima! (I)
shampoo el champú (I)
shape la figura (3)
to share compartir (1)
sharp en punto (I)
sharpener: pencil — el sacapuntas (II)
to shave afeitarse (II)
shaving cream la crema de afeitar (II)
she ella (I)
sheet of paper la hoja de papel (I)
shelf el estante (II)
shelter el refugio (7)
shirt la camisa (I)
  T- la camiseta (I)
shoe el zapato (I)
  high-heeled —s los zapatos de tacón
alto (I)
  — store la zapatería (I)
to shoot fireworks lanzar *(z → c)* fuegos
artificiales (II)
shooting el tiroteo (10)
to shop hacer las compras (II)
shopping:
  to go — ir de compras (I)
short *(height)* bajo, -a; *(length)*
corto, -a (I)
shorts los pantalones cortos (I)
shot la inyección, *pl.* las inyecciones (II)
  to give a — poner una inyección (II)
should deber + *inf.* (I)
show el programa (I)
  game — el programa de concursos (II)
  home shopping — el programa de
compras (II)
to show *(movie or TV program)* dar (I);
mostrar *(o → ue)* (II); indicar
(c → qu) (II)

English-Spanish Vocabulary   535

shower: to take a — ducharse (II)
shrimp el camarón, *pl.* los camarones (II)
shy tímido, -a (II)
sick enfermo, -a (I)
   to feel — sentirse *(e → ie)* mal (I)
sidewalk la acera (2)
to **sign up** inscribirse (1)
silly tonto, -a (I)
silver la plata (II)
   (made of) — de plata (II)
simple sencillo, -a (II)
since desde (que + *verb*) (II)
   it's been *(time)* **—** hace + *(time)* +
     que (I)
sincere sincero, -a (1)
to **sing** cantar (I, II)
singer el / la cantante (II)
single *(unmarried)* soltero, -a (II); *(room)*
   individual (II)
sink el fregadero (II)
sir señor (I)
sister la hermana (I)
sister-in-law la cuñada (II)
sitcom la comedia (I)
situated situado, -a (2)
six seis (I)
   — hundred seiscientos (I)
sixteen dieciséis (I)
sixth sexto, -a (I)
sixty sesenta (I)
size el tamaño (II); *(clothing)* la talla (II);
   (shoe) el número (de zapatos) (II)
skate el patín, *pl.* los patines (II)
to **skate** patinar (I)
   to ice — patinar sobre hielo (II)
ski el esquí, *pl.* los esquíes (II)
   — cap el gorro (I)
to **ski** esquiar *(i → i)* (I)
skill la destreza; la habilidad (9)
to **skin-dive** bucear (I)
skirt la falda (I)
skyscraper el rascacielos, *pl.* los
   rascacielos (2)
slave el esclavo, la esclava (11)
to **sleep** dormir *(o → ue)* (I)
sleeping bag el saco de dormir (II)
sleepy: to be — tener sueño (I)
sleeve la manga (II)
slide *(photograph)* la diapositiva (II);
   (playground) el tobogán, *pl.* los
   toboganes (II)
slow lento, -a (6)
small pequeño, -a (I)
smoke detector el detector de humo (II)
snack *(afternoon)* la merienda (I)
   for a — de merienda (I)
snake la serpiente (I, II)
sneakers los tenis (I)
to **sneeze** estornudar (II)

snow la nieve (I)
to **snow** nevar *(e → ie)* (I)
   it's —ing nieva (I)
soap el jabón (I)
   — opera la telenovela (I)
soccer el fútbol (I)
social service el servicio social (7)
social studies las ciencias sociales (I)
social worker el / la asistente social (12)
society la sociedad (7)
sock el calcetín, *pl.* los calcetines (I)
sofa el sofá (I)
soft drink el refresco (I)
solar solar (II)
sold: to be — venderse (II)
to **solicit** *(donations)* solicitar (7)
to **solve** resolver *(o → ue)* (1)
   has solved haya resuelto (8)
some unos, unas (I); alguno (algún), -a (I)
someone, somebody alguien (I, II)
something algo (I)
   — else algo más (I)
sometimes a veces (I); de vez en cuando
   (II)
son el hijo (I)
   —s; —s and daughters los hijos (I)
song la canción, *pl.* las canciones (II)
sorry: I'm — lo siento (I)
to **sort** separar (I)
so-so así, así; regular (I)
soup la sopa (I)
soup kitchen el comedor de
   beneficencia (7)
sour agrio, -a (II)
souvenir el recuerdo (I)
sowing la siembra (5)
space el espacio (II, 2)
   — heater el calentador (II)
spaceship la nave espacial (8)
Spanish español, -a; *(language)* el
   español (I)
Spanish speaker el / la hispanohablante
   (11)
to **speak in sign language** hablar por
   señas (12)
special especial (II)
   by — delivery por correo urgente (6)
   daily — el plato del día (I)
   — effects los efectos especiales (II)
Special Olympics las olimpiadas de
   minusválidos (7)
specialty: house — la especialidad de la
   casa (I)
speed la rapidez (6)
spell: how do you — . . . ? ¿cómo se
   escribe . . . ? (I)
to **spend** gastar (II)
spicy picante (I)
spider la araña (II)

spinach las espinacas (II)
spine *(on plant)* la espina (II)
spite: in — of (the fact that) a pesar
   de (que) (8)
splendor el esplendor (5)
spoiled *(child)* consentido, -a (II)
spoken: is — se habla (II)
spoon la cuchara (I)
sports los deportes (I)
   — program el programa deportivo (I)
spring la primavera (I)
square cuadrado, -a (I)
squirrel la ardilla (II)
stadium el estadio (I)
stage el escenario (II); *(in a process)* la
   etapa (3)
stairs la escalera (II)
stamp el sello (I)
to **stand** soportar (II)
   to — in line hacer fila (II)
standing de pie (3)
stapler la grapadora (II)
star la estrella (5)
to **start** empezar *(e → ie) (z → c)* (I)
to **state** afirmar (8)
statement la afirmación (8)
station la estación, *pl.* las estaciones (I)
statue la estatua (5)
to **stay** quedarse (I)
   to — in bed quedarse en la cama (I)
   to — healthy mantenerse *(e → ie)*
     sano, -a (II)
steak el bistec (I)
stereo el equipo de sonido (I)
steward, stewardess el / la auxiliar de
   vuelo (II)
stewed guisado, -a (II)
still todavía (I); tranquilo, -a (1)
still life la naturaleza muerta (3)
sting *(insect)* la picadura (II)
to **sting** *(insect)* picar *(c → qu)* (II)
stingy tacaño, -a (I)
to **stir** revolver *(o → ue)* (II)
to **stitch** *(surgically)* hacer puntadas (II)
stitches las puntadas (II)
stomach el estómago (I)
   —ache el dolor de estómago (I)
stone la piedra (II, 8)
stopover la escala (II)
stop sign la señal de alto (II)
store la tienda (I)
   clothing — la tienda de ropa (I)
   department — el almacén, *pl.* los
     almacenes (I)
   discount — la tienda de descuentos
     (I)
storm la tormenta (II)
story *(of a building)* el piso (I)
stove la estufa (I)

strange extraño, -a (8)
strawberry la fresa (II)
street la calle (I)
stress la presión, *pl.* las presiones (2)
striped a rayas (II)
strong fuerte (II)
to **struggle** luchar (10)
student el / la estudiante (I)
— **council** el consejo estudiantil (II)
to **study** estudiar (I)
stuffed animal el animal de peluche (II)
style el estilo (3)
subconscious el subconsciente (3)
subject *(in school)* la materia (II); el tema (3)
subjective subjetivo, -a (4)
suburbs las afueras (2)
subway el metro (I)
— **station** la estación del metro (I)
successful: to be — tener éxito (II)
such as tal como (4)
sufficient suficiente (II)
sugar el azúcar (I)
to **suggest** sugerir *(e → ie)* (II)
suit el traje (I, II)
bathing — el traje de baño (I)
to **suit: it suits me** convenir *(e → ie)*: me conviene (9)
suitable for the whole family apta para toda la familia (4)
suitcase la maleta (I, II)
summer el verano (I)
sun el sol (I)
to **sunbathe** tomar el sol (I)
Sunday domingo (I)
on — el domingo (I)
sunglasses los anteojos de sol (I, II)
sunny: it's — hace sol (I)
sunrise el amanecer (II)
sunset el atardecer (II)
suntan lotion el bronceador (I)
supermarket el supermercado (I)
to **support (each other)** apoyar(se) (1)
to **suppose** suponer (8)
sure: to be — estar seguro, -a (8)
to **surf** hacer surf (II)
surfboard la tabla (de surf) (II)
to **surprise** sorprender(se) (10)
surprise party la fiesta de sorpresa (I, II)
surrealism el surrealismo (3)
suspect el sospechoso, la sospechosa (10)
sweater el suéter (I)
turtleneck — el suéter de cuello alto (II)
sweatshirt la sudadera (I)
sweatsuit el chandal (II)
sweet dulce (II)

to **swim** nadar (I)
swimming pool la piscina (I)
swing el columpio (II)
syllable la sílaba (5)
symbol el símbolo (5)
symptom el síntoma (II)
synagogue la sinagoga (11)
synthetic sintético, -a (II)
system el sistema (II)

table la mesa (I)
to clear the — quitar la mesa (I)
night — la mesa de noche (II)
to set the — poner la mesa (I)
tablecloth el mantel (I)
tablet la pastilla (I)
taco el taco (I)
to **take** llevar; sacar; tomar (I)
to — **a bath** bañarse (II)
to — **charge of** encargarse *(g → gu)* de (9)
to — **off** *(clothes, make-up, etc.)* quitarse (II); *(aircraft)* despegar *(g → gu)* (II)
to — **out** sacar *(c → qu)* (I)
to — **pictures** sacar fotos (I)
to — **a shower** ducharse (II)
to — **time (to)** tardar (en) (2)
to — **a walk** ir a pasear (I)
to **talk** hablar (I)
to — **to each other** hablarse (II)
talk show el programa de entrevistas (I)
tall alto, -a (I)
tape player el tocacintas, *pl.* los tocacintas (II)
tape recorder la grabadora (I)
task la tarea (9)
to **taste** probar *(o → ue)* (I)
tasteless soso, -a (II)
tasty sabroso, -a (I)
taxes los impuestos (2)
taxi el taxi (I)
tea el té (I)
iced — el té helado (I)
to **teach** enseñar (I)
teacher el profesor, la profesora (I)
team el equipo (II)
technician el técnico, la técnica (II)
technology la tecnología (II)
teddy bear el oso de peluche (II)
teeth las muelas (I); los dientes (II)
telegram el telegrama (6)
telephone el teléfono (I); *see also* **phone**
— **office** la oficina telefónica (II)
video — el teléfono con video (II)
television la tele(visión) (I)
— **set** el televisor (II)
to watch — ver la tele(visión) (I)
to **tell** decir (II)

temple el templo (I, 5)
ten diez (I)
tennis el tenis (I)
— **racket** la raqueta de tenis (II)
— **shoes** los tenis (I)
tent la tienda (de acampar) (II)
to pitch a — poner una tienda (II)
terrible terrible (II)
terrorism el terrorismo (10)
test el examen, *pl.* los exámenes (II)
medical — el análisis, *pl.* los análisis (II)
Thanksgiving el Día de (Acción de) Gracias (II)
thanks to gracias a (5)
thank you gracias (I)
that que (I); ese, esa (I, II); aquel, aquella (II)
isn't — **so?** ¿verdad? (I)
— **one** ése, ésa, (I, II); aquél, aquélla (II)
—**'s too bad!** ¡qué lástima! (I)
—**'s why** por eso (I)
the el, la, los, las (I)
theater *(movie)* el cine; el teatro (I)
their su, sus (I); suyo, -a (II)
theirs el suyo, la suya, los suyos, las suyas (II)
them *dir. obj. pron.* los, las; *after prep.* ellos, ellas; *ind. obj. pron.* les (I)
then luego (I); entonces (6)
theory la teoría (8)
there allí (I)
— **is / are** hay (I)
— **it is** allí está (I)
— **used to be** había (II)
— **was / were** había (II); hubo (II)
— **will be** habrá (II)
therefore por eso (I)
these *adj.* estos, -as (I, II); *pron.* éstos, -as (II)
they ellos, ellas (I)
thief el ladrón, *pl.* los ladrones; la ladrona (II)
thing la cosa (I); el objeto (5)
to **think** creer; pensar *(e → ie)* (I); parecer (que) (II)
I (don't) — **so** creo que sí (no) (I)
to — **about** pensar en (I)
third tercer, -a (I)
thirsty: to be — tener sed (I)
thirteen trece (I)
thirty treinta (I)
this este, esta (I, II)
— **one** éste, ésta (II)
thorn la espina (I)
those *adj.* esos, -as (I, II); aquellos, -as (II); *pron.* ésos, -as; aquéllos, -as (II)

thousand mil (I)
threat la amenaza (I)
three tres (I)
   — hundred trescientos (I)
   —-ring binder la carpeta de argollas (I)
throat la garganta (I)
   sore — el dolor de garganta (I)
   — lozenges las pastillas para la garganta (I)
through por (II); a través de (11)
to **throw out** echar (II)
Thursday jueves (I)
   on — el jueves (I)
ticket la entrada (I); el boleto (II)
tidy ordenado, -a (I)
tie la corbata (I, II)
to **tie** *(in scoring)* empatar (II)
tiger el tigre (I)
tight *(clothing)* apretado, -a (II)
tile el azulejo (11)
time la hora; el tiempo; la vez (I); *(period)* la época (3)
   at the same — a la vez (I)
   at —s a veces (I)
   at what —? ¿a qué hora? (I)
   to have a good / bad — pasarlo bien / mal (I, II)
   many —s muchas veces (I)
   on — puntualmente (I)
   what — is it? ¿qué hora es? (I)
tired cansado, -a (I)
to a (I)
   in order — para + *inf.* (I)
toast el pan tostado (I)
toaster el tostador (II)
today hoy (I)
   not — hoy no (I)
toe el dedo del pie (I)
token la ficha (6)
to **tolerate** soportar (II)
toll booth el peaje (2)
tomato el tomate (I)
   — soup la sopa de tomate (I)
tomb la tumba (5)
tomorrow mañana (I)
ton la tonelada (8)
tone *(in a painting)* el tono (3)
   dial — el tono (6)
tongue: mother — la lengua materna (12)
too también (I); demasiado (I)
   — many demasiado, -a (4)
toothache el dolor de muelas (I)
toothbrush el cepillo de dientes (II)
toothpaste la pasta dentífrica (I)
top:
   on — arriba (3)
   on — (of) encima de (I)

torn roto, -a (II)
tortilla la tortilla (I)
touched: to be — *(emotionally)* emocionarse (4)
tourist el / la turista (II)
   — office la oficina de turismo (II)
tower la torre (11)
town el pueblo (II)
   — square la plaza (I)
toy el juguete (II); *adj.* de juguete (II)
track la huella (8)
tradition la tradición, *pl.* las tradiciones (5)
traffic el tráfico (II)
   — jam el atasco (2)
   — light el semáforo (II)
train el tren (I)
   — station la estación del tren (I)
training el entrenamiento (9)
to **transform** transformar(se) (3)
to **translate** traducir *(c → zc)* (12)
translation la traducción, *pl.* las traducciones (12)
translator el traductor, la traductora (12)
transportation el transporte (II)
to **travel** viajar (12)
traveler el viajero, la viajera (II)
   —'s check el cheque de viajero (II)
to **treat (well / badly)** tratar (bien / mal) (9)
tree el árbol (I, II)
tricycle el triciclo (II)
   to ride a — montar en triciclo (II)
trip el viaje (II)
   short — la excursión, *pl.* las excursiones (II)
truck el camión, *pl.* los camiones (II)
true cierto, -a (8)
trumpet la trompeta (II)
truth la verdad (II)
to **try** probar *(o → ue)* (I)
   to — on probarse *(o → ue)* (II)
   to — to tratar de (3)
T-shirt la camiseta (I)
Tuesday martes (I)
   on — el martes (I)
turkey el pavo (II)
to **turn** doblar (II)
   to — off apagar *(g → gu)* (I, II)
   to — on encender *(e → ie)* (II)
turnover la empanada (II)
turtle la tortuga (II)
tutor el tutor, la tutora (II)
to **tutor** dar clases particulares (1)
twelve doce (I)
twenty veinte (I)
twice dos veces (I)
twig el palito (II)
twin el gemelo, la gemela (I)
two dos (I)

— hundred doscientos (I)
type la clase (I)
typical típico, -a (I, II)

ugly feo, -a (I)
umbrella el paraguas (I)
unbelievable increíble (8)
uncle el tío (I)
uncomfortable incómodo, -a (I)
under 17 not admitted without an adult prohibida para menores (4)
under(neath) debajo de (I)
to **understand (each other)** entender(se) *(e → ie)* (1)
understanding comprensivo, -a (1)
to **unfasten** desabrocharse (II)
unfriendly antipático, -a (I)
to **unite** unir (7)
university la universidad (II)
unjust injusto, -a (7)
unknown desconocido, -a (8)
unmarried soltero, -a (II)
to **unpack** deshacer la maleta (II)
unpleasant antipático, -a (I)
until hasta (I)
to **upset** *(one's stomach)* hacer daño a (II)
us *obj. pron.* nos; *after prep.* nosotros, -as (I)
to **use** usar (I)
   used:
     to be — for servir *(e → i)* para (8)
     what's it — for? ¿para qué sirve? (8)
useful útil (12)
usually generalmente (I)

vacation las vacaciones (I)
   to go on — ir de vacaciones (I)
to **vacuum** pasar la aspiradora (I)
vacuum cleaner la aspiradora (I)
vain vanidoso, -a (1)
Valentine's Day el Día de los Enamorados (II)
valley el valle (II)
value el valor (3)
to **value** apreciar (12)
VCR la videocasetera (I)
vegetable la verdura (I)
   — soup la sopa de verduras (I)
very muy (I)
vest el chaleco (II)
veterinarian el veterinario, la veterinaria (II)
victim la víctima (II)
video el video (II)
   — game el videojuego (I)
video conference la conferencia por video (6)
viewers el público (4)
vinegar el vinagre (II)

violence la violencia (II)
violent violento, -a (II)
violin el violín, *pl.* los violines (II)
virus el virus (II)
to **visit** visitar (I)
vitamin la vitamina (II)
voice: in a loud / soft — en voz alta / baja (6)
volleyball el vóleibol (I)
to **volunteer** trabajar como voluntario (II)
to **vomit** vomitar (II)
to **vote** votar (7)
voyage el viaje (II)

to **wait (for)** esperar (6)
to **wait on** atender *(e → ie)* (a) (9)
waiter, waitress el camarero, la camarera (I)
to **wake up** despertarse *(e → ie)* (II)
walk la marcha (7)
walk: to take a — ir a pasear (I)
to **walk** caminar (II)
walking a pie (I)
wall la pared (II)
wallet la cartera (II)
to **want** querer *(e → ie)* (I)
   they wanted to ellos quisieron (3)
   we will want querremos (6)
war la guerra (II)
to **wash** lavar (I)
   — one's face, hair, etc. lavarse la cara, el pelo, etc. (II)
washer:
   clothes — la lavadora (II)
   dish— el lavaplatos (II)
to **waste** gastar (II)
watch el reloj (pulsera) (I, II)
to **watch** ver (I); vigilar (10)
water el agua *f.* (I)
   — pistol la pistola de agua (II)
   to — ski hacer esquí acuático (II)
   — skiing el esquí acuático (II)
waterfall las cataratas (I)
watermelon la sandía (II)
we nosotros, -as (I)
weapon el arma, *pl.* las armas (10)
to **wear** llevar (I); usar (II)
weather el tiempo (I)
   the — is nice (bad) hace buen (mal) tiempo (I)
   — forecast el pronóstico del tiempo (I)
   what's the — like? ¿qué tiempo hace? (I)
wedding la boda (II)
   — anniversary el aniversario (de boda) (II)
Wednesday miércoles (I)
   on — el miércoles (I)
week la semana (I)
weekend el fin de semana (I)

to **weigh** pesar (8)
weight el peso (8)
weights las pesas (II)
   to lift — levantar pesas (II)
welcome: you're — de nada (I)
well bien (I); *(to indicate pause)* pues (I)
well-mannered (bien) educado, -a (II)
western la película del oeste (I)
wet mojado, -a (II)
whale la ballena (I, II)
what ¿qué? (I); lo que (II)
   —'s it used for? ¿para qué sirve? (8)
wheel la rueda (8)
wheelchair la silla de ruedas (II)
when cuando (I)
when? ¿cuándo? (I)
where donde (I)
where? ¿dónde? (I)
   from —? ¿de dónde? (I)
   (to) —? ¿adónde? (I)
whether si (I)
which? ¿cuál? (I)
   — ones ¿cuáles? (I)
while mientras (II)
white blanco, -a (I)
   in black and — en blanco y negro (I)
who que (I)
who? whom? ¿quién(es)? (I)
who's calling? ¿de parte de quién? (6)
why? ¿por qué? (I)
   that's — por eso (I)
width el ancho (8)
wife la esposa (II)
wild *(animal)* salvaje (II); *(plant)* silvestre (II)
to **win** ganar (II)
wind el viento (I)
window la ventana (I); *(plane)* la ventanilla (II)
to **windsurf** hacer surf de vela (II)
windy: it's hace viento (I)
winter el invierno (I)
with con (I)
   — me conmigo (I)
   — you contigo (I)
to **withdraw** *(money)* sacar *(c → qu)* (I)
without sin (II)
witness el / la testigo (10)
wolf el lobo, la loba (I, II)
woman la mujer (I)
   young — la joven (I)
wonderful fantástico, -a; ¡genial! (I); ¡una maravilla! (2)
wood la madera (I)
   (made of) — de madera (I)
woods el bosque (II)
wool la lana (II)
work el trabajo (7)
   — of art la obra de arte (3)

to **work** trabajar (I); *(machines)* funcionar (II)
world el mundo (11); mundial (12)
world-wide mundial (12)
to **worry** preocupar(se) (10)
worse peor (I)
worst el / la (los / las) peor(es) (I)
   the — (thing) lo peor (1)
worthwhile: it's (not) — (no) vale la pena (I)
would be: it — sería (12)
wow! ¡vaya! (I)
to **wrap** envolver *(o → ue)* (6)
wrist la muñeca (II)
   — watch el reloj pulsera (I, II)
to **write** escribir (I, II)
   to — to each other escribirse (II)
writer el escritor, la escritora (II)
writing la escritura (5)
wrong equivocado, -a (6)
   to be — no tener razón (I)
   what's —? ¿qué tienes? (I)

X-ray la radiografía (II)
   to take an — sacar *(c → qu)* una radiografía (II)

to **yawn** bostezar *(z → c)* (4)
year el año (I)
   to be . . . —s old tener . . . años (I)
   New —'s Day el Año Nuevo (II)
   New —'s Eve el fin de año (II)
   New —'s Eve party la fiesta de fin de año (I)
yearbook el anuario (II)
yellow amarillo, -a (I)
yes sí (I)
yesterday ayer (I)
yet: not — todavía no (I)
you *fam.* tú; *formal* usted (Ud.); *pl.* ustedes (Uds.); *dir. obj. pron.* lo, la, los, las; *fam. dir. obj. pron.* te; *ind. obj. pron.* le, les; *fam. after prep.* ti (I)
young *adj.* joven (I)
   —er menor, *pl.* menores (I)
   — lady la joven (I)
   — man el joven (I)
   — people los jóvenes (I)
your tu, tus *fam.;* su, sus *formal & pl.* (I); tuyo, -a; suyo, -a (II)
yours *fam.* el tuyo, la tuya, los tuyos, las tuyas; *formal & pl.* el suyo, la suya, los suyos, las suyas (II)
yuck! ¡qué asco! (I)

zero cero (I)
zipper la cremallera (II)
zoo el zoológico (I)

English-Spanish Vocabulary   539

Más práctica y tarea

Aquí tienes una oportunidad adicional de practicar el vocabulario y la gramática de *PASO A PASO 3*. Escribe todas tus respuestas en una hoja aparte.

PASODOBLE

Escuela San Martín (página 2)

 El primer día de clases Escribe la letra de la frase que mejor conteste las preguntas sobre el primer día de clases.

1. ¿Qué materia es la más interesante para ti?
2. ¿Tienes mucha tarea en la clase de español?
3. ¿Estudias otro idioma?
4. ¿Cuál es la tarea de álgebra?
5. ¿Piensas escribir para el club literario?
6. ¿Conoces a mucha gente?
7. ¿Qué materia es la menos interesante?
8. ¿A qué hora sales de las clases?

a. Por suerte, no tengo mucha esta noche.
b. O para el periódico escolar.
c. Sí, tengo muchos amigos en todas las clases.
d. El día escolar termina a las tres.
e. Para mí, la historia.
f. Tenemos que hacer los problemas 10–12 en la página 6.
g. La geografía es la menos interesante.
h. Sí, alemán.

(Practice Workbook PD-1)

¿Qué están haciendo? (página 3)

 ¿Qué hacen? Escribe lo que hacen estas personas antes de y después de las clases, usando el presente y el presente progresivo del verbo entre paréntesis.

¿Patina (patinar) bien Elisa?
Sí, está patinando ahora.

1. ¿____ (terminar) Jorge el proyecto?

2. ¿____ (bailar) bien Lourdes?

3. ¿____ (jugar) básquetbol todos los días Daniel y Nacho?

Escuela San Martín (p. 2)
Exercise 1
1. e
2. a
3. h
4. f
5. b
6. c
7. g
8. d

¿Qué están haciendo? (p. 3)
Exercise 1
1. Termina / Sí, está terminando el proyecto ahora.
2. Baila / ... está bailando ahora.
3. Juegan / ... están jugando ahora.
4. Gana / ... está ganando ahora.
5. Estudiamos / ... estamos estudiando ahora.
6. Caminas / ... estoy caminando ahora.

¿Qué clase de persona eres tú? (pp. 4–5)

Exercise 1
1. Juan se despierta a las siete.
2. María Teresa se cepilla los dientes a las siete y media (treinta).
3. Tú te duchas a las siete y cuarto (quince).
4. Yo me lavo la cara a las seis y cuarenta y cinco.
5. Mis hermanas se visten a las seis y media (treinta).
6. Verónica y yo nos peinamos a las ocho.

La moda (pp. 6–7)

Exercise 1
1. era
2. coleccionaba
3. tenía
4. jugábamos
5. gustaba
6. llamaba
7. encantaba
8. salíamos
9. llevaba
10. era

Exercise 2
1. prefiere
2. esta
3. ése
4. este
5. Este
6. esos
7. esta / esa
8. ésa

---

4. ¿___ (ganar) muchos partidos tu equipo?

5. ¿___ (estudiar) nosotros después de las clases?

6. ¿___ (caminar) tú mucho?

(Practice Workbook PD-2)

¿Qué clase de persona eres tú? (páginas 4–5)

1 **¿A qué hora?** Escribe cuándo estas personas se preparan para el día.

yo/levantarse/6:30   *Me levanto a las seis y media.*

1. Juan/despertarse/7:00
2. María Teresa/cepillarse los dientes/7:30
3. tú/ducharse/7:15
4. yo/lavarse la cara/ 6:45
5. mis hermanas/vestirse/6:30
6. Verónica y yo/peinarse/8:00

La moda (páginas 6–7)

1 **De pequeña** Escribe la forma apropiada del imperfecto de cada verbo entre paréntesis.

Cuando yo __1__ (ser) pequeña, yo __2__ (coleccionar) animales. Yo __3__ (tener) más de veinte animales grandes y pequeños, de todos los tamaños y colores. Mis hermanos y yo __4__ (jugar) con los animales día y noche. A mí hermano le __5__ (gustar) un dinosaurio que se __6__ (llamar) Rey. Y a mí me __7__ (encantar) un elefante morado, Violeta. Cuando mi familia y yo __8__ (salir), yo siempre __9__ (llevar) a Violeta. ¡Violeta __10__ (ser) mi mejor amiga!

2 **Ir de compras** Completa este diálogo con la palabra más apropiada entre paréntesis.

1. Vendedora: ¿Qué década de moda (prefiere/prefiera) Ud., los años 70 o los 90?
2. Tú: Prefiero (esta/esa) década.
3. Vendedora: ¿Le gusta este abrigo o (ése/aquella)?
4. Tú: No me gusta ése, pero me encanta (esta/este) abrigo negro.
5. Vendedora: (Este/Esta) chaleco es muy popular. ¿Ud. quiere probárselo?
6. Tú: Sí, y quisiera probarme (esas/esos) pantalones negros también.
7. Vendedora: Ud. necesita una camisa. ¿Prefiere (esta/este) camisa blanca o (esa/ese) camisa roja?
8. Tú: Prefiero (aquello/ésa), gracias.

(Practice Workbook PD-3)

542   Más práctica y tarea

Caricaturas (páginas 8–9)

1 **Celebraciones y posesiones** Escribe la letra de la palabra que no esté asociada con las otras palabras.

1. **a.** el cumpleaños   **b.** el tostador   **c.** el aniversario
2. **a.** el árbol   **b.** el nieto   **c.** el abuelo
3. **a.** apagar   **b.** felicitar   **c.** celebrar
4. **a.** el microondas   **b.** el fregadero   **c.** el sótano
5. **a.** la pulsera   **b.** la secadora   **c.** la lavadora
6. **a.** el televisor   **b.** el control remoto   **c.** el reloj

Nuestros pasatiempos (página 10)

1 **Los pasatiempos** Usando el pretérito, escribe los días en que Vicente, Eva y Tomás hicieron estas actividades.

trabajar en el hospital
Eva trabajó en el hospital el miércoles.

	lunes	martes	miércoles	jueves	viernes
Vicente	café	auditorio	parque	auditorio	parque
Eva	café	gimnasio	hospital	gimnasio	plaza
Tomás	biblioteca	centro	biblioteca	casa	plaza

1. patinar en el parque
2. estudiar en la biblioteca
3. hacer ejercicio en el gimnasio
4. jugar ajedrez en la plaza
5. tocar la trompeta en el auditorio
6. comer unos sandwiches en un café
7. ver la televisión en casa
8. ir de compras en el centro

(Practice Workbook PD-4)

El día de fiesta que más me impresionó (página 11)

1 **La fiesta de cumpleaños** Escribe el verbo del recuadro que mejor complete cada frase. Usa cada verbo sólo una vez.

di	jugué	se divirtieron	sirvió
encendiste	pidió	servimos	tuviste
encontró	pusieron	se vistió	

Caricaturas (pp. 8–9)
Exercise 1
1. b
2. a
3. a
4. c
5. a
6. c

Nuestros pasatiempos (p. 10)
Exercise 1
1. Vicente patinó en el parque el miércoles y el viernes.
2. Tomás estudió en la biblioteca el lunes y el miércoles.
3. Eva hizo ejercicio en el gimnasio el martes y el jueves.
4. Eva y Tomás jugaron ajedrez en la plaza el viernes.
5. Vicente tocó la trompeta en el auditorio el martes y el jueves.
6. Vicente y Eva comieron unos sandwiches en un café el lunes.
7. Tomás vio la televisión en casa el jueves.
8. Tomás fue de compras en el centro el martes.

El día de fiesta que más me impresionó (p. 11)

Exercise 1

1. se vistió
2. pidió
3. encendiste
4. di
5. jugué
6. servimos
7. pusieron
8. tuviste
9. encontró
10. se divirtieron

Los tiempos cambian (pp. 12–13)

Exercise 1

1. El mío es muy grande también.
2. El suyo es viejo también.
3. La suya es muy buena también.
4. El nuestro funciona bien también.
5. La mía es roja también.
6. Las suyas son muy caras también.

Tesoros del mundo hispano (pp. 14–15)

Exercise 1

1. Se venden recuerdos.
2. Se hace cerámica.
3. Se ven tesoros mayas.
4. Se pide chocolate caliente.
5. Se hablan español e inglés.
6. Se compran tarjetas postales.

Ricardo ___ el helado.   *sirvió*

1. Cata ___ de ropa elegante.
2. Arturo ___ un pastel de chocolate.
3. Tú ___ las velas.
4. Yo le ___ un regalo estupendo.
5. Yo ___ damas.
6. Nosotros ___ los refrescos.
7. Clara, Rebeca y Manuel ___ los regalos encima de la mesa.
8. Tú ___ que salir temprano.
9. El próximo día Guillermo ___ más tarjetas.
10. Todos los invitados ___ mucho.

(Practice Workbook PD-5)

Los tiempos cambian (páginas 12–13)

1 **¿Cómo son los aparatos?** Contesta las preguntas con uno de los pronombres posesivos del recuadro.

la mía	la nuestra	la suya	el suyo
el mío	el nuestro	las suyas	la tuya

La lavadora es muy grande. ¿Y tu lavadora?
La mía es grande también.

1. Mi televisor es muy grande. ¿Y tu televisor?
2. Tu secador de pelo es viejo. ¿Y el secador de tu mamá?
3. Esta lavadora es muy buena. ¿Y la lavadora de Emilia?
4. Este calentador funciona bien. ¿Y el calentador de tu familia?
5. Mi bicicleta es roja. ¿Y tu bicicleta?
6. Sus joyas son muy caras. ¿Y las joyas de tus hermanas?

Tesoros del mundo hispano (páginas 14–15)

1 **¿Qué se encuentran aquí?** Contesta las preguntas con el *se* impersonal.

¿Qué se reparan aquí? / (joyas)
Se reparan joyas.

1. ¿Qué se venden aquí? / (recuerdos)
2. ¿Qué se hace aquí? / (cerámica)
3. ¿Qué se ven aquí? / (tesoros mayas)
4. ¿Qué se pide aquí? / (chocolate caliente)
5. ¿Qué se hablan aquí? / (español e inglés)
6. ¿Qué se compran aquí? / (tarjetas postales)

(Practice Workbook PD-6)

La salud (páginas 16–17)

1 **Muchos accidentes** Usando el imperfecto progresivo y el verbo *caer,* escribe lo que estaban haciendo estas personas cuando se cayeron.

Juan Carlos/patinar   *Juan Carlos estaba patinando cuando se cayó.*

1. Luisa/esquiar
2. tú /montar en bicicleta
3. yo/bailar
4. Eduardo/jugar vóleibol
5. Carla y Susana /correr
6. el profesor Rodríguez/usar muletas

(Practice Workbook PD-7)

Nuestras películas favoritas (páginas 18–19)

1 **La película de ciencia ficción** Completa el diálogo escribiendo la forma correcta del imperfecto o del pretérito de cada verbo entre paréntesis.

¿(Ir) tú al cine ayer?   *Fuiste*
Sí, (ser) muy tarde cuando fui.   *era*

Enrique: ¿ _1_ (Ver) tú ayer la nueva película del director Jaime Santos?
Alicia: ¿La película en que _2_ (haber) muchos efectos especiales?
Enrique: La película en que los extraterrestres _3_ (llegar) a Chile.
Alicia: Ah, sí. _4_ (Ser) las cuatro de la mañana cuando llegaron.
Enrique: ¿Te _5_ (gustar) mucho esa película?
Alicia: Sí, porque _6_ (ser) original. ¿A ti te _7_ (gustar)?
Enrique: ¡Sí! La actuación del actor principal _8_ (ser) fabuloso.

(Practice Workbook PD-8)

Las muchachas nunca deben romper las reglas (páginas 20–21)

1 **Los opuestos** Escoge la letra de la palabra que tiene el significado opuesto.

1. alguien
2. algo
3. algún
4. alguna
5. siempre
6. también

a. nunca
b. ninguna
c. nadie
d. tampoco
e. ningún
f. nada

2 **¡Qué negativo!** Escribe estas frases de nuevo, cambiándolas al negativo.

¿<u>Alguién</u> compró jabón?   *¿Nadie compró jabón?*

1. ¿Compraste <u>algo</u> especial?
2. Andrés <u>siempre</u> va a los bailes.
3. ¿Hay <u>alguna</u> máquina de afeitar por aquí?
4. Isabel y Cristina llevan este perfume <u>también</u>.

La salud (pp. 16–17)
Exercise 1
1. Luisa estaba esquiando cuando se cayó.
2. Tú estabas montando en bicicleta cuando te caíste.
3. Yo estaba bailando cuando me caí.
4. Eduardo estaba jugando vóleibol cuando se cayó.
5. Carla y Susana estaban corriendo cuando se cayeron.
6. El profesor Rodríguez estaba usando muletas cuando se cayó.

Nuestras películas favoritas (pp. 18–19)
Exercise 1
1. Viste
2. había
3. llegaron
4. Eran
5. gustó
6. era
7. gustó
8. era

Las muchachas nunca deben romper las reglas (pp. 20–21)
Exercise 1
1. c
2. f
3. e
4. b
5. a
6. d

Exercise 2

1. ¿No compraste nada especial?
2. Andrés nunca va a los bailes.
3. ¿No hay ninguna máquina de afeitar por aquí?
4. Isabel y Cristina no llevan este perfume tampoco.
5. ¿Nadie encontró tu lápiz de labios?
6. Ninguno de los chicos tendrá un cepillo.

¡Vamos de vacaciones! (pp. 22–23)
Exercise 1

1.
2. habla
3. lee
4.
5. compra
6. no vayas
7. no traigas
8. ten
9.
10.

El siglo XXI—unas predicciones (pp. 24–25)
Exercise 1

1. Escribirá una novela.
2. Trabajará en una clínica para animales.
3. Será médico.
4. Tocarán en una orquesta famosa.
5. Se casarán.
6. Correrás en los Juegos Olímpicos.
7. Aprenderé japonés.
8. Protegeremos a las víctimas.

5. ¿<u>Alguién</u> encontró tu lápiz de labios?
6. <u>Alguno</u> de los chicos tendrá un cepillo.

¡Vamos de vacaciones! (páginas 22–23)

 ¡A viajar! Busca el verbo en cada frase y escríbelo si es un mandato con *tú*.

Compra tus cheques viajeros.   *compra*

1. Primero, tienes que decidir adónde vas.
2. Habla con tus amigos y parientes.
3. Lee unos libros sobre tu destinación.
4. Puedes aprender mucho de tu destinación.
5. Compra temprano tu boleto.
6. ¡No vayas tarde al aeropuerto!
7. Y no traigas demasiado equipaje.
8. Ten cuidado con tu bolsa.
9. Si sigues estos consejos, estarás preparado.
10. ¡Te vas a divertir mucho!

(Practice Workbook PD-9)

El siglo XXI—unas predicciones (páginas 24–25)

 ¿Qué serán? Escribe lo que será cada persona en el futuro. Escoge una frase apropiada del recuadro y cambia el infinitivo al futuro.

A Samuel le gustan los coches.   *Reparará coches.*

aprender japonés	reparar coches
casarse	ser médico
correr en los Juegos Olímpicos	tocar en una orquesta famosa
escribir una novela	trabajar en una clínica para animales
proteger a las víctimas	

1. A Manolo le encanta escribir.
2. A Francisca le encantan los animales.
3. Martín siempre sacaba buenas notas en las ciencias.
4. Diana e Inés estaban en la banda por ocho años.
5. Julio y Ana se quieren mucho.
6. ¡Tú corres tan rápido!
7. Yo hablo cuatro idiomas.
8. Armando y yo hacemos mucho trabajo voluntario.

(Practice Workbook PD-10)

Aquí tienes una oportunidad adicional de practicar el vocabulario y la gramática de cada capítulo. Escribe todas tus respuestas en una hoja aparte.

CAPÍTULO 1

Vocabulario para comunicarse (páginas 30–35)

1 **Antónimos** Escribe frases que digan lo contrario de estas frases, reemplazando las expresiones subrayadas por sus antónimos.

1. Pedro es muy <u>vanidoso</u>.

2. Nosotros estamos <u>nerviosos</u>.

3. Mi madre es una persona <u>comprensiva</u>.

4. ¡No seas tan <u>irresponsable</u>!

5. El guión fue <u>lo mejor</u> de la película.

6. Tener dinero es <u>lo menos importante</u>.

7. Es bueno <u>llevarse bien</u> con los enemigos.

8. <u>Nunca</u> vamos al cine los fines de semana.

2 **Definiciones** Empareja cada palabra o frase con su definición. Escoge la letra de la respuesta correcta.

1. hacer caso   **a.** lo que tiene una persona graciosa

2. nervioso   **b.** permitir que otra persona use una cosa tuya

3. mudarse   **c.** las otras personas

4. sentido del humor   **d.** ayudar

5. compartir   **e.** que dice la verdad

6. sincero   **f.** que no está tranquilo

7. los demás   **g.** obedecer, no ignorar

8. apoyar   **h.** cambiarse de casa

(Practice Workbook 1-1, 1-2)

Vocabulario para comunicarse (pp. 30–35)
Exercise 1
1. modesto
2. tranquilos
3. incomprensiva
4. responsable
5. lo peor
6. lo más importante
7. llevarse mal
8. Siempre

Exercise 2
1. g
2. f
3. h
4. a
5. b
6. e
7. c
8. d

Tema para investigar
(pp. 36–39)
Exercise 1
1. inscribirse
2. higiene
3. orfanato
4. esgrima
5. influye

Gramática en contexto
(pp. 44–49)
Exercise 1
1. Inscríbete en un club.
2. Comparte tus juegos con él.
3. Múdate a otra casa.
4. Habla con tu profesora.

Exercise 2
1. Di
2. Haz
3. Sé
4. sal

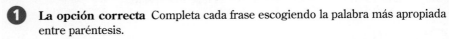

Tema para investigar (páginas 36–39)

1 **La opción correcta** Completa cada frase escogiendo la palabra más apropiada entre paréntesis.

1. Para ser miembro de un club, uno tiene que (inscribirse / quejarse).

2. La (redacción / higiene) es muy importante para estar sanos.

3. Los niños que no tienen padres viven en el (orfanato / asilo).

4. La (campaña / esgrima) es un deporte que no se ofrece en la escuela.

5. Lo que hacemos mejor (adquiere / influye) en el trabajo que escogemos.

(Practice Workbook 1-3, 1-4)

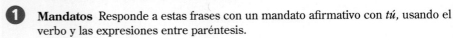

Gramática en contexto (páginas 44–49)
Los mandatos afirmativos con *tú* (página 45)

1 **Mandatos** Responde a estas frases con un mandato afirmativo con *tú*, usando el verbo y las expresiones entre paréntesis.

Tengo mucha hambre. (comer / un taco)
Come un taco.

1. No tengo muchos amigos. (inscribirse / en un club)

2. Tengo muchos juegos y Roberto no tiene ninguno. (compartir / tus juegos con él)

3. No me gusta mi casa. (mudarse / a otra casa)

4. No participo mucho en clase. (hablar / con tu profesora)

2 **Más mandatos** Completa las frases con uno de los mandatos del recuadro.

di	sal
haz	sé

1. ___ siempre la verdad.

2. ___ caso a tus padres.

3. ___ considerado con las demás personas.

4. Para llegar a tiempo a la escuela, ___ temprano de tu casa.

(Practice Workbook 1-5)

Los complementos directos e indirectos (páginas 46–47)

3 **¿A quién?** Escoge el complemento directo o indirecto *[me, te, le(s), lo(s), la(s)* o *nos]* que mejor complete cada una de estas frases.

1. Jorge ___ manda una carta a Arturo.

2. Mi abuela ___ llama por teléfono a nosotros frecuentemente.

3. No ___ hago caso a las personas agresivas.

4. A mí, mis amigos ___ respetan.

5. ___ voy a escribir a Ángela.

(Practice Workbook 1-6, 1-7)

Otros usos de *lo* (páginas 48–49)

4 *Lo* o *lo que* Completa estas frases con *lo* o *lo que*.

1. ___ mejor del verano es que puedo ir a la playa.

2. ___ peor de estar enfermo es no poder ver a mis amigos.

3. ___ más me gusta es ir al cine.

4. Escucha siempre ___ dice el profesor.

5. ¿Sabes ___ mis padres me van a regalar por mi cumpleaños?

5 **¿Qué aprendiste?** Pon en orden estos grupos de palabras para hacer frases completas.

1. los / piensa / demás / en

2. apoyarse / necesario / entre / amigos / es

3. amigos / somos / íntimos / Guillermo / yo / y

4. les / no / hablar / a / voy /

5. considerado / sé / con / hermanos / tus

(Practice Workbook 1-8, 1-9)

Exercise 3
1. le
2. nos
3. les
4. me
5. Le

Exercise 4
1. Lo
2. Lo
3. Lo que
4. lo que
5. lo que

Exercise 5
1. Piensa en los demás.
2. Es necesario apoyarse entre amigos.
3. Guillermo y yo somos amigos íntimos.
4. No les voy a hablar.
5. Sé considerado con tus hermanos.

Vocabulario para comunicarse (pp. 62–67)

Exercise 1

1. segura
2. Los peatones
3. la acera
4. los atascos
5. sano
6. peligroso
7. senderos

Tema para investigar (pp. 68–71)

Exercise 1

1. presión
2. paisaje
3. las afueras
4. población
5. atasco

CAPÍTULO 2

Vocabulario para comunicarse (páginas 62–67)

1 **La opción correcta** Completa cada frase escogiendo la(s) palabra(s) más apropiada(s) entre paréntesis.

1. Me gustaría vivir en una ciudad (segura / peatón).

2. (Los peatones / Las cercas) caminaban rápido en la ciudad.

3. Caminamos por (la acera / el ruido).

4. Tardábamos mucho en llegar al trabajo por (los atascos / los rascacielos).

5. A mi abuelo le gustaba lo (lleno / sano) del campo.

6. El tráfico en la autopista era (aislado / peligroso).

7. En el campo, había muchos (rascacielos / senderos).

Tema para investigar (páginas 68–71)

1 **La respuesta correcta** Completa cada frase usando una palabra apropiada del recuadro.

atasco	paisaje	presión
las afueras	población	rural

1. No me gusta la ___ de la vida en la ciudad.

2. El ___ del campo es hermoso.

3. Hay oportunidades abundantes para vivir en ___.

4. ¿Crees que la ___ de San Antonio es mayor que la de El Paso?

5. Hay un ___ en la carretera porque hubo un accidente.

(Practice Workbook 2-1, 2-2)

2 **Definiciones** Empareja cada palabra con su definición. Escribe la letra de la respuesta correcta.

1. escaparse	**a.** mucho, suficiente
2. jardín	**b.** dinero que todos pagan
3. ofrecer	**c.** dar voluntariamente
4. abundante	**d.** ir lejos de
5. impuestos	**e.** cada día
6. diario	**f.** donde hay flores

(Practice Workbook 2-3, 2-4)

Gramática en contexto (páginas 76–83)

El imperfecto (páginas 77–79)

1 **En el pasado** Escribe la forma apropiada del imperfecto de cada verbo entre paréntesis.

1. Antes, María (hablar) ___ español con Marcos todos los días.

2. De niño, yo (comer) ___ chocolate por las mañanas.

3. Cuando era joven, mi abuelo (vivir) ___ en el campo.

4. Cuando vivía cerca del mar, Marta (ir) ___ con Juan a la playa.

5. En el pasado (haber) ___ menos contaminación.

(Practice Workbook 2-5, 2-6)

Otros usos del imperfecto (páginas 79–81)

2 **Mis amigos y yo** Cambia los verbos al imperfecto.

1. (Soy) una muchacha activa. Siempre 2. (juego) tenis o fútbol con mis amigos. Nosotros 3. (jugamos) los sábados por la mañana. Después, 4. (trabajo) tres horas en mis tareas. En la tarde 5. (vamos) todos al cine y mientras 6. (vemos) la película 7. (comemos) chocolates y 8. (bebemos) refrescos. Después 9. (hablamos) un rato y a las 9:00 de la noche 10. (nos despedimos).

Exercise 2
1. d
2. f
3. c
4. a
5. b
6. e

Gramática en contexto (pp. 76–83)

Exercise 1
1. hablaba
2. comía
3. vivía
4. iba
5. había

Exercise 2
1. Era
2. jugaba
3. jugábamos
4. trabajaba
5. íbamos
6. veíamos
7. comíamos
8. bebíamos
9. hablábamos
10. nos despedíamos

Exercise 3

1. pensaba
2. vivías
3. era
4. decía
5. ibas
6. veíamos

Exercise 4

1. contaminado
2. dormido
3. escondidos
4. rota

Exercise 5

1. decorado
2. situada
3. abiertas
4. encendidas
5. aislados

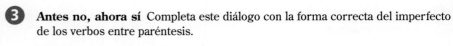

3 **Antes no, ahora sí** Completa este diálogo con la forma correcta del imperfecto de los verbos entre paréntesis.

Daniela: Yo (pensar) _1_ que tú (vivir) _2_ en otra ciudad.

Miguel: Sí, antes yo (ser) _3_ agente de viajes en Montreal, pero ahora vivo aquí.

Daniela: ¡Qué bueno! Yo siempre te (decir) _4_ que tú (ir) _5_ a vivir cerca de mí.

Miguel: Sí. Antes no nos (ver) _6_ mucho. Ahora nos veremos siempre.

(Practice Workbook 2-7)

El participio pasado como adjetivo (páginas 81–83)

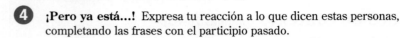

4 **¡Pero ya está…!** Expresa tu reacción a lo que dicen estas personas, completando las frases con el participio pasado.

1. Ángel: Vas a contaminar el medio ambiente.
   Tú: ¡Pero el medio ambiente ya está _____!

2. José: Miguelito va a dormir a las 8:00.
   Tú: ¡Pero él ya está _____!

3. Andrés: ¿Van ellos a esconderse?
   Tú: ¡Pero ellos ya están _____!

4. Patricio: ¡Cuidado! Vas a romper la ventana.
   Tú: ¡Pero la ventana ya está _____!

5 **¿Cómo está…?** Completa cada frase usando un participio pasado apropiado del recuadro.

abiertas	decorado	situada
aislados	encendidas	

1. El salón está ___ para la fiesta.

2. Mi casa está ___ en una comunidad muy bien cuidada.

3. En el verano, las ventanas siempre están ___.

4. Durante el día, las luces no están ___.

5. Gracias a los teléfonos y las computadoras, no estamos ___ de los otros países.

(Practice Workbook 2-8, 2-9)

CAPÍTULO 3

Vocabulario para comunicarse (páginas 96–101)

1 **La intrusa** Para cada uno de estos grupos de expresiones, escribe la palabra que no pertenezca a este grupo.

1. paleta / pincel / arriba

2. reflejado / mural / obra

3. de pie / retrato / sentado

4. centro / estilo / forma

5. naturaleza muerta / autorretrato / sombra

6. primer plano / tema / fondo

7. tono / forma / galería

8. abajo / vivo / apagado

2 **El trabajo del (de la) artista** Completa cada frase con una palabra o expresión apropiada del recuadro.

abajo	fondo	paleta	reflejados
apagados	mural	pincel	retrato
autorretrato	naturaleza muerta	primer plano	temas

Un(a) pintor(a) necesita una __1__ para trabajar con los colores para hacer una pintura. Con un __2__ aplica los colores. Los __3__ de una pintura pueden ser variados: si el (la) artista pinta a una persona, se llama un __4__. Si pinta una composición con frutas sobre una mesa, se llama una __5__. Cuando la pintura se hace en una pared, se llama un __6__.

(Practice Workbook 3-1, 3-2)

Vocabulario para comunicarse (pp. 96–101)

Exercise 1
1. arriba
2. reflejado
3. retrato
4. centro
5. sombra
6. tema
7. galería
8. abajo

Exercise 2
1. paleta
2. pincel
3. temas
4. retrato
5. naturaleza muerta
6. mural

Tema para investigar
(pp. 102–105)

Exercise 1

1. b
2. e
3. f
4. c
5. d
6. a

Exercise 2

1. época
2. criticar
3. imágenes
4. impresionista
5. surrealismo

Gramática en contexto
(pp. 110–115)

Exercise 1

1. puse
2. pusimos
3. puso
4. pusiste
5. puso

Tema para investigar (páginas 102–105)

1 **Definiciones** Empareja cada expresión con su definición. Escribe la letra de la respuesta correcta.

1. el siglo   **a.** representa sólo las cosas como se ven

2. el punto de vista   **b.** cien años

3. el impresionismo   **c.** presenta imágenes desde más de un punto de vista

4. el cubismo   **d.** explora temas del subconsciente

5. el surrealismo   **e.** manera específica de ver las cosas

6. el realismo   **f.** reproduce las sensaciones creadas por el color y la luz

2 **La mejor opción** Completa cada frase con la palabra más apropiada.

1. Los nuevos estilos rompen las tradiciones artísticas de una (época / imagen).

2. No es nada fácil (criticar / tratar) una obra de arte.

3. Picasso presentaba (imágenes / inspiraciones) desde varios puntos de vista.

4. El movimiento (impresionista / realista) trataba de reproducir sensaciones creadas por el color y la luz.

5. Los pintores del (cubismo / surrealismo) pintan con temas de los sueños.

(Practice Workbook 3-3, 3-4)

Gramática en contexto (páginas 110–115)

Repaso: El pretérito del verbo *poner* (páginas 111–112)

1 **¿Dónde está?** Completa las siguientes frases con la forma apropiada del pretérito del verbo *poner.*

1. Mi abuela a veces se preguntaba "¿Dónde ___ yo mis anteojos?"

2. Nos ___ contentos al oír la buena noticia.

3. Dolores ___ los libros sobre el escritorio.

4. ¿Te ___ triste cuando tus padres se fueron de viaje?

5. Emilia se ___ un suéter porque tenía frío.

(Practice Workbook 3-5)

El pretérito de los verbos *influir* y *contribuir* (páginas 112–113)

2 **Las influencias** Completa las frases con la forma correcta del pretérito de los verbos *influir* o *contribuir*.

1. La cultura mexicana ___ mucho en las obras de Frida Kahlo.

2. Tú ___ muy poco al trabajo de tu grupo; la próxima vez debes hacer más.

3. Los colores vivos ___ para hacer más bonito el mural que pintamos.

4. Todos nosotros ___ a la fiesta.

5. Yo ___ mucho en la decisión de Ana de ser pintora.

(Practice Workbook 3-6)

Repaso: El imperfecto progresivo (páginas 113–114)

3 **¿Qué estabas haciendo?** Completa las frases con la forma correcta del imperfecto progresivo del verbo entre paréntesis.

1. ¿Qué (hacer) ustedes después de las clases?

2. Nosotros (mirar) los murales del patio.

3. Mis hermanos le (pedir) algo a Mamá.

4. El detective los (seguir) por toda la ciudad.

5. ¿(leer) tú el periódico cuando te llamé?

(Practice Workbook 3-7, 3-8)

Repaso: El uso del pretérito y del imperfecto progresivo (páginas 114–115)

4 **Estaba hablando cuando...** Pon en orden las palabras para formar frases lógicas.

1. ¿ / qué / cuando / llamaron / te / tú / haciendo / estabas / ?

2. de pie / puse / estaba / me / cuando / yo / la profesora / hablando

3. favorito / viendo / mi / estaba / programa / cuando / se / yo / un ruido / oyó

4. estaban / leyendo / la prima / llamó / cuando / ustedes

5. llegó / visitando / nosotros / la galería / el artista / estábamos / cuando

(Practice Workbook 3-9)

Exercise 2
1. influyó
2. contribuiste
3. contribuyeron
4. contribuimos
5. influí

Exercise 3
1. estaban haciendo
2. estábamos mirando
3. estaban pidiendo
4. estaba siguiendo
5. Estabas leyendo

Exercise 4
1. ¿Qué estabas haciendo tú cuando te llamaron?
2. La profesora estaba hablando cuando yo me puse de pie.
3. Yo estaba viendo mi programa favorito cuando se oyó un ruido.
4. Ustedes estaban leyendo cuando llamó la prima.
5. Nosotros estábamos visitando la galería cuando el artista llegó.

Vocabulario para comunicarse (pp. 128–133)

Exercise 1
1. menores
2. positivo
3. subjetivo
4. emocionarse
5. apta para todos

Exercise 2
1. multa
2. recientemente
3. grabar
4. demasiados
5. alquilar

Exercise 3
1. apto para toda la familia
2. sólo para mayores
3. apto para toda la familia
4. apto para toda la familia
5. sólo para mayores

CAPÍTULO 4

Vocabulario para comunicarse (páginas 128–133)

1 **Antónimos** Escribe palabras o frases que significan lo contrario de estas expresiones.

1. mayores

2. negativo

3. objetivo

4. aburrirse

5. prohibida para menores

2 **La respuesta correcta** Completa cada frase con una palabra apropiada del recuadro.

alquilar	grabar	recientemente
demasiados	multa	reportaje

1. Tuve que pagar una ___ por no devolver la película a tiempo.

2. ¿Qué has visto ___ en la tele?

3. ¿Es ilegal ___ programas de la televisión?

4. Hay ___ rascacielos en esta ciudad.

5. ¿Quieres ___ un video esta noche?

3 **¿Apto para toda la familia?** Decide si cada programa de televisión es *Apto para toda la familia* o es *Sólo para mayores*.

1. *Música para todos*

2. *Temas adultos*

3. *Las noticias deportivas*

4. *Las aventuras de Michito el gato*

5. *Violencia en las calles*

(Practice Workbook 4-1, 4-2)

Tema para investigar (páginas 134–137)

1 **Definiciones** Empareja cada palabra con su definición.

1. entretener
2. clasificar
3. el público
4. la censura
5. manipular

  a. el control sobre lo que se puede ver
  b. divertir
  c. poner en categorías diferentes
  d. influir en alguien
  e. las personas que ven un programa

2 **La mejor opción** Completa cada frase con una palabra o expresión apropiada del recuadro.

censura	percepción	se ha dicho
derecho	se entretienen	tal como

1. ___ que la televisión es mala para los jóvenes.

2. Los niños ___ mucho al ver los dibujos animados.

3. En muchos países hay ___ y por eso la gente no puede ver algunos programas.

4. Celestina dice que tiene ___ a escoger los programas que puede ver.

5. Lo que vemos en la televisión influye en nuestra ___ del mundo.

6. La televisión casi nunca muestra la vida ___ es.

(Practice Workbook 4-3, 4-4)

Gramática en contexto (páginas 142–149)

El presente perfecto (páginas 143–145)

1 **¿Qué han hecho?** Completa las siguientes frases usando el presente perfecto de los verbos entre paréntesis.

1. Ellos (alquilar) un coche.

2. ¿(escoger) tú el libro que vas a leer?

3. El pobre niño (caerse) del árbol.

4. Nosotros no (pagar) ninguna multa por un video todavía.

5. Yo nunca (ir) a San Francisco.

(Practice Workbook 4-5)

Tema para investigar (pp. 134–137)

Exercise 1
1. b
2. c
3. e
4. a
5. d

Exercise 2
1. Se ha dicho
2. se entretienen
3. censura
4. derecho
5. percepción
6. tal como

Gramática en contexto (pp. 142–149)

Exercise 1
1. han alquilado
2. Has escogido
3. se ha caído
4. hemos pagado
5. he ido

Exercise 2
1. he dicho
2. han visto
3. ha muerto
4. ha hecho
5. ha escrito

Exercise 3
1. pude
2. estuvo
3. Estuvieron
4. tuvo
5. pudieron
6. Tuviste

Exercise 4
1. Ellos dijeron que estaban ocupados.
2. Yo no dije nada.
3. Tú me diste muchos problemas.
4. ¿Puedes repetir lo que tú dijiste?
5. José le dio un regalo a Ángela.

Los participios pasados irregulares (páginas 145–146)

2 **Hemos...** Escribe la forma correcta del presente perfecto de cada verbo subrayado.

1. Siempre les <u>digo</u> la verdad a mis padres.

2. Elisa y Camila <u>ven</u> la película que ganó el Óscar.

3. El único árbol de mi jardín se <u>muere</u>.

4. La contaminación nos <u>hace</u> daño a todos.

5. Jorge me <u>escribe</u> varias veces.

(Practice Workbook 4-6, 4-7)

Repaso: El pretérito de *poder, tener* y *estar* (página 147)

3 **¿Qué hicieron?** Completa las frases con la forma correcta del pretérito de los verbos *poder, tener* o *estar.*

1. Yo no ___ ir anoche a la fiesta.

2. Andrea ___ en Uruguay el año pasado.

3. ¿ ___ Guillermo y Manuel en la reunión de la semana pasada?

4. Emilia ___ que ir al dentista.

5. Los estudiantes no ___ terminar el examen a tiempo.

6. ¿ ___ (tú) que salir temprano?

(Practice Workbook 4-8)

Repaso: El pretérito de *decir* y *dar* (página 148)

4 **El pasado** Escribe frases lógicas con la información de abajo. Cambia los infinitivos *decir* y *dar* al pretérito.

1. decir / que / estaban / ellos / ocupados

2. nada / no / yo / decir

3. dar / problemas / tú / me / muchos

4. ¿ / repetir / puedes / decir / lo que / tú / ?

5. regalo / le / José / a Ángela / dar / un

(Practice Workbook 4-9)

CAPÍTULO 5

Vocabulario para comunicarse (páginas 162–167)

1 **Sopa de letras** Pon en orden las letras para formar palabras del vocabulario.

1. o a g ó q o u r l e

2. c r n d ó i i t a

3. o t e l p m

4. u e t t s a a

5. n o c e c u

2 **La respuesta correcta** Completa cada frase usando una palabra del Ejercicio 1.

1. Una ___ es algo que hacen con frecuencia los miembros de una cultura.

2. El ___ es una clase de plato.

3. El ___ era el centro religioso de algunas civilizaciones.

4. Un ___ estudia las cosas enterradas de las civilizaciones antiguas.

5. La escultura de una persona o animal es una ___.

3 **Definiciones** Escribe la palabra correcta que corresponda a las definiciones.

1. casa pequeña hecha de árboles, hojas y otras cosas naturales

2. construcción sagrada

3. hábitos, costumbres

4. lugar donde están enterrados los muertos

5. hacer un edificio

6. una forma de escribir con dibujos

(Practice Workbook 5-1, 5-2)

Vocabulario para comunicarse (pp. 162–167)

Exercise 1
1. arqueólogo
2. tradición
3. templo
4. estatua
5. cuenco

Exercise 2
1. tradición
2. cuenco
3. templo
4. arqueólogo
5. estatua

Exercise 3
1. choza
2. templo
3. tradiciones
4. tumba
5. construir
6. jeroglíficos

Tema para investigar
(pp. 168–171)

Exercise 1

1. c
2. d
3. e
4. b
5. a

Exercise 2

1. siembra
2. cosecha
3. legados
4. precolombinas
5. estrellas

Gramática en contexto
(pp. 176–181)

Exercise 1

1. hace
2. Hace
3. Hacía
4. Hace
5. Hacía

Tema para investigar (páginas 168–171)

1 **Parejas** Empareja cada palabra con su definición.

1. el quiché	**a.** representación de algo
2. actual	**b.** que existía en América antes de 1492
3. el calendario	**c.** idioma de los mayas
4. precolombino	**d.** que existe en el momento presente
5. el símbolo	**e.** sistema de división del año

2 **La mejor respuesta** Completa cada frase con una palabra apropiada del recuadro.

cosecha	excavar	precolombinas
estrellas	legados	siembra

1. La ___ es la etapa en que se prepara para cultivar maíz y otros productos.

2. En la época de la ___ es cuando se recogen los frutos cultivados.

3. La lengua, la religión y la arquitectura son ___ importantes de las culturas antiguas.

4. Las civilizaciones ___ construyeron templos impresionantes.

5. Los planetas y las ___ se observan desde un observatorio.

(Practice Workbook 5-3, 5-4)

Gramática en contexto (páginas 176–181)

Hace ... que / Hacía ... que (páginas 177–178)

1 **Hace mucho tiempo** Completa las frases con *hace* o *hacía*.

1. Nicolás, ¿cuánto tiempo ___ que estudias español?

2. ___ tres años que Miguel vive en América Central.

3. ___ cinco meses que no llovía cuando llegó la tormenta.

4. ___ unas semanas que los arqueólogos excavan cerca de Chichén Itzá.

5. ___ mucho tiempo que no lo veía, hasta que nos encontramos ayer.

(Practice Workbook 5-5, 5-6)

El pluscuamperfecto (páginas 178–179)

 Cuando... Combina las dos frases para formar una, usando *Cuando... ya...* Cambia el verbo de la segunda frase a la forma correcta del pluscuamperfecto. Sigue el ejemplo.

Llegaron los españoles. La civilización maya fundó ciudades como Tikal y Palenque.
Cuando llegaron los españoles, la civilización maya ya había fundado ciudades como Tikal y Palenque.

1. Construyeron el templo. Los mayas empezaron las ceremonias.

2. Los arqueólogos llegaron. Algunas personas excavaron las ruinas.

3. Visité México. Tú estuviste allí muchas veces.

4. Fui a buscar a Armando. Él se fue.

5. Entraste. Yo terminé de comer.

6. Descubrieron la ciudad. Algunos objetos sagrados de las tumbas desaparecieron.

(Practice Workbook 5-7, 5-8)

El verbo *seguir* y el presente progresivo (páginas 180–181)

 Sigo hablando. Escribe las frases de nuevo, cambiando el verbo subrayado a la forma correcta del verbo *seguir* y el presente progresivo. Sigue el ejemplo.

Cuando estoy enfermo, trabajo.
Cuando estoy enfermo, sigo trabajando.

1. Es de noche y estudio.

2. Durante el día, los arqueólogos excavan.

3. Los arqueólogos descubren más ruinas.

4. Ellos dicen lo que piensan.

5. Celebramos las tradiciones de nuestros antepasados.

6. Tú bailas aunque es muy tarde.

(Practice Workbook 5-9)

Exercise 2

1. Cuando construyeron el templo, los mayas ya habían empezado las ceremonias.
2. Cuando los arqueólogos llegaron, algunas personas ya habían excavado las ruinas.
3. Cuando visité México, tú ya habías estado allí muchas veces.
4. Cuando fui a buscar a Armando, él ya se había ido.
5. Cuando entraste, yo ya había terminado de comer.
6. Cuando descubrieron la ciudad, algunos objetos sagrados de las tumbas ya habían desaparecido.

Exercise 3

1. Es de noche y sigo estudiando.
2. Durante el día, los arqueólogos siguen excavando.
3. Los arqueólogos siguen descubriendo más ruinas.
4. Ellos siguen diciendo lo que piensan.
5. Seguimos celebrando las tradiciones de nuestros antepasados.
6. Tú sigues bailando aunque es muy tarde.

Vocabulario para comuni-carse (pp. 194–199)

Exercise 1

1. operadora
2. hacer una llamada
3. a cobro revertido
4. cuelgue
5. el tono
6. marque

Exercise 2

1. c
2. e
3. a
4. d
5. b
6. f

CAPÍTULO 6

Vocabulario para comunicarse (páginas 194–199)

❶ **La conversación** Completa cada frase del diálogo con la palabra o expresión más apropiada entre paréntesis.

ALEJANDRO:	¿Aló?
TINA:	Sí, habla la __1__ (remitente / operadora).
ALEJANDRO:	Quisiera __2__ (hablar en voz baja / hacer una llamada).
TINA:	Muy bien. ¿Cómo la quiere pagar?
ALEJANDRO:	Es una llamada __3__ (a cobro revertido / por formulario).
TINA:	Si quiere, puede hacerla por menos dinero. Primero, __4__ (mande / cuelgue) para empezar de nuevo. Espere __5__ (el tono / la ficha). Finalmente, __6__ (marque / mande) el número 10-10-PASO.
ALEJANDRO:	Gracias. Usted es muy amable.
TINA:	De nada.

❷ **Definiciones** Empareja cada palabra o expresión con la definición más apropiada.

1. remitente
2. contestador automático
3. fax
4. sobre
5. cartero
6. teléfono inalámbrico

a. Un documento que se manda electrónicamente por teléfono.

b. Una persona que lleva cartas y paquetes a las casas.

c. La persona que manda una carta o paquete.

d. Donde escribes la dirección y el nombre de la persona.

e. Aparato para dejar recados si la persona no está en casa.

f. Se usa para hablar si uno quiere moverse por la casa.

(Practice Workbook 6-1, 6-2)

Tema para investigar (páginas 200–203)

1 **La mejor opción** Completa cada frase con una palabra o expresión apropiada del recuadro.

correo electrónico	cualquiera	interactivas
creará	esperar	privadas

1. ¿Cuántos días más tengo que ___?

2. Yo creo que la nueva tecnología ___ más problemas que soluciones.

3. ¿Sabes que ___ puede usar las nuevas computadoras?

4. Las computadoras ___ nos permiten conseguir toda clase de información.

5. Desde mi computadora puedo mandar cartas por ___.

(Practice Workbook 6-3, 6-4)

Gramática en contexto (páginas 208–213)

Repaso: El futuro (páginas 209–210)

1 **¿Qué pasará?** Escribe la forma correcta del futuro de cada verbo entre paréntesis.

1. En el año 2025, la gente (comer) más productos naturales.

2. Con la nueva tecnología, el correo electrónico (ser) mucho más rápido.

3. El próximo año nosotros (visitar) a nuestros amigos frecuentemente.

4. Ellos (llevarse) muy bien en el futuro.

5. Después de graduarme yo (hablar) español perfectamente.

(Practice Workbook 6-5)

Tema para investigar
(pp. 200–203)
Exercise 1
1. esperar
2. creará
3. cualquiera
4. interactivas
5. correo electrónico

Gramática en contexto
(pp. 208–213)
Exercise 1
1. comerá
2. será
3. visitaremos
4. se llevarán
5. hablaré

Exercise 2
1. Haré
2. Habrá
3. saldrá
4. Tendremos
5. pondrá
6. podré

Exercise 3
1. Teresa no te los prestará.
2. Eduardo y Juana nos los mandarán por correo.
3. Nunca se lo diré a usted.
4. Dímelo por favor.
5. Magda me las enviará por correo urgente.

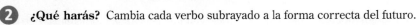

El futuro: Continuación (páginas 211–212)

2 **¿Qué harás?** Cambia cada verbo subrayado a la forma correcta del futuro.

1. <u>Hago</u> muchas llamadas.

2. <u>¿Hay</u> apartados postales en esta oficina de correos?

3. La cartera <u>sale</u> del correo muy tarde.

4. <u>Tenemos</u> clases de historia.

5. Juan <u>pone</u> los libros en la mesa.

6. Creo que no <u>puedo</u> ir a jugar.

(Practice Workbook 6-6)

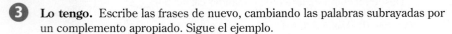

Uso de los complementos directos e indirectos (páginas 212–213)

3 **Lo tengo.** Escribe las frases de nuevo, cambiando las palabras subrayadas por un complemento apropiado. Sigue el ejemplo.

Mi tío me enviará <u>el documento</u> por fax.
Mi tío me lo enviará por fax.

1. Teresa no te prestará <u>los libros</u>.

2. Eduardo y Juana nos mandarán <u>los cheques</u> por correo.

3. Nunca le diré a usted <u>el secreto</u>.

4. Dime <u>el secreto</u> por favor.

5. Magda me enviará <u>las cartas</u> por correo urgente.

(Practice Workbook 6-7, 6-8, 6-9)

CAPÍTULO 7

Vocabulario para comunicarse (páginas 226–229)

1 **La mejor opción** Completa cada frase usando la palabra o expresión más apropiada del recuadro.

los candidatos	gente sin hogar
el centro de rehabilitación	juntar fondos
la Cruz Roja	responsabilidad

1. Un problema social serio es que hay ___.

2. ___ es una organización que ayuda a la gente.

3. Todos tenemos una ___: servir a la comunidad.

4. En ___ ayudan a las personas a recuperarse de los accidentes.

5. En la escuela vamos a ___ para las víctimas del terremoto.

6. ___ promèten resolver los problemas sociales.

2 **Sinónimos** Escribe palabras con el mismo significado.

1. pedir

2. quejarse

3. ofrecer

4. incapacitado

5. ayudar

6. institución

7. persona de mucha edad

8. regalar

(Practice Workbook 7-1, 7-2)

Vocabulario para comunicarse (pp. 226–229)

Exercise 1
1. gente sin hogar
2. La Cruz Roja
3. responsabilidad
4. el centro de rehabilitación
5. juntar fondos
6. Los candidatos

Exercise 2
1. solicitar
2. protestar
3. prometer
4. minusválido
5. colaborar
6. organización
7. anciano
8. donar

Tema para investigar
(pp. 230–233)

Exercise 1
1. c
2. b
3. f
4. a
5. e
6. d

Exercise 2
1. ayuda
2. en contra
3. Las leyes
4. unirnos
5. manifestación

Gramática en contexto
(pp. 238–245)

Exercise 1
1. Mi mamá quiere que mi hermano no juegue fútbol en la casa.
2. La señora Rodríguez pide que su esposo le compre un regalo por su cumpleaños.
3. El candidato espera que los ciudadanos voten por él.
4. Es necesario que ellos respeten las leyes.
5. ¿Sugieres que los pobres soliciten ayuda?
6. Recomendamos que los ancianos coman en el restaurante.

Tema para investigar (páginas 230–233)

1 **Definiciones** Empareja cada palabra con su definición.

1. ejército — **a.** te da el derecho de vivir y votar en un país

2. unirnos — **b.** reunirnos

3. obtener — **c.** fuerza militar

4. ciudadanía — **d.** ahora, hoy en día, en nuestros días

5. obligatorio — **e.** que se tiene que hacer

6. actualmente — **f.** conseguir

2 **La mejor opción** Escoge la palabra apropiada entre paréntesis para completar cada frase.

1. La Cruz Roja ofrece (manifestaciones / ayuda) cuando hay terremotos o desastres.

2. Estoy (a favor / en contra) de la nueva ley, y por eso estoy protestando.

3. (Las causas / Las leyes) son necesarias para que la sociedad funcione bien.

4. Para tener más fuerza, tenemos que (unirnos / garantizarnos).

5. La (manifestación / ciudadanía) fue para protestar contra los nuevos impuestos.

(Practice Workbook 7-3, 7-4)

Gramática en contexto (páginas 238–245)

El subjuntivo (páginas 239–241)

1 **Quiero que...** Combina estas frases usando la forma apropiada del subjuntivo.

1. Mi mamá quiere que / mi hermano no juega fútbol en la casa.

2. La señora Rodríguez pide que / su esposo le compra un regalo por su cumpleaños.

3. El candidato espera que / los ciudadanos votan por él.

4. Es necesario que / ellos respetan las leyes.

5. ¿Sugieres que / los pobres solicitan ayuda?

6. Recomendamos que / los ancianos comen en el restaurante.

(Practice Workbook 7-5, 7-6)

El subjuntivo: Continuación (páginas 241–242)

 Es mejor que... Completa estas frases con la forma apropiada del subjuntivo.

1. Es necesario que yo te (explicar) mis opiniones.

2. Será mejor que los pobres (ir) al comedor de beneficencia.

3. Es muy importante que Andrea (saber) la verdad.

4. Su mamá exige que Patricio (hacer) su tarea antes de salir a jugar.

5. Sugiero que ustedes (acostarse) en este momento.

6. Insistimos en que tú nos (decir) lo que hiciste ayer.

7. Eduardo espera que Juana le (dar) el dinero que él le prestó.

(Practice Workbook 7-7, 7-8)

La voz pasiva: *Ser* + participio pasado (páginas 243–245)

3 **Fue donado por él.** Escribe estas frases en la voz pasiva. Sigue el ejemplo.

Mi equipo de fútbol ganó el partido.
El partido fue ganado por mi equipo de fútbol.

1. La Cruz Roja organizó una campaña para juntar fondos para las víctimas del huracán.

2. El gobierno garantizó los derechos de los ciudadanos.

3. Nuestro candidato ganará las elecciones.

4. Santiago sacó al perro a pasear.

5. Los incas construyeron muchos templos.

6. El arqueólogo descubrió la tumba del líder del grupo religioso.

(Practice Workbook 7-9)

Exercise 2
1. explique
2. vayan
3. sepa
4. haga
5. se acuesten
6. digas
7. dé

Exercise 3
1. La campaña fue organizada por la Cruz Roja.
2. Los derechos fueron garantizados por el gobierno.
3. Las elecciones serán ganadas por nuestro candidato.
4. El perro fue sacado a pasear por Santiago.
5. Muchos templos fueron construidos por los incas.
6. La tumba del líder del grupo religioso fue descubierto por el arqueólogo.

Vocabulario para comuni-carse (pp. 258–263)

Exercise 1

1. redonda
2. misteriosos
3. geométrico
4. gigantesca
5. falsa
6. extrañas

Exercise 2

1. Los extraterrestres
2. mide
3. Los geólogos
4. huellas

Exercise 3

1. El casco sirve para proteger la cabeza.
2. La noticia es increíble.
3. El teléfono sirve para llamar a otras personas.
4. El pincel sirve para pintar.
5. La nave espacial es ovalada.

CAPÍTULO 8

Vocabulario para comunicarse (páginas 258–263)

1 **Los misterios** Escribe el adjetivo del recuadro que mejor corresponda a cada palabra de abajo.

extrañas	geométrico	misteriosos
falsa	gigantesca	redonda

1. rueda
2. extraterrestres
3. diseño

4. piedra
5. noticia
6. huellas

2 **¿Lo crees?** Escribe la palabra o expresión que mejor complete cada frase.

1. ___ llegaron en una nave espacial.

2. La piedra es gigantesca: ___ 30 metros de alto.

3. ___ calcularon el diámetro de los diseños en el desierto.

4. Las ___ que dejan el Yeti son enormes.

3 **¿Qué son?** Escribe frases completas, escogiendo la expresión de la segunda columna que mejor complete la frase de la primera columna.

1. El casco
2. La noticia
3. El teléfono
4. El pincel
5. La nave espacial

a. sirve para pintar
b. es ovalada
c. sirve para proteger la cabeza
d. es increíble
e. sirve para llamar a otras personas

(Practice Workbook 8-1, 8-2)

Tema para investigar (páginas 264–267)

1 ¿Qué sabes? Escribe la letra de la respuesta correcta para cada pregunta.

1. ¿Cuánto pesan las cabezas de piedra encontradas en La Venta?
   a. Entre 11 y 24 kilos.   **b.** Entre 11 y 24 toneladas.

2. ¿Quiénes eran los olmecas?
   a. Dioses extraterrestres.   **b.** Los habitantes de La Venta.

3. ¿Qué se puede encontrar en el desierto de Nazca, Perú?
   a. Un fenómeno inexplicable.   **b.** Muchos monos y arañas.

4. ¿Por qué no creen los arqueólogos que se haya resuelto el misterio de Nazca?
   a. Porque no hay datos suficientes.   **b.** Porque ya no hay dudas.

(Practice Workbook 8-3, 8-4)

Gramática en contexto (páginas 272–279)

El subjuntivo con expresiones de duda (páginas 273–274)

1 **Es posible que...** Escribe la forma correcta del verbo entre paréntesis para cada frase.

1. Es posible que (existen/existan) los extraterrestres.

2. Estoy seguro de que tu bicicleta (mide/mida) dos metros de largo.

3. Mi hermana duda que la ciencia (puede/pueda) explicarlo todo.

4. Nosotros no creemos que esa piedra (pesa/pese) diez toneladas.

2 **No lo creo.** Escribe las frases de nuevo, empezando cada una con *No creo que . . .*

1. Los científicos trabajan día y noche para resolver el misterio.

2. Mi padre conoce a todos los gobernadores.

3. Cada día se descubren nuevas ruinas arqueológicas.

4. Mis compañeros estudian mucho para los exámenes.

(Practice Workbook 8-5, 8-6)

Tema para investigar (pp. 264–267)

Exercise 1
1. b
2. b
3. a
4. a

Gramática en contexto (pp. 272–279)

Exercise 1
1. existan
2. mide
3. pueda
4. pese

Exercise 2
1. No creo que los científicos trabajen día y noche para resolver el misterio.
2. No creo que tu padre conozca a todos los gobernadores.
3. No creo que cada día se descubran nuevas ruinas arqueológicas.
4. No creo que tus compañeros estudien mucho para los exámenes.

569

Exercise 3

1. duermas
2. esté
3. vayamos
4. sean
5. sepan

Exercise 4

1. Es necesario que ella duerma.
2. Es mejor que tú seas generoso.
3. Es importante que ustedes sepan cómo llegar.
4. Espero que tus amigos estén preparados.

Exercise 5

1. Es probable que la policía haya arrestado al ladrón.
2. Es posible que ellos hayan visto esa película.
3. Espero que tú hayas encontrado lo que buscabas.
4. Dudo que ustedes hayan llegado a tiempo.

El subjuntivo: Verbos irregulares (páginas 275–276)

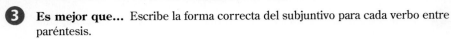

3 **Es mejor que...** Escribe la forma correcta del subjuntivo para cada verbo entre paréntesis.

1. Espero que tú ___ (dormir) bien esta noche.

2. Dudamos que Mariela ___ (estar) en casa.

3. No creo que nosotros ___ (ir) a la ceremonia de graduación.

4. Es posible que las noticias no ___ (ser) ciertas.

5. Es probable que los geólogos ___ (saber) la respuesta.

4 **¿Qué debe hacer?** Escribe una frase completa para completar cada diálogo. Cambia el infinitivo a la forma apropiada del subjuntivo.

1. —Juana está muy cansada.
   —es necesario que / ella / dormir

2. —No quiero prestarle mi motocicleta a mi primo.
   —es mejor que / tú / ser generoso

3. —Vamos a ir a las montañas, pero no conocemos el camino.
   —es importante que / ustedes / saber cómo llegar

4. —Mis amigos quieren participar en el campeonato de fútbol.
   —espero que / tus amigos / estar preparado

(Practice Workbook 8-7, 8-8)

El presente perfecto del subjuntivo (páginas 277–279)

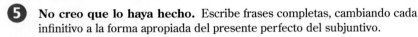

5 **No creo que lo haya hecho.** Escribe frases completas, cambiando cada infinitivo a la forma apropiada del presente perfecto del subjuntivo.

1. es probable que / la policía / arrestar al ladrón

2. es posible que / ellos / ver esa película

3. espero que / tú / encontrar lo que buscabas

4. dudo que / ustedes / llegar a tiempo

(Practice Workbook 8-9)

CAPÍTULO 9

Vocabulario para comunicarse (páginas 294–299)

1 **La mejor opción** Escribe la letra de la palabra que mejor complete cada frase.

1. Un ___ para ser salvavidas es saber nadar.
    a. requisito   **b.** habilidad   **c.** cita

2. El jefe sólo ofrece el ___ máximo si tienes entrenamiento en computadoras.
    a. maduro   **b.** solicitud   **c.** sueldo

3. Si no tienes ___, no te van a dar trabajo como cocinero.
    a. anuncios   **b.** tarea   **c.** experiencia

4. Un vendedor debe tratar bien a los ___.
    a. modales   **b.** clientes   **c.** anuncios

2 **¿Cuál es más importante?** Escoge la característica del recuadro que sea importante tener para cada profesión.

> Hablar bien
> Saber idiomas
> Ser amable
> Ser cuidadoso(a)

1. intérprete

2. recepcionista

3. abogado(a)

4. médico(a)

3 **¿Cómo se llaman?** Escribe la profesión descrita en cada frase.

1. Protege a las personas en la piscina.

2. Se encarga de administrar un negocio.

3. Lleva los productos a las tiendas.

4. Representa a un país en otro país.

(Practice Workbook 9-1, 9-2)

Vocabulario para comunicarse (pp. 294–299)

Exercise 1
1. a
2. c
3. c
4. b

Exercise 2
1. Saber idiomas
2. Ser amable
3. Hablar bien
4. Ser cuidadoso(a)

Exercise 3
1. salvavidas
2. gerente
3. repartidor(a)
4. diplomático(a)

Tema para investigar
(pp. 300–303)
Exercise 1
1. b
2. a
3. a
4. b

Gramática en contexto
(pp 308–313)
Exercise 1
1. Espera el momento oportuno para pedir un aumento de sueldo.
2. No te preocupes por la entrada de cine, yo te invito.
3. No descanses hasta que consigas lo que quieres.
4. Ven cuando estés preparado para la entrevista.

Exercise 2
1. Despiértame temprano los fines de semana.
2. No pidas una entrevista antes de llenar la solicitud.
3. No traigas una carta de recomendación.
4. Pídele trabajo al gerente.

Tema para investigar (páginas 300–303)

1 **La respuesta correcta** Escoge la letra de la respuesta apropiada.

1. ¿Para qué sirve la experiencia de trabajar en una oficina?
   a. para ser cortés   **b.** para dedicarse a tareas administrativas

2. ¿Qué cualidad personal se desarrolla gracias al trabajo?
   a. la puntualidad   **b.** la impaciencia

3. Saber usar y mantener archivos, ¿es una destreza o una cualidad personal?
   a. una destreza   **b.** una cualidad personal

4. ¿En qué momento hay que hablar con el jefe para pedirle un aumento?
   a. ahora mismo   **b.** en el momento oportuno

(Practice Workbook 9-3, 9-4)

Gramática en contexto (páginas 308–313)

Repaso: Mandatos afirmativos y negativos con *tú* (páginas 309–310)

1 **¿Sí o no?** Completa estas frases cambiando el verbo entre paréntesis al mandato afirmativo o negativo con *tú*.

1. (esperar el momento oportuno) ... para pedir un aumento de sueldo.
2. (preocuparse) ... por la entrada de cine, yo te invito.
3. (descansar) ... hasta que consigas lo que quieres.
4. (venir) ... cuando estés preparado para la entrevista.

2 **¿Debes hacerlo o no?** Cambia los mandatos afirmativos al negativo y viceversa. Sigue el ejemplo.

Ponte un vestido informal para ir a la oficina.
No te pongas un vestido informal para ir a la oficina.

1. No me despiertes temprano los fines de semana.
2. Pide una entrevista antes de llenar la solicitud.
3. Trae una carta de recomendación.
4. No le pidas trabajo al gerente.

(Practice Workbook 9-5, 9-6)

572 Más práctica y tarea

El subjuntivo con cláusulas adjetivas (páginas 311–312)

3 **¿Existe o no?** Completa estas frases escribiendo la forma apropiada del verbo entre paréntesis.

1. Estamos buscando a alguien que (saber) usar una computadora.

2. ¿Conoces a alguien que (querer) ser salvavidas?

3. Yo tengo un amigo que (querer) ser hombre de negocios.

4. No hay nadie en mi escuela que (tener) mejores notas que yo.

5. ¿Hay alguna persona aquí que (poder) trabajar de noche?

4 **Siempre dices lo contrario.** Escribe cada frase en la forma negativa usando el subjuntivo. Sigue el ejemplo.

Conozco a alguien que es muy puntual.
No conozco a nadie que sea muy puntual.

1. Conozco a alguien que busca un trabajo de tiempo parcial.

2. Tengo un amigo que trabaja de repartidor.

3. Conozco a alguien que escribe novelas.

4. Conozco a un vendedor que trata bien a sus clientes.

(Practice Workbook 9-7, 9-8)

El subjuntivo con *cuando* (páginas 312–313)

5 **¿Cuándo van a hacerlo?** Contesta estas preguntas usando el subjuntivo con *cuando* y la expresión entre paréntesis. Sigue el ejemplo.

¿Cuándo vas a buscar trabajo? (tener tiempo)
Cuando tenga tiempo.

1. ¿Cuándo van a venir (ustedes) a visitarnos? (terminar los exámenes)

2. ¿Cuándo vas a llenar la solicitud? (encontrar un lápiz)

3. ¿Cuándo vas a pagarme? (tener dinero)

4. ¿Cuándo vamos a ir al cine? (haber una película buena)

(Practice Workbook 9-9)

Exercise 3
1. sepa
2. quiera
3. quiere
4. tenga
5. pueda

Exercise 4
1. No conozco a nadie que busque un trabajo de tiempo parcial.
2. No tengo ningún amigo que trabaje de repartidor.
3. No conozco a nadie que escriba novelas.
4. No conozco a ningún vendedor que trate bien a sus clientes.

Exercise 5
1. Cuando terminemos los exámenes.
2. Cuando encuentre un lápiz.
3. Cuando tenga dinero.
4. Cuando haya una película buena.

Exercise 1
1. Arrestó al sospechoso.
2. Mató a una persona.
3. Cuidaba el edificio.
4. Fue secuestrado.
5. Se piensa que es culpable.
6. Vio el crimen.

Exercise 2
1. asesinato
2. lugar de los hechos
3. tiroteo
4. secuestró
5. rehén
6. lucharon

Exercise 3
1. c
2. b
3. b
4. a

CAPÍTULO 10

Vocabulario para comunicarse (páginas 328–333)

1 **¿Qué hizo cada persona?** Escribe la descripción del recuadro que mejor corresponda a cada persona de abajo.

Arrestó al sospechoso.	Fue secuestrado.	Se piensa que es culpable.
Cuidaba el edificio.	Mató a una persona.	Vio el crimen.

1. el policía   **4.** el rehén

2. el asesino   **5.** la acusada

3. la guardia   **6.** el testigo

2 **¿Puedes describir lo que pasó?** Completa el párrafo usando palabras o expresiones apropiadas del vocabulario.

Ayer hubo un __1__: un hombre mató a un guardia. El asesino trató de escaparse, pero la policía llegó al __2__. El __3__ fue intenso. Para protegerse, el asesino __4__ a una persona. Sin embargo, el __5__ era un boxeador. Los dos __6__; el boxeador era más fuerte y por eso la policía pudo arrestar al asesino.

3 **La respuesta correcta** Escribe la letra que corresponda a la respuesta correcta para cada pregunta.

1. ¿Cómo se llama la persona que cuida un edificio?
   a. Asesino(a).   **b.** Abogado(a).   **c.** Guardia.

2. ¿Adónde van los asesinos después de la sentencia?
   a. De vacaciones.   **b.** A la cárcel.   **c.** Al jurado.

3. ¿Quién decide las penas para los criminales?
   a. La policía.   **b.** El (La) juez.   **c.** El (La) terrorista.

4. ¿Quiénes deciden si el acusado es culpable?
   a. El jurado.   **b.** Las víctimas.   **c.** Los testigos.

(Practice Workbook 10-1, 10-2)

Tema para investigar (páginas 334–337)

1 **La mejor opción** Escribe la letra de la palabra o expresión que mejor complete cada frase.

1. Los terroristas no querían ___ a los rehenes.
   a. rescatar   **b.** poner en libertad   **c.** evitar

2. Las campañas de ___ son muy necesarias.
   a. inseguridad   **b.** seguridad pública   **c.** temor

3. Todos los días hay ataques ___ en la ciudad.
   a. a mano armada   **b.** atentado   **c.** las armas

4. Hay personas que creen que hay que dar penas más ___ a los criminales.
   a. corporal   **b.** arriesgadas   **c.** severas

(Practice Workbook 10-3, 10-4)

Gramática en contexto (páginas 342–349)

Mandatos afirmativos y negativos con *Ud.* y *Uds.* (páginas 343–345)

1 **Eso es lo que deben hacer.** Escribe la palabra correcta para el mandato con *Ud./Uds.*

1. ¡(Castiguen / Castigan) al asesino!

2. ¡No (tiene / tenga) miedo, que ya vienen los guardias!

3. ¡(Vigila / Vigile) bien el edificio!

4. ¡(Protegen / Protejan) los derechos de las víctimas!

5. ¡No (secuestren / secuestran) a los niños!

2 **¿Qué consejos dieron?** Escribe frases completas cambiando los verbos entre paréntesis a un mandato afirmativo con *Ud.* o *Uds.*

(tener cuidado)   Señora, ...   *Señora, tenga cuidado.*

1. (llamar una ambulancia)   Señor García, ...

2. (arrestar al sospechoso)   Señorita, ...

3. (defender a las víctimas)   Señor, ...

4. (hacer justicia)   Señores del jurado, ...

(Practice Workbook 10-5, 10-6)

Tema para investigar (pp. 334–337)

Exercise 1
1. b
2. b
3. a
4. c

Gramática en contexto (pp. 342–349)

Exercise 1
1. Castiguen
2. tenga
3. Vigile
4. Protejan
5. secuestren

Exercise 2
1. Señor García, llame una ambulancia.
2. Señorita, arreste al sospechoso.
3. Señor, defienda a las víctimas.
4. Señores del jurado, hagan justicia.

Exercise 3

1. haya
2. quiera
3. estén
4. castigue
5. sepas

Exercise 4

1. Sentimos que el testigo no quiera hablar.
2. La abogada teme que el sospechoso sea inocente.
3. Me alegro de que los policías protejan nuestra ciudad.
4. Es evidente que la juez quiere ayudar a las víctimas.

Exercise 5

1. Nos asombra que el acusado no quiera defenderse.
2. Me preocupa que haya más violencia cada día.
3. Me da miedo que los asesinos tengan la culpa.
4. Nos alegra de que los castigos para los ladrones sean hoy más severos.

El subjuntivo con expresiones de emoción (páginas 346–348)

3 **¿Y qué piensas tú?** Escribe la forma correcta del subjuntivo para cada verbo entre paréntesis.

1. Es una lástima que ___ (haber) tantos crímenes.

2. Me preocupa que nadie ___ (querer) formar parte del jurado.

3. Nos gusta que los rehenes ___ (estar) en casa finalmente.

4. Es triste que el juez no ___ (castigar) más severamente a los terroristas.

5. Me sorprende que tú no ___ (saber) defender tus derechos.

4 **Díganme cómo se sienten Uds.** Escribe frases completas cambiando los verbos a la forma más apropiada. Sigue el ejemplo.

a mí / dar miedo / los terroristas / volver a recurrir a la violencia
Me da miedo que los terroristas vuelvan a recurrir a la violencia.

1. nosotros / sentir / el testigo / no querer hablar

2. la abogada / temer / el sospechoso / ser inocente

3. yo / alegrarse de / los policías / proteger nuestra ciudad

4. ser evidente / la juez / querer ayudar a las víctimas

5 **Reacción personal** Escribe una reacción para los comentarios usando la expresión entre paréntesis. Sigue el ejemplo.

Hay muchos crímenes en esta ciudad.
(temer)
Temo que haya muchos crímenes en esta ciudad.

1. El acusado no quiere defenderse.
   (asombrarnos)

2. Hay más violencia cada día.
   (preocuparme)

3. Los asesinos tienen la culpa.
   (darme miedo)

4. Los castigos para los ladrones son hoy más severos.
   (alegrarnos)

(Practice Workbook 10-7, 10-8)

CAPÍTULO 11

Vocabulario para comunicarse (páginas 366–371)

1 **La respuesta correcta** Completa cada frase usando una palabra apropiada del recuadro.

castillo	iglesia	mezquita	rey
cristianos	judío	musulmanes	sinagoga

1. La estrella de David es un símbolo ___.

2. Mohamed fue el profeta de los _____.

3. Los católicos, los protestantes y los luteranos son todos ___.

4. Un ___ es el líder de una nación.

5. El templo de los judíos es la ___.

6. Los musulmanes van a la ___ para sus ceremonias religiosas.

7. Los católicos van a la ___ para dar gracias a su dios.

2 **La sopa de letras** Pon en orden estas letras para formar palabras del vocabulario.

1. l a t a l a b

2. s e r d v i d d a i

3. c z e r a l m

4. o l b e u p

5. g o r a s

6. o i e e c n t n t n

7. o e j u l z a

8. l o c s a i l t

Vocabulario para comunicarse (pp. 366–371)
Exercise 1
1. judío
2. musulmanes
3. cristianos
4. rey
5. sinagoga
6. mezquita
7. iglesia

Exercise 2
1. batalla
2. diversidad
3. mezclar
4. pueblo
5. rasgo
6. continente
7. azulejo
8. castillo

Exercise 3
1. batalla
2. rasgos
3. poesía
4. reconquistar
5. mezclar
6. hispanohablante

**Tema para investigar
(pp. 372–375)**
Exercise 1
1. lengua
2. mestiza
3. esclavizaron
4. se compone
5. europeos

Exercise 2
1. africano
2. fusión
3. establecer
4. resultado

3 **Definiciones** Escribe las palabras a las que se refieren las siguientes definiciones.

1. Lucha entre dos ejércitos.

2. Características de alguien o algo.

3. Arte que consiste en componer con palabras.

4. Conquistar otra vez.

5. Unir las partes de dos cosas o más.

6. Que habla español.

(Practice Workbook 11-1, 11-2)

Tema para investigar (páginas 372–375)

1 **La mejor opción** Escribe la(s) palabra(s) que mejor complete(n) cada frase.

1. La (raza / lengua) es necesaria para la comunicación.

2. La raza (mestiza / duradera) es resultado de la mezcla de españoles con indígenas.

3. Los españoles (esclavizaron / establecieron) a los indígenas.

4. La población de las Américas (se compone / se rebela) de gente de muchas culturas diversas.

5. Los españoles son (encuentros / europeos).

2 **Analogías** Escribe palabras del vocabulario para completar cada analogía.

1. europeo → Europa; ___ → África

2. mezcla → separación; ___ → diversidad

3. producir → crear; fundar → ___

4. mezcla → mestizo; causa → ___

(Practice Workbook 11-3, 11-4)

Gramática en contexto (páginas 380–385)

El imperfecto del subjuntivo (páginas 381–382)

1 **Reacción personal** Combina estas frases usando la forma apropiada del imperfecto del subjuntivo.

1. No fue necesario que / Antonio compró esos objetos de arte.

2. Los conquistadores dudaban que / los indígenas se rebelaron contra ellos.

3. Me sorprendió que / Estela se mudó en junio.

4. Me gustó que / Emilia adoptó a dos niños.

5. No fue justo que / Cristóbal le trató así a su hermano.

(Practice Workbook 11-5, 11-6)

El imperfecto del subjuntivo: Los verbos irregulares (páginas 382–384)

2 **¿Qué querían que hicieran?** Empezando cada frase con *Querían que,* cambia estas frases usando el imperfecto del subjuntivo.

1. Norberto y yo dijimos la verdad.

2. Augusto vino por la mañana.

3. César y Claudio trajeron un regalo.

4. Rosa fue al hospital.

5. Tú supiste lo que pasaba.

(Practice Workbook 11-7, 11-8)

El subjuntivo en frases con *para que* (páginas 384–385)

3 **Lo hicieron para que ellos...** Completa estas frases con la forma apropiada del imperfecto del subjuntivo de los verbos entre paréntesis.

1. Los indígenas escondieron el oro para que los conquistadores no los (robar).

2. Los misioneros vinieron para que los indígenas (aprender) la religión cristiana.

3. El profesor nos pidió que estudiáramos para que (sacar) buenas notas.

4. Julio se sentó para que Juliana lo (perdonar).

5. Nos callamos para que la reina (poder) hablar.

(Practice Workbook 11-9, 11-10)

Gramática en contexto (pp. 380–385)

Exercise 1
1. No fue necesario que Antonio comprara esos objetos de arte.
2. Los conquistadores dudaban que los indígenas se rebelaran contra ellos.
3. Me sorprendió que Estela se mudara en junio.
4. Me gustó que Emilia adoptara a dos niños.
5. No fue justo que Cristóbal le tratara así a su hermano.

Exercise 2
1. Querían que Norberto y yo dijéramos la verdad.
2. Querían que Augusto viniera por la mañana.
3. Querían que César y Claudio trajeran un regalo.
4. Querían que Rosa fuera al hospital.
5. Querían que supieras lo que pasaba.

Exercise 3
1. robaran
2. aprendieran
3. sacáramos
4. perdonara
5. pudiera

579

Exercise 1
1. asistente social
2. banquero(a)
3. traductor(a)
4. lenguaje por señas
5. periodista

Exercise 2
1. traductor(a)
2. corresponsal
3. bibliotecario(a)
4. contador(a)
5. diplomático(a)

CAPÍTULO 12

Vocabulario para comunicarse (páginas 400–405)

 La respuesta correcta Completa cada frase usando una palabra o expresión apropiada del recuadro.

asistente social	lenguaje por señas	redactora
banquero	periodista	traductor

1. Una persona que trabaja con los pobres o ancianos es una ___.

2. Mi tío Marcos trabaja en un banco. Él es ___.

3. Estudié idiomas en la universidad. Soy ___.

4. El ___ permite comunicarse a las personas que no pueden hablar.

5. Me gusta entrevistar a las personas. Creo que seré ___.

2 **Mi futura carrera** Escribe los nombres de estas profesiones.

1. Ayuda a la gente a entender algo que está en otro idioma.

2. Envía noticias desde otros países a un periódico en su propio país.

3. Ayuda a las personas a encontrar libros en la biblioteca.

4. Se encarga de los negocios financieros de sus clientes.

5. Representa a su país en otro país.

(Practice Workbook 12-1, 12-2)

Tema para investigar (páginas 406–409)

1 **Definiciones** Empareja cada palabra con su definición.

1. armonía
2. frontera
3. lengua materna
4. inmigrante

a. límite entre países
b. paz; cuando no hay conflictos
c. primer idioma que se aprende
d. una persona que se muda a vivir a un país

2 **La mejor opción** Escoge la palabra apropiada entre paréntesis para completar cada frase.

1. Siempre he (apreciado / expresado) lo que tú haces por mí.

2. Para participar (oficialmente / activamente) en un mundo multicultural, hay que saber hablar otras lenguas.

3. Para tener una buena educación, es necesario (diversificar / viajar) lo que estudiamos.

4. Poder conocer otras culturas es un (beneficio / contacto) de estudiar lenguas extranjeras.

5. Una (armonía / frontera) es algo que separa a dos países.

(Practice Workbook 12-3, 12-4)

Gramática en contexto (páginas 414–419)

El condicional (páginas 415–416)

1 **Sería mejor.** Combina estas frases cambiando el verbo subrayado al condicional. Sigue el ejemplo.

para ser profesor / <u>es</u> necesario tener paciencia
Para ser profesor, sería necesario tener paciencia.

1. Guillermo me dijo que / <u>vino</u> por la tarde

2. para trabajar en un banco / <u>tuviste</u> que estudiar matemáticas

3. Ernesto, / <u>¿vas</u> conmigo a la biblioteca?

4. pensábamos que / <u>era</u> útil seguir estudiando español

Tema para investigar
(pp. 406–409)
Exercise 1
1. b
2. a
3. c
4. d

Exercise 2
1. apreciado
2. activamente
3. diversificar
4. beneficio
5. frontera

Gramática en contexto
(pp. 414–419)
Exercise 1
1. Guillermo me dijo que vendría por la tarde.
2. Para trabajar en un banco, tendrías que estudiar matemáticas.
3. Ernesto, ¿irías conmigo a la biblioteca?
4. Pensábamos que sería útil seguir estudiando español.

Exercise 2
1. podría
2. Habría
3. podrías
4. tendríamos
5. dirían

Exercise 3
1. sería
2. pagaras
3. dijeras
4. estudiaría
5. trataríamos
6. tendría

2 **¿Qué harían?** Completa estas frases con la forma apropiada del condicional de los verbos entre paréntesis.

1. Yo no (poder) hacerlo tan bien como tú.

2. (Haber) menos atascos si la gente caminara más.

3. ¿Me (poder) abrir tú la puerta de la biblioteca?

4. Nosotros (tener) que estudiar más.

5. ¿Qué le (decir) los candidatos al periodista?

(Practice Workbook 12-5, 12-6)

El imperfecto del subjuntivo con *si* (páginas 417–418)

3 **Si fuera posible...** Completa estas frases con la forma correcta del imperfecto del subjuntivo o del condicional del verbo entre paréntesis.

1. Si pudiera escoger, yo (ser) redactor en una revista.

2. Nosotros estaríamos más contentos si tú nos (pagar) más por el trabajo que hacemos.

3. Si tú (decir) la verdad, tendrías más amigos.

4. Si tuviera facilidad para trabajar con la gente, Matilde (estudiar) para asistente social.

5. Si estuviéramos en tu lugar, nosotros (tratar) de estudiar más.

6. Si esa universidad fuera menos cara, (tener) más estudiantes.

(Practice Workbook 12-7, 12-8)

Examen cumulativo

Aquí tienes una oportunidad de ver si has aprendido bien el vocabulario y la gramática de *PASO A PASO 3*. Escribe todas tus respuestas en una hoja aparte.

I. Escoge la letra que corresponda a la mejor respuesta o que mejor complete cada frase.

1. Quiero participar en unas actividades más interesantes.
   a. ¿Por qué no practicas la esgrima?
   b. ¿Por qué no resuelves el problema?
   c. ¿Por qué no se apoyan?
   d. ¿Por qué no mantienes discusiones más civiles?

2. En este mundo se necesitan más oportunidades de empleo.
   a. Sí. Hay muchas cercas aquí.
   b. Quiero vivir en un lugar más sano.
   c. Son abundantes en la ciudad pero no en el campo.
   d. El paisaje es una maravilla.

3. ¿Te gusta este retrato realista?
   a. Las imágenes de las montañas son bastante bonitas.
   b. No comprendo la interpretación del perfil.
   c. Sí, pero el estilo es muy abstracto.
   d. Sí, la naturaleza muerta es muy interesante.

4. Recientemente se han evaluado las opiniones del público.
   a. No. Son demasiado fáciles.   c. Se ha dicho que la percepción es todo.
   b. Pero son sólo para mayores.   d. Se emocionan mucho.

5. Se había desarrollado mucho esa civilización.
   a. Sí. Gracias a las excavaciones sabemos mucho.
   b. Sí. Los mayas usaban sílabas.
   c. Sí. Las chozas son el centro de la cultura.
   d. Sigue aceptando la religión de los otros.

6. Hay diferentes medios de comunicación.
   a. No necesito un apartado postal.
   b. Prefiero el correo electrónico y las conferencias por video.
   c. ¿Quién es el destinatario?
   d. Se equivocó, señor.

7. Eres una persona muy responsable.
   a. Sí. Hay que juntar fondos.   c. Sí, mis padres exigen que actúe como
                                              un buen ciudadano.
   b. No es justo.   d. Prometo donar más.

Examen cumulativo
I.
1. a
2. c
3. b
4. c
5. a
6. b
7. c

8. b
9. a
10. a
11. d
12. a

II.
1. a
2. a
3. d
4. a

8. Hay bastante evidencia de que existe el Yeti.
   a. Es improbable comprenderlo todo.
   b. Dudo que las huellas enormes pertenezcan a esa criatura.
   c. A pesar de eso, no hay datos.
   d. Hay toneladas de ruedas.

9. ¿Cuáles son las cualidades necesarias para ser diplomática?
   a. Hay que tener destreza en mantener relaciones positivas.
   b. Hay que realizar sus metas.
   c. Hay que merecer el sueldo.
   d. Hay que ser productiva.

10. El inocente fue acusado del asesinato.
    a. ¿Crees que tiene la culpa?   c. La sentencia fue severa.
    b. El guardia tiene que vigilar la exposición.   d. No lo van a poner en
                                                        libertad.

11. Hay una fusión de culturas en España.
    a. No vamos a la sinagoga hoy.   c. No es bueno esclavizar
                                                        a nadie.
    b. Hay que rebelarse de vez en cuando.   d. Hay rasgos hoy de muchas
                                                        influencias.

12. Casi no me confundo ahora en español.
    a. Entonces, eres completamente bilingüe.
    b. Es la dificultad de dominar la lengua.
    c. Los redactores también.
    d. ¿Por qué sueñas con ser corresponsal?

II. Escribe la letra de la palabra o expresión que mejor complete cada frase.

1. No son amigos. Casi nunca ___ bien.
   a. se llevan   c. se quejan
   b. se enojan   d. se llaman

2. Si no queremos tener un accidente con los coches, debemos caminar
   por ___ en la ciudad.
   a. la acera   c. el puente
   b. la granja   d. el sendero

3. Van a pintar ___ en la parte exterior de un edificio.
   a. la naturaleza muerta   c. el autorretrato
   b. el perfil   d. el mural

4. Si no quieres comprar el video, siempre lo puedes ___.
   a. alquilar   c. reír
   b. grabar   d. hacer daño

5. Se han interpretado ___ divididos en meses, similares a los nuestros.
   a. los jeroglíficos
   b. los símbolos
   c. los calendarios
   d. los orígenes

6. —¿Cómo puedes tener un número equivocado?
   —¿Por qué no vuelves a ___ el número?
   a. marcar
   b. sonar
   c. colgar
   d. descolgar

7. Mi sueño es ser ___ de ese país un día.
   a. ciudadano
   b. campaña
   c. comedor de beneficencia
   d. candidato

8. Muchas veces ___ es una explicación para un fenómeno natural.
   a. un fantasma
   b. una huella
   c. una nave espacial
   d. un mito

9. Para su edad, es muy ___. Siempre cumple bien con sus responsabilidades.
   a. cuidadoso
   b. honesto
   c. maduro
   d. adecuado

10. Los criminales ___ a los clientes del banco y ahora son sus rehenes.
    a. hirieron
    b. secuestraron
    c. castigaron
    d. vigilaron

11. Quisiera saber más sobre los orígenes de la ___ africana.
    a. mestiza
    b. esclava
    c. raza
    d. reja

12. Nuestro país ___ porque hay gente de otras culturas.
    a. se diversifica
    b. se expresa
    c. traduce
    d. habla por señas

III. Escribe la letra de la palabra o expresión que mejor complete cada frase.

Me gusta vivir y hacer mis quehaceres en la ciudad. _1_ bueno de vivir en la ciudad es que las tiendas están _2_ en el centro. La semana pasada yo _3_ por el centro cuando _4_ por primera vez tres nuevas tiendas. Eran unas tiendas enormes y había una selección muy grande de artículos. Nunca _5_ tantos lugares tan magníficos. En el futuro mis amigos y yo _6_ que ir al centro para comprar todo lo que se necesita. Espero que mis amigos _7_ que el centro es tan seguro como el campo. Cuando _8_ al centro en el futuro, _9_ importante enseñarles que la ciudad es un buen lugar para ir de compras. En total, me gusta la ciudad porque ofrece una variedad de tiendas.

5. c
6. a
7. a
8. d
9. c
10. b
11. c
12. a

III.
1. b
2. d
3. a
4. d
5. b
6. b
7. b
8. b
9. d

IV.
1. los
2. pueda
3. dijeron
4. escritos
5. lucharan
6. será
7. mantener
8. Saquen
9. se escriben

V.
1.
1. buscar
2. sepa
3. me llevara
4. tratar
5. busque
6. podré
7. diré
8. fueran
9. realizaremos

1. a. El
   b. Lo
   c. La
   d. Los

2. a. situado
   b. situada
   c. situados
   d. situadas

3. a. estaba caminando
   b. estaba entrando
   c. estaba cayéndome
   d. estaba mintiendo

4. a. veo
   b. voy
   c. fui
   d. vi

5. a. había ido
   b. había visto
   c. estaba viendo
   d. he ido

6. a. podremos
   b. tendremos
   c. haremos
   d. saldremos

7. a. sean
   b. sepan
   c. hayan
   d. tengan

8. a. vamos
   b. vayamos
   c. fuimos
   d. íbamos

9. a. es
   b. fue
   c. era
   d. será

IV. Completa cada frase con la forma apropiada de la palabra entre paréntesis.

1. ¿Los libros? Se ___ (lo) daré a Eduardo.
2. Trabajo mucho para que mi familia ___ (poder) comer bien.
3. Anoche Catalina y Patricia nos ___ (decir) la verdad.
4. Los exámenes fueron ___ (escrito) por los profesores anoche.
5. Sería mejor que ellos ___ (luchar) más para integrar la tecnología en el estudio de los idiomas.
6. En 20 años la inmigración ___ (ser) posible para muchos inmigrantes.
7. Es importante ___ (mantener) una perspectiva multicultural del mundo moderno.
8. La profesora dijo: "___ (sacar) Uds. la tarea inmediatamente."
9. Teresa y Paulina ahora ___ (escribirse) mucho.

V. Escribe la forma apropiada del verbo entre paréntesis para completar estos párrafos.

1. Antes de _1_ (buscar) un trabajo es necesario que yo _2_ (saber) más del mundo administrativo. Sería necesario que yo _3_ (llevarse) bien con los clientes y los gerentes. Es una buena idea _4_ (tratar) bien a la gente. En el futuro cuando yo _5_ (buscar) trabajo en la ciudad, _6_ (poder) usar mis destrezas en el trabajo. Yo les _7_ (decir) también a los empleados que sería bueno que _8_ (ser) productivos. Así todos nosotros _9_ (realizar) nuestras metas.

2. La violencia es prevalente en la sociedad moderna. Se ha __1__ (decir) que es una reacción contra las normas de la sociedad. Personalmente he __2__ (hacer) muchas cosas para evitar conflictos. Hace tres años que sigo __3__ (trabajar) con otros para resolver conflictos cuando ocurran. Dudo que se __4__ (haber) resuelto todos los problemas de la violencia social. ¿Y la violencia personal? En el futuro, (nosotros) la __5__ (eliminar) cuando (nosotros) __6__ (comprenderse) mejor. Insistiría en que todos nosotros __7__ (ayudarse) en vez de pelearnos.

2.
1. dicho
2. hecho
3. trabajando
4. hayan
5. eliminaremos
6. nos comprendamos
7. nos ayudáramos

ÍNDICE

In most cases, structures are first presented in the *Vocabulario para comunicarse*, where they are practiced lexically in conversational contexts, or in the *Tema para investigar*, where they are practiced in narrative contexts. They are explained later, usually in the *Gramática en contexto* section of that chapter. Light-face numbers refer to pages where structures are initially presented or, after explanation, where student reminders occur. Bold-face numbers refer to pages where structures are explained or otherwise highlighted.

ACKNOWLEDGMENTS

Illustrations   Iskra Johnson Lettering: pp. **I, III, VI-XIII, 428;** Mapping Specialists Ltd.: pp. **XIV-XIX;** Joe Fournier: pp. **4-5, 51, 417;** Tom Tierney: p. **6;** Anthony Sigala: p. **6;** Shawn Banner: p. **7;** Don Morrison: p. **7;** Lane Gregory: p. **7;** Genine Smith: p. **10;** George Thompson: p. **11;** Iskra Johnson: pp. **12-13;** Andy Lendway: pp. **16-17;** Janet Darby: p. **18;** Chuck Passarelli: pp. **20-21;** Cheryl Cook: pp. **30-31, 32, 34, 47, 48-49, 57, 121;** Rob Magiera: pp. **52-53;** Mitch O'Connell: p. **55;** Scott Snow: pp. **62-63, 64-65, 66-67, 78-79, 80, 82, 91, 390-391, 392-393, 394-395, 406-407, 417;** Susan Aiello: p. **75;** Bryan Peterson: pp. **85, 315, 359;** Laszlo Kubinyi: pp. **87, 264, 272;** Tatjana Krizmanic: pp. **89, 422;** Jim Owens: pp. **96-97, 98, 111, 112, 114-115, 123;** Rod Vass: pp. **110, 342;** Phil Cheung: p. **117;** Barbara Callow: p. **118;** John Zielinski: pp. **128-129, 130-131, 133, 145, 147, 148, 157;** Wayne Vincent: pp. **150-51;** David Diaz: p. **155;** Sandie Turchyn: pp. **162-163, 164-165, 167, 171, 179, 181, 189;** Mary Lempa: pp. **172-3;** Karen Nigida: p. **182;** Mary Jo Phalen: pp. **183, 366-367, 368-369, 384, 395;** Dennis Dzielak: p. **187;** Jannine Cabossel: pp. **194-195, 196-197, 209, 210, 213, 221;** Gary Krejca: p. **214;** Hiro Kimura: p. **215;** Mark Stearney: p. **218;** Tom Bachtell: pp. **226-227, 228-229, 240, 245, 253, 393;** Tom Nachreiner: p. **238;** Matt Foster: p. **247;** Bob Gleason: p. **250;** Jim Starr: pp. **258-259, 260-261, 262-263, 276, 278-279, 289;** Paul Rodgers: p. **281;** Garth Glazier: p. **287;** Mitchell Heinze: pp. **294-295, 296-297, 303, 310-311, 323;** Bill Scott: p. **300;** Jane Mjolsness: pp. **317-19;** Susan Blubaugh: p. **321;** Robert Burger: pp. **328-329, 330-331, 333, 344-345, 347, 348, 361;** Ruth Brunke: p. **345;** Steve Salerno: p. **351;** Ted Burn: pp. **353-57;** Jeff Marinelli: p. **380;** Tuko Fujisaki: p. **387;** Neverne Covington: pp. **389-91;** Dan John Sandford: pp. **431-435;** Patti Green: pp. **437, 439, 464-467;** Clyne: pp. **445, 447, 453;** Evan Schwarze: pp. **454-457;** Joe Joe VanDerBos: pp. **462-463;** Troy Thomas: pp. **468-475;** Marlene Kay Goodman: pp. **476, 481;** James Mellet: pp. **482-487;** James McMullen: pp. **488-491;** James Learned: pp. **492-497.**

Photography   **Front Cover:** Stewart Aitchison/DDB Stock Photos; **Back Cover:** ©Buddy Mays/Travel Stock **II:** ©Byron Augustin/DDB Stock Photos; **IV:** (tl)Museo del Templo Mayor, Mexico City; (tr)(b)Museo Nacional de Antropología, Mexico City; **VI:** Museo del Templo Mayor, Mexico City; (CNCA-INAH-MEX); **XVIII-1:** ©Frerck/Odyssey/Chicago; **3:** (tl)©Frerck/Odyssey/ Chicago; (tc)Cameramann International; (tr)(bl)David R. Frazier Photolibrary; (br)©Joe Viesti; **8:** (t)©Jacques Faizant/courtesy ¡Hola!; (bl)©José Luis Martin-Mena/courtesy Semana; (br)©Hoviv/courtesy ¡Hola!; **9:** ©Alcacer/courtesy Semana; **12:** Arthur Tilley/FPG International; **13:** ©Frerck/Odyssey/Chicago; **14:** (t)Museo de América, Madrid; (b)Museo del Templo Mayor, Mexico City; (CNCA-INAH-MEX); **15:** (tl)(b)Museo Nacional de Antropología, Mexico City; (tr)Museo del Templo Mayor, Mexico City; **18:** Everett Collection; **19:** (t)The Kobal Collection; (b)Everett Collection; **22-23:** O'Brien & Mayor Photography/FPG International; **22:** ©Peter Menzel; **23:** (t)©Michele Burgess / Photo Bank, Inc.; (b)©Jerry Alexander/Tony Stone Images; **24:** (tl)©Kent Knudsen/Photo Bank, Inc.; (bl)©Ken Fisher/Tony Stone Images; (br)©Frerck/Odyssey/Chicago; **25:** (tl)©Bruce Ayres/Tony Stone Images; (tr)©Frerck/Odyssey/ Chicago; (b)FPG International; **26-27:** ©Rick Reinhard; **28:** ©Bob Daemmrich/Stock Boston; **29:** (t)©Bob Daemmrich / Stock Boston; (b)Don Smetzer/Tony Stone Images; **33:** Joan Miró, "Self-Portrait," (1919), Musée Picasso, Paris, Photo ©R.M.N.; **35:** ©Robert Fried; **36:** (l)©Michael Newman / Photo Edit; (tr)©Dave Black/Sports Photo Masters, Inc.; (br)©Tony Freeman/Photo Edit; **37:** ©Beryl Goldberg Photographer; **38:** ©Peter Menzel; **39:** ©Beryl Goldberg Photographer; **40-41:** Courtesy La Peña Cultural Center, Berkeley, CA/Photo by Irene Young; **40:** ©Beryl Goldberg Photographer; **41:** ©Beryl Goldberg Photographer; **42:** ©Beryl Goldberg Photographer; **43:** ©Bob Daemmrich/The Image Works; **45:** ©Beryl Goldberg Photographer; **46:** Giraudon/Art Resource, NY; **50:** (l)©Robert Fried; (c)©Chip and Rosa Maria de la Cueva Peterson; (r)©Robert Fried; **51:** Illustration by Carol Lay, reprinted with permission.; **54:** Art Resource, NY; **56:** ©David Wells/The Image Works; **58-59:** ©Peter Menzel; **60:** ©Ulrike Welsch; **61:** (t)Inga Spence/The Picture Cube, Inc.; (b)©Frerck/Odyssey/Chicago; **68:** (t)Art Museum of the Americas/Courtesy Organization of American States; (b)Yale University Art Gallery, Gift Collection of Société Anonyme; **69:** ©Frerck/Odyssey/Chicago; **70:** Reprinted with permission of Artists Right Society; **72:** ©Ulrike Welsch; **73:** ©Robert Fried; **74:** (t)©Gene Dekovic; (b)©Bill Bachmann/Photo Edit; **76:** Jon Bradley/Tony Stone Images; **78:** ©'93 Mug Shots/The Stock Market; **81:** ©Alfredo Arreguín; **83:** (t)©Ulrike Welsch/Photo Edit; (b)Philadelphia Museum of Art. Purchased by Nebinger Fund; **84:** (t)M. Algaze/The Image Works; (b)Chad Ehlers/Tony Stone Images; **87:** Darius Koehli for ScottForesman; **90:** ©Jack Stein Grove/Photo Edit; **92-93:** Schalkwijk/Art Resource, NY; **94:** ©Diane Joy Schmidt; **95:** (t)©William Dyckes; (b)©Wendy Walsh Photography; **99:** Erich Lessing/Art Resource, NY; **100:** BOTERO, Fernando. <u>The Presidential Family</u>. 1967. Oil on canvas, 6'8 1/8" x 6'5 1/4" (203.5 x 196.2 cm). The Museum of Modern Art, New York. Gift of Warren D. Benedek. Photograph ©1999 The Museum of Modern Art, New York; **102:** (t)© <u>Composición surrealista</u>, (1927-28) Fundación Gala-Salvador Dalí, Figueres, Spain; (b) <u>Paysage, Juan-les-Pins</u>, (1920) Musée Picasso, Paris/Photo © R.M.N., Paris ©ARS, NY; **104:** <u>Violin</u>, (1915) Pablo Picasso, Musée Picasso, Paris/Photo ©R.M.N., Paris ©ARS, NY; **105:** DALÍ, Salvador. <u>The Persistence of Memory</u> {Persistance de la mémoire}. 1931. Oil on canvas, 9 1/2 x 13" (24.1 x 33 cm). The Museum of Modern Art, New York. Given anonymously. Photograph ©1999 The Museum of Modern Art, New York; **106:** (l)Los Angeles County Museum of Art/LA County Funds; (r)Private Collection, Courtesy CDS Gallery, New York, NY; **107:** ©1995 Fernando Botero/Licensed by VAGA, New York, NY/Photo ©1994 Chicago Tribune. Reprinted by permission. All rights reserved.; **108:** (t)Museum of Art, Rhode Island School of Design; Nancy Sayles Day Memorial Fund; (b)María Izquierdo "El Alhajero." oil on canvas; 65x95cm. Collection: Banco Nacional de México; courtesy of Fomento Cultural Banamex, a.c.; **113:** Art Resource, NY; **117:**

Índice/Acknowledgments 591

(l)AP/Wide World Photos; (r)Rene Burri/Magnum Photos; **118:** (l)The Phillips Collection, Washington, D.C.; (r)©ARS, NY Collection Tappenbeck Mouzay, France/Giraudon, Art Resource, NY; **119:** Washington University Gallery of Art, St. Louis University Purchase, Kende Sale Fund 1946; **122:** Scala/Art Resource, NY; **124-125:** ©Larry Boyd/Impact Visuals; **127:** (t)©David R. Frazier Photolibrary; (b)Rob Cousins/Panos Pictures; **134:** (tl)Courtesy Coral Picture Corporation/Radio Caracas Televisión, Venezuela; (tr)©Joe Viesti; (bl)©Rick Reinhard; **137:** Walter McBride/Retna; **141:** (t)Richard Emblin/Black Star; (b)D. Goldberg/Sygma; **142:** (tl)Alvaro Camacho/AP/Wide World Photos; (tr)Alyx Kellington/DDB Stock Photo **144:** ©David R. Frazier Photolibrary; **149:** ©David R. Frazier Photolibrary; **152:** ©Chip Simons; **158-159:** Digital reconstruction by Doug Stern based on photography by Enrico Ferorelli and David W. Wooddell/National Geographic Society Image Collection; **158-161:** design bar ©Frerck/Odyssey/Chicago; **160:** (l)©Bob Daemmrich/The Image Works; (r)©Frerck/Odyssey/Chicago; **161:** (t)©Bob Daemmrich/The Image Works; (b)©Frerck/Odyssey/Chicago; **166:** (l)©Macduff Everton/The Image Works; (r)©Bob Daemmrich/ The Image Works; **170:** Thomas Hoepker/Magnum Photos; **174:** ©Richard Lord/The Image Works; **175:** D. Donne Bryant/DDB Stock Photo; **176:** (tl)©VIREO/J. Dunning; (cl)Paulo Fridman/Sygma; (b)David Hiser/Tony Stone Images; **180:** H. Gans/The Image Works; **181:** ©Tony Freeman/Photo Edit; **183:** (tl)Jean Pragen/Tony Stone Images; (tr)David Sutherland/Tony Stone Images; (b)©Frerck/Odyssey/Chicago; **184:** N.T.B./Sipa Press; **186:** A.G.E. FotoStock; **190-191:** ©Roger Ressmeyer/Starlight (Image intentionally flopped to fit design format.); **192:** Leo de Wys, Inc./Fridmar Damm; (inset)©David R. Frazier Photolibrary; **193:** (t)©Beryl Goldberg Photographer; (b)David R. Frazier Photolibrary; **203:** R. Crandall/The Image Works; **204:** Advertisements courtesy of Motorola; **216:** AT&T Archives; **220:** Clifford Hausner/Leo de Wys, Inc.; **222-223:** ©Bob Daemmrich Photography; **224:** Jeff Greenberg/The Image Works; **225:** (t)David Young Wolff/Photo Edit; (b)©Richard Lord/The Image Works; **230:** (l)The Museum of the City of New York; (tr)S. Perry/Gamma-Liaison; (br)©Alyx Kellington/DDB Stock Photo; **233:** Alyx Kellington/DDB Stock Photo; **234:** ©David R. Frazier Photolibrary; **235:** AP/Wide World Photos; **236:** ©Bob Daemmrich/Stock Boston; **237:** Courtesy Habitat for Humanity; **242:** ©Steven & Monica Ferry; **243:** ©Chip and Rosa Maria de la Cueva Peterson; **246:** ©Richard Lord/The Image Works; **248-249:** Courtesy of Jessica Ramos; **254-255:** ©Donald Nausbaum/Tony Stone Images; **256:** ©John Mead/Science Photo Library/Photo Researchers, Inc.; **257:** (t)©Robert Fried; (b)Bates Littlehales/©National Geographic Society Image Collection; **261:** Photofest; **263:** The Kobal Collection; **264:** (t)©Frerck/Odyssey/Chicago; (b)Robert Frerck/Woodfin Camp & Associates; **266:** ©Frerck/Odyssey/Chicago; **268:** ©Frerck/Odyssey/Chicago; **269:** (t)©Buddy Mays/Travel Stock; (b)D. Donne Bryant/DDB Stock Photo; **270:** Museo del Oro, Banco de la República, Bogotá; **272:** ©Richard Nowitz/ National Geographic Society Image Collection; **273:** ©Buddy Mays/Travel Stock; **274:** ©Ulrike Welsch; **277:** Courtesy of Galería Fernando Quintana, Bogotá, Colombia; **280:** AP/Wide World Photos; **283:** Jeff Greenberg /Photo Researchers, Inc.; **284:** Tom McHugh/Photo Researchers, Inc.; **290-291:** ©The Detroit Institute of Arts, Founders Society Purchase, Edsel B. Ford Fund and Gift of Edsel B. Ford. (Acc. No. 33.10.N); **292:** ©Suzanne Murphy Larronde; **293:** (t)©David R. Frazier Photolibrary; (b)©Chip and Rosa Maria de la Cueva Peterson; **299:** (t)Courtesy, Marcela Abadi; (b)©Peter Menzel; **300:** ©Bob Daemmrich Photography; **305:** (t)©Peter Menzel/Stock Boston; (b)Owen Franken/Stock Boston; **306:** ©John Newbauer/Photo Edit; **312:** David Joel/Tony Stone Images; **313:** Vince Streano/Tony Stone Images; **314:** ©Bob Daemmrich/Stock Boston; **322:** (l)©Norman Prince; (r)©Robert Fried; **324-325:** ©Ulrike Welsch; **326:** ©Chip and Rosa Maria de la Cueva Peterson; **327:** (t)©David R. Frazier Photolibrary; **334:** (t)©Cindy Reiman /Impact Visuals; **338:** Courtesy of the Trustees of Dartmouth College. Photography by Jeffrey Nintzel; (b)Scala/Art Resource; **337:** Josef S. Martin/Artothek; **338:** J. Sarapochiello/ Bruce Coleman, Inc.; **339:** ©Carrion/ Sygma; **341:** ©Bob Daemmrich/The Image Works; **343:** ©Walter Weissman /Envision; **349:** SIQUEIROS, David Alfaro. Echo of a Scream. 1937. Enamel on wood, 48 x 36" (121.9 X 91.4 cm). The Museum of Modern Art, New York. Gift of Edward M.M. Warburg. Photograph ©1999 The Museum of Modern Art, New York; **362-363:** ©D. Donne Bryant/DDB Stock Photo; **364:** (l)A.G.E. FotoStock (r)©Beryl Goldberg Photographer; **365:** (t)©Beryl Goldberg Photographer; (b)©Frerck/ Odyssey / Chicago; **368:** A.G.E. FotoStock; **370:** (tl)©Frerck/Odyssey/ Chicago; (tr)©Peter Menzel; (cl)A.G.E. FotoStock; (cr)©Frerck/Odyssey/Chicago; (bl)©Abbas/Magnum; (br)©Frerck / Odyssey / Chicago; **372:** ©Frerck/Odyssey/Chicago; **374:** Field Museum of Natural History (Neg.# 109101c) Chicago; **376:** ©Suzanne Murphy Larronde; **377:** (t)©Frerck / Odyssey / Chicago; **378:** ©Chad Ehlers/Tony Stone Images; **378:** ©Miriam Lefkowitz/ Envision; **379:** Tony Arruza/Bruce Coleman, Inc.; **381:** Jean Higgins/Envision; **382:** Biblioteca Nacional, Madrid/PhotoMas; **386:** ©Beryl Goldberg Photographer; **394:** ©Frerck / Odyssey/Chicago; **396-397:** Courtesy of Concordia Language Villages/Photo by John Borge; **398:** ©Gifford / Gamma-Liaison; **399:** (t)©Ken Laffal; (b)©David R. Frazier Photolibrary; **406:** (t)©David R. Frazier Photolibrary; (c)Antonio Ribeiro/Gamma-Liaison; (b)Piero Guerrini/ Woodfin Camp & Associates, Inc.; **408:** Bob Daemmrich/Tony Stone Images; **410:** Courtesy of Concordia Language Villages/Photos by John Borge; **411:** (l)Courtesy of The Center for Cuban Studies Archives, New York; (r)Reprinted by permission of the artist, Lorenzo Homar and Instituto de Cultura Puertorriqueña; **412:** ©Frerck/Odyssey/Chicago; **413:** Alan Carey/The Image Works; **421:** Stephen Jaffe/Gamma Liaison; **426:** ©Frerck /Odyssey/Chicago; **436-439:** ©Telegraph Colour Library/FPG International; **440:** ©Wendy Walsh Photography; **441:** ©Jack Parsons; **442:** (t)©Jack Parsons; (c,b,)©Wendy Walsh Photography; **443:** ©Jack Parsons; **458-459:** Tony Stone Images; **460-461:** Lorentz Gullachsen/Tony Stone Images.

Text: Para leer readings and additional realia   Chapter 1, p. 39: "¡Vivan los voluntarios!" from ¡OYE!, Volumen 3, Número 5, March/April 1994 issue, p 3. Copyright©1994 by Scholastic Inc. Reprinted by permission of Scholastic Inc.   **Chapter 1, p. 51:** "¡Al concierto!" from ¡OYE!, Volumen 3, Número 5, March/April 1994 issue, p.8. Copyright©1994 by Scholastic Inc. Reprinted by permission of Scholastic Inc.   **Chapter 1, pp. 52-53:** Adaptation of "El color de tu personalidad" from ¡OYE!, Volumen 3, Número 5, March/April 1994 issue, p. 11. Copyright©1994 by Scholastic Inc. Reprinted by permission of Scholastic Inc.   **Chapter 2, pp. 86-87:** Adapted abridgment of "Benvinguts a Càlig" from VOCES DE CAMBIO by Martha E. Heard, pp. 1-3. Reprinted by permission of the author.   **Chapter 3, pp. 118-119:** Adapted from "El Poeta Del Realismo Mexicano" by Annick Sanjurjo Casciero from AMÉRICAS, Volumen 42, Número 4, 1990, pp. 44, 46, and 47. Reprinted by permission from AMÉRICAS, a bimonthly magazine published by the General Secretariat of the Organization of American States in English and Spanish.   **Chapter 4, p. 138:** "En Los Próximos Cinco Años: 'Una de Cada Tres Familias Chilenas Tendrá TV Cable'" by Pilar Segovia Isasi from EL MERCURIO. Sábado 31 de Diciembre de 1994. Reprinted by permission of EL MERCURIO   **Chapter 4, p. 138:** Chart, "El Nuevo Invitado De People Meter" from EL MERCURIO, Sábado 31 de Diciembre de 1994. Reprinted by permission of EL MERCURIO.   **Chapter 4, p. 140:** "Apuesta Por El Satélite" from CAMBIO16, Enero 16, 1995, No. 1.208, p. 18. Reprinted by permission of Cambio16.   **Chapter 4, pp. 152-153:** Adapted from "Alejandra Vallejo-Nágera" from TIEMPO, Abril 1994, p. 90. Reprinted by permission of Ediciones Tiempo, S.A.   **Chapter 5, pp. 184-185:** Elizabeth Burgos Debray, ME LLAMO RIGOBERTA MENCHÚ. Habana, Cuba: Ediciones Casa de las Américas, 1983, pp. 113-114.   **Chapter 6, p. 206:** "Interactivo" from CAMBIO16, Enero 16, 1995, No. 1.208, p. 17. Reprinted by permission of Cambio16.   **Chapter 6, p. 207:** "El Hogar Inteligente" from CAMBIO16, Enero 16, 1995, No. 1.208, p. 17. Reprinted by permission of Cambio16.   **Chapter 6, pp. 216-217:** Abridgment of "El Mejor Amigo Del Hombre" by Elizabeth Mora-Mass from HOMBRE INTERNACIONAL, Año 18, No. 10, Octubre 1993, pp. 73-74. Copyright©1993 by Editorial América, S.A. Reprinted by permission of Editorial América, S.A. **Chapter 7, pp. 248-249:** Interview with Jessica Ramos by Martha Heard. Reprinted by permission of Jessica Ramos.   **Chapter 9, p. 304:** "El Machismo" from CAMBIO16, Enero 16, 1995, No. 1.208, p. 36. Reprinted by permission of Cambio16.   **Chapter 9, p. 304:** "El Hombre En Casa" from CAMBIO16, Enero 16, 1995, No. 1.208, p. 37. Reprinted by permission of Cambio16.   **Chapter 9, p. 306:** Figure, "En México Se Necesita . . ." from MUY INTERESANTE, Año XI, No. 10, p. 17. Copyright©1994 by G + J España Ediciones, S.L.S. en C. Reprinted by permission.   **Chapter 9, p. 306:** Figure, "Los 40 principales" from MUY INTERESANTE, Año XI, No. 10, p. 17. Copyright©1994 by G + J España Ediciones, S.L.S. en C. Reprinted by permission.   **Chapter 9, p. 307:** Graph, ". . . desempleados" from MUY INTERESANTE, Año XI, No. 10, p. 16. Copyright©1994 by G + J España Ediciones, S.L.S. en C. Reprinted by permission.   **Chapter 9, pp. 316-319:** Adapted abridgment of "¿Qué tipo de inteligencia tienes?" from TU INTERNACIONAL, Año 14, No. 8, Agosto 1993, pp. 47, 48, and 49. Copyright©1993 by Editorial América, S.A. Reprinted by permission of Editorial América, S.A. **Chapter 10, pp. 352-357:** From "Hasta aclarar el misterio" by Robert Wernick from SELECCIONES DEL READER'S DIGEST, March 1995, pp. 61-66. Reprinted by permission of the author.   **Chapter 11, pp. 388-391:** "La tercera raíz de México" by Luz María Martínez Montiel from EL LEGADO DE ÁFRICA EN MÉXICO. Copyright © 1993 by Institución Smithsonian. Reprinted by permission of Smithsonian Institution Traveling Exhibition Service. **Chapter 12, pp. 422-423:** "Nieve" from DE CÓMO LAS CHICAS GARCÍA PERDIERON SU ACENTO by Julia Álvarez, pp. 167-168. Copyright©1991 by Julia Álvarez. Publicado en español por Ediciones B., S.A., Barcelona, España. Reprinted by permission of Ediciones B., S.A.

Fondo literario (supplementary readings)   **Chapter 1, pp. 430-435:** Adapted from EL CONDE LUCANOR by don Juan Manuel.   **Chapter 3, pp. 440-443:** Adapted abridgment of "La Persistencia De La Memoria: El Arte Viviente" by Patricia Harris and David Lyon from AMÉRICAS, Volumen 45, Número 6, 1993, pp. 26 and 28-29. Reprinted by permission from AMÉRICAS, a bimonthly magazine published by the General Secretariat of the Organization of American States in English and Spanish. **Chapter 4, pp. 444-453:**

592   Acknowledgments